The Ar

Andrew Ayers

The Architecture of Paris
An Architectural Guide

Edition Axel Menges

© 2004 Edition Axel Menges, Stuttgart/London
ISBN 3-930698-96-X

All rights reserved, especially those of translation
into other languages.

Reproductions: Bild & Text Joachim Baun, Fellbach,
and Gábor Mocsonoky, Budapest
Printing: Druckhaus Münster, Kornwestheim
Binding: Dollinger GmbH, Metzingen

Design: Axel Menges

Contents

- 7 Foreword
- 7 How to use this guide
- 8 Introduction

- 19 1st *arrondissement*
- 56 2nd *arrondissement*
- 64 3rd *arrondissement*
- 76 4th *arrondissement*
- 103 5th *arrondissement*
- 120 6th *arrondissement*
- 134 7th *arrondissement*
- 151 8th *arrondissement*
- 164 9th *arrondissement*
- 177 10th *arrondissement*
- 183 11th *arrondissement*
- 188 12th *arrondissement*
- 201 13th *arrondissement*
- 216 14th *arrondissement*
- 227 15th *arrondissement*
- 236 16th *arrondissement*
- 254 17th *arrondissement*
- 257 18th *arrondissement*
- 266 19th *arrondissement*
- 281 20th *arrondissement*

- 287 21 Saint-Denis
- 293 22 Roissy-en-France
- 296 23 Ecouen
- 299 24 Maisons-Laffitte
- 302 25 Poissy
- 306 26 Neuilly-sur-Seine
- 308 27 La Défense
- 316 28 Saint-Germain-en-Laye
- 319 29 Boulogne-Billancourt
- 327 30 Saint-Cloud
- 330 31 Garches/Vaucresson
- 333 32 Versailles
- 349 33 Charenton-le-Pont
- 350 34 Vincennes
- 355 35 Le Raincy
- 357 36 Marne-la-Vallée
- 368 37 Vaux-le-Vicomte
- 374 38 Fontainebleau

- 381 The Métropolitain and the Réseau Express Régional (RER)
- 384 Arcades and passages
- 390 Seine bridges
- 395 Parisian housing, 1400–1900
- 401 Street furniture

- 404 Selected bibliograpy
- 405 Glossary
- 406 Index
- 416 Photo credits

Foreword

The Architecture of Paris does not set out to be a comprehensive survey of the city's buildings, but is rather a careful selection of some of the more interesting architectural sights to be found in Paris and its hinterland. Where wide coverage often results in frustratingly brief entries, the aim here was to provide more detailed – and thus with any luck more satisfying – analysis of a limited number of sites and buildings. Selection criteria included: works internationally recognized for their excellence, whether anonymous (e. g., Notre-Dame (4.2), Saint-Denis (21.2)) or by »greats« such as Pierre Lescot, François Mansart, Ange-Jacques Gabriel, Auguste Perret, Le Corbusier, etc.; some early or lesser works by such masters; lesser buildings that illustrate particular Parisian or French architectural trends and tendencies; »monuments« that through their great size or impact indelibly modify the cityscape; buildings whose great antiquity makes them interesting in the Parisian context; sites and buildings that illustrate particular type-forms, such as industrial structures, department stores, apartment buildings, etc.; and, last but not least, a handful of curiosities and eccentricities. Furthermore, since this is a guide to a *city*, the definition of »architecture« was widened to include urban infrastructure such as parks, cemeteries, street furniture, and so on.

Although writing is generally a very solitary activity, still it would not be possible without others' help. The author would like to thank Michael Robinson for setting the whole thing up, the staff of the Centre de Documentation du Pavillon de l'Arsenal, Axel Menges and Dorothea Duwe, the publishers, for their patience, and all the friends who have offered advice, support and practical aid (especially David Bundy for his I.T. input). Warm thanks are also due to the following architects and institutions who supplied images for reproduction in the book: Tadao Ando, Paul Andreu, Architecture Studio, Pierre Du Besset and Dominique Lyon, Ricardo Bofill, Michel Bordeau, Frédéric Borel, Centre Culturel d'Art Georges Pompidou, C+H+ (Paul Chemetov, Borja Huidobro), Philippe Chaix and Jean-Paul Morel, Jean-Paul Deschamps, François Deslaugiers, Adrien Fainsilber, Massimiliano Fuksas, Franck Hammoutène, Christian Hauvette, Michel Kagan, Pablo Katz, Michel Macary, Richard Meier, Xavier Menu, Marc Mimram, Jean Nouvel, Office for Metropolitan Architecture, Renzo Piano Building Workshop, Christian de Portzamparc, Richard Rogers Partnership, Patrick Rubin, Francis Soler, Bernard Tschumi, Charles Vandenhove, Manuel Nuñez Yanowsky, and Aymeric Zublena.

How to use this guide

The Architecture of Paris is intended for use in the field as well as the armchair, and is hence organized geographically for practical convenience. Arbitrary though they are, the current French administrative divisions have been used: the 20 *arrondissements* of the Ville de Paris, and the different *villes* and *communes* surrounding Paris proper (whose names are generally those of the villages they once were). The entries are divided into four sections: the first covers Paris *intra muros* by *arrondissement*; the second is devoted to the city's near suburbs (within a 25 km radius), starting to the north of Paris and working round anticlockwise; the third section proposes a couple of excursions further afield; while the final part of the guide is devoted to »themed« entries covering subjects that do not fall into particular geographical divisions: the bridges of the Seine, the Métro, street furniture, and so on. Within each *arrondissement* or *commune*, entries are arranged according to approximate geographical sequence; public-transport details (Métro, bus, train or tram) appear at the head of each entry. To find your way around the region, buy one of the pocket street maps of Paris and its suburbs (*banlieue*), which are readily available from kiosks, newsagents and bookshops.

A glossary is provided at the end of the guide, giving definitions of French words and expressions not usually used in English and therefore not to be found in an English dictionary. Also included are definitions of some of the more obscure architectural terminology employed. American and Canadian readers should note that the European system of counting floors has been used, i.e., ground floor, first floor, second floor, etc. »First floor« should thus be read as »second floor« in North-American usage, »second floor« as »third floor«, and so on.

If you are planning to visit Paris in September, look out for the Journées du Patrimoine (Open House Days), which usually take place one weekend towards the middle of the month. Many buildings not normally open to the public take part. The Ministry of Culture publishes a list of participating sites a couple of weeks in advance – try their website, www.culture.fr.

Introduction

With nearly 11 million inhabitants (10,925,000 according to the 1999 census) and a gross domestic product higher than those of Australia, the Netherlands and India, the Paris region is continental Europe's biggest metropolis, ranking somewhere around 18th world-wide in terms of population and fifth in the EU's league table of GDP per capita. At the centre of this vast conurbation, known as the Ile-de-France, is the Ville de Paris itself, which today counts around 2.1 million inhabitants.
A few more vital statistics will help to get the measure of the place: nearly 19% of France's population lives in the Paris region, 22% of its jobs are to be found there, 28% of the country's riches are produced there and a quarter of its students study there. As for the role of the Ville de Paris within the conurbation, it is home to 40% of the region's jobs, ensuring that every day over 1 million commuters descend on the city centre, and is the principal tourist attraction of a country that proudly claims the title of »World's No. 1 Tourist Destination«. For as well as a modern megalopolis, Paris is also a historical treasure trove, few other cities of its size having managed to conserve so much of their pre-20C fabric. Over 1,500 years' worth of rich and frequently world-class architectural history is to be found there.

View from the Eiffel Tower

One of the fundamental factors to influence the character of a town or city is of course the materials used to build it, and Paris has its own unique set of particularities. Until well into the 17C, much of the city was constructed from wood, which was by far the cheapest available material given the abundant forests of the Ile-de-France. There were also copious stone deposits, Paris being blessed with beds of warm, honey-coloured limestone whose cheery hues are one of the most striking characteristics of today's city. Until the 14C, all Paris's stone needs were supplied locally (many quarry tunnels can still be found underneath the 14th *arrondissement*), but as of the 15C other types of stone began to be brought in from elsewhere. Until the 17C, the principal edifices built entirely of stone were churches, fortifications, palaces and aristocratic *hôtels particuliers*, although the wealthier of the merchant classes could also afford all-stone houses. By Louis XIV's time, prosperity had grown to the extent that streets of entirely stone-fronted buildings began to appear. Those who could not afford ashlar built wood or rubblestone structures, perhaps with stone bases, quoins and window surrounds. Since the Paris region was rich in gypsum deposits, which were exploited from Antique times onwards to produce plaster (see 19.2), non-ashlar structures were traditionally protected with a layer of render. Much of today's city outside of the »beaux quartiers« remains stucco-fronted, and modern constructions are often given a plaster coating so as to blend in with the

existing fabric. The Ile-de-France also contained clay deposits, but apart from a brief period of favour in the first half of the 17C, brick was little used in Paris, essentially because stone, which came to be considered the more noble material, was as readily and cheaply available. Clay was for a long time used to make roof tiles, but during the 17C, again as a consequence of taste, slate became the preferred roofing material, even though it had to be imported from outside the region. The spectacular technological developments of the 19C and 20C entirely overturned the traditional palette of materials, with iron, steel, zinc (for roofing), brick and, from the early-20C on, concrete becoming ever more present. Until the mid-20C, however, limestone remained the favoured facing material within Paris's richer *quartiers*, although it was no longer regional but national production that supplied the demand. Today glass seems to have become the pet cladding material of contemporary architects working in Paris.

Paris before the second millennium
The cradle of modern-day Paris was the Ile de la Cité (4.1), a then 9 ha island in the middle of the Seine that was colonized in the 2C BC by the Parisii, a Celtic tribe that probably migrated there from the Rhinelands. Although today's city bears their name, the settlement was originally known as Lutetia. Control of the Ile de la Cité meant control of the river and all the traffic and merchandise that passed along it; this, in tandem with the natural resources available in the region, made the Parisii extremely prosperous. It was not, however, for Lutetia's wealth that the Romans conquered the settlement in 52 BC, but rather for its strategic importance as a gateway to the north. The Roman occupation lasted four centuries, during which time the Celtic village was entirely transformed into a Roman town. The forum, baths, theatres and main areas of housing were situated on the Left Bank, while the Ile de la Cité was home to the principal administrative edifices (including the governor's palace (see 1.1)). Roman Lutetia still makes itself felt in modern-day Paris through the two major monuments it left behind (the Arènes (5.11) and the Thermes (5.3)) and in certain aspects of the city's street plan. Thus the north–south-running Rue Saint-Jacques (5th) corresponds to the old Roman *cardo* (principal street) on the Left Bank, the Petit Pont and the Pont Notre-Dame (see feature on Seine bridges) still cross where the two Roman bridges crossed, and the Rues Saint-Martin and du Faubourg Saint-Martin (4th, 3rd and 10th) follow the old Roman road that connected Paris to the north.

By the second half of the 3C, the decline of the Roman Empire began to be felt in Lutetia through the increasing number of Barbarian attacks, and the population retreated to a certain extent to the Ile de la Cité, which was fortified by the building of an enormous wall around its perimeter. The empire's hold on Paris finally collapsed in the late-4C. Relatively little is known of Paris's history during the 5C, although in 451 Saint Geneviève is supposed to have saved the town from Attila the Hun. She is also credited with building the shrine that would later grow into the powerful Abbaye de Saint-Denis (21.2). By the turn of the 6C, Paris had become part of the Merovingian kingdom of the Franks, and in 508 King Clovis made the city the seat of his realm. Christianity had come to Paris in the mid-3C and firmly established itself during the 4C, but under the Merovingians it truly flourished with the building of numerous religious edifices. Many of today's ecclesiastical buildings owe their origins to the Merovingians, for example Notre-Dame (4.2), which stands on the site of the old Merovingian cathedral of Saint-Etienne, the Panthéon (5.8), which was built to serve the Abbaye Sainte-Geneviève founded by Clovis, and Saint-Germain-des-Prés (6.4), which was founded by Clovis's son Childebert I. The Merovingians were succeeded by the Carolingians in the 7C, and Paris lost its pre-eminence to Aachen, where Charlemagne fixed his court. The city entered a period of relative decline, exacerbated in the 9C by devastating Norman raids, which again caused the population to retreat to the Ile de la Cité. It was not until the end of the 10C that stability returned, and henceforth the town would expand principally onto the Right Bank rather than the Left.

Medieval to Renaissance Paris
In 987, Hugues Capet, Comte de Paris, was elected king of the tiny realm that then constituted »France«, making the city central to the kingdom's affairs. Throughout the 11C, Paris gradually picked itself up from the ruins and expanded in territory and importance. A measure of its success can be got from the fact that this period saw the construction of the city's first defensive wall on the Right Bank. Today almost nothing survives of 11C Paris, although many of the city's churches owe their origins to 11C architects and a good number of its outlying abbeys were rebuilt or extended at this time. Among them was Saint-Germain-des-Prés, which is one of the few to conserve anything of its 11C structure today. Although Norman architecture was very influential on the Paris region (Normandy being the great church- and abbey-building power of the time), Saint-Germain exhibits certain characteristically Francilien features that depart from the Norman model – most notably its thin walls – whose use would pave the way for the development of Gothic architecture in the following century. Saint-Martin-des-Champs (3.10), another abbey rebuilt in roughly the same period, marks a further step towards the development of early Gothic.

While the 11C had been a time of economic growth and physical expansion for Paris, the 12C proved to be the most glorious period in the city's history to date. Architecturally it was marked by the flowering of early Gothic, the debut of a building revolution that began in Paris and the Ile-de-France and later spread across most of Europe. The most important early-Gothic edifices in the Paris region were Abbot Suger's choir at

Introduction 9

Saint-Denis, which continued the line of experimentation begun at Saint-Martin-des-Champs, and, of course, the cathedral of Notre-Dame, which was begun in the 1160s to replace the old and inadequate Saint-Etienne. The power and expansion of the church in Paris made the city a centre of scholarship and learning, leading to the development of the Latin Quarter with its many colleges, which, by the turn of the 13C, had joined forces to become Europe's principal university, ahead of Bologna and Oxford. It was during the reign of Philippe II Augustus (1180–1223) that Paris reached the apogee of its power, for two principal reasons. Firstly, the king fixed administration of his kingdom in the city, making it a capital in the modern sense of the word, with all the economic and urbanistic benefits this status implies. Secondly, Philippe vastly extended his realm, making it, and by default his capital, extremely wealthy. As a result, by the end of his reign, Paris had expanded to become the Occident's biggest city, growing from approximately 25,000 inhabitants in 1180 to over double that figure by 1220. Tangible expression of this growth was provided by Philippe's new city fortifications, built much further out than the 11C walls, whose battery of defences included the impregnable donjon that was the original Louvre (1.8). But despite its riches almost nothing now remains of Philippe's city, apart from certain portions of the original medieval street plan that survive in the central *arrondissements*. Likewise, the Paris of his illustrious successor, Louis IX (reigned 1226–70) is no more, bar edifices such as the refectory of Saint-Martin-des-Champs and the palace chapel of Saint-Germain-en-Laye (see 28.1), and the major monuments that are Notre-Dame's splendid filigree transept fronts, Saint-Denis's luminous nave and the extraordinary, glass-walled Sainte-Chapelle (1.2). These latter three realizations mark the development of the Rayonnant style, the Paris region's answer to »High-Gothic« architecture, with their perfection and paring down of the Gothic structural system to a vaulted stone skeleton defining glass-filled voids. Philippe IV the Fair's reign (1285–1314) left us with a secular Gothic monument in the form of the Salle des Gens d'Armes in the Palais de la Cité (1.1).

Paris continued to grow exponentially throughout the 13C and early-14C, and by 1328 its population may well have been over 200,000 souls, four times its level just a hundred years before. To put this figure into a wider context, Venice, Genoa and Florence hovered just below 100,000 inhabitants at the time, while other big French towns only counted between 20,000 and 50,000 people. The peace and burgeoning trade that had led to Paris's supremacy would be shattered over the next century by the interminable Hundred Years' War (c. 1338–1453), fought between the English and French monarchies for control of France. As a result, many of the surviving monuments from this period are military, such as Jean the Good's additions to the Palais de la Cité and Charles V's Châteaux de Saint-Germain-en-Laye (28.1) and de Vincennes (34.2). Charles was also responsible for construction of a new city wall on the Right Bank, further out than Philippe Augustus's, which still makes itself felt today in the course of the *grands boulevards* (see below), and of which the infamous Bastille was a part. The few remaining aristocratic *hôtels particuliers* of the period, such as the Hôtel de Clisson (see 3.5) and the Tour Jean-sans-Peur (2.1), reflect the troubled times in which they were built through their heavily fortified exteriors, a characteristic that persisted as late as the 1490s in buildings like the Hôtel de Sens (4.6).

By the end of the Hundred Years' War, due to both the conflict and the plague epidemics that swept across Europe during this period, Paris's population had fallen to between 80,000 and 100,000, half its early-14C level. Many simply quit the city, including the court, which migrated to the Loire valley. With the peace that followed defeat of the English, however, growth and prosperity returned, and by 1500 Paris had regained a population level of around 200,000, which rocketed to nearly 350,000 by the mid-16C. The years 1450–1550 were a period of rebuilding and expansion, and many of the city's churches were either partly or entirely reconstructed at this time. Under English influence, Rayonnant High Gothic had mutated into the even more pared-down but also much more decoration-orientated Flamboyant style, good examples of which can be seen at the Tour Saint-Jacques (4.12), Saint-Merri (4.13), Saint-Gervais-Saint-Protais (4.10), Saint-Nicolas-des-Champs (3.9) and Saint-Germain-l'Auxerrois (1.0). That the Flamboyant style was not just a question of churches is demonstrated by the splendid Hôtel de Cluny (5.4). Where the mass of the people was concerned, however, the French capital remained a medieval, half-timbered city, of which next to nothing now survives.

François I's reign (1515–47) would prove decisive for Paris's future, since the king brought the court back to the city. As a result, he began a whole spate of château building in the Paris region, concentrating his efforts to the west of the capital around the area's many hunting forests, which included the Bois de Boulogne (29.1). This was to have lasting repercussions on the city's development, since instead of building their homes in the capital's east, as they had done in the later medieval period when the court was fixed at Vincennes, Paris's ruling classes began to move westwards. Today the city still preserves a noticeable divide between the rich, *haut-bourgeois* west and the more working-class east, although the municipality has done much to blur the distinction over the last 30 years through post-industrial gentrification schemes. The reigns of François I and his son, Henri II, saw the beginnings of a tentative French Renaissance, which, where architecture was concerned, was mostly a question of applying Classicizing decoration to medieval building types. Good Paris-region examples of early French Renaissance buildings include hybrid efforts such as Saint-Eustache (1.21), Saint-Etienne-du-Mont (5.7), the Hôtel Carnavalet (see

3.1), the rebuilt Château de Saint-Germain-en-Laye and the Château d'Ecouen (23.1), and the much more accomplished Fontaine des Innocents (1.23) and Lescot wing of the Louvre. The Château de Fontainebleau (38.1) was important for its Italianizing innovations in interior décor. 16C Paris also saw a change in the way the city was perceived, again under the influence of Italian ideas, with urban aesthetics becoming a matter for royal and municipal concern. Prior to the Renaissance period, »urbanism« in the French capital had been a question simply of practicalities such as the improvement of river crossings and traffic circulation, the avoidance of fires, the amelioration of hygiene, and so on. As of 1500, however, urban embellishment projects began to be implemented, such as the widening and regularization of façades in the Rue de la Juiverie (1508, since demolished), the straightening out of the Rue d'Autriche in front of the Louvre (c. 1528), and Charles IX's 1564 decree that redevelopment of the Hôtel de Tournelles as housing be effected using standardized, repeating façades (as indeed it was, but under Henri IV and as the Place des Vosges (see below)). This interest in Paris's general physical appearance would gather ever greater momentum over the centuries that followed, reaching its apogee in the Second Empire under Baron Haussmann (see below).

During the latter half of the 16C, Paris was once again beset by armed conflict, this time the Wars of Religion that opposed France's Catholic majority against its Protestant minority. Economically the city went into steep decline, and its population dropped significantly.

The age of Absolutism – from Henri IV to the Revolution
Once Henri IV (reigned 1589–1610) had finally brought peace to France and taken possession of his capital, Paris's population levels picked up again, and at Henri's death stood at around 300,000. Enlightened despot that he was, Henri set about improving and embellishing the medieval city he had inherited, although his reign was too short for the realization of all his plans. Nonetheless he left us with the splendid Place des Vosges (4.19) – probably Europe's first entirely regular square, a new urban type-form that would go on to have a long history –, the imposing ensemble formed by the completed Pont Neuf (see feature on Seine bridges) and the Place Dauphine (1.3), and the model sanatorium that was the Hôpital Saint-Louis (10.4). Henri's reign also marked a further step towards the centralization of France's administration that would culminate in the absolutism of Louis XIV, a development of direct benefit to the capital since it was there that the necessary state machinery was concentrated. Consequently, the 17C saw the emergence of a new »middle« class in the form of the *noblesse de robe*, who built fine *hôtels particuliers* in the Marais, Paris's traditional aristocratic *quartier* (situated in today's 3rd and 4th *arrondissements*). Over the course of the 16C, the *hôtel particulier* had begun to take on standardized form, models such as the Hôtel Carnavalet and Philibert De l'Orme's house (see the Hôtel de Donon, 3.2) setting the trend. But it was in the 17C, in tandem with the flowering of French Classicism, that the *hôtel particulier* took on its definitive form, which would be reproduced *ad infinitum* until the end of the *ancien régime*. Paris has been lucky to conserve many fine examples, and the evolution of the type-form can be traced through buildings such as the Hôtel Lamoignon (4.18), the Hôtel de Sully (4.20), the Hôtel Tubeuf (2.3), the Hôtel d'Avaux (3.7) and the Hôtel de Guénégaud (3.6).

A study of the *hôtel particulier* would also provide a good introduction to the development of French Classicism during the 17C, although to complete the picture one must look to aristocratic and royal châteaux and to the rash of new Parisian convents and monasteries built under Louis XIII (reigned 1610–43) and Louis XIV (reigned 1643–1715) in response to the Catholic Counter Reformation. Where châteaux were concerned, the century saw the emergence of a specifically French type that combined certain aspects of traditional medieval fortified manors with a national interpretation of Italian Classicism. Given the capital's importance, the Paris region is of course especially rich in good examples. The trend had begun in the previous century with buildings such as Ecouen, and can be traced through edifices such as the Palais du Luxembourg (6.8), the original Château de Versailles (32.1), the Château de Maisons (24.1), the Château de Vaux-le-Vicomte (37.1) and the Château de Champs-sur-Marne (36.5). Another important 17C development, again initiated in the 16C, was the advent of the professional architect, which gave rise to a sort of »star system« of greats such as Salomon de Brosse, François Mansart, Louis Le Vau and Jules Hardouin-Mansart. It was of course these men who were responsible for many of the principal developments in the Classicization of ecclesiastical architecture over the 17C. During the 16C, the French church had rather lagged behind the civil sector where the lessons of the Renaissance were concerned, but with the advent of the Counter Reformation in France, directed from Rome itself, Italian influence became ever more palpable. One of the earliest examples was the west front of Saint-Gervais-Saint-Protais, which set the standard for all that followed. It was picked up in the Jesuits' Saint-Paul-Saint-Louis (4.7), which successfully combined local Gothic tradition with the Roman Il Gesù model. This was to be the pattern for most of Paris's 17C churches, developed in buildings such as the chapel of the Sorbonne (5.5) and the Abbaye du Val-de-Grâce (5.9) and standardized by the end of the century in edifices such as Saint-Louis-en-l'Ile (4.4), Saint-Roch (1.15) and Saint-Sulpice (6.5).

Louis XIV's bellicose reign made France Europe's most powerful nation, and its capital expanded to over 400,000 inhabitants. Where urbanism was concerned, the Sun King's two most important contributions to Paris's topography were the demolition of the city's medieval fortifications (see the Porte Saint-Denis, 10.1) and the creation of a suburban centre of power at Versailles (32.1). The 1640s and 1650s had been marred by armed conflict between France's different ruling factions, but by the 1660s all opposition to central royal authority had been crushed. As a result, defence of the realm was pushed out to its frontiers, and Paris's fortifications became theoretically redundant. That the Sun King so actively pursued their demolition did not just reflect his desire to embellish the city, for depriving Paris of the ability to defend itself meant that the troublesome capital could less easily rise up against its sovereign. In 1676 Charles V's wall on the Right Bank was dismantled and replaced by what became known as the *grands boulevards*, a series of wide, tree-lined avenues. Their unprecedented breadth and regularity caused a sensation, and inspired Baron Haussmann's avenues and boulevards in the 19C. In 1704 it was the Left Bank's turn, Philippe Augustus's old walls making way for today's Boulevards de l'Hôpital, Auguste-Blanqui, Saint-Jacques, Raspail and des Invalides. In the absence of constraining fortifications, Paris was able to expand organically out across the surrounding plains. One of the factors that encouraged it to develop ever further westwards was the establishment of Louis XIV's power base at Versailles, a move largely motivated by the king's deep mistrust of the Paris mob. As of 1682, the entire court was confined to the suburbs, a tactic designed to keep the aristocracy in gilded subser-vience. Versailles also provided a showcase for the fruits of the state-administered artistic machine set up by Louis's chief minister, Jean-Baptiste Colbert, which was controlled through the newly founded academies and nourished by the Ecole des Beaux-Arts (see 6.1), whose importance in the development of French architecture over the next two centuries cannot be overestimated.

Despite the move of the court and government to Versailles, Paris still remained France's effective capital, in part because of its size and economic and manufacturing importance (then, as now, the city was a centre of luxury-goods production), and in part because the kingdom's administrative structures remained centred there. The capital's development under Louis XIV included both the renewal of old *quartiers* – the rebuilt Marais being one of the most striking examples – and the urbanization of entirely virgin areas, such as the Ile Saint-Louis (see 4.4 and 4.5). Greater wealth and new urban regulations meant that by the turn of the 18C the majority of Paris's medieval, half-timbered, jettied, gable-fronted houses had disappeared, new structures being in rubblestone or ashlar and presenting eaves to the street (see feature on Parisian housing 1400–1900). But the medieval system of narrow plots remained, and many of the new buildings were simply variations on an old theme, while others that appeared new were in fact medieval structures dressed up in modern garb. For despite the ever increasing awareness of the city as a reflection of the nation's prestige, and for all Louis XIV's centralized power, the crown could not intervene in Paris to the extent it might perhaps have liked. At Versailles, at least initially, the Sun King managed to keep very tight control of the town's development (see 32.6), but state urbanism in Paris was limited essentially to a handful of isolated projects and monuments such as the Collège des Quatre-Nations (6.2), the Places des Victoires (2.2) and Vendôme (1.13), the east front of the Louvre (see 1.8), the remodelled Jardin des Tuileries (1.10), the Invalides (7.12), and the Hôpital de la Salpêtrière (13.1). Nonetheless, the combined forces of the crown, the church and the aristocracy managed to build an entirely new, Classical Paris in the 17C, whose splendour rivalled Rome's and prompted Germain Brice to publish the first ever architectural guide to the French capital in 1684 (which stayed in print until 1752). Although the era has subsequently been given the label »Baroque«, even the Paris region's grandest architectural realizations, such as Versailles or the Invalides, retained a Classical coolness and majesty that had nothing to do with the formal convolutions of Rome, France having evolved a grand manner all of its own. This was also the great age of French gardens, of which Vaux-le-Vicomte, the Tuileries and of course Versailles provide some of the most splendid examples.

Paris's population remained stable in the first half of the 18C, but climbed sharply in the second half to somewhere around 600,000 by the Revolution. The city continued to expand westwards towards Versailles, the new aristocratic *quartier* being the Faubourg Saint-Germain (today part of the 6th and 7th *arrondissements*), which superseded the Marais. On the Right Bank, financiers and the *noblesse de robe* developed the Faubourg Saint-Honoré. Despite Baron Haussmann's having knocked the Boulevard Saint-Germain bang through its middle in the 19C, the Faubourg Saint-Germain still conserves an extraordinary collection of 18C *hôtels particuliers*, many of which, due to the proximity of the Assemblée Nationale (7.4), are now home to government ministries. Again, one could trace the continuing evolution of French Classicism largely through an examination of these aristocratic residences. The early-18C saw the development of the Rococo, which was essentially a question of interior decoration (see the extraordinary Hôtel de Soubise (3.5)), although it was accompanied by greater sophistication in internal planning and a simplification of external massing and detailing, tendencies that are well illustrated in buildings such as the Château de Champs-sur-Marne, the Hôtel Matignon (7.14), the Hôtel Peyrenc de Moras (Musée Rodin, 7. 13) and the Petit Luxembourg (6.9). This trend towards simplification arguably culminated in the mid century with pared-down creations such as Ange-Jacques Gabriel's Petit Trianon (32.4). The final years of the *ancien régime* were marked by a move towards ever greater neo-Classicism, most spectacularly in ecclesiastical architecture with Soufflot's extraordinary Sainte-Geneviève (now Panthéon, 5.8) and lesser, but nonetheless notable, buildings such as Saint-Philippe-du-Roule (8.7) and Saint-Louis-d'Antin (9.8). In secular architecture men such as Gondoin (the Ecole de Chirurgie, 6.6), Brongniart, and Peyre and De Wailly (Théâtre de l'Odéon, 6.7) pushed the neo-Classical idiom ever further, although none went in quite the fantastic direction of Claude-Nicolas Ledoux (see 3.8, 8.9, 11.7 and 19.13). Likewise, the awesome neo-Classical fantasies of Ledoux's teacher, Etienne-Louis Boullée, remained unbuilt (see, nonetheless, 8.3). Where the ordinary inhabitant was concerned, the later 18C saw the emergence of the apartment building, a phenomenon linked to the ever growing tendency towards land speculation.

The spiralling indebtedness of the French crown in the 18C meant that Louis XV and XVI were largely unable to implement the kind of prestige urban projects that Louis XIV had gone in for, the century's only big state-driven schemes in Paris being Sainte-Geneviève, the Place de la Concorde (8.1), the Hôtel des Monnaies (6.3) and the Ecole Militaire (7.9). On a more minor but nonetheless significant note, the medieval houses that crowded onto Paris's bridges were demolished in the 1780s to open up views of the river. Another significant development came with the new building regulations of 1783, which established maximum building heights in relation to street width (see 1.17). One state-implemented scheme that had a profound effect on the lives of Paris's inhabitants was the tax wall, or *barrière*, built by the Fermiers Génereaux around the capital in the 1780s, which defined the city's then limits (see 19.13) and was a good measure of the extent to which it had expanded (today its course can be traced in the ring of avenues known as the *boulevards extérieurs*).

Expansion and reorganization in the 19C city – Napoleon, Rambuteau and Haussmann
The turmoil of the French Revolution and its aftermath resulted in economic stagnation and a drop in Paris's population, which stood at approximately 550,000 at the turn of the 19C. Under Napoleon numbers rose dramatically and had reached 700,000 by 1817. This exponential growth continued under subsequent regimes, reaching 800,000 by 1831 and probably hitting the million mark in the mid 1840s. The capital's hinterland was still relatively sparsely populated at this time, though, with only Versailles, Saint-Germain-en-Laye and Saint-Denis counting over 10,000 inhabitants. When considering the enormous upheavals in Paris's fabric effected from the 1840s onwards, we should bear in mind that this population explosion had occurred with relatively little extension of the city's territory beyond its late-18C limits, with the result that population density approached 1,000 souls per hectare in some central *quartiers*. The cramming of this multitude into a narrow, congested street network that was still essentially medieval engendered all the appalling sanitary and traffic headaches one might imagine, including devastating cholera outbreaks in the 1830s and 1840s.

Great modernizer and reformer that he was, Napoleon (First Consul 1799–1804, Emperor 1804–14) was well aware of the need to overhaul Paris's topography to make the city fit for modern living. He also wanted a capital that would reflect in built form the imperial glory he claimed for France and her dominions. Grandiose plans were drawn up during his reign, which included a new, monumental east–west road axis, a vast imperial palace on the Chaillot hill (see 16.7) and a new university centre on the Ile aux Cygnes (in today's 15th) grouping together the Université de Paris, the Ecole Normale, the Ecole des Beaux-Arts, the national library and the national archives. Romanizing neo-Classicism and the sophistication of the Empire style became the expression of official taste, as exemplified by the work of his preferred architects Charles Percier and Pierre-François-Léonard Fontaine (see 1.8 and 1.9). But the economic crisis of 1812 and the emperor's subsequent fall meant that few of Napoleon's urbanistic ambitions were actually realized. His principal achievements were the initial section of the Rue de Rivoli (1.11), creation of the Place du Châtelet (1.4), and a handful of new public buildings and monuments that included the Bourse (2.8), the Madeleine (8.2), the remodelled Palais Bourbon (7.4) and of course the Arc de Triomphe (16.1, which was not completed until much later in the century). Much of Napoleon's efforts concerned sanitization of what was at best a malodorous and at worst a pestilential city, and it is thanks to him that Paris's current sewer network was begun and that its putrid inner-city graveyards were replaced by modern, hygienic cemeteries outside the then city walls (see the Cimetière du Père-Lachaise, 20.2). The unrealized plans drawn up at the emperor's behest would not go to waste, since it was they that inspired his nephew, Napoleon III, and Baron Haussmann in their thorough reconfiguration of Paris in the 1850s and 1860s.

The Napoleonic era was also a time of technological change, with new stone-cutting techniques, improved cements and greater use of iron changing the way buildings were constructed. Unlike in England, iron was scarce and expensive in early-19C France, which is why all-metal structures were uncommon before the 1840s; the Pont des Arts (see feature on Seine bridges) and the Bourse du Commerce (1.20) were precocious Parisian examples. It was also under Napoleon that Paris's canals were planned, notably the Canal Saint-Martin (which runs through today's 19th and 11th *arrondissements*), although, as with so many of the emperor's schemes, it was not until after his fall that they were actually realized.

Napoleon's defeats in 1814 and 1815 meant that, for the first time since the 15C, Paris was invaded. Deprived of any kind of fortification since the 17C, the city could offer no resistance. As a result, in the aftermath of the empire and in a continent that was becoming ever more politically unstable, calls began to be heard for the building of a new city wall around Paris. This project would not become reality until 1840–44, under Louis Philippe. Known as the Thiers fortifications after the minister who pushed them through parliament, the walls encircled the capital and its outlying villages with

Introduction 13

94 bastions and a 250 m-wide glacis. Their presence profoundly affected the city's future development, since not only did they encourage urbanization of the villages just inside their limits (which were formally made part of Paris in 1860), but they also rendered impossible any »organic« continuity with the hinterland beyond. Today the *boulevard périphérique* (see below) has taken their place, and consequently Paris still preserves a strange separateness and discontinuity in relation to its suburbs.

During the 30 odd years between the first and third Napoleons, the character of Paris's fabric, inherited almost intact from the *ancien régime*, began to change. Many of the city's former religious houses, which had been seized by the state and sold off during the Revolution, were demolished and redeveloped speculatively. A new building-type that flourished as a result was the covered arcade (see feature on arcades and passages), initially a phenomenon of spectacular success but superseded later in the century by the department store (see, e.g., 7.15, 9.9 and 9.10). Fashionable new districts such as the »Nouvelle Athènes« and the Quartier d'Europe went up in the city's northwestern sector around the Chaussée d'Antin (8th and 9th), while the east fell ever further from grace, the *hôtels particuliers* of the Marais being divided up into tenements and workshops. In the 1840s railways began to appear, thereby revolutionizing Paris's hinterland as new settlements and industrial installations grew up along the tracks, while the city *intra muros* added a new building type to its collection in the form of the railway terminus (see 8.5, 10.5, 10.7, 7.1 and 12.4). Indeed as the century wore on a whole host of other new public-building types began to appear in Paris: *mairies d'arrondissement* (see 10.3), libraries, post offices (see 1.19), bank headquarters (see 9.2 and 9.11) and, at the turn of the 20C, telephone exchanges (see 9.1). Factories also became a major component of the 19C townscape, but the post-industrial period of the late-20C has seen to it that very few Parisian examples now survive (see 13.4).

Architecture in the period between the two Napoleons was marked by the generalization of the apartment building, whose façades remained Classical but became ever more richly ornamented. Where churches were concerned, the neo-Classical tendencies initiated in the 18C were explored further in buildings such as Notre-Dame-de-Lorette (9.5) and Saint-Vincent-de-Paul (10.6), while at the same time a very hesitant Gothic revival began to make itself felt in France (e.g. Sainte-Clothilde, 7.3). France's medieval heritage, disdained throughout the 18C, suddenly found itself back in favour, and enormous restoration programmes were begun on edifices such as the Sainte-Chapelle, Notre-Dame and Saint-Denis. It was in this context that the French Historic Monuments Commission was founded and that modern notions of heritage and conservation were developed. The period was also noteworthy in matters of urbanism, thanks to the interventions of Claude-Philibert Barthelot, Comte de Rambuteau. Appointed Prefect of the Seine (head of the *département* that at the time included Paris in its territory) in 1833, he began implementing a series of improvements intended to decongest the capital's outmoded street network. Alignment policies were introduced, whereby projecting façades had to be demolished to ensure that streets were the same width all the way along, and in 1841 a law was passed allowing expropriation of property by the Prefect for the purposes of widening existing streets and knocking through new ones. But Rambuteau was hindered by a modest budget (unlike his successor, Baron Haussmann, he could not get the city into debt) and his actions were thus relatively limited: two new streets were opened up on the Ile de la Cité, while on the Right Bank the Rues Rambuteau and du Pont-Louis-Philippe, the Boulevard Morland and the first section of the Boulevard de Strasbourg were cut through.

In comparison to what followed, Rambuteau's interventions pale into insignificance. During Napoleon III's Second Republic (1848–52) and Second Empire (1852 to 1870), upheavals of a scale never seen before or since changed the old fabric of Paris beyond recognition. Victor Hugo's plaintive cry »Le vieux Paris n'est plus!« (»Old Paris is no more!«) was arguably a gross understatement. It was of course the notorious Baron Haussmann, appointed Prefect of the Seine in 1853, who was the driving force behind these momentous developments. But Haussmann could not have acted without the emperor's backing, nor without the new, pumped-up expropriation laws introduced by Napoleon III in 1852. This revised legal framework also made the operation financially viable, authorizing the municipality to expropriate the land at its pre-development market price and sell it again after development for a much higher sum. Indeed, as ever, finance was at the heart of the matter, since Napoleon III believed that in order for Paris to flourish economically its infrastructure would first have to be thoroughly overhauled. There was also the equally important matter of the remodelled city's representative power, since it was intended to reflect, amplify and legitimize the ascendancy of the regime responsible for its creation. Before becoming emperor, Napoleon III had spent much of his life in exile, including a period in London where he had admired the British capital's wide, pavemented streets, its gas lighting, its sewer network and its splendid parks and gardens. Surpassing London on all these counts was thus his goal. He also, at least to start with, aimed to do something about the plight of Paris's poor, initiating France's first social housing schemes (see the Cité Napoléon, 9.4). But ultimately his policy towards the less-privileged tended towards reliance on the trickle-down effect, and many of Haussmann's Parisian improvements were really acts of gentrification, slum neighbourhoods simply being demolished and the problem displaced elsewhere (generally to the outer, industrialized *arrondissements* or to the industrial areas springing up in the suburbs, such as at Saint-Denis).

The most notorious example of slum clearance occurred on the Ile de la Cité – site of some of the worst early-19C cholera outbreaks –, whose network of tiny medieval streets was entirely razed, slashing the island's population from 15,000 to just 5,000 inhabitants overnight. Demolishing the rookeries had the added advantage of wiping traditional centres of crime and civil unrest from the map.

At the basis of Haussmann's transformations was a thorough restructuring of Paris's traffic and sanitary organization. Before he came on the scene, the principal streets crossing the city from top to bottom and side to side where the Rues Saint-Jacques, Saint-Martin and Saint-Denis (north–south) and Saint-Antoine and Saint-Honoré (east–west), which, due to their extreme narrowness, were woefully inadequate for the volume of traffic they bore. Haussmann's first intervention was thus construction of the Grande Croisée (literally »Great Crossing«) which provided new, infinitely wider north–south and east–west axes in the form of the vastly extended Rue de Rivoli and the Boulevards de Strasbourg, Sébastopol, du Palais and Saint-Michel. The cross was boosted in its lateral sense by the quayside roadways, which were connected to the Croisée via the greatly enlarged Place du Châtelet. Through thoroughfares such as the aptly named Boulevard Haussmann, the Boulevard Saint-Germain and the Boulevard Henri-IV, the baron aimed to extend the network of historic boulevards out as far as the Place de l'Etoile (see 16.1) in the west and the Place de la Nation in the east on both sides of the Seine, creating, in tandem with the *boulevards extérieurs*, a system of concentric rings running round the capital. He was ultimately thwarted in his aim, however, most notably on the Left Bank where the Avenue Duquesne stops dead at the Rue Eblé, never having managed to link up with the Boulevard des Invalides because of the presence of an aristocratic property that even expropriation could not touch. To link the rings together and provide rapid cross-town access, diagonals such as the Avenue de l'Opéra, the Boulevard Raspail and the Boulevard Voltaire were opened up. It was not just slum neighbourhoods that disappeared in the path of these broad new boulevards, large chunks of aristocratic and bourgeois Paris also falling to the demolition man's hammer (a few of the choice spoils ending up at the Musée Carnavalet, 3.1). On the sanitary front, Haussmann's interventions included the expulsion of Paris's abattoirs and other polluting activities from the city centre to the periphery (see 19.6 and 19.7), and a thorough reconfiguration of its water and drainage systems. Although the first Napoleon had made efforts to expand Paris's sewer network, the city remained woefully under-equipped, and consequently, under Haussmann's direction, the engineer Eugène Belgrand constructed hundreds of new kilometres of drains (by 1878 it was calculated that the city possessed some 600 km of sewers, compared to only 20 km at the turn of the 19C). Haussmann and Belgrand also saw to it that capacity of the city's water-supply system was greatly expanded to meet the ever-increasing demand.

Much of Haussmann and Napoleon III's œuvre was an attempt to monumentalize Paris into an imperial capital, whence the taste for imposing structures placed at junctions and the end of road axes, such as the Palais Garnier (9.13), Sainte-Trinité (9.7), Saint-Augustin (8.6), and the Tribunal du Commerce (see 4.1). The new boulevards were aggrandized by the extremely strict façade regulations that governed the apartment buildings erected along them (see feature on Parisian housing 1400–1900), measures which, despite the monotony they often produced, were intended to bring dignified imperial consistency to the cityscape rather than mere uniformity. With the boulevards came wide pavements, at the time something of a novelty in the French capital, which added a host of new street furniture to the gas lighting that had begun to appear in the 1840s (see feature on street furniture). Parks and gardens were also a major component of Haussmannian Paris, the most notable examples being the remodelled Bois de Boulogne (29.1) and de Vincennes (34.1), the Parc Monceau (8.9) and the Parc des Buttes-Chaumont (19.2). Where official architecture was concerned, the era produced the »style Napoléon-III«, of which the Palais Garnier was by far the most celebrated example, although the Sénat's Salle des Conférences (see 6.8) and the Louvre-Tuileries super-palace were also noteworthy. Railways, population growth and ever-burgeoning commerce gave rise to the grand, luxury hotel, whose interiors imitated the ostentation of official taste (see 9.12). With the creation of the Boulevard Malesherbes and the Avenue de l'Impératrice (today Avenue Foch), residential development was encouraged along the Avenue des Champs-Elysées and to its north on the Plaine Monceau. These areas attracted the wealthy and the ruling classes, who, aping the imperial taste for opulent display, produced buildings such as the Hôtels de la Païva (8.13) and Jacquemart-André (8.8). Meanwhile, the outer *arrondissements* (bar the rich 16th and 17th) became ever more industrialized.

Paris as we know it today is the direct product of Haussmann and Napoleon III's vision, all subsequent development having been coloured by their decisions. The model of urbanity they produced, developed from the French Classical tradition, was subsequently exported the world over. Despite Haussmann's reputation for destruction, his interventions caused more to be built than was torn down. Between 1853 and 1870, 27,500 houses and apartment buildings, representing some 117,000 dwellings, were demolished, but in their stead 102,500 new buildings, representing some 215,000 dwellings, went up. Until the automobile explosion of the last 30 years, Haussmann's boulevards managed to absorb all Paris's traffic needs, although the error of leaving the Halles Centrales in the city centre was long regretted for the traffic jams it produced.

The Second Republic and Second Empire also saw the flowering of the age of iron in Paris, a material that was for a long time viewed with suspicion and considered fit only for »industrial« use. Hence iron's most spectacular incursions in the capital, outside of factories, were limited to utilitarian structures such as Eugène Flachat's record-breaking Gare Saint-Lazare (8.5) or Victor Baltard's celebrated Halles Centrales (see 1.22 and 19.6). Henri Labrouste, however, managed to introduce iron into a more »noble« building in his Bibliothèque Sainte-Geneviève (5.6), and as a result secured himself the commission for the iron-vaulted Bibliothèque Nationale (2.4). Theatres had long used iron for its fire resistance (see 1.16), and even a seemingly all-lapidary palace such as the Opéra Garnier was in fact constructed using an iron frame. Meanwhile, iron made a surprisingly bold eruption into ecclesiastical architecture in the form of Saint-Eugène (9.3) and was again used by Baltard at Saint-Augustin; Notre-Dame-du-Travail (14.1), however, would turn out only to be a curiosity, in part because reinforced concrete afterwards superseded iron as the preferred technology of the French construction industry. Commerce latched on to the potential of metallic construction with buildings like Au Printemps (9.9) and Société Générale's *agence centrale* (9.11). The apogee of the Parisian iron age was reached at the 1889 Exposition Universelle with two new record breakers: the fabled Galerie des Machines (Dutert and Contamin, destroyed) and, of course, the Eiffel Tower (7.8).

In 1870, at the fall of the Second Empire, Paris and its hinterland counted 1,850,000 souls, a figure that had risen to the 2-million mark by 1877 and rocketed thereafter. The population of Paris *intra muros* reached its height on the eve of WWI, when just under 3 million people were squeezed into the city's boundaries. With its suburbs the figure reached over 9.3 million, making the Paris region the world's third largest city at the time, after London and New York. While the capital *intra muros* was subject to the strict urban regulations of Haussmann and his successors, the suburbs sprang up entirely without any planning or control. Urbanistically the period was marked by the rebuilding of the monuments destroyed during the 1871 Commune (see 1.1, 1.8, 4.11 and 7.1), the continuation of Haussmann's unexecuted plans (some new streets not being completed till the 1920s), the construction of social housing (see 6.10 and 15.4), and the building of the Paris Métro (see feature on the Métro and the RER). Architecturally, besides the overwrought neo-Renaissance and crashing, Garnier-inspired neo-Baroque of many apartment buildings, theatres and official and commercial edifices (see, e.g., 2.5, 2.6, 4.11, 7.1, 8.14 and 8.15), the period saw the advent of Art Nouveau, which, in Paris at any rate, was more question of decoration than of architecture *per se* (an exception being the Samaritaine, 1.5). One of Art Nouveau's greatest French exponents was Hector Guimard, who amongst other Parisian buildings left us the Castel Béranger (16.11), his own *hôtel particulier* (16.14) and, of course, his world-famous Métro entrances. Where ecclesiastical architecture was concerned, the late-19C saw the fashion for Romano-Byzantine historicism, as exemplified by the Sacré-Cœur (18.2; see also 12.12, 16.3 and 17.2). But, with hindsight, the Belle Epoque's most significant development was the invention of reinforced concrete, which, at least initially, was an entirely French affair. Amongst the pioneers of this new building method were the engineer and constructor François Hennebique and the architects Anatole de Baudot (Saint-Jean-de-Montmartre, 18.4), Auguste Perret (Rue-Franklin apartment building, 16.8, Théâtre des Champs-Elysées, 8.12), Paul Guadet (*hôtel particulier*, 16.17), and Stephen Sauvestre (factory building and bridge at the Chocolaterie Menier, 36.6).

Paris since WWI
Where the Paris region's demographics are concerned, the last 90 years have witnessed a phenomenon of population loss in the city *intra muros* – 2.9 million in 1921, 2.7 million in 1965 and 2,152,000 in 1990 – and massive population growth in the city's suburbs and hinterland: the immediate suburbs (known as the *petite couronne*) now count 6.1 million inhabitants, while a further 2.7 million are to be found in the wider hinterland (the *grande couronne*). In the interwar period, while Paris proper stagnated, the suburbs literally exploded: where, in the period 1850–1914, c. 3,000 ha of land had been developed, in the ten years from 1920–30 over 15,000 ha of countryside (twice the surface area of Paris *intra muros*) were swallowed up by building, without any masterplan to oversee the process. The depressing sprawl that characterizes much of Paris's hinterland today was the result. Amongst the newly developed areas were industrial suburbs such as Boulogne-Billancourt (see 29.6) and Issy-les-Moulineaux.

In Paris, the major urbanistic development was the demolition of the 19C fortifications, which were replaced with a ring of social housing, parks and sports facilities (see the Cité Universitaire, 14.8). Where architecture was concerned, the period was of course marked by the emergence of the Modern Movement and the development of the International Style. Concrete was the miracle material that inspired much of the era's architectural invention, as well as becoming one of the staple building materials of the industrial sector. Where the architectural *avant garde* was concerned, the two key players on the Parisian scene were Perret, who built what was probably the world's first raw-concrete church (Notre-Dame du Raincy, 35.1) and also developed a highly original »concrete Classicism« (see, e.g., 13.12, 16.6 and 16.9), and, of course, Le Corbusier. As the city where he was based, Paris is particularly rich in Corbusian buildings and possesses some of the most famous, including the Villa Savoye (25.2), the Villa Stein-de Monzie (31.1), the Pavillon Suisse (14.10) and the Maisons Jaoul (26.2). Other Parisian Modernists of the inter-war period included Robert Mallet-Stevens (16.2 and 16.12), Pierre Chareau (7.17) and Jean Ginsberg (16.15 and 16.16). But the mass of building in the French capital remained essentially conservative, either reproducing the heavy Classicism of the Belle Epoque or dressing up 19C building types in jazz-age streamlining (1.5, 2.10, 8.11) or Classically inspired, moderne garb (7.6, 12.13, 16.4, 16.7 and 29.5).

Thanks to General von Choltitz, who could not bring himself to carry out Hitler's order to destroy Paris, the city emerged from WWII more or less intact. Much of the rest of France had not been so lucky, however, and a general reconstruction plan was drawn up, which also took into account the Paris region's future development. The 1950s were the era of zoning projects in the capital's hinterland that included the *grands ensembles* (vast Modernist housing estates) and the business district of La Défense (27.1). Then, in 1965, a proper masterplan was at last drawn up for the Ile-de-France: the Schéma Directeur d'Aménagement et d'Urbanisme. One of its most significant recommendations was the creation of five new towns encircling the capital (see Marne-la-Vallée, 36.1), which have gone on to absorb 55% of the region's population growth in the last quarter century. The 1960s and 1970s were also a time of huge transport developments programmed by General de Gaulle's government to make the agglomeration work logistically. They included the suburban train network, the RER (see feature on the Métro and the RER), the urban ring motorway known as the *boulevard périphérique*, the *voies express* running along the banks of the Seine in central Paris, several motorways radiating out of the capital to link it to the provinces, and of course the city's two major airports, of which the first was Orly in the south (Henri Vicariot, 1957–61) and the second Roissy Charles-de-Gaulle in the north (22.1). Today transport has become a major headache for the region, with saturated airports (there is talk of building a third one but nobody can agree on where to put it), congested roads (17 million car journeys are made per day in Paris and the Ile-de-France, compared with 3.5 million in 1960), and equally congested public transport: during rush hours in the capital, 80% of journeys are assured by the RATP and the SNCF. As a result of the exponentially growing traffic, pollution has become a significant issue in the region.

As far as Paris *intra muros* is concerned, the central part of the city remains today essentially as it was in the 19C, apart from the redevelopments of Beaubourg (see 4.15) and Les Halles (see 1.22). Half of Paris's current housing stock dates from the period 1850–1914, against a third built since 1945. It is the city's peripheral *arrondissements* that have changed the most, their redevelopment having been the result either of the renewal of sub-standard 19C housing or of post-industrial clean-up and land reclamation. Large swathes of the 13th, 15th, 19th and 20th *arrondissements* were comprehensively redeveloped in the 1970s and 1980s, while the last two decades have witnessed redevelopment of the former Citroën factories in the 15th (see, e.g., the Parc André-Citroën, 15.8), creation of the Parc de La Villette (19.7) and related projects on the site of former abattoirs in the city's north, and the enormous ZACs

Bercy (12.7) and Paris-Rive-Gauche (13.2) in the east. In tandem with this rebuilding programme came the renovation of Paris's historic *quartiers*, the most spectacular transformation taking place in the Marais, whose restoration was begun in the 1960s when the then culture minister, André Malraux, declared the area a conservation zone. Unlike London, Paris has remained subject to firm building-height restrictions, at least where the city centre is concerned; towards the periphery the rules were frequently bent in the 1960s and 1970s for projects such as La Défense and the redevelopment of the outer *arrondissements*. The most notorious waiver concerned the Tour Montparnasse (15.1), whose central positioning provoked a public outcry. Since the presidency of the resolutely anti-tower Valéry Giscard d'Estaing, however, there have been no more waivers (the case of the Institut du Monde Arabe, 5.13, is particularly revealing). Devolution of power in 1977, which gave Paris an elected mayor and greater control of its own destiny, has helped produce an ever-increasing complication of building regulations in the city (see, e.g., 20.3).

Architecture throughout this period has been characterized by its internationalism; buildings are much less region- and city-specific than ever before, although the weight of the past in Paris is so strong that the city has been able to absorb this development without losing anything of its very specific character. The last 50 years in France have of course been dominated by Modernism and all its variations and fall-out effects. One of the more minor strands in Paris was Brutalism, which, although it arguably originated in the French capital with buildings like Le Corbusier's Maisons Jaoul and Maison du Brésil (14.9), had much more impact elsewhere. The brave new »High«-Modernist era of the 1950s and 1960s produced such politically or technically utopian Parisian schemes as the UNESCO building (7.10), the C.N.I.T. (27.3), Jussieu (5.12), the Parc des Princes (16.18), the C.A.F. building (15.11), and Oscar Niemeyer's French Communist Party Headquarters (19.1), as well as spawning the towers of La Défense and Montparnasse and countless boring, banal, horizontally accented, balconied apartment buildings. Since the late 1970s, the reaction against High Modernism (whose excesses were both celebrated and deliciously sent up in Jacques Tati's 1967 film *Playtime*, set in an *après*-Plan-Voisin Paris) has taken the form of increased respect for the 19C Haussmannian city. This change of heart was in large part triggered by the much-lamented destruction of Baltard's iron pavilions at Les Halles. Where housing was concerned, one of the most talked-about products of this shift in sensibility was Christian de Portzamparc's Rue-des-Hautes-Formes social-housing scheme (13.10), which proposed an alternative to the slab blocks and towers with which the 13th *arrondissement* had up till then been redeveloped. In the decade that followed a certain school of municipality-commissioned, vaguely Purist-inspired architecture began to emerge, characterized by its orthogonal, formal com-

Introduction 17

plexity and ubiquitous white tiling. Postmodernism in its kitsch, revivalist forms had relatively little impact in France, apart from the phenomenon that was Ricardo Bofill and his gigantic neo-Classical housing schemes (see 14.2 and 36.2). The search for an alternative to the High-Modernist slab block that would work in the Haussmannian context, coupled with the ever-increasing complexity of Parisian building regulations, has produced some very inventive, context-conscious apartment buildings over the last 20 years: examples include Architecture Studio's Rue-du-Château-des-Rentiers social housing (13.9) and Rue-de-l'Orillon sheltered housing (11.2), Renzo Piano's Rue-de-Meaux social housing (19.14), Massimiliano Fuksas's Candie-Saint-Bernard redevelopment (11.6), a trio of apartment buildings from Frédéric Borel (11.3, 20.1 and 20.5), Herzog & de Meuron's Rue-des-Suisses social-housing scheme (14.13) and Michel Bourdeau's »Couple-Plus« building (20.3).

Perhaps, as some would have it, in substitution for the West's declining religions, and certainly in response to the increased leisure time that much of society now enjoys, the late-20C has seen the inexorable rise of the museum and related cultural institutions, with maybe nowhere embracing this vogue quite as much as Paris. The first big project was of course the Centre Georges Pompidou (4.15) in the 1970s, which was followed in the next decade by the Musée d'Orsay (7.1), the gargantuan Grand Louvre (1.8), the Institut du Monde Arabe, the Fondation Cartier (14.4), the Cité des Sciences (19.10), and the American Center (12.9). After this frenzy of museum-building, the 1990s were inevitably a bit quieter, but still produced the revamped Musée Guimet (16.5) and the as-yet-uncompleted Musée du Quai-Branly (7.7). This rash of cultural construction of course reflected the tourist industry's significance for Paris, whose importance was both boosted and underlined by the siting of EuroDisney (36.7) in the region. The latest addition to the museum club will be the Musée Pinault (29.7) in Boulogne-Billancourt. Many of the aforementioned museums were part of the state-driven programme of »grands projets« launched by President Mitterrand's socialist government in 1981, which also included the Grande Arche de La Défense (27.4), the Opéra Bastille (12.1), the Ministère des Finances (12.5), the Cité de la Musique (19.5) and the highly controversial Bibliothèque Nationale de France (13.3). Although the architectural impact of these »grands projets« was limited, their potency as symbols of urban renewal was undeniable. In this same vein, and as a city with world-class pretensions, Paris could not remain indifferent to the late-20C phenomenon of the international architectural star system, and consequently now displays its own collection of signature projects by architects such as Tadao Ando (7.11), Frank Gehry (the American Center), Richard Meier (15.10), Bernard Tschumi (19.7 and 36.4) and, although one might not at first realize it, Norman Foster, who designed the city's bus shelters (see feature on street furniture). Regular star contributors have included Renzo Piano and the home-grown talents of Jean Nouvel and Christian de Portzamparc. Another late-20C cultural phenomenon has been the transformation of professional sport into a global entertainment industry, which in Paris produced the giant stadia that are the Parc des Princes and the Stade de France (21.1).

One of the strands of Modernism that has caught the attention of both France's architects and its public alike is Hi-tech. In Paris, it is the Hi-tech preference for glass as an essential building material that seems to have most attracted designers. This interest can be traced back to the 1950s, in projects like the C.N.I.T. and the C.A.F with their translucent curtain walls, and was of course boosted by the experimentation in all-glass façades in the skyscrapers of La Défense. The 1980s saw the development of bravura cable-tensed glass structures, pioneered in the greenhouses of the Cité des Sciences and in the Louvre pyramid. The dream of minimum structure and maximum glazing (famously codified in Mies van der Rohe's 1921 proposal for a skyscraper in Friedrichstraße, Berlin) has been actively pursued in late-20C Paris with buildings like the Institut du Monde Arabe, the Fondation Cartier, and the extremes of Dominique Perrault's Hôtel Industriel Berlier (13.5) and Bibliothèque-Nationale-de-France towers, and Francis Soler's colour-transfer-adorned apartment building in the ZAC Rive-Gauche (see 13.2). Even the king of PoMo himself, Ricardo Bofill, has gone in this direction with his Marché Saint-Honoré office block (1.14). The eastern part of the city, either side of the Seine, is now being redeveloped along all-glass lines, giving rise to a crystal citadel that contrasts strangely with the plaster and stone metropolis of the centre and west. Perhaps this vogue for lean structure and maximum glazing is only a product of the region's history: this is, after all, where the skeletal stone-and-glass marvel of Gothic architecture was developed, 800 years before.

1st *arrondissement*

1.1 Palais de la Cité, today Palais de Justice
Boulevard du Palais
Earliest extant buildings begun c. 1240
(Métro: Cité, Pont Neuf; RER: Saint-Michel Notre-Dame)

What better place to begin a guide to Paris than here, a site continuously occupied since the Parisii tribe of Celts first settled on the Ile de la Cité (4.1), around 250 BC, and which has been of the foremost historical importance to both Paris and France for over 1,000 years? Geographically and politically, the Ile de la Cité was the heart of Paris, and the Palais, as the seat of government, was the city's secular nerve centre. Recurrently added to and rebuilt from the 11C AD right up until the early-20C, today's Palais de la Cité is an extraordinary palimpsest, a fascinating *mélange* of medieval, Louis-Seize, Second-Empire and Third-Republic buildings.

1.1 Palais de la Cité, today Palais de Justice. Engraving by Boisseau, 17C

Origins of the Palais
Information on this site prior to the 11C AD is scant, but we know that during the period of Roman occupation the governor's residence was established here. Flavius Claudius Julianus, governor of Gaul from 355 until 360 AD (when he was proclaimed Roman Emperor by his troops on the Ile de la Cité), mentions the Palais in the very brief description he left of the island, and a painted room and fragments of capitals from the Roman period were uncovered during building work at the Palais in 1845. After the fall of the Roman Empire and throughout the Dark Ages, the governor's residence was occupied by the local rulers. Clovis (reigned 481 to 511), founder of the Frankish kingdom and father of the Merovingian dynasty, made the Palais the seat of his realm. After his death, it lost its pre-eminence, a result of the division of the kingdom between his sons, although it retained its royal status. The incestuous infighting of the Merovingians eventually led to their fall and the rise of the Carolingian Empire, in the second half of the 8C, when the power base moved to Aachen. It was not until 987, when the Comte de Paris, Hugues Capet, was elected king of France, that Paris and the Palais once more became of central political importance. Capet established his advisory body, the Curia Regis, in the Palais, as well as various departments of his administration.

The medieval Palais
Capet was succeeded by his son, Robert II the Pious (reigned 996–1031), who carried out extensive building work at the Palais in the early 11C. At this time the edifice consisted essentially of a quadrilateral castle defended by round towers. Robert's successors each added elements to the Palais, none of which survives today: Louis VI the Fat (reigned 1108–37) built the Chapelle Saint-Nicolas and rebuilt the keep, Louis VII (reigned 1137–80) added an oratory and built a church just outside the palace walls, while Philippe II Augustus (reigned 1180–1223) carried out considerable restoration and embellishment work. Philippe also made the Palais his more or less permanent home, fixing the court there and breaking with the itinerancy that had characterized his ancestors' reigns. It was Louis IX (reigned 1226–70, later canonized as Saint Louis) who built the earliest of today's surviving structures, the Sainte-Chapelle (which replaced the Chapelle Saint-Nicolas), and who was probably also responsible for the Tour Bonbec. Extraordinary when built and still astonishing today, the Sainte-Chapelle is one of France's most important surviving medieval edifices, and thus has its own separate entry in this guide (see 1.2). The Tour Bonbec is the westernmost of the four medieval towers that punctuate the Palais's northern façade, and for centuries was infamous because of the torture chamber it contained (»bon bec« means »good beak« – torture would make you open your beak, i. e. confess). Heavily restored and raised by one storey in the 19C, today's tower has little in common with the 13C original. Of Louis IX's other extensive additions to the Palais, nothing now remains.

Philippe IV the Fair (reigned 1285–1314) was as prolific in his modifications to the Palais as Saint Louis, and substantial parts of his buildings survive today. Work was carried out under the direction of his chamberlain, Enguerrand de Marigny, who was charged with rebuilding the main *logis* containing the king's quarters. The centrepiece of Marigny's interventions was the impressive Grand-Salle (c. 1302–15), which was the Palais's principle banqueting hall, a huge chamber covered by two parallel pointed wooden barrel vaults and decorated with wooden statues of the kings of France. Destroyed by fire in 1618, the Grand-Salle, which was situated at first-floor level, was rebuilt as today's Salle des Pas Perdus (see below). The original ground-floor level buildings that supported the Grand-Salle still stand, however. They are guarded on the Palais's northern façade by the twin Tours d'Argent and de César, which together form an ensemble of distinctly forbidding aspect. Immediately behind the towers is what is known as the Salle des Gardes, a vaulted chamber heavily, and heavy-handedly, restored in the 19C. The capitals of its central pillar are thought to represent the mythic lovers Héloïse and Abélard. Leading off the Salle des Gardes is the famous Salle des Gens d'Armes, which sits immediately under the Salle des Pas Perdus. 64 m long by 27.5 m wide and rising 9 m to the apex of its stone vaults, this is Europe's largest surviving medieval-period chamber, built as a refectory for the 2,000 members of the palace staff. It is much darker today than when first completed, the windows on its southern side having been blocked by the addition of later buildings, while those on its northern and western walls are partially obscured because of the rise in ground level engendered by construction of the Quai de l'Horloge in 1580–1610. The Salle's quadripartite vaults are divided into nine bays longitudinally and four bays laterally and are supported on solid round piers decorated with foliage capitals, except the central row, which was heavily reinforced in the 19C (and consequently lost its original capitals) after one of the vaults collapsed in 1812. (The old Grand-Salle was vaulted in wood, but its replacement following the 1618 fire was vaulted in stone, the weight of which eventually proved too much for the medieval structure underneath.) Despite the clumsiness of the reinforced piers, the Salle des Gens d'Armes appears remarkably airy, and the ensemble effect of its forest of piers and soaring ribs is impressive. The rather unfortunate row of supports running in front of the eastern section of the Salle's northern wall was installed in the 19C to hold up the monumental staircase in the Salle des Pas Perdus. Set into the Salle's massive walls, the four huge fireplaces that originally heated it can be seen.

The Conciergerie

The part of the Palais comprising the Salle des Gardes and the Salle des Gens d'Armes is known as the Conciergerie, after the *concierge* (literally »warden«), whose original role as palace intendant increased over the centuries to include administration of justice over those living within the Palais's walls. The Conciergerie consequently came to be used as a prison, and later proved especially useful for holding detainees prior to their judgement by the Paris Parlement, which sat in the Grand-Chambre upstairs (the Parisian and provincial *parlements* constituted the chief judicial authority in France under the *ancien régime*). By the time of the 1776 fire, which destroyed a significant section of the Palais (see below), the Conciergerie's cells were old and dilapidated. As part of the rebuilding programme following the fire, they were entirely remodelled by Jacques-Denis Antoine and Pierre Desmaisons, and can still be seen immediately to the south of the Salle des Gens d'Armes. During the Revolution, the Conciergerie became especially infamous, serving as a detention area for the Revolutionary Tribunal. The Salle des Gens d'Armes was used as a communal jail for those who could not afford to pay for incarceration in the cells,

1.1 Palais de la Cité, today Palais de Justice

while the latter welcomed, amongst others, Charlotte Corday, Marie-Antoinette and Robespierre. Most prisoners did not stay long; the carts that took the condemned to the guillotine left from the Palais's Cour du Mai (see below), from which entry to the Conciergerie was originally gained.

The Palais under Jean the Good

Immediately north of the Salle des Gens d'Armes is the one remaining storey of the enormous medieval kitchens installed by Jean II the Good sometime around 1350. Located directly on the river, thereby facilitating the arrival of produce, the kitchens originally rose two floors, the upper level serving the Grand-Salle and the lower level the Salle des Gens d'Armes. Square in plan, the lower-level kitchen is covered by quadripartite vaulting and contains four giant hooded fireplaces, one in each corner, an arrangement common in the kitchens of medieval castles. What is unusual here is that the chimney hoods are each supported by a sort of flying buttress linking them to the nearest pier. Jean II was also responsible for the Tour de l'Horloge, the rectangular tower that defends the corner of the Palais at the intersection of the Boulevard du Palais and the Quai de l'Horloge. It is a good deal taller than its elder sisters, suggesting that it was intended as a watchtower. The original *horloge* (clock) after which it was named was installed by Jean's son, Charles V, in 1370, and was Paris's first public timepiece. It was replaced in 1585 by the current clock (which retains its 16C mechanism), the work of Germain Pilon.

Jean the Good's reign, which was dominated by the Hundred Years' War, would prove decisive for the Palais's destiny. In 1356, Jean was captured by the English at the battle of Poitiers; his son Charles was left to assume control in his stead and to raise the enormous ransom. The Parisian middle classes, who had been paying for the war through ever-increasing taxes levied by the crown, rose in revolt against a regime that itself paid nothing and, to boot, had been defeated. Events took a bloody turn in 1358 when an armed crowd, led by Etienne Marcel, leader of the city's mer-

20 1st *arrondissement*

chants, invaded the Palais, killed the Dauphin's two unpopular advisers in front of him, and forced him to wear the red-and-blue Parisian cap, while Marcel himself donned the Dauphin's own hat. Although circumstances subsequently turned against Marcel, who was killed by the mob later that year, Charles never forgot his humiliation and, on becoming king, forsook the Palais for the Louvre (1.8) and the Hôtel Saint-Pol (destroyed). Jean the Good was thus the last sovereign to reside in the Palais.

The Palais from the late-14C to the mid-18C
No longer the seat of the monarchy, the Palais nonetheless remained home to the judiciary, and it was this role that shaped its subsequent development. The Palais at this time was also home to the Chambre des Comptes (treasury) and the chancellery, as well as to various other departments of the royal administration. Successive monarchs added to and embellished the Palais between the 14C and 17C, generally to supply much-needed space to the ever-growing official bureaucracy. Nothing survives from this period, swept away either by fires or by the 19C rebuilding (see below), but it is worth mentioning Louis XII's redecoration of the Grand-Chambre, in 1502, whose elaborate, pendanted ceiling was so thoroughly gilded that the room became known as the Chambre Dorée (golden chamber). In the 19C, the memory of this room would inspire the current Première Chambre Civile (see below). We should also mention Henri IV's sacrifice of the Palais's garden – which formerly occupied the western tip of the island beyond the Palais's walls and which, in medieval times, had supplied the king's table – for the creation of the Place Dauphine (1.3), in 1607. Finally, it is worth giving a brief description of the Palais's external aspect during this period so that subsequent developments can be put into context. The diverse buildings that made up the Palais occupied only a part of its current site, the southern flank of the island still containing streets and houses. The thoroughfare that would become the Boulevard du Palais did not follow today's straight path, but wiggled irregularly and was fronted on its Palais side by houses, amongst which nestled two fortified medieval gatehouses accessing the palace complex. Behind this sheltering wall of dwellings was a large open space, the Palais's courtyard, which was partially divided in two by the protruding bulk of the Sainte-Chapelle. The southern section of this space, today closed off and known as the Cour de la Sainte-Chapelle, was flanked to the west by the Chambre des Comptes and to the south by further houses, while the northern part of the courtyard, known as the Cour du Mai after the May-Day ceremonies performed there every year, was delimited by the Sainte-Chapelle and the Trésor des Chartes (the crown archives) to the south, the Grand-Salle to the north, and the Galerie Mercière to the west. The Galerie Mercière, originally built to link the king's apartments to the Sainte-Chapelle, had become the principal entrance to the Palais, accessed via a grand staircase leading off the Cour du Mai. Behind the Galerie stood Louis VI's keep, as well as various structures disposed around courtyards and stretching as far as the Rue de Harlay. The river frontage was cadenced by the medieval towers already described, between which nestled diverse buildings of mostly undistinguished aspect.

Following the 1618 fire that destroyed the Grand-Salle, Queen Marie de Médicis charged her preferred architect, Salomon de Brosse, to rebuild the chamber (now the Salle des Pas Perdus). Completed in 1626, Brosse's *salle* was itself badly damaged in the fire of 1871 (see below), and what we see today is a reconstruction of the original. Built above the Salle des Gens d'Armes and therefore of the same enormous dimensions, Brosse's *salle* remained faithful to the spirit of its Gothic predecessor, and is divided longitudinally into two barrel-vaulted halves by a row of columns, just as Philippe the Fair's chamber had been. Where the original vaults had been in wood, those of the new *salle* were in stone, pierced by oculi and enclosing sizeable fanlights in their tympana. The walls and piers supporting them are dressed up as a Doric arcade, and the impressively august result appears very Roman, both in its size and in its cold and rather severe grandeur.

The 18C rebuilding of the Palais
In 1776, another fire broke out, this time destroying the old Galerie Mercière and its surrounding structures. The disaster was used as a pretext to speed up a general rebuilding plan, and large sections of the old fabric, including the ravaged Galerie and Louis VI's keep, were demolished. Reconstruction was carried out by three architects – Jacques-Denis Antoine, Guillaume-Martin Couture and Pierre Desmaisons – in 1782–86. As well as the remodelled Conciergerie, mentioned above, the Cour du Mai was entirely rethought and regularized, and took on the form we see today. The buildings fronting the courtyard were demolished so that it was now open on its boulevard side and separated from the street only by a magnificent wrought-iron gateway, designed by Desmaisons and the ironsmith Bigonnet. The Galerie Mercière was rebuilt on its old site with a new grand staircase but, in place of its former, rather picturesque façade, it now wore an august Doric portico, which bore no pediment but was surmounted by a sizeable attic, the latter coiffed with a bulbous *toit à l'impériale*. Furthermore, lower, lateral wings, dressed on their boulevard façades with the same Doric order as the portico, closed the courtyard on both its northern and southern sides, thereby rudely obscuring the Sainte-Chapelle's northern elevation. Construction of this southern wing had also necessitated demolition of the Trésor des Chartes, which had mirrored the Sainte-Chapelle in miniature to its north. Its destruction was carried out despite the fact that it had escaped the fire untouched, and despite protests from the Sainte-Chapelle's canons, who cited the building's antiquity and historical interest in its defence.

The Revolution and the 19C rebuilding of the Palais
If the *ancien régime* was capable of such indifference to its Gothic heritage, the Revolution proved even worse. To the revolutionaries' Enlightenment-educated eyes, a building such as the Sainte-Chapelle was to be thoroughly despised, representative only of the hated Catholic church that for centuries had tyrannized the country with its lurid superstition. The Sainte-Chapelle consequently suffered badly during this period, while the rest of the Palais slowly deteriorated from lack of upkeep. By the time of Napoleon's empire, the buildings were in very poor shape. It was not until the July Monarchy, however, that a renovation and enlargement programme was finally drawn up, by Jean-Nicolas Huyot. His death, in 1840, retarded its implementation, and Louis-Joseph Duc and Honoré Daumet (sometimes spelled »Dommey«) were subsequently commissioned to revise and execute the rebuilding plans. It was at this point that the Chambre des Comptes and other non-judicial state institutions still housed in the Palais were moved elsewhere, leaving the way clear for the development of the Palais de Justice as we know it today. Duc and Daumet's comprehensive reconstruction programme involved the demolition and replacement of the vast majority of the Palais's existing structures as well as extension of the complex to the south, for which the houses fronting the Quai des Orfèvres were to be destroyed. Another decade would go by before work actually started, due to interminable wrangles between the newly created Commission des Monuments Historiques, which advocated respect for the context of the Sainte-Chapelle, and the architects, who intended to obtain as much extra surface area as possible by reducing the size of the Palais's courtyards. Duc thought the contemporary »craze« for the Middle Ages »outmoded and ridiculous«, a view shared by the Conseil Général de la Seine, which was financing the project, whose members considered the exterior of the Sainte-Chapelle entirely »without interest«. After the *coup d'état* of 1852, the new regime lost no time imposing its view, which was on the side of the architects and, as of 1853, the latter gained a powerful ally in Baron Haussmann, for whom the rebuilding of the Palais was a major element in his reconfiguration of the Ile de la Cité as a whole.

Duc and Daumet's Palais de Justice was to be a rationally organized judicial machine, laid out on a rectilinear basis around internal courtyards. Too bad if older, less orderly elements got in the way. Already squashed up on one side against the southern Antoine-Couture-Desmaisons wing, the Sainte-Chapelle now found itself on its other side rather incongruously adrift in a courtyard of severe and utilitarian aspect, whose alignment took no account of the older building's orientation. The Grand-Salle was more easily incorporated into the masterplan, but required the installation of a massive staircase to link it to the Tribunal de Grande Instance (district court) to the north, which, as we have seen, necessitated the introduction of a rather unfortunate row of supports in the Salle des Gens d'Armes below.

The Tribunal de Grande Instance (TGI), which occupies the area above the Conciergerie between the Salle des Pas Perdus, the Tour de l'Horloge and the Tour César, was the first part of the new Palais to be completed, in 1859. In deference to the 13C elements framing its façades, and despite their hostility towards medievalist nostalgia, Duc and Daumet dressed up the TGI's regularly ordonnanced and rather banal elevations with various medievalizing elements: Gothic arches, heavy buttressing, stone mullions, pinnacled dormers and a tall, steep-pitched roof. The result is nonetheless rather dry. A similar formula was used for the short section of the Cour de Cassation (appeal court) that sits between the Tours d'Argent and Bonbec, although here with slightly more success. For the greater stretch of the Cour de Cassation that runs from the Tour Bonbec to the Rue de Harlay, Duc borrowed from French 17C and 18C sources, including the Louvre's Pavillon de l'Horloge which served as the model for the Cour's frontispiece. Where Duc and Daumet's work may sometimes have lacked sensitivity and inspiration, it was certainly not wanting in confidence, and nowhere is this more evident than in the Palais's Rue-de-Harlay façade, designed by Duc and inaugurated in 1869. The basic river elevations are carried round and repeated, but interrupted at their centre by a vast, nine-bay-wide *avant-corps*, whose general disposition Duc is said to have borrowed from the Temple of Dendera, in Egypt. His use of compressed arcades with engaged columns renders the composition flat, solid and rather stodgy in its monumentality. The detailing is eclectic, Italian-Renaissance motifs rubbing shoulders with Macedonian quotations, but the ensemble impresses more in its size than in its architectural qualities, as does the huge, full-height vestibule it encloses. Access to the vestibule is gained by a rather elephantine staircase that dominates the immediate foreground. If the presence of this imposing composition on such a narrow street seems surprising (and we should remember that, when the Rue-de-Harlay façade was completed, the eastern side of the Place Dauphine was still standing), it should be noted that Duc and Haussmann originally hoped to demolish the Place Dauphine and replace it with an open piazza. Had this plan been realized, Duc's composition would have dominated the riverscape for miles around.

Work on the Palais was in full swing when the Franco-Prussian War erupted, in 1870. Following the French defeat came the Paris Commune, one of the city's bloodiest periods. In addition to the thousands of human casualties, a good number of the capital's major public buildings were burned to the ground, including the Palais de Justice. Started in the Salle des Pas Perdus, the Communard fire quickly spread, destroying large sections of the Palais, including the newly finished Cour de Cassation. The vaults in the Salle des Pas Perdus collapsed along half their length, and the Salle des Gens d'Armes was only saved because a water tank

belle-époque façade is remarkable only for the oversized medievalizing tower marking its western extremity. With the completion of this wing ended the enormous rebuilding programme, after 50 years' work and expenditure of over 60 million francs, an astronomical figure in the currency of the day.

The Palais today
Covering a total of 5 ha and containing over 24 km of galleries and corridors, the Palais de Justice is currently frequented by around 15,000 people daily. Despite its immense dimensions, it is too small, and no less than four annexes have already been opened at sites all over Paris. Working conditions in the Palais are difficult, it no longer conforms to fire and building regulations, and a great deal of time is wasted travelling to and from the different annexes. At the end of 1999, the government announced its remedy: Paris's Tribunal de Grande Instance (TGI) is to be transferred from the Palais to a new *cité judiciaire*, scheduled for inauguration in 2006, which is to be built either at the ZAC Paris-Rive-Gauche (13.2) or in the 15th *arrondissement*. The departure of the TGI will allow the institutions remaining in the Palais room to breathe and expand and, once the transfer is complete, the old buildings will be entirely renovated and modernized. The Palais will remain home to the Cour de Cassation, France's highest appeal court, and will thus continue as the country's seat of justice, a role it has fulfilled for over one millennium.

1.2 Sainte-Chapelle
4, boulevard du Palais
Architect unknown, 1241(?)–48
(Métro: Cité; RER: Saint-Michel Notre-Dame)

Even amongst the other extraordinary achievements of the medieval period, the Sainte-Chapelle stands out, and its capacity to amaze remains undiminished after over seven-and-a-half centuries. It was an exceptional project commissioned by an exceptional man – the revered and popular Louis IX (reigned 1226–70), whose piety and Christian fervour ultimately resulted in his canonization, in 1297. Leader of the Seventh and Eighth Crusades, Louis attempted to establish the Capets as the foremost dynasty in Christendom, an ambition which prompted the purchase, in 1239, of what was believed to be the Crown of Thorns and other supposed relics of the Passion from the Byzantine emperor Baldwin II. Possession of the crown of the king of kings was intended to demonstrate the legitimacy of the Capetian line and its pre-eminence over other royal houses. Such a precious relic evidently required a suitable home, and to this end Louis ordered the demolition and rebuilding of the old Chapel of Saint Nicolas in the Palais de la Cité (today the Palais de Justice (see 1.1)). Begun sometime between 1241 and 1244, the Sainte-Chapelle was put up at astonishing speed and consecrated in 1248, the haste being due to Louis's impatience to embark on the Seventh Crusade. Besides its principal function of reliquary for the Crown

1.2 Sainte-Chapelle. After Decloux, *La Sainte Chapelle*, 1865

burst in the inferno, flooding the Palais's lower levels. Miraculously, the Sainte-Chapelle remained untouched.

Following the return to order, Duc and Daumet began the long rebuilding process, as well as continuing their expansion plans. As a result of the fire, most of the interiors we see today date from the Third Republic. One's impression moving round the Palais's circulatory spaces is of endless stone vaulted and colonnaded corridors disappearing off into infinity. The courtrooms were decorated in a heavy, rather overcharged French-Renaissance style, as was then fashionable for official commissions. Amongst them was the Première Chambre Civile, which replaced the old Grand-Chambre destroyed in the fire, for which Duc drew inspiration from the original 16C décor. Duc died in 1879, and Daumet carried on their work alone, although it was Daumet's successor, Albert Tournaire, who built the final phase of the new Palais – the Tribunal Correctionnel on the Quai des Orfèvres, erected in 1911–14. Tournaire's eclectic,

1st *arrondissement* 23

of Thorns, the Sainte-Chapelle was also conceived as the palace chapel of the king and the royal household.

To acquire the Crown of Thorns, Louis had paid the then-astronomical sum of 135,000 *livres*. The Sainte-Chapelle, by comparison, came cheap at only 40,000 *livres*. The name of its architect is not known with any certainty due to the total absence of documentation relating to its construction, and the craftsmen responsible for its adornment remain entirely anonymous. It was for a long time attributed to Pierre de Montreuil (designer, amongst others, of the southern-transept façade of Notre-Dame (see 4.2)), but alternative authors have since been proposed, namely Robert de Luzarches and Thomas de Cormont, whose work on Amiens Cathedral (1220s onwards) strongly resembles some aspects of the Sainte-Chapelle. We must also credit three further names for the building as we see it today: Félix Duban, Jean-Baptiste Lassus and Emile Boeswillwald, who successively conducted the massive restoration programme of 1836–63, the latter two seconded by Eugène Viollet-le-Duc. Indeed the Sainte-Chapelle is almost as much a 19C monument as it is a medieval one, so extensive was the damage it sustained over the centuries and hence so all-encompassing its renovation. Victim of several fires and also of flooding, the chapel suffered most during the Revolution when its sculptures were deliberately destroyed, its furnishings dispersed and the fabric neglected. Between the 1790s and the 1830s it served as a club room, a flour warehouse and as home to the archives judiciaires. By the time of the July Monarchy, the Sainte-Chapelle was in a pitiful state. Following the upheavals of France's recent past, Louis-Philippe's government attempted to reconcile the country with the legacy of the *ancien régime* and with the church. A whole campaign of restorations of châteaux and religious edifices was ultimately programmed, but, as an initial, pilot scheme, it was the Sainte-Chapelle that was undertaken. The first operation of its kind on this scale, work on the building was carried out with meticulous attention to detail, superb craftsmanship and, wherever possible, according to scrupulous archaeological principles. The lessons learnt along the way – and the craftsmen trained for the job – were put to good use in later renovation projects, including that of Notre-Dame.

Programmatic form and exterior design
In its essential programmatic form, the Sainte-Chapelle is derived from a palace-chapel type-standard that developed in the Middle Ages and which consisted of a two-storey structure containing an upper-level chapel for the nobles and a second, ground-floor chapel for the personnel. What made the Sainte-Chapelle distinctive was its added – and primary – role as a reliquary. Reliquaries were generally housed in crypts, but at the Sainte-Chapelle the shrine was placed in the king's chapel, on the upper storey. This choice was no doubt partly inspired by Louis's reluctance to hide his grade-1 relics in a dingy crypt, and also by a desire to establish

1.2 Sainte-Chapelle. Apse

a clear symbolic link between the king and Christ; indeed Louis's very personal association with the Sainte-Chapelle is illustrated by the fact that the upper chapel was originally accessed via a passageway connecting it directly to his private apartments. It was the Sainte-Chapelle's role as a shrine, moreover, that dictated both its physical form and decorative treatment: it was conceived to evoke on a monumental scale the work of goldsmiths and jewellers, whose gem-encrusted reliquary boxes were considered the highest form of church art by virtue of their association with saints and altars. These reliquary boxes were in turn inspired by religious architecture, and often resembled mini-chapels, complete with gabled arcades, pinnacles and roofs.

In its external aspect, the Sainte-Chapelle resembles just such a box, both in its proportions – the building is very compact, and, in relation to its length (36 m), is very tall (42.5 m to the roof ridgeline) – and in its ornamentation: the four bays of its nave are surmounted by richly decorated gables, like those found on Mosan shrines, as are the seven bays of its curved, east-end apse. The massive buttressing that characterizes the majority of vaulted buildings of the period (e.g., Notre-Dame) is absent from the Sainte-Chapelle; its regular buttresses, which set the rhythm of the exterior and give it a strong vertical emphasis, appear far too slender to impede the enormous lateral thrusts of the upper chapel's high vault. The secret of the Sainte-Chapelle's sturdiness and compactness and, as we shall see, of its extraordinary fenestration, is iron. A veritable system of »reinforced stone« was employed to hold the blocks in place, each course being clamped together with iron hooks. Furthermore, two courses of iron tie rods run round the upper chapel, bracing the entire structure, with further such rods located in the roof space above the vault.

Like most religious edifices of the period, the Sainte-Chapelle was intended both to reach up towards heaven and to evoke the heavenly Jerusalem, the paradise home of the saved following the Last Judgement. Thus the vertical thrust of its buttresses is continued by richly carved pinnacles, which form a sort of celestial city of towers, while its high, steep-pitched roof is surmounted by an elaborate spire rising 34 m above the ridgeline. Put up in 1853–55, this spire is the Sainte-Chapelle's fifth: the first two were rebuilt, the third was destroyed by fire while the fourth was dismantled during the Revolution. The current structure was designed by Lassus who, in the absence of detailed documentation on the Sainte-Chapelle's original *flèches*, produced a new design in the style of the 15C. Erection of his spire, which is constructed from cedar wood, was a considerable technical feat. The result is a great artistic success and magnificently captures the spiky spirit of Gothic forms. Encrusted with crockets, finials, gargoyles and angels, it is decorated at its base with sculptures of the twelve apostles, of which the face of Saint Thomas, the patron saint of architects, was modelled on Lassus.

As in most church buildings, the west end contains the principal entrance to the edifice. A two-storey, vaulted porch fronts the doorways to the upper and lower chapels, forming a transitional space between the secular world and the holy realm of the chapel. Both entrances are richly carved – the lower chapel's doorway is dedicated to the Virgin, while the upper-chapel portal depicts the Last Judgement – and date from the 19C, replacing originals destroyed in the Revolution. The upper portion of the west façade, rebuilt by Charles VIII in the decade 1485–95, is dominated by a 9 m-diameter rose window whose sinuous Flamboyant tracery replaced an earlier rose. It is surmounted by a balustrade whose supports take the form of fleurs-de-lis and which carries Charles VIII's monogram, flanked by kneeling angels. Either side of the west façade rise narrow staircase towers disguised, for most of their height, as buttresses. Only at their summits do they flower into monumental pinnacles, punctuating the composition, each one encircled by carvings of the royal crown of France and the Crown of Thorns. In comparison to the remainder of the elevation, the gable end is rather plain, pierced by a small rose, which lights the attic, surrounded by three blind quatrefoils. The balustrades, pinnacles and gargoyles adorning the summits of the Sainte-Chapelle date mostly from the 19C and replaced lost or badly worn originals.

Brief mention should also be made of the royal oratory, known anachronistically as the »Oratoire de Saint-Louis«, which occupies the space between the buttresses of the last bay of the nave's southern façade. Probably dating initially from the 14C, it is accessed from the upper chapel and is supported by a vaulted arch. In the early 16C its façade was remodelled in the form of a monumental gateway, with an imposing tracery-filled gable rising above the arch and a fleur-de-lis balustrade, which carries the crowned initial »L« (probably the monogram of Louis XII), coiffing the ensemble. The statue of the Virgin and Child between the gable and the balustrade, and the statues of Saint Louis and an anonymous bishop standing in elaborately carved niches either side of the arch, all date from the 19C.

The lower chapel
As with many Gothic buildings, the Sainte-Chapelle's exterior is to a large extent the logical product of its interior, which came foremost in the design process. More specifically, it was the interior of the upper chapel which took precedence over everything else, including, inevitably, the lower chapel. Indeed, structurally speaking, the lower chapel is nothing more than a vaulted support for the upper chapel, and is consequently rather incommodious. With its very low vault – only 6.6 m at the apex – and mean fenestration, which lets in little light, it strongly resembles a crypt. Given the proximity of the river, it must also have been extremely damp (indeed in the winter of 1689/90, the Seine burst its banks, flooding the lower chapel and causing considerable damage). Although only 10.7 m wide, the lower chapel is not spanned by a single vault but, presumably to provide a more solid base for the upper chapel and also to avoid dangerously shallow vaulting, is instead divided into a central nave with two very narrow side aisles. The vaults are supported by slender columns that carry not only the main-vault arcades but also the aisle-vault arches running along the exterior envelope. This envelope is in turn animated by a series of blind arcades, and the resulting forest of supports dazzles the eye, obfuscating the limits of the space and alleviating the sense of constriction. The columns' intricate crocket capitals constitute the principal sculptural decoration, although there are also elaborate braces that reinforce the aisle vaults against the thrust of the nave vault, helped in their task by exposed iron tie rods. Despite its tiny windows, the lower chapel is saved from oppressive gloominess by its sumptuous polychromy. The original paint scheme was almost entirely obliterated in the 1689/90 flood, and today's décor is the work of Boeswillwald and his team, who followed what little remained of the original but had for the most part to invent afresh. Rendered primarily in red, blue and gold, the ensemble effect is magnificent. The principal motifs are the royal fleur-de-lis and the castle-

tower emblem of Blanche de Castille, Louis IX's formidable mother. On the side-aisle walls are enamel-and-plaster medallions of the twelve apostles, each one adorned with paste jewels to simulate the decorative treatment of reliquary boxes.

The upper chapel
In contrast to the dinginess of the lower chapel, the upper chapel is breathtakingly luminous. The trend in Gothic church buildings to minimize structure and maximize fenestration here reached its apogee; the upper chapel features almost no walls and is constructed instead as a series of giant glazed arcades. Its vast windows, rising to 15.4 m in the nave, cover a surface area of over 650 m² (not including the rose), and, as the chapel is built as a single vessel, nothing obstructs their brilliance. Here we have the most accomplished and most extravagant expression in medieval architecture of the idea that »God is light«. No clumsy iron tie rods divulge the mystery of how the building stands up since they are dissimulated amongst the glazing bars of the windows, and simultaneously serve to strengthen the glazing against the wind. Like most Gothic church buildings, the upper chapel is very narrow (10.7 m) in relation to its height (20.5 m to the apex of the vault), producing an impression of soaring verticality which is all the more forceful thanks to the uninterrupted fenestration. In comparison to the complexity of cathedrals and churches, with their often multiple aisles, ambulatories and projecting chapels, the Sainte-Chapelle seems impressively simple and coherent, and must certainly rank as one of the formally purest of medieval Gothic structures. However, all is not as regular as it at first appears. Because narrower, the apse windows are almost 2 m shorter than those in the nave, a phenomenon both aggravated and in part dissimulated by the vault design. By maintaining the springing points of the radiating vault at the same level as those of the nave vaults, the chapel's architect achieved overall unity, but had to accept shorter apse windows. So forceful is the regulating effect of the vaulting, however, that one does not immediately perceive this height difference, especially as from many viewing angles the window summits are obscured by the vault arches. Furthermore, the apse-window springing points are artificially maintained at the same height as those of the nave windows, thus assuring additional coherence. The chapel's designer further demonstrated his skill in manipulating optical perception in the configuration of the nave bays: the westernmost bay is a good 35 cm narrower than the others and, when viewed from the apse, the perspective thus appears elongated and the rose consequently seems all the more enormous.

In contrast to the apparent simplicity of its structure, the upper chapel's decoration is remarkable in its richness. Even more than the lower chapel, the upper chapel is intended to resemble a reliquary box, and its jewel-casket décor, unique among major medieval Gothic buildings, dazzles in its gilding and colour. In comparison to the lower chapel, the upper chapel's polychromy was reasonably well preserved at the time of its restoration, and Lassus and his team fixed what remained with a coating of wax, which also served to revivify the colours. Where the paint had been lost, it was replaced according to the original design, and the entirety of the chapel's gilding was renewed. As in the lower chapel, a low wall decorated with blind arcades runs round the chapel's base. Here, most of the polychromy was gone, and the restorers devised the paint scheme we see today, as well as composing the décor underneath the rose, which had disappeared following the installation of an organ (removed in the 18C). Red, blue and gold predominate – especially gold, which is the base colour for the structure of the arcades and of the vaults – although green is also prominent. The royal fleur-de-lis is once more omnipresent, although the ceiling, *fleurdelisé* in the lower chapel, is here bespangled with a galaxy of golden stars to render the high vault yet more celestial. The sculptural elements include statues of the twelve apostles, mounted on the chapel's piers in reference to the apostles' metaphorical significance as pillars of the church. Removed and disfigured during the Revolution, some statues were nonetheless restorable and were remounted by Lassus, who also repainted them according to the remaining traces of polychromy. (Those too badly damaged for restoration were replaced by copies; the originals are in the Musée de Cluny (see 5.4).) Outside of the apostles, sculpture is limited to the crocket capitals of the blind arcades and vault responds – masterpieces of naturalist Gothic art, carved with recognizable leaf species – and to the arcade spandrels, across which a host of angels and vegetal motifs run riot. The sole survivor of the chapel's furnishings is the reliquary tribune, where the precious relics themselves were kept, which dominates the east end. Mostly rebuilt in the 19C, it almost constitutes a work of architecture in itself, and features two particularly fine 13C angel figures.

Over and above its fantastic gilt and carvings, it is the chapel's stained glass, the *raison d'être* of its daring structure, that astounds. Miraculously, two-thirds of the glazing we see today is original. Although many of the panels show signs of having been executed in haste, the ensemble effect is transcendent. The intense reds, blues and purples of the 13C nave and apse windows contrast with the subtler and more varied colours of the 15C rose. Restoration of the glass, which included copying panels that were too delicate to remain *in situ* (the originals are in the Musée de Cluny) and creating new ones to replace those that were lost, was so accomplished that it is difficult to distinguish between the medieval originals and the 19C additions. Rendered as small-scale scenes of a type usually reserved for low aisle windows, the iconographic content of much of the Sainte-Chapelle's glass is consequently undecipherable to the naked eye because too high up. The essential themes are the story of the Hebrews and the childhood and Passion of Christ, cleverly interwoven with references to Louis IX in a way that celebrates the crusades and glorifies Louis as a descendant of the Old-Testament kings, vicar of Christ and spiritual leader of his people.

Contemporary commentators on the Sainte-Chapelle were unstinting in their praise, comparing it to the heavenly Jerusalem and to Solomon's temple, where harmony and beauty reign in glory. Perhaps because of its unique function, the Sainte-Chapelle contributed little to the stylistic development of French Gothic and, as far as its decorative treatment was concerned, remained a glorious one-off. It did, however, become a model for French palace chapels, and an example of its lineage can be seen at the Château de Vincennes (34.2).

1.3 Place Dauphine
Architect unknown, 1607–10
(Métro: Pont Neuf, Cité; RER: Saint-Michel Notre-Dame)

The second of Henri IV's projects for public piazzas in Paris (see the Place des Vosges, 4.19), the Place Dauphine formed part of a general scheme of urban improvement that included the completion of the Pont Neuf (see feature on Seine bridges) and the creation of the Rue Dauphine on the Left Bank to open up the Faubourg Saint-Germain. Situated at the westerly tip of the Ile de la Cité (4.1), where it meets the Pont Neuf, the new *place* was guaranteed commercial success: the Palais de la Cité (1.1) was just next door, and direct access to the rest of Paris could be gained via the bridge.

The *place* was built following a masterplan possibly by Louis Métezeau, Architecte du Roi. Plots were sold

1.3 Place Dauphine

off and 32 identical houses erected around a piazza which, due to its promontory site, forms an isosceles triangle in plan. Entry to the piazza was gained at the triangle's apex and the centre of its base. The houses were more modest than at the Place des Vosges, each comprising two arcaded shops on the ground floor, between which a passage led to an interior courtyard accessing the two upper floors and attic. As at the Place des Vosges, the façades were in brick with stone dressings. The *place* has been much modified, only the two apex houses now preserving their original appearance. Set alight during the Commune, the base of the triangle was demolished in 1872, opening up views onto the Palais de Justice.

1.4 Place du Châtelet
Begun 1808
(Métro: Châtelet; RER: Châtelet-les-Halles)

Given its situation on the river opposite the Ile de la Cité (4.1) – home of the medieval royal palace (1.1) – and at the head of the Pont au Change (see feature on Seine bridges), the earliest bridge linking the Right Bank to the island, this spot could not but have been of strategic significance. In the 9C, it was the site of a wooden tower defending the bridge, afterwards replaced, in 1130, by a stone structure known as the Grand Châtelet (*châtelet* means »little castle«). With the building of Philippe II Augustus's defensive circuit of 1190, the fortress lost its initial *raison d'être* and became home to Paris's military police, until, in the 17C, it was turned into a formidable prison by Louis XIV. By the 19C, the site's strategic importance as a traffic thoroughfare had become paramount, and Napoleon consequently ordered the demolition of the Grand Châtelet to improve access to the Ile. In place of the fortress, a small piazza was created, in 1808–10, decorated at its centre with an imposing fountain, one of 17 commissioned by the emperor who desired that his capital splash with water in the manner of imperial Rome.

Designed and built by the engineer François-Joseph Bralle, with sculptures by Simon Boizot, the fountain, which is dedicated to Victory, fully reflects Napoleon's colonial ambitions. In keeping with the Egyptomania then sweeping France, it features a Nubian-temple style column, inscribed with the names of Napoleon's principal conquests, at whose summit stands a winged, gilded Victory holding out laurel wreaths towards the Palais de la Cité opposite. Female personifications of Vigilance, Justice, Strength and Prudence ring the column's base, while its pedestal is adorned with the imperial eagle and also with four cornucopia spouting water into the basin below. Despite its monumental aspirations, the ensemble is not without charm.

Inevitably, the Place du Châtelet was a prime target for Baron Haussmann who, in 1855–58, enlarged it by several times its original size so as to incorporate it into the »Grande Croisée« (»great crossing«), the principal north–south and east–west traffic axes so fundamental to his plans for Paris. Bralle's fountain was preserved, but moved to the centre of the new square and aggrandized by the addition of a supplementary pedestal adorned with sphinxes disgorging water into an enlarged basin. Work was carried out by Gabriel Davioud, who was also responsible for the two imposing theatres of 1860–62 that sit either side of the square, both commissioned by Haussmann to replace auditoria destroyed for the creation of the Place de la République. To the west is the huge Théâtre du Châtelet – at the time Paris's biggest auditorium, with a capacity of 2,500 – and to the east the smaller Théâtre de la Ville. Davioud dressed up both buildings in a matching garb of Italian-Renaissance inspiration which, virulently criticized by contemporaries, is notable only for its rather hollow grandiosity. In 1967/68, the Théâtre de la Ville was gutted, and its 19C interior replaced with a functional, modern auditorium by Jean Perrotet, which takes the form of a single, enormous tier of seats, entirely free of sight obstructions. The Théâtre du Châtelet, on the other hand, has kept its splendid Second-Empire interior, of which the impressive, horseshoe-shaped auditorium is particularly noteworthy. Held up by admirably slender supports, its four balconies are topped off by the inevitable domed arcade, and the ensemble glitters with gilt and blushes with crimson plush just as a 19C theatre should. At the time of its inauguration, the auditorium was endowed with state-of-the-art lighting and backstage machinery that allowed spectacular simulations of earthquakes, shipwrecks and other disasters.

On the northern side of the Place du Châtelet, the memory of the Grand Châtelet lives on in the form of the Chambre des Notaires (J. A. Pellechet and Charles Rohault de Fleury, 1855–57), whose distinctly uninspired, Classical façades were constructed from stone recovered from the demolished fortress.

1.5 Samaritaine
19, rue de la Monnaie
Frantz Jourdain, 1904–10, 1912; Frantz Jourdain and Henri Sauvage 1925–28, 1930
(Métro: Pont-Neuf)

Like all the big Parisian department stores, Samaritaine, founded in 1870 by Ernest Cognacq, started out small but quickly grew to occupy several prime parcels of real estate. In 1883, Cognacq met the architect Frantz Jourdain, and so began a life-long collaboration. At first Cognacq merely required Jourdain to knock together the pre-existing buildings that he had progressively acquired (Magasin no. 1 is still of this type) but, by 1904, he was able to offer the architect something more challenging: a total rebuild of Magasin no. 2, which occupied a large chunk of land between the river and the Rue de Rivoli (1.11). Jourdain, whose avant-garde tendencies had first manifested themselves in his youthful admiration for Viollet-le-Duc, produced an extraordinary building for Cognacq in which he compellingly demonstrated his conceptions of Art Nouveau. These consisted chiefly of aiming for a synthesis of architecture, painting and

1.5 Samaritaine

the decorative arts, using industrial materials, with a view to popularizing art and bringing it into the street.

Entirely in iron, which allowed the maximum floorspace to be squeezed out of the site (especially as all piping was carried inside the hollow supports), with no facing or cladding, Jourdain's building was essentially a utilitarian, orthogonal warehouse, but one to which a fantastical decoration of enamel painting, ceramic tiles and, especially, elaborate iron and copperwork (by Edouard Schenck) was applied. Colour was paramount, the structural ironwork being painted a bright shade of blue both inside and out, while the paintings – like the metalwork, in the form of floral and vegetal motifs – introduced splashes of brilliant orange and yellow. The intention was to grab the attention of passers-by with a modern evocation of an oriental bazaar, which also served as publicity (a form of expression dear to Art Nouveau), the store's name and the goods it sold featuring prominently amongst the décor. To extend the fantasy element and further attract attention, Jourdain added round towers coiffed with florid metalwork domes to either extremity of the southern façade (demolished when the shop was extended in the 1920s (see below)). Today, only the Rue-de-la-Monnaie frontage testifies to Jourdain's original concept, and this but partially as the decorative metalwork and most of the ceramic tiling were removed in the 1930s. (Jourdain also remodelled the Rue-de-Rivoli façade of Magasin no. 1 in similar style, in 1912, and this conserves certain decorative elements as well.) Inside the store, to bring daylight to the retail spaces, Jourdain hollowed out a vast, central atrium, rising the full height of the building, at whose centre he placed a monumental, balconied staircase. The atrium survives intact, conserving both its paintings and decorative metalwork, although one half has been disfigured by the installation of extraordinarily clumsy escalators, while the other is seemingly treated by the display designers as an old-fashioned embarrassment that must be hidden, rather than as an exploitable asset.

Reaction in official circles against Jourdain's rainbow-coloured iron extravaganza was so strong that, when Cognacq acquired the plot of land between his store and the river in the 1920s, Jourdain called in his long-time friend and associate Henri Sauvage to help design the new wing, fearing that his own name alone on the plans would only garner instant planning refusal. Dreading the worst, the authorities kept a close eye on the design, prohibiting all colour or structural metalwork (perceived as vulgar and commercial) on the river frontage and insisting that stone cladding be used to harmonize with the Louvre (1.8) and the other historic buildings that make up the riverscape. The result, despite its fine Art-Déco detailing, is rather ponderous. Jourdain and Sauvage were also responsible for Magasin n° 3 (today no longer part of Samaritaine), built a few years later to the east of Magasin n° 1 on the Rue de Rivoli. In similar style to the river building, it was put up in only eight months – a record at the time – thanks to Sauvage's well-tried system of prefabrication.

1.6 Saint-Germain-l'Auxerrois
2, place du Louvre
Architects unknown, current building begun early-12C
(Métro: Louvre-Rivoli)

Built on a site occupied by a Christian edifice since the late-6C, Saint-Germain-l'Auxerrois is, like so many of Paris's ancient religious buildings, a complex agglomeration of parts from different periods, in this instance spanning the 12C to the 16C. The earliest surviving element is the 12C tower, whose round-arched openings and simple detailing are unmistakably Romanesque. Originally external, the tower was swallowed up by successive enlargements. Having become too small for its growing congregation, Saint-Germain was entirely rebuilt in the 13C, when it took on the Notre-Dame-inspired

1.6 Saint-Germain-l'Auxerrois with Mairie du 1er (1.7) centre and left

plan we see today: semicircular apse-ambulatory heading a choir slightly longer than the nave, non-protruding transepts, double aisles with side-chapels. Of this 13C church survive the west entrance, the outer of the two southern nave aisles (Chapelle de la Vierge), and the main vessel of the choir and its inner aisle. Construction seems to have begun at the west end, sometime in the first half of the 13C, and proceeded eastwards: the choir was begun around 1250 and the Chapelle de la Vierge and the apse were erected in 1285–1300. Subsequent modifications, including the »Classicization« of its lower levels in the 18C, have robbed the choir of its original High-Gothic character. The west-entrance carvings are perhaps the most interesting remnants of the 13C church, all the more so in that very few examples survive in Paris, most having been destroyed during the Revolution. Saint-Germain's west-end doorways retain their 30 archivolt figures, which include angels, wise and foolish virgins and the twelve apostles, as well as the six statues adorning the jambs of the central opening, amongst which are King Childebert and Queen Ultrogothe, the church's supposed founders. The central doorway's tympanum carving and original centre jamb, which featured a statue of Saint Germain himself, were removed in the 17C to facilitate processions; the tympanum is lost but Saint Germain survives and can be seen inside the church.

In 1420–25 the nave and the two northern aisles were rebuilt. The 15C nave elevations are extremely sober, with only two storeys and Flamboyant-period, fused mouldings without capitals or other detailing. A splendid Flamboyant rose window fills the west end. Saint-Germain's five-arched porch, unique amongst Parisian churches and inspired by Burgundian examples, was added in 1431–39. The final building campaign, c. 1500–70, involved construction of the choir and apse chapels, which latter, because of the presence of the Rue de l'Arbre-Sec behind, flatten out at the east end and eat into the outer aisle.

Restored by Jean-Baptiste Lassus in 1839–55, Saint-Germain is famous for having pealed out the signal for the Saint-Bartholomew's-Day massacre in 1572, a notoriety that was to help save it from demolition by Baron Haussmann – see 1.7.

1.7 Mairie du 1er
4, place du Louvre
Jakob Ignaz Hittorff, 1855–60; Théodore Ballu, 1858–62
(Métro: Louvre-Rivoli)

Between Saint-Germain-l'Auxerrois (1.6) and the nearby Louvre (1.8), there was once a jumble of streets and houses. In the 18C, calls began to be heard for the creation of a public square in front of the palace's east façade, Perrault's colonnade having by then earned its reputation as *the* masterpiece of French Classicism. Steps towards this end were made in the early-19C when small clearings were established in front of both the Louvre and Saint-Germain, but it is to the indefatigable Baron Haussmann that we owe today's Place du

Louvre. Begun in 1853, the square is framed by buildings of Rue-de-Rivoli type façades (see 1.11), with Saint-Germain sitting to one side of it on a slight diagonal. This asymmetry was considered distinctly vexing, and was put forward as an argument in favour of the church's demolition, grandiloquent plans having been made to drive a straight avenue in the axis of the Louvre as far as the Hôtel de Ville (4.11). Haussmann considered Saint-Germain of little artistic value, and had no qualms about sacrificing it on these grounds, an opinion shared by most contemporaries, including Napoleon III's chief minister, Achille Fould, who was in favour of the avenue scheme.

Two factors saved the church: its recent restoration – public money should not be seen to be wasted – and the fact that its bells had rung the signal for the 1572 Saint-Bartholomew's-Day massacre, during which 70,000 Huguenots were murdered. Haussmann feared that, because of his and Fould's Protestantism, the church's demolition would be perceived as latter-day Huguenot revenge, and therefore refused to condemn the building. Instead, to get round the problem of its misalignment, he commissioned Hittorff to build the Mairie du 1er to its north, directing that the new building's general dispositions mimic those of the church but without reproducing its style. Hittorff complied, and his edifice, in hybrid Gothico-Renaissance dress, does indeed mirror Saint-Germain's general form (porch, gable and rose window) and skewness in relation to the *place*. As a result, it is not one of the architect's better compositions. Moreover, because a thoroughfare ran between the church and the Mairie, Saint-Germain's misalignment was still patently visible; the street was thus sacrificed for the erection of a structure that would unite the two buildings and hide Saint-Germain's northern flank. A bell tower seemed like a good idea, and Haussmann commissioned Ballu to design one: the 40 m-high Gothicizing result is so floridly silly that contemporary Parisians nicknamed it the *huilier-vinaigrier* (oil-and-vinegar bottle). Together, church, *mairie* and bell tower form a composition that, though quite preposterous, is delicious in its symmetrical absurdity. While Saint-Germain comes out worse off for the association, the Louvre colonnade is rendered all the more serious in comparison.

1.8 Palais du Louvre
The Louvre's principal entrance is via the pyramid in the Cour Napoléon; there is another entrance at the Porte des Lions on the Quai des Tuileries
Begun 1190
(Métro: Palais-Royal Musée du Louvre)

First fortress, then palace, and now museum, symbol of French monarchy, nation and culture, centre-stage in much of French history, the Louvre is, on top of it all, an extraordinary palimpsest of Gallic official architecture from the Middle Ages to the 21C. Major building campaigns have been carried out at the palace in four of the last five centuries, producing the vast edifice we see

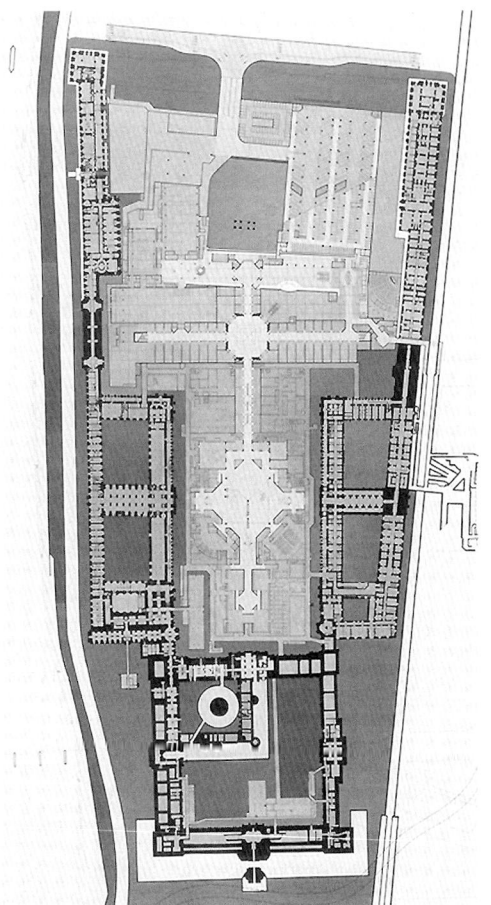

1.8 Palais du Louvre. Basement-level plan

today. Initially part of Philippe II Augustus's Parisian defensive circuit, the Louvre was transformed into a royal residence by Charles V. Too small and medieval for the humanist taste of François I, the old fortress was scheduled for demolition during his reign and a new château begun under his successor, Henri II, in 1549. The initial section of the new palace – the southwestern corner of today's Cour Carrée (»square court«) – was designed by Pierre Lescot and completed under Henri IV in the 1590s. Its western section, known as the Aile Lescot, marked an important point in French architectural history, showing both an advanced understanding of the new Classical idiom coming in from Italy, but also demonstrating a uniquely French interpretation of Classicism that would greatly influence subsequent national output. As the Aile Lescot was being finished, Henri IV was drawing up ambitious plans for the Louvre, known as the »Grand Dessein« (literally »great design«), that would determine the palace's future development. His

30   1st *arrondissement*

proposals consisted in duplicating Lescot's wings to form the Cour Carrée, establishing a riverside wing to link the Louvre to the nearby Palais des Tuileries (see the Jardin des Tuileries, 1.10), and demolishing the streets and houses that separated the two palaces. It would be another two-and-a-half centuries before Henri's vision came to completion, during the reign of Napoleon III.

Henri began realization of his plans with the riverside wing, known in French as the Aile de la Grande Galerie, which was built in 1595–1610 and which was the only part of the Grand Dessein he saw completed. Work continued under Louis XIII, who charged Jacques Le Mercier, his Premier Architecte, with construction of the remaining parts of the Cour Carrée; by the time of his death, in 1654, Le Mercier had completed the north-western corner of the courtyard, including the famous Pavillon de l'Horloge. He was succeeded under Louis XIV by Louis Le Vau, who initially built the eastern halves of the southern and northern wings of the Cour Carrée, but who was foiled by Colbert, Louis's chief minister, when it came to building the courtyard's eastern wing, and especially its city-side façade. For some reason that history has not recorded – personal animosity perhaps, or a feeling he was not up to the job –, Colbert did not want Le Vau to work on the east front, which, as the façade facing the city centre, would have the greatest symbolic weight. After soliciting, and then rejecting, several designs from Italian architects (including the great Bernini), Colbert appointed the three-member »Petit Conseil« in 1667 to supply a scheme. Comprising Le Vau (despite Colbert's hostility still the king's Premier Architecte), the painter Charles Le Brun and the amateur architect Claude Perrault, the Petit Conseil proposed a grandiose design based around a giant colonnade. Although the exact attribution of input will never be known, the east front is generally »given« to Perrault, in large part because its great originality seems unlikely to have come from Le Vau or Le Brun. With its typically Gallic mix of gravity, grandeur and graciousness, this imposing composition soon came to be viewed by many as the summit of French monumental Classicism, a reputation that remains unchallenged today.

Louis XIV had little affection for the Louvre and turned all his energies and attention to Versailles (32.1), abandoning the Grand Dessein for good in 1678. The carcass of the Cour Carrée was now more or less complete, but parts of it were not yet roofed and would remain in this state for over a century, until the advent of Napoleon. In 1757/58, Jacques-Germain Soufflot completed the second floor of the Cour Carrée's eastern wing, and attempts were made to create a square in front of the colonnade. But apart from these relatively minor attentions, the Louvre was essentially abandoned, no royal personages residing there and its apartments being farmed out to the royal academies. The only 18C development of any real importance came with the turmoil of revolution: the opening of the Musée Central des Arts in the palace, in 1793, to display to the French nation works from the royal collections or that had been confiscated from the church or émigré aristocrats. As we now know, it was this institution that would one day become synonymous with the Louvre.

Unsurprisingly, Napoleon's imperial ambitions found their measure in the Grand Dessein, and the emperor duly commissioned his favourite architects, Pierre-François-Léonard Fontaine and Charles Percier, to see to its continuation in 1804. The illustrious pair would work on the project for no less than 44 years, until 1848. As well as roofing the Cour Carrée and completing its décor, both inside and out, they were responsible for the Arc du Carrousel (1.9) and for the first part of a new wing on the Rue de Rivoli (1.11) intended to link the Palais des Tuileries to the Louvre on its northern flank, mirroring the Aile de Grande Galerie to the south. Percier and Fontaine were succeeded by Félix Duban, who carried out an important series of restorations at the Louvre. Then, in 1852, a *coup d'état* gave France another emperor, nephew of the first, who ruled under the name of Napoleon III. His architectural ambitions were no less vainglorious than his uncle's, but with the difference that he succeeded where his uncle had failed, both in the transformation of Paris and in the completion of the Grand Dessein. In 1848, on becoming president of France, the future Napoleon III had commissioned Ludovico Visconti to draw up plans for the Louvre, whose execution could finally be begun in 1852. Visconti died in 1853 and was succeeded on the project by Hector-Martin Lefuel, who would devote 27 years of his life to the Louvre, until his demise in 1880. Lefuel followed the essential outlines of Visconti's masterplan: demolition of the sizeable *quartier* of streets and houses that still stood between the Louvre and the Tuileries, construction of a significant chunk of new accommodation to the north of the Aile de la Grande Galerie, and continuation of Percier and Fontaine's Rue-de-Rivoli wing all the way from the Tuileries to the Louvre so as to join the two châteaux together into one enormous super-palace. Although in plan this megalomaniacal double-château could never be symmetrical – both because of the Louvre's off-axis positioning in relation to the Palais des Tuileries, and because of the divergence towards the west of the courses of the Seine and the Rue de Rivoli – Visconti's scheme attempted to iron out all irregularities and fool the observer into believing the ensemble to be Classically symmetrical, with the Rivoli wing closely mirroring the plan and volume of the southern. As a result, the Louvre-Tuileries's centre consisted of a vast, empty courtyard, the narrower part of which (the Cour Napoléon) was planted with central, railing-surrounded gardens like a London square, while its wider, western portion (the Place du Carrousel) served as a parade ground (today transformed into the Jardin du Carrousel). Lefuel's interventions on the Louvre's old fabric included the complete remodelling of its outer, western façades and the demolition and rebuilding of the western end of the Aile de la Grande Galerie, a liberty for which posterity has not forgiven him.

By 1857, although the *travaux* were not yet over, the Grand Dessein could finally be considered complete, 263 years after it had first been proposed. But it was not destined to last long. In 1870, the Franco-Prussian war resulted in the downfall of the Second Empire and was followed in Paris by the bloody Commune. The violence of this sombre page in French history brought about the destruction of many of Paris's public buildings, and both the Louvre and the Tuileries palaces were set alight by the Communards in 1871. While the fire in the Louvre was prevented from spreading, the Tuileries conflagration raged unchecked and the palace was reduced to a shell overnight. Its ruins crumbled forlornly for over a decade while the authorities decided what to do with them, until finally, in 1882, the government of the Third Republic demolished them as an antiroyalist gesture. Whence the rather peculiar »pincer« formation exhibited by the Louvre and its long wings today. It was following the fire that France's finance ministry moved into the Louvre's Rivoli wing, where it would remain for over a century. Lefuel continued to work on the palace following the empire's fall, rebuilding the fire-damaged Pavillons de Richelieu and de Marsan and doubling in width Percier and Fontaine's section of the Rivoli wing, a task that was never completed due to lack of funds.

Very little of significance changed at the Louvre during the century following Lefuel's death until, in 1981, President François Mitterrand and his socialist government launched the enormous Grand-Louvre project. After years of neglect, the Musée du Louvre had fallen into a pitiful mess, and, gallant man of culture that he was, Mitterrand determined to deliver this damsel in distress from her fate. Over 7 billion francs were spent converting the entire palace into museum space: the finance ministry was expelled from the Rivoli wing into new premises (see 12.5), the old fabric was overhauled and where necessary converted to its new function, vast underground spaces were dug in the palace's courtyards to provide supplementary accommodation, and the Louvre was given a brand-new, monumental entrance – Ieoh Ming Pei's notorious pyramid. The result of this Herculean effort (still not quite finished at the time of writing) is, we are proudly told, the world's largest museum in terms of surface area. It is also, despite the many criticisms that can be levelled at it, a quite extraordinary achievement, a museum of indubitably world-class stature, both for its collections and the galleries that house them.

It is worth pointing out at this stage that the architectural history of the Louvre as recounted by historians both ancient and modern has been almost exclusively a question of façades. The palace does not consciously concern itself with the effects of volume and massing, its form having arisen from the practical and chronologically sequential needs of the plan (the primacy of the plan in the design process being a French bias that reached its apotheosis in the 19C *beaux-arts* design system). Conceived as a series of long and narrow rectilinear wings, the Louvre consequently presents acres of flat-fronted elevation (11 ha in fact!), whose relationship to what lay behind seems to have been of little concern to anyone. This is as true for the Aile Lescot as it is for the east front, and the 19C structures are no exception either. Instead, functioning according to their own autonomous and internal logic, these elevations' role was essentially to convey to the onlooker a variety of political messages, such as the cultured humanism and modernity of François I and Henri II (the Aile Lescot), the mightiness of France's king and her new found dominance in the arts (the east front), or the legitimacy of France's emperor (demonstrated in Napoleon III's Louvre through the use of a variety of historical, royally associated styles). Even the Grand Louvre is often reduced simply to its pyramid, which many commentators read as François Mitterrand's personal bid for immortality.

Philippe II Augustus's fortress and Charles V's palace
Although the original Louvre was swept away in the 16C and 17C for the building of the current palace, it is worth describing its aspect because its foundations survive, and, as part of the Grand-Louvre project, have been excavated and incorporated into today's museological circuit. Surmounted by a ponderous ceiling of raw plank-shuttered concrete and dramatically lit by spotlights, they constitute one of the highlights of the new museum.

When Philippe II Augustus came to the throne, in 1180, sizeable chunks of what is today France were still in the hands of the English crown, which was a source of constant friction between the two countries. This was also the time of the crusades, and during one of their periods of peace Philippe and the English king, Richard the Lion-Heart, organized the 1191 Third Crusade together. Ever mistrustful of his Plantagenet neighbours, however, Philippe decided that before leaving he should protect his capital, and in 1190 ordered construction of a defensive circuit all around Paris. Were the English to attack they would arrive from the northwest, and to defend the most vulnerable point, where the defensive circuit met the river on the Right Bank, Philippe built a particularly solid fortress just outside the walls – the original Louvre. Completed by 1202, the castle occupied the southwestern corner of today's Cour Carrée. It too was square in plan and comprised an outer crenellated and machicolated curtain wall, 2.6 m thick and defended by ten round towers, and a massive round keep, 15 m in diameter, 30 m high and with walls 4 m thick, that was set towards the northeastern corner of the castle's courtyard. The curtain wall was surrounded by a water-filled moat, while the keep was defended by a deep, dry ditch, with stone counterscarps at the castle's base to hinder any attempts at scaling it with ladders. Accommodation was provided by the vaulted chambers of the keep and by *corps de logis* built against the inside of the curtain wall. The use of round towers and especially of round keeps was characteristic of French castles of Philippe's reign, the circular plan having been adopted because it had the advantage over square or rectangular ones of avoiding »dead angles« (i.e. the diagonals radiating from each corner along which attackers could approach out of firing range). Round keeps proliferated all over France during this period, but few matched the size of the Louvre's. Known as the Grosse Tour, it became the symbol of the French monarch's power, and was referred to in the allegiance oath sworn to the king right up to the end of the *ancien régime* (even though it was demolished in 1528).

As we have said, the original Louvre was intended as a fortress and not a royal residence, the monarch's Parisian home being the Palais de la Cité (1.1). Charles V's transformation of the castle into a palace, in the 1370s–80s, came after he abandoned the Palais de la Cité because of a humiliation suffered there, and also followed the building of a new defensive circuit around Paris that negated the Louvre's original military value by bringing it within the city limits (part of this new defensive wall can now be seen in the Galerie du Carrousel – see the Grand Louvre, below)). To make the fortress suitable for royal occupation, Charles opened up windows in its walls, built new *corps de logis* in the courtyard and coiffed the ensemble with elaborate chimneys, turrets and pinnacles. A good idea of what the finished result was like can be got from the famous painting of *The Month of October* in the Duc de Berry's *Très Riches Heures* (1413–16). The reconfigured Louvre was especially celebrated for its spiral *escalier d'honneur*, known as the Grand Vis, which today survives only in the lively accounts of it left to us by enthusiastic contemporaries.

Visiting the remains of Philippe and Charles's Louvre today, one walks down the moat past the middle tower of the northern curtain wall and up to the northeastern-corner tower (known as the Tour de la Taillerie), and then down alongside the eastern curtain wall to the double towers of the castle's city-side entrance (note the drawbridge pier), after which one passes through into the ditch encircling the keep. From there one is taken to a room in one of the courtyard's *corps de logis*, which is known as the Salle Saint-Louis because of the vaults added to it *c.* 1240–50 during the reign of Louis IX.

The Renaissance château of François I and Henri II
In the decades following Charles V's reign the Louvre fell from grace, as later did Paris, subsequent French sovereigns preferring the Loire valley over the troublesome capital. It was François I (reigned 1515–47) who brought the monarchy back to Paris, and as a result began a spate of château building in and around the capital. He decided to rebuild the Louvre as a modern residence, and as a first step towards this demolished the Grosse Tour in 1528. More interested in the Châteaux de Madrid (destroyed), de Saint-Germain-en-Laye (28.1) and de Fontainebleau (38.1), however, he did not actually get round to doing anything about the Louvre until the end of his reign. A year before his death, in 1546, François gave the go-ahead for construction of a new *corps de logis* designed by the »amateur« architect Pierre Lescot. The west wing of the old Louvre was demolished, and the building of Lescot's scheme in its stead begun in 1549 under Henri II.

Lescot's initial project had consisted of a two-storey-high, one-room-wide *corps de logis* interrupted at its centre by a sizeable, three-storey *avant-corps* containing the *escalier d'honneur*, whose presence divided the building's apartments into two distinct halves. At Henri II's request, the staircase was moved to the northern end of the *corps de logis* to allow for one huge assembly room on each floor. Presumably to maintain central emphasis, Lescot conserved the central *avant-corps* (even though, devoid of the *escalier d'honneur*, it no longer served any practical purpose) and designed a new end pavilion to contain the displaced staircase. In the interests of symmetry this pavilion was duplicated at the building's other extremity. Through this accidental process emerged a façade articulation that would become a staple of French Classical architecture from the 17C to the 19C: the symmetrical division of elevations into five parts comprising two identical end pavilions, two identical *arrière-corps* and a central *avant-corps*. Although at first glance circumstance was largely responsible for this, there may well also have been a good deal of conscious or subconscious influence from the articulation of French castles, with their corner and central towers. Another change to Lescot's initial scheme came in the early 1550s with the raising of the *corps de logis* to three storeys, the final, attic storey replacing the high, inter-pavilion roofs originally planned. Instead the Aile Lescot was uniformly coiffed at fourth-floor level with a precocious example of what would become another staple of French building: the double-slope roofing today known as a mansard (after the 17C architect François Mansart). The elaborate lead decoration adorning the summit of the Aile Lescot's roof, which reads as a ridgeline, in fact conceals the roof's hip. It was presumably to achieve a more Italianizing effect of horizontality that Lescot chose this roofing form over the traditional French lofty attics of the era.

Today the original northern façade of the Aile Lescot is no more, having been replaced in subsequent building campaigns, but the 16C Cour-Carrée façade survives and is considered a masterpiece of the French Renaissance. Lescot was not an architect overly concerned with the articulation of volumes, his talent instead lying in the design of surface decoration, a bias borne out by his several collaborations with the sculptor Jean Goujon. It is essentially on the Louvre's extraordinarily rich and accomplished applied décor, carved by Goujon and his atelier, that Lescot's reputation rests today. Lescot, it seems, did not go to Rome until very late in his career, and his knowledge of ancient-Roman and contemporary Italian architecture must therefore have been limited to engravings. This may well explain the hybrid nature of his work, which at the Louvre is convincingly Roman and Antique in its detailing but thoroughly un-Italian in its overall deployment. First and foremost the Aile Lescot displays a use of the orders that was astonishingly »correct« for French architecture of the day, but the subordinate, decorative effect they serve is thoroughly un-Italian. It is the windows and not the orders that seem to have defined the façade articulation, in reversal of Italian practice. Italian buildings of the period tended towards exaggerated monumentality, comprising powerful volumes with massive walls containing sparse fenestration; the Aile Lescot, on the other hand, is all ornamental beauty, its Cour-Carrée elevation consisting of a flat, decorative screen featuring almost as much window as wall. Where contemporaneous Italian buildings generally relied on multiple repetition of standardized elements for their overall effect, the Aile Lescot flaunts its wealth of diverse detailing. And where horizontals were usually strongly emphasized in early-16C Italian edifices, Lescot did all he could to break the ascendancy of the orders' entablatures and introduce dominant verticals, perhaps in subconscious recollection of native Gothic architecture. The Aile Lescot displays a sophisticated use of Mannerist devices, including open-bed pediments, broken entablatures and projecting column bases, that all contribute to this vertical thrust. Other knowing games include the variation of intercolumniation on the pavilions – thereby creating pairs of columns that again contribute to a dominant vertical –, the alternation of pediment types, and countless subtle variations in detail to make each floor very different from the next. The façade's richest decoration is reserved for the pavilions and the central *avant-corps*, where instead of the pilasters of the *arrière-corps* we find engaged columns, statue-filled niches and a garlanded-medallion motif whose future in France would be long. There is also a notable Gallicism in the way the décor becomes more exuberant the further up the façade one goes, as if the French medieval taste for elaborate ornamentation only at eaves level had here been transposed into Classical language. And then there was the explicit political message encapsulated in this décor: bas-reliefs exalting France's military might, prosperity, and artistic and scientific know-how, and the clear aspiration to Antique imperial culture.

Inside the Aile Lescot was just as innovative as outside. Its principal room, known today as the Salle des Cariatides, was on the ground floor, and is famous for the musicians' gallery supported by four caryatids that gives it its name. These huge and highly accomplished statues, of a form hitherto unknown in France and little used even in Italy, were sculpted by Goujon from casts supplied by Lescot (history has not recorded where Lescot got the casts from, however). At the other end of the room was the king's tribune, whose rather imperial vaults were supported by a set of 16 beautifully

1.8 Palais du Louvre. From left to right: Aile Lescot, Pavillon de l'Horloge, Aile Le Mercier

carved and richly ornamented Doric columns. The *escalier d'honneur*, with its elaborately sculpted stone barrel vaults, led up to the Salle des Gardes on the first floor, through which the king's *appartements d'apparat* were reached. Although the king's bedchamber no longer survives, its remarkable ceiling was remounted in the east wing by Percier and Fontaine and still testifies to Lescot's originality. Carved by the Italian sculptor Francisque Scibec de Carpi to Lescot's directions, the ceiling's elaborate décor marked an epoch in French interior design, contrasting totally as it did with traditional native beamed and painted ceilings.

Lescot's interventions at the Louvre did not end with the Aile Lescot. During the reigns of Henri II's successors, François II and Charles IX (*c*. 1559–67), the architect demolished the southern wing of the old château and replaced it with a duplication of the Aile Lescot. His intention was presumably to create a four-sided château of the same dimensions as the medieval Louvre articulated in the manner of Ecouen (23.1), that is to say with a third, identical wing to the north and a lower, entrance wing on the eastern side. Today the Lescot half of the southern wing no longer follows exactly the disposition of the Aile Lescot, Percier and Fontaine having modified its attic storey to match those of the 17C wings to the east and north. Lescot was also responsible for beginning the Aile de la Petite Galerie jutting out from the Louvre towards the Seine, which today is famous for the Galerie d'Apollon begun under Louis XIV.

Work on the Louvre stopped in the late 1560s, interrupted by the Wars of Religion, but in the meantime another building began to go up that would have a profound influence on its future development: the Palais des Tuileries. Commissioned by Catherine de Médicis in 1564, the Palais was situated well to the west of the Louvre outside of Charles V's defensive circuit. It was almost certainly Catherine herself who first put forward the idea of connecting the two châteaux via a gallery running along the river, an arrangement that would not only be convenient shelter-wise but would also allow the monarch to flee any troubles in the capital and escape over the city walls out of sight of the mob.

The Grand Dessein: the Louvre of Henri IV
In 1594, Henri IV effectively put an end to the Wars of Religion by converting to Catholicism, and was at last able to take possession of his capital, Paris. During the remainder of his reign he instigated an ambitious building programme in the city that inevitably included grandiose plans for the Louvre. The Grand Dessein was first put forward in October 1594: as well as Catherine de Médicis' idea of linking the Louvre to the Tuileries, it also proposed the quadrupling in size of the Cour Carrée by replicating Lescot's wings fourfold. Where Lescot's plans for the Louvre would have produced a relatively modest château no bigger than the ilk of Ecouen, the Grand Dessein postulated a truly megalomaniacal palace at least five times as large. As we have seen, Henri got no further than the river wing, but this was already a significant achievement when one considers that the Aile de la Grande Galerie is nearly $1/2$ km long! Firstly, in 1595, the one-storey-high Aile de la Petite Galerie was given an upper floor in which was created the Galerie des Rois, to display the portraits of France's kings and queens. That same year, the first part of the Aile de la Grande Galerie was begun, running from the Aile de la Petite Galerie as far as today's Pont du Carrousel. Its architect is thought to have been Louis Métezeau, who covered the wing's long, flat, sparsely fenestrated Seine-side elevation with a riot of Mannerist carving: a pilastered base whose station was indicated by intricate vermiculated rustication, a narrow mezzanine floor of small rectangular windows and cassettes, and finally the *piano nobile* containing the Grande Galerie itself, where we find a reprise of the column-pairing of Lescot's Cour-Carrée pavilions as well as the alternation of round and triangular pediments of his *arrière-corps*, here used to coiff the ensemble at eaves level. Elaborate sculptures fill every available spare space, but this still does not hide the fact that the basic bay disposition has been repeated 14 times over, and that all this lapidary activity, however virtuosic, is no more than surface decoration.

The second half of the Aile de la Grande Galerie, running from the Pont du Carrousel to the Pavillon de Flore, was probably the work of Jacques II Androuet Du Cerceau. Its façades repeated the double-column, alternating pediment disposition of the first half of the wing, but adapted it better to the building's scale by using a colossal order rising the entire height of the elevation. The result was, however, a little on the clumsy and monotonous side. Today Du Cerceau's creation is no more, having been entirely rebuilt in the 19C by Lefuel, who chose to reproduce the general disposition of Métezeau's façades, presumably in the interest of greater coherence and uniformity. For an idea of what the original was like, however, one can look to the courtyard elevations of Fontaine and Percier's section of the Rue-de-Rivoli wing, since, in the interests of symmetry, Napoleon's architects faithfully copied Du Cerceau's façades. It was also probably Du Cerceau who built the monumental Pavillon de Flore terminating the ensemble, the original of which was yet another victim of Lefuel's demolition-lust. The rebuilt Pavillon de Flore follows the general dispositions of its predecessor, but along considerably more grandiose lines. Inside the Aile de la Grande Galerie nothing now survives of the original décor, and Lefuel even amputated a sizeable chunk off the gallery's western end to build today's Pavillon des Etats.

Under Louis XIII, Henri IV's successor, building of the Grand Dessein progressed slowly. In the space of 30 years, Jacques Le Mercier, the new king's Premier Architecte, managed to complete only the second half of the Cour Carrée's western wing and to begin construction of the first half of its northern, each time faithfully duplicating Lescot's elevations. At the centre of the western wing, to the north of the Aile Lescot, he erected a monumental pavilion, known today as the Pavillon de l'Horloge because of the clock added to it in the 19C. Its first three storeys respected the style and dimensions of the Aile Lescot, but on top of them Le Mercier tacked a giant upper floor on whose Cour-Carrée façade he disposed four pairs of enormous caryatids – no doubt inspired by Goujon's – surmounted by a very Mannerist superimposition of three pediments. The caryatids were a clever way of getting round a thorny question of Classical correctness engendered by Lescot's use of the Corinthian order at ground-floor level and the Composite on the first floor. If one stuck to the rules, no order could be used on any of the floors above since the Composite was always supposed to be the last in the hierarchy; whence Le Mercier's cunning substitution of caryatids for columns. As if his upper-storey extravaganza were not enough, he then coiffed the ensemble with the Louvre's first *toit à l'impériale*, which imitated the bulbous roofing of the Palais des Tuileries's central pavilion (the Pavillon de l'Horloge's current *toit à l'impériale* is by Lefuel, and is, of course, considerably more elaborate than the original). Le Mercier was also responsible for fitting out the ground floor of the Aile de la Petite Galerie as a summer apartment for Anne of Austria, Louis XIV's mother. Today all that survive of this intervention are the vault

1.8 Palais du Louvre. East front

paintings (1655–58) by Giovanni-Francesco Romanelli and their elaborate stuccowork frames, which were created by the sculptor Michel Anguier.

Reluctant grandeur: Louis XIV and the Louvre
Louis XIV was never very fond of Paris, his mistrust and dislike of the capital stemming from a childhood trauma when, at the age of five, he was forced to flee the city's bloodthirsty mob and take refuge at Saint-Germain-en-Laye (28.1). On reaching manhood he spent as little time in Paris as possible, and eventually forsook it entirely for Versailles. Nonetheless, the city remained the seat of the realm, and, at least initially, Louis did not question the policy adopted by his forefathers whereby royal power was best expressed through grandiose Parisian building projects. He was aided and encouraged in this by the man who acted as his chief minister from 1661, Jean-Baptiste Colbert, who set out to perfect the system of absolutist government begun under Henri IV and Louis XIII. As well as building up the enormous administrative machinery this required, Colbert began to institutionalize the arts in the service of the king, a process that included the founding of the royal academies with a view to creating state-defined artistic orthodoxies. This policy was two-pronged: not only would it allow for better expression of the sovereign's power at home, it would also provide an efficient artistic machine that would allow France at last to challenge Italy's dominance of cultural and luxury production (stimulating French foreign exports) and proclaim France's glory as the most powerful nation in Europe. *Reine des arts* as it was, architecture would play a major part in this campaign, a role explained by Colbert in a letter he wrote to his sovereign: »Your majesty knows that, next to glorious military feats, nothing speaks so eloquently of princely intellect and grandeur than the affluence of buildings; posterity will always appraise a ruler with reference to the buildings erected in his lifetime.« Colbert consequently implemented a whole programme of Parisian building that included the Portes Saint-Denis and Saint-Martin (10.1 and 10.2) and the Invalides (7.12); still officially the principal royal residence, the Louvre was the key element in this campaign.

Civil unrest and political instability had halted further building at the Louvre in the early part of Louis XIV's reign, but as of 1661 his Premier Architecte, Louis Le Vau, was able to continue work on the Cour Carrée. By 1668, when he quit the palace to concentrate entirely on Versailles, Le Vau had completed the carcasses of both the courtyard's northern and southern wings, and rebuilt and enlarged the Aile de la Petite Galerie following its partial destruction by fire. The Galerie des Rois had been lost in the blaze, and in its stead Le Vau and the painter Charles Le Brun created the famous Galerie d'Apollon, their first collaboration in the service of the king following their requisition from Vaux-le-Vicomte (37.1). Le Brun repeated the formula that had so impressed Louis XIV at Vaux, namely elaborate, Italian-style gilded-stucco ceilings framing virtuosic allegorical paintings, only on a bigger and even more ostentatious scale. With the Galerie d'Apollon we have one of the first instances of Louis XIV's personal identification with the sun god, which would become the dominant symbolism at the Château de Versailles. Indeed with hindsight Le Brun's work on the gallery can be regarded as a try-out for Versailles, since it prefigured his work there and because he too was taken off the Louvre project to work on the suburban centre of power. Unfinished in Louis XIV's time, the Galerie d'Apollon was not finally completed until the 19C under Duban, when it received its famous central painting by Delacroix.

Whatever the Galerie d'Apollon's splendour, it was without doubt the Louvre's east front that was Louis XIV's principal legacy at the palace. Several of the manifold projects put forward for this elevation (including one of Bernini's) had proposed the creation of a monumental colonnade, and this idea was retained by the Petit Conseil. The initial plan was to transfer the king's apartments to brand-new accommodation in the east wing, whose giant, *piano-nobile*-level columns would thus regally signal the presence of the royal person. But things did not turn out quite as intended. At the time, the city's dense fabric extended right up to the Louvre's walls on all sides bar the river, and, in order to create the monumental square the east façade clearly demanded as a setting, time-consuming and expensive expropriations and demolitions were needed. Already more interested in Versailles than the Louvre, Louis XIV lost heart, and abandoned all attempts at acquiring the necessary land (today's Place du Louvre dates from the 19C (see 1.7)). As a result, security of the royal person could not be guaranteed if the king's apartments were in the east wing, and it was thus decided to leave them where they were in the southern wing but to double this part of the building in width so as to provide new accommodation. Le Vau's time being entirely taken up with Versailles, it fell to Perrault to see to these modifications, which also involved reconfiguring the Petit Conseil's design for the east front, since with the widening of the southern wing the east front's total length increased significantly. The east front's definitive design can thus be given to Perrault, who was also responsible for the new southern elevation as well as for rebuilding the north wing's outside, city-side façade.

Although the colonnade was completed in Louis XIV's reign, the wing it fronted was not, remaining unroofed until Napoleon's time. Moreover, because the royal apartments were no longer to be situated there, Perrault replaced the fenestration originally planned for the *piano nobile* with statue-filled niches (it was Percier and Fontaine who completed the east wing and opened up the windows we see today). Thus, at the time of its construction this gigantic creation was in reality no more than a blind, cardboard-thin backdrop whose chief and only purpose was the representation of royal power. But what a backdrop! Never before had an attempt been made to transpose Roman temple architecture to a palace façade of this measure. Like the Aile Lescot, the east front is divided into five parts, but at this scale the majesty of the five-part arrangement takes on its full significance, proving its ability to cadence a very long elevation. At ground-floor level we find an extremely plain basement on which sits the giant colonnade, whose columns rise the full height of the next two storeys up to the roof line. But, for the first time in a French Classical château, there is no roof, the high attics up till then characteristic of French architecture having here been replaced by a continuous balustrade (an innovation possibly inspired by Bernini's unexecuted east-front projects). This highly Romanizing balustrade is the most obvious example of a general move towards stricter Classicism throughout the east front's design. Another is the famous colonnade, whose subtle handling encapsulates all the genius of the east front's composition. Both Italian and French architects up to this point had generally always used pilasters, or at the most engaged columns, to decorate a façade, never a free-standing colonnade of this nature. Beautifully carved with typically French crispness, the colossal Corinthian columns are organized rather un-Classically in pairs along the main body of the façade's *arrière-corps*, which was a good way of ensuring the wide intercolumniation needed for fenestration (and which was presumably maintained by Perrault, despite the disappearance of the windows, because of its powerful visual effect). To mark the dominance of the pedimented central *avant-corps*, the rear wall breaks forward almost as far as the columns, and the order's intercolumniation subtly widens in the central bay to take on the tall arch of the palace's main entrance. Likewise, on reaching the pavilions the order metamorphoses into corner-delineating pilasters decorating solid wall, while at the pavilions' centres we find a wider, arch-filled bay recalling the central bay of the *avant-corps*, which recedes in the manner of the *arrière-corps* and thereby allows for free-standing flanking columns. The plasticity of the principal run of the colonnade is thus reproduced in the pavilions and a unifying sense of depth is maintained across the entire façade. Cadencing the solid-wall parts of the elevation are pilasters that echo the colonnade in front, while in between them are pedimented openings surmounted by a string course at first-floor level, and, at second-floor level, garlanded medallions that are a direct quote from the Aile Lescot, inflated in size and containing Louis XIV's monogram. Altogether the east front presents a uniquely French combination of the Baroque (the dramatic scale of the colonnade's height and depth, the coupling of its columns, the order's varying rhythm and expression) and the Classical (the clearly expressed, simple massing, the free-standing columns, the straight severity of the roofline and unbroken entablatures, the precision and tautness of the carving) that seems perfectly to express the unbending majesty of absolutism. One might also argue that, gigantic, impersonal and rather cold as it is, the east front also well expressed the anonymous state bureaucracy that was absolutism's chief apparatus. Whatever one's take, there is no doubt that the colonnade's influence was enormous; to cite just two examples in Paris one could mention Gabriel's Place-de-la-Concorde buildings (see 8.1) and Garnier's Opéra (9.13).

Perrault's plans for the east front were never completed in their entirety, the high attic storeys he had proposed for each of the end pavilions not being realized. This may have been due to lack of funds, although it is also possible that the omission was deliberate: by the late-17C the tall pavilions and lofty roofs that had up till then characterized French architecture, and which were an inheritance from the towers of medieval castles, were fast going out of fashion. The same can be said for the east front's dry moat, which was built according to plan but then immediately filled in again; another staple of French château architecture inherited from castles, moats went out of fashion in the same period. In 1964, as part of a restoration campaign at the Louvre, the east front's moat was opened up again. Of the moats originally surrounding the other three sides of the Cour Carrée's external perimeter, nothing survives bar part of the counterscarp built by Le Vau in front of the Pavillon de l'Horloge, which was rediscovered during the Grand-Louvre excavations and today serves as a rather splendid gateway to the museum's subterranean galleries.

Perrault's interventions were not limited to the Louvre's outside elevations, for it is thought to have been him who made an important modification to the façades of the Cour Carrée. Colbert and his officials decided that in place of Lescot's attic storey there should be a fully fledged, pilastered third floor terminating in a flat balustrade like the east front. To get round the problem of Classical correctness, this rebuilt floor would sport a brand new »French order«, for which Perrault is though to have won a competition in 1671. In the end, however, the third storey as built incorrectly sported a Corinthian order and, as far as the central pavilions were concerned, coiffed itself with a simple triangular pediment in place of the elaborate upper levels of the Pavillon de l'Horloge. The presence of this new second floor, especially where the central pavilions are concerned, produces a much greater feeling of unity in comparison to the somewhat additive look of the Lescot/Le Mercier western wing, and also appears more conventionally Classical. Only the Cour Carrée's western wing now sports the old, Lescot-designed upper floor, all the others having been modified to match Perrault's design.

The two Napoleons – completion of the Grand Dessein
Napoleon's reasons for resurrecting the Grand Dessein were clear. Like Louis XIV and Colbert, he believed that princely intellect and grandeur were best expressed through an affluence of building, and went even further than them by deliberately seeking to emulate imperial Rome. The Louvre was perhaps the one exception in

this, since the decision to respect the palace's existing architecture set its symbolic weight within the Bourbon dynasty's lineage, directly recalling the grandeur of the 17C. But revival of the Grand Dessein was not only about architectural representation. As an emperor, Napoleon needed a court, in the sense of both a hierarchy of people of which he was head and of a physical backdrop against which his august person would be set. Moreover, as chief of the executive, he needed ministries and other administrative organizations near at hand. The obvious example of exactly this kind of absolutist power base was of course Versailles. But the sun had set for good on Louis XIV's suburban palace, and, again essentially for politico-symbolic reasons, Napoleon chose the Tuileries as his principal residence. Reviving the Grand Dessein was thus the perfect way of creating a Versailles-style administrative centre in the heart of the city.

The first task the emperor set Fontaine and Percier was completion of the Cour Carrée, which they achieved by 1810. The northern, eastern and southern wings were roofed, the missing carving on the palace's façades supplied, and a start made on the interior, including the vaulting of the Salle des Cariatides. Napoleon actively championed the Musée du Louvre and ordered the reconfiguring of the Grande Galerie, which was where the paintings where exhibited. During the 18C the painter Hubert Robert had suggested blocking the gallery's windows and instead installing roof lights to provide better viewing conditions, an idea taken up by Percier and Fontaine, who also supplied the Corinthian order and transverse arcades cadencing the gallery's length today. In 1810, the emperor ordered construction of new accommodation in the form of the Louvre's Rivoli wing; work continued on and off until 1824, at which point it stretched from the Tuileries as far as the roadway running through the Place du Carrousel.

The fall of the First Empire essentially put a stop to furtherance of the Grand Dessein, but Fontaine and Percier continued working on the Louvre's interiors, producing much of the décor we see today. In 1818, under Louis XVIII, they built monumental staircases in each of the east wing's pavilions; during the reign of Charles X (1824–30), they decorated the first floor of the Le-Mercier wing to house the Conseil d'Etat, and also created a first-floor suite of rooms on the courtyard side of the southern wing to display the Egyptian antiquities recently acquired by the museum; and in the early 1830s, under Louis Philippe, they fitted out the Galerie Campana on the southern wing's Seine side, again to provide exhibition space for the museum. Inventors of the »Empire style« under Napoleon, Fontaine and Percier were arguably more accomplished as interior designers than as architects *per se*, and their Louvre rooms, especially the Egyptian galleries (which today house ancient-Greek artefacts), amply demonstrate the exquisite neo-Classical décor for which they were famed. Delicate mouldings and an inspired use of colour characterized their work, which also relied heavily on painted scenes: those realized by Ingres in the Egyptian galleries are especially celebrated.

Despite the four decades they devoted to the Louvre, Fontaine and Percier's interventions pale into insignificance beside the enormous *travaux* realized by Lefuel, who transformed the palace beyond recognition. On seizing absolute power, Napoleon III revived his uncle's ambitions, organizing his court in exactly the manner of the First Empire's and transferring his official residence from the Elysée (8.16) to the Tuileries. Completion of the Grand Dessein was thus a question of building the Versailles-style power base his uncle had planned. The Louvre-Tuileries super-palace inaugurated by Napoleon III in 1857 provided, amongst others, private imperial apartments and state *salons d'apparat* in the Tuileries, accommodation for the interior ministry and the ministry of police and telegraphs in the Louvre's Richelieu wing (the new chunk of the palace built by Lefuel to link Percier and Fontaine's Rivoli wing to the Cour Carrée), an imperial riding school and attendant stables disposed around the Cour Lefuel (part of the new buildings erected between the western, external façade of the Cour Carrée and the northern, internal façade of the Aile de la Grande Galerie), as well as barracks for the imperial guard and countless other royal and governmental facilities. And then of course there was the museum, which not only retained its previously won territory but gained extra space. It fell to Lefuel to provide a suitable *visage* for the newly completed parts of this imperial city, whose principal component was the Cour Napoléon. With the notable exception of Perrault, the Louvre's architects up to this point had respected absolutely, even to the point of slavishly copying, the palace's 16C architecture, and many contemporaries expected Lefuel to do the same. It is to his credit that he did not, instead choosing to take the palace's historic elevations as a reference point from which to create a style all of his own. In the Cour Napoléon, for example, Lefuel reproduced the basic disposition of the Pavillon de l'Horloge's Cour-Carrée façade on all the pavilions, but inflated it with countless minor aggrandizements (a twinned instead of a single order, freestanding columns rather than pilasters, a superabundance of sculpture filling every available space) to produce an effect of sumptuous ostentation that was quite different from the original. Lefuel's Louvre may be pompously overblown, it may have eschewed 19C technological developments, it is certainly historicizing, but it is undeniably unique to its era. References to France's history and especially to royal architecture everywhere abounded, from the staircase in the Cour Lefuel (via which horses entered the riding school), directly recalling Fontainebleau, to the statues of illustrious Frenchmen standing in rather comic watch atop the Cour Napoléon's ground-floor arcades.

The reconstructed Louvre came in for virulent attack from many contemporary critics, whose tenor is perhaps best summed up by Louis Veuillot's comments: »Our new Louvre is grandly ostentatious and frivolous;

colossal, but not *grand* [*grand* in French meaning both »big« and »great«]. The colossal is as far from the *grand* as the pretty is from the beautiful ... [The palace] appears like a vulgar self-made man, all laden with trinkets and very pimply ...« The inherent snobbery of Veuillot's remarks perhaps hits at a certain truth, namely that, for the first time in French history, the members of the nation's court were almost exclusively drawn from the commercial bourgeoisie, both the French and Industrial Revolutions having put power in their hands. But their taste still aspired to the *ancien régime*, especially where the representation of a new, and somewhat parvenu monarchy was concerned. Simply aping the old regime was not enough however, the new one felt obliged, out of pride in its riches and probably also a snobbish feeling of inferiority and illegitimacy, to go one better in ladling on the magnificence. This tendency was especially marked in Second-Empire interiors, of which the Louvre of course has many. By far its most celebrated are the Appartements Napoléon-III in the Richelieu wing, which were created as the official residence of the interior minister: gargantuan chandeliers, swathes of red velvet, acres of ceiling paintings, an explosion of mouldings and several kilos of gilt make for an environment of truly overwhelming opulence.

The Grand Louvre – 1981–20??
At the dawn of the third millennium, museums occupy an unprecedented position in world culture, having become perhaps the only globally recognized institution, whose buildings are the temples of a new, secular, non-doctrinaire religion. It was in this context that the enormous Grand-Louvre project was launched. At the time, the sorry state of the Musée du Louvre was a national scandal. Due to understaffing, many of its galleries were permanently closed and the entire museum was forced to shut on certain days. The provision of visitor facilities was pitiful, with only two lavatories and no parking, cars and coaches fighting for space in the neighbouring streets. Much of the collection was in storage due to lack of gallery space, and there was an acute shortage of »backstage« areas (conservation workshops, administrative accommodation, etc.). Visitor levels had fallen and were well below the numbers attracted by the Centre Pompidou (4.15) and a perceived lack of popular accessibility led to charges of elitism. There was not even a clearly marked entrance!

The idea of allowing the museum to expand into the entire palace was not new, but had previously been stymied by the finance ministry's stubborn refusal to leave. From the museum's point of view, however, the advantages of such a scheme were obvious: instead of being a kind of tenant in the palace, it would become the Louvre, the identity of the two concepts – museum and palace – thus fusing as one to form France's most prestigious cultural institution. President Mitterrand liked to put it another way: as well as providing the museum with the extra space it needed, the Grand-Louvre project would continue the work of the Revolutionaries and open up the whole palace to the people. On the one hand this was an attack by France's socialist president on the country's *énarque*-led establishment (expelling the arrogant finance ministry from its prestigious home), but on the other, as we shall see, the Grand Louvre represented the president's own personal ambitions as a statesman and was as much about proclaiming France's greatness to the world as it was about providing her people with access to what was theirs anyway.

On the practical, architectural front, the extension of the museum into the finance ministry's premises engendered a logistical conundrum: because of the palace's U-shape, the inclusion of the Richelieu wing in the museological circuit would result in the farthest galleries being 1.5 km apart, a distance considered unacceptably great. As the palace consisted of symmetrical, stage-set architecture, it would be extremely difficult to make any surface additions to the building, besides which its listed status and the weight of public opinion against external modifications would make such an intervention impossible. Therefore the only viable way of linking the museum's farthest galleries was to go underground and excavate the Cour Napoléon (again, not a new idea), an option that also had the advantage of providing supplementary space where backstage activities could be housed, thus leaving the surface buildings entirely free for galleries. As well as new galleries in the Richelieu wing and new underground accommodation, the parts of the palace already occupied by the museum would be overhauled and the building's fabric cleaned and restored.

For this, the most cherished of his »grands projets« (at least until the launch of the Bibliothèque Nationale de France (13.3)), Mitterrand eschewed the usual design competition, instead personally appointing his chosen architect, the Sino-American Ieoh Ming Pei, whose extension to the National Gallery in Washington the French president had greatly admired. The project's essential outlines were already determined, but there remained the tricky question of the museum's entrance. The building's various, unmarked points of entry were considered unsatisfactory, and for the sake of symbolic and monumental *convenance* a single, easily perceptible entrance was called for. Pei's response to this aspect of the brief has become legendary: a huge glass pyramid filling the centre of the Cour Napoléon and lighting a subterranean hall linked by radiating passages to the surrounding wings. The pyramid was intended as a »beacon« to visitors, as well as providing a suitably grandiose portal for the Louvre in thoroughly modern shopping-mall/atrium/airport mode. Public reaction to Pei's proposal took the form of unbridled uproar. Many were incensed at what they perceived as a ploy by Mitterrand to create a personal mausoleum out of one of France's most important historic monuments, the pyramid's obvious pharaonic associations earning him the sobriquets Mitteramsès I and Ton Ton Khamon (»ton ton«, meaning »uncle«, already being one of his nicknames). For others, the pyramid, or any intervention of

1st *arrondissement* 39

1.8 Palais du Louvre. Cour Napoléon

its kind, would be a nasty modern excrescence on a cherished national symbol. And then there was a more pragmatic school of criticism that questioned the wisdom and necessity of having a single main entrance of this sort: given the Louvre's great size, and given that its collections cover fields which in London, for example, are split between three museums (the British Museum, the National Gallery and the Victoria & Albert Museum), was it not far more sensible to provide the building with multiple smaller entrances allowing quick access to specific collections? The enormous queues that today build up outside the pyramid, and the opening of the Porte-des-Lions entrance (Yves Lion and Alan Lewitt, 1999) in an attempt to alleviate the problem, bear witness to the sagacity of those who originally proposed multiple entrances. But the Grand Louvre was not simply about providing a working museum, it was about grand gestures of state power and national greatness, and Pei's scheme was pushed through against all objections.

As one French critic pointed out, in a modern republic only museums can aspire to royal majesty, and the Cour Napoléon as remodelled by Pei is a truly magisterial urban space. Gone are the miserable gardens and finance-ministry cars of 20 years ago, replaced by a vast mineral expanse of diamond-patterned paving, whose blankness and austerity emphasize the palace's immensity. In the centre of the void sits the pyramid, an immaculate, »Platonic« object of the type that so appealed to Mitterrand, surrounded by triangular pools which in summer sport impressively powerful fountains. Because of the Louvre's famous skewness in relation to the *grand axe* (the triumphal way departing from the Jardin des Tuileries), Pei placed a reproduction of Bernini's equestrian statue of Louis XIV in front of the pyramid, in the line of the axis, in the hope that it would, as he put it, »ameliorate an incoherent composition«. The pyramid itself, like that at Gizah, is proportioned according to the golden section. 35 m wide by 21 m high, it supports 86 tonnes of lozenge-shaped glass panels on a stainless-steel welded frame that stands up thanks to a secondary network of tensed cables connected by hand-crafted nodes, whose manufacture was entrusted to a Massachusetts firm specialized in high-tech yacht riggings. The pyramid's specially made laminated glass has none of the greenish iron-oxide tinge present in commercially available glass, and thus ensures minimum colour distortion when the Louvre's façades are seen through the pyramid. Great care was also taken to avoid physical distortion when fitting the glass, the structure being pre-stressed with a set of weights, each of which was lifted off as its corresponding pane was installed. Whether or not one approves of the pyramid (and, despite the initial negative hype, most people do), one cannot but admire its splendid engineering and the way it manages to be both solid and immaterial all at once, providing a focal point for a previously banal space and somehow ennobling Lefuel's overwrought façades.

On entering the pyramid's bottleneck entrance (much criticized because it ruins the perfect geometric form), one arrives on a little platform with plunging views down to the Hall Napoléon, the museum's basement entrance concourse. One can either descend via the escalators to the right, or take the bravura spring-form stainless-steel spiral staircase to the left, which also contains at its centre a space-age piston lift for disabled visitors. If the pyramid's entry and descent are clearly inadequate for the 6 million annual visitors, the concourse itself is made to their measure, a vast cubic space floored and clad in honey-coloured limestone, except for its coffered concrete ceilings, which at first glance one might not recognize as concrete at all. Enormous effort was made to ensure the concrete would be as »noble« as the stone it coiffs: specially dredged Nièvre-Valley sand was used to achieve the same golden hue as the limestone, the shuttering was assembled with cabinetmaker's precision from hand-selected, knot-less strips of Oregon pine, and the set concrete was twice sanded and then waxed to achieve a flawless finish.

Building of the Hall Napoléon was but phase 1 of the Grand-Louvre operation. Phases 2, 3 and 4 involved the gutting of the Richelieu wing to install brand-new galleries in place of the finance ministry's vacated offices, the excavation of all the land under the Place du Carrousel to provide car parks, multi-purpose exhibition spaces, auditoria and a major shopping mall (the Galerie du Carrousel, whose revenues were intended to recoup some of the Grand Louvre's cost), and, last but not least, the refurbishing and extension of the galleries in the old part of the museum. All the Richelieu-wing galleries are extremely slick and chic, their lighting and *mise en scène* often brilliantly thought through. Highlights include the courtyards, which were glassed over with an extremely elegant Peter-Rice-designed metallic structure to display large-scale sculpture, the top-floor painting galleries, whose ingenious cross-shaped rooflights let the sky in but keep harmful sunshine out, and the full-height set of monumental central escalators. The Galerie du Carrousel, built by Michel Macary in association with Pei, was realized along the same lines as the Hall Napoléon, with just as much care, to produce an equally slick and overwhelmingly beige environment. Here the parallels between museum-going and shopping are made abundantly clear. Where the Galerie's main axes meet, daylight is introduced via the »pyramide inversée«, a humorous reference to its bigger, right-side-up sister upstairs. Another Peter-Rice-designed structure, it has all the technological bravura of its surface confrère as well as the added property of bevelled edges that refract light and create magical rainbow effects across the Galerie's floor. Further drama is provided at the Galerie's western entrance by the remains of Charles V's defensive circuit, which was rediscovered during excavation work and incorporated into the circulatory route. As for the museum's original galleries, the last decade has seen refurbishment of more than 15,000 m^2, much of which is beautifully realized, and another 8,000 m^2 are to be reconditioned by 2005. But this will almost certainly not be the end of it, for the Musée du Louvre is now so huge that, like the Forth Bridge, it will be forever *en travaux*.

1.9 Arc du Carrousel
Place du Carrousel
Pierre-François-Léonard Fontaine and Charles Percier, 1806–08
(Métro: Palais-Royal Musée du Louvre)

The construction of a triumphal arch in the Place du Carrousel was decreed in 1806 by Napoleon to commemorate his victories in Europe and to honour the soldiers of the Grande Armée. The arch was also intended as a monumental gateway to the Palais des Tuileries (see 1.10), and was just one of a number of edifices planned by the emperor in his desire to endow Paris with monuments in the manner of imperial Rome. Fontaine and Percier, his chosen architects, were called upon to realize the scheme.

Modelled on the Arch of Constantine (perhaps an unfortunate choice given the latter's distinction as the last victory monument completed before the disintegration of the Roman Empire), the Arc du Carrousel is of classic three-bay design, decorated with pink-marble Corinthian columns and relief sculptures by Joseph Chinard depicting Napoleon's campaigns overseas. Crowning the edifice is a chariot drawn by replicas of the famous antique horses of St. Mark's in Venice; the originals, carried off as booty after Napoleon's conquest of the city, adorned the arch until their return to Venice in 1815. The detailing and craftsmanship of the work are superb.

The arch's dimensions were deliberately restricted so as not to overwhelm the Palais des Tuileries, and as a result it lacks presence. Napoleon was disappointed, and considered the Porte Saint-Denis (10.1) more suitably imposing. Since the enlargement of the Louvre

1.8 Palais du Louvre. Cour Puget

1st *arrondissement* 41

1.9 Arc du Carrousel

(1.8) and the destruction of the Tuileries, the Arc du Carrousel seems more than ever out of scale with its context.

1.10 Jardin des Tuileries
Begun 1566
(Métro: Palais Royal Musée du Louvre, Tuileries, Concorde)

The setting for some of the most turbulent events of French history, the Jardin des Tuileries is today one of the biggest and loveliest parks of Paris *intra muros*. It was created for Queen Catherine de Médicis who, in 1564, began construction of a palace just outside the western walls of the capital, which took the name of the tile factories (*tuileries*) it displaced. Her chosen architect was Philibert De l'Orme, who was succeeded by Jean Bullant in 1570. Completed in its initial state in the 1580s, the palace consisted of a symmetrical row of five classical pavilions, the central one sporting a bulbous *toit à l'impériale*. After construction of the Grande Galerie du Louvre (see 1.8), another pavilion was built onto the Palais des Tuileries, in 1608–10, linking it to the Louvre's Pavillon de Flore. This arrangement was duplicated to the north by Louis Le Vau in 1659–66, bringing the palace's façade to its maximum width of 300 m. In the 19C, the two Napoleons joined the Tuileries to the Louvre to create one, huge super-palace; this megalomaniacal project was barely completed when, during the bloody weeks of the 1871 Commune, the Palais des Tuileries was burned to the ground. Its ruins lingered on until 1882, the year of their demolition as an anti-royalist gesture by the government of the Third Republic.

In front of Catherine de Médicis' new palace, the Florentine gardener Bernard de Carnessechi had created a garden of formal parterres covering a total of 28 ha. Six of these parterres were tended by a certain Pierre Le Nôtre, whose son, Jean, became head gardener in the early 17C, a position he passed on to his own son, André, in the 1630s. The great André Le Nôtre was thus brought up and educated at the Tuileries, although his reputation as a landscape gardener was made elsewhere (see Vaux-le-Vicomte, 37.1). In 1664, his brilliance now recognized, Le Nôtre was asked to remodel the Jardin des Tuileries in preparation for Louis XIV's return to Paris following a period of withdrawal to Versailles (32.1). The new gardens, realized in tandem with Le Vau's extensions to the palace, were thus conceived with the express purpose of glorifying the monarch.

Work lasted over a decade, during which time Le Nôtre totally changed the aspect of the Tuileries, putting the majesty of perspective at the service of the king. The wall separating the palace from the gardens was removed and replaced with a flight of steps uniting the two. The central walkway bisecting the terrain was widened to prioritize the principal axis, and was endowed with two large pools, one near the château and one at the gardens' western extremity. The latter pool was made bigger than the former to counteract the diminishing effect of distance. Moreover, the pathways encircling each pool were contrived so as to correct the effects of foreshortening – when viewed from the château, the pools looked as though at the apparent centre of the circular paths. Le Nôtre was here applying the rules of Descartes's *Dioptrique*, and Descartes himself subsequently asked for plans of the Tuileries to help him when teaching pupils. The part of the gardens nearest the château was laid out with geometric parterres around two further pools, while the central area was planted in a less formal manner with trees.

At the gardens' western end, Le Nôtre cut a central opening in the rampart separating them from their environs to open up the perspective onto the surrounding countryside. Handsome, curved ramps were built, framing the opening and providing access to the ramparts, from where one could look back over the gardens or out towards the Chaillot hill. At Le Nôtre's suggestion, the king bought up the land beyond the gardens, which Le Nôtre then landscaped, creating a 2.3 km-long, straight avenue of trees which continued

1.10 Jardin des Tuileries

the gardens' axis all the way up to the horizon. The royal prerogative was thus symbolically extended into infinity while, conversely, visitors approaching Paris were presented with a magnificent perspective converging onto His Majesty's palace. The axis became today's Avenue des Champs-Elysées; Le Nôtre also laid out the Rond-Point and the basis of the Etoile (now Place Charles-de-Gaulle (see 16.1)). In his day, the land nearest the gardens between the axis and the Cours-la-Reine was filled with staggered rows of trees.

Although replanted in the 19C to suit the tastes of the era, the Jardin des Tuileries still retains the general outline of Le Nôtre's masterplan. In 1991–95, as part of the Grand Louvre project, the gardens were renewed by the landscape architects Pascal Cribier and Louis Bénéch. At the same time, the Jardin du Carrousel – created within the Louvre's Place du Carrousel after demolition of the Palais des Tuileries – was redesigned by Jacques Wirtz, with rows of yew hedges radiating out from the Arc du Carrousel (1.9) towards the Jardin des Tuileries. In addition, the Avenue du Général-Monnier, which formerly separated the Tuileries from the Carrousel, was sunk into an underpass, allowing the two gardens to be physically joined.

The Tuileries are home to both the Musée de l'Orangerie and the Galerie Nationale du Jeu de Paume. The neo-Renaissance-style Orangerie was built in 1853, and now houses the Walter-Guillaume collection, as well as Monet's waterlillies. In 1861–64, the Jeu de Paume (real-tennis court) was built as a pendant to the Orangerie by the architect Viraut. For many years the repository of the nation's Impressionist collections, it was transformed into a gallery of contemporary art in 1987–91 after the Impressionists' move to the Musée d'Orsay (7.1) in 1986. Antoine Stinco, the architect responsible for the conversion, gutted the interior and installed a suite of cool, white galleries, top-lit on the first floor. A generous, full-height entrance hall, entirely glazed within the fabric of the existing building, leads to an *escalier d'honneur* situated in a sort of »canyon« on the building's southern flank, with fine views out onto some of the most famous monuments of the Parisian skyline.

1.11 Rue de Rivoli
Pierre-François Léonard Fontaine and Charles Percier, begun 1804
(Métro: Concorde–Louvre Rivoli)

One of Paris's major traffic axes and famed the world over, the Rue de Rivoli has a long and complex history. After completion of the Place de la Concorde (8.1) in the 1770s, many projects were put forward for a uniform street running from the *place* to the Louvre alongside the Jardin des Tuileries (1.10), usually in conjunction with schemes to unite the Louvre and Tuileries palaces. It was Napoleon who finally authorized construction of such a street, and who took the first steps towards creating a Tuileries-Louvre super-palace (see 1.8). The emperor turned to his official architects, Fontaine and

1.11 Rue de Rivoli

Percier, for the realization of this major urban development.

As well as constituting a Louvre–Concorde link, the street was also intended to provide a suitably august backdrop to the Jardin des Tuileries and to unite the majestic *grand axe* of which the gardens were a part. This was a speculative scheme, in the tradition of Henri IV's Place des Vosges (4.19): owners of plots could build upon them as they pleased provided their façades conformed to Fontaine and Percier's master-design. The architects' elevations featured prominent ground-floor arcades, probably inspired by the Rue des Colonnes (2.7) and also by Italian arcaded streets, above which rose three restrained floors coiffed by a curved zinc attic. Almost entirely free of ornament and animated only by window surrounds and first and third-floor balconies, the façades are sober but nonetheless charming. As well as the Rue de Rivoli itself, the scheme involved the cutting through of the Rue de Castiglione (to link up with the Place Vendôme (1.13)) and also of the Rue and Place des Pyramides. Very slow off the ground, due to the building slump of the 1800s and 1810s, the project was not completed until the mid-1830s.

Napoleon I's Rue de Rivoli ended at the Place du Palais-Royal; it was Napoleon III who had Baron Haussmann extend the street to its current 3 km length in the 1850s. This was one of Haussmann's first and most cherished projects which, in tandem with the north–south run of the Boulevards de Sébastopol and Saint-Michel, formed the east–west axis of the Grande Croisée (»great crossing«) so fundamental to his plans for Paris. Large hotels were amongst the new buildings lining the extended street, and the project was rushed through to be ready in time for the Exposition Universelle of 1855. Fontaine and Percier's by then old-fashioned façades were repeated for the sections running parallel to the Louvre (parts of which were also under construction). In this way, Napoleon III presumably hoped to identify his regime with the glory of his uncle's, but repetition on this scale resulted only in extreme monotony.

gular windows, alternated with framed niches, and a garland motif fills the blank space at its base. Considerably more successful than the exterior, the interior is regulated by twinned, colossal Corinthian pilasters, while the coffered dome is adorned at its apex with a fresco by Charles de La Fosse depicting the Assumption of the Virgin.

1.13 Place Vendôme
Jules Hardouin-Mansart, begun 1698
(Métro: Opéra, Tuileries)

The Place Vendôme was one in a succession of royally-inspired speculative developments, which began with Henri IV's Place des Vosges (4.19). In 1685, Louis XIV bought up the Hôtel de Vendôme from the near-bankrupt duke of the same name with the intention of using the site to build an arcaded square to house the royal library and academies. The façades of this project were built, but financial difficulties necessitated a change of plan and, in 1698, the king sold the land to the municipality. Under Louis's supervision, a new scheme was devised: after demolition of the extant building work, new façades of a square to a design by Hardouin-Mansart would be erected and the plots behind sold off for the construction of *hôtels particuliers*. The project thus constituted a regularized urban stage set, boasting royal assent, behind which the wealthy could build as they chose.

1.12 Notre-Dame-de-l'Assomption

1.13 Place Vendôme

1.12 Notre-Dame-de-l'Assomption
263 bis, rue Saint-Honoré
Charles Errard, 1670–76
(Métro: Concorde, Madeleine)

In 1622, at the bidding of Cardinal de La Rochefoucauld, the Ladies of the Assumption installed themselves in the Rue Saint-Honoré. Nothing now remains of their convent buildings bar the chapel, designed by the first director of the Académie de France in Rome. Both painter and architect, Errard was the great rival of Charles Le Brun, who conspired to get Errard sent to Rome in order to distance him from prestigious commissions back home. Errard was not present for the construction of the chapel, but sent plans which were executed by a M. Cheret, and the latter may be accountable for some of the peculiarities of the finished building.

Originally framed by the convent courtyard, the chapel now stands alone on a small square. One is immediately struck by the huge domed drum surmounting the edifice, which is so disproportionate to the domestic-scale buildings below that waspish contemporaries nicknamed it the »sot dôme« (»sot« means »stupid«, and when pronounced quickly with »dôme« sounds like »Sodom«). The combination of portico and dome was clearly inspired by the Roman Pantheon, and the portico itself was probably directly influenced by the Sorbonne (5.5). The drum is pierced by eight, large, rectan-

The open arcades of the original scheme were abandoned and the size of the enclosure reduced in order to render the project commercially viable. All four sides of the square were built where before there had only been three – the fourth had been left open to frame the Couvent des Capucines (now demolished) – and attic storeys were added where previously there were none. The inclusion of diagonal elevations at the intersections of the square avoided dingy corners and maximized the surface area to be sold.

The *place* is entered at only two points, where it is bisected by a north–south thoroughfare. Hardouin-Mansart's handsome façades show Baroque influence but are restrained by Italian standards of the day, in keeping with French notions of *bon goût*. A rusticated podium of false arcades supports upper storeys decorated with colossal Corinthian pilasters, which become engaged columns on the pedimented *avant-corps* at the centre of each of the two longest façades and in the corners of the square. The whole is surmounted by a sturdy entablature, and the mansard roof is lit by alternating dormer and *œil-de-bœuf* windows (many of the latter were later enlarged into dormers to provide more light). Despite the prestige the square has always enjoyed, it spawned no successors in Paris (a comparable project is the slightly earlier, circular Place des Victoires (2.2), also by Hardouin-Mansart).

Of the mansions behind the façades, the most interesting are the Hôtel de Crozat (1703) and the Hôtel d'Evreux (1706) at nos. 17 and 19 respectively, both by Pierre Bullet. The plan of the Hôtel d'Evreux, whose frontage extends only partially across one of Hardouin-Mansart's corner pediment façades, ingeniously solves the problem of creating a symmetrical building behind an awkward exterior. The latitude of Bullet's room layouts in both *hôtels* anticipated Rococo developments. No. 15, built in 1705, was converted into a hotel in 1896 by Charles Mewès for the hotelier César Ritz, whose name it now bears. Mewès' luxurious Louis-Seize interiors set the trend for Edwardian hotel design and established modern standards of hotel comfort.

The Place Vendôme originally provided the setting for an equestrian statue of Louis XIV dressed *à l'antique*, destroyed during the Revolution. In 1806, Jacques Gondoin and Jean-Baptiste Lepère erected the Colonne Vendôme in honour of Napoleon's victory at Austerlitz. It was cast from metal obtained by melting down the 1,250 Austrian and Russian cannons captured during the battle. Its form is borrowed from Trajan's Column in Rome, and Napoleon's military campaigns are depicted upon it in spiralling bas-reliefs, in imitation of its Antique predecessor. A statue of the emperor by Antoine-Denis Chaudet crowns the column which, toppled during the Commune, was rebuilt in 1873.

In 1991/92, the square was given a 54-million-franc facelift under the direction of Pierre Prunet, Architecte en Chef des Monuments Historiques. Its entire surface was repaved in light-grey granite, parking of cars was

1.14 Annexe to Banque Paribas headquarters

prohibited, and a riot of reproduction Second-Empire candelabra planted across it in straight lines. Not a leaf now disturbs the severe chic of this hard and very French urban environment.

1.14 Annexe to Banque Paribas headquarters
Place du Marché Saint-Honoré
Taller de Arquitectura Ricardo Bofill, 1989–97
(Métro: Pyramides, Tuileries)

Once the focal point of its neighbourhood, this little market square was built on the site of the confiscated Couvent des Jacobins in the 1800s. Later in the 19C, the centre of the square was covered with four iron-and-glass market pavilions, which survived until the 1950s when they were swept away to be replaced by an ugly multi-storey car park. This decision was soon bitterly regretted, and when the lease on the car park finally expired, in 1985, the Ville de Paris seized the chance to make amends. Before any potential clients had even been found, the municipality approached Ricardo Bofill and asked him to draw up plans for a mixed-use complex of shops and offices to replace the car park. Banque Paribas came in at a later stage, and worked closely with Bofill and his team to ensure they got the kind of building that would suit the firm's sober image.

In both its form and external materials – the façade is entirely in steel and glass – Bofill's building pays

1st *arrondissement* 45

homage to the market halls of 19C Paris. What we have here is 90s Bofill: no more elephantine PoMo Classical borrowings (e. g. »Les Echelles du Baroque«, 14.2), but instead a slick, elegant structure inspired by Hi-tech and early-Modernist neoclassicism. Based on the form of a Greek temple, the building's otherwise smooth, sheer façades feature projecting fins signalling the phantom presence of base, columns, entablature and pediment. Prior to the advent of the car park, the Place du Marché Saint-Honoré was bisected by a thoroughfare, a layout which has been restituted by Bofill, thus dividing his building in two. The resulting covered street is reminiscent of the arcades which proliferated in Paris in the first half of the 19C (see feature on arcades and passages), and indeed was designed to be lined with shops (in the eventuality, the majority of the boutiques were let to only a limited number of retailers, producing a very different ambience). The covered arcade, which is closed at night, is traversed above by steel footbridges, linking the divided halves of the Paribas offices. The latter (15,000 m²), fitted out by Bofill, are sleek and coolly minimal.

One of the most immediately striking features of this building is the pristine finish of its materials, from the polished white concrete of its slender pillars to the ubiquitous glass which envelops the offices in a double skin, 75 cm apart for better thermal and acoustic insulation. This is not profound architecture, but the building is nonetheless highly effective, an immaculate crystal cathedral, all glittering transparency and light, in the midst of a huddle of narrow old streets. Moreover, its basement storeys provide parking for 1,000 cars, thus filling the gap left by its unlamented predecessor.

1.15 Saint-Roch
296, rue Saint-Honoré
Various architects, principally Jacques Le Mercier, 1653–1740
(Métro: Pyramides, Palais-Royal Musée du Louvre)

The church of Saint-Roch as we see it today owes its existence to the proximity of the Louvre (1.8) and the Palais des Tuileries (see 1.10). As the court became increasingly present at these two neighbouring palaces, so the surrounding *quartier* attracted the rich and influential, who made known their desire to rebuild the modest, original Saint-Roch in a style more befitting their illustriousness. Begun in 1653 to designs by the then Premier Architecte du Roi, Jacques Le Mercier, the new church is typical of its era in that it is a Classical adaptation of the traditional, local, Gothic type-form. Thus in plan Saint-Roch is modelled directly on Notre-Dame (4.2), with the same apse-ambulatory and non-projecting-transept layout. Just as in a Gothic church, low, chapel-lined side-aisles flank the tall main vessel, whose two-storey internal elevations comprise a Doric arcade coiffed by a clerestory rising into the high barrel vault above. At the crossing, standing in for a Gothic rib vault, we find a shallow saucer dome floating on pendentives. Indeed, so much is Saint-Roch a product of the Gothic tradition that externally, on its functional lateral elevations, it even displays flying buttresses, albeit Classically remodelled ones.

Work on Saint-Roch progressed slowly but steadily, and by the turn of the 18C the church was complete bar its high vault and main entrance façade. The Premier Architecte du Roi of the day, Jules Hardouin-Mansart, was called in to complete the edifice, but instead of seeing to the missing elements he decided to enlarge the church by adding the Chapelle de la Vierge and its pendant Chapelle de la Communion at the rear of the building. Begun in 1706, two years before Hardouin-Mansart's death, the chapels were completed by Pierre Bullet and inaugurated in 1710. Theatrically Baroque, the two-storey, domed, oval Chapelle de la Vierge is enveloped by a circular, one-storey ambulatory (which runs directly off the apse ambulatory) leading to the Chapelle de la Communion. Bullet modified Hardouin-Mansart's plans so that the rear of the Chapelle de la Vierge opens onto the ambulatory behind, thereby creating an extraordinary perspective when viewed from the choir. In the 1750s, the then vicar, Jean-Baptiste Marduel, undertook an ambitious programme of decoration at Saint-Roch that included the Chapelle de la Vierge's elaborate *gloire*, modelled on that at St. Peter's in Rome, and its dome painting, by Jean-Baptiste Pierre, which represents the Assumption.

1.15 Saint-Roch

46 1st *arrondissement*

Saint-Roch was only finally vaulted in the 1720s (the choir-vault and crossing paintings are later, dating from the 19C), and had to wait until the 1730s for the construction of its principal façade. Designed by Robert de Cotte (Hardouin-Mansart's brother-in-law and former assistant), it breaks with the twin-tower composition originally planned by Le Mercier and instead returns to the Roman, Jesuit model that had inspired Parisian churches of the first half of the 17C, for example the Sorbonne (5.5) and the Val-de-Grâce (5.9). A grand, two-storey affair in the Gesù tradition, Saint-Roch's entrance façade broke with the relative delicacy of its predecessors in its heavily projecting, central *avant-corps* and in its exclusive use of ponderous engaged columns instead of the more usual pilasters. De Cotte's design was criticized in its day for its abundant carvings, most of which have since been lost.

The final major addition to Saint-Roch came in 1754 as part of Marduel's programme of improvements. Onto the rear of the church Etienne-Louis Boullée tacked a Chapelle de la Calvaire, which featured at its centre a sort of rocky grotto with a sculpture of the crucifixion dramatically illuminated from a hidden light source above. Sadly, Boullée's work was essentially destroyed in the 19C when the chapel was rebuilt and enlarged to serve as a Chapelle des Catéchismes, although the central niche was preserved *in situ* and, on the rare occasions when the Chapelle de la Communion's shutters are open, still terminates the extraordinary *enfilade* of spaces of which Saint-Roch is composed.

1.16 Palais-Royal
Place du Palais-Royal
Various architects, begun c. 1634
(Métro: Palais-Royal Musée du Louvre)

The complex of buildings today known as the Palais-Royal stands on the site of the former Palais-Cardinal, the sumptuous residence Cardinal Richelieu built for himself in the 1630s after becoming Louis XIII's chief minister. Situated not far from the Louvre (1.8), thereby allowing Richelieu quick access to the king and the court, the Palais-Cardinal was famous for its lavish interiors and for its splendid gardens, as well as for its two theatres, the bigger of which later became home to the Paris opera. Long before his death, Richelieu bequeathed the palace to Louis XIII, reserving for himself only the usufruct, probably in a political move to pre-empt the king's eventual jealously over the magnificence of his chief minister's residence. Following Richelieu's demise, the Palais-Royal, as it was thereafter known, did not become the seat of government as the cardinal had hoped, but was allocated to royal personages of second importance – firstly Louis XIII's widow, then the exiled Queen Henrietta Maria of England and afterwards, in the 1660s, to the dukes of Orléans, who shaped the building we see today. In the 19C, following the fall of the Second Empire, the palace became home to the Conseil d'Etat and the *sous-secrétariat aux Beaux-Arts*; the Conseil is still housed within its walls,

1.16 Palais-Royal

but the Ministère de la Culture has now taken the place of the *sous-secrétariat*. The palace's thespian tradition continues, two theatres still forming part of the complex: the Théâtre du Palais-Royal and the Comédie-Française, France's prestigious national playhouse. Nothing now remains of the palace as Richelieu knew it, his buildings having been entirely replaced during a series of reconstruction campaigns carried out during the 18C and 19C. Despite this, the cardinal's legacy lives on in the layout and general disposition of the current complex and especially in its beautiful gardens, which are one of Paris's more surprising secrets.

Richelieu's palace was disposed around two courtyards, one giving onto the Rue Saint-Honoré (known today as the Cour de l'Horloge) and the other opening out onto the garden (generally referred to as the Cour d'Honneur), an arrangement which the current building retains. The oldest surviving structure in today's ensemble is the northern section of the Rue-de-Valois wing, opposite the Place de Valois (whose buildings originally housed the servants and services of the Palais-Royal). This part of the palace was built in the 1750s by Pierre Contant d'Ivry for the then Duc d'Orléans, Louis-Philippe the Fat, and completed a partial reconstruction campaign that had been begun earlier in the century. Contant's designs stand midway between the Rococo flamboyance of the early-18C and the more sober Classicism of its latter half, and this hybrid quality is well illustrated at the Palais-Royal. His *avant-corps* on the Rue de Valois, with its giant balcony brackets and rather inventive detailing, combines Rococo-style decorative charm with a certain Classical solidity in its massing. The two surviving interiors by Contant in this part of the building – the Duchesse d'Orléans's dining room (now the Salle du Tribunal des Conflits of the Conseil d'Etat) and another of her former chambers (today the Conseil's Salle des Finances) – also illustrate this duality: the dining room is Classically bedecked with pilasters, while the more delicate adornment of the Salle des Finances recalls French-Regency-period interiors.

1st *arrondissement* 47

The next great wave of reconstruction at the Palais-Royal came in 1763, when a fire destroyed the bigger of Richelieu's theatres, home to the Paris opera. As the municipality was responsible for the opera, the cost of its rebuilding fell partly on the shoulders of the councillors, who consequently imposed their own architect, Pierre-Louis Moreau-Desproux, for the job. Louis-Philippe the Fat used the disaster as a pretext for rebuilding the principal sections of the palace, and commissioned his own architect, Contant d'Ivry, to this end. Moreau and Contant worked together on the rebuilding project, the former designing the opera and the façades of the new Cour de l'Horloge, while the latter was responsible for the interiors of the reconstructed *corps de logis* and for the façades of the Cour d'Honneur. Moreau's opera no longer survives, but the Cour de l'Horloge that we see today is essentially his. Its elevations continue 16C and 17C French traditions of secular building but with a lightness of touch that is characteristic of Louis XV's reign. Their domestic scale and use of rather weedy superimposed orders contrast with the grand manner of the 17C, everything here being designed to give an impression of quiet good taste where nothing sticks out or destroys the harmony of the whole. In the hands of a master like Ange-Jacques Gabriel, Louis XV's Premier Architecte, this approach could produce quite sublime buildings (e.g. the Petit Trianon, 32.4), but at the Palais-Royal the result is rather dull. Contant's garden-side façades pack a little more punch, and his splendid *escalier d'honneur*, with its domed covering and dramatic curved descent, is justly famous.

In 1780, Louis-Philippe the Fat, who had secretly married a commoner, Mme de Montesson, forsook the pomp of the Palais-Royal in order to be able to live more privately with his wife, and consequently left the palace to his son, the then Duc de Chartres (who became Duc d'Orléans on his father's death, in 1785). It was under Chartres's tenure that the Palais-Royal reached the apogee of its fame. Always short of cash, the duke decided to exploit the potential of his precocious inheritance by building six-storey apartment buildings with ground-floor colonnades of shops around three sides of the palace's garden. To this end, three new streets were constructed in front of the 17C houses that originally overlooked the garden, bearing the names of Montpensier, de Beaujolais and de Valois, after the duke's sons. Chartres's chosen architect for the new apartment buildings was Victor Louis, who had won fame with his design for the Théâtre de Bordeaux (1772–80). Begun in 1781, work progressed rapidly, and the buildings were inaugurated in 1784. Louis's principal façades are quite extraordinary in that very narrow bays (whose width was determined by the cadence of the palace itself), adorned with a colossal Composite order, are repeated over 200 times around the periphery of the garden. Without the obscuring filter of the garden's trees the effect would be monotonous in the extreme, despite the almost Bacchanalian richness of the decoration which, as well as the Composite order – the most elaborate of all – includes trophy medallions above the first-floor windows, swags and brackets adorning the entablature and giant urns topping off the balustrade. At any rate this architectural exuberance proved entirely appropriate to the hedonistic abandon promoted by the Duc de Chartres at the Palais-Royal. The public flocked there in droves, attracted by the winning combination of luxury commerce, gambling, *filles de joie* and absence of policemen (the Duc de Chartres was such an important personage that he could prohibit the police from entering his property).

Just four days before Louis received approval for his Palais-Royal colonnades, Moreau-Desproux's opera was destroyed by fire, much to the chagrin of the Duc de Chartres who had been banking on the opera's serving as a draw for his new development. Moreover, following the conflagration, the municipality decided not to rebuild on the same site. Not to be deterred, the duke decided to construct a new theatre at the palace anyway, and commissioned Louis to provide a design. Instead of having the auditorium rebuilt on its original site to the east of the palace, the duke directed that the new theatre be constructed to the west of the complex (which involved the destruction of the remaining 17C sections of the palace), thereby allowing the Rue de Valois to open directly into the Rue Saint-Honoré and thus better integrating the palace's colonnades into the urban fabric. Work on the new theatre (today's Comédie-Française) began in 1786 and was completed in 1790. The site was so cramped that Louis was forced to adopt the ingenious disposition of placing the entrance foyer under the auditorium. Although in many respects his design was traditional, in one aspect it was revolutionary: iron frames were used for the roof, the floors and the boxes, essentially in the interests of fireproofing. Externally the building paraded dull, repetitive façades whose only intent was not to stand out from the Palais-Royal proper (the theatre as we see it today was extended in the 19C and rebuilt internally after a fire in 1900). The Théâtre du Palais-Royal (at the northern end of the Rue de Montpensier) was also originally by Louis, but was reconstructed by Louis Regnier de Guerchy in 1830. It is chiefly interesting for its elaborate iron fire escapes, added by Paul Sédille in 1880.

As well as the colonnades and the new theatre, the Duc de Chartres's interventions at the Palais-Royal were to have included the building of new wings onto the palace itself, one to replace the old buildings to the west of the Cour d'Honneur and another, brand-new wing closing this courtyard on its northern side. But funds ran out and the duke was never able to finish the work. The foundations of the northern wing had already been completed, and in a move to protect them from the elements and also to exploit further the commercial potential of the Palais-Royal, the duke granted a certain M. Romain (or Romois) the right to build a temporary, wooden structure on the site to house shops and boutiques. Put up in 1786, Romain's building, which became known as the Galeries de Bois, was an instant hit with the public, and is often cited as one of the precursors to the craze for covered arcades that swept Paris in the early-19C (see feature on arcades and passages). The Galeries de Bois were later replaced by what became perhaps the most famous of Paris's covered arcades, the Galerie d'Orléans, built by Pierre-François-Léonard Fontaine and Charles Percier in 1828–30. The Galerie d'Orléans was demolished in the 1930s, but the parallel colonnades that delimited its lateral extremities still stand between the Cour d'Honneur and the gardens.

Like all other aristocratic property, the Palais-Royal was confiscated during the Revolution, but it was returned to the Orléans clan at the time of the Bourbon Restoration, in 1814. In 1817, the then duke – who later became King Louis Philippe – drew up a plan with Fontaine to complete the building work left unfinished by his father. Fontaine's most significant contribution, apart from the Galerie d'Orléans, was the western wing of the Cour d'Honneur, known as the Aile de Montpensier. Following its completion in 1830, no more major external building work was carried out at the palace until the creation of the highly controversial Colonnes de Buren in 1985/86. Brainchild of the then culture minister, Jack Lang, the Colonnes were the work of the artist Daniel Buren. Although often presented as art for art's sake, they were actually commissioned to dissimulate a change in the Cour d'Honneur's ground level engendered by the construction of a basement extension to the culture ministry's premises. The ventilation and other outlets of these new subterranean spaces were also to be masked by the installation, which replaced the car park that formerly occupied the courtyard. Officially entitled *Les Deux Plateaux*, Buren's work takes the form of a conceptual grid imposed on the courtyard, whose intersections are marked by candy-striped, black-and-white columns of different heights poking up from the courtyard's floor like sticks of seaside rock. Some of the columns continue below ground level in deep, water-filled channels. In one sense the installation can be read as an exploration of the perception and intellectual projection of space. Its construction provoked a national outcry, the project being attached for its cost, its »unsuitability« in the context of a »national monument« and because Lang ignored the directives of the Commission des Monuments Historiques, which was opposed to the scheme. Given the harmlessness of the result (deliberate – Buren wanted a monument that would not dominate), the fuss seems excessive, although on the financial front the columns have proved not only expensive to install but also to maintain.

1.17 Apartment building
33–35, rue Radziwill and 48, rue de Valois
Giraud de Talairac, 1781
(Métro: Palais-Royal Musée du Louvre)
Nicknamed the »tallest house in Paris«, this nine-storey monster was a speculative block erected by a master

1.18 Hôtel de La Vrillière or de Toulouse, now Banque de France

mason. Its excessive height – extraordinary when one considers its date – served not only to maximize rents but also to attract the attention of the rather louche crowd that frequented the fashionable Palais-Royal (1.16) just next door. The building's plain exterior hid a shady dive which was reached by a double spiral staircase (still extant), ideal for those who wished to avoid undesired encounters when arriving or leaving. The building also contained the entrance to the Passage des Bons-Enfants, a glass-covered shortcut linking the Rue de Beaujolais and the then Rue des Bons-Enfants, that prefigured Paris's covered arcades (see feature on arcades and passages).

Two years later, in 1783, possibly in direct reaction to Talairac's giant, legislation was passed limiting for the first time the height of buildings erected in Paris. A royal declaration ordered that henceforth new streets be a minimum 30 feet (roughly 9.6 m) wide and fixed building heights in relation to the width of the street and the materials used for construction. Old streets less than 30 feet wide were to be widened as new buildings were constructed, which explains the discontinuity in the building line observable in many pre-1783 thoroughfares. The effects of these regulations were far-reaching. Not only did they alter the dynamics of the property market, capping maximum profitability, but they also produced an aesthetic effect of greater uniformity. The appearance of Paris is governed by height restrictions to this day.

1.18 Hôtel de La Vrillière or de Toulouse, now Banque de France
1, rue de La Vrillière
François Mansart, 1635–40
(Métro: Bourse)
Commissioned by the Marquis de La Vrillière, this was probably the first private residence built by Mansart in Paris, and in its epoch was considered the epitome of modernity. The simplicity and sobriety of its elevations, and the harmony of its separate volumes, were much admired. Occupation by the Banque de France has al-

1st *arrondissement* 49

1.19 Hôtel des Postes

1.19 Hôtel des Postes
48–52, rue du Louvre
Julien Guadet, 1880–86
(Métro: Les Halles, Louvre-Rivoli)

As an academic at Paris's Ecole des Beaux-Arts (6.1) for over 50 years and, from 1894, its Professor of Theory, Julien Guadet was highly influential. His most illustrious pupils were Tony Garnier and Auguste Perret, and through them his ideas were passed on to the emerging architects of the Modern Movement, including Le Corbusier. Often portrayed as the epitome of academicism, Guadet was an advocate of Rational Classicism, with its emphasis on construction, and also championed an »Elementarist« approach to design whereby typified architectural forms were rationally combined according to the precepts of axial composition. His theories were published in 1902 as the voluminous and dense *Eléments et Théories de l'Architecture*, based on his lecture courses.

Guadet's academic activities left little room for actual building, and the Hôtel des Postes is his one major realization. Although conceived long before he became professor, it displays many ideas that would later be integrated into his teachings. Built on a substantial, wedge-shaped site, the Hôtel is organized around large central spaces intended for the sorting of mail (30,000 sacks per day in the 1880s) and storage of over 100 horse-drawn vehicles. To achieve the wide spans necessary for these activities, a metal frame was used. In its construction and planning, the Hôtel is thus rigorously rational, although it is dressed up in a rather sterile stone wrapping, whose heavy Classicism is of diverse inspiration. Guadet's son, Paul, subsequently showed some of the potential of his father's teachings in his house on the Boulevard Murat (16.17).

tered the house to the point of unrecognizability today. Its most celebrated room was the long gallery running the entire length of the garden wing, and this gallery now constitutes the principal interest of the building. Lit by six enormous windows and covered with a shallow barrel vault, the gallery was unostentatiously decorated in Mansart's time, except for the magnificent allegorical ceiling frescoes by François Perrier.

Purchased in 1713 by the Comte de Toulouse, whose name it then took, the house was remodelled by Robert de Cotte and the gallery redecorated in 1718/19 by François-André Vassé. His gilded carvings, which gave the room the name »Galerie Dorée«, are a masterpiece of Rococo exuberance, and make allegorical reference to the Count's status as both Grand Amiral and Grand Veneur (master of the royal hounds).

Confiscated after the Revolution, the house was assigned to the Banque de France in 1808, and its long decline began. Extensions were added and the original fabric neglected to the extent that, by the 1860s, the Galerie Dorée was in danger of collapse. At the initiative of Empress Eugénie it was entirely rebuilt in 1870–75, including the copying of Perrier's frescoes onto canvas.

1.20 Bourse du Commerce
2, rue de Viarmes
François-Joseph Bélanger, 1806–12; Henri Blondel, 1886–89
(Métro: Louvre Rivoli, Les Halles; RER: Châtelet-Les-Halles)

The Bourse du Commerce as we find it today is the product of several epochs. Its oldest element is the curious astronomical tower in the form of a massive Doric column abutting the southeastern elevation, sole vestige of the Hôtel de Soissons built by Jean Bullant for Catherine de Médicis in 1574–84. After demolition of the *hôtel* in 1748, the property was bought by the Prévôt des Marchands who, in 1763–67, had an *halle au blé* (corn exchange) built on the site to a design by Nicolas Le Camus de Mézières. Circular in plan, the building enclosed a large central courtyard more than 120 feet (37 m) in diameter, which, in 1782/83, Jacques-Guillaume Legrand and Jacques Molinos covered with a wooden-framed dome. At the time of the dome's construction François-Joseph Bélanger had put forward an alternative design in iron – an extremely avant-garde proposal for the era – and, in 1802, when the wooden

50 1st *arrondissement*

structure was destroyed by fire, he submitted proposals for a cast-iron replacement. The Conseil des Travaux Publics was not enthusiastic, declaring Bélanger's project unbuildable and opting instead for a replacement in stone. When, however, it transpired that a stone structure would necessitate massive strengthening of the walls, and after pressure from the Minister of the Interior, they gave way and accepted the scheme.

Engineering projects of this kind were not Bélanger's usual territory (see, e. g., the Château de Bagatelle, 29.2) and for this, the first ever iron dome, he engaged F. Brunet to help him with the necessary calculations. Their collaboration was one of the earliest instances of a clear distinction between the roles of architect and construction engineer. The dome's design did not push the technological capabilities of iron, instead imitating timber forms of construction in the new material. Costs proved considerable, as iron was still an exceptional and relatively scarce material in France at that time. Originally clad in copper, the dome was partially glazed in 1838.

Use of the corn exchange diminished as the century wore on and, in 1886, Henri Blondel was engaged to make the old *halle* suitable for use as a financial exchange, to relieve the cramped Palais Brongniart (2.8). Work involved the sinking of a basement floor and demolition of Mézières's building, which was replaced with a new, deeper structure in heavy neo-Baroque style. The *architecture d'accompagnement* surrounding the edifice dates from this time. Bélanger's dome was conserved and its upper section glazed, revealing its fine, elegant structure, while the lower section was tiled in slate and decorated on the interior with an enormous

1.20 Bourse du Commerce

fresco, covering more than 1,500 m^2, on the theme of commerce around the world. Restored in 1994/95, the dome still serves today nearly two centuries after its construction.

1.21 Saint-Eustache
1, rue du Jour
Possibly attributable to Jean Delamarre and / or Pierre Le Mercier, 1532–1640
(Métro: Les Halles; RER: Châtelet-Les-Halles)

Paris's population grew rapidly in the late middle ages, and many is the church within the city's limits that was rebuilt or extended in the 14C and 15C to accommodate an expanding congregation. Saint-Eustache, which started out life as a modest chapel constructed in 1210, would have been one of these, were it not for the fact that the densely built neighbourhood in which it was situated made its enlargement physically impossible. Seven side-chapels were tacked on to the original structure during the 14C, but apart from these minor additions the church remained essentially as built for over three centuries. Consequently, as the faithful became ever more numerous, so Saint-Eustache became ever more inadequate. By the 16C nothing had changed, and it took the intervention in the late 1520s of the king himself, François I, to rectify the problem. François had announced, in 1528, his desire to make Paris his permanent residence (the capital having been neglected for over a century by French monarchs in favour of the Loire valley), and, »architecte manqué« that he was, set out to express his authority in the city's built environment. But François's real passion was for châteaux, and he had already invested heavily in several homes in the Paris region. By personally taking an interest in Saint-Eustache's plight, and by using the royal prerogative to expropriate surrounding properties and thus allow its reconstruction, he was able to influence the design of a major new edifice without touching the crown exchequer, it being the parish that would pay for the church's rebuilding.

As a result of this conjunction of circumstances – the original impossibility of enlarging Saint-Eustache, and François I's using it to make his mark on the capital – the building has the distinction of being the only major church to have been entirely conceived during the early French Renaissance (the Wars of Religion having put a stop to most building activity in the later part of the 16C). As far as architecture was concerned, the early French Renaissance was essentially a question of applying Classicizing decoration to established medieval building types, and Saint-Eustache, which was designed at a time when no Classical Italian churches of its scale had yet been realized, would follow this trend. Indeed in its plan and massing Saint-Eustache looks back two centuries to Notre-Dame (4.2), with which it set out to compete in importance. Many Parisian churches were loosely modelled on the city's cathedral right up into the Flamboyant period, but at Saint-Eustache the resemblance is especially close, both in lay-

1st arrondissement 51

1.21 Saint-Eustache

out and dimensions: Saint-Eustache is 44 m wide and 34 m high under its main vault (compared to Notre-Dame's 48 m width and 35 m height) and, like the cathedral, is organized on a Latin-cross plan with non-projecting transepts, an apse/ambulatory east end and equal-height double aisles. Only in its length does Saint-Eustache's basic plan differ markedly – 105 m in comparison to Notre-Dame's 130 m –, the important thoroughfares that were the Rue du Jour and the Rue Montmartre preventing its expansion in this direction. François I, it seems, wanted a church in the new style, associated with his name, that would directly and obviously rival with the prestige of the old Notre-Dame.

We do not know with any certainty the name(s) of the architect(s) of the new Saint-Eustache. It seems likely that whoever designed it had been trained in the Paris region and had worked on the extension, begun in 1525, of the church of Saint-Maclou in Pontoise, which presents similar traits. Two possible names fit the bill: Jean Delamarre and Pierre Le Mercier, who worked together on Saint-Maclou. The foundation stone of the new Saint-Eustache was laid in 1532, but it was not finally completed until over a century later, in 1640. Despite this lengthy gestation (which was partly due to a 30-year interruption in building work, c. 1586–1615, occasioned by the Wars of Religion), the original plan was stuck to all the way through. Construction began with the crossing and the chapels of the choir, which were built around the original 13C church (the latter remaining in use throughout and not being destroyed until the late 1620s). Next came the nave, bar its clerestory and high vault, in the period 1545–86. When building recommenced in the 17C, it was with the west front, until 1624 when the main part of the choir was begun. The transepts and the nave were vaulted in 1633–37, after which the new church was consecrated; work carried on, however, with the building of the lady chapel and the northern transept's façade, which is marked with the date 1640.

Although Saint-Eustache's plan followed the Notre-Dame pattern, in other respects the church differed markedly. On entering Saint-Eustache, one cannot fail to be impressed by the enormous height of its main-vessel arcades, and consequently of its aisles, which are so tall that they have their own clerestory above the openings to the low side-chapels. This was a configuration borrowed from High-Gothic French churches such as Bourges Cathedral (c. 1200–55) and, as a result, Saint-Eustache is extremely light inside. This luminosity is further aided by its Rayonnant-style glazed triforium, which reproduces the type pioneered at Saint-Denis (21.2). Moving on in time, but still thoroughly Gothic, are Saint-Eustache's high vaults, which, with their complicated multitude of liernes and elaborate and daringly long crossing and choir pendants, are characteristically Flamboyant. Where the early French Renaissance makes its mark at Saint-Eustache is in the Classicizing design of the piers, arcades and carved detailing. The piers are still composite in the old Gothic manner, but the elements forming the agglomerate

52   1st *arrondissement*

have been Classicized: some piers feature shafts carved as a weird superimposition of enormously stretched bases, Doric pilasters and engaged Corinthian columns, the piers in the crossing comprise ridiculously elongated Corinthian pilasters, while elsewhere cornices have replaced arcade capitals and string courses. The church's arcades (and its windows) are round-headed, except in the apse, where, in order to maintain the narrower arches' springing points and apexes at the same levels as the rest of arcade, pointed, elongated forms had to be used. Almost nothing about Saint-Eustache's detailing is Classically »correct«, and its rather freakish, hybrid quality goes a long way to explaining why it was never copied. Viollet-le-Duc put it more caustically, describing the church as »a Gothic skeleton clad in Roman rags«. Rather than Classical, much of Saint-Eustache's detailing appears almost Romanesque, and it may well be that some of the more Roman-looking of French Romanesque-period churches influenced its design.

Externally, Saint-Eustache fully displays its Gothic origins, with generous glazing, a multitude of flying buttresses and a wealth of carved detail. Because of the church's situation on the Les Halles market (see 1.22), it was the south front, rather than the west, that acted as the building's main entrance, and thus constituted the main façade. In its composition the south front is entirely Gothic, modelled on the famous southern-transept façade of Notre-Dame. But in the execution of the detailing the façade's sculptors tried to Classicize their medieval piling up of ornament, with very bastard results. Gone is the extraordinary filigree and geometric patterning of Notre-Dame, replaced with a much heavier, more solid elevation whose rose window has been straightened out into a rather static wheel, whose carvings attempt to Classicize typically Gothic forms and subjects, and from which Classical detailing (such as Corinthian capitals) pokes in surprising places. Elsewhere the church appears more typical of the early French Renaissance, for example in the narrow towers flanking the north-transept façade, or in the treatment of the lady chapel (especially when viewed from the Rue Montmartre) with its high roof and tall lantern, all of which recalls François I's Château de Chambord (c. 1518–37) in the Loire valley.

The west front we see at Saint-Eustache today is 18C. 15 years after the church's completion, in 1655, Jean-Baptiste Colbert, Louis XIV's chief minister, ordered the addition of two chapels to the base of the original west front's towers. Unfortunately, this intervention weakened the structure to the extent that, in 1688, the western façade had to be demolished. Since the south front served as the main entrance, there was no hurry to rebuild the western elevation, and the current west façade was only begun in 1754. It was designed by Jean Hardouin-Mansart de Jouy, whose two-tower composition – which is a Classical adaptation of a typically Gothic configuration – is based on the type devised by Sir Christopher Wren for St. Paul's Cathedral in London (1675–1711), which had already been copied in Paris by Giovanni Niccolò Servandoni in his 1736 design for the west façade of Saint-Sulpice (6.5). At Saint-Eustache, the collision of this blind, rather dry Enlightenment-era mastodon with the busy Renaissance-period church behind does not make for a happy cohabitation. Like Saint-Sulpice's, the west front of Saint-Eustache was never completed, building work stopping for good in 1778 with the south tower barely begun; on its Rue-Rambuteau flank, one can still see stone scaffolding supports (which normally would have been removed once work was over) projecting from the middle of the otherwise smooth ashlar blocks.

1.22 Jardin, Forum and Nouveau Forum des Halles
Rues Pierre-Lescot, Rambuteau and Berger
Various architects, 1977–87
(Métro: Les Halles; RER: Châtelet-Les-Halles)

For over 800 years, until its relocation in 1969, Paris's principal produce market stood on this spot. The site was twice comprehensively redeveloped, first in the mid-19C and then again in the 1970s following the market's move. This second metamorphosis was the catalyst for a radical and lasting change in Paris's planning and urbanism policies. The saga of Les Halles, as the area is now known, began during the reign of Louis Philippe, when the government decided to rebuild the disparate collection of structures that made up the market complex. The architects Victor Baltard and Félix Callet were appointed to the job in 1845 but, due to the 1848 Revolution, construction of their scheme did not begin until 1851. By 1853 the new building, a traditional masonry structure, was nearing completion when work was suddenly stopped by order of Napoleon III. It seems that the inauguration that same year of Eugène Flachat's Gare Saint-Lazare (8.5) – a daring iron shed that spanned 40 m in a single volley, a world record at the time – had reflected unfavourably on Baltard and Callet's massive stone building, making it seem heavy and clumsy by comparison and thus unacceptable to

1.22 Nouveau Forum des Halles

1st *arrondissement* 53

public and imperial pride. »Umbrellas, only umbrellas!« and »Iron, nothing but iron!« were the emperor's new instructions for the market buildings and, with the backing of Baron Haussmann, Baltard produced an entirely new scheme designed to seduce imperial aspirations. The famous Halles Centrales were born.

In its final form, Baltard's project consisted of two groups of six wrought-and-cast-iron pavilions joined together by covered streets. The first two were completed in 1854, the next four in 1858, another two in 1860 and then in 1874, while the final pair was only realized in the 1930s. Although not technically revolutionary for their time – the distances spanned were considerably less than those already achieved by Flachat – Baltard's pavilions caught the public imagination as symbols of the prowess of the industrial age, inspiring authors such as Zola and Verlaine, who described their delicate ironwork as »Vulcan's lace«. The pavilions' success was such that they became something of a standard model for market halls all over France. But whilst their architecture may have drawn praise, their location was the subject of criticism. Situated in the heart of Paris, their presence caused enormous traffic problems, and the constricting urbanity around them precluded any possibility of expansion. It was these factors that finally prompted the market's relocation to Rungis, outside Paris proper, in 1969.

Before the wholesalers had even left, the fate of Baltard's pavilions was sealed: demolition and redevelopment. Paris was at that time busy constructing her suburban train network (the RER – see feature on the Métro and the RER), and Les Halles, because of its location bang in the city centre, was chosen as the site of a major subterranean rail/Métro interchange. Construction of the station was to be open cast, making the market pavilions' removal unavoidable. In their stead, a vast new complex was to be built that would include a shopping-and-leisure centre. This decision, taken by De Gaulle's government, launched a decade-long battle waged by local residents and conservationists against the state. The conservation campaign garnered world-wide attention: as well as protest marches in Paris, there were demonstrations at the French consulate in New York, and the *Washington Post*, the Metropolitan Museum of Art, Mies van der Rohe and Max Ernst all publicly called for the preservation of Baltard's pavilions. A bomb was even set off at Père-Lachaise (20.2) in the name of the conservation campaign, but to no avail; the authorities remained firm, and destruction of the 19C market buildings began in August 1971. As many conservationists pointed out, an alternative to demolition would have been to dismantle the pavilions and reconstruct them following completion of the opencast work, but this solution was rejected as too costly. Besides, veneration of the past was not in the tenor of the times, at least not at government level; indeed the ultra-Modernist President Pompidou and his officials seem to have been fervently opposed to any kind of conservation, refusing even to meet the American millionaire who offered to buy the pavilions and transport them to the States. However, grace was accorded to one example, *halle* no. 8, which was taken down and re-erected at Nogent-sur-Marne in Paris's eastern suburbs, where it now serves as a cultural centre (Pavillon Baltard, 12, avenue Victor-Hugo, RER: Nogent-sur-Marne). Many commentators have suggested that, had they been judged in today's climate of heritage conservation, Baltard's pavilions would never have been demolished. It was, however, precisely their destruction and the public reaction it provoked that contributed to this change of attitude.

Work on the rail interchange began in 1972, and Parisians were appalled and fascinated in equal measure as an enormous hole appeared where the market had once stood. The *trou des Halles*, as it was dubbed, subsequently entered the city's mythology. As it grew, so did the polemic about what to do with it once the station was completed. Several projects came and went before work even began, and hesitation continued as late as 1979! However, one project that was conceived at the outset and completed in substantially its initial form was the Forum des Halles (Claude Vasconi and Georges Pencréac'h, 1973–79), the shopping centre that occupies the eastern section of the former produce market. Organized around an open patio sunk four storeys below grade, the Forum comprises a warren of wide but low underground passages lined with shops. Inside it is banal and rather depressing, while outside the clumsy curves of its flimsy-looking metal-and-glass covering are a particularly feeble-minded example of 1970s futurism. Its surface buildings are even worse, evocative of some rusty seaside arcade in a tacky resort. That this sorry ensemble should occupy the heart of Paris ought to be a source of national shame.

In the meantime projects came and went for the rest of the site. On his election in 1974, President Valéry Giscard d'Estaing cancelled his predecessors' schemes for the western part of the *trou* and ordered the creation of a park there, naming Ricardo Bofill as its architect. Later, in 1978, Giscard announced plans for a »Palais de la Musique« to be built under the park. But he had not counted on the 1977 devolution of power in the capital, when Paris got her first elected mayor since the 19C. The city's new boss was Jacques Chirac, who set about wresting control of Les Halles from the state, famously declaring, in 1978, »L'architecte en chef des Halles c'est moi!« Under his aegis, Giscard's two projects were scrapped (a half-completed Bofill building even being demolished) in 1979; the idea of a park was retained, but Bofill would not be the architect, while the spaces underneath it were to become home to the »Nouveau Forum des Halles«, a mixture of more shops, public amenities – a swimming pool, a gym, a *vidéothèque* and an auditorium, amongst others – and an attraction, in the form of the »Parc Océanique Jacques Cousteau«. (Cousteau's aquarium was built but eventually went bust and was replaced in the late 1980s by a

1.23 Fontaine des Innocents

Ciné-Cité cinema complex.) Louis Arretche and François-Xavier and Claude Lalanne were appointed architects of the Jardin des Halles, as the park became known, while Paul Chemetov was named architect of the »Nouveau Forum«.

Completed in 1986, the Nouveau Forum has received much better press than its older sister. Working in raw concrete, Chemetov strove both to echo the Gothic forms of Saint-Eustache just above (1.21) and to bring a Piranesian dignity to the vast subterranean spaces he had been asked to fit out. »Chunks of a collapsed town imprisoned below ground« was how he imagined the new forum's aesthetic. In places his strategy comes off magnificently – for example the grandiose swimming pool with its powerful concrete vaults – and his five-storey-high public-circulation areas avoid the nasty sense of compression of the Vasconi-Pencréac'h sections. However, despite their spaciousness and dramatic concrete girders, there is something of a grey, troglodyte, underground-car-park feel to the main public spaces, not helped by the rather tacky lighting and detailing that accompany them. As for the Arretche/Lalanne park, it is a rather uninspired 20C updating of classic French garden design, with lots of trees lined up in rows. Monumental trellis constructions, intended to recall 19C iron-and-glass market-hall architecture, mark the entrances to the Nouveau Forum and also serve to distract from the rather intimidating escalators descending into the depths. Pleasant though lacklustre, the Jardin des Halles is, unusually for a Parisian park, not fenced or gated, and consequently suffers from security problems at night.

Despite the often virulent opprobrium heaped on it over the years, the Les-Halles redevelopment is an undeniable commercial success. Thanks to its situation at the hub of the Ile-de-France's regional rail network, the shopping centre receives over 100,000 visitors a day. But it is not the up-market mall originally hoped for by the authorities; directly connected to Paris's vast hinterland, it now attracts huge numbers of out-of-towners from the capital's less-privileged suburbs.

1.23 Fontaine des Innocents
Place Joachim-Du-Bellay
Pierre Lescot (?) and Jean Goujon, 1547–49
(Métro: Les Halles; RER: Châtelet-Les-Halles)

Although today of distinctly dubious reputation, the Rue Saint-Denis was once Paris's most prestigious thoroughfare, linking the nation's centre of power on the Ile de la Cité (4.1) to the royal abbey of Saint-Denis (21.2). The »Voie Royale«, as it was known, was thus the traditional setting for the monarch's formal entry into the capital. For Henri II's arrival on 16 June 1549, as well as the usual temporary decoration, one permanent structure had been erected – the Fontaine des Innocents. Authorship of the edifice remains contested. Some credit the entire work to Goujon, who we know was definitely responsible for the bas-reliefs decorating the fountain, while others suggest co-authorship with Lescot, with whom Goujon later collaborated on the Louvre (1.8).

As originally built, the fountain was a rectangular structure, situated at the street corner formed by the Rues Saint-Denis and Berger, two bays wide on the latter and one bay wide on the former. Its design – almost certainly inspired by a triumphal arch in the fourth book of Sebastiano Serlio's influential architectural treatise – consisted of a small, arcaded loggia, from which important personages watched the king's arrival, perched upon a high podium whose walls carried water spouts. In the late-18C, the fountain was rebuilt as a freestanding, square structure (fourth, southern side by Augustin Pajou), with water splashing from the former loggia down a podium of cascades. The fountain became famous for Goujon's reliefs of nymphs and sea gods, considered masterpieces of French Mannerism; copies adorn today's fountain, the originals now being in the Louvre.

2nd *arrondissement*

2.1 Tour Jean-sans-Peur
20, rue Etienne-Marcel
Architect unknown, 1409–11
(Métro: Etienne Marcel)

This imposing tower is all that now remains of the *hôtel particulier* of the dukes of Burgundy, which once covered a vast area of land delimited by today's Rues Etienne-Marcel, Montorgueil, Pavée-Saint-Saveur and Saint-Denis. Begun by Robert d'Artois in 1270, the *hôtel* – which passed into the hands of the dukes of Burgundy through marriage – was built just outside the then city walls (erected by Philippe II Augustus in 1190–1202), and abutted them on its southern flank. On 23 November 1407, in a struggle for power, the Duc Jean sans Peur had his cousin, Louis d'Orléans, brother of Charles VI, assassinated, an act which unleashed a terrible civil war. Jean was forced to flee Paris, but returned the following year and not only acknowledged the murder but boasted of it as confirmation of his valour and might. Like many a usurper before and since, he sought to proclaim and consolidate his authority through architecture. A substantial new *corps de logis* was added onto his *hôtel*, punctuated on its southern side by the tower, which was constructed right on top of the old city walls (Philippe Augustus's fortifications had by then been superseded on the right bank by Charles V's wall of 1356–60). With this commanding structure, orientated towards the city centre and visible for miles around, the duke clearly signalled his ambitions.

Rising to four or five storeys – it is uncertain whether or not today's unusually tall second floor was initially divided in two – the tower is surmounted by machicolations and probably originally terminated in a crenelated platform (the current roof dates from the 18C). The top two floors contain fortified bedchambers with attached latrines, of which the uppermost is reputed to have been Jean's refuge in times of trouble. The generous spiral staircase serving the lower floors is crowned by a magnificent stone vault, unique in France, which is carved to represent intertwining oak branches radiating out from its central support, with sculpted oak, hop and hawthorn leaves decorating its surfaces. Miraculously preserved, given the tower's chequered history, the vault is of exceptional quality and must have been created at considerable expense. What is now the tower's second floor is covered by a quadripartite rib vault whose springing points, on the external walls, are marked by angel figures carrying Jean sans Peur's coat of arms. Above the tower's principal entrance can be seen a much-worn allegory of the triumph of the House of Burgundy over Orléans and his clan.

A fascinating and unique survivor of its epoch, the Tour Jean-sans-Peur was »rediscovered« in the 19C following the cutting through of the Rue Etienne-Marcel. It became the property of the municipality in 1884, and was finally restored and opened to the public in 1999.

2.2 Place des Victoires
Jules Hardouin-Mansart, begun 1685
(Métro: Sentier)

The creation of the Place des Victoires, the first of two Parisian piazzas constructed during Louis XIV's reign – the second was the Place Vendôme (1.13), also by Hardouin-Mansart –, was an act of sycophancy on the part of the extravagant Duc de La Feuillade. Having commissioned the sculptor Martin Desjardins to carve a marble statue of the king, which had greatly pleased the monarch when presented to him, the duke ordered a copy in bronze with the intention of displaying it publicly in a befitting setting. He acquired land to the north of his *hôtel particulier* and, in conjunction with financial backers and the municipality, commissioned Hardouin-Mansart to design a piazza to accommodate the effigy.

The architect devised a circular *place* with a radius of 39 m, which, in relation to the 12 m-high statue, gave a viewing angle at the circumference of 18°, considered ideal by theoreticians. The choice of a circular plan for an urban project of this kind was innovative. Hardouin-Mansart's façades were set pieces, behind which purchasers of individual plots could build as they pleased. A *piano nobile* and second floor united by a

2.1 Tour Jean-sans-Peur

giant Ionic order sit atop a rusticated base of false arcades, the ensemble being coiffed by a mansard roof with heavy dormer windows. The architect would subsequently repeat much the same formula, to better effect, at the Place Vendôme. The *place* did not form a complete circle, encompassing as it did two pre-existing buildings either side of the Rue Aboukir, the Hôtel de Pomponne and the Hôtel de Rambouillet. In the interests of symmetry the latter was modified to resemble the former.

The statue itself was a flamboyant affair. The king was represented in coronation costume, trampling a three-headed monster and crowned from behind by a winged Victory. Four figures of slaves encircled the statue's pedestal, which was decorated with bas-reliefs. Moreover, the *place* was lit by four enormous lanterns, which were mounted on columned supports hung with medallions depicting the life of the king. Statue and lanterns were dismantled during the Revolution and the royal effigy melted down, but the other elements of the composition are preserved in the Louvre (1.8). The equestrian statue of Louis XIV which currently adorns the piazza is by François-Joseph Bosio, and was commissioned by Louis XVIII in 1822.

The Place des Victoires was much mutilated in the 19C, firstly with the widening of the Rue de La Feuillade (1828) and the Rue Croix-des-Petits-Champs (1837), and then, most damagingly of all, with the cutting-through of the Rue Etienne Marcel under Haussmann. The latter entailed demolition of the Hôtel de Pomponne and rebuilding of the eastern sections of the *place*, and, consequently, it is now difficult to appreciate fully Hardouin-Mansart's original concept.

2.3 Hôtel Duret-de-Chevry or Tubeuf
8, rue des Petits-Champs
Jean Thiriot, 1635–41
(Métro: Bourse)

This imposing *hôtel particulier*, built at the close of Louis XIII's reign, is one of the last and most impressive Parisian examples of the brick-and-stone style so popular in early-17C France. Commissioned by Charles Duret, *seigneur* of Chevry, the *hôtel* was still unfinished when, in 1641, it was acquired by the financier Jacques Tubeuf, who subsequently sold it to Cardinal Mazarin, in 1649. Mazarin incorporated it into his vast palace, which, by the mid-19C, had mutated into the Bibliothèque Nationale (2.4), of which the Hôtel Duret is now part.

Thiriot's building is of classic *hôtel particulier* design, with a principal *corps de logis* giving onto a garden behind and separated from the street by a courtyard, originally closed on all sides (the current gateway dates from the 18C). At the time of the *hôtel*'s

2.2 Place des Victoires

2.3 Hôtel Duret-de-Chevry or Tubeuf

construction, the picturesque brick-and-stone combination had already been driven out of fashion by a trend towards Classical purism – which insisted on all-stone façades – and was used here only at the specific request of Duret, who wanted to be reminded of his country château. Thiriot was a past master of this polychromatic style, and here took great delight in picking out exaggeratedly heavy rustication against a background of dark-red bricks, set off with elaborate bas-relief carvings. The comparatively simple courtyard façades contrast with the more ambitious garden front, with its two lateral pavilions and grand, central *avant-corps*, which originally contained the *escalier d'honneur*. Of the hôtel's 17C interiors, nothing now remains bar a painted ceiling on the first floor.

2.4 Bibliothèque Nationale
58, rue de Richelieu
Various architects, extant buildings begun 1644
(Métro: Bourse)

France's national library has its origins in the royal collections founded by Louis XI in the 15C and in the decree signed by François I, in 1537, ordering that a copy of each new book printed and sold in the kingdom be deposited at the royal library (an obligation known as the *dépôt légal*). Today the nation's volumes are housed in a brand-new and highly controversial building at Tolbiac in eastern Paris (see the Bibliothèque Nationale de France (13.3)), but for over 250 years, from 1721 to 1998, the collections were kept here at the former Palais Mazarin.

Inhabited by the illustrious cardinal from 1643 until his death in 1661, the Palais Mazarin was a collection of buildings occupying an entire city block within the same limits as today's Bibliothèque-Nationale complex. Mazarin acquired the ensemble from Jacques Tubeuf who, amongst other building work, had completed the unfinished Hôtel Duret-de-Chevry (2.3), which is now part of the library. The cardinal in his turn also carried out considerable construction work, including the building, in 1644–46, of a garden wing containing two superimposed galleries. This wing, along with the Hôtel Duret,

is all that now survives of the 17C complex. Designed by François Mansart and dressed up externally in the same brick-and-stone garb as the Hôtel Duret, the garden wing is essentially interesting for its interior décor. The Galerie Mansart on the ground floor, where the cardinal exhibited his collection of Antique sculpture, conserves only vestiges of its original decoration (*grisailles* by Giovanni-Francesco Grimaldi), but the Galerie Mazarin on the first floor, where the cardinal's paintings were displayed, retains its magnificent vaulted ceiling, decorated with mythological scenes by Giovanni-Francesco Romanelli, as well as niche and window landscapes by Grimaldi.

Following the cardinal's death, the Palais Mazarin was divided between his inheritors, the western section becoming known as the Hôtel de Nevers. It was here, after the ensemble had come into crown possession, that the royal library and *cabinet des médailles* were installed in the 1720s and 1730s. The arcaded wings to the north and east of the *cour d'honneur* on the Rue de Richelieu were put up to designs by Robert de Cotte and his son Jules-Robert in the 1730s. The size of the library's collection increased greatly in the 18C – over 300,000 confiscated documents being added during the Revolution – and, with the ever-continuing influx of the *dépôt légal*, the accommodation at the Hôtel de Nevers became increasingly ill-adapted to its task. It was not, however, until the Second Empire, when crisis point had been reached, that action was finally taken. Henri Labrouste, who had made a name for himself with the ground-breaking Bibliothèque Sainte-Geneviève (5.6), was called in by Napoleon III to carry out a major restoration and rebuilding programme encompassing the entire site, which began in 1854 with the renovation of the Hôtel Duret and the Mazarin galleries. Labrouste received approval for his proposed new buildings, which replaced the majority of the existing structures on the site, in 1859, and the first phase of construction, which included his famous reading room and book stacks, was completed in 1867. The Rue-de-Richelieu façade was inaugurated in 1873, two years before Labrouste's death, after which he was replaced by Jean-Louis Pascal, who completed the last of the new structures – the periodical reading room on the Rue Vivienne – in 1906.

Externally Labrouste's interventions are undistinguished, sporting rather dull, historicizing stone garb, but internally all the invention and daring that he showed at the Bibliothèque Sainte-Geneviève are again apparent. The main reading room is realized in cast iron – the material Labrouste had so triumphantly exposed to the public gaze at the Bibliothèque Sainte-Geneviève and whose fire resistance made it ideal for library construction – and demonstrates his Structural-Rationalist precepts, its structure being given full, unambiguous expression and all decorative elements being subservient to and/or derived from the form of the construction. Surrounded on three sides by adjoining buildings, the reading room disposes of only one fenestrated wall, and in order to provide sufficient daylight for reading (in an era that predated the invention of efficient artificial lighting) Labrouste was obliged to introduce glazing into the roof. He consequently contrived a series of laterally intersecting domes, with openings at their apexes, that are supported on 16 tall and astonishingly slender iron columns, thereby freeing up the maximum amount of space for the readers. The lattice work and rivets of the arches supporting the domes are left exposed for their natural decorative effect, while the domes' interiors are clad with white enamel panels that gently augment the light entering them through reflection. These airy umbrellas must have appeared quite astonishing to contemporaries, for nothing quite like them had ever been built before. For the book stacks, which are separated from the reading room by a monumental glazed archway, Labrouste took inspiration from Sydney Smirke's British Library (1854–57) and, dispensing entirely with historicism, produced a functional iron cage whose stripped aesthetic anticipated 20C developments. In their original form (they have since been altered), the stacks consisted of a top-lit space containing superimposed iron galleries whose grilled flooring allowed light to penetrate to the lowest levels. The rigour and appositeness of the book stacks were much admired, and dispositions of this type subsequently became standard for department-store stockrooms and for warehouses. Although Labrouste's work at the Bibliothèque Nationale did not mark a significant technical advance on what

2.4 Bibliothèque Nationale. Floor plan of reading room

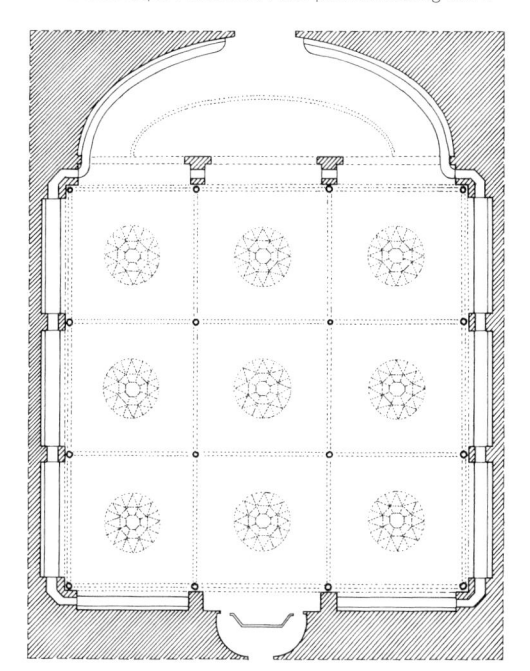

2.4 Bibliothèque Nationale. Reading room

he had achieved at the Bibliothèque Sainte-Geneviève, it nonetheless displayed great formal invention.

Inevitably, with the passing of time and the continued collection of the *dépôt légal* (whose yearly volume has consistently increased), Labrouste's Bibliothèque Nationale eventually became too small to fulfil its function, prompting the decision to build the Bibliothèque Nationale de France at Tolbiac. The old complex has retained the national collections of prints, maps, manuscripts and coins and medals, which now have room to expand, and, as of 2006, will accomodate the library of the newly created Institut National d'Histoire de l'Art in Labruoste's reading room.

2.5 Crédit Lyonnais
17–23, boulevard des Italiens
William Bouwens Van der Boijen, 1876–78 and 1880 to 1803; William and Richard Bouwens Van der Boijen, André Narjoux and Victor Laloux, 1895–1913
(Métro: Richelieu Drouot)

As much a phenomenon of the industrial revolution as railways or factories, deposit banking first took off in France during the Second Empire and soon became a powerful force in the nation's economy. To enhance their prestige and consolidate their new-found authority in the public consciousness, all the major banks built substantial headquarters in the capital, of which the Crédit Lyonnais building was one of the earliest. Initially occupying only a corner of the current site, Crédit Lyonnais progressively acquired adjoining plots of land until, by the time the final building phase began, an area of over 1 ha had been assembled. With 45,000 m² of office space in the finished edifice, this was Paris's biggest civil building.

piece that is a reworking by Van der Boijen senior of the Louvre's Pavillon de l'Horloge (see 1.8), while inside he produced an *escalier d'honneur* based on the famous double-spiral staircase at the Château de Chambord, built for François I in the 16C.

In 1996, while Crédit Lyonnais was under investigation regarding a financial scandal, a fire began in its Parisian headquarters that conveniently destroyed all its archives as well as two thirds of the building, leaving only the façades standing on the southern half of the site. Miraculously, the *escalier d'honneur* and the Louvre frontispiece escaped untouched. Since that time the building has been divided in two (intact northern section and gutted southern part) and sold. At the time of writing, reconstruction of the southern part has just been completed.

2.6 Opéra Comique
Place Boïeldieu
Louis Bernier, 1893–98
(Métro: Richelieu Drouot)

Today's Opéra Comique is the third on this site, the first two having burnt down, in 1838 and 1887; following a long period of hesitation after the second fire, it

2.6 Opéra Comique

2.5 Crédit Lyonnais

Situated in Paris's 19C financial heart between the Bourse (2.8) and the Opéra (9.13), the Crédit Lyonnais building developed on a grander scale a type-form that had come into existence in the mid-19C, and in doing so set the trend for later bank headquarters (see, e.g., the Comptoir d'Escompte and Société Générale buildings, 9.2 and 9.11). This type-form consisted essentially of an imposing glazed hall, where public banking activities were carried out, around which were arranged the back offices (which thus benefited from the natural daylight available on the façades), while the strong-rooms were located in the basement. At Crédit Lyonnais, the glazed hall (whose ironwork was manufactured by the firm of Eiffel) took the form of an impressive, three-storey gallery, rather like a covered street, running down the building's centre. With the 1895–1913 building campaign, this gallery was doubled in length and acquired a huge glass dome at its centre. But the banks did not only employ state-of-the-art iron-and-glass technology, they also insisted on ostentatious stone historicism. Crédit Lyonnais, by making what can only have been deliberate reference to French royalty (despite the advent of the Third Republic), broadcast its ambitions: on the principal, Boulevard-des-Italiens façade we find an entrance frontis-

was finally decided that the Opéra should be rebuilt on the same terrain, despite its constrictedness. A competition was launched, in 1893, which was boycotted by the more avant-garde architects because of political disputes within the profession. With a jury that counted five winners of the Academy's Grand Prix de Rome, including Charles Garnier, the contest attracted mostly academicians and became a triumph of official taste.

Bernier's building is standard *beaux-arts* fare, with a galleried, horseshoe-shaped auditorium of a pedigree stretching back to the 17C. Unlike some of the other competitors, who had daringly revealed the iron that figured as part of their proposals' structures (for reasons of fire resistance, iron had been used in theatre construction since as early as the 1780s (see 1.16)), Bernier hid his building's innards behind a heavy layer of stone. The stolidly monumental principal façade, rendered in crashing neo-Baroque, is singularly of its era, as are the almost photo-realist allegorical paintings commissioned to adorn the Opéra's foyers. Despite a limited budget, the theatre's decorators managed to produce an interior of overbearing opulence, especially in the lavishly histrionic, gilt-dripping stuccowork of the auditorium. Unsurprisingly, contemporary critical reactions were widely divergent: the Opéra was vehemently attacked by those of Rationalist persuasion, while its defenders saw its delirious frivolity as the natural complement to the operettas for which it was created.

2.7 Rue des Colonnes
Nicolas-Jacques-Antoine Vestier and Joseph Bénard, begun 1793
(Métro: Bourse)

2.7 Rue des Colonnes

Constructed during the Terror, the Rue des Colonnes is a curious survivor from a period when very little building work was undertaken. The site's owners, a group of speculators (one of whom was later guillotined), decided to create a street of shops and apartments linking the now-demolished Rue des Filles-Saint-Thomas to the Théâtre Feydeau (also since demolished). They engaged Vestier to draw up plans, which were then executed by Bénard. This was the first street of covered shopping colonnades to be built in Paris, and was no doubt partly inspired by the success of the Palais-Royal colonnades (see 1.16) and also by Italian arcaded streets.

The design of the arcades themselves is unusual, reflecting the mania for pre-Roman sources peculiar to the epoch. Vestier's inspiration was ancient Greek: squat Doric columns, with neither base nor entasis, and palmettes and glyphs adorning the distinctly un-Greek arches linking the columns. Decorative elements are confined to the commercially important arcades; the contrasting austerity of the upper-storey façades anticipates 20C stripped Classicism. It is now hard to appreciate the original perspective effect of the street as its initial 90 m length has been much reduced, firstly by the cutting-through of the Rue de la Bourse in 1824, and subsequently by the building of Haussmann's Rue du 4-septembre in 1864, which entailed demolition of the southern end. The Rue des Colonnes, which was probably one of the sources of inspiration for Fontaine and Percier's Rue de Rivoli (1.11), today sadly lacks the thriving commerce which was its principal *raison d'être*.

2.8 Palais de la Bourse (Palais Brongniart)
Place de la Bourse
Alexandre-Théodore Brongniart, 1808–13; Eloi Labarre, 1813–26; Jean-Baptiste-Frédéric Cavel, 1901–05
(Métro: Bourse)

Despite its considerable economic importance, Paris at the turn of the 19C was one of the few major European cities without a permanent, purpose-built home for its financial exchange. This state of affairs clearly could not continue and, as part of general plans to improve and embellish his imperial capital, the Emperor Napoleon undertook the construction of just such an edifice. The building, he insisted, must be an isolated monument surrounded by a square; the confiscated Couvent des Filles-Saint-Thomas was chosen as the site. Brongniart, anxious to end a long and sometimes difficult career with a prestigious public commission,

2.8 Palais de la Bourse (Palais Brongniart)

spontaneously submitted a project which greatly pleased the emperor and was accepted.

Napoleon's admiration of imperial Rome and his ambitions for his own empire here found expression in a vast Corinthian temple enclosing a vaulted and arcaded central hall, home to the main exchange, and a secondary chamber serving as the Tribunal de Commerce. Brongniart's colonnaded elevations, behind which he placed façades articulated by two storeys of arcades, were probably inspired by his master Boullée's unexecuted project for the Bibliothèque Nationale. Admired at the time, Brongniart's scheme has since been attacked for academicism and dullness. After his death, in 1813, the building was completed by Labarre: already diluted by modifications imposed by the authorities, Brongniart's initial design was further weakened by Labarre's alterations. Too small by the 1860s, the Bourse was eventually extended in the 1900s by Caval, whose two new lateral wings did nothing to improve the reputation of this uninspiring monument.

2.9 Industrial building
124, rue Réaumur
Attributed to Georges Chédanne, 1904/05
(Métro: Sentier)

Haussmann's Rue Réaumur – which remained unexecuted until 1897–1905 – traverses Le Sentier, one of the centres of Paris's textile trade. The buildings erected along the new street were mostly mixed-use edifices of a type which originated in the 1870s, and which featured shops on the ground floor, workshops, warehouses or offices on the intermediary floors, and apartments in the upper storeys. As natural light is essential when working with textiles, the Rue-Réaumur buildings were provided with large areas of glazing on the intermediary floors, often framed in iron. Contemporary taste and desire for prestige nonetheless prescribed quantities of stone and florid detailing, of both which no. 118 (Charles de Montarnal, 1900) provides a good example.

What a shock, then, must have been no. 124 when first built. Even today the boldness of its riveted, all-metal exterior surprises (all metal bar the final, residential storey, in brick, and its mansard roof). The attribution to Chédanne is based solely on his having applied for building permission for no. 124, whose façade could not be further from the *belle-époque* eclecticism of which he was a past master (e.g. the Elysée-Palace Hotel, Avenue des Champs-Elysées, 1898/99). Only no. 124's sensual Art-Nouveau curves and bulging bay windows are at all reminiscent of his usual output. The building's interior spaces were entirely undivided, leaving tenants the freedom to install partitions as necessary. No. 124's simplicity, expression of structure, and free plan prefigure many Modern-Movement concerns, although French fire regulations and reinforced concrete subsequently made this type of metallic construction rare.

2.10 Cinéma Rex
1–5, boulevard Poissonnière
Auguste Bluysen, Maurice Dutrêne and John Eberson,
1930–32
(Métro: Bonne Nouvelle)

Commissioned by the music hall impresario Jacques Haïk, the 3,300-seat Rex was, at the time of its inauguration, one of the biggest cinemas in Europe. (The largest was the magnificent 6,000-seat Gaumont-Palace at the Place de Clichy, built by Henri Belloc in 1930 and sadly demolished in 1972.) Haïk called on the talents of architect Auguste Bluysen for the shell, and engineer John Eberson and decorator Maurice Dufrêne for the interior. Bluysen's ungainly façades are almost entirely blind, relieved only by the confectionery tower in metal and cement which turns the corner into the Rue Poissonnière. The projector cabin is separate from the main auditorium and cantilevered out above the street. The enormous blank panel on the boulevard elevation was intended for luminous animated publicity displays but was never used, by order of the Prefect of Police, who was worried at potential distraction of motorists.

In contrast to the monumental moderne of the Gaumont-Palace, Haïk sought to wow the public with France's first »atmospheric« auditorium which, extraor-

2.9 Industrial building

2.10 Cinéma Rex

dinarily, has survived intact. Eberson, responsible for countless atmospheric cinemas in the United States, here concocted a fantasy of Hispano-Moorish architecture which he stuck onto the auditorium walls and topped off with a celestial ceiling replete with painted clouds and twinkling stars (the management claims still to receive complaints from myopic film-goers perturbed at finding themselves in an open-air cinema!). The building's basement, originally home to a café, a nursery, kennels and even a small hospital, has since been converted into seven further, small-scale auditoria.

2nd *arrondissement* 63

3rd *arrondissement*

3.1 Musée Carnavalet
23, rue de Sévigné
Various architects, begun 1547
(Métro: Saint-Paul)

Founded in 1866 as the museum of the history of Paris, the Musée Carnavalet is a must for anyone interested in the city's architecture, since its collections include a remarkable number of interiors and even parts of exteriors that were rescued from reconfigured or demolished buildings, mostly during the period of Haussmann's rebuilding of Paris. Countless historic views of the city, essentially in the form of oil paintings, and a good number of architectural models also enrich its considerable collections, which further include, amongst others, portraits, furniture, around 2,000 sculptures, 10,000 drawings and over 300,000 engravings and photographs. Moreover, the buildings in which the museum is housed are themselves of great architectural interest. The principal structure is the Hôtel Carnavalet, which, in its original form, was built for Jacques de Ligneris, *avocat au Parlement* and ambassador to the Council of Trent, in around 1547–53. The Hôtel Carnavalet as we see it today is the product of both a rebuilding campaign carried out by François Mansart in the 1650s and a restoration programme executed by Victor Parmentier in the 1860s, which latter aimed to return the building at least in part to its 16C state. These subsequent developments are described in greater detail below, but for the moment we shall concentrate on the design of the house as originally built.

The Hôtel Carnavalet
The Hôtel Carnavalet is important historically in that it is a rare survivor, albeit in modified form, of an aristocratic residence of Renaissance-period Paris, most houses from this era having been entirely demolished and rebuilt at a later date. Evidence suggests that the house may have been designed by Pierre Lescot (of Louvre fame (see 1.8)), although there is no reliable documentation to support this. In plan the building precociously followed what would later become the classic schema for Parisian *hôtels particuliers*, that is to say it featured a principal *corps de logis* running parallel to the street that was sandwiched between a garden at the rear and a *cour d'honneur* at the front, the latter surrounded on its other three sides by service buildings and accessed via a central *porte-cochère*. The *hôtel*'s stables were originally disposed around a small courtyard that was located where the righthand wing of the *cour d'honneur* now stands, and were separated from the *cour d'honneur* by a wall that may have taken the form of a dummy façade mimicking the opposite elevation of the courtyard. This layout had the advantage of allowing the stables to be accessed both from the *cour d'honneur* and directly from the street, and would be repeated in numerous subsequent *hôtels particuliers* from the Hôtel Salé (3.3) to the Hôtel Matignon (7.14).

Apart from its long gallery, the Hôtel Carnavalet's principal rooms were all located in the *corps de logis*, which, as was then usually the case, was only one room thick. Each floor consisted of a suite of interconnecting rooms, with vertical distribution being assured by staircases that rose in the two pavilions projecting from the *logis*'s courtyard façade (the staircases were later displaced by Mansart). As we see them today, the façades of the *corps de logis* are essentially 19C creations (see below), although the famous series of bas-reliefs of the Four Seasons on the courtyard front is original, and may well have been carved by Jean Goujon, who worked with Lescot on the Louvre. The lefthand wing of the *cour d'honneur* originally comprised an open arcade (subsequently filled in by Mansart), coiffed by a high attic, which, lit by dormers, contained the long gallery. The remainder of the structures that made up the original Hôtel Carnavalet were located on the eastern (entrance) side of the *cour d'honneur*, fronting the Rue de Sévigné, and comprised principally the kitchens and stables, which flanked the building's celebrated *porte-cochère*. Although we have no conclusive proof regarding the identity of the designers of either the *hôtel* or its portal, one contemporary commentator attributes the *porte-cochère* directly to Lescot and Goujon, and from its style this attribution seems likely. A tripartite, heavily rusticated composition, the portal is clearly of Italian inspiration, and recalls the work of Giulio Romano, and also the Grotte des Pins (*c*. 1543) at Fontainebleau (38.1), which is attributed to Primaticcio. Lescot's talent was essentially for the decoration of plane surfaces rather than the architectonic articulation of masses, and the complex detailing of the Hôtel Carnavalet's *porte-cochère* is in exactly this mould. As an anecdotal aside, it is worth mentioning one aspect of this detailing, namely the carnival mask on the portal's keystone that sits underneath a personification of Abundance. This was almost certainly added by Françoise de Kernevenoc'h (or Kernevenoy), known as Mme de Carnavalet, who was the owner of the *hôtel* from *c*. 1570 to 1602. The mask was clearly a punning reference to her name, by which the building is still known today.

Reconfiguration of the Hôtel Carnavalet by François Mansart
In 1654, the Hôtel Carnavalet was bought by Claude Boyslesve (sometimes written Boylesve or Boislève), *sieur* of La Guérinière and later Comte de Gonor, who engaged François Mansart to enlarge his new home. Completed in 1661, this was one of Mansart's last realizations. He left the old *corps de logis* more or less as it was, his interventions consisting primarily in building a new, righthand wing in the *cour d'honneur* on the site of the old stable courtyard, extending the lefthand wing through the addition of a supplementary storey and similarly rebuilding the *hôtel*'s street façade on the Rue

de Sévigné so as to provide extra accommodation. Following his reconfiguration, the *hôtel* was endowed with grand, first-floor apartments on all four sides of the *cour d'honneur*. This was unusual – principal rooms were generally restricted to the *corps de logis* – and resulted from the lack of space at the Hôtel Carnavalet. Mansart's recourse to this solution recalled a similar arrangement used by Le Vau at the Hôtel Lambert (4.5). In the *cour d'honneur*, Mansart bent himself to the Hôtel Carnavalet's 16C architecture by mimicking the façade dispositions of the old lefthand wing on his new righthand courtyard elevation (the arcades of the righthand wing served to store carriages) and by decorating both wings with bas-reliefs in the manner of the Renaissance carvings on the *logis*. On the righthand wing we find the Roman goddesses Juno, Hebe, Diana and Flora in what may be an allegory of the *Hours of the Day*, sculpted by the Flemish artist Gérard Van Obstal. The identity of the author of the lefthand wing reliefs, which consist of personifications of the Four Elements, is unknown. For added cohesion in the courtyard, Mansart coiffed both wings and *logis* with uniform mansard roofs that united the building's disparate styles under one horizontal band of dark slate.

Mansart was also sensitive to his 16C forbears on the *hôtel*'s street façade. He preserved the famous portal, embedding it in a grand composition that sought not only to avoid competing with its predecessor but also to enhance its effect. Critics have commented on the extreme delicacy and subtlety of the result, which manages to be at once both exuberant and restrained. Like the portal itself, Mansart's façade is tripartite, with substantial side pavilions flanking the central *arrière-corps* containing the *porte-cochère*. The scale of the new elevation is much bigger than that of the portal, and in this respect the latter loses impact, but otherwise Mansart achieved a surprisingly good blend of old and new. Taking his cue from the portal, he devised a Classical temple composition featuring a rusticated base (the lower levels of the side pavilions are rusticated to match the portal) surmounted by a

3.1 Musée Carnavalet

piano nobile decorated with Ionic pilasters. Subtle retrocessions ensure that what would otherwise be a very plane surface is never dull. The central grouping of pilasters does not, as would have been the obvious configuration, sport a pediment, so as not to compete with that of the portal below, but the two sets of pavilion pilasters do each carry a pediment, thereby setting up a diagonal tension across the façade. Carved decoration is abundant yet never overwhelming and includes two bas-reliefs by Van Obstal, representing Force and Vigilance, which help ensure the cohesion of the portal in its new setting. On the Rue-des-Francs-Bourgeois elevation of the southern pavilion, Mansart configured a clever *decrescendo*, repeating certain elements of the principal façade such as the brackets and cornices but otherwise paring down the detailing to ensure the transition from the richness of the main entrance façade to the very plain elevation on the Rue des Francs-Bourgeois.

Creation of the Musée Carnavalet
In 1866, the Hôtel Carnavalet was acquired by the Ville de Paris, on the initiative of Baron Haussmann, with a view to housing the municipality's historic collections there. The building's restoration was entrusted to the architect Victor Parmentier, who undertook to return it, at least in part, to a supposed 16C state based on 17C engravings by Jean Marot. As far as the *corps de logis* was concerned, this involved putting back the original stone window mullions (although the window frames, which had been lengthened in the 17C to match those of the courtyard wings, were not returned to their original dimensions), replacing Mansart's mansard roof with the high steep variety that originally coiffed the *hôtel*, adding dormers and a balustrade that appear in Marot's engravings but probably never actually existed in the 16C, and, most drastically of all, rebuilding the garden front in ashlar with a frontispiece inspired by Ecouen (23.1), even though the original had always been in rendered rubble stone. The chimneys we see today are also a pure invention of the 19C, as are the balustrades on the courtyard's lateral wings, which replaced the uniform mansard roofs that Mansart had installed around the courtyard. The restitution of the attic storey and separate roofing of the two staircase pavilions fronting the *logis* was also carried out by Parmentier. Archaeologically speaking, the overall result is evidently highly unsatisfactory, and not only does the *hôtel* now appear in an historically »inaccurate«, half-16C/half-17C state, but Mansart's creation has been disfigured. On the other hand, the 19C interventions are interesting in their own right, representative as they are of the historiographic and aesthetic preferences of their day.

The works carried out in the 19C were not just limited to the restoration of the existing fabric, but also included the building of new wings, in eclectic Renaissance style, around the *hôtel*'s garden (Félix Roguet and Joseph-Antoine Bouvard, 1871–90). Incorporated into their façades are vestiges of Parisian buildings that were demolished or reconfigured during the 19C. The archway on the Rue des Francs-Bourgeois is actually a part of the Palais de la Cité (1.1), known as the Arc de Nazareth, which was originally built in 1552–56 by Guillaume Le Breton to link the Chambre des Comptes to its archives; the southern half of the western garden wing of the museum features, on the garden side, the frontispiece of the merchant drapers' guild, built by Jacques Bruand in 1660, which is notable for its exuberant sculpture; and the central pavilion of the arcade running across the middle of the garden is in fact the principal *avant-corps* of the Hôtel Desmarets, built in 1710 by an unknown architect.

The Hôtel Le Peletier de Saint-Fargeau
As its collections grew, the Musée Carnavalet began to feel the squeeze in the Hôtel Carnavalet and, in 1989, following five years' conversion work, took over the neighbouring Hôtel Le Peletier de Saint-Fargeau (29, rue de Sévigné), where its 19C and 20C collections are now displayed. The Hôtel Le Peletier was built in 1686–90 by Pierre Bullet for the *conseiller d'Etat* and *intendant des finances* Michel Le Peletier de Souzy (it was later inherited by Louis-Michel Le Peletier de Saint-Fargeau, whence its current name). The *hôtel* was much admired by contemporaries, and is still striking today in its extreme and rather severe sobriety. String courses, the simplest window surrounds and the odd touch of rustication are all that animate its monumental façades. Internally, its equally restrained *escalier d'honneur* survives, and is noteworthy for its balustrade in cast iron, designed by Bullet, which was a very early example of the use of this technique (most 17C metal balustrades are in wrought iron). The Hôtel Le Peletier has also conserved its orangery, a rare 17C survivor in Paris, which now houses part of the Musée Carnavalet's Gallo-Roman collections.

The museum's collections
Although an exhaustive run-down of the many interiors on display at the Musée Carnavalet is impossible within the scope of this book, it is worth mentioning some of the highlights. One of the oldest rooms in the collection is the *cabinet* of the Hôtel Colbert de Villacerf (in the southwestern corner of the Hôtel Carnavalet), which dates from around 1655. With its rich decoration consisting of gilded carvings and polychromatic painted allegories, it is a charismatic example of the décor of its era. The painting of *Apollo and the Seasons* adorning the summit of the *cabinet*'s ceiling is attributed to the studio of Eustache Le Sueur. Nearby, in the west wing of the museum, are the *grand cabinet* and *grande chambre* of the Hôtel de La Rivière, which also date from the 1650s, and which are notable for their paintings by Charles Le Brun. Moving on to the 18C, the *escalier d'honneur* of the Hôtel de Luynes (in the northern wing of the Hôtel Carnavalet) is remark-

able for its architectural *trompe-l'œils*, painted by the Italian artist Paolo Antonio Brunetti in 1748. Leading off it on the ground floor is the *salon de compagnie* of the Hôtel d'Uzès, whose beautiful panelling, designed by Claude-Nicolas Ledoux in 1767, features gilded carvings of tree trunks sporting musical instruments (note the real strings of the lyres). Just next door is the décor created by Ledoux for the Café Militaire (1762), whose name and military clientele prompted him to conceive Romanizing carvings of arms and armour. By a quirk of history, there are almost no 19C interiors in the Musée Carnavalet, although the small *salon* designed by Henri Sauvage for the Café de Paris in 1899 (first floor of the Hôtel Le Peletier) can just be counted in this category. It is a fine example of Art Nouveau, as is the neighbouring shop interior created by Alphonse Mucha for Georges Fouquet's Rue-Royale jewellery boutique in 1900/01. Mucha's ensemble constitutes a *fin-de-siècle* total environment of quite spectacular impact and, unsurprisingly, went out of fashion very quickly, being removed as early as 1923. For those enamoured of the Art-Déco period, the ballroom of the Hôtel de Wendel (also on the first floor of the Hôtel Le Peletier) is not to be missed. Its painted décor, realized in 1924, was the work of the Catalan artist José Maria Sert y Badia. On a background of white-gold leaf he realized a fantastical *grisaille* in varnish that represents the departure of the Queen of Sheba, headed for her mythic *rendezvous* with King Solomon. Badia's inspiration was clearly Baroque painting, and especially Tiepolo, in what is a composition of quite deliquescent delirium.

3.2   Hôtel de Donon (Musée Cognacq-Jay)

3.2 Hôtel de Donon (Musée Cognacq-Jay)
8, rue Elzevir
Architect unknown, c. 1575
(Métro: Saint-Paul)

Built in the then-aristocratic Marais on land acquired in 1575, this handsome *hôtel particulier* was the home of Médéric de Donon, Contrôleur Général des Bâtiments du Roi. Historians have noted the great similarity between Donon's home and the Parisian residence of Philibert De l'Orme, which the famous architect designed for himself (now destroyed), and although De l'Orme could not have built the Hôtel de Donon – he died in 1570 – his work must certainly have influenced its design. Circumstantial evidence suggests that Jean Bullant may have been responsible for Donon's *hôtel*. De l'Orme's residence, known to us through published engravings, defined a type-standard for the more modest Parisian *hôtel particulier* that was adapted to the narrow plots into which much of the city was divided and that would continue to be employed in its basic disposition until the late-18C. Thus at the Hôtel de Donon we find the classic *hôtel-particulier* schema, with a *corps de logis* that runs parallel to the street and is sandwiched between a garden at the rear and a courtyard at the front, the latter surrounded by service buildings and accessed via a *porte-cochère*, the whole disposed with logical regularity. If in its organization the Hôtel de Donon is an evergreen classic, in its external aspect it clearly belongs to its era, with its mullioned fenestration, lofty hipped roofs and Renaissance-period detailing in the form of arched and pedimented dormer windows.

Restored by the Ville de Paris, the Hôtel de Donon is today home to the Cognacq-Jay collection of furniture.

3.3 Hôtel Aubert-de-Fontenay or Salé (Musée Picasso)
5, rue de Thorigny
Jean Boullier de Bourges, 1656–59; Roland Simounet, 1976–85
(Métro: Saint-Paul, Saint-Sébastien-Froissart, Chemin Vert)

This enormous *hôtel particulier*, one of the Marais's biggest, was built for Pierre Aubert de Fontenay, who made his money collecting salt taxes – hence the building's nickname of Hôtel Salé (literally »salty house«) and an ironic comment on Fontenay's private life). Fontenay's chosen architect, Jean Boullier de Bourges, is today rather an obscure figure, but in his time was evidently well up to date with all the latest developments in *hôtel particulier* design. Although the site's unusually generous width could have allowed him experimental latitude, Bourges chose to respect the traditional *hôtel particulier* schema, and simply scaled it up to the plot dimensions he was given. We thus find the classic disposition of a principal *corps de logis* sandwiched between a garden at the rear and a *cour d'honneur* at the front, the latter also accessing service buildings and being connected to the street via a central *porte-cochère*. Bourges chose a plan variation that had already been used at the nearby Hôtel d'Avaux (3.7), and that would be notably repeated at the Hôtels de Rohan (3.4) and Matignon (7.14), whereby the service buildings are grouped to one side of the courtyard, with the result that the courtyard façade of the *corps de logis* is considerably narrower than the garden front. As at the Hôtel d'Avaux, a dummy elevation closes the courtyard's other (in this case southern) side. In the laying out of the courtyard and the design of the *porte-cochère* – which features a semicircular cutaway around its opening to facilitate the passage of carriages – Bourges showed his familiarity with fashionable developments, but it was in the design of the *logis* that the *hôtel*'s modernity was really displayed. Here we find a double thickness plan in place of the traditional single *enfilade*, an innovation that had been pioneered by François Mansart in the 1640s and which had the advantages of allowing a more flexible layout and ensuring greater independence of access to individual rooms. Externally the *hôtel* is also reminiscent of Mansart's work in that the orders are absent (Mansart never used them on *hôtel particuliers*) and all effect is reliant on the articulation of windows and detailing – string courses, window surrounds, rusticated quoins, etc. However, the subtlety of Mansart's work is absent, and the Hôtel Salé is much more showy than anything he ever produced. A busyness of detail characterizes the courtyard front, which is dominated by a giant, semicircular, sculpture-laden pediment plonked in front of its high attics. The garden front is more austere and, thanks to its enormous width and the generous grounds it fronts, has all the allure of a château.

The various uses to which the Hôtel Salé was put in the 19C and early-20C ensured that very little today remains of its original interior decoration, bar some 18C carvings and mouldings and, luckily for posterity, Fontenay's magnificent *escalier d'honneur*. One of Paris's best-preserved and most impressive 17C staircases, it is accessed via a triple arcade leading off to the right of the grand vestibule by which one enters the *hôtel*. An initial, free-standing central volley leads up to

3.4 Hôtel de Rohan

a half landing, where the path splits into two flights that hang off the sides of the vast double-height volume that contains the staircase. Its walls and ceiling were decorated by the Flemish sculptor Martin Desjardins, and his elaborate carvings include cherubs, eagles and Atlases, as well as Jupiter and Juno with her peacock, the whole united by exuberant swags and cornice mouldings. The ensemble is completed by a beautifully crafted balustrade in wrought iron, a material that came into fashion around this time in place of traditional stone (a good example of a contemporary stone balustrade can be found at Mansart's nearby Hôtel de Guénégaud (3.6)). The staircase's florid splendour is in distinct contrast to the white, rather minimalist »Cubist« interiors created by Roland Simounet as part of the Hôtel Salé's conversion to house the Musée Picasso.

3.4 Hôtel de Rohan
87, rue Vieille-du-Temple
Pierre-Alexis Delamair, 1705–08
(Métro: Rambuteau, Saint-Paul)

In 1705, François de Rohan, Prince de Soubise, gave his son, Armand-Gaston, Bishop of Strasbourg, a plot of land adjoining his Parisian *hôtel particulier* so that the bishop could build himself his own residence in the capital. The previous year, on Armand-Gaston's recommendation, the prince had hired Pierre-Alexis Delamair to rebuild the Hôtel de Soubise (3.5), and Armand-Gaston in his turn commissioned Delamair for the realization of his new house.

Delamair's Hôtel de Rohan is very different in character to his Hôtel de Soubise, no doubt in part because of the much smaller site into which the Hôtel de Rohan is squeezed. It is approached via a *cour d'honneur* which, as at the Hôtel de Soubise, curves round in a gracious semicircle from the entrance gateway to meet the *hôtel* at right angles, although on a considerably smaller scale than its neighbour. At four storeys, the Hôtel de Rohan is much taller than the Hôtel de Soubise and, with its superposition of hierarchically proportioned floors and very shallow roof, appears more archetypally »Classical« and less specifically French than its cousin. Despite the fact that the garden front, which extends across the entire width of the building, is considerably broader than it is tall, it appears very vertical, due to the narrow and lofty ground- and first-floor windows and to its apparent division into a nine-bay *corps de logis* flanked by two-bay wings, an effect achieved solely through the use of quoins. A false, central *avant-corps*, adorned with columns and pilasters and coiffed with a delicate pediment, completes the composition. The courtyard façade, which is given similar treatment, is half the width of the garden front, and is displaced to one side in relation to it in order to allow the stables to be squeezed in next to the *cour d'honneur*, thus ensuring the traditional relationship of an *hôtel particulier* to its outbuildings. Sculpture at the Hôtel de Rohan is discreet, apart from Robert Le Lorrain's magnificent *Chevaux du Soleil* (c. 1735), a bas-relief decorating the entrance to the stables which depicts Apollo's horses taking a drink at sunset.

For many years home to the Imprimerie Nationale, the Hôtel de Rohan was badly mistreated until becoming part of the National Archives complex in 1927. What little remains of its interior dates from the time of the second occupant, Armand de Rohan, Cardinal de Soubise. Delamair's imposing staircase, destroyed by the Imprimerie, was rebuilt in the 1930s. Also of note are the Salon de Musique on the first floor, the painted *chinoiserie* of Christophe Huet's Cabinet des Singes (1749/50), and Germain Boffrand's Cabinet des Fables, originally installed in the Hôtel de Soubise, which depicts fables by Aesop and La Fontaine.

3.5 Hôtel de Soubise
54–60, rue des Francs-Bourgeois
Begun 1375; Pierre-Alexis Delamair, 1704–09;
Gabriel Germain Boffrand, 1732–40
(Métro: Rambuteau)

Hailed as a masterpiece of French Classicism, the Hôtel de Soubise was the result of an 18C reworking of much older buildings, and has itself been considerably altered since becoming home to the National Archives in the 19C. The edifice dates back to 1375, when Olivier de Clisson, Constable of France, built himself an *hôtel particulier* on the site, situated in the new *quartiers* created by the extension of Paris's boundaries under Charles V. Constructed during an era of political instability and violence, the Hôtel de Clisson was semi-fortified to resist possible attack by armed gangs. Its gatehouse still stands, at the western extremity of today's Hôtel de Soubise, and is a rare Parisian survivor of 14C civil architecture. It is similar to the gatehouse of the Hôtel de Sens (4.6), although over a century older, and features a lanceted entrance flanked on either side by corbelled corner turrets. The juxtaposition of this medieval fragment with the refined Classicism of the Hôtel de Soubise makes for an exotic contrast.

In 1553, the Hôtel de Clisson was bought by the powerful Guise family, who undertook substantial modifications. The chapel was remodelled for the Duc François de Guise around 1555 by the Italian painter and architect Francesco Primaticcio. Obliterated in the 19C, all that remains of the chapel's Renaissance aspect is its courtyard façade. The Guises' first-floor *salle des gardes* also survives, a room whose impressive dimensions are reputed to have witnessed the planning of the horrific Saint-Bartholomew's-Day Massacre of 1572.

The family line having died out by the end of the 17C, the Hôtel de Guise was put up for sale and bought, in 1700, by François de Rohan, Prince de Soubise. François quickly tired of the discomfort of the old house, and embarked on a major rebuilding programme. On the advice of his son, Armand-Gaston de Rohan, Bishop of Strasbourg, François hired the talents of a young and relatively unknown architect, Pierre-Alexis Delamair. Due to a combination of setbacks and machinations on the part of jealous rivals, Delamair's career never fulfilled the potential of his talent, and he was ultimately fired from the Hôtel de Soubise project by Hercule-Mériadec de Rohan, son of

3.5 Hôtel de Soubise. Salon de la Princesse

3.5 Hôtel de Soubise. *Cour d'honneur*

François, who found his plans for the interior – a series of grand ceremonial apartments laid out in axial perspective – old-fashioned and uncomfortable. His brilliant treatment of the exterior, however, was instantly recognized as a masterpiece, and has ensured his lasting fame. While working on the Hôtel de Soubise, he was also commissioned to build the Hôtel de Rohan (3.4) for the bishop, on an adjoining plot of land. The palaces of father and son thus faced each other across spacious gardens, forming a monumental ensemble, a relationship today destroyed by the addition of supplementary structures in the 19C.

The external remodelling of the Hôtel de Soubise essentially required an updating of its façades to suit modern tastes. Delamair went further than a mere make-over job, however, by reorientating the entrance to the south, thus allowing him the use of unbuilt land between the house and the Rue des Francs-Bourgeois on which he created a magnificent *cour d'honneur*, almost certainly inspired by the nearby Hôtel du Grand Prieur du Temple (Pierre Deslisle-Mansart, 1667, destroyed). Access to the courtyard is gained via an imposing gateway, which curves back from the street line, and which was formerly endowed on its southwestern corner with a large public fountain (now the Archives' boutique). Despite the evident grandeur of the *hôtel*'s approaches, the visitor is unprepared for the splendid perspective which opens up before him once the gateway's threshold has been crossed. The vast courtyard is laid out with lawns and bordered by a peristyle of twinned Composite columns which curves gently away from the onlooker to meet the *hôtel* at right angles over 50 m later. To ensure complete cohesion between the house and its setting, the columns and cornice of the peristyle continue across the ground floor of the *hôtel*'s façade and, despite the quickening rhythm of the intercolumniation across the central *avant-corps*, the flow remains unbroken. The façade itself is deceptively simple. Only two storeys high, and surmounted by a tall, French-style roof, it features two sets of three, wide bays extending either side of the three-bay *avant-corps*. The latter, which sports columns on the first as well as the ground floor, is crowned by a plain pediment. Its delicate elegance is contrasted with the more robust treatment of the flanking bays which, gently arched and rusticated on the ground floor, feature enormous, widely spaced windows on the upper floor, the whole topped off by a cornice-level balustrade. In its simplicity and the disposition of its elements, the façade is reminiscent of the work of François Mansart. Delamair clearly paid great attention to the proportions and interrelationship of façade and courtyard to ensure a harmonious ensemble, and the splendour of the finished result is all the more remarkable in that it avoids overblown theatricality. The façade is also notable for its sculpture, sparingly but judiciously applied, which includes personifications of Glory and Magnificence crowning the pediment, and incarnations of the Four Seasons decorating the first floor, the latter by Robert Le Lorrain (today replaced by copies).

After dismissing Delamair, Hercule-Mériadec engaged the services of Germain Boffrand to realize the interior of the palace. Today recognized as the greatest of French Rococo architects, Boffrand twice decorated the Hôtel de Soubise. While nothing remains of his first set of interiors, the second, created in the 1730s following Hercule-Mériadec's marriage to Marie-Sophie de Courcillon, are justly famous. The two oval salons in the little pavilion he built adjoining the principal wing are especially renowned. Boffrand assembled an impressive team of artists to work on the project, including the sculptors Lambert-Sigisbert Adam and Jean-Baptiste Lemoyne, and the painters François Boucher, Charles Natoire, Jean Restout, Charles Trémolières and Carle Van Loo. Despite the many unfortunate modifications carried out in the 19C, the state apartments still retain much of their magnificence, and have recently been restored.

The prince's rooms are located on the ground floor, to the rear of the building. One arrives first in his *chambre d'apparat*, which is richly, though in comparison to other rooms in the house, sparingly decorated with Rococo panelling and plasterwork. In all of Boffrand's interiors at the Hôtel de Soubise one notices the Rococo tendency to avoid architectonic elements of decoration, the design proceeding instead from a base of blank, neutral walls to which elaborate, almost nebulous sculptural fantasies are applied. Nonetheless, in comparison with the fanciful freedom of much subsequent German and Austrian Rococo, Boffrand retains a strict, quasi-architectural control over his forms, the rationality and restraint of which seem very French. The prince's bedroom leads into his oval *salon*, which is charmingly decorated in white and *eau-de-Nil* plasterwork, with bas-reliefs on themes such as truth, arithmetic and astronomy. The *grand cabinet* which follows has lost most of its original décor.

The princess's apartments are situated on the first floor, and are reached after climbing the impressive staircase to the right of the vestibule, which was rebuilt in 1844 and redecorated with an allegory of *France Snatching her Archives from the Mists of Time* by Félix Jobbé-Duval. Situated directly above the prince's apartments, the princess's rooms are even more extravagantly decorated than her husband's, and include her *chambre d'apparat*, hung with deep red silk and dripping with gilded mouldings, and the most celebrated room of all, the princess's *salon*. Here Boffrand surpassed himself. The oval space is cadenced by a series of large, arched openings containing either windows, mirrors or doors, between which are narrow panels decorated in white and gold plasterwork. A cycle of irregularly shaped paintings by Natoire, depicting the legend of Psyche, fills the spandrels between the walls and the gently domed, blue-painted ceiling. Elaborate, gilded mouldings in the form of putti and vegetal-derived motifs unite the ensemble and fuse the separate elements into a seamless, deliquescent continuity. Despite the richness of the decoration, the salon retains a lightness and delicacy which thoroughly justify its reputation as the summit of French Rococo achievement.

It was Napoleon who, in 1808, decreed that the French National Archives should be deposited at the Hôtel de Soubise, initially on a temporary basis. Money was never found for the planned purpose-built archive, and Louis Philippe eventually ordered that the Hôtel de Soubise be modified to render it suitable for proper storage of the documents. To this end, in 1838, the architects Dubois, Lelong and Gréterin erected the imposing wing that now stands between the Hôtel de Soubise and the Hôtel de Rohan. During the Second Empire, the private apartments of the Rohans were demolished and replaced by the aggressive, bastion-like building which runs along the Rue des Archives and the Rue des Quatre-Fils, the work of the architect Janniard. The most recent addition to the archive complex is the new reading-room block, built by Stanislas Fiszer in 1983–88, which successfully if anonymously blends in with its more illustrious neighbours.

3.6 Hôtel de Guénégaud-des-Brosses
60, rue des Archives
François Mansart, 1651–55(?)
(Métro: Rambuteau)

Of the surviving handful of Mansart's Parisian *hôtels particuliers*, the Hôtel de Guénégaud is the best preserved, along with the later Hôtel Carnavalet (3.1). Built for a member of the *noblesse de robe* – Jean-François de Guénégaud, *sieur* of Brosses – this deceptively simple building shows the architect at his most austere and is often quoted as the first example of the French *style sévère*. It follows the standard pattern for Parisian *hôtels particuliers*, with a main *corps de logis* giving onto a garden behind and separated from the street by a courtyard, the latter surrounded on its other three sides by service buildings and accessed via a *porte-cochère*. Despite having previously experimented with the sophisticated plan possibilities of double-width *logis* (an innovation that began to appear in the 1640s), Mansart here reverted to the traditional single-width plan, consisting simply of a suite of interconnecting rooms. Guénégaud's apartment was on the ground floor, while his wife occupied the *piano nobile*.

The building's external décor is of extreme sobriety, bereft of the orders – as was Mansart's wont for *hôtels particuliers* –, its effect relying on the perfectly proportioned play of solid and void, in the form of walls and windows, heightened by the application of subtle and beautifully judged decorative elements – string course, window surrounds, rustication, brackets, cornice, etc. Today's street frontage is perhaps even more simple than the original, which probably featured a pedimented attic storey. When Guénégaud acquired the site, it was already occupied by two houses, one bordering the Rue des Archives and the other facing onto the Rue des Quatre-Fils, both of which were incorporated by Mansart into the new *hôtel*. This explains the difference in width between the north and south courtyard wings, invisible from the *cour d'honneur*, but fully apparent on the garden front, where the pavilions are consequently also of unequal width. In the interests of symmetry – and perhaps of humour – Mansart provided the narrower northern pavilion with blind fenestration and a half dormer, visually continuing it into the neighbouring plot. The impressive garden front was remodelled in the 18C, when the first-floor windows were lowered (the courtyard façade retains the original window proportions).

In Mansart's time, the *hôtel*'s interior was decorated with extreme simplicity, and is of little interest today, apart from the splendid *escalier d'honneur* in the southern courtyard wing. Built entirely of stone, it leads to madame's apartments and is supported only on the outer walls of the stairwell, the steps themselves being held up by a continuous, geometrically complex vault, a masterpiece of stereotomy. Despite the restricted space, Mansart achieved a real sense of monumentality, terminating the composition in a bravura flourish of curved treads that spill out ever wider into the hall below.

3.6 Hôtel de Guénégaud-des-Brosses

3.7 Hôtel d'Avaux or de Saint-Aignan (Jewish Museum)
71, rue du Temple
Pierre Le Muet, *c*. 1644–50
(Métro: Rambuteau)

It was probably on the strength of his work at the Châteaux de Chavigny and Pont-sur-Seine that Pierre Le Muet secured the commission for this *hôtel particulier*, built for Claude de Mesmes, Comte d'Avaux. Mesmes wanted a residence that would reflect both his ambitions and his learning, since neither his leading political position (he helped negotiate the treaty of Westphalia) nor his cultured humanism found expression in the family's old, unfashionable Parisian home, which he demolished to make way for the new edifice. Le Muet's building is remarkable for its sense of grandeur, achieved through surprisingly economic means, and for its ingenious use of a difficult site. Screening the *cour d'honneur* from the road is an impressively monumental entrance façade, dominated by a gigantic rusticated arch containing the *porte-cochère*, and one is thus unprepared for the richness of the courtyard. Two storeys high with arcades running all around the ground floor, the courtyard's façades are cadenced by a giant Corinthian order in the form of pilasters applied to all four elevations. Not only were giant orders comparatively rare on Parisian *hôtels particuliers*, but their use was usually confined just to the *corps de logis*; the application of colossal pilasters to all four sides of the courtyard of the Hôtel d'Avaux, in the Italian manner, was thus a bold novelty in the Parisian context. The pilasters were originally to have been fluted and the sculptural decoration generally more florid, but a shortage of funds prevented this. Rather than reducing the courtyard's effect, if anything this simplification of aspect augments its grandeur, which is achieved through only the rhythmic articulation of the fenestration and the plastic qualities of the colossal order and other façade detailing (string course, arch mouldings, balustrades, etc.). Despite the courtyard's Italianizing regularity, there are concessions to French tradition, most notably in the dropped roofline and balustrade- and cornice-free entablature of the front sections of the lateral elevations, which thus coiffed have the appearance of subordinate pavilions.

All is not as regular as it seems in plan, either. The southern (lefthand) courtyard elevation is in fact a dummy, merely masking the neighbouring plot. The *corps de logis* as seen from the courtyard contains only a fraction of the *hôtel*'s accommodation, the majority being incorporated in a wing running off to the north that fills a projecting irregularity in the contours of the site. Consequently, the garden front is much longer than the courtyard elevation, but Le Muet managed to ensure a symmetrical aspect for both while at the same time masking the misalignment of the façades' axes in the plan. The stables and other service buildings are also cleverly squeezed into a plot irregularity, and the casual observer remains oblivious to these asymmetries. Inside, the principal rooms are lined up in simple *enfilades*.

Today the Hôtel d'Avaux is often referred to as the Hôtel de Saint-Aignan, after Paul de Beauvilliers, Duc de Saint-Aignan, who acquired the building in 1688. Nothing now survives of its 17C interiors following its subdivision in the 19C for a variety of light-industrial purposes. Acquired by the Ville de Paris in the 1960s, the *hôtel* was slowly restored and its original external appearance recreated with the removal of extra storeys added in the 19C. In 1986, the Ville and the French government decided to create a Musée d'Art et d'Histoire du Judaïsme at the Hôtel d'Avaux, for which the building was entirely restored a second time by Bernard Fonquernie, Architecte en Chef des Monuments Historiques. Opened in 1998, the new institution's museographic *mise en scène* was designed by the architects Catherine Bizouard and François Pin. Working with spaces that did not always lend themselves to their allotted task, Bizouard and Pin managed, with considerable skill, to create a unified and elegant environment for the objects displayed. Although refined, their sober palette of materials, no doubt inspired by the Grand Louvre (see 1.8) and including light oak, natural plaster and bare stone, tends towards a rather overwhelming sensation of beige.

3.8 Hôtel d'Hallwyl
28, rue Michel-le-Comte
Claude-Nicolas Ledoux, 1766/67
(Métro: Rambuteau)

Despite his prolific production, extant buildings by the extraordinary Claude-Nicolas Ledoux are now rare, especially where his residential output is concerned. This *hôtel particulier* is the only surviving Parisian example of one of his private commissions. An early work, realized when he was just 30 and still unknown, the Hôtel d'Hallwyl is in fact a remodelling of an older building, the 17C Hôtel de Bouligneux. Seeing it today, one would never suspect these antecedents, so much does the edifice appear a product of the Age of Enlightenment. It was the Hôtel d'Hallwyl that launched Ledoux's career, and many of the themes he would go on to develop in later output can already be discerned here. Following a long period of neglect, the building was recently restored and converted into flats.

Externally, the *hôtel* is characterized by a sobriety that verges on the severe, and it is this that instantly distinguishes it from its more commonplace neighbours on the Rue Michel-le-Comte. Franz-Joseph d'Hallwyl, a Swiss army officer and Ledoux's patron on this job, rented the *hôtel* from Jacques Necker, a partner in the Thélusson bank whose offices were just next door, and it was perhaps with this connection in mind that Ledoux conceived the rusticated street frontage, which is reminiscent of the stronghold-style architecture common to banking institutions and to prisons. Its forceful horizontals, which are all the more powerful in that the street's narrowness allows them to be seen only in perspective, are interrupted at their centre by a giant *porte-cochère*, whose disunity of scale is an early example of a classic Ledoux device. Although he preserved its traditional arched form, Ledoux modernized the *porte-cochère* by filling it with a pair of Doric columns topped by a straight lintel carrying carved figures. Interestingly, in Ledoux's engravings of the street façade, certain mannerisms do not appear, such as the windows' dropped keystones or the subtle retrocessions of the cornices that follow the equally delicate articulation of the façade into lateral pavilions, central *arrière-corps* and portal.

The *cour d'honneur* is even more sober than the street façade, and it is astonishing that Ledoux managed to create such a powerful impression with so extreme an economy of means. Façade animation is essentially limited to banded rustication, which attempts to counter the tall verticality of the old Hôtel de Bouligneux. Virtually all that breaks the rustication's monotony, apart from the ground-floor and roof-line cornices, is the area of smooth wall surrounding the fenestration of the courtyard's main façade (where theoretically the principal rooms should have been, although in fact they were not), and the pediments coiffing the first-floor windows of this group. Internally,

3.8 Hôtel d'Hallwyl

the plot's narrowness did not allow, in plan at least, the traditional French division into *corps de logis* and subordinate pavilions, and *enfilades* of rooms were thus lined up around its different wings. Of Ledoux's interiors, nothing now remains bar the *escalier d'honneur* in the left-hand courtyard wing, whose austere architectonics mirror those of the *hôtel*'s exterior.

However, elements of fantasy were not entirely banished from the Hôtel d'Hallwyl, but instead concentrated in the garden. Ledoux decided that it was too small to accommodate greenery, and therefore opted for an architectural composition to fill the space. Tuscan colonnades, which given the garden's cramped dimensions inevitably make one think of the atrium of a Roman villa, flank the area on either side and frame a nymphaeum that occupies its farthest wall. Heavily rusticated, the latter features pedestals decorated with carved conduits from which flows sculpted stone water, a precursor of the famous motif used by Ledoux at the Arc-et-Senans salt works (1773–79). But the feature of the garden that most impressed contemporaries has today disappeared: on the blind wall of the property on the other side of the Rue de Montmorency, Ledoux painted an enormous *trompe-l'œil* depicting an Ionic colonnade with garden greenery receding behind it, thus virtually continuing the *hôtel*'s grounds beyond their temporal limits.

3.9 Saint-Nicolas-des-Champs
254, rue Saint-Martin
Extant buildings begun early-13C
(Métro: Arts et Métiers)

Today a sizeable parish church in the city centre, Saint-Nicolas-des-Champs started out as a modest chapel, which was successively enlarged as its congregation grew. The first known mention of the building dates from 1119, when it was a small place of worship built by the Prieuré Saint-Martin (3.10) for the little community that had established itself outside the priory walls, situated, as its name suggests, in the fields north of Paris. In 1184, the chapel was promoted to the rank of parish church, and in the early-13C it was entirely rebuilt. At this time it was still fairly modest in size, comprising a central nave flanked by single side-aisles with lateral chapels, its bell tower standing on the outermost corner of the west façade. All that remains of the 13C church today are the pillars of the first six bays of the side-aisles and the lower parts of the bell tower, the edifice having been radically altered in subsequent rebuilding campaigns. The first of these was undertaken around 1420, and included the remodelling of the nave, the west front and the tower, which was now enclosed within the church's fabric. The 15C nave elevations are exceedingly sober, with no triforium – the arcade and the clerestory are separated by a band of blank wall – and almost no modelling of the piers, contrasting strongly with the crisply carved shafts of the 13C supports visible in the southern aisle.

3.9 Saint-Nicolas-des-Champs

In 1541, further building work was begun by the master mason Jean de Froncières, who built a second side-aisle on the church's southern flank in place of the old lateral chapels, with new side-chapels extending the church further outwards. This disposition was repeated on the northern side either by Froncières or afterwards in 1574, when the next phase of building work was begun. The effect of this doubling of the aisles is rather peculiar, since the new, outer aisles are taller than the inner ones. Froncières was also responsible for the charnel house (of which only parts now remain) and the small dwelling on the church's southern side.

Executed by order of the Paris *parlement*, the 1574 building campaign, which was completed in 1586, doubled the length of the nave by the addition of four extra bays, somewhat higher and wider than their predecessors and with considerably taller arcades, topped off with roundheaded rather than pointed arches. The new clerestory windows were also roundheaded but, despite these Renaissance concessions to Classicism, the later sections of the church remain fundamentally Gothic. It was probably also at this time that the rather fine Renaissance doorway was built on the southern façade, its richly carved composition inspired by a portal designed by Philibert De l'Orme at the Hôtel des Tournelles (destroyed) in 1559. Work on the church ceased for almost 30 years, until 1613, when the last two bays of the main vessel and the semicircular apse-ambulatory were begun. Completed in 1615, their design is the same as that of the 1574 to 1586 campaign. Extra height was added to the tower in 1668, and sometime in the 18C – perhaps around 1745 – the choir was dressed up in Classical garb, fluted columns and Ionic pilasters replacing its original rather Romanesque-looking supports.

Despite the many different phases of its construction, and even despite the varying sizes and styles of its constituent parts, the interior of Saint-Nicolas appears coherent, thanks to the fact that successive builders stuck to a master scheme probably devised by Froncières. In plan, the church is essentially a smaller-scale version of Notre-Dame (4.2), without transepts. The organ casing obscuring the west window was installed in 1587–1613 and modified in 1635 (the actual working organ is later) and is one of Paris's handsomest. Its underside delimits the church's entrance vestibule and sports some remarkable carved angels. Saint-Nicolas's exterior is undistinguished, although its west front and the first few bays of the southern façade feature fine Flamboyant carvings and detailing.

3.10 Prieuré Saint-Martin-des-Champs, now Conservatoire National des Arts et Métiers
270–292, rue Saint-Martin
Earliest extant buildings begun c. 1060
(Métro: Arts et Métiers, Réaumur-Sébastopol)

A charter dating from around 709/10 contains the earliest surviving mention of the Priory of Saint-Martin-in-the-Fields, although a religious community may have existed on this site as early as 558. Sacked by the Normans in the 9C, the old priory was probably in an advanced state of ruin when, in 1060, Henri I rebuilt the complex and installed a community of canons there. Seven years later his successor, Philippe I, inaugurated the new church, and subsequently gave the priory to the powerful Abbey of Cluny, in 1079. In the late-15C, the priory regained its autonomy, and continued to thrive until the 18C. At the Revolution it was dissolved, but unlike the majority of confiscated religious buildings was not sold off. Instead it was given to the Conservatoire National des Arts et Métiers (CNAM), an organization created in 1794 by the Convention at the suggestion of Abbé Grégoire. The Conservatoire's original role was to improve national industry by acquiring and teaching the workings of new inventions; today it has evolved into an international higher-education and research organization. The Musée des Arts et Métiers, founded under Abbé Grégoire for the display of new inventions, is home to an astonishing collection of scientific and technical instruments, machines, models and drawings. After eight years of restoration and renovation work carried out by Bernard Fonquernie, Andrea Bruno and François Deslaugiers, the museum reopened in March 2000.

Despite the major modifications carried out in the 19C for the Conservatoire's benefit, substantial portions of the old priory survive intact to this day. Founded in troubled times, the complex was originally fortified around its entire perimeter: the mid-13C round tower at the corner of the Rues Saint-Martin and du Vertbois, and the contemporaneous section of crenellated wall running along the latter, testify to this need for security. Another tower can be seen in the nearby Rue Bailly (it now serves as the stairwell of no. 7), which is today entirely disassociated from the rest of the site as a result of the later cutting-through of the Rue Réaumur.

By far the oldest surviving part of the priory is the church, which was situated at the centre of the original site, and now flanks the Rue Réaumur. The building is of simple nave-choir layout, and its nave foundations and lower sections, constructed from rubble stone set in mortar, are characteristic of 11C building methods. Abutting the church's southern elevation, at the junction of the nave and the choir, are the remains of its bell tower which, judging from surviving sculpted elements, must date from around 1100. Shorn of its upper levels in 1807/08, the tower's two remaining storeys were subsequently heavily (and rather freely) restored at the beginning of the 20C, and are now really only of archaeological interest. The church's choir, on the other hand, built around 1132–40, is of great architectural and historical significance. It is famous as a precursor of Gothic architecture, and may well have influenced Abbot Suger's rebuilding of the choir at Saint-Denis (21.2). Its layout follows the classic apse-ambulatory-with-radiating-chapels disposition by then common all over France, although with some particularities that were probably modelled on the mother church at Cluny, for example the evocation in its plan of Cluny's major and minor transepts, the latter expressed at Saint-Martin in the form of a trefoil-shaped axial apsidiole. Where Saint-Martin is revolutionary is in the treatment of its radiating chapels, which constitute a major departure from the precedents at Cluny or anywhere else. In the majority of French Romanesque churches, radiating chapels are clearly disassociated, often with a section of ambulatory wall physically separating them; at Saint-Martin, however, the architect squashed his semicircular radiating chapels hard up together. In theory, each pair should thus share a sizeable section of lateral wall but, instead of building them as individual units separated by masonry, the Saint-Martin architect merged the radiating chapels, introducing a second, concentric row of piers behind that of the apse-ambulatory interface and constructing only the chapels' outer walls. The result reads visually as a second ambulatory, although liturgically it served as a set of discrete spaces, each with its own altar. In comparison to traditional, compartmentalized east ends, Saint-Martin's is a paragon of fluidity and airy spaciousness, although the exceptional number of irregularities in the laying out

3.10 Prieuré Saint-Martin-des-Champs, now Conservatoire National des Arts et Métiers

of the piers, largely due to the site's topographical particularities, results in comically crooked vaulting and general formal incoherence. The slightly later Saint-Denis choir would be a much more accomplished realization of the ideas first tried out at Saint-Martin.

Despite the poor setting out of the plan, Saint-Martin's plan presents some interesting subtleties of layout, notably the way in which the principle axis is emphasized through the spacing of the columns, and the hierarchization of space achieved through lowering the level of the ambulatory in relation to the apse proper. Saint-Martin's choir is also noteworthy for its historiated capitals and for its vaulting systems. While some of the capitals are treated in the manner of illuminated books, others are inspired by Norman examples, with those in the apsidiole being particularly fine. In its vaulting, Saint-Martin's choir presents two principle varieties: Romanesque groin and »scoop« vaulting in the ambulatory and radiating chapels, and – what had by then become the more standard modern system – quadripartite rib vaulting in the apse and the apsidiole. The buttressing of the high apse vault is particularly interesting, comprising as it does deep and narrow slabs of masonry that rise on the ambulatory vault and poke out slightly above the ambulatory roof, stopping just at the springing point of the apse vault. It was unusual for buttressing to take this form and to rise so high, and many architectural historians have interpreted the Saint-Martin system as a precursor of flying buttresses.

The nave we see today at Saint-Martin, built on 11C foundations, dates essentially from the mid-13C, although its west end, roofing and polychromatic painted interior are 19C. It consists of a simple, wooden-vaulted space lit by tall, high-set windows, and is characteristic of a trend for deliberately sober church buildings that emerged in France in the Rayonnant period alongside the elaborate cathedrals for which the era is famed. Today the church is part of the Musée des Arts et Métiers, with a spectacular mise en scène by François Deslaugier. Following the creation of the CNAM in the 18C, the church was used for the operation of large-scale machinery and later served for the display of the museum's aircraft collection. Deslaugier wanted to recreate something of the atmosphere of these former activities, and to this end installed a multi-storey steel structure in the nave on which hang various motorized vehicles and from whose summit aeroplanes suspended from the nave ceiling can be admired at close quarters.

Saint-Martin-des-Champs is famous not only for its 12C choir but also for its 13C refectory, which today serves as the Conservatoire's library. It is often attributed to Pierre de Montreuil (who is also credited with the southern-transept façade of Notre-Dame (see 4.2)), although there is no documentary evidence supporting this. Moreover, the refectory's window design suggests it was constructed sometime around 1230–40, i.e. before Montreuil was active. A single, rectangular volume measuring approximately 43 x 12 m on its exterior,

it is especially celebrated for the astonishingly slender columns holding up the common springing points of its two longitudinal rows of quadripartite vaulting. These soaring supports would later inspire 19C architects working in iron: they were directly copied by Louis-Auguste Boileau at Saint-Eugène (9.3), and the general disposition of the refectory must have been in Henri Labrouste's mind when he created the Bibliothèque Sainte-Geneviève (5.6). The refectory has conserved its elaborate, balconied pulpit, as well as the sculpted doorway (today the library's main entrance) that originally connected it to the cloister (since destroyed). Because of the 19C addition of a lecture theatre on the refectory's southern flank, the building's windows are now blind on this side.

Of the other surviving priory buildings, it is worth noting the long, sober, brick-and-stone edifice running parallel to the Rue Saint-Martin at the site's centre, which was constructed in the early-18C to plans by Pierre Bullet. Its monumental, central escalier d'honneur was added by François Soufflot in 1786. It was around the axis of this staircase that Léon Vaudoyer, who was the principal architect behind the transformation of the priory into the CNAM we see today, disposed his additions. On the Rue-Saint-Martin side he created today's cour d'honneur (1839–50), with a neo-Renaissance entrance façade on the street (replacing the houses that originally stood there), the old refectory to the south and, closing the courtyard to the north, a building whose external aspect mirrors that of the refectory opposite. He was also responsible for the rather ungainly, monumental avant-corps plonked in front of the escalier d'honneur, which constitutes the courtyard's focal point. Vaudoyer's plans were pursued by his successor, Auguste Ancelet, in 1876–94, who was responsible for the completion of the Rue-Saint-Martin elevations and for the long wing that closes the complex at the rear.

4th *arrondissement*

4.1 Ile de la Cité
(Métro: Cité, Pont Neuf, Saint-Michel; RER: Saint-Michel Notre-Dame)

At the beginning, this small island – today covering 17 ha, but originally probably no more than 9 ha in size – was Paris. Colonized by the Parisii tribe of Celts around 250 BC, it was situated between two important river confluences – the meeting-points of the Oise and the Marne with the Seine – on an ancient trade route linking Germania and Hispania. Easily defended against attack, the island was also surrounded by cultivable land rich in gypsum (used as fertilizer) and stone reserves. The Parisii settlement consequently flourished and grew wealthy, as attested by the exquisite gold coins produced there. Known in Latin as Lutetia, which means »mid-water dwelling«, the settlement was of prime importance in Julius Caesar's conquest of Gaul, constituting as it did a strategic point of access to the north of the country. Taken by the Romans in 52 BC, Lutetia remained under the empire's control for over four centuries. Following Caesar's victory, the town was rebuilt along Roman lines and extended onto the Left Bank, covering the summit and northern flank of today's Montagne Sainte-Geneviève. The Ile became home, amongst others, to the port (remains of which can be seen in the Crypte Archéologique du Parvis Notre-Dame), the governor's residence (which evolved into today's Palais de Justice, 1.1), an extensive vaulted basilica (whose exact function remains unknown), the forum and probably also a temple of some kind, situated towards its eastern extremity. Two bridges linked the island to the mainland, located where today's Pont Notre-Dame and Petit Pont cross the river (see feature on Seine bridges), together continuing the *cardo* (which descended the Montagne Sainte-Geneviève where today's Rue Saint-Jacques stands) and joining up with the main road north (today's Rue Saint-Martin).

Sometime in the 2C AD, a defensive wall was built round the Ile, which was strengthened in the early-4C following barbarian attacks at the end of the 3C. Judging from pieces of carving uncovered during excavation work and archaeological digs, it seems that the major buildings of the Left Bank were pillaged for their stone to reinforce the Cité's wall, the mainland town having been largely abandoned because impossible to defend. Around the middle of the 4C, a sizeable cathedral was built towards the eastern end of the island; the secular power represented by the governor's palace at the Ile's western tip was now complemented at its opposite extremity by a centre of religious authority. An important monastic community subsequently grew up around the cathedral which, in the 12C, was rebuilt as today's Notre-Dame (4.2). At the same time, the city's principal hospital, the Hôtel-Dieu, was reconstructed to the south of the small piazza that had been created in front of Notre-Dame, fronting the river. Between the cathedral in the east and the palace to the west was a tight jumble of densely built streets packed with houses, chapels and churches: this was essentially the configuration the island would retain for the next seven centuries.

Significant changes between the 12C and the 19C mostly occurred at the Ile's periphery. By 1840, eight bridges connected the island to the mainland with a ninth linking it to the neighbouring Ile Saint-Louis. In the mid-16C, two small islands at the Ile's western tip were joined to it – today's Square Galant occupies part of their surface – and in the 1650s an island just off its eastern promontory – today's Square de l'Ile-de-France – was also attached. The Ile's surface area was thus significantly increased, and grew further with the building of the quaysides, begun by Henri II in the 1560s and finally completed in the early-19C.

Although by the mid-19C the island's densely-built street pattern had changed little since the medieval period, its demographic character had altered radically. The Cité's narrow streets and alleys, however picturesque, contained some of the worst slums in Paris, immortalized in fiction by writers such as Eugène Sue, Balzac and Victor Hugo. Tuberculosis was rife, and the cholera epidemics that struck the French capital in the early-19C were particularly devastating on the Ile. This was clearly a situation that Napoleon III and Baron Haussmann, great sanitizers and modernizers that they were, could not allow to continue. Haussmann's solution when confronted with slums was demolition. His plans for the Ile were far more ambitious than a mere renewal of its crumbling, sordid housing, however. Instead he planned to turn the island into a public utility, making it home to courts, barracks and a vastly extended Hôtel-Dieu, while also retaining the religious centre that was Notre-Dame. To achieve his goal, he demolished nearly all the original fabric of the Ile, a deed which earned him considerable notoriety and which was viewed by many contemporaries as an act of unprecedented vandalism. The island's population dropped overnight from 15,000 inhabitants in 1850 to only 5,000 at the end of the Second Empire. 16 churches were amongst the thousands of buildings destroyed; for many the capital had been literally disembowelled. Mme Baroche described Haussmann as the »Attila of expropriation«, and Baudelaire lamented: »Le vieux Paris n'est plus« (»Old Paris is no more«). Only a small section of the Ile's original fabric was spared, to the north of Notre-Dame (see below). The heart of the island was entirely gutted, and the streets and houses fronting the quaysides to the east and south of Notre-Dame and to the south of the Palais de Justice were also swept away.

Haussmann and his planners divided up the resulting *tabula rasa* into rectilinear plots of land, which they filled with three imposing public buildings (four including the extensions to the Palais de Justice) as well as an open piazza for the city's flower market (the Place Louis-Lépine), a vastly enlarged square in front of Notre-Dame (six times the size of the original) and, to the south and east of the cathedral, public gardens. By far the largest of the new edifices was the rebuilt Hôtel-Dieu (Stanislas Diet and Jacques Gilbert, 1867–77), which was given an enormous city block stretching from the new Place du Parvis Notre-Dame as far as the river to the north. Arranged around a giant internal cloister with external projecting wings, Diet and Gilbert's building was designed to ensure the maximum possible penetration of air and daylight to the wards, in accordance with the »hygienist« thinking of the time which saw lack of light and ventilation as one of the main causes of disease. The central cloister, despite its scale and the monumental chapel dominating its northern extremity, is charming, and the new hospital was a big improvement on its cramped and crumbling predecessor. Given its prime location opposite Notre-Dame, however, it was rather disappointing in its tired utilitarian Classicism and, on its lateral elevations, it is distressingly reminiscent of a prison. The Hôtel-Dieu at least has the merit of being a little more self-effacing than Victor Calliat's lumpen Préfecture de Police (1862–65), which sits directly opposite the cathedral and which originally served as a barracks for the Garde Républicaine. Only its comically overblown entrance portal is worthy of note. The most interesting of Haussmann's new edifices on the Ile is the Tribunal de Commerce (Antoine-Nicolas Bailly, 1860–65), which sits on the island's northern bank between the Place Louis-Lépine and the Boulevard du Palais. Prior to its construction, the business courts sat in the Palais de la Bourse (2.8), which quickly became too small for the ever-growing volume of cases. In deciding to relocate the Tribunal to the Ile, opposite the Palais de Justice, Haussmann was acting on a logical, functional impulse to concentrate judicial activities in one area. In his stipulations for the design of the building, however, Haussmann acted on quite another motive. Bailly's Tribunal de Commerce is situated directly in the axis of the Boulevard Sébastopol, which is part of the Grande Croisée, the north–south/east–west »great crossing« that was the linchpin of Haussmann's reconfiguration of Paris's traffic circulation. As any visitor to Paris will have noticed, Haussmann liked to terminate the distant perspectives of his long straight boulevards with imposing monuments, and it therefore fell to the Tribunal de Commerce to fulfil this role for the southern end of the Boulevard Sébastopol. When standing on the boulevard, at the level of, say, Les Halles (see 1.22), one does indeed see the Tribunal's prominent if rather weedy dome filling the centre of the vista. On approaching the edifice, though, one notices that there is something rather strange about its configuration: its dome appears singularly off-centre in relation to the mass of the building. This is because the Tribunal was designed around its dome, whose positioning was determined by the axis of the Boulevard Sébastopol. Dressed up as a Classical palace, the Tribunal would logically have had a monumental, symmetrical façade fronting the river, but the dome's relative asymmetry, which affects only the river and Rue-de-Lutèce façades, made this impossible. The building therefore presents what clearly reads as a side elevation to the Seine, despite the presence of a monumental *avant-corps* occupying the western half of the river façade, from which entry to the Tribunal is gained. Besides this fascinating quirk, which is revealing of the almost comical extremes to which Haussmann was prepared to push his urban aesthetic, the Tribunal's exterior is undistinguished; the Boulevard-du-Palais façade presents the symmetrical, eclectic, monumentalizing elevation one would expect. The Tribunal's courtrooms are organized around a central, full-height, glass-covered atrium, and the building has conserved its opulent, Renaissance-style Second-Empire interiors, which include an impressive if rather overwrought *escalier d'honneur* located under the dome.

Whatever one's opinion of Haussmann's transformations of Paris, it is hard to like his rebuilding of the Ile de la Cité. The vibrant living heart of the capital was sacrificed to officialdom, and the result is dry, academic and barren. The only exception to this are the gardens around Notre-Dame which, however contrary to the cathedral's original medieval context, produce one of the most sublime urban prospects anywhere when viewed from the Left Bank. It is tempting, too, to regret the tangle of old streets swept away at the baron's behest, although one can gain some idea of what the Ile was once like from the small section of the original fabric that survives to the north of Notre-Dame. The area has changed considerably even since Haussmann's time, but retains its picturesque medieval street pattern as well as several interesting buildings. This part of the island originally belonged to the monastery attached to Notre-Dame, as evidenced by several canons' houses that survive, including nos. 22 and 24, rue Chanoinesse, which both date from the 16C. At no. 8, rue Massillon can be seen the Hôtel Roger-de-Gaillon, home to the choir school of Notre-Dame since 1455. The current building dates from 1740 and features a rather pretty Rococo *porte-cochère*. Also of note is the charming medieval house that backs onto the Rue des Ursins where it links up with the Quai aux Fleurs (en-

4.1 Ile de la Cité

trance to the house is gained via a 17C structure at 12, rue Chanoinesse), which was sympathetically restored in the 1960s by the architect Fernand Pouillon for Prince Karim Aga Khan. Finally, we should mention the remains of the Chapelle Saint-Aignan, which is one of only three religious buildings to survive out of the 23 that formerly occupied the Ile de la Cité (the other two are Notre-Dame itself and the Sainte-Chapelle (1.2)). This tiny chapel was built for Etienne de Garland, Dean of Saint-Aignan d'Orléans and Archdeacon of Notre-Dame, in 1115–18, and as such is the oldest surviving Romanesque structure in Paris after Saint-Germain-des-Prés (6.4). It has lost its chancel, but the two bays of its main vessel survive. Its rib-vaulting is held up by composite piers, whose unusual historiated capitals feature fleurs-de-lis, lions, acanthus leaves and fabulous creatures. They are all the more interesting in that few examples of Romanesque sculpture survive in Paris. Entry to the chapel is gained via no. 19, rue des Ursins, and it can be visited on appointment by contacting the Séminaire de Paris at 15, rue des Ursins.

4.2 Notre-Dame de Paris
Place du Parvis Notre-Dame
Architect unknown, begun c. 1160
(Métro: Cité, Saint-Michel; RER: Saint-Michel Notre-Dame)

If the Eiffel Tower (7.0) has become an instantly recognizable symbol of France, the Cathedral of Notre-Dame is the definitive symbol of Paris, an iconic example of the Gothic splendours of the Ile-de-France. In its day it was the most ambitious French cathedral yet attempted and, with vaults rising to over 33 m, held the height record for over 30 years (it was finally surpassed by the 37 m-high vaults of Bourges and Chartres, both begun in the 1190s). In the 19C its celebrity was assured by Victor Hugo's *Notre-Dame de Paris* (1831), which not only made the cathedral famous the world over but also mobilized French public opinion in its favour, thus helping to save it from almost certain ruin. Quite apart from its historic and literary fame, Notre-Dame's intrinsic beauty, its complexity, and the sheer marvel of its construction make it an absolute must for any visitor to Paris.

The cathedral was built over a period of 160 years, from the 1160s to the 1320s. Most of Notre-Dame was complete by the 1220s and, despite three changes of architect, was remarkably homogeneous, the later masters having remained generally faithful to the first architect's design. The cathedral of 1160–1220 can be classed as a masterpiece of the early-Gothic period, chronologically subsequent to Abbot Suger's rebuilding of Saint-Denis (21.2), by which it was greatly influenced, but coming 30 years before the »High-Gothic« era of Chartres, Reims, Amiens and Bourges (1190s–1250s). From the mid 1220s on, Notre-Dame was largely remodelled in an attempt to modernize the cathedral in response to subsequent stylistic developments. These later modifications are especially manifest on the exterior, and it would not be wholly unjustified to say that today's cathedral is a 12C building in 13C dress. The final round of major work came in the 19C when, following a century of neglect and the brutal vandalism of the Revolution, the edifice was restored by Jean-Baptiste Lassus and Eugène Viollet-le-Duc. Nearly all the cathedral's decorative elements date from this time.

Conception of the cathedral
The current building is not the first religious edifice on the site. It is thought that in Roman times a temple of some kind was situated at the eastern extremity of the Ile de la Cité (4.1), and a church was certainly established there by the mid-4C AD. Notre-Dame's immediate predecessor, the Cathedral of Saint-Etienne, was a grand affair for its era, reputedly the largest church in Gaul, with a nave approximately 70 m long flanked by double aisles. In the 9C, a monastery was founded there, which by the 12C had become an important and influential community. The complex that grew up around the cathedral included, as well as monks' accommodation, the bishop's palace and the Hôtel-Dieu, a hospital run by the church. In tandem with the creation of the monastery came a cult of the Virgin, with the result that the church of Saint-Etienne was increasingly referred to as »Sainte-Marie« or »Notre-Dame«.

At the same time as the monastery grew in importance, so did the city of Paris. By the 12C, as well as the seat of the realm, it had become one of Europe's intellectual capitals, a pre-eminence that must have rendered the antiquated Saint-Etienne unacceptable to the pride of the bishop and his monks. Competition between dioceses was fierce, and the rebuilding of Saint-Denis would have been perceived as a direct challenge to Paris's position, especially given Saint-Denis's royal connections. Consequently, in 1160, Paris's newly invested bishop, Maurice de Sully, took the eventful decision to replace the city's cathedral. In keeping with his diocese's status, Maurice planned big: the new building would be the largest of its kind yet constructed, 127.5 m long, 40 m wide and 33.1 m high under the main vault (the previous height record for vaulting being 32 m, at Cambrai, begun c. 1150). But his ambitions did not end with the cathedral. His urban redevelopment scheme – for it was in truth exactly that – included the building of a brand-new bishop's palace to the south of the cathedral, as well as the cutting of a new, straight street through the tight jumble of houses in front of Notre-Dame's west façade. The widest in Paris, at 6 m, this street was designed to link the complex to the north–south road crossing the Ile de la Cité, thereby ensuring connection with the mainland, and would also facilitate delivery of raw materials to the building site. The Rue Neuve Notre-Dame, as it was named, was aligned with the axis of the cathedral's central portal, and opened out onto a *parvis*, or square, in front of the edifice, which served as a transitional space between the secular world and the house of God. Although only a fraction of the size of Notre-Dame's current *place*, this *parvis* was exceptionally large for its era, at a time when the majority of cathedrals did not benefit from any interval between them and the surrounding urbanity. To add to the expense of Sully's plans, the creation of the Rue Neuve Notre-Dame necessitated the destruction of the old Hôtel-Dieu and, in consequence, a new, larger hospital was built on the island's south bank abutting the southwestern corner of the *parvis*.

Apart from the cathedral, nothing now remains of Maurice de Sully's *grands travaux*: the bishop's palace was destroyed during rioting in 1831, the old Hôtel-Dieu was demolished and rebuilt to the cathedral's north by Haussmann, and the baron also destroyed the houses surrounding the cathedral for the creation of the current *place*. One can nonetheless get an idea of the congested setting in which Notre-Dame once stood from the marks on the surface of today's Place du Parvis Notre-Dame, which outline the contours of the old *parvis* and of the Rue Neuve Notre-Dame.

The cathedral of 1160–1200
None of the copious documentation that would have accompanied the building of Notre-Dame survives, and its architect's name is consequently unknown to us. Even the date when building work began is uncertain – traditionally quoted as 1163, it now seems likely that construction was started earlier. The cathedral's architect must have been a master of considerable experience and vision, for not only was he attempting an edifice on a massive scale but his design also included some innovative departures from established practice. In plan, Notre-Dame was unusual. For one thing its choir, which terminates in the traditional, continental apse-ambulatory layout, is uncommonly long, having almost the same dimensions as the nave. Nave and choir are flanked on either side by generous double aisles of equal height (most probably inspired by the double aisles of the old Saint-Etienne), which, as initially built, were remarkable for the total absence of any projecting chapels (the current chapels are later additions – see below). The covering envelope of the 1160–1220 cathedral would thus have been very different from what we see today, more uniform, coherent and readable both on the interior and the exterior.

Like the majority of Gothic great churches, Notre-Dame's principal vessel, only 12.5 m wide, is very narrow in relation to its enormous height. This was partly due to the technical difficulties in vaulting broader spans, but also partly motivated by aesthetic concerns, as these tall, narrow spaces give an impression of soaring verticality rising towards heaven. In their original form, Notre-Dame's main-vessel elevations were divided into four »storeys«: firstly, a comparatively low arcade; on top of the arcade a generous tribune gallery; above the gallery a row of oculi opening into the tribune roof space; and finally a row of short clerestory windows just under the vault. The oculi were later removed to allow downward extension of the clerestory windows (see below) but, during the 19C, they were restored in the transepts and in one bay of the nave and the choir by Viollet-le-Duc. Although his restitution is inaccurate, one nonetheless gains a good idea of the initial appearance. Four-storey elevations had been, and would remain, unusual; three storeys (arcade, tribune gallery/triforium, clerestory) were the norm, and later developments would tend towards the expansion of the arcade and clerestory at the triforium's expense. The interior of Notre-Dame, with its very generous, vaulted tribunes and tiny clerestory windows, was thus at odds with later thinking. The reasons for the presence of such spacious tribune galleries are unclear. They were almost certainly not built to house altars – a disposition found in many pilgrimage churches – since they are accessed only by two tiny spiral staircases, but they may have been included for purposes of structural stability: the combination of arcaded aisles and galleries stacked together formed an aqueduct-like structure, and tribune vaults often served to counterbalance the thrust of the high vault. Notre-Dame's wide, vaulted tribunes may thus have been designed to support its record-breaking main vault, although many historians think the cathedral of 1160–1220 probably used flying buttresses for this purpose, in which case the explanation of the galleries as vault supports is less convincing. It could be that tribune galleries were included simply out of respect for tradition (large tribunes having been a standard feature

4.2 Notre-Dame de Paris. East end

of northern French great churches for decades) and/or from an appreciation of their aesthetic qualities.

These wide galleries needed, of course, to be roofed externally, and the tribune roofs originally took the form of a steep-pitched framework built up against the main vessel's walls. Clearly, where the tribune roofs abutted the main vessel, no windows could be cut through, resulting in a blank strip of wall on the cathedral's interior elevations, between the galleries and the clerestory. It was here that Notre-Dame's first architect pierced oculi to animate a space which in the main vessels of many Romanesque cathedrals was left »dead«. In comparison to its Romanesque predecessors', Notre-Dame's internal elevations are rather flat, and these oculi, opening as they did onto the dark attic space above the tribune vaults, would have given a more traditional feeling of depth to the nave walls. (Viollet-le-Duc's glazed oculi produce a very different effect.) They may also have had symbolic value: in French they are referred to as *roses*, and since roses are an emblem of the Virgin, Notre-Dame's chain of oculi may have been intended to represent a rosary.

The quest for altitude in early- and High-Gothic great churches stemmed from a desire to reach ever further towards heaven, and it was this that prompted the evolution in internal-elevation articulation associated with the style. In his treatment of Notre-Dame's choir elevations, the cathedral's first architect did much to break with the traditionally horizontal emphasis of Romanesque great churches and instead put the accent on the interior's upward movement. Thus, unusually for the time, the main vessel's responds rise all the way to the vaults without interruption, contrasting singularly with a building like Laon Cathedral (1160s–90s, almost Notre-Dame's exact contemporary), where Romanesque-style shaft rings and annulets are used to create an effect of horizontal banding. Also innovatory was the first master's decision not to use alternating responds for his sexpartite vaulting. Following the example of Sens (begun *c*. 1140), sexpartite vaults became a characteristic feature of late-12C Gothic, primarily because they required less stone and were therefore less heavy, but also because their rib arches were pointed (unlike the round rib arches of quadripartite vaulting), thereby allowing stylistic continuity. Sexpartite vaults have the particularity of producing irregular thrusts on their springing points, the four outer points being subject to greater forces than the two inner ones. The earliest examples of sexpartite vaulting expressed this inequality in their piers, with alternate heavy and light columns and vault responds advancing along the main vessel. Alternate columns seem to have been disliked, and were soon dropped, but it remained the norm to express the unequal vault thrusts through the responds, by employing heavier capitals and greater agglomerations of shafts for the heavier loads. At Notre-Dame, however, no distinction is made between outer- and inner-vault responds, except on the springing capitals in the choir (the nave, built by the cathedral's second and fourth architects, does not even feature this distinction). This departure from usual practice seems explicable only by a desire for greater uniformity. In comparison to earlier Gothic churches, Notre-Dame's main vessel is more rhythmically fluent and even, its piers drawing one inexorably along towards the high altar at a brisk, regular pace. In one respect, however, Notre-Dame's internal elevations were archaic, namely in the use of rather chunky columns to support the main-vessel arcades. These columns, with their giant capitals carved into foliage forms that project outwards to receive the vault responds, curiously break the vertical emphasis established elsewhere on the main vessel's elevations, and one wonders why compound piers, which would have been more suitable for the expression of upward movement, were not employed. Notre-Dame's master may have been inspired by Saint-Denis's choir, where rather stumpy columns were used to match the piers of the 8C nave, or may have wanted to recreate something of the ambience of the old Cathedral of Saint-Etienne.

Where its east end is concerned, Notre-Dame features an unusual innovation in its ambulatory. The semicircular ambulatories popular on the continent were extremely difficult to vault, complex geometry being required to force the essentially rectilinear form of the vaulting round the curve of the apse, with often horribly clumsy and awkward results. At Notre-Dame, the task was made even more difficult by the ambulatory's double aisles. Aided in part by the lack of radiating chapels, the cathedral's first master found a simple and elegant solution to the problem. In place of the quadripartite vaulting used in the straight sections of the aisles, he introduced a system of diagonal arches in the ambulatory, with the result that the vault is made up of identical triangular compartments which zigzag round the apse. Despite its felicity, this disposition remained unique to Notre-Dame.

Construction of the cathedral, which began at the east end and advanced westwards, progressed at considerable speed. The first architect, who was probably replaced sometime in the 1170s, completed all of the apse and choir and part of the transepts, although he did not build the choir's high vault. The second architect was no less swift, completing the east end in 1182 – the year the high altar was consecrated – and building all but the two westernmost bays of the nave, before his replacement sometime around 1200. Technically, the second master's work was extraordinarily accomplished. Already, in comparison to preceding buildings, the first architect's structure was extremely lean. Where the rubble walls of Romanesque great churches can reach up to 8 m in thickness, Notre-Dame's smooth ashlar walls are, for most of their height, under 1 m in width. This achievement did not, of course, occur in a vacuum, for Paris-region architects had been experimenting for some time with thin-wall structures, for example at Saint-Pierre-de-Montmartre (18.3) and in the choir of Saint-Denis. In the parts of Notre-Dame for which he was responsible, the second master put up a structure whose supports, in relation to the weight they carry, are amongst the thinnest of any surviving building of the Gothic era. Not until the iron buildings of the 19C would such ratios be bettered.

One of the ways in which the second master achieved such slenderness was through extensive use of stone *en délit*. Notre-Dame is built of limestone which, as a sedimentary rock, forms in horizontal strata, or beds. Normally, when building load-bearing structures with limestone, the strata are maintained in the horizontal position, as the rock is best able to resist pressure orientated this way. On the other hand, by using limestone *en délit* (literally »against the bed«), that is to say with the strata orientated vertically, one can produce much thinner members, although at the risk of their shattering if too great a pressure is exerted upon them. The second architect consequently used stone *en délit* only for minor components, for example in the tribune galleries – compare the two breathtakingly slender colonnettes of each nave-tribune arcade with the single, fatter supports used in the choir – and in the aisles, where he alternated single columns with compound piers formed from a slender core surrounded by twelve colonnettes *en délit*. The thinness of Notre-Dame's structures resulted in another aesthetic difference in comparison to Romanesque great churches, for in the absence of a massive masonry envelope the cathedral displays none of the thick-wall games that Romanesque architects liked to play in their buildings, such as hollowed-out passages or layering of supports. Instead, Notre-Dame's tracery-filled clerestory and oculi dramatically highlighted the fact that the interior and exterior surfaces had now coalesced into one thin, simple membrane.

The west front and the 13C nave
Around 1200, attention moved from the still-uncompleted nave to the cathedral's west front, which was begun by a third architect, who completed it up to the top of the Galerie des Rois. Sometime in the decade 1210–20, a fourth architect took over, building the façade's upper parts and starting the towers. Notre-Dame's west elevation has today become one of the most celebrated images in Gothic architecture, a highly graphic, almost iconic distillation of the classic two-tower formula, achieved in part through the unusual flatness and relative sobriety of its surfaces. In comparison to the overcharged, overwrought and almost shambling composition of some other French-Gothic west fronts, it is a model of clarity and simple, harmonious proportions. The two-tower scheme it adopts had by this time become standard in northern France, no doubt partly because of its symbolic division into three parts, representing the Trinity. It also clearly reflects the building's basilical interior with a central nave flanked by double aisles, the latter's twofold thickness being signalled in the pairing of the façade's window openings. Notre-Dame's west front is divided horizontally into five bands, which, as well as articulating its huge surface area, allow a progressive upwards tapering of storeys towards the heavenwards-reaching spires that must originally have been intended to coiff each tower. The lowest band contains three entrance portals, the southernmost of which, known as the Portail Sainte-Anne, was originally created *c.* 1148 for the old Saint-Etienne and re-used, in modified form, on the new cathedral. Its 12C carvings are considered masterpieces of early-Gothic sculpture. The northern portal, known as the Portail du Couronnement, features kings, prophets and the Virgin, amongst others, while the central portal depicts the Last Judgement on its tympanum, as was common. In their quality, Notre-Dame's 13C sculptures are exceptional. Above the portals we find the famous Galerie des Rois, a decorative, balconied colonnade containing statues of the kings of Judah, who were the supposed ancestors of Mary. We should not forget that all this profusion of carving was originally painted, and that colour was also applied to the upper parts of the façade.

Over the Galerie des Rois, at roughly the centre of gravity of the whole composition, we find the west front's 9 m-diameter rose window, which lights this end of the nave. The west façade's rose is symbolic not only of the Virgin but also, as a circle inscribed within a square, of the relationship between heaven and earth: with its four corners signifying the four elements, the square is the temporal realm, while the circle, a »perfect« form with neither beginning nor end and no rup-

4.2 Notre-Dame de Paris. West front

ture or contradiction, represents divinity; together the two forms evoke the mystery of the Incarnation, of God made man. The miracle of the Incarnation is further underlined by the statue of the Virgin and Child sitting atop the middle of the Galerie des Rois: if you stand at the entrance to Notre-Dame's original *parvis*, you will see that the façade's proportions were calculated so that, when viewed from this spot, the statue appears at the exact centre of the rose window above, which thus forms an enormous halo around the figures' heads. This kind of scholastic symbolism is present throughout the cathedral: its twelve doors recall the twelve tribes of Israel and the twelve apostles, its towers, pinnacles and spire evoke the Heavenly Jerusalem, and so on. It has been suggested that the insistence on the Incarnation present in Notre-Dame's west front may have been a display of orthodoxy intended to counter the ideas of the heretic Cathares, who refuted exactly this aspect of Catholic doctrine.

After completing the rose level of the west façade, Notre-Dame's fourth architect turned his attention to the nave, building the two missing bays after the west front. He took an important liberty with the elevation design established by his predecessors, introducing modifications almost certainly inspired by Chartres, whose innovations were to prove very influential. The fourth master built piers based not on the columnar form up till then used at Notre-Dame, but on the compound form employed at Chartres. He did, however, graduate the transition so that the stylistic rupture would not appear too brutal: on the easternmost of his bays we find columnar-core piers with only responds descending down their surface, whereas on the last, westernmost bay we find the full Chartrain model, with a columnar core flanked by both responds and arcade colonnettes. Aesthetically, of course, these compound piers provide a vertical thrust that lends itself much more to the nave's soaring *élan* than the old, columnar model.

Modification and completion of Notre-Dame c. 1220–60
Even though Notre-Dame's west front was still far from finished, in the decade 1220–30 attention shifted to the parts of the cathedral already built, and more precisely to its upper levels, which were entirely modified. The reason for this sudden decision to reconstruct a building that, in medieval-cathedral terms, was brand new, was the rebuilding of the nave at Saint-Denis, which, art historians agree, saw the birth of a new style: the Rayonnant. The most striking characteristic of Saint-Denis's reconstructed internal elevations was the extremely high proportion of glazing in comparison to wall area, the stone-work having been reduced to an absolute minimum to produce surfaces almost entirely of glass. Notre-Dame had long suffered on a practical front from the dinginess of its interior, but now, in comparison to the dazzling, luminous nave at Saint-Denis, its prestige was also dulled by this obscurity. To get more light into Notre-Dame, the high aisle roofs were removed and replaced with flat coverings, and the clerestory windows lowered into the space formerly occupied by the oculi above the tribune galleries (looking at the cathedral's exterior, one can still see the clerestory's original base where the colonnettes flanking each window stop). Extending the clerestory windows was not as simple as one might imagine, however, since it gave rise to a whole set of difficulties concerning the draining of rainwater from the nave roof, which dumped all its load onto the now flat aisle coverings, which could not cope. To resolve the problem, the nave roof was rebuilt with a steeper pitch and a gutter running all along its base, to which were attached numerous »flying buttresses«, which in fact are not buttresses at all but stone conduits that carry rain water out to gargoyles which eject it well beyond the cathedral's perimeter. Thus Notre-Dame's quintessentially Gothic external appearance, cadenced by slender, soaring arcs, actually has nothing whatever to do with the Gothic structural system so admired by Structural Rationalists of the last two centuries!

It is thought that a fifth architect was responsible for the modifications to the cathedral's upper levels, but whoever it was was well versed in the new techniques of »reinforced stone«, whereby iron clamps and tie rods are employed to hold together slender masonry structures that could never otherwise stand up. This method was used to build the splendid filigree arcade running across the west front at the base of the towers, which serves to obscure the gable end of the nave roof without entirely closing the space in between, thereby grading the transition between solid and void. As for the towers themselves, they were completed in their current state by 1245, the spires originally planned for them never being realized. Reinforced stone was again used to spectacular effect in the following decade when Notre-Dame's transept fronts were rebuilt, beginning with the northern which was undertaken by Jean de Chelles in the 1250s, the southern being completed by the famous Pierre de Montreuil in the 1260s after Chelles's death. Quite why new transept façades were constructed is uncertain, but, given that the entrances they enclosed were reserved exclusively for the use of Notre-Dame's canons, we can be sure that the order's prestige and standing had something to do with it. This interpretation is further borne out by the fact that Notre-Dame's new transept fronts were clearly inspired by, and set out to surpass, the rebuilt transept elevations at Saint-Denis (the southern of which, moreover, was the work of none other than Pierre de Montreuil). Notre-Dame's two transept elevations are very similar in their general handling, although the southern is generally considered the more accomplished. Sandwiched between heavy side buttresses coiffed by monumental pinnacles, each comprises an arrangement of niches and gables at ground-floor level enclosing the central portal, a glazed, balconied colonnade rising above, then an enormous rose window filling the entire width of the façade and set within a clearly defined square, and finally, terminating the ensemble, a gable end filled with a smaller rose lighting the attic space. Structurally the main roses were built as part of a huge round-headed arch, the lower spandrels of the squares containing them being glazed but their upper ones being in solid, tracery-decorated masonry. The circle-within-a-square, Incarnation symbolism present on the west front was thus made the principal theme on the transepts, especially on the southern whose rose division is based on the figure twelve, which, as well as the twelve tribes of Israel and the twelve apostles, represented God made man (twelve is the product of the figure three, symbolic of God and the Trinity, and the figure four, representative of creation). Although based on Saint-Denis's, Notre-Dame's transept fronts developed the Saint-Denis model further, with much greater adornment and a blurring of the distinction between solid and void through the use of tracery. The result is a stunning screen of diaphanous filigree that spawned many imitations and descendants, from Strasbourg to London to Clermont-Ferrand.

The cathedral from the mid-13C to the present day
Although following completion of the southern transept façade Notre-Dame could essentially be considered finished, work at the cathedral carried on until well into the next century with the building of side-chapels all round its perimeter (bar, of course, the west and transept fronts). Originally altars had simply been placed against the aisles' outer envelope, but as their number grew they produced such an effect of disorder that it was decided they should be placed in discrete chapels. Constructed in between its buttresses, Notre-Dame's side-chapels were delimited by a continuous wall, giving the cathedral's ground floor a smooth, homogeneous external aspect that would subsequently be imitated in many Parisian churches. The first side-chapels were built round the nave, Pierre de Montreuil put up choir chapels sometime in the 1260s, while the architect Jean Ravy built the apse's side-chapels in 1296–1325. Ravy also reconfigured the apse's drainage system, constructing the splendid flying arcs we see today, which span a whopping 15 m in one go.

Until the turn of the 18C, Notre-Dame preserved intact its medieval state. But the Age of Enlightenment was to prove disastrous for the cathedral. Things started out innocently enough with the redecoration of the choir by Robert de Cotte in 1699–1715. But afterwards, in the mid-century, the cathedral's stained glass was destroyed (bar, thankfully, in the three roses) and replaced with clear glazing in an attempt to produce a brightly lit interior of the kind then so fashionable. 20 years later, in 1771, Jacques-Germain Soufflot destroyed the central jamb and part of the tympanum of the west front's central portal to facilitate the entry of processions. These acts of vandalism were of course to be followed by far worse during the Revolution, which saw the loss of all the cathedral's furnishings, the destruction of its spire, and the brutal mutilation of the south, north and west front's sculptures, the kings of Judah being decapitated because, it seems, popular ignorance thought them representations of the Bourbon monarchs (the heads were rediscovered in the 20C and are now on display in the Musée de Cluny, 5.4).

By the early-19C, when Hugo wrote *Notre-Dame de Paris*, the cathedral was in a pitiful state, its masonry crumbling and threatening to collapse in places, its sculptures mutilated and its gargoyles gone. Fortunately, the reign of Louis Philippe saw a change in attitude towards France's medieval heritage, which was boosted by the king's desire to reconcile the country to its royalist, Catholic past. As a result, a whole series of restoration programmes was undertaken, Notre-Dame's commencing in 1844 under the direction of Lassus and Viollet-le-Duc. Work lasted exactly 20 years, Viollet-le-Duc acting alone after Lassus's death in 1857. Consolidation was the first task, much of the fabric being entirely rebuilt. But the restorers' ambitions went further than simply saving the cathedral, for they undertook to restitute its missing sculpture and furnishings – arguing that without them it could not be understood –, and did not hesitate to invent where historical documentation was lacking. Viollet-le-Duc was especially cavalier in his attitude towards historical accuracy, and once sole master of the project went much further than Lassus would probably have let him. It was often, however, when they were least constrained by archaeological exactitude that Lassus and Viollet-le-Duc's work was at its most brilliant: the fantastical beasts populat-

4.2 Notre-Dame de Paris. Nave

4.3 Mémorial des Martyrs de la Déportation

ing the cathedral's upper realms, for example (of which the »stryge« has achieved iconic status), or Viollet-le-Duc's spectacular crossing spire, which is a much grander affair than the descriptions of the 13C *flèche* on which it was supposed to be based. Humility was not in the restorers' nature, either, for two of the replacement kings of Judah bear their features, and Viollet-le-Duc had himself modelled as Thomas, patron saint of architects, in the group of statues descending from the spire. Indeed almost as much as the original medieval builders, it was Lassus, Viollet-le-Duc et al. who were responsible for the cathedral we see today.

4.3 Mémorial des Martyrs de la Déportation
Square de l'Ile-de-France
Georges-Henri Pingusson, 1961–62
(Métro: Cité)

Of the millions of visitors who flock to Notre-Dame (4.2) every year, how many walk past this extraordinary memorial without even noticing its presence? Situated at the eastern tip of the Ile de la Cité (4.1), where Paris's morgue once stood, the memorial was commissioned by an association of concentration-camp survivors, the Réseau du Souvenir (»Remembrance Network«), as a secular monument to the 200,000 French deportees who died in Nazi hands.

Sunk below ground level, the memorial is invisible from the surrounding quaysides, the only sign of its presence on the river being a small opening in the embankment wall just at the point of the island. A garden separates the monument from the Quai de l'Archevêché and acts as a transitional space between it and the everyday world. Wedge shaped, following the contours of the island, the memorial is accessed via two staircases, one at either extremity of the wedge's base. From the garden, all one perceives of the monument are these staircases and a large concrete slab bearing inscriptions dedicated to the 200,000 victims. Narrow and sunk between sheer concrete walls, the staircases open out into a bare, mineral space hollowed out of the island's tip, from within which the city is hidden entirely from view. All that can be seen is the sky, rather as one imagines the desolate view from a prison court-

yard. The only sign of life is the river, visible through the small opening in the embankment wall, but inaccessible and barred off by a barbed grill, giving it the allure of some Underworld Styx. Entering this space, one feels a sharp sensation of disorientation, sudden loss, and isolation.

Directly opposite the river grill, on the garden side, two upright slabs of concrete enclose a narrow opening that leads into the memorial's crypt. One first enters a pivotal, octagonal space bearing inscriptions, including the names of all the death and concentration camps. To the left and right are small rooms containing soil and human remains brought back from several of the camps, while ahead of one, in the principal axis of the monument, is a long corridor that glitters in the light of 200,000 illuminated quartz rods. At the corridor's entrance is the tomb of the Unknown Deportee. Above the crypt is a gallery, never opened to the public but originally intended to house a museum.

An intense architectural experience produced with a minimum of means, the Deportation Memorial was conceived in a spirit of commemoration and reconciliation; its concrete contains stones from all the mountainous massifs of France, a metaphor for national unity that complements the inscription above the exit to the crypt which reads »pardonne, n'oublie pas ...« (»forgive, don't forget ...«).

4.4 Saint-Louis-en-l'Ile

84 4th *arrondissement*

4.4 Saint-Louis-en-l'Ile
19 bis, rue Saint-Louis-en-l'Ile
Principally Louis Le Vau, begun c. 1656
(Métro: Pont-Marie, Sully-Morland)

Inhabited as of the 1610s, the Ile Saint-Louis was initially provided with a small chapel for the spiritual welfare of its residents, but as the island's population grew it became clear that a full-size church would be needed. Louis Le Vau, who was heavily involved in the island's development, provided the plans for the new building, whose foundations were begun c. 1656. Construction started with the choir, which was completed in 1679, after Le Vau's death. Doubts had been raised regarding the solidity of the structure, and a report was commissioned from two leading architects, Daniel Gittard and Libéral Bruand. Their conclusions were, to say the least, surprising, and included the recommendation that »certain parts, recognized as Gothic, with no order, beauty or charm«, should be rebuilt »in the manner of our beautiful modern architecture«. Exactly what was behind these remarks remains a mystery. Professional jealousy from Gittard and Bruand? Negligence on the part of Le Vau? Consciousness of an evolution in taste? Nonetheless, when work on the church recommenced under the direction of Gabriel Le Duc, in 1702, it was the designs left by Le Vau that guided completion of the building. Le Duc died before the work was finished, and in the end it was Jacques Doucet who completed the church, in 1726.

Squeezed into the urban fabric like any other construction, Saint-Louis does not benefit from any special *mise en scène* and is externally rather undistinguished, apart from its unusual steeple. Completed in 1765 in place of a crossing tower destroyed by lightning, the current steeple, with its series of circular openings, recalls some Baroque-period London churches, and may have been inspired by cross-Channel spires. The name of the steeple's architect is not recorded, and thus the source of its design remains unknown. The grand western entrance to the church designed by Le Duc was never executed, and entry is in fact gained via a rather modest portal on the Rue Saint-Louis-en-l'Ile.

Inside, Le Vau's design reveals itself to be a typically 17C French hybrid of traditional Gothic and more »modern« Classical architecture. Saint-Louis follows the traditional Gothic articulation of high nave, low side aisles, crossing, transepts and choir, with arcades, clerestory and stone vaulting, but is dressed up in Classical garb, the vaulting and arcades being roundheaded rather than pointed and the latter sporting a sumptuously carved Corinthian order expressed in pilaster form. Indeed the church derives its effect less from the qualities of its architecture than from its opulent decoration, which as well as its elaborate sculpted décor includes abundant gilding, especially in the crossing and choir vaults. The carvings in the choir and the transept were realized by Jean-Baptiste de Champaigne, nephew of the more famous Philippe.

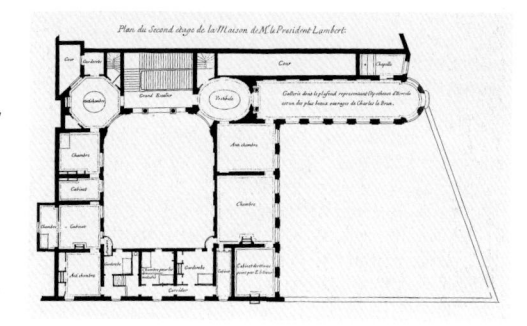

4.5 Hôtel Lambert

4.5 Hôtel Lambert
2, rue Saint-Louis-en-l'Ile and 1, quai d'Anjou
Louis Le Vau, 1640–44
(Métro: Sully-Morland)

In 1639, Jean-Baptiste Lambert, *seigneur* of Sucy and Thorigny and *conseiller* and secretary to the king, bought a chunk of land at the eastern tip of the Ile-Saint-Louis, which was then undergoing development. He engaged the young and relatively unknown Louis Le Vau who, with his brother François, was heavily involved in property construction on the island, to build him an *hôtel particulier* on the site. The result, which was unanimously praised in its time, is today almost certainly the most magnificent and best-preserved example of a mid-17C *hôtel particulier* in Paris. It is important not only for its ingenious architecture, which made Louis Le Vau's reputation, but also for its interior décor, realized in the late 1640s by, amongst others, Eustache Le Sueur, François Perrier and Charles Le Brun. The quality of the Hôtel Lambert's decoration wowed contemporaries, and is today of even greater value in that it remains essentially intact. Some of the *hôtel*'s decorative elements have been removed, but almost all survive (the majority of those removed being in the Louvre, 1.8) and could, theoretically, be returned one day to their original setting. Unfortunately, this is unlikely to happen as the Hôtel Lambert is in private hands and is not even open to the public. This is all the more sad in that not only is the *hôtel* of considerable intrinsic value, but it also marks an important turning point in the history of French artistic creation, for it launched the careers of both Le Vau and Le Brun, the two figures later responsible for Vaux-le-Vicomte (37.1) and Versailles (32.1).

Architecturally, the Hôtel Lambert does not announce its illustrious successors, for in its domestic scale and above all in the exigencies of its site it is of quite a different order. Perhaps its most unusual and remarkable feature is its total departure from the classic Parisian *hôtel-particulier* schema. The vast majority of the capital's aristocratic residences are organized sequentially around a main *corps de logis* that gives onto a garden at the rear and a courtyard at the front, the latter abutting the street and being accessed via a *porte-cochère*. At the Hôtel Lambert this pattern is entirely rearranged so as to take into account the site's topography. To have preserved the usual *cour d'honneur-corps de logis*-garden sequence, it would have been necessary to situate the *hôtel*'s entrance on the quayside, at the head of the site's longest dimension, but this would have meant that the garden and, more importantly, the principal rooms of the house would have been deprived of a view of the riverscape, thereby denying the site's foremost attribute. Instead, Le Vau placed the garden at the open, river end of the plot, and installed the *cour d'honneur* at the site's closed end, accessing it laterally from the Rue Saint-Louis-en-l'Ile. The Hôtel Lambert has no *corps de logis* in the traditional sense of the term, the private apartments being disposed in the courtyard's western wing and the *appartements d'apparat* in its eastern, overlooking the garden. The northern side of the court (that opposite the *porte-cochère*) is almost entirely occupied by a monumental *escalier d'honneur* which, as well as providing access to the east and west wings, also leads directly to a long, narrow wing running along the garden's northern side, in which the *hôtel*'s library and famous long gallery were situated. With this arrangement Le Vau managed to make the most of the site's advantages in a way that maintained a processional, hierarchical distribution of the building's principal accommodation. His plan also showed rather Baroque ingeniousness in the disposition and dissimulation of the more mundane parts of the house, for example the stables, which were hidden behind the library/long-gallery wing at the quayside end – thereby giving them direct access to the outside world – and were connected to the *cour d'honneur* via a narrow rear courtyard leading to a passage just next to the staircase. No space was wasted at the Hôtel Lambert, the chapel, for example, being squeezed into the gap between the library and the party wall of the neighbouring building, on top of the stables.

The *escalier d'honneur* was the linchpin of the composition and constituted the principal entrance to the house. It is highly unusual, with few antecedents and almost no successors in French architecture. Reminiscent of Genoese staircases, it consists externally of a two-storey, open loggia (today glazed) coiffed with a pediment and a tall pavilion roof. The treatment of the staircase itself is highly theatrical: the visitor first ascends a single flight in relative obscurity, is then presented with a bifurcation and, on choosing the right-hand course which leads up to the *appartements d'apparat*, gradually emerges into a spacious, luminous volume at the top of which, when the doors are open, stretches a dramatic vista through the long gallery out to the riverscape beyond. The principal apartments are located in what, in the courtyard, are the first and second floors but which on the garden front become the ground and first floors. To turn the corner from the *escalier d'honneur* into the suites of rooms in the lateral wings, Le Vau installed oval and octagonal vestibules and *antichambres*, hidden behind which rose service staircases accessing the attics. At the street end of the garden wing, on the garden's ground and first floors respectively, were the Cabinets de l'Amour and des Muses, whose painting cycles (now in the Louvre) were realized by Le Sueur. Only the Cabinet des Muses has retained anything of its original décor, including its splendid vault frescoes. By far the most celebrated of the *hôtel*'s interiors, however, was the long gallery, which has survived intact. It is known as the Galerie d'Hercule because of the decorative elements depicting the Antique hero: stucco reliefs, set within elaborate carvings, showing the Labours of Hercules, and, on the gently vaulted ceiling, a huge fresco by Le Brun, again dedicated to Hercules, which at the time was the most ambitious example of Baroque illusionistic painting yet realized in France. This magnificent gallery, masterminded by Le Vau, amply demonstrates that as a *metteur en scène* of lavish, colourful effects he was without equal in mid-17C France.

Externally, the Hôtel Lambert is not quite as dextrous as inside and exhibits the lack of Classical rigour for which Le Vau is often criticized. Where, for example, his great contemporary François Mansart would have considered the building as a unified three-dimensional whole, Le Vau saw it as a series of unrelated façades that he treated rather as flat, theatrical backdrops. Thus the entrance elevation is rusticated and somewhat severe, the *cour d'honneur* sports two rather weedy, superimposed orders (Doric and Ionic) and is coiffed with a roof, while the garden front is articulated with giant, Ionic pilasters and surmounted by an attic storey. Classical pedants would also take issue with some of his detailing, for example the elongated pedestals on which the courtyard's Doric order stands. On the other hand, those prepared to see things in a less Classical and more Baroque way would read his façade treatment as a hierarchical progression: no orders on the entrance façade in its narrow side street, single-storey orders in the private intimacy of the courtyard, and a giant order on the public garden elevation, whose riverscape setting meant it had to be readable from afar. Apart from

4.6 Hôtel de Sens

the powerful entrance elevation, the *hôtel*'s exteriors are rather lacking in punch, but their discretion may well have been deliberate for a client who seems to have preferred exquisite luxury over ostentatious splendour.

4.6 Hôtel de Sens
1, rue du Figuier
Architect unknown, begun c. 1498
(Métro: Pont-Marie, Saint-Paul)

A rare survivor of late-medieval civil architecture in Paris, the Hôtel de Sens is a tardy example of a semi-fortified *manoir* dressed up in the Flamboyant style. In the days when Paris was still only a bishopric, powerful archbishops from other French cities maintained residences in the capital to ensure access to and influence upon the court. The archbishops of Sens lost their hereditary home in 1364, when Charles V expropriated it for inclusion in the Hôtel Saint-Pol (since destroyed), but were given in return the old Hôtel d'Hestomesnil. Just over a century later, the extravagant and disreputable Etienne-Tristan de Salazar, archbishop from 1474–1519, demolished the crumbling Hôtel d'Hestomesnil and built in its stead a brand-new residence, the current Hôtel de Sens. Salazar undertook major works at Sens Cathedral, carried out by Martin Chambiges, and it is possible that the latter was responsible for the new *hôtel*.

Remarked upon by contemporaries for its luxury, the Hôtel de Sens soon came to seem old-fashioned with the dawning of the French Renaissance in the early 16C. Even in comparison with the concurrent Hôtel de Cluny (5.4), it seems a relic of a previous age with its fortress-like aspect. It remained the property of the archbishops of Sens until the Revolution, when it was seized by the state. Sold off in 1797, it was badly mutilated during the 19C and subdivided for a multitude of uses. After decades of public pressure it was finally saved by the Ville de Paris in 1911, which undertook an ambitious restoration programme between 1933 and 1961. The *hôtel* is now the home of the Bibliothèque Forney.

In its layout – a *corps de logis* sandwiched between an entrance courtyard and a garden – the Hôtel de Sens, like the Hôtel de Cluny, prefigures an arrangement that would become standard for Parisian *hôtels particuliers* from the 17C on. The building as we see it today is largely a reconstitution of the original, based on drawings dating back to the 17C. The garden front, the courtyard façades, the majority of the Rue du Figuier wing, the window pinnacles and much of the other detailing are all new. The main staircase tower, however, with its corner machicolation, is original, as is the wonderfully picturesque entrance front. Framed by two corbelled corner turrets, which allowed both the Rue du Figuier and the Rue de l'Hôtel de Ville to be surveyed, it features a lanceted gateway whose tympanum formerly contained a lavish carving of the arms of the archbishops of Sens, destroyed during the Revolution. Of the interior, only a handsome fireplace in the ground-floor hall

4.7 Saint-Paul-Saint-Louis

survives. Despite its somewhat fanciful restoration, the Hôtel de Sens is nonetheless an evocative remnant of medieval Paris.

4.7 Saint-Paul-Saint-Louis
99–101, rue Saint-Antoine
Etienne Martellange and François Derand, 1627–41
(Métro: Saint-Paul)

Built under the patronage of Louis XIII and his chief minister, Cardinal de Richelieu, this splendid church originally served the *maison professe* of the Jesuit order in Paris, whose buildings were begun in 1619 (and still survive as part of the Lycée Charlemagne, visible at the church's rear in the Rue Charlemagne). While most of the complex was hidden from the general gaze at the centre of the city block or on back streets, the church was placed on the most public part of the site, fronting the Rue Saint-Antoine, which at the time was the main road into Paris from the east and one of the capital's chief processional thoroughfares. Designed by the Jesuit monk Etienne Martellange, who built edifices all over France for the order, Saint-Paul-Saint-Louis was begun in 1627 under Martellange's supervision but, as of 1629, became the responsibility of another Jesuit architect, François Derand. Derand completed the building to Martellage's plans except for the entrance elevation, which he designed himself.

4th *arrondissement* 87

The Jesuits' mother church in Rome was Il Gesù (Giacomo Barozzi da Vignola and Giacomo della Porta, 1568–84), and historians have naturally looked to this prototype to explain the design of Saint-Paul-Saint-Louis. While Martellange's scheme can be said to follow the general outline of the Roman original – a Latin-cross plan with barely projecting transepts, a vaulted, four-bay nave flanked by side-chapels and without aisles, a domed crossing and a single-bay, apse-ended choir – it differs fundamentally on numerous counts. In many respects Saint-Paul is thoroughly within the French Gothic tradition, with a very tall (and thus proportionately narrow), three-storey central vessel featuring an arcade, tribune gallery (useful for packing in an expanded congregation) and substantial clerestory, side-chapels that are considerably lower than the main vessel, stone groin vaults in the nave and choir and a radiating rib vault coiffing the choir's apse. Moreover, the side-chapels are interlinked in such a way as to confer on them all the functions of traditional aisles, while in the transepts we find enormous oval windows that are a Classical adaptation of the usual Gothic rose. All these features, as well as the almost total absence of blank wall space in the main vessel, contrast strongly with the very Roman, Baroque interior of Il Gesù. The concessions to Classicism at Saint-Paul are to be found in the giant Corinthian pilasters decorating its piers – whose entablature, despite its strong horizontality, does nothing to break the main vessel's vertical emphasis –, its round-headed arcade and transverse vault arches and its drum-mounted, lantern-lit crossing dome. Indeed, internally at least, the handsome dome is the only convincingly Italianate part of the church.

Saint-Paul's crossing dome was one of the first of its kind in Paris, erected contemporaneously with Le Mercier's at the Sorbonne (5.5), but externally, with its tall, narrow drum, elongated profile and very tall lantern, the effect at Saint-Paul is more Gothic than Italian, unlike the Sorbonne's which appears much more authentically Roman. Moreover, Saint-Paul's dome does not play a major role in the cityscape, its narrow drum being partially obscured by the church's high slate roofing and, when viewed from the entrance elevation, both drum and dome disappear completely behind Derand's multi-storey façade. This latter is very French, employing the same solution used by Salomon de Brosse at Saint-Gervais-Saint-Protais (4.10) to adapt Classical, Italian-style façades to the elongated Gothic proportions of French churches. Where Saint-Paul differs is in its scale, the entrance elevation being considerably bigger than De Brosse's, and in its much more elaborate and lavish carved decoration, all of which was intended to demonstrate in built form the Counter-Reformatory zeal and splendour of the Jesuit order. This ostentation continued inside the church, which in its day was probably Paris's most richly adorned. It has since lost most of its sumptuous furnishings (for example the high altar's huge, tripartite reredos and its silver tabernacle), but has retained its abundant internal carvings.

4.8 Hôtel d'Aumont

1, rue de Jouy
François Mansart (?), begun c. 1630
(Métro: Saint-Paul, Pont-Marie)

For a long time erroneously attributed to Louis Le Vau, the design of this handsome *hôtel particulier* is now thought possibly to be by the great François Mansart. Commissioned by Michel-Antoine Scarron, a member of the *noblesse de robe*, the initial building was realized in two stages: the eastern half was completed sometime between 1630 and 1648, while the western half, which faithfully followed the already completed eastern sections, was built by Michel Villedo in 1649/50. In its disposition, the *hôtel* is a classic example of its genus, with a shallow *corps de logis* giving onto a garden at the rear and separated from the street by a courtyard, the latter surrounded on its other three sides by service buildings and accessed via a central *porte-cochère*. The street façade is rather severe, the only decoration consisting of a grimacing faun above the entrance, and one is thus unprepared for the charm of the *cour d'honneur*. As in most *hôtels* of the day, the separate elements – stables, kitchens, *corps de logis*, etc. – are expressed as discrete volumes, but there is nonetheless a sense of unity and homogeneity, aided in part by the short, full-height lateral wings of the *logis*. The decorative treatment of the courtyard façades is of great delicacy and refinement, especially in its sculpted elements. None of the original interiors survives, bar a very well-preserved French-style ceiling in the eastern courtyard wing, rediscovered during restoration in the 1940s. Its exposed beams are painted with still lifes and Scarron's monogram.

In 1655, the *hôtel* became the property of Scarron's son-in-law, the Duc d'Aumont, who subsequently had the interiors modernized, in keeping with his reputation for splendour. From this period survives the duke's bedchamber, the principal room of the house, with a fine Italian-style ceiling – then the height of fashion – on a theme of *The Apotheosis of Romulus*. Attributed to Charles Le Brun, it has sadly lost its central canvas, but retains intact the finely moulded stucco lions and sym-

4.8 Hôtel d'Aumont

bols of war which decorate its shallow vault, as well as its brown-and-gold monochromes depicting heroic events from Romulus's life. In 1703, the second duke had the *corps de logis* extended eastwards by the architect Georges Maurissart. His intervention involved the altering and lengthening of the garden front, resulting in a rather dry and ungainly composition which has none of the charm of Mansart's original. The *cabinet neuf*, with its white-and-gold panelling sculpted with musical instruments, is also from this period.

When purchased in 1936 by the Ville de Paris, the Hôtel d'Aumont was in a pitiful state and in need of major restoration. Interrupted by war, conversion of the building to house the Tribunal Administratif de Paris was not finally completed until 1963.

4.9 Hôtel de Beauvais
68, rue François-Miron
Antoine Le Pautre, 1654–60(?)
(Métro: Saint-Paul)

This remarkable building has long been famous in architectural histories for its atypicality within the French canon and for the Baroque ingeniousness of its plan, which broke entirely with the traditional *hôtel-particulier* schema. The house was commissioned by Catherine-Henriette Bellier, first chambermaid to the Queen Mother and wife of a certain Pierre de Beauvais, who won favour thanks to her talent for giving enemas! To build herself a home, she acquired a highly irregularly shaped plot on what was then the Rue Saint-Antoine, the principal artery leading east out of the capital (in the 19C the Rue Saint-Antoine was widened, straightened and connected to the Rue de Rivoli (1.11), and the left-behind section of the street in which the *hôtel* is situated was renamed the Rue François-Miron). The brilliance of Le Pautre's design lay in the manner in which he masked the site's crookedness, making the building seem symmetrical, while at the same time supplying accommodation that both respected the usual *convenances* and provided a high degree of practical comfort.

The *corps de logis* of the vast majority of Parisian *hôtels particuliers* of the era were separated from the street by a courtyard, but at the Hôtel de Beauvais Le Pautre chose to inverse this order and build the *logis* on the road with the courtyard behind, in the manner of Italian urban palaces. Carriages reached the courtyard via a central passageway, which was flanked on the street elevation by arcades that were let as boutiques, again as found in Roman palaces. This arrangement, which was partly derived from the configuration of Parisian merchant-class housing, was almost certainly adopted in response to the *hôtel*'s situation on the Rue Saint-Antoine, one of the capital's principal processional routes. With the *logis* on the street, the house's occupants had a ringside view of passing processions from the main apartments, which were even provided with balconies for this purpose – in 1660, the Queen Mother watched Louis XIV's entry into Paris from the

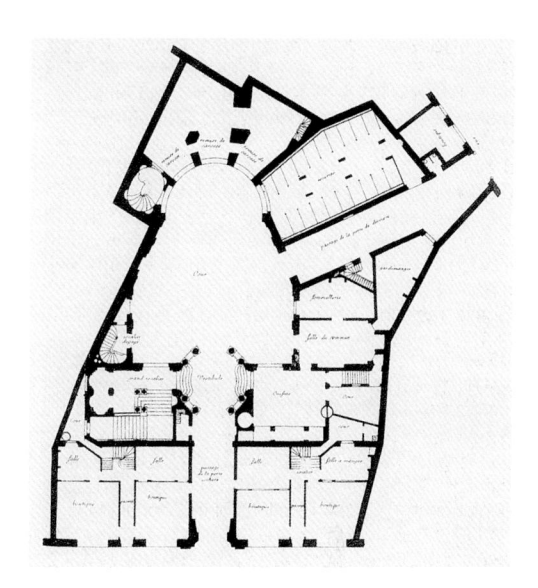

4.9 Hôtel de Beauvais

Hôtel de Beauvais's windows. This arrangement also had other practical benefits, taking advantage as it did of the deeper and more orthogonal portion of the site for the installation of the *logis*, and also allowing visitors to alight from their carriages under cover from the elements in the passageway, which communicated directly with the *escalier d'honneur* via a circular vestibule. On the other side of the courtyard were the stables, which were connected by a second passageway to the *hôtel*'s small portion of street elevation on the Rue de Jouy, thus ensuring that the main entrance was reserved only for the masters of the house and their visitors.

Roughly pentagonal, the courtyard owes its highly unusual but nonetheless symmetrical form to the irregularities of the plot, and much of its lefthand (eastern) elevation is in fact a dummy masking the neighbouring party wall. The convex projection of the vestibule is subtly echoed by the concave depression closing the courtyard at its apex. Due to the plot's restrictedness, Le Pautre was forced to build densely, and all the courtyard elevations are consequently very tall. They are united at *piano-nobile* level by a giant order sitting on a rusticated basement coiffed with a prominent, bracketed cornice, the ensemble making for a highly animated composition whose exaggerated plasticity is rare in a French building of the period. Also atypical was the latitude of Le Pautre's room layouts, for not only did his plans bend themselves rather eccentrically to the nooks and crannies of the site, but the first-floor sequence took absolutely no account of what was underneath it at ground level. Thus, on consulting the 17C plans, we find almost the whole of the ground floor given over to commerce (the boutiques) and ancillary spaces – kitchens, stables, coach-house, etc. – while the first

4th *arrondissement* 89

floor comprises Bellier's apartments. Here we find the double-thickness *logis* divided up fairly regularly, but the lateral portion of the building is much more adventurous: over the stables are squeezed a long gallery, a suspended garden and a bathroom (a rare luxury for the day), while at the courtyard's apex, sitting above the coach-house, is the *hôtel*'s chapel. On his visit to Paris, Bernini, who was distinctly sparing in his enthusiasm for French architecture, praised the Hôtel de Beauvais for the layout of its apartments, which he found greatly superior to the traditional Parisian plan of single-width, repetitive *enfilades*. Of its original interiors the *hôtel* conserves only its grandiose *escalier d'honneur*, whose profuse decoration was the work of the Flemish sculptor Martin Desjardins. Amongst its motifs are rams' heads carrying the letter B, the symbol of the house's mistress (*bélier* = »ram«).

In the 18C, the Hôtel de Beauvais was twice modernized and reconfigured, first in 1704 and then again in 1730–39. In the 19C its fortunes fell, and it was converted into flats, which involved, amongst other indignities, the division of the *piano nobile* into two floors. Thereafter the building's condition became more and more sorry, until by the end of the 1990s it had fallen into an advanced state of dereliction. In 2000–03, a major restoration programme was undertaken with a view to installing Paris's administrative appeal court in the *hôtel*. Work was supervised by Bernard Fonquernie, Architecte en Chef des Monuments Historiques, whose approach was to return the building, wherever possible, to its condition *c*. 1730–39, which is the best-known historical state in terms of surviving plans and drawings. This decision proved highly controversial, with some critics condemning the work as more of a rebuilding than a restoration (on the street façade alone over 40% of the stonework was replaced), others bemoaning the impossibility of attaining historical accuracy due to gaps in our knowledge (the design of the balconies, for example, had to be invented from scratch), and everybody complaining of the enormous cost of the operation – 18.6 million euros. Others take the attitude that at least the building has been saved from ruin and opened to the public.

4.10 Saint-Gervais-Saint-Protais
Place Saint-Gervais
Various architects, current building begun 1494
(Métro: Hôtel de Ville)

Saint-Gervais as we see it today is the fourth church on a site that has been occupied by a place of worship since at least the late-6C. Destroyed by the Normans in 886, the first church was quickly reconstructed but, by the 13C, this second edifice had become too small for its growing congregation and was in its turn replaced by a new building. Of this third church, consecrated in 1420, only the lower levels of the tower now survive, the rest having been demolished for construction of today's building, again for reasons of population growth, in 1494. Work on this fourth church continued on and off for over 150 years, until 1657 when the last of the chapels and the upper storeys of the tower were completed. Despite the long building period, the initial plans were respected, thereby ensuring internal coherence.

Saint-Gervais's designer remains unknown to us, although a speculative attribution has been made to Martin Chambiges (architect of, amongst others, the transepts of Beauvais Cathedral), based on his having been a parishioner. Certainly Saint-Gervais anticipates several characteristics of Beauvais and, given its quality, must have been the work of an experienced master. The building's interior exhibits a wonderful purity of line, which was achieved through the Flamboyant devices of fusion of elements such as vault responds and pier shafts and omission of disruptive components such as capitals. As is often the case in Flamboyant churches, the deliquescent simplicity of the elevations contrasts with the florid vaulting, with its multiple ribs, a particularly elaborate and technically accomplished example being found in the axial Lady Chapel (Chapelle de la Vierge). Externally Saint-Gervais is one of Paris's more picturesque churches, in part because it still preserves something of its original context, including the cemetery bordered by galleries on its northern flank.

Whatever the qualities of the main church, it is for its west front that Saint-Gervais is famous. Following com-

4.10 Saint-Gervais-Saint-Protais

4.11 Hôtel de Ville

pletion of the nave, in 1615, the churchwardens decided to build the west façade in a »new« style, and commissioned several proposals. The scheme they selected, which is generally attributed to Salomon de Brosse and dates from 1616–21, was the first important example of French church architecture of the Baroque period. It was of course to Italy, and more particularly Rome, that French architects of the era looked, but Roman churches, with their two-storey façades designed for Classically proportioned edifices, could not provide a readymade answer for a building with the lofty, Late-Gothic dimensions of Saint-Gervais. To overcome the problem of grafting a Classical façade onto a building of distinctly un-Classical proportions, De Brosse turned to a tried-and-tested French formula for the frontispieces of châteaux (of which a good example is the façade of the Château d'Anet (see 6.1)), which consisted essentially of a superimposition on three levels of the Doric, Ionic and Corinthian orders in the »correct« sequence as defined by theoreticians. This solution allowed him to gain the extra height necessary to cover the volume of the nave, but he was forced to leave out the aisles in his composition (they terminate at the west end in a simple rounding-off and remain visible on either side of the main façade) because to have included them would have rendered the elevation considerably wider, and thereby unacceptably taller once the correct proportioning had been applied. De Brosse's Italianizing adaptation of an Anet-type frontispiece at Saint-Gervais produced a hybrid result that was uniquely French and had great influence on subsequent national output – at the slightly later Saint-Paul-Saint-Louis (4.7), for example, it was consciously imitated. With its sturdy twinned columns, majestic verticality and bold terminal pediment, it is a handsome landmark in the cityscape, and in its time drew unanimous praise – Germain Brice considered it »the most beautiful piece of architecture there is at present in Europe, in which the simple and majestic regularity of admirable Antiquity makes itself again felt ...«, and Voltaire was a subsequent admirer.

4.11 Hôtel de Ville
Place de l'Hôtel-de-Ville
Théodore Ballu and Pierre Deperthes, 1873–82
(Métro: Hôtel de Ville)

Paris's current, 19C *hôtel de ville* stands on a site that has been home to the seat of municipal power in the city since 1357. The building we see today replaced an edifice whose construction was begun in 1533 by Pierre Chambiges to plans by the Italian architect Domenico da Cortona, and which had been extended by Hippolyte Godde and Jean-Baptiste Lesueur in the 1830s. One of the many real-estate casualties of the Communard uprising of 1871, the old town hall was burnt literally to a shell in a conflagration that lasted nearly a week. Although, miraculously, its walls were still standing after the disaster and could have served in the rebuilding, the authorities opted to demolish and start again from scratch. They did, however, stipulate that the original 16C frontispiece should be reproduced in

4.12 Tour Saint-Jacques

the new edifice, thereby setting the historicist tone for the final design.

Chosen by competition, Ballu and Deperthes's town hall remained faithful to the old Hôtel de Ville as it had appeared just before its destruction. Thus, at the centre of the enormous 120×50 m site we find the *corps de logis* and high, lateral pavilions of the original 16C building, reproduced more or less faithfully, while flanking this group are supplementary wings punctuated by pavilions in the manner of Godde and Lesueur's extensions. The town hall attributed to Cortona was, despite the architect's Italian origins, in a northern-European mould, that is to say that although dressed up in Renaissance garb it was inspired by Gothic models (some suggest that Cortona's plans may have been modified by an unknown, northern-trained architect in the mid-16C). In its verticality, central belfry and sculpture-encrusted surfaces the old Hôtel de Ville recalled numerous Flemish town halls of the Flamboyant-Gothic period. Ballu and Deperthes's frontispiece remained faithful to this general outline and to much of the original detailing, but the iconographic content of the façade was entirely reworked in the spirit of Republicanism – anti-royalist heroes such as Etienne Marcel, personifications of French towns (to demonstrate the Republic's unity), and so on. The wings flanking the main frontispiece and the lateral and rear elevations of the building were dressed up in a neo-Renaissance style inspired by the original 16C building, and the resulting enormous, principal façade on the Place de l'Hôtel-de-Ville takes on all the allure of a mock château. Ballu and Deperthes's creation is a quite spectacular pastiche whose artifice and florid detailing tip it towards the kind of gorgeous kitsch embodied by the castle of Neuschwanstein.

Behind its fairytale façades, the Hôtel de Ville is organized around three courtyards (the *cour d'honneur* is now glass covered), with its principal, public rooms on the first floor. These include the Salle du Conseil (council room), which is symbolically located at the centre of the main elevation to emphasize the importance of democratic representation in Paris. No expense was spared on the Hôtel de Ville's interior decoration, and as a result it constitutes an extraordinary monument to the taste for display that marked its era. More than 150 artists and craftsmen worked on the building for nearly 30 years. Neo-Renaissance was the principal style adopted for its décor, which was in keeping both with its exterior and with the official taste of the day. Highlights include the very grand, twin *escalier d'honneur*, the polychromatic and heavily gilded Salon des Arcades, and the outrageously opulent *salle des fêtes*, which has been described as »the Republic's Hall of Mirrors«.

The Hôtel de Ville's *mise en scène* – the enormous square fronting it, the Avenue de Victoria running off in the axis of its façade, and the Rue de Rivoli grazing its northern flank – was the work of Baron Haussmann and his architects and was completed in 1865. The Place de l'Hôtel de Ville has been closed to traffic since 1982 and, framed with fountains by Claude and François-Xavier Lalanne, now constitutes a magnificent pedestrian space in the car-choked city.

4.12 Tour Saint-Jacques
Square de la Tour-Saint-Jacques
Jehan de Felin, 1508–22
(Métro: Châtelet; RER: Châtelet-les-Halles)

This remnant of late-medieval Paris is the sole vestige of Saint-Jacques-de-la-Boucherie, church of the butchers' guild and last in a series of ecclesiastical edifices on this site. Confiscated and sold off during the Revolutionary period, the church itself was demolished in 1797, but the tower was saved for its »artistic value« through the intervention of the Conseil des Bâtiments Civils. In the 1850s, as part of Haussmann's Rue-de-Rivoli project (see 1.11), the tower was restored, by the architect Théodore Ballu, and the square around it created.

Felin's building is a very late example of the Flamboyant style, at a time when Renaissance influence was beginning to make itself felt. Inspired by English churches, the Flamboyant style was concerned almost exclusively with decoration, and the heavily buttressed tower is encrusted on its upper parts with the florid tracery and mouldings beloved of Flamboyant masters. At its summit are the symbols of the four evangelists, and Saint Jacques himself crowns the staircase turret on the northwest corner (all heavily restored). Elongated gargoyles complete the ensemble.

The Tour Saint-Jacques's current isolation was deliberate, as Haussmann wanted to turn it into a spectacular piece of street furniture, a beautiful urban ornament to mark the junction of Paris's north–south and east–west traffic axes, the »Grande Croisée«. Emptied of all meaning, the tower appears like a curious piece of freestanding sculpture. The considerable cost of its preservation was partly justified by its use as a meteorological station, a function it still fulfils.

4.13 Saint-Merri
78, rue Saint-Martin
Architect unknown, c. 1510–52
(Métro: Hôtel de Ville)

This handsome parish church is the third structure on a site that has been occupied by a religious edifice since at least the 7C and where Saint Merri (or Merry or Medericus), a 7C abbot, is buried. It is a tardy example of the Flamboyant style, and exhibits none of the Renaissance influences that were beginning to be felt in the 16C when its construction was undertaken. The church was nicknamed »Notre-Dame la petite«, in part because it was served by seven canons from the nearby cathedral of Notre-Dame (4.2), but also perhaps because in plan it reproduces in miniature its bigger sister's layout. Like Notre-Dame, Saint-Merri has a round-ended apse-ambulatory choir that is almost as long as its nave and, at ground level, nothing projects beyond its continuous external envelope. The church has the singularity of featuring on its northern flank a single aisle lined with side-chapels but on its southern side a double aisle with no chapels. This was partly the result of practical concerns: as the choir was occupied by the Notre-Dame canons and therefore unavailable for use by parishioners, the southern flank's second aisle provided extra space for them.

The church's internal elevations display all the quiet, deliquescent sobriety of French Flamboyant-period churches, having no triforia or capitals and featuring fused shafts. Exuberance is limited to the elaborate window tracery and the splendid crossing vault, with its multiple liernes and tiercerons and central pendant. Note the treatment of its principal, diagonal ribs: because the crossing was unevenly laid out, all but one miss their natural springing points and crash into the crossing arches, but instead of being concealed, their wayward trajectory is affirmed in the carving, a delicious acknowledgement of human imperfection. Externally the church is suitably pinnacled and flying-buttressed, although the carvings on its elaborate west front date from the 19C and replace originals destroyed during the Revolution.

Changes in religious practice in the 18C resulted in the addition of communion chapels to many churches, and Saint-Merri's, designed by Germain Boffrand, was built onto the southern flank of the nave in 1743–45. It consists of a succession of three shallow domed vaults, open at the top in the manner of the Roman Pantheon and themselves coiffed with handsome glass domes. Considered too austere by the standards of the day, Saint-Merri was redecorated in 1751–54 by the Slodtz brothers. Michel-Ange Slodtz was responsible for the marble cladding in the choir and for the splendid Baroque glory above the main altar, while his brother, Paul-Ambroise, produced the extraordinary palm-tree pulpit that stands in the nave. The impressive organ buffet dates in part from 1647 (its initial builder being Germain Pilon), and as such is Paris's second oldest.

4.14 IRCAM
1, place Igor-Stravinsky
Renzo Piano and Richard Rogers, 1973–77; Renzo Piano Building Workshop, 1987–89
(Métro: Rambuteau, Hôtel de Ville)

Founded by the composer Pierre Boulez at the behest of President Pompidou, who wanted a musical component to the arts centre that bears his name (4.15), the Institut de Recherche et de Coordination Acoustique-Musique (IRCAM) carries out state-of-the-art sound and

4.13 Saint-Merri

music research, pioneering the use of up-to-the-minute computer technology. (An example of the institute's work that reached a wide public was the creation of the castrato voice for the film *Farinelli* (1994).) Conceived by Piano and Rogers in tandem with the Centre-Pompidou project, the institute's home is a subterranean complex below the Place Igor-Stravinsky to the south of the Centre. IRCAM was initially to have been built above ground, but once the school that originally occupied its site had been demolished, the architects decided that the piazza they had inadvertently created – which frees up the northern façade of Saint-Merri (4.13) and provides breathing space for the Centre Pompidou's southern flank – was indispensable. An underground solution (which has the added benefit of better acoustic isolation) was thus adopted. Of the millions of tourists who visit this little square every year, how many are aware that below their feet is a whole series of sound workshops descending as far as 15 m, not the least of which is an experimental concert hall of modifiable configuration and volume? The only surface clue to the existence of subterranean structures is the glass roof running along at ground level on the square's western side, which lights the spinal corridor around which the Institut is organized.

There is, however, another, more allegorical indication of the Institut's presence in the form of the Fontaine Stravinsky, which was commissioned by Boulez to coiff the complex after he discovered the work of Jean Tinguely in 1977. Created by Tinguely and his partner Niki de Saint-Phalle and completed in 1983, the fountain features Tinguely's Heath-Robinsonesque contraptions and Saint-Phalle's rainbow-coloured grotesques in a sort of sprinkler *danse-macabre* that was inspired by the music of Stravinsky, a composer especially dear to Boulez. 16 figures, set in a large, rectangular sheet of water, evoke themes from, amongst others, *The Rite of Spring*, *The Firebird*, *Petruchka* and *Ragtime*. Whatever one thinks of Tinguely and Saint-Phalle's work, one has to admire the way their fountain makes an event out of an otherwise rather lacklustre public space, introducing a cheeky note of colour into the cityscape and attracting tourists in droves.

Ten years after its inauguration, IRCAM was beginning to feel the squeeze in its underground home and commissioned Piano to build an extension. The only available space was a tiny plot of land at the Place Igor-Stravinsky's northwestern corner, between the 19C school building fronting the square's western side (home to IRCAM's library and administration) and the former municipal baths (today the Centre Pompidou's security centre) round the corner. Despite the site's narrowness, Piano managed to contrive a building that not only relieved the Institut's space problems but also gave it presence above ground and endowed it with a more dignified entrance than the glorified hole that previously served this function. A 20 m-high tower at the square's corner, in which the main lifts and staircase are now housed (thereby freeing up extra space in the library building), signals the Institut's existence to the outside world, while on the square an all-glass façade marks the entrance, which is reached by an elegant steel bridge that daintily jumps over the spinal corridor's glass roof. The planning authorities stipulated that brick should be used on the façades of the new structure to harmonize with the school and baths buildings. Mortar not being a part of Piano's Hi-tech vocabulary, he here employed a system whereby perforated terracotta bricks are fixed onto infill panels which are then slotted into the metal frame that defines the building's external envelope. This latter-day brick nogging has become a Piano trademark, cropping up everywhere from the Rue de Meaux (19.14) to Potsdamer Platz in Berlin.

4.15 Centre Georges-Pompidou
Place Georges-Pompidou
Renzo Piano and Richard Rogers, 1971–77
(Métro: Rambuteau, Hôtel de Ville)

A quarter of a century after its completion the popular jury is still out on the Centre Georges-Pompidou (more

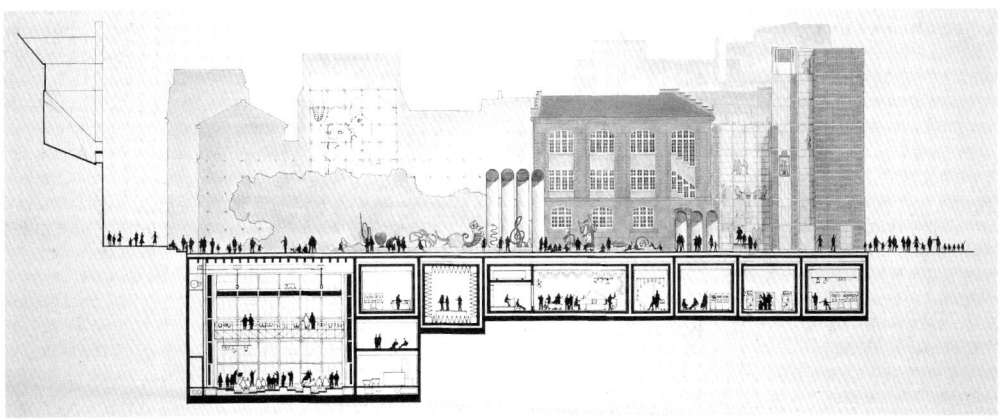

4.14 IRCAM

4.15 Centre Georges-Pompidou

commonly known in France by the name of the *quartier* in which it stands, Beaubourg). Unlike, say, the Louvre pyramid (see 1.8) or even the Tour Montparnasse (15.1), which despite considerable initial controversy have now been accepted in the Parisian landscape, Beaubourg continues to divide opinions. Amongst the general public it is of course the building's uncompromising aesthetics that still manage to provoke, while amongst professionals of the museum world it is certain practical and programmatic aspects of its design that can prompt disaffection. Compared both pejoratively and positively to an oil refinery, a giant Meccano set and a steelworks, Piano and Rogers' building leaves no one indifferent and, although redolent of the bygone era that produced it, remains remarkably fresh. Whatever one's view of its architecture, as an institution the Centre Pompidou has been an overwhelming success, surpassing all expectations: intended to operate with a staff of 300 and welcome 7,000 visitors daily, it currently employs some 1,500 people and is visited by an average of 25,000 per day. The notoriety of the building in which it is housed must surely have contributed in large measure to this triumph.

As its official name suggests, Beaubourg owes its existence to the will of France's Modernist-minded president Georges Pompidou, who in 1969 announced his intention to build a »major museum of contemporary art in all its forms« on the Plateau Beaubourg, an area of land between the Marais and Les Halles that had been empty since the 1930s following slum clearance. The exact remit of the new Centre Pompidou was rather vague, it being hoped that it would become a vital, creative institution that would help effect a renaissance in French contemporary art production. On a more traditional note, it was also intended to house the collections of the Musée National d'Art Moderne (MNAM), which had grown too big for the Palais de Tokyo (16.4) where they were originally displayed. To this initial programme, which essentially concerned the visual arts, was later added a musical component that became the next-door institution of IRCAM (4.14). Architecturally, the president declared, the new art museum should »mark our era«: popular accessibility and avoidance of elitism were to be its founding principles, as stipulated in the 1971 design competition. The nine-member competition jury included the foreign architects Philip Johnson and Oscar Niemeyer and was presided over by the French architect / engineer Jean Prouvé, all three of whom were of uncompromisingly Modernist persuasion. Chosen unanimously out of 681 proposals, the winning project was by the young, Anglo-Italian team of Renzo Piano and Richard Rogers, associated with the engineers Ove Arup (whose team was headed by Peter Rice). Legend has it that Pompidou was not at all enamoured of this choice but, in a rare gesture of presidential humility, accepted the democratic decision of the jury.

Architectural theory in 1960s Britain, where Rogers trained, witnessed a sort of »Futurist Revival« that advocated a technocratic approach in the manner of Buckminster Fuller and was typified by the writings of Reyner Banham and the work of Archigram. It is in this context that Beaubourg's design must be set, and also in the establishment-bashing climate of post-May-1968 France. Piano and Rogers have admitted that their aim was to provoke: extremely young at the time by the standards of their profession, and confident that they would never win the competition, they submitted a proposal that was the architectural equivalent of sticking your tongue out at your elders and betters. Theirs was to be no marble-clad palace of culture, but instead a »supermarket« of artistic activity. It was to the out-of-town, American hypermarket they turned for inspiration, a building type that was a simple container, indifferent to what went on within it and capable of adaptation to a multitude of uses – pure space, as it were. By building an edifice of this sort, and breaking down as much as possible the divisions between it and the outside world, a neutral arena for all kinds of unimagined cultural happenings would, the architects hoped, be produced.

Schematically Piano and Rogers' design was very simple: on top of four basement floors containing car parks and technical and storage spaces rose a six-storey, 166 m-long and 60 m-wide stacking of up entirely unencumbered, and therefore entirely modifiable, floors, constructed using a trabeated steel frame comprising 42 m-high piers and 50 m-wide transversal trusses, the whole being stabilized by a system of external tie rods. To ensure that the floors remained completely clear, all service components – air-conditioning ducts, lifts, escalators, water pipes, etc. – were daringly hung on the outside of the frame and, painted in different colours according to their function, were to provide the centre's only external décor. (It was Rogers, more than Piano, who was attached to this idea, repeating it in later works such as London's Lloyd's Building (1978 to 1986) and prompting the BBC's satirical puppet show *Spitting Image* to portray him with heart, arteries and blood vessels outside his body!) Set within the frame, behind all the service elements, were simple chassis-mounted glass panels protecting the interior from the elements. Piano and Rogers' original intention was to hang loose and modifiable groups of floors and structures within the frame, with the possibility of adding or removing elements according to capacity requirements. But, partly as a result of having to conform to fire regulations, the centre as built is much more fixed and dense than originally intended. The architects did, however, manage to impose their wishes regarding the public square fronting the edifice, setting their building hard up against the traffic artery that is the Rue du Renard so as to create a vast traffic-free piazza on the other side. Alive with street performers and milling crowds, the Place Georges-Pompidou is now a vital component in neighbourhood life.

The Centre Pompidou was, like a real hypermarket, intended to be accessible to all and neutral in its attitude towards both the consumer and the »goods« (artworks) on display within it. It was neutral, also, towards the environment in which it found itself, refusing to engage with or acknowledge it in any way. Although, arguably, Beaubourg subscribes to the Corbusian notion that what is functional and rational is necessarily »beautiful«, it is nonetheless very different from his conception of the »masterly, correct and magnificent play of masses brought together in light«. With its rainbow profusion of ducts on one side and criss-cross of tie rods on the other, its aesthetic effect relies on the »accidental« thrills of a piece of urban infrastructure. Beaubourg also claimed symbolic neutrality, nothing about the building proclaiming it as a cultural centre or attempting to represent »culture«. Yet, in its size, monumentality, total disregard for its surroundings and deliberate »otherness«, it undeniably shouts »institution«. Moreover, certain aspects of its programme were firmly within the 19C tradition of institutional museums, and two elements of the Centre's architecture reflect this: the double-height entrance hall and the monumental escalators snaking up the piazza façade. The *escalier d'honneur* has a long and important history in French public buildings and in museums everywhere, and the Centre Pompidou was not to be without its own example. Following the logic of placing all distributory services on the building's exterior, however, the Centre's staircase was outside, hanging spectacularly off the main façade in a see-through perspex tube. This also allowed continuity between the building's main façade and the piazza fronting it, the movement of crowds across the Place Georges-Pompidou being mirrored in the progression of gallery-goers up the side of the edifice. Affectionately baptized the »caterpillar«, the staircase ironically became the main reason for visiting Beaubourg, droves of tourists being attracted by the futuristic climb with its spectacular views, and not necessarily by the art exhibitions. This may explain why during the Centre's recent refit the staircase was closed to all except paying museum-goers, a modification that has angered Rogers, who held that the ideals of democratic, popular accessibility inherent in the original project should have been maintained, although anti-terrorism security issues must also have influenced the decision.

As two foreign architects working in France, wholly ignorant of French ways of doing things and not, as is usually the case now, associated with a French architectural practice, Piano and Rogers ran into major problems. In the early 1970s the *beaux-arts* system still held sway in France, with its rigid division of professions and tasks: architects produced a design, engineers made it buildable, and constructors put it up, without anyone interfering with another professional's working manner. Piano and Rogers, on the other hand, subscribed to what from a French point of view was considered a more »Anglo-Saxon« working method: for them the role of the architect did not stop at producing a concept, but extended to the technical development of the project and, furthermore, to the planning and logistics of its construction. They saw themselves as the head of a team that involved all the professionals concerned in an almost Arts-and-Crafts spirit of cooperation. Imposing their will in this matter was the first major hurdle, but their persistence paid off in what turned out to be a construction enterprise of heroic proportions.

The French steel industry threw up a second major obstacle when it objected to Piano and Roger's frame design. Their structure required bolts to put it together, whereas in France welding was the preferred method. When fabrication tenders were put out, French steel firms were unable, or unwilling, to produce them within the specified costs, generally giving estimates that were twice as expensive (perhaps also a reflection of France's preference for concrete rather than steel construction). Forced to seek offers outside of France, Piano and Rogers turned to the German firm of Krupp, which was able to fabricate the pieces and meet the deadlines within the budget. Assembling the building's frame was an operation timed with all the precision of a classical ballet and completed in just nine months. The 50 m-long, 75-tonne pre-assembled transverse beams arrived from Germany by train during the day, and then waited at the station until midnight, when huge lorries arrived to take them to the building site. The weight of the convoys was so great that their route had to be specially prepared, huge steel plaques being placed over drains and other subterranean cavities to stop them collapsing, giant magnets afterwards being used to remove the plaques. Once on site, the beams were slowly winched into place by Europe's biggest crane, the whole process being completed by daybreak.

Despite its machine-age imagery, worthy of much Corbusian rhetoric, Beaubourg has nothing to do with mass production. Believe or not, at an engineering level, it is largely a hand-crafted object, more akin in its uniqueness and expense to a Swiss watch than to a production-line prefab. Each of the *gerberettes* (the tapered brackets connecting the main frame to the external tie rods), for example, was individually cast and finished with a hand grinder. As Piano has pointed out, Beaubourg belies its Hi-tech appearance. Nothing about its constructional or operational technology was new or particularly advanced. Describing his and Rogers' original intentions, he has said that the aim was to create a »joyous urban machine« in the heart of Paris that would look like something »straight out of a book by Jules Verne«. This comment is very telling, for it was in the tradition of 19C metal constructions, so rich in France, that the Centre Pompidou was situated. Indeed, in a sorry irony of history, as the steel frame of Beaubourg was going up the next-door iron »umbrellas« of Les Halles (see 1.22) were coming crashing down. Where Beaubourg was innovatory was in the appropriation of this type of »industrial« building for museological purposes, and in the programmatic organization of its functions and infrastructure, visitor flux being concentrated at the building's periphery to allow minimum wasted space and maximum flexibility at its centre.

The flexibility that was at the heart of Beaubourg's design was also responsible for its principal functional flaw, namely its extremely high maintenance costs. As a result of the design decisions taken to ensure entirely unencumbered floor space – building the edifice in steel, leaving its structure uncovered, and placing its service functions on the exterior where they too are exposed –, all its principal components are at the mercy of the elements, which in rainy Paris are not particularly kind. On top of this, its unexpectedly huge visitor numbers further aggravated wear and tear. After only 20 years' service, Beaubourg was in need of a major overhaul, and had to be closed for two years in 1997–99 to allow 576 million francs' worth of renovation work to be carried out. Many critics have questioned the need for such extremes of flexibility in an art institution of this type. Beaubourg's biggest occupant was to be the MNAM, whose collections consisted largely of paintings. Wall space to hang them on should, one would think, have been one of the features supplied by the building, but in fact none was provided, the idea being that the curators could install moveable partitions as they pleased. Seductive in theory, this latitude often stymied curators who had no constraints against which to work. Moreover, suitable lighting, routing and hanging facilities had to be rethought and recreated each time, this part of the job having been entirely ignored by the original architects. Walking around the MNAM today, one is surprised how dull and second rate its spaces seem (this is, after all, a national, prestige collection of world-class importance), having neither the exciting, improvised edge of art works displayed in a real industrial setting, nor the sensual sophistication of a well-conceived, architect-designed gallery.

Piano and Rogers wanted Beaubourg to be a »cultural« continuation of the city at large, attracting all-comers, alive with unexpected encounters and the energy of street art. Its lattice-work façade cries out for posters and electronic billboards to be hung on it, as the architects originally intended, in a celebration of modernity and vital creativity. But, despite the original hopes of the brief, nothing is actually produced at Beaubourg, and programmatically it is no more and no less than a traditional museum. The vague and rather hippie utopian aspirations of total flexibility and artistic renewal that went into its creation turned out to be chimeras, and as an institution it is resoundingly traditional and conservative, tending towards rigid monumentality. Beaubourg's real success, and true legacy, are to be found in a phenomenon that none of its original conceptors seems to have anticipated. By monumentalizing the spectacular and sensationalist image of a Hi-tech cultural machine, as chic as the Citroën DS or Concorde, it made itself emblematic of a nation's pride, attracted tourists in droves and upped the social and economic standing of the neighbourhood around it. This phenomenon has even been given a name: the »Beaubourg effect«, the one that the burghers of Bilbao were so keen for Frank Gehry to repeat with his Guggenheim Museum.

4.16 Atelier Brancusi

4.16 Atelier Brancusi
Place Georges-Pompidou
Renzo Piano Building Workshop, 1995–97
(Métro: Rambuteau)

Although born and brought up in Romania, Constantin Brancusi (1876–1957) made his life and career in Paris, and bequeathed the contents of his studio to the French state. Like many artists of the era, Brancusi had found accommodation in Montparnasse, converting a 19C light-industrial building (at bottom little more than a glorified shed) for his needs. He moved there in 1916 and, as the years went by, acquired adjoining structures, until by the 1940s he had assembled a complex of five spaces. He lived surrounded by his work, making of his studio a highly personalized environment. Finished and in-progress pieces were arranged in harmonious groups whose relationship to each other and to the whole space was carefully considered, as was the studio's lighting. Furthermore, Brancusi allowed nothing to interfere with the studiedly artisanal ambience of his atelier, making many of the everyday objects in it himself and even constructing a new wooden case for his gramophone so that it would be more in tune with the total environment he had created. By the end of his life he refused to exhibit anywhere other than at home.

Unfortunately, Brancusi's studio stood on land earmarked for redevelopment, and was already threatened with demolition before his death. A condition of his legacy (administered by the Musée National d'Art Moderne) was that a facsimile of the building be created to display his bequest in the same conditions as in his lifetime. At first, only a partial reconstitution was established but, following the museum's move to its new home at the Centre Pompidou (4.15), a complete replica was built. Housed in a separate structure outside the main building, its viewing conditions posed security problems, and it was only rarely open. Following floods, in 1990, it was closed entirely, and the museum subsequently decided to rebuild it from scratch. Piano, who had been called in to carry out the Centre Pompidou's 20th-birthday revamp, was also commissioned to design the new Atelier Brancusi.

The architect was faced with two basic and to a certain extent contradictory conditions. His building had to replicate the plan, section and lighting of Brancusi's original studio, as well as conforming to modern curatorial and security requirements. His response to this challenge would prove controversial. Located at the foot of the Centre Pompidou in one corner of the piazza, Piano's Atelier Brancusi is externally discreet. Partially concealed within the rise in level between the Place Georges-Pompidou and the Rue Rambuteau, it presents plain limestone-clad walls to the outside world, the only clue to its vocation being its saw-tooth roof. The building's entrance is reached via a descending flight of steps, which helps smooth the transition from the street's bustle to the atelier's contemplative hush. (This transition would have been even better accomplished if the small walled and tree-planted courtyard next to the entrance had been made part of the arrival route. As it is the courtyard seems rather superfluously tacked on.) The reconstituted atelier occupies the building's centre, the space around it serving as a viewing ambulatory and also enclosing a small gallery area. Presumably at the curators' behest, thick sheets of glass separate the visitor from the reconstitution, and one cannot enter its volumes. It thus becomes rigidified, like a cult object in a temple, constituting a very different experience (for some unacceptably different) to that offered by the original atelier. Flooded from above with natural light, which is cool, white and soft, the building benefits from Piano's usual elegant and sensi-

4.17 Hôtel Amelot-de-Bisseuil or des Ambassadeurs-de-Hollande

98 4th *arrondissement*

tive handling of detail, and constitutes an extremely polished and composed response to the brief. However, this coolness, urbane and sophisticated though it is, was perhaps not the right approach. Far removed from the hand-crafted, reassuringly patinated ambience of Brancusi's original studio, Piano's immaculate white spaces appear somewhat clinical, bleaching out the life from the objects displayed within them. This, combined with their remote, behind-glass presentation, renders the whole experience rather disappointingly frigid.

4.17 Hôtel Amelot-de-Bisseuil or des Ambassadeurs-de-Hollande
47, rue Vieille-du-Temple
Paul Cottard, 1657–60
(Métro: Saint-Paul)

One of the Marais's more picturesque and atypical *hôtels particuliers*, this building was the result of the remodelling and extension by Cottard of an older residence known as the Hôtel de Rieux. Amongst the peculiarities of the finished product is that it does not follow the usual Parisian *hôtel-particulier* disposition of a *corps de logis* sandwiched between a garden at the rear and a *cour d'honneur* on the street; where one would expect to find the garden is another courtyard, of far more imposing dimensions than the *cour d'honneur*. This may partly be the result of the incorporation of sections of the Hôtel de Rieux, but the narrowness and deepness of the site must also have dictated this arrangement, for it would have been difficult to squeeze enough accommodation out of the plot using the traditional disposition. Cottard's latitude earned him comparison with the ingenious Antoine Le Pautre (see the Hôtel de Beauvais, 4.9).

Cottard's work also recalls Le Pautre's in its use of exuberant ornament. The *hôtel*'s *porte-cochère* is one of Paris's finest and, unusually, sports sculptures on both its street and courtyard sides. In the *cour d'honneur*, one finds not only abundant sculpted decoration but also painted adornment, in the form of four sundials. The second courtyard, which is much more informal and vernacularly picturesque than the first, includes an elaborate, architectonic composition of niches and pilasters decorating its blind northern wall. Inside, the *hôtel* conserves some of its original, sumptuously painted interiors, including the Galerie de Psyché by Michel Corneille *père*.

4.18 Hôtel Lamoignon
22–24, rue Pavée and 25, rue des Francs-Bourgeois
Architect unknown, begun *c*. 1584
(Métro: Saint-Paul)

Following her widowhood in 1579, Diane de France, illegitimate daughter of Henri II, lived with her late husband's family until, in 1582, she was created Duchesse d'Angoulême. The new title brought with it considerable wealth, and Diane decided to build herself a home of her own in the then-aristocratic Marais. She acquired several parcels of land at the junction of the Rue des

4.18 Hôtel Lamoignon

Francs-Bourgeois and the Rue Pavée, demolished the existing buildings on the site, and began construction of a magnificent *hôtel particulier* befitting of a princess of the blood. Her choice of architect remains unknown, although Baptiste Androuet Du Cerceau and Thibault Métezeau have been put forward as candidates. It seems likely that work on the *hôtel*, begun in or after 1584, was interrupted by the Wars of Religion, and only completed following a second phase of building in 1611. Diane lived in the house until her death in 1619.

As originally built, the *hôtel* stood alone between its courtyard to the west and gardens to the east, giving it the aspect of a mini-château. The splendid courtyard façade on the Rue Pavée is the only part of the building to survive more or less as Diane knew it. Rising to four storeys above ground, it consists of a five-bay *corps de logis* flanked on either side by one-bay pavilions. Its most immediately striking aspect is the colossal Corinthian order dominating its composition, thought to be the first use of a giant order in Paris. The treatment of the order is highly Mannerist, the entablature broken by tall dormer windows and an odd, Grecian motif linking the capitals. The central bay, which once contained the principal entrance to the building, is crowned by an open-bed pediment. Like her divine namesake, Diane de France was a keen huntress, and the curved pediments coiffing the two pavilions feature relief carvings of hound and deer heads (much restored). Despite the strong Italian influence, the façade, with its tall windows and lofty roof, appears very French.

After Diane's death, the house passed to Charles de Valois who, around 1624, added the northern courtyard wing, possibly by Jean Thiriot. Although radically altering the aspect of the *hôtel*, the new wing harmonizes well with the old building, and features a charming, corbelled turret on the street corner. In 1677, the *hôtel* was bought by the Lamoignons (whence its current name), a family of magistrates who, early in the 18C, had the garden façade entirely rebuilt, in accordance with the rather sober tastes of the day. The original garden front is known to us through engravings – like the courtyard

4th *arrondissement* 99

façade, it was flanked by pavilions, articulated with a giant order, and lit on its final storey by dormers. The Lamoignons demolished the southern pavilion, removed the colossal order and dormers, and altered the rhythm of the bays. The only hint of cheerfulness is provided by the wrought-iron railings at the first-floor windows. In 1718, Marie-Jeanne de Lamoignon added the handsome courtyard gateway, which features carved putti representing Truth (holding a mirror) and Prudence (holding a snake) – the two virtues of a good magistrate.

The Hôtel Lamoignon underwent little change until the 19C when, following the Marais's sharp decline in prestige, it was subdivided and let to a multitude of tenants. Unlike many of its neighbours, however, it survived relatively unscathed and, in 1926, was listed. Bought by the municipality in 1928, it was restored in 1940–75. Since 1969 it has been home to the Bibliothèque Historique de la Ville de Paris, for which the competent but unremarkable buildings to its south were erected in 1964–68. Of the *hôtel*'s original interior, nothing survives bar a few painted joists discovered during restoration and now mounted on the library's reading-room ceiling. The foundations of the grand central staircase (removed during the 17C to allow the creation of a suite of apartments) can still be seen in the cellars.

4.19 Place des Vosges

4.19 Place des Vosges
Architect unknown, begun 1605
(Métro: Bastille, Chemin Vert, Saint-Paul)

When Henri IV came to the throne, in 1594, France was in economic ruin, devastated by the Wars of Religion. After devoting much of his reign to re-establishing order and prosperity, Henri turned to the improvement and embellishment of his capital. Among his innumerable projects were three piazzas, of which the Place des Vosges, originally called the Place Royale, was the first (the second was the Place Dauphine, 1.3, while plans for the third and most ambitious, the Place de France, were scrapped after Henri's death).

The Hôtel des Tournelles in the Marais had been abandoned by Catherine de Médicis after her husband, Henri II, died there following a tournament injury. She had planned to create a development of regular houses on the site, but war interrupted the project. Henri IV, in his desire to create a modern, commodious capital, took up the idea once more. Modern meant Italian, and a master plan for an arcaded piazza of Renaissance inspiration was devised. As well as supplying accommodation for the upper classes, the piazza would provide an open space within the cramped city, which could be used for public festivals. Plots were sold for nominal sums on the condition that the *hôtel* façades conform to the master design. There are several possible candidates for authorship of the latter, but no definite attribution can be made.

The *place* comprises 34 identical pavilions, as well as the Pavillon du Roi on the south side and the pendant Pavillon de la Reine on the north. The standard elevations consist of a squat stone arcade with Doric pilasters, which is surmounted by a lofty first-floor *piano nobile* and a second floor almost as tall, both in red brick with stone dressings. To save money, many constructors used rubble stone plastered to resemble brick. Despite the Italian-Renaissance influence, the square looks very French, thanks, particularly, to its tall, steep-pitched roofs. The *portes-fenêtres* (French windows) were, it seems, without precedent. The Pavillons du Roi and de la Reine are more imposing and richly decorated than the others, marking as they do two of the entrances to the *place*. Two further entrances are located at either end of the thoroughfare traversing the north side of the square. At the *place*'s centre is a 19C equestrian statue of Louis XIII.

Piazzas surrounded by important buildings existed in Italy, as did squares of individual houses in some northern-European towns, but Henri IV's *places* were the first to apply the regularity of Italian façades to a square. Highly successful, the Place Royale spawned several imitations elsewhere in France and, furthermore, provided direct inspiration for Covent Garden in London, the progenitor of all London squares.

4.20 Hôtel de Sully
62, rue Saint-Antoine
Attributed to Jean Androuet Du Cerceau, 1625–30
(Métro: Saint-Paul)

One of the Marais's most handsome 17C townhouses, the Hôtel de Sully was begun by Mesme Gallet, *contrôleur des finances*, who ruined himself gambling and was forced to sell the half-finished house to one of his creditors. It was completed by its subsequent purchaser, Roland de Neufbourg, *conseiller d'Etat*, who afterwards sold it to the Duc de Sully (Henri IV's illustrious chief minister), whose name it still bears. Its architecture is attributed to Jean Androuet Du Cerceau, the last great scion of a dynasty of architects and decorators who influenced French design for almost a century. Today the house is home to the Caisse Nationale des Monuments et des Sites.

In its layout, the building follows the classic *hôtel-particulier* formula, with a shallow *corps de logis* giving onto a garden at the rear and separated from the street by a courtyard, the latter surrounded on its other three sides by service buildings and accessed via a central *porte-cochère*. One of the remarkable things about the Hôtel de Sully today is that it survives in more or less its original state, unlike the majority of its confrères, and thus gives a very good idea of what a grand 17C townhouse was really like. The street façade is punctuated by two imposing, three-storey pavilions: the eastern pavilion originally housed the stables, while the western contained the kitchens. In the *cour d'honneur*, just behind the eastern pavilion, is an open arcade that was used to store carriages. The *cour d'honneur* is remarkably homogenous in comparison to other *hôtels* of the day, due to the fact that its wings are the same height as the main *logis* and are given the same decorative treatment. The profusion of carving that constitutes the *hôtel*'s external décor is its most striking feature: elaborate friezes and sculpture-filled pediments above its windows, bulky dormers decorated with scrolls and coiffed with heavy round-headed pediments punctuating its roofline, and, standing in niches at first-floor level, allegorical figures representing seasons and elements. This exuberant display is a tardy example of Mannerism, closer in spirit to the Hôtel Carnavalet (3.1), completed 70 years earlier, than to contemporaneous *hôtels*.

4.20 Hôtel de Sully

What one cannot perceive from the street, or from the *cour d'honneur*, is that the courtyard wings are of different widths. Du Cerceau was able to hide this on the street frontage by extending the eastern pavilion slightly over into the adjoining plot of land. On the garden front, however, this asymmetry becomes fully apparent, since the façade is an even number of bays wide and its entrance is off centre. The garden front is given the same decorative treatment as the *cour d'honneur*, as is the projecting wing to its west, added in 1660. A substantial orangery closes the garden.

Besides its external décor, the Hôtel de Sully was also rather retrospective in its internal disposition. At the centre of the *corps de logis* is a simple dog-leg staircase, an arrangement common in the 16C, but afterwards abandoned because centrally placed staircases had the disadvantage of cutting the *logis* in two, thus preventing the installation of full-length suites of apartments. Indeed the central staircases of many *hôtels* were subsequently removed (see, e.g., the Hôtel Lamoignon, 4.18) and the Hôtel de Sully's is thus something of a rarity. Of the original internal décor, a French-style ceiling of exposed painted beams survives in the large ground-floor room occupying the western half of the *corps de logis* (today the Caisse's bookshop, very good for volumes on architecture), and the sculpted plaster mouldings decorating the underside of the staircase are still in place. Italian-style ceilings installed by

4.21 Sainte-Marie-de-la-Visitation

François Le Vau, in 1651, can be seen in the western courtyard wing, and the first-floor apartments in the projecting garden wing are among the best preserved of their era in Paris.

4.21 Sainte-Marie-de-la-Visitation
17, rue Saint-Antoine
François Mansart, 1632–34
(Métro: Bastille, Saint-Paul)

Today home to a Protestant congregation, this remarkable church is all that remains of the Catholic Couvent des Filles de la Visitation Sainte-Marie et Notre-Dame-des-Anges, an order founded in 1610 at Annecy and established in Paris in the 1620s. Deprived of its ancillary convent buildings in 1805 when the Rue Castex was cut through, Mansart's small but ambitious edifice now stands alone on a street corner. Its complex design was one of the architect's earliest experiments with centralized-plan-type churches, a configuration imposed by the convent's benefactor, Commandeur Noël Brûlart de Sillery, who had seen and admired the Pantheon in Rome. No doubt much influenced by Philibert De l'Orme's chapel at the Château d'Anet (1549–52), Sainte-Marie's plan comprised a central, circular domed space surrounded by eight subsidiary spaces: an entrance vestibule to the north, a sanctuary containing the high altar to the south, chapels to the east, northeast and northwest, sacristies to the southeast and southwest, and the nun's choir, preceded by a vestibule, to the west. All these subsidiary spaces gave directly onto the main domed volume in a profusion of openings that, like at Anet, contrasted with most Italian domed, central-plan churches where generally only four surrounding spaces led onto the central volume. As at Anet, the four principal subsidiary spaces were curved, bending themselves around the central rotunda, but displayed more complex forms than De l'Orme's, Mansart having here employed what would become his signature »kidney«-shaped chapel layout. Sainte-Marie's subsidiary spaces were, moreover, connected to each other via curved corridors encircling the central rotunda, an innovation of Mansart's that brought a complexity to the spatial relationships that went way beyond the Anet prototype. The result is an »organic« inter-penetration of space that was quite original and thoroughly Baroque in both its peripheral irregularity and its total disregard for the square perimeter containing the church.

As built, Sainte-Marie had the peculiarity that the nun's choir did not have a view of the high altar (giving instead onto the lateral chapel opposite), and therefore to receive communion the sisters had to go down a corridor linking their choir to the sanctuary via the southwestern sacristy. It seems likely from surviving evidence that Mansart's original intention was to organize the church around a central high altar under the dome – which is, after all, the logical disposition for a centralized plan type church – but that for a reason unknown to us this arrangement was abandoned in favour of placing the high altar at the church's rear, where it is orientated south, contrary to usual practice. It is theatrically lit by an oval lantern cut into the sanctuary's vault, producing a wholly Baroque effect for the visitor entering the church since the light source is hidden from view. This disposition is mirrored by the lantern lighting the entrance vestibule, which formerly received further light from a rose window that is today obscured by the church's organ. The main rotunda is lit by two sets of windows, one just under and one cut into the dome, and by the dome's lantern. Further height and dramatic effect is provided by the dark, blank secondary cupola interposed between the main dome and the church's day-lit vertical conclusion. A crisply-carved Corinthian order cadences the rotunda's elevations with Classical rigour, but on the dome and the chapel vaults florid, Mannerist carvings run riot, the many seraphs being a reference to Notre Dame des Anges.

Externally Sainte-Marie is highly original, its entrance frontispiece consisting of a giant, triumphal arch containing a Michelangelo-esque entrance portal, behind which rises a bulbous *toit à l'impériale* coiffed with the entrance vestibule's lantern. The superimposition of the street elevation's three components – the entrance arch with its projecting cross, the *toit à l'impériale* with its lantern, and the main, domed rotunda –, and the elongated nature of the dome, its lantern and the small spire crowning the ensemble, endow Sainte-Marie with a Gothic-style, heavenwards *élan* that is very French.

as a consequence, would be hailed by many contemporaries as the beginning of a great new era. If today its revolutionary qualities are perhaps less easily appreciated, this is partly because Soufflot's original vision has been subsequently much altered, and partly because the spectacular technological developments of the 19C and 20C have largely eclipsed what preceded them.

Churches in France in the century and a half before Sainte-Geneviève had generally featured a standardized, Gothic-derived system of tunnel vaults supported on arcaded piers whose surfaces were dressed up in Classical garb through the application of pilasters (see, e.g. Saint-Roch, 1.15, Saint-Sulpice, 6.5, and Saint-Louis-en-l'Ile, 4.4). This was a tradition denounced by Soufflot because the adaptation of Gothic structure to Classical styling resulted in a massiveness of construction that he considered inelegant and which blocked views across the volume of a church. Moreover, the use of pilasters had been condemned in some quarters, most notably and influentially by Abbé Laugier in his *Essai sur l'Architecture* (1753), as »unnatural« (i.e. Baroque) and irrational in comparison to the rational, »natural«, free-standing column which constituted the most abstracted and philosophically »pure« means of supporting a load. It was, furthermore, the most authentically Antique, if one went back to ancient-Greek architecture as the source of Western tradition. Consequently, in contrast to previous practice, Soufflot determined that the main spaces of the new Sainte-Geneviève would be constructed entirely from free-standing columns bearing lintels in the manner of a Greek temple, an arrangement that would bring to the building's interior a lightness of structure reminiscent of the leanest of Gothic cathedrals, with multiple perspectives being opened up across the entire church. Fidelity to Antiquity was not one of Soufflot's prime concerns, however, since he planned to coiff his columns with complex vaulting, thereby taking his cue from the Gothic cathedral. Indeed the essence of Soufflot's approach was summed up by his collaborator at Sainte-Geneviève, Maximilien Brébion, who wrote: »M. Soufflot's principal objective ... was to combine in one of the most beautiful forms the lightness of Gothic construction with the purity and magnificence of Greek architecture.« Successfully melding the Classical and the Gothic in church design had been an architectural preoccupation since the Renaissance (and would continue to be so into the 20C – see Auguste Perret's rather Soufflot-esque design for Notre-Dame du Raincy (35.1)), and Soufflot was but the latest in a long line of architects to grapple with this problem.

As Soufflot initially designed it, Sainte-Geneviève comprised a perfect Greek cross in plan, with a giant, Corinthian entrance portico covering the entire end of the western-facing arm and a centrally placed altar at the crossing, which was coiffed with a dome. As such it subscribed to a tradition of bravura, centralized-plan great churches that included Bramante's original design for Saint Peter's in Rome (1505/06), Wren's unexecuted Great Model for Saint Paul's in London (designed *c.* 1669; cathedral as built 1675–1711) and, closer to home, Hardouin-Mansart's Dôme des Invalides (see 7.12). Following criticism from the clergy, however, Soufflot altered the plan by making the entrance and east-end arms longer than originally planned through the addition of supplementary elements at their extremities (although the basic bay structure retained the Greek-cross arrangement), thereby bringing the church more into line with traditional French practice where long naves and choirs were crossed by shorter transepts. In this new plan, the high altar was moved to a sort of apse in the east end and Saint Geneviève's shrine placed under the crossing. Soufflot also added two flanking bell towers at the east end, which »medievalized« further the layout of the church. His initial designs had not featured a crypt, but he afterwards added one, firstly a small affair held up with columns clearly inspired by Paestum, and later, in the church as built, an enormous space following the entire upper-level floor plan whose rather Piranesian principal spaces featured low, rusticated vaulting supported on pairs of stumpy, primitive-looking Tuscan columns.

Inside the main church, each arm of the cross comprised a high central vessel, formed from colonnades carrying vaulting, and two lower, flat-roofed flanking

5.8 Panthéon

110 5th *arrondissement*

de Greneuze (1558–82) and finally Christophe Robin, who completed the vaulting in 1586. Another 20 years went by before the west front was begun, to a design by Claude Guérin, and it was not finished until 1622. In 1624 the tower was raised to its current 50 m, and Saint-Etienne was finally inaugurated in 1626.

In plan the church is essentially derived from Notre-Dame (4.2), although with the singularity that its side-chapels remain uninterrupted by its transepts. Its laying-out was extremely irregular, resulting in a choir that is skewed in relation to the nave, an entrance front that cuts diagonally across the nave, and a southern aisle that narrows considerably towards the west. Saint-Etienne is also unusual in that its side-aisles are very tall, rising almost to the springing point of the nave vault, which makes its interior very light and airy but results in a rather stumpy-looking clerestory. Traditional nave/choir-arcade proportions are nonetheless preserved due to the presence of the balcony running round the church at mid-level, which was begun around 1530 (and therefore tacked on to the already completed apse) and features charming *corbeilles* on its aisle side. Unusual in the French context (although to be found in Reims Cathedral (13C)), balconies of this sort were common in contemporary German hall churches. Linked to the balcony by serpentine staircases looping round the crossing piers is Saint-Etienne's famous rood screen (*jubé*), the only one to have survived in a Parisian church, despite attempts by 18C parishioners to have it demolished. Constructed *c.*1530–45 by an unknown architect, the rood screen consists of a low, elongated arch carrying the cross (rood), its balustrade and staircase rails featuring bravura stone fretwork. The splendid choir-aisle doorways either side of the screen were added in 1600–05 with sculptures by Pierre Biard. The choir's pointed arcades exhibit the Flamboyant-period tendency towards highly simplified, fused mouldings, but the later nave arcades have Classically inspired round-headed arches with pier capitals that appear almost Romanesque. Saint-Etienne's elaborately ribbed crossing vault, with its gravity-defying pendant, is also typically Flamboyant. The church is fortunate in that it has conserved much of its magnificent 16C stained glass.

Externally, Guérin's entrance frontispiece is an odd composition, comprising a weird and rather clumsy superimposition of two pediments and a gable (itself adorned with a pediment) that recede back from each other. The ensemble calls to mind some 16C English attempts at Classicizing essentially Gothic structures. Viollet-le-Duc felt the façade was charming in its picturesque and rather eager assemblage of ornament but irritating in its lack of an overall guiding concept. Guérin's creation was heavily restored by Victor Baltard in the 1860s. Running alongside the church's northern flank can be seen galleried charnel houses, built in 1607–09. In 1802–07, the abbey church of Sainte-Geneviève was demolished to make way for the Rue Clovis, thereby freeing up Saint-Etienne's southern flank.

The remaining parts of the abbey – the refectory (13C), the cloister (13C, 17C and 18C), and the church tower (11C and 15C) – are now part of the Lycée Henri-IV across the road.

5.8 Panthéon
Place du Panthéon
Jacques-Germain Soufflot *et al.*, begun 1755
(Métro: Cardinal Lemoine; RER: Luxembourg)

France has always been attached to the idea of the *grand homme* – be he politician, writer, scientist or soldier – whose actions contribute to the greatness of the nation, and it is therefore unsurprising that, in true neo-Antique, Enlightenment style, the country has a pantheon where the remains of its heroes are interred as an example to all. Familiar the world over from picture postcards, the huge, domed and externally rather forbidding building in which the illustrious are laid to rest did not, however, start out life in this capacity. It owes its origin, or so the story goes, to a vow made by Louis XV in 1744 when, seriously ill, he invoked the protection of Saint Geneviève, the patron saint of Paris. The king survived, and afterwards made a pilgrimage to the Abbaye Sainte-Geneviève (see 5.7) where the saint's shrine lay, during which the monks extracted from him a promise to rebuild their old and dilapidated church at crown expense. Louis's word became reality ten years later, in 1754, as part of a whole programme of prestige projects designed to buff up the monarchy's rather tarnished image. The rebuilding of Sainte-Geneviève had the particularity both of promoting cohesion within a divided church and of reinforcing the association between the Bourbon dynasty and Clovis, founder of the Abbaye Sainte-Geneviève and first Christian king of France, thereby symbolically affirming Louis's political legitimacy.

In his capacity of Surintendant des Bâtiments du Roi, it fell to the Marquis de Marigny, brother of the royal mistress, Mme de Pompadour, to oversee the rebuilding project and choose an architect. Tradition and protocol would normally have dictated that the Premier Architecte du Roi – at the time Ange-Jacques Gabriel – be automatically granted this honour, but Marigny, keen to encourage a new, grand style in opposition to Gabriel's quiet, conservative »good taste«, commissioned the comparatively young but nonetheless »hot« Jacques-Germain Soufflot. Marigny was looking to reproduce, in spirit at least, the grand manner of the architecture of Louis XIV's reign, of which one of the most important monuments was Perrault's Louvre colonnade (see 1.8). Soufflot, who (significantly) had been one of the first French architects to visit the temples at Paestum, had become known for what were considered his »radical« views, which included a particular reverence for the column as the linchpin of architectonic expression. By re-examining the fundaments of architecture in a thoroughly Enlightenment spirit of philosophical enquiry, his design for Sainte-Geneviève would entirely break with French tradition to date and,

library, had had to accommodate up to 600 students at a time, a task for which it was distinctly ill-adapted. Labrouste consequently designed a vast reading room for the new building, 85m long by 21m wide, which was also capable of storing 120,000 books. He placed the reading room on the first floor of the library, elevated above street level to ensure sufficient quantities of light by which to work. Bookstacks containing a further 300,000 volumes were housed on the ground floor. This simple, rational plan was enclosed in a simple, easily readable exterior. Constructed in dressed stone, its sober cinquecento style harmonizes well with the Panthéon (5.8) opposite, and is in stark contrast to the showy exuberance of much subsequent Second-Empire output. The plain ground floor, relieved only by a continuous garland of swags, forms a pedestal for the arcaded first floor, whose rhythm corresponds to the structural disposition of the building. The upper portion of the arcades is glazed, while the lower section, which carries bookshelves on the interior, is filled with masonry panels carved with the names of famous writers, piled up like books on a shelf.

A simple archway at the centre of the main façade leads into the vestibule, where one has a first glimpse of exposed ironwork in the form of the shallow-arched girders supporting the ceiling. Labrouste would ideally have liked to create a garden in front of his library, as a transitional space between the noise of the street and the quiet of the reading room, but the cramped terrain made this impossible. As a substitute, he had trees and flowers painted on the vestibule walls, and coloured the ceiling sky-blue. A monumental staircase at the rear of the vestibule leads up to the reading room. The celebrated ironwork of this impressive chamber takes the form of two parallel barrel vaults running the length of the building, supported at their junction by a row of slender iron columns. Widths greater than this had already been covered by single iron spans, but Labrouste was never much concerned with technical prowess. Instead, his two-vault system, whose disposition recalls medieval monastery refectories (see Saint-Martin-des-Champs, 3.10), allowed the volume to be divided up more intimately and permitted full expression of the ornamental possibilities of iron. Moulded into intricate plant-derived motifs, it is combined with polychromatic, decorative frescoes to form a space that is beautifully accomplished.

The Bibliothèque Sainte-Geneviève immediately became a standard model for library buildings and was cited in all the major treatises and encyclopaedias. Its success earned Labrouste the prestigious commission for the Bibliothèque Nationale (2.4). The suitability of iron as a material for library construction, with all its advantages of lessened building costs, freeing-up of space and fire-resistance, was now universally acknowledged. Labrouste had nonetheless cautiously cast the main doors to the Bibliothèque Sainte-Geneviève in bronze (even though the reading-room doors were in iron), in response to the recent scandal at Saint-Vincent-de-Paul (10.6), where parishioners outraged at the use of lowly iron for the church doors had compelled the architect to have them painted to resemble bronze.

5.7 Saint-Etienne-du-Mont
Place du Panthéon
Various architects, current building begun 1492
(Métro: Cardinal Lemoine; RER: Luxembourg)

The first Saint-Etienne-du-Mont was begun in 1222 to serve the populous parish that had grown up around the ancient Abbaye Sainte-Geneviève, founded in 507 and burial site of Paris's patron saint. By the late-15C Saint-Etienne had become too small for its ever-expanding congregation, and a new church was consequently begun in 1492. Like its predecessor, it was built right up against the northern flank of the abbey church, via which entry to Saint-Etienne was originally gained. Construction of the new church took well over a century, beginning with the apse and the tower (under the direction of Etienne Viguier), which latter was completed by 1500. Building work was interrupted for nearly a decade from 1521–30, resuming again in the choir (under the direction of Nicolas Beaucorps), which was completed in 1540. Work on the nave began in 1545, supervised by Pierre Nicolle (until 1558), Thomas

5.7 Saint-Etienne-du-Mont

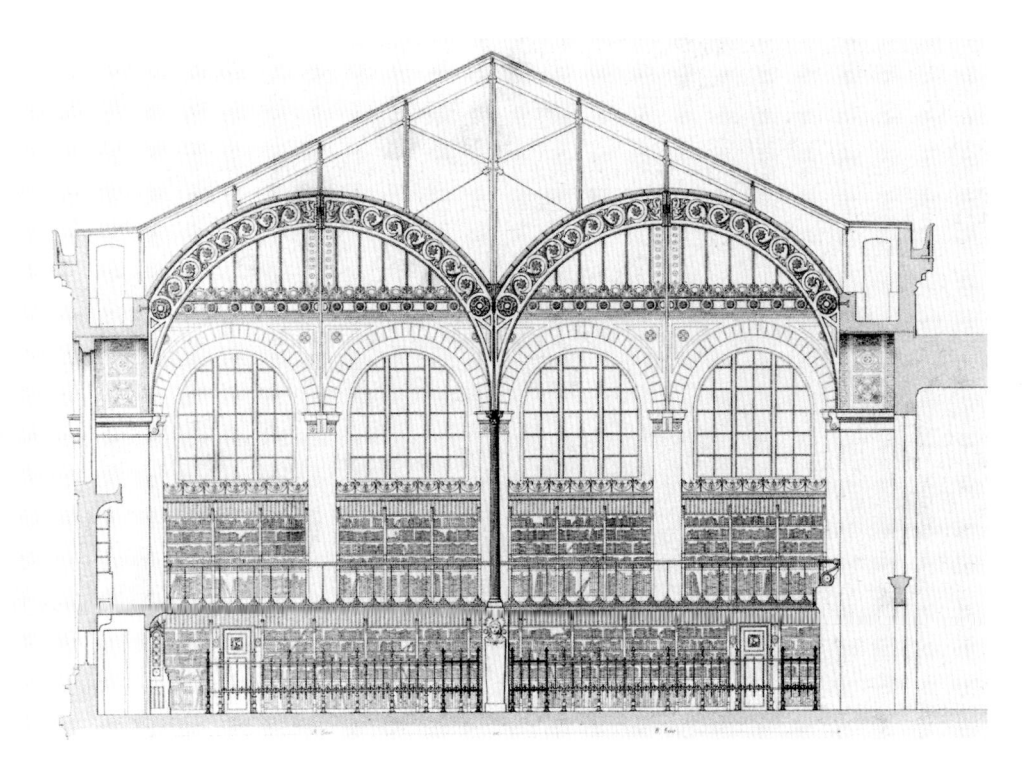

5.6 Bibliothèque Sainte-Geneviève

existence of this second entrance and its picturesque architectonic treatment were highly unusual, contrasting singularly with the western façade. Fronting the northern transept, the college-entrance elevation comprises a pedimented portico surmounted by a sort of triumphal arch coiffed with lofty slate attics, above which rise the church's dome and its dependent side lanterns. The upper elements appear to crush with their weight Le Mercier's funny little, irregularly intercolumniated portico. Inside, the building displays main-vessel elevations that would become standard in French 17C churches: a round-headed colonnade decorated with pilasters and supporting above its cornice a high barrel vault, into which clerestory windows have been cut. The church's pendentive paintings are by Philippe de Champaigne, and Richelieu's tomb was sculpted by François Girardon.

The college buildings that surrounded Le Mercier's church were remarkably plain (although in old photographs they display a picturesque aspect perhaps only sensible to those born after the Modernist era), so much so that Israël Silvestre in his contemporary engravings of the Sorbonne felt compelled to aggrandize them considerably. A call to rebuild them on more ambitious lines was first heard in the Napoleonic era, but it was not until the Third Republic that an architectural competition was launched for their reconstruction and for the college's extension. Nénot's winning design preserved the dimensions of the old courtyard but surrounded it with much more elaborate façades, of 17C-French inspiration, and this same style, although puffed up with crashing monumentality, was employed for the new parts of the college built to the south, on the Rue des Ecoles.

5.6 Bibliothèque Sainte-Geneviève
8–10, place du Panthéon
Henri Labrouste, 1838–50
(Métro: Cardinal Lemoine; RER: Luxembourg)

The Bibliothèque Sainte-Geneviève is generally considered one of the seminal buildings of the 19C, for the rationality of its design and the consequent use of exposed ironwork on the interior, the first time a prestige building dedicated to the arts dared reveal the hitherto despised material in such brazen quantities. Commissioned by the government to restore the former library of the Abbaye Sainte-Geneviève which, since the Revolution, had been part of the Lycée Napoléon (now Henri IV), Labrouste was able to persuade the authorities that complete replacement was a better option than renovation, due to the library's dilapidated state. In doing so he created for himself the opportunity he had so long craved to construct a resolutely modern building.

Originally intended for a handful of aristocratic readers, the old *bibliothèque*, in its new role as a school

out on a corbel. The abbots' private quarters were also situated in this wing.

Although heavily restored in the 19C, the Hôtel de Cluny's exterior is authentically Flamboyant. Its smooth ashlar façades are broken up by string courses and heavily mullioned-and-transomed fenestration, with more ornate, ogee mouldings on the staircase tower and the west-wing arcade. The eaves are marked with a deep cornice sporting grimacing gargoyles and an intricate fretwork balustrade. Most of the ornamentation is reserved for the roof, however, whose steep, slate slopes form the backdrop to enormous and elaborately carved dormers bearing the arms of Jacques d'Amboise, the abbot most probably responsible for the *hôtel*'s construction. In its external ostentation, designed to display power through wealth and not military might, the Hôtel de Cluny further shows its modernity, especially in comparison to a contemporaneous but old-fashioned building such as the Hôtel de Sens (4.6), which still retains a fortress-like aspect.

Inside, the Hôtel de Cluny retains nothing of its original interiors bar the kitchen fireplace (the remainder of its current fireplaces having been rescued from other medieval buildings) and the chapel. The latter is covered by a magnificent, multi-lierned vault supported at its centre by a single, slender pillar. Set up high on the chapel walls are niches which, although they have lost their original statues, still retain their elaborately carved canopies and ledges. Amongst the museum's splendid collections are several architectural fragments, including capitals and a doorway from Saint-Germain-des-Prés (6.4) and statues from the Sainte-Chapelle (1.2) and Notre-Dame (4.2).

5.5 Collège de la Sorbonne
Rues de la Sorbonne, des Ecoles, Saint-Jacques and Cujas
Jacques Le Mercier, 1634–42; Henri-Paul Nénot, 1882 to 1901
(Métro: Cluny-La Sorbonne; RER: Luxembourg)

Today one of Europe's oldest universities, the Collège de la Sorbonne was founded by Robert de Sorbon, chaplain to Louis IX, in 1253. Nothing now survives of the original medieval complex, Cardinal de Richelieu having seen to its complete rebuilding in the first half of the 17C. Begun in 1626, the reconstruction was initially of modest ambition, but following the cardinal's consolidation of his power, in 1630, a much more grandiose scheme was instigated. The new Sorbonne was to be organized around a monumental *cour d'honneur*, at one end of which was to be a magnificent church that Richelieu intended to serve as his mausoleum. Jacques Le Mercier, who had already worked on several of the cardinal's major architectural projects, was called in to design the new church

Le Mercier had trained in Rome, and it was to the Eternal City's S. Carlo ai Catinari (Rosato Rosati, 1612 to 1620), which had been going up while he was there and whose architect may even have been his teacher, that he turned for inspiration at the Sorbonne. His scheme was remarkably faithful to the Roman original, copying S. Carlo's Greek- and Latin-cross plan combination, its typically Roman two-storey west front and its monumental, Italian-style crossing dome, which was the first of its kind in Paris. S. Carlo's dome was still unbuilt when Le Mercier left Rome, but his Sorbonne cupola, with its clustered pilasters and round-headed windows, is remarkably similar to S. Carlo's, and, given that Rosati's design differs in precisely these respects from other Roman domes then extant, it seems likely that Le Mercier had had access to Rosati's plans. On the western elevation, in front of which Richelieu had arranged for the creation of a small square reached via a new street running in the façade's central axis, Le Mercier deployed a composition that clearly follows the type-form developed by Giacomo della Porta – best known for Il Gesù (1571–84) –, with the same vertical division into five bays separated by Baroque groupings of columns and pilasters. In comparison to its Roman forebears, however, the Sorbonne has a feeling of tallness and vertical emphasis – perhaps inspired by local Gothic traditions – and a lightness and elegance of detailing that are very French.

The west front served as the public entrance to the church, while the college's entrance was in the courtyard, which extended to the church's north. Both the

5.5 Collège de la Sorbonne

not been uncovered. On the other hand, the sizeable drain that carried used water to the main city collector just beyond the complex can be still be seen in the cellars.

Viewed from the Boulevard Saint-Michel, the ruins of the *thermes* present two principal rooms to the public gaze. To the north is one of the *palaestrae*, decorated with high, flat-backed niches, while directly south of it is a space that probably served as the *tepidarium* (lukewarm room). Its alternate square and curved niches originally contained individual baths. At the southeastern corner of the complex, on the Rue du Sommerard, are the scanty remains of a *caldarium* (hot room). Various other segments of rooms can be seen, but it is for the impressive, central *frigidarium* and *natatio* (pool) leading off it, whose structures survive intact, that the Thermes de Lutèce are famous. Measuring an enormous 20 x 12 m, the *frigidarium* is covered with two lateral barrel vaults at either extremity and, at its centre, a groin vault that rises to 13.5 m. The 50 m^2 *natatio*, which sits in a niche directly north of the *frigidarium*, also sports a barrel vault. Baths were damp places, and therefore concrete vaulting was used instead of the cheaper and more usual wooden roofs to avoid problems of rot. Vaults were also a more architecturally grandiose covering than timber roofs for what was the principal edifice in Roman public life, baths being the main forum of social intercourse. The surface of the *frigidarium*'s splendid vaulting has been scarred by the passage of time, but in the basement one can still see vaults that bear traces of the wooden coffering used to cast them. Despite the excellent state of its structure, the *frigidarium* has lost all vestiges of its décor, apart from two brackets at the springing points of the vaults that are carved to represent ships' prows. Their presence here has led historians to wonder if there was not some special connection between the Thermes de Lutèce and the Corporation des Nautes, the rivermen's guild, and the theory has been advanced that the *thermes* were built by the corporation for its members. This is not the only unresolved question regarding the Thermes de Lutèce. Evidence suggests that the chambers to the east of the *frigidarium* carried a second storey of rooms, although what these may have been used for we do not know. And excavations have revealed that in the 4C part of the building was destroyed by a terrible fire, whose origins and exact consequences remain a mystery.

5.4 Hôtel de Cluny
6, place Paul-Painlevé
Architect unknown, c. 1470–1500
(Métro: Cluny-La Sorbonne)

Today home to the Musée National du Moyen Age, the Hôtel de Cluny started out life as the Parisian *pied à terre* of the powerful abbots of Cluny. The current building replaced an earlier edifice built before 1334 and was no doubt considered too old and dowdy by the late-15C abbots, who wanted a residence

5.4 Hôtel de Cluny

more representative of their prestige. As well as the plot on which the *hôtel* stands, the Cluny order also possessed the next-door Thermes de Lutèce (5.3 above), which at the time were half buried under neighbouring constructions. It was nonetheless the presence of the *frigidarium*, still intact and used by the abbots as a barn, that determined the orientation of the new *hôtel*, whose *corps de logis* was aligned so as to provide direct access to the Gallo-Roman chamber. In the context of modern-day Paris, the Hôtel de Cluny is remarkable both because of the rarity of surviving medieval residences and because of its excellent state of preservation.

It was the demolitions of the second half of the 19C that brought the *hôtel* its current isolation in the cityscape, where formerly it had been integrated into Paris's dense medieval fabric. In plan it is a precocious precursor of what would become the standard arrangement for Parisian *hôtels particuliers* from the 16–18C, with its *corps de logis* sandwiched between a garden at the rear and a courtyard at the front, the latter containing service buildings and being accessed from the street via a *porte-cochère*. It also showed its modernity through the fact that it forms one homogeneous, compact, U-shaped ensemble, where before the residences of the rich had tended to comprise a looser grouping of physically separate structures. This may well have been born of a desire to extract the maximum accommodation out of a constricted site, a concern that would tax the ingenuity of many an *hôtel-particulier* designer to come. The west wing, running alongside the *thermes*, originally contained a long gallery at first-floor level, while its ground-floor courtyard arcades were provided to shelter visitors' servants. The *corps de logis*, where the principal public / reception rooms were located, is irregularly bisected by a semi-embedded octagonal tower that contains the *escalier d'honneur*. Kitchens and other services were located in the eastern wing on the courtyard. At the rear of the building, a small projecting wing contains, at first-floor level, the chapel, whose apse juts

its graveyard. The graveyard was more of a communal rotting ground than a cemetery in the modern sense, and each time it became too full the oldest and therefore most thoroughly decomposed remains were dug up and removed to the ossuary. Saint-Séverin's charnel house is the only surviving example in Paris, and as such is an authentic remnant of the rather macabre funerary practices of the medieval era, despite its heavy restoration in the 1920s, when its current gables were added. The ossuary's first three bays were demolished in 1763 for construction of the oval communion chapel, by Jules Hardouin-Mansart, that leads off the choir.

Saint-Séverin received its current western entrance in the 19C, an addition transported stone by stone from the demolished church of Saint-Pierre-aux-Bœufs (13C) on the Ile de la Cité (4.1), which was sacrificed for construction of the Rue d'Arcole in 1837. Jollied up at the time of its move by the addition of a gable and pinnacles, the doorway is notable for its 13C jamb shafts with their foliage-carved capitals. Saint-Severin's original entrance still exists, under the tower on the Rue Saint-Séverin. For its décor, Saint-Séverin is chiefly interesting for its stained glass, much of which is 15C (although the first three bays of the nave contain 14C glass from the Collège de Dormans-Beauvais, installed in 1857) and for the 15C painted *Last Judgement* adorning the first ambulatory chapel on the northern side.

5.3 Thermes de Lutèce
6, place Paul-Painlevé
Architects unknown, 1st or 2nd century AD
(Métro: Cluny-La Sorbonne)

Lutetia (Lutèce in French), as Roman Paris was known, counted amongst its public amenities at least three bathhouses (Latin *thermae*, French *thermes*), of which the most monumental, known as the Thermes de Lutèce, survive to this day. They are, along with the Arènes de Lutèce (5.11), one of only two structures remaining from the period of Roman occupation of Paris, which lasted from the mid-1C BC to the late-4C AD The *thermes*' relatively good state of preservation makes them the most impressive Roman remains in northern France, and it is a tribute to their builders that they have managed to weather the cares and neglect of over 1½ millennia with such resistance. They owe their survival largely to the fact that for centuries they were half buried behind a whole collection of medieval structures, amongst which was the Hôtel de Cluny (5.4), whose owners used the structure as a barn and even installed gardens on top of its vaults! It was only in the 19C, essentially during the building of Haussmann's Boulevards Saint-Michel and Saint-Germain (c. 1852–69), that the *thermes* were cleared of later structures, excavated and restored. They now form, along with the Hôtel de Cluny, part of the Musée National du Moyen Age, or Musée de Cluny as it is more colloquially known.

No Antique documentation mentioning the *thermes* has come down to us, and all knowledge we have of their construction and use is speculative, based on excavations and examinations of the ruins. Following a major dig carried out in the aftermath of WWII, the late-2C or early-3C AD were proposed as the probable time of construction of the *thermes*, and the theory advanced that they were built in one go in a relatively short space of time. A more recent hypothesis, based on excavations carried out in the 1980s and 1990s, is that the *thermes* may in fact have been erected as early as the Flavian era (69–96 AD), and that they were considerably modified over the next 200 years before being abandoned, probably sometime around the end of the 3C. Equally uncertain is our understanding of how the different spaces in the *thermes* were used, although as far as some are concerned, for example the complex's two *palaestrae* (exercise courts) and its *frigidarium* (cold-ablutions room), there is little doubt.

The standing ruins we see today represent slightly more than half the original complex, which covered over 6,000 m². In plan the *thermes* were organized as an asymmetrical agglomeration of rooms, with entrance being gained on the northern side between the two sizeable *palaestrae*, hot rooms running along the building's southern flank and, occupying the complex's heart, the *frigidarium*. Nearly all the exposed walls currently subsisting were originally internal, and have lost whatever cladding or rendering they originally possessed (a small segment of painted stucco can be seen in one of the basement rooms). As a result, the constructive system used to build the *thermes* – imported into France by the Romans – is clearly visible: concrete walls, made up of mortar and rubble stone, that are faced with small stone blocks and strengthened by regular bands of brickwork running through their entire thickness. Another typical Roman feature is the hypocaust (under-floor-heating) system installed beneath the hot rooms. The considerable quantities of water used by the baths were almost certainly supplied by the main Lutetia aqueduct, the Aqueduc d'Arcueil (remains of which can be seen at Cachan, south of Paris), but its point of connection to the *thermes* has

5.3 Thermes de Lutèce

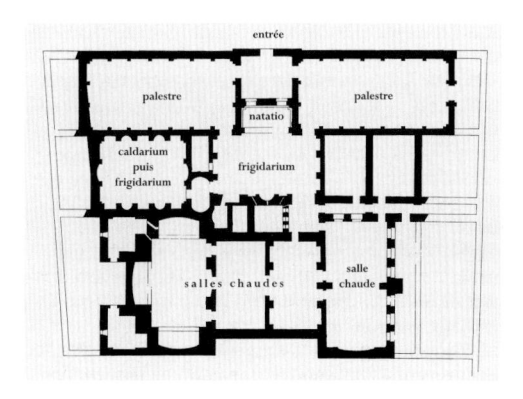

5th *arrondissement*

5.1 Saint-Julien-le-Pauvre
1, rue Saint-Julien-le-Pauvre
Architect unknown, begun *c*. 1165–70
(Métro: Maubert-Mutualité)

This ancient little church was built on the site of a refuge for pilgrims, whose origins went back at least as far as the 6C. The current edifice was erected by the Cluniac monks of Longpont, construction beginning at the choir, which was completed between 1210 and 1220. The dating of the nave is less certain, but it was certainly not finished any later than the choir. In 1651, after a long period of neglect, the first two bays of the nave and the southern aisle were demolished and a new west front constructed. The northern aisle was conserved, its first two bays serving as a sacristy. In 1889, the church underwent extensive restoration during its transfer to Greek-Melchite denomination.

Inspired by the Cathedral of Notre-Dame (4.2) just across the river, which was then also under construction, Saint-Julien-le-Pauvre was never completed in its intended state. The choir (today partially hidden behind an iconostasis) was to have been three »storeys« high, the current clerestory having originally been planned as a triforium. In the nave, a wooden covering stood in for the unconstructed sexpartite vaults (the current vaulting dates from the 17C) and, of the tower that was to have risen on the church's southern side, only the staircase was begun. The church's piers are based on those of Notre-Dame, and its capitals, all carved into foliage bar one representing harpies, form an impressive ensemble. The walls of the three east-end apses were re-used from an older building.

5.2 Saint-Séverin
1, rue des Prêtres-Saint-Séverin
Architects unknown, current building begun early-13C
(Métro: Saint-Michel)

A complex palimpsest of three centuries of French Gothic architecture, Saint-Séverin stands on a site that has been occupied by a religious edifice since the 6C. By the 12C, the church had become the most important on the Left Bank, serving the whole area, and it was presumably because of this pre-eminence that its complete rebuilding was undertaken in the early-13C. The new edifice was a simple vessel eight bays long with single side-aisles, no transepts and a square east end; too small for its growing congregation, it was enlarged in the mid-14C by the addition of supplementary side-aisles. Of this 13/14C church, all that survive are the lower levels of the tower (*c*. 1250), the first three bays of the nave – easily recognizable by the early-Gothic, columnar form of their piers – and the pillars separating the two southern aisles. The triforium in the first three bays, originally blind but glazed in the 18C, is the oldest surviving example in Paris.

Badly damaged by fire some time around 1448, Saint-Séverin was afterwards rebuilt, a process that

5.2 Saint-Séverin

lasted almost a century. The first parts undertaken were the northern side-aisles and the last five bays of the nave, the latter reproducing the disposition of their 13C forbears only with Flamboyant-period, capital-less arcades and ogee tracery. Next, in 1489–95, came the choir, for whose double ambulatory Saint-Séverin is justly famous. At the ambulatory's centre is a curious, twisted column from which spring no less than 14 vault ribs; a similar profusion of ribs characterizes the remainder of its vaulting and forms a delirious shower of stone that has earned the ensemble comparisons with parasols and palm groves. Also worthy of note is the choir's elaborate high vault. The rather unfortunate Classicizing marble cladding adorning the choir arcades was added in 1681 by Jean-Baptiste Tuby, to designs by Charles Le Brun. The final, medieval-era campaign of building work at Saint-Séverin, carried out in 1498–1540, involved construction of the aisle chapels, whose decorated gables cadence the church's exterior. Despite the long period over which the church was built, the end result is remarkably homogenous, both inside and out, essentially because of the 15C builders' decision to repeat the basic dispositions established in the 13C, even though they were by this time rather old-fashioned.

From the same building campaign as the choir are the tower's upper levels and also the sizeable ossuary or charnel house that forms a sort of cloister in front of the church's southern flank, enclosing what was once

aisles. The high vaults were supported by flying buttresses, just like in a Gothic cathedral, but Soufflot Classicized the church's exterior by hiding the aisle roofs, buttressing and all the other working details one normally sees behind high perimeter walls, a trick borrowed from Wren's Saint Paul's. Soufflot rejected traditional Classical barrel vaulting, which has the disadvantage of exerting thrust all along its length, in favour of a much more complex form that was configured to channel thrust into specific areas so as to avoid buckling the columns. Reminiscent of the high vaults to be found in Byzantine churches, the Sainte-Geneviève system consists of a series of saucer domes (also used by Wren at Saint Paul's), each one carried on two transverse main-vessel arches (whose great width in reality turns them into short sections of barrel vault) and two lateral arches. But, unlike in Byzantine churches, or indeed at Saint Paul's, the supporting arches are not allowed to exert the forces they carry all along their bases since they in turn have been hollowed out with further arches, leaving slim piers standing on the entablature, each one placed directly above a column just below. The result is quite wonderfully airy, and could not have been achieved without Soufflot's innovative use of extensive iron reinforcements that stiffen the whole building and clamp its individual blocks of stone together (these reinforcements are today the source of a major headache: two centuries of water infiltration have caused some of them to rust with the result that cracks have begun to appear in parts of the building and stone blocks have even fallen from the vault). The enormous lunettes formed by the lateral arches are entirely glazed, and the resulting clerestory floods the building's upper levels with light. When first completed Sainte-Geneviève must have been quite extraordinarily luminous, since as well as the clerestory windows there were over 30 generously proportioned aisle windows lighting the church laterally. In its current state, however, the building's interior is quite different. As part of Sainte-Geneviève's initial conversion to house the Panthéon (see below), the aesthetic theorist Antoine Chrysostome Quatremère de Quincy blocked all the aisle windows in the interests of the giving the building »a more serious character«, both inside and out. Consequently, light is not allowed to filter through Soufflot's majestic columns as he intended, yet it is a tribute to his vision that, even lit only via the clerestory and crossing, the Panthéon's interior is remarkably bright, and has nothing of the funerary gloom that Quatremère hoped to impose on it. What it does have as a result of this sober overhead lighting – which, moreover, is filtered through frosted glass so as to hide the flying buttresses and outer envelope – is a coldness that, while picking out the crispness of the exquisite carved detailing, renders rather brittle the imperial-Roman grandeur of Soufflot's design.

On Sainte-Geneviève's exterior, Soufflot was just as keen to avoid the use of pilasters as inside, but rejected the obvious solution of a continuous colonnade (probably on grounds of cost) in favour of buttressing projections, rather reminiscent in their effect of pilasters, that cadence the outer envelope. The envelope's surface was further broken up by the many aisle windows, each one being coiffed with a garland to jolly up what were otherwise rather austere façades. In any case, Soufflot knew that it was not the lateral elevations on which the viewer's eye would fix, but on the great, monumental crossing dome, the church's most important and striking external feature. He produced countless different designs for the dome before finally arriving at the definitive scheme in 1777, by which time the rest of the building was already far advanced. The first projects show a rather modest composition with a shallow cupola supported on a small, complex drum, but as time went by Soufflot's proposals became bigger and more traditional. As built, the Panthéon's dome subscribes externally to a lineage going back to Bramante's Tempietto (S. Pietro in Montorio, Rome, 1502) and aggrandized to this scale via Wren's Saint Paul's, and derives internally from the example of the Invalides (7.12). Indeed a concern to rival London, and of course Rome, where Saint Peter's enormous dome had long been one of the wonders of Western architecture, was probably among the factors that prompted Soufflot to modify his initial designs. Perched up on the Sainte-Geneviève hill, the Panthéon's dome dominates the Parisian skyline through its imposing height – reminiscent in aim of the Gothic spire –, which is achieved by the presence of a giant drum and through the elongation of the dome itself which, in comparison to earlier examples, thrusts towards the sky in a most un-Euclidean manner. But, countering this tendency and bringing to the composition a massive breadth is the colonnade surrounding the drum (directly derived from the Tempietto and Saint Paul's), which also allows prominent expression of the freestanding columns that were so essential to Soufflot's conception of architecture at Sainte-Geneviève. (In terms of monumentality, however, Saint Paul's perhaps has the upper hand, for Wren's un-Classical use of filled-in walls every fourth bay gives his drum a solidity that Soufflot's pure colonnade lacks, leaving the Panthéon's dome to spin rather aimlessly on its base.) Inside, Soufflot's dome recreates the clever (and rather Baroque) disposition used at the Invalides, whereby a system of two superimposed shells is employed, the upper one being lit by hidden fenestration (visible externally as the round-headed windows on the drum's attic) and viewed through a hole cut into the top of the lower shell, a trick of which the observer below remains wholly ignorant without prior knowledge of the design. Soufflot's dome goes one step further than the Invalides's in that the external covering, which at the Invalides is constructed from a traditional wooden framework, is in fact another, independent stone shell covering the lower ones like a bowler hat.

Because Soufflot had conceived Sainte-Geneviève in terms of columns, i.e. points on a plan, his approach to the church's crossing was rather different to that of previous architects faced with a similar situation. Obviously columns alone could not hold up the dome's enormous weight, but he determined to treat the piers he designed to support it rather like columns: only four in number, they were to be as slender as possible, allowing the visitor to see around and behind them. Four enormous arches with pendentives would carry the entirely glazed drum, above which would rise the lower, grandly coffered dome, whose central opening was to frame the fresco of the upper dome, illuminated by its hidden light source. Soufflot's scheme was daringly experimental for its era, and was not without its critics. His later career was marred by a very public wrangle over his design initiated by the architect Pierre Patte who, in 1770, attacked Soufflot in print, claiming that the planned 0.9 m-wide piers could not possibly support the dome's enormous weight. Although his scheme was defended by the engineers of the Ecole des Ponts et Chaussées, Soufflot nonetheless modified the piers, but as early as 1776, before the dome was even completed, cracks appeared that set off the whole polemic again. In the end it was proved that faulty workmanship was the culprit and Soufflot was exonerated, but, after the architect's death, fissuring began once more. Although faulty workmanship was again to blame, it was decided that the crossing piers should be strengthened, a task carried out by Jean-Baptiste Rondelet, one of Soufflot's pupils, in 1806–12. Soufflot's original piers had been slender triangular supports squeezed in between, and engaging with, the columns holding up the main-vessel vaults, and had been decorated on their crossing-side elevations with pilasters, despite Soufflot's scruples. Rondelet replaced the engaged columns with solid corner buttresses onto which he moved the pilasters, thereby leaving much wider areas of blank pier in the crossing. The result is more monumental than Soufflot intended, and provides a suitable backdrop for rather pompous commemorative sculptures.

Soufflot died in 1780, and was replaced by his second in command, Brébion. Ten years later, in 1790, just before the full fury of the French Revolution set in, Sainte-Geneviève's carcass was completed. Much of the décor and carvings had yet to be commenced, however, and events saw to it that most of the original programme would never be executed. In 1791, by order of the National Assembly, Sainte-Geneviève became the Panthéon. The idea had first been put forward by the influential Marquis de Villette, who, looking for a suitable resting place for his illustrious friend Voltaire, had declared »... to bring us closer to the Greeks and Romans, ... to set an example for Europe, let us have the courage not to dedicate this temple to a saint. Let it become the FRENCH PANTHEON!« This sentiment was summed up by the inscription placed on the building's entrance pediment at the time of its conversion: »Aux grands hommes la patrie reconnaissante.« On the one hand the choice of Sainte-Geneviève clearly signalled the Revolutionaries' declaration of war on the Catholic church, but on the other the building's neo-Classicism and breach with former French ecclesiastical architecture meant that, apart from its cross-shaped plan and perhaps its monumental dome, nothing about its design made it immediately associable with the Catholic faith. Alterations were nonetheless considered necessary to make the edifice suitable for its new function and, as we have seen, Quatremère de Quincy was called in for the job. In addition to blocking the aisle windows, he demolished the east-end bell towers – superfluous to the building's new function and an unnecessary excrescence on the purity of its external lines –, and replaced the entrance pediment's bas-relief with a new one of more Revolutionary iconography. Of all his interventions, both minor and major, it was the filling-in of the aisle windows that had the most profound consequences, not only, as we have seen, on the interior, but also on the exterior which became blind, monolithic and distinctly bleak.

Throughout the 19C, in step with the changes of political regime, Soufflot's *magnum opus* oscillated back and forth between its roles of church and pantheon; the latter has had the upper hand since 1885. As a result its decor is a hotchpotch of secular and religious and royal and republican iconography straddling over a century of artistic creation. Of particular note are David d'Angers's entrance-pediment relief (1837) depicting *La Patrie* distributing laurel wreaths to the illustrious, Antoine-Jean Gros's dome fresco (1811–24) of *L'Apothéose de Sainte Geneviève*, and the late-19C cycle of aisle-wall paintings showing the life of Geneviève and other saints, whose presence unfortunately makes it highly unlikely that the building's lateral windows will ever be opened up again.

The Place du Panthéon surrounding the monument, which includes a generous semicircular space in front of the entrance portico, was laid out to plans by Soufflot. In his lifetime he only managed to complete the Ecole de Droit at no. 12 (1771–74), the pendant Mairie du 5e at no. 21 not being built until 1844–50. Designed to provide a suitable backdrop to Sainte-Geneviève, these buildings' sober, curved façades, which step back from their centres in a sort of *decrescendo* that nimbly turns the street corners, are dominated by giant Ionic porticoes that act as a counterpoint to the church's elaborate Corinthian entrance. Today's Rue Soufflot, which connects the Panthéon to the Jardin du Luxembourg (see 6.8), was also planned by Soufflot, but was not cut through until the early-19C.

5.9 Abbaye du Val-de-Grâce
277, rue Saint-Jacques
Various architects, notably François Mansart and Pierre Le Muet, 1624–69
(RER: Port Royal)

Commissioned by the pious Anne of Austria, wife of Louis XIII and mother of Louis XIV, the Abbaye du Val-de-Grâce was Paris's most ambitious 17C ecclesiastical building project and one of the most concrete expressions of Counter-Reformatory zeal in France. Begun in 1624 by an unknown architect, it was initially a modest construction, a place of refuge for the queen consort in times of difficulty. But, after becoming Queen Regent of France on the death of her husband, in 1643, Anne was able to complete the complex and lavish all the funds on it she could muster. Her marriage had been a difficult one, marred by two decades of barrenness, and during her childless years she had vowed to build a magnificent monument to the glory of God if only he would grant her a son, which miraculous event finally occurred in 1638. Two years after Louis XIII's death, in 1645, the seven-year-old Louis XIV laid the foundation stone of the Abbaye's new church, the *pièce de résistance* of the whole complex and the expression of Anne's faith and piety. She had hired the great François Mansart to build it, but after less than two years fired him, a dismissal generally attributed to unexplained delays, potentially spiralling costs and the architect's difficult character. He was replaced by the Premier Architecte du Roi, Jacques Le Mercier, who worked on the Val-de-Grâce until 1648, when the troubles of the Fronde halted building work. Just at the moment when order had been restored and construction could begin again, in 1654, Le Mercier died. He was replaced by Pierre Le Muet, seconded by Gabriel Le Duc and Antoine Broutel du Val, who together brought the project to completion in 1669, the year of Le Muet's death. Anne of Austria never lived to see her cherished abbey entirely finished, dying in 1666.

Today the Val-de-Grâce has the distinction of being the only intact, unmodified monastic complex to survive in Paris of the scores formerly found in the city. Its oldest parts, dating from the first phase of work carried out c. 1624–40, are to be found in the lower storeys of the northern, eastern and western wings of the large, rectangular cloister. Mansart had proposed demolishing the original constructions and starting afresh – amongst his early proposals was a scheme showing the church at the centre of a vast palace (so vast it disappeared off the edges of his paper) forming an ensemble clearly reminiscent of the Escorial – but whether because too expensive for the queen or too ostentatious for the modest nuns, his project was never adopted. A compromise solution was thus implemented for the abbey's secular parts, the old cloister being completed and vertically extended during the two-and-a-half decades following Louis XIII's demise to produce the rather hybrid result we see today. On its courtyard sides it comprises a superimposition of two arcaded, vaulted and externally buttressed galleries at ground- and first-floor level that are surmounted by two modest »attic« storeys crowned by a mansard roof. The kitchens, refectories, infirmary wards and other principal rooms and apartments were situated on the outer façades of the cloister and accessed via the courtyard galleries, while the nuns' dormitories were located in the attic stories. Solid and elaborately coiffed pavilions, added by Le Muet after 1654, stand at each of the cloister's external corners. The marriage of the old, arcaded and buttressed parts of the cloister from the first phase of work, whose design is clearly in a medieval tradition, with upper storeys, roofing and pavilions of much more modern aspect was not altogether successful from a Classically-correct point of view, but makes for a very picturesque result. Anne of Austria's apartment was initially at the centre of the cloister's garden façade on the first floor (hence the wrought-iron balcony), but as of 1656 she took up residence in the newly built northeastern pavilion, from whose northern elevation projects a picturesquely rusticated, column-mounted chamber in which she installed her oratory. The full-height pavilion to the west contains her handsome staircase.

For the church of the Val-de-Grâce, which is situated to the north of the old cloister, Mansart contrived a combination of an Italianizing, centralized, domed plan, suitable for a private votive chapel, and the traditional French Latin-cross-with-nave-and-choir plan used for parish churches and cathedrals. This compromise ingeniously adapted Italian prototypes to the specific local needs of the Val-de-Grâce, which had to accommodate the nuns, the general public and the private worship of the queen. The church forms a Latin cross comprising a three-bay, western-orientated nave

5.9 Abbaye du Val-de-Grâce

followed by a domed crossing (containing the high altar at its rear) from which projects the queen's chapel to the north, a Chapelle du Saint-Sacrament to the east, behind the altar, and the nun's choir (of much bigger dimensions than the queen's chapel) to the south. The nave has no aisles but side-chapels that are treated like aisles, with further chapels to be found in the corners between the crossing arms. Mansart experimented throughout his career with the possibilities of the domed, centralized-plan type, firstly at the church of the Visitation (4.21), then at the Val-de-Grâce, and afterwards in unexecuted proposals that would influence Jules Hardouin-Mansart's design for the Invalides (7.12). In the Val-de-Grâce's crossing we find the same profusion of openings as at the Visitation, Mansart having cut diagonal access through the crossing piers to link the corner chapels directly to the main space, an innovation in relation to contemporary Italian centralized-plan churches where generally only the four principal subordinate spaces gave directly onto the main rotunda. The Val-de-Grâce's crossing is rendered yet more complicated and Baroque in its form by the semicircular, cutaway spaces that precede the entrances to the queen's chapel, the Chapelle du Saint-Sacrament and the nuns' choir. This polymorphism in turn necessitated complicated contortions from the giant Corinthian order adorning the crossing's wall surfaces, whose pilasters curve along concave elevations, bend and fold round corners and double up with half-shared capitals. Further elaboration comes in the form of the theatrical balconied niches filling the space between the pendentives and the corner-chapel openings. In the Roman-style, three-bay nave we find Mansart opting for much simpler, more Classical elevations, with plain, round-headed arcades separated by pilaster-carrying piers.

At the time Mansart was sacked from the Val-de-Grâce project the nave rose as far as the entablature but the crossing piers were only half built. All the evidence suggests that, apart from enlarging the Chapelle du Saint-Sacrament and simplifying the design of the nun's choir, Le Mercier contented himself with continuing Mansart's scheme. When work stopped, in 1648, the crossing had reached entablature height and the Chapelle du Saint-Sacrament was roofed: the design of its beautiful, spiral-coffered dome, clearly inspired by Philibert De l'Orme's chapel at the Château d'Anet (1549–52), is attributed to Le Mercier. Le Muet, on the other hand, on succeeding Le Mercier in 1654, completely revised Mansart's proposals for the upper parts of the edifice (perhaps partly in the interests of cost cutting), producing a design that had very little to do with Mansart's intentions and which the disgraced architect considered distinctly inferior. Only on the upper storey of the entrance façade did Le Muet respect the intent of his predecessor's scheme. In place of the high and complicated nave covering probably planned by Mansart, he instead installed a simple barrel vault, in the Roman manner, although it is pierced with clerestory windows as was standard practice in France. The latter are, however, of much smaller dimensions than was usual, thereby producing a hybrid effect halfway between the Italian and French traditions, and the vault is rendered yet more unusual by the lavishly carved compartments decorating its surface, which recall French-Renaissance wooden ceilings. At the crossing, where Mansart's plans showed a complicated, elongated, double dome whose insides had very little to do with its exterior, Le Muet opted for a much more traditionally Italianizing design, which may well have been inspired by Michelangelo's original scheme for the dome at Saint Peter's in Rome. Internally we see a 16-light drum on which rises an uninterrupted hemisphere, whose enormous fresco (depicting God in heavenly glory), one of the biggest of its kind in France, was painted by Pierre Mignard. In fact the internal dome rises only within the height of the external drum, while the dome we see outside is an entirely separate, wooden structure whose base sits above the apex of the internal cupola. In some respects Le Muet's dome design recalls Le Mercier's for the church of the Sorbonne (see 5.5), especially externally in the treatment of the upper parts, which bristle with statues and urns, and the pepper-pot lanterns that cluster round the dome and fill the corners of the square base on which it stands. Returning inside, we should note the splendid pendentive carvings by Michel Anguier (depicting the four Evangelists), the very imperial-Roman coffering of the *cul-de-four* crossing-arm vaults, which terminate in huge, glazed lunettes, and the splendid high altar with its elaborate, twisted-column baldaquin. Inspired, of course, by Bernini's high altar at Saint Peter's, the baldaquin was the joint work of Le Muet and Le Duc, and though more formally complex is lighter in effect than the Italian original. The overall impression made by the Val-de-Grâce's crossing is one of regally restrained richness, and, even if Mansart and his many partisans considered Le Muet's modified crossing design inferior, it must be admitted that his work perfectly matches the stern opulence to be found in the built parts of Mansart's scheme.

Externally, the main entrance façade, although its upper-level detailing was modified by Le Muet, can be more or less attributed in its entirety to Mansart. His elevation is in the two-storey Roman, Gesù (Giacomo della Porta, 1571–84) tradition, and recalls more specifically Carlo Maderno's S. Susanna (1597–1603). The façade has the same central emphasis and vertical thrust as S. Susanna's, but Mansart's genius is palpable in the way the pedimented entrance portico projects forward from the façade while the central portion of the upper storey above actually recedes, bringing a highly plastic, three-dimensional, architectonic quality to the elevation that is entirely lacking in the flat, two-dimensional compositions found in Rome at that time. Despite its open-bed upper pediment and paired columns, Mansart's façade somehow seems more Classical and much less Mannerist than its Roman counterparts, for example in the way the ground-floor order progresses from pilaster, to engaged column to column in the round. Equally innovatory was the church's *mise en scène*, which in its general conception is attributable to Mansart, although its specificities must be given to Le Muet. Flanked by arcaded parlours it is preceded by a huge *avant-cour* whose sides are delimited by dummy elevations that terminate on the Rue Saint-Jacques in square pavilions. In other words it is treated rather in the manner of an *hôtel particulier*, but with the difference that in place of the high wall that would have closed off a private residence from the street we find wrought-iron railings that render the whole majestic composition visible to the public gaze. Today we are used to seeing the church from the vantage point of the Rue du Val-de-Grâce (running in the axis of the composition), which neatly frames the dome and the entrance façade; but this viewpoint has only been possible since 1797, when the street was cut through, and it is interesting to note that Le Muet calculated the relation of dome to façade so that, when viewed from the entrance to the *avant-cour*, the dome entirely disappears behind the façade, all except its terminal cross which appears to crown the apex of the façade's upper pediment.

Contemporaries were unstinting in their praise of the Val-de-Grâce (even while criticizing some of Le Muet's interventions), and it was considered one of the wonders of its time, proof that France was capable of just as much magnificence as Rome. Today the Val-de-Grâce, if not exactly forgotten, is rather overshadowed by later realizations, and its quality and the extent of its influence are generally under-appreciated.

5.10 Grande Mosquée de Paris
1, place du Puits-de-l'Ermite
Maurice Tranchant de Lunel, Robert Fournez, Charles Heubès and Maurice Mantout 1920–26
(Métro: Monge)

100,000 Muslim soldiers died fighting for France in WWI and, following the conflict, the French government decided to express its gratitude by building a mosque in central Paris. Given the 1905 law forbidding the French state from subsidizing religious worship, this was no small gesture, and the creation of an *institut musulman* within the confines of the mosque was used to circumvent this legal conundrum. A 7,500 m² site was donated by the Ville de Paris, and Maurice Tranchant de Lunel, Inspecteur Général des Beaux-Arts in Morocco, was asked to draw up the plans, which were then executed by Fournez, Heubès and Mantout. As well as the mosque proper and the *institut*, the complex includes a hammam, a souk and a tea room (which is very popular in the summer). For the building's layout, over half of which comprises courtyards and gardens, Lunel took inspiration from mosques in Fez, while the Mosquée's décor is an eclectic mix of Hispano-Moorish influences. Notable features include the 33 m-high minaret, the beautiful marble-floored courtyard (inspired by the Alhambra) that leads to the prayer room, and the traditional gardens, whose layout symbolizes paradise. The building's reinforced-concrete structure is masked by a wealth of decorative detail, executed by North-African craftsmen, that includes traditional geometric-motif ceramics, elaborate ironwork and intricate wooden *moucharebiya*. At its best, Paris's Grande Mosquée is an extraordinarily accomplished pastiche, in which one really does feel transported to another land, but there is also a rather kitsch quality to its lavishness that some may find overly *Arabian Nights*.

5.11 Arènes de Lutèce
49, rue Monge and 6, rue des Arènes
1st century AD
(Métro: Monge, Cardinal Lemoine, Jussieu)

The thriving Gallo-Roman town of Lutetia, which spread out across the Left Bank where the Latin Quarter now stands, was endowed with a number of important public buildings, among them the *thermes* (5.3) and the Arènes. An arena/amphitheatre, the Arènes were capable of seating around 15,000 spectators and rivalled those at Arles and Nîmes. Completed some time in the 1C, the building was abandoned during the 3C following barbarian attacks on the area. Still visible in the 12C, when they were pillaged for their stone, the ruins were subsequently buried and their precise whereabouts forgotten. The Arènes were finally rediscovered in 1869 following building work conducted on the site by a local bus company. Public sentiment prevented their destruction, but they were not properly excavated until 1917–18 after the departure of the buses.

Comparatively little survives of the original structure, and what does subsist has been heavily restored (part of the amphitheatre lies under the Rue Monge and thus remains unexcavated). Terraces rising to a third of their original height surround an oval arena sunk to a depth of 2 m. Because the builders took advantage of the hillside site to construct the terraces – thereby minimizing the masonry vaults necessary to

5.12 Faculté des Sciences de Jussieu

support them – the stage is situated to the north at the slope's lower end. Extremely long (41 m), it carries traces of the niched and originally highly decorated *sceana frons*, while animal cages can be discerned under its podium. The site is now a public park, the arena serving admirably for games of *boules*.

5.12 Faculté des Sciences de Jussieu
Place Jussieu
Edouard Albert, Roger Seassal, Urbain Cassan, René Coulon and Louis Madeline († 1962), 1955–71
(Métro: Jussieu)

Following bombing during WWII, this prime riverside site was scheduled for redevelopment as a brand-new science faculty to relieve Paris's overcrowded universities. Seassal, Cassan, Madeline and Coulon were initially assigned to the job, and produced the rather dull Quai-Saint-Bernard and Rue-Cuvier slab blocks, completed in 1961. They had planned to fill the remaining space with similar buildings, but in 1962 André Malraux, Ministre des Affaires Culturelles, decided otherwise, imposing Edouard Albert as head of the design team and asking him to provide a new scheme. A devotee of metal construction, Albert had developed a standardized, prefabricated steel-tube system that had the advantages over concrete construction of being lighter, cheaper, leaner – allowing gains of up to 3% on useable surface area over concrete buildings – and quicker to build. Moreover, plumbing and wiring could run inside the tubes, thereby saving further space and labour. For the Jussieu campus, Albert conceived a grid of rectangular courtyards, vaguely inspired by the Escorial, standing on a marble-paved platform that overcame the unevenness of the terrain and allowed dark spaces, such as particle accelerators, to be housed under it. Mounted on *pilotis* carrying elegant, gondola-shaped beams, the surface buildings were divided internally into L-shaped units, with classrooms in the shorter courtyard arms and laboratories in the longer. Circular concrete towers at the grid's intersections served both to contain vertical communication and to buttress the metal structures enveloping them. Cadenced by the structural tubes – which, according to Albert, were a direct transposition of the traditional Classical colonnade – the delicately proportioned façades were clad in glass and marble. An 85 m-high tower at the centre of the campus's *cour d'honneur* housed the faculty's administrative spaces.

Albert died in January 1968, his campus still unfinished, and the events of May that year ensured it never would be, the frightened government deeming it unwise to allow such a high concentration of students in one spot in central Paris. Of the 22 courtyards originally planned, only 13 were completed; the site's integration into the surrounding city, as Albert had proposed, was never carried out (indeed if anything it was deliberately segregated), and the administrative tower was built to a mediocre design entirely lacking the subtlety of Albert's original. Ironically, despite the government's fears, the unfinished Jussieu soon saw an influx of some 30,000 students, a third more than the original project in its unbuilt entirety was intended to accommodate. It is a tribute to Albert's design that it was able to cope with this radical programmatic change without any external modification or extension.

But, for all its rationalist integrity and elegant economy of means that have gained it the praise of Modernist sympathisers, Jussieu has a relentless, inhuman side in its infinitely extendable monotony (nothing is more monotonous or frightening than infinity) and wind-swept micro-climate, seemingly always several degrees colder than the surrounding city. No relief from the elements, green or otherwise, is provided on the 20,000 m² marble platform, and consequently few linger in the inhospitable courtyards which were nonetheless supposed to provide places of public interaction and animation. Indeed in this respect Jussieu can be said very much to be in a French Classical tradition of enormous, mineral, windswept open spaces, exemplified by the Place de la Concorde (8.1). Jussieu also has another very inhuman side that only fully came to light years after its inauguration. A metal structure of the type designed by Albert is a big fire risk, and hence needs to be well insulated: the material used for this insulation was asbestos. 70 cases of asbestos-related illnesses and deaths directly attributable to Jussieu have now been proven, and painstaking work, evaluated at nearly 4 billion francs, has begun to clear the site. Given this state of affairs, calls have been heard for the campus's demolition, essentially from those who find its architecture ugly and heartless. Contrarily, Modernist sympathizers have asked that this »chef-d'œuvre des sixties« be listed as a historic monument.

5.13 Institut du Monde Arabe
1, rue des Fossés Saint-Bernard
Jean Nouvel, Gilbert Lézérès, Pierre Soria and Architecture Studio, 1981–87
(Métro: Cardinal Lemoine, Jussieu, Sully-Morland)
One of the first of President Mitterrand's *grands projets*, this was the building that brought Jean Nouvel international stardom. Founded in 1974 by the French government and 19 Arab countries, the institute's mission was to further understanding of Arab culture and civilization in France. A site, an architect and a design were chosen, only to be promptly dropped when the socialists came to power in 1981. The new regime selected another, more prestigious site on the Left Bank next to the Seine, and launched a limited national competition for the building. Entrants were asked to provide accommodation for a museum of the Arab world, as well as a *médiathèque* comprising a 40,000-volume library, film and sound archives, an image bank, and an auditorium.

The winning team looked to British and Japanese Hi-tech for inspiration in a design that endeavoured to marry ultra-modern aesthetics with allusions to traditional Arab building forms. The building also had to attempt a marriage between old and new Paris, situated as it is between the Ile Saint-Louis and the relentless orthogonality of the Jussieu campus (5.12). Nouvel had been struck by the use of light in Arab architecture, and the team made this a central element of the design. Constructed entirely from aluminium and glass, the institute's largely transparent exterior consists of two parallel wings, joined at their eastern end. The lower, northern wing is devoted entirely to the museum, and follows the curve of the quayside road to finish dramatically in a sharp prow at its western extremity. To its south is the second, taller wing, shared by the museum and the *médiathèque*, which takes the form of a Cartesian slab, like the Jussieu buildings around it. A narrow, canyon-like »cleft« separates the two wings, which at fourth-floor level becomes a courtyard faced in white marble panels, situated at the heart of the building. Cleft and courtyard are intended to symbolize the »interiority« of much Arab architecture although, as built, neither has much of the intimate

5.13 Institut du Monde Arabe

charm one finds in traditional Arabian buildings. (The courtyard was to have contained an oriental-style garden and fountains, dropped due to budget cuts.) The quayside façade of the building is animated by a whizzing aluminium lattice and, in a somewhat absurd attempt to relate the building to the old city, features profiles of traditional Parisian building types etched onto the glass, almost imperceptible to the passer-by. Entrance to the institute is gained via a large, blank (rather too blank) piazza separating the building from the Jussieu campus. It is here that the design raises to the sun its *pièce de résistance*, a 2,000 m^2 glass curtain wall which controls the amount of light entering the building by way of 27,000 photosensitive shutters, arranged in such a fashion as to evoke the patterns of Arabian *moucharebiya*. The effect is stunning, especially on the interior, which glitters and scintillates like a winking jewel. Costly to construct, the wall has proved equally costly to maintain, and the shutters frequently seize up.

On entering the building, one is struck by the lowness of the ceilings, a result of the planning authority's refusal to waive the local height restrictions, thereby forcing the architects literally to compress their design. Extensive use of double-height spaces alleviates the otherwise inevitable claustrophobia. The Hi-tech aesthetic is continued and, as outside, aluminium and glass dominate. Connecting the floors of the *médiathèque* is a free-standing concrete book-tower, visible through the transparent walls of the western façade, which spirals gratuitously but gloriously towards heaven like a latter-day Tower of Babel. Light is all-important, filtered through the criss-crossing layers of the staircase or the marble panels of the courtyard, rendering complex a structure which in plan is a model of simplicity and clarity. Indeed light is the key motif of this flawed but brilliant building, whose showbiz *éclat* and consequent media coverage put France firmly back in the architectural limelight.

5.14 Jardin des Plantes and Muséum d'Histoire Naturelle
Quai Saint-Bernard, Rue Buffon, Rue Geoffroy-Saint-Hilaire and Rue Cuvier
Various architects, founded 1626
(Métro: Gare d'Austerlitz, Jussieu)

Today one of the world's most venerable natural-history museums, this fascinating complex started out as the royal botanical gardens, founded in 1626 by Louis XIII for the cultivation of medicinal plants. Later in the *ancien régime* it came to include the Cabinet Royal d'Histoire Naturelle, whose collections consisted primarily of mineral samples. Today the Jardin des Plan-

5.14 Muséum d'Histoire Naturelle. Galerie d'Evolution

118 5th *arrondissement*

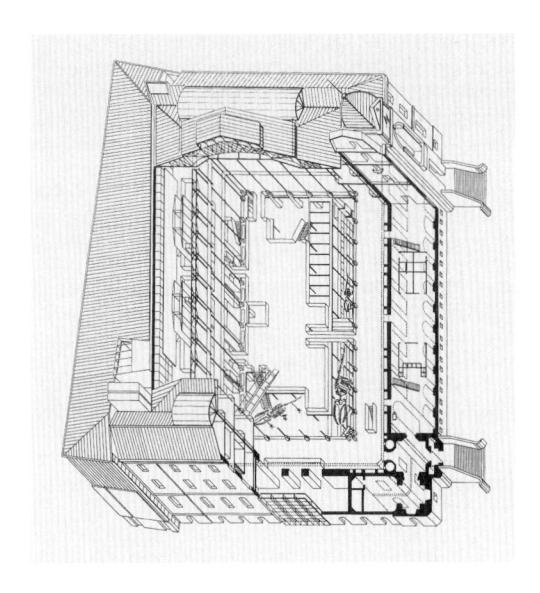

5.14 Muséum d'Histoire Naturelle. Axonometric view

tes contains over 10,000 species (the oldest specimen being a false acacia planted in 1636) in a variety of environments including formal, French-style parterres, a more naturalistic Alpine garden, a rosery, and tropical hothouses. The oldest surviving section is the yew-tree maze, originally created at the end of the 16C and enlarged to its current size by the celebrated naturalist Georges-Louis Leclerc, Comte de Buffon, who was *intendant* of the Jardin from 1739–88. It is crowned by a cast-iron gazebo erected by Edme Verniquet in 1787, which is almost certainly the earliest surviving all-metal construction in Paris.

In 1793, after the fall of the monarchy, the Muséum d'Histoire Naturelle was founded at the Jardin des Plantes by order of the Convention, part of its mission being to look after the neglected animals of the royal menagerie left behind at Versailles (see 32.1). Today the Ménagerie is Paris proper's only zoo (the city's principal zoo is out in the Bois de Vincennes – see 34.1), and it still conserves its original glass-roofed, brick-and-stone elephant house (*rotonde des éléphants*) built by Jacques Molinos in 1802–12. Later in the 19C the Muséum was enlarged by Charles Rohault de Fleury, who built the soberly Classical Galerie de Minéralogie (1833–38) running along the Rue Buffon, which takes the form internally of a 187 m-long, top-lit space lined with drawers and display cases. Fleury also rebuilt the glasshouses opposite on the other side of the formal garden, and planned to construct a Galerie de Zoologie at the head of the site on the Rue Geoffroy-Saint-Hilaire, between the mineralogy building and the glasshouses and at the culmination of the gardens' main axis, thereby symbolically putting the animal kingdom at the top of the hierarchical pile. He

never got to complete his plan, however, and it was Jules André, favourite pupil of Henri Labrouste, who built the zoology building we see today in 1877–89. André's rather flatly pompous stone façade facing the Seine, with its eclectic mix of mostly 17C-French references, affirms the building's institutional vocation but is otherwise unimpressive. Hiding behind this stolid exterior, however, is a minor wonder of 19C metal construction in the form of a three-storey-high, galleried, iron-framed exhibition hall, whose wide, all-glass roof stands on admirably slender colonnettes. Used to display the museum's collection of stuffed animals, the hall suffered from neglect post-WWII and had to be closed in the 1960s on public-safety grounds. It did not re-open again until 1994 after being transformed by the architects Paul Chemetov and Borja Huidobro, winners of a 1987 design competition, into today's splendid Galerie d'Evolution, realized in collaboration with the stage designer René Allio. Lovingly restored, André's structure has been left essentially as was, with supplementary space being gained by excavating the basement. The Galerie's *mise en scène*, very French in its deliberate, chic artificiality, makes liberal use of steel and glass and is especially *soignée* in its lighting, which includes a sky simulator that goes from dawn to dusk in 1 hour 40 minutes.

The 19C's last major addition to the Muséum was the Galerie de Paléontologie (on the Rue Buffon where it joins the Boulevard de l'Hôpital), built by Ferdinand Dutert in 1894/95. Dutert was one of the architects of the famous Galerie des Machines built for the 1889 Exposition Universelle (destroyed), whose 107 m width was covered in a single span by an iron-and-glass vault, a world record at the time. For the Galerie de Paléontologie, he designed an equally lean and elegant iron-and-glass hall, which is, however, belied by its eclectic brick-and-stone exterior, whose ponderous monumentality is in striking contrast.

6th *arrondissement*

6.1 Ecole Nationale Supérieure des Beaux-Arts
14, rue Bonaparte and 11–17, quai Malaquais
Extant buildings begun early-17C; various architects, chiefly Félix Duban, 1832–72
(Métro: Saint-Germain-des-Prés)

The Ecole des Beaux-Arts as we know it today has its origins in the Académie Royale de Peinture et de Sculpture, founded under Louis XIV in 1648. One of the academy's functions was the teaching of these disciplines, which were later joined, following the founding of the Académie Royale d'Architecture in 1671, by the *reine des arts* herself. As the official, state-created and state-sanctioned fine-arts institute in a highly centralized, absolute monarchy, the school and its parent academies held almost total sway over French artistic production. Students could compete for various prizes, the most prestigious of which was the Prix de Rome (created in 1663), whose winners were sent to the eternal city to study its artistic treasures. Even after the school gained independence from the academies, in 1863, the Prix de Rome continued, until the student uprising of May 1968 caused the whole *beaux-arts* education system to be called into question and subsequently reformed. The Prix de Rome was then abolished and the teaching of architecture at the school discontinued, new institutions being set up for this purpose in its stead. It would be hard to underestimate the Ecole des Beaux-Arts' importance in the history of French architecture, so great was its authority, especially in the 19C. The teaching methods and planning and design principles developed there came to constitute a doctrine of composition and building whose influence made itself felt well into the 20C, not only in France but all over the world.

In the aftermath of the French Revolution, the Ecole des Beaux-Arts was transferred to the Collège des Quatre-Nations (6.2), but was expulsed by Napoleon in 1805 and did not find a new home till 1816, when the emperor allotted it the buildings of the former Couvent des Petits-Augustins next door. Begun in the early-17C at the behest of Marguerite de Navarre, the convent was not particularly illustrious architecturally, but included two cloisters (the larger of which survives in modified form – see below), the small and simple Eglise des Petits-Augustins (begun in 1617 and to be found to the right of the school's entrance on the Rue Bonaparte), the domed, hexagonal Chapelle des Louanges (begun in 1608 and now attached to the church), and a large garden. The convent buildings had of course lost their religious vocation in the Revolution, but afterwards found another one that would go on to have a particular resonance for both the Ecole des Beaux-Arts as a physical object and the teaching of architecture there. In the 1790s, Alexandre Lenoir set up his Musée des Monuments Français in the convent, an institution that rescued sculptural and architectural fragments of buildings – chiefly churches and châteaux – destroyed either in whole or in part by Revolutionary vandalism. Amongst his collection were the frontispiece of the Château d'Anet (Philibert De l'Orme, *c.* 1545–50), part of the façade of the Château de Gaillon (architect unknown, *c.* 1508–10), and columns from the tomb of Anne de Montmorency (*c.* 1568). The convent's garden contained rescued funerary monuments and was consequently rebaptized the »Jardin Elysée«. Inside the museum, objects and sculpture were piled up willy-nilly in a Romantic gloom of picturesque eclecticism that probably had much of the aura still found today in the near contemporaneous Sir John Soane's Museum in London. This interest in national production of the Gothic and Renaissance eras went against the then academic canons which valued only Greek and Roman Antiquity and the Italian Renaissance, and both the Musée's collections and their *mise en scène* would influence a subsequent generation of artists and architects. After the institution's closure, some of its collections were returned to their original homes, while the remainder was inherited by the Ecole des Beaux-Arts.

Following Napoleon's decision to transfer the school to the convent, the architect François Debret was appointed to oversee conversion of the buildings for use by their new occupant. His principal intervention was

6.1 Ecole Nationale Supérieure des Beaux-Arts. Frontispiece of the Château d'Anet

to construct a large edifice known as the »Palais des Etudes« on the site of the former convent's garden, a monumental rectangular affair organized around an internal courtyard. Debret was also responsible for the Bâtiment des Loges (1820–29) to the south of the Palais des Etudes, which was built to house students. In 1832 he quit the Ecole des Beaux-Arts for the Abbaye de Saint-Denis (21.2), on whose restoration he was to work, and left the school in the hands of his pupil and brother-in-law Félix Duban, a holder of the institution's own Grand Prix de Rome. Duban would devote almost his entire career to the school until his death in 1872. His first and most significant intervention was to create a monumental entrance piazza in front of Debret's Palais des Etudes by demolishing all the structures that had hitherto separated it from the Rue Bonaparte: the houses fronting the street, the southern part of the larger cloister, which was thus considerably reduced in size, and the whole of the smaller cloister. He then used the fragments of building inherited by the school from the Musée des Monuments Français to turn his entrance piazza into an open-air museum of the history of French architecture. The centrepiece, around which the whole composition revolved, was the fragment of façade of the Château de Gaillon, which Duban set up in the manner of a free-standing triumphal arch in front of the Palais des Etudes, which latter he even raised by one storey so that it would be visible from the street above the Gaillon fragment. The Gaillon façade closed the first, narrower section of the piazza turning it into a sort of *avant-cour*; the part beyond it, in front of the Palais des Etudes, thus became the school's *cour d'honneur*. This division is now less demarcated than in Duban's day since, in the 1970s, the town of Gaillon reclaimed its heritage and the façade fragment went back to join the other parts of the château still standing *in situ*. Low walls in the school's piazza mark the spot where it once stood.

The Gaillon façade, which dated from the very beginning of the French Renaissance, was noteworthy for its sculpted decoration, the work of Italian craftsmen. Duban's insistence on giving it such a prominent place at the Ecole des Beaux-Arts went against the will of the authorities, especially the Conseil des Bâtiments Civils, which considered the Gaillon façade to be of little aesthetic or historical interest. Of the other architectural fragments with which Duban adorned the school, the most famous is the frontispiece of the Château d'Anet, still in place where the architect plonked it, on the gabled entrance elevation of the Eglise des Petits-Augustins. The château, part of which still stands *in situ*, was commissioned by Diane de Poitiers, mistress of the future Henri II, from Philibert De l'Orme, who became Henri's Surintendant des Bâtiments on his accession to the throne. De l'Orme's frontispiece, which consists of a three-storey superimposition of orders, marked an important step in the French context towards greater »Classicization« of architecture. In contrast to previous French efforts, his orders were con-

6.1 Ecole Nationale Supérieure des Beaux-Arts. Palais des Etudes

siderably more archaeologically correct, and their superimposition was effected in the »right« order as advocated by Italian theorists (based on the Colosseum in Rome). There is of course something rather pathetic about the Anet frontispiece's current situation, pinned to the wall of the church like some desiccated insect. In the interest of symmetry, Duban built another gable front directly opposite on the other side of the courtyard, which he hoped to fill with a rescued church front of suitable worth. Unfortunately (or perhaps fortunately if you take the side of the hypothetical church façade), no candidates were ever found. On the blank walls of the courtyard beyond the gables, Duban erected stone arcades that were intended to harmonize with the applied Renaissance architectural fragments and which also served as a frame for rescued sculpted elements, such as those from the Hôtel Le Gendre (or de La Trémoille) mounted on the southern side (*c*. 1500).

Through this *mise en scène* of architectural fragments, Duban turned the entrance courtyards into a sort of *via sacra* along which the visitor passed both in space and in time (the history of architecture) before reaching the Palais des Etudes, which Duban made into a museum of the visual arts where the school's collections of paintings and plaster casts were displayed. As well as raising Debret's structure by one storey, he dressed it up as a quattrocento Florentine palace and later, in 1863, covered its galleried, central courtyard with a very elegant iron-and-glass roof supported on slender, Classically moulded iron columns. It was at this time that the courtyard received its splendid Italian-Renaissance-inspired polychromatic décor and that its first-floor, entrance-façade gallery was converted by Duban to house the school's library, all of whose furnishings and fittings were designed by the architect himself. As of 1874 the covered courtyard became home to the Academies' outstanding collection of plaster mouldings of Classical statues and architecture, which included a full-size corner of the Parthenon (following the upheavals of 1968 the collection was moved to the Petites Ecuries at Versailles – see 32.6). To the west of the courtyard and terminating the *via sacra* of the entrance piazza is the Hémicycle d'Honneur, a semicircular auditorium where the school's prizes were presented. It is decorated with an enormous painting by Paul Delaroche depicting *La Renommée distribuant des couronnes* (completed 1841).

As we have seen, the creation of the school's entrance courtyards necessitated the partial rebuilding of the former convent's larger cloister, which Duban turned into a sort of Roman-style arcaded atrium painted in »Pompeian« colours and decorated with copies of Classical statues. These latter were intended to ensure students' instruction even while they were at leisure in the cloister's leafy shade. This sylvan penumbra was due to the fact that Alexandre Lenoir had planted a Chinese mulberry tree in the cloister, which is today consequently known as the Cour du Mûrier. As for the other significant surviving part of the convent, the Eglise des Petits-Augustins, it is now home to the school's collection of plaster casts of sculpture and copies of paintings. During the 1850s, in need of supplementary accommodation, the school bought the plot to the north of the Cour des Mûriers on the quayside, where Duban erected the Bâtiment des Expositions (1858–62). Conceived for exhibiting students' work, it was built with an iron frame which allowed for the ample glazing we see on its northern, quayside façade, necessary to admit sufficient quantities of cool, steady light by which to view the works displayed (today, of course, the windows tend to be blocked in favour of artificial lighting). The quayside façade was criticized by contemporaries as appearing too »industrial« and austere, despite its monumental stone cladding and carved dormers, which are a quote from and reference to the Louvre (1.8) opposite on the Right Bank. The building's principal hall lies behind the quayside galleries and is a top-lit, double-height volume. In 1884, still in search of extra space, the school acquired the neighbouring Hôtel de Chimay, which stands at nos. 15–17, quai Malaquais. Built in 1740–56 by François Debias-Aubry for the Duc de Bouillon, it is of classic Parisian *hôtel* design, with a *cour d'honneur* built up on three sides on the quayside and closed by a colonnaded screen, while the handsome garden front displays the typical French division into *arrière-corps* flanked by lateral pavilions and adorned with a central, pedimented *avant-corps*. The *hôtel*'s interior was almost entirely gutted by the school for the installation of artists' studios. Between its garden front and the Palais des Etudes is the charming Jardin Lenoir, created in memory of the Musée des Monuments Français and home to, amongst others, the ground-floor arcade of the Hôtel du Faur (or de Torpanne), which was built in the Marais around 1567, and the columns of the Montmorency tomb. The most recent structure to be found at the school – the slab block of studios standing between the Hôtel de Chimay and the Bâtiment des Expositions – dates from 1945–47 and is by Auguste Perret.

6.2 Institut de France (former Collège des Quatre-Nations)
21, quai de Conti
Louis Le Vau, 1662–70; François d'Orbay, 1670–88
(Métro: Louvre-Rivoli, Pont-Neuf, Mabillon)

Following the deaths of Cardinal Richelieu and Louis XIII (in 1642 and 1643 respectively), and thanks to his intimate relationship with Anne of Austria (mother of Louis XIV), Cardinal Mazarin (1602–61) rose to become virtual ruler of France, a position he retained throughout the Sun King's minority. He was also one of the country's wealthiest men, and directed in his will that part of his great fortune be used for the foundation of a boys' college giving scholarships to pupils from the »four nations« – a term then used to describe territories recently acquired by France – as well as taking paying students. The college's chapel was, moreover, to serve as Mazarin's mausoleum, and he also left his considerable library (today's Bibliothèque Mazarine) to the institution. Jean-Baptiste Colbert, who had been the brain behind Mazarin's wealth and who subsequently became Louis XIV's chief minister, was one of the five executors of the will, and he manœuvred to get the college built, appointing Le Vau as architect. The latter, who was at that time working on the Cour Carrée and south front of the Louvre (1.8), proposed building the college opposite the new sections of the palace, on the other side of the river, thereby providing the king with an agreeable view from his future apartments. Drawn up with great alacrity, Le Vau's plans were pronounced »fort beau« by the sovereign, and building work began. Progress was slow but, by the time of Le Vau's death in 1670, the carcass was virtually complete. Le Vau's draughtsman, François d'Orbay, continued the work, and the college finally opened in 1688.

Inevitably, the institution was closed down at the Revolution, and its buildings served briefly as a prison and as the headquarters of the Comité du Salut-Public before being given over to the Ecole des Beaux-Arts (see 6.1). It was at this point that the Pont des Arts (see feature on Seine bridges), linking the Louvre to the college, was built, thereby realizing Le Vau's initial intention which had been to unite his Louvre and college façades as one monumental ensemble. The light, iron structure of the Pont des Arts was a far cry from the heavy, stone construction imagined by Le Vau, however. In 1805, Napoleon decreed that the Institut de France be transferred to the college, and the architect Antoine Vaudoyer was charged with converting the buildings. His interventions included a thorough remodelling of the chapel, in which a false ceiling and tribune galleries were installed to convert it for use as the Institut's assembly hall. It was only in 1961/62, as part of a general restoration programme, that the chapel regained more or less its original aspect.

Le Vau's design is one of the few by a 17C French architect to have been tangibly influenced by Roman Baroque. Although the river frontage is perfectly symmetrical, one soon realizes on gaining the rear of the building that the site is in fact highly irregular, pared away by the Rues Mazarine and de Seine and consisting of a very long, narrow plot of land departing at an oblique to the river frontage. The working college thus shelters behind a façade that is essentially a spectacular stage set. At its centre is the chapel, in the axis of the Louvre opposite, fronted by a full-height pedimented portico and surmounted by an imposing circular drum crowned with a dome. Long, curved, full-height wings stretch out either side of the chapel, forming a semicircular piazza in front of the college, which is prolonged by the two rectangular pavilions that terminate the composition at either extremity. The pavilions are coiffed with lofty French-style roofs that punctuate the façade and counterbalance to a certain extent the central vertical of the drum and dome. The result recalls the work of Pietro da Cortona and Borromini – especially the façade of the latter's Sant'Agnese in Agone (begun 1653) in Rome – and, although less exuberant than Italian buildings of the period, is a good deal warmer and more charming than most contemporary French realizations (the east and south fronts of the Louvre opposite – 1668–78, chiefly the work of Claude Perrault – make for an especially striking contrast). The delight of Le Vau's river front lies in its human scale, in the extravagant use of curves and in the picturesque massing and detailing. The double projection of the chapel façade and the transition of its giant Corinthian order from round to square columns and then to engaged pilasters, as well as their syncopated grouping, constitute a highly accomplished handling of Baroque devices. The giant order is repeated, in shallow-pilaster form, on the end pavilions, while the curved wings carry Corinthian pilasters at first-floor level and an Ionic order on the ground floor. True to hierarchy, the drum is cadenced by twinned Composite pilasters. Its huge arched windows are echoed by the continuous arcades running along the ground floor, interrupted only by the chapel façades. Filled in the 19C with doors and windows, the arcades were originally open and let out as shops. Aside from its luxuriant capitals, the river front is also decorated with various bas-relief carvings, including the elaborate allegorical representation of the Institut de France under the portico (realized in the early-19C, the original sculptures having been destroyed during the Revolution), as well as the flamboyant urns topping the cornices of the lateral pavilions. These urns were originally complemented on the chapel's attic by statues of evangelists and churchmen, all of which have since disappeared.

The college is entered via a doorway at the centre of its eastern wing, which leads into the *cour d'honneur*, whose axis is at 45° to that of the chapel. Oblique elevations in the courtyard's lateral extremities cleverly ensure a regular form (in the event an elongated octagon) while avoiding the necessity of adding an irregular extension to the chapel's side façade. In comparison to the richness of the river front, the courtyard is a simple, almost austere space – as was considered befitting for a college – animated only by two pedimented, pilastered porticos situated opposite each other at the furthest extremities of the octagon. The easternmost portico accesses the Bibliothèque Mazarine, while its western counterpart leads into the chapel. To the southeast of the *cour d'honneur* is a second, very long courtyard, flanked on its western side by an undistinguished building which originally housed the college schoolrooms and dorms, and which fronts the Rue Mazarine on its other side. This second courtyard was originally much bigger (the buildings on its eastern side date from the 19C) and served as the college's recreation area. A small third courtyard prolongs the college even further to the southeast.

Entry to the chapel is gained from the *cour d'honneur*, the river-façade entrance today being used only for visits to the Institut by the French president. Symmetrical about its longitudinal axis, the chapel is divided into three: a generous vestibule behind the river entrance; the main »nave«, which leads off the vestibule and which is surmounted by the drum and dome and flanked by six small side-chapels, three on either side; and finally the chancel, which is coiffed with its own smaller dome and also flanked by side-chapels, through one of which one enters the chapel. The niche at the rear of the choir, where a statue of Napoleon

6.2 Institut de France (former Collège des Quatre-Nations)

now stands, formerly contained the high altar. On entering the nave, one is surprised to discover that although externally the drum and dome are round, inside they, and also consequently the nave, are elliptical in plan, a Baroque trick that had the practical advantage of allowing staircases to be installed inside the wider parts of the drum to access the interior spaces of the dome and its lantern balcony. Ellipses seem to have been something of a leitmotiv in Le Vau's œuvre, for it was he who introduced the oval salon into France (see Vaux-le-Vicomte (37.1)). Furthermore, where externally the drum is pierced by arched windows, its internal elevation presents alternate arched and straight-headed windows. Despite its soaring verticals, the chapel's interior seems rather constricted, due to the compartmentalization of its spaces and the fact that the nave's oblique elevations are closed, so that the gaze has only the narrow archway leading to the chancel through which to travel, before halting abruptly at the altar niche. The chapel's decoration is sharp and rich, although monochrome, bar the punctuating presence of white-veined, red-marble columns in the arcades adorning the chancel, side-chapels and vestibule. Its domes are bare, the paintings planned for them never having been executed.

The centre of the nave is today occupied by a sunken amphitheatre, used for the Institut's assemblies, but was originally intended by Le Vau to receive Mazarin's tomb. Commissioned in 1689, the cardinal's effigy, which was designed by Jules Hardouin-Mansart, was in fact installed in the chancel's western side-chapel, thus terminating the vista leading from the chapel's courtyard entrance. Despite its quality, the tomb seems something of an afterthought, and certainly not the Baroque spectacle that Le Vau presumably envisaged.

6.3 Hôtel des Monnaies
11, quai de Conti
Jacques-Denis Antoine, 1767–75
(Métro: Pont Neuf, Mabillon)

Universally admired when completed, the Hôtel des Monnaies (royal mint) is a fine example of the rational neo-Classicism of the Enlightenment period, and was the building that launched Antoine's international career. The old mint having long since outgrown its cramped home, a new building was commissioned, in 1766, for the Place de la Concorde (8.1), then under construction. Antoine had already drawn up plans (in collaboration with Ange-Jacques Gabriel, designer of the square's palace-front façades) when the original project was cancelled and the current site, nearer the business district, selected. Instead of a mere »factory« squeezed behind somebody else's elevations, Antoine now had the chance to design an entire, monumental edifice on a prime riverside location next to Le Vau's Collège des Quatre-Nations (6.2).

Inversing French tradition, which tended to preface the »noble« parts of a great building with a cour d'honneur surrounded by structures of a lower, service-related nature, Antoine placed the principal wing containing the offices and appartements d'honneur directly on the Seine, thus making the most of the prestigious site. Behind this enormous block, which rises three very tall storeys and extends across a frontage of 117 m, shelter the minting workshops, ingeniously disposed around several courtyards to overcome the site's irregular contours. The river frontage was an extraordinary composition for its time, its originality stemming from the challenge of creating a suitable image for a building of hybrid rank. Essentially a factory, and therefore unworthy of palatial décor, the mint nonetheless had to express the power and prestige of the state it served. Partially inspired by some of Gabriel's more sober designs (e.g. the Ecole Militaire (7.9)), the river front is so austerely decorated over most of its surface – window surrounds, ground-floor rustication, bracketed balconies every third window at first-floor level – that only the hierarchical proportioning of the floors provides any animation. The extreme horizontal emphasis that results is partly contradicted and partly reinforced by a five-bay, central avant-corps which, in the absence of the usual lateral pavilions, is the sole element interrupting the façade's linearity. Its colossal Ionic columns are topped off, probably for the first time in France, not by a pediment but by a squat attic storey that reaffirms the building's horizontality, aided by an exaggeratedly large cornice whose proportions are in fact incorrect for the order it coiffs. The impressively solemn result is of Roman grandeur, although contemporary commentators considered it too »luxurious«, preferring the more modest Rue-Guénégaud façade, which is entirely rusticated in keeping with the fortress aspect reserved for buildings where money was stored. Antoine's plans to rebuild the quayside as a monumental, heavily rusticated bastion – thus making the river the mint's moat – were sadly never realized.

Inside the river wing, the Romanizing vestibule with its Doric columns and coffered barrel vaults is noteworthy, as is the very grand but rather cold escalier d'honneur, which leads up to the Cabinet de l'Ecole des

6.3 Hôtel des Monnaies

Mines on the first floor. This two-storey-high chamber, situated at the river wing's centre, originally served as the mint's council room and is consequently lavishly decorated, again in a Romanizing manner, with Corinthian columns, *trompe-l'œil* coffering and myriad mouldings. It is also architectonically inventive, its upper storey signalled by a balcony above which rises a shallow dome with domed semi-rotundas at each corner. Behind the river wing, in the axis of the main entrance, is the *cour d'honneur*, which presents a similar aspect to the Rue-Guénégaud elevation and appears charmingly intimate after the hugeness of the river façade. The change of scale is acknowledged on the river-wing courtyard front by the shallow pediment containing a clock that adorns this side of the projecting attic. The entrance axis continues into the main minting hall, a curious chamber whose southern extremity takes the form of a domed, semicircular apse shielding a statue of Fortune, giving the hall the air of a religious sanctuary, like some secret temple of mammon.

6.4 Saint-Germain-des-Prés
Place Saint-Germain-des-Prés
Architects unknown, earliest extant buildings begun c. 1000
(Métro: Saint-Germain-des-Prés)

This ancient structure, today a mere parish church standing alone in the cityscape, was originally the linchpin of an important abbey complex founded by King Childebert in the 540s. Legend has it that following an expedition against the Visigoths in Spain, Childebert came back with two important relics – the tunic of Saint Vincent of Saragoss and a silver reliquary designed to hold a fragment of the True Cross –, and created the Abbaye Sainte-Croix-Saint-Vincent, as it was then called, to house them. Childebert was buried in the abbey church, as was, in 576, the man he had appointed as bishop of Paris, Germanus (French »Germain«), who was later canonized. By the mid-8C the abbey had taken on the local saint's name, with the suffix »des prés« indicating that it was out in the meadows beyond the city limits. Although nothing now survives of the 6C church, its spirit lives on in the plan of today's building, the current crossing occupying the position of the original, the main vessels of the nave and the choir being the same width as the 6C chancel, the porch-tower marking the limits of the first nave, and the transepts having Merovingian foundations.

Sometime around the year 1000, the Abbot Morard (in office 990–1014) built what is now the oldest part of the church, the porch-tower at the west end. Solidly constructed and heavily buttressed, it features a chapel above its entrance porch, which, until the installation of today's organ, opened onto the nave. The arcaded belfry coiffing the tower is later, probably dating from the 12C. Also from this latter period (*c.* 1160) is the tower's entrance portal, which originally adorned the church's southern flank until it was moved here in the

6.4 Saint-Germain-des-Prés

17C. At the Revolution its statues were destroyed and the saints on its lintel decapitated. Abbot Morard was probably also responsible for the two flanking towers nestling between the choir and the transepts, an arrangement that was unusual in the Ile-de-France but which recalled German Rhineland practice. The towers' arcaded upper storeys, which had become unsafe, were taken down by Etienne-Hippolyte Godde during his restoration campaign of 1819–25. To the south of the entrance tower is the rectangular Chapelle Saint-Symphorien, again probably the work of Abbot Morard, which replaced a Merovingian funerary chapel where Saint Germain was initially buried.

Sometime later in the 11C, after Morard's interventions, Saint-Germain's nave was rebuilt. It is difficult to date with any precision, but was probably realized under Abbot Guillaume de Volpiano around 1025–30. Unlike the thick, rubble-stone walls of most French Romanesque churches of this size, Saint-Germain's nave elevations are built of thin ashlar, a phenomenon explained by the fact that the nave originally had a flat wooden roof and hence did not need massive walls capable of supporting vaulting. The vaults we see today were added by Christophe Gamard in 1644–46 and were designed to match the 12C vaulting of the choir (see below). Saint-Germain's nave elevations are very simple, comprising a round-headed arcade surmounted by a tall, blank wall pierced with generous clerestory windows set high above the aisle roofs. Semi-engaged buttressing shafts run up the wall between each bay (their capitals are 17C), an unusual feature for an era when horizontal rather than vertical emphasis in nave-elevation design was the norm. The large areas of blank wall would have been painted with some kind of decoration from the outset; the murals we see today were realized in the 19C, and include religious scenes by Hippolyte Flandrin. By far the most remarkable feature of the nave is its fine set of historiated capitals, whose iconography is most unusual and whose quality of carving, although mixed, testifies to the renewal of stone-sculpting techniques in this period. During the 19C restoration campaigns, twelve of the original capitals in the nave were moved to the Musée de Cluny (see 5.4) and replaced by copies.

Like the nave, the crossing and its transepts are difficult to date. They are almost certainly 11C and were realized after Morard's interventions but not at the same time as the nave. Their vaulting and large end windows are 17C. The early-Gothic choir was built at the behest of Abbot Hugues III in the 1140s to replace the old Merovingian structure which was then still standing. It was begun shortly after completion of Abbot Suger's choir at Saint-Denis (21.2), and is a simplified version of the latter. Saint-Germain's choir comprises the by-then classic apse-ambulatory-with-radiating chapels organization, a high quadripartite rib vault and typically early-Gothic piers made up of heavy, squat columns whose capitals are the point of departure for composite shafts. It appears more modern than the later Notre-Dame (4.2) because in place of the traditional tribune galleries it has a triforium opening onto the aisle attics, an arrangement that would become standard in High-Gothic churches. Today it appears even more High Gothic than when initially built because its clerestory windows were lengthened in the 17C (something of the original arrangement can still be seen in the first bay of the choir after the crossing, where the flanking towers rose). The marble colonnettes decorating the triforium are Merovingian and were almost certainly re-used from the original, 6C choir. In one respect Saint-Germain's new choir appears archaic in comparison to that at Saint-Denis, in that its radiating chapels are built as separate, agglomerated units rather than being fused together to form what, at Saint-Denis, almost becomes a second ambulatory. It has been suggested that this seemingly retrograde feature was deliberate and was introduced so as to provide a suitably solid base for the choir's heavy flying buttresses, which otherwise would have been very deep and hence possibly unstable.

In the 1630s the abbey became the headquarters of the order of Saint-Maur, and considerable building work was carried out at the church to make it suitable for its new occupants. Although the Maurists interventions were often harmful from an archaeological point of view, they were at least carried out with respect for the spirit of the original buildings, something that was very rare for the period. As well as the vaulting of the nave and the transformations carried out to the choir windows and the crossing that we have already mentioned, they built the Chapelle Sainte-Marguerite in the right arm of the crossing (thereby demolishing its original apsoidal ending), with capitals imitating the style of those in the nave aisles. The extremely mannered southern entrance portal also dates from this time.

At its dissolution in 1790, the Abbaye de Saint-Germain-des-Prés covered almost the entire city block delineated by today's Boulevard Saint-Germain, Rue Jacob, Rue Saint-Benoît and Rue de l'Echaudé. The Revolutionary regime installed a saltpetre refinery in the complex, and the consequent and numerous accidental explosions resulted in the eventual destruction of most of the abbey buildings and nearly got the better of the church itself (it was the shockwaves of the explosions that weakened the choir/transept towers and made the demolition of their upper storeys necessary). Today, all that remain of significance are the northern side of the 17C cloister running along the church's southern flank and the handsome Palais Abbatial, at 1–5, rue de l'Abbaye, which was the residence of Saint-Germain's abbots. Built by Guillaume Marchand in 1586 for the then abbot, Cardinal Charles de Bourbon, the brick and stone Palais displays a Mannerist penchant for grotesquely inflated, cornice-breaking quoins. A later occupant, Cardinal Egon de Fürstenberg, added a new staircase to the Palais and rebuilt its stables to the north (c. 1699), whose courtyard survives as today's Place de Furstemberg.

6.5 Saint-Sulpice
Place Saint-Sulpice
Various architects, chiefly Daniel Gittard and Giovanni Niccolò Servandoni, begun 1646
(Métro: Saint-Sulpice)

Following the rapid expansion of the parish of Saint-Germain in the early-17C, the 12C parish church of Saint-Sulpice became woefully inadequate and, despite several extensions, was condemned to destruction so that a new, bigger edifice could take its place. A design was produced by the *architecte voyer* of Saint-Germain, Christophe Gamard, in 1636, construction of which began ten years later. But the political upheavals of the Fronde slowed work down to such an extent that by the late 1650s only the Lady Chapel was standing. In 1655, Louis Le Vau proposed a new design – an enlarged version of Gamard's plan –, but it was Daniel Gittard who, in 1660, produced the scheme that would be adhered to over the church's long building period, essentially a reworking of the Gamard-Le Vau plan. By 1678, when work stopped again due to lack of funds, the choir and part of the crossing were complete; construction started again in 1719, the nave being completed in 1736 and the church finally being consecrated in 1745.

In plan, Saint-Sulpice, like so many Parisian parish churches, is based on Notre-Dame (4.2). It is also typical of French 17C church design in that it is a Classical adaptation of traditional Gothic structures. Viollet-le-Duc, in his *Paris-Guide* (1867), attacked it for precisely this, bemoaning the fact that the Classical barrel vault exerted pressure all along its length and consequently necessitated enormous, resource-wasting and view-obstructing piers, for him a stupid anomaly in comparison to the structurally lean churches of properly Gothic design. That said, Saint-Sulpice is handsome, its cathedral-like proportions set off by a crisply carved Corinthian order and its generous clerestory flooding the interior with light. Externally, on all but its western elevations, the church displays essentially workaday façades that are the logical product of its interior structure.

In 1732 a competition was launched for Saint-Sulpice's west front, which was won by the Florentine-born Giovanni Niccolò Servandoni, who had already rebuilt the church's Lady Chapel in 1729 (its sumptuously theatrical, Baroque interior is later, however, by Charles de Wailly (1774)). It was not to his Italian homeland that Servandoni turned for inspiration but to London, his west-front proposal being a reworking of the entrance façade of Wren's Saint Paul's Cathedral. The splendid and, in the Parisian context, highly unusual result comprises two superimposed colonnades

6.5 Saint-Sulpice

flanked by side towers – a configuration derived from Gothic cathedrals – and entirely screens the 17C church behind it. Servandoni's original design was even closer to Saint Paul's than today's façade, with elaborate belvederes coiffing the towers' drums and a monumental pediment crowning the upper colonnade. The pediment was in fact built but was dismantled after being struck by lightning in 1770, a happy event for its Classically correct critics who deplored the fact that, unlike at Saint Paul's, its dimensions were based on those of the entire front (i.e. as if it were supported by a non-existent giant order) and not on those of the upper colonnade on which it stood. Without its pediment and belvederes the west façade is much more augustly Roman than Servandoni's initial design and is also closer in spirit to that touchstone of French Classicism, the Louvre's east front (see 1.8). Unfinished on Servandoni's death in 1766, Saint-Sulpice's entrance front was continued by the obscure Oudot de Maclaurin, who built the (still-uncompleted) south tower to Servandoni's design, while the north tower (1777–80) was erected by Servandoni's pupil, Jean-François Chalgrin. Chalgrin modified his master's scheme, producing a less Baroque and more squarely Classical result, but was thwarted in his plans to rebuild the south tower with the coming of the Revolution. He also designed the church's august organ casing.

The Place Saint-Sulpice was begun in 1752 by Servandoni, who had planned a regular, semicircular backdrop to the church. All he managed to complete was his own house at no. 6. The fountain decorating the square's centre is by Ludovico Visconti and dates from 1843–48.

6.6 Ecole de Chirurgie
12, rue de l'Ecole-de-Médicine
Jacques Gondoin, 1769–86
(Métro: Odéon)

In its day this fine example of Enlightenment-period neo-Classicism was one of the most talked-about buildings in French architectural circles, heralded by many as the first example of a »new wave« in French architecture that, eschewing national tradition, sought renewal in a study of Antiquity. It was designed by a man who, although trained in architecture and sent to Rome by the Academy, had built nothing to date. Indeed the Ecole de Chirurgie (school of surgery) would remain Gondoin's single major building, the only other architectural projects he is definitely known to have worked on being the Colonne Vendôme (see 1.13) and the rebuilding of the Palais de Justice (1.1). For many years he held the post of Inspecteur des Meubles de la Couronne, designing furniture for Marie-Antoinette and the royal household.

At the beginning of the 18C, many in France still considered surgery the preserve of barbers, but as the century wore on the discipline grew in prestige, a royal academy of surgery being founded in the 1730s. Under pressure from his Premier Chirurgien, Germain de

6.6 Ecole de Chirurgie

La Martinière, Louis XV gave the go ahead for a new school of surgery to be built in the Rue de l'Ecole-de-Médecine, just up the road from the old, 17C home of the former Confrérie des Chirurgiens (whose circular, domed anatomy theatre, designed by Charles and Louis Joubert in 1691–95, still stands at no. 5). As well as a new anatomy theatre, the school was to include lecture chambers, laboratories and a small hospital ward. Gondoin organized his building in the manner of an *hôtel particulier* around a *cour d'honneur* – which allowed him to mask the irregularity of the plot –, with the anatomy theatre occupying the place of honour at the rear of the site, where the *corps de logis* of an *hôtel* would have stood. What was novel about his design was not its configuration, however, but the architectonic treatment of the different parts. Externally the most striking element was the screen running along the street, comprising a flat-topped upper floor sitting on an open, Ionic colonnade whose entablature lacks its architrave, producing a virile effect that went against all the established orthodoxies of ideal beauty. Contemporaries were furthermore astonished to see such a straight, horizontal composition entirely without the usual French division into lateral pavilions, *arrière-corps* and central *avant-corps*. The multiplication of columns was also novel, the colonnade being continued all around the courtyard and the anatomy theatre being signalled by a Corinthian portico. As »a monument to the beneficence of the King«, wrote Gondoin, the school »should have the character of magnificence relative to its function; a school whose fame attracts a great concourse of Pupils from all nations should appear open and easy of access. The absolute necessity of columns to fulfil these two objects is alone sufficient to protect me from the reproach of having multiplied them unduly.« Others were not convinced, the author Louis-Sébastien Mercier, for example, complaining in his *Tableau de Paris* (1781–88) that modern buildings all resembled one another behind their proliferation of columns, and reproaching Gondoin for having hidden his anatomy theatre behind a colonnade.

If the columns received mixed press, the anatomy theatre did not, being almost universally praised. Gondoin's stroke of inspiration was to combine the form of an Antique amphitheatre with an open dome derived from the Pantheon, thereby producing a top-lit space that allowed everyone a clear view under abundant natural light. The drama of the theatre's Euclidean volumes and coffered dome is perhaps not surprising from a man who counted Piranesi amongst his friends. Such was the theatre's impact on contemporaries that its basic form was much copied in the post-Revolutionary period, most notably at the Assemblée Nationale (7.4) and the Sénat (6.8). In the end though, the school would not prove as influential as its contemporary admirers believed, technological advances providing the real architectural revolution in the century to come.

6.7 Théâtre and Place de l'Odéon
Marie-Joseph Peyre and Charles De Wailly, 1767–89
(Métro: Odéon)

Squeezed into a tiny and rather primitive theatre that had been their home since 1689, the actors of the Comédie-Française were badly in need of a new venue by the time Louis XV got round to commissioning one, in 1767. It would be another 16 years, however, before they actually took up residence in their new theatre, due to a whole series of events, both political and administrative, that retarded its construction. Peyre and De Wailly had been commissioned at the outset to build the new theatre on the site of the demolished Hôtel de Condé; following various changes of site and of architect (construction of a rival scheme was even begun, in 1774), their initial proposal, albeit in slightly modified form, finally won out. The theatre was begun in 1779 and inaugurated by Marie-Antoinette in 1782, the piazza and housing that constituted the remainder of the Hôtel-de-Condé redevelopment scheme being finished by 1789. Today's theatre is not exactly as Peyre and De Wailly intended since it was rebuilt twice following two fires, one in 1799, after which Jean-François Chalgrin saw to the reconstruction, and another in 1818, whose damage was repaired by Chalgrin's successor, Baraguey.

The Odéon has a very special place in the history of Parisian theatres because it was the first to be treated as a free-standing monument in the cityscape. Parisian playhouses had formerly been squeezed into party-wall sites just like any other construction in the capital's narrow, densely built streets, and were hidden behind façades barely distinguishable from the residential buildings flanking them. How different then was the Odéon, conceived as the jewel in the crown of a prestigious urban redevelopment scheme and benefiting from an island site and a specially conceived piazza designed to show it off to best effect. In this Enlightenment age, beauty was ideally combined with utility, and the island site had the practical advantages of facilitating access for the public, actors and technicians, and also of isolating a fire-prone building type from neighbouring constructions. Five streets radiate out from the semicircular Place de l'Odéon, between which are plain-fronted, uniform apartment blocks with high, rusticated bases containing boutiques, the whole forming a suitably monumental backdrop for the playhouse. The *place* is conceived rather like an urban, Antique-style theatre, with the Odéon itself as the *scaena frons* and its entrance portico providing a covered stage for arriving and departing playgoers.

Occupying the place of honour in this composition, the Théâtre de l'Odéon is dressed up as a temple of thespianism. A heavily rusticated, rectangular box, its Palladio-inspired principal façade has a Tuscan portico, an order which, according to the architects, was the one most representative of Apollo, god of the arts. Originally, one enormous hipped roof covered the whole of the theatre, encompassing the fly-tower within its bulk, but Chalgrin's reconstruction gave the building its current, twin-roofed covering with a terrace terminating the principal façade. Inside, the theatre aimed to be just as revolutionary as outside. This was an age when French drama took on greater naturalism, and the architects made their Italian-style, oval auditorium deliberately shallow in comparison to the old Comédie Française so as to bring the public closer to the action. The Odéon was also one of the first French theatres to feature seating in the stalls, a *nouveauté* that was hotly contested at the time. Although many complained that the auditorium's oval form allowed only partial views of the stage from its sides, it did afford the audience very good views of each other, an important aspect of the social spectacle of 18C theatre. With this in mind, Peyre and De Wailly also conceived a generous, two-level foyer organized around an open central gallery, an arrangement that allowed for multiple perspectives between the crowd. Today the Théâtre de l'Odéon – in any case much reconfigured since it first opened – hardly seems exceptional, but at the time it was a dramatic pioneer.

6.8 Palais du Luxembourg (Sénat)
15, rue de Vaugirard
Salomon de Brosse *et al.*, 1615–45; Jean-François Chalgrin, 1799–1805; Alphonse de Gisors, 1835–56
(Métro: Rennes, Odéon; RER: Luxembourg)

Daughter of the Grand Duke of Tuscany, Marie de Médicis became queen consort of France on her marriage to Henri IV in 1600, but, on his death ten years

6.7 Théâtre de l'Odéon

6.8 Palais du Luxembourg (Sénat)

later, acceded to the much more powerful position of regent (her son, Louis XIII, being only nine at the time). As a mark of her newly found independence, and in order to leave the Louvre (1.8) for which she had little affection, Marie decided to build herself a brand-new, made-to-measure palace, a move that was perhaps also intended to consolidate her hold on power, building being the time-honoured way of expressing the solidity of one's place in society. The queen regent had never forgotten her Florentine homeland, and asked her aunt to send her plans of the Palazzo Pitti (various architects including Bartolomeo Ammannati, 1458 onwards), on which she intended to model her new home. Impatient for results, however, she sent an architect (probably Louis Métezeau) to Florence only eight days after writing to her aunt, charging him with the commission of bringing back detailed drawings of the Pitti. Marie's alacrity would nevertheless be thwarted by the Parisian property market, four years going by before she managed to assemble the necessary quantity of land, on the southern edge of the city, for the creation of château and garden. In the end, it was not Marie's Florentine envoy who built her new palace but Salomon de Brosse, who had already worked for her on the Château de Montceaux. He would not see the work completed, though, and nor would she. Following a dispute with Marie over pay and deadlines, De Brosse was sacked from the project in 1624 (construction was continued by his master mason) and died two years later in 1626. As for Marie, her political machinations eventually resulted in her being exiled from France by her own son, Louis XIII, in 1631, with her palace still unfinished. Curiously, it is not her name that has stuck to the building but that of a certain François de Luxembourg, one-time owner of the adjoining *hôtel particulier* (6.9) that today forms part of the Sénat complex.

The generous plot of land assembled by the queen regent meant that, unencumbered by neighbouring constructions, the Palais du Luxembourg could spread out as it pleased, a first for a royal palace in the urban context of Paris. What Marie had initially asked for was a Florentine palazzo; what she actually got was a French château dressed up in rustication vaguely inspired by the Pitti. De Brosse's plan was thoroughly French, of a type already current a century earlier (see, e.g., the Château d'Ecouen (23.1)) and directly descended from the fortresses of the medieval era. Organized around a rectangular courtyard, it comprises a principal *corps de logis* opposite the entrance, with substantial side wings running up to the entrance front, which latter is closed by a one-storey-high screen (whose current windows are later additions) interrupted at its centre by a monumental, three-storey gateway. On the building's outer corners, which in a castle would have been marked by bastions, we find large,

130 6th *arrondissement*

square pavilions. Despite its inherent conservatism, De Brosse's plan did include some innovation. His *corps de logis* was treated as separate and hierarchically superior to the lateral wings, whose subordination was expressed in their lower height and by the fact that the *logis* had pavilions on its inner as well as outer corners, bringing the total number of pavilions to six in place of the usual four (following subsequent modifications there are now eight – see below). This arrangement had the advantage of allowing discrete apartments to be installed in each of the *logis*'s pavilions, but had the disadvantage, from a Classicist's point of view, of producing asymmetrical lateral elevations. Although in his *hôtels particuliers* De Brosse had been known for placing his staircases in side wings to allow an uninterrupted suite of rooms in the *logis*, at the Palais de Luxembourg he resorted to the traditional arrangement, with a central *escalier d'honneur* cutting the *logis* in two. Behind it, extending into the garden-front *avant-corps* at first-floor level, was the palace's chapel. State rooms were lined up either side, with the queen regent occupying the western half of the building, the eastern being reserved for her son, Louis XIII, whenever he came to visit. The first floors of the lateral wings comprised long galleries: for the western, Marie commissioned Rubens to create the famous painting cycle glorifying her regency (now in the Louvre), while the eastern was to have contained paintings celebrating Henri IV. Stables and services were to have been located in buildings planned for either side of the palace on the street but unfinished at the time of Marie's banishment.

Although inspired by the Palazzo Pitti, De Brosse's treatment of the Luxembourg's façades has little to do with the Italian original. His rustication is much more soberly French than the dramatic bossages of the Pitti, and is essentially surface decoration in comparison to the Pitti's more three-dimensional modelling. The general effect at the Luxembourg was rather ponderous, not only because of the ubiquitous rustication but also thanks to the palace's bulky massing, its lofty French roofs originally rising much higher than today, and its corner pavilions projecting much further than was usual in French châteaux. De Brosse's domed entrance gateway, almost as tall as the pavilions flanking it, is impressive. The sober courtyard-front *avant-corps* recalls the Louvre's Lescot wing, while the more extravagant garden-front *avant-corps*, although roundly modelled and coiffed with a *toit à l'impériale*, appears rather too weedy in relation to the hefty lateral pavilions. All in all, De Brosse's design makes for a suitably majestic edifice, even in the absence today of the roofline statues, high, decorated chimneys and gilded ridgeline motifs that originally enlivened its attics.

The Palais du Luxembourg remained in royal hands until the Revolution, at which time it was still essentially as Marie had left it. After serving as a prison, it became home to the Directoire (1795), and later, in 1799, was occupied by the *sénat conservateur*, France's then second chamber (the role of upper house being one it would retain on and off until the present day; since 1958 it has been home to the Sénat of the Fifth Republic). To make it suitable for its new function, the architect Jean-François Chalgrin demolished Marie de Médicis' *escalier d'honneur* and replaced it at first-floor level with an assembly chamber (which also required the destruction of Marie's chapel). He then built a new and very neo-Classical *escalier d'honneur* in the west wing – thereby destroying Marie's long gallery – in the form of a monumental single flight surmounted by an Ionic colonnade coiffed with a coffered barrel vault. Following the 1814 Bourbon restoration, the palace kept its status of upper house, becoming the Chambre des Pairs (*pair* = peer). By the 1830s, the number of peers had grown to such an extent that extension of the palace was deemed necessary. The nobles in question wanted a building that would fully express the importance of their station, and the architect Alphonse de Gisors was appointed to the job. His solution was simple: the *corps de logis* was more than doubled in width on its southern side to accommodate a new debating chamber and library, with Marie de Médici's garden façade being rebuilt, complete with new lateral pavilions, in front of the additions. Externally, Gisors's pastiche is so accomplished that one cannot, at first glance, tell it apart from its 17C forbears. Internally, the semicircular Salle des Séances (debating chamber) is pompously august, while the more accomplished library was decorated by Eugène Delacroix. But Gisors's most spectacular internal intervention came later, during the Second Empire, when at the behest of Napoleon III he knocked together the first-floor suite of rooms on the courtyard side of the *corps de logis* to form today's Salle des Conférences and its attendant *salons*. Their extraordinarily overbearing decoration, inspired by the Louvre's Galerie d'Apollon, would set the tone for official interiors during the rest of the emperor's reign, including the Palais Garnier (9.13).

Stretching out to the sides and rear of the palace is the famous Jardin du Luxembourg, originally the queen regent's private garden but now a public park. In Marie's time, the Couvent des Chartreux, whose occupants refused to sell up, blocked the gardens to the south, and the creation of any kind of grand axis converging on the château's southern façade was thus impossible. With the dissolution of the monasteries at the Revolution, however, destruction of the *couvent* became reality, and it was Chalgrin who laid out today's monumental, tree-lined Avenue de l'Observatoire. Gisors's advancement of the garden façade necessitated the rearrangement of the parterres in front of the palace, and it was essentially he who was responsible for the park as we see it today. Marie's garden had been punctuated at its eastern end by a rusticated grotto, attributed to Alexandre Francine, which, in the 19C, was transformed into today's delightfully overwrought Fontaine Médicis.

6.9 Petit Luxembourg
17–17 bis, rue de Vaugirard
Initial architect unknown, c. 1550; Gabriel Germain Boffrand, 1710–13
(Métro: Rennes, Odéon; RER: Luxembourg)

Today home to the Présidence of the Sénat (France's upper chamber), this ancient *hôtel particulier*, whose exterior aspect is charmingly modest and domestic in scale, is chiefly interesting for what remains of the grand interiors realized in the early 18C by Germain Boffrand, the greatest of French Rococo designers. Of obscure origin, the *hôtel* took the name of François de Luxembourg, a one-time owner, but was re-baptized the »Petit Luxembourg« following construction of Marie de Médicis' neighbouring Palais du Luxembourg (6.8). In 1709, the *hôtel* became the property of Anne of Bavaria, Princess Palatine, who commissioned Boffrand to enlarge and aggrandize the building to accommodate her considerable household.

Boffrand fundamentally reorganized the old *hôtel*, demolishing the 16C service buildings west of the courtyard and replacing them with a brand-new wing to house the Palatine officers. He was also responsible for the imposing gateway between street and courtyard which links the old building to the new. For the exterior of the new wing, Boffrand imitated the modest style of the old *hôtel*, both out of a concern for harmony and from a love of contrast between simple exteriors and sumptuous interiors. Although he preserved the façades of the old *corps de logis*, he entirely remodelled its interior to create a magnificent suite of first-floor rooms for the princess.

On the ground floor of the old wing, Boffrand installed a modest vestibule lined with Ionic columns, which acts as a transitional space between the courtyard and the princess's apartments. The vestibule opens directly onto the *escalier d'honneur*, considered by contemporaries as one of the most beautiful of its time. Sweeping down in a single flight, the staircase is contained in a huge, double-height hall surmounted by a coffered vault and richly decorated with a Composite order and elaborate carvings, the ensemble painted to resemble white marble. For added grandeur, Boffrand built the balustrade in stone, in place of the customary wrought iron. The princess's apartments lead directly off the staircase landing. The first room of the series has lost its original décor, but is followed by the Salon des Tapisseries, which retains Boffrand's ceiling, cornices and frieze, as does the adjoining Grand Salon. Despite 19C interventions, one can still fully appreciate the subtlety of Boffrand's designs, especially in the Grand Salon, whose delicate, almost ephemeral gilded mouldings appear to float on their white background, drifting off across the vast, gently vaulted ceiling. The two final rooms, including the princess's bedroom, are more sober in style.

Incorporated into the new wing are vestiges of the Couvent des Filles-du-Calvaire, founded by Marie de Médicis in 1622. The cloister survives, converted into a winter garden, as does the lavish, Mannerist interior of the Queen's Chapel.

6.10 Apartment building
22–28, rue Vavin
Henri Sauvage with Charles Sarazin, 1912/13
(Métro: Vavin, Notre-Dame-des-Champs)

The demographic correlation between instances of tuberculosis and densely built and inhabited areas of cities was one of the factors which made fresh-air-and-sunshine cures a staple of TB treatment in the early 20C. In Germany, special sanatoria had been built for tuberculosis patients, featuring stepped-back terraces allowing maximum exposure to light and air. Such ideas caught the imagination of Sauvage who, as a founder member of the Société des Logements Hygiéniques à Bon Marché (Low-cost, Hygienic Dwelling Company), was much concerned with the question of housing the working classes. Sauvage transferred the idea of stepped-back terraces to apartment buildings – in an urban context this had the advantage over traditional building forms of allowing more light to penetrate to street level and, problems of orientation aside, afforded every resident his/her own mini-solarium. Aesthetically, the plastic possibilities of such a type were

6.10 Apartment building

an attractive alternative to the canyon-like monotony of many Parisian streets. Sauvage became convinced that the future of urbanism lay in stepped-terrace buildings, and even patented the idea.

Eager to implement his theories, but unable to secure a commission for workers' housing, Sauvage and a group friends decided to build a stepped-terrace apartment building for themselves, under the auspices of the Société Anonyme des Maisons à Gradins (Stepped-terrace Housing Company Ltd.), founded for the purpose. Situated in a small, typically Parisian street, the building provides a variety of accommodation, from artists studios to large apartments, and included collective facilities (games room, etc.). Sauvage's office was also housed in the building. The street line is respected, and the terraces do not begin until second-floor level. The angle of their descent is fairly steep and an impression of verticality persists, strengthened by the prominent central *avant-corps*. That Sauvage was a past master of Art Nouveau (his Villa Majorelle in Nancy (1898) is considered a key work of the movement), is evident in the picturesque massing and detailing of the building. Its concrete frame is hidden behind white, bevelled »Métro« tiles – the outward expression of his obsession with hygiene – enlivened by dark-blue tiles which hint at details such as string courses and impost blocks. Each terrace has a built-in flower box, and when fully planted the building becomes a kind of vertical garden city.

Sauvage finally got the chance to construct stepped-terrace social housing after WWI (see 18.10), although the building type never caught on in the way he hoped. One reason was no doubt its reliance on the traditional city-block approach to urban planning, a model which later Modernists would challenge and reject. The Rue-Vavin flats were nonetheless influential. Their »air, light, health« doctrine prefigured Corbusian preoccupations, and they are cited as an inspiration for Sant' Elia's *casa a gradinata* in his *Città Nuova* design of 1914.

6.11 Institut d'Art et d'Archéologie
3, rue Michelet
Paul Bigot, 1920–27
(Métro: Vavin; RER: Port-Royal)

An exuberant and late example of eclecticism, the Institut d'Art et d'Archéologie was designed by an architect who built very little, and whose *magnum opus*, which took twelve years to complete, was a relief plan of 4C Rome rendered at a scale of 2 mm/metre. The Institut was commissioned by the University of the Sorbonne (5.5), whose new buildings, completed in 1901, were already too small after only a decade. Bigot's competition-winning design took the form of a perimeter building organized around a central courtyard. Programmatically and conceptually this was standard fare, with exhibition and library space on the ground floor, and classrooms and lecture halls on the other floors. What surprises about the Institut is the treatment of its

6.11 Institut d'Art et d'Archéologie

façades, of a type rarely seen in Paris. Bigot imagined a fantasy mélange of Moorish, Byzantine and vaguely »Mesopotamian« references, the ensemble rendered in bright-red Gournay brick, a material guaranteed to stand out from the honey-coloured stone of which so much of Paris is built. The principal elevation is cadenced by a monumental, ten-bay arcade, surmounted by a blind storey animated with relief patterns in brick. Indeed the entire exterior is textured with different brick effects, which serve to distinguish the composite elements of the façades from one another. Flame-shaped crenellations animate the roof-line, while running along the building's base is a continuous terracotta frieze featuring copies of famous sculpture from the ancient-Greek to the Renaissance eras, including reliefs from the Parthenon, figures from the façades of Reims and Senlis cathedrals, and so on.

7th *arrondissement*

7.1 Musée d'Orsay
2, quai Anatole-France
Victor Laloux, 1897–1900; Act-Architecture, 1979–86, with Gae Aulenti, 1980–86
(Métro: Solférino; RER: Musée d'Orsay)

The ruins of the Palais d'Orsay, the first occupant of this site and one of several victims of the 1871 Commune, crumbled picturesquely beside the Seine for nearly 30 years until it was finally decided in 1896 to raze them to make way for a railway terminus and hotel, the Gare d'Orsay. The new station would receive passenger traffic that previously terminated at the Gare d'Austerlitz, which was now considered too far from the city centre, especially for the flood of visitors expected to attend the Exposition Universelle of 1900. Laloux's competition-winning design was much admired at the time for its »sensitivity« to the urban landscape surrounding this prestigious site opposite the Louvre (1.8) – in other words, the ambiguity of the epoch towards its industrial technology was here exhibited by the architect's deliberate decision to hide all ironwork from view and encase the train-shed in a pompous stone pompadour. Long and squat, the main façade comprises a seven-bay arcade flanked by outsized pavilions, each one dominated by a vast illuminated clock. Magisterial personifications of the towns of Bordeaux, Toulouse and Nantes – the principal destinations served by the Paris–Orléans railway company – sit enthroned on the parapet (the face of *Nantes* was modelled on Mme Laloux). The hotel is clearly defined as a separate element, lighter but no less grand. The ostentation continued inside: the main arcade opened onto seven enormous domed and sky-lit vestibules serving almost no purpose other than access to the platforms, while the trains arrived under a glorious iron and glass barrel vault, 137 m long, 40 m wide and 29 m high, coffered with plaster medallions. The hotel interior was a florid *mélange* of Louis Quatorze and Louis Quinze.

Too small for the larger trains of the 1930s, the station was practically abandoned in 1939 and there followed a long period of decline. By the 1960s its fate appeared sealed: demolition to make way for a luxury hotel. The architectural press proclaimed that no one would mourn this inelegant *pâtisserie*, detested, according to the tenets of the era, for its »dishonesty«, »decadence« and pretension. However, nobody could agree upon a replacement scheme and, by the early 1970s, especially after the much-lamented destruction of Les Halles (see 1.22), public opinion had turned, and the station was added to the list of historic monuments in 1973. But what use was to be found for it?

President Giscard d'Estaing's government proposed the idea of a museum of the art of the 19C: a competition was launched and the winning scheme by the group Act-Architecture chosen by the president himself in 1979. The paradoxical demands of the brief

7.1 Musée d'Orsay

called for respect towards Laloux's architecture while increasing surface area from 30,000 to 43,000 m². Weaknesses in the scheme and interminable wranglings with the curators (worsened by interference from the president) led to the appointment in 1980 of the Italian interior designer Gae Aulenti, with a view to introducing some rigour to proceedings. The museum was finally opened by President Mitterrand in 1986, three years behind schedule and millions of francs over budget.

Enormously popular with the public – no doubt because home to the Impressionists – the completed project has not been a critical or museological success. Reorientated along its longitudinal axis to make the most of its nave-like qualities, the train-shed now contains a central, gently sloping ramp running along its entire length, flanked by newly inserted structures housing exhibition space. Stone-clad and pharaonic in inspiration, the overall effect is of a Vegas Valley-of-the-Kings, extremely ill at ease in its *belle-époque* setting. Apologists for Hi-tech – surely the late-20C equivalent of 19C iron technology – will be horrified by the clumsy PoMo pastiches of industrial forms. Worst of all, much of the gallery space is second-rate and disjointed. Only the spacious and airy Impressionism gallery in the attic really succeeds. Outside of the stylistic errors, one wonders if a better solution could have been found; the paradoxes of the brief appear simply too great to be satisfactorily surmounted.

7.2 Hôtel de Salm / Palais de la Légion d'Honneur
64, rue de Lille
Pierre Rousseau, 1782–88
(Métro: Solférino)

Not content with the absolute power he wielded back home in his German principality, Friedrich III von Salm-Kyrburg tried, largely unsuccessfully, to gain influence and prestige at the French court, one of his tactics being to build this grandiloquent residence whose expense nearly ruined him. In its general dispositions the building follows the classic *hôtel-particulier* schema, with a main *corps de logis* giving onto a terrace behind and separated from the street by a courtyard, the latter flanked laterally by service buildings and accessed via an axial *porte-cochère*. To this traditional layout Rousseau brought a rather cold dignity and forceful sense of grandeur – and this despite the *hôtel*'s compact stature – in an ambitious design that quoted liberally from several distinguished 18C Parisian buildings. The majestic entrance screen on the Rue de Lille was clearly inspired by the Hôtel de Condé (today Assemblée Nationale (7.4)) – the rather severe courtyard colonnade recalls Gondoin's Ecole de Chirurgie (6.6), and the plan was evidently influenced by Claude-Nicolas Ledoux's mythic Hôtel de Thélusson (*c*. 1777–81, destroyed). The same long axial sequence of rooms that characterized the Hôtel de Thélusson is reproduced at the Hôtel de Salm, although where Ledoux's oval *salon* – a staple of French aristocratic architecture since its introduction from Italy in the 17C (see Vaux-le-Vicomte (37.1)) was on the entrance front, Rousseau put it back in its more traditional position at the centre of the rear façade. If this elevation, now overlooking the Quai Anatole-France, seems inappropriately villa-like and domestic today, we should remember that the *hôtel* predates the quayside, and originally headed gardens that descended down to the river. Thus, as was traditional for garden fronts, it is considerably more decorated than the courtyard elevation, providing a contrast that is all the more marked in that the austerity of the Hôtel de Salm's entrance façade was unprecedented in French domestic architecture.

Although it did little to advance the aspirations of its occupant, Rousseau's building impressed contemporaries, including Thomas Jefferson (American minister to France from 1784–89), who was inspired by it for the rebuilding of his Monticello residence (1768–1809). The unfortunate Friedrich von Salm-Kyrburg ended his days on the guillotine, and his *hôtel* subsequently became home, in 1804, to the Légion d'Honneur, shortly after its founding by Napoleon. The building's size and pomp lent themselves perfectly to the pageantry of this kind of official institution, and the only major modification was a later extension along the Rue de Solférino

7.2 Hôtel de Salm / Palais de la Légion d'Honneur

7.3 Sainte-Clotilde-Sainte-Valère

(*c*. 1866) to provide supplementary office accommodation. Set alight by the Communards in 1871, the *hôtel*'s exterior miraculously withstood the conflagration, but its interiors were gutted and afterwards refitted in crashing Third-Republic style. Also at this time, the garden front's dome was rebuilt rather more prominently than Rousseau's original.

7.3 Sainte-Clotilde-Sainte-Valère
23 bis, rue Las-Cases
Franz Christian Gau, 1846–53; Théodore Ballu, 1853–57
(Métro: Solférino)

Initially inspired by Romantic-Movement figures such as Goethe, Schlegel and Chateaubriand, the Gothic Revival became a force to be reckoned with in England but, interestingly, never took off to the same extent in France, the country that originally invented the style. Planned as of 1839, the church of Sainte-Clotilde is chiefly notable as one of the earliest French Gothic-Revival buildings, designed, tellingly, by a German. Indeed something of a war had broken out between Revivalists and the staunchly neo-Classical authorities, and the church was only built thanks to the influence of the Comte de Rambuteau, Prefect of the Seine and an enthusiastic Gothicist, who personally pushed the project

7.4 Assemblée Nationale

through despite three refusals by the Conseil des Bâtiments Civils.

Gau's design is a rather literal pastiche of a 13C French Gothic church in idealized form. The principle façade was probably inspired by Saint-Nicaise in Reims (13C, destroyed). Contemporaries were quick to criticize the »incorrectness« of the interior's blind triforium and the general dryness of the ensemble. Gau died before Sainte-Clotilde was completed and Ballu, his assistant, finished the job. When Ballu took over work was already too far advanced for major alterations to be made and he contented himself with enriching the decorative elements – especially the towers and the porches – in a bid to quell the critics. The result is consequently more picturesque than Gau intended but is still little appreciated; many see it as the epitome of colourless 19C historicism. It is nonetheless a dignified evocation of the High-Gothic style and was realized with superb craftsmanship.

7.4 Assemblée Nationale
126–128, rue de l'Université and 29–35, quai d'Orsay
Various architects, begun 1726
(Métro: Assemblée Nationale)

Like the vast majority of the country's governmental institutions, France's national assembly is housed in an aristocratic palace confiscated by the state at the Revolution and afterwards converted piecemeal to fulfil its new function. In fact the parliament is housed in two such structures: the Palais Bourbon, which contains the assembly proper, and the Hôtel de Lassay, which is the home of the parliament's president. The buildings were originally constructed simultaneously (1726–30) by Jean Aubert, the Palais Bourbon for a daughter of Louis XIV, Louise-Françoise de Bourbon, and the Hôtel de Lassay for her close friend, the Marquis Armand de Lassay. They were for a long time attributed to Jacques V Gabriel, but it is now thought that his role was merely that of a consultant and that the true architect was Aubert. Both residences have been so radically altered since their conception that their builders would have difficulty recognizing them today. It is worth remembering that in the early-18C this site was on the edge of the countryside, and the houses were designed with this semi-rural location in mind: only a single storey high, in the manner of garden pavilions, they were set in sizeable grounds, hidden from their service buildings by copses of trees. By far the bigger and grander was the Palais Bourbon, clearly inspired by the Grand Trianon (32.2), its façades articulated by arched windows, engaged columns and pilasters and coiffed with a balustrade and statuary. The Hôtel de Lassay was in a similar vein, but on a more modest scale. Both houses enjoyed river views from terraces constructed on their northern façades. Of their fine Rococo interiors by Jules Degoullons and Mathieu Le Goupil, only certain elements survive in the Hôtel de Lassay.

It was the Prince de Condé, after acquiring the residences in the 1760s, who was responsible for the first round of alterations, considerably enlarging the Palais Bourbon. The work (c. 1764–75), principally carried out by Antoine-Michel Le Carpentier, included the extension of the Palais's projecting wings as far as the Rue de l'Université, thereby creating a vast courtyard, the construction of the entrance colonnade (essentially the one we see today) based on a design by Marie-Joseph Peyre, and the building of the semicircular piazza opposite, to provide an august urban setting for the Palais. It was also under Condé that the gardens disappeared, replaced by the monotonous service buildings still visible today.

In 1792, both residences were confiscated by the revolutionaries, serving for a time as a prison before, in 1795, the Palais Bourbon was allocated to the Conseil des Cinq-Cents, France's newly constituted lower chamber. Jacques-Pierre Gisors and Emmanuel-Chérubin Leconte were commissioned to build an assembly chamber at the Palais, which involved the total reconstruction of the *corps de logis* on the courtyard side. The result, inaugurated in 1798, appeared rather provisory, with the new assembly chamber sticking up awkwardly above the Palais's façades. The building did not, however, remain in this state for long: in 1806, the Emperor Napoleon charged Bernard Poyet with bringing it into line with imperial aspirations. This involved the embellishment of parts of the interior, and – Napoleon's principal intervention – the construction of a new, monumental river façade. Besides making the Palais more suitably august, this new elevation was designed to mask the roof of the assembly chamber and to dissimulate the Palais's skewness in relation to the Pont and the Place de la Concorde (see feature on Seine bridges and 8.1, respectively). It furthermore served to complete the enormous urban composition formed by the square and its surroundings. Poyet raised a vast, almost totally blind wall perpendicular to the bridge, on which he stuck a gigantic Corinthian portico, thereby satisfying Napoleon's taste for architecture of imperial-Roman flavour and creating a southern pendant to the Madeleine (8.2) then going up to the north of the Place de la Concorde. Despite its grandness, Poyet's composition somehow misses the mark, no doubt partly because of its blankness and the fact that today the giant portico serves only as a secondary entrance, betraying its rather hollow theatricality. It is decorated with monumental sculpture, including a bas-relief by Rude (*Prometheus and the Arts*, 1835) and Cortot's pediment (1838–41) depicting France flanked by, amongst others, Liberty and Order. In comparison to later 19C riverside parliaments (one thinks immediately of Westminster and Budapest), France's assembly rather lacks clout.

By the 1820s, Gisors and Leconte's chamber had fallen into an advanced state of dilapidation, and Jules de Joly was called in to rebuild it. His interventions, carried out in 1829–43, produced the complex we see today. Like his predecessors, Joly created an assembly chamber in the form of a hemicycle; the result, with its red-velvet trappings, elaborate ceiling, tribune set under a sort of proscenium arch and balconies hung behind Ionic pillars, appears very theatrical in the most literal sense of the word. Joly was also responsible for the three new *salons* preceding the hemicycle on the courtyard side as well as for the elaborate vaulted library. Both the library and the Salon du Roi were decorated by Eugène Delacroix (1833–37 and 1838 to 1847 respectively), and his paintings, which include allegories of Legislation, Philosophy and Theology, are counted by critics amongst his masterpieces. The considerable alterations to the Palais carried out under Joly involved the widening of the *corps de logis* on the courtyard side and the rebuilding of the corresponding façades. Joly's Corinthian colonnaded elevations include an elongated entrance portico that attempts to marry the single storey of the function rooms with the enormous bulk of the assembly chamber behind. The latter's positioning and plan are mirrored in the semicircular ramp leading up to the portico. In 1843, when the Hôtel de Lassay once again came into state hands (it had been repossessed by the Prince de Condé after the Restoration), Joly set about linking it to the Palais by means of a gallery – today's Galerie des Fêtes – and raised the *hôtel* by one storey to accommodate the private apartments of the assembly's president.

7.5 Conservatoire de musique Erik-Satie and sheltered housing

135, rue de l'Université and 7, rue Jean-Nicot
Christian de Portzamparc, 1981–84
(Métro: Invalides)

An early work by Portzamparc, who is now a Pritzker-prize winner and one of France's star architects. The redevelopment programme for this site combined two entirely unrelated projects: sheltered housing for old people and a municipal music school, whose pupils are for the most part children. Portzamparc sensibly decided to separate these two activities, placing the *conservatoire* at the corner of the site on the noisy Rue de l'Université – where it has the opportunity to act as a municipal monument – and the sheltered housing round the corner on the quieter, more anonymous Rue Jean-Nicot. Between the two he placed a small courtyard giving onto the street, which opened up the city block and revealed an old tower that had previously been hidden from view (the tower has since been demolished as part of a redevelopment scheme next door). The sheltered-housing block, which occupies the bigger chunk of the site, continues the planarity of neighbouring constructions and although, with its atypically disposed fenestration and corner tower, it stands out from the crowd, the block nonetheless remains soberly respectful to its context.

The *conservatoire*, on the other hand, presents a much more arresting and flamboyant visage to the passer-by. Portzamparc described the urbanity surrounding his building as »spatially sad« – i.e. characterized by long straight streets lined with unadventurous, building-line-respecting façades – and deliberately set out to liven it up a bit. Standing alone at the street intersection, the *conservatoire* is essentially a big cube on stilts, but the articulation of elements that contradict its inherent orthogonality ensures that it is anything but square. As was then fashionable, the *conservatoire*'s elevations sport various ironically handled PoMo Classical quotations, such as the semicircular and triangular pediments crowning its two principle façades, the latter of which is cheekily (or tiresomely, depending on your point of view) subverted by a historicizing circular staircase tower that has been plonked in front of it. Both pediments and tower contradict the *conservatoire*'s cubic rigidity, as do the flight of steps spilling out from behind the tower and the curiously shaped window cut into the upper part of this elevation. There is here a certain youthful over-enthusiasm for knowing, contrived effects that Portzamparc would drop in subsequent projects, paring down his vocabulary to leave

7.5 Conservatoire de musique Erik-Satie and sheltered housing

7.6 Apartment building

only the abstract, rather enigmatic expressionism – the hallmark of later works such as the Cité de la Musique (19.5) – that is already strongly present at the *conservatoire*. It is this that saves the building from the rather Legoland quality that mars so much 1980s Postmodernism. Inside the *conservatoire*, space is handled with fluid dexterity, especially in the upper-storey *salle de danse*.

Frédéric Borel (see 11.3, 18.8, 20.2 and 20.5) cut his architectural teeth as Portzamparc's assistant on this project.

7.6 Apartment building
89, quai d'Orsay and 22, rue Cognacq-Jay
Michel Roux-Spitz, 1928–31
(Métro: Alma-Marceau)

Michel Roux-Spitz was one of a number of architects in inter-war Paris producing high-quality moderne architecture, for the most part luxury housing for the wealthy. Others included Jean Ginsberg, Pierre Patout and Robert Mallet-Stevens (see 16.15 and 16.16, 15.5, and 16.2 and 16.12, respectively), and Roux-Spitz himself talked of an »Ecole de Paris« in relation to their work and the period. He viewed their production as specifically French, in a tradition of Rational Classicism that favoured restrained elegance and clarity over the »Expressionist« exaggeration of some foreign schools.

All these architects' buildings are characterized by their suave styling, and Roux-Spitz's Quai d'Orsay flats are typically slick. Programmatically they are directly descended from their 19C forbears, and are divided internally into service, reception and private areas. Externally Roux-Spitz updated the image of the bourgeois apartment for the children of the automobile age, seducing his leisured clientele with luxuriously crafted, streamlined façades. A concrete frame allows maximal glazing on the principal Seine frontage, which is given the horizontal emphasis then *de rigueur*. There was, however, no question of expressing the building's frame on the exterior, and it is instead hidden behind a skin of white Hauteville stone, so finely machined that the joints are barely visible. Roux-Spitz's by-then trademark bow windows dominate the composition, highlighting the importance of that middle-class institution, the sitting room. Despite its jazz-age geometry and lack of ornamentation, this building is controlled by strict symmetry and proportions that situate it firmly within the legacy of French Classicism.

7.7 Musée du Quai Branly
29–55, quai Branly
Jean Nouvel, 1999, due 2004
(Métro: Alma Marceau; RER: Champ de Mars)

French presidential »grands projets« arguably began with De Gaulle who, although he bequeathed no architectural monuments, was behind prestige projects such as the ocean liner *France* and the supersonic jet *Concorde*. Pompidou, of course, built his Centre (4.15), and Mitterrand was famous for his multiple *grands travaux*. So far, Jacques Chirac has shied away from the pharaonic precedent set by his predecessor, and this 1.1-billion-franc museum is the only architectural scheme for which he is directly responsible. If the institution's name says nothing about its contents, this is because nobody could agree on what to call a museum whose collections will comprise what is colloquially – and perhaps pejoratively – known as »primitive« or »primal« art. Non-European civilizations are the subject of this institution, with all five continents (Africa, Asia, Oceania and the Americas) being represented. To a certain extent it will unite existing collections previously split between the Musée de l'Homme and the Musée des Arts Africains et Océaniens (see 12.13), although new acquisitions are also being made. Research and education will be essential aspects of the museum's work, and rather than merely presenting objects for their aesthetic value it will attempt to encourage fundamental reflections on the nature of humanity and civilization.

The museum's site has been the subject of much controversy, as it was originally to have been home to the ill-fated Centre de Conférences Internationales de Paris (CCIP), the last of President Mitterrand's »grands projets«. Located on the Seine just upstream from the Eiffel Tower (7.8), the 2.5 ha plot was cleared of its original occupant (former government offices) for construction of the CCIP in 1991, but since the conference centre's cancellation in 1993 has remained empty. An all-star international competition was held in 1999 to find an architect for the museum, from which the home-grown talent of Jean Nouvel emerged victorious. Perhaps in a bid to appease the vociferous residents' associations who largely contributed to the CCIP's downfall, Nouvel proposed a building that effaces itself on both its Seine and Rue-de-l'Université façades, hiding at the site's centre behind a thick screen of enveloping greenery that will cover nearly 2 ha. Designed by the landscape gardener Gilles Clément, the Seine-side garden will be densely planted with oaks, maples and creepers, providing the museum with its very own primal forest to prepare arriving visitors for the contemplation of works conceived in an entirely non-urban context. In the manner of Nouvel's Fondation Cartier (14.4), a full-height glass wall running along the street line (baptized the »palisade« by the architects) will mark the museum's entrance on the quayside, both protecting the garden from automobile pollution and further mystifying the external aspect of the museum building proper. The latter will be stuck up on 12 m-high *pilotis*, its whizzing curved profile following the bend of the river. Access will be gained via a ceremonial ramp whose course will continue inside the »grande galerie« that will constitute the essential element of the museum's exhibition spaces. Crowning the building will be a generous terrace and a squashed glass dome housing a panoramic restaurant. Wood, glass and stucco are the principal materials in which the building will be clothed.

Respect for the urban context was one of the brief's stipulations, and the museum will consequently rise no higher than its neighbours, while the three ancillary structures intended for its offices will engage with and mask the rear light wells of the neighbouring 19C apartment buildings. The brief's space requirements are evidently not fulfilled by the rather sparse surface constructions, and consequently an important underground component, containing space for temporary exhibitions, a *médiathèque* and an auditorium, also forms part of the proposal. Nouvel's scheme is intended as the antithesis of a showy, »prestige« museum such as the Louvre (1.8), and, at least in its current, conceptual form, aims instead to shape an emotional environment of »otherness« that will constitute a shrine to the exotic objects to be housed there.

7.8 Eiffel Tower
Champ de Mars
Gustave Eiffel, Maurice Koechlin, Emile Nouguier and Stephen Sauvestre, 1885–89
(Métro: Trocadéro; RER: Champ de Mars)

As Roland Barthes once pointed out, the Eiffel Tower has become so much a symbol of Paris, indeed of France, that it is hard to imagine a time when it did not exist. Its genesis lay in the Exposition Universelle of 1889, held to commemorate the centenary of the Revolution, for which the government wished to find a project that would stun public imagination. Eiffel made this known to his team of engineers, two of whom, Nouguier and Koechlin, in collaboration with the architect Sauvestre, drew up plans for a tower 300 m high, an astonishing figure for the time given that the world's then tallest monument, the Washington Obelisk, measured a mere 169 m. Eiffel was initially uninterested in his colleagues' proposal, but soon changed his mind and patented the design in their three names in December 1885. The Ministre de l'Industrie had already decided in favour of Eiffel's scheme but, for form's sake, held a competition in 1886, which Eiffel won by unanimous decision of the jury. Aside from a 1.5-million-franc subsidy, the tower was to be erected at Eiffel's own expense, and he would benefit from its exploitation for a period of 20 years after which time it was to be demolished.

Prior to the tower, Eiffel's biggest successes had been with his daring iron railway viaducts, especially those at Oporto (1875/76) and Garabit (1880–84), which had brought him considerable fame. The tower was essentially an overgrown viaduct pylon, and Eiffel and his team used all the skill and knowledge they had amassed during construction of the viaducts for the design and assembly of the tower. Eiffel had frequently won commissions because his proposals were substantially cheaper than competitors', and the system of girders employed at the tower provides maximum resistance for minimum structure. Oscillation of the tower's summit never exceeds 12 cm and, despite its 7,000-tonne weight, pressure per cm^2 of its four *piliers* on the ground is equivalent to that exerted by a man sitting on a chair. Components were prefabricated to a high degree of precision at Eiffel's foundry in Levallois-Perret and once on site had merely to be riveted into place. The cranes used to lift them were mounted on rails, which afterwards carried the three sets of lifts essential for rapid transportation of visitors to the tower's summit. Construction began in January 1887; 26 months later in March 1889, one month ahead of schedule, Eiffel climbed to the top of the completed tower where he ceremoniously raised the Tricolore.

7.7 Musée du Quai Branly

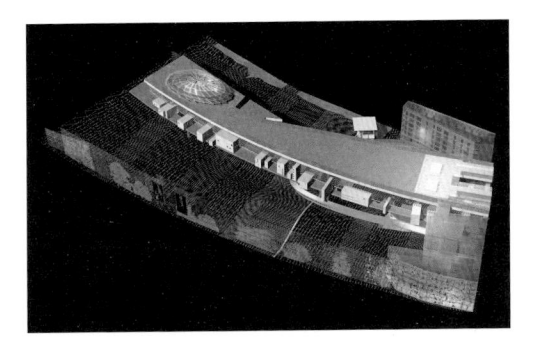

7.8 Eiffel Tower

The age of iron reached its apogee at the 1889 exhibition, which boasted two world records: that for height, in the form of the tower, and also that for width in the form of Dutert and Contamin's Galerie des Machines (sadly demolished in 1909), whose 107 m-wide central hall was covered in a single span by an iron-and-glass vault. The tower retained the height record until construction of the Chrysler Building in the 1930s. Haunted by the idea that his progeny would one day be demolished, Eiffel installed a meteorological station at its summit in an attempt to save it from its fate. In the eventuality it was the telegraph that rescued the tower, which, in 1904, became the signalling station for military communications. By 1906 messages were transmitted over distances of up to 3000 km, and in 1934 the first French television broadcasts were beamed from the tower's peak.

The tower was, from the outset, an enormous success, although not to everyone's taste. Before building work even started a group of eminent artists and academicians published an open letter condemning »the useless and monstrous Eiffel Tower«. Afterwards, Guy de Maupassant, one of the signatories, frequently lunched at the tower's first-floor restaurant because, as he explained, it was the only place in Paris where he could not see it. Public imagination was indeed stunned by this unimaginable structure, whose graceful silhouette has since passed into myth.

7.9 Ecole Militaire
Place de Fontenoy and Champ de Mars
Ange-Jacques Gabriel, begun 1751
(Métro: Ecole Militaire)

Brainchild of Joseph Pâris-Duverney, who petitioned the king for its creation, the Ecole Militaire was conceived as a military training college for young cadets »without fortune, sons of officers disabled or killed in the king's service«. Louis XV, anxious to reward the *noblesse d'épée* for services rendered in the War of Austrian Succession and eager to create an institution of the same impact and calibre as his great-grandfather's Invalides (7.12), enthusiastically approved the idea.

A site was provided on the Plaine de Grenelle, downstream from the Invalides, and Gabriel, Louis's Premier Architecte, was charged with the commission. Accommodation for 700 people was required, as well as the multiple service buildings – armouries, stables, kitchens, hospital wards, etc. – necessary for this type of institution. And it went without saying that the Ecole's architecture should express the power and prestige of France and her monarchy.

Gabriel's initial plans for the complex were clearly inspired by the Invalides: separated from the river, like Bruand's building, by a generous esplanade (which was to serve as the school's training ground, whence its current name of Champ de Mars), Gabriel's institution was an Escorial-type building laid out as a series of rectilinear courtyards grouped around a central, dominating church. The majority of these courtyards, surrounded by low, barracks-type buildings, had been completed by 1756, but thereafter work slowed down until, in 1760, cash ran out and the project was halted. Gabriel's initial scheme was written off as too expensive, and he was asked to provide a re-design. This essentially meant replacing the church with a less costly structure, and Gabriel came up with the building today known as the »Château«, which occupies

7.9 Ecole Militaire

the centre of the composition and carries all the institution's symbolic weight. Constructed in 1769–73, the Château contained the school's *état-major* and a sizeable chapel that replaced the abandoned church. In his initial, 1751 plans, Gabriel had placed the complex's main entrance on the Champ de Mars, but in his redesign the orientation was reversed and the Ecole took on the classic ordonnance of a French château: approached from the semicircular Place de Fontenoy, also laid out by Gabriel, the school is disposed around a generous *avant-cour* that is flanked laterally by the barracks buildings (like the service buildings of a real château) and which leads the visitor to the central Château building via its *cour d'honneur*. The Château's rear façade thus gives directly onto the Champ de Mars, like a genuine château fronting its garden. Gabriel's courtyard elevation is a classic French composition, consisting of a main *corps de logis* sporting end pavilions and a central, pedimented *avant-corps*, whose attic is coiffed with a bulbous *toit à l'impériale*, one of the staples of French state architecture from the 16C to the 19C. More unusual are the superimposed colonnades screening the *logis's arrière-corps*, which recall both the east front of the Louvre (see 1.8) and the Invalides's courtyard arcades. On the garden front, on the other hand, the Château breaks somewhat with the French tradition. The *corps de logis* has no end pavilions and is animated only by the rhythm of its fenestration and the detailing of its window surrounds, all interest consequently being concentrated on the elegant central *avant-corps*, which serves to anchor the composition in the landscape. Gabriel's design, fitting for a building of hybrid status that was not a royal château but nonetheless represented the state, would prove influential.

Internally, the Château is noteworthy for its handsome stone *escalier d'honneur*, of a type whose pedigree goes back to François Mansart's staircase at Blois (c. 1635–38). Its beautifully executed stonework is matched by its fine wrought-iron balustrade, also by Gabriel. The architect's Classicism, which broke with Rococo airiness, is clearly illustrated in the Romanizing coffering and august sobriety of the staircase. The chapel is also quietly solemn, as befitted a military institution. To visit the Ecole, prior written agreement should be obtained from the *commandant*.

7.10 UNESCO
7, place de Fontenoy
Marcel Breuer, Pier Luigi Nervi and Bernard Zehrfuss, 1954–58; Bernard Zehrfuss 1962–65
(Métro: Ségur)

Arguably one of the greatest contributing factors to the hegemony enjoyed by Modernism in the middle years of the 20C was WWII, not only because of the enormous amount of reconstruction necessary once hostilities had ended, but also because of the desire to build a new, better world that followed in the wake of the conflict. It is therefore unsurprising that UNESCO (the

7.10 UNESCO

United Nations Educational, Scientific and Cultural Organization), which was conceived in this brave new, post-apocalypse era, should have wanted to reflect this sentiment when building its headquarters. Having accepted an offer by the French government of a 3 ha site behind the Ecole Militaire (7.9), the organization commissioned an international team of architects, all of Modernist persuasion, to design its new home and moreover charged a committee of five further Moderns – Lucio Costa, Walter Gropius, Le Corbusier, Sven Markelius and Ernesto Rogers – to approve the plans (Eero Saarinen was also consulted). The result, while perhaps not entirely at the *hauteur* of the talents that went into its creation, is nonetheless a showcase of quality 1950s design and today charms in its manifestation of a certain Cold-War-era chic.

The scheme adopted by the UNESCO architects was similar to that devised for the UN headquarters in New York (Wallace K. Harrison *et al.*, 1947–53), but with modifications that were made largely in response to the stipulations of the Parisian planning authorities. As in New York, the site was treated as a blank page on which the two principal structures – the secretariat and the assembly-hall building – were placed, like freestanding sculptures in a field. Again as in New York, it is the secretariat – the bureaucratic component of the organization – that dominates the ensemble, a rather telling comment on the make-up of this kind of institution. But while a tower was the obvious and inevitable form chosen for the New York secretariat, the Paris version was constrained by planning regulations to rise no more than eight storeys. Unable to build a skyscraper, the architects turned to that other great standard of Modernism, the Corb-style bar on *pilotis*, although here again modifications were made to the basic model to keep the planners happy. The project brief demanded that due respect be shown to the Ecole Militaire, and this meant paying special attention to the Place-de-Fontenoy aspect of the new building since the semicircular piazza, laid out by Gabriel, formed the backdrop to the Ecole's southern façade.

7th *arrondissement* 141

Although observing the street line went against the Modernist grain, the UNESCO architects made a concession on the Place de Fontenoy, closing the western side of the piazza with a curved elevation that echoed the semicircular layout of the *place*. It was presumably from this starting point that the curved elevations of the secretariat's other two façades were derived, producing the final Y-shaped building. Oscar Niemeyer would later take inspiration from the form and layout of the UNESCO building for his French Communist Party Headquarters (19.1).

Le Corbusier described the UNESCO secretariat as a »Janus building«, because it can be said to look back in time on the Place-de-Fontenoy façade, where traditional, planar cladding in travertine was used (again in respectful reference to the Ecole Militaire), while its other two elevations are rather more futuristic. Although the building's principal entrance is nominally on the Place de Fontenoy, this façade reads rather as a rear elevation, and the building is best approached from the Avenue de Suffren. Here one is presented with the full sweep of the southwestern façade, a magnificent display of glass and *brise-soleils* and undoubtedly the building's best feature (the eastern façade was given similar treatment but, because of its orientation, comprises fewer *brise-soleils*). The secretariat's expressively powerful *pilotis*, designed by Nervi, are visible at either extremity but are enclosed behind glass along the rest of the façade's length to form an entrance foyer. Marking the point of entry is a bravura, free-standing concrete porch, also by Nervi, which the subcontractors initially refused to construct because they feared it would not stand up. The secretariat's 4,550 offices – all identical 5.5 x 3 m cells each of which, thanks to the bar design, is naturally lit – are accessed via a central bank of elevators situated at the intersection of the building's wings.

Silhouetted against the secretariat when viewed from the Avenue de Suffren, the assembly-hall building is constructed entirely from raw reinforced concrete that bears the marks of the shuttering used to cast it. Rather intimidatingly bunker-like from outside, it features a swooping, copper-covered roof whose form makes it appear as if broken in the centre and whose massive fluting is continued on the end elevations. Inside, however, the bunker-like aspect disappears and in the main assembly hall, which occupies the northwestern half of the structure, one is wowed by the soaring, columnless, fluted envelope whose undulations are not merely structural and aesthetic but were also designed to improve the hall's acoustic properties. At the building's centre the huge span of its roof is supported by a row of massive *pilotis* around which a circulatory *hall des délégués* is disposed. Smaller assembly halls and conference rooms occupy the other half of the building, including the official meeting room of UNESCO's executive council, which was decorated by Philip Johnson and features chairs specially designed by Eero Saarinen.

Even at the time of their inauguration, critics were heard to say that the new UNESCO headquarters were too small, and as the number of member countries increased the provision of additional space became a pressing necessity. Despite the extended emptiness of the institution's grounds, the French planning authorities would not allow it to build any visible structures on them, and UNESCO's executive council therefore came up with a plan to realize an underground extension in front of the secretariat and the assembly-hall building. Designed by Zehrfuss and opened in 1965, it is organized around six sunken patios which provide air and light to the offices and conference rooms giving on to them. It is worth poking around the interiors for their James-Bond period charm – daring star-form exposed concrete roofs in the conference rooms, ubiquitous Scandinavian wood panelling and futuristic hooded telephone booths.

Given the cultural aspect of its mission, it was only natural that UNESCO should commission artworks for its new headquarters, and the building and its grounds contain a number of specially realized pieces. Among the mid-century giants who contributed to its embellishment were Picasso (*The Fall of Icarus* in the *hall des délégués* of the assembly-hall building, not one of his better works), Miró (*The Wall of the Moon* and *The Wall of the Sun*), Giacometti, Henry Moore, Alexander Calder and even Le Corbusier (reproduction as a tapestry of a sketch by Corb inspired by the Breuer/Nervi/Zehrfuss building and entitled *Unesco*; hangs in the *hall des délégués*). Between the secretariat and the Avenue de Ségur, the Japanese landscape architect Isamu Noguchi created the serene Garden of Peace, whose running water, undulating relief and different-coloured rocks and gravel – imported from Japan, as were the cherry trees and other plants – ensure that it remains delightful all year round. Since the inauguration of its headquarters, UNESCO has continued to collect and commission artworks, and there are notable later pieces by Erik Reitzel (*The Symbolic Globe*, 1995, on the Avenue de Suffren), Vassilakis Takis (*Aeolian Signals*, 1993, next to the Garden of Peace), Dani Karavan (*Square of Tolerance*, 1996, on the Avenue de Saxe) and most famously Tadao Ando, whose Meditation Space nestles between the secretariat and the assembly-hall building – see 7.11.

7.11 Meditation Space
Garden of UNESCO, accessed either via the Place de Fontenoy or the Avenue de Suffren
Tadao Ando, 1994/95
(Métro: Ségur)

Commissioned by UNESCO (7.10) to symbolize peace and commemorate the 50th anniversary of the adoption of its constitution, Tadao Ando's *Meditation Space* occupies a sunken corner of space nestling between the institution's secretariat and assembly hall. In a manner comparable to the Deportation Memorial (4.3), Ando has created architecture of powerful effect with

7.11 Meditation Space

a minimum of means, although here, rather than the anguish of alienation, it is the serene timelessness associated with traditional Japanese design that suffuses the work.

Announced by a free-standing wall in Ando's usual precision-cast concrete, the installation is reached via a ramp descending in a hairpin to the hollow of space. Both ramp and hollow are paved in granite that was exposed to the atomic blast at Hiroshima. Once in the hollow, the ramp leads across flowing waters (not always operational) to the meditation chamber itself. A simple concrete cylinder, pierced by two openings, the chamber is closed above by a disc, of slightly smaller diameter than the cylinder, that is fixed at only four points, thereby allowing light to filter down through the gap between disc and wall. In this way the elements light, air, stone and water are united in the design. Four high-backed metal chairs are the chamber's only furnishings, and all that animates its surfaces are the regular lines and points left by the shuttering and a spiral incised on the floor. This may not sound like much, but this simple space has a magical aura of protected calm that induces one to stay and quietly ponder.

7.12 Invalides
Place des Invalides
Libéral Bruand, 1671–78; Jules Hardouin-Mansart, 1676–1706
(Métro/RER: Invalides)

This enormous complex, which dominates the Seine even from the retreat of its vast esplanade, was founded by Louis XIV as a home for old and invalid soldiers. Prior to its creation, the fate of disabled veterans had been a major social problem, since the religious institutions that were supposed to take them in were reluctant to do so, and many ex-servicemen turned to begging or joined bandit gangs simply in order to survive. Situated on a flat, green-field site, just outside the then limits of Paris, the new institution was conceived as a city without the city, comprising dormitories for up to 3,000 men with all the attendant service facilities they could need: kitchens, refectories, infirmaries, workshops (idleness was frowned upon and useful employment encouraged) and, of course, a church. The latter was to comprise two elements: a working nave for the inhabitants of the complex, which was to be directly accessible from the dormitories, and a more ceremonial building, entered via the rear of the site, that would be reserved essentially for royal visits. While Bruand's designs for the secular parts of the institution were approved and building work quickly begun, the several schemes he submitted for the church were all rejected by the authorities. The Marquis de Louvois, who as Ministre de la Guerre was in charge of the Invalides project, had already made known his discontentment with Bruand for what he saw as the architect's slowness in conducting the building works, and eventually brought in another man, the young, unknown and ambitious Jules Hardouin-Mansart, to design the church buildings. Bruand was later sacked completely, and Hardouin-Mansart took over responsibility for the entire project. While Bruand's portion of the complex sometimes rather unfortunately demonstrates his limitations, Hardouin-Mansart's church is perhaps his finest creation, as well as being one of the most important examples of French Baroque.

Like Le Vau's contemporaneous Salpêtrière (13.1), on which Bruand worked following Le Vau's death, the Hôtel des Invalides ultimately owes its organization to the Escorial, whose influence had made itself felt in France through Jesuit colleges and hospitals. The basic layout of the Escorial is replicated, that is to say a grid of courtyards grouped around a main *cour d'honneur* and dominated by a church at the rear situated on the complex's principal axis. Bruand's 195 m-long entrance façade, behind which sheltered the administrative spaces of the Invalides, is articulated in classic French style with a central *avant-corps* and lateral pavilions, but is stretched to proportions of a measure rarely employed. The result is unwieldy and repetitive in the extreme, the task of handling this enormous stretch of masonry seemingly having been too much for Bruand. Only the dormer windows, cleverly and originally treated as armour-clad busts, bring any relief to the monotony of the building's *arrière-corps*, whose sobriety suggests more lack of imagination than military rigour. Charges of unoriginality cannot be levelled at the central *avant-corps*, however, which, breaking entirely with the rest of the façade, is a most peculiar composition. A giant and presumably triumphal arch, held up visually by twinned Ionic pilasters (an order which, critics complained, was feminine and therefore inappropriate for a military institution), frames a tripartite elevation comprising the windows of the *salle d'honneur* and the main entrance to the complex. The arch's enormous tympanum is unfenestrated and filled with a bas-relief of a cavalier in profile (Louis XIV, of course, who consequently dominates the building), a form of royal effigy that had been popular in the Renaissance period but which had entirely gone out of

7.12 Invalides. Cour Royale

fashion by the second half of the 17C. In specifying an effigy of this type for this space, Bruand may have been wanting to renew with an older tradition, although his detractors have been quick to write the sculpture off as an awkward archaism on the architect's part. The king's image was only finally carved in stone in 1734 by Guillaume Coustou (replacing a provisory wood-and-plaster sculpture), although what we see today is actually for the most part a 19C creation, the original having been destroyed during the Revolution.

From the four-storey entrance façade one passes into the *cour d'honneur*, known as the Cour Royale, which is articulated as a two-storey composition. Here Bruand had an easier task – the proportions remain manageable – and the courtyard has none of the awkwardness of the entrance elevation. Longer than it is wide, the Cour Royale is bordered by arcaded galleries whose repetition is broken by central porticos on each side and by projecting corner pavilions. The dormers are treated in a similar fashion to those on the entrance façade, thereby ensuring thematic continuity. On either side of the courtyard, on the ground floor, are the four huge soldiers' refectories (the officers dined apart), while on the first floor we find the former infirmaries (all now serve as gallery space for the Musée de l'Armée, which is housed at the Invalides). The soldiers' accommodation was disposed around the four courtyards that flank the Cour Royale, and offered an unusual level of comfort by the standards of the day. Infantrymen were assigned to small, unheated dormitories containing four to six beds, while the officers were housed in twos or threes in rooms that benefited from a fireplace. The Invalides's staircases were built with wide, low steps to make their negotiation easier for the disabled, and over 200 privies were distributed throughout the complex. Hardouin-Mansart enlarged Bruand's original scheme by adding the single-storey buildings at the rear of the site (either side of the church) in 1679 (east flank) and 1691 (west); supplementary officers' accommodation was built onto the latter in the 1750s by Robert de Cotte.

In many ways, life at the Hôtel des Invalides was modelled on that at monasteries and convents, and the soldiers' church, the institution's principal place of congregation, was at the heart of things. Access to it was gained via the Cour Royale, and its entrance is marked by a portico whose twin-columned décor is considerably more elaborate than that of the courtyard's other three examples. Hardouin-Mansart's design for the everyday section of the church is so different from the royal chapel adjacent to it that from the 18C on many historians mistakenly attributed the former to Bruand, even though the surviving documentation clearly shows that Hardouin-Mansart was responsible for the entire structure and that he intended it to operate as a unified whole. The soldiers' part of the church was referred to as the »choir«, a designation based on the fact that it was conceived to perform a similar function to the choir of a monastery church, that is to say it was a »private« space for the residents of the institution. It is organized like the nave of any parish church and, like the majority of French 17C naves, is a Classical adaptation of an essentially Gothic type-form. Its long, tall, barrel-vaulted central vessel is flanked by low side-aisles, but where one would expect to find the clerestory in a Gothic church there is a gallery, a configuration already established in Jesuit churches (see, e.g., Saint-Paul-Saint-Louis (4.7)) and employed here to ensure sufficient space for the large congregation. As a result, the clerestory is pushed up into the high vault itself in the form of transverse »dormer« vaults. A colossal, crisply-carved, pilaster-form Corinthian order marches round the main vessel and decorates its piers, while giant arches terminate its extremities, one filled with an elaborate Baroque organ, the other leading to the oval sanctuary, which sits between the soldiers' »choir« and the royal section of the church. Since the installation in the 19C of Napoleon's tomb in the royal section (see below), Hardouin-Mansart's original double-church arrangement has been entirely disrupted, the soldiers' choir now being closed off from the rest of the structure by a glass screen and provided with its own high altar; initially, however, the two sections of the building shared a main altar that sat in the oval sanctuary linking the two parts of the edifice. There are almost no direct precedents for this configuration, and it seems to have been an invention of Hardouin-Mansart's based on the specific requirements of the Invalides.

The soldiers' choir, which was necessary for the functioning of the Invalides, was finished with relative alacrity by 1679; the royal half of the building, on the other hand, a less pressing and much more elaborate and costly construction, was not completed until well into the 18C. Where Bruand's entrance façade failed to radiate the glory that Louis XIV claimed for his reign, Hardouin-Mansart's spectacular *dôme*, like the majority of his other royal projects, was conceived essentially with this aim in mind. In choosing a *dôme* Hardouin-Mansart was subscribing to a lineage of centralized-plan churches that included amongst its antecedents Saint Peter's in Rome, Santa Maria della Salute in Venice and, closer to home, the church of the Visitation (4.21), designed by his great-uncle François Mansart. The interest of centralized plans of this type was that in their immaculate, in-the-round symmetry, where no one axis has priority over another, they symbolized divine (and perhaps, in this case, royal) perfection, as well as reaching up to heaven with their enormous domes, whose exteriors constituted an unmissable landmark in the cityscape and whose interiors provided a dizzying spectacle that could be heightened by the application of edifying frescoes. Quite why Louis XIV insisted on building a huge and lavish church of this kind at the Invalides has never been satisfactorily explained, although many commentators have suggested that it was initially intended as a burial chapel for the Bourbons. Legend has it that Hardouin-Mansart was given only a week to draw up the design for the Dôme des Invalides, clearly insufficient time to prepare a building of such complexity. It is almost certain that he »recycled« a never-executed scheme (c. 1665) for a Bourbon funerary chapel at Saint-Denis (21.2), designed by his great-uncle, whose drawings he had inherited and whom he claimed as his master (he added »Mansart« to his surname so as to benefit from his illustrious ancestor's reputation). Mansart had devoted considerable energy to developing the centralized-plan/domed type, and Hardouin-Mansart incorporated features from other such designs by his great-uncle (most notably the Val-de-Grâce (5.9)), thereby paying tribute to Mansart's genius. But, as we shall see, the Dôme des Invalides was not just a mere synthesis of the best of Mansart's designs, for Hardouin-Mansart introduced several original features of his own which pushed further the ideas developed by his great-uncle.

In plan the Dôme des Invalides comprises a Greek cross (with a circular crossing) set within a square, each of whose four corners is filled with a circular chapel. This is a simplified version of the early-16C scheme proposed by Bramante for Saint Peter's, which had gone on to inspire numerous successive centralized-plan/domed churches, including Mansart's. Traditionally, the corner chapels were accessed from the arms of the cross and were not in any way directly linked to the crossing, at whose four corners stood massive piers holding up the dome. One of Mansart's innovations in his domed-church designs had been to cut diagonal links through the crossing piers in order to connect the chapels directly to the central space, thereby opening up the crossing, bringing the chapels into the heart of the composition and pushing forward the logic of the centralized plan. But Mansart's chapels were always »dead ends«, i.e. they could only be accessed from the crossing; Hardouin-Mansart, at the Dôme des Invalides, combined his great-uncle's plan with the traditional arrangement by restituting the connections between the corner chapels and the arms of the Greek cross, and in doing so created a space of even greater fluidity and complexity where multiple perspectives open up before the eye.

As in the soldiers' choir, a giant Corinthian order adorns the walls of the *dôme* (indeed it is the same order carried through), only here it is expressed as twinned pilasters and, in the crossing, as full, disengaged columns, and thus consequently dominates the space in a much more exaggerated manner than in the choir, imbuing the *dôme* with an imperial grandeur that is nowhere to be found in previous French domed churches. Perching on the enormous arches of the crossing and their attendant pendentives is the drum of the great dome. Mansart had tended to compress or even remove entirely the drums of his domes on the interior of his churches (although they were present on the exterior), but Hardouin-Mansart took the more traditional approach, providing the Invalides's crossing with a generous, twelve-windowed drum that ensures an abundant supply of natural light, as well as pushing the dome itself further away from the viewer and thereby rendering the vertical perspective even more dramatic. Yet further theatre is to be found in Hardouin-Mansart's handling of the dome's lighting, which follows an innovatory system designed by his great-uncle for the Saint-Denis funerary chapel. The traditional manner of lighting a dome was to pierce it at its summit with a circular opening on top of which perched a lantern. This method had two major disadvantages: the dome's frescoes were interrupted at their centre, i.e. at what should generally have been the culminating point of the pictorial composition, and they

7.12 Invalides. Dôme

were to a certain extent silhouetted against the light, whose central source was also inclined to produce reflections on some parts of the painting. In the Mansarts' system, two domes are employed, one superimposed on the other, the lower of which is truncated so as to provide a circular opening at its summit giving onto the central portion of the second dome, which is lit by windows concealed behind the lower dome. The presence of two domes is invisible to the uninitiated visitor, but the painting on the interior of the upper dome – in this case *Saint Louis Presenting his Sword to Christ* by Charles de La Fosse – appears bathed in a mysterious light, a splendid visual trick of wholly Baroque cunning. De La Fosse chose to leave a blank area of painted sky at the centre of his composition, thereby rendering the dome's apogee yet more celestial.

The interior of the Dôme des Invalides was of course a major opportunity for a display of French mastery in the decorative arts, and an army of artists and craftsmen worked on the project. Sculpture is abundant inside the *dôme*, but, in comparison to, say, the Val-de-Grâce, remains discreet. Several of the principal sculptors of Louis XIV's reign worked on the Invalides, including Antoine Coysevox, Nicolas Coustou, Pierre Legros and Corneille Van Clève. The high altar, which sits in the oval sanctuary attached to the northern arm of the crossing, is, as at the Val-de-Grâce, protected by a baldaquin that was inspired by Bernini's at Saint Peter's in Rome. Lack of funds meant that the original design was only ever executed in wood and plaster, and it subsequently disappeared at the Revolution. The black-marble baldaquin we see today was installed by Ludovico Visconti in 1853, and is closely modelled on Bernini's.

If the Dôme des Invalides was not intended as a Bourbon funerary chapel, it may instead have been conceived as a pantheon of military heroes. At any rate that is what it has become, with the burial there of various generals and, of course, the Emperor Napoleon. His tomb occupies the centre of the *dôme*, and was built to designs by Visconti in 1840–61. Visconti's scheme was chosen because it did not disrupt views of the high altar nor overwhelm the other monuments in the *dôme*, an exploit achieved by excavating a central hole to contain the imperial sarcophagus (which necessitated the destruction of much of the fine 17C marble flooring). Surrounded by a covered gallery, the 15 m-diameter, 6 m-deep circular opening sits bang under the main dome, and in its rather cold neo-Classical garb, which includes poker-faced winged Victories and bas-reliefs depicting key events of Napoleon's reign, contrasts uneasily with the Baroque church above. The ridiculously oversized sarcophagus (Napoleon was, after all, famously diminutive) is in red quartzite, no doubt chosen for its resemblance to porphyry, a favourite material of the Romans. Many are the critics of Visconti's intervention who point out the harm it does to Hardouin-Mansart's architecture, not only because it competes for attention with the splendours of the dome but also because it prevents the visitor from standing at the edifice's centre, which is after all from where a centralized plan is best viewed.

While the interior of the Dôme des Invalides was strongly influenced by the designs of François Mansart, the exterior is a much more original creation on the part of Jules Hardouin. In essence it consists of three simple, Platonic volumes: a cube on top of which stands a cylinder that is coiffed with a hemisphere. To ensure the marriage of the rectilinear cube with the curvilinear cylinder, Hardouin-Mansart covered the cube in such a way that its roofing is invisible from the ground, thus avoiding a complicated transition. The cube's pedimented lateral elevations are comparatively plain, and all interest is concentrated on the principal façade and its elaborate frontispiece. Despite at first glance seeming fairly Classical, the latter nonetheless has some features that can only be classed as Baroque. The rather free grouping of its columns and the central emphasis thereby given to the façade is one example of this, another being the manner in which the orders »step out« from the rear walls of the elevation the further one gets towards the centre of the composition, a manipulation that would not have been found in the architecture of, say, Palladio or Vignola. The frontispiece's proportions also bear little relation to what is actually going on inside the building, whence the masonry »niche« coiffing the first-floor-level window, which masks the internal barrel vault behind it (see the lateral elevations for the real window profile). But the greatest external innovations are to be found on the drum, which was highly unorthodox in comparison to previous examples, on several counts. Firstly, it was provided with an attic storey (whose windows light the upper of the two internal domes), which was most unusual but was also to be found on Mansart's designs for the Bourbon funerary chapel. Secondly, the handling of its buttressing was quite original. Unlike, for example, Saint Peter's in Rome or the Val-de-Grâce, where we find a regular alternance of buttresses and fenestration, the Dôme des Invalides's drum is provided with buttresses only where they are structurally most necessary, that is to say above the piers of the crossing. They are organized as four pairs, each pair framing a window and being separated by two windows from the next pair. The choice of this configuration resulted in the third singularity of the drum, which is that a solid – and one which, moreover, is adorned with a pair of columns of the Composite order encircling the drum – rises above the apex of the main elevation's pediment, instead of the void that Classical purists would have called for. The line of this solid is carried all the way up to the apex of the dome, where, in a raspberry-blowing demonstration of his unorthodoxy, Hardouin-Mansart placed a square belvedere (in place of the usual lantern), which presents to the viewer not one of its openings, as one would expect, but one of its piers, thereby confirming the choice of alignment of the drum. The switch from void to solid between the frontispiece and the drum does not disrupt the central emphasis of the composition, however, and this, combined with the many »storeys« with which the exterior is composed, the subtle elongation of the dome and the presence of the belvedere with its needle-like spire terminating at 105 m above the ground, results in an upwards thrust and vertical emphasis of almost Gothic character, an effect that is certainly quite unlike anything ever seen in the Renaissance or Antiquity. The Dôme des Invalides is a typically French interpretation of Baroque, the embodiment of what Pevsner described as that »specific combination of grandeur and elegance« that French masters excelled in, cooler and less illusionistic than the Italian Baroque it drew inspiration from, more Classical, but nonetheless just as spectacular.

The exterior of the Dôme des Invalides was as much an opportunity for the display of French sculpture as the interior, and the same team artists that worked on the latter were responsible for the external carvings. If the sculpted elements of the main façade seem discreet today, it should be borne in mind that a whole crowd of statues originally populated the *dôme*'s balustrades and cornices, the majority of which have since been lost. By far the most splendid external decorations are the elaborate trophies adorning each segment of the dome, which, like the belvedere and the spire, are generously gilded. In 1989, to celebrate the bicentennial of the French Revolution, the Dôme des Invalides was thoroughly restored, including the regilding of its external décor: over 12 kg of gold leaf were needed to return to its original gleaming radiance.

7.13 Hôtel Peyrenc-de-Moras or Biron (Musée Rodin)
77, rue de Varenne
Jean Aubert, 1727–32
(Métro: Varenne)

In the early years of Louis XV's reign, the Faubourg Saint-Germain experienced unprecedented growth, replacing the Marais as Paris's aristocratic quarter. A spur to this development was the building of the Invalides (7.12), for which Louis XIV reconstructed the

7.13 Hôtel Peyrenc-de-Moras or Biron (Musée Rodin)

road linking the new institution to Saint-Germain proper. It was along this street, rebaptized the Rue de Varenne, that some of Paris's finest 18C *hôtels particuliers* were built. In contrast to their 17C forbears, many benefited from considerable grounds, thanks to the abundance of space available in the new neighbourhood.

This handsome example was commissioned by the wigmaker-turned-financier Abraham Peyrenc de Moras (whom contemporaries considered something of a parvenu), who wanted a residence that would reflect the magnitude of his newly acquired fortune. His taste was clearly not, however, *nouveau riche*, for the house he built is charming and externally rather understated; it is only in its splendid, entirely detached isolation in the middle of exceptionally generous grounds that its owner's wealth is displayed. The *hôtel* was for a long time attributed to Jacques V Gabriel, but it is now thought that its builder, Jean Aubert, was the true author, Gabriel's role, if any, being that of a consultant. Essentially conceived as a mini château, the *hôtel* is approached via a generous *cour d'honneur*, to the right of which originally stood the kitchens and other outbuildings (since demolished). The house presents classic French façades on both the courtyard and garden fronts, the *corps de logis* sporting pedimented *avant-corps* and side pavilions. The Rococo-period tendency towards fusing the separate elements into a continuous envelope, in contrast to the rather »assembled« look of many 17C French buildings, is clearly evident (although slightly contradicted by the *hôtel*'s disjoined roofing). In plan the building shows another 18C departure from 17C precedents in that its internal load-bearing walls are transversal rather than longitudinal, permitting a more flexible room layout.

Amongst the *hôtel*'s subsequent owners was the Maréchal de Biron (1753–88), whose name it thereafter took. In 1829, it became home to a convent school, which sold off the fine Rococo panelling and wrought-iron fittings. Following the separation of church and state, in 1904, the convent was expelled and the *hôtel* let to a number of artists, amongst whom was Auguste Rodin (1908–17). When he bequeathed his collections to the nation, he requested that a museum be created for them in the Hôtel Biron; in 1919, two years after his death, this wish was fulfilled. Since that time parts of the *hôtel*'s original panelling and décor have been bought back and reinstalled. The magnificent gardens, which were remodelled and replanted by the landscape architect Jacques Sgard in 1993, form a splendid setting for some of Rodin's large-scale works.

7.14 Hôtel Matignon
57, rue de Varenne
Jean Courtonne, *c.* 1722–25
(Métro: Varenne)

Today famous as the official residence of France's prime minister, the Hôtel Matignon was celebrated in its time for the subtleties of its plan and the splendour of its decoration. It was commissioned by the Prince

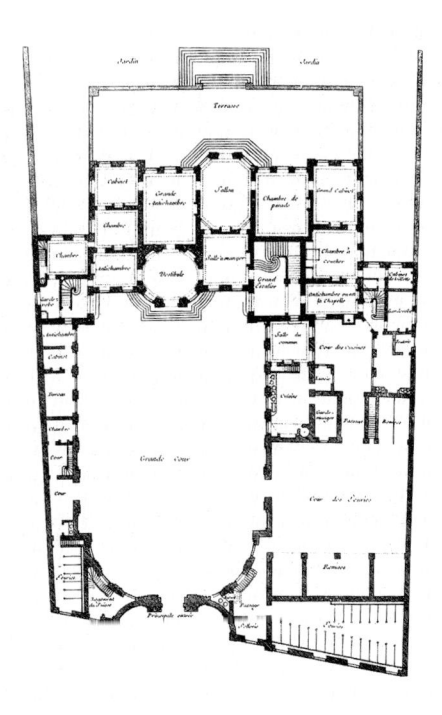

7.14 Hôtel Matignon

de Tingry, but was sold uncompleted because the prince had run out of money. Bought by Jacques de Matignon, Comte de Thorigny, in 1723, the *hôtel* was finished and decorated by its new owner. For reasons that remain obscure, Courtonne was sacked by Matignon at the eleventh hour, and the finishing touches to the building were executed by his replacement, Jean Mazin. Today the *hôtel* remains essentially as Matignon left it externally, although various internal changes were made by the Duc de Galliera, who acquired the residence in the 1850s.

Situated in grounds of 3 ha (an enormous area for Paris), the Hôtel Matignon benefited from more breathing space than was usual for this type of residence, but is nonetheless hemmed in by neighbours. The house follows the traditional *hôtel-particulier* pattern, with a principal *corps de logis* giving onto a garden at the rear and separated from the street by a courtyard, the latter surrounded on its other three sides by service buildings and accessed via a central *porte-cochère*. Courtonne's plan became famous for the way in which, on a restricted site, he cleverly juggled the conflicting needs of symmetry and *commodité* (a term that designated convenience, in the sense of accommodating the practicalities of elegant living). First of all there was the problem of the non-alignment of the building's two principal façades. Because *commodité* dictated that the stables were best placed next to the *cour d'hon-neur*, the courtyard front was considerably narrower than the garden façade which, in the absence of impinging service buildings, could run freely across the width of the site. Symmetry demanded that each elevation be given central emphasis, but the lateral push of the stables on the courtyard front meant that the façades' axes did not coincide. This discordance had to be dissimulated in the house's internal layout so that it would not in any way affect the smooth run of room sequences either from back to front or laterally. Furthermore, there was the difficulty of the *escalier d'honneur*: it had to be directly accessible from the exterior so that the first-floor apartments could be reached discretely, but also had to be out of the way enough not to disrupt the sequence of rooms on either floor. Courtonne gracefully overcame all these problems, ingeniously fitting his *cabinets*, *salons* and *vestibules* together like pieces in a puzzle, helped by the unusually wide site, which allowed him to light some of the rooms laterally. The *hôtels* of the French-Regency period are generally considered the acme of the type for their sophistication, and it was plans of this quality that were perhaps the greatest achievement of the French Rococo.

Rococo influences are also discernible in Courtonne's façades. They feature the traditional French arrangement of a *logis* with end pavilions and a central *avant-corps*, but the separate elements are less distinct than in earlier French architecture, the wall surface having been treated as one single bulging and swelling entity pierced with numerous, regularly spaced windows. This impression is reinforced by a continuous balustrade at roof level. Much blank wall is in evidence, sculpture being limited essentially to the window lintels, although extra exuberance is expressed on the central *avant-corps*, especially on the courtyard side, which was originally crowned with Matignon's coat of arms. (Contemporaries criticized this reversal of the traditional arrangement – usually it was the garden front that was more flamboyant.) Inside, the remaining original decoration is limited to the oval vestibule and the Grand Salon, both Rococo in style although today somewhat overloaded with 19C additions. The current *escalier d'honneur* was installed by the Duc de Galliera in the 1850s, and features paintings by Paul Baudry and the brothers Paul and Hippolyte Flandrin.

7.15 Bon Marché
22–36, rue de Sèvres
Alexandre Laplanche, 1869–72; Louis-Charles Boileau (with Louis-Auguste Boileau), 1872–76; Louis-Hippolyte Boileau, 1920–24
(Métro: Sèvres-Babylone)

Although not the first of Paris's big department stores, Bon Marché is today the city's oldest surviving example (founded in 1852 by Aristide Boucicaut), and was perhaps the first to encapsulate all the features that characterized this most 19C of institutions: free entry, fixed, marked prices, right of return on goods, benefits for employees and philanthropic activities. As such it was one of the principle sources for Emile Zola's *Au Bonheur des Dames* (1882), a novel which described a fictional retail palace in all its bustling detail. Two factors opened the way for the emergence of the Parisian department store: the abolition of the corporations, in 1791, and the development of the railway network, which, converging on the capital, concentrated commerce in central Paris to an extraordinary degree. Architecturally, the department stores were to an extent descendants of the covered arcade (to whose commercial downfall they certainly contributed – see feature on arcades and passages), as the model of iron-framed, top-lit spaces was one they appropriated. Paris's first department store organized around a central atrium of this type was Au Coin de Rue (1864), and it was a feature that soon became *de rigueur* for subsequent shops, allowing as it did the commercialization of deep sites by bringing daylight into their hearts.

Where Bon Marché's selling methods were progressive, its architecture initially was not, Laplanche's first rebuild in 1869 consisting of a traditional masonry structure of banal aspect. Hardly had the paint dried on the new shop than Boucicaut commissioned its extension from Louis-Charles Boileau, whose father, Louis-Auguste – also involved in the project – had won renown for Saint-Eugène (9.3), probably the very first

7.15 Bon Marché

7.16 Fontaine des Quatre-Saisons or de Grenelle

iron-framed church. At Bon Marché the Boileaus designed an all-metal structure (albeit faced in stone) in collaboration with the firms Moisant and Eiffel, who manufactured the ironwork. Louis-Charles saw it as something of a manifesto of iron construction, declaring that where stone gave rise to an architecture of solids, iron engendered an architecture of voids. Rising three storeys (taller shops only became possible with the development of the lift), the store's interior featured a series of monumental glass skylights covering almost the entire upper floor and two handsome central atria. Skylights and atria are still in place, although the latter have lost the flying footbridges and Baroque central staircase that so wowed contemporaries. A set of escalators now replaces the stairs, thankfully designed with a little more care than those at Samaritaine (1.5).

The *nouveau magasin* on the other side of the Rue du Bac is by Louis-Hippolyte Boileau, son of Louis-Charles. Its palatial Art-Déco halls were sadly destroyed in 1979, and only the detailing of the principal entrance now hints at the interior's former splendour.

7.16 Fontaine des Quatre-Saisons or de Grenelle
57–59, rue de Grenelle
Edme Bouchardon, 1739–45
(Métro: Rue du Bac)

Following the rapid expansion of the Faubourg Saint-Germain, which usurped the Marais as Paris's aristocratic quarter in the early-18C, the municipality commissioned a fountain to embellish the new neighbourhood. Bouchardon, a sculptor by profession, was given the job, and produced this Baroque extravaganza to the glory of the city and her councillors.

The fountain's already considerable dimensions are rendered yet more commanding by its concave plan and tall podium. Under the Ionic portico of the imposing central *avant-corps* sits the City of Paris. Royally dressed, she is being paid homage by the Seine and the Marne (the two principal rivers of the region), who lie at her feet. In niches either side of the *avant-corps* stand the four seasons, each bearing seasonal produce to demonstrate Paris's year-round abundance. With its magisterial, beautifully proportioned composition, its crisp execution and its evocation of commerce, plenty and mastery over nature, the fountain makes for a magnificent monument to civic genius. Indeed so pleased were the city councillors with the result that they granted Bouchardon a handsome pension.

In some respects, however, the fountain backfired. Although its architecture garnered unanimous admiration, the total absence of any cascades or jets of water (two little taps, for domestic use, are all it possesses) was vehemently criticized, and its rather surprising situation in such a narrow street found to be equally ludicrous. Unfavourable comparisons were made with the abundant gush and piazza settings of Rome's fountains, and the municipality's competence in matters of urbanism and water provision called into question.

7.17 Maison de Verre
31, rue Saint-Guillaume
Pierre Chareau with Bernard Bijvoët, 1928–32
(Métro: Rue du Bac, Sèvres Babylone, Saint-Germain-des-Prés)

One of the most audacious houses of the interwar period and much admired by Le Corbusier (who was inspired by it for his Immeuble Molitor (29.4)), the Maison de Verre was Chareau's only major construction. It was commissioned by his long-time patrons Dr and Mme Dalsace, who had acquired an 18C *hôtel particulier* whose courtyard positioning made it so dark inside that lamps had to be lit during the day, even in summer. Devotees of modern design, they decided to demolish and build anew *in situ*. Chareau and Bijvoët's extraordinarily bold proposal was a house with walls entirely of glass. To build it, Chareau drew upon all his experience as a furniture maker and his knowledge of industrial materials and processes, to the extent that many have wondered whether the project is better understood as a house or a piece of furniture, a home or a *machine à habiter*.

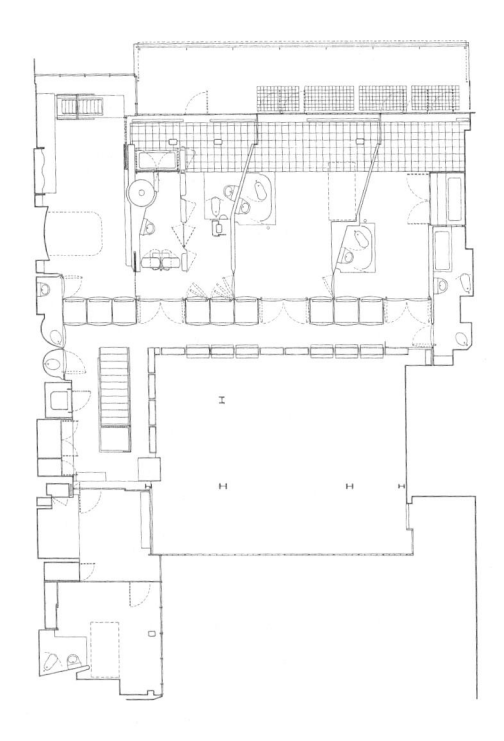

Construction was undertaken in rather *ad-hoc* fashion, and plans were constantly modified after almost daily on-site visits by the clients. An initial difficulty was encountered when the third-floor tenant of the original house refused to move out. Her apartment was left in place, the floors below it being demolished and supplanted by the steel frame of the new house. Chareau and Bijvoët enclosed the structure in a skin of translucent, but not transparent, glass bricks, thereby ensuring the occupants' privacy. The doctor's surgery is located on the ground floor, reception rooms on the first and bedrooms, etc. in the final storey. Kitchens and servants' quarters were housed in a smaller wing in the courtyard. State-of-the-art services, including air-conditioning, were centrally grouped in the basement.

The Maison de Verre has very few windows. By day the interior is bathed in a soft, milky, but cold light, as though underwater, and at night it is floodlit from without to simulate daylight. The interior includes a magnificent double-height living space, reached by a bravura staircase orientated to exploit to the maximum the dramatic effect of the glass walls. The majority of the furniture was designed by Chareau, much of it built in and mechanically ingenious – folding stairways, pivotable bidets etc. – sometimes verging on the Heath Robinson. Many of the spaces are modifiable, equipped with moveable screens and partitions. Every detail received Chareau's meticulous attention in his desire to create a total environment.

Chareau regretted that the Dalsaces did not live according to the rhythm of the house, thereby revealing its principal flaw. Like so many Modernist projects, the Maison de Verre suffers from its intransigence towards its users. Its occupants must adapt to its exigencies; the masters of the house become its servants. Although spawning few direct imitators, the house has been highly influential, especially since its »rediscovery« in the mid-1960s.

7.17 Maison de Verre

8th *arrondissement*

8.1 Place de la Concorde
Ange-Jacques Gabriel, 1755–75
(Métro: Concorde)

By far Paris's most monumental square, the Place de la Concorde was, as every schoolchild knows, commissioned to the glory of absolutism before serving as the theatre of its downfall, when Louis XVI was guillotined there in 1793. The origins of the *place* date back to 1748, when the Ville de Paris decided to erect an equestrian statue of Louis XV. A competition was launched to design a setting for the effigy, for which one of the participants proposed a square situated at the western extremity of the Jardin des Tuileries (1.10), on what was then parkland forming part of the great westward axis designed by Le Nôtre in the 1660s (today's Avenue des Champs-Elysées). Although on the then outskirts of the city, this site presented the advantage of already mostly belonging to the crown, thus minimizing expropriation costs, and would serve to encourage the westward expansion of Paris's wealthy *quartiers*. Following this decision, a second competition, limited to members of the Académie Royale d'Architecture, was organized in 1753; afterwards, Ange-Jacques Gabriel, Premier Architecte du Roi and head of the Academy, was asked to draw up a final project incorporating the best of the competition proposals. Gabriel's plans were approved in 1755, the statue inaugurated in 1763 and the square, initially baptized the Place Louis-XV, finally completed in 1775.

Rectangular in shape, with its longer axis running north–south parallel to the Tuileries, Gabriel's new *place* was truly enormous – 84,000 m² – and consequently required a very different approach to previous squares. Where Paris's small-scale, older piazzas were essentially architectonic creations defined by the buildings surrounding them, the Place de la Concorde was to be more a work of landscaping than of architecture *per se*. It is built on only one side – the north – its eastern extremity being defined by the Tuileries, its southern by the river and its western by the trees of the Champs-Elysées. In laying out the square this way, Gabriel maintained the continuity of Le Nôtre's east–west axis, while at the same time creating a vast stage set, complete with architectural backdrop, on which to display Louis XV's statue. The latter was of course placed at the exact centre of the *place*; so that it would not appear too forlorn in the middle of this huge space and to emphasize royal might, Gabriel surrounded it with a set of 20 m-wide grassed moats, delineated by balustrades and punctuated with guard houses. Within the space thus defined, all the pageant of the court could be deployed for the monarch's ceremonial arrivals at and departures from the Tuileries. A favourite haunt of prostitutes, the moats were filled in, in the 1850s, to increase available space for public gatherings, but their outer balustrades and the guard houses still stand.

8.1 Place de la Concorde

As originally planned, the Place de la Concorde was to be entered at five principal points: from the Rue Royale, running northwards in the longitudinal axis of the square, from the Champs-Elysées and two avenues leading off diagonally on either side of it (the Cours la Reine and a second, proposed thoroughfare that never got off the drawing board), and from the quayside (the Pont de la Concorde came later – see feature on Seine bridges). The north side of the square was thus bisected by the Rue Royale; had this not been the case, a monumental structure with a central focus would have been the obvious scheme for the buildings erected here. Instead, Gabriel built two identical structures either side of the Rue Royale, which are without central focus but which are punctuated by sizeable pavilions at either extremity. This solution cleverly maintains central emphasis, as the middle of the composition is framed by two of the pavilions, which also act as a monumental gateway to the Rue Saint-Honoré, then Paris's principle east–west thoroughfare. For the design of the buildings, Gabriel looked to Claude Perrault's east front of the Louvre (1.8), one of Louis XIV's most potent architectural legacies, in a deliberate move to identify Louis XV's reign with the glory of his great-grandfather's. Like the Louvre, the Place-de-la-Concorde buildings feature a colossal colonnade, although theirs are more Classical in that the columns are single and not twinned as in Perrault's design. Gabriel's detailing is also lighter and more festive than Perrault's: the basement arcades feature English-Palladian-style rustication, swags and garlands run between the first and second floors and, even when using direct quotations from the Louvre (e.g. the oval garlanded medallions adorning the pavilions), Gabriel avoided any hint of heaviness or severity. Given their setting, Gabriel's buildings are also admirably modest in scale, making them considerably friendlier than the massive, bombastic Louvre. On the Rue Royale, their lateral façades wind down in a gentle *decrescendo* the further they get from the *place*.

Initially reserved by the crown to house the state collection of furniture, the square's righthand building became home to its current occupant, the Ministère de la Marine, in 1789. Its interiors were designed by Jacques-Germain Soufflot and Jacques Gondoin and, although restyled in the mid-19C, some of the original décor survives. Of particular note are the *escalier d'honneur*, the Salon des Sacrifices – with decorative elements inspired by both Piranesi and Wedgwood! – and the Galerie Dorée. The square's lefthand building was also intended for state use, but in the end its site was divided into four plots that were sold off for the construction of *hôtels particuliers*, the money thus raised being used to offset the construction costs of the square. Amongst the buildings on this side of the *place* are the Hôtel de Crillon, which conserves an exceptional ceiling from the 1770s designed by Pierre-Adrien Pâris, and the Automobile Club, whose interiors were decorated by Gustave Rives in 1912.

The Place Louis-XV was an inevitable target for Revolutionary iconoclasm, and the statue of the sovereign was duly destroyed in 1792. During the Terror, its empty pedestal witnessed the guillotining of over 1,000 people, including Louis XVI and Marie-Antoinette. Following the Bourbon restoration, a monument to the decapitated Louis was begun in the square, but work was abandoned after the fall of Charles X, in 1830. In 1831, the Viceroy of Egypt offered France two 23 m-high obelisks from the palace of Ramses III in Luxor. In a bid to wipe away memories of the Black Widow, Louis Philippe's government decided to install one of the obelisks at the centre of the square, which was to be refurbished to accommodate it, appointing Jakob Ignaz Hittorff to carry out the work. A 230-ton pink-granite monolith, the obelisk, at over 3,000 years old, can be said to be Paris's most ancient monument. Erected at the *place* in 1836, it caused a good deal of controversy because of its damaged summit, which was considered unaesthetic; everyone agreed that it should be repaired, but opinions differed as to how. After studying the monument, Hittorff concluded that its pyramidal zenith must originally have supported a metal covering. He proposed fitting the obelisk with a new hat in gilded bronze, but was rebuffed by the authorities who preferred to remould the summit in granite-coloured mastic. The mastic soon began to crumble, and was subsequently removed, leaving the obelisk in its original damaged state. 160 years later, in 1998, Hittorff's idea was finally adopted and the monument coiffed with its current gilded-metal pyramid; when the weather permits, its summit now glitters as it must formerly have done under the ancient-Egyptian sun.

Work on the refurbishment of the Place de la Concorde was begun immediately following erection of the obelisk, and completed in 1840. On either side of the monument, Hittorff installed magnificent fountains, allegories of sea and river navigation intended to celebrate French naval know-how. Cast in iron, they were painted to resemble bronze and generously gilded, but faded with time to a dull, uniform grey. Recently restored, they have now regained all their original exuberance. Around the *place*, Hittorff planted 20 rostral columns – thus continuing the naval theme and also symbolizing Paris, whose emblem is a ship's prow – and 80 candelabra, again all cast in iron (see feature on street furniture). The lavishly ornamented columns were designed so that the top of their capitals are as high as the ground floor of Gabriel's buildings, and their spheres at the same level as his balustrades. Finally, to complete the ensemble, eight statues of important French towns were installed on top of Gabriel's guard houses.

Unfortunately, none of the conceptors of the Place de la Concorde could foresee the invention of the motor car. One of Paris's three principal traffic interchanges, the square today is a nightmare environment of speeding, belching vehicles; crossing to view the obelisk and the fountains can be a near-death experience. In 1999, in what was largely perceived as a municipal-election ploy, the outgoing mayor put forward a scheme to reduce the space given over to the automobile by 80%, thereby re-establishing the connection between the *place* and the Tuileries. Despite the major traffic repercussions, police consent was obtained. The new administration, however, has opted to maintain the status quo, and the plans have sadly been dropped.

8.2 Madeleine
Place de la Madeleine
Various architects, principally Pierre Vignon, 1757–1842
(Métro: Madeleine)

Commissioned by Louis XV in 1757, the Eglise de Sainte-Marie-Madeleine was conceived in tandem with creation of the Place de la Concorde (8.1) since it was intended to close the perspective of the Rue Royale as seen from the square. Work was initially entrusted to Pierre Contant d'Ivry, who laid out the enormous piazza around the church, but who completed little of the actual building work before his death in 1777. He was replaced by Guillaume-Martin Couture, who wasted much time modifying Ivry's plans, although he preserved the basic elements of the initial idea: the church was to have been an enormous domed basilica, a pendant on the Right Bank to the Panthéon (5.8) on the Left. But, when the Revolution broke out, halting building work, only the foundations and a handful of columns had been erected, after 30 years' activity!

The church remained in this state for another decade and a half. Various proposals were put forward for alternative schemes incorporating its foundations, including an assembly building, a national library and a financial exchange. In 1806, Napoleon announced his decision to erect a temple to the glory of the Grande Armée on the foundations, and the following year commissioned Pierre Vignon, a pupil of Ledoux's, to carry out the job. Evidently aware of the emperor's taste for architecture that recalled imperial Rome, Vignon proposed an enormous Corinthian temple (a choice that would be repeated a year later by Brongniart for his Palais de la Bourse (2.8)). Vignon was still working on the project at the time of Napoleon's fall; Louis XVIII kept him on, but decreed that the building should become a church, as originally planned by his grandfather. After his death in 1828, Vignon was replaced by Jean-Jacques-Marie Huvé, who finally completed the edifice in 1842.

What immediately strikes one most forcibly about the Madeleine are its enormous dimensions, in part necessary to give it presence when viewed from the Concorde, but no doubt also intended to flatter the imperial ego. The building measures a colossal 108×43 m, its oversized columns rising 20 m. Externally at least, Vignon's church is an authentic peripteral temple, and no windows disturb its intimidatingly august severity. This choice forced Vignon to introduce light internally from above, and the interior consequently comprises a series of three shallow domes, coffered and open at the top in the manner of the Roman Pantheon, as well as a semicircular apse at the northern end containing the altar (the church is not orientated). Each dome is carried on four Corinthian arches with pendentives, all treated in a grand imperial-Roman manner. This, combined with the opulent décor (including sculptures by Rude), produces a rather overwhelming effect of ostentation.

8.2 Madeleine

8.3 Hôtel Alexandre or Suchet

8.3 Hôtel Alexandre or Suchet
16, rue de la Ville-l'Evêque
Louis-Etienne Boullée, 1763–66
(Métro: Madeleine)

Famed for the awesomely monumental neo-Classical fantasies he produced towards the end of his life, Louis-Etienne Boullée was also a practising architect with both private and public clients. His built œuvre was not, however, enormous, and this *hôtel*, constructed for the financier André-Claude-Nicolas Alexandre, is the only example of Boullée's work to survive more or less intact.

One of his earliest projects, begun when he was just 35, the house follows the usual pattern for an *hôtel particulier*, with two principal façades, one giving on to the *cour d'honneur* on the street, the other overlooking the garden. Like other fashionable Parisian *hôtels* of the day, the two façades differ markedly: the courtyard façade comprises a colossal order rising from the ground floor, obscuring the internal divisions of the building, while the garden front is articulated with pilasters rising from the first floor. The courtyard façade is particularly delightful, monumental yet intimate and beautifully proportioned. A garland motif, popular at the time, is repeated on both façades, uniting the exterior thematically and bringing a charming touch of gaiety to the *hôtel*.

Apart from the later addition of a mansard attic in place of its roof terrace, the Hôtel Alexandre's *corps de logis* appears essentially as Boullée intended. Its context has changed radically, however. Incorporated into the headquarters of Suez-Lyonnaise des Eaux, it now decorates the atrium of a monumental steel-and-glass office building by Delaage Tsaropoulos Architecture Carvunis Cholet (1998–2001).

8.4 Chapelle Expiatoire
29, rue Pasquier, Square Louis-XVI
Pierre-François-Léonard Fontaine, 1815–26
(Métro: Saint-Augustin, Saint-Lazare)

Opened in 1721, the Cimetière de la Madeleine started out as a modest parish graveyard, but earned notorie-

8th *arrondissement* 153

0.4 Chapelle Expiatoire

ty during the Revolution. In 1792 it received the Swiss Guards killed during the storming of the Tuileries and later, because of its proximity to the Place de la Concorde (8.1), played host to many of the Black Widow's victims, including the most illustrious of all, Louis XVI and Marie-Antoinette. Following the Terror, the cemetery was sold off to a royalist sympathizer, who faithfully tended it for the next 20 years. After the Bourbon restoration, Louis XVIII ordered the removal of his brother and sister-in-law's remains to the royal necropolis at Saint-Denis (21.2) and, at his own expense, built this chapel, dedicated to all victims of the Revolution, on the site of the cemetery. Fontaine, who with his partner Charles Percier had been Napoleon's private architect, here worked alone, Percier having refused to collaborate on a project whose political content ran against his convictions.

The two main organizing principles of Fontaine's scheme consisted in placing the chapel above the spot where Louis XVI had been buried and enclosing the cemetery in the manner of an Italian *campo santo* (cloistered graveyard), thereby emphasizing the »sacred« character of soil that contained the remains of »martyrs« of the Revolution. Luckily the supposed site of the king's former resting place was at one extremity of the cemetery, allowing Fontaine to create a processional sequence culminating in the royal chapel. In place of the mid-19C square enclosing the ensemble today, we should imagine the building's original context, which was much less dense and included an avenue of trees leading up to the main entrance. On arrival, the visitor is confronted with an imposingly blank elevation whose austerity and limited decoration (funerary wreaths, etc.) herald what is to come. An imposing flight of steps within the generous entrance vestibule leads up to the cemetery, which is bordered on either side by gabled arcades. These recall as much French medieval charnel houses as Italian cloistered graveyards, an impression strengthened by their decoration, which includes winged hour glasses, carved stone »bargeboards« featuring the leaves of different tree species – intended to symbolize the diversity of social classes amongst the Revolution's victims – and tomb stones commemorating the massacred Swiss Guards. Just as the »sacred« ground of the graveyard was raised above the entrance gateway, so the royal chapel is elevated above the cemetery proper, which one must cross to reach it.

Externally the chapel is severe, a crisp assemblage of simple volumes consisting of a central, domed cube from which project half-domed, semicircular apses on three sides, the fourth side facing the cemetery sporting a solemn Doric entrance portico. The impression of cold, neo-Classical geometry is reinforced by the total absence of openings in the chapel's blank walls and by the minimal decoration. The exterior's hardness belies the gracious interior; inside, the edges separating the individual volumes have been bevelled away (the central dome sits on pendentives above an irregular octagon) so that the different spaces run into each other as one fluid whole. Top lit, the chapel is richly and crisply carved on its upper levels, including coffering and rosettes within the domes and religious allegories in the pendentives, all picked out by the gentle light filtering down from above. This upper-level splendour is complemented below by the richly inlaid floor. At once grand and intimate, cold and affecting, the chapel clearly reflects the heritage of Boullée and the Enlightenment era.

Opposite the entrance is the high altar, while in the side apses are two famous sculpture groups – to the south *Marie-Antoinette supported by Religion*, by Jean-Pierre Cortot, and to the north *Louis XVI called to immortality supported by an angel*, by François-Joseph Bosio. Behind these effigies, staircases descend to the narrow crypt where, underneath the high altar, there is a small devotional chapel above the supposed site of Louis XVI's original burial.

8.5 Gare Saint-Lazare
108, rue Saint-Lazare
Alfred Armand, 1841–43; Eugène Flachat, 1851–53; Juste Lisch, 1885–87
(Métro: Saint-Lazare)

The original Gare Saint-Lazare was Paris's first railway station, erected for the Paris–Saint-Germain-en-Laye line in 1836/37. It was rebuilt to the south of the original site in the 1840s by Alfred Armand, whose structure forms the nucleus of the present edifice. Eugène Flachat, the company engineer, added several iron-and-glass train-sheds to Armand's station in 1851–53, of which the largest spans 40 m without intermediary support, a world record at the time. This achievement was made possible by developments in iron lamination techniques, which rendered the metal stronger. Highly impressed, Napoleon III subsequently ordered that

8.5 Gare Saint-Lazare

8.6 Saint-Augustin

the new Halles Centrales (see 1.22) be constructed in iron rather than stone, as previously planned.

In preparation for the 1889 Exposition Universelle, the station underwent a major programme of rebuilding and enlargement, in 1885–87, directed by Juste Lisch, an architect who specialized in stations. His pompous stone pavilions, in *faux*-17C style, hide the working station behind their grandiloquent anonymity. Lisch also added five new train-sheds, to extend the existing structures which were considered too short. In addition, the Gare Saint-Lazare became the first Parisian station to which a large hotel was attached, as was common practice in London – Lisch's lavish Hôtel Terminus (now Concorde Saint-Lazare). Situated in front of the main station, and connected to it by a covered footbridge for first-class passengers, the hotel was intended to welcome the influx of visitors to the 1889 exhibition. Monet immortalized the Gare Saint-Lazare in his series of paintings of the station executed in 1877.

8.6 Saint-Augustin
46, boulevard Malesherbes
Victor Baltard, 1860–71
(Métro: Saint-Augustin)

At the beginning of the 19C, the *quartiers* to the northwest of the Madeleine (8.2), today so solidly prosperous, were the site of a notorious rookery, nicknamed »la Petite Pologne«. Napoleon drew up plans to drive an avenue straight through the middle of the area and so open it up to redevelopment on more middle-class lines, but his dream was not realized until 50 years later by Baron Haussmann. The Boulevard Malesherbes was duly inaugurated on 13 August 1861 with much pomp and ceremony, and the area subsequently underwent rapid expansion. A new parish, dedicated to Saint-Augustin, had been created in 1851, and a temporary wooden church erected for worship. The site chosen for its replacement, in keeping with the Second-Empire predilection for placing monumental public buildings at major traffic intersections, is on the Place Saint-Augustin, at the head of the southern section of the boulevard. It is said by some, although there is no evidence to support this theory, that Napoleon III intended to install his family mausoleum in the new church.

Situated at the junction of two diagonally converging thoroughfares, the site is wedge-shaped and extremely narrow, especially where it meets the Place Saint-Augustin, and thus did not lend itself to construction of a church. The municipality's chosen architect was Victor Baltard, whose famous Halles Centrales (see 1.22) were just going up. Their futuristic iron construction had fired public imagination, and Baltard proposed that Saint-Augustin also be built of iron. This material offered two distinct advantages over traditional stone technology: on such a narrow site, it would avoid the need for space-consuming buttressing and, furthermore, it would considerably reduce the cost and duration of construction. Although it may have seemed appropriate to expose the ironwork of utilitarian buildings such as market halls to the general gaze, this was out of the question for a church, especially one situated in such an up-and-coming area, and Saint-Augustin was therefore to be clad in stone.

The configuration of the site and the demands of monumental urbanism did not allow the usual east–west church orientation, and the main entrance to the building is thus on the Place Saint-Augustin, facing southeast. Baltard's design consists of an eight-bay nave, with tapering side aisles that follow the contours of the site, culminating in a huge square chancel surmounted by a giant dome rising to 80 m. The chancel is flanked by wide side-chapels, and a small, rounded apse protrudes from its rear. Four pepper-pot bell-towers cluster round the dome. The treatment of the exterior is a curious *mélange* of Byzantine, Romanesque and Renaissance influences, with even a hint of Gothic for the principal façade, in the form of the large rose window and the sculpted representations of Christ and the Apostles (by François Jouffroy) which fill the upper sections. All ironwork is banished, bar the rose window and the lantern of the dome. Viewed from the southern section of the Boulevard Malesherbes, the church appears singularly tight and top heavy, especially in the absence of transepts, and the dome seems to weigh down clumsily on the nave below.

In contrast to the exterior, the interior of the church attempts no dissimulation of its structure. This was

8.7 Saint-Philippe-du-Roule

not the first Parisian iron-framed church – Saint-Eugène (9.3) had been completed in the previous decade – but was on a much bigger scale than anything before. The nave of Saint-Augustin is constructed from a series of iron arches supporting shallow transverse vaults. The finely cast iron supports are painted and gilded and, at the springing point, sport angels moulded by Louis Schroeder. Decoration of the church was entrusted to Charles Lameire, one of the best-known interior designers of the day. The result, though sumptuous, is not altogether successful. Lameire called on the talents of a host of other artists and craftsmen, including the illustrious William Bouguereau, who contributed the paintings of Saint Peter and Saint Paul hidden up above the eastern side-chapel.

8.7 Saint-Philippe-du-Roule
154, rue du Faubourg Saint-Honoré
Jean-François Chalgrin, 1764–84
(Métro: Saint-Philippe-du-Roule)

Following the commencement of Soufflot's Sainte-Geneviève (now the Panthéon (5.8)), mid-18C France saw a move away from traditional Gothicizing church design – still clearly evident in buildings like Saint-Roch (1.15) and Saint-Sulpice (6.5), completed in the early-18C – to a more Classical, »basilical« model, of which Saint-Philippe-du-Roule was one of the first and most celebrated examples. The inspiration for this new generation of churches came from early-Christian places of worship, whose form was directly derived from Roman secular basilicas. By appropriating this model, 18C architects were able to build Classicizing churches that avoided the stylistic conflict inherent in buildings such as Saint-Roch and Saint-Sulpice, and could also claim a return to the roots of Christianity, in doing so prefiguring the neo-Classical tendencies of the late-18C.

Chalgrin's design for Saint-Philippe was not a slavish copy of early-Christian basilicas but a liberal adaptation of the type to suit the sophisticated Classicism of 18C France. As originally built, Saint-Philippe presented a classic, single-storey basilical plan, with a barrel-vaulted nave that was flanked by side aisles and that terminated in a semicircular, half-domed apse, where the high altar was located. A tightly intercolumniated Ionic order supported the nave vault and was carried round into the apse as engaged columns, with niches filling the blank wall space between them. Visual unity and a sense of Roman grandeur were achieved through the coffering applied to the nave vault and the apse dome which, for reasons of economy, were realized in wood rather than the stone planned by Chalgrin. The aisles were plain and without side-chapels, although they terminated just before the apse in discrete chapels reminiscent of transepts. The overall result must have appeared both refreshingly straightforward and urbanely august, and contemporary critics praised the unity of plan and articulation that Chalgrin had achieved. Externally, the church was sober to the point of austerity, all interest being concentrated in the broodingly monumental Doric entrance façade. If Saint-Philippe now appears modest, one should bear in mind that when built it towered over the then semi-rural neighbourhood.

Today, although the church preserves much of its former allure, it is hard to appreciate the clarity of Chalgrin's original design because of the considerable modifications carried out in the 19C. The most far-reaching of these was Hippolyte Godde's 1846–50 extension of the church's apse end through the addition of an ambulatory – separated from the apse by freestanding columns – and the Chapelle de la Vierge, which prolongs the building in its longitudinal axis. Godde was also responsible for the windows that pierce the nave's barrel vault, and for the removal of the apse coffering to make way for Théodore Chassériau's fresco of the *Descente de la Croix*.

8.8 Musée Jacquemart-André
158, boulevard Haussmann
Henri Parent, 1869–75
(Métro: Miromesnil)

Often compared to London's Wallace Collection and New York's Frick Collection, the Musée Jacquemart-André is, like its British and American counterparts, remarkable not only for its world-class paintings and objects but also for the building that houses them. The splendid Hôtel André was Nélie Jacquemart and Edouard André's private home, and has preserved intact all its Second-Empire, *haut-bourgeois* magnificence. A prominent figure in Napoleon III's coterie, André chose to build his residence on the Plaine Monceau, an area targeted for expansion by Baron Haussmann that became popular among high-ranking imperial partisans. Initially conceived for the *mondain* pomp of court life, the *hôtel* only found its vocation as a showcase for art following the fall of the empire, when André devoted himself whole-heartedly to collecting. He was subsequently aided in this by the painter Nélie Jacquemart, whom he married in 1881, and together they created the museum we see today, with a view to bequeathing it to the nation.

What is especially interesting about the Hôtel André is the unique insight it gives into the lives of the Second Empire's *haute bourgeoisie*. André had acquired a generous site on the newly laid-out Boulevard Haussmann, which his architect, Parent, filled across its entire width with the *hôtel*. The building is treated more in the manner of a mini château than an *hôtel particulier*, and does not hide behind blank walls as its 17C and 18C forbears would have done, instead giving full rein to the desire for display that characterized the era. To give the building more privacy, and also more prominence, Parent set it well back from the street line, elevated on a basement that respects the site's perimeter and evens out the change in level between the rear and street façades. Curiously, Parent chose to inverse the usual château/hôtel-particulier orientation by placing the garden front – complete with a mini strip of garden that sits atop the basement – on the street (i.e. public) side, the *cour d'honneur* being situated at the rear of the site and reached by two lateral *portes-cochères* leading under the house. Parent's elevations are in the exuberant Louis-Seize style favoured by the Empress Eugénie, the garden front featuring at its centre a semicircular, domed *avant-corps* whose pedigree in French architecture goes back to Vaux-le-Vicomte (37.1).

Inside, the principle rooms are situated on the (conceptual) ground floor, with the *grands salons* grouped together to the west and the more intimate *petits salons* and private apartments occupying the house's eastern half. This layout, which breaks with the traditional arrangement of public rooms *en enfilade*, allowed Parent to install an ingenious system of hydraulic jacks in the basement on which the walls separating the *antichambre*, *salon-rotonde* and *grand hall* can be lowered, uniting these three reception spaces as one on the occasion of grand balls. The *pièce de résistance* of Parent's interiors is the *escalier d'honneur*, situated, rather awkwardly from a practical point of view, at the western extremity of the house, but in being so placed becoming the climax of the reception rooms. Parent had taken part in the competition for

8.8 Musée Jacquemart-André

pensive frivolity, and when work was finally completed, in 1780, the garden had been entirely transformed into a fantasy wonderland of follies and *fabriques*. Amongst these were a pagoda, a Dutch windmill, a dairy, a pyramid, Greek and Gothic ruins, temples of Mars and Love, and a feature known as the »Naumachie«, which consisted of a sizeable oval pool of water partly surrounded by a semi-ruinous Corinthian colonnade. The latter's 28 columns are thought to have come from the never-completed Valois funerary chapel at Saint-Denis (21.2), commissioned by Catherine de Médicis in 1575 and designed by Jean Bullant.

In 1788, the duke's garden was enclosed within the wall of the Fermiers Généraux (see the Rotonde de la Villette, 19.13), and a toll house or *barrière* built just inside its limits by the brilliant Claude-Nicolas Ledoux. Situated at the northern entrance to today's park, the toll house takes the form of a circular temple whose debt to Bramante's Tempietto at San Pietro in Montorio in Rome (1502) is clear, although it has none of the daintiness of the Italian original. Instead, through characteristic handling of vocabulary including baseless, Greek-Doric columns and a broodingly oversized cornice, Ledoux managed to imbue his *barrière* with the aggressive virility that behoved its function. The building's upper storey was fitted out as a belvedere for the duke, who had contributed to the cost of its construction.

8.9 Parc Monceau

8.10 Saint-Alexandre-Nevski

the Opéra (9.13), and his staircase at the Hôtel André is reputed to be his riposte to his rival's flamboyant stairway at the Palais Garnier. He certainly excelled himself, producing a bravura double descent in marble whose lightness contrasts with the heavy stone polychromy of the winter garden in which it is set.

The rest of the décor at the Hôtel André consists essentially of first-rate period pieces acquired with a view to showing off André's superb collection of artwork in suitable surroundings. For her collection of Italian-Renaissance art, Nélie created the museum on the first floor. It was its combination of outstanding masterpieces – including works by Uccello, Rembrandt, Botticelli and Mantegna – and the extraordinary setting in which they are displayed that inspired Cocteau to dub the Jacquemart-André »le musée des chef-d'œuvres et le chef-d'œuvre des musées«.

8.9 Parc Monceau
Various architects, begun 1769
(Métro: Courcelles)
The origins of the Parc Monceau go back to 1769, when the Duc de Chartres (later Duc d'Orléans) acquired a sizeable portion of the Plaine Monceau on which he built a *pavillon d'agrément* surrounded by a French-style garden. Soon growing tired of his new park, the Duc commissioned Louis Carrogis, known as Carmontelle, to remodel it along more exciting lines in 1773. Aristocratic taste of the day inclined towards ex-

158 8th *arrondissement*

Orléans's garden fell into abandon following the Revolution and, after changing hands several times, was finally bought by the Ville de Paris in 1860, the year of the annexation into the capital of its outlying villages. In a lucrative deal, Baron Haussmann sold off a sizeable chunk of the park to the banker Emile Pereire for the development of luxury housing (many of the resulting Louis-Seize-style mansions still stand), and resolved to turn the remaining 9 ha into a public promenade for the wealthy *quartiers* then planned for the newly created 8th and 17th *arrondissements*. Work was carried out by the Service Municipal des Promenades et Plantations, headed by Adolphe Alphand, and completed in 1861. All that had remained of the Duc d'Orléans's *fabriques* were the Naumachie, which was restored, and the pyramid, which was converted for use as a tool shed. Sinuous, naturalistic paths were laid out, a cascade and an artificial cave created, and the whole garden replanted, with many exotic species making an appearance. To close the park, the architect Gabriel Davioud designed a magnificent set of wrought-iron gates and railings in Louis-Quinze style. In the 1870s one bay of the courtyard of Paris's original Hôtel de Ville (designed by Domenico da Cortona, known as Le Boccador, in the 16C – see 4.11) was re-erected in the park following the building's 1871 destruction by fire.

It is interesting to compare the Parc Monceau with its contemporary pendant in the more working-class east of Paris, the Parc des Buttes-Chaumont (19.2). Not only was the latter more than twice the size of Monceau, it was also considerably more elaborate and, with café-restaurants and other amusement facilities, dedicated to leisure. The Parc Monceau, on the other hand, was devoid of such *divertissements* and, with its stately railings, appeared more aristocratic and staid (indeed it preserves a reputation for primness to this day). Plans to rectify Haussmann's oversight in the provision of sufficient green open space for northwestern Paris are currently under discussion; a proposal has been put forward to cover part of the *boulevard périphérique* in the 17th *arrondissement* for this purpose.

8.10 Saint-Alexandre-Nevski
12, rue Daru
R. Kuzmin and I. Strohm, 1859–61
(Métro: Ternes)

This rather surprising incursion of Byzantine Russia into the heart of Haussmannian Paris was financed by the French Russian community, with help from Tsar Alexander II and the Russian holy synod, to replace the cramped chapel in the Rue de Berri that had formerly welcomed imperial expatriates. Saint-Alexandre-Nevski, which has the status of a cathedral, was designed by the chief architect to the imperial court, R. Kuzmin, whose plans were sent to Paris to be realized by I. Strohm (who, like Kuzmin, was a member of the Academy of Fine Arts in Saint Petersburg).

8.11 Office building

Kuzmin's cathedral respects orthodox tradition by liberally borrowing from Russia's architectural past. It has the centralized, Greek-cross-derived plan and internal division into three parts – vestibule, nave and sanctuary, the latter separated from the nave by an elaborate iconostasis – characteristic of Russian orthodox churches and is crowned, as was usual practice, with five towers consisting of a main, central vertical (that rises to 48 m) surrounded by four subordinates. In place of the onion domes traditionally associated with Russian religious buildings, Kuzmin used *shatyory*, squat, octagonal »tent« spires that in the 17C became a common form for church bell towers (e.g. Saint Basil the Blessed in Moscow) and were also sometimes used, as here, on the nave. Saint-Alexandre-Nevski itself has no bell tower, nor any of the other protrusions often to be seen on Russian churches. Its décor is suitably gilded and includes a reproduction above the main entrance of the mosaic depicting Christ at Sant'Apollinare Nuovo in Ravenna (6C).

8.11 Office building
116 bis, avenue des Champs-Elysées
Jean Desbouis, 1928–32
(Métro: Georges V)

In Paris, perhaps more than in many other cities, circumstances often conspire to reduce the external expression of buildings to a question of planar façades. The narrowness of Parisian plots, the economic im-

8.12 Théâtre des Champs-Elysées

perative to build a site to maximum capacity, and the stringency of Parisian building regulations – which, in the past, as well as restricting height, stipulated respect for the street line and encouraged homogeneity – all contribute to this situation. A building's exterior thus becomes a mere surface between two party walls, and the means of architectural expression are consequently limited: the disposition of windows and openings, the interplay of materials, the application of decoration and/or of projecting elements. For a building to stand out, either ingenuity or a talented decorator are required.

Desbouis faced just this problem when building these offices on the Champs-Elysées for the radio station »Poste Parisien«. The client's identity may have inspired the sharp, radio-age geometry of the façade, which is constructed as a series of zig-zagging oriel windows, producing a highly Expressionist, concertina effect. Desbouis's unconvincing pretext for this solution was that it increased light penetration and allowed views both up and down the avenue. The luxurious use of materials – polished travertine cladding, blue Labrador granite for the base and supports, chromed handrails – did nothing to alleviate the violent polemic provoked by the design. Disfigured by advertizing hoardings, which hide the podium and the lowest storey of windows, the façade now appears squatter than

intended, and its panache is further violated by ill-considered neon lettering.

8.12 Théâtre des Champs-Elysées
13–15, avenue Montaigne
Auguste Perret, Henry van de Velde and Roger Bouvard, 1906–13
(Métro: Alma Marceau)

Like his apartment building in the rue Franklin (16.8), the Théâtre des Champs-Elysées is considered one of Perret's seminal pre-war works, an inspiration to younger architects in its use of reinforced concrete. At the time of its construction, it was the subject of a major architectural scandal. The impresario Gabriel Astruc had decided to create a theatre dedicated to opera, dance and music that would be resolutely modern (Diaghilev's notorious Ballets Russes would première there). Envisaging a structure of iron, he commissioned first Henri Fivaz and then Roger Bouvard to draw up plans. Not confident in Bouvard's capacity to handle such a complex project, Astruc later brought in Henry van de Velde, the Belgian architect, designer, theorist and leading Art-Nouveau exponent. Van de Velde was ostensibly hired to decorate the theatre, but his interventions went much further than this and he tacitly became chief architect. Realizing that ferro-concrete construction would be best suited to the restricted site (37 x 95 m), van de Velde engaged Perret Frères to execute his design. This was to prove a fatal error: Perret impugned the logic of van de Velde's scheme and submitted his own, modified design, which was accepted. Van de Velde was demoted to *architecte-consultant* and subsequently resigned. The dispute over authorship persists to this day.

Because of its multiple parentage, the theatre is a case of »design first, structure afterwards«. The enormous auditorium is circular and suspended within eight columns and four bowspring arches, and is integral to a continuous trabeated frame delineating the entire building. The frame is a work of art in its own right and resembles a piece of complex carpentry, reflecting Perret's admiration for timber construction. The enormous main façade, clad in white Auvergne marble, only partly mirrors the underlying structure, contrary to Perret's usual practice. Inside, however, structural elements are emphasised and concrete left exposed, which provoked a scandal when the building was opened. Sinuous, suspended balconies demonstrate the daring suppleness of concrete in the main chamber.

Van de Velde held high-minded socialist ideals, amongst which was a belief in the unifying power of theatre, which he considered the most elevated form of social and cultural expression. It was at his behest that artists such as Maurice Denis and Emile-Antoine Bourdelle, amongst others, were engaged to decorate the theatre. The Classically inspired paintings and reliefs presents a lively if rather stilted evocation of mythological Antiquity. Perret's Classicist tendencies find expression in the proportions of the building as well as in the handling of details – the residual expressions of base, capital and architrave in the foyers, for example. Given the collaborative difficulties encountered during construction, the overall result is remarkably coherent. Restored in 1986/87, the theatre was coiffed in 1990 by a much-criticized panoramic restaurant.

8.13 Hôtel de la Païva
25–27, avenue des Champs-Elysées
Pierre Manguin, 1856–66
(Métro: Franklin D. Roosevelt)

Until the early-20C, when Paris's westward expansion brought business and commerce to the area, the Avenue des Champs-Elysées was essentially residential, lined with the mansions of the very wealthy. Rather like London's Park Lane and New York's Park Avenue, the Champs-Elysées have since seen their opulent 18C and 19C town houses torn down and replaced by commercial buildings. One of the very few survivors of the avenue's residential past is this lavish *hôtel particulier*, built for the social-climbing Marquise de la Païva.

The Marquise was famous for her *mondain* marriages – her commoner first husband was succeeded by the noble but impoverished Marquis de la Païva, and she later wed her long-time lover, the fabulously wealthy Count von Donnersmarck – and also for her literary salon. It was therefore unsurprising that her home (paid for by Donnersmarck, long before their marriage, to the tune of 6 million francs) should reflect some of its mistress's flamboyance. Manguin, who had made a name for himself at the 1855 Exposition Universelle, devised a fantasy extravaganza combining Italian- and French-Renaissance styles, whose opulence is only hinted at by the modestly scaled, carving-encrusted Champs-Elysées frontage. The real splendour lies inside: in a desire for »modernity«, the Marquise commissioned original furniture, fixtures and fittings for the entire house, and a team of craftsmen, led by Manguin, created interiors of astonishing opulence in which gilt, polychromy and coloured marbles feature prominently. The result rivals, on a domestic scale, the Palais Garnier (9.13), and is a splendid example of Second-Empire ostentation.

8.14 Grand Palais
Avenue Winston-Churchill
Henri Deglane, Charles-Louis Girault, Louis Louvet and Albert Thomas, 1896–1900
(Métro: Champs-Elysées-Clémenceau)

The Grand Palais, and its smaller sister the Petit Palais (8.15), were conceived as the centrepiece of the 1900 Exposition Universelle. The impetus for their creation came from the proposed Pont Alexandre-III (see feature on Seine bridges) which was to link the Invalides (7.12) to the Cours-la-Reine, opposite the Palais de l'Industrie and the Pavillon de la Ville de Paris. Survivors of the 1855 and 1878 exhibitions respectively, both these latter buildings had become essential to the artistic life of the city but, hastily erected and ill-adapted to their usage, were far from ideal. The exhibition organizers, anxious to make their mark in a capital crowded with legacies from previous world fairs, proposed their

8.14 Grand Palais

demolition and the erection in their stead of permanent, purpose-built replacements either side of a grand avenue connecting the bridge to the Champs-Elysées.

Where the 1889 exhibition had been a celebration of engineering prowess, that of 1900 was to be a glorification of the arts. The Grand Palais was conceived as a *palais des beaux-arts* to provide gallery space for the various *salons* which marked the artistic calendar of the Parisian year, a role previously assumed by the Palais de l'Industrie. The latter had also hosted the annual *concours hippique* (horse show), as well as other events such as flower shows, and these too were to be transferred to the Grand Palais. To the difficulties of such a highly complex programme was added an extremely short deadline – a joint architectural competition for both *palais* was launched only in 1896. Its very detailed brief prescribed even the limits of the contours of both buildings: given the huge surface-area requirements of the Grand Palais, entrants had little choice but to adopt this plan. It consisted of three parts: the main building on the new avenue, a smaller, parallel wing to the west, and an intermediary section joining the two. Unfortunately, the competition proved indecisive; while Girault's proposal for the Petit Palais easily won, to general acclaim, the organizers declared all the short-listed schemes for the Grand Palais unexecutable. A compromise was reached, whereby the project was divided up between the finalists: Deglane was given the main building, Thomas the parallel wing, and Louvet the intermediary section, while Girault was appointed co-ordinating architect to ensure unity between the two *palais*.

The Grand Palais takes the form of an enormous iron-and-glass hall, designed as a hippodrome but also used to exhibit sculpture, which is encircled by discrete galleries for displaying paintings. Further halls and galleries are located in the westerly wing. Since the main hall is entered at the centre of its longitudinal elevation, the architects built a transept opposite the entrance to provide a suitably impressive perspective for arriving visitors. A resplendent iron staircase by Louvet, successfully combining Classicism and Art Nouveau, links the transept to the westerly wing, while a shallow and elegantly immaterial dome covers the crossing. The main hall is undeniably festive and, although criticized by many contemporaries, is generally admired today. Not so the exterior, which has been universally attacked for its clumsiness and pomposity. Even more than its exact contemporary, the Gare d'Orsay (7.1), the Grand Palais highlights the frequent *fin-de-siècle* rift between stale academic façadism, literally petrified in stone, and the vitality of creation in newer materials. It is paradoxical that the same architects were here responsible for both.

Despite its difficult gestation, the Grand Palais functioned perfectly in its intended role until the installation, in 1937, of the Palais de la Découverte (science museum) in the westerly wing, from when on it suffered a slow decline. Since 1993, after a piece fell from the vault, the main hall has been closed. The subsequent engineers' report revealed that the building was subsiding towards the Seine and generally deteriorating from decades of neglect. After years of hesitation, during which demolition of the Grand Palais was seriously considered, restoration work has now begun and is due for completion in 2005.

8.15 Petit Palais
Avenue Winston-Churchill
Charles-Louis Girault, 1896–1900
(Métro: Champs-Elysées-Clémenceau)

Erected for the 1900 Exposition Universelle, the Petit Palais was conceived, with its bigger sister the Grand Palais (8.14), as the centrepiece of the exhibition. Designed to replace the Pavillon de la Ville de Paris, a legacy of the 1878 exhibition which had never been entirely satisfactory, it was to receive the municipality's collection of paintings and provide gallery space for temporary exhibitions.

Girault's design forms a trapezium in plan, and encloses at its centre a very pretty semicircular courtyard encompassed by a Doric peristyle. Built in an age when artificial lighting was still little used, the Palais features large areas of glazing. Like its bigger sister, its principal façade on the Avenue Winston-Churchill con-

8.15 Petit Palais

8.16 Palais de l'Elysée

sists of a domed central *avant-corps* flanked by colonnaded wings. The dome and the frontispiece were inspired by Bruand and Hardouin-Mansart's Invalides (7.12) across the river, and the remainder of the exterior is derived from an eclectic mix of 17C French references. Internally, the Palais is divided into galleries following its contours, rendered in splendidly torrid Baroque. Encrusted with mouldings, the ceilings feature largely second-rate frescoes depicting high-minded allegories and scenes from the history of Paris. Virtuoso staircases in reinforced concrete – the one overt concession to modern construction techniques – swoop down in gravity-defying curves in each of the two rotundas punctuating the rear elevation.

The Petit Palais was received to great acclaim by contemporaries, and is certainly less cumbersome than the Grand Palais. King Leopold II of Belgium was so impressed that he afterwards appointed Girault as his official architect.

8.16 Palais de l'Elysée
55, rue du Faubourg Saint-Honoré
Armand-Claude Mollet, 1718–20
(Métro: Champs-Elysées-Clémenceau)

Famous today as the official residence of France's president, the Palais de l'Elysée originally bore the name Hôtel d'Evreux, after Henri-Louis de La Tour d'Auvergne, Comte d'Evreux, who commissioned the building. His chosen architect was Armand-Claude Mollet who, although in royal employ, seems to have built little else. Mollet produced a handsome residence very much in the manner of the times, its disposition being that of the traditional *hôtel particulier* with a principal *corps de logis* giving onto a garden at the rear and separated from the street by a courtyard, the latter surrounded on its other three sides by service buildings and accessed via a central *porte-cochère*. What distinguished the Hôtel d'Evreux were its truly vast grounds, which allowed Mollet to give it something of the air of a mini château. His façades were of classic French design, the *logis* sporting side pavilions and a central *avant-corps* on both the courtyard and garden fronts. Sober and yet charming, Mollet's elevations relied for their effect on their delicate proportions and on the subtle interplay of details such as differently profiled window headings (since lost on the garden front). Jacques-François Blondel (one of the most influential architectural theorists and teachers in 18C France) found the *hôtel* to have an »air of magnificence« and considered it »the most beautiful *maison de plaisance* in the Paris region«.

Inside, the building's double-thickness *logis* was divided up so as to provide both an axial sequence between the courtyard and garden fronts and a suite of state rooms running along the latter. Mollet's task was made considerably easier by the abundance of space available to him, and he was not required to employ the kind of ingenuity shown by Courtonne at the Hôtel Matignon (7.14). Blondel admired Mollet's plan for its regularity and *commodité*. Between the 1750s and the 1840s, the *hôtel* changed hands more than half-a-dozen times, and since the 1870s has been home to France's President. Each new owner left his or her mark on the building, and the interior thus conserves only elements of its original décor and disposition. Rococo panelling and plasterwork can still be seen in the Salon des Ambassadeurs, the Salon des Aides de Camp and the Salon Pompadour. In the 1770s, Etienne-Louis Boullée carried out a major redecoration campaign for the financier Nicolas Beaujon, but little remains of his interventions which were effaced by Pierre-Adrien Pâris for the Duchesse de Bourbon. Under Napoleon III, the house was again entirely redecorated (Empress Eugénie's bathroom can still be seen) and the outbuildings extended as far as the perimeter of the site, while during the Third Republic the exuberant Salle des Fêtes (Eugène Debressenne and Adrien Chancel, 1889–1900) was added on the garden front.

9th *arrondissement*

9.1 Telephone exchange
17, rue du Faubourg-Poissonnière
François Le Cœur, 1911–14
(Métro: Bonne Nouvelle)

Following the commercialization of the telephone in the 1880s, and until as recently as the 1980s, telephone-line commutation was performed manually. Turn-of-the-century exchange equipment consisted of a very long apparatus at which telephonists sat in a row on one side, and which was accessible to engineers on the other. To house these machines, large, open, well-lit and -ventilated spaces were needed. From the late-19C on, exchange buildings appeared all over Paris, often associated with post offices as the telephone system was run by the mail service. No dominant type or style emerged, and their appearance was as varied as other industrial or office edifices. Indeed, as they were of strategic communications importance and therefore potential targets of attack, their anonymity was often deliberately preserved.

This handsome exchange is thus unusual in that it draws attention to itself. The brief called not only for space for the exchange machinery but also for standard office accommodation. Taking a rational, functional approach, Le Cœur made the most of the corner site and separated the two activities, placing the exchange halls on the Rue Bergère, where the greatest frontage was available, and siting the offices to their north, on the Rue du Faubourg-Poissonnière. The exchange halls are easily distinguished by their huge windows, which contrast with the offices' more standard fenestration. To achieve the wide spans of the exchange halls, each of which covers a surface area of 600 m², Le Cœur used concrete piers – visible on the Rue-Bergère façade – and reinforced-cement floors. The building's walls are rendered in orange-red brick, beautifully laid, which adds warmth to the rather austere elevation turning the street corner. Here, defiantly, rises an enormous, blind wall, no Expressionist caprice but programmatically necessary as all the incoming cables were attached to it on the interior. Le Cœur nonetheless softened its functionalist severity by adding an elaborate, wrought-iron clock, executed by the sculptor Szabo to Le Cœur's designs, which features the signs of the zodiac. A monumental, coved cornice, decorated on its underside with mosaics, crowns the exchange-hall block, whose roof was laid out as a terrace for employees' recreation. Access was gained from the final storey of the office wing, which contained a canteen and restrooms.

Many contemporaries found the building overly plain, uncompromising and »industrial«, but to today's eyes it is a visual delight. Its massing, at once majestic and picturesque, its decorative elements – besides the clock and cornice there are Szabo's superb wrought-iron grills on the ground floor and a magical canopy, in glass bricks, above the entrance – and the quality of

9.1 Telephone exchange

the workmanship all contribute to a building of aristocratic grandeur and finesse. Following WW1, Le Cœur added the post office which now prolongs the Rue-Bergère wing to the west.

9.2 Former Comptoir National d'Escompte de Paris, now Banque Nationale de Paris
14, rue Bergère
Edouard-Jules Corroyer, 1878–82
(Métro: Bonne Nouvelle)

A floridly fanciful example of late-19C eclecticism, this building was, like the Crédit Lyonnais and Société Générale buildings (2.5 and 9.11), intended not only to provide office space for banking activities but also to demonstrate tangibly the solidity and financial might of the commissioning institution. Rather in the manner of Charles Garnier, with whom he shared a love of polychrome effects in stone, Corroyer browsed through the back catalogue of Europe's Classical tradition to put together a building of startling effect and lavish ornamentation. Making the most of the site's position perpendicular to the Rue Rougemont, which renders it visible from the *grands boulevards*, he created a monumental frontispiece of Roman grandeur that attracts the eye of any passer-by. Exaggeratedly tall, it consists essentially of a triumphal arch coiffed with a pediment, pyramidal roof and bell tower, its lower parts teeming with sculpture, carvings and vermiculated rustication. Amongst these, Aimé Millet's female personifications of *Prudence* (above the main entrance), *Commerce* and *Industrie* are particularly prominent.

Inside, the Roman theme continues with the vast, public banking hall, which is delimited by colossal Doric arcades and covered with a giant, coloured-glass skylight. However, the *pièce de résistance* must surely be the *escalier d'honneur*, whose single flight rises dramatically into an arcaded hall in polychrome stone, decorated with sumptuous golden mosaics. Opulence is manifested not only through the quantity but also the luxurious quality of the building's decoration.

The extensions to the bank, flanking Corroyer's frontispiece, are by Constant Bernard and date from 1903.

9.3 Saint-Eugène
4 bis, rue Sainte-Cécile
Louis-Auguste Boileau and Louis-Adrien Lusson, 1854/55
(Métro: Bonne Nouvelle)

Commissioned by the Ville de Paris to serve a growing neighbourhood, the Eglise Saint-Eugène was France's first iron-framed church, and indeed one of the first iron churches anywhere. The rather avant-garde decision to build a religious edifice in iron – then considered an industrial material – seems to have been made at the suggestion of Abbé Coquand, vicar of the new parish. He astutely realized that use of iron rather than

9.2 Former Comptoir National d'Escompte de Paris, now Banque Nationale de Paris

9.3 Saint-Eugène

stone would greatly reduce costs, thus making viable the small budget allocated by the municipality, as well as allowing a greater amount of useable space to be squeezed out of the restricted site. The Abbé was not an aesthetic revolutionary, however, and directed that the church be styled in the manner of the 13C. Lusson was initially commissioned to design the building but was afterwards replaced by Boileau, and the degree of input of each architect is now unclear. Both claim it in their memoirs, but it is generally thought that the church should be »given« to Boileau.

Saint-Eugène's modest exterior belies its revolutionary interior, and one is left unprepared for its airy spaciousness and the soaring elegance of its iron supports. True to the brief, Boileau did not attempt the daring spans possible in iron, but faithfully reproduced the essentials of a stone, Gothic structure in the new material, with the technical difference that the iron frame is self-supporting, needing almost no buttressing. The hollow piers are also much thinner than most of their stone equivalents, although they were in fact copied from a 13C model: the amazingly slender, stone supports of the refectory at the Priory of Saint-Martin-des-Champs (3.10), whose »metallic allure« suggested their appropriateness as a prototype to Boileau. Four rows of piers support Saint-Eugène's iron vaults and divide it longitudinally into five: a nave and two tall side-aisles, both flanked by an outer row of side-chapels. All ribs and mouldings are faithfully reproduced in iron. Despite its 13C styling, Saint-Eugène's interior is not like any church of the 1200s, as Boileau adapted traditional Gothic forms to the possibilities of iron, creating an atypical hybrid. Not only is the slenderness of the piers unusual, but so too are the full-height, balconied side-chapels, and also the narrow clerestory, which is lit by oculi placed directly under the central ribs of the domical, sexpartite nave vault, thus expressively demonstrating the technical capabilities of iron. Perhaps inevitably, the interior is polychrome – the metal had to be painted against rust – and, despite the medievalizing vegetal motifs in warm dark greens and reds, seems very 19C, as do the luridly coloured stained-glass windows and the elaborate furnishings.

The use of iron at Saint-Eugène fulfilled all expectations, allowing the church to be put up in only 20 months and at half the cost of an equivalent stone structure. Stone is present, but restricted to the external envelope, with almost no structural significance. In his writings on Saint-Eugène, Boileau makes it clear that the medieval styling was imposed on him by the client, and insinuates that he would have preferred a more radical, avant-garde aesthetic exposing the building's true nature. This may partly explain the mediocrity of the exterior, although the lack of funds must also have limited available options. Saint-Eugène exposes two façades to the public gaze: the principal, entrance front, and the western, lateral elevation (the church is not orientated, and the entrance front faces south). The western elevation, in plaster with stone dressings, is entirely unadorned, and appears almost »industrial«, its form being simply the logical, functional product of the interior. The entrance front makes more of a stab at grandeur, although the composition (essentially an enormous gable end articulated according to the internal divisions and dressed up with a monumental portal and sparing Gothic detailing) lacks conviction. One wonders what Boileau would have made of Jules Astruc's singular Notre-Dame-du-Travail (14.1), whose interior is also in iron, but with a deliberately industrial aesthetic.

9.4 Cité Napoléon
58, rue de Rochechouart
Marie-Gabriel Veugny, 1849–53
(Métro: Cadet)

Louis-Napoléon Bonaparte, Prince-President of France from 1848 and, after 1852, Emperor Napoleon III, was an unusual politician for his era in that he took a serious interest in the fate of the working classes. In 1844 he published a book entitled *L'Extinction du Paupérisme* in which he argued that while industrialization, economic progress and wealth creation would be the motors of a general improvement in living standards, on their own these forces were not enough to help society's poorest members, and special measures were therefore necessary to improve their fate. Of particular concern were their living conditions, a subject on which Louis-Napoléon developed progressive opinions. While in exile in London he visited Henry Roberts and George Clark's Streatham-Street apartments (1847), an early British experiment in social housing by which he was greatly influenced (in 1850 he had Roberts' book *The Dwellings of the Labouring Classes* translated into French and distributed to relevant institutions). Calls were being voiced in France for the construction of similar dwellings and, on becoming president, Louis-Napoléon attempted to get the ball rolling by personally donating 500,000 francs for the realization of just such an edifice. The Cité Napoléon, Paris's very first example of specially conceived social housing, was the result.

The presence of nearby gas works employing migrant workers was one of the deciding factors in the choice of site for the new estate. Veugny's design (which was inevitably influenced by Roberts), and the criticisms it attracted, were telling of the attitudes of the day. The Cité comprises four separate buildings accessed via a generous, planted courtyard, and originally provided nearly 200 separate dwellings ranging from one-room bedsits to three-bedroom apartments. Communal facilities were a feature of the estate and included lavatories on each landing, a laundry, a crèche, workshops and a meeting room that also served as an employment centre. Perhaps because this was a showcase development, the estate's stuccoed exteriors exhibit bourgeois standards of architectural pretension, with mouldings, cornices and pilasters. Three of the blocks are unremarkable, but the building on the Rue de Rochechouart, via which entry to the estate is gained, is more unusual. Deeper than the others, it is organized around two glass-covered atria containing staircases and access footbridges – already we see a manifestation of the formula »light + air = health and hygiene« that would influence social-housing schemes until well into the 20C (e.g., Henri Sauvage's Rue-Vavin flats (6.10)). Today, however, the atria appear rather depressingly dingy, and the loose grouping of the blocks seems a much better way of achieving the light-and-air goal. But it must be remembered that the spacious and comparatively well-lit atria were also conceived in opposition to the dark, narrow staircases of many cheap apartment buildings, in the hope that

9.4 Cité Napoléon

»immoral« encounters would thus be avoided. Indeed the whole ethos of the estate was imbued with this kind of determinism, as it was supposed to effect a moral re-education of its residents.

Despite its advantageous rents and facilities, the Cité Napoléon was not a financial (or critical) success. The three-bedroom apartments were too expensive for their target families and, since it was out of the question for more middle-class residents to cohabit with the lower orders, they remained empty. Moreover, the Cité's regulations were strict (including a 10 pm curfew) and it was under police surveillance, which no doubt deterred a good number of potential tenants. As an architectural form the estate stood out in the cityscape (critics were fond of likening it to a barracks) and some residents may therefore have felt stigmatized. All these factors, as well as the bourgeoisie's fear of concentrating the poor in one spot in this way, ensured that small, individual houses for the working classes would be the norm in 19C France. It was not until the turn of the century that large, collective estates began to be built once more in Paris (see, e. g., 15.4).

9.5 Notre-Dame-de-Lorette
18 bis, rue de Châteaudun
Hippolyte Lebas, 1823–36
(Métro: Notre-Dame-de-Lorette)

In the early-19C, the area to the north of the *grands boulevards* underwent rapid expansion, and the building of a church to serve the parish of Notre-Dame-de-Lorette – whose original place of worship had been demolished during the Revolution – became a pressing necessity. An architectural competition for the new edifice was organized in 1823, and Lebas, a pupil of Percier's, emerged the victor. Notre-Dame-de-Lorette was to be his one major work.

Lebas's design follows the French trend, begun in the late-18C and exemplified by Saint-Philippe-du-Roule (8.7), for building Classical, basilical churches that were directly inspired by early-Christian places of worship. Where Chalgrin's Saint-Philippe-du-Roule was a fairly free interpretation of the early-Christian basilical form, Lebas's church was a more literal adaptation of the type, and it seems likely that two models in particular influenced his design – Rome's Santa Maria Maggiore (432–40) and San Crisogono (731–41 and 1123 to 1130). Notre-Dame-de-Lorette presents a classic, basilical aspect, with a simple, flat-roofed nave that is separated from its side-aisles by an entablatured Ionic colonnade and that terminates in a monumental archway. Beyond the latter is the choir, which is an embellishment by Lebas on the basilical model in that it consists of a sizeable, domed volume, although ultimate termination is achieved in the form of the usual semi-circular apse.

Externally the church is extremely sober, all interest being concentrated in two elements – the Italianate bell tower that rises above the choir, and the monumental, Corinthian entrance portico, which rises the full height of the nave and thus appears almost grotesque in its exaggerated scale. Indeed it is so tall that the figures of Faith, Hope and Charity coiffing its pediment are difficult to appreciate from street level. The church's blank exterior walls are in stark contrast to the interior, where a polychromatic *horror vacui* holds sway. The competition brief for Notre-Dame-de-Lorette was unusual in that it specified, for the sake of »harmony and good order« in the church's decoration, that all statues and paintings be created expressly for pre-determined spaces, rather than being installed as an afterthought. Lebas went further than even this implied, for the church was decorated as it was built, under his supervision. Paintings and frescoes dominate in a carefully calculated iconographical circuit. The nave depicts Mary's life on earth, the choir her apotheosis, various saints populate the aisles, while the four corner chapels are dedicated to the sacraments of Baptism, Communion, Marriage and the Anointing of the Sick. Browns dominate in the lower-level background colours, symbolizing the earth, blues occupy the middle levels, representing the infinite ether, while heaven is designated in the domes by substantial background gilding. The result is impressively lavish, too much so for contemporaries who thought its sumptuousness lacked spirituality.

9.6 Synagogue
44, rue de la Victoire
Alfred Philibert Aldrophe, 1865–76
(Métro: Le Peletier, Notre-Dame de Lorette)

It was the French Revolution, so disastrous for Catholicism, that emancipated another religion: in 1791, France's Jews were made full citizens and allowed to celebrate publicly their cult. Where synagogues had once been clandestine, they could now be built openly, although for a long time following enfranchisement Parisian synagogues displayed extreme external discretion. By the 1850s, times had changed, and grandiose, monumental synagogues began to appear. Given the Diaspora and historical repression of the Jews, no tradition of Jewish architecture existed, and suitable forms and iconography for France's new synagogues had thus to be invented. The two recurrent sources to which architects turned were the Temple of Solomon in Jerusalem – of which little remained following its destruction in 586 BC – and Christian churches. This latter choice may seem surprising, but it had both a practical and a political basis. On the practical side, churches were the principal example of a building type designed specifically to hold a congregation, while on the political side their symbolic significance was attractive. Churches and cathedrals were powerful emblems of national identity and belonging; having opted for assimilation, but nonetheless wanting to proclaim their own identity, French Jews perhaps saw a happy compromise in the appropriation of an architectural language that would be readily understandable to Catholic France.

9.6 Synagogue

The huge synagogue in the Rue de la Victoire, today Europe's biggest, was one of two built in Paris in the 1860s with state help, which took the form of land, provided by Haussmann's Préfecture de la Seine. Unlike many of their German and Alsatian counterparts, which benefited from generous and sometimes entirely detached sites, Paris's synagogues were hidden away in narrow back streets (indeed legend has it that the Rue-de-la-Victoire synagogue was not allowed an entrance on the more prestigious Rue de Châteaudun because Empress Eugénie refused to pass a Jewish place of worship on her way to Sainte-Trinité (9.7)). When the *préfecture* was involved with construction, as it generally was, it reserved the right to select the architect from amongst its ranks, with the result that non-Jews were mostly appointed. Here, for once, a Jewish designer was nominated, who also happened to be architect to the Rothschilds, who were financing the synagogue.

Aldrophe's building crystallized contemporary trends in Parisian synagogue design and became a type-standard that spread all over France. His building is basilical in form, thus contrasting with German and Alsatian practice, which favoured centralized plans. The basilical form is both a borrowing from church design and a reference to the Temple of Solomon, itself essentially basilical in plan. In Aldrophe's synagogue, segregation of the sexes is achieved by reserving the nave for the men and by placing the women in the tribunes. Many synagogues featured ancillary buildings containing sacristies, function rooms, etc., an arrangement impossible on this constricted site. Aldrophe got round this difficulty by placing these facilities between the principal façade and the nave, set above an imposing porch that ensures access to the main vessel. The question of style was also tricky, Aldrophe's first proposal being rejected on the grounds that it looked too much like a church. On the other hand, the orientalizing style popular in Germany and Alsace was to be avoided because, in Paris, it was associated with bathhouses and *cafés-concerts*. In the end, Aldrophe opted for solid neo-Romanesque spiced up with vaguely Byzantine details. Despite his redesign, the sumptuous interior, with its basilical plan, semicircular apse and barrel vault, still appears very church-like. The enormous street façade, with its central triple arcades and vast, semicircular gable end, faithfully expressing the vault behind it, is more unusual. Specifically Jewish iconography is limited to decorative details, such as inscriptions and the sculpted Tables of the Law crowning the gable.

Another, remarkably similar synagogue of this type can be seen at 21 bis, rue des Tournelles, 4th (Marcellin Varcollier, 1873–76), featuring exposed ironwork in the nave, designed and manufactured by the firm of Eiffel.

9.7 **Sainte-Trinité**
Place d'Estienne-d'Orves
Théodore Ballu, 1861–67
(Métro: Trinité)

A good example of Haussmannian urbanism, this enormous church was conceived essentially as a piece of civic stage scenery to decorate one of the baron's traffic developments. To improve access to and from the Gare Saint-Lazare (8.5), Haussmann widened the western sections of the old Rue Saint-Lazare and, to avoid the latter's narrow, vacillating eastern stretches, cut a new street, today's Rue de Châteaudun, straight through to meet up with the Rue Lafayette, via which the outskirts of the city could then directly be gained. It so happened that several other streets converged at the junction of the Rue Saint-Lazare and the Rue de Châteaudun, including the Rue de la Chaussée-d'Antin, which provided a direct link to the *grands boulevards* to the south, and three other thoroughfares leading to the exterior boulevards to the north. In order to facilitate traffic interchange at this junction, Haussmann created a generous square (today's Place d'Estienne-d'Orves) which, as was his wont for this kind of space, he determined to embellish with a grandiose public building, in the event a church. According to his memoirs, it was Haussmann himself who drew up the general outlines of the scheme, dictating that the building should feature a prominent tower to close off the perspective as viewed from the Rue de la Chaussée-d'Antin, and stipulating that the church's entrance should be provided with a covered porch for carriages. It was also he who conceived of the garden and fountains in front of the edifice. To realize his ideas, the baron called on a trusted collaborator, Théodore Ballu.

Haussmann advised Ballu to avoid committing himself to any style when designing the church, a command which the architect interpreted as a call for eclecticism. He had perfectly understood that the southern, entrance façade (the church is not orientated) giving onto the *place* would have to be the *pièce de résistance* of the whole edifice, and devised an elaborate *mélange* of Italian- and French-Renaissance borrowings with a central bell tower rising over 60 m. The tripartite division of the façade's central *avant-corps* and the repetition of a triple-arcade motif are clearly intended to signify the Trinity to which the church is dedicated, and Ballu's choice of iconography in the form of the statues adorning the building also went in this sense. If the southern elevation appears more Low-Countries town hall than church, it only underlines its fundamentally civic rather than spiritual vocation. In contrast to this exuberant display, the rest of the building's exterior is decidedly low key, not to say dull.

Like his confrère Victor Baltard, who was building another enormous Haussmannian church, Saint-Augustin (8.6), at the same time as Sainte-Trinité was going up, Ballu turned to iron technology for the structure

9.7 Sainte-Trinité

9.8 Saint-Louis-d'Antin and the Lycée Condorcet (former Couvent des Capucins)

of his building, but unlike Baltard he did not allow any of it to be seen anywhere. Haussmann had wanted a »modern, commodious, elegant« church, which in Second-Empire speak seems to have meant grandiose theatricality. Just as striking as the *mise en scène* of the southern façade is the church's interior, which wows firstly in its dimensions – a colossal 90 x 34 m (for what is not a cathedral but a mere parish church) with an iron-framed barrel vault rising to 30 m –, secondly in the dramatic disposition of its choir, which is elevated above the level of the nave, and thirdly in its sumptuous, polychrome decoration, whose completion took another ten years following the inauguration of the building in 1867. A similar eclectic mix to that employed on the exterior is to be found inside the church, the essentially Renaissance-style nave terminating in a distinctly Gothic apse that serves as a Lady Chapel.

Ballu was also responsible for the apartment buildings flanking Sainte-Trinité, which were conceived as part of the urban ensemble of the Place d'Estienne-d'Orves. Further up the Rue Blanche, at no. 78, is the *hôtel particulier* in which he lived and died, and which was probably built to a design by the architect himself.

9.8 Saint-Louis-d'Antin and the Lycée Condorcet (former Couvent des Capucins)
65, rue de Caumartin
Alexandre-Théodore Brongniart, 1779–82
(Métro: Havre-Caumartin)
Created to absorb a part of Paris's ever-growing population, the new *quartier* of the Chaussée-d'Antin was begun by royal decree in 1720 and, by the 1780s, had become extremely chic. It remained, however, without a place of worship, and it was only through the efforts of an influential resident, Mme de Montesson, and after cajoling by the king himself that the Capuchin order of monks was persuaded to set up a monastery there, whose church would also serve for parish needs. Brongniart, who was awarded the commission, had, until that date, made a name for himself designing

fanciful gardens and elegant *hôtels particuliers* for the wealthy. Faced with the renowned austerity of the Capuchins, he showed himself capable of a surprising asceticism, and produced arguably his finest building.

The monastery is organized around a central cloister, originally built on only three sides, the fourth, western side having been closed by a free-standing colonnade leading to the garden. To the north were the monks' living quarters and to the south the church, while the eastern, linking wing contained parlours as well as the monastery's principle entrance. The severely neo-Classical, baseless columns of the cloister's peristyle, which were thought, erroneously, to have been modelled on Paestum, became famous, and probably inspired the architectural setting of Jacques-Louis David's celebrated *Brutus and His Dead Sons* (1789). Controversy still reigns as to whether they should be classified as Tuscan or Doric. The church is very simple in plan, consisting of a plain, arcaded, barrel-vaulted nave, with one aisle to the south. The aisle, which widens towards the west, cleverly dissimulates the irregularity of the terrain, and was originally to have contained semicircular chapels in each bay, although only one, the Chapel of the Virgin, was actually realized. Decoration was restrained, limited principally to the Doric order.

Of similar restraint was the monastery's street façade which, apart from two tiny windows above the northern doorway and an open lunette above the central, principal portal, was entirely blind. Rigorously symmetrical, it consists of solid, pedimented *avant-corps* at either extremity, one forming the entrance to the church, the other the entrance to the monks' living quarters, with a lower, longer elevation linking the two. The visitor's impression is of a mute, blank wall pierced only by three imposing doorways, the embodiment of solemn piety. The *avant-corps'* entrances are coiffed by simple round-headed pediments, while the impressive central portal is flanked by powerful columns of the same type as the cloister, which are united by an entablature and set against the open lunette to emphasize further their massiveness. Brongniart here used some of the tricks that Ledoux would later master (see, e.g., 19.14), the façade's effectiveness largely relying on the disparity between the heavy architectural features and the flat, empty wall on which they are set. The Couvent des Capucins is nonetheless still far from the exaggerated grotesqueness of Ledoux's work, governed as it is by Brongniart's usual elegant proportions, its severity softened by the decorative treatment of the façade, which is gently rusticated and animated by niches. The long, horizontal panels either side of the central portal originally contained bas-reliefs by Clodion, destroyed during the Revolution at the time of the monastery's closure.

Following its dissolution, the former *couvent* was subdivided and let, although the church remained, intermittently, in use. In 1804, Napoleon decreed that the monastery buildings should be converted for use as a *lycée*, and charged Brongniart with the commission. The architect duly added a fourth wing on the cloister's western side in 1806–08, and further extensions were built by Joseph-Louis Duc in the 1860s. The church was also much modified during the 19C, including the addition of wall paintings and the reorganization of the choir and the chapel. Moreover, Brongniart's bold and uncompromising street elevation was disfigured by the addition of windows, which, happily, were removed in a recent restoration programme that returned the façade to its pre-Revolution state.

9.9 Printemps
64–70, boulevard Haussmann and 2, rue du Havre
Paul Sédille, 1881–89; René Binet, 1907–11
(Métro: Havre-Caumartin; RER: Haussmann Saint-Lazare, Auber)

Founded in 1865 by a former employee of the Bon Marché (7.15), the Magasins du Printemps initially occupied only three floors of a building situated at the street corner of the Rues du Havre and de Provence, but quickly expanded to fill almost the entire city block. Following a fire, in March 1881, that destroyed the majority of the buildings on the site, a replacement scheme encompassing the whole plot was immedi-

9.9 Printemps

ately drawn up. Paul Sédille's design, construction of which was begun with considerable alacrity later that year, became something of a model for subsequent department stores.

In the interests of economy and profit, Sédille used an iron frame in place of a traditional stone, load-bearing structure, thereby maximizing the amount of useable space. His building was essentially of a type perfected for warehouses and its façades do not quite manage to conceal their industrial origins, despite their elaborate décor, which includes a stone dressing of applied orders and carvings, female personifications of the four seasons and colourful mosaics. The domed corner towers were imposed by the municipality in order to provide a monumental elevation to terminate the Rue Tronchet. Although Sédille's plans included electric lighting – Printemps was the first ever department store to be entirely lit by electricity –, natural lighting was still necessary and, consequently, Sédille created a long, three-storey-high atrium at the building's heart, a veritable cathedral in iron. The first at this scale in a department store, the atrium's soaring volume, florid ironwork and coloured-glass ceiling created a dazzling impression of extravagant luxury and set the pace for future stores. Criminally, Sédille's hall was destroyed in the 1960s to allow new storeys to be constructed on top of the old building and to squeeze the maximum floor space out of the original volume. In consequence, the interior of this section of the shop is now devoid of interest.

By the early 20C, business had expanded to the extent that, in 1907, construction of a new building on the next city block along was begun. In the interests of continuity, Sédille's façades were duplicated, with the difference that the corner towers were made bigger and more prominent. Inside, where Sédille's atrium had risen only three floors, the use of electric lifts allowed the new building's atrium, designed by René Binet, to rise a full six storeys. Even more ostentatious than its predecessor, Binet's hall was an octagonal fantasia of Art-Nouveau ironwork with open lift cages clinging to its sides. Further building work was in progress in 1921 when a fire broke out and badly damaged Binet's wing; today, all that remains of his magnificent atrium is the elaborate dome, on the sixth floor, decorated by the glass-smith Brière.

9.10 Galeries Lafayette
38–46, boulevard Haussmann
Georges Chédanne, 1906–08; Ferdinand Chanut, 1910–12; Pierre Patout, 1932–36
(Métro: Chaussée d'Antin (Lafayette); RER: Haussmann Saint-Lazare)

Founded in 1895, the Galeries Lafayette, like their neighbour Printemps (9.9), started out humbly but soon grew to occupy several large chunks of the cityscape. Unlike its neighbour, the store's external aspect is, for the most part, distressingly unattractive – standard Haussmannian elevations groaning under the

9.10 Galeries Lafayette

weight of subsequently added floors. Only a small section of the Rue-de-la-Chaussée-d'Antin façade, by Ferdinand Chanut, has anything of the Art-Nouveau charm one would expect from a large shop of its era. Pierre Patout's 1932 plans to turn the entire exterior into a marble ocean liner were abandoned after only a small portion (to the north of Chanut's elevation) had been completed; stripped of its Lalique bow windows, it is a sorry sight today. The Galeries' theatrical plate-glass display windows, with their heavy, polished-granite surrounds, caused a sensation when installed by Chanut in 1926/27.

Inside, the store is more fortunate, as it has conserved the main Art-Nouveau atrium constructed by Chanut in 1910–12 (its smaller sister disappeared in the 1950s). A rare surviving example of *belle-époque* extravagance, it was less innovatory in form than René Binet's contemporary hall in Printemps, but nonetheless avant-garde in terms of structure, as it is entirely in reinforced cement. Circular in plan and rising four storeys, it is encrusted with elaborate, orientalizing mouldings and ironwork, by Edouard Schenck (who also worked at Samaritaine (1.5)), and is surmounted by a vast, coloured-glass dome. The *escalier d'honneur*, which formerly spilled sensuously from the first floor to the ground floor, was removed in 1974.

9.11 Société Générale, Agence Centrale

9.11 Société Générale, Agence Centrale
29, boulevard Haussmann
Jacques Hermant, 1906–12
(Métro: Chaussée d'Antin (Lafayette), Opéra; RER: Auber)

Although constructed in the early-20C, Société Générale's *agence centrale* belongs firmly in spirit to the 19C, the age of soaring, secular, iron cathedrals. Founded, like its great rival Crédit Lyonnais (2.5), during the Second Empire, the bank had outgrown its old headquarters by the turn of the century, and, in 1905, acquired a prestigious building occupying an entire, wedge-shaped city block behind the Palais Garnier (9.13). Erected between 1867 and 1871 by Charles Rohault de Fleury, the building, whose façades were identical to those of its neighbours, formed part of the *architecture d'accompagnement* surrounding the opera. Jacques Hermant was charged with converting it into a suitable home for the bank.

Apart from modifying the arcades and adding a monumental pedimented *avant-corps* to mark the main entrance on the Boulevard Haussmann, Hermant left the façades untouched. Inside, however, he completely gutted the building, sank four basement floors to house the strongrooms, and constructed a glorious iron-and-glass central hall. Almost five storeys high and crowned by a dome 24 m in diameter supported at only four points, the hall is totally superfluous to the requirements of a banking institution. As if this magnificent expression of the power and prestige of 19C mercantilism were not in itself enough to convince investors of the bank's solidity, the hall is decorated with bronze medallions and stained-glass panels depicting the arms of major French towns where the bank was present. Happily, unlike most others, Société Générale's glass hall has survived the passage of time entirely unscathed.

9.12 Grand Hôtel
1, rue Scribe
Alfred Armand, 1861/62
(Métro: Opéra; RER: Auber)

Familiar to all today, the grand, luxury hotel capable of accommodating several-hundred guests was initially an American phenomenon of the early-19C. Linked in Europe with industrialization and the coming of the railways, the first Parisian example was the Hôtel du Louvre (Charles-Hubert Rohault de Fleury, 1854/55), built for the 1855 Exposition Universelle. With its 700 bedrooms and imposing reception rooms it set the tone for future institutions, including the Grand Hôtel (built with the 1867 exhibition in mind), which aimed to outdo its older rival in size and opulence.

As a fruit of the rebuilding of the *quartier* engendered by construction of the Opéra (9.13), the Grand Hôtel benefited from an entire island site with frontage on the new Place de l'Opéra, but had to content itself with the standardized façades imposed by the authorities. 1,000 bedrooms were initially planned, but only 800 were actually built, arranged so that, if desired, several could be joined to form a suite. But, the luxury of its bedrooms aside, it was the ostentation of its public spaces that brought the hotel renown. Orientated towards the Boulevard des Capucines, they included a glass-covered *cour d'honneur* where carriage passengers could alight protected from the elements (converted, in 1905, into a tea-room with an unusual glass canopy imitating draped fabric) and the vast dining room/salon in the form of a three-storey-high semi-rotunda. The salon's astonishingly opulent Second-Empire-Baroque décor is rivalled only by Garnier's Opéra.

The florid Café de la Paix, also decorated by Armand, occupies the hotel's Boulevard-des-Capucines façade.

9.13 Palais Garnier
Place de l'Opéra
Jean-Louis-Charles Garnier, 1860–75
(Métro: Opéra, Chaussée d'Antin (Lafayette); RER: Auber)

»What is this? It's not a style: it's neither Louis Quatorze, nor Louis Quinze, nor Louis Seize!«, exclaimed an irritated Empress Eugénie on being shown Charles

9.13 Palais Garnier. Main façade

Garnier's plans for the new Paris opera. »Why Ma'am, it's Napoléon Trois«, retorted Garnier, »and you're complaining!« Thus, so anecdote has it, was the design of this iconic building defined by its architect, a definition that remains undisputed, so much does the Palais Garnier seem emblematic of its time and of the Second Empire that created it. A giddy mixture of up-to-the-minute technology, rather prescriptive rationalism, exuberant eclecticism and astonishing opulence, Garnier's opera encapsulated the divergent tendencies and political and social ambitions of its era.

Napoleon III's decision to build a new opera house in Paris was essentially taken for reasons of state security. In 1820, the opera's then home in the Rue de Richelieu had been demolished in a rather extreme gesture of respect for the dead after the Duc de Berry, heir to the throne, was assassinated there. A hastily put together, provisory auditorium, which re-used large sections of the demolished Rue-de-Richelieu theatre, had afterwards been constructed in the Rue Le Peletier. It remained in use much longer than anyone had initially anticipated and, in 1858, was the scene of another assassination attempt, this time against Napoleon III: 8 people died, 148 were injured and the imperial couple narrowly escaped death. It afterwards transpired that the Rue-Le-Peletier auditorium's location in a narrow, densely built street had greatly facilitated the assassin's task. Construction of a new opera house was thus made an urgent priority: in the interests of security, it was to be freestanding on an island site; and in the interests of the empire's prestige, it was to be as splendid as possible.

A site for the new edifice was chosen in the Quartier de la Chaussée-d'Antin, an area at the western extremity of the *grands boulevards* that had already been singled out for redevelopment by Baron Haussmann. Rather forgotten and under-exploited in comparison to the rich neighbourhoods bordering it, the Quartier de la Chaussée-d'Antin would, it was hoped, become the new prestige district of Paris; the presence there of the opera, and the *mondain* society that patronized it, could only encourage this outcome. Situated within a triangle delimited by the Louvre-Tuileries palace (see 1.8 and 1.10), the Bourse (2.8) and the Gare Saint-Lazare (8.5), which linked Paris's wealthy western suburbs to the city centre, the Quartier de la Chaussée-d'Antin was already connected to the old commercial districts by the *grands boulevards*, and was to be integrated into the expanding city by the Boulevard Haussmann and the Rue Lafayette. It would, furthermore, be directly linked to the imperial power base in the Louvre-Tuileries palace by a triumphal avenue, whose summit, in typical

Haussmannian fashion, would be marked by a monumental structure, namely the Opéra.

A competition to find a design for the building was launched in late 1860. Rumour has it that Viollet-le-Duc, protégé of Empress Eugénie, had already been unofficially chosen as architect, and that the competition was organized for form's sake to avoid accusations of favouritism. This would certainly explain Eugénie's subsequent annoyance since, at the announcement of the first round of winners, Viollet-le-Duc's project had not been retained and, after submission of detailed schemes, it was the unknown Charles Garnier who emerged victorious, by unanimous decision of the jury. Although a holder of the prestigious Grand Prix de Rome, Garnier had but one building to his credit. The opera would occupy him almost exclusively for 15 years and, although he later became one of the grand old men of French architecture, his subsequent career was surprisingly devoid of notable work. The Palais Garnier was his one, extraordinary *magnum opus*.

Indeed it was largely due to Garnier's dogged perseverance that the Opéra was ever completed at all. Constant official haggling over the budget, unforeseen costs, hard winters and the fall of the Second Empire in 1870 all slowed down work and threatened the fragile will to complete what was, after all, not strictly a utilitarian facility. A major problem was encountered right at the start, when it was discovered that the Quartier de la Chaussée-d'Antin's water table was extremely high and the Opéra's site therefore sodden. This was particularly unfortunate given that the Palais Garnier needed much deeper basements and foundations than more common building types. Months were spent pumping, but still the ground would not dry up. In the end Garnier was forced to construct, at great expense, an enormous cement damp-proof course underneath the entire building, whose central cistern gave rise to the persistent legend that the Opéra was built above a subterranean lake. Once the foundations had been completed, work on the carcass could finally go ahead, the main façade on the Place de l'Opéra being inaugurated in 1867 for that year's Exposition Universelle. Public reaction was decidedly mixed, and the building's ostentatious appearance fuelled the polemic regarding its cost. Then, following Napoleon III's fall and the establishment of the not-entirely-legitimate Third Republic, calls were heard for the demolition of this extravagant symbol of the previous regime, whose completion, it was held, would be a needless expense. It was only the 1873 destruction by fire of the Rue-Le-Pelletier opera that saved Garnier's building, which was finished in haste for inauguration in early 1875.

Garnier's design for the opera
What the competition judges of 1861 had particularly admired in Garnier's scheme was the clarity of his plan, which was a brilliant example of the *beaux-arts* design methods in which both he and they were thoroughly versed. The parcel of land reserved for the opera was at the centre of a large square, orientated as a diamond in relation to the future opera's principle axis, and the plot thus consisted of a long rectangle with further space at either side. *Beaux-arts* teaching directed that at the centre of the plan should be placed what was termed the *dominante*, a room or space that would distil the essence of the whole building. Thus, at the centre of his site, Garnier positioned the Opéra's horse-shoe-shaped auditorium. Around the *dominante*, so the theory went, the secondary elements of the edifice should be axially disposed and articulated in the most practical sequence possible. At the Opéra we thus find, working along the building's principal axis from front to rear at *piano-nobile* level: the foyer, the *avant-foyer* and the *escalier d'honneur* preceding the auditorium, followed, behind the stage, by the fly tower, the *foyer de danse* (ballet rehearsal room) and finally the theatre's dressing rooms and administrative spaces. Garnier also made use of the extra lateral spaces available to him: on the western side, in the transversal axis of the auditorium, is the domed Pavillon de l'Empereur – a special entrance originally reserved, in the interests of rank and security, for the head of state (today the Opéra's library) – while to the east, duplicating the emperor's pavillon, is the Pavillon des Abonnés, an entrance for season-ticket holders that also included a covered porch under which those arriving by carriage could alight. Garnier had avoided mixing carriage and pedestrian entrances on the main façade, as other competition entrants had done, both for the practical purpose of rendering life more agreeable for those arriving on foot, and also because he considered an imposing flight of steps, in the manner of a temple, a more suitable base for his opera than a common roadway.

Again in keeping with *beaux-arts* teaching, the different parts of the plan were clearly articulated in the Opéra's massing, a revolutionary measure in comparison to older theatres such as the Odéon (6.7), where everything was subsumed under one huge roof. Thus, approaching the Palais Garnier from the Place de l'Opéra, we see in the foreground the façade and roofing of the foyer and the *escalier d'honneur*, then, rising behind them, a domed rotunda signalling the location of the auditorium – not strictly necessary since the auditorium rises no higher than the foyer and the *escalier d'honneur*, although the rotunda's bulk did allow the auditorium's giant chandelier to be winched up into it –, and finally, providing a backdrop to the whole composition, the enormous gable end of the fly tower. The two *pavillons* stand out clearly on either side, while at the Opéra's rear we find more conventionally fronted buildings containing the dressing rooms and administrative spaces. Although often classified as neo-Baroque, Garnier's Opéra has none of the distortions or illusionism often found in Baroque architecture, instead being all rational, readable clarity, inside as well as out. What is undeniably Baroque about the building, however, is the way it was intended to be seen from one particular, fixed spot, namely from the central entrance to the

9.13 Palais Garnier. *Escalier d'honneur*. Engraving, 1880

Place de l'Opéra. Garnier's main façade is justly famous, a stunning combination of elaborate articulation, sculpture and polychromy. With its *piano-nobile* level colonnaded loggia it recalls the east front of the Louvre (see 1.8) or Gabriel's Place-de-la-Concorde buildings (see 8.1), but the introduction of a second, subordinate order in between the twinned colossal columns was clearly inspired by Italian models, such as Palladio's town hall in Vicenza (1549–1617). The heavily emphasized end pavilions are consistent with traditional national practice, and the round-headed pediments coiffing them are a quote from the Louvre's Aile Lescot. On the other hand, the lack of a central *avant-corps* broke with the usual French way of doing things, thus making the colonnade seem more Italianizing. While the colonnade's eclectic references may have given rise to a certain *déjà vu*, the extraordinary ensemble composition with the rotunda and the fly tower was quite unlike anything ever seen before, constituting a new theatre type-form that would be much copied thereafter. Garnier's one regret was the tall attic storey, which he found weighed down too heavily on the colonnade below. Indeed he had only added it after building work started, when he learned that the edifices surrounding the Place de l'Opéra were to be raised from 17.5 m to 23 m, which prompted him to aggrandize his monument through extra upwards bulk.

If the Palais Garnier's plan and articulation were influential, its exuberant external décor was less so, and thus remains entirely redolent of Napoleon III's France. Sculpture and ornamentation everywhere abound, as was *de rigueur* for a Second-Empire state commission, from the busts of famous composers adorning the colonnade, to Carpeaux's scandalous group *La Danse* at entrance level, to the statue of Apollo – god of music and all the arts triumphantly raising his lyre – that crowns the summit of the fly tower. What most shocked contemporaries was the building's gaudiness, a characteristic forgotten until 2000, when, for the first time ever, the Palais Garnier's façade was cleaned. The transformation was astonishing: what had formerly been a dark, grey, rather brooding edifice, despite the exuberance of its décor, was suddenly revealed as a brilliant, glittering, multicoloured extravaganza comprising no less than six varieties of different-hued stone. A partisan of the theory (since proved correct) that ancient-Greek temples were polychrome, Garnier wanted to give the façade of his building – which, he said, »... was after all like a temple, having art for its divinity« – the allure of a tapestry. »May a bit of colour rouse our grey skies!«, he exclaimed, although many, brought up on the severe, monochrome Classicism of buildings such as the Louvre, were not at all ready for this awakening.

Much has been made of the fact that Garnier's Opéra was an almost exact contemporary of Wagner's revolutionary Festspielhaus in Bayreuth, opened in 1876, and many is the historian who has attempted a comparison of the two. Where Garnier's Opéra was charged with symbolizing the power, wealth and *éclat* of Napoleon III's regime, Wagner's opera house was conceived solely as a theatrical instrument from which anything unnecessary to the appreciation of the operatic works performed there was banished. Wagner told his architect, Gottfried Semper, that he wanted a very clear distinction made between the »real« world of the spectators and the »unreal« world of the stage. Garnier, on the other hand, wanted to include the auditorium, the foyers and – most importantly – the audience in what would be a *Gesamtkunstwerk* of all the arts: music, drama, architecture, painting, sculpture and even fashion, for the Opéra was expressly designed as a place where society could see and be seen, a glittering temple of Western culture in which, as Garnier put it, »the shimmer of ladies' toilettes, the *éclat* of their jewels ... the variety of outfits, the movement of the audience and the sort of quivering of a whole crowd, which observes and knows itself observed« could be displayed to best effect. This is why more than a third of the building was given over to foyers, salons and public circulation spaces, the epicentre of which was of course the celebrated *escalier d'honneur*. Symbolic of the climb to the higher realms of art and opera, it was influenced both by the staircase of Victor Louis's Grand Théâtre de Bordeaux (1772–80) and by Versailles's famous Escalier des Ambassadeurs (see 32.1). From the former it borrowed its vaulted, top-lit, colonnaded stairwell, its division into three flights and its caryatid-supported central doorway opening into the stalls, while the latter inspired its marble polychromy. After the brilliance of the *escalier d'honneur*, the Palais Garnier's auditorium can seem a little disappointing. It too owes a big debt to Bordeaux, being in classic Italian style but conforming to French usage in the way everything has been arranged so that the audience can see both the stage and itself, as social display demanded. By using iron (see below), Garnier was able to achieve much wider spans for his balconies than had Louis 80 years before.

Garnier's intention in building the Opéra was to create a magical fantasy realm that would act upon spectators' consciousness and lift them out of the everyday world from whence they had come into an exalted state appropriate to musical drama. This was why, in addition to theatrical architectonics, decoration was so important in the conception of the Palais Garnier. Literally hundreds of artists and craftsmen worked on an interior that, as well as paint, gilt, stucco, bronze, and mosaic, comprised no less than 33 different varieties of stone. Garnier again spoke of creating a tapestry effect of polychromy, whose inspiration was clearly the mythicized Orient so popular at the time. He chose what he called the »palette of Veronese«, with a dominance of red so as to reflect a flattering, rosy hue on the ladies' décolletages. Amongst the myriad elements fighting for attention, it is perhaps the countless lighting fixtures that most stand out, representative as they are of the era's taste for elaborate whimsy that just stopped short of the grotesque. Most spectacular of all is the auditorium's 7-tonne crystal-and-bronze chandelier, created at Garnier's insistence, even though the Opéra's management would have preferred wall lights and a flat, luminous ceiling. Mention should also be made of the overbearingly opulent, 54 m-long foyer, whose ceiling paintings by Paul Baudry were triumphantly scandalous when first unveiled.

What all this lavish, essentially historicizing décor served to conceal was just how much advanced technology went into creating the Palais Garnier. Despite appearances, the building is in fact largely iron framed, and indeed could not have been otherwise since the volume demands Garnier made on it could not have been satisfied using the massive load-bearing walls of traditional masonry construction. Both the auditorium and the circular Vestibule des Abonnés on which it sits were realized using slender iron beams and columns whose points of contact with the ground cover a mere 12 m². But Garnier was cautious with regard to a material that the French had hitherto used almost exclusively for enveloping structures such as train sheds and market halls, rather than for the load-bearing role he required of it, and consequently made his iron members 20 times stronger than engineers' calculations reckoned necessary. For the stage machinery, he replaced all the traditional fire-prone wooden apparatuses with brand-new designs in iron, and installed up-to-the-minute heating and ventilation systems throughout the building. He stopped short of fitting electric lighting, however, considering it better to wait until the technology had progressed beyond its infancy.

The Place and Avenue de l'Opéra

As the Palais Garnier went up, so did the setting designed to display it, the Place de l'Opéra and its subordinate streets being built in 1862–68 and the Avenue de l'Opéra knocked through in 1864–79. Where the Place de l'Opéra was concerned, the stage-set façades that lined it were conceived long before the monument they were supposed to frame. Set down in an imperial decree of 1860, they were in an inoffensive Louis-Seize style articulated so as to permit the mixing of commerce, office space and residential accommodation in the same building without too much visual rupture. To achieve suitably imperial grandeur, a colossal order was used on the two principal floors. Garnier complained about the banality of this *architecture d'acommpagnement*, but it was precisely its uniform blandness that allowed his Opéra to stand out so spectacularly. Framing the entrance to the Avenue de l'Opéra, Henri Blondel designed two rotundas that exploit the theme with slightly more character.

As well as providing a triumphal way between the Palais Garnier and the Louvre, the Avenue de l'Opéra was an important part of Haussmann's traffic network, linking the Rue de Rivoli to the *grands boulevards* and thence to the wealthy *quartiers* then going up in northwestern Paris. Furthermore, its course was driven bang through the Quartier de la Butte-des-Moulins, at the time a notorious rookery. As if demolition was not enough, the hillock (*butte*) that had given the *quartier* its name was flattened to make way for the new thoroughfare. The completion of the Avenue de l'Opéra (originally to have been called Avenue Napoléon) in the aftermath of France's defeat by the Prussians was welcomed as a symbol of national pride, a sign that the country could and would overcome its humiliation. In tandem with the Opéra that crowns it, it is perhaps the most iconic production of Haussmannian Paris.

10th *arondissement*

10.1 Porte Saint-Denis
Junction of the Rues Saint-Denis and du Faubourg
Saint-Denis and the Boulevards Bonne-Nouvelle and
Saint-Denis
Nicolas-François Blondel, 1672
(Métro: Strasbourg Saint-Denis)

Louis XIV's France rose to become the most powerful nation in Europe as the king reaped victory after victory in endless warmongering. Bellicosity abroad brought greater security at home and, in 1670, the king ordered the demolition of Paris's defensive circuit. Charles V's ramparts to the north of the city had become a popular place of promenade, and were thus replaced with broad avenues, which became known as the *grands boulevards* (derived from the German *Bollwerk*, meaning »bastion« or »bulwark«). With the increasing centralization of power in the personage of the sovereign, Louis's minister and Superintendent of Buildings, Jean-Baptiste Colbert, sought to express and consolidate the royal prerogative in the built environment, concentrating his efforts on Paris. Temporary triumphal arches had often been put up for the king's official entries into the city, and Colbert now undertook the creation of permanent structures. The Porte Saint-Denis was the first, erected to the glory of the monarch and celebrating his recent victories in Holland. Its site was 50 m to the north of the demolished medieval gateway, at the crossroads of the new *grands boulevards* and the Rue Saint-Denis, which then served as the Voie Royale running directly between the ancient centre of power on the Ile de la Cité (4.1) and the royal abbey of Saint-Denis (21.2).

10.1 Porte Saint-Denis

10.2 Porte Saint-Martin

Colbert commissioned Nicolas-François Blondel, first head of the Académie Royale d'Architecture (which Colbert had founded in 1671) to build the arch. Blondel was more of a theoretician than practising architect, and the Porte Saint-Denis is his major surviving work. He preached a doctrine of Vitruvian inspiration that was rigorously Classical and rational, as codified by his lectures, published in 1675. A good mathematician, he developed complex theories of proportion, and the *porte*'s dimensions were calculated entirely from multiples of the numbers three and four. The main elevations are composed within a perfect square, each side 23 m long, which is divided vertically into three equal parts and encompasses a single arch. The orders are absent, and the structure is decorated with applied sculpture, the work of François Girardon and Michel Anguier. Engaged obelisks either side of the arch carry symbols of war, while bas-reliefs over the arch, styled *à l'antique*, depict the siege of Maastricht (north side) and the crossing of the Rhine (south side). The inscriptions at the base of each obelisk were composed by Blondel, in Latin, a language he considered more proper to grandeur than French.

The Porte Saint-Denis has been criticized for heaviness and gracelessness, but unlike »prettier« structures (see, e.g., the Arc du Carrousel, 1.9), its brooding bulk and imposing proportions are a powerful expression of royal might and aggression. Through the influence of the Academy, the *porte* became the model for triumphal arches throughout France.

10.2 Porte Saint-Martin
33, boulevard Saint-Martin
Attributed to Pierre Bullet, 1674
(Métro: Strasbourg Saint-Denis)

The Porte Saint-Martin was the second Parisian triumphal arch erected in honour of Louis XIV's military victories. Bullet was a pupil of Nicolas-François Blondel's, and his work in executing his master's design for the neighbouring Porte Saint-Denis (10.1) is thought to

10.3 Mairie du 10ᵉ

have secured him the commission for the Porte Saint-Martin. It is, however, possible that Blondel was responsible for both arches.

Situated 60 m north of the old medieval gate, the Porte Saint-Martin commemorates Louis's capture of the Franche-Comté. Like the Porte Saint-Denis, its main elevations are composed within a perfect square (18 m each side), but encompassing three arches in contrast to the Porte Saint-Denis's solitary opening. Because of the lesser importance of the Rue Saint-Martin in relation to the Rue Saint-Denis, which held the status of Voie Royale, the Porte Saint-Martin is not so richly ornamented as its neighbour. The spandrels of the principal arch are decorated with bas-reliefs: on the northern elevation *The Capture of Limbourg* on the left, by Pierre Legros, and on the right *The Defeat of the Germans* by Gaspard Marsy; on the southern elevation *The Capture of Besançon*, by Martin Desjardins, on the right and, on the left, *The Rupture of the Triple Alliance* by Etienne Le Hongre, in which the king appears as a semi-naked, bewigged Hercules. Despite its rougher, rusticated garb, the Porte Saint-Martin is less intimidating than its neighbour – partly because of its shorter stature –, but is nonetheless a convincing expression of royal potency.

10.3 Mairie du 10ᵉ
72–74, rue du Faubourg Saint-Martin
Eugène Rouyer, 1889–96
(Métro: Château d'Eau)

In 1795, the administrative division of Paris was reorganized into a system of twelve *arrondissements*, which carved up the city into areas of roughly equal population. With the annexation of outlying settlements into the municipal boundaries in 1859, the map had to be redrawn, and the current system of 20 *arrondissements* was introduced. Each *arrondissement* needed its *mairie*, and the municipality undertook a building programme that lasted over 50 years. The *mairie* was the administrative centre of the district, and also where civil marriages were performed. As well as the requisite office accommodation, each *mairie* included a *salle des fêtes* and a *salle des mariages*, and was usually organized around a central courtyard or hall. To symbolize the state power they represented, the new *mairies* were given monumental form and dressed up in an eclectic mix of French Classical styles, 16C and 17C references proving especially popular.

One of the most extravagant, the Mairie du 10ᵉ replaced an earlier structure that was considered too small. Rouyer had come second in the competition for the rebuilding of the Hôtel de Ville (4.11), and his design for the Mairie du 10ᵉ was inspired by Paris's old Renaissance town hall. Internally, the building is disposed around a lavish, *beaux-arts* style atrium, whose imposing *escalier d'honneur* leads up to the function rooms. Externally, the *mairie* is a riot of applied decoration, the work of Antoine Margotin. Charles Garnier was one of the two principal competition judges for the Mairie du 10ᵉ, and his influence is palpable.

10.4 Hôpital Saint-Louis

10.5 Gare de l'Est

10.4 Hôpital Saint-Louis
40, rue Bichat and 2, place du Docteur-Fournier
Claude Chastillon (?) and Claude Vellefaux, 1607–11
(Métro: Goncourt, Colonel Fabien)

Throughout the 16C and early-17C, Paris was regularly hit by the plague, two outbreaks proving particularly fatal: that of 1561/62, when over 68,000 people died, and that of 1606, which was equally catastrophic. On both occasions, Paris's hospitals were saturated, and the disease quickly spread to other patients. A good method of reducing its progress was to isolate sufferers from the uninfected population, and during the 1580 outbreak a village of tents was installed outside the city for this purpose. Following the 1606 disaster, Henri IV, ever eager to improve and modernize his capital, ordered the building of a permanent plague sanatorium beyond the city walls in the fields north of Paris.

Authorship of the hospital, whose design was selected by the king from a choice of three, remains contested. While it is certain that Vellefaux built it, he was probably not the designer, and evidence suggests that Chastillon was in fact the true architect. The Hôpital Saint-Louis is a fascinating example of the type of rational approach later championed in the 18C, for example in Jeremy Bentham's »Panopticon« prison (1791). Indeed the hospital strongly resembles a prison, and patients were literally incarcerated there, deprived even of contact with the ground. Square in plan, the complex was surrounded by high walls, of which only parts now survive. Gatehouses guarded entrances at the centre of each wall, and small pavilions at each corner of the outer perimeter ensured security. Inside the walls were extensive vegetable gardens, making the hospital more or less self sufficient and minimizing the need for exterior contact. Four buildings set into the eastern and western perimeter walls provided accommodation for the staff, their bracket-shaped plan defining the limits of a second, inner square. An internal street separated them from the large, two-storey quadrangle at the centre of the complex, which contained the wards. These were located on the first floor above vaulted storerooms, thus entirely isolating the patients from the outside world. The hospital buildings are in the style of the time, with tall, narrow upper-storey windows and steep French roofs, their rubble walls decorated with stone quoins and either plastered or brick-faced. Set into the northern perimeter wall is the simple hospital chapel, probably intended for use by staff and not by patients. The quadrangle's formally planted, central courtyard is a delightful haven of peace in the bustling city.

In the event, there was little call for Henri IV's plague sanatorium, and it served a variety of other purposes until, in 1772, it became a permanent hospital following a fire at the Hôtel-Dieu (see 4.1). Happily, extensions added at various times during the 20C were built within the old hospital gardens, thus leaving the original edifices intact.

10.5 Gare de l'Est
Place du 8-mai-1945
François-Alexandre Duquesney, with Pierre Cabanel de Sermet, 1847–52; Bertaut, 1924–31
(Métro: Gare de l'Est)

Built to head the Paris–Strasbourg line (opened in 1849), the Gare de l'Est is the French capital's oldest surviving station, and as such is a rare example of the first generation of French railway termini. At the time of its completion, it was hailed as something of a model of its kind, and inspired several imitations abroad. In its initial state, it consisted of an iron-and-glass train-shed spanning five lines, around which were symmetrically disposed Italianate pavilions housing waiting rooms, goods stores, company offices, and so on. Externally, the train-shed was expressed by way of an enormous pediment, which enclosed at its centre a half rose window. Unlike almost every other 19C Parisian station, the Gare de l'Est did not employ Polonceau-type trusses for the train-shed, but instead used a system of tied arches, which was much admired for its graceful proportions and technical sophistication. Careful attention was paid to the station's iconographic content, which includes a magisterial personification of the town of Strasbourg crowning the pediment and, decorating the columns of the entrance arcade, capitals carved with agricultural products grown in the regions through which the line passes.

The early confidence of the railway age was clearly manifested by the monumental form of the Gare de l'Est, whose pediment and rose window proudly proclaimed the presence of the train-shed in the city centre. Following the station's completion, work was begun on the Boulevard de Strasbourg (1852–54), which terminates at the Gare de l'Est, and which was designed to give it a suitably grandiose setting, as well as improving traffic circulation to and from the station. Under Haussmann, the Boulevard de Strasbourg was incorporated into the »Grande Croisée« (great crossing) so fundamental to Second-Empire ambitions for the capital, and the Gare de l'Est consequently found itself at the head of one of Paris's two principal traffic axes.

The Gare de l'Est inevitably proved too small before the century was out, and was extended several times towards the east. In the 1920s, the number of lines was increased to 30, necessitating major building work. The old station was exactly duplicated a couple of hundred metres to the east, and the new and old halls linked by a two-storey hotel building, styled *à l'italienne* in the manner of the original station's pavilions. The resulting palace-front façade is reminiscent of the Gare du Nord (10.7) which, in its turn, was probably inspired by the initial Gare de l'Est. By now too cramped to house platforms, the old train-shed was converted into a departure hall, and was truncated at its northern end. One can nonetheless get a good idea of what the original station must have been like, in the pioneering days of steam.

10.6 Saint-Vincent-de-Paul
Place Franz-Liszt
Jakob Ignaz Hittorff and Jean-Baptiste Lepère, 1824–44
(Métro: Poissonnière)

Something of an archaeological scholar with a passion for ancient-Greek architecture, Hittorff achieved notoriety when he published his discovery that Hellenic

10.6 Saint-Vincent-de-Paul

buildings were originally polychrome, a concept then considered rather shocking. Saint-Vincent-de-Paul, his *magnum opus*, became a manifesto of his theories of polychromy, whereby painting, sculpture and architecture were to be united through colour in a sort of a *Gesamtkunstwerk* of the visual and decorative arts. Situated on land formerly occupied by the Prieuré Saint-Lazare, where Vincent de Paul himself had lived in the 17C, the church was built to serve a rapidly expanding *quartier*. Begun by Hittorff's father-in-law, Lepère, only its foundations were complete when Hittorff took over in 1831.

Conceptually, Saint-Vincent-de-Paul is modelled on paeleo-Christian basilical churches, themselves directly derived from the Roman administrative buildings in which early Christians worshipped. The French vogue for neo-Roman churches began during the *ancien régime* (see, e. g., Saint-Philippe-du-Roule (8.7)) and, fuelled by neo-Classical thinking, continued under the Restoration, the aim being to return to the roots of Christianity. Saint-Vincent-de-Paul is thus of classic basilical design, with a high (28 m), galleried nave lit by clerestory windows, low side-aisles, a semicircular, half-domed apse and a double-pitched ceiling. Despite its Grecian attire, the church's exterior expresses this basilical form, except on the principal elevation, whose situation dominating the Rue Lafayette encouraged something more grandiose. Hittorff devised a twin-towered, Italianizing façade set at the top of a wide flight of steps flanked by curving ramps – an ensemble inspired by the famous SS. Trinità dei Monti in Rome. Plonked uneasily onto the façade is an enormous, twelve-columned portico (symbolic of the twelve apostles) of Greek inspiration, whose Ionic order breaks with the Corinthian usually favoured in Paris. The pediment sculptures by Charles Lebœuf-Nanteuil, representing the glorification of Saint Vincent de Paul, are in the round as opposed to the more usual bas-relief: in Hittorff's eyes, sculpture in the round on pediments had the advantages over bas-relief of being more authentically Greek, and aesthetically superior, because easily readable from afar. It was also cheaper (as it does not need to be carved *in situ*) and more robust than bas-relief.

Despite its theatricality, the church's exterior does nothing to prepare one for the lavishness of the interior. Partly to restrict the number of artists who could work on the décor and thereby ensure stylistic unity, and partly to rival the magnificent neo-Roman churches then going up in Munich, Hittorff insisted that wax painting (an elaborate technique then little used) be employed for the nave murals, and that the windows be executed in painted glass (an equally esoteric skill). The nave paintings, on a background of pure gold, were the work of Hippolyte Flandrin and François Picot. Flandrin's 92 m-long friezes – depicting processions of saints filing towards Picot's Christ in the apse – are particularly acclaimed. Gold and colour are everywhere, from the richly moulded, coffered ceilings to the intricate Ionic and Corinthian capitals of the nave columns. The impact of all this polychromy is today hard to appreciate, partly because of the blackening effect of time and incense, and partly because the church is extremely dark. Fenestration is sparse, and Charles-Laurent Maréchal's splendid painted windows exclude much light; indeed, contemporary parishioners, unable to read their prayer books, insisted that at least the windows' borders be lightened. Hittorff caused further congregational indignation with his neo-Renaissance nave doors, cast in ignominious iron, which parishioners insisted be painted to resemble bronze (they were perhaps unaware that the church's gilded furnishings, largely designed by Hittorff, are also in cast iron). The biggest scandal, however, was caused by Hittorff's treatment of the porch walls – his theory of polychromy extended equally to the exterior of buildings, and for the porch he commissioned a cycle of brightly coloured paintings in weatherproof enamel, a recently invented technique. Put up in 1860, public opinion against them was so strong that Baron Haussmann ordered their removal barely a year later, in 1861.

10.7 Gare du Nord
Place Napoléon-III
Jakob Ignaz Hittorff, Lejeune and Léon Ohnet, 1857–66
(Métro/RER: Gare du Nord)

Built to serve the Paris–Lille–Brussels line in 1846, the first Gare du Nord was already woefully inadequate after less than ten years, following enormous growth in passenger traffic. Permission for its reconstruction was finally given in 1857, and the architects of the Compagnie des Chemins de Fer du Nord, Lejeune and Ohnet, drew up preliminary plans. It seems that they, and not (as previously thought) Hittorff, were responsible for the basic design of the station, Hittorff's involvement probably only beginning in 1861. The company wanted a monumental building that clearly expressed its function and that was not dissimulated behind another edifice, unlike, for example, the London stations hidden behind their hotels. With this in mind, the company decided its offices should be housed in an entirely separate structure nearby.

Ohnet and Lejeune devised a plan for the station in which the principal façade, heading the platforms on the Place Napoléon-III, served as the entrance for suburban passengers and railway personnel, while access to the mainline trains was gained via the lateral elevations, with departures on the western side and arrivals to the east. Probably inspired by the nearby Gare de l'Est (10.5), their design for the main elevation consists of an enormous gable end, following the contours of the principal train-shed behind, at the centre of which is a huge arched window, flanked by two smaller glazed arches. Two-storey wings stretch out on either side, and pedimented pavilions, also containing glazed arches, punctuate the composition at either extremity. Hittorff's contribution was probably limited to the façade's »Roman-Empire« styling – crisp colossal Ionic pilasters which aggrandize the central gable and the pavilions, with sober Doric columns for the sub-order. No less than 23 feminine personifications of European cities, the work of some of the most renowned sculptors of the day, complete this imposing ensemble. Despite the uneasy effect produced by the application of a giant order to a gable end in a rather unorthodox manner (the diagonals of the gable crash uncomfortably into the horizontals of the entablatures), the façade successfully monumentalizes the building's function, while at the same time clearly expressing the form of the train-shed behind it. It is all the more remarkable in that nothing quite like it existed before, the architects having invented a new and spectacular type-form which, albeit overwrought, somehow looks as one thinks a station ought to look. The façade has unfortunately been disfigured by the subsequent addition of a glazed canopy along its entire length.

The iron-and-glass train-sheds, entirely the work of Hittorff and his office, are structurally separate from the stone façades surrounding them. 35 m wide, the principal shed is constructed from Polonceau-type trusses supported by slender 38 m-high, cast-iron columns. Hittorff cut his teeth assisting Bélanger with the dome of the Halle au Blé (1.20), and consequently became an adept of iron construction; the structure of the Gare du Nord is characteristically light and economical. Hittorff was also a pioneer of the theory that ancient-Greek buildings were polychrome, and the ironwork of the train-sheds, today a uniform sea-green, was originally multicoloured. On the station's eastern flank, which was formerly scarred by an ugly 1972-vintage car park, a new Métro/RER interchange has just been built (1999–2001), whose twin glazed halls cover an impressive light / stair-well descending three floors below ground.

Contemporary critical reactions to the Gare du Nord were wildly divergent, with some proclaiming it a temple of steam, while others considered it an architectural abomination. Anatole de Baudot, a pupil of Viollet-le-Duc and a fervent partisan of Structural Rationalism, praised the train-sheds but attacked the façadism of the elevations attached to them. 140 years later, in a world less morally upright and grown accustomed to ubiquitous curtain walling, his arguments seem less pertinent. Unlike many of its confrères, the Gare du Nord has resisted major alteration, and remains a magnificent legacy of the confidence and inventiveness of the railway age.

10.8 Théâtre des Bouffes du Nord
37 bis, boulevard de la Chapelle
Louis-Marie Emile Leménil, 1875/76
(Métro: La Chapelle)

Hidden away within a city block and invisible from the street, this little theatre is one of Paris's lesser-known delights. Built in a working-class area far from the theatre district, it was intended as a local, popular playhouse, but never really found the clientele it was seeking. Following countless changes of ownership, it closed its doors, seemingly for good, in 1952. It was rediscovered in the 1970s by the director Peter Brook, who established his company there, and is now an acclaimed fixture of the Parisian theatre scene.

Leménil's auditorium is reached via a passageway from the street, and hence has no foyer. Elliptical in shape, it is tall and narrow, with three balconies and a maximum depth of only 16 m. The balconies are supported by slender, full-height, cast-iron columns that terminate in arcades, which in turn support a dome decorated with cast-iron filigree panels. The theatre's beauty comes partly from its intimate proportions and elegant ironwork, and partly from Brook's inspired restoration. In fact it was more of a consolidation than a restoration, as the romantic decrepitude into which the theatre had fallen has been preserved, peeling paint and all. The new furnishings have a temporary feel about them, as though squatting in the ghost of the old playhouse. By removing the original stage and allowing the performance area to spill out beyond the proscenium arch into the stalls, Brook has created a very direct relationship between audience and actors, heightening the theatre's intimacy.

10.7 Gare du Nord

11th *arrondissement*

11.1 Cirque d'Hiver
110, rue Amelot
Jakob Ignaz Hittorff, 1852
(Métro: Filles du Calvaire, Oberkampf)

Commissioned by the impresario Louis Dejean, the Cirque d'Hiver was intended to complement his Cirque d'Eté on the Champs-Elysées, also by Hittorff (1840/41, destroyed). Dejean's extravagant horse shows at the Cirque d'Eté attracted large crowds in summer, but the circus was considered too far from the city centre for use in winter. Having acquired an inner-city site in the popular theatre district, Dejean asked Hittorff to build him a new, 4,000-seat circus which, for minimum expense, would have the appearance of opulence and monumentality necessary to attract the public in large numbers.

Put up in record time – just over seven months – Hittorff's building consists essentially of a 20-sided regular polygon, 41 m in diameter, constructed from rubble-stone and covered in a single span by a wooden-framed roof. Although an adept of iron construction, Hittorff used wood for the roof frame for reasons of economy. Designed so that none of its structure is apparent on the interior, the roof gives an impression of weightlessness that was much applauded by contemporaries. To enhance this effect, Hittorff decorated the ceiling with a *trompe l'œil* painting depicting a richly coloured canopy, in imitation of the coverings of Antique circuses.

Rendered in inexpensive plaster, the circus's exterior is Greek in inspiration, and was originally highly polychrome. Animated by an engaged Corinthian order, it features bas-relief friezes on an equestrian theme, and cast-iron statues of an Amazon on horseback and a mounted warrior frame the entrance. Circuses still perform in this building to this day, 150 years on.

11.2 Sheltered housing
16–20, rue de l'Orillon
Architecture Studio, 1994–96
(Métro: Belleville)

Walking around the rather lugubrious, run-down streets of this neighbourhood, one is surprised suddenly to come across this bright and inventive building by Architecture Studio, which respects the surrounding 19C urbanity while adding a dash of contemporary colour. Commissioned by the municipality, the complex provides 83 studio flats for pensioners and an underground car park. The architects observed the street line by building around the perimeter of the site, but opened it up to its surroundings by means of a central garden-courtyard giving onto the Rue de l'Orillon. Thus the building is divided into two wings that run down the site's longer sides, with a linchpin structure containing vertical circulation connecting them at the rear of the plot. Lined up along the lateral street façades, the flats, which benefit from street-side balconies, are

11.1 Cirque d'Hiver

accessed via corridors running along the courtyard elevations. The latter, with their streamlined curves opening out towards the street and sleek, all-glass façades that reveal rows of brightly coloured front doors, make the semi-public/semi-private space that is the garden-courtyard a visual delight for passers-by. This attractiveness is all the more admirable in that it is achieved with a remarkable economy of means. Some critics have wondered why the flats were not placed on the courtyard or orientated according to sun exposure, and it can be argued that to a certain extent residents' convenience was sacrificed in the interests of contextual tact. Civically minded and urbane, this project inserts a colourful clearing into a dense and dingy area of the city.

11.3 Post office and postal-workers' housing
113, rue Oberkampf
Frédéric Borel, 1989–93
(Métro: Parmentier)

At the end of the 1980s, the Poste Française embarked on a major Parisian building campaign to provide rent-controlled housing for its employees as well as new neighbourhood post offices. A policy of engaging young, relatively unknown but upcoming architects paid off handsomely, with the results garnering much

11.2 Sheltered housing

interest and praise (see also 20.3). Of all the schemes, that which attracted by far the most attention was this complex of 80 apartments designed by Frédéric Borel, whose star has been firmly in the ascendant ever since.

The site allocated to Borel's post office housing was typically Parisian: narrow and deep (20×87 m) with party walls either side rising up to 23 m. The traditional development pattern of such a plot would have included a tall, street-line-respecting structure on the road with a courtyard and other, lower buildings behind. As a result of this Parisian tendency to build canyon-like streets, much of the city is hidden; behind the standardized façades of the avenues and boulevards is a whole other world, which in the working-class east historically included not only courtyards but also factories, ateliers, warehouses and workshops, all realized in a multitude of forms and materials. Pushing further ideas he had first developed at nearby 100, boulevard de Belleville (20.1), Borel took this topography of the secret heart of the city block as his starting point, aiming to reproduce its formal and material diversity while opening it up to the world at large. He made clear his debt to Surrealism when, quoting Isidore Ducasse, he said »we should promote wherever possible the Surrealist principle of ›the fortuitous encounter of an umbrella and a sewing machine‹, or recreate, using different forms, the emotion produced by the confrontation at a street corner of a factory chimney and housing, the surprise of a gigantic warehouse juxtaposed with small ateliers in a courtyard.« Just as the Surrealists tried rationally to create irrationality, so Borel planned to create unplanned urban »chaos«.

Closing the party-wall gap at 113, rue Oberkampf is a massive, Haussmannian-scale block, whose complicated contours are organized in a symmetrical triptych – just about the only symmetry one finds in the entire complex. The ground floor of this block is left open, forming a covered public space that accesses the post office and allows views over the rest of the site. A private, sunken garden fills the centre of the plot, various structures line its sides, while two slender, free-standing towers dramatically terminate the perspective as viewed from the street (their complementary volumes are intended to point to sky and earth). Behind them, closing the site's rear, is a courtyard delimited by a low-rise, curved, vaguely Classicizing façade. Myriad details enrich the ensemble: multiform volumes and profiling, numerous passageways and walkways – including a high-altitude flying footbridge and a swooping free-standing staircase –, a multitude of different types of fenestration and an equally impressive array of materials and finishes. Indeed so complexly »chaotic« did Borel's design appear to the planning authorities that they pronounced it »unbuildable«. But despite their scepticism and despite the strict and complicated Parisian building regulations, which he respected to the letter, Borel managed to produce an ensemble of extraordinary richness and variety. That this was done within the limits of the budget and without sacrificing quality of workmanship makes the achievement even more remarkable. Inside the diversity continues, with quirky, individualized, adaptable apartments, which some critics have complained are too small and unorthodox.

Dramatic, exciting, sculptural, oneiric, Cubist, mannered; these are just some of the adjectives that have been used to described 113, rue Oberkampf. Borel's debt to Christian de Portzamparc (for whom he worked at the start of his career) is evident in the project's sculptural wilfulness and slightly forced expressionism, while similarities to Zaha Hadid's work can be found in the penchant for volumetric distortion (e.g. the trapezoid towers). But whatever its influences, Borel's building remains a *tour de force* of inventiveness and an admirably site-specific creation.

11.4 Commercial units, offices and apartments
25, rue Saint-Ambroise
Louis Miquel with Georges Maurios, 1965
(Métro: Saint-Maur, Saint-Ambroise)
Following the destructions of WWII, France embarked on a programme of mass housing, one of whose fruits was Le Corbusier's famous experimental Unité d'habitation in Marseilles (1945–52). In all, four *unités* were built (plus a fifth, in Berlin), none of which were located in the Paris area. Aside from the Maison du Brésil (14.9), the closest the capital came to a genuine, Corb-style *unité* was this mixed-use block, designed by Corb's former assistant, Louis Miquel.

Where Corb's *unités* were to form part of a »Ville Radieuse«, standing alone in open parkland, Miquel had to deal with the exigencies of a cramped Parisian plot with a pre-determined street line and encroaching party walls. Corb himself had faced a similar situation when building the Salvation Army's Cité de Refuge (13.6), and had opted to break with the street line, orientating his building towards the sun. Miquel, on the other hand, accepted the conventions of city planning and, through economic necessity, abandoned the use of *pilotis*, reserving the ground floor for glass-fronted commercial units. The first-floor office space is signalled on the exterior by a *brise-soleil* – which Corb recommended in rainy Paris as protection against precipitation – and the duplex apartments on the upper floors, stacked according to Corb's »bottle-rack« principle, manifest themselves through wide loggias. Like the *unités*, the building is in raw concrete, although with none of the brute power of Corb's handling of the material. Unlike many of Corb's buildings, however, the block was clearly well constructed, and looks remarkably fresh after nearly four decades' existence.

11.5 Crèche
56, rue Saint-Maur
Christian Hauvette, 1988–90
(Métro: Saint-Maur)

Because of the system of narrow plots that predominates in Paris and the building regulations that stipulate respect for the street line, much Parisian architec-

11.3 Post office and postal-workers' housing

11.4 Commercial units, offices and apartments

ture comes down in its street-side expression to a question of façades, the art of filling the plane between two party walls. Thus many Parisian buildings tend towards expressing themselves as a two-dimensional mask stretched across the gap in the urban fabric into which they are inserted. For this municipal crèche, which is sited in just such a context, Christian Hauvette pushed Parisian façadism to its logical limit, creating a building that literally hides behind a free-standing carapace. To decipher Hauvette's crèche, it is best to read it from back to front. The horizontally emphasized rear façade, which gives onto a small outdoor play area, is entirely glazed, with even its balcony railings consisting of large sheets of outwardly inclined glass, high enough to prevent toddlers climbing over them. The basic crèche building is a simple stacking of floors, whose curved ceiling profiles allow services to run through their centre while keeping their façade width to an elegant minimum. Staff accommodation occupies the first floor, while the ground and upper floors contain the crèche proper. These latter spaces have essentially been left clear for the crèche personnel to arrange as they choose. Standing in front of the stack of floors, on the street side of the building, is a concrete perimeter frame, inside which are suspended the building's staircases (the lift rises in its own separate tower, cut into the stack of floors). And hovering in front of the circulation frame, sitting on an oversized concrete I-beam, is the crèche's free-standing street façade.

It is onto this mask that Hauvette, a former pupil of Roland Barthes's, has loaded all the building's signification. Realized *à la* Tadao Ando in plates of raw, grey, carefully cast concrete with shuttering holes still apparent, the street façade consists of two largely blind, curved screens, whose undulations serve in part to obfuscate the misalignment of the buildings either side of the crèche. Cut into these concrete screens are various openings: traditional windows that echo the 19C-

11.5 Crèche

block next door, horizontal and vertical regulating strips, a central breach and, here and there, gratuitous incisions that emphasize the façade's two-dimensionality. Hauvette's intention in creating this powerful, enigmatic, rather forbidding concrete shield was to evoke both the muscled defences of a bunker and the feminine bulges of protective maternity. Parents were to be reassured and child molesters deterred. But what signals does this building send out to the disinterested passer-by? And if security really is the major issue, is the aesthetically aggressive, visual mythology of fortress architecture actually appropriate here, or would banal anonymity provide a better defence?

11.6 Candie-Saint-Bernard redevelopment
Massimiliano Fuksas, 1987–98
(Métro: Ledru Rollin)

Densely built and cut off from the avenues and boulevards for which Paris is famous, this working-class area in the Faubourg Saint-Antoine (formerly the centre of Paris's furniture-making industry) had become distinctly dilapidated by the late 1980s, abandoned by the activities that had originally shaped its fabric. Pursuing its policy of gentrification of the working-class east, the Ville de Paris stepped in and commissioned the upcoming Italian architect Massimiliano Fuksas to rebuild and regenerate a sizeable chunk of the *quartier*. The first, biggest and most spectacular of Fuksas's interventions concerned the 150 m-long site running along the Passage Saint-Bernard between the Rues Charles-Delescluze and de Candie, which was ear-marked for public-sector housing. Residents' associations originally wanted a public garden included in the redevelopment, but a fear that it might become a hang-out for drug dealers prompted its metamorphosis into a sports centre, presumably with the intention of beneficially occupying the local youth. In a gesture designed to symbolize the supplanting of the industrial age by the electronic one, Fuksas imagined a building that represented a main-frame computer spewing out an enormous sheet of computer paper which, unfurling itself across the cityscape, would literally rewrite the area's history. Revisions imposed by the planners and by residents (who insisted that the sports centre be partially sunk below ground to reduce its bulk) modified this original concept, but the development remains an unusual and startling creation.

At the head of the site on the Rue Charles-Delescluze is the residential part of the complex, comprising 33 apartments, its street façade consisting of an imposing and rather severe Haussmannian-scale block, whose gently curved profile only hints at what takes place behind. Once round the corner in the Passage Saint-Bernard one sees that Fuksas's sheet of paper has been transformed into an enormous »zinc wave«, the street block's rear and the curvy back-extension building undulating out of it having been clad in this typically Parisian, hard-nosed material. Next, sitting on top of an underground car park, comes a series of open-air ball-games areas, with high chain-link fencing that is very inner-city NYC. This vocabulary is continued at the rear of the site with the sunken sports hall, whose bridge-like roof provides further open-air games space. The »wave« is continued both inside the hall, in the form of a concrete elevation mirroring the form of the curvy back-extension building (complete with blind »fenestration«), and in the swoop of the sports-hall roof itself. Large, ground-level windows light the hall and allow passers-by a ringside view of the activity in its Brutalist interior. Across the road, on the other side of the Passage Saint-Bernard, a miniature version of the main Rue-Charles-Delescluze block provides further apartments. The ensemble effect of this first phase of Fuksas's redevelopment is very »ghetto chic«, and in its quintessential urbanity presents a convincing alternative to bland gentrification schemes.

For his second intervention in the area – a building containing six apartments on a minuscule site at 19, impasse Charrière – Fuksas took an entirely different approach to that employed for the sports centre. In response to the site's position sandwiched between two existing structures, he opted for some contextual »urban stitching«. On a plot only a few metres wide, he managed to make reference to both the metal-and-glass and brick architecture traditional to the area, effect a transition from a tall building on one side to lower structures on the other, provide individualized, spatially inventive apartments, create an attractive, dynamic and plastically picturesque exterior, and all this without resorting to pastiche or whimsy. His final project in the *quartier* – a fourth apartment block, this time opposite the sports centre at 17, passage Saint-Bernard – was in another mould again: contextual materials were once more employed, but here in a much more sober and orthogonal manner. The common theme throughout these developments was the provision of individualized, inventive and spatially challenging accommodation, whose risk-taking is generally rare in the public sector.

11.7 Barrière du Trône
Place de la Nation
Claude-Nicolas Ledoux, 1787
(Métro/RER: Nation)

When Louis XIV made his triumphal entry into Paris in 1660, the processional route was decorated with *arcs de triomphe* and other temporary structures including, on the road from Paris to Vincennes, a royal throne. The spot became known as the Place du Trône, and when in the 1780s the Fermiers Généraux decided to extend the limit of their customs barrier encircling Paris (see 19.13), it became the site of one of the principal customs houses. The design and execution of these *barrières* had been entrusted to Ledoux, who paid particular attention at the Place du Trône because, as the land still belonged to the crown, his proposal was subject to the direct approval of Louis XVI. Not limiting himself to a mere functional interpretation of the brief, Ledoux used the Fermiers' commission to endow Paris with the monumental gateways he felt the city deserved.

11.6 Candie-Saint-Bernard redevelopment

11.7 Barrière du Trône

The volume of traffic on the road to Vincennes necessitated construction of two four-storey pavilions, one on each side of the highway. Identical, they demonstrate Ledoux's genius for the fantastic and grotesque. Surmounted by colossal projecting pediments, the pavilions feature giant, gaping entrance arches which frame doors ridiculously tiny in comparison to their cavernous enormity. In addition, Ledoux planted two towering Doric columns in the middle of the roadway, which, in 1843, were crowned with statues of Philippe II Augustus and Saint Louis. The columns' excessive height and the general exaggeration of Ledoux's scheme make this a truly magisterial entry to the city.

12th *arrondissement*

12.1 Opéra Bastille
2–6, place de la Bastille
Carlos Ott, 1983–89
(Métro: Bastille)

In 1977, François Bloch-Lainé, Inspecteur des Finances, published a damning report on the Paris opera, criticizing the Palais Garnier (9.13) for its profligacy, expense and prohibitive ticket prices. As a remedy he advocated the construction of a brand-new, 3000-seat opera house. In the flush of election success, the new socialist regime headed by President Mitterrand took up the challenge. Although traditionally elitist, opera, so the rhetoric went, was largely concerned with the heroic themes of liberty and should thus be democratized. Of available sites, the Place de la Bastille, traditional rallying ground of the left, was chosen for the new auditorium: opera would be offered to the masses at the very spot where the patriciate had first been challenged, and the project would form the centrepiece of celebrations of the bicentenary of the French Revolution in 1989.

A major problem at the Garnier was that for much of the season the theatre was dark, incapacitated by changeovers between productions. If turnaround time were shortened, spectator numbers could be increased and costs diminished. For the new auditorium the *mission* overseeing the project devised a revolutionary turntable system, to be installed deep below the stage, on which several sets could be stored simultaneously and simply jacked into place when needed – theoretically the theatre need never close. It was to be a »Renault de l'opéra«, an opera factory that would run like clockwork with the greatest efficiency, open to everyone at affordable prices and offering quality performances in state-of-the-art surroundings.

The technical specifications drawn up by the *mission* were so detailed that for the architectural competition entrants had merely to design a wrapper for a pre-determined piece of theatrical machinery. The wedge-shaped site, home to a redundant railway station, was cramped for a project of this size. Symbolic exigency required the main entrance to be placed on the Place de la Bastille, to which the opera was supposed to bring some coherence. The quality of the competition results was disappointing, and Mitterrand grudgingly chose Ott's proposal more because of deficiencies in other finalists' schemes than for merits of its own.

Ott's opera is organized around the site's longest axis. It was such a tight fit that the foyers had to be squeezed into the leftover space around the edges. The façade is composed of a mixture of glass curtain walling, stainless-steel panels and stone cladding (which earned notoriety when it started to fall off). Projecting semi-cylindrical elevations soften the bulk of the behemoth and signal its principal public and staff entrances. Out of scale with its surroundings, the opera has an uneasy relationship with the Place de la Bastille. The main entrance, at an oblique to the *place* and hemmed in by an 18C building, is somewhat divorced from its context. In an attempt to rectify this problem, Ott placed a free-standing, black-granite portal in front of the opera, following the curve of the road. Too small to constitute a truly monumental entrance, but with pretensions to it, the portal is ineffectual. The opera's coolly elegant and functional interior has been criticized for its lack of flamboyance, although this was deliberate as Ott wanted to create an opera for Everyman whose public spaces would, in opposition to the Garnier, be easily comprehensible, transparent and welcoming. The result, gigantic and cold, is in truth rather intimidating, although the acoustics and technical capacities of the main auditorium are to be praised. 2,700 people can be seated within its huge volume which, roofed without intermediary support, is entirely free of sight-line obstructions. In repudiation of the Garnier's famous staircase, the Bastille's *escalier d'honneur* is hidden behind aluminium panels which zigzag across the otherwise transparent façade, a sadly missed opportunity to exploit the theatricality of a public crowd and interact with the surrounding city. Indeed, the entire project seems something of a missed opportunity, and the question »What is a people's opera?« appears never to have been asked.

12.2 Viaduc des Arts
1–129, avenue Daumesnil
Patrick Berger and Philippe Mathieux, 1988–99
(Métro: Bastille, Gare de Lyon, Daumesnil)

Opened in 1859, the Paris–Strasbourg railway line terminated in the capital at the Place de la Bastille, tra-

12.1 Opéra Bastille

12.2 Viaduc des Arts

12.3 Municipal office building

versing the then working-class 12th *arrondissement* on its way eastwards towards Alsace. To lessen its impact on the urban fabric and overcome the uneven terrain, the inner-city sections of the line were mounted on a handsome brick-and-stone viaduct, more than 1 km in length and comprising over 80 arches. A century later, in 1969, the metropolitan stretch of the line, rendered superfluous by the construction of the RER A (see feature on the Métro and the RER), was decommissioned and sold to the Ville de Paris. The station was eventually demolished to make way for the Opéra Bastille (12.1), but the viaduct remained, impossible to replace as many adjacent buildings faced directly onto it, preventing new construction. The question remained of what to do with it. Slowly crumbling into ruin, its arches sheltered a whole variety of garages, warehouses, downmarket cafeterias and other urban undesirables. The municipality opted for gentrification. The viaduct is situated near the Faubourg Saint-Antoine, an area historically famous for its cabinet makers, metal workers and other craftsmen. In a bid to nurture new talent, the Ville decided that the viaduct should be fully restored and its arches cleared out and refurbished as ateliers, to be let at attractive rents to up-and-coming young designers and artisans. Furthermore, the top of the viaduct and the remainder of the old railway line would be converted into a planted walkway, stretching 4.5 km from the Bastille to the *périphérique*.

Patrick Berger's competition-winning design proposed a standardized infill façade for each arch, bringing a high degree of coherence to the ensemble and emphasizing the viaduct's regular rhythm. Set well back from the edges of the viaduct, the façades feature large expanses of glazing, framed in hardwood and divided horizontally at first-floor level. The set-back and the abundant use of glass preserve the viaduct's visual three-dimensionality and ensure that the arches still read as arches, an impression strengthened by the use of glass for many of the rear façades. Basement floors sunk below each arch provide storage space and house sanitary facilities, and many arches feature mezzanines for increased floor area. 61 of the remaining 71 arches were convertible, and tough selection criteria have been employed when choosing occupants from amongst the queues of hopefuls.

Philippe Mathieux's *promenade plantée* has proved just as successful, as witnessed by the crowds of strollers thronging the viaduct, especially at weekends. The narrowness of the space – only 9 m – left little choice but for a central walkway, which is bordered with vegetation and punctuated by lime trees planted at each pier. Monotony is avoided through regularly-spaced thematic gardens, which frame the views of the cityscape available from this charming elevated Eden.

12.3 Municipal office building
94–96, quai de la Rapée
Aymeric Zubléna, 1987–92
(Métro/RER: Gare de Lyon)

Commissioned by the Ville de Paris, this building was initially intended to house a *préfecture*, one of the administrative institutions of French government. In response to what was basically a call for banal office space, Zubléna chose to make a grand yet succinct civic gesture that would mark the building's municipal character in the cityscape. Dominating its riverside setting, the eleven-storey, aluminium-clad edifice essentially consists of a solid, orthogonal box built right up to the site's perimeter. But the river front, across two thirds of its length, curves sensuously away from the street line to form a 140 m², concave entrance piazza, punctuated on one side by a pair of slinky, aluminium lift towers. Fronting the piazza and rising almost the entire height of the building is an enormous, 900 m², stainless-steel-framed sliding glass gate, weighing 85 tonnes and operated by hidden motors. By opening at 9.00 am and closing again at 6.00 pm sharp, it marks the solemn rhythm of officialdom. Despite the building's change of use (a municipal department now occupies the edifice), decided after construction had begun, this ingenious symbol of civic potency was retained.

12.4 Gare de Lyon

Sadly, Zubléna's building has not aged and weathered especially well. The giant gate's glazing has been removed (presumably on safety grounds), and consequently, bereft of the ability actually to seal off the entrance piazza, it loses much of its force. Moreover, the building's aluminium cladding is caked in a layer of brown grime, dulling its Hi-tech sheen and rendering it prematurely dowdy.

12.4 Gare de Lyon
20, boulevard Diderot
Marius Toudoire, 1891–1902
(Métro/RER: Gare de Lyon)

The capital's first Paris–Lyons–Marseilles-line terminus was completed in 1852, a low-key, functional affair that was enlarged four times before its complete replacement was decided in the 1890s. Not only was the old station unable to cope with the ever-increasing volume of passengers, but its visage was considered too dowdy for the forthcoming Exposition Universelle of 1900. In the event, work fell behind schedule, and the new station was not inaugurated until two years after the exhibition, in 1902.

The double-span, iron-and-glass train-shed, which covers a total of 13 lines (in contrast to the previous seven), was not designed by Toudoire but by a team of engineers, a reflection of *belle-époque* schizophrenia concerning engineering and »architecture«. The working station is entirely dissimulated behind a monumental stone extravaganza of eclecticism, whose references range from French 17C to northern-Italian Renaissance. The latter is exhibited in the form of the extraordinary, 64 m-high clock tower (today bereft of its lantern, statues and gilding), which is situated so as to be visible from the Place de la Bastille. Articulated around its staircases, which divide it vertically, the station's main façade sports at roof level regal personifications of the cities of Paris and Marseilles, and is also adorned with female bas-relief allegories of mechanics, navigation, steam and electricity, which appear more soft-porn than technological. Despite the station's pomposity, there is a holiday air to its extravagance, reminiscent of seaside resort buildings. The Gare de Lyon is also home to the lavish, neo-Baroque »Train Bleu« restaurant.

12.5 Ministère des Finances et de l'Economie
1, boulevard de Bercy
Paul Chemetov and Borja Huidobro, 1982–89
(Métro: Bercy)

The Ministry of Finance, France's largest and most powerful government department, was housed from the 1870s onwards in the Richelieu wing of the Louvre (1.8) after its former headquarters in the Rue de Rivoli were burnt down during the Commune. President Mitterrand's 1982 decision to make the entire Palais du Louvre into a museum meant that a new home had to be provided for the ministry. In consultation with the Ville de Paris, a site was chosen in the then ungentrified eastern section of the city, between the Gare de Lyon (12.4) and the ZAC Bercy (12.7), in the hope that implantation of such an institution would kick-start the area's economy and property market. A national competition was held in which entrants were asked to provide 225,000 m² of office space in a building constituting a »grand gesture« and capable of updating the ministry's working practices for the 21C. No prototype existed for government buildings in France – since the Revolution ministries had traditionally been housed in palaces confiscated from royalty and the aristocracy, or more recently in anonymous corporate blocks – and it was thus up to competitors to invent a suitable iconography for the edifice.

The site was awkward: roughly T-shaped and divided in two by the Rue de Bercy, it comprised a narrow strip of land running alongside the railway tracks behind the Gare de Lyon and a longer, wider tract running down to the Seine by the Boulevard de Bercy. The height restrictions operational in Paris precluded the obvious solution of a tower. Chemetov and Huidobro's winning proposal ran with the constraints of the site, partly allowing them to dictate the form of the building. Their scheme did indeed constitute a grand gesture. A narrow block occupying the terrain next to the railway is the springing point for an enormous ten-storey »viaduct« which, after traversing the Rue de Bercy, careers onwards for several hundred metres before planting itself firmly into the bed of the Seine. Inspired by the Métro overpass which sits atop the Pont de Bercy (see features on Seine bridges and the Métro

12.5 Ministère des Finances et de l'Economie

and RER), the viaduct, said the architects, was their solution to the problem of creating a riverside landmark on such a narrow frontage. The viaduct thus constitutes the principal façade of the ministry, confronting the suburbs like a fortress and compelling motorists entering Paris from the east to pass under its imposing bulk. A formally planted »moat« separates it from the boulevard, and it is coiffed by an outsized helicopter pad. Sheltering behind the viaduct are low-storey buildings arranged around courtyards, including two 19C pavilions surviving from the *barrière* (toll house) which once occupied the site. Internally, the building is organized along a spinal corridor of power, flanked on either side by offices and culminating in the apartments of the minister himself, directly over the river. The office space was designed to be as adaptable as possible, deliberately low-tech to cope with unforeseen changes of use. Deep plans were avoided so that all offices are naturally lit and, at the request of ministry staff, all windows can be opened. The entire building derives its proportions from a 0.9 m² base module repeated *ad infinitum* to build up larger units.

The Ministère des Finances received a mixed press. It was likened to fascist and Stalinist architecture and unfavourably compared with a motorway tollgate. Indeed its viaduct form evokes the *barrières* which formerly encircled Paris, an obvious metaphor for the tax-collecting activities of the building's occupants. This is not an edifice concerned with openness, transparency and other qualities often used architecturally as signifiers of democracy and accountability, and it eschews the modern cult of Hi-tech. Instead, the use of stone, with its connotations of weight and permanence, the aggressive manner in which the building confronts the Seine and cuts across the Rue de Bercy, its deliberately ponderous aesthetic and even the ostentation of is helicopter pad, all serve as reminders of the pervasive power of the state.

12.6 Palais Omnisports de Paris-Bercy
2, boulevard de Bercy and 1, rue Romanée
Pierre Parat, Michel Andrault and Aydin Guvan, 1979–83
(Métro: Bercy)

Programmed in the context of Paris's bid to host the 1992 Olympics, the Palais Omnisports de Paris-Bercy (POPB) was conceived as a modifiable sports arena capable of accommodating between 3,500 and 17,000 spectators for over 24 different types of sporting activity, from basketball to boxing to water games. Recognising that sports tournaments alone would not be enough to make the project financially viable, the municipality also required that the new building be capable of hosting arts events, including rock concerts, musicals and even opera. A site was found for the Palais Omnisports on the edge of Paris's redundant wine-warehouse complex, soon to become the ZAC Bercy (12.7), to which the sports facility was intended to give a kick start. With regard to the building's external form, the brief stipulated that the POPB's surface bulk should be kept to a minimum and that it should project an image compatible with the future Parc de Bercy (12.8), whose site was just next door.

Parat, Andrault and Guvan's winning scheme, selected from a limited consultation of 16 practices,

12.6 Palais Omnisports de Paris-Bercy

takes the form of a gigantic sawn-off pyramid, with the rectangular arena at its centre and training areas, changing rooms and other ancillary services sheltering under its eaves. Four entrance halls, lit by space-frame-mounted glazing, are cut into the pyramid's sides. To limit the building's height, the arena was partially sunk below ground level. A horizontal roof, the architects concluded, would provide maximum internal flexibility, which explains the pyramid's truncated profile. The four massive, 6 m-diameter and 30 m-high concrete pillars poking out of the building's summit support the blue-painted steel girders coiffing the ensemble, from which the roofing is hung. Designed by the architect and engineer Jean Prouvé, the roof girders feature a considerable external cantilever which allows them to span 80 m internally without intermediary support and also to carry the weight of all the sound and lighting equipment necessary for the diverse events put on at the POPB. The arena's impressive technical capacities are deployed in a no-nonsense, functional interior, whose robust allure stresses that the POPB was conceived foremost as a facility and not as a monument.

Externally however, lest their concrete-and-steel behemoth seem nonetheless too monumentally Brutalist, the architects attempted to soften its image by clothing its flanks in well-watered grass. This was presumably also a sop to the planned greenery of the Parc de Bercy. While the presence of all this turf hardly disguises the building's bulk, it does reinforce its sporty image, as though Wimbledon and several football pitches had been stacked up in a sort of megalithic mound. Unsurprisingly, the result seems rather incongruously bleak in the context of today's very urban Bercy. Mystery: how do they mow these vertical lawns?

12.7 ZAC Bercy
Various architects, 1985–2000
(Métro: Bercy, Cour Saint-Emilion)

Until the 1860s, when the extension of Paris's limits as far as the Thiers fortifications changed its contours for good, the city was surrounded by a *barrière*, or duty boundary, by means of which taxes were levied on goods entering the capital (see also the Rotonde de La Villette, 19.13). Alcohol, which arrived in barrels by boat, was of course one of the main sources of revenue. It was thus at Bercy, on the banks of the Seine just beyond the limits of the *barrière*, that stockage of alcohol and especially wine began to concentrate, leading to the gradual creation of an enormous warehouse complex. Even after the boundary change, Bercy remained the centre of Paris's wine trade. Tree-lined, cobbled streets running down to the river were fronted by small stone warehouses, known in French as *chais*, that resembled little terraced houses, their gable ends facing onto the roadway. A system of rails allowed barrels to be transported around the complex by horse-drawn waggon. It was the rise of the château system, whereby storage, blending and distribution were all organized at the point of production, that rendered Bercy's facilities redundant, and by the 1970s most of the traders had packed up and gone.

All 39 ha of the site belonged to the Ville de Paris, which began the process of deciding what should be done with this derelict chunk of prime real estate. Redevelopment as a new *quartier* of the city, with a mixture of residential and business areas, was the solution retained, and the project was given ZAC status (see glossary for a definition of the term »ZAC«). In line with the municipality's policy of increasing public green open space within Paris, the operation was to be organized around a sizeable park of roughly 12.5 ha – the future Parc de Bercy (12.8). To the north of the park housing was programmed, while to its southeast a business and commercial development was planned. At the start it was decided that as many as possible of the site's existing trees would be preserved, and old cobblestones were to be re-used for the new pedestrian thoroughfares. By the late 1980s most of Bercy's original fabric had been demolished in preparation for the new developments, but a small group of warehouses was saved *in extremis* from the demolishers and subsequently became the Bercy-Village shopping centre (12.10). Before the redevelopment operation had even been officially launched, the municipality built its new Palais Omnisports (12.6) at Bercy so as to kick start the future ZAC, and it later manœuvred to get both the prestigious Ministère-des-Finances (12.5) and American-Center (12.9) buildings sited there. When the Métro Météor (see feature on the Métro and the RER) was being planned, the line was deliberately routed via Bercy to ensure the ZAC's connection to the rest of the city and thus its potential economic success. Indeed Line 14's tardy completion badly affected Bercy's economic growth, but since its inauguration in 1998 financial results have more than fulfilled expectations.

Although perhaps the most lucrative for its developers, the business section has proved the most disappointing architecturally. Its coordinating architect, Michel Macary, essentially followed the model of the

1990s suburban business park, although on a tighter and denser urban scale. The business sector's buildings provide a good back-catalogue of French commercial architecture of the past decade: slick, effective, but mostly not especially inspiring. Amongst them are Macary's own all-glass, four-star Sofitel (1992–2001) and his horizontally emphasized, *pilotis*-mounted Bercy-International building, Francis Soler's glass-and-stone ministry-of-finance boxes opposite on the other side of the Place des Vins-de-France and, buffering the southeastern extremity of the development from the railway depot beyond, the 360 m-long steel, concrete and glass rampart of Henri La Fonta's Cap-Val building (1990–93). Also known as Zeus-Paris-Bercy (Zeus, the name of the development group, officially stands for »Zone d'Evolution Urbaine de la Seine« but is also an anagram of Suez, the group's principal shareholder), and baptized the »Banana« by locals, the Cap-Val building included 92,000 m² of commercial showroom space, known as Bercy-Expo, which was intended as a trade centre for wine and food producers. Unfortunately, this bid to continue, at least partially, Bercy's traditional activities fell foul of the Parisian property crisis of the early 90s, and Dionysus's followers were so few in taking up residence at Bercy-Expo that Zeus was later obliged to rent the entire building as banal office space.

Where the business section of the ZAC is disappointing architecturally and urbanistically, the residential part, especially the portion fronting the Parc de Bercy, is much more interesting. Over 2,000 dwellings were planned under the co-ordinating aegis of Jean-Pierre Buffi. Bercy's development came in the wake of the comprehensive redevelopment schemes of the 1960s and 1970s whose urbanistic choices had been called into question, and Buffi wanted to avoid the errors of recent predecessors. It had been decided in advance that things would be done the traditional way: instead of one architect producing a megalomaniacal design for the entire site, it would be divided up into lots each of which would be contracted out to different developers, architects and builders. Buffi's job was to bring coherence to the whole. Looking to renew with tradition when planning the 400 m of southwestern-orientated park front, he examined two 19C streets that enjoy similar park-side positioning: Percier and Fontaine's Rue de Rivoli (1.11) overlooking the Tuileries (1.10), and the Haussmannian buildings fronting the Champ de Mars. From the Rue de Rivoli he retained the idea that the park-front buildings should provide a decorative backdrop to the greenery, but he rejected the uninterrupted bar of Percier and Fontaine's terrace in favour of the fragmentation of the Champ-de-Mars blocks, which allowed the pleasures of the park to be enjoyed by those further back from its limits. The terrain was thus chopped up into multiple lots with three side streets (including the already extant traffic artery that is the Rue Joseph-Kessel) connecting the front of the development to the Rues Pommard and Gabriel-Lamé at the rear. A third reference was Giuseppe Terragni and Pietro Lingeri's Casa-Rustici apartment building (1933–36) in Milan, whose organization as a courtyard fronted by slender, footbridge-style terraces struck Buffi as way of maintaining the urban-screen effect of the Rue de Rivoli while avoiding the hierarchical duality of Haussmannian-era Paris, where city blocks are bordered on the street by a solid barrier of »noble« buildings that hide what are often »ignoble« spaces and constructions behind. At Bercy, the street-over-city-block-interior pecking order was to be abolished: the front-of-park façades would be broken up into discrete »pavilions« linked visually by flying terraces thereby forming a sort of lattice through which the garden-courtyards behind them would be visible. This was also supposed to effect something of a »democratization« of views over the park, allowing the apartments within the courtyards to benefit from the views enjoyed by the front-of-park flats.

From these precepts, Buffi determined a standard model for each chunk of land: a U-shaped, perimeter-following ensemble of buildings on the sides and rear and, on the park front, a pair of pavilions united visually to the rest of the ensemble by evenly spaced flying terraces. Like Terragni before him, Buffi was trying to effect a synthesis of an older tradition with more Modernist ways of doing things. To his regret, however, the older tradition in question already had the upper hand in that volume-to-site-area ratios and building heights had been pre-determined by planning regulations, and he was thus unable to give his edifices the proportions he would have considered appropriate for the site. This, coupled with the high density required of the apartment buildings, meant that all the architects were forced to build up to the height limit, thus precluding picturesque variations in roofline. On the other hand, the resulting horizontal alignment of parapets was perhaps a more coherent and traditionally Parisian way of doing things. One of Buffi's main concerns was to avoid the façadism of 19C Paris and create truly three-dimensional architecture where space, as well as

12.7 ZAC Bercy

12th *arrondissement* 193

volumes and elevations, would be paramount. The spaces in question were essentially those between each block and the interior courtyards; to ensure their proper handling, Buffi divided up the plots so that architects building flats on the lateral roads would be responsible for both sides of the street, while those building directly on the park front would also have responsibility for the courtyard behind. Volume, proportions and the positioning and horizontal emphasis of the flying terraces were thus all pre-determined by Buffi; besides these formal dictates he also specified, in the interest of further coherence, two material details: that white-stone cladding should be used for the park-front and Rue-de-Pommard/Rue-Gabriel-Lamé façades, and that all the flying terraces should sport the same matte-black metal handrails whose design he himself produced. The choice of a white stone was rather un-Parisian and broke with Frank Gehry's decision to use local limestone for his neighbouring American Center, although the result obviously appears more Purist and Modernist than the honey-coloured rock of which the 19C city is built.

The architects lined up to build the park-front structures were a fairly illustrious lot, and included a subsequent Pritzker-Prize winner (Christian de Portzamparc) as well as holders of the French *grand prix national* and *équerre d'argent*. The big question was thus to see how they would cope with the constraints and teamwork imposed by this unusual commission, whose ensemble playing Buffi likened to a symphony orchestra. Beginning at the American Center, the first of the series one encounters is by Franck Hammoutène, and faces the blind eastern wall of the Center on the Rue Jean-Renoir. Hammoutène gave presence to his otherwise sober façades through the application of bay windows sporting cantilevered, wire-mesh-fronted balconies that are complemented in their tough inner-city chic by the spiralling fire escapes on the roofline. Next come Philippe Chaix and Jean-Paul Morel's twin front-of-park pavilions, where the spacing of the flying terraces imposed by Buffi was used to create double-height, glass-fronted rooms on the park, a generous and urbane gesture that none of the other architects thought of. This had the added merit of requiring far less stone cladding than for the neighbouring buildings. Chaix and Morel were also the most adventurous with regard to their rooflines, coiffing the lefthand pavilion with a metal spiral (containing a penthouse) *à la* Tower of Babel. The rear building of their plot is a balcony-fronted, soberly horizontal affair. Fernando Montès was responsible for the next plot along, which includes, at its rear, a glass-fronted neighbourhood school and dustmen's flats. On the park side, cantilevered, glass-fronted balconies and emphasized vertical lines counteract the overwhelming horizontality of Buffi's flying terraces. Adjacent to Montès's constructions comes the first pair of blocks fronting a two-sided thoroughfare (the Rue George-Gershwin), which were designed by Yves Lion. Although his pebble-dash-fronted slabs are essentially symmetrical, their windows were disaligned in relation to each other to avoid direct sightlines between the blocks. F. Ceria and Alain Coupel's front- and rear-of-plot buildings, which are next in sequence, recall Montès's up the road, displaying a similar play of fenestration and cantilevers, only here the emphasis is horizontal rather than vertical, especially in the extremely sober garden-courtyard. The buildings either side of the Rue Joseph-Kessel which follow were the work of Fabrice Dusapin and François Leclercq; they display unremittingly utilitarian elevations, except when turning the corner into the park, where yet more cantilevered balconies relieve their planar monotony.

Following in line on the other side of the park, we find Christian de Portzamparc's front- and rear-of-plot buildings. The most immediately striking feature on the park elevation is the use of a peachy-coloured stone (in contravention of Buffi's directives), which provides a welcome relief from the sometimes rather dreary white of the rest. Perhaps perversely, his park elevations feature much less glazing than those of his confrères, but the rooms here are probably much cooler in summer as a result and he was able to play with the pattern of his fenestration in a way denied the other architects. He also filed away his park pavilions in concertina step back to allow increased diagonal views of the park from within the garden-courtyard. The rather cheap-looking plaster elevations of the latter were perhaps a consequence of the extra added cost of the park-front peach stone. At the rear of the plot, on the Rue Gabriel-Lamé, Portzamparc's construction splits in two to allow preservation of a centenarian tree, and dons all-glass corners to mark the event. For the moment, the final buildings in the series are Henri Ciriani's two transversal slab blocks either side of the Rue de l'Aubrac. Their splendidly graphic and glazed park fronts, which neatly punctuate the opening of the street, contrast very uneasily with the dull, mean and shabby plaster-fronted lateral elevations. At the time of writing construction of the last plot in the sequence has just begun, thereby ending a six-year quarrel between residents and the municipality over whether or not the local secondary school should be built there. It was the municipality that won, and new apartment buildings will stand here as of late 2004.

What is immediately striking about the Bercy front-of-park development taken as a whole is the extent to which coherence has been achieved despite the very different characters of the participating architects. So often attempts at imposing neighbourhood unity and harmony result in boring monotony, especially in the Modernist absence of the fussy detailing with which our forefathers enlivened their frequently repetitive cities. But here, while still upholding the Modernist moral stand against criminal ornament, Buffi and his team have managed to create a visually varied yet united ensemble whose architectonic qualities lie in the play of solids, voids, projections and horizontal lines.

Some of the architects felt that Buffi's prescriptions were too detailed and left them no room for manœuvre, although Buffi himself considered that his confrères did not make full use of the liberty accorded them, especially when designing the front-of-park pavilions, which he had imagined as being more adventurous than the orthogonal boxes actually produced. Criticism has been levelled at the overall stiffness of the very French »Classical Modernism« in which the flats are garbed, although its dry rigour is clearly within the Parisian tradition. Also in the Parisian tradition is the fact that the hierarchy of noble and ignoble has not been entirely banished as promised: the flats' side, rear and courtyard façades generally display cheaper materials and much less in the way of architectonic inventiveness than the front-of-park elevations. One further doubts, given the high accommodation density and hence building volume, that the democratization of park views talked about has really been achieved. But the greenery-filled courtyards compensate for this to an extent, and the openings in the park-side façades allow for a very urbane play of solids and voids and for extra light penetration into the spaces behind them.

The front-of-park development at Bercy has attracted a lot of attention from the French architectural press, most of it very positive. Whether, as one commentator wondered, future generations will view it as a latter-day Weissenhofsiedlung remains to be seen, but the 90s New Order introduced by Buffi and Co. may yet inspire similar initiatives elsewhere.

12.8 Parc de Bercy

Marylène Ferrand, Jean-Pierre Feugas, Bernard Le Roy, Bernard Huet et al., 1987–97
(Métro: Bercy, Cour Saint-Emilion)

Long before any of the details of the ZAC Bercy (12.7) had been worked out, one element was sure: that the redevelopment of Paris's former wine warehouses would be disposed around a major new park, in a bid to redress the city's shortage of green open space. A 710 x 190 m rectangle on the banks of the Seine, cut in two towards its southeastern end by the Rue Joseph-Kessel, was earmarked for this purpose. Old cobbled streets, scattered remnants of the mostly demolished wine-warehouse complex, and hundreds of mature trees were contained within the confines of this rather arbitrarily imposed perimeter. The 1987 Europe-wide design competition specified in its brief that as well as providing a community amenity for the surrounding quartiers, the park should constitute an event of city-wide significance. However, entrants were asked to favour »the everyday and the intimate rather than the spectacular«.

The winning team proposed a »Jardin de la Mémoire« that would celebrate the site's history by integrating vestiges of past activities into its fabric. Consequently, the team's first move was to see what of the elements already present on the site could be re-used in the park. Over 200 trees (some more than two centuries old), the cobbled thoroughfares of the wine-warehouse complex and a handful of surviving buildings were thus retained, giving the landscape architects a good amount of greenery and pathways and several potential follies to work with. To reconcile the different and varied expectations of the park's future users, the designers divided the terrain into three parts. The first, just next to the Palais Omnisports (12.6), consists of open, tree-dotted lawns that are accessible 24 hours/day and where picnicking and ball games are permitted, a rare liberty in Parisian gardens. The second is divided up into nine parterres, each planted on a different theme: kitchen garden, rosery, orchard, seasonal gardens and so on. Intended to recall the summer villas that occupied the site in the 18C, these domestic-scale gardens include a surviving wine warehouse, converted for use as a gallery, and a modern orangery, conceived for overwintering non-hardy plants. The central parterre contains the former Pavillon des Gardes, which now houses a gardening education centre. Baptized the »Jardin Romantique« by its architects, the third and largest section of the park spreads out either side of the Rue Joseph-Kessel. Water is the unifying theme of this garden, in the form of a canal that opens out at its southeastern end into a circular pool, at whose centre is an island containing an 18C wine merchant's house. Ruined arches saved

12.8 Parc de Bercy

from the Marché Saint-Germain, a planted hillock (in fact a cleverly disguised water tower), as well as the merchant's house, the pool and the canal all contribute to the picturesque aspect of the Jardin Romantique. Footbridges perched high on embankments that hide the Rue Joseph-Kessel from the park unite the garden's separated halves. Sadly, the planned foot tunnels were never realized.

Criss-crossing the entire park, like unifying *tracés régulateurs*, are two sets of pathways. The first comprises the old cobbled thoroughfares of the wine warehouses and their waggon rails, via which barrels were once transported. When built, these roadways were perpendicular to the Seine, but since the realignment of the quayside in the 20C their relationship to the river has been skewed. The second set of paths was added by the landscape designers and continues the orthogonal street pattern created by the ZAC's planners to the northeast of the park, which runs perpendicular to today's river bank. Built up slightly above ground level, the new routes are literally superimposed on the old, creating a palimpsest that is intended to read like archaeological strata. The designers had also planned to install a sort of memorial to the former Bercy wine trade with vats, waggons and barrels grouped around the Pavillon des Gardes, a feature whose potential effect they likened to the scattered remains of Pompeii. Subsequent funding cuts, however, meant that this idea had to be abandoned.

Despite the park's riverside setting, any connection with the Seine was rendered impossible by the presence of the multi-lane Voie Georges-Pompidou on the river bank, whose width and 800 m length alongside the park made its burial in a tunnel financially prohibitive. Moreover, this monument to the automobile age was a major noise and pollution nuisance. To deal with the problem, the park's designers built a 14 m-wide and 8 m-high embankment – inspired by the rampart separating the Jardin des Tuileries (1.10) from the Place de la Concorde (8.1) – alongside the motorway as a sight-and-sound barrier. As well as preserving the park's interior intimacy, the embankment provides an elevated, tree-lined walkway that offers fine views over the river and the surrounding areas, thus allowing the visitor to place the park in its city-wide context. Furthermore, a car park, lavatories and various other facilities are housed in the embankment's volume. The planned Tolbiac footbridge (see feature on Seine bridges) should one day connect the embankment, and thus the park and the whole Bercy neighbourhood, to the ZAC Rive-Gauche (13.2) across the river. The pathways of the park's open lawns converge on the point from which the bridge is programmed to depart, and a monumental water cascade on the embankment itself heroically marks the scheduled event.

Unlike the contemporaneous Parc André-Citroën (15.8), the Parc de Bercy does not attempt to make a grand gesture in the cityscape, but instead seeks inspiration from a more domestic source, evoking both private urban gardens and cottage gardens like Monet's at Giverny. Fragmentation, variety, movement and surprise are interwoven in a collage where narration – both of the site's history and of the changing seasons – is the uniting principle. Plants and planting, as well as the built elements, are a vital component in the park's charm, and in this it brilliantly succeeds where the Parc de La Villette (19.7), another example of 1980s park design, fails. Paris's elevated population density ensures that any green space is immediately saturated, but the Parc de Bercy seems to be especially appreciated.

12.9 Palais du Cinéma (former American Center)
51, rue de Bercy
Frank O. Gehry, 1988–94
(Métro: Bercy)

Who is not now familiar with the name of Frank O. Gehry, designer of the astonishing Guggenheim Museum in Bilbao (1991–97), a building that passed into myth before it even opened? Over the last decade or so, Gehry has produced a series of extraordinary buildings that defy established architectural conventions and, through his use of computer-aided design, has extended the limits of what was previously considered possible. His American Center in Paris is slightly atypical within this canon: site constraints and planning regulations did not allow him the *carte blanche* his runaway imagination is usually granted, and the challenge was to create the usual madcap Gehry spectacle within the restrictions of the Parisian planning code.

The American Center's mission is to further understanding between France and the U.S. through a programme of cultural events such as film, theatre and exhibitions. Looking to expand and unable to do so in its original location (where the Fondation Cartier (14.4) now stands), the Center accepted a virgin, island site in the ZAC Bercy (12.7) on the edge of the new Parc de Bercy (12.8). The French authorities offered the site on advantageous terms, hoping that the presence of a prestige institution in a landmark building would boost growth of the ZAC and contribute to the area's sense of identity. A compact rectangle with one corner lopped off on the diagonal, the site did not permit the organic, tentacular plans common to Gehry buildings, especially as within its confines he was expected to squeeze, amongst others, a 400-seat theatre, a 100-seat cinema, 1,000 m^2 of gallery space, an audio-visual centre and a car park. A perimeter-respecting plan was thus really the only option, one which also suited Gehry's desire to draw inspiration from the Parisian context, where street-line-observing buildings are the norm. He also had to work within certain conditions imposed by the planners, which included respecting the scale and context of the Rue de Bercy on the northern elevation and not allowing any of the Center's public spaces to overlook the apartment block situated to its east.

In homage to Haussmannian town planning, whose basic system featured street-line-respecting buildings enclosing more loosely developed city-block interiors, Gehry organized the American Center as a series of volumetrically different structures lined up at the site's periphery and clustering around the open centre of the city block. In further deference to the 19C city, he used traditionally Parisian materials for the exterior: stone, glass and zinc. On the eastern façade stone is about all we see, since Gehry put as little fenestration there as possible, as stipulated by the planners (indeed it is so blank that he even talked about growing ivy up it!). For the northern façade, which was supposed to integrate into the Rue de Bercy, he took his cue from the cliff-like elevations and repetitive fenestration of many 19C Parisian streets, although with certain joky modifications: articulation as two separate blocks joined by a garage, deeply recessed windows giving the impression of a solid-stone structure, and a cheeky »skirt« flaring out on the corner block, like the escarp of a castle moat. Glass elevations immediately under the skirt further send up traditional stone architecture by confounding our notions of the weight of masonry and the bearing of loads. Fittingly, it was the Center's administrative spaces that were housed behind the monotonous windows of these parts of the building.

While the eastern and northern façades read as »backstage«, it is on the park elevations, where Gehry could operate without restriction, that the spectacle occurs. Gehry wanted the Center to be »just like Paris ... full of dance and music and activity«, and consequently organized a freak show of bizarrely shaped architectural elements on these sides of the building. On the western elevation, plonked next to the flared-skirt corner block, is a blank stone box carrying what Gehry baptized the »pineapple«, a series of irregular, curvy volumes where visitors' apartments were located. Situated on the site's cut-off corner and coiffed by a sort of stone hillock is the building's principal entrance, roofed in a skirt-like swathe of zinc (entering buildings under ladies' skirts is a favourite Gehry trick, also found at Prague's »Fred and Ginger« building (1992–97)). Behind it rises the deformed bastion of the building's lift-and-stair tower. Finally, on the southern side of the building,

12.9 Palais du Cinéma (former American Center)

we find a cascade of glass, falling in watery shards, that lights upper-level spaces and the theatre foyer. There is of course something rather gratuitous about all this formal latitude, which, according to Gehry, was intended to evoke Paris's ramshackle roofs and courtyards, as well as, in its planning-regulated frame, providing a metaphor for the creative vitality of a New World less encumbered with building restrictions than the Old. Inside, the floor plan is just as complex as the building's external contortions, especially given all the different volumetric demands of the varied facilities. Everything was articulated around a bravura, two-level, top-lit entrance lobby, which occupies the forefront of the building and the centre of the city block. As an architectural experience this is perhaps the Center's best feature: light-filled and featuring a majestic *escalier d'honneur* (*de rigueur* in any self-respecting French public building), it allows views through its skylights to the deformed volumes above in a Dalí-esque distortion of traditional Parisian glazed courtyards.

Building the American Center was a technical and organizational challenge, especially since only 18 months were allotted for construction. Because of the design's complexity, plans took three times longer to draw up than would have been the case for a more conventional project. As this is France, concrete rather than steel was the material chosen for construction, and the building is in fact one enormous, homogeneous, reinforced-concrete shell structure, entirely cast *in situ* bar the pre-stressed beams spanning the theatre. For the building's cladding, Gehry and the planners wanted an authentically Parisian stone, and consequently chose Saint-Maximin limestone (to be seen, for example, at the Palais-Royal (1.16)). For most of the building's surface, standard 3 cm-thick panels were used, laid in staggered courses, but the curved sections of façade demanded individually shaped slabs. These are up to 6 cm thick since they are in fact flat on their undersides, the curvature having been carved onto their outer surfaces. Cutting of the curved panels was originally to have been performed by computer-controlled saw, but the machine in question proved problematic and in the end the blocks were shaped by hand. Ironically, although garbed in this most Parisian of materials, Gehry's building looks curiously out of place in its context, partly because none of its neighbours is similarly clad, and partly because the surface pattern created by the staggering of the stone panels is unwonted in the Parisian context. In the decade following its completion the building has weathered into quite a different animal from the pristine creature initially unveiled. Each stone joint is now darkly stained by mould, with the singular result that the cladding resembles the heavy blocks of a cartoon medieval castle.

Much was expected from this particular American in Paris, but many critics were disappointed with the finished Center. It was not Gehry enough, it was too dry, it didn't entertain as a Gehry building should. To a certain extent this was simply because the constraints imposed on the architect did not permit the unbridled spectacle we have come to require of him; the site was just too small to accommodate all the ideas everyone wanted to pack into it. Context was forced on Gehry as an issue, but his response to Parisian planning was not very convincing: the back-and-front nature of the design is highly unsatisfactory in a building that clearly also wants to be an autonomous object and, rather than integrating into its surroundings, it seems only to be beating a retreat. Also – and this was a fundamental error of judgement – the context was not Haussmannian Paris, as Gehry nostalgically chose to see it, but the 90s New Order of the ZAC Bercy (which, moreover, was still an unbuilt vacuum when the American Center was designed). The subtleties of contextual couture are not what Gehry is famous for, and it was perhaps unfair to expect it of him here, since, paradoxically, his project was to a certain extent supposed to define the context. That nobody subsequently picked up on the cues he gave was not his fault.

In 1996, just two years after its inauguration, financial difficulties forced the American Center to sell off Gehry's building. Acquired by the French state, it is now being gutted for installation of the dark spaces necessary for a *palais du cinéma* that will group together the Cinémathèque Française, the Henri-Langlois Cinema Museum and the Bibliothèque du Film, which were formerly scattered across Paris in unsatisfactory accommodation. Launched by the Culture Ministry in 1998, the project has been considerably delayed by ministerial hesitation and in-fighting between the different institutions concerned. But, if further squabbles can be avoided and building work keeps to schedule, this new palace of the Seventh Art should open in autumn 2003.

12.10 Bercy Village
Cour Saint-Emilion
Denis Valode and Jean Pistre, 1997–2000
(Métro: Cour Saint-Emilion)

For almost 200 years Bercy was the site of Paris's centralized wine-warehouse complex, which grew up just outside the limit of the *barrière* (duty boundary) that formerly encircled the city (see the Rotonde de la Villette, 19.13). Organized around a system of tree-lined, cobbled streets, the warehouses (known in French as *chais*) took the form of rows of small, stone, gable-ended buildings featuring deep cellars for the storage of the wine. Barrels arrived by boat on the Seine and were distributed in waggons running on rails. Closed in the 1970s, the wine-warehouse complex was subsequently scheduled for redevelopment in the guise of the ZAC Bercy (12.7) and, by the end of the 1980s, most of the original buildings had already been swept away. It was only through the actions of a local pressure group that the last surviving examples – the 41 *chais* of the Cour Saint-Emilion (c. 1840) and the Lheureux warehouses (1886) to their north – were listed as historic monuments, thus preventing their destruction. The Lheureux buildings, it was afterwards decided, would be renovated to house a fun-fair museum and a bakery school, while the Cour Saint-Emilion was to metamorphose into a picturesque shopping centre to serve the new neighbourhoods then going up north of the Parc de Bercy (12.8).

At least that was the proposal for which planning permission was granted. But the company overseeing the development, Altaréa, felt that the Bercy-2 shopping centre (33.1) just the other side of the *périphérique* would pose too much of a competitive threat, and hence opted for a different development concept. In place of the neighbourhood shopping parade initially planned, Altaréa proposed a themed leisure complex, based on American »family-entertainment centres«, which they baptized »Bercy Village«. Food and relaxation were to be the key activities, disposed in a quaint, car-free, »heritage« setting. To this end, the Cour Saint-Emilion's *chais* were beautifully restored and extended at their rears to provide a total of 24,000 m² of retail space. The wood-and-glass extensions were designed to present a visage at once Hi-tech, rural and industrial and to ease the transition in scale from the vast neighbouring Zeus buildings to the Lilliputian *chais*. Within the confines of the Cour Saint-Emilion, the cobblestones were re-laid complete with their original waggon rails, which were filed down for the comfort of high-heeled punters. Rumour has it that the architects even asked that a few dandelions be planted in the paving cracks for extra added authenticity. Lined with trees and abounding in outside restaurant tables, the very successful result is in essence an up-market adaptation of Disneyland's Main Street, USA (see 36.7).

Dominating the southern end of Bercy Village, like a cathedral commanding its close, is the complex's commercial *pièce de résistance*, a UGC Ciné-Cité multiplex cinema, designed by Alberto Cattani (UGC's principal architect) in collaboration with Valode and Pistre. With a total of 18 screens and 4,500 seats, this

12.10 Bercy Village

is Paris's biggest movie theatre. Its siting was no accident: forming a sight/sound barrier between the Cour Saint-Emilion and the multi-lane expressway running along the river, it benefits from the facilities on offer at the Village while at the same time proclaiming its presence to the thousands of motorists who pass it everyday on its other side. The planners stipulated that the multiplex should be divided in two either side of a central glazed atrium prolonging the thoroughfare of the Cour Saint-Emilion, which was originally to have continued across the river via a footbridge (a project later cancelled). Ticket counters, bars and a café are all housed in this mall-like central space, whose access circuits are designed to extract maximum dramatic effect from crowd movement, with flying staircases and footbridges configured so that departing cinephiles do not cross paths with those arriving. Outside, the auditoria are stacked up like boxes, with copper and stainless-steel slats masking their raw-concrete exteriors in *faux*-Hi-tech facing. It may not be profound, it's certainly commercial, but it works.

12.11 Collège Jean-François Oeben (former Collège Arago)
17–23, rue de Reuilly
Jean-Paul Deschamps, 1992–95
(Métro: Faidherbe-Chaligny, Reuilly-Diderot)

Rather like Christian Hauvette's municipal crèche (11.5), this is another example of protectionist, keep-out architecture from the Ville de Paris. A rebuilding of a secondary school, Deschamps scheme orientates itself around the trees of the neighbouring plot. A quarter-circle classroom block embraces a first-floor level playground and hides from the street behind a discrete structure housing the school's administration. Passers-by arriving from the Rue du Faubourg Saint-Antoine are confronted with an entirely blind, raw-concrete wall (the rear of the administrative block) perched on a raw-concrete, rusticated podium (rustication signalling fortification). Although pedestrians approaching from the other direction see a lot more glass, they nonetheless encounter the grey, perforated-metal gates and fencing surrounding the building, whose tough, inner-city allure would not appear out of place in a prison. In a gesture of civility, there is an all-glass entrance elevation, but it is safely set well back from the dangerous street behind the metal fencing.

Viewed from the playground, the school presents an entirely different visage. Glass as far as the eye can see, from the sleek surfaces of the administrative block to the whizzing, *brise-soleil*-coiffed classroom fenestration, floods the building with light and, according to Deschamps, opens it up to the city at large. But, and in this the school recalls Le Corbusier's Salvation-Army hostel (13.6), all this glazing also facilitates surveillance. Considered thus, the playground becomes an arena monitored by the sentinel watchtower of the administrative block. Transparency, too, can be put to good use in the architecture of security and control.

12.11 Collège Jean-François Oeben (former Collège Arago)

12.12 Saint-Esprit
186, avenue Daumesnil
Paul Tournon, 1926–34 and 1954–61
(Métro: Daumesnil)

The Sacré-Cœur (18.2) is generally thought to have prompted the spate of neo-Romanesque and Byzantine churches constructed in Paris in the inter-war years. For the Byzantine style, the ultimate model was of course Hagia Sophia (532–37) in Istanbul; many Parisian architects referred to it (see, e.g., Sainte-Odile (17.2)), but none more obviously than Paul Tournon at the Eglise du Saint-Esprit. In his writings on the project, Tournon, a devout catholic, makes no mention of the church's Justinian prototype, instead describing in semi-mystical terms his source of inspiration: »When I was told that the planned church would be dedicated to the Holy Ghost, I had an immediate impression of a vast dome, a human image of the universe, with the Holy Spirit at the zenith. This form in itself would have been enough to express the universality of our faith ...«

Be that as it may, Saint-Esprit is a fairly faithful interpretation of Hagia Sophia, realized on a Parisian scale in reinforced concrete. It was built to serve an *arrondissement* that had grown massively in population in the late 19C, and is situated on one of the principal thoroughfares traversing the area. Following the separation of church and state, in 1905, new churches no longer benefited from the prime, often island sites they had been guaranteed by 19C planners, and now had to fight for space on the commercial market. Saint-Esprit's situation is consequently rather awkward, on a site cobbled together from two separate plots, with only a very narrow frontage on the avenue, the majority of the land being obscured behind adjoining buildings.

Tournon was left with little choice but to build the church on the principle plot and then signal its presence with a separate structure directly on the avenue.

Rectangular rather than square like Hagia Sophia, Saint-Esprit's nave is dominated by its 22 m-diameter central dome, supported at only four points, which was put up in a mere 27 days. As at Hagia Sophia, the dome is flanked by four half-domed apses which, although not structurally necessary in a concrete construction, help stabilize the main dome against strong winds. Internally, the concrete is left raw and partly decorated with mosaics set into it when it was poured, thus saving time and making the décor a more integral part of the whole. Principally lit by rows of windows running round the domes, Saint-Esprit's interior appears impressively mysterious, its Euclidean forms rendered strangely massive and heavy by the semi-gloom, not at all like Hagia Sophia's soaring, airy volume. Either side of the nave, Tournon introduced stacked double colonnades, each with a total of twelve columns; structurally unnecessary, they block views of the side-apses, but recall a similar disposition at Hagia Sophia, as well as forming part of an iconography in which numbers take on symbolic significance: four pendentives for the four prophets of the Old Testament and the four evangelists of the New, twelve arches for the twelve apostles, etc. Frescoes retracing the history of the Church decorate the nave's lower sections, the work of a team of artists led by Maurice Denis. Externally, Saint-Esprit is clad in a skin of Burgundy brick, decorated with rather Expressionist false buttresses crowned with pinnacles carrying statues.

To signal the church's presence on the avenue, Tournon designed a bell-tower, a task he seemingly found rather difficult: following many redesigns the tower was only finally begun in the 1950s. Tournon's original idea consisted of a streamlined spire, clearly based on Perret's Notre-Dame du Raincy (35.1), surmounted by a powerful lamp so as to act literally as a lighthouse for lost souls. The final version of the tower was less floridly evangelizing and more pragmatic: a substantial building containing apartments and meeting rooms coiffed with a Perret-esque belfry. Linking church and bell-tower is a narrow narthex, which overcomes a difference in ground level as well as cleverly masking a change in orientation through use of a half-rotunda.

12.13 Palais des Colonies (former Musée des Arts Africains et Océaniens)
293, avenue Daumesnil
Albert Laprade with Léon Jaussely, 1928–31
(Métro: Porte Dorée)

For the 1931 Exposition Coloniale, organized to vaunt the glory of France and her empire, one permanent structure was commissioned – the Palais des Colonies. Situated at the entrance to the exhibition, it housed displays on the history of colonialism and the civilizing benefits brought by France to her domains.

12.13 Palais des Colonies (former Musée des Arts Africains et Océaniens)

Because of the permanent nature of this piece of propaganda, the organizers had ruled out pastiche and eclecticism when commissioning the museum, calling instead for an original »création française«,

Architectonically, there is nothing very original about Laprade's building, an axially planned, *beaux-arts* palace. It is the decorative treatment of the museum, in stripped but opulent neo-Classicism, that proved influential on a whole decade of official and luxury creation. The sparsely fenestrated main façade sports a flimsy colonnade bearing an outsized cornice, and is covered with an enormous 1,128 m² bas-relief. The work of Alfred Janniot, the relief took three years to complete, and depicts the prosperity of the French Empire. Inside, the central *salle des fêtes* is decorated with an elaborate fresco in similar style and on a similar theme, as are the circular Salons de l'Afrique and de l'Asie at either extremity of the main façade. The *salons* were furnished by Jacques-Emile Ruhlmann and Eugène Printz respectively. Considered retrograde by some, for others the museum represented a renewal of tradition and the *rappel à l'ordre* of a world still scarred by the Great War. Emptied of the collections of African and Oceanic art they housed until 2003, the Palais's flamboyant interiors look set to become home to a museum of 20C decorative arts in 2007.

13th *arrondissement*

13.1 Hôpital de la Pitié-Salpêtrière
47, boulevard de l'Hôpital
Various architects, extant buildings begun 1658
(Métro: Gare d'Austerlitz)

Founded as a poorhouse following an edict of 1656 that ordered the round-up of Paris's homeless, the Salpêtrière hospice was so named because it was initially installed in the buildings of a former gunpowder factory (*salpêtre* = saltpetre). The new institution was already too small when it opened, and an enlargement programme was drawn up by Antoine Duval, in 1658. The first phase, financed by Cardinal Mazarin (and consequently known today as the Mazarin building), was completed in the early 1660s, but thereafter work stopped due to lack of funds. In 1669, Louis XIV decided to pay for a church at the Salpêtrière, for which he imposed his official architect, Louis Le Vau. The latter went further than simply designing a place of worship for the hospice, instead drawing up a new, comprehensive redevelopment programme.

Like Libéral Bruand's contemporaneous Invalides (7.12), Le Vau's plan consisted essentially of a grid building in the manner of the Escorial near Madrid, with dormitories disposed around square courtyards, the whole dominated by the church. Built at one extremity of the Mazarin building, the church was to be flanked on its other side by a duplicate of Duval's wing, thus forming a monumental entrance façade. When Le Vau died, in 1670, only the church's foundations had been finished, and Louis XIV commissioned Libéral Bruand to complete the building, which opened in 1677. Further wings were built to the north of the Mazarin block in the 1680s, but it was not until 1756 that the Lassay building, the symmetrical pendant of the Mazarin wing, was erected to plans by Germain Boffrand, thus completing Le Vau's entrance elevation. In the late-18C, the hospice gained its current entrance portal. Since the early-20C, the Salpêtrière has been part of a major hospital complex, for which many further buildings have been erected.

13.1 Hôpital de la Pitié-Salpêtrière

A long, three-storey-high block flanked at either end by imposing pavilions, the Mazarin building (that to the left of the church on the entrance façade) sports the lofty slate roofs fashionable in France in the 17C, and encloses at its centre a gateway decorated with the arms of the cardinal. The ensemble effect of the Mazarin-building-church-Lassay-block sequence is undeniably monumental, although the repetition of elements engendered by the duplication of Duval's wing makes it rather fussy and incoherent, despite the relative simplicity of the individual components. Behind the Mazarin building are the dormitories of the Cour Mazarin and the Cour Sainte-Claire; parts of the latter may possibly date from before Duval's initial interventions. The courtyards planned for the rear of the Lassay wing were never realized.

By far the most interesting and impressive feature of the Salpêtrière is the church, which is dedicated to Saint Louis. The hospice's 3000 inmates included mad women, prostitutes, epileptics, geriatrics and criminals, and Le Vau's main concern in designing the church was to ensure that these different groups could attend mass at the same time whilst being physically segregated from each other. Saint-Louis's plan consequently consists of a central octagon, containing the high altar, around which are disposed four naves and four chapels, thus providing eight individual congregational spaces (in the event the nave behind the altar was never used as such, serving instead as a grain store and today as the hospital's archive). The church's dimensions are truly vast, made doubly striking by the severe sobriety of the décor, splendour evidently not having been considered necessary for the poor. Although its walls are bare, the church's volumes are nonetheless splendid, especially the central octagon, whose powerful arcades, which support the drum and dome, appear positively Piranesian. Externally, the church is just as sober, except on the entrance façade, where a triple arcade (one of Le Vau's favourite motifs), decorated with Ionic pilasters, acts as the building's porch. Libéral Bruand evidently enjoyed himself designing the church's roofing, which is composed of improbably tall, slate-covered forms, including the gloriously bulbous dome with its oversized lantern.

13.2 ZAC Paris-Rive-Gauche
1991–2011
(Métro: Gare d'Austerlitz, Quai de la Gare, Bibliothèque François-Mitterrand; RER: Gare d'Austerlitz, Bibliothèque François-Mitterrand)

Paris, like many other European cities (most notably London), was historically divided east/west, with the majority of its industry and poorer populations being concentrated in its eastern half, while the *beaux quartiers* of the rich were to be found in the west. One explanation often given for this phenomenon is that the prevailing winds in Europe blow west–east (the rich would therefore naturally situate themselves in the west to avoid everybody else's smoke and pollution), although local factors often contributed to the divide. In London, the presence of the port in the east made it logical that industry and commerce should congregate in this sector of the city, while in Paris François I's decision in the 16C to privilege his châteaux in the west (those in the east falling into comparative disgrace) encouraged the court and aristocracy to follow suit and build their mansions on the capital's western outskirts. Whatever the causes, the result, in today's post-industrial age, has been the same: both Paris and London have found themselves with underprivileged eastern sectors that have been progressively abandoned by the industry that was once their economic *raison d'être*, and both cities have undertaken major reorientation and redevelopment programmes intended to rectify this imbalance. Paris began even earlier than London, in the 1960s (the comprehensive rebuilding of large chunks of the 13th, 19th and 20th *arrondissements*, the Jussieu (5.12) and Gare-de-Lyon redevelopments) and, following the recent completion of the ZAC Bercy (12.7) just across the river on the *rive droite*, is now bringing this process to a close with the huge building site that is the ZAC Paris-Rive-Gauche, the city's biggest urban operation since Haussmannian times. (For an explanation of the term »ZAC«, please refer to the glossary.)

At the time of writing the ZAC Paris-Rive-Gauche has already passed the halfway stage in its 18-billion-franc realization, although it has not entirely left behind the controversy and polemic that dogged its beginnings. Paris's urbanists had had their eye on this sector of the city for decades, but it was not until the late 1980s that plans for the ZAC began to crystallize. The stimulating impetus came in 1988, when President Mitterrand, at the suggestion of Paris's then mayor, Jacques Chirac, decided to build the new Bibliothèque Nationale de France (BNF, 13.3) at what would become the centre of today's ZAC, a riverside site formerly occupied by a railway freight terminus. The presence of such a prestigious institution in this forgotten part of town would, it was hoped, act as a spur to the redevelopment of the area. Four years later, in 1991, the municipality officially launched the ZAC-Paris-Rive-Gauche project, which encompassed the entire swathe of land running alongside the Seine from the Gare d'Austerlitz as far as the *boulevard périphérique* – over 130 ha in total. A considerable chunk was occupied by the railway lines departing from the Gare d'Austerlitz, and the municipality consequently raised the possibility of moving the station to free up the land for development, a suggestion that the SNCF ultimately rejected. Not to be deterred, the municipality then came up with the positively pharaonic proposal of covering the railway tracks with a huge concrete platform – 32 ha in size – on which a quarter of the new neighbourhood would be built. The ZAC was to be organized around a major, 40 m-wide traffic axis, baptized rather grandiloquently the Avenue de France, which would run northwest–southeast down the middle of the site, connecting the Pont Charles-de-Gaulle (see feature on Seine bridges) on the Quai

13.2 ZAC Paris-Rive-Gauche

d'Austerlitz to the Boulevard Masséna at the city limits. Streets running perpendicular to this principal axis would ensure its connection to the pre-existent residential areas of the 13th *arrondissement* to the north and to the river and its quayside artery to the south. In other words, turning their back on contested 20C planning policies as codified by the Charter of Athens, the ZAC's conceptors looked to the 19C Haussmannian city for inspiration, producing a thoroughly *beaux-arts* grid of streets bisected by a boulevard and mixing traffic and pedestrians in the traditional manner. The only glitch came where the concrete platform had to link up with the pre-existing Rue du Chevaleret, 10 m below it, a connection which, it was decided, would be achieved using picturesque, Montmartre-style flights of steps. So that the new neighbourhood would not remain a forgotten and inaccessible outpost of urbanity, a major RER/Metro interchange was planned for it, with a new station being opened up on the RER C (which already ran across the ZAC) and the creation of a stop on the brand-new express metro line, the Météor (now referred to rather more prosaically as Line no. 14 – see feature on the Métro and the RER), which would put the *quartier* at only twelve minutes from the Madeleine.

So much for the ZAC's outlines and infrastructure, what was actually going to be built on this re-conquered and reconnected terrain? This was one of the first points of polemic, for the answer was essentially offices. The figures currently stand at no less than 700,000 m² of office space, 430,000 m² of apartments (roughly 5,000 separate dwellings), 405,000 m² of shops, commercial units and community facilities (schools, crèches, etc.), 210,000 m² reserved for a new university campus (principally the Université Paris-VII – see the Quartier Masséna below), and 100,000 m² of green open space. In other words, over a third of the total 1,745,000 m² of floor space are to be devoted to offices. Economically this is hardly surprising; 57 % of the total cost is being financed by the municipality, the remainder being divided up between the state, the region, the SNCF and private developers, and office rents are thus the only viable way of recouping the enormous sums invested.

The Avenue de France
2.5 km long, symbol, spine and principal artery of the ZAC Rive-Gauche, the Avenue de France was, so its planners recount, inspired by New York's Park Avenue where it runs over the tracks terminating at Grand Central Station. It was also intended, according to the developers, to become for eastern Paris what the Champs-Elysées are for the west. If today's visitors may have difficulty seeing the parallel, they will surely not fail to notice that in one aspect at least the two avenues are very alike: both are almost entirely lined with offices. While on the Champs-Elysées this was the result of market forces, at the Avenue de France it was a deliberate planning decision taken in response to the thoroughfare's location above railway lines: because of potential noise and vibration problems, no housing could be built on it, and it was thus the tertiary buildings of the ZAC that would be sited there. Shops, cafés and other commercial outlets were to line its pavements. Paul Andreu, architect of airports (see 22.1), was called in to ensure its overall coherence.

At the time of writing, the Avenue de France extends from the Pont Charles-de-Gaulle as far as the southeastern entrance to the Bibliothèque-François-Mitterrand RER station, although only the section between the station and the Rue de Tolbiac has buildings on both sides, the remainder, in the absence of the southwestern part of the concrete platform, featuring office blocks on the river side only. In a bid to counter criticisms of the original project, where the avenue seemed to have been conceived almost solely as an automobile expressway, its breadth has been divided into three: two roadways and a central reservation area containing trees, pavements and cycle paths. Perhaps in a deliberate ploy to recall the Champs-Elysées, the avenue's developers asked the architect Jean-Michel Wilmotte to design street furniture for it, which he did by recycling and completing the line he had produced for the Champs-Elysées revamp (see feature on street furniture). His slick, stylish traffic lights, lampposts and benches bring a sense of unity to the entire ZAC. There is also a remarkable sense of homogeneity, not to say monotony, in the office blocks lining the Avenue de France. From Christian Hauvette's Caisse-des-Dépôts-et-Consignations building (1999–2002), next to the Gare d'Austerlitz, to Fabrice Dusapin and François Leclercq's Accenture block (1998–2001) at the corner of the Rue Emile-Durkeim, to Marc Rolinet's Réseau-Ferré-de-France building (2000–2003), 92, avenue de France, nearly all the structures lining the avenue wear the same Cartesian, orthogonal, horizontally orientated steel-and-glass uniform, displaying a maximum of transparent glazing and a minimum of visible structure. Walking along the half-completed street today, it is as though the film sets of Jacques Tati's *Playtime* (1967) had been made real. Even Jean-Michel Wilmotte's 14-screen MK2-Cinema complex (2000–03), just behind the all-glass towers of the BNF, sports enormous, entirely glazed façades held up by slender concrete *pilotis*: two of the screens are located in boxes clearly visible through the transparent elevations, while the remainder are located in the basement, protected from railway vibrations by a spring-mounted suspension system. Nor does Chemetov and Huidobro's Collège Thomas-Mann (2000–03) manage to offer much variation on the general theme, despite its programmatic differences. At this rate the Avenue de France will be a very slick and sorry place indeed.

The future of the as-yet-unbuilt southeastern side of the avenue, between the Gare d'Austerlitz and the Rue de Tolbiac remains, at present, in suspense. Because of the difficulties of integrating the Gare d'Austerlitz's splendid train-shed with a concrete platform that would crash into it at about mid-height, the municipality seems to be on the verge of abandoning the idea of covering the railway tracks around the station, and instead may simply instigate some sort of cosmetic landscaping programme to tidy up the view from the avenue. For the even bigger section of ZAC between the Boulevard Vincent-Auriol and the Rue de Tolbiac behind the BNF, the all-encompassing concrete platform has again been called into question, partly because of its enormous cost and technical difficulties (source of some of the most virulent criticisms of the Paris-Rive-Gauche project), and partly because of the presence on the Rue du Chevaleret of the Halle des Messageries Ferroviaires (also known as the Halle Sernam). Built by the engineer Eugène Freyssinet, pioneer of reinforced-concrete construction and father of vibration-compacting and pre-stressing techniques as we know them today, the Halle des Messageries (1927–29) is a handsome structure comprising three, very long, juxtaposed »naves« that are covered by elegantly economical, tie-rod-tensed concrete vaults. Few of Freyssinet's buildings still stand, and the Halle des Messageries is thus a rare survivor of concrete's early days. The ZAC's developers want to demolish it since it gets in the way of proposed structures and would be difficult to reconcile with the concrete platform, while local residents and Freyssinet fans are eager to see at least its partial preservation, suggesting its conversion for use as a covered market and/or transport museum. In the meantime, railway tracks still dominate this sector of the ZAC.

The Quartier Tolbiac
Already five years old, this sector of the project was the first to rise from the ground. The presence of the BNF – adrift in an industrial wasteland and badly in need of neighbouring constructions and services to humanize it –, the fact that the land was free of obstructions and ready to build on, and last but not least the highly visible riverside site – long-term, politically vulnerable projects need good PR –, made it the obvious starting point. The architect Roland Schweitzer was given the job of overseeing and co-ordinating development of the *quartier*, which divides naturally into two chunks, one either side of the BNF, delimited by the Boulevard Vincent-Auriol to the northwest and the Rue de Tolbiac to the southeast. His approach took inspiration from the 19C city, and more specifically the Haussmannian tendency to build tall, »noble« constructions at the periphery of city blocks, behind which shelter lower-rise, more intimate structures and activities at the blocks' centres. Thus in the Quartier Tolbiac we find perimeter bar blocks, intended to be deliberately bastion like so as to protect the neighbourhood gardens behind them from the aggressive monumentality of the BNF. To emphasize further this defensive, curtain-wall effect, Schweitzer determined that all the perimeter buildings should be orthogonal slabs without projecting structures, although he did insist on multiple »breaches« in the form of subsidiary thoroughfares to avoid too intimidating an effect. Inside the city blocks, however, architects were given a little more volumetric latitude.

At the head of the *quartier*, on the Avenue de France, we find office buildings, but the more minor streets are lined with rent-controlled apartment blocks. All display the same orthogonal, Cartesian horizontality as the offices, although with greater diversity of materials, finishes and fenestration and with the added ingredient of balconies. In general the result is visually rather impoverished, perhaps imputable to the limited construction budgets available, although some architects found ingenious ways of introducing a bit of variety: for example Jacques Ripault and Denise Duhart's internal courtyards and wooden shutters on their Jardin-James-Joyce blocks (1994–96), or Philippe Gazeau's equally inventive play of shutters in the Jardin Georges-Duhamel (on the corner of the quayside and the Rue Emile-Durkheim, 1994–97). The Jardin James-Joyce also has the distinction of sheltering within its pleasant but lacklustre confines the ZAC Rive-Gauche's very first church, a small, discreet, brick-faced affair by Pierre-Louis Faloci, aptly named Notre-Dame-de-la-Sagesse (1997–2000). To find the most-talked-about building in this sector of the ZAC, we must return to the Jardin Georges-Duhamel, on whose northwestern side stands Francis Soler's much-published apartment building (9–19, rue Emile-Durkheim, 1994–97). Soler has long been personally concerned with the dream of maximum transparency that seems to have seduced so many of the other of the ZAC's architects, and set the tone with this block. Essentially a simple stacking of floors, a configuration designed to cut construction costs, the building avoids volumetric tedium through its upper-level step-downs and *jardin*-side irregular projections. The façades, which feature floor-to-ceiling glazing along the length of each storey, could also have been very boring were it not for their Hi-tech, finely detailed balconies, which also act as *brise-soleils*, and the controversial window transfers reproducing cherubs and other motifs from Guilio Romano's fresco *The Feast of the Gods* at Mantua's Palazzo del Te. Soler intended these transfers to provide colourful net curtains that would render life in his goldfish-bowl apartments a little less exposed, proof that even he recognizes that his bravura, »degré zéro« architecture of cling-film-wrapped floor space is not necessarily for everyone.

The Quartier Masséna
The southeastern sector of the Quartier Masséna, running alongside the river, looks set to become by far the most interesting part of the whole ZAC Rive-Gauche. In the late 1990s, at the height of a property slump which, critics claimed, would make the 900,000 m² of office space originally planned for the ZAC unsellable, the municipality changed tack and negotiated with the state for the building of a new university campus here. The principal institution will be the Université Paris-VII Denis-Diderot, which is severely short of space in its current accommodation. Following a mini-competition in 1995, Christian de Portzamparc was nominated to coordinate development of the area, and will see realization of the campus and adjoining neighbourhoods through to their scheduled completion in 2005.

One of the challenges of this sector of the ZAC will be the renovation and integration of a number of already extant structures, which include the derelict SUDAC plant (13.4), Halle-aux-Farines warehouse building and Grands Moulins de Paris (at the time of their opening, in 1921, the world's biggest mill complex), as well as the Frigos, a former refrigeration building that has been an artists' squat since the 1980s. Municipality and developers originally wanted to demolish all of these (bar the SUDAC plant, which is listed), but local associations fought and won for their preservation. The Frigos have now been legitimized by being bought up by the municipality, which leases space to the resident artists at very favourable rents, while the Halle aux Farines and the Moulins are awaiting conversion for use by Paris-VII. As for the SUDAC plant, Frédéric Borel is getting ready to turn it into the Ecole d'Architecture de Paris Val-de-Seine.

Meanwhile, a new chunk of urbanity is nearing completion in the area circumscribed by the Seine, the

Avenue de France, the Rue de Tolbiac and the Grands Moulins. Besides the offices on the avenue, apartment buildings, student accommodation, a school and a couple of mini-parks constitute the essential of the area's amenities. Portzamparc's masterplan comprises four-to-eight-storey buildings organized around internal streets and courtyards in a configuration intended to respect the spirit of Paris's traditional urbanity but also open up the city block to today's light and air requirements. Equal importance is given both to building volumes and the voids around them, and views and sightlines are carefully controlled. Refreshingly, the all-glass mania that has swept much of the rest of the ZAC has been dropped here in favour of an architecture of varied volume and fenestration, multiple materials and, here and there, bright colours. Architects as different as Ricardo Bofill, Antoine Stinco, Olivier Brenac, Xavier Gonzalès, Pierre Bolze and Simon Rodrigues-Page have all contributed buildings to the patchwork, which enjoys a formal richness entirely lacking elsewhere in the ZAC Rive-Gauche.

At the time of writing, the eastern extremity of the Quartier Masséna, where the Avenue de France hits the Boulevard Masséna, remains the ZAC's most uncertain sector. Quite how the avenue will link up with the boulevard, and, eventually, with the suburbs beyond, has not been decided. The situation is greatly complicated by the difficult nature of the cityscape in question, which is occupied by the *boulevard périphérique*, a spaghetti-junction-style interchange and, of course, railway lines. One proposal that has prompted much comment is Yves Lion's scheme to build a series of 25-storey office towers in the sector, an approach based on the logic that only large-scale structures of this kind could possibly work in such a hostile environment. Since the 1970s, stringent height restrictions have prevented this sort of development in Paris, and Lion's proposal has divided reactions into two principal camps: a minority who find the current legislation too constraining, and a majority that fears a waiver will prompt an unstoppable flood of tower-building across the French capital.

13.3 Bibliothèque Nationale de France
11, quai François-Mauriac
Dominique Perrault, 1989–95
(Métro: Quai de la Gare, Bibliothèque François-Mitterrand; RER: Bibliothèque François-Mitterrand)

Last of President Mitterrand's »grands projets« and the building that shot Dominique Perrault to fame, the Bibliothèque Nationale de France (BNF) was also one of the most controversial and talked-about French architectural projects of the 1990s. The sheer scale of the scheme and its enormous cost – nearly 8 billion francs –, the cultural and political concerns at stake, the haste and authoritarianism with which the project was realized, and the spectacular teething problems from which the finished building suffered ensured that copious column inches were filled with its ups and downs throughout the decade. The story began back in the early 1980s when it became clear that the »BN« – the old Bibliothèque Nationale (2.4) in central Paris – had finally reached saturation point and could no longer fulfil its allotted task. Space was the primary resource lacking: space to house the ever-growing influx of the *dépôt légal* (by law France's national library receives copies of every book published in the country), space to accommodate the ever-increasing number of readers, and space to carry out the book-restoration, administrative and other activities that are part and parcel of a library's work. Due to its situation in a historically sensitive, densely built neighbourhood, expansion on the old site was impossible, and it was evident that new premises would have to be built at another location. In 1988, a press communiqué, symbolically issued on Bastille day, announced that a new library was to be built at Tolbiac in eastern Paris. It would not replace the old BN, but would provide supplementary space, the collections post-1945 (around 3 million volumes) moving to the new building, while the remainder would stay put in the Rue de Richelieu. But the new facility was not to be just a modest annexe, either: Mitterrand spoke of an »entirely new kind« of library that would be »open to all, use the most modern cataloguing and retrieval technologies«, be consultable on-line and »connected with other European libraries.« In other words, it was to be the library of the 21C, or so the rhetoric went.

Situated on the banks of the Seine and formerly home to a railway freight depot, the 7.5 ha site allocated to the BNF was offered by the Ville de Paris, who hoped that the presence of this prestigious institution

13.3 Bibliothèque Nationale de France

in the area would kick start its pharaonic ZAC-Paris-Rive-Gauche project (13.2). An international architectural competition was held in 1989 to find a design for the new library, from which the very young (36) and relatively unknown Dominique Perrault emerged victorious. His design appealed to the jury – and Mitterrand – because of its clarity and boldness. Ignoring the surrounding environment, but conscious of the need for monumentality in a prestige, riverside institution, Perrault designed an enormous, half-buried rectangular building filling the entire site, at whose centre was a »hole« the size of the Jardin du Palais-Royal (see 1.16), which was to be filled with gardens. Reading rooms were to be disposed round this introverted »cloister«, while the building's exterior would be entirely blind, treated like a giant, plank-covered temple plinth with monumental steps rising on three sides. As for the books, they were to be housed in four 79 m-high, L-shaped towers rising from the plinth, whose form, Perrault said, was intended to recall an open book. They would define an enormous void, »a place not a building«, as he put it, an anti-monument that would offer the nation the one luxury that crowded Paris cannot usually provide: space.

Many are the grandiose architectural projects that have never made it off the drawing board due to political opposition, and Mitterrand had sussed out in his first term of office that the key to avoiding such an outcome is speed. In its initial stages a project is vulnerable to changes of government, budget cuts, etc., but once building work has progressed beyond a certain point there is generally nothing that can stop its completion. Hence the precipitation with which the BNF was executed: competition in 1989, start of construction in 1991, delivery of the building in 1995, full opening of the library in 1998 – less than ten years from start to finish. To measure the phenomenal speed of the operation one only has to look across the Channel to the British Library, a project of almost identical programme, size and complexity, that took over 30 years to realize! For the in the end the BNF mutated from a simple annexe into a full national library, accommodating France's entire collection of around 12 million volumes. This decision was taken after the architectural competition had been held, when outraged academics, incensed by the arbitrariness of the 1945 split, successfully persuaded the authorities that an all-or-nothing solution was the only option. Thus a design intended for 3 million volumes suddenly had to adapt itself to four times that number; fortunately, Perrault's scheme proved flexible enough to absorb this capacity change without calling into question the initial concept.

There was worse to come, however. Perrault's competition proposal had specified that the towers would be in glass so as to »show off the ›book‹ to advantage, with a random manner of occupation in the towers appearing like an accumulation of knowledge, a knowledge never completed, a slow but permanent sedimentation.« What this seemed to be saying was that, in a new variant of the clichéd architectural metaphor that transparency equals democracy, the nation's written heritage would be put on display in enormous glass bookcases and offered up at least visually (if not in practice) to the man in the street. This immediately sparked off uproar from librarians and experts the world over, who pointed out that the paper from which books are made is light sensitive, and that consequently book stacks are best placed underground where it is dark and cool, not in glass greenhouses where they would literally cook. It is astounding enough that the ministry overseeing the library did not point out that storing books under glass is a bad idea, and that the winning architect did not discover this elementary fact for himself, but that the project was pushed ahead even once this howling flaw had been acknowledged seems beyond comprehension. Presumably there were not time or resources enough to start the design process again from scratch, since the resulting setback could have jeopardized the whole project. Presidential push was behind this baby, and it would go ahead come what may.

Still, it would have been a shame to let the nation's written heritage crumble into dust, and a compromise was consequently reached. The library's administrative services were to be moved out of the podium, where they appeared in the competition proposal, to the towers, and the freed-up underground space given over to book storage. In this way, only 40% of the collection would be housed in the towers, and those books that were placed under glass would be protected from the sun's rays by heavy wooden shutters, kept permanently closed. It is these that give the library's towers their brown, rather retrograde, 1970s allure when viewed from afar. (Perrault later claimed that he never meant that the books would be on view but that »the wood [presumably of the shutters] would be visible through the glass«, which latter constituted »a protecting element.« But why, in that case, go to all the expense of building crystalline glass towers only to close them again?) What nobody realized was that dividing the administrative spaces up amongst the towers would give rise to a fairly serious operational problem: situated at each of the building's corners, they are about as far away from each other as is possible, and, because there are no communication routes running either across or underneath the garden, the time necessary to get from one tower to its diagonal opposite is quite considerable. As a result, staff complain bitterly about the enormous distances they have to cover every day, made worse by heavy, hard-to-open fire doors.

It is not only the staff that complained, but also the public arriving at the library. The tropical-wood-covered podium (much criticized by environmentalists) presents an intimidating bank of steps that is not easy to climb, and quite what readers with mobility problems are expected to do is not at all obvious. Once on top of the plinth, one finds oneself in a bleak, inhospitable space that suffers badly from the Venturi effect, with winds gusting down around the towers. Bushes in cages are lined up along each of the plinth's shorter sides in a particularly sadistic-looking example of Nature subjugated, while mean-looking lighting pylons accentuate the urban-wasteland feeling. Lingering up here is frequently not an option, but then trying to get off the plinth can be hazardous too, for in wet or frosty weather it becomes a giant slippery skating rink that has got the better of many: in the first winter of operation alone, multiple complaints were filed for falls and fractures. And, to add insult to injury, having made all the effort to climb up the plinth, one then discovers that to get into the library one must descend again, via escalators leading down into the garden hole. One can only wonder if this initiation rite was not in fact a deliberate ploy to put people off and deter all but the most serious researchers, thereby providing built-in protection against overuse (even the library's siting in a peripheral and, at the time, underdeveloped area of Paris could be interpreted this way). At least now the Avenue de France (see 13.2) has been built, the podium steps can be avoided.

While on the plinth, an intriguing vision of what might have been is provided by a closer examination of the towers. Their curtain-wall façades are consummately minimalist, with a simple aluminium lattice containing 3.6 x 1.8 m double-glazed panels into which cooled air is pumped to prevent internal, greenhouse-effect overheating. To avoid the greenish tinge of commercially available glass, the manufacturer Saint-Gobain provided 6,000 tonnes of specially made, very white glass, which renders the façades wonderfully transparent and crystalline. What a pity that all this effort was expended to procure a perfect view of wooden shutters. The plinth also provides a good view of another controversial element of Perrault's design, namely the garden. Many were surprised that the library turned its back on its riverside setting, but Perrault wanted to offer readers a cloistered oasis of calm. Gardens and knowledge have of course been inextricably linked in Western consciousness since Eden, and Perrault wanted the BNF's to resemble a chunk of wild, virgin nature, the primeval forest that covered the Ile-de-France long before Paris ever existed. To achieve this he transplanted mature pines from Normandy and arranged boulders and undergrowth in imitation of the Forêt de Fontainebleau. The original idea was that researchers would be able to take breaks in this sylvan setting, and even meet for a chat in little cabins. But then someone pointed out that trees attract wood-eating insects, and that insects that like wood are also quite partial to paper, and as a result, in the interests of protecting the books, the garden façades were hermetically sealed and access to the mini-forest denied. As a result, it has been reduced to a role of expensive backdrop, a rather surreal simulacrum of nature that ironically demonstrates man's total domination of his environment.

Entering the library via the garden's parapet, one arrives in what is known in BNF jargon as the *haut-de-jardin*. Socialist president that he was, Mitterrand had promised that the BNF would be egalitarian and open to all; but the library's management, fearing an uncontrollable flood of users, refused to give just anyone access and continued their policy of restricting entry only to serious researchers. As a compromise, a 1,650-seat, free-access library for the general public was created in the upper part of the building (the *haut de jardin*), while the »real« BNF, with its 1,900 researchers' seats (compared to only 600 at the old BN), was situated downstairs in what is known as the *rez-de-jardin*. Despite the many criticisms of their configuration, Perrault's interiors are the library's most successful feature, realized with a lavishness unusual in the public sector. Determined that his building »would not have the atmosphere of an airport« while still remaining resoundingly Modern, the architect set about contrasting the luxury of highly *soigné* design (desks, chairs, lighting, etc.) with the rougher and more surprising charms of »industrial« materials used out of context. Raw concrete and huge sheets of metal mesh, in places stretched tightly across the walls and in others hung in swathes from the ceiling, provide a backdrop for the sleek, sophisticated furniture. To avoid the alienating coldness that could have resulted, large amounts of chestnut-coloured wood and acres of squirrel-red carpet (chosen, legend has it, by Mitterrand himself) were introduced, bringing a womb-like, rosy hue to the BNF's interiors. In general Perrault sought to avoid the sensation of gigantism, but to reach the *rez-de-jardin* one must take monumental escalators that plunge into a 30 m-high, metal-mesh-covered »canyon«, whose Piranesian volume, some mean-spirited wags suggest, perfectly expresses the chasm between the plebs upstairs and the exclusive researchers' club below. Indeed the *rez-de-jardin*'s reading rooms have all the cocooned hush and luxury appointment of a London clubhouse, with beautifully conceived desks featuring built-in lighting consoles and lap-top terminals, and especially regal, solid-wood researchers' chairs, which sparked off a national scandal when it was revealed that readers' bottoms were to be supported for 3,000 francs apiece.

The BNF was billed as the library of the 21C. What this meant in practice was the mechanization and automatization of all its services, with, of course, computers controlling everything. Cataloguing, ordering volumes for consultation, air-conditioning, the Télédoc automated book-transportation system, the movement of readers around the building via electronic key-cards (whose total control extends to preventing one's departure if one's books have not been returned), every aspect of the library's use is administered by computers in a virtual architecture of electronic barriers, regulation, movement and flux. All this was intended to make the BNF a perfectly efficient book-delivery machine, considerably reducing costs, time and effort expended. At the library's opening it turned out that, in large part because the BNF's extremely complex software was far from ready, exactly the opposite was true, books taking up

13.4 Compressed-air plant

to 48 hours to arrive in comparison to 45 minutes at the old BN. The on-line catalogue was badly conceived and difficult to use, Télédoc frequently jammed and, because of its hermetically sealed automatization, trapped books within its transporters, and readers were confounded at every turn by the electronic-card system. The building's architecture, with its huge distances, impractical arrangement and under-podium staff areas whose mean, windowless spaces contrasted singularly with the reading rooms' luxury, did nothing to help. Moreover, costs had actually significantly increased, the BNF's electricity consumption equalling that of a town of 30,000 inhabitants. Highly experimental in every domain, the BNF fell foul of its ambitions and the undue haste with which it was realized. The long process of trying to put it all right has but begun.

13.4 Compressed-air plant
13, quai Panhard-et-Levassor
Joseph Leclaire, 1890–91
(Métro: Bibliothèque François-Mitterrand)
The Compagnie Parisienne d'Air Comprimé (Parisian Compressed Air Company, later the Société Urbaine de Distribution de l'Air Comprimé, or SUDAC), was founded in the 1880s by the Austrian Victor Popp, and provided Paris with a city-wide supply of compressed air. A pulse every minute drove the capital's public clocks, and compressed air was also used to power hydraulic lifts and pneumatic communication systems. SUDAC's compressors were still operating as late as 1994.

The plant, built in the heart of the city's eastern industrial sector, originally consisted of an iron-and-glass boiler hall, served by two brick chimneys, and a 70 m-long main compressor hall. In the 1920s the old boiler hall was replaced with a concrete-framed structure, and one of its chimneys demolished. The other chimney survives, however, as does the compressor hall, an impressive metal-framed structure with brick and glass infill, surmounted by a shallow metal barrel-vault. The frame features trellis beams in the form of Saint-Andrew's crosses, which were a common feature of industrial buildings of the period and which were used in modified form at the Centre Georges-Pompidou (4.15). The northern façade carries the arms of the Ville de Paris in stained glass, and was originally surmounted by a »master clock« which regulated the municipality's time-keepers.

The SUDAC plant is one of the last remaining examples of this type of structure in Paris, and the chimney and compressor hall have consequently been listed. Following a decade of dereliction, the building is now set to become part of the ZAC Rive-Gauche's new architecture school, designed by Frédéric Borel (see also 13.2).

13.5 Hôtel Industriel Berlier
26, rue Brunesseau
Dominique Perrault, 1986–90
(Métro: Porte d'Ivry, Quai de la Gare; RER: Bibliothèque François-Mitterrand)
Fearful that light-industrial and artisanal businesses would leave its territory for ever in search of cheaper suburban rents, the Ville de Paris instituted a programme of construction of *hôtels industriels* in the 1980s with a view to encouraging this sort of enterprise to stay. *Hôtel industriel* is a rather vague term signifying a multi-purpose, adaptable space capable of simultaneously fulfilling the roles of warehouse, workshop, office, laboratory, and so on. One of the results of the

13.5 Hôtel Industriel Berlier

Ville's programme was this building, designed by Dominique Perrault of Bibliothèque-Nationale-de-France fame (see 13.3). The *hôtel*'s site, which belongs to the municipality, is bang in the middle of a chaotic jumble of motorways, railway tracks and post-industrial wasteland (although the Ville's ZAC-Paris-Rive-Gauche project (13.2) is now aiming to change all that), and it is one of the strengths of Perrault's design that it manages to make an impact in this ungrateful environment.

Perrault's work has been described as »style-less«, a term to which one should naturally take exception but which tries to characterize a certain abstract neutrality or would-be universality in some of his buildings, where orthogonal geometry, technique and use of materials dictate the design, and site- and/or function-specific composition and expression do not enter the equation. This approach was arguably ideal for the Hôtel Industriel Berlier, whose function was entirely unspecific and whose setting was so diverse as to give no cues for the building's design. Formally and programmatically Perrault's scheme is very simple: a stack of floors encased in a breathtakingly transparent glass box – floor space surrounded by solid air, or shrink-wrapped in cling-film, if you will. A minimalist glass brick into which everyone can see, the building arguably avoids the problems of expressing function and purpose as it simply takes on the identity of the activities carried out inside it. But then on the other hand, given that computers have made the workspace at least superficially similar in many different types of industry, the casual observer might be none the wiser (by way of illustration, the Hôtel Industriel Berlier's occupants have included a printing works, a photo agency, a homeopathic lab and Perrault's own practice). Nonetheless, the *hôtel*'s immaculate, shiny, Hi-tech exterior confers a sexy, sophisticated image on the activities carried out inside it, one of the paradoxes of this building being that such extreme formal simplicity requires great technical accomplishment. The vertical glass panels are glued into place (opening windows are not one of the *hôtel*'s features) and, to keep floor thicknesses to a minimum and save space, all services (cables, pipes, air conditioning etc.) run round the building's perimeter, inside the glass skin, in tandem with a system of *brise-soleils* that ensure relief from the sun's rays. Aesthetically this produces strong horizontals that complement the vertical orientation of the glass panels. The perimeter grouping of services is essentially the same solution as that used at the Centre Pompidou (4.15), but in Hi-tech, minimalist form as opposed to Piano and Rogers' exaggerated, multi-coloured extravaganza of ducts and shafts.

By day, the Hôtel Industriel Berlier is alternately transparent and alternately opaque, depending on the lighting conditions and the amount of sky it reflects, and by night it is brilliantly lit from within like a jeweller's display case. Whatever the external conditions, the building's occupants can always see out, with plunging views out onto the *péripherique* or towards central Paris in the west. Some have suggested that this archi-

13.6 Cité de Refuge de l'Armée du Salut

tectural »degré zéro«, made of simple volumes and glass, is the future of building, and certainly several recent Parisian housing schemes have emulated its daring. But transparency is not for everyone. Perrault subsequently tried to repeat this feat of limpidity in the towers of the Bibliothèque Nationale de France, using better-quality, whiter glass with a view to displaying the national collections of knowledge for all to see. This approach had notorious practical repercussions, and the library's towers as built are rendered opaque by solid wooden shutters.

13.6 Cité de Refuge de l'Armée du Salut
12, rue Cantagrel and 37, rue du Chevaleret
Le Corbusier and Pierre Jeanneret, 1929–33
(Métro: Bibliothèque François-Mitterrand, Porte d'Ivry)
A keen patron of music, whose protégés included Fauré, Stravinsky, and Debussy, Princess Winaretta de Polignac probably met Le Corbusier through his brother, the composer Albert Jeanneret. She began championing the architect and, after donating a considerable sum towards the Salvation Army's proposed new 500-bed hostel, secured him the commission for the building. The Army had begun an ambitious programme of social welfare after WWI, culminating in the Cité de Refuge. Its mission included training and re-educating the homeless in its care and, as well as accommodation facilities, the hostel was to provide workshops where residents would be employed. A site was offered by the Ville de Paris in the working-class 13th *arrondissement*. Le Corbusier's highly experimental final project was more than a simple response to the demands of the brief – as a synthesis and manifesto of ideas put forward in his plans for the Ville Radieuse (1928–31), it constituted a showpiece of the Corbusian city of the future.

In deliberate opposition to the traditional urban fabric surrounding the hostel, Corb ignored the street line, orientating his building transversally to catch the southern sun. The concrete-framed main dormitory block, a precursor of his famous *unités d'habitation*, is mounted on *pilotis* to overcome the hillside terrain, and rises eleven

13.7 Maison Planeix

storeys, the maximum height permitted by the regulations. The leftover space to the south contains low-rise buildings housing administration and arrival facilities, and also a small garden. Entry to the Cité is gained via a flight of steps leading up to a hollowed-out cube bearing the Salvation Army's name, from which a covered footbridge crosses to the low-rise structures – an architectural promenade of great dignity. Once inside, a circular entrance hall takes one through to a larger space which acts as a sort of orientation turntable, providing access to the rest of the building. A meeting room (where the spiritual well-being of residents was attended to) is situated below, while kitchens and ateliers are located in the ground floor of the dormitory wing. Ever an apostle of the automobile, Corb included a garage in the basement.

The buildings of the Ville Radieuse featured maximum glazing to let in the life-giving rays of the sun, and were to be sealed off from the outside world and entirely air-conditioned, a form of total climate control which Corb dubbed »respiration exacte«. The Cité de Refuge became the experimental prototype for these ideas. As originally built, the southern façade of the dormitory block was one vast, 1,000 m² all-glass curtain wall, double glazed and without a single opening window. Air-conditioning was unknown in France at the time, and Corb's audacity proved simply too precocious. Of the building's many teething problems, the most serious was the inadequacy of the air-conditioning and heating systems, with the result that residents froze in winter and boiled in summer. Less than two years after the Cité's inauguration, following recriminations between client and architect, Corb was forced to introduce opening windows along the entire façade. Shattered by a German bomb in 1944, the façade was rebuilt in the early 1950s along more traditional lines, although, at Corb's suggestion, each of the new windows incorporates a *brise-soleil*, one of his later leitmotifs.

In its original state, the Cité de Refuge was exemplary of Corb's engineer's aesthetic of the 1920s, a building made to look industrially produced, with its steel-and-glass curtain walling and ubiquitous glass bricks and tubular steel railings. It also resembled one of his Purist paintings, with the Platonic forms of the entrance and administration buildings set against a backdrop of glass. Its styling incited the inevitable comparisons with ocean liners, an analogy all the more apt given its role as a mini-city within the metropolis. This machine imagery, and the surveillance-facilitating transparency of the original design, take on a slightly disturbing aspect when one remembers the building's function as a centre of »social redemption«, where less well-adapted citizens were »normalized« and rendered useful and productive.

13.7 Maison Planeix
24 bis, boulevard Masséna
Le Corbusier and Pierre Jeanneret, 1924–28
(Métro: Porte d'Ivry)

A keen amateur painter and devotee of modern architecture, Antonin Planeix owed what wealth he had to his funerary-monument business, and struggled to find the cash to build this house. The Maison Planeix is thus unusual amongst Corb's private commissions in that it was not constructed for a rich, indulgent patron but for a man of more modest means, who was keen to maximize the potential for commercial exploitation of his investment. It was also atypical in Corb's œuvre in that, like the Maison Cook (29.3), it was one of the rare houses he built that was not free-standing but instead subject to the constraints of party-wall urbanism. This in turn influenced the design, and partly explains the »cubic« solution chosen for the principal façade. Historians have seen this as the first in a series of Corbusian cubic compositions that culminated in the Maison Cook and the Villa Stein (31.1).

Although the Maison Planeix predates the codification of Corb's famous »five points of a new architecture«, the house was conceived with them in mind. Two central *pilotis* appear on the ground floor, which was originally to have been left entirely clear for the later installation of undetermined rental activities. In the event, at the suggestion of Pierre Jeanneret, Planeix opted for the current disposition of two discrete, double-height artist's studios either side of a central garage. It was also Jeanneret who introduced the Maison-Citrohan-style external staircase at the rear of the building to facilitate access and maximize flexibility in the event of later subdivision of the house. (Although its exterior remains virtually unchanged since Planeix's day, the house's interior has now been divided into flats.) Planeix's living accommodation was originally on the first floor, while the second and final floor was given over to his painting atelier, which was lit by glazed saw-tooth roofs à la Maison-atelier Ozenfant (14.7). Around the latter, a token *toit-terrasse* was disposed. The plan was of course free, emphasized by beams and supports that stopped just short of the equally free façades. Décorwise, the house was fitted out with full Purist austerity.

For the street frontage, Corb did not seek to fight the planar façadism implied by the house's party-wall context, but treated the elevation as a canvas on which he could freely dispose openings and projections, thereby demonstrating its non-load-bearing nature. Classically symmetrical, the façade features a central suspended cube that divides it into three, breaking the run of the first-floor strip windows (another of the »five points«) and providing a symbolically »royal« balcony for the atelier above. The street elevation only really »works« when seen face on from a distance, which is unfortunately difficult today with the heavy traffic and obscuring trees of the Boulevard Masséna.

13.8 Médiathèque Jean-Pierre Melville
93, rue de Tolbiac
Canal: Daniel and Patrick Rubin, 1984–89
(Métro: Tolbiac, Porte d'Ivry)
With 3,500 m² of floor space and a collection of over 100,000 books, CDs and videos, this is Paris's largest municipal library. Its prominent corner plot is situated in a heavily redeveloped residential area which presents a rather chaotic range of building styles and heights. When briefing the architects, the Ville de Paris stipulated only that the library should fully express its »civic importance«.

13.8 Médiathèque Jean-Pierre Melville

In terms of size, the Canal team reverted to tradition, producing a four-storey building of Haussmannian proportions. Their two fundamental design elements were flexibility of use and abundant natural light. By using a frame system which allowed extremely wide spans and placing services at the periphery, the architects achieved entirely unencumbered floor spaces of 400 m² on each level. As well as permitting organizational freedom (the furnishings, also by Canal, are deliberately unfixed), this also maximizes daylight penetration into the building. As luck would have it, the library's principal façade faces north – books do not fare well in sunlight, so southern exposure would have posed problems – allowing a splendid, all-glass exterior. The short, southern façade, hidden away in a back street between two party walls, is given over to the librarians' offices, thus insulating the building's interior from treacherous solar rays.

The principal façade, constructed from a fine aluminium lattice, is gently bowed, and terminates at its eastern extremity in a tight curve which, as well as elegantly turning the street corner and signalling the building's entrance, encloses a free-standing spiral staircase. The all-glass frontage serves a double purpose: it floods the library with daylight, but also allows the activities within to be observed from without, a deliberate move by the architects to break with the intimidating aspect of many traditional libraries and entice passers-by into their building. Located next to the façade, where there is most light, the reading areas feature floors which have been whittled away to almost nothing through bevelled ceiling profiles and 50 cm floor-level step-downs. The result, viewed from the exterior, is magnificent: the readers appear as if suspended in mid-air within an enveloping glass bubble. The eastern elevation is treated in a similar fashion, but also features a giant aluminium frame, set away from the façade, which is used to display enormous photographs, printed on semi-transparent canvas and stretched across the void. This »urban window« satisfies the law stipulating that all new public buildings must devote 1 % of their budget to art works.

Through its shiny glass exterior, the Médiathèque Jean-Pierre Melville both announces its civic presence and demonstrates its function. For once the architectural cliché that transparency equals openness and user-friendliness seems justified; expected to attract 20,000 readers in the first two years, the library welcomed over 15,000 in its first six months.

13.9 Social housing
106, rue du Château-des-Rentiers
Architecture Studio, 1985–87
(Métro: Tolbiac, Nationale)
Architecture Studio have compiled a list of around 1,000 »leftover« sites in Paris – tiny plots of land, often at junctions, that are generally the unwanted result of redevelopment schemes and are considered too small and awkward to build on – and proposed their exploita-

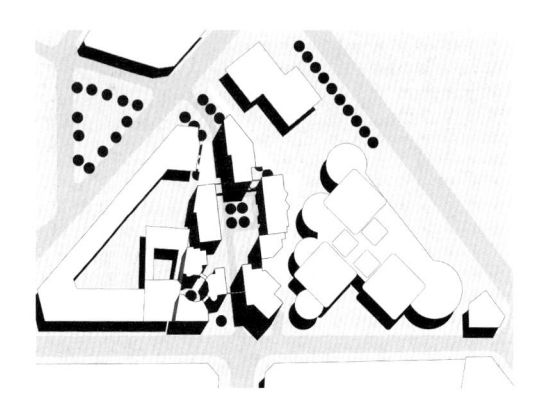

13.10 Social housing. Site plan

tion as a way of »repairing« the urban fabric and countering land shortage in expensive central districts. Here they demonstrated their ideas on a wedge-shaped site of less than 100 m², over which looms a 13-storey apartment slab, one of the fruits of the intensive but piecemeal postwar redevelopment of this neighbourhood. Into this space, Architecture Studio successfully squeezed 25 flats and created a building that re-establishes a sense of the street pattern in this rather chaotic environment. A striking feature of their scheme is the sort of Meccano tower at the building's »prow«, which is in fact the remains of the crane used to construct it. Since the site was too small to accommodate an ordinary crane, the architects built their own which, to save time and money, was designed to form part of the final structure. To mark its central importance, they cut away the building's upper levels to reveal the crane's frame and also exposed its lower parts to serve as an entrance porch. The building's elevations are tiled and feature, on the Rue-Jean-Colly façade, a map of the surrounding area that dissimulates monotonous fenestration. Although this building's rather Legoland aesthetic is not perhaps for everybody, it nonetheless intelligently demonstrates the possibilities of building on a restricted site.

13.10 Social housing
Rue des Hautes-Formes
Christian de Portzamparc with Giorgia Benamo, 1975–79
(Métro: Tolbiac, Nationale)

This relatively modest development (209 apartments) is widely credited in France with having entirely transformed contemporary attitudes towards the question of collective housing and the built form it should take. Indeed it was its deliberately un-monumental modesty that was the scheme's key attribute. Located in an area of the 13th *arrondissement* that was comprehensively redeveloped in the 1960s and 1970s, for the most part with high-density bar and tower blocks as was then the French norm, the site was itself originally destined to become home to two towers. Portzamparc's project set itself up in direct opposition to this logic of »functionalism, international architecture and mass construction seemingly produced by machines«, and instead proposed a made-to-measure ensemble of seven non-identical buildings arranged around a small square. This approach took inspiration from the traditional Parisian city block, which is generally built up around its perimeter but open at the centre. Trying to spread out two tower-blocks' worth of accommodation over a site of only 4,000 m² meant building fairly densely, and to avoid totally covering the available surface Portzamparc's blocks were obliged to rise a still slightly intimidating twelve storeys. Loosely grouped, the buildings are contrived so as to offer different apartment configurations and to display different heights, profiles and fenestration on their exteriors, with round towers, cutaway corners, arches and double-height windows making a rather random appearance. The somewhat gratuitous, »Postmodern«-looking beams and arches connecting individual blocks to each other are in fact the residue of an attempt to get round the original *réglementation* concerning the site, which stipulated that only two ensembles should be constructed there.

In opting for artificial, contrived-vernacular variety, the scheme clearly set out to reject the socialist egalitarianism of much postwar housing where production-line repetition ensured that everybody had and was shown to have the same. The architects also tacitly rejected the Puritan Modernist axiom that a building's internal logic should be reflected on its exteriors, although they

13.10 Social housing

did not go to the fantasy extreme of, say, Ricardo Bofill's »Versailles-for-the-people« palace-fronted housing estates (see 14.2 and 36.2), where internal function and layout are entirely obfuscated. The make-believe here was limited to the right to visual variety which the architects claimed for the future residents of their scheme. But variety is not necessarily a guarantee of individuality or a sense of place, or even of a visually interesting result (repetition can also be interesting – see, e. g., Renzo Piano's Rue-de-Meaux social-housing scheme (19.14), where attention to detail ensures success), and the Rue-des-Hautes-Formes estate does not manage to avoid the rather anonymous blandness that is the lot of many social-housing schemes. Moreover, the architects' »anti-functionalist« approach could not escape the laws of economics. The multiplication of blocks in place of the two towers originally proposed meant a considerable increase in façade surface area, but the budget for the façades' finishing remained the same. Consequently, instead of the more *soigné* exterior that would have been possible under the tower-block solution, Portzamparc was obliged to resort to a cheap render that weathers badly and is expensive to maintain. This is not the only disappointment of the scheme as built. Many housing estates suffer from a »ghettoization« problem, and by creating an internal square that is not strongly integrated into the surrounding urbanity and through which no one but residents has really any business to pass, the Rue-des-Hautes-Formes's architects arguably fell into just this trap. The internal square is not a private, gated garden in a swish development, nor is it an animated public space. Instead it appears rather emptily forlorn and even slightly sinister, like a De Chirico painting. Bringing commerce into the space might have been one way of avoiding this problem.

Although Portzamparc and Benamo's project did not resolve all the questions raised by the stance its architects took, its critique of Modernist doctrine did help re-launch the debate on contemporary urbanism in France, and arguably contributed to a renewal of its forms.

13.11 »Grand Ecran« building
18–20, place d'Italie
Kenzo Tange with Michel Macary and Xavier Menu, 1985–91
(Métro: Place d'Italie)

Comprehensively redeveloped in the 1960s and 70s, the 13th *arrondissement* today bristles with high-rises that cohabit sometimes rather uncomfortably with vestiges of the area's older, more low-rise fabric. Nowhere is this better illustrated than at the Place d'Italie, where the towers of the redeveloped sector face the *arrondissement*'s 19C *mairie*. Indeed the *place* was originally to have received its very own tower, a 180 m-high monster baptized the »Tour Apogée« that would have marked the entrance to the Italie-2 shopping centre. The anti-high-rise, anti-Modernist President Giscard d'Estaing (whose urban policies were diametrically op-

13.11 »Grand Ecran« building

posed to those of his predecessor, Georges Pompidou) cancelled planning permission for the tower in 1975, sparking off a law suit that was not resolved until ten years later when the municipality acquired the still-vacant site. At this time the very Japanophile Jacques Chirac, then mayor of Paris, offered Kenzo Tange a choice of locations in the French capital to construct what would be the architect's first building in Europe. All of the proposed sites were in the city's eastern sectors, in line with the municipality's bid to gentrify the poorer *arrondissements*. Tange selected the Place d'Italie, initially wanting to remodel the whole piazza, an offer that was politely refused. Confined to just the Tour-Apogée site, he was asked to design a building that would house a new, ambitious film centre, comprising cinemas and up-to-the-minute audio-visual production facilities. Billed as a »Centre Pompidou du cinéma«, it was intended to promote Paris's self-styled position as capital of the seventh art, hence its name of »Grand Ecran« (»big screen«).

But as so often with such developments, things did not turn out quite as planned. Just as the final scheme had at last been accepted (after 20 redesigns), the municipality decided it could no longer finance the building and sought to off-load the project onto the private sector. The consortium that took it on conveniently forgot about the film centre, and what Paris finally got was a commercial office building with a cinema in its basement. Added to this disappointment was the anticlimax of Tange's design. What we have here is not the Pritzker-Prize-worthy architect of the Tokyo-Olympics stadia (1960–64), but rather late-period Tange, Grand Ecran being an example of the slick, commercial and ultimately rather bland granite-and-glass architecture that has constituted the bulk of his output for the last 20 years. The building was intended to act as a pacifying link between the traditional urbanism to the north of the Place d'Italie and the towers to the south, and in this respect at least, with its varied volumes and middle-range height, succeeds rather well. Following the site's perimeter, Grand Ecran is organized around a generous, glass-covered atrium, which serves little purpose other than lighting the offices (14,000 m^2 of them) around it. The atrium's lower levels provide access to the Italie-2 shopping centre and to the Gaumont cinema, but otherwise one is not encouraged to linger in its rather oddly terraced spaces, a sadly missed opportunity, for this could have been a lively public space. Indeed considerably more animation is to be found on the plaza fronting the building on the Place d'Italie.

It is on the Place-d'Italie façade that all interest is concentrated (the lateral elevations are soporifically bland), with its slightly retro, 1950s feel and impressive glass curtain wall. The building's most arresting feature is its glass lift tower, extended to a height of 55 m by a kinetic sculpture, designed by Thierry Vidé, that is intended to represent cinema. If indeed it moved it might achieve this but, despite installation of the necessary machinery, the sculpture was never switched on. As it is it forms a sort of prominent Meccano campanile.

Despite their disappointment, most critics recognized that Grand Ecran could have been worse, and that it is at least well-bred and urbane. In one respect the building does live up to its promise: France's biggest cinema screen (24 x 10 m) is housed in its basement.

13.12 Garde-Meuble du Mobilier National
1, rue Berbier-du-Mets
Auguste Perret, 1934–36
(Métro: Gobelins)

Originally founded under Charles V (1337–80) to house and maintain the state collections of carpets, tapestries and furniture, the Garde-Meuble du Mobilier National owes its current, purpose-built abode to the 1937 Exposition Internationale, for which the institution's then home was demolished to make way for exhibition pavilions. Auguste Perret, who had initially been called on by the government to draw up a masterplan for the Exposition (for which he was not paid), was awarded the commission for the Garde-Meuble's new buildings in recompense for the dropping of his exhibition proposals. With this project, constructed in only twelve months, Perret refined his own very personal reinforced-concrete-construction style and developed ideas that would form the fundament of his Parisian masterpiece, the Palais d'Iéna (16.6), which was begun the same year as the Garde-Meuble's completion.

Perret was trained in the *beaux-arts*, Classical tradition, and this is immediately apparent in his design for the Garde-Meuble. The brief called for repair workshops, warehouse space for the reserves, office space for the administration, and exhibition areas to display pieces of furniture that were not currently in use in state property. The site (next to the Gobelins tapestry factory) slopes steeply, dropping 4 m from one side to the other, a feature some architects would have used as a starting point for their design. True to his schooling, however, Perret chose instead to establish an artificial, conceptual ground level, to this end installing an enormous concrete platform, supported on 28 m-long concrete beams, across the entire site. Under it he placed the reserves which, because of the sloping terrain, are easily accessed by lorry, while above the platform, symmetrically organized around a generous *cour d'honneur*, are the conservation workshops, offices and, where the *corps de logis* would stand were this a château, the exhibition building. The Garde-Meuble is arranged and massed like an 18C *hôtel particulier* and, as with many Classically inspired edifices, the proportional relationships of the different structures to each other are determined by the golden section (which, for Perret, brought »humanity« to a building). A pronounced cornice crowns the Garde-Meuble and visually unites its wings, while at an intermediary level a second cornice coiffing the lower structures achieves a similar purpose by running round the courtyard as a canopy and then topping off the curved, twin-columned colonnade that closes the courtyard's entrance. This colonnade, the only light note in an otherwise extremely sober, orthogonal design, is a typical Perret gesture. Although he pronounced himself against curved forms in concrete, on the grounds that since they need elaborate shuttering they are expensive to produce and thus do not constitute a rational, economic use of materials, he nonetheless systematically broke his own rules in his projects for the sake of curvaceous expressionism, which is here rendered all the more effective by the dryness of the trabeated façades against which it is set.

13.12 Garde-Meuble du Mobilier National

13.13 Stade Sébastien-Charléty

Apart from the entrance colonnade's columns, the the Garde-Meuble exhibits no free-standing supports. The members of its concrete frame are nonetheless clearly expressed, and the concrete infill panels between them are treated as just that. Perret experimented with a structural system that he would later adapt and refine at the Palais d'Iéna, consisting of a megastructure supporting the roof and the floors, with a secondary framework holding in place the windows and infill panels. Each panel is slotted into grooves cast into the supporting framework, and the same system was used for the windows. Perret's usual care and attention are apparent in the composition, casting and finishing of the concrete which, although entirely unrendered, has aged well. The building's interior is also in bare concrete, with elaborate concrete roof domes lighting the repair workshops and exhibition spaces. The Garde-Meuble du Mobilier National is one of Perret's drier realizations – perhaps deliberately so to reflect its utilitarian vocation –, but what it lacks in pizzazz it makes up for in the quiet, rigorous elegance of its design.

13.13 Stade Sébastien-Charléty
Avenue de la Porte de Gentilly
Henri and Bruno Gaudin, 1988–94
(Métro: Porte d'Italie; RER: Cité Universitaire)
The revival of the Olympic Games at the end of the 19C was instigated by the French, worried they lacked enough fit men to fight a potential war. Ever mindful of anniversaries, Jacques Chirac, then mayor of Paris, decreed that the city should be provided with a brand-new athletics complex, to be inaugurated in the centenary year of the founding of the Olympic Committee. The complex was to replace an outmoded and dilapidated stadium dating from 1939 and occupying an 8 ha site on the edge of Paris, bounded on one side by the notorious *boulevard périphérique*. A 20,000-seat replacement arena was but one element of the programme: amongst other facilities to be provided were covered tennis courts, training areas, administrative accommodation including the headquarters of the Olympic Committee, leasehold office space, and a public garden on the roof of the underground car park.

Client and architects were anxious to avoid the problems of other stadia, such as the Parc des Princes (16.18), whose attitude they considered too introspective and brutal towards its surrounding neighbourhoods. They wanted instead to create an arena that would be open to its environs, a kind of »urban clearing« to aerate the dense city. Oval in shape and partially submerged, the Stade Charléty is constructed from a skeleton of concrete trusses, which support the terraces and from which the roofing elements are suspended. The trusses rise well above the tops of the terraces, leaving a dramatic breach between roof and seating. At one point the terraces sink low enough for passers-by on the boulevard Kellerman to have a clear view through to the racetrack. Despite the extra-terrestrial massiveness of its members, the whole structure has a light, airy feel. The roofline, which gently undulates with the changes in terrace height, is topped off by four huge lighting pylons, poised above the arena like giant fly swatters and visible for miles around; they have since become the building's trademark.

Four staircases fan out from the main spectator gallery onto the esplanade at the junction of the boulevard Kellerman and the Avenue de la Porte de Gentilly, forming a sort of *cour d'honneur*. The bar of administrative buildings which runs the length of the avenue terminates at the esplanade with the prow of the Olympic Committee building, rendered in ocean-liner style. Indeed the whole complex, with its lean engineering and limited palette of whites and greys, has a rather nautical air: before becoming an architect, Henri Gaudin was a mariner. The administrative buildings are raised off the ground on *pilotis*, permitting tantalizing glimpses of the stadium beyond. The Stade Charléty, like an alien spacecraft landed in Paris, is a popular and dynamic addition to the cityscape.

14th *arrondissement*

14.1 Notre-Dame-du-Travail
59, rue Vercingétorix
Jules Astruc, 1892–1902
(Métro: Montparnasse)

Is this the logical conclusion of the current set in motion by Louis-Auguste Boileau's groundbreaking Saint-Eugène (9.3) in the 1850s? Probably not. This church, situated in an area of Paris that in the late-19C was predominantly working class, has a floor entirely in reinforced cement and – a feature unprecedented at the time and probably unrepeated since – exposes an all-metal structure on the interior that is entirely unadorned and undissimulated, thus conserving a purely industrial aesthetic. At the time of the church's construction, the desire for economy was evoked as justification for this choice, but it seems certain that there was also a highly ideological motive behind the decision. The vicar of the parish wanted a building that would provide an ambience familiar to his congregation, and the church's factory aesthetic was thus presumably an attempt to fulfil this request, borne out by its dedication to workers everywhere (the English translation of its name is »Our Lady of Work«).

Astruc's design remains faithful to the basilical form of a traditional Gothic church, with a tall central nave that is lit by a clerestory and flanked by lower side-aisles. The aisles, whose side-chapels are topped off by a balcony running the length of the building, were probably a direct quote from Saint-Eugène. Unlike Saint-Eugène, however, Notre-Dame-du-Travail is not vaulted, and makes no attempt at plastic artistry, graphic movement being provided purely in the form of bracing struts. The result is certainly refreshingly rigorous, although perhaps misguidedly patronizing in its original intentions.

14.2 »Les Echelles du Baroque« social-housing scheme
Place de Catalogne
Taller de Arquitectura Ricardo Bofill, 1979–85
(Métro: Gaîté)

Earmarked for comprehensive redevelopment after WWII, the area behind the Gare Montparnasse, which was made up of poor-quality 19C housing and light-industrial buildings, was finally given over to the demolition men in the early 1970s. For the rebuilding of a substantial chunk of the *quartier*, the municipality called on Ricardo Bofill, who had cut his teeth on French soil with grandiloquent housing schemes in Paris's satellite *villes nouvelles* (see »Les Espaces d'Abraxas«, 36.2). Here, in place of the huge green-field sites and relaxed planning requirements of the new towns, Bofill was faced with the exigencies of dense Parisian urbanity and its attendant regulations. The challenge was thus to adapt his model of social housing to this restrictive environment.

14.1 Notre-Dame-du-Travail

Redevelopment of the neighbourhood was organized around the circular Place de Catalogne, Paris's biggest new piazza since Haussmannian times (which sadly is rather a non-place, despite its monumental water feature by the sculptor Shamaï Haber). Les Echelles' irregular site gives onto the *place* and is bisected by the Rue de Vercingétorix, which is enclosed within the estate as a pedestrian walkway and accessed from the piazza via a monumental gateway. Bofill divided his scheme around this natural axis, with to the west of the Rue de Vercingétorix an enclosed space in the form of an amphitheatre and to the east a big oval piazza, also entirely enclosed, baptized the Place de Séoul. Thus the estate's 272 public-sector apartments occupy the leftover areas between the four different public spaces (Place de Catalogne, Amphithéâtre, Rue de Vercingétorix and Place de Séoul), following their perimeters. This Baroque approach, which masks the site's irregularities, displays a certain sophistication absent from the bombastic, axial layouts of Bofill's new-town estates. Rising only seven storeys, as stipulated by the planning regulations, the buildings' façades exhibit the same Legoland, »Versailles-for-the-people« Classicism as his new-town housing – lumpen, prefabricated cornices, giant orders, pediments and triglyphs, all in sophisticated concrete, as well as, on the Place de Séoul, crude, colossal Doric columns in mirrored glass that act as bay windows for the apartments they front. Bofill's simplistic and tyrannical façadism has much in common with the regimented uniformity of Second-Empire apartment buildings.

However, where in the new towns the arrogant hugeness of the Bofill estates makes them brutal and overwhelming, here, on a more human scale, his kitsch Classicism seems almost innocuous, a plastic PoMo-palace wrapping whose humour is not inappreciable. Moreover, unlike the new-town estates stuck out in the middle of nowhere, Les Echelles integrate well into the surrounding urbanity. You may not be able to hang a window box on the mirrored-glass columns, but you can at least look out onto the charming gardens below, and the residents seem to like it that way.

14.3 Cimetière du Montparnasse
3, boulevard Edgar-Quinet
Begun 1824
(Métro: Edgar Quinet, Raspail)

The Cimetière du Sud, as the Montparnasse cemetery is officially known, was the second of three cemeteries created outside the then boundaries of Paris by order of the Prefect Nicolas Frochot in a bid to sanitize the capital's funerary practices (see the Cimetière du Père-Lachaise, 20.2). Between Frochot's edict of 1801 and the cemetery's inauguration in 1824, the municipality bought up land around the confiscated residence of the Frères de la Charité – already the site of a small cemetery – until a square-shaped parcel of 10 ha had been assembled. Not only the regularity of its boundaries but also the flatness of its terrain distinguished the new cemetery from the romantic dells of Père-Lachaise, and it was consequently laid out in a formal, »Classical« system of walkways, under the direction of Etienne-Hippolyte Godde. In 1847, the cemetery's size was increased to its current 18 ha; no further extensions were possible after its inclusion within the boundaries of the Ville de Paris in 1859.

Surrounded by high walls, the cemetery is entered at the centre of its north–south axis, which leads to a pivotal *rond-point*. This, together with a satellite orbital path are the only curves in an otherwise rectilinear plan. The pathways are bordered with regular rows of trees. Perhaps because of its smaller size, the chapels

14.2 »Les Echelles du Baroque« social-housing scheme

14.3 Cimetière du Montparnasse

and mausolea at Montparnasse tend to be less monumental and architectonic than their counterparts at Père-Lachaise. It is, however, a treasure-trove of sculpture, and includes work by Arp, Brancusi, Carpeaux, Dalou, Laurens and Rodin.

14.4 Cartier Building
261, boulevard Raspail
Jean Nouvel and Emmanuel Cattani, 1991–94
(Métro: Raspail, Denfert-Rochereau)

Unable to expand in its former home and looking to move, Cartier S.A. struck a deal with insurance giant GAN. Cartier would lease a prestigious site on the Boulevard Raspail belonging to GAN, provided that GAN commissioned Cartier's preferred architect – Jean Nouvel – to build their new headquarters there. As well as the usual offices, the new building was also to house the Fondation Cartier de l'Art Contemporain. The site was »sensitive«, jealously defended by residents' associations and home to several mature trees, including a Cedar of Lebanon, planted by Chateaubriand (a former resident) in 1823, dominating the central foreground. Nouvel and Cattani's response was to blur the boundaries of garden and building in a deliberately simple design which, like Nouvel's Institut du Monde Arabe (5.13), is perceived as complex through the play of transparency and light.

14.4 Cartier Building

The architects erected two four-storey-high metal-and-glass screens along the street line, which frame the cedar in the central void between them. Visitors must pass under the tree to gain entry to the building, whose principal façade consists of a sheer Cartesian wall of glass, extended out above and beyond the limits of the main structure. The rear elevation is treated in the same way, and the Cartier Building is thus made up of a succession of reflecting glass screens, which confuse the gaze of the uninitiated. Are the trees inside or outside? Where does the building begin or end? What is sky and what is glass? In fact the building is a simple orthogonal box, with eight floors above ground and another eight below. The *fondation* occupies the double-height ground floor and the first basement storey. A single space, broken only by a small central mezzanine above the entrance, the ground-floor gallery is entirely glass-walled, and can be opened completely onto the garden. An all-glass gallery is clearly not suitable for some types of exhibit, and traditional white-box space is provided in the basement below. Rising above the gallery are seven floors of offices, while below it are storage and technical areas and four floors of parking. There are no internal staircases, and both lifts and fire-escapes are externalized to save space, the latter snaking down between the projecting glass wings of each façade. The building's structure is deliberately pared down to give an impression of virtuality.

Nouvel and Cattani's approach is a rather literal architectural interpretation of cinematic techniques such as superposition and sequential framing, and the building's flat glass screens have something of the flimsiness of a film set. Once its illusory mechanisms have been divined, their power diminishes. The building's magic is less effective than the Institut du Monde Arabe's, but it is nonetheless an elegant and imaginative response to the brief.

14.5 Observatoire
61, avenue de l'Observatoire
Claude Perrault, 1667–83
(Métro: Denfert-Rochereau, Saint-Jacques; RER: Port-Royal)

France's first national observatory, founded by Louis XIV in 1667 at the instigation of his chief minister, Jean-Baptiste Colbert, was planned in order to provide a permanent home for the Académie des Sciences (itself founded a year earlier by Colbert and the king). As well as a platform for scrutinizing the heavens, the new observatory was to be a place where academicians could meet and carry out experiments pertaining to all manner of physical phenomena. Louis's military and administrative ambitions were behind the Observatoire's creation, for he was desirous that accurate maps of his territory be drawn up with the help of the astronomers' calculations. Claude Perrault (of Louvre-colonnade fame – see 1.8), who was a physicist and a doctor before he was an architect, was commissioned to design the edifice, construction of which was begun on 21 June (the summer solstice) 1667. This date was not merely symbolic: the observatory was to be bisected by a meridian (baptized the Paris Meridian), which was traced on the ground at midday on the solstice and served to orientate the new building.

The site chosen for the observatory was out in the fields south of Paris at the edge of a fairly high-lying plain, and thus presented ideal observation conditions since the surrounding horizon was free of obstructions.

The edifice was intended to be not just a shelter for the academy's activities but also a scientific instrument in its own right. To visualize the observatory in its original state, we should imagine it without its low-lying side wings, which were added in the 1830s. Perrault's building consists essentially of a square *corps de logis* which, thanks to the meridian, is rigorously orientated according to the cardinal points. Entry is gained via a central tower on the northern façade, while on the southern front there are two octagonal towers, one at either extremity, whose facets indicate the positions of the sun at the solstices and equinoxes. For solidity's sake, the observatory was constructed entirely from precision-cut ashlar and no wood was used in the carcass, the floors all being built on stone vaults. The observatory rises three storeys on its northern façade but only two on its southern front, the ground floor becoming a basement on this side due to the presence of an enormous terrace on which experimental machines were built and operated. Each storey is taller than the one below it and is articulated by a string course, almost the only animation on otherwise extremely sober façades – a sobriety intended to convey the observatory's serious scientific purpose. The building's flat roof (originally in cement but since covered with inclined stone tiles because of drainage problems) provided an elevated observation platform, a feature superseded in the 19C by the domed copper telescope housing (1845) coiffing the southeastern tower, which mechanically turns 360° to orientate the viewing apparatus.

Inside, the building provided laboratories and meeting rooms on the ground and first floors, while the second floor houses the Cassini Room, conceived by the observatory's first director (whose name it bears) and dedicated to the Paris Meridian. The latter is materialized in copper on the floor and is surrounded by carved marble plaques representing the zodiac. An opening in the room's southern wall allowed the sun's rays to be focussed onto the meridian. Cassini was also responsible for the 55 m-deep »zenithal well«, intended for experimental purposes, that runs through

14.5 Observatoire

14.6 Hôtel Lemordant

the entire building from the roof down to the quarry tunnels over which the observatory is built (Foucault swung his first pendulums here). Also of note is the observatory's handsomely sober stone staircase, whose suspended vaults are masterpieces of stereotomy.

The magisterial Avenue de l'Observatoire, which runs along the Paris Meridian and links the observatory and the Luxembourg (6.8), was laid out in 1811. Its sumptuous gardens were realized by Gabriel Davioud in the 1860s and feature Carpeaux and Frémiet's famous Fontaine des Quatre Parties du Monde.

14.6 Hôtel Lemordant
50, avenue René-Coty
Jean-Julien Lemordant with Jean Launay, 1927–31
(Métro: Alésia; RER: Cité Universitaire)

Does architecture exist for the blind? One is tempted to reply that, in the ordinary course of events, the answer is no. Construction yes, but not architecture, if one accepts its definition as construction plus some kind of »artistry«. This »artistry« is almost always expressed visually – and is therefore imperceptible to the non-sighted – and without the faculty to perceive it as such architecture surely becomes an impossibility. But being blind does not prevent one from imagining spatial relationships and visual combinations in one's head, and this is how this curious house was designed. Its conceptor, Jean-Julien Lemordant, had studied architecture but made his career as a painter, until WWI changed his life forever – on his return from service he was blind. In 1927, he acquired the Avenue-René-Coty site, which had remained unbuilt since its creation 40 years before because of its awkward nature: very long and narrow and rising steeply behind the street line. Through the use of strips of wood attached to a board, he communicated the plans of the house he wanted built there to the architect Jean Launay, who oversaw their execution.

Given the manner of its creation and the difficulties of the site, Lemordant's house is quite extraordinary. Its lower level, which contains only a garage and the concierge's lodge, is almost entirely blind to overcome the sloping terrain, and the dwelling therefore perches on a sort of bastion. On the first floor, which runs the entire length of the site, Lemordant placed the kitchen and guest bedrooms: the site's extreme narrowness left him little choice but to line up his rooms along the avenue façade with a long, rear corridor for access. Four further floors rise above this second storey, but only at the wider end of the site. As a result, the building takes on something of the look of an ocean liner, with the bridge and superstructure of the upper stories surveying the hull and bow of the lower. On the second floor are Lemordant's dining and living rooms, the third floor is entirely given over to his studio – whose huge, glazed roof dominates the superstructure –, a mezzanine occupies the fourth floor, while the final storey contained Lemordant's bedroom, an isolated eyrie with its own private roof garden.

Aside from its unusual distribution and massing, what is especially striking about this building is the extreme sobriety of its exterior. Lemordant himself cannot have been familiar with the International Style, but Launay would clearly have been aware of it. The »ocean-liner« aesthetic of the period is here stripped down to its absolute bare essentials – rendered walls and blank openings for the windows – and consequently the house actually resembles less the work of, say, Le Corbusier or Robert Mallet-Stevens, with their emphasis on strip windows and machine-age references, and more that of Adolf Loos. In its nudity, although not in its picturesque massing and asymmetry, the Hôtel Lemordant recalls Loos's Steiner Haus (1910) in Vienna, which Lemordant may have known. He was certainly up to date with modern construction techniques, and his house displays its use of a concrete frame through its cantilevered balconies and corner windows. Indeed Lemordant – or perhaps Launay? – paid great attention to the aesthetic possibilities offered by this manner of construction, skilfully manipulating the distribution of openings and the placing of projections, which constitute the façade's only animation.

In an irony of history, Lemordant died of tear-gas poisoning in the May 1968 uprisings, and quit this world without ever explaining why, as a blind artist, he had built a huge, naturally lit studio for himself that he could not use. Visitors to the Hôtel Lemordant were astonished by their host's ability to give detailed tours of his house, during which he would lead them to particular paintings to explain their colours. In his almost maniacal, total control of his environment – necessitated by his blindness – he mirrored the design attitude of many Modern-Movement masters.

14.7 Maison-atelier Ozenfant
53, avenue Reille
Le Corbusier and Pierre Jeanneret, 1922–24
(Métro: Porte d'Orléans; RER: Cité Universitaire)

Le Corbusier's first realization in Paris, this house/artist's studio was built for his friend and collaborator Amedée Ozenfant, with whom he developed Purism – a »post-Cubist« painting movement that glorified the heroic, Platonic qualities of certain everyday objects – and cofounded the magazine *L'Esprit Nouveau*, in which they published their ideas. It was thus only to be expected that Corb would attempt to apply some of his and Ozenfant's Purist principles and vocabulary to his friend's house/studio project, although his aspirations were greatly restricted by the site.

Taking the form of an extremely narrow, irregular pentagon, the plot was hemmed in on three sides by party walls, and thus left very little room for manœuvre. Despite these constraints, Corb made what he could of the commission. The terrain was so cramped that a »free plan« could be established using conventional load-bearing walls (and the unseen party walls of the Ozenfant house are indeed of this type), but Corb nonetheless employed a slender, full-height concrete

14.7 Maison-atelier Ozenfant

column at the intersection of the two external walls so that their façades might be »free«. Corb treated these two elevations in a manner reminiscent of his Maison-Citrohan project (c. 1920–22). A deliberate pun on »Citroën«, the Citrohan house was an idealized »machine for living in« and, with its concrete frame, *pilotis*, double-height living space, »industrial« fenestration and white-washed Platonic forms, anticipated his later »five-point« villas. In the manner of the Citrohan, the Ozenfant house presents a cuboid, white-washed exterior. Its ground floor was originally given over to a garage (since removed) and services, as at the Citrohan, and its first-floor accommodation is, like the Citrohan's, reached directly via an external staircase (in the form of an elegant spiral because of the cramped terrain). As at the Citrohan, »industrial« fenestration is used including, at first-floor level, the strip windows that would become a Corbusian leitmotif. Corb applied all his usual rigour to the arrangement of the building's deceptively simple elevations, employing the Classical device of regulating lines to govern their proportions.

At the Maison Citrohan, the double-height living space had recalled an artist's studio; at the Ozenfant house, Corb was required to supply the real thing. It perches at the top of the building and is clearly signalled by its ample glazing. The house's roof terrace, seemingly such a Corbusian motif, is not in fact original (it was added in 1946), and replaced saw-tooth skylights – an industrializing form borrowed directly from the factory – that formerly lit the atelier. Besides the changes already listed, the house has also had an extra floor added at the rear of the terrace and has seen alterations to its first-floor entrance; all these modifications make it difficult today to appreciate the clarity of Corb's original concept.

14.8 Cité Universitaire
1–83, boulevard Jourdan
Various architects, begun 1923
(RER: Cité Universitaire)

Constructed at great expense in the aftermath of Napoleon's defeat and the allied occupation of Paris, the Thiers fortifications (1840–45), named after the minister who proposed them, encircled the capital with 94 bastions and a 250 m-wide glacis. They served but once, in 1871, resisting only four months against the invading Prussians. Half a century later, WWI conclusively demonstrated that modern warfare had rendered such installations obsolete, and destruction of the Thiers ring was duly voted by parliament in 1919. In 1920, at the initiative of the then education minister, André Honnorat, 28 ha of the land thus recovered – bastions 81–83 and the glacis that went with them – were reserved for the construction of a *cité internationale universitaire*. Conceived in the aftermath of the Great War, the Cité was intended to provide low-cost accommodation for students of all nationalities studying at Parisian universities, in a spirit of pacifism and fraternity. Brought together at the Cité, the world's future elite, it was hoped, would come to a better understanding of each other and, once back in their native countries, would champion global peace and co-operation.

Honnorat's scheme might never have taken off had it not been for the generosity of a wealthy industrialist, Emile Deutsch de la Meurthe, who pledged 10 million *francs-or* for the construction of accommodation for 350 French students. The Fondation Deutsch-de-la-Meurthe (Lucien Bechmann, 1923–35) was thus the first realization at the Cité. Meurthe had called for a garden-city approach to the design, and Bechmann duly proposed six pavilions loosely grouped around a seventh building that served as a sort of »town hall« for the community. For the façades, the architect employed a Cotswolds pastiche directly inspired by Oxford colleges. As well as the Fondation Deutsch-de la Meurthe, Bechmann was responsible for the Cité-U masterplan, which, on the site of the demolished bastions, provided for the construction of low-rise halls of residence loosely scattered in a garden setting, while the glacis, in keeping with municipal directives on the redevelopment of the fortifications, was reserved for parkland and sports facilities.

Between 1925 and 1939, 19 new halls were built at the Cité, for the most part financed by foreign governments invited to participate in the scheme. Architects were encouraged to express »nationality« in the pavilions, thereby producing a disparate collection of buildings that was criticized by some for disunity and for the lack of inter-pavilion dialogue, and praised by others for its pluralism and diversity. Examples of »nationalizing« pavilions are the Fondation Hellénique (Nicolas Zahos, completed 1932), whose concrete frame sports Classical stone garb with an entrance portico inspired by the Erechtheion, the Collège d'Espagne (Lopez Otero, 1927–35), whose silhouette recalls Salamanca University and the Escorial, and the Collège Franco-Britannique (Pierre Martin and Maurice Vieu, 1929–37), in Tudorbethan Oxbridge style. The enormous Maison Internationale (Bechmann and Jean-Frédéric Larson, 1929–36), which houses a library, a restaurant, a theatre and other communal facilities, is a pastiche of Fontainebleau (38.1). Two buildings from this period stand out in their uncompromising Modernity and in the quality of their architecture: Dudok's Pavillon Néerlandais (14.11) and Le Corbusier's seminal Pavillon Suisse (14.10).

Post war, a further 17 pavilions were added, bringing the total to the current 37. In contrast to their interwar predecessors, almost all were entirely Modernist in concept, the best known being Le Corbusier's Brutalist Maison du Brésil (today the Fondation Franco-Brésilienne, 14.9). In comparable mood is the last pavilion built at the Cité, the former Maison de l'Iran (Mossem Foroughi, Hedar Ghiai and Claude Parent, 1961–69), today the Résidence Avicenne. In response to the brutalism of the *boulevard périphérique* (1960–73), which cuts across the edge of the Cité, the architects sus-

14.10 Pavillon Suisse. South front

pended two four-storey blocks from a massive grey-steel frame, an arrangement intended to be easily comprehensible from a fast-moving car. A monumental spiral staircase counterpoints the frame's orthogonal rigidity on the boulevard side of this harsh, hard-nosed building.

14.9 Fondation Franco-Brésilienne (former Maison du Brésil)
7L, boulevard Jourdan
Le Corbusier and Lucio Costa, 1954–59
(RER: Cité Universitaire)

20 years after Le Corbusier completed the Pavillon Suisse (14.10), Lucio Costa – one of several South-American architects who had been greatly influenced by Corbusian ideas – was presented with almost exactly the same brief when he was asked to build a student residence for his native Brazil at the Cité Universitaire (14.8). Needing the help of an architectural practice *in situ*, and in deference to his master, Costa asked Le Corbusier to collaborate with him on the execution of the design, also hoping that this gesture would bury a long-standing disagreement between them over paternity of the Ministry of Education in Rio (1936–43). Unfortunately, this second collaboration was not to be a happy one either.

Costa's initial idea was based very closely on the Pavillon Suisse, with a principal bar on *pilotis* containing the student rooms, and connecting low-rise structures at ground-floor level housing the Maison's other facilities. Like the Pavillon Suisse, the Maison du Brésil was to be steel-framed and panel-clad, although unlike its predecessor it was to perch on slender rather than massive *pilotis*. Costa also reworked the design of the Pavillon Suisse's northern façade for his new building, adding a sensual bulge to its orthogonality and disposing the square corridor openings in chequerboard alternance, as well glazing the whole of the central section. The first setback to the faithful translation into reality of Costa's initial concept came from the Cité-U authorities, who wanted the building's orientation reversed (Costa had intended that the bedrooms face west and the access corridors east; the Cité-U board wanted the student rooms to face east). This change meant that, as originally conceived, the ground-floor buildings no longer functioned. Costa's initial reaction was to insist on starting again from scratch taking into account the new orientation, but Corb managed to persuade him that the ground-floor spaces alone could be reconfigured, and undertook the task himself, entirely redesigning the areas in question. Nor did Corb's interventions stop there. He subsequently insisted on the addition of substantial *brise-soleils* (at the time his favourite leitmotif) to the bedroom windows, pleading their utility as *brise-pluies* that would protect the window frames against Parisian precipitation. Costa reluctantly agreed, but asked that their inner surfaces be painted in the colours of the Brazilian flag, which was

14.10 Pavillon Suisse. North front

done. More radically yet, Corb next demanded that the building be realised entirely in raw concrete, and set about remodelling its exterior in line with his then-favoured Brutalist aesthetic, making the *pilotis* cumbersomely massive and replacing Costa's smooth surfaces with rough-cast concrete panels. For Costa this was too much, the building Corb had produced was, he felt, »anti-Brazilian«. »We like clear and natural solutions«, he wrote to Corb, »and that which is simple and harmonious, we are sensitive to grace. We do not like that which is brutal, forbidding and complicated. We do not like jagged, angular and aggressive forms.« Despite his convictions, Costa eventually gave in but, no longer recognizing his work in the finished product, renounced all claim to authorship. Nor did the Maison itself benefit from its mixed parentage: although a representative example of Corb's Brutalist period and the closest thing to a *unité d'habitation* to be found in Paris, it is not considered one of Corb's masterpieces.

The building's fate following its completion was just as turbulent as its conception. In 1971, the Brazilian government massively cut the Maison's funding, with the result that the Cité-U authorities were eventually forced to step in and take partial control (hence the change in name). In the meantime, the building's fabric suffered from the resulting lack of upkeep, to the extent that, in 1997, the Maison had to be closed for safety reasons. In 1998–2000, a huge renovation programme was undertaken to consolidate its deteriorating concrete and bring the accommodation up to modern standards. One bedroom was restored to its original state, complete with Charlotte-Perriand furniture, and is open to the public.

14.10 Pavillon Suisse
7K, boulevard Jourdan
Le Corbusier and Pierre Jeanneret, 1930–33
(RER: Cité Universitaire)

Like Le Corbusier's contemporaneous Salvation-Army hostel (13.6), this seminal building prefigured his famous *unités d'habitation* and was partly conceived as both a manifesto and a life-size experimental mock-up for ideas put forward in the utopian Ville-Radieuse project (1928–31), his most developed conception of the machine-age city. Paradoxically, it also marked the turning point in Corb's thinking and aesthetic from crisp, sleek, industrially mass-produceable and universally applicable *objets-types* towards a more individualized, low-tech, ponderously sculptural and workman-produced architecture.

Programmatically the Pavillon Suisse was like all the other pavilions at the Cité Universitaire (see 14.8), providing basic accommodation for international students studying in Paris, but it stood out in its uncompromising Modernism, which contrasted strongly with the nationalizing historicist dress adopted by most of its confrères. As at the Salvation-Army hostel, Corb chose a simple orthogonal bar for the principal part of the building, orientated to catch the southern sun, with the student rooms lined up along the meridional façade, which is entirely glazed. In contrast, the northern elevation, along which run access corridors, is perforated with small square openings. The lifts and staircase are separate from the main building, enclosed in a discrete volume jutting out from the northern façade. Behind it extends a single-storey structure housing the building's foyer, a common room and accommodation for the concierge.

The famous »five points of a new architecture« are clearly demonstrated in the Pavillon Suisse: the main part of the building is lifted off the ground on *pilotis*, horizontally orientated glazing is used (albeit no longer in strip form), the façades are non-loadbearing and »free«, the final storey includes a roof terrace, and a free plan is demonstrated on the ground floor. Corb originally intended to construct the Pavillon's frame entirely in steel – thereby demonstrating the prefabrication possibilities of the *objet-type* it was supposed to represent – but the presence of quarry tunnels under the site compelled him to use concrete for the *pilotis*, although the floors above are metal framed. These *pilotis* are one of the many departures from Corb's Purist vocabulary to be observed at the Pavillon Suisse. In contrast to the insubstantial, cylindrical supports of his Purist buildings, those at the Pavillon are massive (thinner *pilotis* would no doubt have appeared too flimsy under the heavy bulk of the main slab) and subtly modelled, and their concrete is entirely bare and untreated. For the lift/staircase tower, Corb used an irregular curvilinear volume (that contrasts nicely with the rectangularity of the main bar rather as in a Purist painting) instead of one of the Euclidean solids that formerly made up his repertoire. More uncharacteristic still, the principal unglazed parts of the building are clad in stone (not a material one associates with Corb) and, although it is precision machined and mounted, the presence of its joints (which reflect the building's structure) and grain constitute a distinct deviation from the Platonic purity sought in the pristine white villas of the 1920s. (Corb's use of stone at the Pavillon may partly have been prompted by the weathering and maintenance problems he had experienced with his stucco constructions.) A much greater variety of materials is exhibited at the Pavillon than in previous buildings, including, as well as the aforementioned stone cladding and raw concrete, glass bricks and, on the projecting ground-floor volume, rubble-stone walling, whose technological primitivism and picturesqueness are a far cry from the sophisticated machined image of his 1920s output. All these modifications to Corb's vocabulary herald his Brutalist buildings of the 1950s, of which good Parisian examples are the Maison du Brésil (14.9) and the Maisons Jaoul (26.2).

Despite these changes there is still continuity with previous preoccupations. The *objet-type* aspect of the Pavillon is clearly manifested in the fact that, with its narrow rectangular volume sitting on low legs, the main bar resembles a piece of furniture, a chest of drawers for living in that can be moved around anywhere. This furniture metaphor can be taken further when one considers the building's structure: the steel frame is divided up into bays each of which is the width of a student bedroom, and the latter can be conceived of as structurally separate from the main building, slotted into it like bottles in a rack. This cellular composition prefigures both the *unités* and the monastery of La Tourette near Lyons (1957–60). The concern to ensure maximum exposure to the life-giving rays of the sun expressed in the Ville-Radieuse project is here taken care of by the abundant southern glazing and the roof terraces, and the *pilotis* allow the greenery of the Cité Universitaire, visually at least, to flow uninterrupted through the building at ground level, emblematic of Corb's desire to create anti-street, parkland cities that would, he hoped, banish the ills of the chokingly mineral, 19C townscape. But even as he experimented with the Pavillon Suisse, Corb was losing faith in the ability of machine-age, production-line architecture to solve every urban problem.

Contemporary reaction to the Pavillon was, in some quarters, extremely hostile. Criticism centred on its representational muteness – considered inappropriate for a building that many thought should transmit some idea of »Swissness« – and on its sobriety, which some found shockingly severe. This is partly explicable in that the Pavillon Suisse is certainly drier and more utilitarian than Corb's Purist projects, lacking their otherworldly aesthetic; nor does it have the ponderous power present in so much of his later work. It is nonetheless a sleek, neat and elegant solution to the brief, and was much imitated. Moreover, for a building that is now 70 years old, it has aged and weathered extraordinarily well, in stark contrast to many of Corb's other projects. Indeed it is hard to believe that the Pavillon dates from the early 1930s, for it resembles more a building of the 1960s or 1970s – the period when the Corbusian legacy was at its most influential –, and it

14.11 Pavillon Néerlandais

224 14th *arrondissement*

may simply be that it was too ahead of its time to be properly appreciated when first completed.

14.11 Pavillon Néerlandais
61, boulevard Jourdan
Willem Marinus Dudok, 1928–38
(RER: Cité Universitaire)

Dudok's contribution to the Cité Universitaire (14.8) for his native Netherlands is a suave example of the International Style, of which he was a noted exponent – his town hall at Hilversum, near Amsterdam (1926–28), had already garnered considerable renown by the time of the Cité-U commission. In Paris he employed the same streamlined vocabulary as at Hilversum: clearly defined planar slabs arranged in elegant compositions, their surfaces cadenced by metal strip windows whose horizontality is set off against carefully juxtaposed verticals, the whole coated in a layer of white render that dissimulates the building's structure and emphasizes the abstract quality of its volumes. Arranged around a central courtyard containing a sizeable ornamental pool, the Pavillon features two tall wings on its boulevard side that protect the courtyard from traffic noise, the blocks to the rear being more domestic in scale. Communal areas give onto the courtyard, while student rooms occupy the floors above. Despite the problems associated with rendered buildings, the Pavillon has aged well, and appears as coolly sleek as when it first opened.

Like the work of his French contemporary Rob Mallet-Stevens (see 16.2 and 16.12), which is in a similar vein, Dudok's œuvre lacked the social, utopian and moral concerns that characterized the buildings of the »greats« of the International Style. His machine-age aesthetic is simply that, with none of the experimentalism of the radical Modernists. This said, their underlying conventionality does not make his buildings any the less thoughtfully designed or suitable for their purpose.

14.12 Institut National du Judo
25, avenue de la Porte-de-Châtillon
Architecture Studio, 1988–2001
(Métro: Porte d'Orléans)

Judo has become increasingly popular in France over the last 20 years, and this project, jointly commissioned by the Ville de Paris and the Fédération Française de Judo (FFJ), was intended to provide a permanent home for the country's national judo competitions. Besides the 1,800-seat dojo itself, the brief called for training and education facilities, offices for the federation, accommodation for visiting competitors, and press/conference rooms. The site selected for the Institut was out on the city's edge in a ring of parks and sports facilities occupying the former glacis of Paris's 19C fortifications (see also 14.8). A design competition was organized in 1988 and won by Architecture Studio.

The new Institut's site was triangular, delimited on one side by the Avenue de la Porte-de-Châtillon, on another by the Montrouge Cemetery, and on the third by the notorious *boulevard périphérique*, Paris's orbital motorway. This was not the only time Architecture Studio had been faced with the *périphérique* problem – their university hall of residence (18.9) on the city's northern boundary also borders the motorway – and, as in the 18th, they were forced to make the presence of this major nuisance a principal consideration in the design. A sports hall necessitates less acoustic isolation than dwellings or offices, so here it was simply a question of running the dojo building along the *périphérique* and keeping the offices and competitors' accommodation away from the motorway. Grouped together in a long bar, the offices, etc. were placed on the cemetery edge of the site, running up to the motorway, and separated from the main hall by a semi-covered street, an arrangement that allowed the dojo building to be fully displayed on the city (avenue) side. Designed to convey externally all the civic importance of the Institut and fix its identity in the cityscape, the dojo building took the form of an enormous, copper-covered quarter dome, an easily comprehensible form that could be slipped into the apex of the triangle and would provide a homogeneous umbrella for all the varied spaces to be housed under it.

Such, at least, was the scheme at the time of the competition. In the 13 years between design and completion, radical changes in programme were introduced that almost sank the whole operation. As is so often the case, it was financing, or rather lack of it, that prompted these modifications. The FFJ simply could not afford the building, and consequently, in order to provide much-needed rental income, dictated the addition of a 357-room hotel, the provision of space on the avenue side for a sports-equipment retailer (in the event the chain Go Sport), and modification of the jodo so that it could accommodate sports other than just judo and seat 2,500 instead of the 1,800 initially planned. The resultant increase in occupational density led the firemen in charge of safety regulations to require increased security measures for the basement car park, which nearly engendered a costly redesign that would have jeopardized the entire scheme. Luckily, the architects found a clever way round the problem, and their basic concept was flexible enough to allow addition of extra elements without being entirely distorted. Thus, the office bar could be enlarged to include the hotel and the jodo could be rotated by 90° under its dome to make possible the capacity increase and also to allow squeezing in of the Go Sport store.

Within this new commercial context, the blind, black-concrete wall of the jodo building on the *périphérique* could handily be turned into a giant billboard advertising the Go Sport store. If the cemetery bar may have suffered from the redesign – its rather distressing lack of external finesse is probably imputable to budgetary juggling –, the jodo's interior actually benefited from the rethink occasioned by the modifications. Reorientated, it now makes better use of the dramatic interior curve of the dome, whose soaring profile ennobles this building both inside and out.

14.13 Apartment buildings and housing
17–19, rue des Suisses
Herzog & de Meuron, 1996–2000
(Métro: Plaisance)

So far this is the only Parisian project by the celebrated Swiss team headed by Jacques Herzog and Pierre de Meuron, winners of the 2001 Pritzker Prize and best known for London's vast Tate Modern (1995–2000). During the firm's 20 years' existence its output has been extremely varied, but a common thread can be traced throughout Herzog & de Meuron's œuvre, essentially in the often rather earthy minimalism of their buildings, their concern for surface effect and their use of rough, »industrial« materials in unexpected contexts. All these traits are to be found in this unusual complex of 57 public-sector dwellings, built for the Ville de Paris.

Situated in a partly redeveloped area of the 14th *arrondissement* that is still essentially 19C in character, the complex occupies a sizeable chunk of land in the middle of a city block, with two stretches of street frontage – a narrow band on the Rue Jonquoy and a more substantial tract on the Rue des Suisses. The architects chose to respect the surrounding urbanity by inserting seven-storey-high buildings into the gaps on each street, thereby closing the block in the manner of the 19C city. All semblance between Herzog & de Meuron's buildings and their older neighbours ends here, however. The street blocks are essentially very simple: a regular stacking of thin, cantilevered floors with all-glass façades that are recessed to leave narrow balconies on both the street and rear fronts. What makes these elevations other than banal is the outer skin the architects have devised for them: a series of unpainted, metal-mesh sunscreens, which concertina out of the way when open but which, when closed, entirely veil the buildings behind their forbidding, grey impenetrability. The effect is disconcerting to the point of intimidation, reminiscent of prisons or the keep-out vocabulary of American gated communities. Rather like Christian Hauvette's concrete-shielded crèche (11.5), Herzog & de Meuron's building plays with notions of public v. private and security v. insecurity. As well as sending out »back-off« signals to would-be burglars, the shutters act as industrial-strength net curtains that hide the activities going on inside the buildings and even camouflage their architectural form, which becomes lost behind the relentless grid of the shutters' metal mesh. Counteracting the severity of this on the Rue-des-Suisses frontage are kinks in the building's alignment, which mirror the shutters' concertina action and also constitute a cheeky raspberry blown at traditional, street-line-respecting urbanism.

As well as the two street buildings, a third structure within the city block completes the housing complex. Here the tone changes entirely. Behind the towering metal barricade of the street buildings shelter distinctly domestic-scale dwellings in a garden context. The city block's interior measures a rather awkward 150×21 m, and the architects wisely chose to go with this, filling the space with a narrow, three-storey building, divided vertically into individual houses, that runs the entire length of the site. Herzog & de Meuron originally wanted to park it up against the neighbouring structures to the northeast, but residents insisted that it be moved out into the middle of the plot. The architects turned this to their advantage, using the space gained behind to add one-storey projections that contain the houses' kitchens and bathrooms and serve to delimit small private gardens. The building thus exactly mimics the disposition of 19C British terraced housing. In the treatment of its exterior envelope, however, it could not be less like its cross-Channel forbears. The principal, southwestern façade is entirely glazed and features continuous verandas whose warm wooden decking and roll-down shutters contrast dialectically with the hard-nosed metal-mesh of the street buildings. So, too, does the treatment of the city-block building's side and rear façades. The raw concrete from which they are cast has been left exposed, but will not remain so for long: rope trellises have been stretched across these elevations and climbing plants will soon provide them with a living, green, camouflaging overcoat.

14.13 Apartment buildings and housing

15th *arrondissement*

15.1 Tour Montparnasse
Place Raoul-Dautry
Eugène Beaudouin, Urbain Cassan, Louis Hoym de Marien and Jean Saubot, 1959–73
(Métro: Montparnasse-Bienvenüe)

As Paris proper's first and only real skyscraper, the 57-storey, 210 m-high Tour Montparnasse – in its day Europe's tallest building – was bound to be the subject of considerable controversy. Indeed nearly a decade went by between the announcement of its construction, in 1959, and the granting of planning permission for the building, in 1968, and it was only due to the personal backing of the ultra-Modernist, pro-tower President Pompidou and his culture minister, André Malraux, that it got built at all. The Tour Montparnasse was but one element in a comprehensive redevelopment scheme concerning the 19C Gare Montparnasse, which the SNCF had been wanting to replace since the 1930s. By the 1950s, the 14th and 15th *arrondissements* were suffering badly from the industrial decline that marked the mid-20C, and the public authorities controlling Paris decided to join forces with the SNCF to create a new business district on the site of the old station, which, they hoped, would revitalize the area's fortunes. The redevelopment was to be carried out in two phases: firstly the station would be demolished and rebuilt to the south, with a complement of office buildings and housing, and secondly a shopping centre and further office accommodation would be erected on the site of the old terminus. Over 480,000 m² of space were programmed, which had to be squeezed into a site of only 8 ha; recourse to a tower was thus the obvious, although not the only, solution to this conundrum.

Construction of the station and the 50 m-high bar blocks surrounding it was carried out in 1960–69 without a murmur of protest from anywhere. Meanwhile, phase two, which comprised the shopping centre and tower, was continuously stalled due to the polemic surrounding the building of a skyscraper in central Paris. The objections were obvious – an unnecessary and costly excrescence, the tower would spoil the views, irrevocably alter the character of old Paris by imposing its brooding bulk on the city and, worst of all, set a dangerous precedent. In the event, the 1973 oil crisis and resulting property slump, combined with the anti-tower policies of President Giscard d'Estaing, Pompidou's successor, ensured that the proliferation of Tour Montparnasses feared by many Parisians never occurred.

As towers go, the Tour Montparnasse is not a bad example. Because of their inevitable hugeness, skyscrapers are best treated as boldly and simply stated free-standing objects; any attempt to smother them in detail or break up their bulk usually fails. On the other hand, less is more can be overdone, resulting in crass, bland, monotonous monsters. The Tour Montparnasse

15.1 Tour Montparnasse

avoids both these pitfalls. Its rectilinear profile and chocolate-brown, bronzed-glass facing ensure that it dramatically marks the horizon, rather in the manner of one of Stanley Kubrick's mysterious *2001: A Space Odyssey* monoliths, while its gently curving principle façades, introverted side elevations and varied cladding detailing – whose upright elements emphasize the tower's verticality – confer enough subtlety and elegance to avoid accusations of cheapness or crudity. Built on foundations that descend 70 m to the bedrock below, the tower comprises a central concrete core (containing the lifts and staircases) from which are suspended cantilevered steel floors that carry the metal-framed, curtain-wall façades. A high degree of prefabrication was used in the tower's construction, thereby allowing it to rise at the very rapid rate of six floors per month.

Visited by over 700,000 tourists annually, who are attracted by the views from its summit, the Tour Montparnasse has become an accepted, if not loved, part of the Parisian cityscape, and no longer raises much in the way of comment. It certainly seems a good deal less offensive today than the distressingly bland and repetitive office bars surrounding the rebuilt Gare Montparnasse. Special planning dispensation was needed to build the tower and station, and it is unlikely in today's climate that such a waiver would be granted again. Strict height restrictions will thus ensure that the Tour Montparnasse remains Paris's only skyscraper.

15.2 Former editorial offices of Le Monde

15.2 Former editorial offices of *Le Monde*
13–15, rue Falguière
Pierre Du Besset and Dominique Lyon, 1988–90
(Métro: Falguière)

Compelled by financial circumstances to sell its old headquarters in central Paris, the famous national daily *Le Monde* decided to rationalize its activities by moving its printing and commercial departments out to the suburbs at Ivry and finding a new, smaller Parisian home for the editorial department. A property developer proposed leasehold office space in a disused garage near Montparnasse, an offer the newspaper accepted on the condition that it be allowed to commission an architect of its own choosing to carry out conversion of the garage. The developer agreed, and *Le Monde* duly organized a limited architectural competition to find a suitable proposal, inviting young, unknown talent to compete. In the brief, the newspaper called for a scheme that would facilitate the free circulation of people and ideas, provide an image consistent with its no-nonsense, pared-down style, and be realizable within the extremely tight deadline – less than 20 months from competition to handover.

Apart from strengthening its floors, Du Besset and Lyon's winning scheme left the garage's interior essentially as was to provide flexible office space that could be modified as the journalists wished. The site was deep, and to get light into its middle the architects replaced the garage's ramp, which occupied the building's centre, with a generous, glass-roofed atrium that also served to access the editorial offices, via balconies. In the airy, glass-fronted entrance hall, which is linked to the atrium by an escalator, they paid special attention to the effects of light, using flooring fabricated from recycled industrial glass and wall paint containing microscopic glass beads to impart a touch of opalescence to its surfaces. However, their principal gesture was external: in place of the garage's anonymous curtain walls with their regulation upper-floor step-backs, Du Besset and Lyon conceived perfectly smooth, aluminium-and-glass façades that link the ground floor to the roof-line in one continuous, sweeping curve

of 42 m radius, thereby producing a strong street presence that is both simple and bold. The façades' streamlined profile posed a technical challenge in terms of both surface effect – great precision was required to achieve the immaculate smoothness desired – and waterproofing, the upper levels acting as roofing rather than as an elevation. Most of the contractors approached pronounced the façades unbuildable, especially given the tight deadline, and Durand, who accepted the job, ran into difficulties that ultimately delayed completion by a couple of months.

Although delighted with its new home, *Le Monde* found that the separation of editorial and commercial services was too costly in terms of wasted time and duplicated jobs, and consequently gave up its lease on the Rue-Falguière building in 1996 for bigger premises. Du Besset and Lyon's offices now house the Institut d'Aménagement et d'Urbanisme de la Région d'Ile-de-France

15.3 Notre-Dame-de-l'Arche-de-l'Alliance
81, rue d'Alleray
Architecture Studio, 1985–98
(Métro: Convention)

A brand-new church for a brand-new parish, Notre-Dame-de-l'Arche-de-l'Alliance (Our Lady of the Ark of the Covenant) posed a third-millennium dilemma: how, in this sophisticated, secular age, can one create buildings of convincing spiritual and religious ambience without resorting to a pastiche of traditional church forms? During the 18C and especially the French Revolution, Enlightenment extremists characterized the Catholic church as a dangerous force of lurid superstition to be replaced by the rational precepts of a reasoned religion, as exemplified by free-masonry. Here, in this late-20C building, we find a Catholic church building that appropriates forms and imagery associated with the Enlightenment tradition to appeal to a generation that is the product of over two centuries of French rational thinking and administration.

At the core of Architecture Studio's church is a perfect cube, a Euclidean, Enlightenment solid *par excel-*

15.3 Notre-Dame-de-l'Arche-de-l'Alliance

lence that also recalls the Heavenly Jerusalem (as all medieval churches were supposed to do), whose plan, in the Bible, is described as forming a perfect square. In their perfection, cubes can also be said to represent the divine. Perched on twelve *pilotis* (a number chosen to represent both the apostles and the tribes of Israel, and also a further reference to the Heavenly Jerusalem), the church is enveloped in a stainless-steel grid framework that materially extends its presence while blurring the exact division between the building and its surroundings. This grid can also be seen to constitute, by extension, the base of some Cartesian conception of infinite (and therefore Godly) space. Almost the only external reference to traditional church architecture at Notre-Dame is the »virtual« bell tower, which is also constructed from aluminium trellising. In what is a slightly facile gesture, it signals the building's function both through its form and through the cross contained within its upper levels. The cube of the church proper is clad in orange-brown wood-fibre/resin panels which, on closer inspection, turn out to be serigraphed with the text of the *Ave Maria* in French. According to the Old Testament, the Ark of the Covenant was a gold-plated, acacia-wood coffer containing the stone tablets of the Ten Commandments, and was symbolic of the presence of the Almighty; in both its form and cladding, the central cube of the church is intended to recall this ancient, holy casket, although in its pristine, plasticky smoothness it is clearly of the Hi-tech era.

Entrance to Notre-Dame can be gained either via the baptistery, which nestles between the *pilotis* underneath the principal cube, or via the imposing steps (there is also a lift) leading up to the eastern side of the church. The principal internal space has been given the form of a three-dimensional Maltese cross, one of whose arms takes the form of a semicircular apse behind the altar. Nestling under the roof, in the space subtracted from the main cube to form the Maltese cross, are parish rooms and accommodation for the clergy, reached via hidden spiral staircases. A sunken roof terrace forms a sort of suspended cloister. The main space is clad in the same panels as the exterior (although without the stencilling) and is lit via large, lateral, stained-glass windows and a central funnel directed at the altar. Rather gratuitously, the external aluminium trellis intrudes into the church at the level of the altar, thus forming a sort of rudimentary rood screen. And since this is the age of electricity, the cross behind the altar is a projection, God being, of course, light.

Serious, sober and thoughtful, Notre-Dame-de-l'Arche-de-l'Alliance is a worthy attempt to build a »rational« church. Somehow it does not quite come off, though: the interior gives the impression of a studio theatre, despite the lighting effects designed to dress it up with a bit of religious mystery, while the exterior seems overly flimsy and mannered. Cubic, Cartesian, orthogonal – a hymn to the right angle – it appeals to the intellect, forgetting that religious belief is largely a question of emotions.

15.4 Social housing

15.4 Social housing
5, rue de la Saïda
Auguste Labussière, 1912–19
(Métro: Porte de Versailles)

Commissioned by the Groupe des Maisons Ouvrières (until the creation, in 1914, of the Office Public d'Habitation de la Ville de Paris, the provision of social housing in the French capital was entirely in the private sector), this estate was intended for large, very-low-income families who had previously been living in slums. Rents therefore had to be kept to a minimum, meaning that in order to make the scheme financially viable initial investment also had to be minimal. The challenge facing Labussière was thus to provide sanitary and dignified dwellings on a very tight budget.

Five storeys high and therefore fairly densely populated, Labussière's scheme is divided into symmetrically disposed, agglomerated pavilions (rather in the manner of a French château), thus ensuring that all the apartments receive plentiful light and air, conditions considered necessary not so much for the residents' pleasure as for their health (dark and airless accommodation being thought to propagate tuberculosis). This manner of grouping the estate also avoided the monotony of orthogonal bars, and its picturesque massing is complemented by the external, open-air staircases that connect the different pavilions, creating a play of solid and void. For the buildings' structure, Labussière chose an exposed, trabeated reinforced-cement frame with brick infill and flat, cement roofs, a rational and economic choice of materials and construction. Handsomely proportioned, the result is sober but not dull, and appears surprisingly »modern« given its vintage.

The apartments themselves, which were all identical with a surface area of 56 m² and three bedrooms, were organized around a communal kitchen/living room that constituted the linchpin of the design. Well lit and ventilated, it was suitable for the exercise of cottage industries (which were encouraged), and allowed the rest of the flat (i.e. the children) to be surveyed at one glance. It was also considered the »moral« heart

15.5 Apartment building

of the home. (Apartments for better-off working-class families tended to have separate kitchens and living rooms and be disposed around an access hallway.) While each flat had running water and its own lavatory, the bathing facilities were communal; this was not only for reasons of economy, but also to encourage hygienic habits by exposing residents' behaviour to the gaze of their neighbours. This was also why the staircases were open air – »immoral« encounters were less likely to take place in broad daylight in front of other residents, and there was an added advantage in that cleaning costs were reduced. In its architectural determinism, the Rue-de-la-Saïda estate took its cue from pioneering projects such as the Cité Napoléon (9.4). As a result of the experience he gained with the Groupe des Maisons Ouvrières, Labussière was later appointed *architecte voyer* in charge of social housing for the Ville de Paris.

15.5 Apartment building
3–5, boulevard Victor
Pierre Patout, 1929–34
(Métro: Balard)
Trained as an architect, Pierre Patout first made a name for himself as an interior designer at the 1925 Exposition des Arts Décoratifs, in collaboration with the furniture maker Jacques-Emile Ruhlmann. Their exhibition success brought the commission for the dining room of the ocean liner *Ile-de-France* (1926/27) and, following the *Atlantique* (1928–30), their nautical career culminated with the famous dining room of the equally celebrated *Normandie* (1934/35), for which Patout also designed the swimming pool and chapel. Perhaps because of his marine experience, Patout championed the »ocean-liner« style in his realizations on terra firma.

This speculative block, of which Patout was also developer, stands on a wedge-shaped site that was reputed »unbuildable«. Sandwiched between the boulevard and a railway embankment, it narrows from 10 m at its widest point to a mere 2.8 m at its apex. Patout nonetheless managed to squeeze in 3,200 m^2 of floor space, including his own triplex apartment at the building's »prow«. Given the site's shape, it was perhaps inevitable that the finished block should resemble a ship, but Patout deliberately strengthened the comparison. The building's »waterline« is delineated by the projecting upper floors, the »hull« is designated by an area of vertical fenestration, while the »superstructure«, signalled by horizontal bands of windows, descends in a series of terraces to the »bow«. The uppermost floors are cadenced in a manner reminiscent of funnels. This is an elegant solution to the challenge of a difficult site, despite the ugly embankment elevation, which did not receive the suave finishing of the principal façades.

15.6 Cité des Artistes
230, rue Saint-Charles and 69, rue Leblanc
Michel Kagan, 1989–92
(Métro: Balard)
Commissioned by the Ville de Paris as part of the Citroën-car-factory redevelopment, this complex comprises 38 subsidized artists studios with attached dwellings, as well as twelve ordinary public-sector apartments. The site allocated to the *cité* is at one extremity of a long path that diagonally traverses the Parc André-Citroën (15.8), and it thus fell to Michel Kagan's building both to close the perspective in a suitable manner and constitute a fitting entry to the park. With this in mind, the planning authorities had imagined a semicircular edifice whose convex façade would give

15.6 Cité des Artistes

onto the park and mask the rears of 19C buildings on the Rue Leblanc. It soon became clear, however, that the requirements of the brief could not be squeezed into the planners' crescent, and Kagan was forced to ask for more space. The idea of curvature was retained, though, with the semicircle becoming a central rotunda in the built composition. Kagan clearly rose to the challenge of the awkwardly shaped site, and produced a building that revels in the difficulties of its context.

Like Richard Meier, whose Canal+ headquarters (15.10) stand at the other end of the Parc André-Citroën's diagonal path, Kagan's work takes inspiration from Le Corbusier, more particularly the master's immaculate white Purist creations of the 1920s. Also like Meier, Kagan has a proclivity for extreme formal complexity which is not to be found in Corb's œuvre. Indeed both Meier and Kagan's output can be viewed as a mannerist, aestheticized appropriation of Corbusian form, divested of the social ideals that shaped the original. At the Cité des Artistes we find a whole gamut of Corbusian vocabulary put together in what Kenneth Frampton (one of Kagan's champions) aptly described as a Chinese puzzle. Divided amongst four separate buildings – one triangular, one circular, one square and the final rather amorphous – the studios and apartments were all individually designed and contrived so that the ateliers face north and the living spaces west, a *tour de force* of logistical ingenuity. In its interaction with the 19C buildings on the Rue Leblanc, the *cité* becomes part of a traditional Parisian city block with a courtyard at its centre, a good-mannered neighbour whose urbanism has nothing to do with Corbusian planning doctrine. Instead Corb's influence is felt in a host of formal features: all-white, concrete finish, obsessive horizontality, strip windows, glass bricks, slender *pilotis*, ocean-liner handrails, and so on. But Kagan's building is plastically diverse in a way that Corb's creations are not, to the extent that it looks completely different on each façade. There is not a dull moment anywhere, and although overworked the *cité* is a tribute to Kagan's keen eye for the dramatic possibilities of light, shade, layering and juxtaposition.

15.7 Hôpital Européen Georges-Pompidou
20, rue Leblanc
Aymeric Zublena, 1983–2000
(Métro: Balard; RER: Boulevard Victor)

Billed as the hospital of the 21C, this giant complex was designed to replace four existing hospitals, with a catchment area of more than 570,000 people. Economies of expenditure and furtherance of interdisciplinary co-operation were the main motivations behind the creation of the Hôpital Européen Georges-Pompidou (HEGP), whose 120,000 m² and 827 beds came in at the enormous total cost of 1.8 billion francs. Programmed as part of the vast Citroën-car-factory redevelopment, the hospital is well connected transport wise, standing as it does between Métro and RER sta-

15.7 Hôpital Européen Georges-Pompidou

tions and at a stone's throw from the *boulevard périphérique* and the riverside expressways. The site is both long and deep, and one of the architect's priorities was to get as much daylight as possible into the building, which he did by articulating it as a series of intersecting wings of varying heights organized around a glazed, spinal »street« running the site's full length. The Parc André-Citroën (15.8) flanks the hospital on its northern façade, and Zublena made sure that all the patient rooms are on this side of the building, to take advantage of the abundant greenery and avoid the hot summer sun.

Intended to operate as an efficient, lean medical machine, the HEGP uses state-of-the-art computer technology to control everything from prescriptions to radio imaging to the air conditioning. The hospital's architecture was conceived to facilitate its running, both present and future. Studies abroad had shown that over a ten-year period the cost of converting existing hospital buildings to accommodate new technology and practice was often as high as initial investment. Zublena therefore tried to make his building as flexible as possible, for example by limiting structural floor divisions or building in cavities to the hospital's frame to allow potential supplementary vertical circulation. Escalating delays in the HEGP's construction, however, meant that even it was a victim of this problem: part of

15.8 Parc André-Citroën

the unfinished building had to be demolished to allow installation of an unforeseen, new-generation scanner. A whole host of features is designed to facilitate hygiene at the HEGP – ubiquitous hard-wearing, wipe-down, anti-fungal and anti-bacterial wall and floor surfaces, avoidance of germ-harbouring projections in operating theatres, minimalist shower installations in the bedrooms and even specially designed sink units with laser-operated soap and water dispensers so that human hands need never touch the bowl. Money was not unlimited, though, and Zublena worked hard to achieve the elegant economy of means so prized by early Modernists, with both the hospital's interior and exterior exuding a sleek, no-nonsense, utilitarian sheen.

The HEGP has proved extremely controversial. Years behind schedule and way over budget, it was beset by considerably more than the usual amount of teething problems, the worst of which was an outbreak of legionnaire's disease.

15.8 Parc André-Citroën
Jean-Paul Viguier, Alain Provost, Patrick Berger, Gilles Clément and Jean-François Jodry, 1988–95
(Métro: Javel, Balard; RER: Javel, Boulevard Victor)
Traditionally very dense and lacking the green »aeration« of cities such as London or Berlin, Paris has been the object of an ambitious programme of park creation in recent years, which aims to ensure that no inhabitant need travel further than 500 m from home to find a public garden of some sort. In line with this policy, three major new parks have been created as part of the redevelopment of large, redundant industrial sites on the city's periphery: the Parc de La Villette (19.7) in the north, the Parc de Bercy (12.8) in the east, and this example, in the southwest, which covers 13 ha of the former Citroën-car-factory site. Linchpin of the ZAC-Citroën redevelopment, the Parc André-Citroën's sphere of influence is both local and city wide: as well as providing a community amenity for the surrounding quartiers it was also intended to play the kind of monumental urban role effected by illustrious predecessors such as the Champ de Mars (see 7.9) and the Esplanade des Invalides (see 7.12) further upstream. The competition brief called for a break with both traditional gardens and with the architectonics of La Villette. Two teams jointly won the competition, and their proposals were combined to produce the Parc André-Citroën as we see it today.

Within its irregular contours, the park is divided into distinct zones, of which the principal is the rectangular central esplanade descending down to the Seine. The landscape architects here attempted a modern updating of the Champ-de-Mars / Invalides-type riverside garden by reproducing the geometric, formal framing of such spaces but using informal planting that includes generous lawns intended for leisure activities. The esplanade is also unique of its kind in Paris in that it extends all the way to the waterfront, a feat achieved by burying the quayside roadway in a tunnel and elevating the RER onto an elegant concrete bridge, which unfortunately still fuzzes the relationship between park and river. At the esplanade's head is a paved piazza framed by two monumental, Hi-tech, temple-like greenhouses by Patrick Berger; the piazza itself is home to a water feature baptized the »Peristyle«, which consists of 80 pre-programmed, variable jets that attract hordes of splashing kids in the summer. Water is present everywhere in the park, in the form of the long canal running down the esplanade's southern side, in the cascades that cadence its opposite flank, or in the murky depths of the Seine itself. In tandem with the often monumental architectural features that contain them, the water features structure space in the park, as does a long, diagonal path running across the entire extent of the terrain. At the eastern corners of the park are »white« and »black« theme gardens with suitably coloured architectural features and vegetation. Along the esplanade's northern flank, between the cascades, is a whole series of sunken gardens themed on metals and the senses: the red garden, for example, represents both copper and taste, the orange garden iron and touch, and so on. A wild »garden in movement« sits at the park's northwestern corner.

Inevitably, the Parc André-Citroën has proved enormously popular, its esplanade filling up at the first hint of a ray of sunshine, its water features attracting hordes of screaming children and its more intimate gardens harbouring lovers' sighs. Inventive, multi-faceted and fun, it is yet somehow disappointing. Despite its bid for resolute modernity, the design suffers from its abstract, intellectualizing approach, inherited from Baroque-period gardens. Great in drawings, the beautiful plan is perceived quite differently from the ground; graphic coherence on paper becomes visual confusion in the field, especially in the absence of the regulating vegetation that was the generator of classic French gardens. The Parc André-Citroën's architectonic and water features seem overly contrived and gratuitous, and on their own are not enough to create an overall sense of place. As a result the main esplanade lacks punch, and is sadly overwhelmed by the questionable architecture surrounding the park.

15.9 Bibliothèque Gutenberg
8, rue de la Montagne-d'Aulas
Franck Hammoutène, 1987–91
(Métro: Balard)

One element in a major redevelopment scheme concerning the former Citroën car factory, this children's library stands out markedly from its neighbours. In its wilful dissociation from its surroundings, Hammoutène's building appears like some alien object fallen from outer space. The means of achieving this effect are cunningly simple, coming down essentially to the library's *mise en scène* as a discrete, box-shaped object and the clever choice of external materials: black concrete, against which are set stainless-steel panels arranged in the manner of angular, enveloping ribbons. Apart from the glazed entrance, which signals the building's public nature and allows glimpses of the activity within, hardly any fenestration disturbs the self-sufficiency of the external façades, a deliberate move to isolate the interior from its surroundings. On entering the library, one discovers that it is organized around a central, circular garden-courtyard, open to the sky, whose walls are entirely in glass, thus ensuring abundant natural light but precluding any contact with the outside world. The space between the courtyard and the building's outer perimeter, whose surfaces are painted in a manner resembling raw, plank-shuttered concrete, contains the working library, and is subdivided by giant, triangular partitions propped against the external walls to create »caves« that serve as reading areas. The strong, sculptural nature of this building seems rather bizarrely out of tune with its function, both practically – the spaces appear poky, awkward and ill-adapted to the furnishings they contain – and aesthetically, the cheeriness of the children's library contrasting oddly with its sombre, cyclopean container.

15.10 Canal+ headquarters
101, quai André Citroën and 2, rue des Cévennes
Richard Meier & Partners, 1988–92
(Métro/RER: Javel)

After less than ten years' existence, the phenomenally successful independent television company Canal+ commissioned itself a permanent, purpose-built home. The architect selected by the management was Richard Meier, a choice inspired by their desire for a resolutely modern abode, expressive of the channel's with-it image. When ordering a Meier, one usually has a fair idea of what one is getting. Although he has frequently said that the form of a building should be adapted to its environment, his aesthetic remains unflinching. From Malibu to Frankfurt, from Harbor Springs to The Hague, the studied geometry of his gleaming, Purist-inspired volumes is always covered with the same trademark white-enamelled metal panels. For this, his first (and as yet only) building in Paris, he made no exception.

Meier's task was complicated by the constraints of the site. L-shaped and sandwiched between the Parc André-Citroën (15.8) and the 1970s tower-block chaos of the Front de Seine, it was, to Meier's astonishment, subject to stringent height restrictions. This not only exacerbated the problem of squeezing the client's surface-area requirements into the available space, but also posed difficulties for the building's relationship to the river, from which it is separated by a road, railway and quayside sand depot. Meier's solution was rigorously schematic. The two primary activities of Canal+ personnel – production and administration – are clearly separated: the company studios are housed in a low, wide wing running perpendicular to the Seine, while the river wing consists of a narrow, eight-storey blade of offices, glazed along its entire frontage. A generous, glass-roofed atrium, situated at the pivot of the resulting L, serves as the entrance hall. The administrative blade drops from eight to five storeys at its southern end, as dictated by the regulations; Meier fought with the authorities to be allowed to continue visually the roofline of the building with what he dubbed an »urban window« which, in tandem with the prominent satellite dishes at the northern end, assures the building's riverside presence. The scheme's rigid functional segregation was imposed, Meier has said, by purely practical concerns – given their very different spatial and lighting requirements, it seemed only natural to separate administration and production. In an attempt to avoid any consequential staff division and conflict, Meier created architectural routes through the building which force the two camps to mix.

The Canal+ headquarters dazzle the eye with their whiteness, but it is only in this that they stand out from other commercial architecture in the area. Meier's

15.9 Bibliothèque Gutenberg

15.10 Canal+ headquarters

meticulous attention to detail is, as usual, superb, and the generous budget shows in the finishes, but the building is disappointingly banal; the plastic poetry of much of his other work is missing here, perhaps stifled by the exigency of the site.

15.11 Caisse d'Allocations Familiales (CAF)
10–20, rue Viala
Raymond Lopez and Marcel Reby, 1955–59
(Métro: Dupleix)

Not to be missed by lovers of brave-new-world 1950s design, this building, which is today the subject of quite some controversy, was commissioned to house Paris's social-security services. The site allocated to the CAF was classified as being »for immediate redevelopment«, meaning that it was exempt from the usual Parisian step-back and street-line-respecting regulations. The architects were therefore able entirely to ignore the surrounding urbanity and build an eleven-storey-high, sun-orientated, *pilotis*-mounted office block in the middle of the site, around which are grouped lower-level ancillary structures and gardens. But it was not so much for its formal characteristics as its technical capacities that this building was considered noteworthy. By all accounts the CAF was at its most striking during construction, before the addition of its curtain walling, when the elegant flared and cantilevered beams of its steel frame were silhouetted against the sky. Load and dilatation must be taken into account when using this kind of metal structure and, to allow them to contract and expand in total liberty, the CAF's lightweight aluminium-framed façades were suspended from the roof (just like real curtains) which, at this scale, was a first in France and probably Europe. Although they do not appear so externally, the façades are in fact entirely diaphanous, the panels below the strips of opening windows being made from extremely light (8 kg/m^2) polyester resin that is 40 % translucent (see the building by night, when lit from within, for the full effect). Weight watching was also a consideration for the floors, which are fabricated from ribbed sheet metal whose load is only 35 kg/m^2, a tenth of the then norm. For maximum flexibility, the office space was divided up using moveable partitions in lightweight, plastic-covered reinforced plaster, most of which were also partially glazed to allow maximum daylight penetration into the building. Despite its industrialized, utilitarian design concept and consequently aspect, the CAF does feature touches of flamboyance such as the flying staircases accessing its main foyer and the bubble domes lighting the employees' canteen. And its elegantly economical engineering exudes a certain subtle panache, full of postwar, Modernist optimism and confidence in technological progress.

But technological innovation can backfire, and the CAF was not without its malfunctions. Its lightweight façades were poorly insulated, the problem being especially acute in summer when internal temperatures could rise to 40° C. Lopez subsequently added external *brise-soleils* to the most sun-exposed parts of the building to counter this difficulty. A 1965 change in fire regulations made the CAF's steel *pilotis* illegal, with the result that, because it could not easily be modified to conform with the new law, firemen were permanently assigned to the site. These problems aside, the building functioned quite normally with nothing but routine maintenance for 30 years. The controversy currently surrounding it arose as a result of the 1992 decision to decentralize the Parisian social-security services, which consequently decided to rid themselves of the Rue-Viala edifice. Because of its problems, demolition seemed the best solution. But this was without reckoning on the Modernist enthusiasts' lobby, from amongst whose ranks figures such as Paul Chemetov, Marc Mimram and Rémi Lopez (son of Raymond) spoke up in the CAF's defence. Their action initially paid off, with the building being listed as a *monument historique* in 1998. But the social-security services appealed and, in a landmark 1999 judgement, got the listing overturned. The court ruled that the grounds given for the CAF's protection – the historical and technological interest of its metal structure and curtain walling, both of which would need radical modification in any redevelopment scheme – were of insufficient merit, and in its decision was probably only following popular sentiment: this is a building that appeals to cognoscenti but not, in general, to the layman (or, frequently, journalist), who is apt to find it ugly. Today facing an uncertain future, the CAF symbolizes the dilemmas of a recent-heritage debate that can only intensify as more 1950s buildings obsolesce.

15.12 Lycée Camille-Sée

15.12 Lycée Camille-Sée
11, rue Léon-Lhermitte
François Le Cœur, 1931–34
(Métro: Commerce)

An ever-growing shortage of space in Paris's existing schools and their inequitable concentration in the city centre prompted the building of four new *lycées* in the 1930s, all situated in the outer *arrondissements*. The first was the Lycée Camille-Sée, which turned out to be François Le Cœur's last building (he died in 1934). Unanimously praised in the architectural press of the era, it was an honourable ending to a distinguished career (see also 9.1), and set the tone for its three successors.

Le Cœur was known for his unbending rigour and sober Rationalism, an approach that would prove opportune in the case of the Lycée Camille-Sée. The school was conceived to accommodate 1,800 pupils, a number for which the theorists of the day recommended a site of around 20,000 m², loosely grouped low-rise buildings surrounded by plenty of recreation space being considered the ideal configuration. However, because of the high cost of land in central Paris, the new *lycée* was allocated a plot of only 5,800 m², and Le Cœur found himself faced with the conundrum of trying to squeeze a high density of pupils into a small site while still observing the light and air requirements demanded of such an institution. Building high was evidently the only option, and the school consequently rises seven storeys, five above street level and two below. Its wings follow the perimeter of the site and give onto a central courtyard whose floor is sunk one storey below grade to allow the upper of the basement levels to be naturally lit. The courtyard opens out on its southern side towards the trees of the Square Saint-Lambert opposite, and the classrooms are all grouped round it in order to benefit from the sunshine and greenery on offer. Running around the outer perimeter of the building are generous circulation spaces that were conceived in part to make up for the lack of recreation space – the courtyard on its own is evidently insufficient for 1,800 pupils – and which also contained the escalators that were installed to facilitate vertical circulation of pupils in what was then an exceptionally high-rise school. Further recreation space was provided on the roof, where terraces were created for gymnastics lessons.

A pupil of Anatole de Baudot's (see 18.4), Le Cœur shared with his master a passion for concrete, and the Lycée Camille-Sée is entirely realized in this material. His rectilinear and rather dryly monumental façades are in unfaced, bouchardé concrete and, devoid of all but the simplest detailing, appear very Scandinavian. A note of bravura appears in the form of the charming circular entrance pavilion situated at the centre of the Rue-Léon-Lhermitte elevation, with its geometrically arranged beams, glass-brick dome and colourful mosaic floor.

16th *arrondissement*

16.1 Arc de Triomphe
Place Charles-de-Gaulle
Jean-François Chalgrin *et al.*, 1806–35
(Métro/RER: Charles-de-Gaulle-Etoile)

Ever since, in the 1660s, André Le Nôtre created the great westward axis (today's Avenue des Champs-Elysées) that departs majestically from the Tuileries (1.10), this spot, at the summit of the Chaillot hill and therefore the termination of Le Nôtre's avenue when viewed from Paris, was the subject of countless plans for some kind of landmark monument. It was not until 1806, however, that the Emperor Napoleon finally decreed that a triumphal arch, dedicated to the glory of the Grande Armée, should be built on the site. Napoleon was impatient: plans were hurriedly drawn up by Jean-François Chalgrin and Jean-Arnaud Raymond, and the first stone of the new arch laid on 15 August 1806, the emperor's birthday. By 1807, although the foundations were complete, a definitive design was still not established, as Raymond and Chalgrin had subsequently submitted rival proposals. In the end, Chalgrin prevailed, and was named sole architect of the monument in 1808. He continued work on the Arc until his death, in 1811, when he was succeeded by his pupil, L. Goust. Napoleon's first defeat, in 1814, closed the building site; nothing more was done for almost ten years, and the uncompleted Arc was even threatened with demolition. Finally, in 1823, by order of Louis XVIII, work resumed, with Goust and Jean-Nicolas Huyot overseeing proceedings. In 1830, Goust retired, and Huyot continued alone, before being dismissed in 1832 and replaced by Guillaume-Abel Blouet, who completed the monument in 1835.

Despite the many changes in regime and in architect between 1806 and 1835, Chalgrin's 1808 project was adhered to, at least in its general outline, and the Arc de Triomphe can therefore be »given« to him. His design is of the Arch-of-Janus (Rome, early-4C) type, with a single, monumental opening in the axis of the Arc's main façades, as well as two smaller, lateral arches that meet the principal opening perpendicularly. Napoleon's architectural projects all make clear his desire to identify his regime with the glory of imperial Rome, but the Arc de Triomphe also invites comparison with the reign of Louis XIV, as its principle elevations are reminiscent of the Sun King's Porte Saint-Denis (10.1). The measure of Napoleon's unabashed ambitions can be got from the Arc de Triomphe's size: a colossal 45 m wide by 50 m high, making it almost certainly the biggest triumphal arch in the world. Given its huge dimensions, it comes as no surprise to learn that one of Chalgrin's teachers was Etienne-Louis Boullée.

The division of the Arc's principle façades into threes, both vertically and horizontally, is reminiscent of the distribution of the west front of Notre-Dame (4.2), and produces a similar impression of calm and majesty.

This effect is also due to the relative sobriety of the Arc, whose sculptural elements are clearly contained and delineated, leaving large areas of blank wall. Chalgrin's original intention was to dress up the structure with columns, but this proposal was rejected by Napoleon in order to cut down on costs. As a result, today's monument appears far more quietly powerful and imposing than did the initial projects. In 1810, when the Arc barely rose above its foundations, Chalgrin was commissioned to construct a life-size, *in-situ* mock-up of the final project for the wedding of Napoleon to Marie-Louise de Habsbourg-Lorraine. Realized in painted canvas hung from a wooden frame, the mock-up gave Chalgrin the opportunity to correct his design, including adding greater emphasis to the Arc's cornice and attic so that the monument would stand out against the Parisian sky when viewed from afar. Because of the presence today of the towers of La Défense (see 27.1) on Paris's western horizon, it is hard to appreciate the Arc's original impact on the cityscape, when it was the most prominent and massive object for miles around, a hegemony it retained until the building of the Eiffel Tower (7.8) in the 1880s.

Napoleon was rather coy about his motives for building the Arc de Triomphe – which was one of at least four triumphal arches he was planning for Paris (besides the Arc de Triomphe, only the Arc du Carrousel (1.9) was completed) –, declaring in a letter to his interior minister, »Triumphal arches would be futile structures without result if they were not a means for encouraging architecture«, and, »With these four arches I intend to sustain sculpture in France for 20

16.1 Arc de Triomphe

Gloire des Arts, and the statues surrounding the piazza's pool, all of which are now lost bar Dejean, Drivier and Guénot's reclining nymphs. Mention should also be made of Antoine Bourdelle's spiky bronze *Génie de la France* which presides over the skateboarders who have now colonized the Palais's public spaces.

The state's modern-art collection quit the west wing of the Palais de Tokyo for the Centre Pompidou (4.15) in the 1970s, and since then the fortunes of this half of the building have been rather chequered. Various institutions came and went until in the early 1990s the ministry of culture decided to install a museum of cinema at the Palais. 80 million francs were spent on the preliminary stages of converting the west wing for this purpose before a change in minister precipitated the project's cancellation. As a result, this part of the building remained an empty, gutted shell for many years. Finally the decision was taken to install a Centre d'Art Contemporain at the Palais, and the architects Anne Lacaton and Jean-Philippe Vassal were charged with making the west wing ready for its new occupant. Lacaton and Vassal are known for their minimalist, *arte povera* approach, which is essentially what secured them the contract since the budget was so limited (20 million francs, compared to the 300 million that were allocated to the cinema museum) that little besides basic consolidation work was possible. Reopened in early 2002, the west wing thus remains in a raw, stripped state so as to lend a little *faux*-industrial chic to the happenings and art events now programmed there.

16.5 Musée Guimet
6, place d'Iéna
Charles Terrier, 1888/89; Henri and Bruno Gaudin, 1994–2001
(Métro: Iéna)

A rich industrialist who was passionate about Asia, Emile Guimet amassed a stunning collection of objects from across the entire continent, which he opened to the Parisian public in a purpose-built museum in 1889. Occupying an irregular, wedge-shaped site whose contours it followed, Terrier's building was organized around a central courtyard and signalled its presence on the Place d'Iéna by a domed rotunda. For reasons that remain obscure – contrariness perhaps? or love of contrast? –, the architect chose to dress up this museum of Asian art in a Hellenizing outfit that would not have been out of place in 19C Athens. Guimet's private institution later became the Musée National des Arts Asiatiques, and its collection expanded into one of the richest in the world. As it did so, new galleries were squeezed into every available spare inch of space, including the courtyard, until by the late-20C the museum had become a bewildering, forgotten rabbit warren whose dusty, chaotic displays attracted few visitors. In 1994 the museum's directors decided that a major revamp was in order: two years of preliminary studies and proposals went by before work started, in

16.5 Musée Guimet

1996, and it was another five years before the museum reopened its doors. The result of this long renaissance has garnered universal praise, and the Musée Guimet is now one of Paris's star museological attractions.

The architects could have chosen to gut the museum, preserving only the façades (which are listed), and start from scratch inside, but they eschewed this *tabula rasa* approach for a more subtle reworking of the existing fabric. The building is thus still organized around its central courtyard which, glassed in on its lower levels, is now one of the institution's more impressive galleries, home to the Khmer collection. Here we have a good example of the Gaudins' use of a subtle palette of grey polished marbles that complement the objects on display. Despite its central position, the Khmer gallery is not the linchpin of the museum, this role being fulfilled by the magnificent double *escalier d'honneur* which the Gaudins have installed behind the rotunda. Curvilinear flights of stairs hanging dizzyingly in mid air connect the different parts of the museum and provide multiple cross views onto the diverse richness of the collections. Wherever possible the galleries receive natural light – albeit veiled and filtered to protect the objects displayed – and to this end shafts and openings have been cut through between floors, adding to the inter-textuality encouraged by the many

»windows« between galleries which encourage visitors to consider the historical links between the different cultures displayed. The museum's layout is still disorientatingly Byzantine, but rather than detracting from the visit the complexity adds a supplementary delight to this labyrinthine palace of treasures.

16.6 Palais d'Iéna
1, avenue d'Iéna
Auguste Perret, 1936–46; Paul Vilmond, 1960–62;
Gilles Bouchez, 1993–95
(Métro: Iéna)

Although less well known than the ground-breaking Théâtre des Champs-Elysées (8.12) and Notre-Dame du Raincy (35.1), this building is perhaps Perret's *magnum opus*, a mature and assured development of his very personal style. Conceived to house a Museum of Public Works, the Palais was commissioned in the wake of the 1937 Exposition Internationale, and was almost certainly given to Perret as consolation for the dropping of his exhibition proposals (as was the Garde-Meuble du Mobilier National (13.12), which prefigured certain aspects of the Palais). The brief called for an edifice providing gallery space, to display models of state engineering projects, and a purpose-built lecture hall. Perret's ambitions went beyond these mundane requirements, and he set out to build a Classical palace entirely in unadorned reinforced concrete with a new, modern order to rival that of the Parthenon – in short a manifesto of his architectural dogmas. The building we see today is unfinished – war interrupted work after completion of only one wing, and although Perret subsequently realized the lecture hall work thereafter was abandoned –, but enough was built to demonstrate fully the rigour and elegance of his ideas.

For Perret, reinforced-concrete technology was the miracle breakthrough that would allow the 20C to produce masterpieces comparable to those of the Antique and medieval eras. He believed that concrete, since poured in wooden shuttering, should imitate wooden forms, as had ancient-Greek structures. He generally argued against curved or irregular forms in concrete as they needed elaborate formwork and were thus expensive to produce, violating his conviction that design should be determined by a rational, economic use of materials. He nonetheless often permitted himself curved forms for the sake of expressiveness. An ardent admirer of Antique and especially ancient-Greek buildings, Perret aimed to do what he felt »our ancestors would have done in our place with the means at our disposal«. These principles, largely inherited from his *beaux-arts* training, formed the basis of his dry, rigorous, orthogonal, Classically inspired style.

In a typical example of *beaux-arts* planning, the contours of Perret's design for the Palais followed those of its triangular, island site, thus producing a three-wing, symmetrical building with a central courtyard. Situated halfway down the Chaillot hill, the terrain drops steeply, a feature some architects would have used as a starting point for their design. True to his schooling, however, Perret conceived a rigidly isometric, regular building for which he established an artificial, conceptual ground level, partially burying the edifice on the Avenue du Président-Wilson and, conversely, exposing the basement storey on the Avenue d'Iéna. He designed exhibition halls running in a continuous loop around the ground floor, while at the triangle's apex he placed the lecture hall, in the form of an amphitheatre. The amphitheatre is expressed externally as a half-rotunda, serving both to turn the corner gracefully and to signal the principal entrance to the Palais. For the building's structure, Perret employed a system of his own devising, for which he coined the term »abri souverain« (»sovereign shelter«), consisting of a megastructure of colossal, external columns supporting the roof, with a separate structure underneath holding up the floors. The main advantage of this rather contrived arrangement was that it allowed an uninterrupted giant order that was not merely decorative but also structurally useful, in the manner of the ancient-Greek temples he so admired. Another, secondary advantage was that the top floor of a building constructed in this way was entirely free of columns or supports.

Perret's unorthodox structural system is clearly visible on the Avenue-d'Iéna wing, which exhibits the colossal columns of his new order. Reversing usual practice, the columns taper inwards towards their bases, a form inspired by palm trees he had seen in Egypt. He justified its use on the grounds not only that it occurred in nature but also because he felt it expressed the indissoluble and continuous relationship of the different parts of a concrete structure to one another. The columns thus widen towards their summits to take on the dimensions of the beam they support – rather like furniture legs – and, to effect a smooth transition from the beam's orthogonal shape to the columns' cylindrical one, Perret designed a sort of flared, ornamented capital, which he insisted was not a capital but a »link«. That this was all rather fanciful becomes clear on examining the columns' bases

16.6 Palais d'Iéna

which, despite being embedded in the concrete structure below, just as the summits are integral to the beam above, are not made to blend smoothly into their concrete bed, presumably because it represents conceptual ground level and they are therefore to be read as standing on terra firma. Above the columns rises a beautifully detailed, graphically drawn cornice, which adds weight and presence to the composition and makes for a truly monumental order. Indeed, the whole façade is admirably proportioned and impeccably sharp, the only weak note being the capitals, which seem inappropriately whimsical. Behind the colonnade, the non-load-bearing walls feature large areas of glazing, their solid parts consisting of concrete breeze blocks. The exterior of the rotunda is treated in essentially the same fashion as the Avenue-d'Iéna wing, but on a smaller scale.

The Palais d'Iéna has been described as a »hymn to concrete«, an epithet inspired by Perret's loving handling of the material. Not for him the »mediocre« practices of cladding or plastering (indeed he proudly boasted that not a single sack of plaster entered the Palais's building site): concrete was enough on its own. But where at Le Raincy Perret had been obliged to use a cheap and ultimately disastrous mix, he here produced exquisitely composed and worked concrete of the finest quality that has aged astonishingly well. Green porphyry and pink marble were amongst the constituents used to achieve the desired colours. After removal of the shuttering, the concrete was finished by hammering and, to give an impression of fluting on the columns, smooth ridges were made by polishing the surface with carborundum brick. The breeze blocks, in two different shades, were also finished by hammering and were laid with all the care of cut stone, the joints being carefully pointed to give a graphic effect that sets off the pattern created by the different-coloured blocks. The result is exceptional and proves that concrete, if made with enough care, can be as noble a material as stone.

Not only is the exterior of the Palais in unadorned concrete, so is the interior. On entering the building by the rotunda, one is led along a curved ascent, with views onto the surrounding cityscape, up to the level of the exhibition halls. The one completed section is a handsome space, glazed on either side, its double row of columns (here more powerful for the absence of capitals) marching along majestically, the warm colour of its concrete complemented by wooden coffering on the ceiling and marble flooring. The famous *escalier d'honneur* is situated at the building's fulcrum opposite the amphitheatre, whose curved form it echoes. Set against screens of concrete tracery (one of this building's leitmotifs), the staircase is a dizzy display of gravity defiance, full of movement, its two curved primary descents whizzing round to join for one final downward lunge. This daring demonstration of concrete's technical capabilities contrasts in its curvaceousness with the dry trabeation of the galleries in a typically Perret-style *coup de théâtre*. So does the amphitheatre, which is covered by a shallow, concrete half-dome whose frame is filled with glass bricks. The sensation of airiness and light is somewhat diminished by the concrete umbrella that Perret considered necessary to protect the dome, and artificial lighting is needed when the amphitheatre is in use.

The Museum of Public Works opened in the one completed wing of the Palais in 1939 but by 1956 had been closed, expelled in favour of the Assemblée de l'Union Française. This latter institution was in its turn moved out, in 1959, to be replaced by the current occupant, the Conseil Economique et Social. In 1960, the Conseil engaged Paul Vilmond, a former student of Perret's, to build the Avenue-du-Président-Wilson wing to provide further office space. Vilmond did not pastiche his master's work but nonetheless respected its spirit, employing the same materials and reproducing the proportions of Perret's original. By the 1990s, extra space was again needed, and Gilles Bouchez was commissioned to build the third and final wing on the Avenue Albert-de-Mun. His design owes nothing to Perret's Classical tradition and, with its white-concrete façade featuring horizontal strip windows, appears very »machine-age« Modern. Yet Bouchez's structure is functional and discreet and does not seek to draw attention to itself, the only flamboyant note being the black *brise-soleils* that whizz round the façade's curved profile.

Architecturally, the Palais d'Iéna was the culmination of Perret's career to date, and in the body of work he produced between the end of WWII and his death in 1954 he rarely equalled its serenity. The Parthenon may not have had to worry, but the Palais stands as testament to the originality and brilliance of this pioneering Modernist.

16.7 Palais de Chaillot

Place du Trocadéro and 54, avenue de New-York
Gabriel Davioud and Jules Bourdais, 1876–78; Jacques Carlu, Louis-Hippolyte Boileau and Léon Azéma, 1935 to 1937
(Métro: Trocadéro)

The Chaillot hill, with its prestigious position on a bend in the Seine directly opposite the Ecole Militaire (7.9) and the Champ de Mars, was long coveted for its monumental possibilities. Napoleon planned to build a vast palace there, designed by Fontaine and Percier, but work never progressed beyond the excavation stage. Haussmann subsequently contented himself with merely flattening the summit for the creation of a park, signalled by a belvedere, and it was not until 1876 that the government of the day decided to exploit the site's potential by commissioning a combined 10,000-seat opera house and art gallery to act as the centrepiece of the 1878 Exposition Universelle. A rather ungainly Italianate composition in brick, the Palais du Trocadéro, as it became known, was situated at the top of the hill in the axis of the Champ de Mars and comprised an enormous, central, semicircular auditorium (in the event a multi-purpose space seating 5,000), flanked by two narrow towers and also by two long, low, curved wings containing gallery space, each punctuated at either end by imposing pavilions. The hillside embraced by these lateral wings was laid out with gardens, and cascades and fountains descended from the auditorium to the river.

The Palais du Trocadéro initially dominated the surrounding landscape, a hegemony subsequently snatched away from it with the building of the Eiffel Tower (7.8) at the foot of the Champ de Mars. At first a great success, despite the auditorium's poor acoustics, the Palais quickly went out of fashion and, by the 1920s, calls for its demolition began to be heard. In 1933, in preparation for the 1937 Exposition Internationale, the then government commissioned Auguste Perret to design a »Cité des Musées« to replace the ageing Palais. Perret's plans were extinguished in the 1934 political crisis and, in a bid for economy, the new government resolved that the Palais du Trocadéro should no longer be demolished but instead remodelled, including »camouflaging« its exterior. This decision, as well as the irregular circumstances in which the Carlu-Boileau-Azéma team obtained the commission, provoked a public outcry, and a petition signed by eminents such as Picasso, Matisse, Cocteau, Chagall and Braque was drawn up against the project. The scheme nevertheless went ahead and, once completed, was not without its admirers, amongst whom were some of the petition signatories rallied to its cause.

After some hesitation, the architects decided that no verticals should compete with the Eiffel Tower, and consequently took the inspired decision to demolish the Palais's auditorium and its towers, leaving a void, flanked by the curved, lateral wings, in its stead. Traditional doctrine, which dictates that a high point should be marked by an edifice of some kind, was thus reversed. The old Palais's lateral wings were doubled in width and dressed up in streamlined stone façades whose monumental stripped Classicism is reminiscent of Italian, Russian and German totalitarian architecture of the era. A new auditorium, housing the Théâtre National Populaire, was built underneath the piazza that took the old auditorium's place, and the land in front of the piazza excavated to free up the theatre's foyer façade. Between the theatre and the quayside, the architect Henri Expert installed a series of pools and fountains whose centrepiece is the spectacular water cannon that periodically fires enormous jets towards the Eiffel Tower. The new Palais was much praised for its discreet dignity and for its updating of French Classicism, Carlu having expressly sought »lines in the French monumental tradition« that would embody »the horizontality that is the glory of the Place de la Concorde« (see 8.1).

Today, as well as its theatre, the Palais de Chaillot is home to the Musée de la Marine (naval museum) and the Musée de l'Homme (museum of mankind), and its

16.7 Palais de Chaillot

eastern wing is currently undergoing conversion to house a »Cité de l'Architecture et du Patrimoine« (architecture and heritage centre) due for completion in 2005.

16.8 Apartment building
25 bis, rue Franklin
Auguste Perret, 1903/04
(Métro: Trocadéro, Passy)

Revolutionary when constructed, this building is regarded by many historians as one of the seminal works of Modern architecture, a precursor of various later developments. This was not the first use of concrete in a domestic setting, but it was the first instance where the potential of concrete framing was investigated, and almost certainly the first time that such a frame was expressed so blatantly in a non-industrial context. Perret trained at the Ecole des Beaux-Arts (6.1) under Guadet (see 1.19), but quit his studies before completion to join his father's construction firm. The Rue-Franklin flats were erected on land owned by the Perret family, whose home and business, including Perret's personal atelier, were to be installed in the building. The U-shaped plan of the block, open at the front, was a clever innovation of Perret's: by placing the regulation courtyard on the street façade he avoided the usual dingy lightwell, maximized window area and took advantage of views towards the Eiffel Tower (7.8). The façade is clad in white faïence tiling by Alexandre Bigot, but frame and infill are expressed differently, the frame being covered with plain white tiles and the remainder with Art-Nouveau-inspired vegetal motifs. Perret later said that tile coverings were applied because at the time they thought it necessary to protect the concrete's metal reinforcement from the elements. The concrete posts apparent on the ground floor are suggestive of the *pilotis* that would become a hallmark of Modernism, while on the sixth floor the frame breaks free in the form of balconies, pointing towards potential manipulation of form possible with frame construction. The layout of the apartments, unimpeded by load-bearing walls, constitutes an early example of the free plan, although conventional configurations were employed.

Technically the Rue Franklin building did not advance the possibilities of concrete construction. Its trabeated frame/infill structure was directly inherited from timber technology and could, for the most part, be reproduced in wood. Cantilevers and curtain walling would come later. Perret was never to be overly preoccupied with pushing the technological limits of concrete, however. He inherited ideas from French Rational Classicists, such as Choisy, who saw the origin of ancient-Greek architecture as the reproduction of wooden forms in stone. Perret believed that frame construction was the consummate evocation of built form and that concrete was even nobler than stone because of its direct relationship with wood in the form of the shuttering used to cast it. All his work was suffused with Classicism in the French tradition, present at the rue Franklin block in its proportions and trellis/plant tile motif. Through this innovative building, Perret established his reputation, demonstrated an aesthetically acceptable use of concrete framing and influenced a whole generation of younger architects.

16.8 Apartment building

16.9 Apartment building
51, rue Raynouard
Auguste Perret, 1929–32
(Métro: Passy)

A comparison between this building and Perret's Rue-Franklin apartments just up the road (16.8) gives a good idea of the evolution of his techniques in the 30 years separating the two. As at the Rue Franklin, Perret was here both client and architect, designing an apartment block that also included accommodation for his practice (the glass-fronted space on the Rue Berton). Here, however, instead of a party-wall plot, Perret disposed of a superb if rather narrow island site, situated on a hillside. He reserved the upper two floors, which benefit from splendid views, for his own dwelling.

French Classicism remained Perret's source of inspiration throughout his life, and the Rue-Franklin and Rue-Raynouard buildings are similar in both their massing and verticality. The trabeated concrete frame

16.9 Apartment building

that had been so daringly expressed at the Rue Franklin is again visible at the Rue Raynouard, but with the major difference that here it is exposed to the elements, without any protective treatment. Furthermore, the infill panels are now also in unadorned concrete, in contrast to the faïence tiles used at the Rue Franklin. Youthful caution – Perret originally thought that concrete needed to be protected from precipitation – has given way to mature confidence: »When making concrete we are producing stone, nobler and more beautiful than natural stone.« The splendid staircase linking Perret's offices to the main edifice prefigures the magnificent specimen he later designed for the Palais d'Iéna (16.6), the building that was probably the fullest expression of his love affair with concrete.

16.10 Maison de la Radio
116, avenue du Président-Kennedy
Henry Bernard with Jacques Lhuillier, Georges Sibelle and Edouard and Jean Niermans, 1952–63
(Métro: Passy; RER: Kennedy Radio-France)
Programmed by order of General de Gaulle following the creation of France's state-owned radio monopoly, the Maison de la Radio was conceived to provide a single, coherent home for the different departments of Radio France, which were previously dispersed all over Paris. Henry Bernard emerged the winner in the 1952 architectural competition with a proposal that he presented as purely functional and conceived solely on the basis of the systematic processes of radio production. Circular in plan, his building is divided into concentric rings: the outer, which is day-lit, contains offices and the smaller recording studios, the second contains the larger studios, while the third, innermost ring houses the technical facilities, including the broadcasting apparatus and the main control room. At the building's centre, a 65 m-high tower provides space for the radio's sound archives. In other words, programmes are written and developed in the outer ring, recorded in the second, broadcast in the third, and stored at the building's heart. There are also three large auditoria, designed by the Niermans brothers, which occupy the lower levels of the river section of the two outer rings. Bernard claimed that his functional, programmatic approach was all that mattered, even to the point of disdain for the building's exterior: »Once the inside was done, its casing was of little importance to me«, he later declared. Nonetheless, he seems to have put some effort into the Maison de la Radio's external styling, and its no-nonsense streamlining and sleek aluminium cladding have aged extremely well.

16.11 »Castel Béranger« apartment building
14, rue La Fontaine
Hector Guimard, 1895–98
(Métro: Ranelagh; RER: Kennedy Radio-France)
Following several unremarkable œuvres de jeunesse, Hector Guimard – today generally recognized as France's foremost Art-Nouveau architect and world famous for his Paris Métro entrances (see feature on the Métro and the RER) – suddenly produced this building, which set the whole of Paris talking and brought him overnight celebrity. Commissioned by a speculator, the Castel Béranger was a complex of 36 apartments intended to be let at moderate rents. Guimard was given carte blanche to do as he pleased within the limits of the brief and the budget, and seems to have poured the whole of his creative energies into the project, overseeing and designing everything right down to the plumbing. The result is something of a hybrid, for it fuses the philosophy of his early work – a vernacular, anti-Classical rationalism inspired by the theories of Eugène-Emanuel Viollet-le-Duc (whose influence he was eager to acknowledge) – with a new, »irrational« decorative freedom whose flowering was triggered by Guimard's visit, in 1895, to the great Belgian Art-Nouveau architect Victor Horta.

Planning permission for the Castel Béranger had been sought before Guimard's trip to Brussels, and the fundaments of the building were not modified following his exposure to Horta's work. The Castel came as quite a shock to Parisians of the day, breaking entirely as it does with the Classical, symmetrical, dressed-ashlar monotony of Haussmann-regulated façades. Instead we find a vernacular variety of forms, an eclectic range of materials and consequently a whole gamut of colours and textures. A dislike of symmetry was an inclination inherited from Viollet-le-Duc, although whether the Castel Béranger's complex façades are the external expression of interior function, as Viollet-le-Duc would have had it, or whether its picturesque massing was contrived essentially for its decorative effect, is uncertain. Similarly, the extensive employment of bricks and rubble stone as well as ashlar could be ascribed to a Viollet-le-Duc-esque concern for a rational, economic use of materials, but equally the aesthetic qualities of these elements and the ornamental opportunities their combination offered seem to have guided Guimard's handling of them. Inside the building, we find a more faithful translation of Viollet-le-Duc's ideas. Guimard went to the trouble of considering every apartment individually, and no two are alike. However, they all share a Viollet-le-Duc-esque regard for the optimization of available space – long corridors are consequently banished – and their common kitchen-pantry-dining-room sequence was directly borrowed from Viollet-le-Duc's *Histoire d'une Maison* (1873). Guimard oversaw everything connected with the apartments, right down to designing the wallpaper and worrying over the tiniest decorative details, a total-environment approach that became characteristic of Art Nouveau. In a bid for thrift, he eschewed conventional plaster ceiling coverings, instead leaving apparent the uncontrived decorative effect of the

16.10 Maison de la Radio

16.11 »Castel Béranger« apartment building

floors' metal structure, a rational, economic use of materials of which Viollet-le-Duc could only have approved.

It is not, however, for its Structural-Rationalist leanings, which anticipated Modern-Movement concerns, that the Castel Béranger is generally remembered, but for its Horta-inspired decorative elements. Externally, these are chiefly confined to the ironwork, where we see the sinuous, shrinking-and-swelling swirls of »organic« inspiration that are for many are the essence of Art Nouveau. The Castel Béranger's principal, Rue-La-Fontaine entrance, with its elaborate iron gates, is especially celebrated. Guimard's debt to Horta is clear, although he developed his own »line«, more vertical and less cyclical than Horta's. Many have criticized the isolated nature of these Art-Nouveau flourishes in a generally inconsistent design, and it is to Guimard's later, full-blown-Art-Nouveau work (e. g. the Hôtel Guimard, 16.14), produced after his complete absorption of Horta's ideas, that we must turn for a truer estimate of his mature capabilities. Nonetheless, the Castel Béranger struck an appreciative chord with numerous contemporaries, its flats all being let before the building was even finished and its façades winning the annual municipal competition for originality and diversity. Of course, such a boldly unconventional design also attracted a good deal of adverse attention, and critics were quick to nickname it the »Castel Dérangé« (»dérangé« = deranged).

16.12 Rue Mallet-Stevens

Robert Mallet-Stevens, 1926/27
(Métro: Ranelagh)

Neglected until fairly recently and still little known outside his native France, Rob Mallet-Stevens was, in his heyday in the 1920s, ranked at the forefront of the Modernists. The Russian Constructivist Konstantin Melnikov was highly impressed by his work, which he had seen at the 1925 Exposition des Arts Décoratifs, and Le Corbusier was a one-time friend and supporter. Mallet-Stevens's later obscurity was almost certainly due to his relatively early death, the modest extent of his built legacy and, especially, the absence of governing doctrine in his work, and hence of disciples. He also lacked the social utopianism of many of his contemporaries, and has been written off by some as a modern stylist for the wealthy. The Rue Mallet-Stevens was his *magnum opus*, built for the architect himself and a group of his friends. They had jointly acquired a large parcel of land in still undeveloped Auteuil for which Mallet-Stevens designed a *cul-de-sac* surrounded by urban villas, each tailored to the individual owner's requirements. This was a standard form of development in the area at the time – of the many other examples one can cite Le Corbusier's uncompleted Square du Docteur-Blanche (16.13) just up the road. With such a project an architect had the opportunity to design not merely individual buildings but an entire segment of the cityscape.

Programmatically, Mallet-Stevens's approach to the urban environment was conventional and, in terms of the type of accommodation they offered, the villas were unexceptional: as was then usual in the homes of the well-to-do, they were divided vertically into reception, private and service areas. Aesthetically, however, the Rue Mallet-Stevens was uncompromisingly avant-garde, a showpiece of the International Style. Uninterested in the expression of structure, Mallet-Stevens preferred to »sculpt« his houses, as he put it, into an abstract interplay of orthogonal volumes, and thus coated them in a unifying layer of white stucco, hiding their concrete frames. The street line is respected in the Rue Mallet-Stevens, and signalled at the base of each villa by horizontally striped banding. After rising one or two storeys, however, the houses start to fragment into smaller volumes, stepping back into myriad terraces and compositional permutations. This ambiguity towards the role of his buildings in the urban environment, which both respect their context and at the same time behave as if isolated in space, says much about Mallet-Stevens's genteel brand of Modernism, in contrast to other, more radical approaches.

Of the villas in the Rue Mallet-Stevens, most notable are no. 10, built for the sculptors Joël and Jan Martel, whom Mallet-Stevens often commissioned, and no. 12, which the architect built for himself and which also housed his practice. The interior of no. 10 was complex, almost a Loosian »Raumplan«, articulated around a spiral staircase which forms the linchpin of the build-

16.12 Rue Mallet-Stevens

ing's external composition. No. 12, which curves round into the Rue du Docteur-Blanche and thus acted as a sort of ambassador for the street, included a magnificent double-height living space animated by a cantilevered staircase. Mallet-Stevens collaborated with a number of designers, including the glass-smith Louis Barillet, whose work can be seen in the stairwell windows of nos. 8 (built for Mme Reifenberg, pianist) and 10, and the metal-smith (and later architect) Jean Prouvé, who executed the fine grill at the entrance to no. 10. Francis Jourdain was responsible for the interior decor of nos. 3–5 (home of the filmmaker Allatini), 7 and 8, while for the furnishing of his own house Mallet-Stevens collaborated with Pierre Chareau.

The Rue Mallet-Stevens is in a sorry state today. Many of the architect's carefully considered compositions have been disfigured by the addition of supplementary storeys, the stucco is cracked and discoloured, and the whole street crumbles like Sleeping Beauty's castle behind a superabundance of vegetation. Enough remains, however, to give an idea of its former allure and of the extraordinary impression that this unique development must once have made.

16.13 Villas La Roche and Jeanneret-Raaf

8–10, square du Docteur-Blanche
Le Corbusier and Pierre Jeanneret, 1923–25
(Métro: Jasmin)

Had Le Corbusier had his way, the Square du Docteur-Blanche would, like the nearby Rue Mallet-Stevens (16.12), have been an entire, architect-designed

246 16th *arrondissement*

enclave in the city, a *cul-de-sac* surrounded by urban villas conceived together as a manifesto of the *esprit nouveau*. Having heard that the land was coming up for residential development, Corb spontaneously proposed his services to the Banque Immobilière Parisienne (BIP), which was controlling the operation, thus embarking on a long, involved saga. During the course of 1923, he designed at least eight different schemes for the *square* for about as many clients, some of whom he may have invented to lend greater credibility to his proposals. The BIP was sceptical, however, and events conspired to thwart Corb's initial ambitions. In the end he built only two houses: one for the Swiss banker and art collector Raoul La Roche, and one for his own brother and sister-in-law, Albert Jeanneret and Lotti Raaf, and their children. When considering the project as realized, it should be borne in mind that what we see is only part of the whole story, since today's picturesque, asymmetrical composition was originally to have been flanked on the opposite side of the street by at least one other villa, thus forming a much more balanced and monumental ensemble. Nonetheless, this »incomplete« state does not detract from what was one of Corb's pioneering works, a project that served as a »laboratory«, as he put it, in the evolution of his architecture and theories. Now home to the Fondation Le Corbusier, the houses have remained in essentially their original condition, the Villa La Roche being open to the public as a museum and the Villa Jeanneret containing the Fondation's library (accessible only to researchers).

Programmatically, the two villas could not have been more different. Raoul La Roche was rich and single and wanted a house that would be as much a showcase for his considerable collection of Cubist paintings as a home. The Jeannerets were of more modest means, and into a site not even half the size of La Roche's had to fit practical living accommodation for a family of four. Given the restricted nature of the available plots, especially the Villa Jeanneret-Raaf's, Corb was left with little choice but to build the houses as a semi-detached ensemble. No doubt because of this, and despite the very different characters of the two briefs, he chose to combine the two projects as one, a »maison double« as he called it, and externally the demarcation between the two villas is indiscernible without prior knowledge of the design.

The Villa La Roche

According to Raoul La Roche, the impetus for his villa came from Corb himself, who had commented that someone with a painting collection as fine as La Roche's should have a house worthy of it; »Alright then, build me this house«, was the banker's response. Given the nature of the commission and the greater means at La Roche's disposal, it was perhaps inevitable that the Villa La Roche should be the more architecturally impressive of the two villas. Here Corb had the space and freedom to lay on a full *promenade architecturale*, the first example in his œuvre of what would become a major preoccupation in later works (see, e.g., the Villa Savoye, 25.2). The idea of the *promenade architecturale* was that, contrary to Baroque architecture, which was generally designed to be viewed from a single, fixed point, Corb's buildings should be discovered as one moved through them, by means of a carefully programmed route in which form and intent were gradually revealed over time. At the Villa La Roche this begins even before one enters the house, the approaches to the building having been carefully considered. Advancing along the Square du Docteur-Blanche, one's gaze is immediately drawn to a curved white volume, lifted up on *pilotis*, that closes the thoroughfare, which we will later discover is La Roche's picture gallery. When the house was first built cars could drive right up to – and under – the gallery (the railings now obscuring the ground-floor area are later additions), an early demonstration of Corb's urbanistic doctrine whereby the city of the future would be raised up above the ground to facilitate free circulation of vehicles. Indeed this was the first of his built projects to feature *pilotis*, one of the famous »five points of a new architecture« that he would codify a year after completion of the Villas La Roche and Jeanneret-Raaf (see the Maison Cook, 29.3). *Pilotis* had other advantages in Corbusian thinking: they cut contact between accommodation and the dampness of the ground, they reduced costs since less excavation work was needed, and they also allowed space to be reclaimed at ground level, which, if it was not allotted to the motor car could theoretically be given over to gardens. Highlighting this fact, and underlining the central importance of the *pilotis* in Corbusian theory, the single, white, slender central support of La Roche's picture gallery is dramatically set off against the dark vegetation behind it.

A highly sculptural object floating in space, the picture gallery contrasts strongly with the more solid and orthogonal principal mass of building running along the length of the Square du Docteur-Blanche, which one discovers only once one has progressed towards the villas. This main mass of the houses, which is actually symmetrical on its central section, comprises all of the Villa Jeanneret-Raaf – the part up to the mid-point between the two garage doors – and a sizeable chunk of the Villa La Roche. Here we find, at first-floor level, another of the future »five points«, in the form of the horizontal strip windows running the entire length of the façade. Interestingly, we do not yet have full expression of the »free« façade that would later become a Corbusian preoccupation, since the strip windows are regularly interrupted by slivers of solid masonry, instead of the continuous band of glazing with pillars behind that he afterwards employed. The pristine, machined, »industrial« aesthetic that was characteristic of his 1920s output is fully manifested, however, with smooth, rendered, whitewashed volumes and fenestration that is set flush with the walls, giving the impression that the

16.13 Villa La Roche

exterior is a »skin« wrapped round the building. In truth, the white render hides a hand-made trabeated concrete frame with hand-laid brick infill. Likewise, the windows only have the appearance of having been industrially mass-produced. Corb billed his fenestration as the »élément mécanique-type de la maison«, a key component in the »revolution« in domestic architecture that he set out to achieve, but in fact the windows at the Villas La Roche and Jeanneret-Raaf were all specially made. That this does not seem to have bothered anyone too much was no doubt due to the fact that the villas were to a certain extent conceived as rhetorical, manifesto prototypes.

Aesthetically the villas can be said to share certain traits with De Stijl – the horizontality, planarity and almost cardboardy illusion of weightlessness –, but where a building such as Gerrit Rietveld's Schröder House (1923/24) is all projecting and interlocking planes, the villas' composition is rooted firmly in the idea of the single, coherent volume, architecture as »the masterly, correct and magnificent play of masses brought together in light«, as Corb famously put it in Vers une Architecture. The Villas La Roche and Jeanneret-Raaf later featured as the first of his iconic »four compositions« published in 1929, labelled with the caption »Fairly easy type, picturesque, animated. One can however discipline it through classification and hierarchy.« An agglomeration of volumes that ripples gently with projections and recesses, the villas' external form was, to a certain degree, decided by their interiors: »the inside makes itself comfortable and pushes the outside, which forms diverse projections«, as Corb himself described it. The ensemble nonetheless retains a strong sense of unity thanks to the horizontal, linking band of the strip windows and the flat, straight roof parapet. In their cubic whiteness, the villas are immaculate, machine-age adaptations of the housing Corb had admired so much on trips around the Mediterranean.

Entrance to the Villa La Roche is gained via a small section of elevation joining the picture gallery to the principal mass of the ensemble. Above the discreet and rather diminutive front door is a huge picture window which, we discover once inside, lights a full-height entrance hall rising almost three storeys. This space is the linchpin of the villa, around which all the rest of the house is articulated. As behoves such a sequentially important junction, it is given bravura architectural treatment. The first thing one sees on entering the hall is a huge, white, blank wall directly opposite, which, illuminated by the steady northern light of the picture window, was intended for hanging paintings. Display, both in the sense of architectonic ostentation and in the specific instance of La Roche's art collection, is thus immediately presented as the prime objective of the house. Essentially a giant white cube, the entrance hall is animated on its three other vertical sides by a whole series of projections and openings that dematerialize its limits into a complex play of solids and voids. To the right of the entrance are galleries and a staircase occupying the full height of the space, while to the left we find a projecting cubic balcony, the opening of a rising staircase and a seemingly unreachable, top-lit upper gallery (La Roche's library, as we will later discover). Behind, a footbridge runs in front of the picture window, linking the two halves of the house at first-floor level. Movement, through space and by extension through time, was essential to the *promenade architecturale*, and in the Villa La Roche's entrance hall Corb entices the visitor to move by means of a carefully considered *mise en scène*. The presence of the overhanging balcony to the left, and the inviting staircase opening below it, encourage one to mount to this level, from where one is led on into the principal room of the house, the picture gallery. As one does so, one begins to understand how the villa is put together, the constantly changing relationships of its constituent parts, visible both inside and out, allowing one to grasp the architect's intentions.

In contrast to the insistent orthogonality of the rest of the villa, the picture gallery features sensuous curves in the form of its front wall and a ramp sweeping up it, which accentuates the room's length and emphasizes that movement down the space, as in an Elizabethan long gallery, is solicited here. Lit by a sort of clerestory just under the ceiling, the gallery is luminous but enclosed, with no views out. Mood is created through polychromy, the first time Corb experimented with colour in this way, the range of tones used being that of his Purist paintings (some of which figured in La Roche's collection). To leave the gallery and continue the *promenade architecturale*, one must climb the curving ramp, whose steepness Corb badly miscalculated to the extent that rubber flooring had to be laid to stop people from sliding down it! Corb's lack of interest in this kind of detailing is well known, and is further demonstrated at the Villa La Roche in the rather rudimentary and at times downright shoddy finishes. After making the rather uncomfortable climb to the top of the ramp, one arrives at last in Raoul La Roche's library which, perched at the summit of the villa like some Andean eyrie, enjoys plunging views over the entrance hall below. High-placed look-outs requiring a climb to reach them were a feature of Corbusian houses (the Maison Cook, for example, had one), and may well have responded to sympathy on Corb's part with the solitary thinker of Romantic tradition who seeks intellectual inspiration on a mountain top (in the manner of Nietzsche's *Zarathustra*). The Villa La Roche's library is also reminiscent of the bridge of an ocean liner, a form of transport much admired by Corb, whose captains he considered heroes of the modern era. Culmination of the *promenade architecturale* on this side of the house, the library was intended as a place of meditation, from which one must descend to put one's thought into action.

Returning from the library back to the entrance-hall landing and crossing the footbridge in front of the picture window, one arrives at the only public room on the other side of the house, La Roche's dining room. This part of the building is arranged as a simple stacking of rooms, with the garage and concierge's flat on the ground floor, the dining room and attendant spaces on the first floor, La Roche's bedroom and bathroom above, and, crowning the ensemble, a roof terrace. Joylessly, almost shockingly Spartan, the dining room receives flat, even northern light by day from its strip windows, and by night is illuminated with bare bulbs suspended on slender wands attached to the ceiling. This austerity – which permeates the whole house – is a reflection of Corb's strange, rather severe, monastic outlook on life, and is even more patent in La Roche's bedroom (not open to the public). Given that this is the master bedchamber, the space is remarkably meagre and poky, even in comparison to other Corbusian bedrooms, which were generally smaller than those their clients wanted. Clearly, for Corb, a bedroom was a cell for sleeping in, and nothing more (likewise, the bathrooms and lavatories in his houses are frequently very mean). Terminating this section of the house is the partially covered and planted roof terrace, a representation of »nature« that complements the library (symbol of human intellect) crowning the villa's other side.

Raoul La Roche allowed Corb total-environment control by giving him responsibility for all the house's furnishings, right down to cutlery and glassware. Corb's taste for Spartan minimalism equally applied to the contents of a house, but was intellectualized in the notion of the *objet-type*. Where he did not employ furniture of his own devising, he chose industrially mass-produced objects of the type celebrated in his Purist paintings, products that he considered refined almost to essential perfection through a trial-and-error improvement process that, in his rendering of it, was practically akin to natural selection. The Villa La Roche was a Purist manifesto of the *esprit nouveau*, and living in it was not for the faint hearted. Comfort, luxury and individuality were sacrificed in favour of the architect's own Puritanical vision of life, and the occupant was required to conform. Even the picture collection for which the villa was ostensibly built was not entirely at home here, La Roche commenting that the sculptural poetry of Corb's creation was »so beautiful« that it seemed »almost a shame to hang paintings on it«.

The Villa Jeanneret-Raaf
Unlike Raoul La Roche, who gave Le Corbusier *carte blanche* to design his villa as he pleased, Albert Jeanneret and Lotti Raaf had specific ideas about what they wanted in their house. Luckily their requirements and sensibilities coincided with Corbusian concerns, especially those encapsulated by the famous slogan

»une maison est une machine à habiter«. Convenience and practicality were to be the ruling deities in the Villa Jeanneret-Raaf. In a letter to Corb, Albert Jeanneret spoke of his wish that the villa should, like Lotti Raaf's home in Sweden, allow »the mistress of the house to satisfy easily her desire for constant cleanliness, brightness and economy of effort«. The villa's programmatic requirements were standard middle-class fare for the time, and Corb stacked them vertically, as was then common, in the manner of a London town house. In the basement we find services – laundry, boiler room, etc. –, on the ground floor are the entrance, garage, concierge's lodge, maid's bedroom and Jeanneret's music room (Corb's brother was a professional musician), the first floor contained the bedrooms and the bathroom, while the final storey was given over to the living areas: kitchen, dining room and *salon*. This is clearly not quite the traditional stacking order for this kind of house, deliberately so, for by placing the living accommodation on the upper storey Corb ensured not only that it received the maximum amount of light and benefited from the best views but also enabled it to communicate directly with the roof garden above (the villa has no ground-level gardens). It is interesting to note that this is almost exactly the same arrangement used by Paul Guadet in his own *hôtel particulier* (16.17) completed in 1912.

The roof gardens of the Villas La Roche and Jeanneret-Raaf were the first examples in Corb's œuvre of what would become one of the architect's leitmotifs, yet another of the »five points«. Roof gardens were both economic and practical: in a densely built city like Paris they provided an amenity that most inhabitants could only dream of, reclaiming space that had previously been reserved »only for the romantic assignations of alley cats and sparrows« (Corb's words). Furthermore, elevated above the noise and pollution of the street, they provided a more pleasant environment than traditional, earth-bound gardens, one endowed with copious fresh air and sunshine. The virtues of these latter elements, along with the benefits of physical exercise, had been drummed into Corb as a child, and he was always keen to get his clients to use their roof terraces for gymnastics. Lotti Raaf seems especially to have appreciated hers, but more from an interest in sunbathing than sport. She was also thrilled by her 12.5 m-long living room, declaring that »the first impression is one of air, light and gay colours ... It's a symphony created by an artist, a feast for the eyes.« By disposing the dining and living rooms of the villa as adjoining, open and interlocking »Ls«, Corb was able to play on visual continuity and diagonal perspectives to ensure an illusion of spaciousness that would not normally have been possible in rooms of this size. With its stacked plan, almost entirely blind lateral wall and principal fenestration at front and back, the Villa Jeanneret-Raaf constitutes a prototype terraced house, and could easily have been repeated *ad infinitum* in a long street of tacked-together dwellings.

16.14 Hôtel Guimard
122, avenue Mozart
Hector Guimard, 1909–12
(Métro: Michel-Ange-Auteuil)

One of the best surviving examples of Guimard's mature style, this house was built for the architect himself and his wife, the painter Adeline Oppenheim. Begun a full decade after the early, experimental Castel Béranger (16.11), it shows a designer now in full control of his language and vocabulary. Moreover, since Guimard was his own client and therefore restricted only by budget, he was able to create the kind of total-environment *Gesamtkunstwerk* that Art-Nouveau architects at their most zealous strived for.

The site acquired by Guimard was an irregularly shaped corner plot, small enough that he could omit internal load-bearing walls and push the burden out onto the façades, thereby freeing up the interior. Space was at a premium, as Guimard had to accommodate not only his household but also his practice (on the ground floor) and his wife's studio (a large pentagonal space on the third floor, whose big northerly window can be seen on the Villa-Flore façade). The liberty and ingenuity of his plans, which included cleverly disposed oval reception rooms on the first floor, recalled the interior deftness of some Rococo *hôtels particuliers* (e.g.

16.14 Hôtel Guimard

250 16th *arrondissement*

the Hôtel Matignon (7.14)), whose architects had also faced the problem of making the most of a cramped site. (Indeed one could also make a case for a link between the rippling sinuosity of Rococo decorative forms and the »organic«, vegetal-inspired motifs of Art Nouveau.) Guimard's mature mastery of his style is evident in his elevations. Where at the Castel Béranger his budding Art-Nouveau tendencies were expressed as isolated elements in otherwise conventional façades, here he achieved synthesis, designing exteriors that undulate in deliquescent dilatation, their decorative components subservient to an organic whole. In its quasi-Rationalist expression of material and, to a certain extent, structure, the Hôtel Guimard displays its debt to Baudot, Viollet-le-Duc and, ultimately, Gothic architecture.

Guimard attended to every detail of the house's decoration and fittings, from the panelling, plasterwork, lighting and furniture to the design of the carpets, curtains and table linen, which bore the monogram »OG« (Oppenheim-Guimard). New technology was an Art-Nouveau preoccupation and, true to form, Guimard installed a lift in place of the traditional *escalier d'honneur* (thereby saving space), which consisted simply of a base surrounded by two-way mirrors so that his visitors would not be »shut up in a cage«. Following Guimard's death in the 1940s, his widow offered the house and its contents to the French state, but her gift was refused and, sadly, the fittings were dispersed. The Hôtel Guimard's dining-room furniture can now be seen in the Musée des Arts Décoratifs.

Guimard also built the apartment building opposite at 1, villa Flore / 120, avenue Mozart (1924–26), which demonstrates his post-WWI, Art-Déco-influenced style.

16.15 Apartment building
25, avenue de Versailles
Jean Ginsberg and Berthold Lubetkin, 1930/31
(Métro: Mirabeau)

Ginsberg and Lubetkin, former acquaintances in Warsaw, crossed paths again by chance in Paris, completed their studies at the same school – the École Spéciale d'Architecture – and afterwards collaborated on what was for each his first project: an apartment building in the Avenue de Versailles, a development mounted by Ginsberg with capital borrowed from an uncle. Ginsberg went on to develop one of the most prolific Parisian practices of the 20C, while Lubetkin emigrated to England and became a founding father of British Modernism.

As a first project, the Avenue de Versailles block is astoundingly assured. An astute businessman, Ginsberg purchased a site in Auteuil, an area then in full expansion and likely to attract the young, moneyed clientele who patronized modern architecture. The narrowness of the site chosen is explained by his limited means. Nine storeys high and supported at only three points, the apartment building features identical plans on all bar the ground and final floors, with »artists'« studios at the rear and two-bedroom apartments on the street. Both architects were admirers of Le Corbusier (Ginsberg worked with him briefly), and the master's influence is omnipresent. The façade is free, demonstrated by the slender central column behind which the windows curve away to form a small terrace on each floor. The ground floor is borrowed from Corb's Maison Cook (29.3), although the Parisian building code did not allow the total liberation of the floor space permissible in Boulogne. Lubetkin had to fight with the authorities to retain even a 1.5 m setback of the ground-floor street façade, regarded by the Prefect of Police as a likely shelter for snipers in the event of a riot! The windows, of German manufacture, are given the horizontal emphasis recommended by Corb and, in accordance with his preaching on the beneficial effects of fresh air and sunshine, are operated by a complex mechanism allowing them to disappear entirely into the walls. This theme is continued on the roof-terrace, intended as a solarium and for the practice of Swedish gymnastics, and hence equipped with a communal shower. Rendered in classic ocean-liner style, with beautifully crafted, »aerodynamic« handrails, the terrace was, at the time of construction, the highest point in Auteuil, with splendid views upriver towards the Eiffel Tower (7.8).

Despite the district architect's derisive description of the building as »Bolshevik«, it was a great success, and all the flats were let before it was even completed. Ginsberg and Lubetkin's attention to detail and the finesse of the finishes have attracted particular admiration. One of the first apartment blocks built to Corbusian principles, it was widely published in the architectural press – thanks, in part, to Ginsberg's gift for self-promotion – and made the reputations of its two young architects.

16.16 Apartment building
42, avenue de Versailles
Jean Ginsberg and François Heep, 1933/34
(Métro: Mirabeau)

Ginsberg's third project and second apartment building in the Avenue de Versailles (see 16.15), this was, like no. 25, a speculative development mounted by Ginsberg himself. On this occasion he collaborated with François Heep. Situated on a street corner, the site is built to maximum capacity as permitted by the regulations. The plans are standardized, comprising four small apartments per storey, except for the ground floor, occupied by a boutique and servants' quarters (since modified), and the eighth and ninth floors, which together form a penthouse. As at no. 25, great attention was paid to convenience and detailing, including, for example, placing all utility meters in the stairwell outside the apartments, thus allowing access without disturbing residents.

What makes this building special, however, is the treatment of the exterior. Shadow and relief are subtly

16.16 Apartment building

contrasted with light and plane in the form of the balconies on the avenue frontage and the smooth, flat elevation on the Rue des Pâtures. A semicircular »tower« joining the two façades elegantly turns the corner and acts as the hinge of the composition. The curvature of the tower windows is superbly accomplished. Small cantilevered balconies punctuate the Rue des Pâtures frontage, and asymmetrical projecting volumes crown the edifice. Weathering and alterations have taken the aerodynamic edge off the building, but it has nonetheless aged well.

Heep later emigrated to Brazil, while Ginsberg's subsequent output never quite matched the plastic artistry of no. 42. His postwar career, devoted almost exclusively to property development, produced mostly disappointingly uninspired slab blocks.

16.17 Hôtel Guadet
95, boulevard Murat
Paul Guadet, 1912
(Métro: Porte de Saint-Cloud)

Son of Julien Guadet, who was professor of theory at the Ecole des Beaux-Arts (see 1.19), Paul Guadet studied architecture under his father, and counted amongst his fellow students Auguste Perret. He later became, like Perret, a devotee of concrete construction, and turned to this material when designing himself a home, as well as to the expertise of his former classmate – who ran his own construction company specializing in concrete technology – to build it. Put up six years after Perret's seminal Rue-Franklin flats (16.8), Guadet *fils*'s house, which is something of a curiosity, takes up Perret's transposition of traditional timber trabeation to concrete, an approach that was derived partly from Guadet *père*'s theories of Rational Classicism and partly from the ideas of Auguste Choisy. On its boulevard façade, the Hôtel Guadet displays an elegant grid of thin concrete posts and beams, decorated with ceramic tiles, whose voids are mostly glazed, with brick panels providing the necessary areas of wall surface. Through its proportions and detailing – for example the lintel tiling that recalls a Doric frieze or the cornice surmounting it – the *hôtel* makes clear its debt to the Classical tradition. Its distribution is eminently rational: Guadet's practice and studio were on the tall ground floor, the shorter first floor contained bedrooms, while the second floor, which is as tall as the ground floor and from which the roof garden could be reached, housed the living and dining rooms. Inside, Guadet's enthusiasm for concrete went even as far as casting his bed in the stuff!

16.18 Parc des Princes
Avenue du Parc-des-Princes and 24, rue du Commandant-Guilbaud
Roger Taillibert, 1967–72
(Métro: Porte de Saint-Cloud)

At the time of its inauguration and until completion of the Stade de France (21.1) in 1998, this was France's biggest stadium, where all the country's major soccer and rugby finals were played. Its construction was an unexpected by-product of the building of Paris's ring road, the *boulevard périphérique*, whose course happened to lop off a chunk of a 19C stadium that originally occupied the site. The municipality seized this opportunity to strike a bargain with the state for the realization of a brand-new, national stadium to replace the old, local one. The technical specifications set out in the brief were challenging: into an area of only 4 ha – under part of which ran the *périphérique* – Taillibert was asked to squeeze 50,000 covered seats and to ensure that no supporting pillars or other obstructions obscured the view of the pitch from anywhere in the stadium. In its formal and technological response to these demands, the new Parc des Princes was something of a revolutionary pioneer.

In its basic conception Taillibert's design is daringly simple, comprising two tiers of seats, the lower of which sits on the ground while the upper is suspended from a series of giant concrete brackets ringing the stadium; these brackets also carry the huge, cantilevered span of the roof, which at its widest extends a breathtaking 48 m without intermediary support. Rising to different heights according to the length of roof they carry (externally the stadium is oval in plan, but the internal roof perimeter is rectangular, following the contours of the pitch), the 50 brackets, each 12 m apart, give the stadium its distinctive »open-flower«

or »sliced-melon« look. Their gently curving profile accommodates the slope of the terraces as well as contributing to the building's expressionist aesthetic. Realized in raw, pre-stressed concrete, the brackets, like all the stadium's other principal components, were prefabricated on site and assembled using state-of-the-art computer technology (one of the earliest instances of its application to a major construction project) that ensured accuracy to within a centimetre. In this, as in every aspect of the building, Taillibert seems to have sought the most elegant economy of means, this principle being valid for the stadium's basic structure right down to details such as the lighting units mounted in the thickness of the roof – thereby avoiding projecting pylons – and the rainwater run-off concealed within the brackets. In its 30 years' existence, the Parc des Princes has needed only relatively minor reconditioning. Its success brought Taillibert the commission for the 1976 Montreal Olympic stadium, and he has since gone on to build a number of other stadia in America and the Middle East.

The Parc des Princes was not without its critics, however. In terms of urban infrastructure, especially

16.17 Hôtel Guadet

16.18 Parc des Princes

parking, the stadium is seriously under-equipped, and the surrounding area becomes impassable during matches. Not everyone was enamoured of its architecture either, some finding it rather brutally monumental and closed off from its urban context. (The Stade Charléty (13.13) was one answer to this: also in concrete, it substitutes lean, skeletal forms borrowed from Hi-tech for the rather massive »Modernist Baroque« of the Parc des Princes.) After the launch of the Stade-de-France project, the Parc des Prince's most vociferous opponents (many of whom were local residents) waged a campaign for its demolition on the grounds that it would be rendered superfluous by construction of the new stadium. Happily this has not occurred and, as well as becoming home to the Paris-Saint-Germain football team, the Parc des Princes is planning to diversify its activities to include rock concerts, antique fairs and so on. With this in mind it has recently undergone substantial modifications, including the lowering of the pitch by 70 cm to accommodate extra seating and the construction of an ancillary building to house Paris-Saint-Germain's administration, shop and a restaurant. Designed by Taillibert himself, this new annexe takes the form of a peculiarly humpbacked, curvilinear structure in metal and glass.

17th *arrondissement*

17.1 Salle Cortot
78, rue Cardinet
Auguste Perret, 1928/29
(Métro: Malesherbes)

This intimate little concert hall was commissioned by the pianist Alfred Cortot for Paris's Ecole Normale de Musique. The rather awkward, 9 x 29 m site allocated to the building was formerly occupied by the stables of the 19C *hôtel particulier* in which the school is housed. On being engaged for the job, Perret promised Cortot a space whose acoustic would »ring like a violin«. In the opinion of Cortot, Perret surpassed even this promise, the violin in question being, in the words of the pianist, »a Stradivarius«. Perret had expressed his dissatisfaction with the acoustics of concert halls designed by acoustic engineers, and claimed to derive his inspiration from nature: after appreciating the timbre of a group of pilgrims singing underneath a tree canopy, he concluded »that to obtain the same sonority, it would suffice ... to build a hall that was perforated to the same extent as the covering of trees«.

Contrary to usual practice, the Salle Cortot's orchestra platform is placed at the centre of one of the site's longer sides, a clever move that ensures that none of the seats is further than 17 m away from the musicians. As this is a Perret building, it is of course realized in reinforced concrete, the balconies displaying the same kind of whizzing curvilinear profiles and seemingly weightless cantilevers as at his earlier Théâtre des Champs-Elysées (8.12). A fervent admirer of ancient-Greek temples and a subscriber to the idea that their forms were derived from timber construction, Perret always aimed to imitate the tectonics of wooden buildings in his concrete structures, arguing that there was a direct link between timber and concrete construction because of the wooden shuttering used to cast the concrete. Thus at the Salle Cortot we have a frame structure of beams and supports that could theoretically have been realized in wood, and the grain of the formwork used to cast the concrete is left apparent on its surface. As for the canopy-of-trees idea, the hall is not so much perforated as treated like a giant, resonating sound box, the spaces between the concrete members being filled with 4 mm-thick wooden panels behind which are 3 cm-deep air gaps. In an unusual move for Perret, he painted the interior concrete surfaces of the hall a golden-bronze colour (he usually left his concrete bare), so that it has the appearance of gilded wood and thus harmonizes visually with the wooden panels, giving the impression of an edifice constructed entirely from timber.

Externally, the Salle Cortot displays a blind entrance façade on the Rue Cardinet that masks one end of the hall. It is articulated like a Classical temple with a prominent cornice and a »frieze« that is in fact the grill covering the aeration system's vents.

17.2 Sainte-Odile
2, avenue Stéphane-Mallarmé
Jacques Barge, 1935–46
(Métro: Porte de Champerret)

Launched in 1931 by Cardinal Verdier, Archbishop of Paris, the »Chantiers du Cardinal« (»Cardinal's Building Sites«) were an ambitious programme of church construction that aimed to keep pace with the Paris region's massive population growth, the diocese of Paris having expanded from 750,000 to around 5 million souls in the space of a only century. Over 60 new churches were initially planned, including Sainte-Odile, which was intended for a new parish of around 30,000 people.

Like so many of its interwar confrères, whose architects took their cue from the Sacré-Cœur (18.2), Sainte-Odile is of Byzantine inspiration and, like Paul Tournon at the Eglise du Saint-Esprit (12.12), it was to the ultimate Byzantine church, Hagia Sophia (532–37), that Barge turned for his design. The long, narrow and constricted site with which he had to work precluded a square, centralized, domed plan of the Hagia-Sophia type, and he instead ingeniously stuck together, end to end, three such structures, terminating the composition with a rectangular choir, itself concluding in a semicircular apse. The advantage of this system was that it allowed a vast, unencumbered nave that

17.1 Salle Cortot

Sainte-Odile is constructed entirely in reinforced concrete, faced on the exterior with a skin of dark Belgian brick, but left largely unadorned on the interior, where it is finished with care. This, combined with a certain heaviness of structure and the lack of light, renders the interior impressively cavernous and gloomy. The exterior, with its northern-European bricks arranged in stripes and its spiky crenellation, appears very Expressionist, as does the 72 m-high bell-tower, one of Paris's tallest. Lofty, evangelizing bell-towers for parishes too long godless were favoured by the French Catholic Church at this time, and the standard reference was Auguste Perret's tower at Notre-Dame du Raincy (35.1). Barge here supplied his own streamlined version with fins, which appears very Gotham City. A monumental archway filled with bas-relief sculpture marks the church's entrance although, as with the other decorative elements, it is not of the same quality as Barge's expressive architecture.

17.3 Palais des Congrès
Place de la Porte-Maillot
Guillaume Gillet et al., 1969–74; Christian de Portzamparc, 1994–99
(Métro: Porte Maillot; RER: Neuilly Porte-Maillot)

Eager to exploit the city's potential as a centre for international conferences, Paris's chamber of commerce commissioned this »palace of congresses« at a time when the city was undergoing major transformations at its periphery. The new conference centre was strategically sited to take advantage of these developments. Midway between the old business districts of the 8th and 16th *arrondissements* and the new *quartier d'affaires* at La Défense (27.1), it was located bang on the brand-new *boulevard périphérique*, which, via its link to the A3 motorway, made the Palais directly reachable by car from Charles-de-Gaulle airport (22.1). Moreover, the Palais fronted Paris's prestigious Tuileries–La Défense »grand axis« (see 1.10), and also sat above one of the RER suburban railway lines. To increase further its chances of success, the Palais was to include a 1,000-bedroom hotel and a 15,000 m² shopping centre. Gillet's design clearly separated the hotel from the rest of the Palais, with the conference/shopping centre occupying a low, six-storey building directly on the *grand axe*, while the hotel was located in a 33-storey tower rising behind it. Although an attempt was made to jolly up the hotel with curved façades and indented edges, it is not particularly inspired. Nor, externally, was the conference/shopping centre, which echoed the hotel's convex curves with a concave indentation on the *grand axe*, and whose layered, concrete-balconied façades had a rather timorous, Festival-of-Britain air about them. Internally, however, the centre's functional, 3,723-seat main auditorium was generally considered a great success; its 4,000 m² column-free ceiling and three-level foyer nestling under the seating were bravura feats of concrete construction.

17.2 Sainte-Odile

squeezed the maximum possible surface area out of the limited space, each dome being supported on giant arches spanning the church's width. As it gives onto neighbouring buildings, Sainte-Odile's southwestern flank (the church is not orientated) is blind, consisting of three huge, full-height side-chapels in the form of semicircular domed apses. The southeastern flank, in contrast, is entirely glazed, with one enormous window per bay. Further light is introduced, as at Hagia Sophia, by a row of small windows running round the base of each dome. Despite its substantial glazing, the church's interior is very dark, partly because of its northern exposure and partly because of the heavy, almost opaque stained glass filling its principle windows.

17.3 Palais des Congrès

The chamber of commerce's speculation paid off handsomely, to the extent that by the 1990s demand for bookings at the Palais far exceeded possible supply. Opinion was not so enthusiastic regarding the building's architecture, which was generally considered rather drab and unfashionably dated. The Palais's management therefore decided to kill two birds with one stone by commissioning an extension to the building that would increase its capacity by 41,000 m² and also provide it with a new, modern visage on the *grand axe*. Portzamparc's proposal, chosen from a limited competition, cleverly overcame the rather contradictory demands of the brief. Local residents' associations had managed to impose a restriction on the increase of the Palais's surface area on the ground, with the result that the architect had very little room for manœuvre. In order to achieve the desired surface-area augmentation, he devised a 30°-inclined elevation on the *grand axe* whose summit projects well beyond the building line below, thereby providing supplementary space on the upper floors. The diagonal of the façade's slant is cut midway by a horizontal, in the form of a terrace running along its entire 156 m width; the terrace serves as the building's principal fire escape, with slinky metal staircases connecting it to the ground. In this way dramatic tension was brought to the façade and precious internal space was saved. Further drama is supplied towards the façade's centre in the form of a cutaway that reveals a seemingly free-standing, inversed cone, in which the Palais's three new conference auditoria are housed – where the original building dissimulated its auditorium, the extension celebrates this aspect of its function. An already complex shape that is moreover deformed by the course of the Palais's old façade, the »cone« would have been unbuildable ten years before, but thanks to computer technology the complex calculations required for its cladding were realizable. Portzamparc had originally proposed a glass-fronted building, but later decided that this was expensive and inappropriate for an edifice whose spaces require the shutting out of daylight. Consequently, the steel-framed main elevation is faced with stone-coloured concrete panels, whose dual tint gives an appearance of rustication. As such the Palais takes on a fortress aspect, an inversed, space-age bastion guarding the gates of Paris, whose scale and horizontality were intended to speed the *grand axe* along at automobile velocity.

18th *arrondissement*

18.1 Funiculaire de Montmartre
Place Suzanne-Valadon and Rue du Cardinal-Dubois
François Deslaugier and Roger Tallon, 1990/91
(Métro: Abbesses, Anvers)

Montmartre's first funicular railway was built in 1900 to render less arduous the 200-step climb to the church of the Sacré-Cœur (18.2), then under construction. Initially powered by water, the Funiculaire was electrified in 1935, and the new cars remained in service for 55 years until, worn out and in need of continual repair, their replacement was scheduled in 1990. In view of the ever-increasing passenger numbers – 2,350,000 in 1989 –, the RATP decided that, instead of a mere technological updating, the entire railway should be rebuilt, including its nondescript and dowdy stations. No less a celebrity than Roger Tallon, creator of the TGV and, subsequently, the Métro Météor trains – see feature on the Métro and RER), was hired to design the new cabins, and he engaged François Deslaugier, whose back-catalogue included the lifts of the Grande Arche de La Défense (27.4), to build the replacement stations.

More akin to an inclined elevator than to a traditional funicular, the new railway was designed to halve maintenance costs while more than doubling capacity from 800 to 2,000 passengers/hour. Tallon's slick cabins feature low, panoramic windows to allow good views of the surroundings, and are entirely automated. Unlike their predecessors, they are totally independent of each other, so if one breaks down the other can continue running. They are equipped with weight sensors which, once a certain threshold has been reached, tell the cars to depart, although if after two minutes passenger numbers are not yet sufficient the cars will leave anyway. The 113 m journey lasts 40 seconds (compared to 70 with the old system), the track climbing 36 m at an angle of 35°.

For the stations, Tallon envisaged transparent structures in the spirit of Guimard's famous glass Métro

18.1 Funiculaire de Montmartre

18.2 Sacré-Cœur

canopies. Deslaugier rejected the idea of direct quotation in the form of a »palm-leaf« structure, instead opting for something more audacious. The station buildings are pared down to an absolute minimum, and rendered in streamlined stainless steel. On top of them perch, like membranous wings, soaring steel-and-glass canopies, whose undulations correspond to the direction of travel at either end. The glass membranes are held in tension by double brackets set at the extremities of supporting arms, and are thus entirely free from these arms, above which they rise in a taut curve. The physical interaction of glass and steel is similar to that of bone and flesh, and the resulting structure is both strong and flexible. Deslaugier's »diaphanous vaults«, as he described them, are discreet yet daring, transparent yet tangible, and harmonize well in the surrounding urban landscape. Unfortunately, no one seems to have considered the Parisian climate, which regularly dumps layers of grime onto their pristine surfaces, rendering them rather less than crystalline.

18.2 Sacré-Cœur
Place du Parvis-du-Sacré-Cœur
Various architects, principally Paul Abadie, 1874–1923
(Métro: Abbesses, Anvers)

Paradoxically, one of Paris's biggest tourist draws is hated by many inhabitants of the city. Today the opprobrium boils down essentially to aesthetics, the Sacré-Cœur's architecture frequently being condemned as kitsch, wedding-cakey or simply plain ugly. But this vision of the Sacré-Cœur as the paragon of unsightliness has a long history, one that began at its conception and was rooted as much in its perceived political content as in the supposed transgression of any aesthetic canon. The church was commissioned in the wake of France's 1870 defeat by Prussia, a national catastrophe that certain members of the French Catholic church interpreted as divine punishment for Gallic impiety and decadence. This had begun, of course, at the Revolution, and could no longer continue unexpiated: many priests called on the faithful to ask salvation from the Sacred Heart of Jesus as a sign of national repentance. Numerous dioceses subsequently changed their dedication to the Sacred Heart, and it was in this context that the rich and pious brothers-in-law Alexandre Legentil and Hubert Rohault de Fleury formulated their famous vow to build a pilgrimage church in Paris, dedicated to the Sacred Heart, as a symbol of French penitence. The idea took off, with money being raised through a national subscription. Donations came essentially from conservative, rural France, which was one of the many reasons why the project came to be associated with anti-Communard (the Commune having been a solely Parisian uprising), pro-Royalist and anti-Republican sentiment. The thinly disguised political attitudes of certain prominent clergymen did nothing to appease matters, either. Add to this the Sacré-Cœur's provocative site on the Montmartre hill – supposedly chosen because Saint Denis was executed there, but which also happened to be the spot where the Communard uprising had begun, and which, to boot, conferred on the church an inescapable hegemony in the Parisian cityscape – and you had a recipe for altercation. To complicate matters even further, in 1873 the Assemblée Nationale declared the project to be of »national interest«, thereby conferring on it an official legitimacy that many considered to be at the very least inappropriate.

A national architectural competition was held in 1874 to find a design for the Sacré-Cœur, which was won by the relatively unknown Paul Abadie, a former pupil of Viollet-le-Duc's. It should be noted that, due to its extremely long construction period, the church we see today is not exactly as Abadie intended. He died in 1884 and was succeeded by a total of five other architects, who, although they respected the broad outlines of his original design, made many changes of their own. Work on the Sacré-Cœur suffered from numerous setbacks, the first being due to the fact that the Montmartre hill was riddled with disused quarry tunnels. In order to find firm foundations, the builders had to construct over 80 piles descending 34 m, a massive civil-engineering effort that had not initially been programmed. This considerably pushed up the project's overall cost, which in turn further slowed progress due to the piecemeal nature of the church's financing (which was reliant on the continuous generosity of donors), building work only proceeding when there was money in the bank. Completion of the Sacré-Cœur was yet further delayed by WWI, and the church was only finally finished externally in 1923 and internally in the 1930s.

The competition brief had stressed that the Sacré-Cœur was to be a pilgrimage church, meaning that numerous services would be held in it at the same time, and most of the entrants, including Abadie, therefore turned to the traditional western-European apse-ambulatory plan (which had originally developed for precisely this purpose). The brief also called for towers or a dome, with the majority of the entrants, again including Abadie, prioritizing this latter option. What Abadie understood perhaps better than any of the other competitors was that unlike, say, Gothic cathedrals, where the interior had priority and the exterior was arguably a mere product of the internal design, the Sacré-Cœur, because of its situation on the Montmartre hill, had first and foremost to be an exterior, a spectacular monument of sculpture that would merit its dominating position in the cityscape. The dome was of course the central element in this, so what Abadie did was to take a centralized, square-plan design, in the tradition of the Dôme des Invalides (see 7.12), and tack onto its rear a giant semicircular apse-ambulatory, with a generous crypt underneath ensuring further altar space. Simply placing a dome at the forefront of the composition was not enough, however, its form and decoration needing to be as spectacular as its positioning in the cityscape. Abadie had spent many years working in the Périgord region, restoring (some say rebuilding) cathedrals and churches there, most notably Saint-Front in Périgueux (c. 1120–73), and his design for the Sacré-Cœur was inspired by these examples. Although »Romanesque« in many respects, the Périgord churches are famous for their elaborate »Byzantine« domes and detailing, and it was these that Abadie pastiched at the Sacré-Cœur. Thus at Montmartre we find a cluster of four subordinate domes around the main drum in the manner of Saint-Front, and the same stretched, »peppershaker« lanterns and »fish-scale« treatment of the dome surfaces as in the Périgord originals. The elongated form of the Sacré-Cœur's domes, which bears no relation to the Périgord prototypes and has been much criticized, was not part of Abadie's original design. His domes were much flatter and more hemispherical, the elongation having been introduced by Hervé Rauline (chief architect from 1891 to 1904) on the grounds that traditional domes, when viewed from the base of the steep Montmartre hill, would have lost much of their impact. The stretched domes we see today were thus intended to »correct« the perspective from this viewpoint, ensuring that the church loses none of its soaring *élan* when approached by pilgrims.

Nestling between three of the domes on the main façade is Abadie's Romanesque-style, tripartite frontispiece, sporting lateral turrets and a terminating niche containing a statue of a Sacred-Hearted Christ. The busy multiplication of vertical elements on the principal façade gives the impression of some ethereal citadel, a fantastical, fairytale evocation of the Heavenly Jerusalem. On sunny days the ensemble literally dazzles the eye, thanks to the very hard and white Château-Landon stone from which the church is built. This stone has the peculiarity of bleaching on contact with air, thus making the Sacré-Cœur Paris's only self-cleaning monument! The church's dazzling whiteness has been yet another source of complaint, many finding its virginal fairness just too prissily clean and exhibitionistic. On its lateral façades the Sacré-Cœur presents a rather heterogeneous, assembled aspect, the projecting front and rear elements cohabiting rather disharmoniously with the domed central section. The apse, with its cluster of individually roofed radiating chapels, appears very southern-French Romanesque. Tacked onto its rear, in the line of the church's principal axis, is the Sacré-Cœur's bell tower, which was designed by Lucien Magne (chief architect from 1904 to 1916) and differs markedly from Abadie's proposal. Venetian Byzantine more than the Périgord variety seems to have been Magne's main inspiration, the result being rather reminiscent of 19C water-tower architecture. The bell tower was nearly not built at all because of reservations in certain quarters about placing such a phallic object behind the lady chapel!

Many critics have described the Sacré-Cœur's interior as being more »successful« than the exterior, although what they probably mean by this is that inside the church is more austere and uniform than externally. Coldly grand, the central space seems exaggeratedly vast because the corner-chapel arches have their springing points at the same height as the crossing arches, the result giving one the impression of a Piranesi-designed aircraft hangar. Perched on top of this gargantuan space, the dome, which internally is smaller than externally, appears rather weedily minuscule. The central emphasis one would have expected is lost, all attention being diverted to the oversized apse and its lavish ceiling mosaics, which provide practically the only colour (Abadie's original proposal included considerably more internal décor than we see today). Fenestration is sparse, with the result that the church's interior is extremely dark.

So is the Sacré-Cœur really as awful as its detractors claim? Ultimately it is a matter of personal taste, although many critics have tried to rationalize their dislike. An oft-heard complaint was that the Sacré-Cœur's architecture is bad because it is not convincingly Romanesque and, to boot, is realized in a »non-French« style. But then, on the other hand, this could be viewed positively, for although inspired by already extant buildings the Sacré-Cœur is not a slavish copy but a truly original, 19C-French creation. As for charges of kitchness, a case could certainly be made for the Sacré-Cœur as an example of »gorgeous kitsch«, its external form and styling being essentially intended as crowd-pleasers and having no »profound« *raison d'être*. Whatever the verdict, the late-20C's re-evaluation of 19C buildings, Postmodern camp sensibility and ignorance of and/or indifference to the Sacré-Cœur's original political context are all contributing to an improvement in its reputation.

18.3 Saint-Pierre-de-Montmartre
2, rue du Mont-Cenis
Extant buildings begun 1134
(Métro: Abbesses, Lamarck-Caulaincourt)

One of Paris's oldest surviving churches, this building is all that remains of the Abbaye de Montmartre, a Benedictine nunnery founded by Adélaïde de Savoie, wife of Louis VI the Fat, in 1134. According to legend, Montmartre, whose name is a corruption of *mons martyrium* (martyr's mount), was the site of the beheading of Saint Denis, patron saint of the Frankish monarchy. The nuns were guardians of his shrine, which was a popular place of pilgrimage throughout the Middle Ages. Their abbey church, as well as being an evocative remnant of medieval Montmartre, is an excellent example of the technological advances made by Paris-region builders during this period, advances that ultimately led to the development of the Gothic structural system.

We know very little about the construction history of Saint-Pierre-de-Montmartre, except that, at the time of its consecration in 1147, it was probably not finished. The church suffered badly during the Revolution (when the abbey buildings were demolished) and later became so derelict that in the mid-19C it was threatened with destruction. The building as we see it today is the product of a major restoration programme carried out in 1899–1905.

In plan, the church comprises a four-bay nave flanked by single side-aisles, a crossing and transepts – each of which has a projecting chapel on its eastern side –, and a small chancel terminating in a semicircular apse. Most heavily restored are the transepts, the southern one being essentially a 19C invention. The nave elevations are three »storeys« high, with a pointed-arch arcade (probably influenced by Burgundian churches), clerestory windows cut into the wall and, between the clerestory and the arcade, columned openings leading into the aisle roof space, which originally served as an ossuary. In comparison to most Romanesque churches, Saint-Pierre-de-Montmartre's walls are astonishingly thin, and are constructed through most of their thickness from dressed ashlar blocks, rather than consisting of a rubble-stone infill between two stone skins, as was then generally common. The advantage of ashlar walls was that they avoided the stability problems sometimes caused in rubble walling by poor mortar adhesion, and they are obviously more economical in material. On the other hand, because ashlar walls are less massive, they are unable to support the enormous lateral thrusts of stone vaulting. To get round this problem, the Saint-Pierre architect built huge compound vault responds inside the nave that bear much of the load on their own, the actual walls functioning

18.4 Saint-Jean-de-Montmartre

18.4 Saint-Jean-de-Montmartre
19, rue des Abbesses
Anatole de Baudot with Paul Cottancin, 1894(?)–1904
(Métro: Abbesses)

Viollet-le-Duc's favourite pupil and most dedicated disciple, Anatole de Baudot garnered notoriety as a polemicist, propounding a vigorously moralizing doctrine of Structural Rationalism based on his master's teachings. He railed against what he perceived as the decline of architecture in the 19C, which he blamed on the 17C and 18C (he was of course a Gothicist) and on *beaux-arts* teaching, condemning historical pastiche, the »irrational« use of columns and orders and the continued employment of stone in the face of new technologies. He advocated a reasoned, economic use of materials, and believed that buildings should be »truthful« about their construction; indeed, for him, manifestation of structure was the only legitimate mode of architectural expression. He was not against decoration, provided it complemented an edifice's structure and did not serve to hide it. Besides his writings, Baudot produced a number of buildings, of which the most famous is Saint-Jean-de-Montmartre, his fullest demonstration of his theories. It was also a technological pioneer, being probably the first large-scale construction in reinforced cement, and prefiguring many later developments.

Saint-Jean was commissioned in the wake of Montmartre's population explosion following the village's annexation into the city of Paris in 1860. The site acquired for the church was on steep gravely terrain, thus hampering traditional construction methods, and it was probably for this reason and in a bid for economy that Baudot's proposal was chosen. The architect had realized that reinforced cement, because it could be used as both skeleton and covering (unlike iron), would allow both a lean structure and an economy of materials in the spirit of Gothic construction. He joined forces with the engineer Paul Cottancin, who had patented his own system of reinforced-cement construction, something of a hybrid in that hollow bricks, bound into the cement with wire, formed an integral part of the structure. The rationale behind this was that bricks, which are just as pressure-resistant as cement, obviated the need for costly shuttering, saving time and money. Construction of the church was begun in 1897, but was halted in 1899 because of a planning-regulation infraction. The authorities were also doubtful as to the solidity of reinforced-cement technology, refusing to believe that a single cement slab only 7 cm thick between the crypt and the nave would hold, or that the 25 m-high piers, which measured a mere 50 cm across, would not buckle. Tests were carried out, the floor being loaded with sandbags at 800 kg/m^2 and the piers charged at 1,500 kg/m^2: neither budged. Construction of the building finally resumed in 1902.

Consisting essentially of a wide central nave with low side-aisles, Saint-Jean is constructed from a system of piers and rib vaults whose structure is clearly

merely as infill panels. In doing so he prefigured the Gothic structural system, which, at its most accomplished, consists of a stone skeleton whose voids are filled with glass and non-load-bearing wall.

Sometime around 1180, Saint-Pierre's chancel-apse vault was rebuilt, today's radiating ribs probably replacing a simple *cul-de-four*. The high vault was also rebuilt, sometime in the late-15C, because it was threatening to collapse (the nave and chancel walls still list at quite an angle), and the vault responds were then deprived of their capitals. One bay of the original vaulting remains, however, in the chancel, and constitutes the oldest surviving Parisian example of a rib vault. Its webs (hidden behind a coat of plaster) are, like the walls, constructed from thin ashlar courses, contrasting with the thick rubble webbing then common in northern-French churches; coursed ashlar webs later became the standard method. Saint-Pierre still possesses a good number of its original foliage-carved and historiated capitals, including one (fourth bay, north aisle) representing a man sitting backwards on a billy goat and lifting its tail, a symbol of lust! At the nave entrance are four Merovingian capitals (6C), which came originally from southwestern France. Also of note is the church's roof structure, which is essentially 12C and is one of the oldest surviving examples of its type in France. Externally, the building is less distinguished, much of what we see dating from the church's restoration, except the west façade, which is either late-17C or early-18C.

differentiated, on the interior at least, from the thin vertical infill panels, which are formed from two skins of brick separated by a 7 cm-wide insulating air gap. For the vault coverings, Baudot used two layers of reinforced cement, separated by a 4 mm layer of slag that helps insulate the church's interior against temperature fluctuations. The vaulting demands no extra roofing, unlike traditional vault constructions, the church being essentially a monolithic brick-and-cement structure that stands alone against the elements. Its exterior is faced in a skin of orange brick, the exposed cement portions being decorated with ceramic tesserae. For all Baudot's insistence on the expression of a building's constructive elements, Saint-Jean's structure is not easily decipherable externally. The church is also rather a curious amalgam of Gothic, vaguely Byzantine and Art-Nouveau-inspired forms, the elaborate convolutions of its multi-lierned vaults and overwrought balconies somehow lacking in formal conviction. Baudot tried to demonstrate some of the more daring possibilities of construction in reinforced cement, for example in the glazed compartments of the nave vault or in the open lattice work of the main façade's tower, but his efforts seem timid and irresolute. Despite these shortcomings, Saint-Jean was a brilliant technical achievement that clearly demonstrated the potential of reinforced-cement and, by extension, reinforced-concrete construction.

18.5 Théâtre des Abbesses

18.5 Théâtre des Abbesses
31, rue des Abbesses
Charles Vandenhove with Jacques Sequaris and Prudent de Wispelaere, 1986–96
(Métro: Abbesses)

Postmodernism in its ironical-kitsch and/or historical-pastiche forms is rare in France in comparison to, say, Britain or the U.S., learning from Las Vegas having been an exercise the French mostly considered irrelevant. Some French architects flirted with these brands of PoMo (for example Christian de Portzamparc in his early buildings – see 7.5 and 13.10), but in general when they make an appearance on French soil they are the work of foreigners, Ricardo Bofill being the most famous exponent (see 14.2 and 36.2). This example was produced by a team of architects headed by the Belgian Charles Vandenhove. Commissioned by the municipality, the project included, as well as the 420-seat theatre itself, dance studios and 30 public-sector apartments. The planning authorities stipulated that the scheme should integrate well into the existing fabric and above all should not disrupt the views from the Bateau-Lavoir (Picasso's former studio) just up the hill. Luckily, the terrain on which the complex stands slopes steeply, and the architects could place the theatre at the site's lower end, thereby ensuring that its bulk does not rise high enough to cause complaint. With the auditorium thus located at the rear of the plot, the architects followed the logical course of action and placed the apartments in buildings of a similar scale to their neighbours arranged around a courtyard that is visible from the Rue des Abbesses, whose street line is respected. Public access to the theatre is gained via the courtyard, while the dance studios sit under the auditorium, drawing light from the building's lateral and rear façades.

The complex's street elevations pastiche traditional 19C Parisian architecture: realized in stucco and stone-coloured concrete they sport evocations of Classical detailing (simplified rustication, pilasters, cornices, etc.) and curved zinc roofs with dormers. A variety of building heights is employed, both to reproduce artificially the unplanned diversity of the surrounding area and to ensure visual transition between neighbouring buildings of markedly different dimensions. Reminiscent in some respects of Aldo Rossi's »neo-19C« housing at La Villette (19.4), although without its graphic rigour, the street elevations successfully blend themselves into the existing cityscape, to the extent that one barely notices them. For the theatre proper's principal façade, however, the architects went for something more spectacular: onto an enormous and rather camp pink-stuccoed gable end they plonked a prissily detailed portico (styled by the artist Robert Barry), the ensemble constituting a tongue-in-cheek reference to traditional theatre architecture.

Inside, the theatre combines full-width frontal seating with lateral galleries, whose polychromatic décor is by Olivier Debré. Debré's murals were the subject of considerable controversy, the theatre's first director finding that they diverted attention from the stage and consequently covering them with black curtains during performances. The artist afterwards sued!

18.6 Maison Tzara
15, avenue Junot
Adolf Loos, 1925–27
(Métro: Abbesses, Lamarck-Caulaincourt)

The author of *Ornament and Crime* sojourned in Paris from 1922 to 1928. Of the innumerable designs he produced during this period, including his famous house for Josephine Baker (1927), only two came to fruition and were actually built – the Kniže boutique on the Champs-Elysées (no longer extant) and the Maison Tzara. Loos had first met Tristan Tzara in Zurich in 1917, when the poet was in full Dada fury. By 1925, however, Tzara wished to settle down and build a house for himself and his family. Loos's derisive and satirical attitude towards the fine arts had appealed to Dadaist sensibilities, but Tzara was not looking to live in a Dada manifesto. Impressed by the outspoken Austrian, he described him as »this great architect, the only one today whose work is not photogenic and whose expression is a school of profundity and not a means for attaining illusory beauty«.

The Maison Tzara is situated on a hillside plot in Montmartre in a very un-Parisian avenue of detached houses and villas. The street façade consists of a tall, austere rectangle, whose proportions and horizontal division into two parts, as originally designed by Loos, were obtained using the golden section. The planned sixth floor was never built, and the house thus appears more squat than intended. The lower section of the façade is in rough-hewn stone, while the upper portion is stuccoed. Each section encloses a cavity at its centre and, aside from a second-floor band of windows, all glazing is confined to these openings. The uppermost cavity corresponds to the living areas, and it has been suggested that its positioning and proportions, which also respect the golden section, were inspired by Egyptian tomb design, to signify a link between the life of the house and eternity. The result is certainly unusual, all the more so given that the materials used to such strange effect are entirely commonplace. The garden façade (since modified) was less forbidding than the street frontage, stepping back in terraces and incorporating larger areas of fenestration.

The interior of the house (today entirely altered) was divided vertically into service, reception and private areas, as was then common. Its torturous layout was due to Loos's »Raumplan« design method, which consisted in determining the size, proportions and interrelationship of rooms on a psychological and functional basis according to their use. Changes of level were incorporated into the plan to create spatial flux and distinguish one area of the house from another, a process complicated by Loos's preference for symmetrical exteriors composed of simple volumes. Myriad stair-

18.6 Maison Tzara

cases, which both divided and linked space, articulated the accommodation in the Maison Tzara, whose comfort contrasted, in typical Loosian manner, with the sobriety of the exterior.

18.7 Cimetière de Montmartre
20, avenue Rachel
Opened 1825
(Métro: Place de Clichy)

Last of the three cemeteries created by order of Prefect Nicolas Frochot's 1801 decree (see the Cimetière du Père-Lachaise, 20.2), the Cimetière de Montmartre, or Cimetière du Nord as it is officially known, is situated on a hillside slope that was formerly quarried for plaster. During the Revolution, the site was used as a mass grave for victims of Parisian uprisings (including the Swiss Guards killed at the Tuileries in 1792), and was afterwards bought by the municipality, in 1796, for use as a cemetery. Then only a fraction of its current size, the burial ground quickly filled up and, despite Frochot's decree, attempts to enlarge it failed, leading to its closure in 1808. It was not until 1825 that the current 11 ha of land had been assembled and the cemetery could open once more.

The irregularly shaped terrain is divided up less freely than the contemporaneous sections of Père-Lachaise, but not as formally as the Cimetière du Montparnasse (14.3). Where, in places, the hill drops steeply, picturesque terraces ensure level, usable ground. The cemetery's eastern extremity is marred by the Pont Caulaincourt, a road bridge built in 1888, which oppresses the »Avenue Principale« leading from the main entrance. Family mausolea proliferate, as at Père-Lachaise, although there are fewer monumental structures. Notable tombs include architect Frantz Jourdain's monument to Emile Zola (1902) and Félix Duban's memorial to Paul Delaroche (1856). The cemetery also possesses work by sculptors of renown, including Bartholdi (designer of the Statue of Liberty), Bartholomé, David d'Angers, Rude and Rodin.

18.8 Primary school
1, rue Paul-Abadie and Rue de la Moskova
Frédéric Borel, 1999–2001
(Métro: Porte de Saint-Ouen, Porte de Clignancourt)

This new primary school was programmed in the context of the ZAC Moskova, a global renovation of a forgotten and dilapidated corner of Paris. Situated on a new pedestrian thoroughfare baptized Rue Paul-Abadie, the school fronts one side of a newly created square giving onto the Rue Leibniz. The building had at once to display its official character while integrating with the varied, domestic-scale neighbouring buildings, and also to address the paradox of providing a protected environment for the children while at the same time opening itself up to the city.

As Borel pointed out, everybody remembers their first school, whether good or bad, and its formative influence can thus make itself felt throughout a lifetime. The architect consequently wanted his building to be clear and easily readable to its future pupils, which explains its relative formal simplicity in comparison to his other Parisian projects (which have all been housing schemes – see 11.3, 20.1 and 20.5). Instead of the open, spatially heterogeneous, multi-faceted and multi-finished architecture of his apartment complexes, we find here, fronting the new square, a simple, closed, protecting volume made up of a granite-clad base supporting a white-concrete box. Scaled to the dimensions of its neighbours and finished in sober Parisian colours, Borel's building harmonizes with its context. On the other hand, by treating the school very much as an object standing apart in the cityscape, the architect made sure its institutional character was expressed, an aspect of its image that is further underlined by the serious, exaggerated horizontality of the main façade. Leisure and recreation spaces are contained in the plinth, while the classrooms are situated in the concrete box. Projecting buildings at the school's rear provide, on the Rue-de-la-Moskova side, a one-storey assembly/games hall (whose roof terrace serves as supplementary recreation space) and, on the Cité-de-la-Moskowa side, staff accommodation, this latter wing ensuring a smooth visual transition between the school and the neighbouring apartment blocks. Occupying the space between the two rear projections and spilling out into the remainder of the site is the playground, which is treated rather in the manner of an open-air room, an impression reinforced by the large window in the wall separating it from the Rue de la Moskova.

This window was just one of Borel's many efforts to open up the building to the outside world, which also included the enormous areas of glazing at the centre and ends of the concrete box, and charming touches like the child-height strip window running along the street side of the assembly/games hall. Although Borel felt that Disney-style, »fairytale« architecture would be the built equivalent of gaga baby talk and was therefore best avoided, he did nonetheless include a certain number of slightly zany (and slightly gratuitous) features that were presumably intended to appeal to children: the »Egyptian« profiling of the plinth, the very Libeskind diagonal strip windows on the front and rear façades, the rather odd, oval window with its eyebrow canopy at the righthand end of the main elevation, and the equally peculiar coloured projecting panels in front of the large windows on each of the lateral façades. While adults will no doubt perceive these as playful nods towards a »childish« conception of architecture, one wonders what children will really make of them. Grown-ups may appreciate some of the quotations – we have already mentioned Libeskind, there is also definitely something of Portzamparc (for whom Borel worked at the outset of his career) permeating the ensemble, while the handling of the Rue-de-la-Moskova playground wall seems very Barcelona Pavilion.

Borel wanted the school building itself to contribute to the children's education, in the most basic sense of the word, it being the place where three- to six-year-olds learn the fundaments of sociability and coping with the world outside the home. Let's hope an appreciation of urbane, well-bred, thoughtful architecture, as exemplified by their school, will be one of the things they take away with them.

18.9 Hall of residence
4–8, rue Francis-de-Croisset
Architecture Studio, 1989–96
(Métro: Porte de Clignancourt)

19C Paris was cut off from its hinterland by a formidable defensive circuit comprising 94 bastions and a 250 m-wide glacis. In the aftermath of WWI, it became clear that modern warfare had rendered this sort of installation obsolete, and destruction of Paris's defensive ring was begun in 1920. City and suburbs were reunited for a brief period until, in the 1960s, General de Gaulle ordered construction of the *boulevard périphérique* to cope with the ever-increasing traffic flow

18.9 Hall of residence

in and around the capital. A six-lane, orbital motorway, the *périph'*, as it is colloquially known, follows the path of the old defensive circuit, and is perhaps even more effective a barrier between city and suburbs than were the fortifications, for it adds an extra, nightmarish disruption not provided by the latter: noise. Indeed decibel levels on certain stretches are so invasive that expensive plans are underway to cover the offending sections of motorway. When building this university hall of residence on a site bang up against the *périphérique*, Architecture Studio were left with no option but to take noise control as the central generating element of their design.

To this end, the architects erected their own defensive bastion, a huge 105 m-long and 33 m-high double wall running alongside the motorway, whose principal purpose is to shield the space behind it from the traffic's roar. The gently bowed, prefabricated outer wall, in black concrete, is fixed to the straight, inner wall – which, also in concrete but cast *in situ*, constitutes the building's »true« façade – by a series of tie rods, thereby leaving a gap between the two walls that reaches 5 m at its widest point. The sound shield is thus composed of a sandwich of 35 cm-thick concrete screens and an insulating layer of air. Had it not been for the site's fortuitous orientation – the area protected by the sound shield faces south –, this solution might have proved problematic. The towering black bulk of the sound shield is rendered a little less severe on the *périphérique* side by its curvature, which gives it an aerodynamic sharpness evocative of speed, and by the fluorescent orange hazard stripes decorating its extremities, a tongue-in-cheek reference to road signposting. At night, hundreds of tiny points of light enliven its inert mass.

On the other side of the sound shield, 351 studio apartments are contained in three eleven-storey, prow-shaped buildings that project forward from their protective screen. The prow-shaped form was chosen to allow a maximum of south-facing fenestration, and all the apartments benefit from views across to Montmartre, which would not have been possible with traditional, rectilinear bars. Those apartments furthest from the point of the prow are equipped with projecting, southern-orientated windows which, as well as catching the sun, avoid direct *vis-à-vis* with the studios opposite. All the windows are double glazed, except for those nearest the extremities of the sound shield which are quadruple glazed for added soundproofing. Staircases and other services are grouped at the centre of each block, allowing the apartments to run around the exterior. The clean, streamlined aspect of the studio buildings is emphasized by their swooping roof profile and shiny aluminium cladding.

But although this hall of residence is orientated towards Paris, the southern sun and views of Montmartre, it does not turn its back entirely on its noisy motorway neighbour and the suburbs beyond. The gap between the two walls of the sound shield contains the horizontal circulation connections between the three studio blocks, in the form of gangways running the length of a space that the architects justifiably describe as »Piranesian«. Its drama is further heightened by a huge window in the middle of the outer wall, which serves to light the circulation space and offers plunging views onto the *péripherique* and the hinterland beyond. In this way, this clever and admirably site-specific building, like any good general, turns to its advantage difficult conditions that might otherwise have been construed as defeat.

18.10 Social housing and swimming pool
13, rue des Amiraux
Henri Sauvage, 1919–30
(Métro: Simplon)

A founder member of the Société des Logements Hygiéniques à Bon Marché (Low-cost Hygienic Dwelling Company), Henri Sauvage patented a design for apartment blocks in the form of stepped-back terraces with which he hoped to revolutionize social housing. Well lit and ventilated, his buildings were intended to avoid all the ills of densely built, overcrowded neighbourhoods, then thought to be a major factor in the spread of tuberculosis. Unable to secure a commission for workers' housing, Sauvage tested his ideas by building a private apartment building in the Rue Vavin (6.10) for himself and a group of friends in 1912/13. It was not until after WWI that he finally got the chance to construct stepped-terrace social housing, when the Ville de Paris commissioned him to erect a block of 78 flats in the Rue des Amiraux.

Unlike at the Rue Vavin, the Rue-des-Amiraux site comprises almost an entire city block. Sauvage's building follows its periphery, and consists of eight storeys of stepped terraces on all three sides, articulated around four vertical staircase towers. Despite the »hill-town« qualities of the design, the overall effect is rather forbidding, not helped by the hygiene-evocative »Métro« tiles which hide the building's concrete frame and which, unlike at the Rue Vavin, are without decorative relief. The accommodation consisted of modest three- and four-room flats which, in advance of Le Corbusier, were provided with collective heating, washing and other facilities. Where the Rue-Vavin flats are provided with open terraces, Sauvage here used a system of stepped-back loggias, which garnered the disapproval of the planning authorities. They considered that all the advantages afforded by step-backs would be forfeited if balconies overshadowed the apartments. Nor had Sauvage solved the problem of orientation: because the building respects the street line, and because the resultant pyramidal form created by the stepped terraces prohibits double exposure of the flats, many of the dwellings face north. Despite the authorities' reservations the scheme was eventually accepted, after two redesigns, and although ultimately without successors was considered a victory of heroic innovation over conservative planning policies.

The repetition of step-backs in pyramidal form meant that the building's core consisted of a gigantic void. Sauvage suggested it be filled with a cinema, but the municipality preferred the idea of a swimming pool; work duly began in 1926, after completion of the flats, and the impressive top-lit pool was opened in 1930. Its creation prompted a reversal of attitude on the part of Sauvage. Still obsessed by stepped-terrace buildings, he now saw them as the outer covering for immense internal spaces, and proposed a series of ever more megalomaniacal pyramids – including a »Giant Hôtel« scheme for the Quai Branly – none of which ever came to fruition.

18.10 Social housing and swimming pool

19th *arrondissement*

19.1 French Communist Party headquarters
2, place du Colonel-Fabien
Oscar Niemeyer (with Paul Chemetov), 1965–80
(Métro: Colonel Fabien)

Completed only 20 years ago yet already spectacularly (and fashionably) dated, the headquarters of the Parti Communiste Français (PCF) are a fascinating example of High Modernism at its most baroque. Niemeyer is of course famous for his collaborations with Le Corbusier and for the principle edifices of Brasília, designed and built between 1956 and 1970. A card-carrying communist, Niemeyer fell from political grace in Brazil following the 1964 military coup and was forced into semi-exile. Europe became his base, and he realized a number of buildings there. For the PCF, whose old and dispersed headquarters caused a great deal of time to be wasted travelling from one office to another, Niemeyer waived his fee to make possible the construction of a new, made-to-measure home.

Situated in a densely populated working-class district (scene of many communist triumphs) on a circular, 19C traffic intersection (named after a communist Resistance hero), the site was a far cry from the *tabula rasa* of Brasília. It also presented the inconvenience of being fronted along its rear periphery by a vast, almost windowless party wall in rough-hewn stone. This latter factor precluded Niemeyer's initial idea of building a tower, demanding instead an edifice to mask the offending masonry. Niemeyer thus constructed what is essentially a standard, Corb-inspired slab block, elevated on Brutalist *pilotis* and curtain-walled in glass (by Jean Prouvé). True to his baroque spirit, however, he gave his slab a cheeky kink, rendering the orthogonal sensuously serpentine, and echoing the curvature of the Place du Colonel-Fabien. Lifts and stairs are grouped together in a separate concrete tower at the rear. The slab block contains the PCF's offices, which thus, curiously, become the building's principal emblem, as if bureaucracy were the dominant ideology. The public spaces are invisible externally: strict security requirements ruled out the obvious solution of a glass-fronted foyer between the *pilotis*, and Niemeyer consequently created an underground entrance hall, whose roof forms an undulating esplanade in front of the office bar. Protruding from this esplanade is a white, mammary mound, the uppermost extremity of the PCF's central auditorium, the only perceptible external clue to the existence of subterranean structures. Equally imperceptible without the aid of a model or drawing is that in plan the lift/stair-tower and the esplanade's contours form respectively a hammer and a sickle, the latter embracing the auditorium's womanly bulge.

Surveyed by the office bar, entrance to the building is gained via a rather sinister staircase descending just in front, signalled by a wavy concrete canopy. Windowless and rendered in raw concrete (Niemeyer expressly eschewed luxurious finishes for this »maison du travail-

19.1 French Communist Party headquarters

leur«), the generous public foyer is surprisingly warm and welcoming, its fluid free plan at once enthralling and confusing. Its sinuous floor and ceiling profiles direct one towards the *pièce de résistance*, the main auditorium. Here things become pure *2001: A Space Odyssey*: space-capsule-style sliding doors open into a 9 m-high and 22 m-diameter windowless, domed chamber, whose surface is covered with 121,000 suspended aluminium strips, painted white and lit from behind by neon tubes. The effect is stunning and, in combination with a series of giant ducts under the roof, the strips act as a vast vacuum cleaner, their slightly static surface attracting dust which is then sucked away! A womb-like hush pervades the chamber's embracing volume, in which one feels maternally cocooned. Below the auditorium, three further storeys of basement floors, occupying the entire surface area of the site, provide conference and meeting rooms, television studios and technical and parking space.

In their day, Niemeyer's PCF headquarters were at the forefront of avant-garde design and conformed to the progressive image the party wished to project; that environment shapes character is of course one of the fundaments of Marxist philosophy. Today seemingly as dated as the ideology in whose name it was constructed, Niemeyer's building remains a *tour de force* of sculptural inventiveness, an expressive tribute to its architect's originality.

19.2 Parc des Buttes-Chaumont
Service Municipal des Promenades et Plantations, 1864–67
(Métro: Buttes Chaumont)

This most extraordinary of Paris's parks – a product of Napoleon III's policy of emulating the green open spaces he had so admired in London while exiled there – was created following the 1860 annexation of the capital's outlying villages into its territory. The name »Chaumont« is a corruption of the French for »bald mount«, an apt description of the rocky outcrop that dominated the site. Mined for gypsum from the Middle Ages on, the Buttes Chaumont were also, until 1789, home to Paris's principal gallows. Thereafter the site became an enormous rubbish tip, and by 1860 had degenerated into a pestiferous health hazard whose quarry tunnels sheltered all variety of criminals and undesirables. In an early example of post-industrial land reclamation, the Ville de Paris voted to turn the area, whose topography made it unsuitable for building, into a park for the newly created 19th *arrondissement*.

The engineer Adolphe Alphand lead the team responsible for the site's regeneration, and wisely decided to exploit to the full the pre-existent accidents of terrain, rather than trying to achieve a *tabula-rasa* starting point. It is this accidental topography that made the Parc des Buttes-Chaumont so unlike anything usually seen in French gardens. The site's steeply undulating 23 ha are divided up with sinuous paths and carriageways and planted with naturalistic copses of trees. In the centre of the park are a series of spectacular features created from the debris of the old gypsum quarry. Out of a sizeable lake rise rocky pinnacles and a huge, looming headland (large sections of which are built of artificial rock) whose sheer sides drop cliff-like into the water and whose high point is adorned with an elaborate, circular temple (by the architect Gabriel Davioud) that acts as both beacon and belvedere. Industrial-age technology makes a dramatic appearance in the form of the soaring brick arch and airy suspension bridge that provide access to the headland, while nearby a quarry working now serves as an artificial cave, 14 m wide by 25 m high, decorated with stalactites and containing a thundering cascade whose water falls 32 m from a reservoir above. A Swiss chalet and an English cottage (both by Davioud), intended as café-restaurants, complete the facilities of this fantasy mountain resort in the heart of working-class Paris.

Completed in time for the 1867 Exposition Universelle, the Parc des Buttes-Chaumont was an instant success and today attracts an astonishing 3.5 million visitors a year. Continuing the tradition of late-18C aristocratic landscape follies, as exemplified by Marie-Antoinette's Jardin du Petit Trianon (32.5), it is pure but glorious kitsch, and clearly anticipated 20C, Disney-style popular theme parks (see Disneyland Paris

19.2 Parc des Buttes-Chaumont

19.3 Collège Georges-Brassens

(36.7)). The Parc des Buttes-Chaumont is currently the object of a major, six-year-long restoration programme.

19.3 Collège Georges-Brassens
51–55, rue d'Hautpoul
Manuel Nuñez Yanowsky, 1994
(Métro: Botzaris)

This secondary school was built as part of the ZAC Manin-Jaurès, a ten-year project to redevelop the former La-Villette railway line. The ZAC is a good example of the kind of planning policies adopted by the Ville de Paris since the early 1980s, which, in opposition to the comprehensive-redevelopment programmes of the 1960s and 70s, have aimed to effect a sort of urban »couture«, stitching back together fragmented parts of the cityscape. In this case the railway became the Allée Darius-Milhaud, a 1 km-long landscaped walkway integrated into the existing street pattern. A mixture of housing, offices, light-industrial buildings, schools and other facilities were planned to line it. Various architects worked on the project, with mixed results.

The fun-and-funky Collège Georges-Brassens is one of the ZAC's more startling realizations. Nuñez Yanowsky, who formerly worked with Ricardo Bofill and who was responsible for »Les Arènes de Picasso« (36.3), has, like Bofill, updated his vocabulary for the

19.4 Apartment buildings

Hi-tech 90s. For the college, he wanted a building that would astonish and inspire the pupils. Constructed from very smooth and white *in-situ* cast concrete, it sports quick-cadenced, classically inspired façades at its side and rear, reserving its fireworks for the principal entrance elevation on the playground. Here, whizzing Art-Déco-influenced profiles display a seemingly anarchic array of oddly shaped windows, the whole crowned by a »floating cornice« in the form of a metal trellis girder that lights up at night with neon strips. Rational yet gratuitous, silly yet serious, the *collège* is an event in an otherwise quiet corner of Paris.

19.4 Apartment buildings
1–11, avenue du Nouveau-Conservatoire
Aldo Rossi with Claude Zuber, 1986–91
(Métro: Porte de Pantin)

One may well walk past these buildings without even noticing them, so much do they blend into the Parisian townscape, and certainly nothing immediately suggests authorship by one of the top architectural stars of the 1970s and 1980s. But this is precisely what the late Aldo Rossi intended. Eschewing the egotistical signature building, he preferred to respect context and take his cues from local urban archetypes which, as he rightly pointed out, fashion the character of a place: the London terraced house, the Milanese tenement and, here, the 19C Parisian apartment building.

This is not to say that Rossi-esque preoccupations are not present: the Platonic volumes, repetitional rationality and slick asceticism that characterize his work are all apparent, and the project recalls more specifically his Gallaratese housing block near Milan (1969 to 1976). The same rectilinear arcade, punched-out repetitive fenestration and plain white surface are duplicated. But here the facing is in stone, the most common traditional building material in Paris, the windows have been elongated to Parisian proportions, and the arcade is reminiscent of that most famous of Parisian streets, the Rue de Rivoli (1.11, which was itself influenced by the Italian arcades that Rossi knew so well). Reference to Fontaine and Percier's thoroughfare continues in the curved roof, which is covered with traditional zinc and articulated by dormers and chimneys. Only the absence of balconies departs from the 19C model. Rossi also allowed himself a dash of latitude in the cylindrical corner post-office tower, enclosed within brick elevations and painted bright blue.

19.5 Cité de la Musique
209–223, avenue Jean-Jaurès
Christian de Portzamparc, 1984–95
(Métro: Porte de Pantin)

Programmed in the wake of redevelopment of the redundant La-Villette abattoirs as a major new public park (the Parc de La Villette, 19.7), the Cité de la Musique was designed to provide a new home for the state-run Conservatoire National Supérieur de Musique et de Danse, which was no longer functioning properly in its small and run-down quarters in the Rue de Madrid (8th). As well as accommodation for the conservatory proper, the Cité was to provide space for a Musée de la Musique to display the Conservatoire's fine collection of instruments, offices for the Institut de Pédagogie Musicale, and a medium-sized, adaptable concert hall of up to 1000 seats. There was also talk of building a 3,000-seat auditorium for large-scale symphonic works – a facility sorely lacking in Paris –, but budget restrictions made its realization impossible, although it was nominally retained in the programme in the hope that money might later be forthcoming. A limited, national design competition was organized in 1983–85: its winner, Christian de Portzamparc, was at the time a rising star, and the Cité de la Musique would prove to be the work that made his reputation, weighing heavily in his 1994 Pritzker-Prize victory. His achievement was all the more remarkable in that he brought off a programme of extreme technical and formal complexity on a very tight budget.

The area allocated to the Cité comprised two sites on the Avenue Jean-Jaurès either side of the Place de la Fontaine-aux-Lions (which had formerly served as the principal entrance to the La-Villette livestock market), and it thus fell to the Cité's architect to shape both the *place* and, by extension, the southern entrance to the Parc de La Villette. Portzamparc chose to place the Conservatoire to the west of the piazza, where it would be more integrated into the surrounding urbanity, and the concert hall, museum and Institut de Pédagogie Musicale – the »Pôle Public«, as this part of the Cité is known – to the east on an island site cut off from the townscape. Although the majority of the park's visitors will not be coming for the Cité de la Musique, those arriving from the south cannot but be concerned by Portzamparc's work since it is via his remodelled Place de la Fontaine-aux-Lions that they enter. Whether or not one is a partisan of Portzamparc's idiosyncratic architecture, it must be admitted that his handling of the Place de la Fontaine-aux-Lions is superb. He himself has said that the »voids around an object can be as important, or even much more important, than the object itself«, and the void that is the *place* amply demonstrates this. Intended, as he put it, as »a sort of huge vestibule at the scale of the park«, it brilliantly subverts the dominant, symmetrical axiality of the Grande Halle aux Bœufs (19.6) to create a more subtle, complex space that, despite a relatively low building density, retains a definite sense of enclosure while still remaining open to the park beyond.

Where the Cité itself is concerned, it was also an architecture of voids that to a certain extent prevailed. Portzamparc has made clear his hostility towards the monumental monoliths that often result from the large-scale, bureaucrat-planned projects of the modern era, finding them unnecessarily intimidating and dehumanized. Instead, he proposes, one should aim for variety and fragmentation, looking to the everyday, organically developed fabric of the city for answers. In place of the production-line, Modernist slab block there should be a diversity of forms, materials and spaces that mirror in miniature the diversity of the city itself. »My view was to embrace the richness of the city as a phenomenon which contains the past (in many different epochs), the present, and changes for the future«, he said. While such an approach has obvious appeal for high-density housing schemes (see Portzamparc's Rue-des-Hautes-Formes social housing, 13.10), its application to more institutional projects, for which a strong sense of unity and identity is arguably desirable, seems at first glance a little perverse. But where the Cité de la Musique was concerned this approach turned out to have significant advantages. The programme demanded such a wide variety of spaces and was so often modified during the course of its realization that flexibility proved to be of paramount importance; it was precisely the Cité's »fractioning« into semi-autonomous units that provided this suppleness, allowing the form and capacity of individual elements within the ensemble to be modified without calling into question the whole. Nonetheless, like a film script that has been chopped about by interfering producers and over-zealous *monteurs*, there are trailing plot lines and unexplained disjunctions that mar the Cité's overall coherence.

The Conservatoire National Supérieur de Musique et de Danse
Inaugurated in 1990, the western part of the Cité housing the conservatory was, because of its density and the need for acoustic isolation of the different spaces, the most complex of the two, but is also, paradoxically, by far the more accomplished and fluid. Its facilities include, amongst others, 105 individual practice rooms, 79 teaching rooms, five dance studios, an opera auditorium seating 350–450, an organ hall and a symphonic concert space both seating 250, a library, a gym, accommodation for over 50 students and office space for the conservatory's administration. Portzamparc grouped the ensemble into four strips – expressed on the boulevard side by four pavilions containing rehearsal rooms – so as to allow for greater flexibility in his acoustic-isolation juggling act. The first strip, on the Rue du Nouveau-Conservatoire, contains the library, gym and six storeys of student accommodation coiffed with a much remarked-upon sinusoidal roof, which some have found overly gratuitous in its attempt to express »musicality«, although it does splendidly dramatize an otherwise dull façade. Sheltering behind the ramparts formed by the Avenue-Jean-Jaurès and Rue-du-Nouveau-Conservatoire façades is a garden courtyard, across which run the other strips in various states of fragmentation and deconstruction. With this arrangement we find Portzamparc reinterpreting the classic Haussmannian city block: monumental buildings on the street enclosing more intimate and diverse spaces inside (a theme dear to one of Portzamparc's former assistants, Frédéric Borel – see 11.3 and 20.1). Within the courtyard, the second strip contains the symphonic concert hall, located in the basement to help its acoustic isolation, followed by a sunken patio and garden. In the next strip we find the three other performance spaces, lined up one after the other and partially buried to minimize their surface bulk: firstly an »interdisciplinary« practice hall, then the conic ellipse of the organ hall (a form chosen for its acoustic properties), and finally the opera auditorium, whose fly tower punctuates the ensemble. The fourth strip, truncated due to the presence of older buildings on the site, contains the

19.5 Cité de la Musique

dance studios as well as exhibition galleries. Generous circulation spaces run behind the four rehearsal-room pavilions and in between each strip.

To ensure a strong public identity for this disparate collection of volumes and spaces, Portzamparc united the Avenue-Jean-Jaurès façade under huge concrete eaves lifted straight out of Chandigarh (the first of many direct quotations from Le Corbusier), whose supposed functional justification is that they act as a sound screen. Shallow pools distance the building from the street and further emphasize its institutional character, as does the pale-blonde stone with which it is clad. One crosses a footbridge to enter, and is then attracted down into the main foyer by the light flooding into it, the descent being effected via a dramatic *escalier d'honneur*, as is *de rigueur* in any self-respecting French public building. This thoroughly Corbusian *promenade architecturale* deposits one 3 m below grade, the foyer constituting an intermediary space between the upper part of the conservatory and the subterranean world of the performance spaces. In another rather forced attempt to go beyond the commonplace associations made between music and architecture (rhythm, movement, progression, harmony, dissonance, etc.) and make a specific allusion to musicality, the foyer's outer wall takes on the curve of a grand piano in plan. Despite their basement location, the circulatory spaces leading off it to the performance halls are day-lit thanks to the sunken garden and patio, which in their turn receive southerly sunlight due to the generous »breach« that Portzamparc opened up in the student-accommodation wing. While the other performance spaces were of necessity black-box, practical affairs, the organ hall could be naturally lit and, with its conic form dramatically panelled in acoustic coffering, provides a splendidly baroque setting for its period instrument.

Upstairs, the multiple rehearsal spaces are each contrived as boxes within a box, independent of the main structure so as to achieve acoustic isolation. They are all naturally lit, but Portzamparc avoided direct views out to maintain studious concentration. In contrast, to provide welcome relief from the rather pressure-chamber atmosphere of the rehearsal and performance spaces, he opened up the circulation areas as much as possible to the outside world, and used bright splashes of colour wherever this was not possible. Nonetheless it is not onto the noisy avenue that the Conservatoire gives, but onto its abstractly articulated courtyard, which provides the measured calm of a monastic cloister. It is the Conservatoire's voids – the courtyard and internal circulation spaces – that best demonstrate Portzamparc's talent for banishing repetition and orchestrating a whole symphony of different forms and vistas with sometimes breathtaking bravura.

The Pôle Public
In contrast to the Cartesian boundaries established for the Conservatoire, the site allocated to the public part of the Cité was less conventional: a cheese-shaped wedge, narrowing to a very fine point where the Place de la Fontaine-aux-Lions meets the Avenue Jean-Jaurès. Since acoustic isolation was a much less pressing issue in the Pôle Public than in the Conservatoire, Portzamparc was able to ignore purely practical concerns when drawing up his plan, instead choosing to embody in it the purely symbolic: a spiralling bass clef occupies its centre. For some this gesture was poetic and inspired, for others inappropriately wilful and artificial. The epicentre of the clef, and therefore of the whole complex, is the oval concert hall, around which unwinds a glass-covered, internal street leading out towards the park beyond. But this spiral is not the only movement in the ensemble, for it is contradicted by and wound up against a strong diagonal in the form of an elevated lattice-work girder, under which runs a pathway providing public access to the Cité, whose entrance on the Place de la Fontaine-aux-Lions is handily signalled by one of Bernard Tschumi's red follies. The diagonal movement of the girder and the wedge of the site are reinforced by the ever increasing height of the Pôle Public as one moves away from the *place*, the idea being that one day this rising crescendo will culminate in the hypothetical symphonic concert hall. In the meantime the drama ends rather ignobly in a car park.

The buildings that actually make up the Pôle Public are disposed along the site's perimeter, enclosing the spiral and the girder within them. They are articulated as separate units, with gaps, breaches and even »streets« separating them from their neighbours. Clearly defined roofing for each part, variations in fenestration, multiple wall finishes and a motley use of colour all contribute to the fragmentation of the Pôle Public into a chunk of city within the city. The idea seems to have been to evoke the multihued density of an Italian hillside village, but no real village was ever as knowingly orchestrated as this musical city, and there is inevitably a slightly absurd family resemblance between all the different parts, aggravated by the multiple quotations from late Le Corbusier and the sometimes annoyingly quirky fenestration. Indeed one of the main criticisms of Portzamparc's approach has been that the attempt to recreate overnight the slowly evolved palimpsest effect of the city at large can only ever seem gratuitously contrived. The oval shape of the modifiable concert hall, forming the *dominante* of the whole composition, was imposed by Portzamparc, despite the warnings of sound experts who pointed out how dangerous this form can be acoustically (London's Royal Albert Hall is a particularly notorious example). Portzamparc nonetheless seems to have pulled it off, and the hall, designed in collaboration with the composer and conductor Pierre Boulez, has firmly established itself in the Parisian musical scene. As well as its expressive curves, the oval plan allowed greater flexibility where stage and seating configurations were concerned, with the possibility of placing the performance area either at one end or in the middle. To achieve the right acoustics on a limited budget, raw-plywood panelling was in-

19.6 Grande Halle aux Bœufs

stalled under the balconies and neon-lit to remarkably elegant effect, while a simple but effective system of sound reflectors adorns the hall's ceiling.

While the concert hall is undoubtedly successful, the remainder of the Pôle Public is less so, in large part because of Portzamparc's insistence on making formal gestures that have little or no practical *raison d'être*. While this tendency was curbed at the Conservatoire by the strict functional requirements and the density of the programme, at the Pôle Public the vagueness of much of the brief led to equally vague architecture. The glass-covered gallery curling round the concert hall, for example, is a rather forlorn space that does not go anywhere and along which nobody is obliged to pass, a great pity both because of the opportunity missed and because its absurd redundancy undermines the symbolic significance of the bass-clef motif. Portzamparc had hoped that the Cité's café would find its home in the gallery, thereby turning it into a covered arcade, but the café's management understood that cul-de-sac galleries are never commercially viable and insisted instead on a higher-profile location at the tip of the wedge, with frontage on both the avenue and the *place*. That the café (with a chic interior by Portzamparc's wife, Elisabeth) and its piazza-side terrace are always full testifies to their business acumen. Another rather redundant feature was the lattice-work girder, which Portzamparc had intended to glass in to house part of the Musée de la Musique. As is so often the case, however, the curators had not been consulted in advance and refused the girder on the grounds that it would not provide suitably black-box space, their fragile instruments needing protection from the light. Instead the museum is entirely enclosed within opaque, masonry walls, with sombre interiors and elegant, fibre-optic-lit display cabinets by Franck Hammoutène. As for the girder, the Cité's current director is planning to fit it out as a new *médiathèque*, due for completion in late 2004.

Portzamparc was also responsible for the Holiday Inn on the other side of the Avenue Jean-Jaurès, whose upper levels can be seen rising above the Cité de la Musique (when viewed from the Place de la Fontaine-aux-Lions) in a streamlined mirroring of the Pôle Public's crescendo. With these two edifices overlooking the *boulevard périphérique*, he has thus framed the entrance to this part of Paris. Perhaps, one day, the symphonic concert hall will complete the composition and, with any luck, bring to the Pôle Public the sense of direction it currently lacks.

19.6 Grande Halle aux Bœufs
Place de la Fontaine aux Lions
Jules de Mérindol, 1863–67
(Métro: Porte de Pantin)

Mid-19C Paris counted no less than ten abattoirs, dispersed all over the city, a situation which created the double nuisance of aggravated traffic congestion and unpleasant odours in central and residential areas. The indefatigable Baron Haussmann turned his attention to their rationalization in 1859, creating a series of complexes on the outskirts of the city, linked by an orbital railway. The first and largest of the new Parisian abattoirs was situated at La Villette, and covered 55 ha either side of the Canal de l'Ourcq. It included not only slaughterhouses, but also a large animal market. Louis-Adolphe Janvier, the architect-in-chief of the complex, used the site's pre-existent bisection by the canal to separate these two activities, situating the slaughterhouses to the north and the market to the south, where it was easily accessed from the Avenue Jean-Jaurès.

Designed by Jules de Mérindol, Architecte des Monuments Historiques and therefore a close collaborator of Viollet-le-Duc's, the market consisted essentially of a row of three giant iron-and-glass halls which, covering a total of 27 ha, constituted the largest cast-iron ensemble in Paris. Sheep and calves were auctioned in the two identical lateral halls, while the larger, central hall housed the beef market. Since the destruction of the famous Halles Centrales in the 1970s (see 1.22) and of the sheep and veal halls in the 1980s (sacrificed during creation of the Parc de La Villette, 19.7), the central Halle aux Bœufs has become a rare survivor of the magnificent cast-iron market halls which were the wonder of the 19C.

Mérindol's design for the three halls bore a strong resemblance to, and was almost certainly inspired by, Eugène Flachat's audacious 1851 proposal for the Halles Centrales, which was never realized. A colossal 240 m long, 82 m wide and 19 m high, the Grande Halle aux Bœufs is basilical in form, with a three-bay wide central »nave« lit by roof lights and by a clerestory, which is flanked by triple aisles lit by dormers. Originally entirely open at ground-floor level, the structure consists essentially of a huge roof supported on slender cast-iron columns, recalling Napoleon III's call for iron »umbrellas« for the Halles Centrales. Light, sturdy and economical in its use of material, the Grande Halle aux Bœufs is also a marvellous object, an elemental, iron cathedral of commerce. In 1983–85, as part of the Parc-de-La-Villette project, it was beautifully restored and converted for use as a »polyvalent cultural space« by the architects Philippe Robert and Bernard Reichen. The Place de la Fontaine-aux-Lions (completed in 1867), onto which the Grande Halle faces, was created to provide a suitably monumental setting for it and the other market halls, although the fountain itself is earlier, dating from 1811.

19.7 Parc de La Villette
Bernard Tschumi, 1983–91
(Métro: Porte de Pantin, Porte de La Villette)

It was, of course, the unstoppable Baron Haussmann who was initially responsible for the creation of La Villette. Great sanitizer and rationalizer that he was, he could not leave Paris's abattoirs in the disorganized and unhygienic state that he found them, and consequently decided to concentrate all such facilities on the outskirts of the city, away from the populous centre where they had previously caused traffic congestion and olfactory pollution. Served by the Canals Saint-Denis and de l'Ourcq and also by an orbital railway linking all the new abattoirs together, La Villette was the first and the largest of these installations, its 55 ha comprising not only slaughterhouses but also an important animal market. Opened in the 1860s, the complex included three magnificent cast-iron market halls (one of which survives – see the Grande Halle aux Bœufs (19.6)). A century later, La Villette was badly in need of repair and modernization, and it was the government of another great organizer and rationalizer, General de Gaulle, that took on the task. Millions of francs were invested and a host of new structures begun to replace old and crumbling edifices, including a gigantic new market hall. But the authorities had not foreseen the coming of the refrigerated lorry, whose generalized use rang the death knell of La Villette. Cold-storage transportation allowed animals to be slaughtered where they were produced, in the countryside, and made centralized, urban abattoirs redundant. La Villette's decline was as rapid as its creation, and the complex closed for good in 1974.

Paris suddenly found itself with 55 ha of industrial wasteland ripe for redevelopment, a situation that resulted in five years of political intrigue and fighting between municipality and government. President Giscard d'Estaing's regime eventually emerged victorious, its plans for the site being finalized in 1979. Everyone agreed that the huge market hall begun under De Gaulle and left unfinished at the time of the abattoirs' closure could not be demolished for financial reasons, and the authorities came up with the idea of a science museum to fill it, the future Cité des Sciences et de l'Industrie (19.10). One of the 19C market halls (the Grande Halle aux Bœufs mentioned above) was to be preserved for its architectural value, but the others, which were in an extremely poor state of conservation, would have to go. On the insistence of his sister, Mme du Saillant, Giscard also decided on the creation of a new concert hall at La Villette, an idea that would metamorphose into the future Cité de la Musique (19.5). Between these complementary poles of music and science, a public park of roughly 35 ha would help to redress the lack of green open space in Paris. A 1980 architectural competition provided designs for both the Cité des Sciences and the park, conceived together as a united ensemble by Adrien Fainsilber. A classic association of trees and water arranged in straight lines, Fainsilber's landscape represented an aesthetically conservative, Giscardian vision of France.

Unfortunately for Valéry Giscard d'Estaing, time and political calendars were against him, and his 1981 general-election defeat came before any of his La-Villette projects had even been started. François Mitterrand's socialist government took over the site's redevelopment: while they retained Fainsilber's proposal for the Cité des Sciences, they unceremoniously dropped his plan for the park. His rather dull tribute to Giscardian values was to be superseded by something much more experimental, the only one of Mitterrand's »grands projets« to have a truly socialist, left-wing agenda. An international competition to find a design for the park was held in 1983, with a brief that set revolutionary objectives. The past was to be ignored since, it was held, historical prototypes no longer had any relevance to modern life. Neither bucolic, English-style landscapes, nor Haussmannian primness nor theme-park-style escapist fantasy such as the Parc des Buttes-Chaumont (19.2) provided what today's with-it public needed. Instead this was to be a resolutely urban environment, of a never-before-seen kind, a park for the 21C. Its number-one aim was to act as a link: a link between city and suburbs, between nature and urbanity, between science and the arts, and between people and cultures in multi-racial, modern-day France. Rather than catering for passive relaxation in the manner of the traditional park, the new facility would be devoted to activities: video games, gardening, painting, sports, exhibitions, theatre, and so on, in addition to the music, popular science and »polyvalent culture« on offer within its limits at the Cité des Sciences, the Cité de la Musique and the Grande Halle. In the words of the *établissement public* set up to oversee La Villette's development: »The age of pluralism will find its space at La Villette. This pluralism is that of popular culture, which communicates to everyone and where all tendencies can find expression.« Moreover, the park was to be open 24 hours a day, and consequently would constitute a real, continuous, vital piece of the urban fabric, not some gated, lockable facility that chastely shut out the evil world at dusk, as did almost every other Parisian park.

The competition was a stormy affair which, after much dispute and controversy, produced a winner in the form of the Swiss-born architect Bernard Tschumi. Well known as a theorist and polemicist, he had built nothing to date. His scheme generated great interest within the profession as the supposed first example of Deconstructivist architecture, a claim backed up by no less than the founder of Deconstruction himself, the philosopher Jacques Derrida, who wrote a suitably un-

19.7 Parc de La Villette

readable essay on Tschumi's project. Instead of creating a harmonious environment that would disassociate itself from the city at large in its planned »perfection«, Tschumi wanted to celebrate »real« urbanity in all its dirty, chaotic discontinuity, championing its random juxtaposition of unrelated elements and in-between spaces, which he saw as »the new places of contemporaneousness.« »We are opposed to Olmsted's [Frederick Law Olmsted, co-designer of New York's Central Park] notion, widespread in the 19C, that ›in a park the city is not supposed to exist‹«, Tschumi wrote. »Creating false cliffs to hide a *boulevard périphérique* ignores the force of urban reality.«

La Villette's expanse was already broadly structured by existing features – the Cité des Sciences, the Canal de l'Ourcq bisecting the terrain, the Grande Halle aux Bœufs and the Place de la Fontaine-aux-Lions – and further delimited by the sites of proposed constructions: the Cité de la Musique and the Zénith (19.8). Designing the park was not, therefore, a question of *carte blanche* freedom but of filling in the gaps between these elements, whose rather random scattering represented exactly the kind of accidental urban discontinuity of which Tschumi had spoken. Instead of creating an environment based upon these existing features, Tschumi attempted to increase further the incidence of chance and accident by imposing on the in-between spaces a series of three »autonomous« regulating systems – which he baptized Lines, Surfaces and Points – whose »random« interaction was supposed to recreate the fortuitous encounters of urban chaos. The Lines were essentially the pathways, the systems of communication, which included a major north–south thoroughfare running down one side of the park and linking together the two Métro stations at either extremity, another straight axis running alongside the Canal de l'Ourcq, and a long meandering pathway, the »Promenade Cinématique«, which, unfurling itself across the park like a roll of film, would feature themed gardens along its route. The Surfaces were what actually covered the ground: large areas of grass baptized »Prairies«, the paving of the paths or seating areas, asphalt clearings for athletics, and so on. The Points were an abstract, Cartesian grid system drawn virtually across the site whose intersections, each 120 m from the next, would be marked with a series of red-painted »follies« (25 in all). Each one a »deconstructed« variation on a 10 m-wide cube, the follies, whose aesthetics clearly owed something to Russian Constructivism, would provide containers for the activities put on by the park's management, without in any way being modelled on the uses to which they would be put; or they could simply be left empty as latter-day up-datings of the 18C picturesque ruin. They were intended to create a strong »brand image« for the park in the manner of British phone boxes or Paris Métro entrances, using a symbol otherwise devoid of meaning.

With his superimposition of systems, Tschumi was playing the old Surrealist game (currently very fashionable in architectural circles) of rationally trying to create irrationality and accident. Nonetheless, chance and internal logic were not allowed to reign quite as freely as their architect suggested in his rhetoric. The »neutral« grid of the follies, for example, was placed so that one of its lines just happened to coincide with the park's principal north–south thoroughfare, thus ensuring a street of activity-fillable structures, and another row of follies »fortuitously« stands guard along the Canal de l'Ourcq. Rational criteria clearly dictated the routes taken by the Lines and the siting and nature of the Surfaces. To the extent that their grid spacing meant that the follies sometimes collide with other structures – one folly is embedded in the entrance to the Cité de la Musique while others sprout from the sides of the 19C pavilions flanking the Grande Halle –, one could argue that this regulating system does indeed mimic the accidents of urban discontinuity. But, despite its humour, it smacks of the wilful and the contrived, and, had the architects so wished, the grid could no doubt have been manipulated so that none of the follies came into contact with other constructions. The follies have lived up to expectations in one respect, however: sporting the scarlet livery of London's phone boxes and buses, they have indeed become emblematic of La Villette, providing the photogenic distillation of place that allows the park to exist virtually on the pages of glossy magazines, as all contemporary architecture worth its salt should.

Walking around the Parc de La Villette today one sees a pleasant but visually rather banal green space composed of grass and trees in which people do the things they have always done in parks: picnicking, reading, sunbathing, playing football, and so on. To a certain extent this is unusual in the Parisian context since the »Prairies«, which were expressly intended for ball games and recreation, break with traditional Parisian parks where, until very recently, grass was strictly out of bounds. But providing accessible green open spaces is hardly revolutionary stuff! The follies bring visual diversion, but unless one looks at a map their grid arrangement is not necessarily apparent and one could easily be forgiven for thinking them randomly spaced. Similarly, the Promenade Cinématique is difficult to follow in the field, and its themed gardens seem arbitrarily scattered. Although the Parc de La Villette is supposed to represent the antithesis of the *beaux-arts* tradition, it suffers from one of the main faults imputed to *beaux-arts* design, namely that without prior knowledge of the plan one cannot easily grasp or appreciate the designer's intentions. Furthermore, Tschumi's intellectual, urbanizing approach did not concern itself overly with plants or horticulture, and his use of vegetation is uninspired: 18 ha of grass in the form of the already discussed Prairies and standard species of trees following the major pathways. The themed gardens, of which there are ten in all, are more visually and/or horticulturally interesting and inventive than the rest of the park, but again are hardly revolutionary. They include the Dragon and Dune-and-Wind Gardens, which were conceived by Tschumi as children's play areas, Fujiko Nakaya's Fog Garden, where vaporizers produce hissing clouds of mist (not always operational), Laurence Vacherot and Gilles Vexlard's sunken »Gardening Garden«, and Alexandre Chemetoff's Bamboo Garden, a half-buried micro-climate where lush vegetation flourishes.

Activities laid on in the park, in addition to those provided by the Cités and the Grande Halle, include horse riding, street arts, a »music kiosk«, a video workshop, theatre and a jazz club, and in summer there is also an open-air cinema festival. Of the follies' ability to contain whatever is required of them there can be no doubt: one has already served successively as a gardening workshop, a restaurant and a painting atelier. Because the park is open 24 hours a day, its night-time lighting was important for security reasons. Standard-issue street lamps could have been deployed, but the designers went for something rather more adventurous. A galaxy of stars twinkles on the Place de la Fontaine-aux-Lions, blue neons run along the major pathways, the Dragon Garden is dramatically floodlit, clusters of ultra-violet tubes populate one of the Prairies and sleek lighting rods by Philippe Starck poke up here and there. At night the Parc de La Villette dresses up *en grande toilette*, donning the magic it lacks by day. As for its other furnishings, we find underlit benches with triangular stainless-steel bins by Tschumi, bridges and railings recalling the Cité de la Science's girders, and, the *pièce de résistance*, groups of swivel chairs by Philippe Starck. Attached to the ground at just one point by a tiny pivot and strengthened only by a dorsal fin, the chairs attempt to distil the quintessence of chairness with their seemingly gravity-defying minimalism. Mention should also be made of the wavy corrugated-iron canopy running the length of the principal north–south thoroughfare, which was designed by Rice, Francis and Ritchie (creators of the Cité des Science's stunning greenhouses), as was the elevated walkway/canopy fronting the Canal de l'Ourcq.

On sunny summer days the Parc de La Villette swarms with people and, if judged in terms of frequentation, can only be qualified a resounding success. But given the high hopes of the brief and the promise of Tschumi's rhetoric one cannot help feeling rather disappointed. Despite all the talk about urban edges and celebration of gritty reality, the park seems conventionally park-like and turns its back on the suburbs and the *périphérique* (which is entirely screened by trees). Where the site's history could have been taken as a fruitful starting point (as at the Parc de Bercy, 12.8), it was ignored, Tschumi's scheme claiming to disregard topographical specificities and provide an abstract, supposedly universally applicable system: the follies' grid as an infinitely extendable, plonk-anywhere, Corbusian »free plan«. »Composition« of the park was made »voluntarily impossible« so that chance and accident could work their magic, and yet what we end up with is not the stomach-wrenching excitement of urban fracture but a landscape resembling a playing field. Given its 21C aspirations, it is perhaps fitting that the park should have borrowed from one of the dominant forms of late-20C popular culture, namely the theme park (as exemplified and pioneered by Disneyland – see Disneyland Paris, 36.7). For although none of its conceptors ever explicitly said it, that is essentially what La Villette is, with »pluridisciplinary« culture as the theme. Where, arguably, the Parc des Buttes-Chaumont was a proto-theme park providing Disney-style fantasy but not the activities, La Villette is an activity park without the fantasy. Or perhaps the fantasy is here after all in the Deconstructivist design, with its chimera of urban discontinuity.

19.8 Zénith
211, avenue Jean-Jaurès
Philippe Chaix and Jean-Paul Morel, 1983/84
(Métro: Porte de Pantin)

The impressive list of »grands projets« announced in 1982 by the newly-elected socialist government included a *salle de rock* – brainchild of then culture minister Jack Lang –, which was planned for Paris's Porte de Bagnolet. Impatient for results, Lang meanwhile commissioned a fast-build, temporary rock/pop venue for the Parc de La Villette (19.7) to serve until completion of the Bagnolet project. Initially planned to stay up two to three years, the temporary venue, dubbed the »Zénith«, saw its life-expectancy increased following budget cuts which extinguished the Bagnolet scheme, and is still standing today, 20 years on.

Essentially a Hi-tech big top (total capacity 6,300), the Zénith has all the advantages of a traditional marquee while eradicating some of the disadvantages. Extremely quick to build – twelve months including design – it was also cheap, paying for itself in six years. Its metal frame, spanning 75 m, eliminates the sight-obstructing supports of most marquees and serves to carry 50 tonnes of stage equipment. The building also has better acoustic and weather insulation than traditional canvas-covered structures thanks to its double-thickness, PVC-coated polyester »skin«. (Designed to last 15 years, the Zénith's original covering was replaced in 2000.) Dismantling and re-erection of the Zénith takes three months. For its architects it was proof that light, economic, movable buildings can be as durable and effective as permanent, masonry edifices. On the other hand, its acoustics are not ideal and its space-age-bouncy-castle exterior is not very interesting. Its commercial success has spawned a series of sister Zéniths elsewhere in France.

19.9 Géode
Parc de la Villette, behind the Cité des Sciences
(30, avenue Corentin-Cariou)
Adrien Fainsilber, 1980–85
(Métro: Porte de La Villette)

One of the more startling realizations at the Parc de La Villette (19.7), the Géode was programmed as part of the Cité-des-Sciences project (19.10), and was conceived to house a 26 m-diameter, omnimax cinema screen for the projection of semi-in-the-round films that literally envelop the viewer in their action. The competition brief for the Cité des Sciences did not specify where this screen should be installed, but many of the entrants chose to site it in a discrete structure outside the main volume of the science museum. The screen's hemispherical form evidently suggested a globe-shaped covering, and the opportunity to provide a curvilinear contrast to the long horizontals of the Cité des Sciences was too attractive a temptation to be passed up. Fainsilber's winning proposal included just such a structure, in the form of a free-standing orb floating in front of the park façade of the Cité. A Euclidean solid *par excellence* in the best French Enlightenment tradition, the Géode, as it was soon baptized, was intended to thrill not only through the films shown in it but also through its architecture. As conceived by Fainsilber, it was to be covered in stainless-steel triangles polished to reflect the surrounding park-scape, like an otherworldly, oversize glitter ball. A highly visible event in the landscape, whose realization posed an engineering challenge of considerable difficulty, the Géode would act as a symbol of the science museum and more generally La Villette, while also proclaiming to all who saw it France's industrial and technical savoir-faire. But the spirit of disco was entirely foreign to President Giscard d'Estaing, who declared the Géode »a graceless protuberance contrary to French taste« and ordered its dissimulation within the volume of the Cité des Sciences. More culturally right-on than his predecessor and, as it turned out, a sucker for neo-Classicizing Euclidean solids, President Mitterrand, who came to power in May 1981, promptly ordered the restitution of the original plans, and the Géode thus regained its prime position outside the Cité, whose enormous length it today helps to break.

Fainsilber's edifice consists of two entirely different and independent structures. The working cinema sits on a colossal concrete construction, most of whose weight is supported by one central pier. Popped over the top of it, and structurally separate from it, is a 36.5 m-diameter spherical geodesic space frame that carries the building's outer skin of 6,433 spherical stainless-steel triangles. The laying of these was especially difficult: to achieve the immaculate finish desired, the plates were fixed hard up against each other without any gap, thus leaving no margin for error. If a mistake had been made at the beginning of the fixing process it would have been impossible to close the sphere at the end, and the whole lot would have had to be removed and the procedure begun again from scratch. As it is, the finished result is quite spectacular, reflecting and outlandishly distorting all around it, complemented by the equally reflective sheet of water on which it is set.

The sphere, like the cube and the pyramid, is of course a mythical architectural form, and Fainsilber wanted to avoid cutting an opening into the perfect solid he had created in the Géode (unlike I.M. Pei at the Louvre (1.8), whose pyramid features doors that were much criticized for the disruption they bring to its pure lines). To circumvent the problem, Fainsilber brought the public in from below, through a basement storey connecting the Géode to the Cité des Sciences. One thus enters the edifice via an impressive space underneath the cinema, whose aspect can only be described as Brutalist baroque: below the massive, raw-concrete forms of the theatre's underside, around which the space frame's interior departs into the gloom, four slimline escalators slink up around the central concrete pier, depositing the visitor under the enormous hemispherical screen. Unfortunately, the films shown at the Géode are rarely up to the quality of its architecture.

19.10 Cité des Sciences et de l'Industrie
00, avenue Corentin Cariou
Fournier, Fournier, Semichon and Walrand, 1964–69;
Adrien Fainsilber, 1980–86
(Métro: Porte de La Villette)

Billed as an exciting, up-to-the-minute new science museum, the Cité des Sciences et de l'Industrie was one of the key projects in the redevelopment of the former La Villette abattoirs (see the Parc de La Villette, 19.7). It owed its conception to the presence at La Villette of a gigantic concrete market hall, commissioned by the state in the 1960s but never completed due to the economic downturn that subsequently hit the complex, forcing its closure in 1974. Despite the myriad conflicts that beset the abattoirs' redevelopment, everyone was in agreement on one point: destruction of the unfinished hall was out of the question, not only because of the scandalous sums of money wasted building it, but also because demolition costs would render any new construction on the site prohibitively expensive. The question remained, therefore, of what to do with this monstrous white elephant. In 1977, President Giscard d'Estaing and his government came up with the idea of filling it with a new science museum, which would provide a showcase for French technological expertise and prowess. Concentrating on current innovation, the Cité was intended to stimulate public interest in science, its displays being constantly renewed and »permanent« exhibits having a maximum life span of 10–15 years. The brief also called for an omnimax cinema screen, which ended up taking the form of the superlunar Géode (19.9), outside the Cité proper. A competition to find an architect and a design was held in 1980 and won by Adrien Fainsilber.

Had the museum been programmed from scratch rather than as a filler for a vacant building, it would no doubt have been much smaller. As it was it had somehow to contend with the vastness of the market hall, which covered 4.7 ha on the ground – three-and-a-half times the grade surface area of the Centre Pompidou (4.15) – and rose higher than the Arc de Triomphe (16.1). Furthermore, converting the hall for an entirely different function to that for which it had been conceived was a considerable logistical and technical challenge, one that was yet further complicated by the strict health and safety regulations applicable to public buildings. Floors had to be moved and/or strengthened, the roof girders slid along to a different position, a powerful ventilation system devised and conformity with draconian fire regulations assured. These difficulties were compounded by the vagueness of the original brief – at the time the building was designed nobody knew exactly what it would house – and by conflicts between the architect and the museum's curators. Fainsilber's competition entry had proposed a museum that was largely day-lit and naturally ventilated, an exhibit in itself demonstrating responsible and eco-friendly building. The curators, however, wanted neutral, black-box exhibition space that they could light and configure as they pleased, especially given that exhibits were meant to be temporary. A traditional air conditioning system and artificial lighting were thus imposed on Fainsilber's concept, with the result that it lost much of its original coherence. These kinds of administrative and curatorial quarrels eventually turned out to be so wasteful, and conversion problems so difficult and expensive, that many of those involved in the museum's creation subsequently wondered whether it would not have been better to demolish and start from scratch after all.

Be that as it may, the project went ahead as planned, a child of circumstance and compromise. A closed box seemed to be what the curators required, and Fainsilber dutifully filled in the holes in the market hall's original structure, all the while striving to give his building a hard-nosed »industrial« allure (although with finishes of greater luxury than is the norm for industrial edifices). Factories and workshops were, after all, the places where technology is devised and employed. He also hoped, through the use of »simple architectural forms without mannerism«, as he put it, to avoid the »fugitive modes of current architectural taste« and thus ensure that his project did not date too quickly. The original structure's mighty steel roof girders were exposed and painted cobalt blue, while the massive concrete pillars supporting them were clad in sober grey granite. Glass-and-aluminium façades retreat behind and under this mega-structure partly, as Fainsilber said, to allow the monumental character of the initial building to come through, but no doubt also to reduce, at least a little, the museum's huge interior surface area. As part of his original plan to increase daylight penetration into the building, and also with a view to rendering the museum yet more monumental, Fainsilber left what were originally intended to be the basement storeys of the southern façade exposed (the ground had been exca-

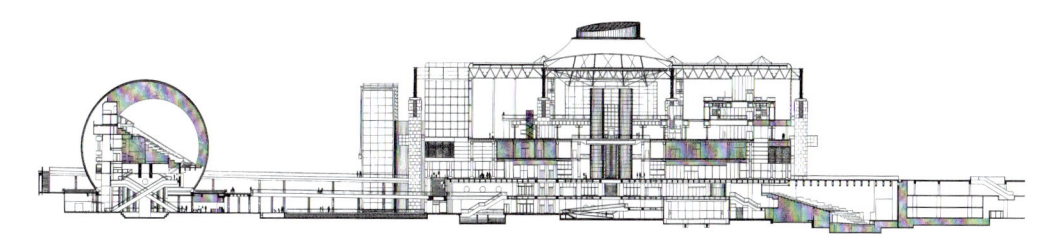

19.10 Cité des Sciences et de l'Industrie with Géode (19.9)

vated for construction purposes but not yet filled back in), and placed sheets of water at the bottom of the resulting »moat«, thereby highlighting the Cité's institutional character and recalling the canals that cross the park. Sitting in front of these moats, on its own pool, is the Géode, whose spherical form provides relief from the relentless horizontals of the Cité and helps to break up the enormity of its 250 m-long façade.

The bays either side of the Géode are filled with projecting all-glass elevations, intended as greenhouses, that were designed by the engineer Peter Rice in collaboration with Martin Francis and Ian Ritchie (RFR, as they called themselves). Fainsilber asked the engineers to create glazing that would be as transparent and »immaterial« as possible, a challenge whose difficulties had a precedent in Martin Francis's design for the curtain walling of Norman Foster's Willis Faber Dumas building in Ipswich (1971–75). The engineers rejected the glass-fin solution employed at Ipswich on the grounds that internal fins would be too visually obstructive, and instead turned to cable trusses for La Villette. The frames from which the glass panels are hung follow the contours of the greenhouses. Each pane is suspended from the one above and the ensemble is stiffened against the wind by the tensed cables. The panes are held in place by connectors whose bolts feature ball bearings in their heads; these bearings prevent the glass from bending under the stress of the trusses and thus ensure that the glazing remains perfectly smooth. The result is stunning: externally one sees only the immaculate surface of the glass, while inside the delicate filigree of the trussing is noticeable only up close. Cable-tensed glass elevations of this kind have today become commonplace, but at the time RFR's realization was truly revolutionary, and it remains a superlative example of its type. Fainsilber wanted the glasshouses to be filled with trees and plants, thereby providing a link with the greenery of the park outside and creating a sort of ecological, »bioclimatic« (as he dubbed it) interface between interior and exterior. The curators did not agree, however, and these splendid structures are today empty.

Entering the Cité des Sciences, one is admitted into a vast, central volume reminiscent of an airport or shopping mall, with giant escalators leading off to galleries on other levels. Grand staircases have long been standard features of big museums, from Schinkel's majestic portico stairway at Berlin's Altes Museum (1823 to 1830) to the Centre Pompidou's cascading »caterpillar«. Fainsilber's example impresses by its size, but otherwise lacks the element of surprise necessary to make it truly exciting. The space containing the escalators is top lit via two »cupolas« (as they were baptized), which were another intervention by RFR designed to demonstrate technological wizardry. They were a hangover from Fainsilber's original proposal for a naturally lit museum, and were intended to show how daylight could be manipulated for precise needs. Mounted on canvas-covered steel space frames, the cupolas take the form of rotating glazed discs equipped with a system of adjustable mirrors and slats. Filtered through the slats (which act like a venetian blind), light is projected into the interior via the mirrors which, thanks to the computer-controlled rotating function, can be directed towards or away from the sun depending on weather conditions and lighting requirements. The mirrors themselves can be choreographed to provide spot-lighting, sunbursts, diffused general light and a multitude of other lighting possibilities.

Snaking everywhere within the vastness of the Cité's vessel are the fat ducts of the air-conditioning system, which reinforce the industrial aesthetic and recall the piping of the Centre Pompidou. Their prominence may also have been a snipe on Fainsilber's part towards the curators who had insisted on this form of ventilation; when filling the exhibition spaces many found that the ducts »got in the way«. Displays are grouped into four big themes: From Earth to Universe, Languages and Communication, Matter and Man's Intervention, and The Adventure of Life. Despite the desire for constant renewal and the emphasis on recent developments, the Cité's remit embodies all the pedagogic paternalism of the 19C museum, and the building that houses it, for all its late-20C industrial allure, is equally the product of a tradition of 19C monumental museum design. Solid, conventional and dependable (a minor miracle given the conversion problems), the Cité des Sciences leaves innovation to its bravura applied elements: the cupolas, the glasshouses and the Géode.

19.11 Municipal street-cleaning maintenance workshops
17, rue Raymond-Radiguet
Renzo Piano Building Workshop, 1988/89
(Métro: Crimée)

A minor building, both in Piano's œuvre and in the hierarchy of the city: storage space and repair workshops

the spaces within its concrete frame. In the hands of less imaginative architects, this could have been the building's only visage.

19.12 Crèche
13 bis, rue de Rouen
Pierre Granveaud with Pablo Katz, 1990/91
(Métro: Riquet)

Over the past decade or so the Ville de Paris has built a whole series of new crèches, each time commissioning young architectural practices selected from limited, invitation-only competitions. The results have been mixed but always interesting (see also 11.5). This little example is squeezed into an awkward site in the heavily redeveloped 19th *arrondissement*, a situation that made its realization an exercise in problem solving. The site's narrowness and the tall adjoining structures meant that building upwards was inevitable, even though the architects felt that ideally crèches should be horizontally organized spaces. And how was one to ensure abundant daylight in a deep plot that has little street frontage and is overshadowed by its neighbours? The architects' solution was to divide their building in two, separating the halves with a sort of »cleft« that runs diagonally across the site and thus allows light to penetrate into its heart, while at the same time avoiding sightlines from the surrounding buildings. Occupying the larger, rear portion of the plot is the two-storey crèche proper, while protecting it on the street is a four-storey structure containing

19.11 Municipal street-cleaning maintenance workshops

19.12 Crèche

for Paris's street-cleaning equipment. And yet Piano lavished considerable attention to detail on this project, raising it above the purely ordinary.

Rather than hide the workshops' supposedly shameful purpose behind solid walls, the architects chose to give it an all-glass street façade, allowing passers-by to see the activities going on inside. As well as providing a bit of street theatre, this was also a practical move, since the maintenance spaces are thus flooded with steady northern light to work by. The handling of this elevation is expressively diverse: hovering before the building's concrete frame is a delicate chassis in galvanized steel – the material from which Paris's dustbins used to be made before their replacement in the 1990s with green-plastic wheelie bins – holding glued glass panels in seamless precision. Galvanized steel makes further appearances in the railings and fire escapes, contrasting with the immaculate sophistication of the glass in its tough, inner-city patina. It is also present in the sculpted totem lighting mast standing at the façade's centre. The monumental entrance canopy, with its individual supporting elements and Tricolore-flying flag-pole, would be standard issue for a school or *commissariat de police*, and confers on the building full civic dignity.

The workshops' rear elevation is much more banal: traditional glazing and red-painted metal panels closing

278 19th *arrondissement*

19.13 Rotonde de la Villette

services and the administrator's apartment. Clad in dark-sandstone panels, the exterior presents a sharp but unintimidating visage to the world, whose sense of fun – which almost certainly appeals more to adults than to children – is expressed through the funky, seemingly randomly placed fenestration, the razor-edge prow of the street building or in details such as the shiny aluminium chimney. This is not »profound« architecture but it is certainly effective.

19.13 Rotonde de la Villette
Place de Stalingrad
Claude-Nicolas Ledoux, 1786/87
(Métro: Jaurès, Stalingrad)

Under the *ancien régime*, taxes on merchandise were the preserve of an appointed group of individuals known as the Fermiers Généraux who, for the purpose of levying duty on goods entering Paris, had encircled the capital with a gated palisade, or *barrière*. By the 1780s, the palisade had become rather ineffectual, and millions of *livres* were being lost every year through smuggling. To prevent further fraud, the Fermiers ordered construction of a new, extended wall around the city, incorporating a no-man's-land 100 m wide on its outer side. Each entry in the wall would be provided with a gatehouse, or *bureau* as they became known, to accommodate the guardsmen and clerks who collected the taxes and to supply warehouse space for confiscated goods.

Ledoux, who had worked for the Fermiers in the past, secured himself the unpopular but lucrative commission to design and build the 55 *bureaux*. Endowed with a generous budget, his schemes were far more than mere functional interpretations of the brief. He used the commission to provide Paris with the monumental gateways he felt the city deserved, naming his creations »Propylées«, after the entrances to ancient-Greek temple precincts. Although no two *bureaux* were the same, they shared a family likeness, in large part due to Ledoux's predilection for grotesque effects in architecture based on his maxim that the smallest object should be offered that which the largest may expect. The resultant exaggerated monumentality served only to increase detestation of the *barrières*, which were regarded as symbols of despotism, and made their architect almost as unpopular. When, by the 1860s, the growth of Paris had made Ledoux's *barrières* redundant, the majority were demolished, and only four now survive: the Barrières du Trône (11.7), d'Orléans (see 8.9), d'Enfer (at the Place Denfert-Rochereau) and de Pantin, or Rotonde de la Villette as it is now known.

The Barrière de Pantin was one of the largest *bureaux*. Ledoux's design was inspired by Palladio's Villa Rotonda, a building he had never seen but of which he had heard much on visits to England, where neo-Palladianism was then at its height. All the *bureaux* were

19th *arrondissement* 279

19.14 Social housing

composed of simple volumes, here a drum-like cylinder set upon a rectangular podium. The drum weighs heavily on its base, violently compressing its four porticoes, which are excessively diminutive in relation to their width. An arcade supported by paired columns marches round the drum, which is surmounted by a colossal Doric cornice. The columns are simple, almost crude supports, topped off by the most rudimentary capitals; those carrying the porticoes are sturdier and square in plan, thus appearing even more primally powerful. Surrounded by extraordinary structures such as this, Paris must once have seemed a strange and forbidding city indeed.

19.14 Social housing
64–66, rue de Meaux
Renzo Piano Building Workshop, 1987–91
(Métro: Bolivar)

With this complex of 220 rent-controlled apartments commissioned by the municipality, Renzo Piano set out to demonstrate that a restricted budget does not necessarily imply an unimaginative, second-rate result. Although generous, the rectangular site was deep with a comparatively narrow street frontage, and the planners originally wanted to run a road down it to open it up. Piano vetoed this idea, preferring instead to organize his buildings around a central garden, which, he argued, would provide a more peaceful and domestic setting for the apartments. These are variations on a standardized two-bedroom unit organized around a generous central living room. They are stacked up in blocks of six storeys, the maximum height permitted by the planning laws, in a perimeter-building solution that ensures that all flats benefit from double exposure onto both the internal garden and the exterior. Piano's basic block model tended towards the rectilinear – as witnessed by the units fronting the street –, but the building regulations imposed step-backs on the lateral façades to allow daylight into the neighbouring sites, and the planners asked that adjoining party walls and building heights be respected, which introduced yet further variety. Nonetheless, the structures display an orthogonal simplicity of line that was a translation of Piano's decision to keep building costs to a minimum (complexity of form generally results in greater expense) and instead spend money on the external finishes.

Hung onto the reinforced-concrete structure on the courtyard façades, and covering their entire surface, are rectilinear frames made from prefabricated, glass-fibre-reinforced concrete (GRC). The rectangles formed by the frames are filled with fenestration, GRC louvers (that protect balconies and stairwells) and red-terracotta tiles set within slender GRC braces. The result is a complex play of perpendicularly intersecting lines, rather like crazy graph paper, in which the industrial grey of the GRC is set off against the warm orange of the terracotta. This palette, which has little to do with the surrounding Parisian urbanity, has become a Piano leitmotif; its use here was justified by its capacity to weather well, thereby reducing maintenance costs and patinating the complex in a manner that will harmonize with the greenery of the courtyard. The latter has been planted with a copse of birch trees, a clever choice given that, although the trees are deciduous, their silvery bark makes them as visually interesting in winter as in summer, its metallic shine complementing the steely grey of the GRC. Despite the relative simplicity of its constituent elements, the courtyard constitutes a quite extraordinarily rich environment, whose effect is not merely the sum of light and volume but also derives from more complex, intangible qualities. Gaps between the street buildings allow the passer-by tantalizing glimpses into this tranquil and beautifully judged space.

20th *arrondissement*

20.1 Social housing
100, boulevard de Belleville
Frédéric Borel, 1985–89
(Métro: Belleville)

Commissioned by the municipality, this modest project for 47 social-sector apartments garnered the then only 30-year-old Frédéric Borel considerable attention and, in its urban and formal concerns, prefigured his much-lauded Rue-Oberkampf apartment complex (11.3). 100, boulevard de Belleville's site is typically Parisian, comprising a relatively narrow street frontage sandwiched between tall, Haussmannian-style buildings with greater room for manœuvre behind, within the city block. Traditionally, a building-line-respecting structure would have closed the site on the street, hiding the city block's interior from view. Borel's initial concern was to open up this secret, private space to the world at large, which he did by organizing his complex around a long courtyard flowing into the street. The bulk of the accommodation is nonetheless invisible from the boulevard because concealed behind pre-existing structures. Despite this, the scheme has a strong street presence thanks to three monumental and very different structures that front the courtyard like ranked sentinels. The startling disparity of their treatment is a manifestation of Borel's second principal urbanistic concern, namely a desire to reproduce in a microcosm the accidental variety of which cities like Paris are composed. This is what gave rise to the multifarious forms, elements and finishes that characterize 100, boulevard de Belleville: the »sin-curve« roof of the main (northerly) block, the metal cladding of the central »sentinel«, the multitude of different window forms, the courtyard's flying footbridge, and so on.

With this approach, expression of structure, »honest« use of form and materials and other such moralizing Modernist tenets are pushed aside in favour of sculptural sensuality, eclecticism and expressionism. Borel has mentioned Surrealism as one of his influences, and 100, boulevard de Belleville can be seen as an »assemblage« of »autonomous« objects, a picturesque juxtaposition of (fake) *objets trouvés*. The fact that these »objets trouvés« are artificially created points to the fact that there is a large degree of gratuitousness in Borel's creation, a mannered, almost Disneyland approach to architecture where external elevations are treated rather like film sets. In opposition to Modernist doctrine, the interior is not the sole generator of external form, although neither is it at the mercy of the exterior. Despite their outlandish exterior, 100 boulevard de Belleville's flats follow conventional norms, and great care was taken with regard to fenestration to ensure that each apartment benefits from carefully considered views and lighting.

Borel started his career working for Christian de Portzamparc, and 100, boulevard de Belleville can be read as a continuation of ideas formulated by Portzamparc at his 1970s Rue-des-Hautes-Formes housing scheme (13.10). Both projects share the same concern to artificially inject variety and accident into the urban environment and to open up the city block to the outside world. Borel went one step further than Portzamparc in that his Boulevard-de-Belleville scheme attempts to reflect the diversity of the city at large, where separate architectural elements engage in a dialogue of fragmentation. Borel's debt to his former employer further comes through in 100, boulevard de Belleville's expressionist, almost figurative quality, inspired by Portzamparc's later work and exemplified by the main block's sin-curve roof (which was in fact designed before Portzamparc's more famous example at the Cité de la Musique (19.5)). Within the limits of his presumably more generous budget, Borel was also able to achieve a variety and a quality of detailing and finishes that were beyond Portzamparc's means at the Rue des Hautes-Formes. 100, boulevard de Belleville's courtyard, however, suffers from similar problems to that at the Rue des Hautes-Formes, namely that it is a rather dead, purposeless space whose troubling emptiness is worthy of a De Chirico painting (Borel would correct this at 113, rue Oberkampf by creating a private garden instead of an empty public courtyard). Like Portzamparc, Borel can be accused of rather wilful mannerism, but his Boulevard-de-Belleville scheme

20.1 Social housing

is so fresh and inventive, especially in the Parisian context, that one is prepared to forgive any over-icing of the cake.

20.2 Cimetière du Père-Lachaise
Boulevard de Ménilmontant
Begun 1804
(Métro: Père-Lachaise)

One of the most visited cemeteries in the world, Père-Lachaise has long been a place of pilgrimage for those wishing to pay homage to the great and the good buried within its walls, while others come simply to marvel at this extraordinary, densely packed city of the dead. Revolutionary when opened, it broke entirely with previous funerary practices in France, and became a model for burial grounds the world over. With its melancholy function and sylvan setting on a hillside overlooking Paris, it caught the imagination of the Romantic age, and many eminent architects and sculptors designed tombs and monuments for the rich and famous laid to rest on its slopes.

Reform of the Parisian burial system had been lengthily discussed throughout the second half of the 18C but, as with so many improvements, was only finally put into practice under Napoleon. From the Middle Ages until its closure in 1780, Paris's principal cemetery was the Saints-Innocents, in the district of Les Halles (see 1.22). Less than 1 ha in size, it became more and more ill-adapted to its purpose as the population grew. Bodies were interred in communal graves in what was essentially a mass rotting ground rather than a cemetery in the modern sense. Funerary monuments were rare, except for the very wealthy or illustrious, and the majority of graves were not even marked. Each time the cemetery became full, corpses were dug up and moved to nearby charnel houses so that the ground could be used again. Furthermore, until the Revolution, French cemeteries were the domain of the Catholic Church, which refused to bury suicides, executed criminals or people of other faiths.

All pre-Napoleonic cemeteries were closed to the public, largely on hygiene grounds, and the Cimetière des Saints-Innocents became increasingly the subject of sanitary scandals as the *ancien régime* drew to a close. Numerous were the complaints regarding the nauseous stench of putrefaction and the infectious miasmas which emanated from its confines. The final straw came in 1780, when a burial pit gave way and semi-decomposed corpses poured into the cellars of neighbouring houses. The Saints-Innocents was closed and, in 1786–88, its contents were transferred to a system of disused quarry tunnels, re-baptized the »catacombes«, in what is now the 14th *arrondissement*. (Approximately 6 million skeletons were removed to the Catacombes from the Saints-Innocents and other Parisian cemeteries, and arranged in macabre piles. The Catacombes are open to the public.) During the turmoil of the Revolutionary period, the pressure on the remaining Parisian cemeteries became intense, but it was not until 1801 that the Prefect Nicolas Frochot announced the creation of three large new cemeteries outside the then boundaries of Paris: the Cimetière du Nord, known today as the Cimetière de Montmartre (18.7), the Cimetière du Sud, better-known as the Cimetière du Montparnasse (14.3), and the Cimetière de l'Est, the official title of Père-Lachaise.

The Cimetière de l'Est, the first and largest of the three, was created on the site of a former Jesuit country residence which took the name of one of its previous occupants, Père François de la Chaize d'Aix, confessor to Louis XIV. Controlled by the municipality, the new cemetery was entirely secular and subject to strict regulations regarding the interment of corpses. Hygiene was now made a priority, which influenced the choice of site, the Ménilmontant hill being selected for its exposure to fresh purifying breezes. Shortly after the inauguration of Père-Lachaise, inhumations in the city centre were banned, the remaining inner-city cemeteries were closed and their contents transferred to the Catacombes. The new cemetery was slow in gaining acceptance, however, in part because the predominantly Catholic population was reluctant to consider burial in unconsecrated ground. Frochot instigated several measures to ensure the cemetery's success. One of the most important, which would shape the future development of Père-Lachaise, was the concession of ground in perpetuity, allowing families the opportunity to erect permanent monuments to their deceased, a bid for immortality previously impossible. To raise the prestige of the cemetery, the remains of several great historical figures were removed to it, including Louise de Lorraine (wife of Henri III), Molière, La Fontaine and the mythic lovers Abélard and Héloïse. Finally, a programme of landscaping was undertaken, directed by the architect Alexandre-Théodore Brongniart.

Père-Lachaise was to be unlike any cemetery before it – sanitarily safe, secular and open to the public. In order to convince the people of Paris, the municipality wanted something out of the ordinary. Influenced in

20.2 Cimetière du Père-Lachaise

part by Masonic ideas and by English landscape gardeners, Brongniart designed a *jardin à l'anglaise* that made the most of the hillside terrain (which rises as much as 25 m), featuring sinuous alleys converging at strategically placed junctions. The effect was wonderfully romantic and picturesque, with tombs and monuments scattered amongst copses and thickets, and flowers growing everywhere in abundance – a garden of eternal rest. Brongniart placed the main entrance to the cemetery in the axis of the old Jesuit residence, which he proposed to replace with an enormous pyramid. Situated at the crest of the hill and visible from afar, the pyramid would have monumentalized the cemetery's vocation, as well as providing a covered hall for funerary ceremonies. Brongniart also proposed that imposing monuments to important personages be erected at the major intersections of the paths. At his death, in 1813, much of the landscaping was complete, but the pyramid had not risen beyond its foundations. It was his successor, Etienne-Hippolyte Godde, who continued work on the cemetery, and who, inspired by Brongniart's designs, erected the entrance gateway in 1818. The pyramid, however, was never completed, due to lack of funds. In its place, Godde built a modest Catholic chapel in 1818–21, paid for by money left in the will of a pious widow. The chapel takes the form of a plain Doric temple, whose austere simplicity is today overshadowed by the elaborate monument to Adolphe Thiers next door.

The cemetery's fame grew rapidly after 1815, and its glory days began. Besides the ever increasing number of burials, Père-Lachaise became a popular place of pilgrimage and promenade, and countless guidebooks were published detailing its charms and listing the celebrities interred there. Paris's population more than doubled in the first half of the 19C (the one-million mark was reached in 1846), despite cholera epidemics in 1832 and 1849 which killed 18,402 and 16,165 people respectively, and these factors alone were enough to increase dramatically demand for space at Père-Lachaise. It was, however, the unexpected popularity of concessions in perpetuity, which far outstripped initial predictions, that rendered pressure on the available space acute. Successive enlargements between 1824 and 1842 took the size of the cemetery from an initial 17.58 ha up to 26.43 ha, but this was still insufficient. In 1850, the surface area of Père-Lachaise was almost doubled with the addition of land to the east of the original burial ground occupying the plateau at the top of the hill, bringing it to its current size of 43.93 ha. The inclusion of Père-Lachaise within the boundaries of the Ville de Paris in 1860 precluded any further extensions.

Partly because of the flatness of the terrain, which did not lend itself to picturesque landscaping, and partly out of a desire to optimize the use of available space, the 1850 extension was laid out in plain, functional grid form. The new sections of the cemetery soon filled up, while the older sections, where tomb density had increased to saturation point, had long since lost the parkland aspect of Brongniart's original creation. Père-Lachaise was becoming distinctly urban in character. By the 1870s, pressure on space was again an issue and, unable to increase further the size of the cemetery, the municipality began to look for other solutions to the capacity problem. In 1885, in anticipation of the legalization of cremation in France, it began construction of a crematorium at Père-Lachaise, to designs by Jean-Camille Formigé. Although pro-cremation laws were passed in 1887, the crematorium was not inaugurated until 1890 and was only finally completed in the 1920s, perhaps a reflection of the unpopularity of cremation in France.

Byzantine in inspiration – a stylistic choice probably influenced more by fashion than any other consideration –, Formigé's crematorium consists essentially of a square, domed hall, whose exterior façades are largely blank but animated by alternate light and dark stone banding. The columned and pedimented entrance elevation is surmounted by a bas-relief carving of a sarcophagus, from which thick smoke escapes, symbolizing the building's function. Three half-domed apses protrude from the rear elevation, which is surmounted by tall, pepper-shaker chimneys. The brick dome is covered with enamelled stoneware tiles, enlivened with palm-leaf motifs. Inside, the *salle des cérémonies* (the crematorium, like the cemetery, is secular) is decorated with stained glass and mosaics which probably date from the 1920s. The two outer apses, which are entirely separate from the main space and originally contained the ovens (since removed to the basement), serve as reception rooms for the families of the deceased. The central apse leads directly off the *salle des cérémonies* and contains a flight of steps at the top of which sits a stone sarcophagus from where the coffins descend to the furnaces.

Formigé was also responsible for the columbarium which surrounds the crematorium on three sides, thus forming a sort of cloister. Based on Italian models, it consists of a covered arcade containing two storeys of funerary niches, the upper storey being reached by way of a gallery running the length of the arcade. Predictably, the niches were quickly filled and, in 1937–42, another columbarium, with space for 24,000 urns, was built under the esplanade in front of the crematorium. The work of Jules Formigé, son of Jean-Camille, it is constructed wholly from raw reinforced concrete, and takes the form of two storeys of passages running off from a central, galleried atrium. The entire ensemble – crematorium and columbaria – forms a dignified and almost exotic setting for this most sensitive of vocations, and has been listed as a national monument.

It is, however, tombs that dominate at Père-Lachaise, and the cemetery consequently provides an extraordinary and fascinating record of changing architectural and tombstone fashions, as well as constituting an important repository of sculpture. While the poor were still buried in communal graves, the middle and upper classes, who could afford either concessions in perpetuity or temporary, renewable concessions, competed in ostentation (in death as in life) with the design of their gravestones. The cemetery authorities imposed no restrictions on tomb design, provided that decorum was respected. Aside from the countless crosses, and the urns, caskets, sarcophagi and broken columns inspired by Antique tombs, many of the earlier funerary monuments reflected the mania for all things Egyptian which swept France at the beginning of the 19C. The Gothic revival was also a big hit, of course, especially for the design of family vaults. One of the first to appear was the tomb of the Greffühle family, erected in 1815 to plans by Brongniart, which established the model for those to follow. At the time, its cost of 50,000 francs was considered outrageously exorbitant but, from around 1830 onwards, family vaults began to proliferate. Varying enormously in size, they nearly all feature a small devotional chapel above ground, built over the actual crypt, and in many parts of the cemetery are so common that they form what look like streets of quaint little houses. As well as chapels and the more commonplace types of gravestone, Père-Lachaise is overflowing with monuments and mausolea. An exhaustive list is impossible within the scope of this book, but amongst the more renowned are: the tomb of Héloïse and Abélard, a Gothic pastiche created at the behest of Alexandre Lenoir (1817); the impressive neo-Classical monument to General Foy, conceived as an explicit political gesture of opposition to the Bourbon regime in power at the time of the general's death (Léon Vaudoyer, architect, and David d'Angers, sculptor, 1831); the extraordinary, vast, conical tower erected to the memory of Baron Félix de Beaujour by the sculptor Cendrier (1836); Albert Bartholomé's intense Monument aux Morts (1895–99); and, one of the most visited monuments of all, Jacob Epstein's ominous, angular angel, carved for the tomb of Oscar Wilde (1911/12).

20.3 »Couple Plus« apartment building
132, rue des Pyrénées
Michel Bourdeau, 1989–95
(Métro: Alexandre Dumas)

Like Frédéric Borel's much-talked-about 113, rue Oberkampf (11.3), this project was one of the fruits of a major building campaign undertaken by the French postal service to provide affordable accommodation for its Parisian employees. Young and innovative architects were expressly sought out, and the results garnered much positive comment. Michel Bourdeau's building was conceived to provide 34 apartments on a restricted site (683 m² with 24.77 m street frontage) sandwiched between a dull 1960s block and an older, Haussmann-style building. Rather like Borel, Bourdeau was eager to break the hegemony of the street-line-respecting, frontally orientated »box«, although his means of achieving this were very different from Borel's. »Couple Plus« was of course subject to Paris's stringent building regulations, which largely concern themselves with façades and their articulation, and Bourdeau's principle strategy was to subvert traditional, Haussmannian notions of the façade and the planning laws they engendered in order to introduce greater flexibility and dynamism into his building.

Suspended within Couple Plus's orthogonal concrete frame is accommodation ranging from studio flats to three-room apartments. Externally, however, this variety is hidden behind a startlingly graphic series of curved, strip shields hung from the plane of the building line. Closed to the north and open to the south, these shields flaunt the conventions of traditional Parisian façades in two ways: firstly, they naughtily project beyond the building line; and secondly (and more importantly), they play on the potential of the oblique view, cleverly exploiting the fact that people rarely look at buildings frontally, in the way elevations are drawn, but instead generally perceive them from an angle. Thus, as one approaches Couple Plus from the north, one sees only the closed carapace of the shields, which give the impression of a conventionally solid façade. From the south, however, the building presents an entirely different visage, with balconied openings sheltering behind what we now see to be the thin skin of the shields, and protruding, angular structures suspended within a section of open concrete frame next to the southern party wall. This latter feature was another attack on traditional façadism, intended to ban-

20.3 »Couple Plus« apartment building

ish entirely planar elevations and notions of front and back and also to introduce extra daylight into the building's lateral parts. Large expanses of olive-green render further underline Couple Plus's unconventionality, setting off the silvery hue of the shields, which were fabricated from a lightweight metacrylate-resin-based composite (concrete would have been too heavy), a mix known for its resistant qualities but never before used on this scale.

Inside the building, Bourdeau grouped together kitchens, bathrooms and entryways in a single block to allow greater flexibility in the disposition of living and bedrooms in the limited space. Views out of the flats are regulated by the shields' narrow strip openings (three strips per apartment) which, ignoring the average eye-level heights of the human body, are supposed to »cocoon« the occupant from the aggressive city outside. A retaliation against the »goldfish-bowl« effect that Bourdeau reproached in much social housing, the strip openings nonetheless seem unnecessarily dictatorial (one can cover up unwanted glazing but one can't cut windows through where there aren't any). The section of open frame is also problematic: essentially an adaptation of traditional light wells, it is an interesting idea, but realized at this tight scale suffers from the dinginess associated with its forbears. Likewise, the balcony openings behind the shields seem rather mean. Although he asked many of the right questions, Bourdeau did not necessarily come up with satisfactory answers.

Furthermore, challenging building regulations can be dangerous. Since the state was Couple Plus's client, it pushed planning permission through even though the accommodation density infringed Parisian regulations. The municipality appealed and won, and Bourdeau's project would have had to be shorn of its upper levels if not for the miraculous availability of a neighbouring plot which, purchased by the post office and developed as green open space, allowed Bourdeau's building to remain unmodified.

20.4 Primary school
99–101, rue Pelleport
Francis Soler, 1986–88
(Métro: Pelleport)

It is fitting that Paris, birthplace of Surrealism, should feature architecture inspired by Breton et al.'s movement. Frédéric Borel wanted to recreate fortuitous encounters of the kind described by Isidore Ducasse (see 11.3 and 20.1), while for this municipal primary school, Francis Soler took inspiration from the assemblages of the American artist Joseph Cornell. Cornell was famous for his boxes, in which normally unconnected objects were juxtaposed in surprising, »thought-liberating« combinations. For Soler, what was important about Cornell's work was the »fugitive expression« of »non-apprehensible spaces« that were bounded by the »material limitation of the box«. To him this was analogous to the confrontation between »the immateriality

20.4 Primary school

of thought« and its often »conventional frame«, or the »paradox of the unstructured minds of our children« set within the official institution that is a school ... Translated into architecture, these ideas became a four-storey, concrete box of a building whose glass-curtain-walled street façade sports an enormous aluminium frame, two of whose sides are missing. A pair of black steel poles, slanting at an irrational angle, prevents the frame from falling to the ground. Graphic black glazing bars and striated, anthracite-finished concrete complete the rather brooding vocabulary of the school's exterior. Inside, clarity of plan and volume and abundant natural light were favoured. While the building's external aspect is certainly powerful and signals its civic and official nature, one wonders if the architect's intended metaphors really come through. The expressionism seems too flimsy and gimmicky, although anything more radical would probably not have been accepted for a school.

20.5 Social housing
15, rue des Pavillons and 131, rue Pelleport
Frédéric Borel, 1994–99
(Métro: Télégraphe)

A decade after his memorable Boulevard-de-Belleville housing scheme (20.1), and five years following his spectacular Rue-Oberkampf apartment complex (11.3), the still-only-39-year-old Frédéric Borel produced this equally extraordinary apartment building, which demonstrates a very different facet of his »cubist« architecture. Situated on a wedge-shaped plot of land at the junction of the Rues Pelleport and des Pavillons, this totem tower of ten rent-controlled flats is but phase one of a complex which, if completed, will ultimately provide 30 dwellings. Its context could not be more different from the Boulevard-de-Belleville and Rue-Oberkampf projects, and it is essentially this that explains its striking dissimilarity to its predecessors. Where the Boulevard-de-Belleville and Rue-Oberkampf sites were

20.5 Social housing

typically Parisian, hemmed in between the towering party-walls so common to the Haussmann-era city, the Rue-des-Pavillons plot was surrounded by a disparate collection of mutually disregarding, detached buildings. At its feet were vestiges of the area's original low-rise, mid-19C fabric, while to the north and east were joyless 70s slab blocks (that to the north rising an intimidating 17 storeys), all of them jostling for position on the heights of the Ménilmontant hill. Borel was consequently left with no choice but to implant yet another free-standing object in this heterogeneous landscape, and the challenge was thus to try to bring some kind of coherence to the surrounding chaos. Perhaps only a building as unorthodox as Borel's could have managed this impossible task, but manage it it did.

Apart from considerations of scale and volume, there was no point trying to take any cues from the site's surroundings. Instead Borel created a building that is as formally complex and multi-faceted as the cityscape that contains it. Logistically, however, his apartment block is very simple: an eight-storey stacking of flats, with lifts and stairs externalized in a free-standing tower to the north. Phase two of the scheme (if it goes ahead) will link up to the other side of the lift-and-stair tower. With vertical access sequestered in this way, Borel was able to construct the apartment tower around a central, load-bearing concrete wall, an arrangement that allowed him the latitude he wanted at the building's periphery. Like Michel Bourdeau's buildings (see 20.3), much of Borel's work aims to break away from the frontally orientated, planar-façaded boxes of which Paris is made up, a feat he achieved here through what he described as an effect of »folding«. The apartment tower is made up of layers of concrete partitions that dance in a complex geometry of inclined verticals, their edges exposed like peeled-back origami pleats, with vertically stressed fenestration sandwiched within the folds of the walls. An impressive symphony of colours and finishes further amplifies the building's unorthodoxy, with pale-orange and pistachio stucco, cream-coloured stone, eau-de-nil glass, aluminium and even tenebrous-green serpentine all hustling for attention. Because it eschews traditional fenestration and rectilinearity, Borel's building looks like nothing else in the vicinity, and it is perhaps this sculptural, rainbow-sharded latitude that ensures its contextual success. As seen from the southern section of the Rue Pelleport, Borel's creation masks the relentless rise of its 17-storey neighbour (which formerly dominated the area), presenting an urban event that terminates the perspective with calm dignity. On its eastern façade it becomes more animated, while the Rue-des-Pavillons elevation is all kinetic, volitant flare.

Inside, the building is as visually unconventional as outside. Its complex morphology meant that no two apartments are alike, and their plans are almost as irregularly angular as the exterior. All the living rooms and kitchens are orientated to the west, where they take advantage of spectacular views over Paris towards the setting sun, while the bedrooms sit on the other side of the central load-bearing wall, orientated east. Eccentrically framed views across the cityscape are afforded on every façade bar the north. Although aesthetically nonconformist, the building is in fact programmatically routine, demonstrating with brio that traditional accommodation does not necessarily imply traditional, unimaginative solutions.

21 Saint-Denis

21.1 Stade de France
La Plaine Saint-Denis
Macary-Zublena and Regembal-Costantini, 1994–97
(RER: Stade de France Saint-Denis, La Plaine Stade de France)

On 12 July 1998, when the World Cup final, hosted by France, was won by the French team, hundreds of thousands of people poured onto the Champs-Elysées for an all-night party. But while the national football team was the toast of the town, it was rivalled by another star of the tournament – the brand-new, 2.6-billion-franc Stade de France, which had been built specially for the competition. Where mythic stadia like Wembley owed their fame to decades of long service and football folklore, the Stade de France achieved instant celebrity, as much for its architecture as for the sporting event for which it was conceived, and earned its designers the prestigious Légion d'Honneur in recognition of their achievement. For not only had they produced an admirable building, but they had done so under extremely difficult circumstances, not the least of which had been the impossibly tight schedule: less than two-and-a-half years from start of construction work to handover.

France first put forward its candidature to host the 1998 World Cup in 1988, and was officially selected by FIFA in 1992. A key element in the French proposal was the promise to build a new, 80,000-seat stadium in the Paris region. Multiple sites were put forward during the four years before France's selection, but it was not until November 1993 that an official choice was made: a 17 ha chunk of land in Saint-Denis, formerly occupied by gas works. The chosen site's advantages were manifold: only 1.5 km from Paris, it could be well served by the RER, a Métro stop was not far, the A1 and A86 motorways passed nearby, and it was on the way to Paris's main airport at Roissy (see 22.1). Moreover, the presence of such a prestige facility in one of Paris's more problematic suburbs would, it was hoped, raise the area's standing and bring in money and jobs. (Indeed an adjunct to the stadium project, in the form of a new *quartier* comprising apartments and offices, was planned concurrently.) And, environmentally, the project would see to the clean-up of a heavily polluted former industrial site.

In February 1994, a national competition was organized to find a design for the stadium, which, to save time, included the novel requirement that architects associate directly with engineering and construction companies to present a joint design/realization proposal. The competition's ultimate judge was the then prime minister, Edouard Balladur, who went against the jury's decision (in favour of a project by Jean Nouvel) and instead selected a joint scheme by two teams of architects – Michel Macary and Aymeric Zublena with Michel Regembal and Claude Costantini – and the consortium Bouyges-Dumez-SGE. Although the result was announced in October 1994, construction of the new stadium could not begin until nearly a year later, in August 1995, due to the depollution work necessary beforehand. As a result, the architects and their consortium disposed of exactly two years and five months to complete the building. Construction was a heroic enterprise that mobilized 200 lorries per day and kept some 15 cranes in permanent action. By far the most difficult part was the roof, which required 2,500 convoys of prefabricated parts from Poland and the services of the world's two biggest cranes, which could only operate in wind-free conditions. When it was discovered that the depollution works had not been entirely successful, the architects designed a 9 m-deep concrete pan to protect the stadium's turf from poisonous hydrocarbons, any pollution that found its way into the pan being pumped out and treated. Despite this and other unforeseen difficulties which yet further complicated construction, the Stade de France was handed over bang on schedule and only slightly over budget.

Since the stadium was going to need to carry on making money long after the World Cup, and as it could not live off national football alone, the competition brief had called for a highly adaptable building capable of hosting both reduced-capacity athletics meetings of around 65,000 spectators and rock concerts, arena-scale operas and other shows of up to 100,000 spectators. The architects were anxious to produce an edifice

21.1 Stade de France

that while monumental would not be cold or intimidating and that would integrate well with its surroundings. Partially sunk below grade to reduce its bulk on the skyline, the elliptical stadium consists essentially of three tiers of seating supported on a massive concrete structure whose giant members flare out in soaring cantilever. In response to the call for adjustable seating permutations, the lowest tier slides away on rails to reveal an athletics track sitting underneath, a neat response to the problem encountered in stadia such as Wembley, whose athletics track distanced football fans from the hallowed turf. To facilitate production of concerts and theatrical events, a sort of subterranean »ring road« was built underneath the Stade de France's tribunes to allow equipment deliveries right into its heart. As is common in oval stadia, the seating rises higher at the building's narrower ends, and the tribunes' upper profile thus undulates in a gentle wave. Below them, a trabeated concrete-framed structure contains the building's many ancillary facilities – spectator boxes, changing rooms, reception rooms, offices, press facilities, restaurants, bars, shops, etc. –, and the stadium's exterior thus presents a sheer glass-and-stainless-steel façade over which projects the flare of the upper tribunes. The three tiers of seating are each accessed separately, the lowest via a ramp leading down to the stadium's basement, the middle via footbridges connecting it to the esplanade surrounding the stadium, and the topmost via 18 bravura free-standing concrete staircases, each of which resembles a ship's bow when seen from behind. Generous circulation spaces ensure that the stadium can be evacuated in as little as six minutes, and its ancillary facilities appear unusually chic in comparison to bog-standard stadia.

But nothing so far described catches the eye or the imagination as much as the stadium's roof, the *pièce de résistance* of the edifice and its primary signifier. Suspended by cables from 18 masts encircling the upper tribunes (which thus do not in any way obstruct views of the pitch), it consists of a giant 6 ha, white-PVC-covered steel-framed canopy floating 42 m above turf level that sticks out far enough on either side both to cover all the seats and the access ring on the stadium's exterior. Whether on days of driving winds and rain this Hi-tech *velum* manages to keep everyone warm and dry is questionable, but it is the building's trademark, as instantly identifiable as Saturn's rings, a sort of flying saucer dropped in industrial Saint-Denis that was intended to suggest openness, hope (in the manner of a Spielbergian close encounter) and of course to demonstrate French flair and engineering prowess. It is especially resplendent at night when lit from underneath, which gives it the spectacular allure of a hovering halo as well as producing agreeable diffuse lighting for the upper tribunes. Despite its impression of soaring airiness, the roof weighs a whopping 17,000 tonnes, but is nonetheless vulnerable to wind action, whence its aeroplane-wing profile which offers the least resistance. The roof's inner ring is in glass, which both allows more light to reach the pitch and filters it, thereby reducing contrast for the television cameras. If the Stade de France lacks typical stadium lighting pylons, it is because all the necessary lamps, and the P.A. system, have been hung within the roof, while unsightly drainpipes were banished by channelling rainwater into the masts' interiors. As is so often the case, a bold, seemingly simple formal gesture in fact required great technical accomplishment to achieve.

21.2 Abbaye de Saint-Denis
2, place de la Légion-d'Honneur
Architects unknown, current buildings begun c.1130
(Métro: Saint-Denis-Basilique; RER: Saint-Denis)

It was of course in the Ile-de-France region that Gothic architecture was born, and by far the majority of histories on the subject begin their tale here, at the Abbey of Saint-Denis. The ambitious and highly innovative choir added to the abbey church by Abbot Suger in 1140–44 marked the turning point in the invention of a new type of architecture, and set the standard for a whole subsequent generation of great churches. But Saint-Denis's importance in architectural history did not end there, for in the 13C, with the rebuilding of its nave, the abbey gave us what became known as the Rayonnant-Gothic style, which would prove even more influential. That one particular abbey church out of the hundreds in France should have been so artistically pre-eminent was no accident, for Saint-Denis, thanks to the prestige of its patron saint, rose to become the most powerful religious house in 12C France. The lurid legend of the saint himself is shrouded in mystery and confusion: he is supposed to have been an evangelizer sent from Rome, who became Paris's first bishop, before being beheaded by hostile locals at Montmartre (Martyrs' Mount) from where he walked some 10 km with his head before falling in field where a pious Christian woman buried him! From the 9C on, Saint Denis's identity became confused with Dionysius the Areopagite and Pseudo-Dionysius, who were all thought to be one and the same person, although subsequent scholarship has re-established Paris's Denis as a separate saint. That the abbey stands at the site of his burial is not contested, but it seems that his final resting place was in fact the cemetery of the Roman settlement of Catulliacus rather than the field of legend.

The first known building at Denis's tomb was a mausoleum built sometime in the early-4C, which was replaced with a larger basilica at the end of the 5C, supposedly at the behest of Saint Geneviève. In the 7C a monastery was established at Saint-Denis, and in 768 to 775 a new abbey church was begun. Several Carolingian monarchs were buried there, establishing a precedent that would take on full significance after Hugues Capet (reigned 987–96), founder of the modern French royal line, chose the abbey as his final resting place: thereafter it became the official royal necropolis, all bar three of the *ancien régime*'s monarchs being laid to rest there. During the reign of Louis VI (1108–37),

Denis was adopted as the patron saint of France, and Saint-Denis's then abbot, Suger, brought the monastery to the peak of its power and influence. It was under Louis VI's patronage that Suger began construction of a new west front at Saint-Denis in the 1130s, which was consecrated in 1140. The abbot's ultimate intention was to rebuild the whole church, both to provide a building big enough to cope with the ever-increasing influx of pilgrims, and because the abbey's prestige demanded a new, modern edifice worthy of its status. But the old 8C church had such a venerable aura about it – especially since it was believed that Christ himself had consecrated it – that Suger dared not replace it too hastily, and for his next campaign of work turned to the east end, where he built his famous new choir under the patronage of Louis VII (reigned 1137–80). Drawing on developments realized in other Ile-de-France churches such as Saint-Pierre-de-Montmartre (18.3) and Saint-Martin-des-Champs (3.10), it combined for the first time in one edifice pointed arches, rib vaults, vault responds and flying buttresses in a coherent stylistic and technical synthesis, and can be considered the first major edifice of the early Gothic. Saint-Denis's close royal connections made its architecture emblematic of the house of France, and of the symbolism elaborated by the monarchy whereby the French king was considered to bear in his person the living image of Christ, and as a result all the kingdom's great churches subsequently looked to Suger's choir for architectural inspiration. After completion of Saint-Denis's east end, work began on a new nave, of which only the foundations, built outside the walls of the old church, had been completed at the time of Suger's death in 1151.

For the next eight decades, Saint-Denis retained its ungainly hybrid state, the modest Carolingian nave being sandwiched between the much bigger, early-Gothic westwork and choir. It was Louis IX (reigned 1226–70), the queen regent, Blanche de Castille, and Saint-Denis's then abbot, Eudes Clément, who set about rectifying this state of affairs and bringing to the royal necropolis the grandeur it lacked. Begun in 1231 by an unknown architect, the new structures included massive transepts designed to contain the royal tombs; to ensure internal harmony, the upper parts of the 12C choir were also entirely rebuilt. Sometime around 1247 the celebrated Pierre de Montreuil took charge of the work, bringing new stylistic and technical developments to what was already a highly innovative design. Finally completed in 1281, Saint-Denis's Rayonnant nave pushed the Gothic structural system to new extremes of leanness, with minimum supports and maximum glazing, and influenced great-church design across the continent for centuries to come.

Until the French Revolution, the abbey church of Saint-Denis remained essentially as the 13C had left it, bar the addition during the 14C of side-chapels on the nave's northern flank (the lack of corresponding chapels to the south was due to the presence of abbey buildings there). In the 16C, Catherine de Médicis began construction of a circular Classical mausoleum on the northern transept front, probably to designs by Jean Bullant, but it was never completed and ended up being demolished in 1719. The 18C also saw the demolition of the original abbey buildings, which were replaced by a new ensemble whose general outlines were designed by Robert de Cotte. Work began in 1701 and carried on piecemeal until 1781, producing the regular, Classical, Invalides-inspired ensemble we see today (see also 7.12). Given Saint-Denis's status as France's royal necropolis and major symbol of its monarchy, not to mention of the equally hated Catholic church, it was inevitable that the Revolution would be particularly cruel to the abbey. The church's roof was stripped of its lead and the vaults left exposed to the elements, while the portal sculptures were decapitated and mutilated. In 1793, by order of the Convention, the royal tombs were destroyed and over 800 corpses of kings, queens, princes and aristocrats tipped into a communal pit. Nonetheless, Alexandre Lenoir was allowed to save the most artistically important funerary monuments, which he transported to his Musée des Monuments Français (see 6.1). Afterwards the church was used for storing grain, and there was even talk of demolishing the nave to build a covered market in its stead.

By the time Napoleon decided to turn the abbey church into his family mausoleum, the building was in a pitiful state. Jacques-Guillaume Legrand was appointed to restore it, and set about Neoclassicizing the interior; afterwards the emperor changed his mind and hired Jacques Cellerier to undo the work of his predecessor. In 1813, François Debret was named architect of Saint-Denis, and spent the next 33 years giving the building a thorough overhaul. A pioneer in the delicate art that is the restoration of historic monuments, he assembled a whole team of craftsmen to carry out the job, which, as well as consolidating the building's fabric, included repairing or replacing damaged or lost sculptures and stained glass, redecorating the chapels and bringing back what remained of the royal tombs to the church. Funerary effigies from other vandalized churches were also brought there, and Saint-Denis today houses the most important collection of tomb monuments in France. Debret was not, however, a rigorous archaeologist, and worked more as a decorator, seeking to establish a general medievalizing ambience that suited the tastes of the day rather than an accurate historical restitution. He was also guilty of sloppiness in technical matters, and was forced to resign after the church's north tower, whose lightning-struck spire he had rebuilt to a new design, began to collapse and had to be demolished. One of his most virulent critics was Eugène-Emmanuel Viollet-le-Duc, who replaced Debret at Saint-Denis in 1846 and worked on the abbey church until his death in 1879. He devoted a considerable amount of energy to undoing as much as possible of Debret's work, and it is essentially to him that we owe Saint-Denis as it appears today.

Saint-Denis before the first millennium
It is in the current abbey church's crypt that the most interesting remains of earlier structures on the site are now to be found. Indeed much of today's crypt is in fact 8C, the original Carolingian structure having been re-used in the 12C rebuilding of the choir. This was where Saint Denis's remains were located and where pilgrims came to venerate his shrine. Today we can still see the semicircular corridor that ran round the saint's sanctuary, as well as fragments of the painted décor that adorned its walls. Also remaining, although much altered by Suger, is the Lady Chapel tacked on to the original crypt by Abbot Hilduin in 832, with its series of low arcades and carved capitals. Other Carolingian capitals and column bases from Saint-Denis can be seen displayed in the upper part of the church or in the Musée de Cluny (see 5.4).

Abbot Suger's rebuilding, c. 1130–50
Today the oldest complete structure at Saint-Denis is the massive westwork, begun by Suger sometime in the 1130s, which became the prototype for a whole series of French great-church west ends. In its general outlines it reproduces the already established Norman twin-tower model, although it also looks back to early-medieval west fronts, for example in the chapels placed above its side entrances. In his *De Administratione*, Suger justified the building of a new westwork both symbolically – its division into three representing the Trinity – and practically, the provision of three doors allowing for easier handling of the crowds of pilgrims that flocked to the abbey. Today, with the north tower gone, Saint-Denis's west façade appears very lopsided and clumsy, not helped by the fact that the towers were, unusually, set back behind a crenellated gallery, which both contributed to symbolizing the Heavenly Jerusalem (which all churches were supposed to represent) and, as Suger put it, could be used, »should circumstances require it, for practical purposes«. The first-floor chapel rising above the central portal was much taller than those either side, and, to fill the gap between its window and the crenellations, Saint-Denis's builders constructed a rose window lighting the tribune. This was one of the very first examples of a centrally positioned rose window on a west front, and would go on to inspire numerous imitations. Although badly mutilated in the 18C and heavy-handedly restored by Debret, Saint-Denis's three entrance portals still testify to something of the originality of the church's sculptural elements, which art historians classify as the very first examples of Gothic carving. The most innovative and influential elements were the larger-than-life jamb statues, which have since been lost. A principal feature of the iconography was the Old Testament kings, thereby highlighting the cult of kingship that Suger helped set up around the French monarchy.

But the innovations of Saint-Denis's westwork were nothing in comparison to those of its choir, which can be considered the touchstone of Gothic architecture.

Today the full impact of Suger's east end can only be conjectured, since the original tribune, clerestory and high vault are gone and no documentation survives regarding the form they took. Nonetheless, there is enough evidence to allow a reasonably trustworthy reconstitution. Whoever designed Saint-Denis's 12C choir must have been extremely sure of what he was doing, for it was completed in the astonishingly rapid period of four years. Certain peculiarities in the design that would not necessarily be repeated elsewhere are explained by the need to take into account the original Carolingian church, and it was for this reason that the east end was built on top of a massive and sturdy crypt, which enveloped the saint's shrine and the old subterranean structures. It was also for this reason that the choir was constructed using slim, columnar supports instead of the compound piers by then generally employed elsewhere in the region, an archaism that reflected the Roman-style columns of the 8C nave, with which, at least initially, the new choir had to harmonize. Since this was a pilgrimage church and Suger's stated aim was to »process« ever greater numbers of pilgrims, the choir took on the by-then classic apse-ambulatory-with-radiating-chapels form, allowing pilgrims to circulate round the ambulatory without disturbing the monks' liturgical space in the chancel. It had one peculiarity though, almost certainly borrowed from Saint-Martin-des-Champs, in that its radiating chapels were not treated as individual, clearly defined units, as was generally the case in French Romanesque churches, but were fused with each other and with the ambulatory to form one continuous, fluid space. Thus in place of the vault-bearing walls that usually separated chapels we find a second row of columns, with the result that Saint-Denis's choir chapels read as a second ambulatory closed by a continuous, coherent envelope. And this continuous external envelope, instead of comprising large areas of solid wall as would have been the case in Romanesque churches, was treated as a glazed arcade, thereby permitting great quantities of light to enter and allowing for a maximum expanse of stained glass.

Indeed stained glass was the choir's principal decorative element, for in comparison to many Romanesque churches its carved stone components – limited to shaft-arches, vaults and foliage capitals – were restrained. But, with the continuous glazed envelope of the radiating chapels and the similar disposition that must have existed in the clerestory, Saint-Denis could sparkle and shine with the deep, jewel-like intensity of coloured glass. Over 700 *livres* were spent on the church's windows, an enormous figure when one considers that the entire choir carcass had cost 1,400 *livres*. In *De Administratione*, Suger devoted a considerable amount of space to justifying the gorgeous and costly artworks he had commissioned for the abbey – which, as well as stained glass, included gilt-bronze doors, gold-and-jewelled reliquary boxes and altar plate –, expounding a neo-Platonic, Pseudo-Dionysius-style philosophy in which these artworks, rather than being merely vulgar and temporal as detractors claimed, were the medium via which our base minds can be raised from the material to a higher, spiritual realm. Suger's scholastic outlook considered that faith must be illuminated by reason and reason via the imagination and the senses: Saint-Denis's splendid stained glass literally illuminated the pictorial messages it carried and expressed the fundamental medieval notion that »God is light«. Scholastic symbolism was, furthermore, incorporated in numerical form into the very fabric of the choir: besides the proportioning systems, such as the golden section, used to design the east end, the twelve columns of the chancel (not including the crossing supports) stood, according to Suger, for the twelve apostles – the pillars of the Church –, and, likewise, the twelve supports of the choir's outer envelope and its internal continuation (again not including the crossing-level piers), could be said to represent the twelve minor prophets. Thus every component of the choir carried symbolic weight and the ensemble formed a complex allegory of Christian doctrine and faith. Today, stripped of its original furnishings and the majority of its original stained glass, the choir's overall effect is greatly diminished; of Suger's glazing, around 15 panels remain in the ambulatory chapels, combined in new compositions by Viollet-le-Duc.

21.2 Abbaye de Saint-Denis

To create this luminous outer envelope of stained glass, Saint-Denis's architect(s) developed a highly economical structural system that privileged voids over solids, and to achieve this it seems extremely likely that they used flying buttresses. Today the choir's upper levels feature heavy vault responds added in the 13C that descend all the way down to the floor, but the original responds would have departed only from the capitals of the chancel columns. These capitals do not project anything like as much as those at Notre-Dame (4.2), for example, and we can thus conclude that the original vault responds were relatively slender and could not have supported alone the thrust of the high vault (as was the case at Saint-Pierre-de-Montmartre). Consequently, some other, supplementary type of support must have been included, and evidence exists to suggest that it may well have taken the form of flying buttresses. If so, then Saint-Denis represents a sudden, complete jump from the hesitant experimentation of earlier Francilien churches to the lean, skeletal Gothic structural system that would afterwards be copied all across Europe. Several great churches built immediately in the wake of Saint-Denis and almost certainly influenced by it display exactly this structural system, and it was thanks to Suger's choir that columnar piers became a staple of early-Gothic architecture before being superseded by the compound pier in the High-Gothic era. Not everything about Saint-Denis was reproduced elsewhere, however, its model of merged radiating chapels never really catching on, probably because this fluid space contradicted the physical separation necessary for liturgical purposes.

One other significant element survives from Suger's time, namely the portal known as the Porte des Valois, which was probably created for one of the abbot's never-completed transepts and was incorporated into the northern transept front in the 13C. Almost certainly commissioned towards the end of Suger's life, it was badly damaged during the Revolution and heavily restored thereafter. Nonetheless it still provides an interesting comparison with the west front, marking the development of Gothic sculpture with more autonomous, naturalistic figures and greater graphic impact. Instead of the west end's round-headed arches we find a fully-Gothic pointed arch head, and the jamb statues are still in place.

The Rayonnant abbey church, 1231–81
If Saint-Denis's choir was the touchstone of Gothic, its 13C nave can be regarded as the culmination of the style, or at any rate the culmination of a certain strand in Gothic that privileged structural leanness over decorative exuberance. Its dispositions were disseminated across Europe by French architects in the employ of foreign powers, and its influence was consequently even greater than Suger's east end. Perhaps the ultimate progeny of the lessons of Saint-Denis (although French historians do not like to admit it) was the cathedral at Cologne (*c*. 1248–1322), which combined the

exaggerated height of High-Gothic churches with the lean elegance of the abbey's nave elevations. The first 13C campaign of work at Saint-Denis was carried out fairly rapidly by an unknown architect in the years 1231 to 1245: at the end of this period the 12C choir had been reconfigured to match the new nave elevations, the northern transept was entirely completed and a start had been made on the southern, and the first three bays of the nave rose as far as the vault springing points. Active at Saint-Denis at least as early as 1247, Pierre de Montreuil continued work on the church until his death in 1267, the southern transept façade being his most significant intervention. Progress after 1245 was greatly slowed down by financial difficulties, which explains why Saint-Denis was only finally completed in 1281.

In the 90 odd years between the consecration of Saint-Denis's choir and the start of work on its nave, the potential of Suger's east end had been developed in a number of French great churches, including Chartres (c. 1194–1220) and Amiens (1220 onwards), and it was only natural that the 13C builders at Saint-Denis should look to these edifices for inspiration. At Amiens a three-storey nave elevation had been employed featuring a narrow triforium sandwiched between a tall arcade and clerestory, with compound piers defining each bay and creating a soaring sense of upwards thrust. It was essentially this model that was adopted at Saint-Denis, but with the difference that the vertiginous heights that had characterized High-Gothic churches could not be reproduced here because of the need to integrate the old, 12C east end, which was of more modest dimensions. Indeed it is a measure of Saint-Denis's influence that after building of its new nave the height race between French great churches, so fierce in the High-Gothic period, began to lose momentum. Instead, Saint-Denis pushed the development of the skeleton-and-void structural system to its limits: unlike Amiens's, its vault responds are not interrupted by string courses and its cruciform piers have no columnar core and thus no capital to interfere with the responds' upwards thrust, thereby accentuating vertical emphasis and the role of the structural elements; its arcade arches almost touch the base of the triforium, thereby reducing residual wall space to a minimum; and, the most important innovation of all, its triforium is entirely glazed, producing a completely light-filled screen above the main-vessel arcade. Furthermore, in place of the complex, domical sexpartite vaults of the early Gothic we find simple quadripartite vaults, which had the advantage of allowing a daringly flat profile that reduced to a minimum obstruction of the clerestory's summit and accentuated the sensation of transparency. In short, Saint-Denis's new nave was designed as a lean, pure, monochrome skeleton for the display of stained glass.

Amiens's principal innovation had been its advanced use of tracery, and Saint-Denis's builders picked up where Amiens's architects left off. The early 13C saw the development of bar tracery in place of plate tracery, a technically more sophisticated system that allowed much leaner members. Plate tracery, to be found, for example, at Chartres, took the form of a stone screen, structurally integral to the rest of the façade, into which openings were cut; bar tracery, on the other hand, was structurally independent of the façade containing it and comprised much less bulky members, held together with iron clamps, that took on more linear, slender forms. At Amiens, we find elaborate bar tracery used to highly decorative effect but in physically discrete units; at Saint-Denis, on the other hand, the builders used tracery to fuse visually the clerestory and the triforium and emphasize the non-structural nature of these spaces. Indeed in the three easternmost bays of the nave constructed in the 1231–45 campaign, the clerestory dimensions were contrived so as to include the triforium in a single unit of classic proportions. Because of the relative darkness of the triforium, however, one does not naturally read the elevation in this way, and in the westernmost bays of the nave Montreuil and his successors consequently gave the clerestory its own, autonomous proportioning in the traditional manner. One wonders why the 1231–45 builders did not do away with the triforium altogether and instead construct a taller clerestory (as would later be done in some Flamboyant period churches – see, e. g., Saint-Nicolas-des-Champs (3.9)). Tradition was no doubt a strong factor in the triforium's retention, and its aesthetic properties were surely also appreciated: in Saint-Denis's nave it provides a graduated transition between the gloom of the main-vessel arcades and the total luminosity of the clerestory.

At Saint-Denis the most spectacular application of bar tracery is to be found in the rose windows terminating each of its transepts. They strike immediately and forcibly in their enormous size, considerably larger than those at, say, Chartres, and in the way the whole of the arch under the vault has been glazed as one continuous unit, with glass-filled lower spandrels and a glazed arcade that carries round visually the main-vessel elevations' triforium. A whole battery of iron reinforcements was needed both to keep these filigree screens up and to strengthen them against high winds. Montreuil's southern rose is arguably the more accomplished, with thinner members and an effect of concentric rings themselves made up of circular elements. Constructed with spokes that travel all the way from their centres to their circumferences – a technical innovation in comparison with earlier circular windows –, these spectacular roses gave the Rayonnant style its name: *rayonner* = to radiate, and Saint-Denis's transept roses radiated both outwards in stone and across their vast expanse with gorgeous, stained-glass-coloured light.

22 Roissy-en-France

22.1 Aéroport Charles-de-Gaulle
Paul Andreu, 1965–2005
(RER: Roissy Aéroport Charles-de-Gaulle)

Gateway to Paris – and indeed to France in most cases – for over 45 million air travellers annually, Roissy Charles-de-Gaulle (CDG) is Europe's third airport after Frankfurt and London Heathrow. Situated on the wide, flat Plaine de France 25 km north of the capital, it constitutes a small town in its own right, sprawling across 3,254 ha and employing over 75,000 people. CDG was programmed, appropriately enough, by General de Gaulle when it became clear that Paris's ever increasing air-traffic volume could not be handled solely by Orly, the capital's other major airport located to the south (Henri Vicariot, 1957–61). Because of its status as an *ouvrage d'infrastructure*, CDG was exempt from the usual planning regulations as well as the architectural competition that traditionally accompanied state commissions. Instead it was an affair of technocrats, its design and construction being assigned to the Corps des Ponts et Chaussées.

Anyone familiar with CDG will know that it comprises three parts of very different character: Terminal 1, Terminal 2 Halls A–D, and Terminal 2 Halls E–F, the two parts of Terminal 2 being separated by an RER/TGV station. What the visitor may be surprised to learn is that all three sections of the airport, and the railway station, are in fact by the same architect. Indeed, following his Ponts-et-Chaussées début at CDG, Paul Andreu went on to become a specialist in airport construction, building over 40 air terminals worldwide in almost as many years. At CDG, the evolution of his approach can be traced through the different phases of construction.

The first part realized was of course Terminal 1, which was completed in 1974. Like Orly, it was not as a work of architecture *per se* that CDG1 was conceived, but as a functional piece of infrastructure capable of dealing as efficiently as possible with the practical demands made of it. No doubt influenced by the ideas of Archigram and their ilk, Andreu and his team took the flow and flux of passenger movement as the basis for the building's design, formalism only coming in at a second stage once the basic passenger-movement circuit had been established. The result was a wide, squat cylinder of a building, approached by roadways that ran underneath and into it, and orbited around two thirds of its circumference by seven satellite boarding pods each capable of handling several planes at once. Chosen to keep distances within the terminal to a minimum, the cylinder form was divided up into strata of activity, with arrivals on one floor, check-in on another, security controls on yet another, and car parking on the roof. For reasons of economy, Terminal 1 was realized as a raw-reinforced-concrete monolith, little attention being paid to its external aspect, which looms over the approaching passenger like some sort of Brutalist camembert. Unlike Orly, which despite its rather dull, functionalist approach at least included large windows and observation terraces, CDG1 was a hermetically sealed transit machine that sucked passengers in, processed them, and pumped them out to the waiting-area satellites

22.1 Aéroport Charles-de-Gaulle. View from the east

22.1 Aéroport Charles-de-Gaulle. View from the west

without their once being given a clue as to their whereabouts in relation to the outside world. After passing through the check-in – whose circular form makes it very disorientating –, one is spewed through perspex tubes running across a fountain-filled hole in the building's centre (which no doubt seemed very futuristic at the time but has not aged well), before again plunging into darkness in the long tunnels linking the terminal building to the boarding satellites. It is only at the end of this initiation rite that one finally emerges into the full daylight of the boarding satellite from where one enjoys sweeping views across the runways and the aeroplanes.

The authorities' original intention was to duplicate Terminal 1 five times over, but when it came to starting work on Terminal 2 they decided that a different approach was needed, economic imperatives requiring a building that could be constructed in stages and come into service progressively, which was impossible with the closed system of the Terminal-1 model. Terminal 1's lack of architectonic panache may also have played a part in the decision not to replicate it. The first section of Terminal 2, Hall B, was inaugurated in 1981, and was followed by Hall A in 1982, Hall D in 1989, and finally by Hall C in 1993. Andreu devised a linear arrangement for the terminal, whose buildings are disposed in pairs either side of a central flyover, with oval viaducts accessing each pair. Curved so as to provide a longer façade for docking aircraft, Halls A–D are a big improvement on Terminal 1 as far as passenger orientation and architectural excitement are concerned. Each one is spanned by a soaring concrete roof that stands up entirely without intermediary supports, with the result that departing passengers always know where they are since the whole volume of each hall can be taken in simply by raising one's head. Glass curtain walls on the docking side allow splendid views out, as well as letting in considerable quantities of natural light, which are augmented by the »bubble« skylights set between each section of the roof vault. The sense of airy spaciousness at Terminal 2 comes as a welcome relief after the dingy, compressed feeling of Terminal 1. In terms of passenger transit, however, Terminal 2 is less efficient than Terminal 1, its linear arrangement meaning that greater distances must be travelled.

A perennial problem at Terminal 1 was the distance of the RER station from the terminal building, rail passengers having to take a bus that shuttles back and forth between the two. The airport authorities determined not to make the same mistake at Terminal 2, and consequently built a railway station at the head of Halls C and D, serving not just the RER but also the TGV network, thereby allowing provincial air travellers to avoid the congestion of central Paris. Designed by Andreu in collaboration with Jean-Marie Duthilleul, chief architect of the SNCF, and the engineering firm RFR headed by Peter Rice, Roissy-Gare, as the station is known, was completed in 1994. Trains arrive in tunnels under the runways that cross the axis of Terminal 2 perpendicularly. At this intersection the architects built a three-storey concourse and interchange above which they constructed a six-storey hotel. Situated underneath this ensemble, the 500 m-long platforms are lit along much of their course by two enormous steel-and-glass space frames that rise up either side of the concourse/hotel ensemble. In order to present a flat, waterproof surface to the elements, the frames feature arched struts whose upside-down orientation in comparison to traditional station structures reflects Roissy-Gare's topsy-turvy, underground location.

Paul Andreu's most recent addition to CDG is the second half of Terminal 2, Halls E–F, commissioned in 1989 (as Andreu has since retired, this is his last realization at Roissy). Hall F came first, its western half being inaugurated in 1998 and its eastern in 1999. The first two thirds of Hall E opened in 2003, and the remainder is due for completion in 2005. Incontestably Andreu's most impressive realization at CDG, Hall F has already entered Paris's mythology, appearing in movies, pop videos and, amongst others, an advert for Louis Vuitton suitcases. If the rest of Roissy can be accused of lacking architectural thrill or denying the excitement of air travel, this cannot be said of Hall F's generous spaces. In their general conception, Halls E and F follow the pattern established at CDG2A–D, being disposed either side of a prolongation of the original central flyover and accessed by an oval viaduct. Instead of building a pair of separate halls each side, however, for Hall F Andreu constructed one enormous concourse from which project two »peninsulas«, as they have been dubbed, around which aircraft dock. Even more than in CDG2A–D, every effort was made to ensure that passengers can easily orientate themselves within Hall F simply through the visual clues provided by the building's form. Thus, all along the roadside entrance to CDG2F runs a full-height space dubbed the »canyon«, which makes clear that arrivals are on the ground floor and departures on the first. Covering the ensemble like an airship hangar is an extraordinary, 400 m-long and 74 m-wide folded concrete vault, into which are incised the beginnings of the peninsulas' steel-and-glass space frames, through whose panes, in the distance, docking aircraft can be seen, leaving no doubt as to where boarding takes place.

Much of Hall F's architectonic excitement is provided by its bravura vault, whose construction demanded considerable ingenuity from its designers. The concrete one sees is not, as one might first imagine, structural, being in fact a 12–28 cm-thick veil hung off a steel frame. Andreu wanted to »reintroduce some mystery ... concrete, deviated from its usual structural role, was used as facing in the form of a thin hull. The advantage of this familiar, mineral material is that it gives an impression of solidity and stability that contributes to users' well-being.« Where, usually, a building's frame is constructed first and its cladding applied after, at CDG2F the process was reversed: the concrete veil's thinness made it highly fragile, so it was cast first, *in situ*, and its supporting frame fixed in place afterwards

as the coffering was taken off. In section the vault has the profile of an aeroplane wing, with a tight, upright curve facing onto the aircraft-docking areas. It was these sections that were cast first, horizontally on pivoting shuttering, each 240-tonne concrete mass afterwards being rotated into its upright position. As well as its daring form, the concrete is notable for its quality, enormous care having been taken to achieve an even finish, a task complicated by the presence of hundreds of little square windows punched into the vault, which, as well as admitting daylight, serve to soften the building's acoustics. Outside, a covering of zinc protects the ensemble.

Where Hall F's vault was given the profile of an aircraft wing, its peninsulas took on roughly the form of an aeroplane fuselage. 130 m long, 48 m wide and rising 22 m at their highest point, each one comprises 14 boarding gates. The work of RFR, the steel-and-glass frames covering them were designed to be as minimalist as possible, the glass being placed directly onto the framework. An externally mounted, perforated-steel *brise-soleil* prevents greenhouse-effect temperature rises, while fibre-optic lighting ensures dramatic illumination at night. The peninsulas' floors do not meet the space frames, which has the practical advantage of keeping sticky public fingers away from the glass and thus reducing maintenance costs, and also gives the impression of a »magic carpet« floating within the frame, »an allegory of flight preceding the flight« as Andreu put it.

Hall F's one major failing was its cost, the difficulties encountered in building the concrete vault taking it 45% over budget. Consequently, for the brand-new Hall E, a less-complex structural system was devised. Formally, Hall E follows pretty much the same pattern as Hall F, except where aircraft docking is concerned, the peninsulas having been replaced by a 650 m-long »jetty« running parallel to the main building. This new configuration will allow a 60% capacity increase over Hall F as well as greater efficiency where security checks are concerned, passengers being funnelled from the check-in hall through a narrow building known as the »isthmus«, where security controls are concentrated, before emerging into the enormous jetty. Although Hall E's check-in building looks pretty much the same as Hall F's, sharp-eyed passengers will spot one essential difference: its soaring vault is in fact in wood, not concrete, a cheaper and easier-to-handle option. And instead of the complex space frames of Hall F's peninsulas, Hall E's jetty uses a similar concrete-veil system to Hall F's check-in, only tubular in form and much lighter since perforated across its entire surface, as well as being clad externally not with zinc but with a glass skin serigraphed to counter the greenhouse effect. These »corrections« to Hall F's design have produced a cheaper, more efficient building that nonetheless preserves the excitement of its airy, light-filled spaces.

23 Ecouen

23.1 Château d'Ecouen
Various architects, *c*. 1538–55
(SNCF: Ecouen-Ezanville, then either a 2 km walk or bus 269, direction Garges-Sarcelles, to Mairie d'Ecouen)

Situated a mere 19 km outside central Paris, this splendid French-Renaissance château is surprisingly little known and little visited, all the more surprisingly given that it is also home to the fine collections of the Musée National de la Renaissance. This is no doubt largely due to its current isolation with regard to the Ile-de-France's major population centres, but its situation did not always seem so parochial. The château occupies an elevated plateau dominating the Plaine de France around it, a strategic position that made it essential in the defence of the realm against invaders from the north and the east. Property of the Barons de Montmorency from at least 1000 AD, the promontory was the site of an older fortress that was demolished to make way for today's château by the illustrious Anne de Montmorency, favourite of François I, who became Constable of France (head of the armies) in 1538. The coincidence of the dates of this change in Anne's fortunes and his decision to reconstruct Ecouen is probably not accidental, and many historians agree that the new château was destined to reflect in built form the increased power and prestige of its *seigneur*.

Ecouen is a contemporary of the famous châteaux of the Loire valley – which at the time was where the court and aristocracy were mostly concentrated –, and it is thus to them that one should look to set Montmorency's building in its historical context. Like its Tourangeaux confrères, Ecouen marks the beginning of the transition from the medieval fortress in which the aristocracy had hitherto lived to the stately home they would occupy in later centuries. In plan Ecouen is still like a castle: square, its four wings enclosing a central courtyard, and its outer corners marked by solid square pavilions that took the place of the bastions one would find in a castle. The use of pavilions was a move towards civil architecture that broke, for example, with François I's slightly earlier Château de Chambord (*c*. 1518–37), but which would afterwards become standard for French châteaux. Surrounding Ecouen are elaborate medieval-style moats comprising grazing-fire emplacements, but it is clear that their function was purely symbolic since not only are the moats dry but they disappear off the side of the promontory to the north. Ecouen again breaks with the Loire-Valley châteaux in that it does not descend directly into its moats as they do but is set back on a sort of platform, another innovation that would become standard in French châteaux thereafter. On Ecouen's north front the platform extends into a sizeable terrace overlooking the village, below which originally stood a real-tennis court (since destroyed).

The built mass of Ecouen is organized as a U-shaped ensemble of three equal-height wings containing the principal accommodation, the fourth, east-facing, entrance side having originally been closed by a wall. This massing was modern and followed a vogue introduced in French chateau design at the beginning of the 16C (and still current over a century later, for example at the Palais du Luxembourg, 6.8). The entrance-side wall was later replaced, in 1546, by a low wing coiffed with less stately roofs than the others but endowed with a grand and elaborate entrance portico. What we see on the entrance side today actually dates from Napoleonic times, the 16C construction having been demolished in 1787; although of little interest, the current structure at least respects the volumes of its predecessor. While Ecouen's external massing followed a by-then-standard pattern, the internal division of its three principal wings was exceptional. The usual arrangement in châteaux both before and after was to place the principal accommodation in the wing opposite the entrance (the *corps de logis*); but at Ecouen this wing, which is narrower than the others, contains only a long gallery, the main apartments being located in the side wings: the monarch's suite in the righthand (northern) wing (Montmorency was so high ranking that he needed to keep separate apartments for the king) and Montmorency's, at least initially, in the left. This configuration was also to be found at Henry VIII's contemporaneous Nonsuch Palace at Cuddington (1538 to 1641) and would crop up again over two centuries later at Versailles (32.1). It had the advantage of allowing the two sets of principal apartments to share the long gallery, which links them with regal grandeur. As a result of this arrangement, Ecouen needed two *escaliers d'honneur*, one for each lateral wing. Both are situated at the centre of their respective wings, with supplementary vertical communication being provided by spiral staircases located in the round towers nestling between the pavilions and the château's *arrière-corps*. Montmorency later moved his apartments to the eastern end of the righthand wing, next to those of the king, but could still access his chapel and library (both in the château's southeastern pavilion) via a long gallery in the entrance wing.

In the absence of surviving documentation, it is very difficult to date precisely the different phases of construction of Ecouen. We also do not know with any certainty the name(s) of its initial builder(s), although some historians have put forward the obscure Pierre Tâcheron, who it seems was in Montmorency's employ. It is thought that the first parts of the château to be built, *c*. 1538–45, were the gallery and lefthand wings and the four corner pavilions. The aspect of these initial portions of the château is sober to the point of severity. Two stories high (three on the pavilions) with lofty slate roofs (which had been the norm in medieval France and would continue to be so until well into the 17C), Ecouen presents solid ashlar walls divided up by a grid of simplified, abstracted pilasters and cornices whose lack of definition makes them almost akin to string courses. Fenestration is relatively sparse, with mullions, tran-

23.1 Château d'Ecouen

soms and architraves of very plain profile. The sole animation is provided by the windows' seemingly rather irregular grouping which ignores the proportions of the pilaster/cornice grid and hence brings some welcome tension to these powerful but otherwise monotonous elevations. Rather like Chambord (whose wall treatment is similar), it is only above its eaves that the initial Ecouen shows a bit of dash, adorning itself with pilaster-flanked, elaborately coiffed dormers (another medieval inheritance) and tall, pilaster-clad chimneys. The dormers on the lefthand wing are more exuberant than those on the gallery wing, especially on the courtyard side, leading some historians to suggest that as work progressed Montmorency began to find the earliest of the château's elevations too severe, and hence ordered more ornament to be applied.

Following these first parts of the château came the new entrance wing, in 1546, whose complicated portal, decorated with superimposed orders and caryatids, may have been the work of Jean Goujon. All that survives of it today are a few fragments of sculpture which can be seen on display inside the château. The introduction of this elaborate element, which broke entirely with the austere, soldierly aspect of the château's earliest façades, has been seen by some as a response to the completion in the late 1540s of several new, and of course »rival« (in terms of their owners' prestige), French châteaux whose exteriors were much more Italianizing than the original Ecouen. Goujon probably also built the first bay of the righthand wing; at any rate its courtyard-side dormers were almost certainly based on his work, since they are very similar to a design he contributed to the illustrations of the 1547 French translation of Vitruvius. While their full-Doric frame is eminently Classical, their inventively and elaborately carved coiffures subscribe to a much more northern-European, medieval tradition. As of the late 1540s, Goujon's time was entirely taken up by his work on the Louvre (1.8), and it was to Jean Bullant that Montmorency turned for completion of the righthand wing, which was finished in its initial state sometime around 1550–52. On the courtyard elevation of this wing, Bullant contented himself with reproducing the basic disposition of the lefthand wing and repeating Goujon's dormers across its entire length. On its external (northern) façade, however, Bullant introduced a decorative treatment that was more modern. In place of the string-course/abstracted-pilaster façade-surface division apparent on the rest of the château, he here employed a full set of superimposed pilasters with cornices in the Italian manner, respecting the »correct« hierarchy as defined by theorists: Tuscan on the ground floor and Doric at first-floor level. Unlike Italian models, however, the orders are not the generators of the façade proportions, but are instead mere applied decoration: the vertically aligned fenestration is what defines the bay division, its dominance being signalled by the way the windows break through the orders' cornices. As well as in the use of orders, this part of the building appears more Classical in its dormers, which sport round-headed pediments similar to those that Pierre Lescot had just applied to the Louvre.

What particularly distinguished the righthand wing's northern façade from the rest of the château, however, was the enormous pedimented *avant-corps* occupying its centre. It was built to contain the principal staircase of this side of the building, which accessed the king's apartments and had thus to reflect fully the illustriousness of this part of the edifice. To this end Bullant made it wide, generous and vaulted, with full landings separating each flight, in contrast to the narrower, quarter-turn-with-winders staircase found in the lefthand wing. Since the righthand wing was not wide enough to contain both staircase and landings, Bullant devised the *avant-corps* to house the latter. It also serves another function, which is to dissimulate the fact that the staircase does not occupy the exact centre of the façade, the enormous length of the royal Salle d'Honneur having displaced it slightly eastwards. Initially, the *avant-corps* enclosed only the first landing, the second forming an open-air terrace terminating the structure. For this first stage, Bullant designed a triumphal-arch-with-pilasters composition, which was made rather awkward by the need to provide low openings at ground-floor level. He was subsequently asked to cover the second landing as well, and simply repeated the triumphal-arch motif, this time with Ionic pilasters and an open-bed pediment. The ensemble result is rather clumsy in its proportions and the constituent parts do not gel, neither with each other nor with the château behind.

Towards 1555 Bullant was again active at the château, modifying the northern and southern courtyard façades by the addition of *avant-corps* to their centres, a commission clearly intended to give these plain, and by then old-fashioned, elevations something of the more modern grandeur of the northern façade. On the righthand wing Bullant had once again to hide the off-centre positioning of the staircase inside, and to this end concocted a weird and, to Classically correct eyes, extremely clumsy two-bay composition featuring superimpositions of twinned, free-standing columns at either extremity and a solid projection at the centre, decorated with niches. In fact this ensemble is not really an *avant-corps* in the strict sense since the fenestration framed by its constituent elements is on the same plane as the rest of the façade; while the entablature of the upper order runs uninterrupted above the void below, that of the lower breaks back to the wall plane. To give his composition central emphasis and a consequent sense of monumentality, Bullant coiffed it with a bizarre agglomeration of Classically styled dormers flanking a blind, pedimented panel. Despite its quirkiness, the ensemble somehow works in its picturesque setting. If his righthand wing *avant-corps* were both criticized for their clumsiness, Bullant's design for the courtyard façade of the lefthand wing is generally considered a much more distinguished affair, probably the closest the French Renaissance got to the spirit of ancient Rome. As well as constituting a pendant to its opposite number on the righthand wing, this *avant-corps* was intended to provide a suitable setting for Michelangelo's two famous sculptures of slaves (now in the Louvre), which were given to Montmorency by Henri II. Like its confrère opposite, it is essentially applied decoration stuck onto a flat wall, this time consisting of a pediment-less portico whose four colossal Corinthian columns are grouped in pairs. This is the earliest-known use of a giant order in France, realized at a time when even Italy counted very few examples. Bullant's design seems of another, much later era, and the effect of this exquisitely carved, faithfully Antique composition (columns copied from the Roman Pantheon, entablature details borrowed from the Arch of Septimius Severus and the Temple of Castor and Pollux) in a setting clearly not intended for it (note the way the surrounding fenestration crashes into it) is rather disconcerting.

Ecouen's interiors are organized as simple *enfilades* of rooms filling the entire width of the wings they occupy – corridors and double-thickness plans would not come until the mid-17C. The principal apartments, except for that reserved for the queen, were at first-floor level. The château was famous for its lavish (and colourful) décor, luxury at Ecouen even going as far as the inclusion of bathrooms, installed in vaulted chambers in the basement. Although none of the original interiors survives intact, enough remains to give a good idea of what the château must once have been like inside. Contrary to usual French practice of the time, none of Ecouen's original fireplaces were sculpted, but instead presented flat plaster surfaces intended to receive painted decoration. Twelve of these survive, their elaborate *trompe-l'œil* frescoes clearly being intended to recreate in two dimensions the ornate stuccowork to be found at Fontainebleau (38.1). Many painted friezes also survive, as well as one painted ceiling in the king's bedroom. In the Salle d'Honneur can be found a very elaborate, sculpted chimneypiece that was made in Italy and given to Montmorency by Cardinal Farnese. The flooring in the château's principal apartments originally comprised decorative tiles, some of which survive to this day, but almost nothing remains of the extensive panelling that covered the château's walls. Also gone is the cycle of stained-glass windows depicting the story of Psyche that formerly adorned the long gallery. The chapel is thoroughly Gothic, although its complicated vaulting, which has retained its original frescoes depicting Montmorency's arms, indicates its late date.

Before leaving Ecouen, we should make brief mention of the Eglise Saint-Acceul, which sits just below the château in the village (32, rue de la Libération). Almost certainly financed by Montmorency, its choir dates from the early 1540s, and its bell tower from the 1550s. This may well have been all there was to the original building, the single aisle on the northern side probably being later. The nave was added in 1730. We do not know the name of the original architect, but some have suggested that Bullant, who is buried in the church, may have built it. Entirely Gothic, the tall and externally very simple choir reproduces in miniature the design of the Sainte-Chapelle (1.2), giving it enormous windows that, fortunately, have kept their original stained glass. Dated 1545, the splendid panels show scenes from the Passion and the life of the Virgin Mary.

24 Maisons-Laffitte

24.1 Château de Maisons
2, avenue Carnot
François Mansart, c. 1630–60
(RER: Maisons-Laffitte)

This splendid château, today little known and under appreciated, is one of the masterpieces of the great François Mansart, considered by many the father of French Classicism and its finest exponent. Of his surviving canon, only the Château de Blois (c. 1635–38) could be said to surpass Maisons. Located on a bend in the Seine about 20 km from Paris, Maisons was built for René de Longueil, an important member of the *noblesse de robe*. Little documentation survives regarding his château, and it is thus very difficult to date precisely. Building work was certainly going on at Maisons in the period 1628–35, but whether this concerned today's château or an earlier building is not clear. All we know for certain is that contracts to provide flooring for the current edifice were signed in 1642. Likewise, a date for final completion is hard to establish: while the carcass was probably finished by 1646, its internal and external decoration continued much longer, and the house's stables may have been constructed as late as the 1660s (if one believes the legend that the young Jules Hardouin-Mansart helped his great-uncle build them). Remarkably, the château proper has remained essentially intact since Mansart's day, the only significant modifications coming in 1779–81 when the Comte d'Artois had François-Joseph Bélanger redecorate some of the interiors.

The same cannot, unfortunately, be said of the château's surroundings. If Maisons today is considerably less well known than Vaux-le-Vicomte (37.1) and Versailles (32.1) – the châteaux it inspired –, this is because it has lost the magnificent gardens and *mise en scène* essential for its proper appreciation. Where Versailles and Vaux remain *Gesamtkunstwerke* of stone, vegetation and water, Maisons is now hemmed in by genteel suburbia and unwieldy road developments, a jewel bereft of its crown, as it were. This transformation

24.1 Château de Maisons

was effected by the banker Jacques Laffitte, who acquired the property in 1818 and sold off the grounds for development. His action almost certainly saved the château from total destruction – many others were lost during this period –, but left us today with only a fraction of the former whole. It was Laffitte who demolished Maisons's splendid stables, thus depriving the château of its processional *avant-cour*, but it was a subsequent owner who, in 1877, brought the Avenue Carnot almost up to the house's front door, sweeping away in the process its *cour d'honneur* and attendant moats. The château itself would have been next in line were it not for the government's acquisition of the building, in 1905, which saved it from destruction. Today Maisons is open to the public, and also houses the Musée du Cheval de Course.

As originally built Maisons sat on a grand, triumphal axis disappearing off towards Saint-Germain-en-Laye on the entrance side and descending on the garden side to the Seine, beyond which it was prolonged towards the horizon on the opposite bank (today the bridge at Maisons ruins the fine river views that originally inspired the château's siting). The château itself was orientated northwest–southeast, the ideal configuration as advocated by theoreticians. As well as riverside gardens, there were formal parterres fronting the château's southern, lateral façade and regularly laid-out copses to its north. Arriving at the château one first traversed a stone-gated, funnel-shaped pre-*avant-cour* delimited by rows of trees, one then entered the *avant-cour* proper, which contained the stables, before crossing the moats surrounding the house to gain the *cour d'honneur*. A very similar layout, almost certainly inspired by Maisons, can be seen at Vaux-le-Vicomte. Maisons's stables, which stood on the *avant-cour*'s northern side, were a grand affair, too grand for the likes of some who felt that *convenance* had not been respected: of considerable dimensions and aggrandized with Doric and Ionic orders (like the château itself), the stables featured a central, pedimented *avant-corps* that rose almost as high as the house to which it was supposedly subordinate. For symmetry's sake, the stables were mirrored on the courtyard's other side by a blind, stage-set wall, Longueil's failure to acquire the land beyond preventing him from erecting a proper pendant building.

Maisons can be seen as constituting a transition stage between the still essentially medieval château type of buildings such as Ecouen (23.1) and the Palais du Luxembourg (6.8) and the villa-like châteaux that emerged at the end of the 17C, such as Champs-sur-Marne (36.5). Maisons borrowed from Ecouen and its ilk the rectangular, moated platform on which it stood, thereby indicating the noble tradition of stately-home design to which it subscribed. But, by the 1640s, the long anterior wings of houses like Ecouen and the Luxembourg, which had contained both state rooms and services, had gone out of fashion, services being placed in substantial basement accommodation, as at

Maisons and Vaux. Mansart nonetheless acknowledged the important compositional role played by anterior wings in traditional château design, contriving for Maisons a clever *decrescendo* from full-height flanking pavilions (whose bulk makes them read as the beginning of wings) to one-storey projections protruding from the pavilions, and then to raised terraces that traced the contours of phantom wing extremities. Although the terraces disappeared at Maisons with the truncating of the *cour d'honneur*, those at Vaux give an idea of what Maisons must have been like.

Sitting at the rear of the moated platform is the château's *corps de logis*, which, like the pavilions, is two storeys high and coiffed with the lofty slate roofs then so fashionable in France (which were yet another medieval inheritance). The *logis*'s centre is decorated with a monumental, three-storey-high frontispiece that is made up of a series of three superimposed *avant-corps*, the first rising two storeys, the second three, and the third being but one floor high. Just as the anterior wings' *decrescendo* demonstrates Mansart's dexterity with massing, so the frontispiece displays his subtle and complex handling of the Classical language. With its stacking of twinned columns, the frontispiece's central section recalls Philibert De l'Orme's famous design for the frontispiece at Anet (see 6.1), but Mansart's composition goes much further than Anet's in its manipulation of the orders. A Doric order runs all around Maisons on its ground floor, being expressed along most of its length as pilasters. On the frontispiece it begins as pilasters on the first *avant-corps*, becomes engaged columns on the second, but returns to pilaster form on the final *avant-corps*. At first-floor level it is the Ionic order that encircles the house, again essentially in pilaster form. On the frontispiece however, it mutates from pilasters on the first *avant-corps* to in-the-round columns on the second *avant-corps*, although its cornice breaks back to pilaster level at the frontispiece's centre. The ground floor's projecting *avant-corps* is thus set off against a receding void at first-floor level. On the frontispiece's third floor there is only one *avant-corps*, whose centre recedes back to the plane of the *logis*, in the process entirely breaking the lower cornice of the pediment surmounting it. This recession is further heightened by the free-standing urns sitting atop the cornice of the Ionic order below. Through these extremely subtle effects of solid and void, projection and recession, Mansart infused a wonderful plasticity into his composition. By crowning the frontispiece with its own enormous roof he made it read as a separate, central pavilion, thereby heightening the splendid pyramidal effect of the entrance front, which rises in stages from the anterior terraces to culminate in the mini, lantern-topped *toit à l'impériale* coiffing the frontispiece's pediment. While fully respecting the Classical language he was using, Mansart managed to bring a very French, Gothic-inherited sense of height and upward movement to Maisons (not unlike that of Paris's 16C Hôtel de Ville – see 4.11), his brilliant synthesis of the two traditions resulting in a composition of great dynamism, alive with horizontal and vertical tension.

Compared to Italian architecture of the period, Mansart's œuvre has a reputation for rather dry Classicism, but on closer inspection we find some very unClassical manipulations at Maisons. If we add to the pediment-breaking recessions of the frontispiece the staccato rhythm of the cornice-level dormers, the varied grouping and intercolumniation of the orders running round the house, and the asymmetrical chimneys punctuating each pavilion, we can see that he was anything but a rule-bound pedant. Rigorous in his intellectual conception of architecture, Mansart treated each of his buildings as a three-dimensional whole, and Maison's lateral elevations carry round the entrance-front dispositions in logical sequence to the garden façade. Here we find essentially the same composition as on the entrance elevation, although with only very slightly projecting, colonnaded lateral pavilions and an aggrandized frontispiece featuring free-standing columns on its third level. Because of its flatness in comparison to the entrance front, the garden façade does not quite so successfully carry off its pyramidal composition, and has the rather assembled look of Louis-Treize and early-Louis-Quatorze châteaux. The terraces descending to the garden give the impression, when seen from the river, that Maisons sits atop an impressive mound of masonry.

Inside, the house is essentially only one room thick (the introduction of double-thickness plans to châteaux would be Le Vau's major innovation at Vaux), the *corps de logis* comprising *enfilades* of *pièces d'apparat*. One enters the house via a richly carved vestibule, which, like the entrances at Vaux and Versailles, was originally open to the air, being closed only by wrought-iron gates. The vestibule's décor is a fine example of Mansart's talent for combining opulent display with imperial-Roman severity. Realized entirely in bare stone with no colour anywhere, it features elaborate Doric columns based on a design by Jean Bullant for the Tuileries (see 1.10) that carry an entablature very similar to Michelangelo's at the Palazzo Farnese (which Philibert De l'Orme had published in France). The splendidly moulded ceiling vault encloses delicate bas-reliefs by Gilles Guérin, while four eagles menace the visitor from each corner, symbolizing the house's owner through their punning presence (eagles are reputed for their distance vision: Longueil = *long œil* = long eye). To the south of the vestibule is the *escalier d'honneur*, pushed to one side out of the central *avant-corps* where it would traditionally have been found. This arrangement had the advantage of not cutting the suite of first-floor rooms entirely in two, therefore allowing for a grand *piano-nobile* chamber (the Salle des Gardes – see below), but carried the disadvantage of taking away the central *avant-corp*'s symbolic significance, since it traditionally signalled the staircase's presence. Thus Maisons's frontispiece becomes somehow »false« as it bears no relation to the château's internal plan (Le

300 Maisons-Laffitte

24 Maisons-Laffitte

24.1 Château de Maisons
2, avenue Carnot
François Mansart, c. 1630–60
(RER: Maisons-Laffitte)

This splendid château, today little known and under appreciated, is one of the masterpieces of the great François Mansart, considered by many the father of French Classicism and its finest exponent. Of his surviving canon, only the Château de Blois (c. 1635–38) could be said to surpass Maisons. Located on a bend in the Seine about 20 km from Paris, Maisons was built for René de Longueil, an important member of the *noblesse de robe*. Little documentation survives regarding his château, and it is thus very difficult to date precisely. Building work was certainly going on at Maisons in the period 1628–35, but whether this concerned today's château or an earlier building is not clear. All we know for certain is that contracts to provide flooring for the current edifice were signed in 1642. Likewise, a date for final completion is hard to establish: while the carcass was probably finished by 1646, its internal and external decoration continued much longer, and the house's stables may have been constructed as late as the 1660s (if one believes the legend that the young Jules Hardouin-Mansart helped his great-uncle build them). Remarkably, the château proper has remained essentially intact since Mansart's day, the only significant modifications coming in 1779–81 when the Comte d'Artois had François-Joseph Bélanger redecorate some of the interiors.

The same cannot, unfortunately, be said of the château's surroundings. If Maisons today is considerably less well known than Vaux-le-Vicomte (37.1) and Versailles (32.1) – the châteaux it inspired –, this is because it has lost the magnificent gardens and *mise en scène* essential for its proper appreciation. Where Versailles and Vaux remain *Gesamtkunstwerke* of stone, vegetation and water, Maisons is now hemmed in by genteel suburbia and unwieldy road developments, a jewel bereft of its crown, as it were. This transformation

24.1 Château de Maisons

was effected by the banker Jacques Laffitte, who acquired the property in 1818 and sold off the grounds for development. His action almost certainly saved the château from total destruction – many others were lost during this period –, but left us today with only a fraction of the former whole. It was Laffitte who demolished Maisons's splendid stables, thus depriving the château of its processional *avant-cour*, but it was a subsequent owner who, in 1877, brought the Avenue Carnot almost up to the house's front door, sweeping away in the process its *cour d'honneur* and attendant moats. The château itself would have been next in line were it not for the government's acquisition of the building, in 1905, which saved it from destruction. Today Maisons is open to the public, and also houses the Musée du Cheval de Course.

As originally built Maisons sat on a grand, triumphal axis disappearing off towards Saint-Germain-en-Laye on the entrance side and descending on the garden side to the Seine, beyond which it was prolonged towards the horizon on the opposite bank (today the bridge at Maisons ruins the fine river views that originally inspired the château's siting). The château itself was orientated northwest–southeast, the ideal configuration as advocated by theoreticians. As well as riverside gardens, there were formal parterres fronting the château's southern, lateral façade and regularly laid-out copses to its north. Arriving at the château one first traversed a stone-gated, funnel-shaped pre-*avant-cour* delimited by rows of trees, one then entered the *avant-cour* proper, which contained the stables, before crossing the moats surrounding the house to gain the *cour d'honneur*. A very similar layout, almost certainly inspired by Maisons, can be seen at Vaux-le-Vicomte. Maisons's stables, which stood on the *avant-cour*'s northern side, were a grand affair, too grand for the likes of some who felt that *convenance* had not been respected: of considerable dimensions and aggrandized with Doric and Ionic orders (like the château itself), the stables featured a central, pedimented *avant-corps* that rose almost as high as the house to which it was supposedly subordinate. For symmetry's sake, the stables were mirrored on the courtyard's other side by a blind, stage-set wall, Longueil's failure to acquire the land beyond preventing him from erecting a proper pendant building.

Maisons can be seen as constituting a transition stage between the still essentially medieval château type of buildings such as Ecouen (23.1) and the Palais du Luxembourg (6.8) and the villa-like châteaux that emerged at the end of the 17C, such as Champs-sur-Marne (36.5). Maisons borrowed from Ecouen and its ilk the rectangular, moated platform on which it stood, thereby indicating the noble tradition of stately-home design to which it subscribed. But, by the 1640s, the long anterior wings of houses like Ecouen and the Luxembourg, which had contained both state rooms and services, had gone out of fashion, services being placed in substantial basement accommodation, as at

Maisons and Vaux. Mansart nonetheless acknowledged the important compositional role played by anterior wings in traditional château design, contriving for Maisons a clever *decrescendo* from full-height flanking pavilions (whose bulk makes them read as the beginning of wings) to one-storey projections protruding from the pavilions, and then to raised terraces that traced the contours of phantom wing extremities. Although the terraces disappeared at Maisons with the truncating of the *cour d'honneur*, those at Vaux give an idea of what Maisons must have been like.

Sitting at the rear of the moated platform is the château's *corps de logis*, which, like the pavilions, is two storeys high and coiffed with the lofty slate roofs then so fashionable in France (which were yet another medieval inheritance). The *logis*'s centre is decorated with a monumental, three-storey high frontispiece that is made up of a series of three superimposed *avant-corps*, the first rising two storeys, the second three, and the third being but one floor high. Just as the anterior wings' *decrescendo* demonstrates Mansart's dexterity with massing, so the frontispiece displays his subtle and complex handling of the Classical language. With its stacking of twinned columns, the frontispiece's central section recalls Philibert De l'Orme's famous design for the frontispiece at Anet (see 6.1), but Mansart's composition goes much further than Anet's in its manipulation of the orders. A Doric order runs all around Maisons on its ground floor, being expressed along most of its length as pilasters. On the frontispiece it begins as pilasters on the first *avant-corps*, becomes engaged columns on the second, but returns to pilaster form on the final *avant-corps*. At first-floor level it is the Ionic order that encircles the house, again essentially in pilaster form. On the frontispiece however, it mutates from pilasters on the first *avant-corps* to in-the-round columns on the second *avant-corps*, although its cornice breaks back to pilaster level at the frontispiece's centre. The ground floor's projecting *avant-corps* is thus set off against a receding void at first-floor level. On the frontispiece's third floor there is only one *avant-corps*, whose centre recedes back to the plane of the *logis*, in the process entirely breaking the lower cornice of the pediment surmounting it. This recession is further heightened by the free-standing urns sitting atop the cornice of the Ionic order below. Through these extremely subtle effects of solid and void, projection and recession, Mansart infused a wonderful plasticity into his composition. By crowning the frontispiece with its own enormous roof he made it read as a separate, central pavilion, thereby heightening the splendid pyramidal effect of the entrance front, which rises in stages from the anterior terraces to culminate in the mini, lantern-topped *toit à l'impériale* coiffing the frontispiece's pediment. While fully respecting the Classical language he was using, Mansart managed to bring a very French, Gothic-inherited sense of height and upward movement to Maisons (not unlike that of Paris's 16C Hôtel de Ville – see 4.11), his brilliant synthesis of the two traditions resulting in a composition of great dynamism, alive with horizontal and vertical tension.

Compared to Italian architecture of the period, Mansart's œuvre has a reputation for rather dry Classicism, but on closer inspection we find some very un-Classical manipulations at Maisons. If we add to the pediment-breaking recessions of the frontispiece the staccato rhythm of the cornice-level dormers, the varied grouping and intercolumniation of the orders running round the house, and the asymmetrical chimneys punctuating each pavilion, we can see that he was anything but a rule-bound pedant. Rigorous in his intellectual conception of architecture, Mansart treated each of his buildings as a three-dimensional whole, and Maison's lateral elevations carry round the entrance-front dispositions in logical sequence to the garden façade. Here we find essentially the same composition as on the entrance elevation, although with only very slightly projecting, colonnaded lateral pavilions and an aggrandized frontispiece featuring free-standing columns on its third level. Because of its flatness in comparison to the entrance front, the garden façade does not quite so successfully carry off its pyramidal composition, and has the rather assembled look of Louis-Treize and early-Louis-Quatorze châteaux. The terraces descending to the garden give the impression, when seen from the river, that Maisons sits atop an impressive mound of masonry.

Inside, the house is essentially only one room thick (the introduction of double-thickness plans to châteaux would be Le Vau's major innovation at Vaux), the *corps de logis* comprising *enfilades* of *pièces d'apparat*. One enters the house via a richly carved vestibule, which, like the entrances at Vaux and Versailles, was originally open to the air, being closed only by wrought-iron gates. The vestibule's décor is a fine example of Mansart's talent for combining opulent display with imperial-Roman severity. Realized entirely in bare stone with no colour anywhere, it features elaborate Doric columns based on a design by Jean Bullant for the Tuileries (see 1.10) that carry an entablature very similar to Michelangelo's at the Palazzo Farnese (which Philibert De l'Orme had published in France). The splendidly moulded ceiling vault encloses delicate bas-reliefs by Gilles Guérin, while four eagles menace the visitor from each corner, symbolizing the house's owner through their punning presence (eagles are reputed for their distance vision: Longueil = *long œil* = long eye). To the south of the vestibule is the *escalier d'honneur*, pushed to one side out of the central *avant-corps* where it would traditionally have been found. This arrangement had the advantage of not cutting the suite of first-floor rooms entirely in two, therefore allowing for a grand *piano-nobile* chamber (the Salle des Gardes – see below), but carried the disadvantage of taking away the central *avant-corp*'s symbolic significance, since it traditionally signalled the staircase's presence. Thus Maisons's frontispiece becomes somehow »false« as it bears no relation to the château's internal plan (Le

Vau got round this problem in his châteaux by placing oval salons in his central *avant-corps*, as at Vaux, an arrangement that was much copied). Rising half in the frontispiece and half in the *arrière-corps*, Maisons's staircase is a splendid affair, with vault-mounted treads hanging off the stairwell walls in daring cantilever, and a very Mansartian system of superimposed domes coiffing the ensemble. The balcony inside the dome's drum links the two halves of the second floor. Again we see Mansart's liking for crisp, naked stone: entirely bare on the ground floor, the stairwell's walls are adorned with first-floor-level Ionic pilasters which enclose projecting panels whose cornices are home to hosts of exquisitely carved gambolling *putti*.

To the north of the *escalier d'honneur*, on the ground floor, is a suite of rooms known as the Appartement des Captifs, which was originally René de Longueil's personal apartment. It takes its name from the monumental carved chimneypiece in the bedchamber, whose reliefs, sculpted by Guérin, include a medallion of Louis XIII carried by two kneeling »captives«. In the ground floor's other half we find the »Appartement de la Renommée«, which probably originally accommodated Mme de Longueil but which was extensively remodelled by Bélanger. As well as the charming Salle des Jeux there is Bélanger's magnificent summer dining room, which is decked out in very Romanizing stuccowork by Nicolas Lhuillier. Moving upstairs to the first-floor *piano nobile*, we find to the south of the *escalier d'honneur* the Appartement des Aigles, today decorated in early-19C style, while to the north is the splendid Appartement du Roi, which contains the château's principal rooms. At the time stately homes like Maisons and Vaux were built, France's kings had a *droit de gîte*, or right of abode, in all their vassals' residences, and it became standard practice to install sumptuous suites of rooms for the sovereign's eventual use. The first chamber in the king's apartment is the giant Salle des Gardes, or des Fêtes, which features a cantilevered musicians' gallery and has conserved some of its 17C window-recess paintings. Like all the rooms in the Appartement du Roi, the Salle des Gardes has a high, wooden-vaulted Italian-style ceiling, an innovation in French aristocratic interiors that began to appear in the 1640s. A major disadvantage of this new kind of magnificence was that the floor above was rendered useless since it was filled up with the ceiling vaults. The curious depressions in the Salle des Garde's ceiling may have been included to improve the room's acoustics. Prolonging the Salle des Gardes via a triple arcade is the Salon d'Hercule, so-named because of the painting of Hercules that formerly occupied the chimneypiece's oval medallion (today replaced by a portrait of Louis XIV). The fireplace has retained all of Guérin's splendid Fontainebleau-style carving (see 38.1), which includes fruit-carrying caryatids, Longueil eagles and drapery-bearing *putti*. From the Salon d'Hercule one enters the king's bedchamber, whose eastern extremity contains a pilastered alcove for the bed itself. Beyond it on the entrance side of the house are the remarkable *chambre à l'italienne* and Cabinet des Miroirs. The *chambre à l'italienne* was so named because of the rather surprising Caryatid-lined dome surmounting it, which is representative of a fashion for such contrivances in the mid-17C. As for the Cabinet des Miroirs, although one of the château's smallest rooms it is perhaps its most delightful: lit by only one window, it features an Ionic order enclosing false windows filled with panels of mirror glass, and is surmounted by a shallow painted-and-gilded dome. Rooms of this sort were very much in vogue in the mid-17C, and Maisons's is one of the earliest surviving examples. This kind of mirror decoration would reach its apogee later in the century in Versailles's famous Galerie des Glaces.

Until the tribulations of the 19C, Maisons enjoyed the highest reputation. Both Bernini and Voltaire were admirers, and the influential theorist Jacques-François Blondel made visits to the château part of his teaching course. In his 1771 *Cours d'Architecture* he praised »the solidity without heaviness, the precision of the stone dressing without dryness, the expression of the moulded profiles which are all excellent right down to the service courtyards«, as well as Maisons's »perfect union of architecture and sculpture« and »the felicitous proportions of the attics in relation to the façades, the handsome disposition of the exterior.« Even the 19C, which treated the house so badly, paid it tribute in the countless town halls that took its frontispiece for inspiration. Today any admirer of French Classicism cannot fail to be touched by its rigour, grandeur and inventiveness.

25 Poissy

25.1 Collégiale Notre-Dame
8, rue de l'Eglise and 7, rue Saint-Louis
Original architect unknown, begun c. 1016
(RER: Poissy)

Poissy has been included in this guide because of the presence there of the Villa Savoye (25.2), but its collegial church of Notre-Dame, which can be taken in either on the way to or coming back from the Villa, is also worth a visit. It was begun in the early-11C by King Robert the Pious, who owned a château nearby (since destroyed), and was probably completed in its initial state by the late-12C. In the 16C the church was much extended, renovated and reconfigured, and it was later heavily restored, first in the 1830s and then again in the 1860s, this latter time by Eugène Viollet-le-Duc. Amongst other interventions, he entirely rebuilt the choir, with some differences in design from the original, and reconstructed much of the southern side of the nave. As a result, the exact configuration of the original building is difficult to establish with any certainty.

A simple basilica in plan with no transepts, the *collégiale* makes its presence felt in the landscape via two prominent towers, one a square tower-porch situated at the church's west end and the other an octagonal belfry rising at the eastern end of the main vessel, just before the lower, apse-ended choir. This double-tower distribution, whose origins dated back to the middle of the first millennium, was still to be found in some late-Romanesque and early-Gothic ecclesiastical buildings in the Ile-de-France despite by then being rather archaic (a variation on this theme can be seen at Saint-Germain-des-Prés, 6.4). Built at the end of the 11C, Poissy's porch-tower is the oldest surviving part of the building: its solid, heavily buttressed square base is prettily coiffed with an arcaded octagon terminating in a short, octagonal, stone spire (which was rebuilt in 1896), an arrangement that would influence other churches in the region. The Burgundian-style, wooden-spired, east-end tower is later, built at the same time as the nave. Thought to date from the second quarter of the 12C, the nave has been much reworked since, and only the first bays before the choir on the southern side still show something of the original aspect: three-storey elevations comprising a round-headed arcade, a tribune gallery with a twin-arched opening under a main tribune arch, and a stumpy clerestory. Notre-Dame's original main-vessel design was probably influenced by Norman examples, especially if, as Viollet-le-Duc's restoration would have us believe, its tribune was originally designed as an externally lit triforium passage and not as a dark triforium giving onto the aisle-roof attic. Only in its relatively thin walls does Notre-Dame show anything of the developments that would lead to the creation of early-Gothic architecture in the Ile-de-France. The other bays of the nave were largely rebuilt in the 16C, especially the northern side, and nothing now remains of the church's original, round-arched rib vaulting (its current vaults date from the 16C and 19C).

The plan of Notre-Dame's east end, with its eastern-orientated flanking chapels, was probably borrowed from Burgundian practice. The church's side-chapels all date from the 16C, as does the double-arched entrance porch on the southern side. Despite its late date nothing of the French Renaissance is to be seen in the porch's design, which is pure Flamboyant. Its portal carvings have survived and include, in the archivolts, angels playing instruments and, in the tympanum, an allegory of the Annunciation. Inside the church can be seen several interesting 12C capitals.

Poissy was famous in the later middle ages as the birthplace of Louis IX – later Saint Louis –, who was baptized in the *collégiale*. In the first chapel to the right of the church's entrance can be seen the remains of the font supposedly used at his christening: its ruinous state is due to the fact that, as a relic connected with the saint, it was incessantly raked by the faithful to produce dust which, when mixed with water and drunk, was supposed to cure fevers!

25.2 Villa Savoye (»Les Heures Claires«)
82, rue de Villiers
Le Corbusier and Pierre Jeanneret, 1928–31
(RER: Poissy)

One of the Modern Movement's most iconic buildings, ultimate and archetypal machine-age creation of Le Corbusier's interwar, Purist period, the Villa Savoye occupies a very special place in the imagination of architects. Over 70 years since its completion, it still has the power to amaze, bewilder and inspire. Viewed by many historians as the culmination of a series of buildings in Corb's œuvre that included the Villa La Roche (16.13), the Maison Cook (29.3), the never-realized Villa Meyer (1925/26) and the Villa Stein-de Monzie (31.1), it synthesized and transcended ideas present in his earlier works to reach a new high point of artistic expression. Programmatically, however, it could not have been more banal: a weekend/summer home for a wealthy French couple, Pierre and Eugénie Savoye, on a tree-filled site in then-rural Poissy. To this prosaic brief Corb brought all the technical, organizational and aesthetic innovation with which he hoped to revolutionize not just architecture but society's whole way of living, thereby producing a mythic building whose influence is still enormous. But, as with so many of Corb's early works, the untried experimentation of the Villa Savoye's groundbreaking design coupled with the architect's notorious disdain for practical matters produced a dwelling that was, in the end, uninhabitable. Uncomfortably cold and damp due to defective heating and rainwater drainage, the house was abandoned by its owners after only a few years. Its subsequent history was nearly one of oblivion: left to rot, it became a barn during WWII and was scheduled for demolition in the 1950s. Only the personal intervention of then culture minister André Malraux, alerted by concerned aficionados, saved it

25.2 Villa Savoye. View from the north

from destruction. Thrice restored (most recently in 1996/97), it is now a historic monument open to the public.

It is that celebrated first, external view of the Villa Savoye in its bucolic setting that still has the greatest power to move and surprise, as one stumbles across this extraordinary object plonked down in the middle of a grassy meadow. A foretaste of what is to come is provided by the white, cuboid concierge's lodge on the roadside, but leaves one unprepared for the full effect as, following the driveway through a dense grove of trees, one is suddenly presented with a complete view of the house. This highly theatrical initiation through dark primal nature out into the light of the clearing lands us in front of a structure that is in total contrast and contradiction with the greenery of the site, a pristine, white, strip-windowed box mounted on the slenderest of *pilotis* and sporting mysterious curved volumes on its upper levels. Already the forewarned visitor will have understood that all of Corb's famous »five points of a new architecture« have here been combined: the *pilotis* that lift the house's main floor off the damp ground and avoid deep foundations, the (supposedly) industrially produced steel strip windows that let in maximum daylight, the free façade which allows this ribbon fenestration to be stretched across its entire length, the free plan signalled by the villa's ground-floor undercroft, and the roof terrace implied by the vaguely nautical volumes at the building's summit. But more than just a manifesto of the *esprit nouveau*, the Villa Savoye is an object of austere, engineered beauty in which these individually prosaic elements have been combined in perfect equilibrium: take any one part away and the whole loses all its substance. Even if one does not subscribe to the theories of absolute and universal laws of harmony and proportion which Corb used to compose his façades, one can appreciate their balanced majesty and enigmatic abstraction. The cuboid volume of the *piano nobile* – one of the primary, Platonic solids of which Corb was so fond – has been affirmed by not allowing the windows to run round its corners, and a subtle game is played with our notions of weight and support, vertical members at times breaking up the glazing and at others disappearing behind the fenestration. Despite its box-like appearance, the Villa Savoye seems anything but static, its pentastyle *pilotis* setting up a march round its circumference like the columns of a temple.

In its divorce from the surrounding landscape, the house subscribes to the Classical tradition of temples – such as those at Paestum which read very much as objects in, rather than integral parts of, the landscape –, Roman and Palladian villas and French châteaux. It also shares with historical villas and country homes their ideological urban/rural opposition, »domestic life set in a Virgilian dream«, as Corb put it. Where the Villa Savoye breaks fundamentally with its forbears, however, is in the materials from which it is built: reinforced concrete, breeze blocks and white render are, historically, entirely alien to the Ile-de-France. When freshly painted the house shines with all the brave new singularity its architect intended, but exposed to Francilien dampness for too long and it turns green with mould, whitewash staying white in the hot, dry Mediterranean climes where Corb first experienced it but not in rainy Paris. Indeed the high-maintenance impracticality of his white Purist villas was no doubt one of the reasons that Corb later switched tack entirely and experimented with more earthy, patina-friendly materials (see, e.g., 14.10 and 26.2). Not that all of the Villa Savoye's exterior is white, however. The walls of the ground-floor undercroft are painted dark green, which prevents them from competing with the dazzling *piano nobile* above and emphasizes the idea that the surrounding landscape can flow under the house, while the solarium on top of the house was originally polychrome.

It was that magic machine-age invention *par excellence*, the automobile, that made weekend villa dwelling possible for the likes of the Savoyes, and Corb paid it tribute in the very design of their house. A double driveway leads up to the villa, allowing cars to progress under its *pilotis*-mounted overhang on its northeastern side, deposit passengers at the front door on the northwestern flank, and then either park in the garages on its southwestern side or carry on back out the way they came. To make this circuit possible, the villa's dimensions were calculated so as to take into account the width and turning circle of a saloon car, which latter dictated the radius of the tight curve defining the ground-floor entrance elevation. Apart from this processional arrival route, no attempt was made to landscape the villa's grounds. Corb explained: »... the view is very beautiful, as are the grass and the forest: we will interfere with them as little as possible. The house will stand in the middle of the grass like an object, without disturbing anything.«

Although externally the Villa Savoye appears to be a simple, *pilotis*-mounted box sitting atop a podium, once inside one realizes how illusory this impression was, for within its rectilinear confines a highly diverse and complex series of spaces has been squeezed. The villa featured as the last of Corb's famous »four compositions«

published in 1929, labelled with the caption: »Very generous, an architectural desire is affirmed outside while inside all functional needs are satisfied.« It was of course the then revolutionary *pilotis*-based concrete-frame system that allowed this complex articulation of space, and *pilotis* are celebrated inside as well as outside the house by being set in front of internal walls and partitions rather than hidden within them. Indeed as one enters the villa via its main door one passes through a second, symbolic portal in the form of a pair of lintel-linked *pilotis*, an almost Stonehenge-style arrangement which could only be contrived by distorting the building's grid of supports. Fully glazed around most of its perimeter to make up for its location under the dark overhang of the *piano nobile*, the entrance hall in which one arrives is a splendidly luminous space where the boundary between outside and in has been subtly dematerialized, the brisk rhythm of the »industrial« window frame enclosing it in railing-like transparency. Hygiene-obsessed Swiss that he was, Corb provided a washbasin at the rear of the hall so that one could shake off the outside world *à la* Pontius Pilot before going up to the *piano nobile* where the Savoyes' apartments were located. The remainder of the ground floor, beyond the basin, is occupied by maids' bedrooms, a laundry and the chauffeur's apartment, which is accessed separately from outside.

Returning to the hall, we find that two routes have been provided up through the house, one prosaic and the other processional. The prosaic, intended for the Savoyes' servants or those in a hurry, takes the form of an elegantly engineered spiral staircase, a free-standing object that rises efficiently and directly up to the roof; the processional, on the other hand, consists of a gently ascending, sharply dog-legged ramp that wends its way slowly through the different levels and provides a picturesque *promenade architecturale* which allows one to »see the sights« of the villa. In volume 1 of his *Œuvre complète* (1937), Corb explained: »... one climbs imperceptibly via a ramp, which is a very different sensation from that produced by a staircase with steps. A staircase separates one floor from another: a ramp connects them.« A much-evolved descendant of the clumsy incline in the Villa La Roche's picture gallery, the Villa Savoye's ramp rises symbolically at the exact centre of the house and traces a path to its summits that could be compared, in the manner of its *mise en scène*, to the climb to the Parthenon, which Corb had much admired. Movement, through time as well as space, was the key to this device, which Corb had also observed in Arab architecture. Again in the *Œuvre complète*, he wrote: »Arab architecture gives a precious teaching. It must be appreciated on foot, walking; it is by walking and moving that one sees the architecture's organization develop. This is a principle contrary to Baroque architecture which is conceived on paper around a theoretical fixed point.« The hairpin spiral of the Villa Savoye's ramp sets up movement at the house's core, the remainder of the accommodation spinning round it

25.2 Villa Savoye. Living room and *jardin suspendu*

in centrifugal dispersal. In this it is arguably analogous to an illustrious predecessor, Palladio's centralized, square-plan Villa Rotonda (1566–70), as Colin Rowe famously pointed out in his 1947 essay »The Mathematics of the Ideal Villa«.

In order to encourage one to move up the ramp, Corb glazed its sides, thereby producing mysterious overhead lighting that draws one forwards. A constantly changing and highly graphic display of light, shadow, solid and void accompanies one's climb. Arriving at the head of the ramp on the first floor, one can either go out onto the terrace which is visible through the glazing to one's left, or carry straight on into the villa's generously proportioned main living space. Corb's natural tendency was to orientate his domestic buildings towards the south so that the main living spaces would be flooded with life-giving sunlight. At the Villa Savoye, however, the principal living room faces northwest so as to take advantage of sweeping views across the neighbouring Seine valley. To introduce sunshine into the heart of the house, Corb created a sort of first-floor courtyard or *jardin suspendu*, as he called it, which features full-height, entirely glazed southern-facing doors separating it from the living room. One of these slides back and allows the division between inside and out to be entirely dematerialized in clement weather. The very large (86 m^2) living room is a plain, almost Spartan space, the only animation coming from its structural beams and *pilotis* and the radiators, shelves and built-in cupboards sitting under its strip windows. A horror of the dark, cluttered interiors of the *fin-de-siècle* period prompted Corb to tidy as much as possible away into streamlined built-in furniture. Just as streamlined is the stainless-steel up-lighter suspended from the ceiling and running down the room's entire length. Although, unusually for the time, the Villa Savoye was entirely centrally heated, the living room nonetheless has a fireplace, which, treated as a prominent free-standing object, is symbolic of that quintessence of »home«, the hearth. Given how low-set the living room's strip windows are, one suspects that Corb must have rather short of stature, for anyone over about 1.60 m cannot see the sky out of them without bending down.

The remainder of the villa's rooms are lined up along its northeastern and southeastern façades. In the corner next to the living room we find the rather cold and clinical kitchen, whose impressive range of built-in sinks and cupboards, the latter in aluminium, anticipated the mass-produced kitchen units we know today. Next in line, separated from the kitchen by a small terrace, is the guest bedroom, with built-in cupboards both under the windows and just inside the door, the latter serving jointly as a wardrobe and as a partition for a very tiny lavatory. Corb usually tried to avoid corridors in his houses but did not quite manage it at the Villa Savoye, access to the next room in the sequence, the Savoyes' son's bedroom at the eastern corner, being gained via a narrow passage. The omission of corridors was part of his policy of reducing as much as possible spaces he considered secondary, such as lavatories or circulatory areas (and even bedrooms, when his clients would let him), so as to gain extra square metres in a dwelling's principal rooms. This explains the mean pokiness of the Villa Savoye's corridor, which feels so compressed that Corb felt obliged to introduce a skylight at its darkest end to render it less unappealing. As well as the son's bedroom, it accesses a bathroom that was shared by both Master Savoye and guests. Moving on round to the villa's southeastern flank we find M. and Mme Savoye's bedroom, which has become famous for its sky-lit en-suite bathroom, with its blue-tiled sunken bath and chaise-longue. Although the description sounds luxurious, the realization is less so, Corb's disdain for precious materials or slick finishing, and his rather weird, monastical attitude towards domesticity, producing an environment that seems rudimentary and Spartan. And this despite the bold polychromy with which he experimented at the Villa Savoye, the master bedroom, for example, featuring one rose-coloured wall, and the boudoir leading off it being painted a deep azure on its far side.

From the boudoir, doors lead onto a small, covered veranda that opens out into the *jardin suspendu*. Treated in the manner of an outside room, with unglazed strip-window openings on its external wall, this courtyard/terrace provides a splendid sun trap sheltered from the winds and enjoys framed views out across the grounds. Flower beds soften its mineral severity, and Corb intended that grass be allowed to grow in the cracks between its paving stones. It also provides some splendid views of the villa itself, and is integrated into the *promenade architecturale* by the axial ramp, which continues its climb outside, rising up one side. The culmination of this *escalade*, as in the ascension to the top of an Aztec temple, is a shrine to the sun, the villa's solarium, which is situated within the mysterious curved volumes we saw from below (which are in fact simple screens). Here, from this vantage point, one can either offer up one's body to the sun or, thanks to an opening cut in one wall, contemplate the splendid view across the Seine valley. Corb's admiration for the monumental machine-age edifices that were ocean liners is here expressed in the nautical treatment of the solarium's railings and in the deckhouse allure of its screens. Like a ship's captain on his bridge, the villa's owners could survey all their property from here.

Given its setting the Villa Savoye could have been conceived as part of a lush garden, perhaps dissolving the boundaries between inside and out and celebrating the earthy joys of country living. But instead Corb chose to make it a self-contained, self-referential object whose »garden« is an abstract, walled, concrete roof terrace, entirely divorced from the reality of the ground and open only to the dreaming sky. One of Corb's justifications for roof terraces was that they recovered precious space for the benefit of garden-deprived urban dwellers, but in the country they were surely redundant. The Villa Stein's terrace was at least connected to its garden by an outside staircase, but no such link with terra firma is provided at the Villa Savoye. As James Ackerman has pointed out, the house »stands alone in the history of the villa by affirming rather than rejecting the conditions of urban life«, its *piano nobile* clearly providing a suitable prototype for a top-floor, high-rise penthouse. Nature is framed, observed and dominated from the Villa Savoye's *piano nobile*, even when one is outside in the *jardin suspendu* or up in the solarium. Raised on its *pilotis* like a table on legs, the villa was treated as a piece of furniture placed in the landscape; since furniture can be reproduced and placed anywhere, it is unsurprising to learn that Corb later designed a whole housing estate of Villas Savoye for an Argentine developer (project never executed).

The Villa Savoye is also paradoxical in that, like nearly all of Corb's Purist buildings, it purports to be a machine-age manifesto put together from mass-produced, pre-fabricated, industrial components, but is in fact a hand-crafted, hand-assembled one-off made to look like an engineered prototype for repeatable housing units. But then more than just a showcase for Corb's urbanistic and architectural theories, more than a simple *machine à habiter*, it was also conceived as a work of art, a *machine à émouvoir*. Today it touches us not only in its plastic artistry, in the intellectual rigour and clarity of its conception, and in the boldness of its futuristic outlook, but also in the nostalgia it evokes for the age of utopias, when people still believed, however naively, that architecture alone could revolutionize the world. We now know how oppressive and absolutist the prescriptions of the Modern Movement could turn out to be, but the Villa Savoye still seduces us into believing in that clean, bright, progressive, sunshiney future that never was.

26 Neuilly-sur-Seine

26.1 Folie Saint-James
32, avenue de Madrid
François-Joseph Bélanger, 1781–82
(Métro: Pont de Neuilly)

An astonishing example of the late-18C taste for frivolity, this *folie* was built for the fabulously wealthy Claude Baudard de Saint-James, who had earned his fortune as General Treasurer of the Colonies. Saint-James engaged Bélanger, who was then working on the nearby Bagatelle (29.2) for the Comte d'Artois, to build him a villa with a *jardin à l'anglaise* to rival the whimsy of his royal neighbour. His only instructions were »Do as you please, as long as it's expensive«.

The villa still stands, a simple brick box dressed up in plaster neo-Classical garb, and preserves some original interiors. Bélanger's garden, with its many *fabriques* (follies), was less fortunate, although the most famous *fabrique* of all, the Grand Rocher, survives. Known in its day as the »Eighth Wonder of the World«, the Grand Rocher was essentially a huge pile of rocks inside of which a grotto, a substantial bathroom with its own reservoir, and a gallery were installed. Externally the rocks were artfully arranged to suggest a cave, whose entrance is filled with an Antique Doric portico, thereby contriving a delirious alliance of civilization and »nature«. The resulting pagan temple of ablutions is a Baroque composition of bacchic fancy, impressive today in its eccentricity, if no longer in its size. An idea of the expense of the project can be gleaned from the fact that 40 horses were needed to transport just one of the bits of rock used in the ensemble. Small wonder that Saint-James went bankrupt shortly afterwards.

26.2 Maisons Jaoul
81 and 81 bis, rue de Longchamp
Le Corbusier, 1951–55
(Métro: Pont de Neuilly)

Just at the moment when the world was pigeon-holing him as the high priest of Modernism, with all the implications of Hi-tech, machine-age wizardry that this label implied, Le Corbusier dumbfounded both admirers and critics alike by producing these two houses, seemingly the antithesis of all that he had preached before. The man who had once mythologized the engineer's craft, turning it into a creed, here produced a pair of buildings that were technologically rudimentary and of deliberately crude construction, externally so raw that the term Brutalist (from the French »brut« – »rough« or »crude«) was coined to describe them. As we shall see, the Maisons Jaoul were not quite such a radical innovation in Corb's œuvre as they at first appeared, but nonetheless constituted a »volte-face« that shocked and fascinated contemporaries.

The houses were commissioned by Corb's friend André Jaoul, who wanted accommodation for himself and his wife and also for his son and his family. Corb proposed two similar, separate structures, one for each family, that were united at basement level by a communal garage. A buffer zone of garden separated the street from the first house, which was aligned parallel to the road, thus creating an intimate, protected space behind. Within this, the second house extended perpendicularly to the first. Jaoul's budget was limited, and this may partly explain the (for him) novel construction-method choices made by Corb. Gone were the »five points of a new architecture«: the Maisons Jaoul have no *pilotis*, their walls are load-bearing and thus as restricted (i. e. not »free«) as their plans, glazing is sparse, strip windows are nowhere to be seen and, instead of carrying a sun terrace, their roofs are turf-covered »Catalan« vaults. It is these vaults that are the linchpin of Corb's design.

Right from the start of his career Corb had been interested in Mediterranean vernacular architecture – the simple vaulted cells of Greece and Spain – and had proposed the adaptation of the type as a cheap-housing model in his Maison-Monol project of 1919. He subsequently returned to the vault motif on several occasions, for example at the Immeuble Molitor (29.4) or in the weekend house he built at La Celle-Saint-Cloud in 1935 (which also anticipated the materiality of the Maisons Jaoul). In tandem with the famous free plan, the idea of an organic, cellular architecture had always been one of Corb's preoccupations, visible in the honeycomb structure of the *unités d'habitation* and implicit in the Monol project. The Maisons Jaoul are essentially a series of juxta- and superimposed Monol-type structures, whose dimensions were calculated using Corb's Modulor proportional system (which was derived from the (idealized) human form). Where the Maison-Monol

26.2 Maisons Jaoul. View from the west

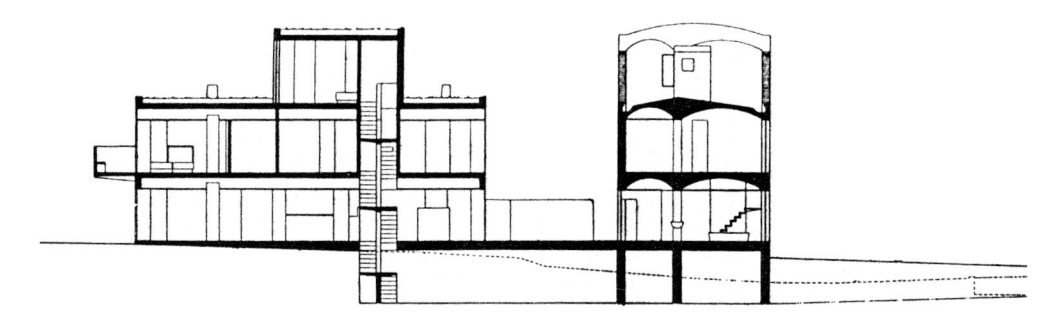

26.2 Maisons Jaoul. Section

vaults were in concrete, those at the Maisons Jaoul were constructed using traditional Catalan methods from three layers of flat bricks held together with plaster. Concrete does make an appearance, chiefly in the form of the vault lintels, whose rough-cast surface provides a tactile contrast with the brick walls. Corb paid particular attention to the effects of surface and texture at the Maisons Jaoul, deliberately using the cheapest, roughest bricks and instructing his skilled craftsmen to introduce the kind of arbitrary irregularity visible in a rubble-stone wall. To achieve this, a different bricklayer was employed every three courses, and the workmen were encouraged to twist and deform the work and to leave trowel marks in the cement. Gone were the pristine white volumes of Corb's Purist villas, replaced by a preoccupation with chance surface effect and contrasts »between precision and accident« that recalled Surrealist concerns. Inside, the houses were divided up in a cellular fashion, without corridors, and painted in saturated monochrome tones which, with the bricks of the vaults, imbued them with a cosy, almost rustic atmosphere.

Corb himself gave no explanation regarding his change of direction at the Maisons Jaoul, and it was left to historians and critics to supply one. Some suggested contrariness – the master's desire to confound expectations and remain one step ahead of the game –, for others the Maisons Jaoul were simply the product of a strain in his thinking that had always been present but never yet fully expressed, while a third theory suggested that this »new« architecture was a reaction against the photographic stranglehold to which the International Style had succumbed. Photography had at first seemed a blessing to the Modern Movement: by banalizing »unique« objects it freed Modernist creations from the constraints of time and space, conferring on them the intemporality and universality that their progenitors claimed were theirs. A sophisticated mechanical/chemical process suffused with the spirit of the machine age, photography idealized Modern-Movement architecture, giving it a credibility it might not otherwise have had. Crumbling, uneven plaster, unattractive weathering and rusting window frames were wiped out in the silvery haze of the gelatinous image. The danger was that architecture would begin to dematerialize through the action of the photographic medium, becoming merely a hollow, virtual image of itself. Architects could either go with this current – as much recent work has done – or resist it, as Corb may have been trying to do at the Maisons Jaoul, by emphasizing the solid, earthy, material qualities of buildings. Whether or not architecture can ultimately withstand the erosive effects of photographic reproduction is still a point for debate. That Corb was a master manipulator of image is certain: one essential similarity between say, the Villa Stein (31.1) – one of his canonical Purist creations – and the Maisons Jaoul is that both were constructed artisanally by craftsmen; the former was made to look sleek and industrially produced, while the latter were deliberately »roughened up« to appear as crudely constructed as possible.

The powerful effect of the Maisons Jaoul, a primal mixture of monumentality and introspection combined with artlessness and sophistication, is compounded by their enigmatic muteness. Their influence was enormous, the shallow vaults becoming, for a good while afterwards, an architectural cliché. The houses were especially appreciated in Britain, inspiring a whole group of young architects, including James Stirling, who were labelled the »New Brutalists«.

27 La Défense

27.1 The business district of La Défense
Master plan drawn up by the Etablissement Public d'Aménagement de La Défense (EPAD), begun 1958
(Métro: La Défense, Grande Arche de La Défense; RER: La Défense)

In the 1660s, as part of a remodelling of the Jardin des Tuileries (1.10) for Louis XIV, André Le Nôtre laid out a triumphal axis disappearing off into infinity towards the western horizon. This *grand axe*, as it is known, has inspired generations of subsequent Frenchmen, with the result that it has now been extended to a whopping 8 km, and plans are afoot to stretch it even further. Of course the simple tracing of this axis on the ground was not enough, it had to be expressed in the built environment, and one of the principal manifestations of that expression is the multi-million-franc international business district of La Défense. Unique in Europe and perhaps in the world, this pharaonic development was conceived during the postwar boom to make up for the short-fall of office space in Paris. Programmed to replace crumbling neighbourhoods of loosely-built suburban housing and light industry, the new business district was able to spread out in a manner impossible in the traditional *quartier d'affaires* of the 8th *arrondissement*. A few vital statistics will help to get the measure of La Défense's success, 40 years on: in an area of 160 ha it provides over 2.5 million m² of office space that are let to more than 1,500 companies, its public-transport interchange is the busiest in Europe with 100 million users per year, 160,000 people work here and 20,000 live here. Dominating the skyline for miles around, its disparate cluster of towers has earned it the nickname »Manhattan-on-Seine«, an entirely positive reference for some and an indication of all its faults for others.

The idea of building a giant new business district at La Défense was first put forward in the 1930s, but it was only with the construction of the C.N.I.T. (27.3) here in the mid-1950s that the government of the day decided to act. In 1958 a state-controlled *établissement public* (acronym EPAD) was set up to oversee development of the portion of the *grand axe* between the Seine and the Place de La Défense. A team of architects and planners was assembled that included Robert Camelot, Jean de Mailly and Bernard Zehrfuss, architects of the C.N.I.T., as well as the urbanists Robert Auzelle and Claude Boistière and the engineer André Prothin, who was EPAD's first director. Together they elaborated a masterplan based on the principal dispositions of the famous Charter of Athens drawn up by Le Corbusier *et al*. in 1933: the total separation of pedestrians and traffic via a raised esplanade (pedestrians on top, cars underneath) and the building of towers to achieve maximum density for minimum surface occupation on the ground. At La Défense, the raised pedestrian esplanade would follow the line of the *grand axe*, while traffic would access the development via a sort of amoeba-shaped ring road, baptized the Boulevard Circulaire, that was modelled on the splitting of Paris's east–west traffic artery either side of the Jardin des Tuileries, which, as Auzelle put it, leaves an »oasis of calm« in the middle. Subsidiary thoroughfares running under the esplanade and meeting at a central roundabout would allow direct access to the basements of the buildings above. Car parks, drains, gas conduits and all other similar services would be contained in the space under the pedestrian platform, thereby avoiding the need for costly excavation and facilitating maintenance access. La Défense was originally intended to be a mixed development of housing and offices: relatively low, ten-storey housing units were to front the *grand axe*, while around 20 office-filled towers of 30 storeys would rise behind. Referred to by the planners as »Palais-Royal« units, the apartment buildings were all to be organized around large rectangular gardens in the manner of the Jardin du Palais-Royal (see 1.16).

Before construction work could begin, the site had to be cleared (more than 8,000 existing dwellings being demolished) and the necessary infrastructure built, including the multiple roadways and the elevated esplanade itself. The very first office block constructed – a building for Esso, since demolished to make way for the Cœur-Défense development (see below) – was completed in 1962. While the apartment buildings went up as planned, construction of the office towers was slower off the ground. It was only with the arrival of the RER rail link (see feature on the Métro and the RER) in 1970 that things really got going. It was also at this time that Jean Millier, who had taken over as head of EPAD in 1969, called into question the original masterplan, arguing that what Paris needed was a greater quantity of office space at La Défense and, in place of the regulation 24×42×100 m towers imagined by the planners, bigger and more individual buildings that would provide immediate visual recognition for the companies occupying them. There was also an economic aspect to his argument, since it had become clear that the enormous state investment in La Défense's infrastructure would not easily be amortized if the original masterplan were maintained. Millier's big-building thinking happened to coincide with the proclivities of France's then president, the ultra-Modernist Georges Pompidou, and EPAD's director obtained permission to increase the planned office space at La Défense from the initial goal of 860,000 m² to a walloping 1,500,000 m². Obviously, since the site was not extended, this increase could only be achieved by building towers, and height limits were thus waived at La Défense with presidential blessing. Besides allowing for a dynamism in the property market that would not have been possible in central Paris, authorizing the construction of skyscrapers at La Défense was a clever way of making sure the French capital displayed these symbols of economic prowess – by then *de rigueur* for any self-respecting financial centre – without actually building them in the historic centre, which remained jealously protected by height restrictions.

As a result of this change in policy, the early 1970s saw a rash of towers rising ever higher from La Défense, of which the most notorious was without doubt the 179 m-high Tour Gan (Wallace K. Harrison and Max Abramovitz with J.-P. Bisseuil, 1970–74). Its 48 floors made its visible for miles around, including from central Paris, where it obscured the sky behind the Arc de Triomphe (16.1). Although the Arc's hegemony in the skyline had long since been lost, the scandal provoked by the Tour Gan was enormous; France's future president, Valéry Giscard d'Estaing, who as finance minister under Pompidou was horrified to see the Tour Gan going up from the windows of his office in the Louvre (1.8), tried in vain to get height restrictions imposed at La Défense. But the march of progress was ineluctable, and more skyscrapers followed. However another scandal, this time financial, halted building work at La Défense soon afterwards, when the 1974 petrol crisis prompted the collapse of the international market, leaving EPAD with thousands of square metres of unoccupied office space and a debt of 700 million francs. Despite calls for state disengagement, the government stood by the operation, whose financial health eventually picked up to the extent that in 1978 authorization was granted for construction of a further 350,000 m² of office accommodation. The decade that followed saw a property boom at La Défense that included the building of a 100,000 m² shopping centre and President Mitterrand's project for the Grande Arche (27.4), which finally brought visual coherence to the development. La Défense was also extended beyond its original limits with the laying out of the Quartier Valmy to the west of the Grande Arche, allowing for the building of yet more office space. Another slump in the mid 1990s was followed by a second boom, with the result that today there is almost no more constructible space left at La Défense, and EPAD is programmed to disappear at the latest in 2007, leaving behind balanced books.

Because of its long building period, La Défense offers a fascinating case study in the evolution of French skyscraper architecture over the last 40 years. It has to be said that the first generation of towers, those conceived under the urban regulations of the initial masterplan such as the Tour Aquitaine (Xavier and Luc Arsène-Henry and Bernard Schoeller, completed 1967, a.k.a. the Tour AIG), the Tour Europe (Delb, Chesneau and Verola, completed 1969) and the Tour Atlantique (Delb, Chesneau, Verola and Lalande, completed 1970), are not very inspired. Their box-like form, imposed by the planners, and the Brutalist cladding displayed by many of them have dated very badly. There is one exception, however, which is the Tour Nobel (a.k.a. the Tour PB31; Jean de Mailly and Jacques Depusse, 1964 to 1967), standing at the esplanade's eastern end like a sentinel announcing La Défense on the Seine. This was in fact the business district's very first tower, which perhaps explains the care with which it was realized. The architect/engineer Jean Prouvé designed both the structure and the curtain walling, finally getting to try out ideas he had put forward as early as 1949. Structurally the tower consists of a central concrete core, containing lifts and other vertical services, off which are suspended steel cantilevered floors. This was the first time in France, and perhaps anywhere, that concrete and steel had been allied in this way, and Prouvé's system afterwards became standard in his homeland (being employed, for example, at the Tour Montparnasse (15.1) and the Tour Gan). It was also the first time in a non-industrial French context that sliding shuttering was used in concrete construction, allowing for very rapid completion. For the curtain walling, Prouvé designed a highly elegant combination of steel, aluminium and glass with streamlined curved corners. Unfortunately, asbestos was used to fireproof the Tour Nobel's structural steel components, and its cladding was consequently entirely renewed during a clean-up operation carried out in 2001–03.

As we have seen, following the 1972 change in masterplan, La Défense witnessed construction of a second generation of much bigger and more spectacular towers that included the 159 m-high, brown-glass-and-aluminium Tour Assur (a.k.a. the Tour Axa; Dufau, Stenzel and Dacbert, completed 1974), the aforementioned Tour Gan – whose cross-shaped plan cleverly avoided deep floors and whose elegant green-glass cladding still seems extremely suave – and the famous Tour Fiat, which at the time of its construction was La Défense's tallest skyscraper. It was the 1974 petrol crisis and the negative reaction of employees to the working environment in this second generation of towers that forced a rethink of tall-building design at La Défense, giving rise to a third generation of skyscrapers in the 1980s. A particularly striking example of this evolution is provided by a pair of buildings standing to the north of the esplanade on the Place de la Coupole: the aforementioned Tour Fiat (completed 1974, today renamed Framatome) and the Tour TotalFinaElf (originally just Elf, completed 1985), both by the same architects, Roger Saubot and François Jullien. The Tour Elf was originally to have been an identical twin to the Tour Fiat, but the economic crisis retarded its construction and prompted a complete redesign. Although programmatically the towers as built are almost identical – each is roughly 180 m high and provides approximately 100,000 m² of office space – their forms and technical capacities could not be more different. Inspired by the enigmatic black monolith of *2001: A Space Odyssey*, the Tour Framatome is a solid box of a building, whose façades were intended to provide as little animation as possible, whence the perfectly smooth and almost unreadable skin of black smoked glass and granite. Each of the tower's floors provides nearly 2,000 m² of open-plan office space, with many who work here consequently finding themselves a long way from a window. By the time the Tour Elf came to be built, on the other hand, the workforce had made known its dislike of open-plan spaces, preferring smaller groupings in divided offices, and its desire for windows for all. To solve this logistical conundrum, the architects »fractioned« the tower into several volumes, thereby avoiding deep plans and maximizing façade surface area and hence fenestration, although they still opted for the same blankness of detailing, this time in 80s mirror glass. The Tour Elf also represented another improvement over its predecessor guaranteed to please the company bosses: it is half as expensive to heat, light and maintain as the Tour Framatome. Saubot has described this contrasting pair as an »opposition of the slender and the massive. Two towers that converse like a woman in an evening dress next to a man in a dinner jacket.«

If »fractioning« of towers to obtain maximum daylight penetration was the fashion in the 1980s, the 1990s saw the advent of the ellipse form to achieve much the same result. Buildings with oval plans allow for lifts and services to be contained in their thick centres while the curved elevations ensure high façade surface area per volume. Examples include Pacific Tower (27.5), the broken half cylinders of Pierre Parat and Michel Andrault's twin Société-Générale towers (completed 1995) and also their Tour Sequoia (completed 1990, today occupied by Cégétel), not to mention the brand-new Tour Hines (Pei, Freed, Cobb & Associates, 1995–2001), home to EDF, whose extremely suave ellipse is highlighted by the daring, 28-storey-high cutaway on its esplanade side that signals its main entrance. Another 90s phenomenon has been the obsolescing of many of the first generation of towers, whose accommodation falls below today's computer-age standards and whose architecture often no longer conforms to safety regulations and/or seems woefully dowdy and dated. As a result, numerous examples have been entirely refurbished, sometimes outside as well as in – e.g. the Tour Nobel – or even entirely demolished, as was the case with the Esso building, whose place has now been taken by the shiny twin towers of the Cœur Défense (Jean-Paul Viguier, 1991–2001). As space at La Défense has filled up, so architects have had to become more formally inventive: the planned Tour CBX (Kohn Pedersen Fox, scheduled for late 2003) narrows to a sharp point in the manner of New York's Flatiron building so as to take advantage of a sliver of land not originally earmarked for construction.

As well as a case study of tower design, La Défense also provides a fascinating example of the full application of Charter-of-Athens-style urbanism, revealing many of its problems and limitations. While the esplanade does indeed furnish 30 ha of pedestrian and planted spaces, as its creators proudly point out, one nonetheless wonders what exactly it was for. Until the Grande Arche arrived and closed it off both visually and physically, it resembled a giant aircraft carrier surrounded by cliffs, and was a nasty wind tunnel in which few wished to linger outside of the summer months. Even now, apart from lunchtime cafés in clement weather, people don't really seem to invest the space, and for

most it is simply territory one must cross to get from office to car or train. Moreover, getting off the esplanade down to ground level or into surrounding neighbourhoods is a daunting experience for those not already familiar with the escape routes. On the practical front, the presence of the esplanade and all its attendant services underneath has enormously complicated construction of new buildings (see, e.g., the Grande Arche and Notre-Dame-de-la-Pentecôte (27.2)), and while it has facilitated service maintenance it has also made these installations more vulnerable to accident (e.g. flooding) and attack. La Défense has also suffered from its physical isolation in the environment, the high-speed, traffic-only Boulevard Circulaire cutting it off from its surroundings with all the aggression of a defensive circuit. With the recent building of a giant tunnel under La Défense connecting the A14 motorway to central Paris, the Boulevard Circulaire now has less reason to be a cars-only expressway, and plans are under discussion to turn it into a more humanized, urban boulevard with trees, pavements (i.e. pedestrians) and cycle paths. Traffic lights have been introduced as a first step towards this. Thus, 40 years on, one of the fundaments of the Charter of Athens – abolition of the traditional street in favour of car/pedestrian separation – is being reversed at La Défense.

Architecturally, La Défense has also proved questionable. The original masterplan combined cutting-edge Modernist infrastructure with rather pompous, *beaux-arts*-tradition layout and massing, the goal being to create a French version of Manhattan where the New York skyline's »chaos« would be transformed into an orderly avenue that Haussmann himself could have been proud of. Following the 1972 change in masterplan and the consequent opening up of La Défense to market forces, the *beaux-arts* tradition was cast to the winds and discontinuity *à l'américaine*, both in scale and massing, allowed free rein. As a result La Défense feels especially weird: one senses that this was a highly planned environment but nonetheless the »American«-style visual chaos the authorities initially wanted to avoid rules supreme. And unlike Manhattan, La Défense is rather lacking in »star« buildings to bring it some world-class *éclat*, while the mediocre structures in between are hardly urbane or neighbourly enough to make up for this deficit. Of course market forces may eventually solve this problem all on their own if the current trend for demolishing older buildings to make way for ever newer, bigger and shinier ones continues.

Today the knock-on effects of La Défense are beginning to be felt in the neighbouring *quartiers*. Huge new residential districts are currently going up to the northwest of the Grande Arche, mostly composed of ten-storey-high apartment buildings in a PoMo, Disney-style garb hitherto unknown in France, which are clearly intended to attract the executives and their families who work at La Défense. The housing that was entirely lacking in the 1972 masterplan is thus being built next door and should, with time, remove the mono-use, ghetto atmosphere pervading La Défense. Today the planners' attention is turned towards the proposed 3.5 km extension of the *grand axe* to the next bend in the Seine, beyond Nanterre, which they intend to line with yet more offices as well as housing and university buildings. The big question now, of course, is how much further can the axis go? Will it one day hit the sea on the Normandy coast? And then what?

27.2 Notre-Dame-de-la-Pentecôte
Parvis de La Défense, to the north of the C.N.I.T.
Franck Hammoutène, 1994–2001
(Métro: Grande Arche de la Défense; RER: La Défense)

Despite the increasing secularization of Western society and the separation of church and state just over a century ago, France remains a largely Christian country, and not even the brave new business district of La Défense (27.1) could be without its place of worship. Realized 40 years after La Défense's founding to replace a small Christian centre that had become inadequate for the thousands of people frequenting the area every day, the building in question, Notre-Dame-de-la-Pentecôte, also happened to be the Paris region's first completed third-millennium church. To the usual problem facing latter-day church designers – how to express faith in this secular age? – was added another: how to put up a modest religious building in a hostile environment like La Défense, where towering temples of commerce dominate the landscape?

Hammoutène's responses were simplicity and orthogonality. Externally the building takes the form of a glass-and-marble-clad cube, Cartesian and instantly comprehensible. Intended to be as much a community centre as a church *per se*, Notre-Dame-de-la-Pentecôte is organized on three levels: under the esplanade, in a sort of »basement«, are meeting rooms, then at esplanade level, where entry to the building is gained, we find a generous vestibule, while sitting on massive pillars inside the vestibule, and set within the enveloping cube of the building's exterior, is a concrete box containing the church proper. Entering the vestibule one finds oneself in a half-day-/half-artificially lit space from which, to reach the church proper, one must climb steep stairs that become progressively darker towards their summit. Once there, after opening the doors into the church, one is dazzled by light flooding in from behind the altar. This is because the church's rear wall is entirely glazed with white frosted glass, serving both to express the idea that »God is light« and to hide the depressing prospect of motorways and construction sites beyond. Outside, frosted glass again makes an appearance, this time in the form of a giant, translucent, freestanding rectangular panel sitting in front of the church, on which is traced a skinny cross. This simple gesture signals the building and its function in the landscape, without resorting either to inflated monumentality or to false modesty.

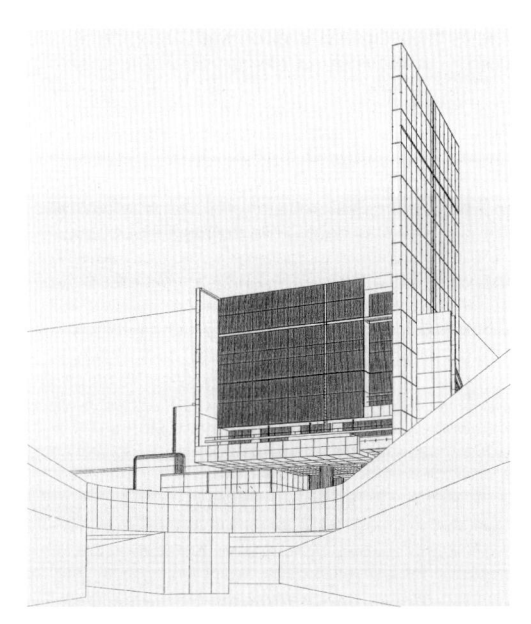

As is so often the case, however, that which looks simple and effortless was in fact extremely complex and difficult to achieve. To start with, there was the problem of the church's foundations. The building does not stand on terra firma, but floats on the Charter-of-Athens-style platform of La Défense, under which run a multitude of services: roads, Métro and firemen's tunnels, drains, electric cabling, gas conduits, and so on. Since the church's positioning was determined by the surface occupation of the platform, it did not take into account all the obstacles that lay underneath. In order to get round them and provide a solid base for the building, 62 micro-piles were driven into the free patches of ground between the different obstacles, many of the piles being inclined by up to 20° so as to avoid further obstacles buried below. Onto the reinforced-concrete foundations cast around the heads of these piles were set six 1.3 m-diameter concrete pillars that carry a concrete box containing the meeting rooms, which in turn carries the upper levels of the church. As a result of this complex system, the foundations alone counted for a third of the building's total cost. Then there was the 35 m-high glass panel. What, formally, could be more simple than this rectangular monolith?; yet what, structurally, could be more complex in the esplanade context of La Défense where it has to resist buffeting winds of up to 200 km/h? In collaboration with the engineering firm Rice, Francis and Ritchie, Hammoutène developed a welded-steel cage frame (necessitating 16,500 welds!), which is capable of bending, onto which the frosted-glass panels were hung. The resulting 55-tonne structure sits on a complex system of supports and is cleverly stabilized at its summit by a series of small water-filled tanks.

27.2 Notre-Dame-de-la-Pentecôte

27.3 Centre National des Industries et des Techniques (C.N.I.T.)
Parvis de La Défense
Robert Camelot, Jean de Mailly and Bernard Zehrfuss, structural engineer Nicolas Esquillan, 1954–58
(Métro: Grande Arche de la Défense; RER: La Défense)

Welcome to the world's biggest concrete vault! This extraordinary, triangular-plan structure covers 22,000 m² (the surface area of the Place de la Concorde (8.1)), with a maximum span of 238 m (206 m across each of its three arched façades) and a maximum height at its apex of 46.3 m. Supported at only three points, the vault also holds the world record for structural leanness in terms of the ratio of the surface area covered to the number of supports. And what is even more astonishing is that this spectacular achievement is already nearly half a century old.

The C.N.I.T.'s genesis dates back to the brave new period of postwar renewal when France, like the rest of Europe, was trying to boost her industrial expansion. Paris at that time lacked a suitable exhibition space capable of holding large-scale trade fairs, and French industrialists consequently joined forces to rectify the problem. A site was selected for a new exhibition centre out to the west of Paris on the Place de La Défense, which was then part of a residential suburb. Land was cheap and plentiful here at the time, and although the C.N.I.T. was initially stuck out in the middle of suburbia, it would not remain stranded for long. The planners had had their eye on La Défense since before the war with a view to developing a business district there, and the building of the C.N.I.T. at precisely this spot was clearly calculated to help kick start the operation (see 27.1). As the state-appointed architects responsible for this sector of Paris's suburbs, it fell to Camelot, Mailly and Zehrfuss to design the new exhibition hall. The plot acquired for the C.N.I.T. was roughly triangular, and the brief given the architects simple: fill as much of the site as was practicable with a giant hall encumbered by as few intermediary supports as possible. Whence Mailly's idea of a triangular vault supported only at its apexes.

At the outset, nobody knew how to build such a structure or even if it was buildable at all. Various ideas were proposed, and both steel and concrete constructors consulted. In the end it was the concrete industry that won out, with a proposal by the engineer Nicolas Esquillan. His scheme comprised three double-skin, wedge-shaped, folded vault sections, each of which fanned out from its point of contact with the ground to meet the others at the vault's centre. Esquillan liked to point out the structure's extreme leanness, which, he said, is »20 times thinner than an eggshell scaled up to the size of the vault«. The miracle innovation at the C.N.I.T., which allowed these hitherto unimaginable dimensions to be realized, was pre-stressed concrete. This technology was not new, having been invented at the end of the 19C, but its development had been slow and its use limited. Esquillan adapted its theory to the specific context of the C.N.I.T.: the building could only stand up because of a system of pre-stressed steel cables running underground that pulled the vault's feet together and prevented them from slipping outwards. The result is truly spectacular, especially when viewed from below: gently fluted fans of concrete soaring above one's head with all the levity of folded paper. Externally, the C.N.I.T. is now partly hidden by the Charter-of-Athens-style esplanade of La Défense, and the true measure of its daring dimensions can no longer be fully appreciated.

27.3 Centre National des Industries et des Techniques (C.N.I.T.)

New innovations in their turn create new problems, and one of those that cropped up at the C.N.I.T. was the question of how to close the sides of the vault against the elements. Obviously, since this was an exhibition hall, light was an important factor, and the building's façades had thus to be as transparent as possible. The renowned architect/engineer Jean Prouvé – a specialist in metal construction – was called in to design them, and produced results that by the standards of the day were quite astonishingly lean and transparent. With a frame realized in stainless steel because of its low maintenance requirements, Prouvé's glass curtain walls were hung off the vault's arches via a sort of corrugated metal rail that allowed them to move with the concrete's dilation, which can reach up to 30 cm. The glass panels overlapped, like fish scales, which allowed for air gaps to ensure ventilation, and the whole structure was stiffened against the wind by footbridges that also gave access for cleaning and repair. The C.N.I.T. as we see it today has been reconfigured and its façades rebuilt (see below), but that on the esplanade side of the building is a replica of Prouvé's original design; this time, however, some of the elements holding the glass panels in place have themselves been realized in glass, rather than the original stainless steel, for even greater transparency.

If Prouvé's façades were conceived with maintenance needs in mind, the vault was not. Its exterior is painted to protect it from the elements, but there is no system of access and skilled mountain climbers have to be engaged for each respraying. Moreover, the underground cables holding the building together are inaccessible along much of their length, which caused great alarm in the early 1990s when it was discovered that some of them had begun to corrode. Were one of them to break, the consequences could be disastrous. Given the uncertainty of the situation and the potential for calamity, the building's owners decided to err on the side of caution and adopted a radical remedy: construction of a second system of pre-stressed-concrete support, this time in the form of pairs of giant bolts that nail the vault's feet into the ground and are capable of resisting the 6,000 tonnes of outward thrust that each foot would exert if its cables ruptured. Deep wells were sunk to ensure their anchorage in the bedrock.

This costly intervention came in the wake of a major overhaul, carried out in 1987–89 by the architects Michel Andrault and Pierre Parat, in which the C.N.I.T. was entirely rid of its original interior and supplied with a brand new, much higher-density filling. For despite the original technical bravura of its architecture, the building had never really been suited to its function. Certainly it could easily accommodate large trade fairs, but the space under the vault was acoustically very poor, difficult to divide up and adapt, and moreover badly lit, this latter problem being due to the fact that in order to make the building financially viable in the first place projecting extensions had had to be built on two of its three façades. Add to this the problems of access, which resulted in interminable traffic jams, and you had a recipe for financial disaster. Andrault and Parat's intervention – much criticized for the tackiness of its detailing and because it no longer allows for unencumbered views of the vault – comprises a mound of concrete floors built up around the periphery of the C.N.I.T.'s interior, which supply shelter for a shopping centre, a hotel and other commercial activities. At the centre of this mound a sort of »crater« provides a covered public plaza, whose star attraction is the soaring vault above. Access to the building has been entirely rethought, including the provision of increased underground parking space. Exhibitions are still held in the C.N.I.T., but have been relegated to a smaller, more isolated and more adaptable space in the basement. Here we have the clue as to why the C.N.I.T.'s world records have gone unbroken for so long: whatever their capacity to thrill and amaze, who really needs giant umbrella structures like this?

27.4 Grande Arche de La Défense

27.4 Grande Arche de La Défense
1, parvis de La Défense
Johann Otto von Spreckelsen with Paul Andreu, 1982 to 1989
(Métro: Grande Arche de la Défense; RER: La Défense)
Of the monumental legacies of the Mitterrand era the Grande Arche de La Défense is one of the most admired and most ambiguous. It was among the nine »grands projets« announced by presidential *communiqué* in 1982 and was conceived around the idea of a »Carrefour International des Communications« (»International Communications Crossroads« or »CIC«), the remit of which was, from the outset, rather vague. An international competition was launched: candidates were asked to produce a monument which would mark the 200th anniversary of the French Revolution in 1989 as the Eiffel Tower (7.8) had marked the centenary, and which would celebrate the utopian ideals of communication. The building was also to provide office space for two government ministries. The panel of luminaries (all of Modernist persuasion) assembled to judge the 400 entries included Richard Rogers, who described the event as the most efficiently organized eight days of his life. Four schemes were submitted to the president, from which he selected that by Spreckelsen, an architect hitherto unknown outside his native Denmark.

The site – at the head of La Défense (see 27.1) and lying on the *grand axe*, the triumphal way running west from the Louvre (1.8) – had long been a source of polemic. Innumerable schemes had been proposed in previous decades, none of which had come to fruition. A question of perennial thorniness divided opinion:

should the axis be terminated or left open at the Tête Défense? Spreckelsen's proposal seemed to do both. It took the form of a giant concrete cube, 105 m square, out of which was hollowed a void the height of Notre-Dame and the width of the Champs Elysées, a »window to the world ... with a view into the future« as the architect fancifully described it. The edges of the void were gently bevelled to lighten the mass of the building – an elegant rather than a brutal monumentality –, its surfaces clad in white carrera marble, the stuff of monuments *par excellence*, and the sides of the cube glazed to planar perfection. Through the impeccable finish of the exterior Spreckelsen sought to bring nobility to his monolith. The detailing of the cladding was also intended to evoke the etching of a microchip, one of man's most extraordinary achievements and the fundament of modern communications technology. Visitors would approach the cube from the esplanade of La Défense and ascend marble steps to the floor of the void (the »plateau«), where they would be protected from the elements by an amorphous glass canopy, which Spreckelsen dubbed the »clouds«. Entrances would lead into the ministries housed in the sides of the structure, while glass lifts ascending on free-standing stanchions would propel visitors up to the attic, where Spreckelsen envisaged restaurants, conference facilities and roof gardens. A circular opening, or »crater« as the architect called it, would lead down into the base of the cube where part of the CIC would be accommodated. Another structure to the north of the Arche, dubbed the »Collines« (hills), was also to house the CIC.

Spreckelsen, whose œuvre to date consisted of three churches, intended his building to be a »Triumphal Arch of Man«, and the vocabulary he used to describe the various elements of the Arche – plateau, clouds, crater, hills – suggests he also wanted it to be some kind of quasi-religious allegory of the universe, in which nature is encompassed by a giant, Cartesian, rational order. Mitterrand was enthusiastic, but hesitant. Future generations would hold him personally responsible for this landmark situated on the *grand axe* and visible from many areas of Paris. At his behest the biggest crane in France was brought to La Défense and a 400 m² gantry, painted to resemble marble, suspended from it at the height of the roof of the future arch. The gantry collapsed before anyone had a proper chance to see it, but Mitterrand decided to go ahead nonetheless.

Because of the complex and problematic nature of the site above roads and railway tracks, the Arche could not be built flat onto the axis, but was instead gently swivelled by six degrees to avoid obstructions below, thus mirroring the *désaxement* of the Louvre at the other end of the triumphal way. A major disagreement arose over the manner of construction. Spreckelsen insisted that the Arche be fabricated by means of a monolithic, Cartesian megastructure of 21 m base dimensions. The engineers, on the other hand, did not see why more traditional methods, which would render construction easier, should not be used. Spreckelsen refused to compromise the purity of his intellectual conception, proclaiming that God would see and judge his creation. The Arche is thus fashioned as a single piece of solid concrete, reinforced in every direction, and weighing approximately 300,000 tonnes. Its promoters boast that a giant could pick it up and carry it away without it disintegrating. It is supported on twelve massive concrete piers, each bearing four times the weight of the Eiffel Tower, its repose cushioned by a layer of neoprene.

Construction had gone ahead without any clear idea of the function of the CIC, and its ever-changing programme necessitated continual redesigns from Spreckelsen (he submitted eleven proposals for the Collines before the end of the affair). The spiralling costs of the project finally led to the cancellation of the CIC in 1986 by Chirac's government, and the Arche was sold off to private investors. Failing health and the prospect of yet further redesigns prompted Spreckelsen to resign; he died before completion of the project. Paul Andreu, his second in command, replaced him, and work was hurried through so that the Arche was more or less fin-

27.5 Pacific Tower

ished by 1989 to host the G7 summit of that year. The Collines were farmed out to the architects Buffi and Lenormand, who produced a rather bland speculative atrium, and the British engineer Peter Rice designed the clouds in the absence of detailed plans from Spreckelsen. Fabric, rather than glass as Spreckelsen had envisaged, the clouds are disappointing stodgy in comparison to the evanescent structures of his initial sketches.

As built, the Grande Arche de la Défense is a curious monument. Denuded of its symbolic function it is, in the crudest terms, no more than a vast square office block with a hole in the middle. Moreover, the office space it provides is poor by commercial standards. The relationship between form and function in Spreckelsen's design was, however, never very strong from the beginning. In a sense the Arche is more akin to sculpture than architecture. The inevitable comparisons with Boullée have frequently been made, and the Arche is a clear descendant of the Arc de Triomphe (16.1) and the Eiffel Tower, neither of which have any function other than the symbolic and monumental. But if the Arc is emblematic of the power and pride of the French State, and the Tower is redolent of 19C industrialism and the age of iron and steam, for what does the Grande Arche stand? As an icon of communications it is hardly convincing, nor does it constitute a showpiece of technical advances. The original intention was to complement the Louvre at the other end of the axis – tomb-temple of history versus centre of progressive technology and window to the future. Instead the Arche sits at the head of La Défense, commanding, enigmatic and mute, irreproachable in its immaculate whiteness. For some it is an expression of the timeless and universal, the play of light on its pure geometry a spiritual experience. To others it seems supremely ironic that a monument to the 20C should consist of a gigantic void.

27.5 Pacific Tower (also known as Japan Tower) and Japan Bridge
Cours Valmy, La Défense
Kisho Kurokawa, 1988–92
(Métro: Grande Arche de la Défense; RER: La Défense)
Situated in the Valmy sector of La Défense (27.1) – an extension of the original business district located behind the Grande Arche (27.4) –, the 26-storey Japan Tower provides 56,000 m² of office space, part of which houses a Franco-Japanese business institute and a Japanese cultural centre. It is accessed on one side by an elevated walkway and circumscribed on the other by seven lanes of motorway. Crescent-shaped in plan, the building echoes the Grande Arche by way of a 19-storey-high, wedge-shaped opening at its centre. Although it may seem entirely gratuitous, this opening does serve a practical purpose, preventing the Cours Valmy from becoming a dead end by way of the footbridge that links it to the Kupka building across the motorway. Construction of Pacific Tower introduced two innovations to French building practice: the use of B60

concrete, whose great strength allows a reduction in wall thickness and in steel reinforcement, and the development of a time-saving system whereby the tower's prefabricated concrete façade panels were mounted before casting of the main structure behind. On the motorway side the building presents a grid of hundreds of square windows set into the granite-effect panels, but on its Cours-Valmy side this same window grid is covered by an enveloping sheet of glass. Construction of the central opening's load-bearing lintel was a heroic operation that involved casting the 500-tonne structure on the ground and then slowly jacking it into place.

According to Kurokawa, Japan Tower's opening represents the symbolic portal at the entrance to a Japanese tea salon, its glass façade is an evocation of *shoji* – the sliding, rice-paper-covered doors of traditional Japanese houses –, while the footbridge was inspired by *taiko bashi* – traditional Japanese curved wooden bridges. But looking at the building, these pronouncements do not seem convincing and come across as marketing spiel intended to »exoticize« what is in fact a typically slick and thoroughly international product of late-20C capitalism. The provision of a Japanese-style garden on the building's roof is merely a gimmick designed to reinforce this rhetoric. From a design point of view, the project's most interesting element is perhaps the spectacular footbridge. 100 m long, it uses tied arches for the main structure because of the inability of its supports to absorb horizontal thrust. To make it stable against lateral winds, the tied-arch form was doubled and braced horizontally, with a plexiglass-covered walkway being mounted in the space between the arches and braces. Although it may not be immediately apparent, the bridge is in fact totally asymmetrical due to the skewness of its supporting buildings in relation to each other. As a result, each of the bridge's component elements is unique, and without sophisticated computer software its design and fabrication would have been impossible.

28 Saint-Germain-en-Laye

28.1 Château de Saint-Germain-en-Laye
Place Charles-de-Gaulle
Earliest extant buildings begun *c*. 1230
(RER: Saint-Germain-en-Laye)

For almost five centuries, from the 1120s to the 1680s, the Château de Saint-Germain-en-Laye was one of France's principal royal residences. Set on the crest of a hill overlooking the Seine, with fine views from its grounds towards Paris in the east, the château was favoured by successive monarchs because of the excellent hunting offered by the forest of Saint-Germain. We know very little about the original château – the first known mention of which dates from 1124, during the reign of Louis VI the Fat – because it was burnt to the ground by the invading English, in 1346. Only the chapel, built by Louis IX in the 1230s, survived. 20 years after the attack, Charles V began construction of a new fortress-château, incorporating the 13C chapel, that was completed in 1367. Today, only the curtain wall of Charles's building survives, the rest having been demolished, in 1539, by François I, who began an ambitious rebuilding programme that was completed by his son, Henri II, in the late 1540s.

François I and Henri II's château remained much as they had left it until the 1680s, when Louis XIV commissioned Jules Hardouin-Mansart to enlarge the residence. The architect added five enormous full-height pavilions, one at each corner of the building, as well as replacing the chapel's roof with a supplementary storey and masking its external façade with an elevation matching those of the rest of the château. No sooner were these modifications complete than Louis XIV abandoned Saint-Germain for Versailles, afterwards giving the old château to the exiled James II of England, in 1688. After James's death, Saint-Germain fell into disgrace, and later served as a prison during the Revolution. By 1862, when the Emperor Napoleon III commissioned Eugène Millet to restore the château to house the Musée des Antiquités Celtiques et Gallo-romains, its buildings were on the verge of dereliction. Millet took the decision to return Saint-Germain to its 16C state, which involved the demolition of Hardouin-Mansart's corner pavilions and the rebuilding of the missing elevations. Much of the surviving original fabric was also rebuilt, and today's château is to a certain extent a 19C facsimile of the 16C building. Millet also undertook a thorough restoration of the chapel. One of his principal historical sources when restoring the château was Jacques Androuet Du Cerceau's engravings of Saint-Germain, published in 1576–79 in *Les plus excellents bastiments de France*. Millet's interventions were completed in 1867, and the Musée des Antiquités Celtiques et Gallo-romains opened that same year, subsequently becoming the Musée des Antiquités Nationales, which still occupies the château.

The chapel
Begun sometime around 1230 and completed in 1238, the Chapelle Saint-Louis, as it is today known (named after its builder, Louis IX, who was canonized after his death), was originally a freestanding structure within the first château's walls. Attributed by many to Pierre de Montreuil (who is also credited with the southern-transept façade of Notre-Dame de Paris (4.2)), the

28.1 Château de Saint-Germain-en-Laye

chapel was described by Viollet-le-Duc as »one of the most characteristic examples of 13C art at the moment of its splendour«. The Saint-Germain chapel was to a degree a precursor of Louis IX's sublime Sainte-Chapelle (1.2), although on a smaller scale. One storey high and measuring 24 m in length by 10 m in width, it is essentially a simple, vaulted chamber, terminating at its east end in a curved apse and originally glazed on all sides. Its square-headed windows are highly unusual, occurring nowhere else in medieval French-Gothic architecture. The enormous, 100 m² rose window dominating the western end was walled up at the time of Hardouin-Mansart's modifications in the 17C. Nothing of the chapel's original decoration survives today apart from the vault bosses, which are carved into faces, that nearest the rose window reputedly representing Louis IX himself. On the courtyard façade, a rather ungainly arcade at the summit of the chapel's walls, added by the 19C restorers, attempts to establish a visual link between the 13C edifice and the two 16C wings framing it. The Chapelle Saint-Louis was the setting, in 1238, of the handover by the Byzantine Emperor Baldwin II of the Crown of Thorns, which had been bought by Louis IX, and for which the king afterwards built the Sainte-Chapelle.

From Charles V's fortress to François I's château
After 20 years' abandonment following its destruction by the English, the château was rebuilt by Charles V, in 1364–67. The foundations of Charles's keep (the square tower at the corner of the garden and entrance façades) may well date back to the 1120s; if so, they are the sole visible vestige of the original 12C château. As for the keep's current façades, they are 19C, rebuilt after the removal of Hardouin-Mansart's corner pavilions. The machicolated curtain wall running round the base of the château, with its *chemin de ronde* (or covered look-out gallery) and its dry moat, is thus the principle authentic remnant of Charles's castle. Its irregular plan, in which none of the principal walls meets any other at right angles, is perhaps a feature inherited from the original 12C château. Further than this we know very little about Charles's fortress, the living quarters having been swept away for François I's rebuilding.

A sophisticated Renaissance patron and indefatigable builder, François was responsible, amongst others, for the new Louvre (1.8), the Château de Fontainebleau (38.1) and the Château de Madrid (destroyed). One of the reasons for this architectural bulimia was his reorganization of the French state along more centralized lines, a process that would reach its apogee with the absolutism of Louis XIV. François suppressed the power of the nobility and, in concentrating authority in the personage of the king, created a system of patronage whereby the court grew greatly in significance. The vastly increased number of courtiers and attendant service personnel meant that, wherever the king resided, a considerable château was needed to accommodate the royal household. In 1539, attracted by the beauty of the setting at Saint-Germain and by the hunting to be had in the forest, François decided to remodel entirely the château. He appointed Pierre Chambiges to oversee the work, later replacing him, in 1544, with Guillaume Guillain and Jean Langeois. According to Jacques Androuet Du Cerceau, however, the king was »so attentive« to the work going on at Saint-Germain »that one could almost not say other than that he was the architect of it«. By the time of François I's death, in 1547, the majority of the new château was inhabitable. Only the west wing remained unfinished, and Henri II, François's son, saw to its completion shortly thereafter.

François I's remodelling involved the demolition of Charles V's old *logis* and the erection, against the medieval curtain wall, of a succession of new wings with, at their centre, a sizeable courtyard of the same irregular shape as the château's perimeter. Rather unusually, the new wings were built in stone dressed with brick, the exact opposite of the brick-and-stone combination that would become so popular in France at the end of the 16C. The design of the new château was more unusual still, and, besides certain similarities shared with other châteaux built by François I, was and would remain unique in France. On the courtyard façades, the structure is clear, essentially two sets of arcades superimposed one on top of the other, their heavy buttressing supporting a vault on the upper floor, which in turn supports the almost flat, stone roof. Encircled by balustrades and invisible from the ground, the château's roofing contrasts strongly with the elaborate, lofty, slate-covered attics generally favoured in France at that time. On the château's moat façades, only the upper of the two arcades is visible, the lower parts of the elevations consisting of Charles V's curtain wall. Six circular towers containing spiral staircases, three in the courtyard and three on the château's exterior, punctuate the intersections of the wings (the moat-façade towers are all 19C, the originals having been demolished for the addition of Hardouin-Mansart's pavilions) and provide a vertical counterpoint to the otherwise dominant horizontals of the elevations. A strong Italian influence is perceptible throughout the design: the arcades and balustrades, the ironwork strengthening the walls (used in a manner imported directly from Italy) and the curious windows of the *piano nobile*, which consist of an arched opening surmounted by a pediment, all recall Italian and especially Veneto buildings. It has been suggested that Sebastiano Serlio (who was familiar with Venetian architecture) may have influenced the design, although his arrival in France in 1541, two years after work on the château was begun, does not quite tally.

Internally, the building's 8,000 m² were divided up into 55 apartments, not horizontally with corridors, as is usual today, but vertically with staircases, each apartment having individual access to the courtyard. The many internal spiral staircases that linked most of the apartments to the ground have since been removed. Besides the staircase towers already mentioned, only the *grand escalier* in the garden wing can still be seen today. It is essentially an imposing dog-leg, vaulted in brick and expressed externally as a tower at the centre of the garden front, said tower containing loggias that lead off the staircase's landings. At the eastern end of the garden wing were the king's apartments – hence the grand staircase – situated on the *piano nobile*, which at Saint-Germain is the second floor (i. e. the floor immediately above the medieval *chemin de ronde*). The positioning of the king's living quarters was no accident, and the attribution of apartments, based on rank and etiquette, was even subject to a written *règlement* of 1585. France's king was obliged to be seen – to demonstrate his power through his physical presence – and the siting of his apartments at the furthest possible point away from the chapel meant that, to attend morning mass, he was obliged to cross the entire courtyard (which was open to the public), thus allowing him to appear before his subjects. Next to the king's apartments and interconnecting with them were of course the queen's living quarters (in the east wing), while on the floor below the king's chambers were those of his mistress, linked to them via a spiral stair.

The château's décor in the 16C was simple to the point of austerity, and the few luxurious *cabinets* installed by Louis XIV in the 17C have since disappeared. The building's interior is thus of little interest today, bar the grand ballroom in the west wing. Occupying the entire area between the keep and the chapel, the ballroom may, judging from the layout of the rooms below it and the thickness of their foundations, have been built on the site of the old medieval castle hall. Uncompleted and still open to the sky at the time of François I's death, the ballroom was afterwards vaulted in brick by the great Philibert De l'Orme, whom Henri II had made his superintendent of buildings. The ballroom's southern external corner was originally cut off on the diagonal, following the irregular course of Charles V's curtain wall. Hardouin-Mansart corrected this »fault« when he added his corner pavilions, and the original layout was not restituted in the 19C because it was considered inelegant (consequently, the entire southern section of the west wing's exterior is pure 19C invention). The ballroom has lost its dais and its original fireplace, the fantastical brick chimney-breast we see today being a later arrangement.

The gardens and the Château Neuf

In François I's time, the château's gardens consisted simply of an area of square parterres laid out in front of the north (garden) wing. In 1557, Philibert De l'Orme began construction of a second château, for Henri II, that was situated due east of the old château on the edge of the hill overlooking the Seine. Greatly enlarged in the 1590s by Henri IV, this new residence (which became known as the Château Neuf) was essentially a sort of sprawling, single-storey villa. It became famous for its fantastic gardens, inspired by those of the Villa d'Este at Tivoli, which descended in terraces to the river and which included elaborate grottoes and waterworks. Abandoned along with the old château, the Château Neuf and its gardens soon fell into disrepair, made worse by the fragility of the subsoil on which they were built. They were finally demolished in the 1770s by their then owner, the Comte d'Artois (brother of Louis XVI), who planned several grandiose replacement schemes, none of which was ever executed. All that remains of the Château Neuf today is its northern river-façade pavilion, baptized the »Pavillon Henri-IV« in the 19C and now part of a hotel (address: 19, rue Thiers). Inside the pavilion, the king's oratory, with its painted dome, can still be seen.

During the 1660s and 1670s, at the command of Louis XIV, André Le Nôtre remodelled the gardens at Saint-Germain, his principle interventions being the creation of the Grand Parterre and the building of the Grande Terrasse. Laid out in front of the north wing of the old château on the site of François I's gardens, the Grand Parterre was decorated with pools and terminated in a wide avenue that penetrated 3 km into the forest of Saint-Germain. This magisterial perspective was ruined in the 19C by the arrival of the Paris-Saint-Germain railway line, which cut right through it, but, since the covering of the railway (now the RER A – see feature on the Métro and RER) in the 1960s, Le Nôtre's composition has regained much of its former splendour. The Grande Terrasse was a major work of civil engineering that took four years to complete (1669–73). 2.4 km long and 30 m wide, it runs northeast along the side of the forest, 62 m above the Seine below, in a straight, uninterrupted line. The perspective effect of this grandiose balcony is heightened by the fact that for the first third of its length it descends in a gentle slope, before levelling out for the remainder of its run.

The town of Saint-Germain-en-Laye

The charming town of Saint-Germain-en-Laye developed because of the presence of the château, its glory days coming in the 17C during the 20 years that Louis XIV was resident there (1660s–80s). Today Saint-Germain is one of Paris's wealthier suburbs, but still retains the feel of a rural town because it is separated from surrounding sprawl by its hillside position and by the 3,500 ha of the forest of Saint-Germain. The current layout of the town centre dates essentially from the 17C, and several of the numerous *hôtels particuliers* built by Louis XIV's courtiers still survive. The main church is the palaeo-Christian-style Saint-Louis, across the road from the château, which was begun in 1766 by Nicolas-Marie Potain and finally completed in its current form in 1848. Also of note is the Musée du Prieuré (2 bis, rue Maurice-Denis), a 17C hospital which became the home of the Symbolist painter Maurice Denis, in 1915. Now a museum dedicated to the Symbolists and the Nabis, it features Denis's studio, built by Auguste Perret in 1912, as well as a chapel decorated by the painter himself.

29 Boulogne-Billancourt

29.1 Bois de Boulogne
(Métro: Porte Maillot, Porte Dauphine, Porte d'Auteuil)
Covering some 865 ha, the Bois de Boulogne is the Paris region's second-largest green open space after the Bois de Vincennes (34.1), its pendant in the east. Famous as the playground of the rich, bourgeois *quartiers* of western Paris, today's Bois is the descendant of an ancient forest, never cleared for cultivation because of the infertility of the soil on which it grew. Common land during the Roman period, the forest became crown property under the Franks, whose kings hunted there. By the time of Charles V (reigned 1364 to 1380), the forest had fallen out of favour, and the king concentrated his activities to the east of the capital, around the Bois de Vincennes. Until the Renaissance period, the Bois de Boulogne, although under royal ownership, received no special attention and was exploited by the neighbouring communities, including the Abbaye de Longchamp (whose windmill, much restored, can still be seen in the Bois).

During the reign of François I (1515–47), the reorientation of Paris's development towards the west was initiated with the reconstruction of both the Louvre (1.8) and the Château de Saint-Germain-en-Laye (28.1). François also built himself a residence in the Bois de Boulogne, the fabled Château de Madrid (demolished in 1792), modelled on houses he had seen while in captivity in Spain. Begun in 1527, and completed for Henri II in 1552, it was entirely clad in majolica tiles and was famed for its lavish interiors. The château never served as a permanent royal residence, but was used as a hunting lodge. To improve sport in the Bois de Boulogne, Henri had the forest walled, thus preventing the escape of game animals as well as the exploitation of the Bois by the local population.

By the 17C, the forest was again out of royal favour, and Louis XIV hunted there only twice, in 1651. However, with the building of Versailles (32.1) from the 1660s onwards, and the court's removal there in the 1680s, the Bois's fortunes changed. Previously isolated from Paris, it now found itself on the principal route between the suburban centre of power and the capital, and the villages around the Bois subsequently became fashionable as a semi-bucolic retreat for the bourgeoisie. Moreover, the to-ing and fro-ing of the court became so frequent that, at the beginning of the 18C, a whole system of roads was built through the Bois, linking Paris to Versailles and Saint-Germain-en-Laye. By the mid-18C, the forest was criss-crossed with straight avenues, which also facilitated Louis XV's and Louis XVI's frequent hunting expeditions there. In the second half of the century, the forest became a popular place of promenade and, from 1775 onwards, horse races were organized there by the very anglophile Comte d'Artois. The 18C also saw the building of several aristocratic and royal residences in the Bois, of which the Château de Bagatelle (29.2, below) and the Folie Saint-James (26.1) survive.

Devastated during the revolutionary period by townspeople in search of firewood, the Bois de Boulogne was restored as a game park under Napoleon. It was again decimated in 1814 by allied troops during the occupation of Paris, restored once more under the Bourbons, but suffered again after the Revolution of 1830. As a result of the rapidly increasing urban population, the Bois became extremely fashionable under the July Monarchy as a place of aristocratic and upper-middle-class recreation. Nonetheless, 89 ha were lopped off its eastern limits for the construction of the Parisian fortifications in 1841, and it suffered further damage at the hands of the urban population after the Revolution of 1848. By the time Napoleon III turned his attention to the Bois in 1852, it was in a sorry state.

The work carried out at the Bois de Boulogne at the behest of France's second emperor lasted six years and employed 1,200 men and 300 horses on a continual basis. Napoleon III's ambition was clear – to endow Paris with a park as splendid as those he had seen in London during his years of exile, and to have as much of it as possible ready for the Exposition Universelle of 1855. Work began under the direction of the architect Jakob Ignaz Hittorff, assisted by the landscape gardener Louis-Sulpice Varé. Apart from the laying out of the majestic Avenue de l'Impératrice (today rebaptized the Avenue Foch), which linked the Bois to the Place de l'Etoile (see 16.1), Hittorff and Varé's plans were low key and respected the natural topography. But the emperor wanted a river like the Serpentine in Hyde Park, and Varé was charged with creating one. Unfortunately, the landscape gardener miscalculated the slope of his 1.5 km-long trench, with the result that it emptied itself at one end while flooding the land around it at the other. Baron Haussmann, who was appointed Prefect of the Seine in 1853, fired Hittorff and Varé and set up the Service Municipal des Promenades et Plantations to complete the transformation of the Bois de Boulogne, engaging the engineer Adolphe Alphand as its director and the gardener Pierre Barillet-Deschamps and the architect Gabriel Davioud as seconds in command. Bas-

29.1 Bois de Boulogne

ing their interventions on the Hittorff/Varé plan, the new team got rid of most of the 18C network of straight roadways, replacing them with sinuous, naturalistic, »English«-style path- and carriageways. Varé's disastrous river was converted into two lakes, the bigger of which was adorned with islands, the area around them was landscaped with lawns, and Davioud supplied the Bois with houses for the gardening staff as well as kiosks, benches, advertising hoardings and all the other necessary furniture, making sure that a strong family resemblance (today we would call it a brand image) was imparted to the different designs (see also feature on street furniture). Work further included the planting of 420,000 trees and the installation of a complex irrigation system (the Bois de Boulogne had long suffered from dryness) in the form of a network of naturalistic streams.

To avoid unnecessary draining of the imperial treasury, Napoleon III made a gift of the Bois de Boulogne to the Ville de Paris, on the condition that the municipality carry out the work planned at its own expense to the designs provided by the state. By buying up the estates of Longchamp and Madrid, in 1855, Haussmann increased the Bois's surface area by 400 ha and extended its limits all the way to the Seine. It was on part of this newly acquired terrain that the Hippodrome de Longchamp was opened in 1857, continuing the tradition of horse racing at the Bois begun by the Comte d'Artois. Later, in 1873, the Hippodrome d'Auteuil opened on the Paris side of the Bois. It was during the belle époque that the Bois de Boulogne reached its peak as a mondain pleasure ground, attracting le tout Paris for trysts, drives and promenades.

Today the Bois faces an uncertain future. Since the building of the boulevard périphérique (Paris's notorious ring motorway) in the 1960s, it has been physically cut off from the city it is meant to serve along much of its eastern frontier. Invaded by leisure and sports facilities, which have eaten up 160 ha, the Bois now only counts about 150 ha of unadulterated woodland. Each morning it is crossed by 13,000 cars (more than on the Autoroutes du Sud and de l'Est put together). Moreover, over 40% of the Bois's surface was devastated by the December 1999 hurricane, which destroyed thousands of trees overnight. A major programme of replanting has begun, and discussions are underway to sort out the Bois's long-term development.

29.2 Château de Bagatelle
François-Joseph Bélanger, 1777–86
(Métro: Porte Maillot, Porte Dauphine, Porte d'Auteuil)
A »bagatelle« is an unimportant trinket, and the first aristocratic house on this site – built for the Maréchal Duc d'Estrées in 1720 – was ironically baptized thus, for despite its small dimensions it cost over 100,000 livres. In 18C France, »bagatelle« was also a euphemism for sex, and the château fulfilled this signification of its name through the efforts of the raunchy Maréchale. It became notorious as a centre of debauchery and court intrigue, a reputation its subsequent owner, the Marquise de Monconseil, did nothing to diminish. She, however, ruined herself through fast living, and the house eventually fell into dereliction. In 1777, following its purchase on a whim by the Comte d'Artois (brother of Louis XVI) in 1775, Marie-Antoinette joked that she would come and dine at Bagatelle in two months, and bet her brother-in-law 100,000 livres that the château would not be ready in time. The Comte rose to the challenge, and 900 workmen toiled day and night to build a new house to designs by the Comte's Premier Architecte, François-Joseph Bélanger. Begun on 21 September, the château was finished on 26 November. The Comte thus won his bet, although decoration of the house and landscaping of the gardens was not completed until 1786. In all, his »trinket« cost over 2 million livres.

The motto above the château's main entrance reads »Parva sed apta«, which roughly translates as »Small but well-adapted«. The vogue for this kind of small-scale aristocratic residence began during the reign of Louis XV, when the king and many of his courtiers sought refuge from the rigid etiquette of Versailles (32.1) in more intimate surroundings. Bélanger's design was delightfully simple. Square in plan and three bays wide on each side, it was articulated symmetrically around a small central staircase, behind which rose the double-height, round salon which half-protrudes from the garden façade. The ground floor contained reception rooms, and was given piano nobile proportions, while the low upper storey contained bedrooms. Treatment of the exterior was light, with banded rustication below the eaves-level cornice, niches either side of the main entrance, and a small attic storey decorated with friezes rising above the central bay. The main entrance, surmounted by a small lunette and columned canopy, appeared more town-house than princely. During the 19C, the exterior aspect of the château was ruined when its then owner, the Marquess of Hertford, raised the height of the first floor, widened the windows and added fussy detailing. In its day, the château was famed for its interior, particularly the count's bedroom, decorated as a

29.2 Château de Bagatelle

military allegory in the form of a tent held up by bundles of spears, with cannon supporting the chimneypiece. Paradoxically, the building containing servants' quarters and services, situated to the south of the *cour d'honneur*, was bigger than the château itself, to which it was linked by a tunnel.

Bagatelle was especially celebrated for its gardens, designed by Bélanger and the Scotsman Thomas Blaikie. Its 14 ha were landscaped *à l'anglaise* – one of the earliest English-style gardens in France – with sinuous pathways and clustered copses, although French love of artifice found expression in the numerous *fabriques* dotted here and there – a Swiss house, a Dutch house, an Indian pavilion, and so on. None survive bar the »grand rocher« (great rock) and its theatrical cascade of water. Hertford subsequently extended the gardens by 10 ha, and had them re-landscaped by Louis-Sulpice Varé, who added further pools and grottoes. The Marquess also built the orangery, the stables, and the Louis-Quinze entrance gateway. His heir, Sir Richard Wallace (of fountain fame – see feature on street furniture), demolished the original services building to lengthen the *cour d'honneur*, and built in its stead the »Trianon« which we see today. Bagatelle was bought by the Ville de Paris in 1905 and its grounds replanted by Jean-Claude-Nicolas Forestier, who, inspired by his friend Monet's garden at Giverny, created the château's famous rose garden in 1906.

29.3 Maison Cook
6, rue Denfert-Rochereau
Le Corbusier and Pierre Jeanneret, 1926/27
(Métro: Boulogne-Jean-Jaurès)

Conceived the same year Le Corbusier codified his famous »five points of a new architecture«, the Maison Cook marked an important breakthrough in the architect's œuvre, for it was the first building to which he applied all these principles together in a tentative but convincing demonstration of his theories. Commissioned by an American friend of Corb's, the journalist and painter William Cook, and situated a stone's throw away from the Bois de Boulogne (29.1), the house occupies a relatively narrow plot enclosed between party walls, meaning that its public face consists of only one, essentially planar façade. The elevation thus defined is roughly square, as is the building's plan perimeter, making the edifice a cube, one of the ideal, »Platonic« forms of which Corb was so fond. But, as is immediately obvious, the Maison Cook has nothing of the primal simplicity of a cube, its orthogonal envelope being merely a virtual regulating principle containing what is in fact an extremely complex layering of space and construction.

Some of the measure of this complexity can be got from a comment made by Corb on the Maison Cook later in his career: »Here are applied with great clarity the certainties from discoveries to date: the *pilotis*, the roof garden, the free plan, the ribbon window sliding sideways. Regulating lines are automatically gen-

29.3 Maison Cook

erated by simple architectural elements at a human scale, which also controls the floor heights, the window dimensions, doors and railings. The classic plan is turned upside down: the underneath of the house is free. The main reception room is right on top of the house. You step directly on to the roof garden from which you have a commanding view of the Bois de Boulogne. One is in Paris no longer; it is as if one were in the countryside.«

The »certainties from discoveries to date« are of course the famous five points, which Corb combined into what he intended to be a generic, universally applicable solution to house-building the world over. The essential of these points was the *pilotis*, and to understand the Maison Cook one must first examine this aspect of its design. Given its limited scale, the house could have been built in basically its current form using only traditional load-bearing walls, but with the crucial difference that its plan would have been restricted by immovable masses of masonry. With the *pilotis* system of concrete-framed construction, the floor plans could take on any form they wanted hindered only by freestanding columns, and Corb made clear this aspect of the Maison Cook's design through the use of curvilinear internal partitions that contrasted in their sinuosity with the building's rectilinear envelope. The use of *pilotis* at the Maison Cook was in fact rather timid, but Corb nonetheless rhetorically highlighted their fundamental importance to his architectural philosophy by exposing one slender central support at the ground-floor entrance to the house. When the Maison Cook was first completed, the ground floor was entirely open apart from the concierge's lodge and main entrance, demonstrating Corb's urbanistic doctrine whereby the city of the future would be raised up above ground to facilitate free circulation of vehicles. *Pilotis* also had other advantages: they cut contact between accommodation and the dampness of the ground, they reduced building costs since minimum excavation work was needed for their construction, and the space reclaimed at ground level could, theoretically, be given over to gardens, a fact suggested at the Maison Cook by the flower box set underneath the overhang. Ground space would also be reclaimed at roof level with terraces and gardens, a complementarity highlighted in the façade composition of the Maison Cook by the diagonal opposition of the main space underneath the house (the garage), at bottom left, with the opening of the roof terrace, at top right. *Pilotis* construction was the way of achieving all of this, hence its emphasis bang in the middle of the composition, further highlighted by the curved volume of the concierge's lodge behind. Exposure of load-bearing supports in this way would subsequently become something of an architectural cliché; the Maison Cook's ground-floor composition was directly reproduced by Ginsberg and Lubetkin in their Avenue-de-Versailles apartment building (16.15), and the device is still much copied today.

Strip (ribbon) windows were another of the five points, employed by Corb ostensibly because they let in maximum light but clearly also because their horizontality contrasted startlingly with traditional, vertically orientated fenestration, producing a sleek, modern, machine-age allure. They also demonstrated another advantage of concrete-frame, *pilotis* construction, namely the liberation of the façade from load-bearing constraints, making it »free«, like the plan, to take on whatever openings, solids or projections the architect desired. At the Maison Cook we see an advance in Corb's techniques over previous buildings: where, for example, at the Villas La Roche and Jeanneret-Raaf (16.13) the strip windows are chopped up by thin slivers of load-bearing masonry, those of the Maison Cook run uninterrupted across the entire elevation, with the central *pilotis* visibly rising behind them. Keen to demonstrate that free façades did not have to be flat, Corb balanced the composition of the Maison Cook's street front with a projecting balcony at top left, like the bridge of an ocean liner, which indicates the presence of the main living room behind. The living room is in fact a double-height space, and was clearly a reproduction of the main living space of the famous Pavillon de l'Esprit Nouveau conceived for the 1925 Exposition des Arts Décoratifs. Contemporary photographs showed its original industrial-age Purist décor: *objet-type* furnishings (oriental rugs, Mapple armchairs and bare light bulbs), immaculate wall and ceiling surfaces and sleek radiator and window engineering. The traditional domestic stacking order was of course entirely reversed at the Maison Cook, with bedrooms, etc. on the first floor and the main living spaces on the second floor, a configuration allowing the latter to connect directly with the roof terrace. In the Corbusian city of the future, roof terraces would replace traditional space-consuming gardens with the added benefits of views and fresher air that their elevation above the noisy street allowed. At the Maison Cook, in contrast to previous Corbusian buildings, the roof terrace's importance is highlighted by its location within the virtual cube defining the volumetric limits of the house. Even more than the earlier Villa Jeanneret-Raaf, the Maison Cook was a manifesto adaptation of traditional terraced-house urbanism (narrow plots defined by the street line and party walls), which, thanks to the miracle of concrete-frame, *pilotis* construction, could be turned upside down and infused with all the benefits of the *esprit nouveau*.

It is worth mentioning the Maison Cook's neighbours, this area of Boulogne constituting a sort of open-air museum of inter-war design. Just next door, at no. 4, is an *hôtel particulier* built by Raymond Fischer in 1927/28 with a contorted interior derived from the application of Adolf Loos's »Raumplan« theory. On the other side of the Maison Cook, at no. 8, is the Hôtel Collinet (1926) by Robert Mallet-Stevens, a good example of his suave brand of the International Style. Together these three villas form a quite extraordinary triptych of early Modernism. The Hôtel Collinet came first, then the Maison Cook and finally Fischer's house; it is interesting to note that while Corb entirely ignored the proportions of Mallet-Stevens's house (except where the regulation-set roofline was concerned), Fischer chose to align his openings and fenestration with those of the Maison Cook. Just up the street from this trio, on the roundabout (junction of the Rue Gambetta and the Avenue Jean-Baptiste-Clément), is a house/artist's studio built by Pierre Patout for the painter Alfred Lombard in 1928. Patout and Lombard met on the project of the ocean liner *Ile-de-France*, which they had been hired to decorate. With a symmetrical, V-shaped plan owing more to the French Classical tradition than to the Modern Movement, Lombard's house is dominated by the glazed box of his studio, which is perched on the building's summit. Moving back up the Avenue Denfert-Rochereau past the Maison Cook, we come to the Immeuble Ternisien, at the junction with the Allée des Pins. It was begun by Le Corbusier as a villa/studio (1923–27) to be realized on a very tight budget. Subsequently finding themselves on the verge of bankruptcy, the owners called in Georges-Henri Pingusson to reconfigure and extend the building (1933–36) into the five-storey apartment block we see today. Its wedge-shaped corner plot evidently suggested a ship, and Pingusson produced a building in what the French call »ocean-liner« style, complete with portholes and roof-top promenade deck. Finally, at nos. 7 and 9, allée des Pins, are the Maison Miestchaninoff and the Atelier Lipchitz (1924/1925), both by Corb and Jeanneret and built for the sculptors Oscar Miestchaninoff and Jacques Lipchitz. Although considered secondary in Corb's œuvre, they present an interesting and essentially unmodified example of his early Purist creations, and the elevations of the Villa Miestchaninoff make clear his reliance on the golden section and other classic proportioning devices when designing his buildings.

29.4 Immeuble Molitor
24, rue Nungesser-et-Coli and 23, rue de la Tourelle
Le Corbusier and Pierre Jeanneret, 1931–34
(Métro: Michel-Ange Molitor, Porte d'Auteuil)

The traditional Parisian speculative apartment building, with its deep plan squeezed between impregnable party walls, has long challenged architects' ingenuity. On the one occasion he was faced with this particular conundrum, here at the Immeuble Molitor, Le Corbusier once again demonstrated his unfailing inventiveness. The site presented one natural advantage in that it was orientated almost exactly east–west – the ideal Corbusian configuration – but otherwise presented all the classic inconveniences of party-wall plots, being narrow (12 m) and deep (24 m). This left Corb little choice but to dispose the apartments back to back and, despite their free plan, they are laid out fairly conventionally. The site's narrowness made light wells unavoidable; to render them fully effective and avoid vis-à-vis across a squalid shaft, Corb faced the light wells' surfaces entirely in glass bricks.

But it was on the building's exterior façades that glass made its most spectacular appearance. No doubt inspired by the Maison de Verre (7.17), on whose building site he had several times been spotted surreptitiously sketching, Corb designed audacious all-glass elevations. Identical on both façades, they improved on Chareau's prototype by including opening, transparent fenestration as well as frosted Nevada glass bricks, the latter being reserved only for the »wall« parts of the elevations. Externally the window/glass-brick contrast reads as solid and void, but internally the apartments are flooded with light across the entire wall surface. The various elements of the façades are held together by a black-painted steel frame, making for a truly engineered aesthetic and adding a certain materiality to the building, an impression reinforced by the cantilevered central projection, whose sides and underneath are opaque. The central cantilever both demonstrates the »freeness« of the elevations (as does the recessed ground floor with its exposed central column) and plays with our notions of gravity and weight, appearing far too heavy to hang where it does. Corb's futurist façades make for a striking contrast with the Immeuble Molitor's stone-clad, stripped-Classical neighbours, for example Michel Roux-Spitz's bow-fronted apartment building (1931) at 22, rue Nungesser-et-Coli (remarkably similar to his Quai-d'Orsay flats (7.6)). But even Corb's steel-and-glass architecture was copied and adapted by Classically minded admirers: for their apartment building at 5, avenue Vion-Whitcomb, 16th (1935/36), Jean Ginsberg and François Heep reproduced the Immeuble Molitor's façades in stone!

Corb reserved the building's last two storeys for his own private studio/apartment, which he occupied until his death. He arranged the rooms so as to eliminate corridors and minimize the number of doors, and covered the ensemble with a shallow barrel vault, a cherished motif which he would famously return to at the Maisons Jaoul (26.2). Corb's apartment is now owned by the Fondation Le Corbusier (see 16.13) and can be visited by appointment.

29.5 Hôtel de Ville
26, avenue André-Morizet
Tony Garnier, with Jacques Debat-Ponsan, 1926–34
(Métro: Marcel Sembat)

Ranked amongst the great theorists of French 20C architecture, Tony Garnier was renowned for his imaginary Cité Industrielle of 1904, a rationally-planned, socialist utopia, which was greatly to influence Le Corbusier. Garnier subsequently became municipal architect of his native Lyons, where he worked almost exclusively until his death. His only built project outside Lyons was the *hôtel de ville* at Boulogne-Billancourt, commissioned by the socialist mayor, André Morizet. Garnier is reputed to have accepted the job by saying that as he

29.4 Immeuble Molitor

29.5 Hôtel de Ville

could never build the town hall of his Cité Moderne in Lyons – because Lyons's old *hôtel de ville* would never be replaced – he might therefore try in Boulogne.

Morizet and his council had fairly specific ideas about what was required. They had been impressed by the town hall of Schaerbeck, in Belgium, which featured a large central hall around which public services were disposed. For ideological and budgetary reasons, Morizet wanted a building devoid of decoration, what he dubbed a »municipal factory«. A prominent clock tower, which was a central feature of Garnier's preliminary proposals, was consequently omitted from the final scheme. The new town hall was originally intended to replace the old *hôtel de ville* of Boulogne, but was subsequently relocated to a new, virgin site at the geographic centre of the *commune*, in a move to unite symbolically the two communities of Boulogne and Billancourt.

Garnier's building is indeed undecorated, to the point of austerity, but nonetheless makes clear its civic consequence through its proportions and imposing dimensions. It is divided into two distinct parts: the smaller, southern section, which houses the council chamber, mayor's office and reception rooms, and which, in keeping with its official character, is faced in stone; and the more functional public-service block abutting it to the north, which resembles Garnier's drawings for the exhibition hall of his Cité Industrielle, and which exposes the reinforced concrete of its rhythmic façade to the light of day. A colossal projecting cornice unites the two sections. As at Schaerbeck, the public services are grouped around a central atrium, thus avoiding the dingy corridors and disorientating floor plans common to so many town halls. The atrium, a magnificent five-storey, galleried space, has preserved its moderne fittings. The offices surrounding it are equipped with moveable partitions, for maximum flexibility, and are entirely day lit. The reception rooms are also modifiable, and are reached by way of an imposing *escalier d'honneur*.

Unanimously praised at the time of its inauguration, Garnier's design is in a tradition of French Rational Classicism which found expression in much official and establishment architecture of the inter-war period. The *hôtel de ville* at Boulogne-Billancourt, which has remained entirely unaltered, admirably fulfils its functions to this day

29.6 Ile Seguin
Redevelopment due to begin late 2003
(Métro: Pont de Sèvres)

Until the aftermath of WWI, this 11.5 ha, crescent-shaped island sitting in a bend in the Seine between Boulogne and Meudon was a haven of greenery, disturbed only by the odd villa here and there or by the river's annual floods. Then, in 1920, Louis Renault, head of the car-manufacturing firm, set his sights on the island; his factory had swallowed up all available land on the Boulogne bank of the river opposite, and the Ile Seguin was the only possible space left onto which his automobile empire could expand. At first it was just a question of providing sports grounds, allotments and other leisure facilities for his workers, but as of 1923 very different plans began to be drawn up. The island was raised by 3 m across its entire surface to provide a flat, flood-free *tabula rasa* onto which a huge new car factory could be built that would allow Renault to fulfil his dream of introducing Taylorist, production-line working methods into France. By the 1930s this dream had become reality: 12,000 men were employed on the island in a six-level industrial citadel that comprised 774,000 m^2 of floor space containing 118 workshops and its own power station to ensure total autonomy. Two bridges allowed raw materials to roll in and 69,300 completed cars to roll out every year. As a built mass the factory presented a quite extraordinary aspect, Renault's ever-increasing space needs having meant that not a square inch of the island was left uncovered, with a heterogeneous assortment of iron-framed and concrete buildings stretching ever on down its longest axis, their generously glazed and white-rendered façades giving the ensemble the air of a cyclopean ocean liner moored precariously in the Seine.

It was the impossibility of expanding in this restricted site and the eccentric working practices that resulted from its topography – cars progressed randomly up and down several levels on their way round the factory – that finally prompted the Ile Seguin's closure in 1992. The question remained, of course, of what to do with this rapidly deteriorating industrial leftover, and Renault and the municipality of Boulogne-Billancourt initially opted for complete redevelopment, making public their plans to demolish the factory and replace it with offices and housing in 1998. Their proposals were not limited to just the Ile Seguin but also included the 31.5 ha of Renault's mainland workshops. But Renault and the local councillors had not counted on the national interest raised by the site nor on the sentimental attachment felt by many towards the island, this having been the spot where numerous French social-employment battles had first been fought and won. It was the architect Jean Nouvel who sounded the alarm in a March-1999 article in Le Monde, in which, comparing the Ile Seguin to a crusaders' castle, he called for at least partial preservation of the existing fabric out of respect both for France's industrial heritage and the thousands who had worked there, and also because its »architectless architecture« was infinitely more exciting than the bland gentrification Renault and the municipality were proposing. But Nouvel had not taken into account a major obstacle, namely that the factory was made up of a disparate collection of cheaply constructed and therefore poor-quality buildings never intended to last, which, moreover, had rapidly deteriorated in the years following the site's closure. Their conservation and conversion were thus for the most part impossible, and replacement was the only option.

Nonetheless, the fuss raised by Nouvel et al. prompted Renault and the municipality to rethink their plans and commission an entirely new redevelopment scheme. At the time of writing nothing has been fixed in stone, but the general outlines of the Ile Seguin's rebuilding have been drawn up. In 2000, millionaire businessman François Pinault struck a deal with Renault and the public authorities to build a new contemporary-art museum on 3.2 ha of the island's northwestern tip (29.7); scheduled for completion in 2005, it will certainly be the pièce de résistance of the whole redevelopment. The municipality has decided to complement this future bastion of the arts with a cité of the sciences, to include university and business premises. In acknowledgement of the island's future dual role, and perhaps in a bid to obscure its industrial (i.e. militant) past, it is to be rechristened »L'île des deux cultures«. Planned for a timeframe of ten years, development will also include rebuilding of Renault's mainland site, which is to become a mixed-use extension of Boulogne-Billancourt's existing fabric. Architect Patrick Chavannes's reconstruction scheme aims to create a leafy neighbourhood whose street plan will follow the cues given by the surrounding urbanity. Also in the pipeline is new tramway to link Boulogne and the Renault redevelopment to the neighbouring areas. As for the Ile Seguin, no less than three new bridges are proposed, one of which has been designed by Marc Barani.

Apart from the Musée Pinault, no detailed designs have yet been produced for any of the Ile Seguin's proposed new or rehabilitated buildings, but a team of architects, urbanists and landscape designers has drawn up reconstruction guidelines. Their proposals consist of five principles: 1. preservation of the island's 3 m-high artificial plinth; 2. creation of a pedestrian quayside round the entire isle; 3. attempted recreation, perhaps through the use of screens and cantilevers, of the bastion-like effect of the Renault factory's sheer walls; 4. opening up of the island's interior with at least 4.5 ha of non-built, public spaces; 5. ensuring visual coherence within the broad context of the Seine valley. Loose in scope, these principles still leave a lot of room for manœuvre, and it is therefore difficult to predict what the final ensemble will be like. One can only hope that the obvious contradiction between points 2 and 3 will not lead to overly unfortunate compromise. And before building work can even begin, the thorny question of who will pay for the hugely expensive initial demolition and depollution works must be resolved, a subject of dispute that could yet scotch the whole scheme.

29.7 Musée Pinault
Northwestern tip of the Ile Seguin, Boulogne-Billancourt
Tadao Ando, 2001–05
(Métro: Pont de Sèvres)

Flagship project in the Ile-Seguin redevelopment scheme (29.6), the 32,000 m², 150-million-euro Musée Pinault is intended to provide a home for the reputedly fantastic collection of contemporary art built up by millionaire French businessman François Pinault. With works reportedly both numerous and prestigious enough to rival London's Tate Gallery, New York's Museum of Modern Art or Paris's own Centre Pompidou (4.15), this will be France's most resplendent private art museum. Tadao Ando's design for its building was chosen from a limited competition in October 2001 and, if all goes ahead as planned, construction will begin in mid 2003 for completion in late 2005. The brief called for a »certain religiosity« in the new museum, which should project a spirit somewhere »between a Romanesque chapel and a Gothic cathedral«, as well as, in Pinault's words, making visitors »feel better on leav-

29.6 Ile Seguin

29.7 Musée Pinault

ing«. Ando's only work in France to date is his Meditation Space (7.11) in the garden of UNESCO (7.10), and it may well be that Pinault, who reportedly favoured Ando above all the other competitors from the outset, was thinking of the powerful effect of this small but emotive building when commissioning his museum.

The site acquired for the Musée occupies 3.2 ha at the northwestern tip of the Ile Seguin facing the Pont de Sèvres, and thus benefits from all the excitement of the surrounding riverscape. 300 m in length and 130 m in width at its broadest point, its shape clearly suggests a ship, and, given its watery setting, a naval form was the obvious solution for any building constructed there (indeed the Renault factories that initially stood here resembled an ocean liner). Ando has not entirely disappointed such expectations, although he prefers to describe his scheme as »aquatic spaceship«. Pinault said he wanted a building that would »escape fashion«, and described Ando's scheme as »timeless« (»intemporel«). Anyone familiar with the Japanese architect's work will know that his calm, reflective, »monumentally minimalist« buildings are a far cry from the fireworks of a Frank Gehry (to whose Bilbao Guggenheim the Musée Pinault's programme has frequently been compared) or the trendy contrariness of a Rem Koolhaas (one of the architects who lost to Ando in the Pinault competition). Ando's museum will be a classic, rational, serene architectural object, whose interior will have been as scrupulously and meticulously thought through as its exterior – in other words the opposite of a Centre-Pompidou-style supermarket of art.

The Musée Pinault is to comprise three principal layers: a concrete podium at water level, inside which will be housed administrative spaces and the museum's library, a ship's-bow-shaped concrete storey at the summit, mounted on *pilotis* and containing the top-lit galleries of the permanent collections, and, sandwiched between the two, an entirely glass-fronted floor comprising temporary-exhibition space. Rising to 28 m, two long, box-shaped volumes in glass will poke out from the building's rear like the superstructure of a ship, overlooking a generous garden. The museum is to follow the contours of the island, taking on its quirks and asymmetries; at the heart of this perimeter plan will be a wedge-shaped, open-air courtyard whose tip will terminate in a circular, glass-roofed atrium that will act as the building's circulation hub. Leading off the atrium and rising between the box-shaped volumes, a monumental *escalier d'honneur* (no French public building should be without one!) will conduct visitors to the upstairs galleries. Echoing this feature externally, at the island's prow, more monumental steps will descend to the water, encased in high, transparent glass walls. Indeed although Ando's favourite material is raw concrete, much of the Musée Pinault will be encased in glass to make it as shiny and reflective as the water on which it will sit. Through the building's form, Ando hopes to evoke the physical memory of the old Renault factory in the interests of »continuity of history«, but avoiding all nostalgia so as to »regenerate« a 20C »industrial fortress into a cultural fortress of the 21C«.

30 Saint-Cloud

30.1 Parc de Saint-Cloud

Antoine Le Pautre, 1664–65; André Le Nôtre, c. 1668 (Métro: Boulogne Pont de Saint-Cloud; the park is across the bridge on the other side of the river)

Situated on a hillside bordering the meandering Seine, the Parc de Saint-Cloud was created for the château of the same name. Probably begun in the 1570s, the château was purchased, in 1658, by Monsieur, Duc d'Orléans and brother of Louis XIV, who began a major programme of enlargement and embellishment. Work lasted almost 50 years and was chiefly carried out by Le Pautre and Jean Girard, with later interventions by Jules Hardouin-Mansart. The château was the setting for several important events in French history, the most spectacular being its destruction in 1870 by the invading Prussians. All that now remain are the stables, kitchens and offices.

Happily, the château's gardens, which were also remodelled at the behest of Monsieur, survive. Amongst the first embellishments commissioned by the duke was the famous Grande Cascade, perhaps the most spectacular 17C fountain in France. Built by Le Pautre (perhaps aided by Le Nôtre), it takes the form of a two-arch, bridge-like structure, from which descends a row of five cascades, terminating in a semicircular pool. The cascade is studded with countless fountains and jets of water, many of which spout from urns or from the mouths of grotesque creatures. Dribbling, dripping rustication accentuates the watery effect, and the ensemble is crowned by personifications of local rivers. A canal, added by Hardouin-Mansart in 1698/99, prolongs the cascade onto the flood-plain of the Seine, thus thematically linking the gardens and the river (a relationship today spoiled by the four-lane motorway on the river bank).

Le Nôtre's interventions, which encompassed the entire park, took the château as one of the focal points. Situated halfway up the hillside, the U-shaped house opened out onto commanding views across the Seine towards Paris in the east. Le Nôtre established no direct relationship between house and river (although autographed plans survive for a grand, terraced avenue linking the château to the Seine), but instead created two magisterial axes which extend from the house towards the northern and western horizons. Despite the often sharp undulations of the hillside site, he not only managed to impose a complex, geometrical system of straight avenues onto the terrain, but also benefited from the landscape's irregularities. The western axis, which departed from the château's garden front, com-

30.1 Parc de Saint-Cloud

prises star-shaped intersections around imposing basins and features, either side of the château's esplanade, jets of water designed to catch the setting sun. The northern axis, which departed from the château's southern wing, is visually the most splendid, commencing with an impressive pool and then climbing sharply up the steep hillside opposite. Le Nôtre skilfully planted the gardens with a combination of trees and parterres to give them a pronounced chiaroscuro effect as they descend towards the river.

30.2 Villa dall'Ava

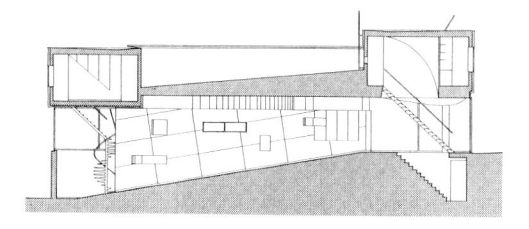

30.2 Villa dall'Ava
7, avenue Clodoald
OMA Rem Koolhaas, 1982–91
(Tram (from La Défense): Les Coteaux; SNCF: Gare Val d'Or)

In the decade following completion of this house, Rem Koolhaas firmly established himself as the high priest of the architectural avant garde, an ironic fate if ever there was one given his professed contempt for the architectural star system. An inspiration to classrooms-full of eager students, his every aphorism, despite famously uncharismatic delivery, is seized upon for debate. Still better known for his provocative theories and publications than for his built output, Pritzker-Prize-winning Koolhaas translates little of his polemic into his architectural projects, essentially because his writings are chiefly concerned with the »undesigned« spaces produced by the market forces of international capitalism, and with the impotence of the architectural profession in the face of this phenomenon. Instead his buildings generally evolve from a raspberry-blowing critique of previous generations of architects' work, in good, old-fashioned rebel-boy style, and as a result it often turns out that what his designs are not is as important as what they are. In this early project, realized in the wealthy western-Parisian suburb of Saint-Cloud, it was suburbanism and the iconic villas of the Modern Movement that provided Koolhaas with suitably provocative grist for his mill.

Saint-Cloud's privileged hillside position overlooking Paris and the Seine led to its development at the turn of the 20C with large, solid, brick-and-stone vernacular villas. Koolhaas's clients, a wealthy couple, had acquired a 650 m² walled garden in the midst of this suburban villadom, on which they wanted to build a resolutely modern house. Commissioning a young, polemical and at the time untried architect says a lot about their pluck. They did not, however, wish to give Koolhaas total *carte blanche* to do as he pleased, and had specific ideas about what they wanted from the house. It was to provide accommodation for them and their teenage daughter, whose rooms were to be autonomous from theirs; the garden was to be respected, and the living spaces were to be glass walled to allow full advantage to be taken of the surrounding greenery; the house was to include a swimming pool, ideally on the roof; and – a tacit requirement – the result should be a »masterpiece« (as Koolhaas ironically put it). This programme was clearly full of inherent contradictions, which no doubt greatly appealed to Koolhaas, genie of the contrary. Firstly, the site was small (650 m²) but the house was comparatively big (250 m² of accommodation). Secondly, the programme was essentially that of an isolated villa in the countryside, but its context was resoundingly suburban. And thirdly, how was one to put a swimming pool on top of living areas made of glass?

Much of Koolhaas's work, both theoretical and built, can be read as a critique of Modernism, and the Villa dall'Ava is no exception. The obvious Modernist precedents for this kind of programme were buildings such as Le Corbusier's Villas Stein-de Monzie (31.1) and Savoye (25.2), Mies van der Rohe's Farnsworth House (1946–51, Plano, Illinois) and Philip Johnson's Glass House (1947–49, New Canaan, Connecticut). But as Koolhaas was well aware, the context of his villa was not that of any of these houses; it could not be a »magical object floating in an infinite landscape«, but had to »find its place in a very dense context, violently anti-modern«, as he described it. It fell to him to devise »the most delicate and minimal way to exploit the site«, which was »so fragile that any brutal form, like a cube, would simply kill it«. A simple, »Platonic« volume the Villa dall'Ava certainly is not, although its highly complex design does include box-shaped elements. For Koolhaas the garden wall was the real limit of the house, the villa itself being but a secondary partition within this primary space. To avoid »killing« the site he devised a long, narrow composition embedded in the slope of the terrain at its rear, alongside which space »flows«, to use Koolhaas's description of the compositional flux. Already we see Koolhaas's spirit of contradiction coming out, for in this basement storey, in pure defiance of expectation and common sense, he placed a family room lit only by a narrow skylight. Elsewhere the house is classically organized, with the main living spaces at garden level and bedrooms etc. on the first floor. This upper level comprises two laterally orientated rectangular accommodation boxes – one for the clients' daughter, on the street, and the other for the clients themselves, at the rear facing onto the garden – that are separated by a more elongated third box running perpendicularly between them and containing the swimming pool. Perched up on the roof with stunning views over Paris and the Eiffel Tower (7.8), the swimming pool should have represented the summit of luxury living. But Koolhaas declared himself to be »annoyed« by its beautiful setting and deliberately made the pool difficult to get to, with only a ladder-like folding metal staircase providing access. Of the »event« created by the swimming pool and its view he said: »Although I find it quite moving, I did everything I could to prevent that moment from becoming the apotheosis of the house. The house is not a single trajectory leading towards that ultimate experience.« In other words, the pool was not to become the climax of a Le-Corbusier-style *promenade architecturale*. Confounding expectations and the teachings of masters is to a certain extent what the Villa dall'Ava is all about.

We see this tendency again in the building's structural system. The swimming pool is supported on a row of *pilotis*, but, as we will find out when we descend to the ground floor, these are mostly hidden and deliberately unexpressed, flouting the Rationalist dogma that structure should be clearly revealed. Structure looks like it is being revealed in the daughter's accommodation box on the street, since a whole forest of skinny *pilotis* rises under it (through which one much pass to reach the front door), but an analysis of the house's design proves otherwise. Although one reads these *pilotis* as traditional load-bearing supports, they are in fact in tension, pulling the accommodation box down towards the ground and preventing it from flying upwards under the effect of the heavy cantilever of the parents' accommodation box at the other end of the building. The imagery of the Villa Savoye's famous *pilotis* is here wickedly subverted. The garden-level floor running underneath the swimming pool and the parents' accommodation box is entirely glass-walled, reproducing the goldfish-bowl living of the Farnsworth and Glass Houses. Its glass envelope can in places be slid entirely back allowing the living room and garden to merge as one. As we have already noted, the pillars supporting the swimming pool are hidden, as it turns out dissimulated within wooden storage units, and we are thus left with the illusion that the pool, which weighs a whopping 40 tonnes when full, is magically hovering on thin partitions of glass, in contradiction of all laws of physics and Structural Rationalism. On seeing the plans, the horrified next-door neighbours complained that all this glazing would infringe privacy regulations, to which Koolhaas responded by proposing the use of frosted glass for the principal section of wall overlooking the adjoining plot. But the neighbours were not satisfied and took the matter to court, no doubt hoping to scotch the whole project, whose uncompromising aesthetic is perhaps hard for some villadom dwellers to swallow. After three years' interruption in building work, the matter was finally resolved in Koolhaas's clients' favour when the Conseil d'Etat, France's highest civil court, ruled that a frosted-glass wall was a wall and not a window, thereby making architectural jurisprudence.

Johnson's Glass House has been described as one of the world's most beautiful yet least functional homes. Koolhaas in his work to date has always shied away from traditional notions of beauty, which, he says, are »lazy« and bound up with conventional responses conditioned by a tyranny of the elegant. If any of his buildings starts to get overly elegant he will deliberately seek to rough it up a little. At the Villa dall'Ava this comes through in his choice of materials – raw concrete, corrugated aluminium cladding, net fencing on the roof and, in an ironic nod towards next-door villadom, stone »crazy-paving« cladding – and in the blandly utilitarian way the house's exterior is put together, in total defiance of the cult of the picturesque that characterizes the surrounding buildings. Even while sharing exactly their programme, the Villa dall'Ava seeks to antagonize its neighbours, reproducing but at the same time parodying the comfortable, domestic middle-classness they represent. But then, as we have seen, the classic Modernist, »design« alternatives to 19C villadom are also subverted in this house. When asked in an interview why he is so famous, Koolhaas replied: »I'm still able to disappoint expectations. That's an important freedom.« But does contrariness make for good architecture? Taken to extremes, probably not, but Koohaas's mild-mannered games could hardly be considered extreme. And while the Villa dall'Ava will annoy all those it was intended to annoy, it will also please all those who share Koolhaas's dry sense of humour.

31 Garches / Vaucresson

31.1 Villa Stein-de Monzie (»Les Terrasses«)
17, rue du Professeur-Victor-Pauchet
Le Corbusier and Pierre Jeanneret, 1926–28
(SNCF: Garches-Marnes-la-Coquette; then follow the Avenues Joffre, Foch and du Maréchal-Leclerc to the town centre, from where the Rue Athime-Rué leads up to the Rue du Professeur-Victor-Pauchet)

One of the iconic buildings of Le Corbusier's Purist period, and indeed of the entire early Modern Movement, the Villa Stein-de Monzie is located north of the Parc de Saint-Cloud (30.1) in the suburb of Garches (now part of Vaucresson), which in the 1920s was still distinctly rural. While the house's original interior is no more, having been subdivided in the 1950s, its façades remain essentially intact, bar certain alterations to the terraces. The villa was commissioned by Michael and Sarah Stein (brother and sister-in-law of Gertrude) and Gabrielle de Monzie as a shared dwelling that would benefit from both the countryside and the nearby capital, which thanks to the recently invented motor car could quickly be reached. The plot acquired for the house was long and narrow and Corb chose to exploit this to dramatic effect by situating the building half way down it, allowing for a majestic approach in the manner of a 17C château yet still providing a sizeable rear garden. A single-storey, white-stucco porter's lodge announces the villa on the street, from where a long, off-centre gravel drive leads up to the house, terminating at the garage door and thereby highlighting the centrality of the motor car in machine-age living. Corb's care with regard to the planting of the grounds, which included preserving existing trees on the site, ensured that the villa's approaches are quite splendid, especially today now that the gardens have matured. But the setting would be nothing if the jewel it contained was not up to par, and Corb made sure to supply a magnificent entrance front.

An enormous rectangle rising four storeys and filling most of the width of the plot, the entrance façade comprises a *tabula rasa* of pristine white render within which various elements are set. At ground-floor level we find the aforementioned garage door, the servants' entrance placed asymmetrically under a little cube-shaped balcony, a large area of industrial-looking glazing lighting the entrance hall, and the principal visitors' entrance, which distinguishes itself hierarchically from the servant's door by its greater size and by the giant canopy suspended above it on steel rods. Clearly a humorous, automobile-age reference to castle drawbridges, the canopy is a rare flash of playfulness from a generally poker-faced architect. At first- and second-floor level are strip windows running the entire width of the façade, right up to its edges, while above them, at third-floor level, is a central balcony sitting alone in an expanse of white stucco, seemingly destined for somebody to bestow a pontifical blessing on the trees below. The villa's entrance elevation reads superficially as a solid mass of masonry, but there are nonetheless indications that this is actually one of Corb's much-vaunted, non-load-bearing »free« façades hung off a concrete frame. The most obvious clue lies in the continuous bands of strip windows which, since entirely unbroken by intermediary or peripheral supports, could not possibly bear the weight of the blank third floor above were it really in solid masonry. This impression of weight supported on a void recalls the massing of the Doge's Palace in Venice and contributes much to the regal aspect of the façade, whose proportions were carefully worked out using regulating lines. The entrance front cleverly fuses the formal, Classically symmetrical with the asymmetrical, »vernacular« Modern, a synthesis which, as we shall see, was one of the generating principles of the entire design.

Unlike the later Villa Savoye (25.2), which sits in open space and whose square plan renders all its elevations of equal importance, the Villa Stein, again like a 17C château, presents only two principle façades – the wide entrance and garden fronts –, with distinctly secondary lateral façades squeezed out at the site's edges. So skipping over the side elevations, let us nip straight round the back to see what the garden front tells us about the building. The difference is striking, the entrance façade's Classical formality having given way to an informal, vernacular mood more suited to an elevation giving onto a private garden. There is thus a duality between front and back that neatly sums up the urban/rural opposition that qualifies the villa as an architectural type. The garden façade makes it quite clear that this is a concrete-framed edifice, since the left-hand side of the building dissolves into a void underneath the canopy of the third floor, considerable areas of glazing hang in a cantilever over the ground floor,

31.1 Villa Stein-de Monzie. Axonometric view

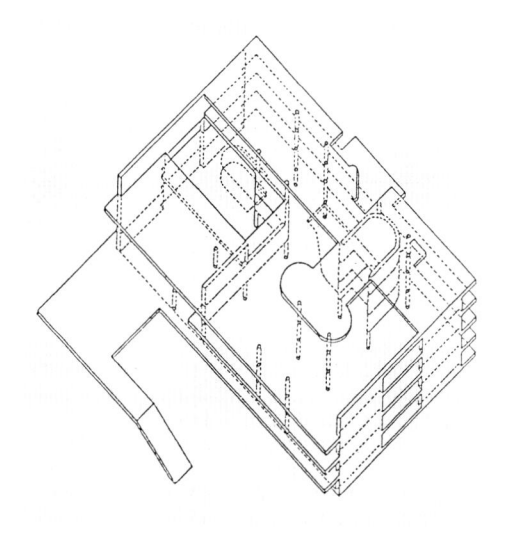

31.1 Villa Stein-de Monzie. Entrance front

and a good portion of the third floor turns out to be open to the sky and populated with asymmetrically placed objects resembling ship's funnels or deckhouses. A projecting terrace leads off the left-hand void and is connected to the ground via a staircase running parallel to the house, marking the final in a depth-revealing sequence of layers defined by the »internal« façades at the rear of the void, the limits of the external envelope and the projection of the terrace/stairs. It is interesting to note that in order to get the stairs to descend at just the right angle within the confines of the house's two central bays, Corb had to raise their base onto a little mound.

For those familiar with Corb's work, what is immediately striking about the Villa Stein is that externally there are no *pilotis* in sight. *Pilotis* were the essential of his famous »five points of a new architecture«, both the elemental supports of his concrete-frame system and a means of raising buildings up off the ground to liberate land for other uses. Interestingly, early schemes for the Villa Stein show a totally open ground floor perched on *pilotis*, like at the Maison Cook (29.3) or the Villa Savoye, but to achieve this Corb had had to place the servants' spaces in a rear, subsidiary wing. In the built project, however, he opted for maintaining a fixed, cuboid envelope into which all accommodation would be squeezed, and the ground-floor spaces consequently filled up with the service areas and the exposed *pilotis* disappeared. Of the remaining five points, three are clearly expressed on the garden elevation – the metal strip windows, the »free« façade, and the roof terrace, which allowed built-upon ground space to be reclaimed at attic level –, while the fifth, the free plan, became immediately evident on entering the house. Accommodation was divided up in classic bourgeois layers at the Villa Stein: main entrance and service spaces on the ground floor, principal »public« rooms on the first floor (traditionally always the *piano nobile* in grand houses), and bedrooms, bathrooms etc. at second- and third-floor level. The building's *pilotis*-supported concrete-frame system allowed each storey's plan to be free and entirely independent from the others, an advantage that Corb exploited to the maximum. Although the ground-floor service spaces were conventionally divided up along an L-shaped corridor, the meandering walls of the entrance hall gave a taste of what was to come. Having begun the villa's *promenade architecturale* by climbing the sinuous *escalier d'honneur*, visitors emerged on the first floor into a showpiece of the *esprit nouveau*. Divided up by only a couple of curving partitions, the main living areas flowed into each other in an airy sequence of spatial flux and *objet-type*

Garches/Vaucresson 331

minimalist furnishings that clearly owed their source to an allergic reaction to oppressively over-decorated and rigidly segregated *fin-de-siècle* interiors. While there was a sharp distinction between the Steins' and Gabrielle de Monzie's private apartments upstairs, the living spaces of the *piano nobile* were entirely shared, and in this respect the villa could perhaps be viewed as an aristocratic microcosm of the communal living that Corb was advocating in his designs for machine-age mass-housing units (one of the paradoxes of his early career being that ideas conceived for universal, mass housing could only be tried out in the rather precious projects of extremely wealthy clients). The living room gave onto the first of a series of terraces at each level of the house, whose significance in Corb's healthy-body-healthy-mind thinking came out in the Villa Stein's formal appellation, »Les Terrasses«. Moving on up, the *promenade architecturale* carried on through second and third floors articulated around eccentrically rambling partitions, until one finally arrived at the ultimate goal, namely the pontifical balcony on the entrance front. Clambering up to climaxes in this circuitous, Acropolis-inspired way was a feature of many Corbusian projects, here also analogous to an Alpine peak, with a seemingly unreachable point signalled on arrival being made the culmination of an arduous climb. Mme Stein allegedly declared she would never attempt the *escalade*, and it was reported that the house's owners had taken to calling it »Mont'là-d'sus« (»climb up there«) instead of »Les Terrasses«.

The Villa Stein featured as the second of Corb's famous four compositions published in 1929, labelled »very difficult (intellectual satisfaction)«. In a series of lectures he explained that what he meant by this was that »the compression of the internal organs inside an absolutely pure, rigid envelope« at the Villa Stein was a self-imposed »constraint« that had required considerable intellectual effort; in other words, rather as Classical architects had often had to use great ingenuity to maintain symmetrical plans within asymmetrical sites, so Corb had had to employ considerable inventiveness to squeeze his asymmetrical, »vernacular« free plan into a symmetrical, rigid container – the fusion of the Classical and the Modern once more. In this respect the Villa Stein contrasted with many of his previous buildings (e.g. the Villas La Roche and Jeanneret-Raaf, 16.13), and reflected a strain in his œuvre that began with the Maison Planeix (13.7) and continued with the Maison Cook, which was designed concurrently with the Villa Stein (although finished first). Both houses have only two principal façades (the Maison Cook is part of a terrace), and both are cuboid compositions where all elements, including roof terraces, are contained within an outer, rectangular envelope. But there is one essential difference between them, namely that the Villa Stein finally shows confident use of the *pilotis* system, whose full potential was exploited with significant peripheral cantilevers all around the building and free-standing supports inside.

Colin Rowe pointed out in his celebrated 1947 essay »The Mathematics of the Ideal Villa« that the grid plan regulating the location of *pilotis* and external walls at the Villa Stein is remarkably similar to that used by Palladio to divide up the interior of his Villa Malcontenta (1560), with the same ABABA sequence running from side to side in both. Although there is no evidence to show that Corb had specifically the Villa Malcontenta in mind when designing the Villa Stein, it is clear that he was well versed in Classical proportioning systems, and he himself said that at Garches, more than in any of his other projects, »proportion ruled absolutely there, as absolute mistress«. But, as we have seen, he seemed to be striving to combine the Classical with a new, freer, vernacular »Modern«, and this can be seen in the plan proportioning, there being a very telling difference between the Stein and Malcontenta villas' proportional systems in their front-to-back sequences. Palladio's runs $1\frac{1}{2}:2:2:1\frac{1}{2}$, thereby maintaining central emphasis, while Corb's runs $\frac{1}{2}:1\frac{1}{2}:1\frac{1}{2}:1\frac{1}{2}:\frac{1}{2}$, the initial and final $\frac{1}{2}$s corresponding to the cantilever of his floors beyond the building's concrete frame, thereby transferring interest to the periphery. The same can be said of the way he divided up the Villa Stein's interiors, which were organized »centrifugally« with, as Rowe put it, »peripheral dispersion of incident« instead of the traditional, Classical central focus.

The Villa Stein was one of the last, and most accomplished, of Corb's Purist-period creations. His aim in building it is perhaps best summed up by a caption in *Towards a New Architecture* (1923) he placed underneath a photograph of an ocean liner: »An architecture pure, neat, clear, clean and healthy.« Duality permeates the whole design, it being both a luxury, craftsman-produced villa and a try-out of ideas for industrially fabricated mass-produced housing, a machine for living in and an aristocratic residence of the most classic variety. At once immaculately automobile-age and Classically neo-Palladian, the building still seems very avant-garde, 75 years on.

32 Versailles

32.1 Château de Versailles
Place d'Armes
Various architects, principally Louis Le Vau and Jules Hardouin-Mansart, begun 1623
(RER: Versailles Rive-Gauche)

»Le faste et la pompe qui entourent les rois font partie de leur pouvoir.« Charles-Louis de Secondat, Baron de La Brède et de Montesquieu

At the beginning, overlooking a rather wild valley covered with forest, heaths and marshes, was a small hillock on whose southern side perched the settlement of Versailles. A modest medieval château and its attendant gaggle of houses were all that was to be found here. Louis XIII loved to come and hunt at this desolate spot and, in 1623, built himself a little hunting lodge on top of the hillock so that he would no longer have to spend the night at the local inn. A brick-dressed-with-stone affair coiffed with slate roofs, it was described by the Maréchal de Bassompierre as »the sickly little château of Versailles, whose construction would not inspire vanity in even the simplest gentleman.« Later, in 1631–34, the château was enlarged by the architect Philibert Le Roy, and at this time comprised a modest, one-room-wide, two-storey-high *corps de logis* flanked by narrow lateral wings on its eastern, entrance front, thereby forming a rectangle each of whose external corners was marked by a protruding square pavilion. The same lofty slate roofs and red-brick-and-stone livery as the original château were once again employed, in keeping with the fashion of the day, and moats, then *de rigueur* in French châteaux, surrounded the edifice. This handsome but unremarkable building would go on to form the nucleus of today's vast ensemble.

It was of course Louis XIV who was responsible for the sprawling palace into which his father's château metamorphosed. His interest in Versailles became apparent in the early 1660s, when he began to use the château as a trysting point for his then mistress Mlle de La Vallière. The affection he felt for the place, and his deep mistrust of Paris (see 1.8), go some way to explaining his initial decision to aggrandize the château into a residence worthy of more sustained royal occupation. We should also note that his interventions at Versailles came after the affair of Vaux-le-Vicomte (37.1), during which the king had discovered the magnificence produced by the teamwork of the architect Louis Le Vau, the painter Charles Le Brun and the landscape architect André Le Nôtre, whose talents would once again be combined at Versailles. The Sun King's initial *travaux* at Versailles essentially concerned the grounds, which were entirely transformed by André Le Nôtre as of 1661. Work on the park and gardens continued unabated for nearly 30 years to produce the magnificent ensemble we see today. As far as the château was concerned, the first major building campaign was launched in 1668 when Louis XIV decided to enlarge the house to make it truly worthy of his presence. He hesitated for a long time over whether or not to destroy his father's residence and rebuild completely, in the end opting for a compromise solution that preserved the original château but allowed for its demolition at a future date if necessary. Designed by Louis Le Vau, the extension was nicknamed the »Envelope« because it literally enveloped the old château on three sides. Its points of contact with the old building were kept to a minimum, however (thereby making destruction of the old château possible without disturbing the new constructions), and no attempt was made to harmonize its aspect with the original fabric, prompting the Duc de Saint-Simon to declare: »The beautiful and the plain, the vast and the choked, were sewn together.« As today's visitor will immediately see, Louis XIII's château was never demolished, and the palace of Versailles thus presents a rather quaint mélange of styles and scales on its entrance side. Inside the Envelope, Le Brun created a suite of state apartments that astonished contemporaries by their splendour.

Despite the magnificence of the reconfigured château, Louis XIV still was not content, and began yet another huge campaign of building work in 1678, this time intended to provide sufficient accommodation for his ultimate goal: the transfer of the entire court and government to Versailles. Eager to break the potentially rebellious power of the aristocracy, Louis set out to confine them to gilded idleness away from the troublesome capital, and, in 1682, his suburban palace duly became the seat of the realm. The architect he hired to effect this transformation was Jules Hardouin-Mansart, who built the enormous Ailes du Nord and du Midi either side of the old château to accommodate France's nobles, and who reconfigured the west front of the Envelope for the creation of the famous Galerie des Glaces (hall of mirrors). To the south of the château on its entrance front he put up a vast quadrangle of service buildings – the Grand Commun, which included the enormous Services de la Bouche (kitchens) where food to feed the entire court was prepared –, and enlarged and extended the long wings in front of the Cour Royale to house government ministries. Hardouin-Mansart also began construction of a new chapel at Versailles, which was completed by his brother-in-law Robert de Cotte in 1710. By the end of Louis XIV's reign, the Château de Versailles had metamorphosed into an enormous Forbidden City that counted 2,143 windows, 1,252 chimneys dotted around 10 ha of roof, and no less than 67 staircases. 3,000 people were housed there permanently, and up to 10,000 flooded its state rooms on special occasions. As well as the château proper there were the huge gardens, the king's private retreat at the Trianon (see 32.2, 32.3, 32.4 and 32.5), an enormous hunting park of over 6,000 ha, and an entire town to the east of the complex that supplied the services without which it could not have functioned (see 32.6). The alacrity with which all this was thrown up was truly astonishing, as were the resources deployed: in the year 1685 alone, 36,000 workers toiled on the various building and landscaping projects at Versailles.

But the *travaux* did not end with Louis XIV's death. Throughout Louis XV's reign the château underwent constant modification, especially where its interiors were concerned, the king's private apartments being entirely remodelled and the queen's state rooms redecorated to suit the tastes of the day. In the 1760s Louis XV determined to provide Versailles with the opera house it lacked: designed by his Premier Architecte, Ange-Jacques Gabriel, and situated at the northern end of the Aile du Nord, the magnificent Opéra Royal was completed in haste for the wedding of the Dauphin and Marie-Antoinette in 1770. A year later, and despite an increasingly depleted treasury, Gabriel managed to persuade the king to undertake building of the »Grand Dessein« (literally »great design«), an idea originally proposed by Hardouin-Mansart whereby the picturesque assemblage of brick-and-stone courtyards of the château's entrance front would be replaced by something much grander and more Classically regular realized entirely in stone. Luckily for the château, the financial difficulties that plagued the last 20 years of the *ancien régime* prevented Gabriel from completing his boring design, the only part actually realized being the rebuilding of the northern wing of the Cour Royale (the pendant end façade on the southern wing was added at the behest of Louis XVIII, for symmetry's sake, by Alex Dufour in 1820). Under Louis XVI, no more building work was carried out on the château, although much furniture was commissioned and some interiors were reconfigured or redecorated, including the queen's apartments at the behest of Marie-Antoinette.

Remarkably, the French Revolution left the château intact, although its sumptuous furnishings were sold off and dispersed for ever. The building was nonetheless threatened by neglect, and although Napoleon began its restoration with the intention of making it his summer residence, it was really Louis Philippe (reigned 1830–48) who saved the château, when, unable to move into the palace himself for political reasons, he created the Musée de l'Histoire de France at Versailles. A propaganda exercise intended to reconcile the French people with their history and monarchy, the museum, dedicated »à toutes les gloires de la France«, displayed historical paintings and sculptures as well as specially commissioned history paintings. To accommodate them, Louis Philippe had the architect Frédéric Nepveu gut the Aile du Midi of its former princely apartments and construct in their stead new, monumental galleries. Despite Nepveu's remarkable interiors, posterity has never quite forgiven Louis Philippe for destroying the Louis-Quatorze and Louis-Quinze décor of the apartments they replaced. Today, as a consequence of his interventions, the Château de Versailles presents a double *visage*: on the one hand the former royal apartments, which have been progressively restored as far as possible to their state at the end of the *ancien régime*, and on the other the 19C-gallery circuit.

For Auguste Perret, writing in the 1920s, the Parthenon was Architecture, but Versailles was not. Versailles was building, with lots of added decoration. Indeed decoration is the key to understanding the palace. Open to all comers, even the most lowly, it was designed as a showcase for the monarch, who, so that his personal cult could be maintained, had to be seen as often as possible by his subjects. The splendour with which he surrounded himself, as well as providing a tangible demonstration of his wealth, and consequently of his power, was also an advertisement for the artistic and manufacturing skill and know-how of France. Italy was the great artistic rival at the time Versailles was built, having dominated the visual and decorative arts for over a century, but Louis XIV's palace became the proof of France's newly acquired leadership in the artistic domain. The Galerie des Glaces, for example, was expressly designed with the intention of wresting hegemony over glass manufacture from Venice. To achieve this domination, artistic production in France was entirely taken over and reorganized by the state, whose vice-like grip further ensured the establishment of artistic orthodoxies that served state needs. Versailles was created as a political tool in the furtherance of absolutism, but without the absolutist system and the state-controlled artistic machine it produced, the palace could not have been built.

We should also remember that the Baroque age in which Versailles was created construed the world in terms of theatre, and nowhere was this theatricality more apparent than in the ceremonies, rituals and dressing-up of Louis XIV's court. A microcosm of the Christian, Classical order that the Sun King's rule aspired to impose on his territory, the gardens and château of Versailles were both a physical expression of these ideas and the backdrop for their acting out, from the ritualization of the king's day – organized around the phases of the sun and beginning with the famous *lever* – to the many sumptuous costumed parties and *fêtes* held by the king, whose execution demanded casts of thousands and the active participation of the entire court, and which often lasted for days at a stretch. Allegory was everywhere, although the iconography changed with time: the initial identification of the Roi Soleil with Apollo, the sun god, later gave way to the king's direct representation amongst the pantheon of divinities, as painted by Le Brun on the ceiling of the Galerie des Glaces.

First metamorphoses, c. 1661–78
Louis XIV's first interventions on the fabric of Versailles were modest: Le Brun created some new interiors (none of which now survives) and, in front of the house on the entrance side, Le Vau constructed parallel buildings containing stables, kitchens and other services that delimited a new *avant cour* – today's Cour Royale. Then, in 1668, came the decision to enlarge the building, and all the hesitation over whether to extend or demolish and start afresh. An extension was begun by Le Vau in 1668, work stopped in early 1669 while the king

32.1 Château de Versailles. Garden front

considered a total-replacement scheme, until finally the enlargement solution was once again adopted a few months later. Le Vau died in 1670, and work was continued by his assistant François d'Orbay, the carcass being completed in 1671.

Although the term »Envelope« was coined to describe Le Vau's enrobing stone extension, his additions really only consisted of two new, one-room-wide lateral wings added on either side of the old château, which projected beyond it on the garden front where they were linked by a ground-floor gallery. At first- and second-floor level was a void reaching back as far as the old château's garden façade, which Le Vau remodelled in stone to match his new additions (as we shall see, the void was later filled in by Jules Hardouin-Mansart for the creation of the Galerie des Glaces). Each of the new wings was fitted out with magnificent state apartments, the king's in the northern and the queen's in the southern (rooms which came to be referred to as the Grands Appartments, while the original royal accommodation in the old parts of the château took on the appellation Petits Appartements). On the château's entrance front, the wings of the Envelope stuck out either side of the old, modest *cour d'honneur*, which retained its original brick-and-stone livery but was aggrandized by the addition of busts, gilded balconies and a sumptuous black-and-white marble floor (whence its current name of Cour de Marbre). It was no doubt this state of affairs that prompted Saint-Simon's acerbic commentary; the ungainly cohabitation of old and new was masked as of 1674 when the stable/service blocks of the Cour Royale were attached to the old château by new constructions and converted for domestic use.

Le Vau's garden front was surprising in the French context, for although it counted some features of clearly national origin it was in the main far more Classical and Italianizing than anything seen before on Gallic soil. Three storeys high, its façade division was reminiscent of the Aile Lescot at the Louvre (1.8), with an arcaded ground floor, a lofty first-floor *piano nobile* and a low, square-windowed attic. Instead of the giant order one would expect to find on a royal palace of this sort, Le Vau provided only a single-storey Ionic order at first-floor level, and terminated the Envelope in a very un-French flat balustrade. Gone were the bulging curves, complicated massing and tall roofs of Vaux-le-Vicomte, replaced by orthogonal simplicity and a dominant horizontality, *à l'italienne*, whose strict, unbroken, unpedimented entablatures contrasted startling with the vertical emphasis up till then found in French Classical architecture. Indeed horizontals were originally even more dominant in the Envelope's design, for above the windows of the *piano nobile*, hiding the ceiling cornices behind, Le Vau placed carved panels like those he used at Vaux-le-Vicomte, which Hardouin-Mansart later replaced with the arched window terminations we see today. The whole design was very »straight«, both literally and metaphorically, with no mannerisms or Baroque games, magnificence being achieved through the scale, the massing and the subtle use of the order to create *avant-corps*. But the aspect of the Envelope that most surprised contemporaries was its flat roofing, hidden behind balustrades in the Italian manner with urns and trophies bristling on the skyline. Le Vau may well have been influenced by Bernini's flat-roofed designs for the east front of the Louvre, and he had in part been responsible for the east front as built, which adopts a similar roofline, but there is nonetheless something rather strange about Versailles's lack of roofs that one does not feel on seeing the Louvre. Saint-Simon summed it up well when he said: »One thinks one is seeing a burnt-out palace whose final floor and roofs are still missing.« There is a precedent for this arrangement in Le Vau's own œuvre, namely at the Hôtel Lambert (4.5), an early work whose garden front sports a squat, flat-topped attic of the same peculiar aspect. But it was not only the lofty roofs of French tradition that disappeared with the Envelope, since Versailles's hereditary moats also vanished at Le Vau's behest, thereby putting them forever out of fashion in French châteaux.

Of the state apartments created by Le Brun in the Envelope during the 1670s, only half-a-dozen or so interiors now survive in anything like their original form, most of them in the Grands Appartements du Roi. As at Vaux-le-Vicomte, it was to Italy that Le Brun turned for inspiration, the suite of rooms he created for the king recalling Pietro da Cortona's »Planet Apartment« (c. 1640–50) in the Pitti Palace in Florence. Le Brun's original scheme was to create an *enfilade* of rooms dedicated to each of the seven known planets and culminating, appropriately enough, with the sun in the form of the Salon d'Apollon at the suite's centre, which was Louis XIV's throne room. This proposal was never realized in its entirety, and some of the interiors that were built were later transformed or destroyed. One such was the famous Escalier des Ambassadeurs, via which the Grands Appartements du Roi were originally reached, demolished by Louis XV in 1752 to enlarge his private apartments. Today the staircase's magnificence lives on in engravings, a model and even a life-size 19C facsimile, built by Bavaria's Ludwig II at his Schloß Herrenchiemsee. At Versailles, one can get an idea of what the Escalier's lavish décor must have been like in the Salons de Vénus and de Diane, each of which headed one of the staircase's two upper flights. The Salon de Vénus in particular, with its splendid red-marble order topped off by gilded capitals and entablatures, its geometric wall panels in green, red and white marble, and its *trompe-l'œil* architectural perspectives painted by Jacques Rousseau, recalls the Escalier's *mise en scène*. But the principal decorative element in the Salon de Vénus, and indeed in all the rooms of the king's apartments, were the elaborate vaulted ceilings. For their design, Le Brun again turned to the formula he had used so successfully at Vaux-le-Vicomte, namely a cooled-down, Gallic interpretation of Pietro da Cortona's work at the Pitti Palace, with carved and gilded stuccowork providing a splendid architectonic framework for highly accomplished, illusionistic vault frescoes. To realize this huge ensemble, Le Brun assembled a whole army of extraordinarily skilled artists and craftsmen that included the painters Jean-Baptiste de Champaigne and Charles de La Fosse, the latter of whom created the magnificent ceiling frescoes in the Salon d'Apollon.

If, the Salons de Vénus and de Diane aside, the king's apartments today seem comparatively plain under their lavish coverings, it is because they have lost their original coloured-marble floors as well as the extraordinary chiselled-silver furnishings that constituted their principal eye-level décor, the whole lot having been melted down by Louis XIV to finance his incessant bellicosity. The silver furniture and the king's collection of paintings were set off against unimaginably sumptuous wall hangings – silk in summer and velvet in winter –, the most famous of which was the Tenture de la Paix, whose surfaces were cadenced by pilasters in gold and silver thread standing out as much as 15 cm from the fabric's surface. It, too, was sacrificed to fill the treasury, this time by Louis XV in 1743. In the absence of his attendant objects and furnishings, it is now difficult to appreciate the full magnitude of the splendour with which Louis XIV surrounded himself.

The Grands Appartements de la Reine have also changed considerably since the Sun King's day. Their layout exactly mirrored that of the king's apartments on the other side of the château, and this arrangement, whereby both the queen's state rooms and her private apartments in the old château had equal emblematic weight and importance to those of the king, has been interpreted by some as symbolizing a »double« monarchy based on Queen Marie-Thérèse's claim to the Spanish throne. Whether or not this can be read into the château's original layout, the symmetrical symbolism was destroyed following Marie-Thérèse's death in 1683 when Louis XIV annexed all the queen's private apartments for his own use (see below). For the decoration of the queen's Grands Appartements, Le Brun employed much the same formula as in the king's state rooms, with Cortona-derived ceilings sporting paintings along similar allegorical lines. Amongst what now remains of Le Brun's first campaign of work in the queen's apartments, we should note the ceiling of the Antichambre du Grand Couvert, with its six splendid *trompe-l'œil* painted bas-reliefs, and the vault paintings of the Salle des Gardes de la Reine: originally produced for the king's Cabinet de Jupiter (destroyed for the creation of the Salon de la Guerre – see below), they were the work of Noël Coypel, whose humorous corner canvasses showing members of the court leaning over a balustrade are a particularly accomplished example of Le Brun's illusionism. The type of whimsy they represent has a pedigree stretching back to Veronese's frescoes of spectators peeping down from balustrades in the Villa Barbaro at Maser (c. 1555–65).

The seat of the realm – Louis XIV's transformations c. 1678–1715

Where extension of the château was concerned, the Sun King's decision to transfer the entire court and government to Versailles posed something of a dilemma.

Because the palace was closed off to the east by the town and to the west by the garden, the only directions in which it could expand were laterally, to the north and the south. Hardouin-Mansart was opposed to this solution, primarily on aesthetic grounds, but also because it would involve considerable earthworks to overcome the steep slope of the terrain. He submitted an alternative proposal whereby the necessary new accommodation would be obtained by building a supplementary storey on top of the château, a solution which, he further believed, would increase the building's majesty. But his scheme was dismissed, perhaps because it could not have supplied sufficient space, and the idea of a north–south extension retained. Once the enormous terraces had been built, Hardouin-Mansart erected new, very long and very wide wings either side of the Cour Royale, on whose garden elevations he repeated Le Vau's façade articulation, stretching it across a whopping total of 670 m. Rather than the discrete, self-contained object it had been before, the palace's garden front now comprised an infinitely extendable agglomeration of repeatable bays, like the units of a ruler, whose measure was given by the countless round-headed French windows. For some, this unlimited repetition can be read as a metaphor for the infinitely extensible power of France's absolute sovereign, stretching both physically across his territory and virtually through more abstract domains. But in terms of the aesthetic effect produced on the château's garden front, Hardouin-Mansart's additions can only seem deeply regrettable, and many is the visitor who will be disappointed on first seeing Versailles from its gardens. Where the Envelope's height and width had been calculated in relation to each other to produce an imposing object that stood out against the skyline and dominated all around it, Hardouin-Mansart's interventions created the effect of a long, low, flat, boring bar disappearing out of view to either side and seemingly unrelated to the magnificent setting it occupied. Moreover, Le Vau's order, whose dimensions had been calculated in accord with the restricted, self-contained scale of the Envelope, came to seem prissy, fussy and weedy when repeated ad infinitum across such a vast expanse. The final effect was of an overdecorated, aristocratic barracks, which is at bottom what the enlarged château really was.

The subtle play of volume that had characterized the Envelope was also ruined by Hardouin-Mansart, who filled in the central void for the creation of the Galerie des Glaces. If externally this intervention was unfortunate, internally it was quite another matter. The suite of rooms made up by the gallery and its attendant antechambers – the Salon de la Guerre to the north and the Salon de la Paix to the south – perhaps represents the summit of the Louis-Quatorze style. Created by Hardouin-Mansart and Le Brun, the ensemble occupies the entire west front of the Envelope and was intended as the culmination of the palace's public rooms. The two salons formed part of the king and queen's public apartments, while the gallery was the setting for important balls, fêtes and state receptions, as well as providing the backdrop for the monarchs' daily procession to mass. Once again the décor's inspiration was Italian Baroque, but once again this was a very French interpretation of Italy's inventions, cooled down and straightened out for more northern tastes, but also imbued with a majesty unique to Gallic soil. Sumptuous marble polychromy, lavish gilded-bronze carvings and monumental vault paintings were the basic decorative elements, combined in compositions governed by regular, easily readable and symmetrically disposed compartments. The Salon de la Guerre is perhaps the most original of the three interiors, its decorative effect relying almost entirely on sculpture, the centrepiece of which is Antoine Coysevox's stucco medallion representing *Louis XIV Victorieux et Couronné par la Gloire*. Its paintings and sculptures depict the Sun King's victories, while the Salon de la Paix's show his more peaceful political manœuvres.

But the pièce de résistance was of course the 73 m-long, 10.5 m-wide and 12.3 m-high Galerie des Glaces: constructed in 1678, it received its marble cladding in 1679, its sculptures were completed by 1680, but another four years went by before Le Brun finished the enormous vault paintings. Two features in particular indicate the Galerie's symbolic significance: firstly, the red-marble order cadencing the room, which is not one of the five Antique orders but a new, »French« order devised by Le Brun, whose capitals combine the essential elements of the Corinthian with the French cock and the Bourbon fleur de lis; and secondly the thematic content of the virtuosic trompe-l'œil vault painting, which, in place of the allegorical events of mythology usually chosen to symbolize royal deeds, directly represents Louis XIV and the principal events and accomplishments of his reign. The Galerie is of course famous for its mirrors, which occupy arched frames corresponding to the windows opposite. Each of the 578 silvered panels measures approximately 90×60 cm, about the maximum size that contemporary techniques allowed. Although mirrors had long been a staple feature of luxury decoration – Philip IV of Spain, for example, created a salon de miroirs in his Alcazar palace in 1651 –, never before had such a great number been assembled in one place, their difficult manufacture and prohibitive cost making such a display beyond the means of all but the most fabulously wealthy. But fabulously wealthy was what France's monarch had become, and these glaces, which, orientated west, caught the golden rays of the setting sun, have become indelibly associated with the Sun King's reign. Once again, to understand the full effect, we should try to imagine the lavish furnishings that accompanied this exuberant décor: white-and-gold brocade curtains, two enormous Savonnerie carpets, and solid-silver tables and guéridons, as well as 41 silver candelabra and 17 crystal chandeliers. Today the Galerie is furnished with copies of a series of candelabra created in 1769 for the marriage of the future Louis XVI and Marie-Antoinette, of which six originals survive, as well as reproduction chandeliers.

In tandem with his vast building campaign on Versailles's garden front, Hardouin-Mansart also carried out significant modifications to the entrance front. He aggrandized the Cour de Marbre through the addition of a new, three-storey high *avant-corps*, whose height and first-floor-level arched windows announced the garden front. A foretaste of the interior decoration was also provided by the eight red-marble columns holding up a generously gilded wrought-iron balcony. In deference to the garden front's flat roofline, Hardouin-Mansart did not coiff the *avant-corps* with a pediment, but instead terminated it with a triangle of lead statues and trophies encasing a monumental clock, the work of the sculptors Marsy and Girardon. The Cour de Marbre's busts, marble columns and balconies were repeated on all the wings leading out towards the Cour des Ministres, giving the whole a coherent but nevertheless very picturesque aspect, amplified by the elaborate dormers and lead roof dressings that were also added at this time. In plainer red-brick-and-stone livery are the ministry wings sitting in front of the Cour Royal. Hardouin-Mansart's interventions made necessary the building of new stables, which he duly supplied on the other side of the Place d'Armes in front of the château (see 32.6). Despite its splendour, everybody, Hardouin-Mansart included, considered Versailles's entrance front a bastardized compromise of only temporary nature. Their objections no doubt stemmed partly from its old-fashioned brick livery and partly from the way the ever receding courtyards lead one from the very big to the very tiny – »the vast and the strangled«. But it is precisely this that is so delightful for the visitor arriving at Versailles, who finds himself caught up in a *decrescendo* of scale but a *crescendo* of sumptuousness, culminating in the intimate, almost domestic but exquisite Cour de Marbre.

Following the death of his consort in 1683, Louis XIV undertook the enlargement and remodelling of his Petits Appartements in the old parts of the château, appropriating for himself the entire suite of rooms surrounding the three sides of the Cour du Marbre. Although the use of corridors and *cabinets* to provide privacy in room layouts had been one of the developments of 17C-French domestic planning, Louis XIV at Versailles was interested only display, and his apartments both »private« and public were consequently organized as long *enfilades* of rooms opening into each other. Mme de Maintenon, his morganatic second wife, complained: »With him, only grandeur, magnificence and symmetry count; it's worth putting up with all the draughts that rush underneath the doors as long the latter are opposite each other.« In 1680, Le Brun had built the Escalier de la Reine, ostensibly as a pendant to the Escalier des Ambassadeurs for the queen to access her apartments, but, with the reconfiguration of the king's Petits Appartements, it soon became the principal staircase in the whole château. Under a vaulted, marble-clad ceiling, the staircase rises in a classic half-turn-with-landings, the stairs themselves being held up on elongated arches. The polychrome, marble-clad walls with their red-marble pilasters and gilded-bronze carvings announce the decoration of the Grands Appartements. This décor is continued virtually in Philippe Meusnier and Jean-Baptiste Blain's *trompe-l'œil* painting of a palace peopled with figures dressed *à l'orientale*. The Salle des Gardes de la Reine, into which the staircase opens, was given polychrome marble cladding to match.

In 1701 Louis XIV took a decision of minor practical but high symbolic importance when he transformed the first-floor room at the centre of the Cour de Marbre (in front of the Galerie des Glaces) into his private bedchamber. The royal person's resting place was thus placed at the epicentre of the palace and, by extension, of the kingdom. It was here that the ceremonies of the *lever* and the *coucher* took place each day. The bedchamber's décor breaks somewhat with the Baroque monumentality of the Grands Appartements, Le Brun's geometric marble polychromy giving way to a much more Classical arrangement of wood-carved pilasters and sculpture finished with uniform gilding. Gone too, is the elaborate ceiling of Le Brun's time, replaced by a plain white vault. Whether these changes are imputable to the bedchamber's more intimate character, an evolution in taste, or simply to the treasury's financial difficulties in the last years of Louis XIV's reign, is a matter for debate. Nonetheless the bedchamber is suitably showy, much of its effect relying on the sumptuous silk wall hangings, bed drapes and chair coverings. The fabrics we see today are reproductions of those created for Louis XV in 1722 for his summer décor (the winter hangings have sadly not been recreated). Accessing the bedchamber to the south is the Salon de l'Œil-de-Bœuf, so named because of the »bull's-eye« mirror interrupting the frieze high up on one wall. Here we see the ageing Hardouin-Mansart (assisted by Robert de Cotte) producing décor that clearly anticipates Louis-XV-period interiors in its use of light, gilded mouldings on a plain white background. Nonetheless, the presence of pilasters, the oversized frieze with its dancing children, and the high vault (reminiscent of François Mansart's work at Maisons, 24.1) put the Salon de l'Œil-de-Bœuf firmly in the tradition of 17C monumental interiors. Today the Salon and the king's bedchamber are the only rooms in the Petits Appartements to look anything like they did during the Sun King's reign, the remainder having been entirely reconfigured by Louis XV and Louis XVI (see below).

Louis XIV's last major intervention at Versailles was the building of the chapel at the southern end of the Aile du Nord. Hardouin-Mansart's design sought inspiration in the French tradition of palace chapels, such as the Sainte-Chapelle (1.2), comprising two levels, the upper for the king and his retinue and the lower for those of more humble station. At Versailles, the upper level became a gallery, overlooking the nave below, in a building that splendidly and intelligently combined the Gothic and the Classical. The gallery, with its resplendent Corinthian colonnade that contemporary commentators likened to the Louvre's east front, is thoroughly Classical, while the lavish decoration, which includes illusionistic vault paintings by Antoine Coypel, Charles de La Fosse and Jean Jouvenet, is exuberantly Baroque. But almost everything else about the chapel is taken from the Gothic tradition: the plan, with its aisles and semicircular apse-ambulatory termination, the very tall, three-storey interior elevations with their nave arcade and clerestory, the barrel vault whose deep window recesses almost make it a groin vault, and the external flying buttresses that support the vaulting. Seen from outside, the chapel dominates the château with its high roof: for some (Saint-Simon included) this is proof that Hardouin-Mansart's scheme to raise the height of the remainder of the palace to match had in fact been accepted, but was never carried out due to the architect's death; for others it demonstrated only God's dominance over the Bourbon dynasty.

Versailles from Louis XV to Louis Philippe
The most far-reaching modifications to the Château de Versailles during Louis XV's reign concerned its interiors. One of the first rooms realized under his aegis was the Salon d'Hercule, which had been begun under Louis XIV by Robert de Cotte in 1712 but left unfinished. De Cotte recommenced work on the Salon in 1729, which was finally inaugurated in 1736 when François Lemoyne completed the enormous ceiling-vault painting. Constituting as it did the link between the Grands Appartements du Roi and Hardouin-Mansart's chapel, and being almost twice the size of any other room in the series, the Salon d'Hercule clearly required monumental treatment. In its wall decoration the Salon displays a tardy but particularly accomplished example of the marble polychromy so characteristic of official taste under Louis XIV, and was already out of fashion by the time of its inauguration. One entire wall was specially configured to receive Veronese's *Repas chez Simon*, which had been given to Louis XIV by the Republic of Venice in 1664. But it was Lemoyne's vault painting that stole the show: one of the largest of its type ever realized (480 m^2), it depicts the Apotheosis of Hercules via a cast of 142 figures floating around in a sea of clouds rising above the illusionistic cornices of an imaginary palace. Louis XV, on seeing it for the first time, made Lemoyne Premier Peintre du Roi on the spot. But the artist never benefited from this honour: worn down by the stress of painting the ceiling, and suffering from paranoia, he committed suicide a few months later.

Unlike his great-grandfather, Louis XIV, who was clearly a born performer, Louis XV hated appearing in public, and consequently spent much of his reign enlarging, embellishing and rendering more commodious his private apartments at Versailles. Away from the constant press of the public in the Grands Appartements, and the stifling etiquette of Louis XIV's bedchamber in the Petits Appartements, he created a whole little world made just to his convenience. This private apartment was situated on the northern side of the Cour de Marbre; by building across the large courtyard that originally separated the old parts of the château from the Envelope, Louis XV was able to add many new rooms. Where Louis XIV's chambers had been organized *en enfilade*, Louis XV delighted in the introduction of new corridors, *cabinets* and staircases that allowed individual access to different rooms and consequently a high degree of privacy and *commodité*. The majority of the new spaces were decorated with panelling designed by Ange-Jacques Gabriel and carved by Jacques Verberckt, and the interiors they created are considered masterpieces of the »style Louis-XV«. Influenced by French Rococo – a style developed in private houses that was the deliberate antithesis of Louis-Quatorze, Versailles-type grandeur –, the panelling features delicate and beautifully accomplished gilded mouldings on plain, white backgrounds under plain, white ceilings. Instead of the pomp of the Grands Appartements, we find intimate interiors designed to seduce and charm the onlooker with their subtle sophistication. Nonetheless, in comparison to French Rococo, Gabriel and Verberckt's work shows a certain august stiffness, and beside the wild creations of Germany and Austria at that time is a paragon of simplicity, clarity and »bon goût«. The best panelling is to be found in the Nouvelle Chambre (1738), the Cabinet de la Pendule (1738), the Cabinet Intérieur (or Cabinet d'Angle, 1738 and 1753), the Pièce de la Vaisselle d'Or (1753–67) and the dining room (1769). Also of note is the Cabinet du Roi (or Cabinet du Conseil), created by Louis XV to the north of Louis XIV's bedchamber, with panelling designed by Gabriel and sculpted by Antoine Rousseau (1755). All these rooms are situated on the first floor of the château (which is the upper floor on the two-storey-high Cour-de-Marbre side), and were semi-public in that courtiers and ministers were admitted to them. But upstairs, in the mansard attic, Louis XV installed a whole warren of entirely private rooms, some of which served to lodge his mistresses. Here we again find examples of Gabriel and Verberckt's panelling, but of a lighter and simpler aspect than in the rooms below, and generally without gilding. Instead delicate colours were used and finished with a technique known as *vernis Martin*, which, requiring up to 16 coats of paint, gave the walls the freshness and shine of porcelain. A good example can be seen in the room now known as the Salle à Manger de Mme du Barry. Further fine examples of Louis-Quinze panelling can be found in what remains of the royal children's apartments on the château's ground floor.

Versailles presents a fascinating case study in the use of space for political manipulation. It was of course the wily Louis XIV who first perfected the system: although his life in the château was almost 100 % public, he also disposed of private houses at the Trianon and Marly (destroyed), to which invitations could be given and refused and favour thus granted or denied. In an absolutist system where nothing could be done without the king's approval, his favour was paramount to success, and Louis XIV did not hesitate to use his power to encourage jealousies and rivalries for his own ends. Etiquette could also be manipulated to express royal displeasure, Saint-Simon for one having felt the full force of the king's disapproval through the invitation system. When a lady was asked to Marly, her husband could automatically accompany her, but this was not the case for the more prestigious Trianon; by consistently inviting the Duchesse de Saint-Simon alone to the Trianon, and denying her applications for Marly, Louis XIV coldly communicated his discontentment with the duke. Louis XV, in remodelling his Petits Appartements, introduced his great-grandfather's system into the château's heart: admittance to the first-floor rooms was a sign of privilege, but invitation to the attic apartments represented the summit of favour. Applications for the attic-apartment gatherings were made to Mme de Pompadour, who presented a list of hopefuls to the king on his return from hunting. He would tick off the names of the chosen few which were then read out to the eager crowd assembled in the Galerie des Glaces at the door to the Cabinet du Roi. Once through, the guests passed from the Cabinet into a corridor containing a tiny oval staircase that led up to the attic, thereby heightening the sense of mystery and exclusivity.

While Louis XV disposed of Grands Appartements, semi-public Petits Appartements and private attic apartments replete with mistresses, his Polish consort Marie Leszczinska had only her Grands Appartements plus a few miserable little *cabinets* running alongside them. Forced to spend considerable amounts of time in them, she consequently modified their décor to suit her tastes. Marie-Antoinette in her turn redecorated the whole lot, and the only room that now appears essentially as it did during Marie Lezsczinksa's time is the Chambre de la Reine. Realized in 1730–35, it was designed by Robert de Cotte and Jacques V Gabriel (father of Ange-Jacques) and executed by the sculptors Degoullons, Le Goupil and Verberckt. It represents something of a hybrid between the official pomp of Louis-Quatorze state rooms and the new, more intimate interior design developed during Louis XV's reign. Nonetheless, the overwhelming profusion of elaborate gilded carving makes clear the bedchamber's representative role. Realizing exactly which side their bread is buttered on, Versailles's curators spent 30 years from 1955 to 1975 restoring the room to almost exactly its state on 6 October 1789, when Marie-Antoinette fled it in the face of the marauding mob, never again to return. Thus the extravagant bed and accompanying silk wall hangings recreate Louis-Seize designs. The corner ceiling carvings also date from Marie-Antoinette's time: sculpted by Rousseau, they feature the Habsburgs' imperial double eagle combined with the arms of France and Navarre.

Louis XV's »grand projet« at Versailles, at least until the Grand Dessein, was the Opéra Royal. When building the Aile du Nord, Hardouin-Mansart had reserved a space for a theatre at the wing's northern extremity, a location chosen because of its proximity to Versailles's reservoirs (important for a fire-prone building type) and because the site's natural slope allowed under-stage areas to be built without expensive excavation works. Gabriel's design for the Opéra is derived ultimately from Palladio's wooden Teatrico Olimpico (1584), which the Italian architect had based on observations of Antique amphitheatres, and which Gabriel sent Nicolas-Marie Potain to draw (Potain also visited the theatres of Bologna, Parma, Modena and Turin). France's first Italian-style auditorium, the Opéra Royal has in common with its cinquecento forbear both its curved plan and the free-standing colonnade under the roof, but differs in its disposition of seating, preferring classic 18C boxes and flat stalls to the amphitheatre-style seating banks used by Palladio. In some respects this arrangement reflects the uses to which the Opéra was put, for its ostentatious décor provided as much a setting for the court to display and observe itself as a place for the production of operas and plays, state balls and banquets often being held there. Indeed the astonishing haste with which the Opéra was built – only 23 months – was due to the impending marriage banquet of the Dauphin and Marie-Antoinette, which duly took place on 19 May 1770 in the just-completed auditorium.

Perhaps appropriately for a theatre, the architecture we see at the Opéra Royal is something of a sham, its interior being, like the Teatro Olimpico, entirely in wood. It is interesting to note in this respect that not only the workmen of the Bâtiments du Roi but also those of the Menus-Plaisirs (the entity responsible for temporary décor and stage scenery for the court) were drafted in for the building's construction. With lashings of gilding, columns painted to look like marble, elaborate carvings and chandeliers, and equally overblown *appliques* mounted on mirrors behind the colonnade, the Opéra gives an overwhelming impression of lavish sumptuousness that prefigures the bombast of 19C theatres. Nonetheless, there is a Classical monumentality and dignity that are typical of Gabriel. The coffered half dome that covers what should have been the royal box was contributed by Charles de Wailly, architect of the Théâtre de l'Odéon (6.7), but was never used by Louis XV. The king's legendary shyness prompted him to a have a little grill-covered space installed underneath instead, behind which he could hide during performances. By all accounts the latter were truly spectacular thanks to the Opéra's sophisticated stage machinery, which was designed by the *machiniste* Blaise-Henri Arnoult, who was also responsible for the ingenious system that allowed the auditorium's transformation into a ballroom. In part because of its wooden interior, the Opéra was also blessed with excellent acoustics.

Hardly had the paint dried on the Opéra than Gabriel began the Grand Dessein. His scheme proposed raising the height of the entrance elevations to three storeys, like the garden front, and hiding the Cour de

Marbre and its attendant excrescences behind a new wing at the western end of the Cour Royale, which would consequently become the château's *cour d'honneur*. Five years later, following Louis XVI's accession (1774) and Gabriel's retirement (1775), work stopped due to the crown's financial difficulties, never to resume. All that had been completed was the rebuilding of the Cour Royale's northern wing, today known as the Aile Gabriel. For its façades, the architect recycled the essential dispositions of his buildings at the Place de la Concorde (8.1), but with engaged columns in place of the long colonnade. Judging from the drawings and the completed wing, the final result would have been august but exceedingly dry. Similarly sober is the monumental staircase at the end of the Aile Gabriel (only completed in its current form, to the architect's plans, in 1985), which was intended to stand in for the polychrome splendour of Louis XIV's Escalier des Ambassadeurs. New projects for completion of the Grand Dessein appeared in the 1780s – including a characteristically oversized neo-Classical fantasia by Etienne-Louis Boullée –, but the exchequer's continuing financial problems prevented any of them ever from being realized.

In the end, despite the many grandiose schemes elaborated for Versailles under Louis XVI, the unfortunate king's reign produced only a handful of new interiors at the palace. The move towards neo-Classicism displayed in what came to be known as the »style Louis-XVI« can clearly be seen in the king's library, in his Petits Appartements, which was decorated on his accession to the throne. The last production of Gabriel and Rousseau's teamwork, the library is quite unlike their previous interiors, everything having become much more sober, rectilinear and architectonic. A similar sober orthogonality can be seen in the queen's *cabinets*, which Marie-Antoinette had redecorated by Richard Mique, especially where her library (1779) and Cabinet de la Méridienne (1781) are concerned. There is nonetheless a feminine daintiness to these rooms' ornament not to be found in the king's apartments. In the Grand Cabinet Intérieur de la Reine (or Cabinet Doré, 1783), Mique ladled on the ornament and gilding more heavily, although still with the same daintiness. His mouldings of winged sphinxes and smoking braziers, inspired by discoveries at Pompeii and Herculaneum, anticipated the Empire style.

The neo-Classicism that started out so delicately in Louis XVI's reign had reached full-blown grandiloquence by the time of Louis Philippe's in the Galerie des Batailles and its attendant rooms. Clearly inspired by Percier and Fontaine's reworking of the Louvre's Grande Galerie, Nepveu's Galerie des Batailles blows up its prototype's scale and decoration to imperial-Roman proportions. We also see the beginnings of 19C historicism and the »battle of the styles« in Nepveu's work at Versailles, his Salles des Croisades, designed to display paintings of the crusades, being dressed up in medievalizing heraldic panelling that seems rather incongruous in the context of Louis XIV's palace.

The gardens at Versailles
On Louis XIV's accession, the grounds at Versailles consisted of roughly 80 ha divided up into a grid of formal parterres. By the end of his reign the château's surroundings comprised 95 ha of remodelled gardens and a further 1,700 ha of landscaped grounds known as the »Petit Parc«, which contained, amongst others, the Grand Canal, the Pièce d'Eau des Suisses and the Trianon. Today the Domaine de Versailles has been reduced to 815 ha comprising the gardens and part of the Petit Parc. While the gardens have conserved essentially their general outlines as Louis XIV knew them, they have lost many of their 17C fountains and follies, although enough remains to get an idea of what the overall effect must have been. Today's visitor should also bear in mind that an ageing tree stock and two disastrous storms (one in 1990 and another, even worse, in 1999) have meant that the majority of the gardens' copses have had to be felled and replanted over the last few years. As a result, the »architectonic« qualities of Le Nôtre's design are currently hard to appreciate. Versailles lost 10,000 trees in the 1999 hurricane alone, and although millions of euros have already been spent repairing the damage, several decades will be needed before the park regains anything of its former aspect. Indeed the park and gardens will never be quite the same as before the storms, the authorities having decided to use the replanting as a pretext to return the grounds to something of their turn-of-the-18C state, as known to us through the voluminous archives.

Like Le Nôtre's gardens at Vaux-le-Vicomte and the Tuileries (1.10), the principal organizing element at Versailles is a giant central alley running in the château's axis, not just on the garden side as at the Tuileries, but also on the château's entrance front, like at Vaux. Again as at Vaux, the entrance-side avenue is flanked by two

32.1 Château de Versailles. Garden

further, diagonally radiating avenues in the manner of Rome's Piazza del Popolo. But while the form of Versailles's axial alley may recall Vaux's, its scale is of quite another order: on the château's entrance side it runs at least 2 km, disappearing off into infinity, while on the garden side it stretches over 4 km, again running all the way to the horizon. In this way Le Nôtre put perspective at the service of the king, visually suggesting the infinite extension of his divine right to rule. On either side the axis is bordered by trees, again as at Vaux, but where in the earlier château's garden we find just plain woods, at Versailles there is a whole grid of *bosquets* (literally »copses«) containing follies, fountains, grottoes and statuary of all kinds. And where Vaux's canal was organized as a hidden surprise, Versailles's gargantuan, 1.65 km-long Grand Canal is the principal landscaping element of the composition, prolonging the central axis almost to the horizon and defining the view from the château atop its hillock. Versailles also differs from Le Nôtre's previous gardens in the way formal parterres are used, since instead of simple grids set in front of the château we find a more subtle arrangement of formal gardens running along an east–west axis either side of the palace. This configuration was partly dictated by the site's topography, since the steep drop in front of the château prevented the usual layout. Instead, leading off the main terrace in front of the palace (the Parterre d'Eau), we find a monumental arrangement of stairs and topiary-planted embankments descending to the Parterre de Latone, from which the Tapis Vert (literally »green carpet«) takes one down to the Bassin d'Apollon and the Grand Canal. Much of the delight of Versailles's gardens comes from the way these formal, open, comprehensible-at-a-glance areas are contrasted with the closed, secret, surprise-filled penumbra of the *bosquets*.

Before going on to describe the gardens in detail it is worth pointing out the gargantuan scale of the earth and engineering works necessary to create them. Vast amounts of manpower were employed constructing the terraces, draining the marshes and bogs that initially covered the valley bottom, digging the Grand Canal and the other ponds and pools, planting the thousands of trees and building all the fountains and follies. Versailles was not a naturally prepossessing site, and the huge efforts expended to make it what it is today, in an age prior to the invention of mechanized earth-moving and engineering equipment, testify to a desire on Louis XIV's part to impose his will on Nature and, through the spectacular transformation of the environment thus effected, demonstrate his temporal power. One perennial problem was the shortage of water, huge quantities being needed to supply the 2,400 fountain jets that splashed and tinkled at Versailles in the Sun King's time. An enormous and ingenious pump known as the Machine de Marly was built on the Seine 7 km away, although its capacity proved disappointing, and a giant aqueduct was even begun (1684–88) to bring in water from the River Eure 110 km away, although, after expenditure of 8 million *livres* and the loss of 227 workers' lives, Louis was forced to abandon the project because the exchequer could no longer support it. As well as a huge civil-engineering and landscaping effort, Versailles's gardens were also a gigantic artistic enterprise, Charles Le Brun having headed an army of sculptors who produced the hundreds of statues and carvings needed to populate the alleys, parterres and *bosquets*. As in the Grands Appartements, the iconography of the statues and fountains seems initially to have been based around the legend of Apollo, and Le Brun clearly intended to dispose the sculptures according to a carefully considered itinerary that would have given a logical, symbolic meaning to the whole. But Louis XIV cared more for immediate aesthetic effect than for rigorously thought-out allegory, and, again as in the Grands Appartements, Le Brun's original concept was subsequently shaken up by Hardouin-Mansart to the point where it lost all its initial sense.

As Anthony Blunt has pointed out to his compatriots, the conception of a garden we find at Versailles »is the exact reverse of that with which the Englishman is now familiar, and it requires as much effort for us to recognize its qualities as to see the beauties of Racine if we have been wholly brought up on Shakespeare«. But some of Louis XIV's French contemporaries had just as much difficulty appreciating Le Nôtre's efforts, Saint-Simon for one, who was characteristically caustic when he wrote: »Louis XIV liked to tyrannize Nature ... The gardens, whose magnificence astonishes, but which when used, even lightly, put one off, are in equally bad taste. One can only reach the cool shade via a vast, torrid area at the end of which, wherever one is, one can only go up or down; and the gardens end with the hill, which is very short. The violence everywhere done to Nature disgusts and repels one despite oneself. The abundance of water forced and gathered up from all over the place makes it thick, green and muddy; it spreads a noticeable and unhealthy dampness, whose smell is even worse.« Saint-Simon's contemporaries generally saw only the magnificence, however, and it was for this reason that Versailles's grounds became a model for princely gardens throughout late-Baroque Europe.

The obvious place to begin our tour of Versailles's gardens is at the Parterre d'Eau in front of the château, so named because of its two large pools, which are lined with bravura bronze statues representing France's rivers, thereby symbolizing the expanse of the Sun King's territory. To the south of the Parterre d'Eau is the formally planted Parterre du Midi, which looks out onto a lake known as the Pièce d'Eau des Suisses after the Swiss Guards who spent four years digging it from 1678 to 1682. In between the Parterre du Midi and the lake is Versailles's orangery, which was constructed by Har-douin-Mansart in 1684 as part of the earthworks need-ed to build the Aile du Midi, and which replaced an earlier orangery by Le Vau. Orientated due south, Hardouin-Mansart's building sits underneath the

Parterre du Midi and features long wings projecting out either side and defining a sort of courtyard. Access to this space is gained via the wings' roofs, which prolong the Parterre du Midi and each terminate in a monumental staircase, known as the Cent Marches (Hundred Steps), which are justly famous. The orangery's courtyard constitutes a splendid sun trap and is so sheltered that in summer orange and palm trees in pots are lined up along its alleys.

Moving back up to the other side of the Parterre d'Eau we find the Parterre du Nord, which is formally planted in a similar manner to the Parterre du Midi, and which leads to the fountain-lined Allée d'Eau that descends via the Bassin du Dragon to a large pool called the Bassin de Neptune. The Bassin du Dragon is a 19C concoction, apart from the dragon itself which was sculpted by Gaspard Marsy in 1667. As for the giant Bassin de Neptune, it was only completed in 1741 under Louis XV, with a splendidly Baroque lead sculpture of the sea god and Amphritite by Lambert-Sigisbert Adam, which appears even more spectacular when its water jets are operational. To the west of the Allée d'Eau is the Bosquet des Trois Fontaines, and to its east the Bosquet de l'Arc de Triomphe; both have unfortunately lost the features that gave them their names.

Now let us return again to the Parterre d'Eau and this time descend the monumental steps fronting it to the Parterre de Latone, so named because of the four-tiered fountain occupying its centre. Sculpted by the Marsy brothers in 1668–70, it shows Latona, Apollo's mother, protecting her children from the insults of Lycean peasants while calling on Jupiter to avenge her, which the god duly did by turning the uncouth bumpkins into toads and lizards – whence the rather comic water-spouting amphibians on the lower tiers. Some have seen in this work an allegory for the plight of Louis XIV's mother during the troubles of the Fronde. Leading off from the Parterre de Latone is the urn- and statue-lined Tapis Vert, which, when its defining trees are tall enough, dramatically narrows the perspective as seen from the château and forces the view down onto the Grand Canal. Completed in its current form in 1671, the canal features a 1.07 km-long transversal extension known as the Petit Canal, making for a total perimeter of 5.67 km. In Louis XIV's time its waters were animated by a whole fleet of barges and ships, whence the small port known as »La Petite Venise«. Between the Tapis Vert and the canal is the Bassin d'Apollon, one of Versailles's most famous fountains. Created by Jean-Baptiste Tuby to designs by Le Brun in 1668–71, it shows the sun god seated in his chariot which four horses are pulling from the sea to climb into the sky and light another day. Interestingly, in relation to the real sun, they are going the wrong way!

To the north and south of the Parterre de Latone and the Tapis Vert are Versailles's principal *bosquets*. As first created by Le Nôtre they were home to a whole series of delightful, fountain-filled fantasia whose charm and whimsy clearly owed much to Italian gardens such as that of the Villa d'Este in Tivoli. Today they are but a shadow of their former selves, having lost such wonders of artifice as the maze, with its 32 fountains illustrating Aesop's Fables, the Théâtre d'Eau, whose fountains formed a semicircular wall of water, and the Montagne d'Eau, whose name says it all. Today the only of Le Nôtre's spectacular inventions to survive intact is the Salle de Bal (literally »ballroom«) or Bosquet des Rocailles (c. 1685), which consists of three shell-encrusted cascades arranged around an oval arena. Equally dramatic, although much less florid, is the Bosquet d'Encelade (c. 1675), featuring Gaspard Marsy's wonderful gilded statue/fountain of the agonizing Titan half buried by the island of Sicily, which Athena has just dumped on top of him. In a rather sillier vein is Hardouin-Mansart's Bosquet de la Colonnade, which features a flimsy circular peristyle enclosing water-splashing bowls. Louis XVI saw to the creation of one spectacular Bosquet in the form of the Bains d'Apollon, realized by the painter Hubert Robert in 1776. It was designed to accommodate Girardon, Regnaudin, Marsy *et al.*'s splendid groups of statues representing Apollo and his horses served by nymphs and Tritons (1672), which had formerly stood in the Grotte de Thétis (demolished for the building of Hardouin-Mansart's chapel). Robert placed them in a wonderfully evocative, waterfall-draped cave that fully demonstrates the period's tendencies towards overblown Romanticism.

32.2 Grand Trianon
Parc du Château de Versailles
Louis Le Vau, 1670; Jules Hardouin-Mansart with Louis XIV and Robert de Cotte, 1687/88
(RER: Versailles Rive-Gauche; if you are arriving by car, the nearest gate is the Porte Saint-Antoine)

The name »Trianon« is all that today survives of the village of the same appellation, which was bought up and demolished by Louis XIV in the late 1660s in order to enlarge his estate at Versailles. Where the settlement had once stood, at the head of the northern arm of the Petit Canal, the Sun King ordered the construction of a »refreshment pavilion«, a place where he and his then mistress, Mme de Montespan, could escape for meals away from the rigid court etiquette at the Château de Versailles (32.1, above). Put up with great alacrity in the summer months of 1670, the Trianon de Porcelaine, as the edifice became known, was Louis Le Vau's last building. It took its name from the blue-and-white ceramic tiles and ornaments that covered its exterior, from the courtyard floor to the roof, and which were supposed to evoke the decoration of Chinese buildings. This architectural caprice consisted of a main, single-storey *corps de logis*, which was flanked on its courtyard by free-standing, subordinate pavilions, each of which served for the preparation of a different meal course. Behind the Trianon was a garden, which the king kept stocked with a dazzling variety of flowers, so many in fact that his head gardener reputedly disposed of 2 million flower pots for their upkeep and rotation.

But like the flowers that adorned it, the charms of the Trianon de Porcelaine were to be but temporary. Cracks rapidly appeared in its ceramic decoration, Mme de Montespan fell from grace, and the king grew bored with his little folly. In 1687 he ordered its reconstruction, on much more grandiose lines, and himself dictated certain features of the final design.

Jules Hardouin-Mansart, in his capacity as Premier Architecte du Roi, was commissioned to carry out the conversion, which he accomplished with almost as much alacrity as his predecessor, work beginning in the summer of 1687 and the king's first »dinner« in the new Trianon occurring in January 1688. Baptized the »Trianon de Marbre« because of the marble columns and cladding decorating its exterior (it was only with the construction of the Petit Trianon, 32.4, that the building took on its current name of »Grand Trianon«), the edifice owes its rather peculiar, asymmetrical ground plan to the fact that the Trianon de Porcelaine's pavilions were incorporated in the new plan, although not its *corps de logis*, which was demolished. One of the reused structures was the former Pavillon des Parfums (where scented flowers had been cultivated), which was situated away from the other buildings of the old Trianon, and which thus, in order to connect it to the new complex, necessitated the building of the long gallery that projects westwards from the northern end of the garden front. Centred around its *cour d'honneur*, the Grand Trianon is divided into two halves – that south of the courtyard housed the kitchens and the apartments of the Grand Dauphin, while that to the north contained the royal apartments – which are linked by a colonnade that forms the linchpin of the composition. This colonnade, which since its creation has been inaccurately referred to as the »Péristyle«, was one of the features imposed by Louis XIV on the Grand Trianon. He had it drawn up by Robert de Cotte, who replaced an ill Hardouin-Mansart during part of the design and building period (de Cotte, who was one of Hardouin-Mansart's assistants as well as his brother-in-law, was also responsible for the Grand Trianon's original interiors). The colonnade, which the king wanted so as to allow views of the garden from the *cour d'honneur*, has the singularity of featuring columned arcades on the courtyard side and free-standing columns on the garden front. It was also Louis XIV who ordered the destruction of the high, French-style roofs that had coiffed the Trianon de Porcelaine, and which Hardouin-Mansart had originally planned to retain in the conversion, because he did not want the building to have the aspect of a »grosse maison«. Louis would not even allow chimneys, which to function properly need a certain amount of height, to protrude beyond the balustrade that crowns the Grand Trianon's elevations, and thus the building's unprecedented, low-slung horizontality, which is one of its most startling and original characteristics, is entirely imputable to the king. We should remember, however, that when built the Trianon's skyline was not quite as austerely nude as it appears today, since it was originally home to a host of statues, urns and other ornaments that have since been lost.

The Sun King also dictated many of the details of the building, including the twinning of the columns on the Péristyle and the choice of materials for the external cladding, the principal of which is pink Languedoc marble, with green Pyrénées marble also making an appearance. Hardouin-Mansart's principal contribution to the building's exterior appearance seems to have been the articulation of its façades. Out of Le Vau's rectangular bays, which were topped off with bas-relief panels, he created round-headed arcades whose summits occupy the space formerly filled by the panels, and descended the glazing to floor level through the use of *portes-fenêtres* (French windows). Never before had French windows been used on a such a large and systematic scale, and it is almost certainly thanks to the Grand Trianon that they became one of the staples of 18C French architecture. Their presence at the Trianon serves to blur the distinction between interior and exterior, making the building a garden palace *par excellence*. The combination of the Trianon's low, unintimidating scale, warm, coloured, marbles and exuberant sculpted detailing featuring festoons and swags creates a delightful mood of gay sensuality, yet the result remains controlled, and the visitor is in no way overwhelmed by its charms. It is safe to say that nothing quite like the Grand Trianon had ever been built before: in place of the imposing, self-contained, agglomerate structures that were French châteaux up till this point, we find a single-storey series of arcades articulated in such a manner as to suggest that they could be extended infinitely in any direction, an open, unresolved structure whose almost vernacular plan stands in stark contrast to the squarely symmetrical and delimited architecture of a building such as Vaux-le-Vicomte (37.1). Indeed so unusual in character was the Trianon that nothing quite like it would be built again in the century following its creation, although elements of its design (such as the aforementioned French windows) were influential, and a few aristocratic villas and *maisons de plaisance* (e. g. the original Palais Bourbon, 7.4) copied

32.2 Grand Trianon

its external aspect. One wing of the Trianon – that which runs northwards from the western end of the gallery, and which is known as the Trianon-sous-Bois – would prove particularly foretelling of future developments. Unlike the rest of the exterior, the Trianon-sous-Bois is not marble clad but instead realized in plain, dressed ashlar, and is divided into two low storeys rather than one tall one. In the austerity of its principal elevations, where the only animation is provided by the fenestration and its very plain surrounds and keystones, the Trianon-sous-Bois anticipates buildings of the second half of the 18C, such as Gabriel's Rue-Royal façades (see 8.1).

Internally, the Grand Trianon is divided up into long suites of rooms running along the garden front, where the principal chambers are located, with parallel suites of rooms running behind on the building's courtyard side. Stripped of its furnishings during the Revolution, the Grand Trianon was rehabilitated under Napoleon and Louis Philippe, and thus presents a curious mélange of Louis-Quatorze and Empire-style interiors. The Salon des Glaces, which is attributed to Robert de Cotte and whose current state (but not its furnishings) is the result of work carried out between 1688 and 1703, is the best example at the Trianon of late-Louis-Quatorze decoration. Realized entirely in mirrors and white-painted panelling (whose relief elements were probably originally intended to be gilded), it prefigures Louis-Seize-period interiors. The room that has probably changed the least since the Sun King's day is the gallery, which is decorated with 22 paintings of the gardens of Versailles (21 by Jean Cotelle and one by Jean-Baptiste Martin), which were commissioned during Louis XIV's reign and thus provide an important documentary record of the palace as he knew it. Also of note is the Chambre de l'Empereur, which was redecorated by Napoleon and features some fine Empire furnishings and hangings. It, along with the other interiors at the Trianon, was beautifully restored in the 1960s.

We should not leave the Grand Trianon without mentioning its gardens, which feature parterres and terraces descending towards the Petit Canal. Although their glory days are over, and Le Nôtre's Jardin des Sources, which prefigured 18C *jardins à l'anglaise*, is no longer extant, the Trianon's grounds retain their charm. The principle feature is the Buffet d'Eau, a fountain created by Hardouin-Mansart, in 1703, whose jets are presided over by Neptune and Amphitrite. Copses of trees surround the gardens and provide a tousled contrast to their manicured horizontality.

32.3 Pavillon Français
Parc du Château de Versailles, Jardin des Trianons, midway between the Grand and Petit Trianons
Ange-Jacques Gabriel, 1749
(RER: Versailles Rive-Gauche; if you are arriving by car, the nearest gate is the Porte Saint-Antoine)
It is interesting to compare this exquisite little pavilion, built by Gabriel as a place of rest for Louis XV in the Tri-

32.4 Petit Trianon

anon gardens, with its nearby senior of 60 years, the Grand Trianon (32.2), and with its other neighbour and successor, the Petit Trianon (32.4), begun by Gabriel more than a decade later. The Pavillon Français stands as something of a midway point between the two. One storey high, like the Grand Trianon, the Pavillon is composed of a central octagon with four projecting wings, forming an Irish cross in plan. Internally, elaborate white-and-gold columns and mouldings and a frieze of farmyard animals decorate its walls, but externally, although it is reminiscent of the Grand Trianon, it presents a much more sober aspect. In place of the Grand Trianon's coloured marbles, we find plain, dressed ashlar, rusticated with rectilinear precision. Decoration is limited to the windows' carved spandrels and keystones and to the flamboyant urns and cherubs that sprout from the building's balustrade (as was originally the case at the Grand Trianon). But despite these touches of gaiety, we can already see a move towards the pared-down restraint of the Petit Trianon. Mme de Pompadour, who was behind the Pavillon commission, played an important role in the simplification of style that culminated in the Petit Trianon, which was also commissioned at her instigation. The results were clearly to the liking of Louis XV, who declared with regard to the Pavillon that »it is in this taste that one should build«.

32.4 Petit Trianon
Parc du Château de Versailles
Ange-Jacques Gabriel, 1762–68
(RER: Versailles Rive-Gauche; if you are arriving by car, the nearest gate is the Porte Saint-Antoine)
Although her physical relationship with Louis XV lasted only five years, Jeanne-Antoinette Poisson, Marquise de Pompadour, maintained a close friendship with the king until her death, and was effective mistress of the royal household for 20 years. She encouraged Louis to take an interest in architecture and the arts, and was a generous patron. She also encouraged Louis's interest in horticulture, with the result that in 1750 the king com-

missioned Claude Richard to create a botanical garden in the grounds of the Grand Trianon (32.2). The king liked to spend time there, away from the intrigues of the court, and Mme de Pompadour consequently persuaded him that they should build a small *pavillon d'agrément* in the garden. Gabriel, as Premier Architecte du Roi, was charged with the task, and produced a masterpiece that is regarded by many as the summit of French Classicism.

Gabriel's œuvre was essentially conservative, a consolidation of trends that had begun in the 17C with the work of Mansart and Le Vau, and nothing about the Petit Trianon was especially original. Its careful, sober simplicity and extremely restrained detailing nonetheless heralded a Classical revival that became known as the »style Louis-XVI«. Perfectly square in plan, the house is five bays wide on all sides, and terminates at cornice level in a balustrade, the lofty roofs so fashionable in the 17C and early-18C being entirely absent. Three storeys high on its southern (entrance) and eastern fronts, the house displays only two storeys on its other two façades, which are surrounded by a low terrace that cleverly gets round the rise in ground level on these sides of the building. The entrance, northern and western façades are all divided vertically into three by the inclusion of an only-very-slightly-projecting central *avant-corps*; since the west front, which gives onto the formal gardens leading to the Grand Trianon, was considered the principal elevation, its *avant-corps* is adorned with colossal Corinthian columns, while the other two sport Corinthian pilasters. The east front, which gave onto the parterres of the botanical gardens, is the plainest of all the four, with neither *avant-corps* nor order.

It is interesting to compare a 1761 set of designs for the house with the edifice as built. Gabriel originally planned a building only three bays wide on the main façades, with swags, medallions, round-headed pediments and other detailing decorating their surfaces. By increasing the house's width he made it more imposing and more august, and by stripping the detailing down to an absolute minimum created a work of quiet »good taste« that is a masterpiece of restraint. Devoid of any of the sculpted protuberances that characterized French luxury architecture up to this point, the Petit Trianon avoids severity only through the extreme refinement and elegance of its proportions.

In comparison to the lavish pomp of the Château de Versailles (32.1), the interior of the Petit Trianon is modest. The principal rooms are all situated on the first floor – which is reached by an imposing *escalier d'honneur* – and follow the perimeter of the house. Their delicately carved panelling, painted in subtle colours with only sparing gilding, reflects the house's garden setting and the king's interest in botany: swags and garlands and the royal monogram rendered in leaves and flowers in the Salon de Compagnie, lilies inside circular wreaths in the Salon de Musique, and bunches of roses in the Cabinet du Roi (later the Chambre de la Reine), all sculpted with vigorous authenticity by Honoré Guibert.

The king's private apartments were in the attic, reached by a discreet staircase.

Mme de Pompadour died before completion of the Petit Trianon, and it was Louis XV's subsequent mistress, Mme du Barry, who first shared its charms with the king. On his accession to the throne, in 1774, Louis XVI gave the residence to Marie-Antoinette, who entirely transformed the grounds (32.5), and with whom the house is now indelibly associated.

32.5 Jardin du Petit Trianon
Parc du Château de Versailles
Richard Mique with the Comte de Caraman and Hubert Robert, c. 1775–85
(RER: Versailles Rive-Gauche; if you are arriving by car, the nearest gate is the Porte Saint-Antoine)

Ill-suited to the rigid ceremony and bitchy intrigue of court life, Marie-Antoinette sought refuge as often as possible in the Petit Trianon (32.4), which Louis XVI had given her on their accession to the throne in 1774. She lived there as a private individual, entirely proscribing etiquette – company was not even required to stand when she entered a room. When she acquired the residence, the grounds to its north and east were occupied by the greenhouses and parterres of Louis XV's botanical garden. Over the next decade, at enormous expense, the queen radically transformed the area into an escapist fantasy world whose charms would banish, at least temporarily, the burden of state affairs.

The last two decades of the *ancien régime* witnessed an aristocratic craze for English and Chinese-style landscape gardens, and Marie-Antoinette commissioned the Jardinier-Fleuriste du Roi, Antoine Richard, to create just such a garden at the Petit Trianon. His designs were not to her liking, however, and she asked the Comte de Caraman, an amateur gardener of some renown, to produce an alternative scheme. His proposal so delighted her that she appointed him »Directeur des Jardins de la Reine«. Richard Mique, as Premier Architecte du Roi, was engaged to make the count's project a reality. Over the course of time Caraman's influence waned, and he was replaced in the

32.5 Jardin du Petit Trianon. Hameau de la Reine

queen's confidence by the landscape painter Hubert Robert, who was appointed »Dessinateur des Jardins du Roi« in 1778.

Directly north of the Petit Trianon, in place of Louis XV's greenhouses, Mique created a small artificial lake, from which flows a brook that meanders all over the garden before terminating in a wide horseshoe in front of the east façade of the house. Sinuous, »naturalistic« paths snake across the terrain, joining up the several *fabriques*, or follies, that are dotted here and there.
To the west of the lake is the Belvedere, designed by Mique and completed in 1779. A small octagonal pavilion with a sumptuous marble floor, it was intended for intimate gatherings, with, as its name suggests, a picturesque view over the garden. Close to the Belvedere is the Rocher (rock), a bucolic assemblage of boulders attributed to Richard, which contains the queen's grotto and from which gushes the »source« that feeds the lake and the brook. On a small island formed by a parting of the brook, almost exactly in the axis of the Petit Trianon's east front, Mique erected the exquisitely detailed, circular Temple d'Amour (1777/78) and he was also responsible for the little theatre to the northwest of the Trianon, completed in 1780, whose stage was destined for the thespian talents of the queen herself. Its intimate oval auditorium recalls, in its general outline, Gabriel's Opéra Royal (see 32.1).

However, by far the most famous of Mique's creations at the Petit Trianon is the Hameau de la Reine (queen's hamlet), built in 1783–85. It was inspired by the hamlet created for the Duc de Bourbon-Condé at Chantilly a decade before. Around a sizeable lake that he dug to the north of the Jardin Anglais, Mique erected a picturesque ensemble of mock-Norman buildings: a mill, a dairy, a dovecote, the Tour de Marlborough, the famous Queen's House – whose rustic thatched exterior belies its refined interior – and, slightly away from the lake, a farmhouse. The Hameau was not simply a cloyingly pretty *mise en scène*, however, because everything worked – the queen churned butter in the dairy, her eldest daughter tended vegetables in the garden and, in the farmhouse, a peasant family was installed to look after the queen's cows, Blanchette and Brunette, and create a bucolic *tableau vivant* for royal delectation. The farm also had a more serious purpose, as it was used to demonstrate the latest agricultural practices and formed part of the royal children's education. Nonetheless, it was essentially extravagant kitsch, and its profligacy in Revolutionary eyes no doubt contributed to Mique's subsequent condemnation to the guillotine.

32.6 Ville de Versailles
(RER: Versailles Rive-Gauche)

A ruined medieval château and a small village originally constituted the settlement of Versailles, both of which disappeared under the encroaching tentacles of Louis XIV's palace (32.1). The town of Versailles as we see it today grew up as a natural pendant to the Sun King's château, providing the services necessary for the everyday functioning of the enormous and populous complex. First established in the 1660s, the new settlement was built to the east of the château either side of the huge Place d'Armes that precedes the château's *avant-cour*. Indeed until the 19C the town of Versailles was really two settlements – the Quartier Saint-Louis to the south of the Place d'Armes and the Quartier Notre-Dame to the north – that were physically separated by the three avenues radiating out from the château's entrance (a disposition almost certainly inspired in part by Rome's Piazza del Popolo), which were initially laid out as tree-lined thoroughfares set in parkland. Until the early-18C the town's development was subject to strict rules of urbanism. Straight streets were laid out with uniformly disposed plots containing detached buildings surrounded by gardens, the dimensions of each construction being subject to regulations intended to ensure a harmonious, dignified setting for the château. Indeed initially the town was more of an extension to the palace than a separate settlement in its own right. The town's first buildings were constructed to house the courtiers, and consisted of identical two-storey pavilions in plastered rubble stone with ashlar dressings, the plaster having been painted to look like brick; in other words, their external livery was exactly that of the château itself at that time. Some historians have chosen to see this initial ensemble of palace and town as one single entity, a sort of *château éclaté* with multiple pavilions spreading out individually from the main construction which, through the height restrictions imposed on subordinate structures, remained dominant in the composition. Very little survives of the original Versailles: the Maison des Fontainiers or des Sources (so named because its upper levels contained a reservoir that supplied the neighbourhood's drinking water) at no. 11, rue Carnot (Jacques IV and Maurice Gabriel, 1683) is almost the only still-extant example of the town's two-storey pavilions, while the brick-built Hôtel de Guise (François d'Orbay, 1670–73) at 24, rue de la Chancellerie (running alongside the Avenue de Sceaux) is a rare example of one of the larger residences built during the period of urban regulation.

It was the northern half of the town that initially developed most rapidly and which consequently became home to Versailles's first church, Notre-Dame (at the end of the Rue Hoche), whose name was afterwards given to the entire *quartier*. Begun in 1684 by Jules Hardouin-Mansart, Notre-Dame follows the traditional plan for a large parish church, that is to say it is a scaled-down version of the Notre-Dame-de-Paris-type layout (see 4.2) comprising a Latin cross with non-projecting transepts and an apse-ambulatory terminating the ensemble. The volumetric relationships and main-vessel elevations also follow the traditional pattern. This essentially Gothic design is Classicized inside with Doric pilasters, round-headed arcades, a barrel vault and a crossing dome. Where the interior is grand but hardly very inspired, the entrance façade, much criticized by contemporaries, is surprisingly clumsy for someone of Hardouin-Mansart's reputation: an Italian-style two-storey elevation, rather lacking in finesse, either side of which the architect plonked outsized bell towers that are not at all integrated into the composition.

After Louis XIV's death, the development of Versailles was left to the much-less-regulated free market, and most of the town as we see it today is 18C or later. The continuing presence of the court and the government ensured that building work was in constant progress, and by the end of the *ancien régime* Versailles had grown to become France's sixth largest town. It conserves many fine stone- and stucco-fronted *hôtels particuliers* and apartment buildings, whose façades demonstrate all the stylistic variety of the reigns of Louis XV and XVI. Developed later, the southern part of the town was more regularly laid out than the Quartier Notre-Dame, essentially comprising a grid of streets that is interrupted by the former market place of the Carré Saint-Louis and by the Place Saint-Louis (off the Rue du Général-Leclerc), both of which mirror similar dispositions in the town's northern half (the elegant Place Hoche and the Marché Notre-Dame). The Quartier Saint-Louis finally got itself a place of worship in the mid-18C with the building of the church of Saint-Louis (now the Cathedral of Versailles) at the head of the Place Saint-Louis on a site roughly pendant to that of Notre-Dame in the north. Begun in 1743 and inaugurated in 1754, Saint-Louis was the work of Jacques Hardouin-Mansart de Lévy de Sagonne, grandson of Jules Hardouin-Mansart. As well as being a geographic and familial parallel to its predecessor, Saint-Louis is also in volumetric symmetry with Notre-Dame since Jacques Hardouin-Mansart based his design on the general disposition of his grandfather's church. Jacques nonetheless learnt from his ancestor's mistakes, at least as far as Saint-Louis's entrance façade is concerned, his main elevation being rather more visually coherent than Notre-Dame's thanks to the Baroque groupings of columns and resultant tightness of composition. Inside, however, Saint-Louis is even more bland and uninspired than its older sister.

Other notable 18C buildings in Versailles include the Ministère de la Guerre and the Ministère des Affaires Etrangères, de la Marine et des Colonies (3 and 5, rue de l'Indépendance-Américaine, respectively), built by Jean-Baptiste Berthier in 1759–61. These buildings had the innovatory particularity of being specifically conceived to house government ministries, although to a large extent their designs were adaptations of pre-existent building types: the Ministère de la Guerre is organized like an *hôtel particulier* around a *cour d'honneur*, while the Ministère des Affaires Etrangères resembles a middle-class apartment building, although with much more lavish external adornment. Inside, however, both featured fire-proof compartments made up of brick transversal walls carrying Mediterranean-style brick vaults that were conceived to ensure protection of the ministries' precious archives. In quite another vein is the Couvent de la Reine (today the Lycée Hoche, 73, avenue de Saint-Cloud), which was begun in 1767 at the behest of Queen Marie Leszczynska, Louis XV's consort, by Richard Mique (better known for Marie-Antoinette's *hameau* at the Petit Trianon – see 32.5), and completed in the early 1770s. The convent is organized around its central chapel, which on initial plans appeared as a traditional basilica but was later entirely re-designed by Mique as a centralized, domed edifice whose distinctly neo-Classical, Euclidean volumes were at least partly inspired by Palladio. Despite Mique's reputation as a »safe« architect, the chapel of the Couvent de la Reine shows his ability to innovate and, in its Enlightenment-era neo-Classicism, anticipates by half a century a building like Fontaine's Chapelle Expiatoire (8.4). Inside, the chapel has retained its original décor, including a highly unusual cycle of bas-reliefs by Joseph Deschamps depicting the life of the Virgin Mary.

It was not only queens but also royal mistresses who got to build at Versailles: where Louis XV's first mistress, Mme de Pompadour, left her mark on the park in the form of the Petit Trianon (32.4), his second *amie*, Mme du Barry, graced the town with the addition of her stables (1772) at 19, avenue de Paris (now the Hôtel de Police). They were built by the great Claude-Nicolas Ledoux, a protégé of la du Barry's, and distinguish themselves on the avenue through their enormous *porte-cochère*, which is essentially a scaled-up version of the architect's design for the portal of the Hôtel d'Hallwyl (3.8). The major difference in the Versailles composition, apart from increased size, is that the portal is here given added monumentality through the addition of a giant stone frame that sets it forward as a central, dominant *avant-corps*.

We should not leave Versailles without visiting the Place d'Armes, which was the geographical and ceremonial hub of the whole palace-town ensemble. It is of course dominated by the château to the west, and is closed to the east by the Grandes and Petites Ecuries, which were built by Jules Hardouin-Mansart in 1679–82 (these appellations dated from the time of François I, the Grandes Ecuries being the stables of the king's riding horses while the Petites Ecuries housed his carriage horses). Because located in between Versailles's radiating avenues (Grandes Ecuries to the north, Petites to the south), the sites reserved for the stables were wedge shaped, which is presumably what suggested to Hardouin-Mansart the horse-shoe-form entrance courtyards around which each building is organized. With their arcaded crescents and lavishly sculpted, pedimented *avant-corps* they form a suitably princely backdrop to the Place d'Armes, which served not only as a monumental esplanade for the palace but also as a parade ground and setting for official royal arrivals at, and departures from, the château. Today, however, the Place d'Armes serves another, more prosaic purpose, being the car-and-coach park for the thousands of tourists who come every year to visit the former palace of the Sun King.

33 Charenton-le-Pont

33.1 Centre Commercial Bercy 2
Rue Escoffier, Charenton-le-Pont
Renzo Piano Building Workshop, 1987–90
(Métro: Liberté)

At bottom this is a fairly bog-standard concrete-framed shopping centre, organized around a long, five-storey-high atrium and sitting on top of an underground car-park. Such was the project for which planning permission had been obtained when Renzo Piano and his team were called in to make things a little more interesting. They took their cue from the building's site, which lies in the no-man's-land that is the intersection between the notorious *boulevard périphérique*, Paris's encircling motorway, and the equally traffic-choked Autoroute de l'Est. In response to this inhospitable environment, they chose to encase the centre in an enormous, aerodynamic shell that both isolates it from its surroundings and also constitutes a strong symbol that is easily comprehended from a speeding motor-car. Reminiscent of an airship, the shell perches on top of the shopping centre and comprises a bent- and laminated-wood frame that is clad in two skins, the outer of which consists of prefabricated, satin-finished aluminium »scales«. This system provides an insulating layer of air around the centre that helps maintain a steady internal temperature. Set into the building's 2 km^2 of roofing are glazed openings to light the public spaces. As well as giving the centre a suitably Hi-tech allure, the aluminium strips serve to reflect sunlight and also recall the zinc roofs of traditional Parisian apartment buildings.

For its whizzing, futurist air to succeed, Bercy 2 needed to remain indefinitely pristine, but unfortunately its shell has not aged well. Piano's more successful Kansai Airport in Japan (1988–94) re-appropriated Bercy 2's sensuous profile.

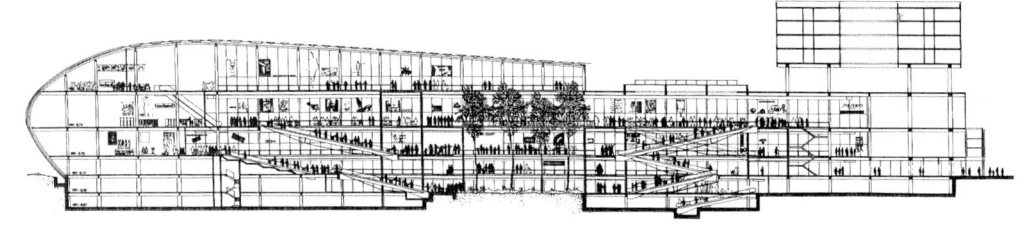

33.1 Centre Commercial Bercy 2. Section and general view

34 Vincennes

34.1 Bois de Vincennes

(Métro: Porte Dorée, Porte de Charenton, Château de Vincennes)

At 995 ha, the Bois de Vincennes is the Paris region's biggest green open space, one of the two »lungs« of the metropolis, in tandem with the Bois de Boulogne (29.1), its counterpart in the west. It is the descendant of an ancient forest which escaped clearance because the ground on which it grew was too stony for cultivation. Acquired by the crown during the 10C, the forest became a hunting ground in the 12C, thereby reflecting Paris's increasing importance as a royal centre: the king needed nearby sport, and the Bois de Vincennes, situated a short distance outside Paris on one of the city's major exit roads, was ideally located. It is thought that a royal hunting lodge was built there during the reign of Louis VII (1137–80), although the first definitely attributable royal residence in the Bois was built under Louis's successor, Philippe II Augustus (reigned 1180–1223), whose fortified *manoir* was successively enlarged by subsequent monarchs to become the present-day Château de Vincennes (34.2). Philippe also erected a wall around the forest to protect it from exploitation by the local population, and stocked it with a variety of game animals.

The forest and its château retained their royal importance until the 1680s, after which Louis XIV moved his court to Versailles (32.1) far away in the west. Following a period of decline, Louis XV had the Bois replanted and renovated, in 1731, to plans by Robert de Cotte. Cotte's transformations included the creation of a system of straight avenues criss-crossing the forest to meet at star-shaped intersections, the principal of which was the Allée Royale, which departed from the southern façade of the château. After completion of the work, Louis XV opened the Bois to the public, commemorating his restoration by the erection of an obelisk at one of the star-shaped junctions, not far from the château.

During the Revolutionary period, the Bois de Vincennes was decimated by the townspeople, who cut down the trees for firewood. Partially restored under the First Empire, it was entirely renewed after the Restoration and became a hunting ground once again. During the July Monarchy, the Bois was much in vogue as a place of promenade. Such peaceful activities conflicted with the needs of the army, however, which had been established by Napoleon in the Château de Vincennes, and which considered the Bois a natural extension of its territory for training and later for defensive purposes. The military's requirements took ever-increasing precedence, and during the 1840s – a politically unstable period in Europe – and afterwards in the 1850s, almost half the then-existing surface area of the Bois de Vincennes was appropriated for use by the armed forces. 166 ha of woodland were destroyed for the creation of an enormous exercise field that cut the Bois literally in two.

With the urban upheavals of the Second Empire, the Bois found itself on the doorstep of the metropolis following the 1859 enlargement of Paris's municipal boundaries, as did the Bois de Boulogne. During his family's exile after the fall of his uncle Napoleon, the future Napoleon III had spent time in London and had admired the British capital's spacious parks and gardens. When, after becoming emperor in 1852, he began to rebuild Paris with the help of Baron Haussmann, he made a gift of the Bois de Boulogne to the municipality, and had it transformed into a *jardin à l'anglaise*. As well as parks, Napoleon III liked symmetry, and, in 1858, decreed that those parts of the Bois de Vincennes not occupied by the army should be remodelled in a similar fashion to the Bois de Boulogne, and made fully accessible to the public. The Bois de Vincennes would thus form an eastern pendant to the Bois de Boulogne, providing the working populations of the east with a similar amenity to that already enjoyed by the wealthy *quartiers* in the west. The first phase of the work was undertaken by the Service Municipal des Promenades et Plantations, an organization originally set up by Haussmann to carry out the transformation of the Bois de Boulogne and headed by Adolphe Alphand, who was seconded by Pierre Barillet-Deschamps and Gabriel Davioud. As at Boulogne, a naturalistic landscape was created, inspired by English parks, with sinuous walkways, open lawns and ornamental lakes. The improvements proved costly and, unable to justify continued state expenditure, Napoleon III transferred possession of the Bois to the Ville de Paris, in 1860, on the condition that the municipality complete the work already begun. The Ville increased the size of the park by buying up land on its periphery, including the Plaine de Bercy, thereby bringing the Bois right up to the gates of the city. In the centre of the former plain, another lake was dug, the impressive Lac Daumesnil, complete with islands and a classical temple perched on a concrete grotto. In 1859, the Paris–Strasbourg railway line was opened (see also 12.2) which, in passing via Vincennes, provided the townspeople with direct access to the Bois. In its new role as a public pleasure park, the Bois was a roaring success, a place of dancing and revelry as well as of picnics and promenade. As at Boulogne, horse racing also formed part of the entertainment, the Hippodrome de Vincennes being opened in 1863 (the race course we see today dates from 1976–83).

During the 1870 Franco-Prussian war, the Bois de Vincennes was again devastated. Although afterwards restored, the army extended its presence and later, during WWI, increased its territory to a total of 350 ha. In the inter-war period the Bois de Vincennes was chosen as the site for the 1931 Exposition Coloniale, which was something of a propaganda exercise designed to glorify French imperialism. 93 ha of parkland round the Lac Daumesnil consequently found themselves overwhelmed by all sorts of pavilions of exotic inspiration. Only the Palais des Colonies (12.13) was intended to be permanent, but the wooden-framed »Grand Pagode«, as it is colloquially known, just next to the lake, also survived, along with two of its smaller sisters. Designed by Louis-Hippolyte Boileau and Léon Carrière, the pavilions were erected to house the exhibits from Cameroon and Togo, and were loosely inspired by the palaces of Cameroonian chieftains found in the Bamoun, Bamileke and Fonschanda regions of the country. Following the exhibition, the pavilions were retained and transformed into a Musée du Bois. After the museum's closure, in the 1970s, they became home to a Buddhist centre, which was enlarged in 1983–85 by the building of a colourful, Tibetan-style temple to designs by Jean-Luc Massot.

One of the biggest successes of the Exposition Coloniale was its zoo, and the government consequently decided to create a permanent zoological establishment in the Bois de Vincennes after the exhibition's closure. Opened in 1934, the zoo is the work of Charles and Daniel Letrosne. In contrast to Berthold Lubetkin's abstract, Modernist interventions at London Zoo, completed around the same time, the Letrosnes decided to create a naturalistic stage set for the animals, albeit out of modern materials. The centrepiece of their design is the extraordinary, 65 m-high chamois rock, visible for miles around, which successfully imitates the mountainous habitat of these creatures. Constructed from a concrete-and-metal frame faced with a 5 cm-thick layer of cement, the rock is hollow, and contains two large water tanks as well as visitor galleries. Its recent restoration included widening the animal paths so that two chamois can now pass each other at the same time.

The second half of the 20C saw two major changes at the Bois de Vincennes: the departure of the armed forces and the increasing encroachment on the wood of sports and leisure facilities. The army was finally persuaded to release its stranglehold on the Bois in the 1950s (modern warfare having made its presence there obsolete), and its former exercise field could thus be replanted with trees. It still hangs on to the Château de Vincennes, however, as well as to two sizeable barracks, one just next to the castle and another to its south, bang in the middle of the Allée Royale (which was recreated in the 1980s). Getting the army to leave and the barracks demolished has so far proved a pipe dream. As for leisure facilities, the Bois is now home to the Parc Floral, created by the landscape architect David Collin in 1969, as well as to numerous stadia and sports grounds, which altogether have swallowed up nearly 120 ha.

Today the Bois de Vincennes faces an uncertain future. Only 110 ha of untouched woodland survive, commuter traffic chokes its thoroughfares, and decades will be needed for its planted environment to recover from the December 1999 hurricane, during which 210 ha were literally devastated and a total of 4,000 trees lost overnight. As a result, large stretches of the Bois de Vincennes now resemble wasteland rather than a wood. An ambitious programme of long-term replanting has been undertaken, and there has been talk of returning as much of the Bois as possible to a »natural« state.

34.1 Bois de Vincennes

34.2 Château de Vincennes
Avenue de Paris
Extant buildings begun 1361
(Métro: Château de Vincennes)

Forbidding fortresses are not what one immediately associates with Paris, but sitting just outside the city boundary in a banal suburb is this splendid example. One of the biggest and best-preserved medieval castles in Europe, the Château de Vincennes has the distinction of being the only medieval-period French royal residence to survive substantially in its original form. Its history is inextricably linked with the Bois de Vincennes (34.1) at whose edge it stands, the first building on this site almost certainly having been a hunting lodge built by Louis VII (reigned 1137–80). Later, Philippe II Augustus (reigned 1180–1223) erected a modest *manoir* here, which, progressively enlarged and improved by successive sovereigns, constituted the nucleus of today's castle. It survived intact until the 17C, and only finally disappeared completely in the 19C. The enormous fortress we see today was built by Jean II the Good (reigned

1350–64) and his son, Charles V (reigned 1364–80), in response to the very real threat of English attack during the Hundred Years' War. First came the huge keep (c. 1361–71), a stone's throw away from the old *manoir*, in which the royal person could be kept safe both from enemy capture and the blood-lust of riotous mobs at home. Then, c. 1373–80, Charles V built an enormous curtain wall encircling 6 ha of land – including the *manoir* and its dependent buildings – and defended by nine towers. He also began the château's beautiful chapel, which was only finally completed in the mid-16C. The name of Jean and Charles's architects have not come down to us, although Raymond du Temple, who worked on the Louvre (1.8) in the same period, has been proposed as a likely candidate.

In the 1650s, Cardinal Mazarin reconfigured the southern end of the château with a view to providing safe accommodation for the young Louis XIV in the event of Parisian uprisings. To this end, Louis Le Vau built two new wings against the eastern and western curtain walls and reconfigured the southern curtain wall as an arcade to allow views out across the Bois and the Allée Royale. Following his majority, Louis XIV often came to Vincennes to hunt, but abandoned the château after installing the court permanently at Versailles (32.1) in 1682. In the 18C the castle entered a period of decline, being used as a prison – notable inmates including Diderot, Mirabeau, and the Marquis de Sade – and a porcelain factory, and briefly housing the Ecole Militaire. Threatened with destruction in 1787 and again after the Revolution, it became home to the Arsenal de Paris in 1796 and was thereafter occupied by the military. Lack of upkeep caused the château's towers to fall into dereliction, and they were consequently demolished to the height of the curtain wall in the early-19C, all except for the Tour du Village. Since the end of WWII, the château has been home to the army, navy and air-force archives.

The keep
Although the keep we see today dates from the reigns of Jean the Good and Charles V, its foundations are in fact older, having been built by Philippe VI, father of Jean the Good, in 1336–40. Begun in the context of the Hundred Years' War, Philippe's *travaux* were almost certainly abandoned due to the financial difficulties engendered by the conflict. An idea of the cost of castle-building can be got from the fact that in the year 1363 alone Jean the Good employed 200 masons, 200 journeymen, 100 labourers and 80 stone cutters at Vincennes, with 300 waggons transporting stone to the building site. Hundreds of men must also have been employed at the quarries, estimates for the total number of people involved in the project being put at between 1,500 and 2,000 at any one time. At this spanking rate the keep proper was completed in just eight years, in 1369, and its defensive circuit in 1371.

It is to Philippe VI's architect that we owe the keep's plan, a square of 16.25 m with four round towers defending it at each corner – thereby avoiding the problem of »dead« angles (the diagonals radiating from the corners along which attackers could approach out of firing range) – and a rectangular latrine tower jutting out on the northern side. Rising a whopping 52 m above ground level and comprising walls 3.25 m thick, Vincennes's keep is almost certainly the largest now surviving in Europe. It sits on a square platform that is defended by a 14 m-deep, heavily counterscarped moat (now dry) and a curtain wall, which is itself defended by round corner turrets and a machicolated *chemin de ronde* (covered look-out gallery), which also probably served as a promenade gallery for the king. An elaborate twin-towered gatehouse with a drawbridge and portcullis provides access to the keep's platform on its eastern side, and is now the only point of entry, the less elaborate western-side gateway having disappeared in the 17C. A small barbican formerly guarded the stone bridge leading to the eastern gatehouse, but has since been demolished. Also gone are the various structures, including the château's chapel, that stood on the platform outside the keep, most of them built up against the platform's curtain wall. That Vincennes was a royal residence and not just a military installation was made clear externally through the gatehouse's sculpted decoration, which included moulded cornices (repeated on the keep itself) and, above the entrance archway, statue-filled niches and the monarch's coat of arms (vandalized during the Revolution).

Entry to the keep was gained at first-floor level via a footbridge connecting it to the gatehouse. Five storeys of accommodation were provided, each bar the last comprising essentially the same layout: a large vaulted room occupying the keep's centre with further chambers in each of the corner towers. Supplementary spaces are to be found within the thickness of the walls, including the principal spiral staircase rising the full height of the structure. Services – kitchens, storerooms, etc. – were on the ground floor, the first floor served as the Salle du Conseil (council room), the second and third floors contained the king's and queen's bedchambers respectively, the fourth floor housed the Dauphin, while the fifth, with its corbelled exterior balcony, formed part of the keep's upper defensive measures, in tandem with the flat roof terrace. At some point after the keep's completion a grand, spiral *escalier d'honneur* was built in the southeastern corner tower to provide access to the king's apartment from the Salle du Conseil. Each of the main chambers is coiffed with four quadripartite vaults supported at its centre by a slender pillar. Almost nothing now survives of the château's sumptuous décor bar the wooden vault panelling still to be seen in some rooms and the many vault carvings, which include elaborate colonnettes, tracery and mouldings on the central pillars, and wall brackets sporting, amongst others, prophets' and evangelists' heads. Monumental carved chimneypieces, of which a fine example can be seen in the queen's bedchamber, also contributed to the building's

34.2 Château de Vincennes. Chapel

adornment. To visualize the castle in all its former glory we should imagine the rich wall hangings, panelling and painted decoration that filled its spaces with colour; traces of red-and-white *fleurs de lis* on a blue background can still be seen in the king's bedchamber (although the other painted décor we see today was the work of 18C prisoners). If the royal apartments seem improbably small, we should remember that Charles had a considerable number of other rooms at his disposal in the buildings constructed outside the keep against its curtain wall, which were accessed via footbridges from the Salle du Conseil.

At the time of writing the keep is undergoing long and painstaking restoration work and is consequently closed to the public. Instabilities in its structure necessitated the construction of a scaffolding corset to hold it up during renovation, and its exterior will probably be thus obscured for a good few years to come.

The curtain wall

Realized astonishing quickly in the space of only seven years, the enormous curtain wall built by Charles V at Vincennes measures exactly 700×1000 feet (228× 391 m). These huge dimensions are more those of a small fortified town than a castle, and it seems that Charles's intention was to create nothing less than a fortified seat of government, an easily defendable and closed-off Forbidden City set sufficiently far away from the troublesome capital to avid the mob, but close enough to oversee the affairs of the kingdom. Christine de Pisan's biography *Le Livre des Faiz et Bonnes Mœurs du Sage Roy Charles V* (1404) affirms: »[the king] liked the Château de Vincennes so much that he formulated the project of building a closed town there; the plans were all ready ... He had thus distributed and assigned places to his courtiers to build there, but his death put a stop to all his fine projects.« Rather than the forerunner of Brasilia that some French historians have suggested, Charles's project, had it been completed, would have been more of a precursor to Louis XIV's suburban seat of government at the Château de Versailles.

2.6 m thick on average and rising 10 m above ground level, the curtain wall terminates in a machicolated walkway which was originally crenellated. Its exterior elevation is notable for the extremely high quality of its stonework, whose realization must have been exceedingly costly. Nine enormous, 43 m-high rectangular towers defended the wall, as well as a huge water-filled moat (today, like the keep's, dry). These towers were not just military installations, however, for their internal dispositions and their décor make it clear that they were designed as residences, which, in the event of attack, could act as separate, self-contained »keeps«. The Tour du Village at the northern flank's centre, the only tower to survive intact, was the largest, and still displays some of its original décor: gabled and pinnacled niches (now devoid of their statues) and the royal coat of arms above the entrance, angels flanking the decorative arch containing the tower's clock, sculpted cornices and gargoyles at roof level, and, inside, vault carvings and sculpted fireplaces. In its size, quality of construction and inhabitable towers, the Château de Vincennes is unlike any other castle, but it is also unlike any walled town, Charles V's architects having invented a new kind of fortress-town specifically tailored to their monarch's needs.

The chapel
Situated opposite the keep, the Sainte-Chapelle de Vincennes owes its off-axis positioning to the fact that it was orientated in relation to Philippe Augustus's *manoir*, which stood to its north. We do not know when the chapel was begun, but by the time of Charles V's death, in 1380, its walls rose as far as the windows' bases. Continued under Charles's immediate successors, the chapel had probably reached the vault springing points by 1410. During the century that followed, the Paris region was essentially abandoned by France's monarchs, who preferred the safety of the Loire valley, and it was not until François I brought the court back to the capital that work began again on Vincennes's chapel. In the 1520s its pinnacles were constructed and its roofing begun, followed by the vaults, which were completed in 1550. Over the next two years the chapel was fitted out with sumptuous furnishings and decoration, almost all of which was destroyed at the Revolution.

Architecturally, Vincennes's chapel reproduces the essential dispositions of the upper level of the famous Sainte-Chapelle (1.2) in the Palais de la Cité (1.1). If the Sainte-Chapelle de Vincennes is only one storey high, and not two as was the tradition for French palace chapels, it is because Charles V had his own private places of worship within the keep complex, Vincennes's Sainte-Chapelle being destined to act more as a sort of »parish church« for the settlement the king planned to create at the château. Like the Palais de la Cité's Sainte-Chapelle, Vincennes's also served as a reliquary, being given a fragment of the »True Cross«, and was run by a chapter comprising a treasurer, 15 canons and various curates and clerks. Unlike the Palais de la Cité's, it still conserves its treasury (*trésor*), which juts out from the rear of its northern flank. In the absence of the lavish décor and polychromy to be found at the Palais de la Cité, Vincennes's Sainte-Chapelle appears even more architectonically »pure«, its soaring single vessel representing for many the summit of the Gothic »skeletal« structural system. Just as at the Palais de la Cité, this »purity« would not have been possible without the considerable battery of iron reinforcements that allows the building to stand up.

If the Sainte-Chapelle de Vincennes owes its general disposition to the architecture of the first half of the 13C, its decoration is mostly of the 14C. While the apse window tracery is Rayonnant in style, that of the nave is Flamboyant, from which we can conclude that construction started at the east end and terminated at the west with the magnificent entrance elevation. Set within the entrance front's elaborately coiffed flanking towers we find a superimposition of three crocketed and tracery-filled gables. The architect's handling of the monumental rose window combined with the delicate filigree of the middle and lower gables produces a splendidly subtle effect of diaphanous layers, like sheets of embroidered muslin hung one in front of the other. Also of note are the portal's beautifully accomplished archivolt carvings, featuring kings, prophets and angels, which are a rare surviving example of Paris-region sculpture from this period.

Modification of the castle under Louis XIV
Louis Le Vau's first intervention at Vincennes consisted in building what is now known as the Aile du Roi, on the château's western flank, in 1654. Inside it contained apartments for the king, the queen mother (regent at the time) and the king's brother, the Duc d'Anjou. Because his façades were set in the context of a fortress, Le Vau made them heavily rusticated, but ennobled the interior elevation with colossal Doric pilasters. In 1658, the architect doubled the accommodation available at Vincennes by building an identical wing on the château's eastern side, which become known as the Aile de la Reine. It was at this time that the *cour d'honneur* was created through the building of a rusticated arcade linking the two wings to the north, and the parallel conversion of the southern part of the curtain wall. What, when viewed from within the curtain wall, appears to be a centrally placed, Doric triumphal arch providing access to the castle, turns out, when viewed from outside the château, to be the 14C Tour du Bois cut down to a fraction of its original height and dressed up in Classical garb; the undisguisable medieval buttressing clearly gives the game away on the external façade.

Little now remains of the 17C décor in the Ailes du Roi and de la Reine, which was realized in 1659–61 by Philippe de Champaigne, Michel Dorigny and Nicolas Loir. Of particular note amongst the surviving interiors is a gilded, painted and panelled *cabinet* in the Aile du Roi, whose monumental stuccowork ceiling was clearly influenced by Italian models.

35 Le Raincy

35.1 Notre-Dame du Raincy
83, avenue de la Résistance
Auguste Perret, 1922/23
(RER: Le Raincy)

One of the iconic buildings of the early-Modern period, Notre-Dame du Raincy was, like Perret's pioneering, concrete-framed apartment block in the Rue Franklin (16.8), technically conservative in its use of the new material but aesthetically revolutionary. Commissioned to serve an expanding suburb and also to commemorate the Battle of the Marne, the church was built on an extremely limited budget, a constraint which led Perret to take a step unprecedented for a religious edifice and construct it entirely from raw reinforced concrete. With this, the first of his many church commissions, Perret stripped his style down to its essentials, creating a building of great rigour and beauty.

In plan, Notre-Dame du Raincy is a simple rectangle, but structurally and visually it is more complex. Perret closely followed the precepts of Auguste Choisy, by whom he was greatly influenced, and created a hybrid building of essentially Gothic inspiration that nonetheless attempts to solve the age-old opposition between Classical and Gothic structural systems, a question that had haunted church designers since the Renaissance.

35.1 Notre-Dame du Raincy. Interior view

His design comprises a tall, central nave, covered by a shallow, concrete barrel vault and flanked by narrower and only very slightly lower side aisles, themselves coiffed by short, transverse vaults. Following the natural slope of the terrain, the nave floor descends gently westward (the church is orientated east–west rather than the usual west–east), which allowed Perret to create a raised choir whose undercroft houses the vestry. Four rows of columns support the vaulting, two on either side of the nave, and dramatically demonstrate the technical capabilities of concrete: some 12 m high, the columns are a mere 43 cm in diameter at the base, thinning to only 39 cm at the summit, and thus appear breathtakingly slender. Perret justified their polygonal profile – which, because of the complex shuttering needed to mould them, made them more expensive than simple rectangular supports – on technical as well as aesthetic grounds. Like a tree trunk, rigidity is ensured from all angles and it was, he claimed, the most suitable form for a member under compression. Polished ridges on the columns produce an impression of fluting and give graphic gradations of shadow. Columns and vaults together form an entirely free-standing, rigid whole, with no load-bearing walls or external buttressing, and, true to Choisy, the structure is visible at a glance, each component pared down to its essence. Despite the columns' lean prowess, the design is not particularly technically advanced: spans much greater than those at Notre-Dame du Raincy had already been achieved in reinforced concrete, and the church could easily have been covered in one go. Perret's choice of structure was thus clearly made on symbolic, aesthetic and ideological grounds – symbolic and aesthetic in terms of the references to traditional church architecture, ideological in terms of Perret's belief in the superiority of structures derived from wooden construction, in the mould of Antique, and especially ancient-Greek, temples. Rather in the manner of Soufflot's Panthéon (5.8), Notre-Dame du Raincy successfully combines the Classical and Gothic systems, managing to be both a roof supported by free-standing columns, like an Antique temple, and at the same time a vaulted basilica, in the manner of a Gothic church.

Because columns and vaults are free-standing, Perret was able to curtain his church in glass – held in place by a concrete filigree of squares, rectangles, circles and lozenges – thus encapsulating the idea, so recurrently expressed in medieval church architecture, that »God is light«. One is immediately struck by the freedom of space produced by Notre-Dame's economical structure and the abundant light flooding in. The stained glass was the work of Maurice Denis who, aided by Marguerite Huré, created a graded progression of colour which culminates in the deep blue of the rear choir wall. The effect is stunning and earned the church the sobriquet of »Sainte-Chapelle du béton« (literally »holy chapel of concrete« but also a reference to Paris's 13C Sainte-Chapelle (1.2), which is famous for its soaring stained-glass windows).

On the exterior, only the church's principal, entrance façade received special treatment – the others, largely hidden behind neighbouring buildings, are simply the logical product of the internal design. For the main elevation, Perret conceived a 50 m-high bell tower (criticized by Le Corbusier as too historicizing) which steps back successively towards its summit. In the interests of economy and speed, Perret aimed for a high degree of standardization of components, and the tower is thus built from the same type of columns as those supporting the vaults. Perret also claimed that the church's vault dimensions had been determined by the necessity of re-using shuttering that his firm had previously employed on another project. While the real degree of »production-line« fabrication may have been less than Notre-Dame's supporters subsequently claimed, Perret's methods certainly presented considerable advantages over traditional technology: total construction time was only 14 months, and the final cost was astonishingly low at 600,000 francs.

Where, cautiously, Perret had tiled the concrete frame of his Rue-Franklin flats to protect the iron reinforcements from the elements, at Notre-Dame du Raincy he boldly left the concrete exactly as was after removal of the shuttering, without even any surface treatment. This was ultimately to prove disastrous, as the poor-quality mix was not waterproof, causing it to crumble and the iron reinforcements to rust, shattering

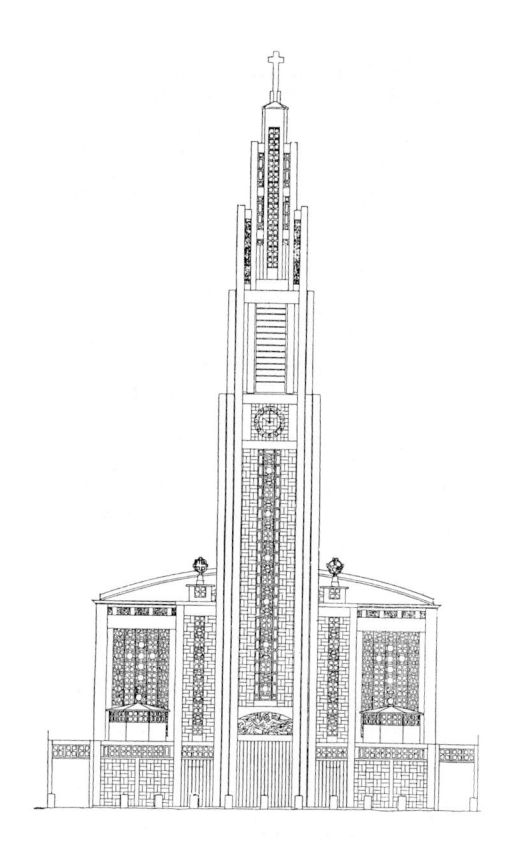

35.1 Notre-Dame du Raincy. Front elevation

the concrete still in place. In 1988–96, a massive and expensive restoration programme was undertaken, which included the application of a waterproof coating. Some argued that it would have been easier and cheaper to demolish the church and build a replica, but the French authorities were insistent that, despite its recent date, the building (listed since 1966) should be treated like any other historic monument. Thus, Perret's masterpiece, which suffered from its precocious audacity, has been given a new lease of life and continues to attract visitors from all over the world. It also lives on through the countless imitations it spawned, both in France and abroad, which include, curiously, a half-sized replica in Tokyo, built by the American architect Antonin Raymond in 1938.

36 Marne-la-Vallée

36.1 The new town of Marne-la-Vallée
(RER: all stations on the A4 line between Bry-sur-Marne and Marne-la-Vallée Chessy)

Planned by General de Gaulle's government in 1965, Paris's five satellite new towns – Cergy-Pontoise, Saint-Quentin-en-Yvelines, Evry, Sénart and Marne-la-Vallée – were intended to decongest the capital and boost the region's economic growth while also avoiding the uncontrolled urban sprawl that threatened to choke a good chunk of the Ile-de-France. Biggest of the five at 15,000 ha, Marne-la-Vallée is also the most unusual urbanistically in that its territory takes the form of a long corridor running along the Marne valley, with no obvious centre or focal point. Instead we find a disparate collection of built-up areas that include pre-existent settlements such as Champs-sur-Marne, Lagny-sur-Marne and Noisiel (see 36.6), which were swallowed up into the new town, and newly constructed areas such as Noisy-le-Grand, the Cité Descartes and Disneyland Paris (36.7). Running along the corridor and linking them all together (and to Paris) are the RER railway line (see feature on the Métro and the RER) and the A4 motorway. There is also a TGV link on the Dijon-Lille line. From a population of 103,000 in 1975, Marne-la-Vallée has grown to an estimated 260,000 souls at the time of writing. Despite the increased urbanization necessary to house all these new inhabitants, much of the town's territory remains sparsely populated countryside.

Paris's new towns were not intended to be dormitory settlements dependent on the capital, but self-supporting communities with their own jobs and industry sufficient to employ all who lived there. Perhaps inevitably, given the expansion of the tertiary sector in the last 30 years and Marne-la-Vallée's proximity to Paris, the town has attracted essentially white-collar employment. Well over 1,100,000 m² of office space are now to be found there, companies having been lured by the town's winning combination of overheads considerably lower than those in Paris and a location nonetheless close and well-connected enough to benefit from the capital's prestige and highly educated workforce. Commuting from the capital to Marne-la-Vallée is thus not unusual.

Although Marne-la-Vallée was conceived in the 1960s utopian era of projects such as Brasília and Chandigarh, it has turned out to be a very different place from these megalomaniacal, single-architect-designed, prestige environments. Instead, developed by bureaucrats along watered-down Modernist-utopian lines, it has for the most part become an incoherent sprawl of soulless zoning, with banal business parks, lacklustre housing estates, Legoland out-of-town shopping centres and the odd attempt at creating »neighbourhood centres«. Disjunction and discontinuity are generally the sorry result, perhaps most shockingly displayed at Noisy-le-Grand, where Marne-la-Vallée's biggest shopping centre fights for attention with *grands ensembles* such as the »Espaces d'Abraxas« (36.2) and »Arènes de Picasso« (36.3), to name but the two most notorious. Having said that, an effort has been made to preserve existing heritage in its unspoilt entirety – forests for example, or some of the many estates and châteaux such as Champs-sur-Marne (36.5) –, and not all the new developments are devoid of interest.

One, which although flawed merits a detour, is the Cité Descartes (RER: Noisy-Champs). A 150 ha *parc scientifique*, the Cité was developed in order to encourage closer links between research institutions and business, being home both to electronics, computer, telecom and construction companies and a number of higher-education institutions, amongst which the Ecole Supérieure d'Ingénieurs en Electronique et Electrotechnique (ESIEE, Dominique Perrault, 1984–87), the Ecole Nationale des Ponts et Chaussées and the Ecole Nationale des Sciences Géographiques (ENPC and ENSG, Philippe Chaix and Jean-Paul Morel, 1989–96), and the Ecole d'Architecture de Marne-la-Vallée (36.4) are noteworthy for the buildings housing them. As a piece of planning the Cité is astoundingly banal, having been divided up into lots in the manner of an industrial estate, each building sitting in splendid isolation in the middle of its site with no attempt to relate it to anything else in the vicinity. Chaix and Morel's ENPC-and-ENSG building (6–8, avenue Blaise-Pascal) opts for a certain Cartesian, minimalist universality in the face of this non-context. Comprising three long, five-storey bars linked by a giant entrance atrium, its strength comes from the rigorous and elegant handling of the façades, which are pared-down steel-and-glass affairs providing maximum glazing and a dash of Hi-tech sophistication. By far the Cité Descartes's loudest building is Perrault's ESIEE (2, avenue Blaise-Pascal and Avenue André-Marie), which is organized as a series of six stubby wings projecting from a huge, 300 m-long building running down the avenue. It is the treatment of the latter that shouts, Perrault having given it a sharp cut-away profile faced in white aluminium, prompting inevitable comparisons with aeroplane wings and computer keyboards. This electronic-age, engineering-aesthetic *architecture parlante* encloses an interior that is all cool, elegant Hi-tech. In front of the school stands Piotr Kowalski's monumental sculpture *L'Axe de la Terre* (1992).

We should not leave Marne-la-Vallée without mentioning one rather minor structure that has become something of a mascot for the town: Christian de Portzamparc's water tower (1971–74) on a roundabout junction between the old and new parts of Noisiel. A sense of place is precisely what is missing from much of Marne-la-Vallée, and a landmark of this sort is invaluable in its power to distinguish an area from the great mass of Anywhere'sville. Such was Portzamparc's thinking when designing the tower, which he saw as challenging Modernism's puritanical prohibition of the monument in favour of the purely functional. His first major work, the 35 m-high water tower was deliberate-

36.1 The new town of Marne-la-Vallée. Water tower

ly intended to recall the Tower of Babel – the mythic mother of all sky-reaching monuments – in its spiralling, decagonal form; that form does not just have to follow function was the message he wanted to get across. He clearly also had The Hanging Gardens of Babylon in mind, since the tower's concrete frame was covered with see-through metal trellising intended to support climbing plants contained in concrete troughs. Unfortunately, in the winter of 1974, the municipal authorities forgot to drain the troughs' irrigation pipes which then burst, with the result that most of the plants subsequently died, never to be replaced. Nonetheless, even without its green covering, Portzamparc's tower is splendidly enigmatic, appearing both solid and immaterial as well as joyously gratuitous.

36.2 »Les Espaces d'Abraxas« social-housing scheme
Boulevard du Mont d'Est and Rue du Centre, Noisy-Le-Grand
Taller de Arquitectura Ricardo Bofill, 1978–83
(RER: Noisy-le-Grand Mont d'Est)

If Ricado Bofill is (almost) a household name today, it is undoubtedly due to his work for the French authorities in Paris's satellite new towns, which brought him worldwide fame and consolidated his international practice. In all Bofill built six social-housing schemes in the Paris region (including the inner-city »Echelles du Baroque«, 14.2), and later went on to construct Montpellier's Antigone development. His first project on French soil was »Les Arcades du Lac« (1972–75) in the new town of Saint-Quentin-en-Yvelines (to the west of Paris), which he followed up with »Le Viaduc« (1978–80), again at Saint-Quentin. While these two early estates already showed the axially planned, monumental approach and use of prefabricated concrete parts that characterized the whole series, it was at Marne-la-Vallée's »Espaces d'Abraxas« (see also 36.1), his third Paris-region realization, that he fully developed the prefabricated Classical vocabulary that would become his trademark.

Plonked in the chaotic environment of Noisy-le-Grand with no attempt to make any connection with the surrounding urbanity, fighting for attention like all the buildings here, Les Espaces d'Abraxas comprise some 591 dwellings and are organized in three principal parts. At the head of the site is the »Palacio«, a 19-storey-high mastodon of superimposed boxes containing 441 apartments; curving in to meet it and define the piazza around which the scheme is disposed is the »Théâtre«, a glass-pillar-fronted amphitheatre of 130 dwellings; while in the piazza's centre is the third element, the »Arc«, a triumphal-arch structure containing 20 further apartments. All three are dressed up in crude, caricatural, kitsch-Classical garb: eleven-storey-high fluted columns, crass evocations of pediments, inhabited cornices, glazing-barred fenestration, and so on. Fixed to an *in-situ* cast frame, this mega-Classical cladding is realized in beautifully crafted, prefabricated concrete for which the project's engineers developed a sophisticated, weather-resistant mix (thereby heralding something of a renaissance in French concrete construction). Inside the buildings is a variety of spacious, well-configured apartments (many in the form of duplexes) that are generally appreciated by residents. Combining Baroque axial planning *à la* Versailles, inflation of scale *à la* Boullée, dramatic chiaroscuro *à la* Piranesi and exaggerated detailing *à la* Ledoux, Bofill's creation was supposed to constitute at once a homage to the Western Classical tradition and an architectural in-joke of oh-so-knowing, PoMo irony.

Bofill's social-housing schemes were billed as an alternative to the dreary postwar estates of slab blocks and towers that had mushroomed all over Europe and were already becoming the despair of many less-privileged Parisian suburbs. But visiting Abraxas it immediately becomes clear that programmatically the estate is exactly the same as the slab-and-tower ensembles it was intended to replace, all that has changed being the configuration of the volumes involved and their external cladding. Sacrificing Modernist, functionalist concerns of sunlight orientation, etc. in the aesthetic interests of Classical symmetry, Bofill created what he later famously described as »Versailles for the people«. One could

36.2 »Les Espaces d'Abraxas« social-housing scheme

read into this remark a whole host of French-Revolutionary and Soviet-style egalitarian overtones, and indeed many critics unfavourably compared Bofill's supposedly ironic use of Classicism with the entirely unironic social housing of Soviet Realism. Terry Gilliam even used Les Espaces d'Abraxas in his film *Brazil* (1985). Certainly the estate sacrifices individuality to the needs of the greater ensemble effect, but in this it could be argued that it is just an updating of very un-Soviet 18C London, where rows of terraced housing were dressed up to look like enormous palace fronts. However, where the London developments were exclusive, very urban(e) residences designed to aggrandize the consenting rich, here it was the less affluent that were allocated these cartoon-château, ghetto-bound apartments out in the suburbs away from the middle-class city centre. For the officials who commissioned them, Bofill's monumental housing estates represented a tempting *rappel à l'ordre* from the »chaos« of postwar Modernism; pronouncing the architect's name was a sort of urbanist's »abracadabra« (a word purportedly invented by the ancient god Abraxas) that would magically tidy everything away into a semblance of ordered, Classical continuity.

36.3 »Les Arènes de Picasso« social-housing scheme
Place Pablo-Picasso, Noisy-Le-Grand
Manuel Nuñez Yanowsky, 1980–84
(RER: Noisy-le-Grand Mont d'Est)
Even for those not familiar with Manuel Nuñez Yanowsky's œuvre, it will come as no surprise on seeing this housing estate to learn that he was a member of Ricardo Bofill's Taller de Arquitectura, working on the Taller's gigantic housing schemes in the Paris region. Just like Bofill's nearby »Espaces d'Abraxas« (36.2), whose programmatic remit they share, »Les Arènes de Picasso« mix prefabrication, gigantism and PoMo Classicism in an estate of 500 dwellings. But where Bofill's historical borrowings were primarily concerned with the Classical language of façade articulation, Nuñez Yanowsky seems to have sought inspiration in the more abstract, Euclidean-solid-based neo-Classical fantasies of Etienne-Louis Boullée. Organized around the octagonal Place Pablo-Picasso, Les Arènes's most striking features are two 14-storey-high, apartment-filled circular slabs whose elevations recall Boullée's famous drawings for an unbuildably enormous Isaac Newton mausoleum (1784). According to Nuñez Yanowsky himself, »What counts most for an architect is the association of simple images and recognizability of forms and

36.3 »Les Arènes de Picasso« social-housing scheme

volumes ... Everyone should feel the presence of a cylinder, a cube, a prism ...« Marking the horizon with their inescapable monumentality, these slabs certainly make their presence felt! Perhaps in a bid to domesticate them, locals have dubbed them the »Camemberts«. As with Bofill's analogous schemes, the best of this project lies in the quality of its prefabricated concrete mouldings, which include rusticated oval window frames and rather Art-Déco inspired arcade detailing. Again like Bofill's schemes, Les Arènes de Picasso do not constitute an alternative to, but merely a variation on the theme of, gigantic, Modernist collective-housing schemes.

36.4 Ecole d'Architecture de Marne-la-Vallée
10–12, avenue Blaise-Pascal, Champs-sur-Marne
Bernard Tschumi, 1994–99
(RER: Noisy-Champs)

Just as hairdressers often have the most appalling haircuts and, according to an old French proverb, only cobblers are poorly shod, so schools of architecture are generally housed in the most awful buildings. Here was a chance to change all that for once: a commission for a brand-new, purpose-built architecture school on a green-field site in Marne-la-Vallée's Cité Descartes (see 36.1). Winner of the architectural »consultation«, Tschumi, dean of Columbia University's architecture school and initially better known as an academic and theorist than as a practising architect, was well placed to understand the needs of an educational institution. His scheme for Marne-la-Vallée was, he claimed, an attempt to »design a space conceived for the age of the modem and mobility, a new type of school that does not take inspiration from the former Ecole des Beaux-Arts, the Bauhaus, American schools or from elsewhere.« Its construction also coincided with the 1998 reform of the French architectural teaching system.

The Cité Descartes is laid out rather in the manner of an industrial estate, with the buildings it contains sitting in splendid isolation from each other surrounded by grounds and parking lots. Context was therefore not an issue for Tschumi's building, which was essentially designed from the inside out. Its central, generating element is a capacious, glazed, galleried, »un-programmed«, »event-orientated« space baptized the »Forum«, around which all the school's other functions are organized. Tschumi wanted the Forum to act as an »events generator«, where spontaneity and chance would be encouraged and the school's social cohesion assured. Enclosed within the Forum's volume is the *pilotis*-mounted box of a 135-seat lecture hall, whose undercroft serves as a café/conversation space, and whose roof, reached via footbridges from the Forum's galleries, supports an inclined dance floor. With this *mise en scène*, it was hoped, the obligatory coming and going of the school's students and teachers (traversing the Forum is unavoidable) would animate the space in a randomly choreographed, cinematic manner, thereby allowing the institution to develop its own autonomous urbanity in this out-of-the-way site far from the »intellectual nourishment« of the city (as Tschumi put it). Tschumi also believed that »real« learning often happens outside the designated spaces, in corridors and hallways, and the Forum is intended to encourage this.

To the sunny south of the Forum are the school's administrative spaces, while to the north, benefiting from the cool, even light, are the design studios. These latter are interspersed with the classrooms in another gesture of architectural determinism, here intended to forestall the schism between teaching and practice. This pedagogical spirit seems also to have influenced the handling of the building's internal and external finishes, a variety of materials having been used in different ways for apparently no better reason than to provide a demonstration of modern construction possibilities. Thus we find cable-mounted glass, *in-situ* cast and prefabricated raw concrete, welded-aluminium cladding panels, metal meshes, wooden flooring and so on and so forth. The building we see today is in fact only half the school as planned, its director having decided that it was financially and politically safer to build it in two phases. As is the school can accommodate up to 500 students; if all goes well and phase two is constructed, capacity will rise to 1,200. The building's second half will prolong the first in the axis of the Forum, with the latter being extended to incorporate a second, 400-seat lecture hall underneath a monumental staircase (whose initial treads are already in place, taking off into thin air at the Forum's rear).

Tschumi's design for Marne-la-Vallée is at bottom a highly rational and pragmatic response to the school's programmatic requirements as they stand today. Some critics were disappointed that the author of *Architecture and Disjunction* had produced such a »traditional« building. But then the school will surely be dispensing »traditional« teaching; the on-line, virtual architecture school of the future will no doubt be a very different place.

36.5 Château de Champs-sur-Marne
31, rue de Paris, Champs-sur-Marne
Jean-Baptiste Bullet de Chamblain with Pierre Bullet, 1703–07
(RER: Noisiel, then either a 20-minute walk or bus no. 220 in the direction of Bry-sur-Marne)

Son of peasants and one-time valet, Paul Poisson de Bourvallais rose to become one of France's foremost financiers in the twilight years of Louis XIV's reign, amassing an enormous fortune that was the envy of many an old noble family. In his new social position he clearly needed a château, and consequently purchased the estate at Champs with a view to remodelling it in his own image. Although Bourvallais's wealth was *nouveau*, his taste was not, and the house and gardens he created there were widely admired for their charm and commodiousness. But Bourvallais did not enjoy Champs for long. Following Louis XIV's death the old nobility had its revenge, and he was disgraced, losing his château in the process. Champs afterwards passed through a variety of hands (including a brief period in 1757–59 when it was leased by Mme de Pompadour) until the Revolution, when it was confiscated by the state, stripped of its contents and saw its gardens ploughed for cultivation. The 19C was no kinder, when the château lost its mansard roof (replaced by a terrace) and generally fell into a sorry state. Salvation arrived in 1895 in the form of the rich banker Louis Cahen d'Anvers, who patiently restored Champs to its former splendour. In 1935, his son donated the property to the French state, and it is now a national monument open to the public. The château and its grounds are a classic example of 18C-French understated refinement, which perhaps explains their attractiveness to filmmakers, for Champs has starred in several period movies including *Dangerous Liaisons* (1987) and *Ridicule* (1995).

To rebuild Champs, Bourvallais commissioned a little-known architect, Jean-Baptiste Bullet de Chamblain, who was assisted by his more famous father, Pierre Bullet. Bullet is known for the innovatory plans of his *hôtels particuliers* at the Place Vendôme (1.13), and in the same way that these latter residences broke with previous practice, Champs marks the turning point between the grandiose, Baroque formality of 17C French châteaux and the externally simplified yet spatially more complex developments of the 18C. This is not to say that display was not still an important part of the château's *raison d'être*, and its *mise en scène* is clearly in the lineage of illustrious forbears such as Maisons (24.1) and Vaux-le-Vicomte (37.1). Thus at Champs we find the château sitting on a majestic central axis, preceded by a generous *cour d'honneur* flanked by service buildings, while a splendid French-style garden continues the axis at the château's rear. The ditch separating the

36.4 Ecole d'Architecture de Marne-la-Vallée

cour d'honneur from the road recalls the moats at Maisons and Vaux, and the courtyard's elaborate railings can also trace their origins back to Vaux. Similarly, the setting of the garden front on a masonry terrace, with steps spilling out onto the central pathway below, recreates comparable dispositions at Vaux and Maisons. Champs is also classically French in its general massing, each of the two principal façades sporting lateral pavilions and central *avant-corps*, that on the garden front taking the form of a semicircular protrusion that was clearly inspired by Vaux's oval salon. But in its decorative aspect, Champs differs greatly from its predecessors. Where, for example, Maisons and Vaux are busy with external detailing and complicated roofing, Champs is sober to the point of austerity. A touch of rustication in the form of pavilion quoins, minimalist window surrounds, a string course and a modest cornice constitute the only animation on the surfaces of the château's *arrière-corps*, all attention being concentrated on the dominant *avant-corps*, and even the latter are plain in comparison to 17C châteaux. The beautifully simple and understated courtyard frontispiece reproduces a design used by Bullet at the Château d'Issy (c. 1680), while the garden-front *avant-corps*, with its full rustication, bracketed balcony and decorative sculpture, is more elaborate – as garden-front *avant-corps* generally were –, but nonetheless could hardly be qualified as showy. Champs also breaks entirely with the rather »assembled« look of most 17C French buildings, whose constituent pavilions, *logis* and other parts were clearly distinguished, and instead displays façades that are treated as one continuous, homogeneous envelope, an impression strengthened by the unifying influence of its horizontal mansard roof. The only contradiction to this sense of unity is the protrusion of the garden front's *avant-corps* above the château's cornice line (which also engenders correspondingly elongated fenestration), a characteristic of many 17C châteaux that was dropped in later 18C buildings in the interests of greater uniformity (see, e.g., the Hôtel Matignon, 7.14).

Comfort was also of greater concern in the new century, and this is expressed at Champs in the organization of its plan. A double thickness of rooms occupies the *logis*, as pioneered by Le Vau at Vaux, and the plan reproduces the transversal and horizontal *enfilades* that governed Vaux's layout. But where rigid symmetry dominates at Vaux-le-Vicomte, at Champs Bullet de Chamblain handled his room sequencing with much greater flexibility to permit the introduction of practical features tailored to the convenience of the château's users. Thus we find a whole series of little corridors and service staircases that allow rooms and suites of rooms to be accessed individually, thereby ensuring privacy and facilitating the unobtrusive movement of servants about the building. Each bedchamber disposed of a cluster of ancillary spaces – studies, *garderobes* and the like –, and very early on Champs was provided with bathrooms. The château also possessed a designated, fixed dining room (conveniently situated above the kitchens in the cellars) which, in the early-18C, was still something of a novelty. All these features point to the fact that Champs was conceived more as a *maison de plaisance* (a concept that came into fashion in the 18C) than as a château in the 17C sense of the term, and Parisian luxury residences such as the Hôtel d'Evreux (today Palais de l'Elysée, 8.16), Hôtel Matignon and Hô-

36.5 Château de Champs-sur-Marne

tel Peyrenc-de-Moras (7.13) were subsequently influenced by it.

This emphasis on pleasure was also reflected in the château's interior décor, which sought to charm rather than to impress. Amongst the surviving original interiors created by Bullet de Chamblain for Poisson de Bourvallais are the two oval salons on the ground and first floors (the principal rooms of the house), both of which feature elaborate panelling carved with Composite pilasters. Connecting these two spaces vertically is the imposing *escalier d'honneur*, which combines the same simple dignity and quiet refinement visible on the exterior of the house. Several of the château's rooms were redecorated during the ownership of the second Duc de La Vallière (1739–63), including the celebrated *salon chinois* (also sometimes referred to as the *salon d'assemblée*) in the northeast corner of the château on the ground floor. The *salon*'s panelling and plasterwork are in fact original, but it is famous for the *chinoiseries* added by Christophe Huet in 1748. These take the form of 58 painted scenes depicting the pleasures of life, represented by assorted monkeys and rather Westernized »Chinamen« in the act of fishing, dancing, gardening and so on. This theme is continued in the small boudoir, again decorated by Huet, on the southern side of the house, where painted blue monochromes show the pleasures of living in Nature – singing, drinking, fishing, etc. Several of the upstairs rooms feature fine Rococo panelling, the most celebrated example being the *chambre d'honneur*, where haughty peacocks and cooing doves disport themselves amongst florid, vegetal-derived motifs. Legend has it that this decoration was created for Mme de Pompadour (whose symbol was a dove), but there is no documentary evidence to support this.

When Louis Cahen d'Anvers acquired Champs, almost all trace of its 18C gardens had disappeared, effaced by a 19C *jardin à l'anglaise*. Plans of the original gardens – which are attributed to Claude Desgots, a great-nephew and pupil of André Le Nôtre – survived, however, and Cahen d'Anvers commissioned Achille Duchêne (assisted by his father, Henri) to recreate them, at least in spirit if not in all their details. Thus the Duchênes reproduced the long central axis, with its delineating rows of trees and terminal circular pool, and the big lateral parterres and elaborate box-hedge topiary directly in front of the house, but not the supplementary parterres that originally accompanied the axis to its conclusion, or the more intimate gardens that once extended east of the château. Instead, the re-created French gardens are framed by the trees and meadows of the remaining parts of the 19C *jardin à l'anglaise*, a contrast that enhances the charm of both. Although the river Marne runs just beyond the northern end of the central axis, in the 18C it was not used to terminate the perspective, as would have been logical, because the river's flood plains did not belong to the Champs estate. The Duchênes disposed of greater room for manœuvre than their 18C forbears, and consequently extended the axis beyond the final pool, but trees still obscure the river, and it falls to an enlarged copy of the *Bain des Chevaux d'Apollon par les Tritons* (the original, by the Marsy brothers, is at Versailles (32.1)) to close the composition.

36.6 Chocolaterie Menier-Nestlé

36.6 Chocolaterie Menier-Nestlé
7, boulevard Pierre-Carle, Noisiel
Various architects, current buildings begun 1860
(RER: Noisiel)

Founded in the early-19C as a producer of pharmaceutical products, the firm of Menier radically changed direction in the 1860s when chocolate – an ingredient it had previously used in some of its medicines – became the company's principal product. Under the management first of Emile-Justin Menier (1826–81), and then his sons Henri (1853–1913) and Gaston (1855–1934), the firm expanded to become one of the world's leading chocolate manufacturers, commanding over half the French market by 1900 when it reached the summit of its glory. As well as the famous factory complex we see today centred around the cocoa-grinding watermill on the river Marne at Noisiel, the Menier empire at its peak included large tracts of land in Nicaragua – where the cocoa necessary to make the chocolate was grown –, another factory in London and a warehouse in New York, the company's headquarters in central Paris, the Meniers' château (since demolished) at Noisiel, and a small company town built by the Meniers to house the 1,000 or so workers employed by them at the Noisiel site. Decline began to set in after WWI, eventually culminating in the firm's takeover by a rival group in the 1960s, at which time the company town was sold off to its inhabitants. The Noisiel factory finally ceased production in 1993, and was converted in 1996 by the architects Bernard Reichen and Philippe Robert to house the headquarters of Nestlé France, the current owners. Three of the surviving buildings are of exceptional interest, and together with the company town the Noisiel

Marne-la-Vallée 363

site constitutes a fascinating and extremely well-preserved example of France's 19C industrial heritage. The factory is unfortunately not open to the public – except on the occasion of the annual Journées du Patrimoine (see How to use this guide) –, but Nestlé has installed a footbridge and public footpaths around the complex that allow good views of the exterior.

Of all the structures that make up the Menier factory, by far the most celebrated is the cocoa-grinding mill that spans the narrower of two branches of the Marne, on a site occupied by a watermill as early as the 12C. The current edifice, which was designed by Jules Saulnier and dates from 1871/72, was commissioned by the Meniers to replace an earlier 19C mill that had become too small. Saulnier's building owes its fame in part to its revolutionary structure: this was in all probability the world's first edifice constructed with an all-metal cage frame (as opposed to a market-hall type structure like Baltard's famous Halles Centrales (see 1.22)). Certainly partly metal-framed buildings had already appeared in Britain and America, but they had not used iron so exclusively, nor exposed it to the public gaze in the manner of Saulnier's edifice. The mill sits on four stone piers, between which turned the three water turbines that powered its grinders. An iron chassis delimits its plan, from which rise the principle elements of its trabeated frame. Daring engineering was not a feature of Saulnier's design, and the frame is essentially a transposition of timber construction into iron, right down to the diagonal braces that strengthen the structure against the wind. Similarly, the use of bricks to fill the spaces between the frame's iron members is simply a reprise of traditional nogging. It is Saulnier's handling of this brick infill that constitutes the building's second extraordinary feature. Having committed himself to the considerable expense of rebuilding the mill from scratch, Emile-Justin Menier did not stint on its decoration, and allocated Saulnier the necessary funds to produce something beyond the merely utilitarian. The mill was, after all, the core element of the factory, and as such was a suitable support on which to proclaim the Meniers' pride and industrial prowess. Saulnier's structural system did not lend itself to the application of sculpture – the traditional adornment of important French buildings – and he therefore decided to create two-dimensional decoration in the form of motifs composed from different-coloured bricks. Paying great attention to the colours used and setting off enamelled bricks against a nankeen background, he created circles, lozenges and vegetal motifs, and included ceramic medallions depicting either the Meniers' »M« or stylized cocoa plants. Saulnier compared his façades to a Persian carpet, the effect from a distance being that of a warm, harmonious ensemble, while closer to a wealth of detail jumps out at the viewer. An elaborately decorated company clock dominates the mill's entrance façade, while below it hangs the bell that rang out the workers' shifts. Although Saulnier's building was widely published following its completion, and garnered praise from Viollet-le-Duc, its direct influence was limited.

In the decade 1880–90, the Noisiel factory was enlarged by the architect Jules Logre to provide new warehouses and other service buildings. Amongst the structures erected at this time was the refrigeration building (1882–84), which stands near the perimeter wall on the Chemin de la Rivière. Its parentage is contested, legend having it that it is in fact a re-used pavilion from the 1878 Exposition Universelle that was designed by the great Gustave Eiffel himself. There is no documentary evidence to support this theory, which is based essentially on the exceptional quality of the building's ironwork. Its elegant structure follows the market-hall type of the Halles Centrales, a form employed so as to allow column-free space for the installation of the four large refrigeration machines that cooled the underground storage rooms. The decorative motifs of Saulnier's watermill are repeated here but in three dimensions and in iron, with cocoa flowers studding the building's cornice and the Meniers' »M« adorning its elaborate columns.

The Chocolaterie Menier reached the peak of its production at the turn of the 20C, when new buildings were added by Stephen Sauvestre and Jules Logre (1905–09). Sauvestre, who is best known for his part in designing the Eiffel Tower (7.8), was responsible for the imposing structure that sits on the island in the Marne just west of Saulnier's watermill, and which was soon baptized by the company's employees the »Cathedral«. It was built in 1905/06 in collaboration with Armand Considère, who had patented the reinforced-concrete system used to construct it, which employed metal coils for the reinforcement elements. The Cathedral's rather ungainly, Classically garbed exterior gives no clue to the building's purpose. It is connected to Logre's moulding-workshop buildings on the other side of the river by a graceful bridge, also by Sauvestre and Considère, whose 44.5 m span, designed on the principle of an inverted suspension cable, constituted a record in reinforced concrete at the time. The Cathedral's monumental Classicism was intended to impress important visitors, who were led into the building via the bridge and then directed via an imposing staircase to an elegantly decorated chamber in black and white that one contemporary described as being like the foyer of an opera. Here, in a display of pure industrial theatre, the cocoa paste produced in Saulnier's watermill, which arrived via underground pipes, was rained down with sugar to form chocolate mix (the columns supporting the roof of the mixing hall even had flared bell bottoms to encourage the mixture to spill out). Afterwards, the chocolate paste was transported across the bridge to the moulding workshops in wagonettes mounted on rails.

As part of Reichen and Robert's conversion of the factory buildings, the Cathedral, its mixing hall and the bridge were all carefully restored, the mixing hall now serving as a function venue. The dispersed nature of the factory buildings at Noisiel made them ideal for housing separately the different divisions of Nestlé France, with the former route of the factory's railway tracks, now glazed over, forming a linking corridor between the individual departments. Reichen and Robert's meticulous and sensitive conversion was closely monitored by the Commission des Monuments Historiques, which itself undertook restoration of Saulnier's mill, where Nestlé's boardroom is now housed.

We should not leave Noisiel without making brief mention of the company town. Founded by Emile-Justin Menier both on sound business grounds and as a laboratory for the social revolution he hoped to promote, it was a rather fanatical example of liberal 19C paternalism, and included a school – several years before the introduction of compulsory education in France – a retirement home and even a model farm intended to meet the alimentary needs of the community. Despite Emile-Justin's liberal idealism, the Meniers' ascendancy at Noisiel was absolute, to the point where deceased workers were even buried in Menier coffins! The town's 360 semi-detached houses and other buildings were built in four principal campaigns between 1874 and 1911 by Louis and Jules Logre. Much influenced by British models, its 11 ha site is divided up into three long, parallel streets that are interrupted by a square towards the factory end of the terrain. The houses follow a prize-winning model for workers' dwellings that had been exhibited at the 1867 Exposition Universelle and praised by Napoleon III. All the structures at Noisiel are in a vernacular brick style whose uniformity is today unfortunately disrupted by the render that has been applied to many of the houses.

36.7 Disneyland Paris
Various architects, 1987–2002
(RER: Marne-la-Vallée Chessy)

The »Sistine Chapel« of American consumer culture – as Umberto Eco memorably described Disneyland, Uncle Walt's nostalgic tribute to fairytale and the mythic America of his childhood – finally came to the Old World in 1992, ten years after the opening of Tokyo Disneyland and nearly 40 years after inauguration of Walt's original theme park at Anaheim, California. In a mere decade, and despite initially catastrophic financial results, Disneyland Paris has become France's undisputed number-one tourist attraction, with an average of 12.3 million visitors every year, just beating the cathedral of Notre-Dame (4.2), its only serious rival. As well as the 56 ha Disneyland proper, Disneyland Paris now counts a second big theme park, Disney Studios – a 20 ha, audio-visual extravaganza of rides and spectacles inspired by American cinema – and a battery of back-up facilities in the form of the Disney Resort, which includes seven hotels providing nearly 6,000 rooms, a conference centre, a major shopping mall and Disney Village, a sort of fast-food-and-bar complex. Disney thought long and hard about where to site its European theme park before finally settling on the *ville nouvelle* of Marne-la-Vallée (36.1), a choice no doubt influenced by Paris's popularity as a tourist destination and by its excellent transport links, Marne-la-Vallée even having its own TGV stop.

Employing film theory when designing buildings has been popular amongst avant-garde architects over the last couple of decades, but if you want to see a whole environment conceived along the lines in which movies are made, come to Disneyland. The team that created the original Disney theme park were all Hollywood art directors (some of whom had trained as architects), and the park was thought out in terms of movie tricks and terminology: frames, shots, scenes, sequencing, forced perspective and all the other illusionism that makes film sets come alive and hides the »real« world lurking behind. Narrative was one of the key elements in the conception of Disneyland, for this was an environment thought out using storyboards, where the visitors are of course the actors. Crowd control and manipulation is also a highly accomplished art at Disneyland, carried out with such skill that one generally remains oblivious to the ruse. Disney's basic precept was that most theme parks, and indeed the real world, are physically tiring and psychologically alienating places in their profusion of choices and lack of visual coherence. Disneyland, on the other hand, would provide the illusion of free will, choice and freedom in what was in fact a highly controlled and eminently reassuring, aestheticized environment. This is why Disneyland does not invent any of the fantasy it serves up for consumption, instead borrowing from myth, fairytale, film and social history. It is the already established popular culture of the broad middle that is on the menu, nerdy popular science, twee nostalgia, action cinema and all. Many have denounced Disneyland's celebration of the American mainstream as superficial, reactionary, repressive, reductionist and racist.

The original Anaheim Disneyland has been read by some commentators as a critique of American car culture, a place where one leaves one's automobile behind to enter a magic never-never land of fume-free pedestrian spaces and nostalgic train rides. France is not America, however, and the SNCF remains a force to be reckoned with. For this reason, most visitors to Disneyland Paris will arrive on the RER, and the laying-out of the park's approaches consequently differs markedly from Anaheim. On leaving the train station one's attention is immediately attracted by three »weenies« (a term coined by Disney to describe visually spectacular features that draw the visitor towards them the way a dog is attracted to a Frankfurter): the gates of Disney Village (see below), the Mickey-Mouse water tower of Disney Studios (see below), and the turreted bulk of the Disneyland Hotel (designed by Robert Stern), which constitutes the entrance to Disneyland itself. Reached via gently descending gardens, the hotel is rendered as a late-19C, candy-floss-pink seaside fantasia clearly inspired by San Diego's wooden Hotel del Coronado (built in 1888 and famously used in the film *Some Like it*

Hot). Thus, with the Mickey-Mouse gardens and the fairytale turrets of the hotel – that recall the fantasy castle we all know awaits us inside – Disneyland Paris begins out in the »real« world, before the park's threshold has even been crossed.

Within their perimeter confines, all the spin-off Disneylands closely follow the plan of the Anaheim original, and Disneyland Paris is no exception. Like its older sisters, it has one single point of entry, a feature that goes against some theories of crowd control but about which Walt Disney was adamant. Multiple entries are confusing, he maintained: in order to find his or her bearings the visitor must refer to only one entrance/exit. At Disneyland Paris, in a classic example of architectural theatre, one leaves the real world by being funnelled down into the dark underneath of the Disneyland Hotel, from where one emerges into the light of the Magic Kingdom. More specifically, one comes out into »Main Street, U.S.A.«, Uncle Walt's nostalgic evocation of the typical small Missouri town in which he grew up. The first thing one encounters in this fictional urbanity is the railway station serving the live-steam trains running round Disneyland's perimeter. Disney was an ardent steam buff, so much so that he installed a scaled-down, live-steam railway in his garden, and it was his interest in model trains that fuelled creation of the original Disneyland. And nowhere illustrates this better than Main Street, whose maniacal attention to detail is clearly the outsized creation of some school-boy, model-railway dream. Trams, a town hall, a saloon bar and various shops and facilities from the 1900s are all recreated with over-wrought perfection. The stage-set illusion is so convincing that one remains oblivious to the fact that the Main-Street façades are in fact confectionery masks stuck onto single concrete-framed mega-structures (one on either side of the road), and not individual buildings. One is also oblivious to the forced perspective used to make Main Street appear longer when viewed from the entrance – the building fronts narrow as one moves along –, or to the fact that the buildings are full scale on the ground floor but only two-thirds scale above. Instead one is entirely absorbed in contemplating the myriad period details, lost in the pleasure of the ersatz. An illusion of participating in the fantasy is provided by the food and gifts on sale, genuine commerce being made to seem like play.

Contrasting with the »close-ups« of the store fronts and their interiors, the view down Main Street was conceived as a »long shot«. Just as at Anaheim Disneyland, the Paris visitor is lured up the street by the weenie that is Sleeping Beauty's Castle towards a circular piazza known by Disney insiders as the »Hub«. Interestingly, the original piazza was inspired by Paris's Place de l'Etoile (see 16.1) and its radiating avenues. The Hub is at the centre of all the Disneylands, with the different »Fantasylands« disposed around it in more or less circular regularity. Disney's »imagineers« (as the theme park's designers are known in-house) thought of it in terms of television: the Hub is like a 1950s TV-channel dial providing viewer (visitor) choice. While within the rides and attractions much effort is made to disorientate visitors and befuddle their sense of space, outside all is logical, rational, graspable clarity, giving »guests« (as visitors are known) the illusion of control in their movement around the park. In fact a clever system of weenies is used to manipulate the public's progression through space, of which the ultimate, now used as Disney's symbol on all its publicity, is Sleeping Beauty's Castle. Weenies tend to be tall pointy things, and the castle is of course the epitome of the type. All the Disneyland castles can trace their origins back to Ludwig II's Neuschwanstein (Christian Jank *et al.*, 1868–92), but each is a variation on the theme. Paris's castle, the tallest of the series, is more surreally elongated and less »realistic« than its predecessors, more Toon Town, with improbable flying buttresses, fantastical fenestration and square trees decorating its gardens. Perhaps the thinking behind this was that the »real thing« is so close at hand in Europe that it was better to offer a purely fantastic creation that could only be found in Disneyland. Visible from everywhere in the park, the castle reminds you that you are not really in a mid-West town *c.* 1900, or in any of the other fantasy realms on offer, but in Disneyland, the magical storybook kingdom.

Disjunction, voids, and environmental chaos are not part of the Disney ethos, and enormous landscaping efforts have thus been made to ensure a smooth transition between the park's different »Lands«, so that the visitor is not confronted with too abrupt a change. Likewise, the »real« world must never be allowed to intrude, which is why Disneyland is surrounded by a high earth embankment, whose tree-covered presence ensures that one cannot see out and also helps create a stable, slightly warmer micro-climate within. One reality that proved impossible to banish from the Magic Kingdom was the fact that most visitors spend more time standing in line than actually sitting on rides, and consequently, to avoid riotous rises in impatience, considerable art was employed to make queuing, if not actually enjoyable, at least bearable. Disney queues never happen in straight lines but always in zigzagging, level-changing *promenades architecturales* that are lined with features and exhibits related to the ride in question. In this irony-free realm of instant make-believe and beauty, of gorgeous, hand-crafted kitsch, the opportunity for private contemplation must be removed; for the dream to work, distraction must be provided at all times. It is this intensified hyper-reality, where the boring, inconvenient bits of the everyday are ironed out, that ensures Disneyland's success.

Besides Main Street, Disneyland comprises four other fantasy realms: Frontierland, Adventureland, Fantasyland and Discoveryland. Frontierland's principal weenies are Big Thunder Mountain – a classic roller-coaster ride through a Rockies gold mine – and the *Psycho*-style Phantom Manor, whose ghost-train ride features cars that pivot and rotate to point the visitor towards different »shots« in the manner of a tracking

36.7 Disneyland Paris

camera. Here, in comparison to Main Street's relatively staid, linear, contemplative narrative, the story (about a jilted »Blood Bride«) is organized as a series of rapidly interposed cinematic jump cuts. Adventureland boasts the impressive weenie that is the »Indiana Jones and the Temple of Doom« ride, whose roller-coaster cars are equipped with »motion simulators« that give riders the sensation of steeper hills, sharper curves and greater speeds than they actually experience. In Fantasyland, the »It's a Small World« attraction includes a good example of the painted »visual-intrusion flats« that are sometimes used to dissimulate the Magic Kingdom's edges: the abstracted towers and turrets they depict direct the gaze upwards to the sky and thereby discourage the onlooker from thinking about what may lie beyond them. Still in Fantasyland, underneath Sleeping Beauty's Castle, we find a fine example of one of Disney's celebrated Audio-Animatronics' robots, in this case a spectacularly »realistic«, teeth-snapping dragon, whose perfection makes clear the exact relation between Disneyland and the ersatz: simply duplicating the real is not the intent, the aim instead being to fabricate the ideal just as we had always dreamed it. Where the future is concerned, however, this can prove problematic, as Discoveryland highlights. In the Anaheim Disneyland, Discoveryland started out as »Tomorrowland«, where a serious attempt was made to give a taste of the possible hereafter. Experience soon showed, however, that the passage of time made yesterday's vision of tomorrow into today's snigger-triggering joke, which thus needed constant and expensive updating. At Disneyland Paris, this problem has been circumnavigated by creating a land that is based on a vision of the future which is firmly rooted in the past – the *fin-de-siècle* futurism of Jules Verne and H. G. Wells –, proving that even tomorrow can be reduced to nostalgia.

Phoney nostalgia is also a big component in Disneyland Paris's second park, Disney Studios, which was inaugurated in 2002. In keeping with its silver-screen, Hollywood theme, the park's attractions are knitted together with Art-Déco architecture of the kind Los Angeles should have been made of but never really was. But as a total-entertainment environment it is much less accomplished than Disneyland proper, in part because many of the attractions, given the art they celebrate, are indoor, theatre-based events. Where, in the original Disneylands, visitors are given the illusion of participation, at Disney Studios they are generally passive spectators. With its single theme, one would have thought that bringing a coherent visual aspect to Disney Studios would have been easier than in Disneyland proper. But visiting the new park, one soon realizes how much the half century of trial and error that went into perfecting the original Disneyland is lacking here. The seamless fantasy that characterizes its older sisters has not been achieved at Disney Studios, and disjunction and voids here and there rear their fantasy-dashing heads. And the fact that the non-theatre attractions rely on fakes of fakes – simulacra of movie sets – introduces a critical distance in the already passive (and therefore critical) visitor that is absent from the original theme parks. As a result, the hyper-reality that ensured the original parks' success is impossible here.

Before leaving Disneyland we should take a quick look at the Disney Resort, whose architect-in-chief was Robert Stern. Centred around an artificial lake in landscaped grounds, it is home to the Disney hotels and conference centre, and also includes Disney Village (originally Festival Disney), which is sited so that one must cross it to reach the other facilities. Designed by no less an architectural luminary than Frank Gehry (see also 12.9), Disney Village was, according to the architect, intended by Disney's management to provide a final attraction in the dark Ile-de-France winter that would encourage departing visitors to spend their last bucks. The Village is Disney's Las Vegas, an unashamedly commercial strip open into the small hours and designed to be seen at night when lit up, an entire street conceived along the lines of an amusement arcade. Where the theme park proper is a land of Ducks, here we find text-book Decorated Sheds, with candy-striped, spangly towers marching past retail hangars dressed up with all kinds of fantasy frontages. Wavering between Duck and Decorated Shed, the five Disney Resort hotels are each based around a different theme: Michael Graves' PoMo Hotel New York is intended to recall the skyscrapers of the Big Apple; Robert Stern's Hotel Cheyenne was made to resemble an American frontier town, or at any rate Hollywood's idea of a frontier town; Antoine Grumbach's Sequoia Lodge was supposed to evoke America's national parks; Antoine Predock's Hotel Santa Fe is intended to recall a New-Mexican *pueblo*; while Stern's Newport Bay Club – one of Europe's biggest hotels at 1,100 rooms – was inspired by late-19C New-England yachting clubs. Many of the Disneyland-based holiday packages propose staying in a Disney hotel with an excursion into Paris; thus, in a curious reversal of roles, Disneyland becomes the real world and Paris the theme park one visits on a day trip.

Marne-la-Vallée 367

37 Vaux-le-Vicomte

37.1 Château de Vaux-le-Vicomte
Louis Le Vau, 1656(?)–61

(Vaux-le-Vicomte is situated 55 km by road from Paris, and is best reached by car. From Paris, either take the A6 to the Fontainebleau exit, then follow the signs to Melun, from where signposts will direct you to the château; or, take the A4 to Melun and follow the N36 and the D215 to Vaux. Alternatively, you can take the RER D, or a main-line train from the Gare de Lyon, to Melun, and then hire a taxi to take you the 6 km from there to Vaux-le-Vicomte.)

An outstanding 17C masterpiece, the Château de Vaux-le-Vicomte is a key work in the history of French architecture, the first full-blown example of the sort of axially-planned magnificence for which France became famous the world over. To build it, three of the era's greatest talents were united: the architect Louis Le Vau, the painter-decorator Charles Le Brun, and the landscape gardener André Le Nôtre. The story of its creation is rendered all the more compelling by the fate of its originator, Nicolas Fouquet. One of the country's richest and most powerful men, and one of its most cultured – benefactor of La Fontaine, Molière, and Corneille, to name but a few –, his destiny was directly linked with the building of Vaux, whose splendour was the catalyst of his downfall.

Genesis of the château

Fouquet acquired the seigniory of Vaux in 1641, while he was Maître des Requêtes (counsel of the Conseil d'Etat). A protégé of Cardinal Mazarin, who was Prime Minister and effective ruler of France during Louis XIV's minority, Fouquet rose to become Surintendant des Finances (finance minister and banker to the king) in 1653. His ever-increasing prestige demanded a château worthy of his position, and he decided to remodel Vaux: the old château, the village of Vaux and two hamlets were razed to make way for his new residence, construction of which is thought to have begun in 1656. Put up at extraordinary speed, Vaux-le-Vicomte was habitable by early 1658, and the embellishment of its gardens and of its interior could then begin. Over the next three years, the château became famous for the lavish receptions held there by Fouquet. The last, given on 17 August 1661 in honour of the young King Louis XIV, who had just established absolute rule, has gone down in history. Molière's *Les Fâcheux* – commissioned only two weeks before – was premièred that evening, and the 6,000 guests, who included the entire court, were treated to a lavish supper followed by a splendid firework display in the brilliantly illuminated gardens. The king complimented his finance minister on the beauty of the latest enhancements at Vaux, and Fouquet retired that night believing himself at the summit of his glory. The blow fell two weeks later, on 5 September; the king, livid with jealously at Fouquet's display of power, wealth, and prestige, and spurred on by Fouquet's rival, Jean-Baptiste Colbert, had his finance minister arrested, charged with embezzlement of state funds. Mazarin had died early in 1661, and Fouquet was left without protection. The trial resulted in Fouquet's condemnation, and he was sentenced to exile. Louis XIV found this punishment too lenient, and used the royal prerogative to change the penalty to life imprisonment in solitary confinement, ensuring that Fouquet would never return. It has been suggested that the disgraced finance minister may have been the famous man in the iron mask.

The architect whom Fouquet hired to build Vaux-le-Vicomte, Louis Le Vau, had made his reputation with the ingenious but relatively modest Hôtel Lambert (4.5). It was at Vaux that Le Vau's talent for combining grandeur and elegance on a large scale was first given full expression. Although Premier Architecte to the king since 1654, he had been given little opportunity to display his skill for the sovereign, and his one full commission for a château (as opposed to renovations or partial reconstructions of existing buildings), at Le Raincy (destroyed), had come 13 years earlier, in 1643. As we shall see, although an *œuvre de jeunesse*, Le Raincy prefigured Le Vau's work at Vaux. It is thought that Fouquet originally hoped to engage the talents of the great Nicolas Poussin to decorate the interior of his new château, but the ageing artist had by then left France with the intention never to return. In the event it was one of Poussin's pupils, Charles Le Brun, whom Fouquet hired. Like Le Vau, Le Brun had earned renown for his work at the Hôtel Lambert and, following his triumph at Vaux, would be appointed Premier Peintre du Roi, in 1662. Of the three greats who created Vaux, only André Le Nôtre had not yet made a name for himself, and the attribution of the gardens to him is not certain, although highly probable. The only definite piece of information we have is that Le Nôtre was living in the château in 1661, at the time of Fouquet's fall from grace; the date of his arrival there is unknown, and others may well have worked on the gardens prior to his intervention.

Le Vau's masterplan and design of the château

Vaux-le-Vicomte is the first full-blown example of a château in the »grand manner« that became so closely identified with Louis XIV's reign. While Louis Le Vau has been criticized for his lack of rigour and seeming insouciance in the handling of detail, his great ability as a *metteur en scène* of striking ensemble effects has never been in question. The château at Vaux is situated towards one end of a magisterial, 1.5 km-long axis, running north–south, which terminates at either end in a set of radiating avenues. In front of the château a huge *avant-cour*, flanked on either side by service buildings, descends in a gentle slope towards the house. The service buildings, which include stables, servants' quarters, the servants' chapel and farm buildings, form a monumental composition in their own right. Decked out in a livery of red brick and

37.1 Château de Vaux-le-Vicomte. Entrance front

stone, they are arranged in the form of two matching quadrangles either side of the courtyard, with substantial two-storey pavilions at the corner of each quadrangle and at the centre of each of their longest sides. Linking the quadrangles visually and closing the *avant-cour* from the road is a long run of iron railings, held up by stern-faced terms and punctuated at either end by false, pedimented gateways. The use of iron railings in place of the usual rubble-stone wall was an innovation that would become standard in French châteaux after Vaux. What one cannot see from the *avant-cour* is that the château proper is constructed on a moated platform, which is accessed by two bridges, one on the entrance and one on the garden front, both aligned with the central axis of the house. This is the first of many features almost certainly borrowed by Le Vau from the Château de Maisons (24.1), built by his great rival, François Mansart. Maisons and Vaux are frequently described as transitional works between the French Renaissance – whose great houses were generally a hybrid of Italian influence and established native practice – and the full-blown French Classicism of the late-17C. Their moats are picturesque throwbacks to medieval fortified residences, and Vaux's may well have been inspired by the old moated château it replaced. On the garden front at Vaux the moat is again invisible, although here the terrain descends away from the château. Improving on a device used at Maisons, Le Vau skilfully landscaped this slope into a cascade of steps and terraces which, in combination with the château's platform, produce the illusion when viewed from afar that the house is built on an impressive mound of masonry. The gardens, laid out either side of the grand central axis, extend ever further backwards away from the château until they hit a sharp, steep, rising slope, up which the axis climbs to the horizon and thus, by analogy, to infinity. Nonetheless, despite the amplitude and magnificence of its setting, the house dominates its environment with all the insistence and haughtiness of a spoilt dowager duchess.

Built at the rear of its platform, the château is heralded on the entrance front by a generous space which fulfils the functions of a *cour d'honneur*. In his setting out of this space, Le Vau made reference to an older generation of French châteaux by including long, raised terraces which extend from either side of the house to the front of the platform. These are clearly intended to evoke the disposition of great houses such as the Palais du Luxembourg (6.8), which featured long wings extending from either side of their entrance façades, thus forming a U shape in plan and delineating the *cour d'honneur*. Vaux's terraces even widen into phantom pavilions at their extremities. These devices are yet further quotations from Maisons, and were originally used by Mansart to indicate that his château was conceived in a noble tradition of French design while at the same time emphasizing its modernity in comparison to predecessors. (The long anterior wings of the older châteaux had generally contained kitchens and other domestic service rooms. The subsequent fashion for placing such rooms in the basement of the *corps de logis*, as at Vaux, rendered these service wings obsolete.) Maisons was also modern in that it was built of stone, unlike the châteaux of the preceding era which were in brick and stone, a combination that went out of fashion in aristocratic circles in the mid-century probably because the middle classes, aping their superiors, had begun to use it. Surviving drawings show that Vaux was originally to have been in brick and stone but, at the last minute, Fouquet and Le Vau changed their minds. As we have seen, although the house was built entirely from stone, the service buildings remained in brick and stone, thus establishing a hierarchy of materials that would remain standard in France for a long time to come. At Vaux, this hierarchy is taken one stage further, since the brick and stone of the main service buildings are preceded by structures in rubble stone and plaster.

As one would expect, the château is centred on the great north–south axis and its elevations are perfectly symmetrical around this axis. Perhaps more surprisingly, its interior disposition is also rigidly symmetrical, on all floors, bar one or two very minor differences in layout between the eastern and western halves. Le Vau's floor plan at Vaux is particularly noteworthy for two features: its double-thickness massing of rooms in the *corps de logis*, and the enormous, double-height, oval Grand Salon which dominates the garden front. Traditionally, the *corps de logis* of French châteaux were only one room wide, greater depth being achieved at their extremities in the form of pavilions (four pavilions were the norm, one at each corner of the *corps de logis*, as at Vaux). Double-thickness plans, which allow a more complex configuration as well as individual access to rooms, had begun to be used in the *corps de logis* of the most modern Parisian *hôtels particuliers*, including Le Vau's own Hôtel Tambonneau (1642–46, destroyed). Le Vau's transposition of this type of plan to the house at Vaux is the first known occasion of its use in a château. The basement and first floor even feature long corridors running the length of the house, ensuring autonomy to the rooms they serve; until the mid-17C, corridors were virtually unknown. The oval salon was also an innovation, in France at any rate, as it was imported by Le Vau from Italy. He never went to Rome, but would have known of the central, oval salons of buildings such as the Palazzo Barberini (Carlo Maderno and Gianlorenzo Bernini, 1625–37) from drawings and engravings. He was the chief exponent of this type of room in France – a type that would go on to have considerable longevity in French architecture – and had already used it to great effect, notably at Le Raincy. Where, at Le Raincy, the salon occupied the entire width of the narrow *corps de logis* and was therefore expressed on both the entrance and garden fronts, at Vaux, with its greater width, the salon is preceded on the entrance side by a generous vestibule, thus delaying and dramatizing the visitor's discovery of this the centrepiece of the house. Only the dome and lantern surmounting the salon, which peek over the ridges of the entrance-façade roofs, hint at its presence to those arriving at the château.

Le Vau's entrance façade is characteristically French, consisting of a succession of receding volumes which draw the visitor in towards the central *avant-corps* whence access to the château is gained. In all, four cuboid volumes, treated as pavilions, crowd round the *corps de logis*. On the ground floor, concave elevations link the *avant-corps* to the two nearest pavilion volumes, softening the rectilinearity of the composition, a device used by both Mansart and Salomon de Brosse. The overall effect is somewhat disparate and disorderly, not helped by the complex and lofty roofing which coiffs the château. Another medieval inheritance, these high roofs, so typical of French buildings of the first half of the 17C, were fast going out of fashion and would not be used by Le Vau again. Indeed drawings exist of Vaux portraying it with low-pitched roofs, probably produced by Le Vau after completion of the house and intended to show it in an ideal state. Although rather ungainly, the entrance façade at Vaux is nonetheless picturesque, in spite, or perhaps because, of its idiosyncrasies. Le Vau's apparent sloppiness – or indifference – with regard to detail is discernible in his treatment of the outer pavilions: Classical purists would call for their division into an odd number of bays, but Le Vau has articulated only two. Laxity becomes crime with the application of colossal Ionic pilasters (Le Vau had a distinct fondness for giant orders) with a pediment; the pediment's apex finds itself sitting directly above the central pilaster. Such latitude attracted a good deal of criticism, as did the curious disposition of the central *avant-corps*, whose entrance portico rises only as far as the first floor, rather than to the roofline as one would expect. Laden with statuary and Fouquet's arms, its resplendent pediment appears somewhat ridiculous perched on top of stumpy little, one-storey, rusticated columns. The explanation for this singularity may lie in the fact that the château's chapel (no longer extant) was situated above the building's entrance, on the first floor: it would have seemed at best in dubious taste and at worst heretical to crown God's domain with the arms of the master of the house. On the other hand, the main entrance clearly required a grand portico carrying the owner's emblems, and thus this eccentric compromise was reached.

Far more successful is the garden front, no doubt in part because of its greater simplicity, although it is no less ambitious. The two flanking pavilions are here a full three bays wide, with the result that the colossal order comes into its own as an element of the composition. The pavilions project only slightly forward from the *corps de logis*, which is dominated by the swollen protuberance of the Grand Salon. Above the salon rises an enormous, bulbous slate dome, the most striking feature of the ensemble. In contrast to the shambles of attics crowning the entrance front, the garden-façade roofing appears perfectly coherent, the high pavilion roofs punctuating the composition and counterbalancing the giant dome. For added grandeur, the latter is surmounted by an imposing lantern. At the centre of the façade, on the Grand Salon's *avant-corps*, Le Vau plonked a two-storey portico, an almost exact copy of the one he designed for the Hôtel Tambonneau. The portico appears rather too dainty for the focal position it occupies, and there is also a certain uneasiness in its relationship to the prominent, womanly bulge of the Grand Salon. Indeed the salon's curves appear generally somewhat uncomfortable within the constraints of Le Vau's otherwise sharply rectilinear composition. Some critics have attributed Vaux's »faults« to the haste with which the château was designed and built, but the attention to detail which Le Vau brought to other aspects of the design does not seem to bear this out. Despite the »gaff« of the two-bay entrance-front pavilions, his use of the orders is sophisticated, with a Doric sub-order running round the building in the form of an entablature at first-floor level and fully expressed in the ground-floor columns of the entrance and salon porticoes. The bas-relief panels above the ground-floor windows, which were and would remain unusual in French buildings, also attest to his capacity for refinement. They are yet another reference to inherited French design traditions, this time the very tall windows which characterized châteaux prior to Vaux and which usually ran the full height of the wall space from floor level to the upper limit of the ceiling. As we shall see, the decorative treatment of Vaux's interior was highly innovatory in France, with vaulted, moulded ceiling profiles in the Italian manner. These ceilings did not permit the intrusion of windows above their cornice line, and thus on the exterior necessitated a substantial gap between the upper limit of the ground-floor windows and those directly above. To integrate the old, French way of doing things with the conflicting requirements of these new ceilings, Le Vau continued the ground-floor window frames up to the level they would traditionally have occupied, and filled the gap between the glazing

37.1 Château de Vaux-le-Vicomte. Garden front

and the top of the frame with the aforementioned bas-relief panels. Besides their appropriateness in the context of French practice, these panels also offered supplementary decorative opportunities, and were carved with Fouquet's insignia. (Interestingly, while the panels are present on the entrance and garden fronts, they were not used on the less-important lateral elevations, nor do they appear in the »idealized« drawings of Vaux.)

On entering the château of Vaux-le-Vicomte from the *cour d'honneur*, one passes through the triple arcade of the grand portico and arrives first in the vestibule, which is decorated with the same Doric order that runs around the ground floor of the house's exterior. A second triple arcade leads from the vestibule directly into the Grand Salon, from which the principle rooms of the house are accessed: to the west Fouquet's *appartement d'apparat* and to the east the Appartement du Roi. The provision of a whole suite of rooms reserved for the eventual use of the king was standard practice in the great houses of the day, since the monarch travelled a good deal. More unusual is the fact that the principal rooms are situated on the ground floor rather than on the first floor, which was traditionally the *piano nobile*. This disposition explains the absence of grand staircases at Vaux, normally an essential feature of French châteaux: as there were no grand apartments on the first floor, a grand staircase was not needed to reach them. There is also no gallery at Vaux, again a standard element in most contemporary châteaux, as it was here replaced by the Grand Salon. Communicating directly with the garden by way of a third triple arcade, the salon was originally closed only by iron gates, as was the vestibule. Thus, in the manner of Maisons, the central vestibule-salon section of the house was open to the air, constituting a sort of grand interior courtyard between the *cour d'honneur* and the garden and allowing perspective views through the house (the current glazed doors were installed in the 18C). This accounts for the decorative treatment of the vestibule and salon, both of whose elevations have the appearance of external façades and are rendered in stone. Dividing the house in two with all the absoluteness of a canyon – which explains the presence of two identical staircases leading to the first floor, one in the eastern and one in the western apartments –, the vestibule-salon duo prevented Le Vau from fully exploiting the potential advantages of the double-thickness *corps de logis*. On the ground floor, he divided up each apartment into a conventional suite of formal rooms on the garden front (*antichambre*, *chambre* and *cabinet*), but did not really seem to know what to do with the space at the front of the house. Likewise, the first-floor plan with its dark corridors seems a wasted opportunity.

The château's décor
The entirety of the décor at Vaux-le-Vicomte was overseen by Charles Le Brun, who arrived at the château in 1658 and lived there until Fouquet's arrest in 1661. Le Brun produced designs for both the painted and sculpted elements of the interiors, which were then realized by a team of artists he had assembled for the project, although he executed the principal paintings himself. This was, it seems, the first time in the history of French art that one, chief artist had directed the decoration of a major building in this fashion. As we have already said, the interiors at Vaux were highly innovative in France, realized in the Italian manner which Le Brun had experienced firsthand in Rome. He was, along with Antoine Le Pautre, the principal exponent of this kind of décor in France, a décor which at Vaux is confined essentially to the ceilings. One room, namely the square, anterior chamber in Fouquet's apartment,

seems to have been decorated before Le Brun's arrival, since it features a traditional, French-style ceiling with exposed, painted beams. It is quite likely that this ceiling, including its frieze of Roman soldiers subsequently added by Le Brun, was only a temporary arrangement and that the intended décor was never realized. Approaching Fouquet's rooms from the Grand Salon, one first enters his antechamber, also known as the Antichambre d'Hercule because of its iconography which seeks to identify the master of the house with the mythic hero. Here we have one of Le Brun's magnificent Italianizing ceilings, although its decoration, for the most part rendered as *trompe-l'œil*, is considerably more restrained than any contemporary Italian examples. Next comes Fouquet's *chambre d'apparat*, also known as the Chambre des Muses, which reveals Le Brun at his most brilliant. The ceiling is again principally rendered as an enormous *trompe-l'œil* painted onto the coved vaults, but with such vigour and freshness that one entirely forgets that this is only a two-dimensional representation. Its central panel, an allegory of fidelity, recalls Fouquet's loyalty to the crown during the troubles of the Fronde (1648–52 – a series of uprisings by the nobility against the growing power of the monarchy), while the muses surrounding it are a reference to his patronage of the arts. Leading off the bedroom is the curious Cabinet des Jeux (games room), decorated with intricate painted and gilded panelling. The signification of many of its allegories is lost to us, although they would have been immediately readable to contemporaries. Fouquet's emblem, the squirrel (chosen by his father because in Anjou, where the family originated, »fouquet« means »squirrel«), crops up regularly, as it does all over the house, but the interpretation of the many grass snakes, (coincidentally?) the emblem of Fouquet's arch rival, Colbert, and especially of one panel in which the snake appears to menace the squirrel, remains controversial.

As we have already seen, the linchpin and symbolic heart of the house is the Grand Salon. Never completed, the salon was conceived as a representation of the universe to the glory of Fouquet. We have already noted that its elevations are rendered in stone and treated architectonically, more precisely with a Composite arcade running round the lower storey and a row of windows (mostly false) encircling the upper. No one opening is privileged over any other, and the chain thus remains unbroken, going round eternally, or to infinity, like the universe it represents. The space around the windows is richly carved with garlands and allegories of gods and continents, as well as with terms representing the twelve signs of the zodiac and the four seasons. On the floor, at the centre of the room, are the remains of a sundial, which was to have found echo in Le Brun's proposed painting for the underside of the dome, intended as the crowning glory of the ensemble. Never even begun (the current, uncompleted composition dates from the 19C, but known to us through preparatory drawings, Le Brun's project for the painting depicted the Palace of the Sun, peopled by gods and seasons, at whose centre shone a new star called the Squirrel. The existence of this extraordinary room, which served no practical purpose other than access and which was intended only to impress, testifies to Fouquet's excessive vainglory.

The finance minister nonetheless humbly ensured that the king's apartments were even more magnificent than his own. The king's antechamber, the first room of the suite, was never completed, but the majority of its splendid ceiling is in place. Here the décor consists not only of *trompe-l'œil* painting but also of moulded, gilded stucco work in a manner then little used in France but prevalent in Italy. The next room, the Chambre du Roi, is even more lavishly decorated, with almost full-relief angels and putti, the ensemble dripping with gilding. Probably inspired by Pietro da Cortona's work at the Pitti Palace in Florence (c. 1637–47), the bedchamber, although to modern eyes inconceivably opulent and unrestrained, is a good deal less exuberant than its Italian precursors. French Baroque gets no more spectacular than Le Brun, but in comparison to contemporary Italian creations it is toned-down Baroque, rendered palatable for cooler northern tastes by avoidance of the extreme theatricality and illusionism dear to the Roman masters. Following on from the Chambre du Roi is a little *cabinet* with a charming, two-tone stucco ceiling and an Italian-style fireplace of a sort used all over the house. These sober fireplaces, with their flues hidden in the thickness of the walls, were a far cry from traditional French chimneypieces, which featured a prominent and often highly ornamented breast. The *cabinet* leads into a suite of rooms redecorated in the 18C and 19C; the only other room of note on the ground floor is the dining room, which dates from Fouquet's time. Prior to the mid-17C, the practice of maintaining a fixed space for eating was exceptional – usually tables would simply be set up wherever seemed appropriate on the day. Vaux's dining room, whose walls are painted with allegories of peace and abundance, is thus an early example. On the first floor, almost none of the original décor survives, bar Fouquet's bedroom, painted with *trompe-l'œil* mouldings and dedicated to Apollo.

The gardens

Vaux's grounds are often referred to as the first example of gardens realized »à la française«. While this is certainly not true – precedents for Vaux can be found in many French gardens of the first half of the 17C –, it was perhaps the first time that all the elements which go to make up a classic French garden were united, and the moment at which consciousness of a truly original, national art form took hold. The central axis regulating the composition, for example, had already been used on several occasions (e.g. at Maisons), but never with the effectiveness, the sense of magnificence, achieved at Vaux. Work on the gardens must have begun long before construction of the château, perhaps as early as 1641 when Fouquet acquired the estate, for the task of clearing, levelling and replanting the landscape was simply enormous. In the absence of supporting documentation, what is attributable to whom is difficult to establish, but it seems almost certain that Le Vau greatly influenced the general outline of the composition. As for Le Nôtre, while the parterres nearest the house are perhaps not his work (although the Parterre de la Couronne is traditionally attributed to him), the farthest sections of the gardens clearly bear his hallmark.

We have already seen how carefully the setting for the château was shaped, how the natural slope of the land was exploited to produce a highly calculated effect. In the laying out of the fountains and parterres, equal care was taken. The parterres nearest the house are planted with the geometric topiary fashionable at the time; those in the gardens' lateral sections are more intricate than those directly in front of the house and are provided with raised walkways to allow better appreciation of their ingeniousness. Great attention was paid to the effects of perspective, and whoever laid out these sections of the gardens must, like Le Nôtre, have been an expert in optics (Le Nôtre studied all the treatises on the subject, including Descartes's *Dioptrique* and the 43 volumes of Père Nicéron's *La Perspective Curieuse ou Magie Artificielle*). Everything is calculated to reduce and »correct« the foreshortening and diminishing effects of distance, it being always assumed, of course, that the point of observation is the château. Thus the pathway occupying the central axis actually widens the further it gets from the house, the farthest parterres are longer than those nearest the château to give an impression of equal surface area, and the pools get bigger as one moves further away. This first section of the gardens terminates in a huge square pool, behind which one can make out a long, stone grotto. The presence of so much water at Vaux – fountains spout everywhere (and there are fewer today than in Fouquet's time) – was certainly something of an innovation, and it is used not just ornamentally but as an organizing element of the composition, and also for its optical effect. One particularly stunning trick can only have been contrived by Le Nôtre. When one reaches the square pool at the end of the central pathway, one discovers, to one's great surprise, that the grotto does not sit directly behind it, as it appeared to do from the house, but that in fact a vast, sunken canal separates the two. 1 km in length, the canal is actually the local river, the Anqueil, dammed to produce this impressive sheet of water. Looking down one sees a rusticated cascade of imposing dimensions descending towards the canal. And if one then turns around towards the château, one finds that the size and position of the square pool have been perfectly calculated so that the house is exactly reflected within it.

Despite its 70 ha, the garden does not seem frighteningly huge – indeed everything is stage-managed on a human scale, but without diminishing the inherent grandeur. The garden's intimacy owes much to the thick woods surrounding it on all sides, planted so as to contrast their naturalness with the artifice of the formal parterres and to give some relief from the flatness of the latter. As in Fouquet's time, the gardens are peopled with statues, although many date from the 19C, the originals having been dispersed after Fouquet's arrest. The grotto, however, is original, and is adorned with personifications of the Nile and the Anqueil – based on Antique representations of the Tiber and the Nile – sitting in caves that drip with rustication. Between the grotto's central arcades, geometricized Atlases symbolically bear the weight of the hillside above. In reality, after climbing one of the curved ramps rising either side of the grotto, one finds that its summit is occupied by a large, circular pool known as the »Gerbe« (»burst« or »shower«) because of the 3 m-high fountain which thundered there in Fouquet's day. Of the 19C sculptures, the giant statue of Hercules which stands at the extremity of the axis at the top of the hill is particularly striking. A statue of the mythic hero was planned for this spot in Fouquet's time, but never realized; unlike the current standing colossus, it was to have portrayed a sleeping Hercules, an allegorical representation of Fouquet resting following the labours of creating the house and gardens.

Fate of the château to the present day
After Fouquet's arrest, his assets, including Vaux, were frozen, and the château's contents subsequently sold off, much being bought by the king. The house was not returned to Fouquet's wife until 1673. Her eldest son having died without heirs, Mme Fouquet sold the property to the Maréchal de Villars, in 1705. His heir ruined himself, and was obliged to sell the château, which was bought by the Duc de Choiseul-Praslin, in 1764, in whose family it remained for almost a century. Vaux was saved from destruction during the Revolution by the astuteness of the then Duchesse, who placed it under the protection of the Commune des Arts. During all this period, the house underwent only minor, interior modifications. By the latter half of the 19C, however, it had fallen into near dereliction, and at one stage was even threatened with demolition. Vaux was bought by sugar magnate Alfred Sommier, in 1875, and entirely renovated. The garden, which had become totally overgrown from neglect, was carefully restored on the basis of 17C plans and engravings; unfinished at the time of Sommier's death, the work was completed by his descendants, in whose hands the château remains today. Almost none of Fouquet's furniture survives, but period pieces have been acquired in its stead. Today the châ-teau and its gardens have regained all the splendour that was formerly theirs. It was Louis XIV himself who paid perhaps the greatest tribute of all to the brilliance of Vaux-le-Vicomte when, immediately after Fouquet's arrest, he engaged the team who created Vaux to aggrandize his small, out-of-the-way château at Versailles (32.1).

38 Fontainebleau

38.1 Château de Fontainebleau
Place du Général-de-Gaulle
Various architects, begun 12C
(SNCF: Fontainebleau; the château is a 20-minute walk from the station along the Rues Aristide-Briand and Grande)

Although a royal residence has stood on this spot since at least 1137, it is for the Renaissance château begun in 1528 by François I that Fontainebleau is now famous. Having moved his court from the Loire valley back to Paris, François needed châteaux in the Ile-de-France region, and consequently began a whole spate of stately-home building. He also needed bases from which to pursue that most royal of sports, hunting, and it was the beautiful Forêt de Fontainebleau that attracted him to this site, 65 km from the capital. He began converting and enlarging Fontainebleau's medieval fortress into what, initially at least, was to be a relatively modest retreat where king and court could amuse themselves in sylvan seclusion. But construction at Fontainebleau never ceased as François continued adding ever more pavilions, courtyards and *logis* to house an expanding retinue, with the result that the château was one vast building site throughout his reign. At his death parts of the building were still under construction, and it was left to his son, Henri II, to complete them. As a result of François's piecemeal reconstructions and additions, Fontainebleau presents a disorientating and highly picturesque sprawl of wings and courtyards that is quite unlike any other French royal residence. Plans by Gabriel in the 18C to regularize the whole lot came to nothing, and the many subsequent additions and modifications only increased the château's romantically disparate aspect.

It was not for its external appearance, however, that François I's château became famous throughout Europe, but for its internal décor, realized by a team of craftsmen that became known as the first school of Fontainebleau. François brought in from Italy the artists Giovanni Battista di Jacopo di Guasparre, known as Il Rosso, and Francesco Primaticcio, known in French as Le Primatice, who together directly imported up-to-the-minute Italian Mannerism into still-largely-medieval France. But in doing so they created a new, highly original type of décor, of which Rosso's Galerie François-I is the most celebrated example. With the bedchamber of the Duchesse d'Etampes (François I's mistress) and the château's Salle de Bal, completed under Henri II, Primaticcio brought his own contribution to the movement.

Modifications to the château continued under Henri II's immediate successors, but the Wars of Religion put a stop to further building work in the last decades of the 16C. At the turn of the 17C, Henri IV turned his attention to Fontainebleau: after François I, he was the monarch who built most at the château. Moreover, his tenure saw the development of a second school of Fontainebleau – this time lead by the French and Flemish artists Toussaint Dubreuil, Ambroise Dubois and Martin Fréminet –, whose principal surviving realization is the Chapelle de la Trinité.

For over a century during the reigns of Louis XIII and Louis XIV, Fontainebleau remained essentially as Henri IV left it, undergoing only relatively minor modifications. This was not the case under the Sun King's great-grandson, however. It is unsurprising that, shy and averse to courtly formality as he was, Louis XV should have particularly appreciated Fontainebleau, where he could indulge his passion for hunting in a more informal setting than Versailles (32.1). As a result, of all the sovereigns who succeeded Henri IV, it was he who most modified the château. His many additions were also accompanied by some regrettable destructions for which posterity has not entirely forgiven him: Primaticcio's famous Galerie d'Ulysse, for example, was demolished to make way for the pedestrian Aile Louis-XV, and the »Belle Cheminée« that had given its name to one entire wing of the château was dismantled for the creation of a theatre. Louis XV's unfortunate successor, Louis XVI, contented himself with the addition of a new suite of rooms, and also ordered some exquisite interiors for his wife, Marie-Antoinette.

Fontainebleau survived the Revolution unscathed apart from losing its furnishings. In the early-19C the château became indelibly associated with Napoleon – it was here that he bade farewell to France before being exiled to Elba –, and his memory lingers on in certain aspects of the interior décor. Since the château was empty when it came into his possession, he had to refurnish it, with the result that Fontainebleau today possesses one of the finest collections of Empire furniture anywhere. By the 1830s, the château's splendours had become distinctly tarnished under the effects of time, and Louis Philippe consequently undertook a major restoration programme. The early-19C's idea of »restoration« was rather different from our own, and comprised a considerable amount of repainting of frescoes, embellishing of surviving interiors and creation of new, historicizing ones where originals were lacking (our more authenticity-conscious age has tried to undo much of Louis Philippe's handiwork where the 16C decorative ensembles are concerned). Napoleon III, the last French sovereign to reside at Fontainebleau, added a new theatre to the château's facilities, and Empress Eugénie installed her Musée Chinois there. The Third Republic opened the château as a public museum.

The informality that characterizes Fontainebleau's layout is perhaps a reflection of the fact that, for all the monarchs who spent time there, the château was a place of leisure, relaxation and amusement. Although its interiors were not lacking in stately splendour, it was nonetheless a very different environment from more forbidding palaces such as the Louvre (1.8) or Versailles. François I loved Fontainebleau so much that he referred to it as »chez moi«, and Napoleon's affection for it was equally strong. He famously described the château,

38.1 Château de Fontainebleau. Aile de l'Escalier-en-Fer-à-Cheval

from the nostalgia of exile, as the »maison des siècles«, the »real home of our kings ... A rigorous architect's palace it might not have been, but it was assuredly a well thought-through and perfectly appropriate dwelling. It was probably the most commodious, fortuitously sited residence in Europe ...«

Before going on to describe the château's development in detail, it is worth giving a brief outline of its extremely complex layout. Fontainebleau comprises a series of courtyards running west–east, the first of which, on the Place du Général-de-Gaulle in the west, is known as the Cour du Cheval-Blanc (after a plaster cast once placed there) or the Cour des Adieux (because Napoleon said his farewells there). Biggest of the château's courtyards, it today serves as its main entrance and *cour d'honneur*. It is closed on its western side by railings, on its northern by the Aile des Ambassadeurs, on its southern by the Aile Louis-XV, and on its eastern by the Aile de l'Escalier-en-Fer-à-Cheval, which, as well as Jean Androuet Du Cerceau's famous »horseshoe« staircase, includes the Pavillon des Armes to the north and the Chapelle de la Trinité. East of the Cour du Cheval-Blanc is the Cour des Fontaines, open on its southern side to François I's enormous carp pond (Etang des Carpes), but closed on its western flank by Ange-Jacques Gabriel's Gros Pavillon and the Aile des Reines-Mères (or des Papes), on its northern side by the wing containing the Galerie François-I, and on its eastern by the Aile de la Belle-Cheminée. North of the Galerie François-I is a garden known as the Jardin de Diane. The Galerie itself runs at its eastern extremity into the château's 12C keep, which commands the Cour Ovale, originally Fontainebleau's principal courtyard. As well as the keep at its western head, the Cour Ovale is closed by state apartments to the north and by the Porte Dorée, the Salle de Bal and the Chapelle Saint-Saturnin to the south. At the courtyard's eastern extremity is a monumental gateway known as the Porte du Baptistère. Running north off the Cour Ovale is the long, narrow Cour des Princes, which includes the superimposed Galeries des Cerfs and de Diane on its western, Jardin-de-Diane side, while east

of the Porte du Baptistère, across a narrow carriageway, is the square Cour des Offices.

François I and Henri II's château, 1538–59
When François I first arrived there, the Château de Fontainebleau consisted of a small medieval fortress, roughly oval in plan and dominated by its square, 12C keep. The keep was the only part of the original structure that François retained intact, both because of its solidity and because many previous French monarchs, including the revered Louis IX (Saint Louis), had resided there. The highly picturesque Cour Ovale which the keep commands owes its irregular plan to the fact that, in view of his initial modest ambitions, François re-used the foundations and bases of the old fortress to construct his new buildings. The reason he built the wing containing the Galerie François-I running westwards from the keep was to link the Cour Ovale to the church of the Couvent des Trinitaires, a religious community that had grown up next door to the château and whose buildings the king appropriated for his own use. In front of the convent, he constructed the Cour du Cheval-Blanc to house the château's servants' quarters, kitchens and other outbuildings.

History has not recorded for us exactly who designed François I's new structures at Fontainebleau, but we know that the master mason Gilles Le Breton was responsible for building them. While some are happy to credit Le Breton with the title of architect, others feel that a more illustrious personage must have been behind them. (The Italian architect Sebastiano Serlio is often associated with Fontainebleau, although he did not arrive in France until 1541 and his interventions at the château seem to have been very minor.) Comprising simple, single-width *enfilades* of rooms, and coiffed with high, medieval slate roofs, the first new structures were built of plastered rubblestone with sandstone quoins, string courses, dormers and pilasters, although the latter are so clumsily put together, with visible cement joints, that they read more as quoins. It was partly the use of local sandstone, whose extreme hardness makes it difficult to shape and carve, that was responsible for this, adding to the buildings' rather vernacular, rough-and-ready allure. The original Fontainebleau can be seen in the Cour Ovale, either side of the keep, on the Aile de l'Escalier-en-Fer-à-Cheval (although much of this façade was later remodelled and parts refaced in limestone), and on the outer, southern elevation of the Porte Dorée. In François I's time, Fontainebleau's principal approach was via the long avenue running up the western side of the Etang des Carpes and culminating in the Porte Dorée, which thus initially constituted the château's *entrée d'honneur*. As such it was given especially *soigné* treatment and presents an interesting record of this transition stage in French architecture. Formally the gatehouse is resoundingly medieval, an adaptation of the classic twin-tower fortress format. The »towers« are linked by three superimposed open bays (the middle one is now closed by glazing) each

Fontainebleau 375

sporting slightly flattened arches, a configuration perhaps inspired by the ducal palace at Urbino (Luciano Laurana, c. 1465–72). Italian influence can also be seen in the use of pilasters and the triangular pediments applied to each window, although the way the top of one pediment cuts into the base of the window above was peculiar to France and seems to express a rather Gothic yearning for verticality. Indeed, despite the Classical trappings, the gatehouse is very un-Italian and appears to have been developed from earlier French models, which would explain why the pilasters' capitals are of a quattrocento type that had long gone out of fashion in Italy. Equally un-Italian is the curious portal François I had carved on the Pavillon des Armes, where, holding up an oddly shaped pediment, we find a pair of terms/caryatids sporting pharaonic headdresses, which are the first known example of Egyptian motifs used in French architecture. Fontainebleau also possesses what may well be the first example of cyclopean rustication in France, in the form of the Grotte des Pins realized c. 1543 at the western extremity of the southern wing of the Cour du Cheval-Blanc, on its garden side. Probably either by Serlio or Primaticcio, it features powerful Atlantases in between its arcades whose form is cleverly combined with the rusticated blocks. While at the Cour du Cheval-Blanc, we should take a quick look at its northern wing, the Aile des Ambassadeurs, which is today the principal surviving element of François I's outbuildings. Here we find established a hierarchy of materials that would be much imitated in subsequent châteaux: while Fontainebleau's noble parts were dressed with stone, its subordinate structures were dressed with brick.

Although charming and historically interesting in the French context, the first exteriors at Fontainebleau were, on a European scale of quality, awkward and provincial. The same cannot be said of the Galerie François-I and the other interiors realized there in the first half of the 16C, which, through the countless engravings made of them, influenced decorators across the continent for decades afterwards. Built c. 1528–30 and decorated c. 1535–40, the Galerie François-I takes the form of a 60x6 m long gallery – one of the earliest surviving examples of its type in France – with windows running all along both sides (those on the north are now blocked following the building of additional structures). In place of a traditional French beamed-and-painted ceiling it possesses a fine coffered covering by the Italian carpenter Francisque Scibec de Carpi, who was also responsible for the handsome wooden panelling on the lower half of the gallery's walls. But it was for the treatment of the walls' upper levels that the room became famous: a series of flat fresco panels, depicting complex allegorical scenes whose theme seems to be fate and kingship combined with allusions to the life of François I, that are set within sumptuous, high relief plaster frames and mouldings. Perhaps partly inspired by Raphael's decoration in the Palazzo Branconio dell'Aquila in Rome (now destroyed), this combination of painting and sculpture was eminently suited to the long gallery it adorned (a type of room not generally found in Italy), the panels setting up a brisk rhythm as one advances and the three-dimensionality of the carvings lending itself to being seen in sharp perspective. Rosso showed great invention and originality in his stuccowork, whose figures vary from Michelangelo-esque youths to lascivious fauns to upright Romans. Flying *putti*, swags of fruit and François I's salamander everywhere abound, but the decorative device that would have the most influence is the ubiquitous strapwork, imitating rolled and cut-out leather, whose generalized use was, it seems, an innovation of Rosso's that is now indelibly associated with the first school of Fontainebleau.

The principal survivor of Primaticcio's work at Fontainebleau during François I's reign is the bedchamber of the Duchess d'Etampes, decorated in 1541–44. In the 18C Louis XV converted it into a staircase (the Escalier du Roi) and under Louis Philippe it was given a carving-laden ceiling that it did not originally possess, but Primaticcio's famous frieze survives intact. It is essentially an adaptation of the same formula used in the Galerie François-I, but with some important stylistic differences that reflected the room's original destination. The more intimately scaled frescoes recount the life of Alexander the Great, whose manly doings are contrasted with willowy nymphs that form part of the elaborate, high-relief stuccowork frame, where strap-work is again an important feature. In comparison to the rather dumpy Graces to be found in the Salle de Bal (see below), the nymphs are elegantly, almost erotically elongated, and, surprisingly, conform much more to our own era's canons of feminine pulchritude than to those usually associated with the Renaissance.

One other important interior survives from the Fontainebleau that François I knew, namely the Chapelle Saint-Saturnin on the southern side of the Cour Ovale, whose construction was begun in 1531. Programmatically it is of the medieval palace-chapel type developed at the Sainte-Chapelle (1.2), comprising a lower chamber for the common household and an upper one for king and nobles. The chapels are unusual in that they terminate in a semicircular apse at both ends. In the upper chapel we find a remarkable coffered wooden vault, dated 1546, of a type uncommon in France, that opens into an octagonal lantern at its centre. The chapel's splendid painted polychromy, featuring seraphs and *trompe-l'œil* rosettes, was realized under Henri IV.

Next to the Chapelle Saint-Saturnin, to its west, stands the impressive Salle de Bal, the château's ballroom. Begun in 1545 and unfinished at François I's death in 1547, it was completed under Henri II. Philibert De l'Orme, Henri's superintendent of buildings, was charged with the necessary building work, and Primaticcio, aided by the fresco painter Nicolo Dell'Abate, saw to the ballroom's decoration. Externally the ballroom presents a new style of construction in comparison to

38.1 Château de Fontainebleau. Cour des Fontaines from the Etang des Carpes

the earlier Renaissance parts of the château, with superimpositions of large-scale arcades and a much greater use of ashlar. This aspect can also be seen on the Pavillon des Armes, and may have been inspired by the rebuilding work carried out by François I at the Château de Saint-Germain-en-Laye (28.1). Inside we see that the ballroom comprises a 30 m-long hall flanked on both sides by enormously thick arcades and with a musicians' gallery at one end. These massive supports were originally intended to carry a stone vault (whose carved and gilded brackets were left in place), but De l'Orme decided to cover the ballroom with a much less costly, Italian-style coffered wooden roof. Constructed by Scibec de Carpi with octagonal coffers, its effect is nonetheless splendid. The opposite end of the room to the musicians' gallery is dominated by De l'Orme's monumental fireplace, which features bronze satyrs copied from Antique originals. Perhaps again in the interests of cost cutting, or maybe because of the room's grand scale, there is much less stuccowork in the ballroom than in the earlier parts of the château, its mural décor consisting essentially of panelling, designed by De l'Orme, and enormous frescoes, designed by Primaticcio and executed by Dell'Abate. Their allegory is today difficult to decipher, but the modern eye can still appreciate the delicacy of Dell'Abate's colours, even if the drawing of some of the figures, especially the Three Graces in the fourth spandrel on the courtyard side, seems a little elephantine.

Philibert De l'Orme's other principal interventions at Fontainebleau were the rebuilding of the Chapelle de la Trinité and the partial reconstruction of the Aile des Reines-Mères; neither today looks much like he intended. For the new chapel he contrived a monumental entrance in the Cour du Cheval-Blanc in the form of an ingenious, horse-shoe-shaped staircase, which gave its name to the wing it accesses and whose memory lives on to a certain extent in the reconstruction it inspired in the 17C (see below). When rebuilding the Cour-de-la-Fontaine façade of the Aile des Reines-Mères, he introduced limestone ashlar for the first time to Fontainebleau, prompting a refacing of the Aile de l'Escalier-en-Fer-à-Cheval that was never completed.

Fontainebleau and the last Valois monarchs, 1559–70
After Henri II's accidental death in a tournament in 1559, the new queen regent, Henri's widow Catherine de Médicis, sacked De l'Orme, who had been the protégé of Henri's mistress, Diane de Poitiers, and replaced him as Surintendant des Maisons Royales with her compatriot Primaticcio. In the decade 1560–70 she completed two important modifications to Fontainebleau: the rebuilding of the eastern wing of the Cour de la Fontaine, which is now known as the Aile de la Belle-Cheminée, and the doubling in width of the Cour

Ovale's northern wing for the creation of new state apartments. She also began refacing the southern façade of the Galerie François-I in limestone ashlar (completed under Henri IV) and had a water-filled moat dug around the »noble« parts of the château (whose course through the Cour du Cheval-Blanc is today marked by balustrades), a reflection of the troubled times in which she ruled. Architecturally, by far the most interesting of these additions was the Aile de la Belle-Cheminée, whose reconfiguration was undertaken in order to enlarge and aggrandize the apartments of Catherine's son, the infant king Charles IX. While the rebuilt wing's eastern, garden-side façade is undistinguished, on its western, courtyard side Primaticcio contrived a very ambitious elevation that broke with everything before realized at Fontainebleau. Rigorously symmetrical, it is articulated around two monumental staircases that reverse the convergence of Michelangelo's stairs in his 1538 design for the senator's palace on the Capitol in Rome, as well as recalling the diverging stairways of some Italian hillside gardens. The lefthand stairway provided a suitably regal entrance to Charles IX's apartments, while the righthand one accessed the Grande Salle that occupied most of the reconstructed wing's length. Although featuring ground-floor rustication, first-floor Tuscan pilasters and dormers all contrived to match those of the Aile des Reines-Mères opposite, the Aile de la Belle-Cheminée produces a very different effect. Primaticcio played a whole subtle game of voids, the void formed by the staircases being matched at the façade's centre by a receding arch, in place of the projecting *avant-corps* one would expect to find, although the illusion of a central pavilion is preserved through the use of a monumental winged and pedimented dormer. The elevation's central part is further monumentalized by yet more voids in the form of statue-filled niches, which find their echo in the side pavilions. Not only is the Aile de la Belle-Cheminée unlike anything seen before in France, it is also, with its strong French influence, unlike anything known in Italy, and remained a glorious one off.

In comparison, the building of a new suite of rooms onto the Jardin-de-Diane side of the Cour Ovale structures, thereby doubling in width their simple *enfilade*, was a much more pedestrian affair. Indeed it has since lost its original façade, which was replaced by an equally undistinguished elevation in the 18C. Paradoxically, given its plain exterior, some of the most important rooms in the château came to be installed in this new structure, while the older parts of the Cour Ovale became antechambers, *salles de garde*, etc. Today the interiors to be seen here constitute an extraordinary palimpsest of styles and epochs, with up to three centuries of décor cohabiting in the same space.

Fontainebleau under Henri IV, 1594–1610
Henri IV's interventions at Fontainebleau, which included both additions and rebuilding, showed a remarkable respect for the original architecture of the château, and testify to his great affection for it. Of his surviving structures, the earliest in date is the 74 m-long wing running north of the Cour Ovale on the Jardin de Diane and containing the Galerie des Cerfs on its ground floor and the Galerie de Diane on its first, which was built *c*. 1600. Henri's Galerie de Diane is no more, having fallen into ruin and been replaced with an entirely new interior in the 19C (see below), but one can still get an idea of what his Galerie des Cerfs was like, even though for the most part what we see today is the result of a reconstruction carried out under Napoleon III. During Louis XV's reign the Galerie had been divided up into apartments, but when these were dismantled in 1863 sufficient traces of the original décor were found to allow a reconstitution. Under a French beamed and painted ceiling is a series of enormous mural frescoes showing aerial views of Henri's principal châteaux, a conceit perhaps inspired by the Vatican's Gallery of Maps. Unfortunately the frescoes cannot be taken as historically accurate records since much of what they depict had to be invented by the 19C restorers, based on surviving documentation.

After constructing his new galleries, Henri next turned his attention to the Cour Ovale, whose eastern end was rebuilt on larger and more regular lines in 1601 to 1605. Instead of its original oval closing, it was given parallel wings terminating in imposing pavilions, between which a monumental gateway was erected, thereby creating a new *entrée d'honneur* to the château that superseded the Porte Dorée. The pavilions are noteworthy for the absolute respect they show to Le Breton's original structures, a rare example of an historically sensitive intervention in an age that was not generally sentimental about the past. As for the gateway, known as the Porte du Baptistère, it is a most unusual and elaborate composition, its quirkiness stemming in large part from the fact that its ground floor, in local sandstone, was originally a drawbridge gatehouse that stood in the Cour du Cheval-Blanc and provided access to the Aile de l'Escalier-en-Fer-à-Cheval across Catherine de Médicis' moat. Having filled in the château's moats, Henri IV decided to re-use this charming exercise in rustication – which had originally been created by Primaticcio in the 1560s – by plonking it in between his new Cour-Ovale pavilions. But on its own it did not appear sufficiently grandiose to constitute the *entrée d'honneur* to the Cour Ovale, so Henri ordered an imposing second storey in limestone, which consists of a sort of vaulted, arcaded, lanterned belvedere with elaborate Victories holding up Henri's arms in its eastern, entrance-side pediment.

Henri's rebuilding of the Cour Ovale's eastern end was part of a larger scheme to re-orientate the château, which up till then had rather rudely turned its back on the town of Fontainebleau that had grown up to serve the royal household. This was brought to fruition with the building of the Cour des Offices in 1609, which replaced François I's Capitainerie. Open on its western flank facing the Cour Ovale, the Cour des Offices presents a typically early-17C-French assemblage of tall pavilions and lower *arrière-corps* on its other three sides, the use of plastered rubblestone and brick dressings clearly signalling that these were subordinate structures to the château proper. The one exception is the monumental gateway at the centre of the northern flank, which is entirely in ashlar and is preceded on its town side by the Place d'Armes (which Henri IV never got round to turning into the monumental pizza he had planned). Visitors entered via the Place-d'Armes gateway, and, if of non-royal rank, descended from their carriages or horses in the Cour des Offices and then proceeded to gain the château proper on foot via the Porte du Baptistère. We do not know who designed the Cour des Offices and its monumental gateway, although the names of Jacques II Du Cerceau and Salomon de Brosse have been put forward as likely candidates; whoever it was knew how to handle theatrical Baroque effects, building a giant example of what is known in French as an *exèdre*, a vaulted niche, here aggrandized through splendidly handled rustication. It is echoed in the courtyard pavilion opposite by a concave façade adorned at its base with three fountains.

There was of course no point building all these splendid new exteriors if one did not provide some new interiors to wow the crowd, and Henri IV did not stint on this aspect of the château's embellishment either. It was he who moved the king's bedchamber out of its traditional home in the keep to Catherine de Médicis' Jardin-de-Diane wing (today Napoleon's Salle du Trône), who created the famed Belle Cheminée and who completed the Chapelle de la Trinité. But time and changing fashion have undone much of Henri IV's work, and relatively little survives by the second school of Fontainebleau. The Cabinet de Théagène (or Salon Louis-XIII), to the north of the keep on the Cour Ovale, gives a good idea of their style, although its original intimate effect was ruined by Louis XV who added four new doorways in place of some of Ambroise Dubois's paintings. We find here the same combination of painting and stuccowork as pioneered in the Galerie François-I, only there is more lavish gilding, a greater profusion of small-scale, detailed ornament, and – an important development – the painting has spread to the ceiling where it is contained in painted stuccowork compartments *à l'italienne*. Moreover, the paintings themselves are very different in style, being realized on wood or canvas which permitted the much darker, chiaroscuro effects dear to northern artists. The second school's abilities in the domain of sculpture were spectacularly demonstrated by the Belle Cheminée; a measure of its lost magnificence can still be got from Mathieu Jacquet's giant marble bas-relief of Henri IV on horseback that now adorns the Salon Saint-Louis (formerly the king's bedchamber) in the keep. The last interior undertaken by Henri IV was the Chapelle de la Trinité, whose redecoration was, according to legend, prompted by the Spanish ambassador, Don Pedro: on being shown round the château in 1608 and asked what he thought, he supposedly replied: »All that is lacking is for God to be as well housed as your Majesty.« Completed under Louis XIII, the chapel provides another spectacular example of late-Mannerist painting and stuccowork, especially on its splendid compartmented barrel vault, whose cycle of scenes on the Redemption of Man are by Martin Fréminet.

Henri IV also devoted considerable effort to embellishing Fontainebleau's gardens, which became famed for their elaborate fountains. Today the only survivors from his time are the 1.2 km-long grand canal and the Fontaine de Diane in the *jardin* of the same name. Henri apparently took great delight in the construction of the canal, spending hours watching the workmen and losing a bet to the Maréchal de Bassompière that it could be filled in two days. Predating its famous successor at Versailles by 60 years, it caused quite a stir at its inauguration. As for the fountain, it features a bronze copy of an Antique Diana disporting on a plinth guarded by urinating hounds, whose pissing posture was modelled by Pierre Biard.

Louis XIII–XVI and Fontainebleau, 1610–1787
Louis XIII's reign saw only one intervention of significance at Fontainebleau, but one that would come to be identified with the château for ever after: Jean Androuet Du Cerceau's building of a new »horseshoe« staircase, in 1632–34, to replace Philibert De l'Orme's original of 1550 which was falling into ruin. Du Cerceau's *escalier*, which has since become emblematic of Fontainebleau, is an elaborate affair, with twin flights cascading in gentle undulations down into the courtyard below.

The early years of Louis XIV's reign were marked by the regency of his mother, Anne of Austria, who carried out a thorough redecoration of Fontainebleau's state apartments c. 1644–50. Today we can still see the beautiful painted ceiling she installed in the queen's bedchamber (now known as the Chambre de l'Impératrice), with gilding carvings by Guillaume Noyers, the rather overcharged gilded ceiling and panelling of the Salle du Trône, and certain remarkable elements of décor in the Aile des Reines-Mères, where she made her apartment after Louis XIV's majority. In comparison, the Sun King's interventions, at least where the château proper was concerned, seem minimal: the building by Jules Hardouin-Mansart of an undistinguished wing doubling the Galerie des Cerfs (1701) to provide extra accommodation for courtiers, and the creation of a comparatively modest apartment for his morganatic second wife, Mme de Maintenon, in the Porte Dorée (panelling with sun motif still to be seen). It was in the château's gardens that he really left his mark, sweeping away Henri IV's *petits jardins* and fountains and commissioning André Le Nôtre and Louis Le Vau to replace them with the regal but not very inspiring pools and parterres we see today.

Louis XV's tenure at Fontainebleau had a much more marked effect on the château's fabric. In search of space for an ever-expanding court, his first intervention was the building of new wings onto that constructed by Hardouin-Mansart to form today's Cour des Princes (Jacques V Gabriel, 1736–38). Still short of space, his next move was to sacrifice the original southern wing of the Cour du Cheval-Blanc for the erection of a more substantial building, destroying Primaticcio's Galerie d'Ulysse in the process. Although this act of vandalism caused consternation in some quarters, the spirit of the age was perhaps more accurately summed up by the Duc de Luynes, who described the gallery as »mauvaise et inutile«. In its stead rose the brick-and-stone Aile Louis-XV (eastern half 1739–40, western half 1773/74, façade design by Jacques V Gabriel), whose distinct lack of *éclat* is partly explained by the cash-strapped king's instructions that every expense should be spared. He was less stingy when it came to rebuilding the pavilion at the carp-pond end of the Aile des Reines-Mères, which was constructed by Ange-Jacques Gabriel in 1750–54; known as the Gros Pavillon, its elevations were directly based on the garden façade at Versailles, thereby giving us an idea of what the Sun King's palace would have looked like with a roof! Inside the château, as well as upsetting, modifying or destroying some of the earlier décor, Louis XV also enlarged and entirely redecorated the Salle du Conseil (1751–54 and 1773) in the Jardin-de-Diane wing. Certain aspects of its treatment, such as the compartmented ceiling with paintings by Boucher, were deliberately anachronistic so as to harmonize better with the neighbouring rooms, although the delicate intricacy of Jean-Baptiste Pierre and Carle Van Loo's exquisite wall panels is clearly a product of the Rococo. Also Rococo was Louis XV's theatre – for whose creation the Belle Cheminée was destroyed – which today, alas, is no more, having burnt down in 1856.

It is to Louis XVI that we owe the obstruction of the Galerie François-I's northern windows, sacrificed for construction a new *enfilade* of rooms that are now home to Napoleon's private apartments (see below). The twilight years of the *ancien régime* also produced some notable new interiors, all realized for Marie-Antoinette. The queen's Salon des Jeux was redecorated by Pierre Rousseau in 1786 with neo-Classical paintings and reliefs, her bedchamber was given new doorways in a matching style, and a new boudoir was created for her next door, again by Rousseau. Famous for its exquisite appointments, the Boudoir de la Reine was realized with the most exacting attention to detail, right down to the ivy-entwined window mechanism by the *bronzier* Pitoin. Marie-Antoinette only got to enjoy her new rooms for one season, for after 1786 the court never returned to Fontainebleau, and it was left to Empress Josephine to hang up the sumptuous silk hangings the late queen had ordered for her bedchamber.

Fontainebleau in the 19C
Although Napoleon's chief contribution to today's château was its furnishings, he also made one important intervention in its built fabric: the demolition in 1809 of the western wing of the Cour du Cheval-Blanc (which was falling into dereliction) so as to turn the courtyard into Fontainebleau's *cour d'honneur* and principal entrance. His plans to create a square with radiating avenues leading off the courtyard came to nothing, however. Inside the château, the most splendid Empire décor is to be found in Napoleon's private apartments, which demonstrate all the bold refinement of the style. The emperor also began refurbishing the Galerie de Diane, whose current configuration, inspired by Percier and Fontaine's design for the Grande Galerie in the Louvre, was the work of Maximilien-Joseph Hurtault. The gallery's rich neo-Classical décor dates from the reigns of Louis XVIII and Charles X.

The modifications effected under Louis Philippe are in a very different mode, since it was from the original Renaissance château that they took inspiration, reflecting the profound change in attitude towards historic monuments that occurred during the Bourgeois King's reign. Besides the restorations already mentioned, some new interiors were created, such as the Salon des Tapisseries, with its 16C-style coffered ceiling, or the Salle des Gardes, whose panelling was painted in the intricate manner of Henri IV's time. Restoration of Fontainebleau continued under Napoleon III, who also added a new theatre in the Aile Louis-XV because he found the 18C auditorium in the Aile de la Belle-Cheminée too narrow and uncomfortable. Constructed in record time by Hector Lefuel in 1854, the Second-Empire playhouse features a charming auditorium that was clearly inspired by Gabriel's opera at Versailles. A decade later, in 1863/64, Empress Eugénie created her Musée Chinois in the Gros Pavillon; a fascinating testimony of the era's growing interest in orientalism, it displays objects looted from the Summer Palace in Beijing and gifts from the king of Siam. With the completion of the Galerie des Fastes in 1867, where historic paintings of the château were assembled, so ended over 300 years of constant building and renewal at Fontainebleau, leaving us the »maison des siècles« as we see it today.

The Métropolitain and the Réseau Express Régional (RER)

At the turn of the 21C, any city aspiring to metropolis status wants its own underground railway system. Indeed one of the chief characteristics of modern urban life is the inordinate amount of time spent in these mass-transit subterranean spaces, whose environmental quality consequently has an enormous impact on city dwellers' lives. Paris has two underground-railway systems: the 14-line Métropolitain, the original and classic Métro which is run by the RATP, and the RER, a suburban train network run by the SNCF whose five lines cross the capital in tunnels. Together they handle over 5 million passengers daily, and have become an essential element in Parisian life. Indeed a whole popular mythology has grown up around Paris's Métro, which has regularly featured in songs, films and literature over the last century, and its Art-Nouveau entrances, designed by Hector Guimard, are now a tourist symbol of the French capital.

Given the magnitude of Baron Haussmann's reconfiguration of Paris – undertaken at just the same time as London was providing itself with the world's first underground-railway network –, it is surprising that the French capital was so sluggish in building its own Métro, since the baron's *travaux* would have provided the perfect opportunity to do so. But Haussmann's lack of interest, followed by a 20 year-long quarrel between the state and the local authority over who should control the new facility, prevented any of the manifold projects from ever getting off the drawing board. In the end it was the prospect of the millions of visitors who would descend on Paris for the 1900 Exposition Universelle that prompted urgent action, as of 1897, when the state gave in and let the city plan a six-line network under the direction of the engineer Fulgence Bienvenüe. Opened in July 1900, the first line completed (today's Line no. 1) ran from the Porte de Vincennes to the Porte de Maillot. Construction was greatly facilitated by Haussmann's wide boulevards, which allowed the cut-and-cover method to be adopted, a much cheaper option than deep tunnelling. As a result, most of Paris's Métro network follows the above-ground road system. Two of the original lines, nos. 2 and 6, were not built in tunnels but on elevated viaducts because their course crossed several overground railways; although a viaduct line cost exactly twice the price of a cut-and-cover one, deep tunnelling was even more expensive, and it was therefore cheaper to traverse the mainline railways via bridges.

By 1914 there were ten lines totalling 92 km, by 1939 158 km of track was in operation, and the network continued to grow in the postwar period. But the Métro was a purely Parisian affair, with only minimal extensions into the neighbouring suburbs, and it became clear that the capital's hinterland needed to be linked up to the underground network. It was thus that Gen-

Métro station Breguet-Sabin

eral de Gaulle's government conceived the RER in the 1960s, which involved integrating already existing suburban train lines with the Métro system via a series of subterranean crossings through central Paris. Although some cross-capital lines already existed, the remainder had to be built from scratch, prompting a huge civil-engineering effort that produced vast and very deep complexes such as Auber station. It was for construction of one of these interchanges, Châtelet-les-Halles station, that Victor Baltard's famous Halles Centrales (see 1.22) were destroyed, making way for a truly awful 1970s dystopia that is worthy of Jacques Tati's *Playtime*. Today the RER has a reputation for crime which its scary stations do nothing to improve.

The end of the 20C saw two new additions to Paris's underground-railway network: the Métro's Line no. 14, conceived to link the Gare Saint-Lazare (8.5) to southeastern Paris, and the RER's Eole (an acronym for *est-ouest liaison express*), more prosaically known as Line E, which links the Gare Saint-Lazare to the Gares de l'Est (10.5) and du Nord (10.7). Both schemes were characterized by the particularly careful attention paid to their station design, intended to do away with the dowdy and, where the RER was concerned, dangerous image the networks had gained in recent years. It now seems likely that Line 14 and Eole will be the last heavy-duty, tunnel-bound transport interventions in Paris, since there is little room or need for expansion in the city centre, and because considerably cheaper alternatives, such as tram lines, could be employed in the suburbs.

The original Métropolitain
Back in 1897, it was public opinion that constituted the chief obstacle to construction of Paris's Métro. Alarmed by some of the more outlandish schemes proposed over the years, Parisians were generally hostile to this new invention, fearing they would be forced underground like moles or that their streets would be scarred with monstrous »industrial« excrescences. Below grade the Métro's builders could do as they pleased since their work was invisible from the street; for the platforms they thus opted for the cheap, no-nonsense solution of facing their elegant, elliptical vaults with »hygienist« bevelled white tiles (which today, especially in some of the less well-maintained stations, give the impression of vast underground lavatories). But where the street-level installations were concerned, they had to tread much more carefully. Charles Garnier, advising the Minister of Public Works, explained: »The Métro, in the eyes of the majority of Parisians, will have hardly any excuse unless it absolutely rejects all industrial character to become entirely a work of art. Paris must not be transformed into a factory; it must remain a museum.« A competition was consequently organized to find designs for the Métro's ticket halls, but none of the results was considered suitable. In the end the banker Adrien Bénard, an ardent admirer of Art Nouveau whose bank was financing the Métro's construction, imposed Hector Guimard (who had just achieved notoriety with his »Castel Béranger« apartment building, 16.11) to build the new underground's street-level entrances. The even more sensitive question of the elevated Métro was delegated by Bienvenüe to Jean-Camille Formigé, chief architect of the Ville de Paris.

Of the two architects, Formigé was much the less radical, and he chose to play safe. While not attempting to disguise the fact that the elevated Métro was a major work of civil engineering, he nonetheless sought to make it more palatable to the public through *soigné* detailing. In true 19C eclectic style, he leafed through the back-catalogue of Classicism seeking forms that could be adapted to this new industrial use. Thus we find a curious mélange of stone piers, whose heavy rustication does nothing to disguise their bulk, and metal Doric columns topped off with vaguely »Assyrian« capitals. The stations' entirely glazed walls exhibit the elegant leanness possible with iron construction, but the swags and garlands decorating them seem a superfluous adornment.

Guimard, on the other hand, was a much more uncompromising character, especially where style and aesthetics were concerned. His early career had been marked by his experimentation with Structural Rationalism *à la* Viollet-le-Duc, to which he later added, after meeting the Belgian architect Victor Horta, the sinuous lines and »vegetality« of Art Nouveau. The Paris-Métro entrances would mark the culmination of this fusion. Using the most economically appropriate material was one of the tenets of Structural Rationalism, and Guimard consequently chose cast iron both because of its cheapness and because it lent itself perfectly to his linear forms. Through a system of standardized prefabricated parts, he developed a series of five different types of Métro entrance, ranging from the most elementary, consisting simply of railings, to the elaborate pagoda-like structures that formerly stood at Bastille and Etoile stations. Standardization created a strong family resemblance amongst the station types, and the brand image was further consolidated by a verdigris paint scheme and Guimard's specially designed Métro lettering. The most common entrance type comprised railings and a pair of alien-eyed lamps carrying a sign indicating the station's name, but it was the »libellules« – covered entrances whose insect-like metal skeleton and projecting tongues of glass recalled the body and wings of a dragonfly – that particularly caught public attention. Contemporary Parisians were surprisingly hostile to these unprecedented, astonishing creations, denouncing their green colour as »German« and their lettering as un-French.

Indeed it is only in the last 30 years or so that Guimard's work has acquired the almost cult following it enjoys today. Prior to this period, it and Art Nouveau in general were considered rather cheesy relics of yesteryear, and were consequently frequent targets of demolishers' bulldozers. Many of Guimard's Métro entrances were destroyed, including those at Bastille and Etoile.

Métro station Châtelet

Around 60 survive today, of which all bar three fall into the two most basic categories of the series. Two, those at Châtelet station (Place Sainte-Opportune, 4th) and at Dauphine station (Avenue Foch, 16th), are of the *libellule*, Model B type, while the entrance at Abbesses station (Place des Abbesses, 18th) is an example of one of Guimard's more rococo designs. The Métro entrances' fate underlined the ephemerality of the Art-Nouveau movement in general, although Guimard himself achieved immortality as the inventor of the »style Métro«.

Into the 21C – Line no. 14 and Eole
Launched simultaneously in 1989 by France's then prime minister, Michel Rocard, Line no. 14 (also known as »Météor« – METro Est-Ouest Rapide) and Eole were intended to relieve the central section of RER Line A, which had reached saturation point. Météor, moreover, would serve the municipality's two huge eastern-Parisian redevelopment schemes, the ZACs Bercy (12.7) and Paris-Rive-Gauche (13.2). Both projects came in for heavy criticism because of their uniquely Parisian routing, which did little for the suburbs, and because of their enormous cost (7 billion francs for Météor and 8 billion for Eole), which ate up all the available financing for a decade, again at the suburbs' expense. This costliness was partly attributable to the new lines' stations, which were realized with a luxury never before seen in Paris's underground network.

Météor was first off the mark with an initial section of seven stations (Madeleine–Bibliothèque François-Mitterrand) being inaugurated in 1998. A prolongation to the Gare Saint-Lazare is due to open in late 2003, while an extension southwards is programmed for 2005/06. Of the initial chunk, six stations were designed by the architect Bernard Kohn, while the seventh, Bibliothèque François-Mitterrand, was the work of Antoine Grumbach and Pierre Schall. Météor has the distinction of being the world's first fully automated, driverless Métro, and the RATP consequently wanted the line's stations to inspire the sense of security that the absence of drivers might otherwise dissipate. Kohn's approach was twofold: introducing as much natural light as possible to counter the Métro's murky image, and giving the passenger the sense of orientation that older stations' labyrinthine tunnels did not. Unfortunately, RATP cold feet and French security bureaucracy in general whittled away his original wide light wells to almost nothing, but he did manage to retain his generously dimensioned circulation spaces and splendid, triple-height platform tunnels. Tiles and naked neon have been banished from his *soigné* stations, where luxurious finishes are combined with carefully calculated lighting effects: the ticket barriers with their illuminated glass fins are a good example of both. Bibliothèque François-Mitterrand, which also includes an interchange with the RER C, is by far the most architectonic of Météor's stations, comprising majestic columned and vaulted spaces, all realized with beautifully crafted concrete in a variety of colours and finishes.

Inaugurated in 1999, the two new central-Parisian Eole stations (Haussmann-Saint-Lazare and Magenta) were designed by Jean-Marie Duthilleul, chief architect of the SNCF. He took a similar approach to Kohn, only on a much grander scale and with more spectacular results. Here we see the full potential of the light-well idea, the ticket concourses leading into glass-roofed, Piranesian volumes filled with monumental escalators and staircases. 30 m below, at platform level, we find splendid concrete vaults coffered with sound-absorbent cushions. Attention to detail is everywhere manifest, from the variety of different concrete finishes to the wood and copper cladding to the white marble flooring, intended to reflect attractively on passengers' faces. Artificial lighting is again carefully managed, with some elegantly evocative examples of contemporary lamp design.

Arcades and passages

One of the fruits of the middle-class, capitalist expansion that was set in motion by the French Revolution, Paris's covered arcades were the talk of their age, providing an unprecedented social and commercial environment whose spectacle attracted both the consumer and the *flâneur* in droves. Originated in the French capital and subsequently exported all over the world, the covered arcade prefigured the 19C department store, and its legacy persists today in the form of shopping centres and malls. At their peak in the mid-19C, Paris's arcades numbered at least 50; today around 20 survive as testimony to this unique phenomenon. Although the arcade subsequently spread outside France, nowhere had such a high concentration as early-19C Paris, and the genus entered the city's collective consciousness, becoming an integral part of its identity that was immortalized in literature by authors such as Balzac and Zola. By the term »arcade« (»passage couvert« in French), we mean a glass-roofed, shop-lined passageway that crosses a city block between two or more streets and is accessible only to pedestrians. In a pre-Haussmann capital that still retained a dense, constricted, medieval street pattern, arcades of this sort were extremely attractive for several reasons. Free of vehicles, they offered refuge from the noise, mud and danger of busy streets without pavements (and sometimes even without cobblestones) and also provided a shortcut for pedestrians wishing to avoid traffic congestion. Shelter from the elements and a clement environment were ensured by their glass roofs and, after nightfall, the glittering gas jets they pioneered provided a cheery contrast to the Stygian gloom of the unlit streets outside. The luxury boutiques with which they were lined offered a feast for the eye, and the stomach could find satisfaction in the cafés and restaurants that also colonized their spaces. For the commercial tenants of the arcades, a large clientele was assured, one which, moreover, would be encouraged to linger by the pleasantness of the setting. And, for the property developer, the construction of an arcade was either a way of maximizing the commercial rents to be squeezed out of a deep site with little street frontage or a means to realize considerable cash profits relatively quickly by selling off the boutiques. Furthermore, because situated on private property at the heart of a city block, the arcade was exempt from highway-authority regulations.

90 % of Paris's arcades were built in the first 50 years of the 19C, in two waves: 1823–28 and 1839 to 1847. The feverish property speculation of which they were a part was given a huge kick start by the Revolution, in whose name vast areas of the city, formerly belonging to the church or the aristocracy, were confiscated and put onto the market. Many arcades were built on the sites of expropriated aristocratic *hôtels particuliers* or of demolished convents. Paris's *passages* were essentially a phenomenon of the city centre, exclusive to the economically vibrant *quartiers* of the Right Bank and often built in proximity to a centre of attraction such as a theatre or the ever-popular *grands boulevards*. Few arcades were constructed during the immediate post-revolutionary and Napoleonic periods due to the political instability of the times, which caused a general property slump, but, following the Restoration, the building boom began. It reached its peak around 1825, only to crash a couple of years later, around 1828. Slowed down by the 1830 Revolution, the market did not pick up again until 1837/38, when the second wave of arcade building began.

It was the emerging middle classes who led the speculation that produced the arcades, and it was also they who constituted the principle clientele of the arcades' luxury boutiques. Towards the late 1780s shops had begun to appear in Paris that aimed to seduce a moneyed public through not only the attractiveness of the goods they offered but also through the lavishness of their interiors and the setting in which their merchandise was displayed. The arcades provided an environment in which such shops could now flourish, and contemporary descriptions of Parisian *passages couverts* often dwell on the splendour of the establishments they housed. It was not only shops and boutiques that were drawn to the new arcades, but also cafés, restaurants, playhouses, dance halls, »panoramas« and baths, in short a whole industry of leisure that installed itself under their sheltering glass. The *passages* consequently became centres of fashion and *flânerie*, a public version of the aristocratic *salon*, where people came to see and be seen. The flip side of the coin was the thriving prostitution that colonized the arcades and which, in reality, was one of their principal attractions. Indeed it was the relative freedom of these spaces, which constituted a sort of urban drawing room where loitering was encouraged and where men and women of all classes mingled freely in an ambience propitious to socializing and chance encounter, that made them so popular. The moral crackdown of the 1830s and 1840s, which resulted in legislation expressly prohibiting *filles de joie* from soliciting in Paris's covered arcades, was certainly one of the factors in their subsequent decline.

It has to be said that even the most lavish of Paris's arcades were not architecturally remarkable, in large part because they remained faithful to the scale of the medieval city. Even the street entrances, though they often rise the full height of the arcade, do not stand out in a city full of tall, elaborately decorated *portes-cochères*. The more upmarket arcades were endowed with an aggrandizing décor of their own from which their shopkeepers benefited, but in the less ambitious it was the shop fronts alone that provided decoration. Decorative motifs tended to be fairly standardized, cornucopia, Mercurys (Mercury was the god of trade) and personifications of Industry and Commerce being the most popular. If the Parisian arcades were of modest aspect, many of the foreign imitations they subse-

Galerie Colbert

quently inspired were of far more spectacular character. England was the first country to build arcades in the French manner, in the 1810s, and one of its earliest, the Burlington Arcade in London (Samuel Ware, 1815 to 1819), was directly inspired by Paris's Passage des Panoramas (see below). From the 1840s on, the phenomenon spread to the rest of Europe and to America (paradoxically just on the eve of its decline in France) and produced much more grandiose specimens than those seen in Paris: Brussels' Galerie Saint-Hubert (Jean-Pierre Cluysenaar, 1846/47), Milan's huge Galleria Vittorio-Emmanuele II (Giuseppe Mengoni, 1865–67), and the vast complex that is Moscow's GUM (Alexander Pomerantsev, 1888–93), to name but three. Unlike these iron-and-glass monsters, which constitute an urban event in themselves, the smaller and more discreet Parisian arcades are best considered together as a phenomenon rather than singly in isolation.

Origins and development of the Parisian arcade
(In the following account of the development of Paris's arcades, those still extant are highlighted in bold. Addresses are given at the end of the feature.)

The origins of the Parisian arcade are obscure, but it must to a certain extent have been inspired by market halls, covered colonnades and, perhaps, Arab *souks* and Ottoman bazaars, discovered by the French at the time of Napoleon's military campaigns in Egypt. The story of the Parisian arcade is usually told beginning in 1781 at the Palais-Royal (1.16), property of the Duc de Chartres, who, to increase his income, commissioned the architect Victor Louis to build a mixed-use development of shops and apartments around the palace garden. Completed in their current state in 1784, Louis's constructions feature a colonnade at ground-floor level under which shelter shop-filled arcaded loggias, probably inspired by Italian arcaded streets. The colonnades (clear ancestors of the *passage couvert*) were an instant success. They surrounded three sides of the garden, the fourth, southern side having been reserved for a new *corps de logis* for the palace proper. Work on this new wing stopped after only the foundations had been completed, due to lack of funds, and the duke subsequently granted a certain M. Romain (or Romois) the right to build a temporary, commercial structure on the site, thereby both maximizing his revenues and protecting the foundations of the uncompleted wing. Erected in 1786, Romain's building, known as the Galeries de Bois (Wooden Galleries), consisted of a pair of boutique-lined passages, lit by clerestorys, the whole constructed entirely in wood. At the galleries' western extremity was a short, shop-lined passage lit by a glazed roof. This first example of a Parisian covered arcade – which also fulfilled the shortcut criterion as the galleries linked the Rue de Montpensier to the Rue de Valois – was an instant hit with the public and, to go by contemporary accounts, soon became the social and political heart of the nation. Its success was in large part due to the Palais-Royal's special status: the Duc de Chartres was such an important personage that he was able to prohibit the police from entering his property, and gambling, prostitution and revolutionary fervour consequently thrived within the Palais-Royal's walls, tacitly support-ed by Chartres. Following the Revolution, he voted in favour of Louis XVI's execution, but subsequently lost his own head in the Terror. Despite their temporary status, the Galeries de Bois outlasted him, and were only finally demolished in 1828 to make way for the Galerie d'Orléans (see below).

Because of their provisory nature and the fact that they were not at the centre of a dense city block, the Galeries de Bois are generally made to concede the title of first Parisian arcade to the Passage Feydeau (Martin Habert-Thibierge, 1790/91. A permanent, masonry structure sited so as to provide a shortcut when walking from the Palais-Royal to the *grands boulevards*, the Passage Feydeau was guaranteed success by its strategic positioning and by its proximity to the Théâtre Feydeau, and some of its resident establishments consequently became famous. Probably lit by a series of openings in its double-pitched, wooden roof, the Passage Feydeau was dingy and architecturally unspectacular, and disappeared with the theatre in the late 1820s. Today Paris's oldest surviving arcade is the **Passage du Caire**, built by a M. Prétrelle in 1798, which is also the city's longest, at 370 m all told. It takes the form of a warren of passages criss-crossing the site of the demolished Couvent des Filles-Dieu. De-

Arcades and passages 385

spite its exotic name, inspired by Napoleon's Egyptian campaign, the arcade was always rather workaday and was a big disappointment to the public of the era. Its regular, arcaded bays at first-floor level have today lost any decoration they may once have had, and its original wooden roof was replaced in the mid-19C by the current rather rudimentary iron-and-glass structure. The curious building at the arcade's Place-du-Caire entrance, which is decorated with Egyptian motifs, probably dates from the late 1820s. Now colonized by Paris's textile trade, the Passage du Caire may lack the charm of later arcades but is nonetheless an interesting survivor.

Much more in the spirit of the classic arcade is the **Passage des Panoramas**, which opened just a year after the Passage du Caire, in 1799. It was built by an American, William Thayer, as an adjunct to a development of a very different nature – a pair of panoramas, an attraction that became extremely popular in early-19C Europe. Brought to Paris by Thayer, who had seen examples in London, the panorama was essentially a giant, in-the-round painting of a landscape, usually an urban or battle scene, rendered with great illusionistic skill. Just as today Paris's Grand-Louvre (see 1.8) or London's Royal-Opera-House developments include shop units to make them economically viable, so Thayer included an arcade of boutiques running between his two panoramas. Ironically, it was the arcade that proved the more durable attraction, as the panoramas disappeared in the 1830s. The arcade's oldest section consists simply of two plain storeys under the roof, which was originally wooden-framed. The current iron-and-glass structure probably dates from 1834, when the arcade was enlarged by Jean-Louis Grisart, who added the short galleries running off the main passage. Some elements of the original décor survive, as well as the florid 19C woodwork of the »Abre à Cannelle« tea-room. Paris's first public trial of gas-lighting was carried out in the Passage des Panoramas in 1816, and the arcade later featured in Emile Zola's *Nana* (1880). It remains popular today due to its proximity to the *grands boulevards*.

Almost a decade later, in 1808, came the Passage Delorme (demolished in 1896), designed by Nicolas-Jacques-Antoine Vestier. It was here, probably for the first time in a Parisian arcade, that an iron-framed roof was used. Iron was a rare and consequently expensive material in France in the early-19C, and arcade roofs up till this point had been in wood. Their glazing had therefore only been partial as their structures were too cumbersome to allow a full glass covering. Through the lightness and slenderness of its members, an iron framework afforded a fully transparent skin, and the Passage Delorme astonished contemporaries by the translucidity of its covering. To maximize light levels in the arcade, mirrors, encased in a décor of mini-pilasters and bas-reliefs, were installed between the shopfronts, an idea taken up in subsequent *passages* and still visible at the **Galerie Véro-Dodat** (see below).

It was during the Restoration that the initial big wave of arcade-building occurred, and the first of this series was the Passage de l'Opéra (François Debret, 1822/1823; demolished 1924). With a simple, elegant iron-and-glass roof and gas-lighting from the outset, this arcade set the basic standard for those to follow. In 1823–26 came the **Galerie Vivienne**, which aimed to outdo all that had preceded it and which today is probably Paris's loveliest arcade. Designed by François-Jacques Delannoy, a pupil of Charles Percier's, the Galerie Vivienne offers more variety in its forms than most arcades due to the fact that it was converted from pre-existing buildings on the site, including an old *hôtel particulier* and its garden. On entering the arcade from the Rue des Petits-Champs, one arrives first in a generous rectangular space, originally the *hôtel's cour d'honneur*, which is followed, after one has traversed the *hôtel's corps de logis*, by a small and rather charming rotunda, included to mask a slight change in direction, and then by the arcade proper. Both the rotunda and the principal stretch of the *passage* were built on the site of the *hôtel's* garden. A flight of steps at the end of this main section takes one down to a second, shorter stretch perpendicular to the first, leading to the Rue Vivienne. The Galerie's main spaces are striking in contrast to previous arcades by their grander scale and by their elaborate décor, which includes elegant Empire-style mouldings and a colourful mosaic floor. The shops themselves are installed in arcaded loggia with a mezzanine under the arch – a standard arrangement for Parisian shops since at least the 17C – and are surmounted by a low storey of apartments. Masonry arches cadence the simple iron-and-glass roof and provide supplementary decorative opportunities. An enormous success with the public when opened, the Galerie Vivienne twice survived demolition threats in the early-20C and has now been entirely restored.

Despite its generous proportions, the Galerie Vivienne is not Paris's tallest arcade; that title goes to the **Passage du Grand-Cerf** (begun in 1824 and probably only completed around 1835), which rises an exceptional 11.8 m. Its roof and shop fronts are almost certainly not original and probably date from around 1845–50. Iron is much in evidence, from the elegant and admirably economical arcs supporting the roof to the shop-front frames, which are entirely glazed across two storeys. Tie beams at mid height support the arcade's light fixtures and are partially disguised by elaborate wrought ironwork. As well as its height, the arcade is unusual for the footbridges crossing it just under the roof, which add an architectonic dimension to an otherwise simple space. Entirely renovated in the late 1980s, the Passage du Grand-Cerf is today a charming place of calm in the bustling city.

1826 was a boom year for the construction of *passage couverts*, and four of today's survivors were begun then. Built in a very short time as a prolongation of the Passage du Caire, the **Passage du Ponceau**, despite some aggrandizing plasterwork, was as downmarket as its neighbour and is today in very poor state, having suffered the indignity of being re-roofed in PVC. Also built and inaugurated in 1826 was the **Galerie Véro-Dodat**, which was at quite the other end of the arcade hierarchy. When opened it provided a very convenient shortcut between Les Halles (see 1.22) and the Palais-Royal, which, in tandem with the proximity of Laffite & Caillard, one of Paris's busiest mail-coach services, ensured an abundant clientele. Architecturally the arcade is undistinguished: narrow with two low storeys under a simple glass roof that is twice interrupted by buildings crossing at second-floor level, rendering the arcade rather dark. It was not, however, for its architecture but for its decoration that the Galerie Véro-Dodat became famous, a décor that survives intact today. The arcade's elegant wooden shop fronts are separated by paired colonnettes enclosing tall mirrors surmounted by cherubs holding cornucopia, its upper storey, coiffed with a frieze of palmettes and glyphs, is painted to resemble marble, and the undersides of the solid sections of its roof are adorned with extravagant paintings of Roman deities. Copper facings on the shop-fronts, burnished to resemble old gold, joined forces with the mirrors to provide a glittering complement to the fiery gas jets that lit the arcade after dusk, astonishing contemporaries by its brilliance. Although it remained popular into the mid-19C, the Galerie suffered from poor ventilation and its reputation declined through comparison with subsequent better-lit and -ventilated arcades.

More successful on this score was the **Passage de Choiseul** (François Mazois and Antoine Tavernier, 1826/27), built up the road from the Galerie Vivienne in proximity to the Théâtre Ventadour (which still survives in the small square to the west of the arcade, now converted into a bank). Rising three tall storeys under the roof (whose current ironwork dates from 1891), the *passage* features arcaded-loggia boutiques in the manner of the Galerie Vivienne and is very simply decorated, apart from clocks and balconies adorning either extremity. Its perspective effect is nonetheless impressive due to its great length. On quite another echelon is the **Galerie Colbert** (J. Billaud, 1826/27), built parallel to the Galerie Vivienne and intended to outdo it in all respects. What we see today is actually a concrete-framed facsimile of the original, constructed in the early 1980s, the old fabric having become too dilapidated to be saved. Like Vivienne, the Galerie Colbert was converted from an *hôtel particulier* (that had once belonged to Jean-Baptiste Colbert, hence the arcade's name) although, through various subtle tricks – sloping the floor gently to mask the change in level, imperceptibly stretching and squeezing the shop-front openings to hide irregularities – Billaud ensured that its internal spaces were considerably more uniform than its neighbour's. For the new arcade's elevations he essentially reproduced the Galerie Vivienne's disposition of arcaded loggias with an upper storey of apartments, but endowed it with a far more elaborate decoration

than its rival. Engaged Corinthian columns separated the shop units, elaborate plaster mouldings adorned the walls and the entire arcade was polychrome, its lower surfaces painted to resemble costly marbles, its upper levels decorated with Pompeiian motifs. The *pièce de résistance*, much remarked upon by contemporaries, was the 15 m-diameter rotunda at the intersection of the arcade's two perpendicular stretches, whose magnificent iron-and-glass roof included *trompe-l'œil* draped velum painted onto its lower sections. Despite the very positive reaction to its grandeur, the Galerie Colbert was never a commercial success, and was always the losing party in its fierce battle with the Galerie Vivienne. With the original polychromy now reproduced in its entirety thanks to paint samples discovered during demolition, today's Galerie Colbert lustres in rather hollow splendour, as the absence of shops – the Galerie now houses the recently created Institut National d'Histoire de l'Art – renders its spaces lifeless and somewhat sad.

Even more sad is the **Passage Vendôme** (Jean-Baptiste Labadye, 1827) which, built on the site of the demolished Couvent des Filles-du-Sauveur near the then theatre district, provided a very handy link between the *grands boulevards* and the nearby Marché du Temple. Despite this highly propitious location, the arcade was never a commercial success, and today, although colonized by several seemingly established businesses, is in a very sorry state indeed. Its older, western section features arcaded loggias and, unusually in a Parisian *passage*, dressed-stone upper storeys, while the western section, rebuilt by E. Soty in 1869 after the creation of the Place de la République, is coiffed by a very elegant iron-and-glass roof of the Galerie-d'Orléans type (see below). Until recently in an equally sorry condition was the **Passage Brady** (1827/28), whose developer originally planned it to be Paris's longest arcade, with 113 shops surmounted by apartments. Existing buildings in too good a state to be demolished prevented accomplishment of this dream, and the arcade was subsequently divided in two by the construction of the Boulevard de Strasbourg in 1854. The eastern section was never covered, and can still be seen in this state. As for the western, covered section, it suffered badly from years of neglect, losing almost all original decoration and falling into a state of semi-dereliction. It nonetheless remained lively due to its colonization by Paris's Asian community, and is currently being restored.

The **Passage du Bourg-l'Abbé** (Auguste Lusson, 1828) has been allowed to fall into an even worse state than the Passage Brady. Built to continue the path of the Passage du Grand-Cerf (see above) as far as the Rue Saint-Martin by linking up with the open-air Passage de l'Ancre, it lost its eastern section with the cutting through of the Boulevard Sébastopol in 1854. The current monumental entrance by Henri Blondel dates from this time, and is adorned with caryatids representing Commerce and Industry. The arcade has a rather charming barrel-vaulted roof in iron and glass, which prefigured that of what was perhaps the greatest Parisian *passage couvert*, the Galerie d'Orléans. Begun the same year as the Passage du Bourg-l'Abbé and completed in 1830, the Galerie was commissioned by the Duc d'Orléans (later King Louis Philippe), the then owner of the Palais-Royal, to replace the crumbling and by this time rather sordid Galeries de Bois. The duke's chosen architects were the prestigious duo of Pierre-François-Léonard Fontaine and Charles Percier, and their arcade, at 70 m long, 8.5 m wide and 9 m high, was one of the biggest ever built in Paris. Their design consisted of a pair of handsome Doric arcaded loggias, containing shop units, united by a bravura iron-and-glass roof in the form of a pointed barrel vault, which featured a raised central ridge to allow ventilation. As well as the roof, extensive use was made of iron, from the staircases and floor supports to accessory items such as candelabra, balustrades and even flower pots. The Galerie was universally admired, and prompted the comment from the novelist duo Erckmann-Chatrian that »when one has not seen this gallery, one knows neither the riches nor the magnificence of the earth«. The Galerie d'Orléans became famous Europe-wide, and directly inspired Brussels' Galerie Saint-Hubert and Milan's Galleria Victor Emmanuele II, as well as subsequent Parisian realizations. It nonetheless suffered from the general decline of the Parisian arcade, and was demolished in 1933–35 in a bid to »aerate« the Palais-Royal. The parallel colonnades that marked its limits still stand.

The second big wave of arcade building began in 1839, and one of the first of these was the modest **Passage Puteaux**, opened that same year. Not far away is the **Galerie de la Madeleine** (Théodore Charpentier, 1845), decorated in solid bourgeois fashion as befits a development in this exclusive neighbourhood. The **Passage du Havre** (1845/46) was more workaday than the Madeleine but commercially more successful due to the proximity of the Gare Saint-Lazare (8.5) and the shops of the Boulevard Haussmann. As part of the Eole railway development (see feature on the Métro and the RER), the original arcade was recently demolished and rebuilt afresh by Michel Macary (see below). At the same time as the Passage du Havre, two of Paris's most celebrated arcades, the **Passage Jouffroy** (Hippolyte Destailleur and Romain de Bourge) and the **Passage Verdeau** (Jacques Deschamps), were going up on the *grands boulevards*. Conceived as one, combined speculative operation, they were begun in 1845 and opened in 1847. The Passage Jouffroy continues the path of the Passage des Panoramas on the other side of the Boulevard Montmartre, and in its turn is prolonged by the Passage Verdeau as far as the Rue du Faubourg-Montmartre. In its design, the Passage Jouffroy's principle, boulevard section owes much to the Galerie d'Orléans, although it takes the Galerie's use of iron one step further. Jouffroy's floor and roof (of which the latter is a direct copy on a smaller scale of the Galerie d'Orléans's) are linked in an all-metal structure, while its iron shop fronts are entirely glazed across two storeys in the manner of those at the Passage du Grand-Cerf. If one enters the Passage Jouffroy after crossing the boulevard from the Passage des Panoramas, one is immediately struck by the more generous dimensions of the newer arcade, by its very handsome glass roof, which provides more light and ventilation than the older arcade's, and by its immaculate tiled floor, which concealed a hypocaust heating system, the first in any Parisian arcade. The Passage Verdeau is built on essentially the same principle as the Passage Jouffroy, although it has always been commercially the less successful of the two due to its separation from the *grands boulevards*.

The last of the arcades of the golden age was the **Passage des Princes** (1859/60) which, in the interests of space rationalization was recently dismantled and rebuilt (1995). Its original boulevard entrance has gone, replaced by a modern building; the coloured-glass dome that prefigures the arcade on this side dates from the 1930s and was incorporated into it from a hotel that formerly stood on the site. Only one storey high under the elaborate ironwork of its glass roof, today's Passage des Princes gives a good idea of how the majority of Parisian arcades must have looked when new, since its meticulous restoration included complete reproduction of the original polychromy. It is now home to the Village des Jouets, a collection of toyshops.

Decline of the arcade
The reasons for the sudden decline of Paris's arcades are elusive, but it is certain that together Haussmannization and the department store contributed to their downfall. From the 1850s onwards very few arcades were built in Paris and, by the 1900s, those that remained seemed to have entered a terminal twilight from which they would never recover. Haussmann's boulevards had brought air, daylight, wide pavements and street-lighting into the heart of the old city, breaking the monopoly the arcades had previously held on these amenities, and rendering them seemingly narrow and dingy by comparison. In a capital that now benefited from rapid circulation of both vehicles and pedestrians, the arcades had become somehow irrelevant, superfluous in the absence of the dense city that had spawned them. Moreover, as we have seen, many suffered physically at the hands of the Haussmannization process, undergoing either total or partial demolition to make way for the baron's new streets. During the same period, the department store began to appear (see, e.g., the Bon Marché, 7.15), posing a direct threat to the arcades' competitiveness by reproducing on a bigger scale their winning formula of a multitude of goods and services available under one roof. The department stores had the upper hand in that they were able to offer commercial advantages to the consumer (right of return on goods, free delivery, etc.) as

well as an enormous range of products that the arcades' little boutiques could not possibly match. Moreover, these giant new stores appropriated the model of top-lit spaces that the arcades had introduced, but endowed it with considerably more grandeur, monumentality and luxury than could be found in even the most ostentatious of Paris's *passages*. Having been at the forefront of avant-garde urbanism, the arcades were now relegated to the sad ranks of yesterday's outmoded relics. The moral climate had also changed, and the rather louche pleasures that had contributed to the arcades' success had been driven elsewhere. The department store, in contrast, aimed to please a respectable and mostly feminine clientele.

Although by the end of the 19C the Parisian arcade as a vital urban form had been relegated to the pages of history, a few developments in the spirit of the *passage couvert* were built in the French capital in the early years of the 20C. The **Cité Argentine** (Henri Sauvage with Charles Sarazin, 1903–07, a mixed-use development of apartments, shops and offices, incorporates at its heart a substantial glazed arcade lined with retail space on the ground floor and office space at first-floor level. Although a *cul-de-sac*, and therefore not a *passage* in the strict sense, Sauvage's arcade owes a clear debt to its 19C forbears. Certain 19C arcades, none of which survives today, were created by glazing over existing pedestrian passages, and this is exactly what was done around 1925 at the **Passage du Prado**. Its iron-and-glass roof is cadenced by rather curious Art-Déco arcs in wood and plaster and it features an octagonal rotunda in the manner of the Galeries Vivienne and Colbert. Briefly popular in the 1930s, the arcade is not in the best of shape today. As Paris's centre of gravity displaced itself ever further westwards, the Champs-Elysées and their hinterland became a thriving commercial area, and several arcade-type developments were built there in the interwar years. The most lavish was the **Arcades des Champs-Elysées** (also known as the Arcades du Lido; C. Lefebvre, M. Julien and L. Duhayon, 1924–26) whose developer freely acknowledged his debt to the 19C *passage couvert* but was nonetheless careful to avoid calling his prodigy a *passage* or a *galerie* so as not to invite association with its disgraced forbears. Laid out as a series of rectangular glazed halls, the arcade is lavishly decorated in a grandiose, Edwardian manner, although its splendid glass lamps by Lalique are pure Art Déco.

More recently it is of course the shopping centre or mall that has appropriated the model of a covered, comfortable commercial environment pioneered by the arcades (one can perhaps detect a move towards this type of development in the wide, generous spaces of the Arcades des Champs-Elysées). Notable Parisian examples include the Forum des Halles (1.22), the Carrousel du Louvre (see 1.8) and, just outside Paris proper, the Centre Commercial Bercy 2 (33.1). The 1990s saw the realization of two Parisian developments that are very close to the concept of the 19C covered arcade: Michel Macary's rebuilding of the **Passage du Havre** (1996/97) and Ricardo Bofill's office building for Banque Paribas in the Place du Marché Saint-Honoré (1.14). The former, now on several levels, is slick but not very distinguished and lacks the charm of its forebears. It nonetheless continues to benefit from the proximity of the Gare Saint-Lazare and the Boulevard Haussmann. Bofill's building is architecturally and aesthetically more successful but, its retail spaces let to only a couple of chains, lacks the variety and animation of a traditional arcade. Both these examples nonetheless demonstrate that there is still life left in the covered arcade as an urban form, two centuries after it first appeared.

Still-extant arcades

Arcades des Champs-Elysées, 78, avenue des Champs-Elysées, 8th.
Cité Argentine, 111, avenue Victor-Hugo, 16th.
Galerie Colbert, 6, rue des Petits-Champs and 4, rue Vivienne, 2nd.
Galerie de la Madeleine, 9, place de la Madeleine and 30, rue Boissy-d'Anglas, 8th.
Galerie Véro-Dodat, 19, rue Jean-Jacques-Rousseau and 2, rue du Bouloi, 1st.
Galerie Vivienne, 4, rue des Petits-Champs, 6, rue Vivienne and 5–7, rue de la Banque, 2nd.
Passage Brady, 43, rue du Faubourg-Saint-Martin and 46, rue du Faubourg-Saint-Denis, 10th.
Passage de Choiseul, 40, rue des Petits-Champs and 23, rue Saint-Augustin, 2nd.
Passage des Panoramas, 11, boulevard Montmartre and 10, rue Saint-Marc, 2nd.
Passage des Princes, 5, boulevard des Italiens and 97–99, rue de Richelieu, 2nd.
Passage du Bourg-l'Abbé, 120, rue Saint-Denis and 3, rue de Palestro, 2nd.
Passage du Caire, 2, place du Caire, 33, rue d'Alexandrie, 237–239, rue Saint-Denis and 14, rue du Caire, 2nd.
Passage du Grand-Cerf, 145, rue Saint-Denis and 10, rue Dussoubs, 2nd.
Passage du Havre, 109, rue Saint-Lazare and 69, rue Caumartin, 9th.
Passage du Ponceau, 119, boulevard de Sébastopol and 212, rue Saint-Denis, 2nd.
Passage du Prado, 16, boulevard Saint-Denis and 16, rue du Faubourg-Saint-Denis, 10th.
Passage Jouffroy, 10–12, boulevard Montmartre and 9, rue de la Grange-Batelière, 9th.
Passage Puteaux, 33, rue de l'Arcade and 28, rue Pasquier, 8th.
Passage Vendôme, 16, rue Béranger and 3, place de la République, 3rd.
Passage Verdeau, 6, rue de la Grange-Batelière and 31, rue du Faubourg-Montmartre, 9th.

Seine bridges

It is of course because of the River Seine that Paris came into existence, its waters being historically vital for defence, transport, commerce, industry and domestic needs. But crossing the river has also always been just as vital, and bridges have existed here from the earliest times. The first were those that connected the Parisii's settlement on the Ile de la Cité (4.1) to the mainland, later replaced with two Roman bridges linking the *cardo* on the Left Bank to the Ile de la Cité and then to the main road north on the Right Bank. They crossed where today's **Petit Pont** and **Pont Notre-Dame** stand, and were almost certainly wooden affairs. From the time of the Roman occupation until the late-16C, bridges came and went in Paris, but they never numbered more than five, each time connecting the Ile de la Cité to either bank. Since space was a precious commodity in the walled medieval city, they all supported constructions of one kind or another, generally shops and houses. Although none now survives, their memory lingers on in the names of their successors.

Today by the far the oldest structure crossing the Seine in Paris is the rather paradoxically named **Pont Neuf** (»New Bridge«), which links up the western tip of the Ile de la Cité with the Right and Left Banks. Commissioned in 1577 by Henri III, it was programmed to relieve the four other Parisian bridges then standing, which had reached saturation point and were the source of constant traffic jams. Designed collectively by a team of experts that included Baptiste Androuet Du Cerceau, Pierre des Illes and Thibault Métezeau, the Pont Neuf was begun in 1578 but was not completed until 1607, under Henri IV, due to a ten-year interruption in work occasioned by the Wars of Religion. Technically it was conservative, with none of the daring of contemporaneous Italian bridges, its massive, heavily buttressed piers supporting no less than twelve arches, the widest of which spanned 19.4 m. Greater spans could be achieved using arches with a flattened profile, but the Pont Neuf's retained the traditional semicircular form. The bridge's decoration also appeared archaic in comparison to Classicizing, Italian structures, with castle-like turrets sitting atop each pier, although its splendid collection of bearded mascarons, all of which are different, reflected the Mannerism of the day. Where the Pont Neuf was highly innovative, however, was in its lack of houses, an absence ordered by Henri IV who wanted to introduce the Classical idea of a riverscape, and show off the newly Classicized Louvre (1.8), to otherwise-medieval Paris. He also made the bridge part of a global urban-redevelopment scheme that included the creation of the Rue and Place Dauphine (1.3). A public piazza was built at the bridge's centre, on the Ile de la Cité, where an equestrian statue of Henri IV was erected, the first example in France of this kind of monumental *mise en scène* of a royal effigy (the current statue is 19C, the original having been destroyed at the Revolution). The Pont Neuf as we see it today is of course the product of four centuries of maintenance and renovation, which included the straightening out of its original humpback in the 19C.

The 17C added three new bridges to Paris's collection with the development of the Ile Saint-Louis (4th), whose pastures began to be urbanized under Louis XIII. One of the initial developers was Christophe Marie, who left his name to the only one of the island's original bridge structures to survive today. The **Pont Marie** was begun in 1614 by the developer himself, but work only really got going as of 1623 when the master mason Rémy Collin took over. Completed in 1630, the bridge was not especially technically advanced, with round arches and heavily buttressed piers. At the time bridge building was far from an exact science, but observation seemed to show that the ratio of pier thickness to arch width should be in the order of 1:5. This did not always ensure stability, however, and the Pont Marie lost its two island-side arches in the Seine's annual floods of 1658. The disaster was especially tragic given that the bridge originally carried houses, 20 of which were swept away. The missing arches were rebuilt with a more modern, flattened profile and without their dwellings, which gave the bridge a rather odd, lopsided allure. This was corrected in the 18C with the demolition of all the remaining houses (see below). Like the Pont Neuf, the Pont Marie had its original, rather pronounced humpback straightened out in the 19C.

One other 17C bridge survives in Paris, the **Pont Royal**, which was built by order of Louis XIV in 1685 to 1689 to link the Left Bank to the Tuileries (see 1.10) and facilitate the aristocratic traffic that plied back and forth between the Faubourg Saint-Germain and Versailles (32.1). Designed by Jules Hardouin-Mansart and constructed by Jacques IV Gabriel, it was technically similar to the Pont Marie but with more modern, slightly flattened arches spanning much greater distances (25 m for the Pont Royal's central arch, compared to 16 m at the Pont Marie) in perfect, elegant symmetry. The king forbade the building of any houses on the bridge, and it was given pavements like the Pont Neuf. Construction was complicated by the difficulty of find-

Pont Neuf

ing a solid riverbed footing on the Tuileries side, a problem solved by sinking a rubble-filled boat at the spot where the bridge's first pier was to be constructed! The Pont Royal is striking in its extreme sobriety and in its elegant lines, which include a flaring out of its roadway at either end (to make it easier for carriages to turn into the bridge) and parapet mouldings that continue round onto the quayside walls. Again, like the Pont Neuf and the Pont Marie, the Pont Royal had its pronounced humpback straightened out in the 19C, which reduced its vault thickness by a third. Before the construction of the Pont du Carrousel and the Pont des Arts (see below), the Pont Royal and the Pont Neuf together defined a river basin running alongside the Louvre that was used for royal water pageants, mock Antique naval battles and other spectacles.

Prior to the 18C it was essentially architects who were responsible for building bridges; Palladio, for example, devoted considerable space to them in his *Four Books of Architecture* (1570). In France the situation began to change with the creation of the Corps des Ingénieurs des Ponts et Chaussées (Corps of Engineers of Bridges and Roadways) in 1716, which produced a schism between architects and engineers that would make itself fully felt in the following century. It was henceforth engineers who designed France's bridges, architects' involvement, if any, generally being limited to aesthetics. Indeed we see this shift in the one 18C Parisian bridge still standing today, the **Pont de la Concorde** (1786–91), which was built by the engineer Jean-Rodolphe Perronet, first director of the Ecole des Ponts et Chaussées (founded in 1747). The research and specialization encouraged by the Ponts et Chaussées brought a new scientific rigour to the art of bridge building, and Perronet was one of the leaders in the field. His Pont de la Concorde marked the apogee of masonry bridge construction, demonstrating an economy of materials that would not be bettered. Constructed by order of Louis XVI to connect the Faubourg Saint-Germain to the Faubourg Saint-Honoré and complete the Place de la Concorde (8.1), the bridge was extremely lean, with piers only 3 m wide and a central arch span

Pont Alexandre-III

ning 31 m. Prior to Perronet, bridges in France had generally been built with massive piers capable of bearing alone all the lateral thrust of an arch, both for reasons of safety – if one arch collapsed the pier would not topple under the thrust of the next – and because the time period over which bridges were built was often very long, piers having to support only one arch for years before the next one along was constructed. Perronet's bridges, however, were built all in one go with arches that counterbalanced each other, as at the Pont de la Concorde. Given its setting, this work of urban infrastructure was »architecturalized« by turning its pier buttresses into chunky Doric columns, whose incorrect proportioning suggests that they descend much further below water level than is actually the case. By an irony of history, the bridge, which was initially baptized »Pont Louis-XVI«, was completed with stones from the recently demolished Bastille. The Pont de la Concorde we see today is more than twice as wide as when first built, its enlargement having been carried out in 1929 to 1931 using traditional masonry techniques and reusing the original façades.

As well as the inexorable rise of the engineer, the Enlightenment era also saw a radical change in attitude towards inhabited bridges. The combined interests of aesthetics, safety and hygiene saw to it that all the buildings standing on Paris's bridges were demolished in the late-18C to early-19C. Aesthetics found these picturesque vestiges of the medieval city contrary to the Classical ideal of sweeping riverscape perspectives, safety disapproved of houses on bridges because they were very accident prone and often collapsed as a result of fire, floods or the shock of an impact, and hygiene called for their removal to allow breezes to blow unhindered up and down the river and thus aerate the stinking city. Paris's bridge inhabitations did not go without a fight, however, since they constituted mini neighbourhoods whose residents were extremely reluctant to move elsewhere. Their demolition profoundly altered the topography of the city.

Viaduc d'Austerlitz

Out of the Enlightenment era came the industrial revolution, which, with its technological advances and population explosion, was of course a great time of bridge building. Over the course of the 19C, Paris saw nearly all of its historic bridges rebuilt and more than 15 new ones constructed. Today the vast majority of its river crossings date from this period, enjoying a longevity that was denied most of their forbears. One of the reasons that many of Paris's pre-19C bridges had had such limited life spans was their massiveness: the combination of thick piers and relatively narrow openings prevented the river's current from flowing normally and caused it to accelerate as it passed through their arches, thereby greatly increasing its erosive capacities. These wide piers and narrow openings also got in the way of water traffic and upped the chances of the bridges being hit by river craft, which could further weaken them. The replacement of Paris's historic bridges in the 19C was carried out either for reasons of safety – the structure was threatening to collapse or made navigation of the river dangerous – or because the bridge in question could not cope with the road-traffic volume it was expected to carry. Many of the new bridge structures were in iron, a material that allowed very wide spans to be built and therefore got round the problems inherent in traditional bridge construction.

Metal bridges had been pioneered in late-18C Britain, whose precocious Iron Bridge at Coalbrookdale (1787) set the standard for what was to follow. Because iron was scarcer in France than in England, metal construction in Gallic climes did not take off until the advent of Napoleon. Paris's very first iron bridge was the **Pont des Arts** (1801–04), which was commissioned to provide a pedestrian crossing between the Louvre and the Institut de France (6.2). Initially planned in stone, it was afterwards programmed in iron, no doubt partly because imperial pride wanted to show that France was capable of matching English expertise. Designed by Louis-Alexandre de Cessart and Jacques Lacroix-Dillon, the Pont des Arts was in fact technically backward in comparison to British bridges of the period, reproducing a wooden structure in cast iron and using stone supports. Although it actually had more piers than its Parisian forbears (eight, where the Pont de la Concorde had four), its lightweight structure did dramatically reduce their bulk and was much less visually obstructive than a massive stone bridge. This abundance of piers was to prove the Pont des Arts' undoing, for they got in the way of river traffic and prompted its demolition, despite listed-building status, in 1981. The original bridge was replaced by a facsimile in steel, identical except for having one arch fewer, in 1982–84.

Metallic bridge construction really took off in Paris with the vogue for suspension bridges that swept the city in the period 1830–50. Realized in cast iron, which proved to be an inherently unsuitable material for this kind of structure, they were all replaced before the 19C wore out. It was of course during the Second Empire, at the time of Baron Haussmann's *grands travaux*, that the greatest number of new Parisian bridge structures was built: 15 in all, of which ten were in stone and five in iron. It was partly aesthetic conservatism, especially where the historic city centre was concerned, and partly the cheaper cost of stone structures (iron was still an innovative and expensive material in mid-19C France) that ensured the continuing construction of masonry bridges. Representative examples of Second-Empire stone bridges include the **Ponts Saint-Michel** (Vaudrey and Lagalisserie, 1857) and **au Change** (Vaudrey and Lagalisserie, 1858/59): conceived as a matching pair to link the Place du Châtelet (1.4) to the Boulevard Saint-Michel and thereby complete Haussmann's Grande Croisée (north–south and east–west traffic crossing), they display lean and elegant Perronet-type structures, soberly finished with Classical detailing and Napoleon III's monogram. Of the Haussmann era's iron bridges, two stand out: the **Pont d'Arcole** (Alphonse Oudry, 1854/55) and the **Pont Sully** (Vaudrey and Brosselin, 1874–76), the latter being planned and designed under the baron's supervision but not actually realized until after the Second Empire's fall. The Pont d'Arcole was originally to have been built by the Corps des Ponts et Chaussées in stone, but a rival scheme in iron was submitted by the company Cadiat. Despite the fact that the iron bridge cost 300,000 francs more than the stone one, the Ministre des Travaux Publics chose the metallic option because it allowed the river to be crossed in one go without any intermediary piers getting in the way of water traffic. He was also conscious that Oudry's daringly low-slung 80 m span would constitute a Parisian record. Realized in wrought rather than cast iron, the Pont d'Arcole originally comprised a series of twelve parallel arcs that were kept under tension via a system of tie rods anchored in the quayside piers. In 1888 some of these rods snapped and the bridge partially collapsed; it was rebuilt along more traditional lines with 14, self-supporting arcs. In contrast, the Pont Sully was much less daring, its cast-iron arches spanning a maximum of only 49.5 m and being supported on stone piers implanted in the riverbed. The bridge has the particularity of crossing the Seine on a diagonal so as to link up with the Boulevard Saint-Germain; Napoleon III disapproved so strongly of this affront to Cartesian rectilinearity that the Pont Sully's construction was delayed until after his downfall.

Paris's first steel river crossing came in 1893–96 with the **Pont Mirabeau**, built by the brilliant engineer Louis-Jean Résal and celebrated in poetry by Apollinaire. Although it has the appearance of a traditional arched structure, the bridge is actually formed from two sets of cantilevers, each half of the 96.5 m central span being counterbalanced by one of the lateral spans, which consequently exert very little pressure on the quayside. Giant bronze allegories of commerce, abundance, navigation and the Ville de Paris decorate its piers. The 1900 Exposition Universelle produced three new bridges: the **Pont Alexandre-III**, the **Pont Rouelle** and the **Passerelle Debilly**. Longest of Paris's crossings at

Passerelle Solférino

370 m, the Pont Rouelle (Moïse, Widmer and Bonnet, 1897–1900) provided a railway link to the Champ de Mars to facilitate visitors' arrival at the exhibition. Its mixed structure includes an impressive 85.7 m span achieved using two giant, parallel iron arches from which the carriageway is hung, the first Parisian example of such a bridge. In complete contrast to this piece of transport infrastructure was the exuberant Pont Alexandre-III (Résal and Amédée Alby with Joseph Cassien-Bernard and Gaston Cousin, 1896–1900), which as well as providing a river crossing was intended to constitute an architectonic work of art. Conceived in tandem with the Grand and Petit Palais (8.14 and 8.15) to form a monumental »exhibition way« worthy of the nearby Invalides (7.12), the bridge was also, paradoxically, expected to efface itself in the landscape, neither obscuring the view of the military hospice nor planting any piers in the riverbed. This presented a technical challenge in that the 107 m span would have to be as low-slung as possible, resulting in enormous thrusts on its quayside piers (825 tonnes/articulation). Résal designed a very elegant structure comprising 15 parallel, moulded-steel arcs composed of riveted voussoirs, which was then dressed up by Cassien-Bernard and Cousin with splendidly crashing neo-Baroque décor, realized by no less than 17 artists. In comparison, the Passerelle Debilly (Résal and Alby, 1899/1900), a footbridge with an arch-and-suspended-roadway structure of the Pont-Rouelle type, surprises in its complete lack of ornament, the criss-cross of its struts and the relief of its rivets supplying the only decoration.

At the turn of the 20C, construction of Paris's Métro (see feature on the Métro and the RER) necessitated the building of two new bridges and the adaptation of a third, already extant crossing. The new constructions were the **Pont de Bir-Hakeim** and the **Viaduc d'Austerlitz** (both by Louis Biette and Jean-Camille Formigé, 1903–05), while the **Pont de Bercy**, a stone bridge of 1863/64, had a masonry Métro viaduct constructed on top of it. The Pont de Bir-Hakeim was also built as a road bridge carrying a second-storey viaduct, but in steel with a cantilever structure of the Pont-Mirabeau type. Architect of the Ville de Paris, Formigé was brought in to make this »industrial« facility acceptable to the wealthy *quartiers* in which it stood, and it was he who was responsible for the fine detailing of its metallic elements and for the very *belle-époque* triumphal arch and terrace at the bridge's centre. It also sports some monumental cast-iron sculptures, which include a naked worker fixing the last rivet! The Viaduc d'Austerlitz, on the other hand, was in a less well-to-do area and carried Métro trains only, thus allowing it to be unashamedly and monumentally »industrial«. Because of the presence of other bridges very close by, it was decided that it should not have any riverbed piers, and it was consequently given a double-arc structure of the Pont-Rouelle/Passerelle-Debilly type. Its splendid, soaring, 140 m span holds the Parisian record, and is rendered all the more majestic by Formigé's decorative cast-iron trophies.

The eve of WWI produced a curious hybrid amongst Parisian bridges, the **Pont Notre-Dame**, whose central section was rebuilt in metal by Résal (1910–14), but whose original lateral arches in stone, parts of which dated back to 1500, were conserved. In the interwar period, reinforced concrete began to be used for bridge construction, and two Parisian crossings were rebuilt in the new material: the **Pont de la Tournelle** (Pierre and Louis Guidetti, 1924–28) and the **Pont du Carrousel** (Gaspard, Morane, Umbdenstock and Tourry, 1935–39). In the interests of respecting their historic context, however, both were clad in ashlar, and it is only in their extremely lean and elegant forms that the truth of their construction can be discerned. The Pont du Carrousel was even given a humpback, buttressed piers and keystones to match its masonry forbears, while the Pont de la Tournelle's 73 m span received Pont-Neuf-inspired turrets, a heavy machicolated cornice and a pylon-mounted, Art-Déco sculpture of St Geneviève decorating one of its piers, the work of Paul Landowski.

Despite the hegemony achieved by concrete construction in postwar France, steel continued to be used for bridge building, with monolithic welded structures making an appearance in the 1960s. Paris's examples are rather lacklustre, with only the **Pont de l'Alma**'s elegantly asymmetrical span (Coste, Blanc, Man Yick, Arsac and Dougnac, 1970–74) coming anywhere near the chic one would expect of the French capital. An effort was made to reverse this tendency with the two most recent additions to Paris's bridge collection, both of which date from the 1990s. The perfect horizontality of the **Pont Charles-de-Gaulle** (Louis Arretche and Roman Karasinski, 1993–96), with its immaculate white aeroplane-wing profiling, was intended to demonstrate both elegance and environmental discretion. Much criticized at the outset because of its enormous cost and the fact that it led nowhere, the bridge was rescued by the ZAC Paris-Rive-Gauche (13.2), which drove its grandiloquent Avenue de France up to its southern extremity. In quite another register was the **Passerelle Solférino** (Marc Mimram, 1992 to 1999), a footbridge built to link the Tuileries, and by extension the Louvre, to the Musée d'Orsay (7.1), thereby connecting Paris's two biggest museums in a riverway tourist trail. Its design was complicated by the requirements that the bridge cross the Seine in a single, 106 m-long span, access both embankment and quayside, and respect the »sensitive« nature of its prestigious site. Mimram rose brilliantly to the challenge, producing an extremely lean, elegant and minimalist structure whose principal arcs not only support a horizontal, upper walkway but also a lower one following their curve, which thereby gives onto the quaysides. Modern steel-cutting techniques allowed an extremely lightweight, springy structure, which, like London's Millennium Bridge, was found by some to be a little too bouncy. Although accusations of instability proved to be entirely unfounded, the Passerelle Solférino's opening was delayed by a year while expensive shock absorbers were installed.

The first Parisian bridge of the third millennium will also be for pedestrians, connecting the Bibliothèque Nationale de France (13.3) to the Parc de Bercy (12.8). A 1999 competition produced an audacious design by the Austrian architect Dietmar Feichtinger, which sets out to challenge the Viaduc d'Austerlitz's record: a 190 m span formed from two arcs, one orientated convexly and the other concavely, that access both embankment and quayside and define a central, airborne oval where boutiques can be installed. Construction has been continually delayed, the current completion date for the Passerelle Bercy-Tolbiac being given as 2006.

Location of bridges mentioned:
Passerelle Debilly, connects the Quai de New-York, 8th, to the Quai Branly, 7th.
Passerelle Solférino, connects the Quai des Tuileries, 1st, to the Quai Anatole-France, 7th.
Petit Pont, connects the Rue Saint-Jacques, 5th, to the Rue de la Cité, 4th.
Pont Alexandre-III, connects the Esplanade des Invalides, 7th, to the Cours la Reine, 8th.
Pont de Bercy, links the Boulevard Vincent-Auriol, 13th, to the Boulevard de Bercy, 12th.
Pont de Bir-Hakeim, links the Boulevard de Grenelle, 15th, to the Rue de l'Alboni, 16th.
Pont de la Concorde, links the Place de la Concorde, 8th, to the Quai Anatole-France, 7th.
Pont de la Tournelle, links the Rue des Deux-Ponts, 4th, to the Quai de la Tournelle, 5th.
Pont de l'Alma, connects the Place de l'Alma, 8th, with the Place de la Résistance, 7th.
Pont des Arts, links the Quai du Louvre, 1st, to the Quai Malaquais, 6th.
Pont du Carrousel, connects the Quais du Louvre and des Tuileries, 1st, to the Quais Voltaire and Malaquais, 6th.
Pont Marie, links the Place du Bataillon-Français-de-l'ONU-en-Corée, 4th, to the Rue des Deux-Ponts, 4th.
Pont Mirabeau, connects the Quai André-Citroën, 15th, to the Quai Louis-Blériot, 16th.
Pont Neuf, connects the Place de l'Ecole, 1st, with the Ile de la Cité, 1st, and the Rue Dauphine, 6th.
Pont Notre-Dame, connects the Rue de la Cité, 4th, to the Quai de Gesvres, 4th.
Pont Royal, runs between the Quai des Tuileries, 1st, and the Rue du Bac, 7th.
Pont Rouelle, railway (RER) bridge connecting the Quai de Grenelle, 15th, to the Avenue-du-Président-Kennedy station, 16th.
Pont Saint-Michel, connects the Boulevard du Palais, 1st/4th, to the Boulevard Saint-Michel, 5th/6th.
Pont Sully, connects the Boulevard Henri-IV, 4th, to the Ile Saint-Louis, 4th, and the Boulevard Saint-Germain, 5th.
Viaduc d'Austerlitz, connects the Gare d'Austerlitz, 13th, to the Right Bank, 12th.

Parisian housing, 1400–1900

No guide to Paris could consider itself complete without discussing the »everyday« buildings that go to make up the city's housing stock. Outside of mansions, palaces and monuments, it is the anonymous mass of ordinary people's dwellings that defines the spirit of a place at any given time. While little remains of the jumble of houses that characterized medieval Paris, other centuries are better represented: tall, narrow, 17C *maisons bourgeoises*, the first, purpose-built apartment buildings of the 18C and, of course, the mighty mansion blocks and *immeubles* of the 19C. Covering all this ground with the seriousness it deserves would be hard even in an extended volume, let alone within the scope of this guide, but we shall attempt a brief survey. Our flight through the centuries will stop at just after 1900, because not only is 20C housing well represented in this guide in individual entries, but the period's ever-increasing internationalism meant that its housing was far less place-specific than that of previous eras.

Medieval Paris, 1400–1600
Although one would never suspect it now, seeing the stone, plaster, concrete and glass metropolis that is modern-day Paris, the city was, until well into the 17C, largely constructed of wood. Given the abundant forests of the Ile-de-France, which covered much

No. 3, rue Volta, 3rd

vaster stretches than today, this was hardly surprising, since wood was by far the cheapest and most readily available material. To envisage Paris as it would have appeared to, say, François I in the early-16C, we should imagine a half-timbered city filled with countless tall, narrow, gabled and jettied houses lining dark, constricted streets. By far the majority were only one room wide, rising up to six storeys (although four was the norm) and enclosing courtyards and outbuildings at the centre of the city block. Cellars and ground floors were in stone, the half timbering was filled with a mixture of small stones and plaster, and roofs were either covered with wooden planks, thatch or tiles. A typical house might have featured a shop on the ground floor, the owner's apartments on the first and second, and perhaps rented accommodation on the upper floors. Often, a narrow staircase tower at the rear of the building assured vertical access.

Unsurprisingly, given the constant renewal Paris has undergone and the less robust nature of wooden structures compared to masonry ones, nothing of consequence now remains of the half-timbered medieval city. There are, however, three surviving houses that provide an evocative idea of what the French capital may have looked like before 1700. All three expose to the public gaze the medieval half-timbering techniques with which they were constructed, and while two of them perhaps date back as far as the 14C the third is almost certainly 17C, demonstrating the tenacious persistence of this type of wooden construction. Often referred to as the »oldest houses in Paris«, nos. 11 and 13, rue François-Miron, 4th, are possibly late-14C, but they have been so often restored and reconfigured that it is impossible to know what is authentically medieval and what is later. The houses do not display the jetties that were common at the time, although it has been suggested that these may subsequently have been removed. On the other hand, their frames are of a type that ceased be used as of the mid-15C, featuring long upright members rising several storeys: by the 1450s there was a shortage of big enough trees in the Paris region to provide supports of this size, which, in tandem with the difficulties of erecting such massive members in narrow, confined streets, prompted the adoption thereafter of frames constructed from single-storey members. Other structures of a similar type survive elsewhere in Paris but hidden behind a coat of plaster: 41, rue Quincampoix, 4th, or 13, rue Vieille-du-Temple, 4th, for example. It now seems certain that another building often credited with the title »oldest house in Paris«, no. 3, rue Volta, 3rd, is in fact mid-17C. It displays a masonry ground floor and half-timbered upper floors constructed using single-storey-high members in the manner that became usual after 1450. Louis XIV's 1667 edict stipulating that all wooden structures must be rendered should have caused the building's frame to disappear from view, but either the regulations were successfully defied or the plaster was removed at a later date (as in the Rue François-Miron).

Pre-17C Paris was not only a wooden affair, however, and, besides the grand stone residences of the senior clergy and the aristocracy, some more modest, merchant-class houses were also built in ashlar. It is to an ashlar structure that the title of »oldest house in Paris« can probably be definitely attributed: the Maison de Nicolas Flamel (51, rue de Montmorency, 3rd), which dates from 1407. A rich alchemist, Flamel built the house as a refuge for the homeless, which explains the Gothic-lettered inscription running across its façade. Only the ground, first and second floors conserve anything of their 15C aspect, the upper storeys having been added at a later date to replace the enormous gable end that originally terminated the street elevation and earned the building the nickname »Maison du Grand Pignon«. The ground floor's sculpted décor was unusual for the time, and is thought to have been the work of a tombstone carver at the nearby church of Saint-Nicolas-des-Champs (3.9).

The »grand siècle«, 1600–1715
Two principal developments left their mark on Parisian housing during the 17C: the capital's increasing size and wealth, which produced an improvement in the solidity of construction of its housing stock, and the emergence of the notion of aesthetics in urbanism, which expressed itself through construction regulations and through a change in sensibility towards the treatment of façades. This process had begun in the 16C, but, slow to find acceptance among the general population, did not bear fruit until the early-17C. During the early-Renaissance period, François I, Henri II and Charles IX had issued edicts banning jettied upper floors and other projections from Paris's houses, essentially on hygiene and safety grounds: jettied floors tended to cut out the light in narrow streets and engendered a greater physical proximity of houses that increased the potential for the spread of fire. But there was also an aesthetic element to the banning of projections, for in an age when regularity was beginning to be considered beautiful the interdiction of disorderly excrescences contributed to a less chaotic-looking cityscape. Enforcing the regulations was another matter, however, and it was not until Henri IV's reign that their effect began to make itself felt. A further example of this is provided by the question of exposed wood on building façades, which was banned twice before Louis XIV's 1667 edict, in 1560 and 1607. The fact that the Sun King had once again to reiterate this provision says much about the difficulties of imposing construction regulations. Like the interdiction of projections, the requirement that wooden houses be plastered could be construed in terms of safety – a coat of plaster protected fire- and rot-prone frames –, but also had a strong aesthetic effect of regularization and, as it were, »demedievalization«.

If attitudes towards façade aesthetics changed over the 16C and 17C, the system of plot division and the type of accommodation supplied by the market did not. In general houses remained narrow and deep with as few as one or two windows on the street and one or two rooms per floor, as in medieval times, façade widths rarely exceeding 9 m (four to five windows). The apartment building as we know had yet to be invented, and houses were either occupied by one single family or, when they were rented out to multiple occupants, were divided up vertically, each tenant taking on as many rooms as he saw fit spread across several floors. Rooms did not have fixed, purposely conceived functions, allowing great flexibility for the coming and going of tenants with different needs and greater or lesser budgets. Apart from the enclaves where the *hôtels particuliers* of the rich were concentrated, social division was much less neighbourhood dependent than now, instead being expressed vertically within each *maison*: the more stairs one had to climb, the cheaper the rent, and hence the lower social standing of the occupant.

Although greater wealth meant a significant increase in the number of houses built entirely in ashlar or in a mixture of ashlar dressings and plastered rubble stone, construction in wood continued for the more modest types of housing right up into the 19C. A typical house at the cheaper end of the scale featured thick, rubble-stone party walls (through which chimneys could be run without too much risk of fire) that supported lightweight, wooden-framed façades filled with a mixture of crushed stone and plaster, with external rendering. As well as its low cost, this system had the advantage of allowing easy insertion of windows and also the addition of extra storeys at a later date if necessary: many is the 17C house that was raised by several storeys over the course of the 18C and 19C. Houses built prior to the 1660s are recognizable by the pronounced bulge (known in French as the *fruit*) they exhibit at the junction between the ground floor/*entresol* and the remainder of the elevation, which slopes backwards up to eaves level. Structural stability was, it seems, the reason behind this, the bulge reducing the likelihood that the façade would collapse into the street. Increasing conformity to Classical regularity meant that this practice was abandoned in the second half of the 17C. The first half of the century saw a revolution in attic-construction techniques, firstly with the dropping of medieval-period street-orientated gable ends in favour of tranversally orientated roofs, thereby avoiding the damp and rot problems caused by party-wall gutters, rainwater instead being thrown off into the street and rear courtyard. Then, in the 1640s, came the generalization of the oh-so-French mansard roof, whose perimeter frame allowed both the roofing of deep plans in one go and the installation of a full extra storey of accommodation in the attic; thereafter, the mansard's broken profile would remain a staple of Parisian architecture right up until the 20C.

Where their façade articulation is concerned, houses of the 17C are recognizable by the presence of pronounced dormer windows in the attic, by the use of real or fake quoins to mark party-wall delimitations, by the horizontal division of elevations by string courses, by the presence of ground-floor arcades containing shops and an *entresol*, or by the use of wrought-iron window balustrades, which began to appear in the 1640s. The bigger houses generally possessed an arched *porte-cochère*, often sumptuously decorated, that allowed carriages to pass into the courtyard behind. As of the mid century, slate became the preferred roofing material for Paris's houses, even being stipulated by royal edict. Many are the streets in the central *arrondissements* that still conserve good examples of 17C and early-18C houses, for example the Rue de l'Arbre-Sec, 1st, the Rue Saint-Honoré, 1st, the Rue Saint-Denis, 1st, the Rue Quincampoix, 3rd and 4th, the Rue Saint-Paul, 4th, the Rue Saint-Louis-en-l'Ile, 4th, or the Rue Monsieur-le-Prince, 6th.

Decline of the ancien régime, 1716–89
The first half of the 18C did not produce any fundamental changes in the nature of Paris's housing stock, the medieval-proportioned *maison bourgeoise* persisting as the dominant type, albeit with some changes in dress from its 17C forbears. The early years of Louis XV's reign saw the building of some very handsome merchant-class houses, for example in the Rue de l'Arbre-Sec, 1st, or the Rue François-Miron, 4th. Realized entirely in ashlar, they often displayed Rococo decorative tendencies: *anse-de-panier* window arches, elaborate shell and curlicue motifs at the keys of soberly carved window frames, impressively detailed balcony brackets, and ever more intricate wrought-iron balustrades. As the century progressed, however, a move towards much greater asceticism, directed from *en haut* by personalities such as Mme de Pompadour and Gabriel (see 32.3 and 32.4), made itself felt in the city's housing stock. The neo-Classical tendencies of the Enlightenment period expressed themselves in a domestic architecture that became much more rectilinear and generally much simpler of aspect. Light, banded rustication was often the only detailing of note, such as is found in the houses surrounding the Place du Marché-Sainte-Catherine, 4th (*c.*1775–80), which were situated towards the lower end of the social scale. But even more *haut-bourgeois* buildings in ashlar frequently show a surprising simplicity, not to say severity, of aspect.

Meanwhile, a typological revolution was tentatively beginning with the appearance in the 1750s of the purpose-built apartment block in the modern sense. This phenomenon was a result of the development of the banking system in the first half of the 18C, and the tendency towards speculation that it produced; many of the biggest development schemes were instigated by cash-strapped aristocrats, for example the Duc de Chartres at the Palais-Royal (1.16) or the Comte de Provence at the Odéon (see 6.7). More modest examples of speculative development included Louis-François Trouard's apartment building at 9, rue du Fabourg-Poissonnière, 9th (1758), whose articulation owed much to the Italian urban palace, despite its Grecian dress, the even more imposing, palace-fronted blocks to be found in the Rue de Tournon, 6th (*c.*1770 to 1780), and Pierre Desmaisons's »flatiron« Immeuble Montholon (58, rue de Seine, 6th, 1771), which prefigured Restoration-period buildings.

At the twilight of the *ancien régime*, Louis XVI introduced construction legislation that would shape the character of Paris's built fabric for over a century to come. Almost certainly drawn up in reaction to what were perceived as speculative excesses (see 1.17), the building regulations of 1783 and 1784 were based on three categories of street width: those less than 7.8 m, those of between 7.8 m and 9.75 m, and those greater than 9.75 m. For the first category, four storeys rising to eaves at 11.7 m were permitted; for the second, five storeys rising to eaves at 14.62 m were allowed; while for the final category, which rarely concerned streets of more than 15 m in width, six storeys up to eaves at 17.54 m were authorized. Above eaves level, attic accommodation of no more than 4.87 m could be built, with a roof slope of 45°. These figures were based partly on the proportions of Classical façade division (for the tallest buildings, a two-storey base followed by three principal floors, an attic storey and a roof storey) and partly on theories of harmonic proportioning of building height to street width. The full effects of the 1784 regulations would not be felt until the 19C, however, political unrest ensuring that not enough construction was undertaken before then to demonstrate their uniformizing potential.

Revolutions and empires, 1790–1852
The Revolution and its aftermath produced two major and far-reaching changes in the character of Parisian housing: the immediate and irreversible decline of both the *maison bourgeoise* and the aristocratic *hôtel particulier* in their traditional forms, and the emergence in their stead of the purpose-built apartment building as the dominant dwelling type, a product of the rapid development of capitalism and the consequent expansion of the middle classes. Through the social, economic and property-market upheavals it instigated, the Revolution created the conditions for an unprecedented building boom in Paris, although the political instability of the post-Revolutionary and Napoleonic eras delayed this process until the 1820s. Two major booms then followed, firstly in the period 1823–28, and again, after a crash and slump, in 1839–47. The feverish speculation of which they were a part produced several entirely new housing developments, of which the two most famous, the Quartier de l'Europe and the Nouvelle Athènes, were situated on the northern outskirts of the city beyond the fashionable *grands boulevards*. Continuing the process hesitantly begun in the 18C, they broke with the traditional building practices of the *ancien régime* through the nature of their instigators – speculators rather than individuals constructing houses for their personal use –, by the model of apartment buildings that they promoted, and through the new form of urbanity they adopted, which featured a mesh of narrow

Haussmann-era apartment building, Boulevard Saint-Germain, 6th

secondary streets divided up by a network of major thoroughfares linked by traffic hubs. This urbanistic approach would of course be extended across the remainder of Paris under Haussmann, a process in fact begun by his predecessor, Rambuteau, whose 13 m-wide Rue de Rambuteau caused a sensation when it was cut through in 1838–40, and whose 30 m-wide Boulevard de Strasbourg (1852–54) was modelled on the 17C *grands boulevards*.

The apartment buildings that lined these new streets or that replaced older houses elsewhere were characterized by the much greater width of the plots they occupied in comparison to pre-1789 housing, by their horizontal division and, as the century wore on, by the monumental and decorative treatment of their façades. Most displayed proportioning systems inherited from the Classical tradition, with a base containing ground-floor shops and possibly a first-floor *entresol*, then a tall *piano-nobile* storey – where the best apartments were situated because neither too near nor too far from the ground – followed by two to three storeys of diminishing height up to a cornice, above the cornice rose an attic storey set slightly back and often distinguished by a balcony, and finally came a low floor in the roof. In comparison to later decorative excesses, the apartment buildings of the Restoration period seem remarkably plain. They took their cue from the traditional stucco sobriety of the *maison bourgeoise* and from the neo-Classical rigour of Fontaine and Percier's Rue de Rivoli (1.11). Walking around parts of the 9th and 10th *arrondissements* today (the Rue Saint-Lazare, the Cité de Trévise, the Rue d'Hauteville) or the 6th (the Rue Bréa, the Rue Madame), we find flat, plaster-fronted façades animated only by repetitive fenestration, string courses and cornices. If it were not for the delicately ribbed shutters that became fashionable in the period, the effect would be monotonous in the extreme. These shutters highlight the dominance that windows had long played in the articulation and generation of façades in French architecture, a hegemony that here reflected both the structural techniques used to construct such apartment blocks – it is once again the massive, rubble-stone party walls that provide stability and allow the street elevation to be pierced so abundantly with fenestration – and the progress of industrialization, glass having become cheap enough that speculators could afford to supply plentiful glazing.

It was not only glass manufacture that was revolutionized by industrialization during this period, but every aspect of the building trade, including stone cutting and carving. Mechanization made these tasks easier and cheaper and the results more precise, and as a result stone became an affordable cladding material for the street fronts of middle-class apartment buildings. Taking their cue from the homes of the aristocracy, speculators began building blocks of flats with all-stone elevations, and as the century wore on carved decoration became an ever more important factor in the bid to attract tenants from the expanding middle classes. In comparison to the plain, plaster façades of the *ancien régime* and the Restoration, many Louis-Philippe-period buildings exhibit florid sculpted details, perhaps the most famous example being the Maison Dorée (1839, now part of the BNP-Paribas building at 16, boulevard des Italiens, 9th), which illustrates the era's penchant for repetitive façade articulation enlivened by intricate detailing. The arrival of sculpted wall surfaces heralded the end of exposed external shutters, which were replaced by folding models that disappeared into the window openings.

Inside, Restoration and Louis-Philippe-period apartment buildings abandoned the vertical fluidity of the *maison bourgeoise* for a strictly horizontal division, a standard apartment building of the time featuring two flats per floor, one on the street and the other on the courtyard behind. If the penchant for stone façades was borrowed from the homes of the aristocracy, so was the tendency to divide apartments up internally into *enfilades* of rooms. Where the aristocratic château or *hôtel particulier* had generally lined up its best rooms along the garden front, the early-19C apartment building lined its up along the street, lesser spaces such as kitchens or privies being relegated to the rear around lightwells. By this token, the second apartment on the courtyard side was of lesser standing than that on the street. The presence of communal courtyards shared by more than one apartment building marked the new tendency to conceive urban space in terms of the city block, rather than simply at the scale of the individual plot of land as had been the case with the *maison bourgeoise*; as the century progressed, so ever more monster buildings on ever wider plots of land appeared.

It was the late 1840s that saw the emergence of the basic model of apartment buildings that would dominate Parisian housing production for the next half century. Ashlar fronted, their façades were divided up into a repetitive grid of openings and blanks, the latter's compositional importance frequently being highlighted by the presence of carved, carpentry-like panels. For a more monumental effect on the grandest streets, colossal orders could be applied. Sculpted elements such as door and window surrounds, balcony brackets and keystones were often mass produced by mechanical stone-cutting saws. The traditional floor division was underlined by continuous balconies at *piano-nobile* and attic-floor level, that on the *piano nobile* highlighting the importance of this floor in the social hierarchy, and that at attic level serving to crown the principal cornice below it. The impact of these balconies, on an entire street of apartment buildings of however different decoration, was to produce strong, unifying, horizontals that brought to the cityscape a perspective effect of forceful cohesion. Rather than volumetric masses in the cityscape, such apartment buildings, with their flat, standardized façades, were conceived to be viewed purely as backdrops, decorative curtains lining the everyday theatre of life that was the street. There was also an economic aspect to this phenomenon: not generally owned by the families that occupied them (in contrast to suburban villas or country houses), apartments and the buildings containing them became a simple unit of monetary exchange, and consequently tended towards greater homogeneity in the manner of counters in a game of Monopoly. Bourgeois capitalism and industrialization found one of their most characteristic modes of expression in the mass-produced type-form that was the mid-19C Parisian apartment block.

Haussmannization and beyond, 1853–1900
By the time Baron Haussmann came on the scene, in 1853, the urbanistic basis of Second-Empire Paris had already crystallized, and it was left to the prefect and his cohorts to systematize it and undertake its dissemination across the entire city. The *immeuble haussmannien* and the urbanism it adorned were inventions of the Restoration and the July Monarchy; what Haussmann brought to these models was a scale of realization and a degree of standardization never before seen. One of the ways he achieved this was through the new building regulations of 1859, whose major innovation, conceived in response to the increasing number of very wide streets, was to elevate the eaves to 20 m above ground level on thoroughfares over 20 m in width, thereby bringing the norm to seven storeys on the new boulevards. However, much of the evident standardization we see in Haussmannian streets was not in fact a result of strictly codified regulations, since on reading the relevant texts we find that many Second-Empire norms – for example, the balconies at *piano-nobile* and fifth-floor level – are not even mentioned. Instead it was the municipality's corps of *architectes voyers* – roughly equivalent to today's planning inspectors – that imposed on developers the remarkable homogeneity that we find in ensembles such as the Avenue de l'Opéra (1st and 9th) or the Boulevard Voltaire (11th). Further, the fact that, because of the expropriation system, the municipality was the landowner where much of the new development was concerned allowed it to stipulate certain aesthetic aspects (construction in ashlar, placing of balconies, etc.) in the sales contracts. Moreover, it was quite common for the authorities to undertake construction of at least one building on a new street, usually on a prominent site such as a junction, so as to set the tone for what would follow.

Within the apartment building we also find a greater move towards standardization during the Second Empire, the fluid and adaptable *enfilade* plans of Louis Philippe's reign being superseded by strictly hierarchized apartment layouts in which the function of each room was determined in advance. A typical upper-middle-class flat of the 1860s featured reception rooms on the street, bedrooms on the quieter, courtyard side of the building grouped in a block away from the »public«

Post-1902 apartment building, Boulevard Henri-IV, 4th

parts of the apartment, and service zones entirely segregated from the principal living spaces. Multiple corridors and vestibules, rare in pre-Second-Empire flats, became standard features. Class distinctions also became more codified and standardized, and as the century wore on ever more effort was expended in rigidly segregating servants from their masters. Where servants had previously lodged with the family, their quarters were now moved up to the attics of big apartment blocks, and back stairs for maids and tradesmen became the norm. This *haut-bourgeois* standard served as the model for flats of lower standing, although economy inevitably meant compromise both where display and segregation of servants were concerned – ornamentation became less rich the further one went down the social scale, the importance given to representational spaces such as staircases and hallways diminished, and, in the cheapest apartments, servants and masters once again cohabited.

Perhaps surprisingly, given its essential animosity to the Second Empire it replaced, the Third Republic carried on Haussmann's work where he had left off, completing unfinished boulevard projects and continuing to impose the apartment-block and façade-articulation type-forms promoted during his tenure: the Avenue de l'Opéra, realized for the most part during the 1870s, is a striking example of this. Haussmann's model of urbanism was not without its critics, however, especially amongst architects, and as the century wore on more and more complaints were voiced regarding the boring, regimented monotony of the new Paris. It was not the fundament of Haussmannian urbanism that gave rise to dissension, however, for on this there seems to have been a general consensus, but rather its formal, plastic and aesthetic qualities. Many were those who called for less planarity, more volumetric latitude and more fantasy and variety in the articulation of Paris's apartment blocks. Changes began to make themselves felt even within the strict limits set by the regulations and the *architectes voyers*, for example in the tendency to add more and more balconies to street façades, thereby introducing greater variety (and also denying the traditional floor hierarchy, each storey now being of equal social standing) and, as of the 1880s, with the appearance of bay and oriel windows (referred to rather incorrectly in French as *bow-windows*), which introduced iron, glass, asymmetry and undulation into otherwise regimented stone façades.

Slowly but surely these trends were reflected by changes in the building regulations. In 1884, the rules concerning attics were modified: instead of the old 45° cut off, roof profiles could now follow a quarter circle above eaves level (which remained at its 1859 figures), effectively allowing for an extra attic floor and bringing buildings on the widest boulevards to a whopping eight storeys. As a result, their monumentality and insistence in the cityscape was increased, breaking with the rather cardboardy weightlessness of many Haussmann-era blocks. Then, in 1893, the rules were modified regarding the planarity of façades, essentially in response to the popularity of bay windows, which could now be built in »permanent« materials (i. e. stone) rather than just the iron and glass tolerated before (iron and glass bay windows, however much they projected, being viewed by the regulations as filling for a void rather than as part of the wall structure). Nine years later, in 1902, a new set of regulations broke entirely with certain fundaments of the Haussmannian city and allowed construction of buildings of a very different nature. Elaborated by the architect Louis Bonnier, the 1902 rules addressed both the desire for greater variety in façade and volumetric articulation and the consequences of an invention that Haussmann had not foreseen in 1859: the lift. Introduced in the second half of the 19C and generalized by the turn of the 20C, the lift overturned the traditional hierarchy of floors, making those at the top of an apartment building – where the best views, the most light and the least noise were to be had – more desirable than those below. The 1902 rules consequently allowed for greater height and variety in the upper parts of buildings: eaves were still maintained at their 1859 levels, but above them the attic storeys could rise in a steep arc that allowed the deepest blocks on the widest thoroughfares to reach 32 m, almost a full 10 m more than the maximum 22.41 m allowed by the 1784 limits. Where façade articulation was concerned, the 1902 regulations showed greater tolerance of projecting elements and allowed the introduction of breaches and set backs in the street line.

The results of these changes were immediate. Façades became much more fluid and undulating, the regulations allowing for the typically Parisian Art-Nouveau-inspired bulges of apartment blocks such as those in the Rue Huysmans (6th), or of the famous Hôtel Lutétia at 45, boulevard Raspail, 6th (Louis Boileau and Henri Tauzin, 1907–11). The receding centre of Auguste Perret's Rue-Franklin apartment building (16.8) would have been impossible before 1902. Above eaves level there soon mushroomed a whole fantasy city of terraces, elaborate dormers, loggias, turrets and *œils-de-bœuf*, highlighting the new-found desirability of Paris's upper floors and bringing yet further top-heavy monumentality to the streetscape. But the *architectes voyers*' attempts to introduce variety of materials into Paris failed – bar a couple of Art-Nouveau exceptions such as Guimard's Castel Béranger (16.11) and Jules Lavirotte's splendidly over-the-top ceramic-decorated apartment building at 29, avenue Rapp, 7th (1900) –, the French capital stubbornly remaining a city of stone and plaster in solid bourgeois tradition. And despite the architectural revolutions of the 20C, many was the middle-class Parisian apartment building that proudly displayed its direct descent from the Haussmannian model right up until the 1950s. Indeed it was only with the revision of the 1902 regulations in 1959 that the hegemony of 19C urbanism was first seriously challenged in Paris.

Street furniture

Although one does not always consciously notice them, the objects surrounding one in the street, be they lampposts, post boxes, telephone boxes, benches or advertizing stands, contribute enormously to the feel and character of a place. They can even, in the case of the most unusual or spectacular, become emblematic of the town or city they equip. Paris is particularly rich in iconic street furniture, much of it dating from the 19C and especially from the time of Haussmann's *grands travaux*. Even in entirely redeveloped, out-of-the-way neighbourhoods the old models are still used, and however recent or futuristic the surrounding architecture you know you are still in Paris because of the standardized tree grills, Wallace fountains, Second-Empire lampposts and so on.

But it was not always so. Prior to the 19C, Paris's only generalized municipal street furniture was lighting, with which the city was first properly equipped under Louis XIV. The Sun King wanted Paris to shine at night primarily for security reasons, and saw to it that 2,700 candle-filled iron lanterns were placed at the city's junctions. In the 18C the candles were replaced by oil lamps sporting reflectors, which were known as *réverbères*; 13,000 of them lined Paris's streets by the early-19C. It

Place de Furstemberg

was in precisely this period that the city's collection of street furniture began to expand and diversify, a result of technological developments that both changed the mode of urban living and made possible the production of new kinds of equipment. Gas lighting started to appear in Paris in the 1820s, an invention born of the industrial revolution but which also contributed to industrialism's continuing development by allowing the city to function 24 hours/day. 200 gas lamps lined Paris's streets by 1837, a number that only eight years later had exploded to 8,000.

Besides the technological advances of the early-19C, it also took a major innovation in the way public space in the city was organized to produce the abundance of street furniture we know today: the introduction of the pavement. Prior to the 19C Paris had almost no pavements, traffic, vendors' stalls and pedestrians all being mixed up in dangerous, dirty chaos in the city's narrow streets. Pavements became generalized in London long before Paris (e. g. the Westminster Paving Act of 1751), and unfavourable comparisons soon began to be made between the French capital and its British counterpart. It was Louis Philippe's Prefect of the Seine, Claude-Philibert Barthelot, Comte de Rambuteau, who, in tandem with his policy of street widening in Paris, first generalized pavements in the city. From only 267 m in 1820 the total length of Parisian pavement rose to 20 km in 1830 and by 1848 had reached 195 km. Mrs. Trollope, an Englishwoman visiting France in 1835, was moved to »bless the dear little pavement which ... borders most of the streets of Paris now«, and was certain that »in a few years ... it will be almost as easy to walk in Paris as in London«. Rambuteau also introduced new street furniture to equip his pavements, which included, amongst others, gas lamps, benches and urinals. Today the most notable survivors from his time are the lanterns designed especially for the Place de la Concorde (8.1) and the Avenue des Champs-Elysées by Jakob Ignaz Hittorff. Besides the elaborate rostral columns monumentalizing the corners of the *place*, Hittorff also produced a smaller-scale cast-iron lamppost that was repeated *ad infinitum* around the square and up and down the avenue. Gas-light lampposts were still very much a new-fangled invention at the time, and the form they took was open to innovation. Since Classicism was the era's dominant mode of expression where state and civic pride was concerned, Hittorff's design comprised a slender Composite colonnette stretched to a suitable length via a richly moulded pedestal and sporting an elaborately coiffed glass lantern at its summit. Unfortunately, the colonnette's tiny capital was made rather ridiculous by the enormous lantern wobbling on top of it, but this did not deter later attempts at adapting Classical columns to lamppost design.

It was of course Baron Haussmann who fulfilled Mrs. Trollope's prophesy through his enormous new avenues and broad boulevards, which introduced hundreds more kilometres of pavement into Second-Empire Paris. It was also under his aegis that the city received its first fully thought-through, extensive collection of street furniture. One of Napoleon III's ambitions in his remodelling of Paris as an imperial capital was to rival London's parks and gardens and bring nature into the heart of the dense city. To this end Haussmann created the Service Municipal des Promenades et Plantations (SMPP), whose remit also included the furnishing of Paris's streets. The SMPP's chief architect was a dedicated civil servant named Gabriel Davioud, and it was he who was responsible for the city's range of street furniture, either designing models himself or issuing directives when others undertook the work. By the time of the Empire's fall in 1870, Paris had equipped itself with an outstanding collection that became a reference in the field; as well as lanterns and lampposts, it included benches, newspaper kiosks, advertising columns, urinals, bandstands and railings. These objects soon came to be so much identified with the City of Light that they were considered an indispensable aspect of its character, and as a result many still furnish its streets today.

It is 19C lantern and lamppost designs that are most commonly found in the 21C city, the stock comprising not only originals but also countless reproductions installed over the past decade as part of a policy of glamming up the Haussmannian townscape. The most numerous and basic type is the Réverbère Oudry, named after its original manufacturer, which is instantly recognisable by its foliage-entwined post design, whose leafy theme brought the emperor's park-and-nature campaign into even the most mineral of neighbourhoods. A variety of lanterns can be found on top of Réverbères Oudry, a distinction having been made during the Second Empire between the *beaux quartiers*, where round lanterns coiffed with castles and cornices were used, and the poorer, peripheral *arrondissements*, where plainer, square lanterns were employed. A three-lantern unit mounted on elaborate brackets could also be placed on top of Oudry-type posts. Moving up in scale, we find the much taller, three / four-lamp models today used for public spaces such as the Place Vendôme (1.13) or the Avenue de l'Opéra (1st/9th). Like the Réverbères Oudry, their forms were clearly inspired by furniture, stair-banister and candlestick design. More lavish, five-branch candelabra can still be seen in the Place de Furstemberg (6th) or in the Place André-Malraux (1st), where the arms carry frosted globes rather than lanterns. At the Place de l'Opéra (9th), we find lampposts designed by Charles Garnier that match lighting-fixture designs within the Opéra (9.13) itself. Although electricity began to replace gas as of the 1860s, the new technology did not at first profoundly affect the form of Paris's street-level lampposts, and it was only in the mid-20C with the invention of powerful bulbs suitable for lighting roadways (as opposed to pavements) that the enormous pylons we know today began to appear. Around 150 different types of lamp currently light the streets of Paris.

Despite the great variety of lamppost designs, they all had two things in common: the arms of the Ville de Paris which were stamped on their bases and the dark-brown paint with which they were protected from the elements. Where the bulkier items of street furniture were concerned, Davioud saw to it that they were given an even stronger family resemblance. The various kiosks that dotted the streets and parks, the bandstands, the advertizing columns and some of the urinals were painted a uniform dark green and coiffed with vaguely orientalizing, »dragon-scale« polygonal domes. Mass-produced in cast iron, they wore lacy cornices and acanthus-leaf plumes and brought a fairytale touch into the otherwise serious city. Today the principal survivors are newspaper kiosks and the advertizing poles known as »Colonnes Morris«. The latter, which have become especially emblematic of Paris, were designed by the printing firm Morris in response to calls from the municipality for a solution to the problem of theatrical bills. Haussmann had provided 144 wall-mounted panels for bill posting, but managing them turned out to be impossible since competitors stuck ever larger posters on top of their rivals'. Bill posting on the Morris Columns, on the other hand, was controlled by the printing firm which charged a fee for the service, advertizers being attracted by the fact that Morris Columns could be given much more prominent positions in the cityscape than traditional billboards. Moreover – and this clinched the contract for Morris –, their interiors could be used to store the tools necessary for the cleaning and maintenance of Paris's streets. Today the Morris Columns have been eclipsed in the tourist imagination by the 50 or so drinking fountains offered to the city by Sir Richard Wallace in the 1870s. The most famous model was by the sculptor Charles Lebourg, which, designed to match Davioud's kiosk style, comprised a dolphin-decorated pedestal sporting caryatids holding up a dragon-scale dome from which fell a constant trickle of water. In an era when only the very rich had running water in their homes, the Wallace fountains were an instant success. Today the chain-attached cups which originally allowed passers-by to drink from them are gone, having been removed in the 1950s for hygiene reasons.

As well as serving to rationalize and sanitize certain activities that were carried out in the street, and on top of its capacity to jolly up otherwise dead spaces, Paris's street furniture was also used to structure, landscape and monumentalize the cityscape. Street corners were punctuated with Morris Columns, railings delimited green spaces from mineral ones, and kiosks provided a focal point at the centre of squares. The *ad infinitum* repetition of lampposts was an especially powerful way of bringing uniform coherence to the street. In narrow thoroughfares lamps were disposed in staggered rows on either pavement, but in the grand boulevards and avenues they were synchronized to produce a processional, perspective effect that brought a third dimension to the flat building façades. To ensure a perfectly even

Sir Norman Foster, bus shelter

prospect, lamp heights were adjusted in relation to each other to take account of unevennesses in the terrain. Trees were an equally powerful tool for monumentalizing the city, and as well as bringing nature into the townscape provided much-needed shade in the summer. Not only were they almost items of street furniture in themselves, but they also required their own furnishings in the form of protective railings for young saplings and grills covering the soil around them. Most of today's grills and railings still follow the SMPP designs, the grills being an especially evocative hallmark of Parisian boulevards. A circular, rose-window filigree around the base of each tree, they are cast in four sections with varying radiuses, narrower grills replacing the larger ones as the tree grows. Their only drawback is that paving stones must be cut to fit round them. When the Boulevard Richard-Lenoir (11th) was repaved in the 1990s, a new, square-edged tree-grill design was introduced, with »crazy-paving« filigree intended to evoke the patterns of sun-dappled foliage.

The management of Paris's enormous stock of street furniture is a daunting task that the municipality could not possibly handle alone. Right from the start many of the facilities were subcontracted out, the most famous example being the Morris Columns. Today the company JC Decaux, which bought up all of its competitors in the 1980s, enjoys a total monopoly on Paris's subcontracted municipal street-furniture. Newspaper kiosks, Morris Columns, public-lavatory cabins, bus stops and advertizing hoardings are all controlled by the Decaux empire. On the one had the company has contributed to the tourist-orientated »museumification« of Paris by reproducing, albeit in modernized and updated form, Second-Empire designs, while on the other it has encouraged contemporary »star« designers to produce new, innovatory equipment. Thus, as well as the few remaining 19C Morris Columns in Paris's streets we also find Decaux-designed modern ones, realized in more hard-wearing materials, glassed over and lit from within; in some cases they even revolve or incorporate telephone booths. Similarly, almost none of Paris's original newspaper kiosks survives, but in the central *arrondissements* rather Disneyfied Decaux adaptations of Davioud's cabins squat in every major thoroughfare. In contrast, however, it is to Decaux that we owe the nonon-sense engineering of the self-cleaning automatic *sanisette* lavatories, as well as the neat discreet design of Parisian bus shelters, the work of Sir Norman Foster no less.

Decaux also landed itself the lucrative contract for the revamp of the Avenue des Champs-Elysées (1989 to 1994), programmed by the municipality in the rather vain hope of bringing some elegance back to this famous thoroughfare and fighting off the fast-food ambience that had set in. Supervised by architect Bernard Huet, the scheme included doubling the pavement width by removing the access alleys that formerly ran up each side, repaving in granite, renewing all the avenue's street furniture, and planting a second row of trees down the middle of the newly enlarged pavements. It was this latter part of the job that turned out to be the most difficult and expensive, all sorts of subterranean obstacles getting in the way – from drains to gas conduits to Métro ventilation shafts – and being extremely time-consuming and costly to move. Nonetheless the architects managed it, and Huet's very classy two-tone paving now graces the avenue, distinguished by details such as the matching car-park entrances or the channel and lip established around tree gratings to stop filthy water from poisoning the soil. For the street furniture, French designer Jean-Michel Wilmotte was asked to provide an entirely new collection: the streamlined lighting pylons, the elegantly minimalist benches and the very slick anthracite-steel traffic lights (which contrast singularly with the rather naff, Second-Empire-styled lights found elsewhere in the city) all carry his signature. But for the street-level lamps the decision was taken to reproduce Hittorff's design, and Decaux refused Wilmotte's newspaper kiosk, advertising column and bus shelter in favour of its own models, arguing that, symbolic of Paris as it is, the Decaux range had to be present in the city's most famous avenue. As a result the Champs-Elysées have a curiously disparate half-heritage/half-futuristic look; to see the full Wilmotte effect one must travel to the 13th *arrondissement* where the designer has provided all the street furniture for the vast new ZAC Rive-Gauche (13.2).

Another bone of contention during the Champs-Elysées project concerned the avenue's litter bins, Wilmotte's design being rejected in favour of the rather brassy Decaux model. Today, however, all the Decaux bins have disappeared from the streets of Paris, removed in the post-11-September climate of fear and replaced by simple pole-mounted rings carrying see-through bin bags. Visually rather makeshift, these new bins also have the practical disadvantage of not holding on tightly enough to their bags, which frequently fall off and dump their load all over the pavement. It remains to be seen whether Decaux will come up with a more effective safety *poubelle* for the 21C.

Selected bibliography

Babelon, Jean-Pierre, *Demeures parisiennes sous Henri IV et Louis XIII*, Hazan, Paris, 1991.
Babelon, Jean-Pierre, and Claude Mignot (eds.), *François Mansart. Le génie de l'architecture*, Gallimard, Paris, 1998.
Beaumont-Maillet, Laure, *Guide du Paris médiéval*, Hazan, Paris, 1997.
Beutler, Christian, *Paris und Versailles*, Reclam, Stuttgart, 1970.
Blunt, Anthony, *Art and Architecture in France, 1500 to 1700*, Penguin, London, 1982.
Boinet, Amédé, *Les églises parisiennes*, Editions de Minuit, Paris, 1958–64.
Braham, Allan, *Architecture of the French Enlightenment*, Thames & Hudson, London, 1980.
Carmona, Michel, *Haussmann*, Fayard, Paris, 2000.
Cortesi, Isotta, *Parcs publics, paysages 1985–2000*, Actes Sud/Motta, Arles, 2001.
Chaslin, François, *Les Paris de François Mitterrand. Histoire des grands projets architecturaux*, Gallimard, Paris, 1985.
Chemetov, Paul, and Bernard Marrey, *Architectures à Paris, 1848–1914*, Dunod, Paris, 1984.
Curtis, William J.R., *Modern Architecture since 1900*, Phaidon, Oxford, 1987.
Delorme, Jean-Claude, and Anne-Marie Dubois, *Passages couverts parisiens*, Parigramme, Paris, 1996.
Des Cars, Jean, and Pierre Pinon, *Paris-Haussmann. »Le pari d'Haussmann«*, Editions du Pavillon de l'Arsenal/Picard, Paris, 1991.
Eleb-Vidal, Monique, and Anne Debarre-Blanchard, *Architectures de la vie privée. Maisons et mentalités, XVIIe–XIXe siècles*, AAM Editions, Brussels, 1989.
Favier, Jean, *Paris. Deux mille ans d'histoire*, Fayard, Paris, 1997.
Frampton, Kenneth, *Modern Architecture: a Critical History*, Thames & Hudson, London, 1985.
Gabriel, André, *Guide de l'architecture des monuments à Paris*, Syros Alternatives, Paris, 1991.
Gleiniger, Andrea, Gerhard Matzig and Sebastian Redecke, *Paris. Contempary Architecture*, Prestel, Munich and New York, 1997.
Hautecœur, Louis, *Histoire de l'architecture classique en France*, Picard, Paris, 1943–1952.
Hautecœur, Louis, *L'histoire des châteaux du Louvre et des Tuileries*, Paris and Brussels, 1927.
Jeannel, Bernard, *Le Nôtre*, Fernand Hazan, Paris, 1985.
Kimpel, Dieter, *Paris – Führer durch die Stadtbaugeschichte*, Hirmer, Munich, 1982.
Laborde, Marie-Françoise, *Architecture industrielle, Paris et environs*, Parigramme, Paris, 1998.
Lambert, Guy (ed.), *Les Ponts de Paris*, Action artistique de la Ville de Paris, Paris, 1999.
Le Moël, Michel, *L'Architecture privée à Paris au grand siècle*, Commission des travaux historiques de la Ville de Paris, Paris, 1990.
Lemoine, Bertrand, and Philippe Rivoirard, *L'Architecture des années 30*, Délégation à l'Action Artistique de la Ville de Paris/La Manufacture, Paris, 1987.
Loyer, François, *Autour de l'Opéra. Naissance de la ville moderne*, Délégation à l'Action Artistique de la Ville de Paris, Paris, 1995.
Loyer, François, *Paris XIXe siècle, l'immeuble et la rue*, Hazan, Paris, 1987.
Lucan, Jacques, *France. Architecture 1965–1988*, Electa Moniteur, Paris, 1989.
Marrey, Bernard, *Le Fer à Paris. Architectures*, Editions du Pavillon de l'Arsenal/Picard, Paris, 1989.
Marrey, Bernard, *Les grands magasins des origines à 1939*, Picard, Paris, 1979.
Marrey, Bernard, and Marie-Jeanne Dumont, *La Brique à Paris*, Editions du Pavillon de l'Arsenal/Picard, Paris, 1991.
Marrey, Bernard, and Jacques Ferrier, *Paris sous verre. La ville et ses reflets*, Editions du Pavillon de l'Arsenal/Picard, Paris, 1997.
Marrey, Bernard, and Franck Hammoutène, *Le Béton à Paris*, Editions du Pavillon de l'Arsenal/Picard, Paris, 1999.
Martin, Hervé, *Guide de l'Architecture Moderne à Paris*, Editions Alternatives, Paris, 1996.
Olsen, Donald J., *The City as a Work of Art: London, Paris, Vienna*, Yale University Press, New Haven and London, 1986.
Pérouse de Montclos, Jean-Marie (ed.), *Le Guide du Patrimoine. Ile de France*, Hachette, Paris, 1992.
Pérouse de Montclos, Jean-Marie (ed.), *Le Guide du Patrimoine. Paris*, Hachette, Paris, 1994.
Pillement, Georges, *Les hôtels de Paris,* Editions Tel, Paris, 1941–45.
Ragot, Gilles, and Mathilde Dion, *Le Corbusier en France*, Electa Moniteur, Paris, 1987.
Sutcliffe, Anthony, *Paris: An Architectural History*, Yale University Press, New Haven and London, 1993.
Texier, Simon (ed.), *Eglises parisiennes du XXe siècle*, Action Artistique de la Ville de Paris, Paris, 1996.
Toulier, Bernard (ed.), *Mille monuments du XXe siècle en France*, Editions du Patrimoine, Paris, 1997.
Wilson, Christopher, *The Gothic Cathedral*, Thames & Hudson, London, 1990.

Glossary

Aile: wing.
Appartement d'apparat: formal or ceremonial suite of rooms in a grand residence. Usually includes a *chambre d'apparat*.
Arrière-corps: see *avant-corps*.
Arrondissement: administrative district of Paris (literally »rounding-up«).
Avant-corps: part of a building projecting forward from the principal block or *corps de logis*. In relation to the *avant-corps*, the remainder of the building is referred to as the *arrière-corps*.
Avant-cour: a courtyard which precedes the *cour d'honneur*.
Barrel vault: the simplest form of vaulting, consisting of a continuous pointed or semicircular vault uninterrupted by transverse vaults.
brise-soleil: device for shading windows from the sun, usually composed of horizontal and vertical fins attached to the window frame.
Cardo: in Roman town planning the principal north–south street of a settlement.
Chambre d'apparat: ceremonial bedchamber.
Clerestory: the upper portion of the walls of the main vessel of a church or basilical-type building, in which windows are set.
Corps de logis: principal part of a building, as distinct from attached wings or pavilions, usually where the most important rooms are situated.
Cour d'honneur: the principal courtyard of a grand or public building, through which official/ceremonial entry is gained.
Enfilade: rooms *en enfilade* are organized in a straight sequence, each one opening into the next.
Escalier d'honneur: the principal and often ceremonial staircase of a grand or public building.
Grands boulevards: »boulevard« is a word derived from the German *Bollwerk* meaning »bulwark« or »bastion«; the term »grands boulevards« is applied to Paris's original boulevards, the series of wide avenues created in the 1670s by Louis XIV on the site of the city's demolished 14C defensive circuit (i.e., today's Boulevards de la Madeleine, des Capucines, des Italiens, Montmartre, Poissonnière, Bonne-Nouvelle, Saint-Denis, Saint-Martin, and Beaumarchais).
Groin vault: a vault formed from two perpendicularly intersecting barrel vaults, different from a quadripartite vault in that it has no ribs.
Hôtel de ville: town hall.
Hôtel particulier: private urban residence, usually used to denote large or grand town houses, as opposed to the apartment blocks which mostly make up French towns.
Mairie: town hall, or the council/administrative body of a town; also the administrative centre and seat of the mayor of an *arrondissement*.
Maison de plaisance: a concept invented in the early-18C denoting a luxury (and hence usually aristocratic) home whose design is intended to facilitate gracious living, maximizing comfort and commodiousness.
Open-bed pediment: a type of broken pediment, whose base, as opposed to its summit, is breached.
Périphérique: abbreviation of »*boulevard périphérique*«, the ring-road encircling Paris, constructed between 1960 and 1973.
Quadripartite vault: a vault divided by ribs into four compartments, a type derived from a groin vault.
RATP: the Régie Autonome des Transports Parisiens, Paris's state-owned transport company, which is responsible for both the buses and the Metro (including the Funiculaire de Montmartre), but not for the RER, which is the domain of the SNCF.
RER: acronym for »Réseau Express Régional«, Paris's express suburban train network run by the SNCF.
Respond: in church architecture, a shaft or agglomeration of shafts connecting the springing point of a vault to the corresponding arcade support below and thus forming a pier.
Salle des fêtes: assembly room, usually of municipal buildings, where conferences, balls, etc. are held.
Salle des pas perdus: term applied to large halls in public buildings (e.g., railway stations) whose principal function is circulatory.
Sceana frons: Latin term designating the often multi-storey, highly decorated architectural backdrop behind the stage of an Antique theatre.
Sexpartite vault: a vault divided by ribs into six compartments (compare quadripartite vault).
SNCF: the Société Nationale des Chemins de Fer, France's state-owned railway company.
Springing point: the point of departure of an arch or vault from its supports.
Stereotomy: the art of cutting stone into three-dimensional shapes.
Term: a pedestal from which emerges a sculpted human, animal or fabulous figure.
Toit à l'impériale: tall roof structure, usually applied to central pavilions of a building, whose flanks and arrises are curved, producing a bulbous, dome-like effect.
ZAC: acronym for »zone d'aménagement concerté«, literally »concerted-development zone«. A ZAC is a legal administrative device that provides a framework for the planning and realization of complex development or redevelopment schemes initiated by a public authority or authorities. The ZAC system allows the public authority/authorities to define the content of a scheme while entrusting its implementation to the private sector, either wholly or in part. In the case of the two principal ZACs featured in this guide – the ZAC Bercy (12.7) and the ZAC Paris-Rive-Gauche (13.2) – implementation of the schemes was carried out by a specially constituted *société d'économie mixte*, a joint-stock company of both public and private ownership in which the public sector retains a controlling interest (between 51% and 65%).

Index

References are given using the entry number or, where the features are concerned, the title. Primary references are in **bold**.

Abadie, Paul 18.2
Abramovitz, Max 27.1
Académie des Sciences 14.5
Académie Royale d'Architecture 6.1, 8.1, 10.1
Académie Royale de Peinture et de Sculpture 6.1
Accenture building 13.2
Ackerman, James 25.2
Act-Architecture 7.1
Adam, Lambert-Sigisbert 3.5, 32.1
Adélaïde de Savoie 18.3
Aéroport Charles-de-Gaulle 17.3, **22.1**
Albert, Edouard 5.12
Alby, Amédée *Seine bridges*
Alcazar Palace 32.1
Aldrophe, Alfred Philibert 9.6
Alexander II 8.10
Alhambra, Granada 5.10
Allio, René 5.14
Alphand, Adolphe 8.9, 19.2, 29.1, 34.1, *Street furniture*
Altaréa 12.10
Altes Museum, Berlin 19.10
American Center *see* Palais du Cinéma
Amiens Cathedral 4.2, 21.2
Ammannati, Bartolomeo 6.8
Ancelet, Auguste 3.10
Ando, Tadao 7.10, 7.11, 11.5, 29.7
Andrault, Michel 12.6, 27.1, 27.3
André, Jules 5.14
Andreu, Paul 13.2, 22.1, 27.4
Anet, Château d' 4.10, 4.21, 5.9, 6.1, 24.1
Angers, David d' 5.8, 18.7, 20.2
Anguier, Michel 1.8, 5.9, 10.1
Anne of Austria 1.8, 4.9, 5.9, 6.2, 38.1
Anne of Bavaria, Princess Palatine 6.9
Antoine, Jacques-Denis 1.1, 6.3
Apartment buildings general: *Parisian housing*; Avenue de Versailles **16.15**, **16.16**, 29.3; Avenue du Nouveau-Conservatoire 18.5, **19.4**; Avenue Mozart / Villa Flore 16.14; Avenue Vion-Whitcomb 29.4; Boulevard Victor **15.5**; Quai d'Orsay **7.6**; Rue des Suisses **14.13**; Rue Franklin **16.8**, 16.9, 16.17, 35.1, *Parisian housing*; Rue Nungesser-et-Coli 29.4; Rue Radziwill **1.17**; Rue Raynouard **16.9**; Rue Saint-Ambroise **11.4**; Rue Vavin **6.10**, 9.4, 18.10
Arc de Triomphe **16.1**, 19.10, 27.1, 27.4
Arc du Carrousel **1.9**, 16.1
Archigram 4.15, 22.1
Architecture Studio 5.13, 11.2, 13.9, 14.12, 15.3, 18.9
Archives Nationales 3.5
Arènes de Lutèce **5.11**
»Arènes de Picasso« social-housing scheme 19.3, 36.1, **36.3**

Armand, Alfred 8.5, 9.12
Arnoult, Blaise-Henri 32.1
Arretche, Louis 1.22, *Seine bridges*
Arsène-Henry, Luc and Xavier 27.1
Artois, Comte d' 24.1, 26.1, 28.1, 29.1, 29.2
Arup, Ove 4.15
Assemblée Nationale 6.6, 7.2, **7.4**
Astruc, Gabriel 8.12
Astruc, Jules 9.3, 14.1
Atelier Brancusi **4.16**
Atelier Lipchitz 29.3
Aubert, André 16.4
Aubert, Jean 7.4, 7.13
Aulenti, Gae 7.1
Automobile Club 8.1
Auzelle, Robert 27.1
Avenue de l'Opéra 9.13, *Parisian housing*
Avenue des Champs-Elysées 1.10, 8.1, 8.11, 8.13, 13.2, 16.1, *Street furniture*
Azéma, Léon 16.7

Bagatelle, Château de 26.1, 29.1, **29.2**
Bailly, Antoine-Nicolas 4.1
Baker, Josephine 18.6
Baldwin II 1.2, 28.1
Balladur, Edouard 21.1
Ballu, Théodore 1.7, 4.11, 4.12, 7.3, 9.7
Baltard, Victor 1.22, 5.7, 8.6, 9.7, *Métro and RER*
Balzac, Honoré de 4.1
Banham, Reyner 4.15
Banque de France *see* Hôtel de La Vrillière
Banque Paribas, annexe to headquarters **1.14**, *Arcades and passages*
Baraguey (architect) 6.7
Barani, Marc 29.6
Barberini, Palazzo, Rome 37.1
Barcelona Pavilion 18.8
Barge, Jacques 17.2
Barillet, Louis 16.12
Barillet-Deschamps, Pierre 29.1, 34.1
Barrière d'Enfer 19.13
Barrière d'Orléans 8.9, 19.13
Barrière du Trône **11.7**, 19.13
Barry, Madame du 32.1, 32.4, 32.6
Barry, Robert 18.5
Barthes, Roland 7.8, 11.5
Bartholdi, Frédéric Auguste 18.7
Bartholomé, Albert 18.7, 20.2
Bassompièrre, Maréchal de 32.1, 38.1
Baudot de Saint-James, Claude 26.1
Baudelaire, Charles 4.1
Baudot, Anatole de 10.7, 15.12, 16.14, 18.4
Baudry, Paul 7.14, 9.13
Beaudoin, Eugène 15.1
Beaujour, Baron Félix de 20.2
Beauvais Cathedral 4.10
Bechmann, Lucien 14.8
Bélanger, François-Joseph 1.20, 10.7, 24.1, 26.1, 29.2
Bellier, Catherine-Henriette 4.9
Benamo, Giorgia 13.10
Bénard, Adrien *Métro and RER*

Bénard, Jacques 2.7
Bénéch, Louis 1.10
Bentham, Jeremy 10.4 12.10, 15.8, 19.7, *Seine bridges*
Bercy Village 12.7, **12.10**
Berger, Patrick 12.2, 15.8
Bernard, Constant 9.2
Bernard, Henry 16.10
Bernier, Louis 2.6
Bernini, Giovanni Lorenzo 1.8, 4.9, 5.9, 7.12, 24.1, 32.1, 37.1
Berry, Duc de 9.13
Bertaut (architect) 10.5
Berthier, Jean-Baptiste 32.6
Besset, Pierre du 15.2
Biard, Pierre 5.7, 38.1
Bibliothèque Forney 4.6
Bibliothèque Gutenberg **15.9**
Bibliothèque Historique de la Ville de Paris 4.18
Bibliothèque Mazarine 6.2
Bibliothèque Nationale 2.3, **2.4**, 5.6, 13.3
Bibliothèque Nationale de France 1.8, 2.4, 13.2, **13.3**, 13.5, *Seine bridges*
Bibliothèque Sainte-Geneviève 2.4, 3.10, **5.6**
Bienvenüe, Fulgence *Métro and RER*
Biette, Louis *Seine bridges*
Bigot, Alexandre 16.8
Bigot, Paul 6.11
Billaud, J. *Arcades and passages*
Binet, René 9.9, 9.10
Bisseuil, J.-P. 27.1
Bizouard, Catherine 3.7
Blaikie, Thomas 29.2
Blain, Jean-Baptiste 32.1
Blanche de Castille 1.2, 21.2
Bloch-Lainé, François 12.1
Blois, Château de 7.9, 24.1
Blondel, Henri 1.20, 9.13
Blondel, Jacques-François 8.16, 24.1
Blondel, Nicolas-François 10.1, 10.2
Blouet, Guillaume-Abel 16.1
Blunt, Anthony 32.1
Bluysen, Auguste 2.10
Boeswillwald, Emile 1.2
Boffrand, Gabriel Germain 3.4, 3.5, 4.13, 6.9, 13.1
Bofill, Ricardo 1.14, 1.22, 13.2, 13.10, 14.2, 18.5, 19.3, 36.2, 36.3, *Arcades and passages*
Boileau, Louis-Auguste 3.10, 7.15, 9.3, 14.1
Boileau, Louis-Charles 7.15
Boileau, Louis-Hippolyte 7.15, 16.7, 34.1, *Parisian housing*
Bois, Emile 16.3
Boistière, Claude 27.1
Boizot, Simon 1.4
Bolze, Pierre 13.2
Bon Marché **7.15**, 9.9
Bonnier, Louis *Parisian housing*
Bordeaux, Grand Théâtre de 1.16, 9.13
Borel, Frédéric 7.5, 11.3, 13.2, 18.8, 19.5, 20.1, 20.3, 20.4, 20.5
Borromini, Francesco 6.2
Bosiot, François-Joseph 2.2, 8.4
Bouchardon, Edme 7.16

406

Boucher, François 3.5, 38.1
Bouchez, Gilles 16.6
Boucicaut, Aristide 7.15
Bouguereau, William 8.6
Bouillon, Duc de 6.1
Boulevard périphérique 13.2, 13.13, 14.8, 14.12, 16.18, 17.3, 18.9, 33.1
Boulez, Pierre 4.14, 19.5
Boullée, Louis-Etienne 1.15, 2.8, 8.3, 8.4, 8.16, 16.1, 27.4, 32.1, 36.3
Boullier de Bourges, Jean 3.3
Boulogne, Bois de **29.1**, 38.1
Bourbon, Cardinal Charles de 6.4
Bourbon-Condé, Duc de 32.5
Bourdais, Jules 16.7
Bourdeau, Michel 20.3, 20.5
Bourdelle, Emile-Antoine 8.12, 16.4
Bourge, Romain de *Arcades and passages*
Bourges Cathedral 1.21, 4.2 1.20, **2.8**, 4.1, 8.2, 9.13
Bourse du Commerce **1.20**, 10.7
Bouvard, Joseph-Antoine 3.1
Bouwens Van der Boijen, Richard and William 2.5
Boyslesve, Claude 3.1
Bralle, François-Joseph 1.4
Bramante, Donato 5.8, 7.12, 8.9
Branconio dell'Aquila, Palazzo, Rome 38.1
Brancusi, Constantin 4.16, 14.3
Brébion, Maximilien 5.8
Brenac, Olivier 13.2
Breuer, Marcel 7.10
Brice, Germain 4.10
Brière (glass-smith) 9.9
British Library, London 2.4, 13.3
Brongniart, Alexandre-Théodore 2.8, 8.2, 9.8, 20.2
Brook, Peter 10.8
Brosse, Salomon de 1.1, 4.7, 4.10, 6.8, 37.1, 38.1
Broutel du Val, Antoine 5.9
Bruand, Jacques 3.1
Bruand, Libéral 4.4, 7.12, 8.15, 13.1
Brun, Joseph-Silvestre 16.1
Brunet, F. (engineer) 1.20
Brunetti, Paolo Antonio 3.1
Bruno, Andrea 3.10
Buffi, Jean-Pierre 12.7, 27.4
Buffon, Comte de 5.14
Bullant, Jean 1.10, 1.20, 8.9, 3.2, 21.2, 23.1, 24.1
Bullet, Pierre 1.13, 1.15, 3.1, 3.10, 10.2, 36.5
Bullet de Chamblain, Jean-Baptiste 36.5
Buren, Daniel 1.16
Burgundy, dukes of 2.1
Burlington Arcade, London *Arcades and passages*

Cabanal de Sermet, Pierre 10.5
Caesar, Julius 4.1
Café de la Paix 9.12
Café de Paris 3.1
Café Militaire 3.1
Cahen d'Anvers, Louis 36.5
Caisse des Dépôts et Consignations 13.2

Caisse Nationale des Monuments et des Sites 4.20
Calder, Alexander 7.10
Callet, Félix 1.22
Calliat, Victor 4.1
Camelot, Robert 27.1, 27.3
Canal 13.8
Canal+ headquarters 15.6, **15.10**
Candie-Saint-Bernard redevelopment **11.4**
Capet, Hugues *see* Hugues Capet
Capitol, Rome 38.1
Capuchin order 9.8
Cap Val building (Zeus-Paris-Bercy) 12.7
Caraman, Comte de 32.5
Carlu, Jacques 16.7
Carnesecchi, Bernard de 1.10
Carpeaux, Jean-Baptiste 9.13, 14.5
Carpi, Francisque Scibec de *see* Scibec de Carpi, Francisque
Carrière, Léon 34.1
Carrogis, Louis (Carmontelle) 8.9
Cartier, Fondation 7.7, 12.9, **14.4**
Casa Rustici, Milan 12.7
Cassan, Urbain 5.12, 15.1
Cassien-Bernard, Joseph *Seine bridges*
Cassini, Giovanni Domenico 14.5
»Castel Béranger« apartment building **16.11**, 16.14, *Parisian housing*
Catacombes 20.2
Catherine de Médicis 1.8, 1.10, 1.20, 4.19, 8.9, 21.2, 38.1
Cattani, Alberto 12.10
Cattani, Emmanuel 14.4
Cellerier, Jacques 21.2
Cendrier (sculptor) 20.2
Centre Commercial Bercy 2 12.10, **33.1**
Centre de Conférences Internationales de Paris 7.7
Centre Georges-Pompidou 1.8, 4.14, **4.15**, 4.16, 7.7, 13.4, 13.5, 13.11, 16.4, 19.10, 29.7
Ceria, F. (architect) 12.7
Cessart, Louis-Alexandre de *Seine bridges*
Chaillot hill 1.10, 16.1, 16.6, 16.7
Chaix, Philippe 12.7, 19.8, 36.1
Chalgrin, Jean-François 6.5, 6.7, 6.8, 8.7, 9.5, 16.1
Chambiges, Martin 4.6, 4.10
Chambiges, Pierre 4.11, 28.1
Chambord, Château de 1.21, 2.5, 23.1
Chambre des Notaires 1.4
Champaigne, Jean-Baptiste de 4.4, 32.1
Champaigne, Philippe de 4.4, 5.5, 34.2
Champ de Mars 7.9, 12.7, 15.8, 16.4, 16.7
Champs-sur-Marne, Château de 24.1, 36.1, **36.5**
Chancel, Adrien 8.16
Chandigarh 19.5
Chantilly, Château de 32.5
Chanut, Ferdinand 9.10
Chapelle de l'Assomption **1.12**
Chapelle Expiatoire **8.4**, 32.6
Chapelle Saint-Aignan 4.1
Chareau, Pierre 7.17, 16.12, 29.4

Charles V 1.1, 1.8, 4.6, 13.12, 28.1, 29.1, 34.2
Charles VIII 1.2
Charles IX 1.8, 38.1, *Parisian housing*
Charles X 1.8
Charpentier, Théodore *Arcades and passages*
Charter of Athens 13.2, 27.1
Chartres, Duc de 1.16, 8.9, *Arcades and passages*, *Parisian housing*
Chartres Cathedral 4.1, 21.2
Chasériau, Théodore 8.7
Chastillon, Claude 10.4
Chateaubriand, François-Auguste-René de 14.8
Chaudet, Antoine-Denis 1.13
Chavannes, Patrick 29.6
Chelles, Jean de 4.2
Chemetoff, Alexandre 19.7
Chemetov, Paul 1.22, 5.14, 12.5, 13.2, 15.11, 19.1
Childebert I 1.6, 6.4
Chinard, Joseph 1.9
Chirac, Jacques 1.22, 7.7, 13.2, 13.11
Choisy, Auguste 16.8, 16.17, 35.1
Chrysler Building, New York 7.8
Cimetière de Montmartre **18.7**, 20.2
Cimetière des Saints-Innocents 20.2
Cimetière du Montparnasse **14.3**, 18.7, 20.2
Cimetière du Père-Lachaise 1.22, 14.3, 18.7, **20.2**
Ciriani, Henri 12.7
Cirque d'Hiver **11.1**
Cité de l'Architecture et du Patrimoine 16.7
Cité de la Musique 7.5, **19.5**, 19.7
Cité de Refuge de l'Armée du Salut 11.4, 12.11, **13.6**, 14.10
Cité des Artistes **15.6**
Cité des Sciences et de l'Industrie 19.7, 19.9, **19.10**
Cité Descartes 36.1, 36.4
Cité Industrielle 29.5
Cité Napoléon **9.4**, 15.4
Cité Universitaire **14.8**, 14.9, 14.10, 14.11
Clark, George 9.4
Clément, Abbot Eudes 21.2
Clément, Gilles 15.8
Clovis 1.1, 5.8
Cluny, Abbaye de 3.10, 16.3
C.N.I.T. (Centre National des Industries et des Techniques) 27.1, **27.3**
Cocteau, Jean 8.8
Cœur Défense 27.1
Cognacq, Ernest 1.5
Colbert, Jean-Baptiste 1.8, 1.21, 6.1, 10.1, 14.5, 37.1
Collège de Dormans-Beauvais 5.2
Collège d'Espagne 14.8
Collège des Quatre-Nations *see* Institut de France
Collège Franco-Britannique 14.8
Collège Georges-Brassens **19.3**
Collège Jean-François Oeben (former Collège Arago) **12.11**
Collège Thomas-Mann 13.2

407

Collin, David 34.1
Collin, Rémy *Seine bridges*
Cologne Cathedral 21.2
Colonnes Buren 1.16
Colosseum, Rome 6.1
Comédie-Française 1.16, 6.7
Commune 1.1, 1.3, 1.8, 1.10, 1.13, 4.11, 7.1, 18.2
Compressed-air plant (SUDAC) 13.2, **13.4**
Comptoir National d'Escompte de Paris (Banque Nationale de Paris) **9.2**
Conciergerie *see* Palais de la Cité
Condé, Prince de 7.4
Confrérie des Chirurgiens 6.6
Conseil d'Etat 1.8, 1.16, 30.2
Conseil des Bâtiments Civils 4.12, 6.1, 7.3
Conseil des Cinq Cents 7.4
Conseil Economique et Social 16.6
Conservatoire de Musique Erik-Satie and sheltered housing **7.5**
Conservatoire National des Arts et Métiers *see* Saint-Martin-des-Champs
Conservatoire National Supérieur de Musique et de Danse 19.5
Considère, Armand 36.6
Constantine, Arch of 1.9
Contamin, Victor 7.8
Contant d'Ivry, Pierre 1.16, 8.2
Cook, William 29.3
Coquand, Abbé 9.3
Corday, Charlotte 1.1
Cormont, Thomas de 1.2
Corneille, Michel 4.17
Cornell, Joseph 20.4
Corporation des Nautes 5.3
Corps/Ecole des Ponts et Chaussées 5.8, 22.1, 36.1, *Seine bridges*
Corroyer, Edouard-Jules 9.2
Cortona, Domenico da 4.11, 8.9
Cortona, Pietro da 6.2, 32.1, 37.1
Cortot, Jean-Pierre 7.4, 8.4, 16.1
Cortot, Salle **17.1**
Costa, Lucio 7.10, 14.9
Costantini, Claude 21.1
Cotelle, Jean 32.2
Cottancin, Paul 18.4
Cottard, Pierre 4.17
Cotte, Robert de 1.15, 1.18, 2.4, 4.2, 7.12, 21.2, 32.1, 32.2, 34.1
Coulon, René 5.12
Coupel, Alain 12.7
»Couple Plus« apartment building **20.3**
Cour de Cassation 1.1
Courtonne, Jean 7.14, 8.16
Cousin, Gaston *Seine bridges*
Cousteau, Jacques 1.22
Coustou, Guillaume and Nicolas 7.12
Couture, Guillaume-Martin 1.1, 8.2
Couvent de la Reine, Versailles 32.6
Couvent des Filles-du-Calvaire 6.9
Couvent/Eglise des Petits-Augustins 6.1
Covent Garden, London 4.19
Coypel, Antoine 32.1
Coypel, Noël 32.1

Coysevox, Antoine 7.12, 32.1
Crèches: Rue de Rouen **19.12**; Rue Saint-Maur **11.5**, 12.11, 14.13
Crédit Lyonnais headquarters **2.5**, 9.2, 9.11
Cribier, Pascal 1.10
Crown of Thorns 1.2, 28.1
Crypte Archéologique du Parvis Notre-Dame 4.1

Dalsace, Dr and Mme 7.17
Dastugue, Marcel 16.4
Daumet, Honoré 1.1
David, Jacques-Louis 9.8
Davioud, Gabriel 1.4, 8.9, 14.5, 16.7, 19.2, 29.1, 34.1, *Street furniture*
Debias-Aubry, François 6.1
Debré, Olivier 18.5
Debressenne, Eugène 8.16
Debret, François 6.1, 21.2, *Arcades and passages*
Decaux *see* JC Decaux
Deglane, Henri 8.14
Degoullons, Jules 7.4, 32.1
Dejean, Louis 11.1
Delaage Tsaropoulos Architecture Carvunis Cholet 8.3
Delacroix, Eugène 1.8, 6.8, 7.4
Delamair, Pierre-Alexis 3.4, 3.5
Delamarre, Jean 1.21
Delannoy, François-Jacques *Arcades and passages*
Delaroche, Paul 6.1, 18.7
Dell'Abate, Nicolo 38.1
De l'Orme, Philibert 1.10, 3.2, 3.9, 4.21, 5.9, 6.1, 24.1, 28.1, 38.1
Dendera, Temple of 1.1
Denis, Maurice 8.12, 12.12, 28.1, 35.1
Denis, Saint 18.2, 18.3, 21.2
Deperthes, Pierre 4.11
Depusse, Jacques 27.1
Derand, François 4.7
Derrida, Jacques 19.7
Desbouis, Jean 8.11
Descartes, René 1.10
Deschamps, Jacques *Arcades and passages*
Deschamps, Jean-Paul 12.11
Deschamps, Joseph 32.6
Desgots, Claude 36.5
Desjardins, Martin 2.2, 3.3, 4.9, 10.2
Deslaugiers, François 3.10, 18.1
Delisle-Mansart, Pierre 3.5
Desmaisons, Pierre 1.1, *Parisian housing*
Destailleur, Hippolyte *Arcades and passages*
Deutsch de la Meurthe, Emile 14.8
Diane de France 4.18
Diane de Poitiers 6.1, 38.1
Diet, Stanislas 4.1
Dionysius the Areopagite 21.2
Disney, Walt 36.7
Disneyland Paris 12.10, 19.2, 19.7, **36.7**
Dommey, Honoré *see* Daumet, Honoré
Dondel, Jean-Claude 16.4
Donnersmarck, Graf von 8.13

Dorigny, Michel 34.2
Doucet, Jacques 4.4
Du Cerceau, Baptiste Androuet 4.18, *Seine bridges*
Du Cerceau, Jacques II Androuet 1.8, 28.1, 38.1
Du Cerceau, Jean Androuet 4.20, 38.1
Duban, Félix 1.2, 1.8, 6.1, 18.7
Dubois, Ambroise 38.1
Dubreuil, Toussaint 38.1
Duc, Louis-Joseph 1.1, 9.8
Ducasse, Isidore 11.3, 20.4
Duchêne, Achille and Henri 36.5
Dudok, Willem Marinus 14.11
Dufour, Alex 32.1
Dufrêne, Maurice 2.10
Duhart, Denise 13.2
Duquesney, François-Alexandre 10.5
Dusapin, Fabrice 12.7, 13.2
Dutert, Charles-Louis-Ferdinand 5.14, 7.8
Duthilleul, Jean-Marie 22.1, *Métro and RER*
Duval, Antoine 13.1

Eberson, John 2.10
»Echelles du Baroque« social-housing scheme 1.14, **14.2**
Eco, Umberto 36.7
Ecole d'Architecture de Paris Val-de-Seine 13.2, 13.4
Ecole de Chirurgie **6.6**, 7.2
Ecole de Droit 5.8
Ecole des Beaux-Arts 1.19, **6.1**, 6.2, 16.8
Ecole Militaire **7.9**, 7.10, 16.7
Ecole Nationale des Sciences Géographiques (ENSG) 36.1
Ecole Normale de Musique 17.1
Ecole Supérieure d'Ingénieurs en Electronique et Electrotechnique, (ESIEE) 36.1
Ecouen, Château de 1.8, 3.1, **23.1**, 24.1
Eiffel, firm of 2.5, 7.15
Eiffel, Gustave 7.8, 36.6
Eiffel Tower 7.7, **7.8**, 16.1, 16.7, 16.8, 27.4
Elysée-Palace Hotel 2.9
EPAD 27.1
Epstein, Jacob 20.2
Erckmann-Chatrian *Arcades and passages*
Ernst, Max 1.22
Errard, Charles 1.12
Escorial, near Madrid 5.9, 5.12, 7.9, 7.12, 13.1, 14.8
»Espaces d'Abraxas« social-housing scheme 14.2, 36.1, **36.2**, 36.3
Esprit Nouveau, L' 14.7
Esquillan, Nicolas 27.3
Estrées, Maréchal Duc d' 29.2
Etex, Antoine 16.1
Eugénie, Empress 1.18, 8.16, 9.6, 9.13, 38.1
EuroDisney *see* Disneyland Paris
Evreux, Comte de 8.16
Expert, Henri 16.7
Exposition Coloniale, 1931 12.13, 34.1

Exposition Internationale, 1937 13.12, 16.4, 16.6, 16.7
Exposition Internationale des Arts Décoratifs, 1925 15.5, 16.12, 29.3
Exposition Universelle, 1855 1.11, 8.13, 8.14, 29.1
Exposition Universelle, 1867 9.13, 19.2, 36.6
Exposition Universelle, 1878 8.14, 8.15, 16.7, 36.6
Exposition Universelle, 1889 5.14, 7.8, 8.5
Exposition Universelle, 1900 7.1, 8.14, 8.15, 12.4, *Métro and RER*, *Seine bridges*

Faculté des Sciences de Jussieu **5.12**, 5.13, 13.2
Fainsilber, Adrien 19.7, 19.9, 19.10
Falguière, Alexandre 16.1
Faloci, Louis 13.2
Farnese, Cardinal 23.1
Farnsworth House, Plano, Illinois 30.2
Fédération Française de Judo 14.12
Feichtinger, Dietmar *Seine bridges*
Felan, Jehan de 4.12
Fermiers Généraux 8.9, 11.7, 19.13
Ferrand, Marylène 12.8
Festspielhaus Bayreuth 9.13
Firestation, Rue Mesnil **16.2**
Fischer, Raymond 29.3
Fiszer, Stanislas 3.5
Flachat, Eugène 1.22, 8.5, 19.6
Flamel, Nicolas *Parisian housing*
Flandrin, Hippolyte 6.4, 7.14, 10.6
Flandrin, Paul 7.14
Flavius Claudius Julianus 1.1
Folie Saint-James **26.1**, 29.1
Fondation Deutsch-de-la-Meurthe 14.8
Fondation Franco-Brésilienne *see* Maison du Brésil
Fondation Héllenique 14.8
Fondation Le Corbusier 16.13, 29.4
Fonquernie, Bernard 3.7, 3.10, 4.9
Fontaine, Pierre-François-Léonard 1.8, 1.9, 1.11, 1.16, 2.7, 8.4, 12.7, 16.7, 19.4, 32.1, 32.6, *Arcades and passages*
Fontainebleau, Château de 1.8, 3.1, 14.8, 23.1, 24.1, **38.1**
Fontaine des Innocents **1.23**
Fontaine des Quatre-Saisons or de Grenelle **7.16**
Fontaine Médicis 6.8
Forestier, Jean-Claude-Nicolas 29.2
Formigé, Jean-Camille 20.2, *Métro and RER*, *Seine bridges*
Formigé, Jules 20.2
Forughi, Mossem 14.8
Fosse, Charles de la 7.12
Foster, Sir Norman 19.10, *Street furniture*
Foucault, Jean Bernard Léon 14.5
Fould, Achille 1.7
Fouquet, Georges (jeweller) 3.1
Fouquet, Nicolas 37.1
Fournez, Robert 5.10
Foy, General 20.2
Frampton, Kenneth 15.6

Francine, Alexandre 6.8
Francis, Martin 19.10
Franco-Prussian War, 1870 1.1, 1.8, 9.13, 18.2, 30.1, 34.1
François I 1.8, 1.21, 2.4, 13.2, 23.1, 28.1, 29.1, 38.1, *Parisian housing*
François II 1.8
Fréminet, Martin 38.1
French Communist Party headquarters 7.10, **19.1**
Freyssinet, Eugène 13.2
Frigos 13.2
Frochot, Nicolas 14.3, 18.7, 20.2
Froncières, Jean de 3.9
Fuegas, Jean-Pierre 12.8
Fuksas, Massimiliano 11.6
Fuller, Buckminster 4.15
Funiculaire de Montmartre **18.1**
Fürstenberg, Cardinal Egon de 6.4

Gabriel, Ange-Jacques 1.16, 5.8, 6.3, 7.9, 8.1, 32.1, 32.2, 32.3, 32.4, 38.1, *Parisian housing*
Gabriel, Jacques IV 32.6, *Seine bridges*
Gabriel, Jacques V 7.4, 7.13, 32.1, 38.1
Gabriel, Maurice 32.6
Gaillon, Château de 6.1
Galerie d'Orléans 1.16, *Arcades and passages*
Galerie des Machines 5.14, 7.8
Galerie du Carrousel 1.8
Galerie Nationale du Jeu-de-Paume 1.10
Galeries Lafayette **9.10**
Gallaratese housing scheme, Milan 19.4
Galliéra, Duc de 7.14
Gamard, Christophe 6.4, 6.5
Garde-Meuble du Mobilier National **13.12**, 16.6
Gare d'Austerlitz 7.1, 13.2
Gare de l'Est **10.5**, 10.7, *Métro and RER*
Gare de Lyon **12.4**, 12.5
Gare du Nord 10.5, **10.7**, *Métro and RER*
Gare Montparnasse 14.2, 15.1
Gare Saint-Lazare 1.22, **8.5**, 9.7, 9.13, *Métro and RER*
Garnier, Charles 2.6, 9.2, 9.13, 10.3, *Métro and RER*, *Street furniture*
Garnier, Tony 1.19, 29.5
Gau, Franz Christian 7.3
Gaudin, Henri and Bruno 13.13, 16.5
Gaulle, Charles de 7.7, 16.10, 19.7, 22.1
Gaumont-Palace cinema 2.10
Gazeau, Philippe 13.2
Gehry, Frank O. 4.15, 12.7, **12.9**, 29.7, 36.7
Geneviève, Saint 5.8, 21.2
Géode **19.9**, 19.10
Germain (Germanus), Saint 6.4
Gesù, Rome 1.15, 4.7, 5.5, 5.9
Ghiai, Hedar 14.8
Giacometti, Alberto 7.10
Gilbert, Jacques 4.1
Gillet, Guillaume 17.3
Ginsberg, Jean 7.6, 16.15, 16.16, 29.3, 29.4
Girard, Jean 30.1

Girardon, François 5.5, 10.1, 32.1
Girault, Charles-Louis 8.14, 8.15
Giscard d'Estaing, Valéry 1.22, 7.1, 13.11, 15.1, 19.7, 19.9, 19.10, 27.1
Gisors, Alphonse de 6.8
Gisors, Jacques-Pierre 7.4
Gittard, Daniel 4.4, 6.5
Giverny 12.8, 29.2
Glass House, New Canaan, Connecticut 30.2
Godde, Etienne-Hippolyte 4.11, 6.4, 8.7, 14.3, 20.2
Gondoin, Jacques 1.13, 6.6, 8.1
Gonzalès, Xavier 13.2
Goujon, Jean 1.8, 1.23, 3.1, 23.1
Goust, L. 16.1
»Grand Ecran« building **13.11**
Grand Hôtel **9.12**
Grand Pagode 34.1
Grand Palais **8.14**, 8.15, *Seine bridges*
Grand Trianon 7.4, 32.1, **32.2**, 32.3, 32.4
Grande Arche de La Défense 18.1, 27.1, **27.4**, 27.5
Grande Croisée 1.4, 1.11, 4.1, 4.12, 10.5, 16.1, *Seine bridges*
Grande Halle aux Bœufs 19.5, **19.6**, 19.7
Grande Mosquée de Paris **5.10**
Grandes et Petites Ecuries, Versailles 32.6
Grands Moulins de Paris 13.2
Granveaud, Pierre 19.12
Graves, Michael 36.7
Grégoire, Abbé 3.10
Grimaldi, Giovanni-Francesco 2.4
Gropius, Walter 7.10
Gros, Antoine-Jean 5.8
Groupe des Maisons Ouvrières 15.4
Grumbach, Antoine 36.7, *Métro and RER*
Guadet, Julien 1.19, 16.8, 16.17
Guadet, Paul 1.19, 16.13, 16.17
Guérin, Claude 5.7
Guérin, Gilles 24.1
Guggenheim Museum, Bilbao 4.15, 12.9, 29.7
Guibert, Honoré 32.4
Guidetti, Pierre and Louis *Seine bridges*
Guillain, Guillaume 28.1
Guimard, Hector 16.11, 16.14, 18.1, *Métro and RER*, *Parisian housing*
Guise family 3.5
Guvan, Aydin 12.6

Haber, Shamaï 14.2
Habert-Thibierge, Martin *Arcades and passages*
Hadid, Zaha 11.3
Hagia Sophia, Istanbul 12.12, 17.2
Haïk, Jacques 2.10
Hall of residence, Rue François-de-Croisset 14.12, **18.9**
Halle aux Farines 13.2
Halle des Messageries Ferroviaires (Halle Sernam) 13.2
Hammoutène, Franck 12.7, 15.9, 19.5, 27.2

409

Hardouin-Mansart, Jules 1.13, 1.15, 2.2, 4.8, 5.2, 5.8, 6.2, 7.12, 8.15, 24.1, 28.1, 30.1, 32.1, 32.2, 32.6, 38.1, *Seine bridges*
Hardouin-Mansart de Jouy, Jean 1.21
Hardouin-Mansart de Lévy de Sagonne, Jacques 32.6
Harrison, Wallace K. 7.10, 27.1
Haus Steiner, Vienna 14.6
Haussmann, Baron Georges-Eugène 1.1, 1.4, 1.6, 1.7, 1.11, 1.22, 2.2, 2.7, 2.9, 3.1, 4.1, 4.2, 4.11, 4.12, 8.6, 8.9, 9.6, 9.7, 9.13, 10.5, 10.6, 16.1, 16.7, 19.6, 19.7, 29.1, 34.1, *Métro and RER*, *Arcades and passages*, *Seine bridges*, *Parisian housing*, *Street furniture*
Hauvette, Christian 11.5, 12.11, 13.2, 4.13
Heep, François 16.16, 29.4
Henrietta Maria, Queen 1.16
Henri I 3.10
Henri II 1.8, 1.23, 4.1, 4.19, 6.1, 23.1, 28.1, 29.1, 38.1, *Parisian housing*
Henri III *Seine bridges*
Henri IV 1.1, 1.3, 1.8, 4.19, 6.8, 10.4, 38.1, *Seine bridges*
Hermant, Jacques 9.11
Herrenchiemsee, Schloß 32.1
Hertford, Marquess of 29.2
Herzog & de Meuron 14.13
Heubès, Charles 5.10
Hilduin, Abbot 21.2
Hilversum town hall 14.11
Hittorff, Jakob Ignaz 1.7, 8.1, 10.6, 10.7, 11.1, 16.1, 29.1, *Street furniture*
Holiday Inn, Avenue Jean-Jaurès 19.5
Honnorat, André 14.8
Hôpital de la Pitié-Salpêtrière 7.12, 1.**3.1**
Hôpital Européen Georges-Pompidou **15.7**
Hôpital Saint-Louis **10.4**
Horta, Victor 16.11
Hôtel Alexandre **8.3**
Hôtel Amelot-de-Bisseuil (Hôtel des Ambassadeurs-de-Hollande) **4.17**
Hôtel André *see* Musée Jacquemart-André
Hôtel Aubert-de-Fontenay (Hôtel Salé, Musée Picasso) 3.1, **3.3**
Hôtel Biron *see* Hôtel Peyrenc-de-Moras
Hôtel Colbert de Villacerf 3.1
Hôtel Collinet 29.3
Hôtel d'Aumont **4.8**
Hôtel d'Avaux (Hôtel de Saint-Aignan, Jewish Museum) 3.3, **3.7**
Hôtel de Beauvais **4.9**
Hôtel de Clisson 3.5
Hôtel de Condé 6.7
Hôtel de Donon (Musée Cognacq-Jay) **3.2**
Hôtel d'Evreux 1.13, 8.16
Hôtel de Guénégaud-des-Brosses 3.3, **3.6**
Hôtel de Guise, Versailles 32.6
Hôtel d'Hallwyl **3.8**, 32.6
Hôtel de la Païva **8.13**
Hôtel de La Rivière 3.1

Hôtel de La Trémoille *see* Hôtel Le Gendre
Hôtel de La Vrillière (Hôtel de Toulouse, Banque de France) **1.18**
Hôtel de Lassay *see* Assemblée Nationale
Hôtel de Luynes 3.1
Hôtel de Rohan 3.3, **3.4**, 3.5
Hôtel de Saint-Aignan *see* Hôtel d'Avaux
Hôtel de Salm (Palais de la Légion d'Honneur) **7.2**
Hôtel de Sens 3.5, **4.6**, 5.4
Hôtel de Soissons 1.20
Hôtel de Soubise 3.4, **3.5**
Hôtel de Sully **4.20**
Hôtel de Thélusson 7.2
Hôtel de Torpanne *see* Hôtel du Faur
Hôtel de Toulouse *see* Hôtel de La Vrillière
Hôtel d'Uzès 3.1
Hôtel de Ville, Boulogne-Billancourt **29.5**
Hôtel de Ville, Paris 1.7, **4.11**, 8.9, 10.3, 24.1
Hôtel de Wendel 3.1
Hotel del Coronado, San Diego 36.7
Hôtel des Monnaies **6.3**
Hôtel des Postes **1.19**
Hôtel des Tournelles 3.9, 4.19
Hôtel Desmarets 3.1
Hôtel-Dieu 4.1, 4.2, 10.4
Hôtel du Faur 6.1
Hôtel du Grand Prieur du Temple 3.5
Hôtel du Louvre 9.12
Hôtel Duret-de-Chevry (Hôtel Tubeuf) **2.3**, 2.4
Hôtel Guadet 1.19, 16.13, **16.17**
Hôtel Guimard **16.14**
Hôtel Industriel Berlier **13.5**
Hôtel Lambert 3.1, **4.5**, 32.1, 37.1
Hôtel Lamoignon **4.18**, 4.20
Hôtel Le Gendre 6.1
Hôtel Le Peletier de Saint-Fargeau *see* Musée Carnavalet
Hôtel Lemordant **14.6**
Hôtel Lutétia *Parisian housing*
Hôtel Matignon 3.1, 3.3, **7.14**, 8.16,
Hôtel Peyrenc-de-Moras (Hôtel Biron, Musée Rodin) **7.13**, 36.5
Hôtel Ritz 1.13
Hôtel Salé *see* Hôtel Aubert-de-Fontenay
Hôtel Tambonneau 37.1
Hôtel Tubeuf *see* Hôtel Duret-de-Chevry
Hoym de Marien, Louis 15.1
Huet, Bernard 12.8, *Street furniture*
Huet, Christophe 3.4, 36.5
Huidobro, Borja 5.14, 12.5, 13.2
Hugo, Victor 4.1, 4.2
Hugues Capet 1.1, 21.2
Hugues III, Abbot 6.4
Hundred Years' War 1.1
Huré, Marguerite 35.1
Hurtault, Maximilien-Joseph 38.1
Huvé, Jean-Jacques-Marie 8.2
Huyot, Jean-Nicolas 1.1, 16.1

Ile de la Cité 1.1, 1.3, 1.4, 1.23, **4.1**, 4.2, 4.3, 5.2, *Seine bridges*
Ile Saint-Louis 4.1, 4.4, 4.5, 5.13, *Seine bridges*
Ile Seguin **29.6**, 29.7
Illes, Pierre des *Seine bridges*
Industrial building, Rue Réaumur **2.9**
Ingres, Jean-Auguste-Dominique 1.8
Institut d'Aménagement et d'Urbanisme de la Région Ile-de-France 15.2
Institut d'Art et d'Archéologie **6.11**
Institut de France (former Collège des Quatre-Nations) 6.1, **6.2**, 6.3, 16.4
Institut National d'Histoire de l'Art 2.4, *Arcades and passages*
Institut du Monde Arabe **5.13**, 14.4
Invalides 1.8, 5.8, 5.9, 7.9, **7.12**, 7.13, 8.15, 13.1, 18.2, 21.2, *Seine bridges*
IRCAM **4.14**, 4.15
Iron Bridge, Coalbrookdale *Seine bridges*
Issy, Château d' 36.5

Jacquet, Georges 16.1
Jacquet, Mathieu 38.1
James II 28.1
Jank, Christian 36.7
Janniot, Alfred 12.13, 16.4
Janus, Arch of, Rome 16.1
Janvier, Louis-Adolphe 19.6
Jaoul, André 26.2
Jardin des Plantes **5.14**
Jardin du Carrousel 1.10
Jaussely, Léon 12.13
JC Decaux *Street furniture*
Jeanneret, Albert 13.6, 16.13
Jeanneret, Pierre 13.6, 13.7, 14.7, 14.10, 16.13, 25.2, 29.3, 29.4, 31.1
Jean-Pierre Melville, Médiathèque **13.8**
Jean-sans-Peur, Duc 2.1
Jean II the Good 1.1, 34.2
Jefferson, Thomas 7.2
Jewish Museum *see* Hôtel d'Avaux
Jobbé-Duval, Félix 3.5
Jodry, Jean-François 15.8
Johnson, Philip 4.15, 7.10, 30.2
Joly, Jules de 7.4
Joubert, Charles and Louis 6.6
Jouffroy, François 8.6
Jourdain, Francis 16.12
Jourdain, Frantz 1.5, 18.7
Jouvenet, Jean 32.1
Judo, Institut National du **14.12**
Jullien, François 27.1

Kagan, Michel 15.6
Kansai Airport 33.1
Karasinski, Roman *Seine bridges*
Karavan, Dani 7.10
Katz, Pablo 19.12
Koechlin, Maurice 7.8
Kohn, Bernard *Métro and RER*
Kohn Pederson Fox 27.1
Koolhaas, Rem 29.7, 30.2
Kowalski, Piotr 36.1
Krupp 4.15
Kurokawa, Kisho 27.5
Kuzmin, I. 8.10

410

La Défense, business district of 16.1, 17.3, **27.1**, 27.2, 27.3, 27.4, 27.5
La Feuillade, Duc de 2.2
La Fonta, Henri 12.7
La Fosse, Charles de 1.12, 32.1
La Martinière, Germain de 6.6
La Roche, Raoul 16.13
La Rochefoucauld, Cardinal de 1.12
La Tourette, monastery of 14.10
La Vallière, second Duc de 36.5
La Vallière, Mlle de 32.1
Laffitte, Jacques 24.1
Labadye, Jean-Baptiste *Arcades and passages*
Labrouste, Henri 2.4, 3.10, 5.6, 5.14
Labussière, Auguste 15.4
Lacaton, Anne 16.4
Lacroix-Dillon, Jacques *Seine bridges*
Laitié, Charles-René 16.1
Lalanne, Claude and François-Xavier 1.22, 4.11
Lalique, René 9.10, *Arcades and passages*
Laloux, Victor 2.5, 7.1
Lameire, Charles 8.6
Landowski, Paul *Seine bridges*
Lang, Jack 1.16, 19.8
Langeois, Jean 28.1
Laon Cathedral 4.2
Laplanche, Alexandre 7.15
Laprade, Albert 12.13
Larson, Jean-Frédéric 14.8
Lassus, Jean-Baptiste 1.2, 4.2
Laugier, Abbé 5.8
Launay, Jean 14.6
Laurana, Luciano 38.1
Lavirotte, Jules *Parisian housing*
Le Breton, Gilles 38.1
Le Breton, Guillaume 3.1
Le Brun, Charles 1.8, 1.12, 3.1, 4.5, 4.8, 5.2, 32.1, 37.1
Le Camus de Mézières, Nicolas 1.20
Le Carpentier, Antoine-Michel 7.4
Le Cœur, François 9.1, 15.12
Le Corbusier 1.19, 7.10, 7.17, 11.4, 12.11, 13.6, 13.7, 14.6, 14.7, 14.9, 14.10, 15.6, 16.2, 16.12, 16.13, 16.15, 18.10, 19.1, 19.5, 25.2, 26.2, 27.1, 29.3, 29.4, 29.5, 30.2, 31.1, 35.1
Le Duc, Gabriel 4.4, 5.9
Le Goupil, Mathieu 7.4, 32.1
Le Hongre, Etienne 10.2
Le Lorrain, Robert 3.4, 3.5
Le Mercier, Jacques 1.8, 1.15, 5.5, 5.9
Le Mercier, Pierre 1.21
Le Monde 29.6; former editorial offices **15.2**
Le Muet, Pierre 3.7, 5.9
Le Nôtre, André 1.10, 16.1, 27.1, 28.1, 30.1, 32.1, 32.2, 37.1, 38.1
Le Pautre, Antoine 4.9, 4.17, 30.1, 37.1
Le Raincy, Château 37.1
Le Roy, Bernard 18.9
Le Roy, Philibert 32.1
Le Sueur, Eustache 3.1, 4.5
Le Vau, François 4.20

Le Vau, Louis 1.8, 1.10, 4.4, 4.5, 4.8, 6.2, 6.3, 6.5, 13.1, 16.4, 32.1, 32.2, 34.2, 37.1, 38.1
Lebas, Hippolyte 9.5
Lebœuf-Nanteuil, Charles 10.6
Lebourg, Charles *Street furniture*
Leclaire, Joseph 13.4
Leclercq, François 12.7, 13.2
Leconte, Emmanuel-Chérubin 7.4
Ledoux, Claude-Nicolas 3.1, 3.8, 7.2, 8.9, 9.8, 11.7, 19.13, 32.6
Lejeune (architect) 10.7
Lefebvre, Julien and Duyahon *Arcades and passages*
Lefuel, Hector-Martin 1.8, 38.1
Legentil, Alexandre 18.2
Légion d'Honneur: 7.2, 21.2
Legrand, Jacques-Guillaume 1.20, 21.2
Legros, Pierre 7.12, 10.2
Leménil, Louis-Marie Emile 10.8
Lemordant, Jean-Julien 14.6
Lemoyne, François 32.1
Lemoyne, Jean-Baptiste 3.5
Lenoir, Alexandre 6.1, 20.2, 21.2
Lenormand, B. 27.4
Leopold II 8.15
Lepère, Jean-Baptiste 1.13, 10.6
Lescot, Pierre 1.8, 1.23, 3.1, 23.1
Les Halles 1.21, **1.22**, 4.15, 7.1, 8.5, 8.6, 19.6, 36.6, *Métro and RER*
Lesueur, Jean-Baptiste 4.11
Letrosne, Charles and Daniel 34.1
Lewitt, Alan 1.8
Lézérès, Gilbert 5.13
Lhuillier, Jacques 16.10
Lhuillier, Nicolas 24.1
Ligneris, Jacques de 3.1
Lingeri, Pietro 12.7
Lion, Yves 1.8, 12.7, 13.2
Lipchitz, Jacques 29.3
Lisch, Juste 8.5
Logre, Jules 36.6
Logre, Louis 36.6
Loir, Nicolas 34.2
Lombard, Alfred 29.3
London Zoo 34.1
Longchamp, Abbaye de 29.1
Longueil, René de 24.1
Loos, Adolf 14.6, 18.6
Lopez, Raymond 15.11
Louis, Victor 1.16, 9.13, *Arcades and passages*
Louis Philippe 1.16, 3.5, 4.2, 32.1, 38.1, *Arcades and passages*
Louis VI the Fat 1.1, 18.3, 21.2
Louis VII 1.1, 21.2, 34.1, 34.2
Louis IX (Saint Louis) 1.1, 1.2, 5.5, 11.7, 21.2, 25.1, 28.1, 38.1
Louis XI 2.4
Louis XII 1.1, 1.2
Louis XIII 1.8, 1.16, 4.7, 5.9, 5.14, 6.2, 6.8, 32.1
Louis XIV 1.4, 1.8, 1.13, 2.2, 4.9, 5.9, 6.2, 7.12, 7.13, 10.1, 10.2, 11.7, 13.1, 14.5, 27.1, 28.1, 29.1, 32.1, 32.2, 32.6, 34.2, 37.1, 38.1, *Seine bridges, Parisian housing, Street furniture*

Louis XV 5.8, 6.6, 6.7, 7.9, 8.1, 8.2, 29.1, 29.2, 32.1, 32.3, 32.4, 32.5, 34.1, 38.1
Louis XVI 8.1, 8.4, 11.7, 29.1, 32.1, 32.4, 32.5, 38.1, *Seine bridges, Parisian housing*
Louis XVIII 1.8, 2.2, 8.2, 8.4, 32.1
Louvet, Louis 8.14
Louvois, Marquis de 7.12
Louvre 1.1, 1.7, **1.8**, 1.9, 1.10, 1.11, 1.15, 1.16, 1.23, 2.5, 3.7, 4.5, 4.15, 5.8, 6.1, 6.2, 6.8, 7.1, 7.7, 7.9, 8.1, 9.13, 12.5, 19.9, 23.1, 27.4, 29.1, 32.1, 38.1, *Seine bridges*
Lubetkin, Berthold 16.15, 29.3, 34.1
Ludwig II 32.1, 36.7
Lusson, Auguste *Arcades and passages*
Lusson, Louis-Adrien 9.3
Luynes, Duc de 38.1
Luzarches, Robert de 1.2
Lycée Camille-Sée **15.12**
Lycée Condorcet *see* Saint-Louis-d'Antin
Lycée Henri-IV 5.6, 5.7
Lycée Hoche, Versailles 32.6
Lyon, Dominique 15.2

Macary, Michel 1.8, 12.7, 13.11, 21.1, *Arcades and passages*
Maclaurin, Oudot de 6.5
Madeleine, Eglise de la 7.4, **8.2**
Madeline, Louis 5.12
Maderno, Carlo 5.9, 37.1
Madrid, Château de 1.8, 29.1
Magne, Lucien 18.2
Mailly, Jean de 27.1, 27.3
Maintenon, Mme de 32.1, 38.1
Mairie du 1er 1.6, **1.7**
Mairie du 5e 5.8
Mairie du 10e **10.3**
Maison-atelier Ozenfant 13.7, **14.7**
Maison Citrohan 13.7, 14.7
Maison Cook 13.7, 16.13, 16.15, 25.2, **29.3**, 31.1
Maison de la Radio **16.10**
Maison de l'Iran 14.8
Maison de Verre **7.17**, 29.4
Maison des Fontainiers/Sources, Versailles 32.6
Maison Dorée *Parisian housing*
Maison du Brésil 11.4, 14.8, **14.9**, 14.10
Maison Internationale 14.8
Maison Miestchaninoff 29.3
Maison Planeix 13.7, 31.1
Maisons, Château de **24.1**, 36.5, 37.1
Maisons Jaoul 14.10, **26.2**, 29.4
Maison Tzara **18.6**
Mallet-Stevens, Robert 7.6, 14.6, 14.11, 16.2, 16.12, 29.3
Malraux, André 5.12, 15.1, 25.2
Manguin, Pierre 8.13
Mansart, François 1.8, 1.18, 2.4, 3.1, 3.3, 3.5, 3.6, 4.5, 4.8, 4.21, 5.9, 7.9, 7.12, 24.1, 37.1
Mantout, Maurice 5.10
Marcel, Etienne 1.1, 4.11
Marchand, Guillaume 6.4
Maréchal, Charles-Laurent 10.6

411

Marguerite de Navarre 6.1
Marie, Christophe *Seine bridges*
Marie-Antoinette 1.1, 6.6, 6.7, 8.1, 8.4, 29.2, 32.1, 32.4, 32.5, 38.1
Marie de Médicis 1.1, 6.8, 6.9
Marie Leszczynska 32.1, 32.6
Marie-Thérèse 32.1
Marigny, Enguerrand de 1.1
Marigny, Marquis de 5.8
Markelius, Sven 7.10
Marly, Château de 32.1
Marne-la-Vallée: new town of **36.1**, 36.2, 36.3, 36.4, 36.5, 36.6, 36.7; Ecole d'Architecture de 36.1, **36.4**
Marot, Jean 3.1
Marsy, Gaspard 10.2, 32.1
Marsy brothers (Girardon and Régnaudin) 32.1, 36.5
Martel, Jan and Joël 16.12
Martellange, Etienne 4.7
Martin, Jean-Baptiste 32.2
Martin, Pierre 14.8
Mathieux, Philippe 12.2
Marie-Antoinette 1.1, 6.6, 6.7, 8.1, 8.4, 36.5
Maupassant, Guy de 7.8
Maurios, Georges 11.4
Maurissart, Georges 4.8
Mazarin, Cardinal Jules 2.3, 2.4, 6.2, 13.1, 34.2, 37.1
Mazin, Jean 7.14
Mazois, François *Arcades and passages*
Meditation Space (UNESCO) 7.10, **7.11**, 29.7
Meier, Richard 15.6, 15.10
Melnikov, Konstantin 16.12
Mémorial des Martyrs de la Déportation, **4.3**, 7.11
Menier family 36.6
Menier-Nestlé, Chocolaterie **36.6**
Menu, Xavier 13.11
Mercier, Louis-Sébastien 6.6
Mérindol, Jules de 19.6
Merri (a.k.a. Merry or Medericus), Saint 4.13
Mesmes, Claude de 3.7
Métezeau, Louis 1.3, 1.8, 6.8
Métezeau, Thibault 4.18, *Seine bridges*
Métropolitain 12.5, 12.7, 13.2, 16.11, 18.1, 19.7, *Métro and RER*
Meuron, Pierre de *see* Herzog & de Meuron
Meusnier, Philippe 32.1
Mewès, Charles 1.17
Michelangelo Buonarroti 5.9, 23.1, 24.1, 38.1
Miestchaninoff, Oscar 29.3
Mies van der Rohe, Ludwig 1.22, 30.2
Mignard, Pierre 5.9
Millet, Aimé 9.2
Millet, Eugène 28.1
Millier, Jean 27.1
Mimram, Marc 15.11, *Seine bridges*
Ministère de la Culture 1.16, 12.9, 16.4
Ministère de la Guerre, Versailles 32.6
Ministère de la Marine 8.1

Ministère des Affaires Etrangères, Versailles 32.6
Ministère des Finances et de l'Economie 1.8, **12.5**, 12.7
Mique, Richard 32.1, 32.5, 32.6
Miquel, Louis 11.4
Miró, Joan 7.10
Mitterrand, François 1.8, 5.13, 7.1, 7.7, 12.1, 13.2, 13.3, 19.7, 19.9, 27.1, 27.4
MK2 Bibliothèque 13.2
MNAM (Musée National d'Art Moderne) 4.15, 4.16
Molière 37.1
Molinos, Jacques 1.20, 5.14
Molitor, Immeuble 7.17, 26.2, **29.4**
Mollet, Armand-Claude 8.16
Monconseil, Marquise de 29.2
Monet, Claude 8.5, 12.8, 29.2
Monsieur, Duc d'Orléans 30.1
Montarnal, Charles de 2.9
Montès, Fernando 12.7
Montespan, Mme de 32.2
Montesquieu, Baron de 32.1
Montesson, Mme de 1.16, 9.8
Monticello, Virginia 7.2
Montmorency, Anne de 6.1, 23.1
Montreuil, Pierre de 1.2, 3.10, 4.2, 21.2, 28.1
Monzie, Gabrielle de 31.1
Moore, Henry 7.10
Morard, Abbot 6.4
Moreau-Desproux, Pierre-Louis 1.16
Morel, Jean-Paul 12.7, 19.8, 36.1
Morizet, André 29.5
Mucha, Alphonse 3.1
Municipal office building, Quai de la Rapée **12.3**
Municipal street-cleaning maintenance workshops **19.11**
Musée Carnavalet **3.1**, 4.20
Musée Cognacq-Jay *see* Hôtel de Donon
Musée de Cluny 1.2, 4.2, 4.6, 5.3, **5.4**, 6.4, 21.2
Musée de la Marine 16.7
Musée de la Musique 19.5
Musée de l'Armée 7.12
Musée de l'Orangerie 1.10
Musée de l'Homme 16.7
Musée d'Orsay 1.10, **7.1**, 8.14, *Seine bridges*
Musée des Antiquités Nationales 28.1
Musée des Arts Africains et Océaniens *see* Palais des Colonies
Musée des Arts Décoratifs 16.14
Musée des Monuments Français 6.1, 21.2
Musée du Cheval de Course 24.1
Musée du Prieuré 28.1
Musée du Quai-Branly **7.7**
Musée Guimet **16.5**
Musée Jacquemart-André **8.8**
Musée National de la Renaissance 23.1
Musée National des Arts Asiatiques *see* Musée Guimet
Musée Picasso *see* Hôtel Aubert-de-Fontenay

Musée Pinault 29.6, **29.7**
Musée Rodin *see* Hôtel Peyrenc-de-Moras
Muséum d'Histoire Naturelle **5.14**

Nakaya, Fujiko 19.7
Napoleon 1.4, 1.8, 1.9, 1.10, 1.11, 1.13, 2.8, 3.5, 6.1, 6.2, 7.4, 7.12, 8.2, 8.6, 9.8, 14.8, 16.1, 16.7, 20.2, 21.2, 32.1, 32.2, 38.1, *Seine bridges*
Napoleon III 1.8, 1.10, 1.11, 1.22, 2.4, 4.1, 6.8, 8.5, 8.6, 8.16, 9.4, 9.13, 16.1, 19.2, 19.6, 28.1, 29.1, 34.1, 36.6, 38.1, *Street furniture*
Narjoux, André 2.5
National Gallery, Washington 1.8
Natoire, Charles 3.5
Necker, Jacques 3.8
Nénot, Henri-Paul 5.5
Nepveu, Frédéric 32.1
Nervi, Pier Luigi 7.10
Neuschwanstein 4.11, 36.7
Niemeyer, Oscar 4.15, 7.10, 19.1
Niermans, Edouard and Jean 16.10
Noguchi, Isamu 7.10
Noisiel company town 36.6
Nonsuch Palace, Cuddington 23.1
Notre-Dame, Collégiale **25.1**
Notre-Dame-de-l'Arche-de-l'Alliance **15.3**
Notre-Dame-de-la-Pentecôte **27.2**
Notre-Dame-de-la-Sagesse 13.2
Notre-Dame-de-Lorette **9.5**
Notre-Dame de Paris 1.6, 1.15, 1.21, 3.9, 4.1, **4.2**, 4.3, 4.13, 5.1, 5.4, 5.7, 6.4, 6.5, 16.1, 21.2, 32.6, 36.7
Notre-Dame de Versailles 32.6
Notre-Dame du Raincy 5.8, 12.12, 16.6, 17.2, **35.1**
Notre-Dame-du-Travail 9.3, **14.1**
Nouguier, Emile 7.8
Nouvel, Jean 5.13, 7.7, 14.4, 21.1, 29.6
Noyers, Guillaume 38.1
Nuñez-Yanowsky, Manuel 19.3, 36.3

Observatoire **14.5**
Office building, Avenue des Champs-Elysées **8.11**
Office for Metropolitan Architecture *see* Koolhaas, Rem
Ohnet (architect) 10.7
Olympic Committee 13.13
OMA *see* Koolhaas, Rem
Opéra Bastille **12.1**, 12.2
Opéra Comique **2.6**
Opéra Garnier *see* Palais Garnier
Oppenheim, Adeline 16.14
Orbay, François d' 6.2, 32.1, 32.6
Orléans, Duc(s) de 1.16
Orly Airport 22.1
Otero, Lopez 14.8
Ott, Carlos 12.1
Oudry, Alphonse *Seine bridges*
Ozenfant, Amedée 14.7

Pacific Tower (a.k.a. Japan Tower) and Japan Bridge 27.1, **27.5**
Paestum 5.8, 9.8, 25.2
Païva, Marquise de la 8.13

Pajou, Augustin 1.23
Palais Abbatial 6.4
Palais Bourbon *see* Assemblée Nationale
Palais Brongniart *see* Palais de la Bourse
Palais-Cardinal *see* Palais-Royal
Palais de Chaillot 16.4, **16.7**
Palais d'Iéna 13.12, **16.6**, 16.9
Palais de Justice *see* Palais de la Cité
Palais de la Bourse (Palais Brongniart)
Palais de la Cité (Palais de Justice) **1.1**, 1.2, 1.3, 1.4, 3.1, 4.1, 6.6, 10.1, 34.2
Palais de la Découverte 8.14
Palais de l'Elysée 1.8, **8.16**, 36.5
Palais de Tokyo 4.15, **16.4**
Palais des Colonies (former Musée des Arts Africains et Océaniens) **12.13**, 34.1
Palais des Congrès **17.3**
Palais du Cinéma (former American Center) 12.7, **12.9**
Palais Garnier 1.8, 6.8, 8.8, 8.13, 9.11, 9.12, **9.13**, 12.1, *Street furniture*
Palais/Jardin du Luxembourg 6.6, **6.8**, 6.9, 14.5, 24.1, 37.1
Palais Omnisports de Paris-Bercy **12.6**, 12.7, 12.8
Palais-Royal: **1.16**, 2.7, 12.9, 13.3, 27.1, *Arcades and passages*, *Parisian housing*; Théâtre du 1.16
Palazzo del Te, Mantua 13.2
Palladio, Andrea 9.13, 19.13, 25.2, 31.1, 32.1, *Seine bridges*
Panthéon 5.6, **5.8**, 8.2, 8.7, 35.1
Pantheon, Rome 1.12, 4.13, 4.21, 6.6, 8.2, 23.1
Parat, Pierre 12.6, 27.1, 27.3
Parc André-Citroën 12.8, 15.6, 15.7, **15.8**, 15.10
Parc de Bercy 12.6, 12.7, **12.8**, 12.9,
Parc de La Villette 12.8, 15.8, 19.5, 19.6, **19.7**, 19.8, 19.9, 19.10
Parc de Saint-Cloud **30.1**
Parc des Buttes-Chaumont 8.9, **19.2**, 19.7
Parc des Princes 13.13, **16.18**
Parc Floral 34.1
Parc Monceau **8.9**
Parent, Claude 14.8
Parent, Henri 8.8
Pâris, Pierre-Adrien 8.1, 8.16
Pâris-Duverney, Joseph 7.9
Parisii 4.1
Paris Meridian 14.5
Parmentier, Victor 3.1
Parthenon, Athens 6.1, 8.4, 16.6, 25.2, 32.1
Parti Communiste Français (PCF) 19.1
Pascal, Jean-Louis 2.4
Passage/Rue des Bons-Enfants 1.17
Passerelle Bercy-Tolbiac 12.8, *Seine bridges*
Patout, Pierre 7.6, 9.10, 15.5, 29.3
Patte, Pierre 5.8
Pavillon de l'Esprit Nouveau 29.3
Pavillon Français **32.3**
Pavillon Néerlandais 14.8, **14.11**

Pavillon Suisse 14.8, 14.9, **14.10**
Pei, Ieoh Ming 1.8, 19.9, 27.1
Pencréac'h, Georges 1.22
Percier, Charles 1.8, 1.9, 1.11, 1.16, 2.7, 8.4, 9.5, 12.7, 16.7, 19.4, 32.1, *Arcades and passages*
Pereire, Emile 8.9
Perrault, Claude 1.8, 5.8, 6.2, 8.1, 14.5
Perrault, Dominique 13.3, 13.5, 36.1
Perret, Auguste 1.19, 5.8, 6.1, 8.12, 12.12, 13.12, 16.6, 16.7, 16.8, 16.9, 16.17, 17.1, 17.2, 28.1, 32.1, 35.1, *Parisian housing*
Perriand, Charlotte 14.9
Perrier, François 1.18, 4.5
Perronet, Jean-Rodolphe *Seine bridges*
Perrotet, Jean 1.4
Petit Luxembourg **6.9**
Petit Palais 8.14, **8.15**, *Seine bridges*
Petit Pont 4.1, *Seine bridges*
Petit Trianon 1.16, **32.4**, 32.5, 32.6; Jardin du 19.2, 32.3, 32.4, **32.5**
Peyre, Marie-Joseph 6.7, 7.4
Philip IV of Spain 32.1
Philippe I 3.10
Philippe II Augustus 1.1, 1.8, 11.7, 34.1, 34.2
Philippe IV the Fair 1.1
Philippe VI 34.2
Piano, Renzo 4.14, 4.15, 4.16, 13.5, 19.11, 19.14, 33.1
Piazza del Popolo, Rome 32.1, 32.6
Picasso, Pablo 7.10
Picot, François 10.6
Pierre, Jean-Baptiste 1.15, 38.1
Pilon, Germain 4.13
Pin, François 3.7
Pinault, François 29.6, 29.7
Pingusson, Georges-Henri 4.3, 29.3
Piranesi, Giovanni Battista 6.6, 8.1
Pisan, Christine de 34.2
Pistre, Jean 12.10
Pitti Palace, Florence 6.8, 32.1, 37.1
Place Dauphine 1.1, **1.3**, 4.19, *Seine bridges*
Place de la Concorde 1.8, 1.11, 5.12, 6.3, 7.4, **8.1**, 8.2, 8.4, 9.13, 12.8, 16.7, 32.1, *Seine bridges*, *Street furniture*
Place de l'Odéon **6.7**, *Parisian housing*
Place des Victoires 1.13, **2.2**
Place des Vosges 1.3, 1.11, 1.13, **4.19**
Place du Carrousel 1.9
Place du Châtelet **1.4**
Place Vendôme 1.11, **1.13**, 2.2, 36.5
Planeix, Antonin 13.7
Playtime 13.2, *Métro and RER*
Poisson de Bourvallais, Paul 36.5
Polignac, Princess Winaretta de 13.6
Polonceau, Camille 10.5, 10.7
Pompadour, Mme (Marquise) de 5.8, 32.1, 32.3, 32.4, 32.6, 36.5, *Parisian housing*
Pompidou, Georges 1.22, 4.14, 4.15, 7.7, 15.1, 27.1
Pont Alexandre-III 8.14, *Seine bridges*
Pont au Change 1.4, *Seine bridges*
Pont Caulaincourt 18.7
Pont Charles-de-Gaulle 13.2, *Seine bridges*

Pont de Bercy 12.5, *Seine bridges*
Pont de la Concorde 7.4, *Seine bridges*
Pont des Arts 6.2, *Seine bridges*
Pont Neuf 1.3, *Seine bridges*
Pont Notre-Dame 4.1, *Seine bridges*
Popp, Victor 13.4
Porta, Giacomo della 4.7, 5.5, 5.9
Porte Saint-Denis 1.8, 1.9, **10.1**, 10.2, 16.1
Porte Saint-Martin 1.8, **10.2**
Portzamparc, Christian de 7.5, 11.3, 12.7, 13.2, 13.10, 17.3, 18.5, 18.8, 19.5, 20.1, 36.1
Poste Française 1.19, 11.3, 20.3
Poste Parisien 8.11
Post office and postal workers' housing, Rue Oberkampf **11.3**, 20.1, 20.3, 20.5
Potain, Nicolas-Marie 28.1, 32.1
Potsdamer Platz, Berlin 4.14
Pouillon, Fernand 4.1
Poussin, Nicolas 37.1
Poyet, Bernard 7.4
Predock, Antoine 36.7
Préfecture de Police 4.1
Primary schools: Rue Pelleport **20.4**; Rue Paul-Abadie/de la Moskova **18.8**
Primaticcio, Francesco (Le Primatice) 3.1, 3.5, 38.1
Printemps **9.9**, 9.10
Printz, Eugène 12.13
Pritzker Prize 7.5, 12.7, 19.5, 30.2
Prix de Rome 6.1
Prothin, André 27.1
Prouvé, Jean 4.15, 12.6, 16.12, 19.1, 27.1, 27.3
Provence, Comte de *Parisian housing*
Provost, Alain 15.8
Prunet, Pierre 1.13
Pseudo-Dionysius 21.2

Quatremère de Quincy, Antoine Chrysostome 5.8

Raaf, Lotti 16.13
Radio France 16.10
Rambuteau, Claude-Philibert Barthelot, Comte de 7.3, *Parisian housing*, *Street furniture*
Raphael 38.1
RATP 18.1, *Métro and RER*
Rauline, Hervé 18.2
Ravy, Jean 4.2
Raymond, Antonin 35.1
Raymond, Jean-Arnaud 16.1
Reby, Marcel 15.11
Regembal, Michel 21.1
Regny de Guerchy, Louis 1.16
Reichen, Bernard 19.6, 36.6
Reims Cathedral 4.2, 5.7, 6.11
Reitzel, Erik 7.10
Renault, Louis/firm of 29.6, 29.7
Renzo Piano Building Workshop *see* Piano, Renzo
RER 1.22, 12.2, 13.2, 15.8, 22.1, *Métro and RER, Glossary*
Résal, Louis-Jean *Seine bridges*
Réseau du Souvenir 4.3
Réseau Ferré de France 13.2

413

Résidence Avicenne see Maison de l'Iran
Restout, Jean 3.5
Rex, cinéma **2.10**
Rice, Francis and Ritchie (RFR) 19.7, 19.10, 22.1, 27.2
Rice, Peter 1.8, 4.15, 19.10, 22.1, 27.4
Richard, Antoine 32.5
Richard, Claude 32.4
Richard the Lion-Heart 1.8
Richelieu, Cardinal de 1.16, 4.7, 5.5, 6.2
Rietveld, Gerrit 16.13
Ripault, Jacques 13.2
Ritz, Charles 1.13
Rives, Gustave 8.1
Robert, Hubert 1.8, 32.1, 32.5
Robert, Philippe 19.6, 36.6
Robert II the Pious 1.1, 25.1
Roberts, Henry 9.4
Robespierre, Maximilien de 1.1
Rocard, Michel *Métro and RER*
Rodin, Auguste 7.13, 14.3, 18.7
Rodrigues-Page, Simon 13.2
Rogers, Ernesto 7.10
Rogers, Lord Richard 4.14, 4.15, 13.5, 27.4
Roguet, Félix 3.1
Rohault de Fleury, Charles-Hubert 1.4, 5.14, 9.11, 9.12, 16.1
Rohault de Fleury, Hubert 18.2
Rolinet, Marc 13.2
Romanelli, Giovanni-Francesco 1.8, 2.4
Romano, Giulio 3.1, 13.2
Rondelet, Jean-Baptiste 5.8
Rosati, Roberto 5.5
Rossi, Aldo 18.5, 19.4
Rosso, Il 38.1
Rotonde de la Villette **19.13**
Rousseau, Antoine 32.1
Rousseau, Jacques 32.1
Rousseau, Pierre 7.2, 38.1
Roux-Spitz, Michel 7.6, 29.4
Rouyer, Eugène 10.3
Rowe, Colin 25.2, 31.1
Royal Albert Hall, London 19.5
Rubens, Peter Paul 6.8
Rubin, Daniel and Patrick 13.8
Rude, François 7.4, 8.2, 16.1, 18.7
Rue de Rivoli 1.7, **1.11**, 2.7, 4.9, 4.11, 4.12, 9.13, 12.5, 12.7, 19.4, *Parisian housing*
Rue des Colonnes 1.11, **2.7**
Rue Mallet-Stevens **16.12**, 16.13
Ruhlmann, Jacques-Emile 12.13, 15.5

Saarinen, Eero 7.10
Sacré-Cœur 12.12, 16.3, 17.2, 18.1, **18.2**
Saint-Acceul, Ecouen 23.1
Saint-Alexandre-Nevski **8.10**
Saint-Augustin **8.6**, 9.7
Saint-Bartholomew's-Day massacre 1.6, 1.7, 3.5
Saint Basil the Blessed, Moscow 8.10
Saint-Denis, Abbaye de 1.21, 1.23, 3.10, 4.2, 6.1, 6.4, 7.12, 8.4, 8.9, 10.1, **21.2**
Saint-Esprit **12.12**, 17.2
Saint-Etienne Cathedral 4.2
Saint-Etienne-du-Mont **5.7**

Saint-Eugène 3.10, **9.3**, 7.15, 8.6, 14.1
Saint-Eustache **1.21**, 1.22
Saint-Front, Périgueux 18.2
Saint-Germain-des-Prés 4.1, 5.4, **6.4**, 25.1
Saint-Germain-en-Laye, Château de 1.8, **28.1**, 29.1, 38.1
Saint-Germain-l'Auxerrois **1.6**, 1.7
Saint-Gervais-Saint-Protais 4.7, **4.10**
Saint-Jacques-de-la-Boucherie see Tour Saint-Jacques
Saint-Jean-de-Montmartre **18.4**
Saint-Julien-le-Pauvre **5.1**
Saint-Louis, Saint-Germain-en-Laye 28.1
Saint-Louis, Versailles 32.6
Saint-Louis-d'Antin (Lycée Condorcet, former Couvent des Capucins) **9.8**
Saint-Louis-en-l'Ile **4.4**
Saint-Maclou, Pontoise 1.21
Saint Mark's, Venice 1.9
Saint-Martin-des-Champs (Conservatoire des Arts et Métiers) 3.9, **3.10**, 5.6, 9.3, 21.2
Saint-Maur, Order of 6.4
Saint-Merri **4.13**, 4.14
Saint-Nicaise, Reims 7.3
Saint-Nicolas-des-Champs **3.9**, *Parisian housing*
Saint-Paul-Saint-Louis **4.7**, 4.10
Saint Paul's Cathedral, London 1.21, 5.8, 6.5
Saint Peter's, Rome 1.15, 5.8, 5.9, 7.12
Saint-Phalle, Niki de 4.14
Saint-Philippe-du-Roule **8.7**, 9.5
Saint-Pierre-aux-Bœufs 5.2
Saint-Pierre-de-Chaillot **16.3**
Saint-Pierre-de-Montmartre 4.2, **18.3**, 21.2
Saint-Roch **1.15**, 8.7
Saint-Séverin **5.2**
Saint-Simon, Duc de 32.1
Saint-Sulpice 1.21, **6.5**, 8.7
Saint-Vincent-de-Paul 5.6, **10.6**
Sainte-Chapelle 1.1, **1.2**, 4.1, 5.4, 23.1, 28.1, 32.1, 34.2, 38.1
Sainte-Clothilde-Sainte-Valère **7.3**
Sainte-Geneviève, Abbaye de 5.6, 5.7, 5.8
Sainte-Geneviève, abbey church of see Panthéon
Sainte-Marie-de-la-Visitation **4.21**, 5.9, 7.12
Sainte-Odile **17.2**
Sainte-Trinité 9.6, **9.7**
Salazar, Etienne-Tristan de 4.6
Salm-Kyrburg, Friedrich III von 7.2
Salvation Army 13.6
Samaritaine **1.5**, 7.15, 9.10
San Carlo ai Catinari, Rome 5.5
San Crisogono, Rome 9.5
Sant'Agnese in Agone, Rome 6.2
Sant'Apollinare Nuovo, Ravenna 8.10
Sant' Elia, Antonio 6.10
Santa Maria della Salute, Venice 7.12
Santa Maria Maggiore, Rome 9.5
Santa Susanna, Rome 5.9
Santi Trinità dei Monti, Rome 10.6

Sarazin, Charles 6.10, *Arcades and passages*
Saubot, Jean 15.1
Saubot, Roger 27.1
Saulnier, Jules 36.6
Sauvage, Henri 1.5, 3.1, 6.10, 9.4, 18.10, *Arcades and passages*
Sauvestre, Stephen 7.8, 36.6
Scarron, Michel-Antoine 4.8
Schaerbeck town hall 29.5
Schall, Pierre *Métro and RER*
Schenck, Edouard 1.5, 9.10
Schinkel, Karl Friedrich 19.10
Schoeller, Bernard 27.1
Schröder House, Utrecht 16.13
Schroeder, Louis 8.6
Schweitzer, Roland 13.2
Scibec de Carpi, Francisque 1.8, 38.1
Seassal, Roger 5.12
Sebille, Georges 16.10
Sédille, Paul 1.16, 9.9
Semper, Gottfried 9.13
Sénat see Palais du Luxembourg
Senlis Cathedral 6.11
Sens Cathedral 4.2
Sequaris, Jacques 18.5
Serlio, Sebastiano 1.23, 28.1, 38.1
Sert y Badia, José Maria 3.1
Servandoni, Giovanni Niccolò 1.21, 6.5
Service Municipal des Promenades et Plantations 8.9, 19.2, 29.1, 34.1, *Street furniture*
Sgard, Jacques 7.13
Sheltered housing, Rue de l'Orillon **11.2**
Silvestre, Israël 5.5
Simounet, Roland 3.3
Sir John Soane's Museum, London 6.1
Slodtz brothers (Michel-Ange and Paul-Ambroise) 4.13
Smirke, Sir Sydney 2.4
SNCF 3.2, 15.1, 22.1, *Métro and RER*
Social housing: Boulevard de Belleville 11.3, **20.1**, 20.5; Rue de la Saïda **15.4**; Rue de Meaux 4.14, 13.10, **19.14**; Rue des Amiraux **18.10**; Rue des Hautes-Formes **13.10**, 20.1; Rue du Château-des-Rentiers **13.9**; Rue Pelleport **20.5**
Société Anonyme des Maisons à Gradins 6.10
Société des Logements Hygiéniques à Bon Marché 6.10, 18.10
Société Générale: agence centrale 9.2, **9.11**; towers 27.1
Soler, François 7.7, 12.7, 13.2, 20.4
Sorbonne, Collège/Chapelle de la 1.12, 1.15, 4.7, **5.5**, 5.9, 6.11
Soria, Pierre 5.13
Soufflot, François 3.10
Soufflot, Jacques-Germain 1.8, 4.2, 5.8, 8.1, 8.7
Spreckelsen, Johann Otto von 27.4
Stade de France 16.18, **21.2**
Stade Sébastien-Charléty **13.13**, 16.18
Starck, Philippe 19.7
Stein, Michael and Sarah 31.1
Stern, Robert 36.7
Stinco, Antoine 1.10, 13.2

Stirling, James 26.2
Stravinsky, Igor 4.14
Strohm, I. 8.10
SUDAC see Compressed-air plant
Sue, Eugène 4.1
Suez-Lyonnaise des Eaux headquarters 8.3
Suger, Abbott 3.10, 4.2, 6.4, 21.2
Sully, Maurice de 4.2
Synagogues: Rue de la Victoire **9.6**; Rue des Tournelles 9.6
Szabo (sculptor) 9.1

Tâcheron, Pierre 23.1
Taillibert, Roger 16.18
Takis, Vassilakis 7.10
Talairac, Giraud de 1.17
Taller de Arquitectura Ricardo Bofill see Bofill, Ricardo
Tallon, Roger 18.1
Tange, Kenzo 13.11
Tate Modern, London 14.13
Tati, Jacques 13.2, *Métro and RER*
Tauzin, Henri *Parisian housing*
Tavernier, Antoine *Arcades and passages*
Teatro Olimpico, Vicenza 32.1
Telephone exchange, Rue du Faubourg-Poissonière **9.1**
Tempietto, San Pietro in Montorio, Rome 5.8, 8.9
Temple, Raymond du 34.2
Temple of Solomon, Jerusalem 9.6
Ternisien, Immeuble 29.3
Terragni, Giuseppe 12.7
Terrier, Charles 16.5
Thayer, William *Arcades and passages*
Théâtre de la Ville 1.4
Théâtre de l'Odéon **6.7**, 9.13
Théâtre des Abbesses **18.5**
Théâtre des Bouffes du Nord **10.8**
Théâtre des Champs-Elysées **8.12**, 17.1
Théâtre du Châtelet 1.4
Thermes de Lutèce **5.3**, 5.4, 5.11
Thiers, Adolphe 14.8, 16.1, 20.2
Thiriot, Jean 2.3, 4.18
Thomas, Albert 8.14
Thomas, Saint 1.2, 4.2
Tiepolo, Giovanni Battista 3.1
Tinguely, Jean 4.14
Toudoire, Marius 12.4
Tour Aquitaine 27.1
Tour Atlantique 27.1
Tour CBX 27.1
Tour Europe 27.1
Tour Framatome (former Fiat) 27.1
Tour Gan 27.1
Tour Hines 27.1
Tour Jean-sans-Peur **2.1**
Tour Montparnasse 4.15, **15.1**, 27.1
Tour Nobel 27.1
Tour Saint-Jacques **4.12**
Tour Sequoia 27.1
Tour TotalFinaElf 27.1
Tournaire, Albert 1.1
Tournon, Paul 12.12, 17.2
»Train Bleu« restaurant 12.4

Trajan's Column, Rome 1.13
Tranchant de Lunel, Maurice 5.10
Trémolières, Charles 3.5
Très Riches Heures 1.8
Tribunal Administratif de Paris see Hôtel d'Aumont
Tribunal de Commerce 4.1
Tribunal de Grande Instance 1.1
Trocadéro see Palais de Chaillot
Trollope, Mrs. *Street furniture*
Trouard, Louis-François *Parisian housing*
Tschumi, Bernard 19.5, 19.7, 36.4
Tuby, Jean-Baptiste 5.2, 32.1
Tuileries 1.8, 1.9, **1.10**, 1.11, 1.15, 8.1, 9.13, 12.7, 12.8, 16.1, 24.1, 27.1, 32.1, *Seine bridges*
Tzara, Tristan 18.6

UGC Ciné Cité Bercy 12.10
Ultrogothe, Queen 1.6
UNESCO **7.10**, 7.11, 29.7
UN headquarters, New York 7.10
Unité d'habitation, Marseilles 11.4
Université Paris-VII Denis-Diderot 13.2
Unsterller, Nicolas 16.3
Urbino, ducal palace 38.1

Vacherot, Laurence 19.7
Val-de-Grâce, Abbaye du 1.15, **5.9**, 7.12
Valode, Denis 12.10
Van Clève, Corneille 7.12
Vandenhove, Charles 18.5
Van Loo, Carle 3.5, 38.1
Van Obstal, Gerard 3.1
Varé, Louis-Sulpice 29.1, 29.2
Vasconi, Claude 1.22
Vassal, Jean-Philippe 16.4
Vassé, François-André 1.18
Vaudoyer, Antoine 6.2
Vaudoyer, Léon 3.10, 20.2
Vaudrey and Lagalisserie *Seine bridges*
Vaux-le-Vicomte, Château de 1.8, 4.5, 8.8, 24.1, 32.1, 32.2, 36.5, **37.1**
Velde, Henry van de 8.12
Vellefaux, Claude 10.4
Vendôme, Colonne 1.13, 6.6
Verberckt, Jacques 32.1
Verdier, Cardinal 17.2
Verlaine, Paul 1.22
Verniquet, Edme 5.14
Veronese, Paolo 32.1
Versailles: Château de 1.8, 1.10, 4.5, 5.14, 9.13, 23.1, 24.1, 29.1, 29.2, **32.1**, 32.2, 32.4, 32.6, 34.2, 37.1, 38.1; ville 6.1, 32.1, **32.6**
Vestier, Nicolas-Jacques-Antoine 2.7, *Arcades and passages*
Veugny, Marie-Gabriel 9.4
Veuillot, Louis 1.8
Vexlard, Gilles 19.7
Viaduc des Arts **12.2**
Viard, Paul 16.4
Vicariot, Henri 22.1
Vicenza town hall 9.13
Vidé, Thierry 13.11
Vieu, Maurice 14.8

Vignola, Giacomo Barozzi da 4.7
Vignon, Pierre 8.2
Viguier, Jean-Paul 15.8, 27.1
Villa Barbaro, Maser 32.1
Villa dall'Ava **30.2**
Villa d'Este, Tivoli 28.1, 32.1
Villa Foscari, Malcontenta 31.1
Villa Majorelle, Nancy 6.10
Villa Rotonda, Vicenza 19.13, 25.2
Villa Savoye 25.1, **25.2**, 30.2, 31.1
Villa Stein-de Monzie 13.7, 25.2, 26.2, 30.2, **31.1**
Villas La Roche and Jeanneret-Raaf 16.12, **16.13**, 25.2, 29.3
Villedo, Michel 4.3
Ville Radieuse 11.4, 13.6, 14.10
Villette, Marquis de 5.8
Vilmond, Paul 16.6
Vincennes: Bois de 5.14, 29.1, **34.1**, 34.2; Château de 1.2, 34.1, **34.2**
Vincent de Paul, Saint 10.6
Vincent de Saragosse, Saint 6.4
Viollet-le-Duc, Eugène-Emmanuel 1.2, 1.5, 1.21, 4.2, 5.7, 6.5, 9.13, 10.7, 16.11, 16.14, 18.2, 18.4, 19.6, 21.2, 25.1, 28.1, 36.6
Visconti, Ludovico (Louis) Tullius Joachim 1.8, 6.5, 7.12
Vitruvius 10.1, 23.1
Volpiano, Abbot Guillaume de 6.4
Voltaire 4.10, 5.8, 24.1

Wagner, Richard 9.13
Wailly, Charles de 6.5, 6.7, 32.1
Wallace, Sir Richard 29.2, *Street furniture*
Ware, Samuel *Arcades and passages*
Wars of Religion 1.8, 1.21, 4.18, 4.19, 38.1, *Seine bridges*
Washington Obelisk 7.8
Wedgwood, Josiah 8.1
Wilde, Oscar 20.2
Willis Faber Dumas building, Ipswich 19.10
Wilmotte, Jean-Michel 13.2, *Street furniture*
Wirtz, Jacques 1.10
Wispelaere, Prudent de 18.5
Wren, Sir Christopher 1.21, 5.8, 6.5

ZAC Bercy 12.5, 12.6, **12.7**, 12.8, 12.9, 12.10, 13.2, *Métro and RER*
ZAC Citroën 15.6, 15.7, 15.8, 15.9, 15.10
ZAC Manin-Jaurès 19.3
ZAC Moskova 18.8
ZAC Paris-Rive-Gauche 1.1, 12.8, **13.2**, 13.3, 13.4, 13.5, *Métro and RER*, *Seine bridges*, *Street furniture*
Zahos, Nicolas 14.8
Zehrfuss, Bernard 7.10, 27.1, 27.3
Zénith 19.7, **19.8**
Zola, Emile 7.15, 18.7, *Arcades and passages*
Zoo de Vincennes 34.1
Zuber, Claude 19.4
Zublena, Aymeric 12.3, 15.7, 21.1

Photo credits

Tadao Ando 7.11, 29.7
The Architectural Review 12.1, 14.13, 27.4
Artefactory 7.7
Jean-Pierre Attal 27.5
Andrew Ayers p. 8, 1.1.2, 1.2.2, 1.3, 1.5,
   1.6, 1.8.2, 1.8.3, 1.8.4, 1.9, 1.10, 1.11,
   1.12. 1.13, 1.15, 1.16, 1.19, 1.20, 1.21,
   1.23, 2.1, 2.2, 2.3, 2.5, 2.6, 2.7, 2.8,
   2.9, 2.10, 3.1, 3.2, 3.3, 3.4, 3.5,1,
   3.5.2, 3.6, 3.8, 3.9, 3.10, 4.1, 4.2.1,
   4.2.2, 4.3, 4.4, 4.6, 4.7, 4.8, 4.10, 4.11,
   4.12, 4.13, 4.17, 4.18, 4.19, 4.20, 4.21,
   5.2, 5.4, 5.5, 5.7, 5.8, 5.9, 5.10, 5.12,
   6.1.1, 6.1.2, 6.2, 6.3, 6.4, 6.5, 6.6,
   6.7, 6.8, 6.10, 6.11, 7.1, 7.2, 7.3, 7.6,
   7.8, 7.9, 7.10, 7.12.1, 7.12.2, 7.13, 7.15,
   8.1, 8.2, 8.3, 8.4, 8.5, 8.6, 8.7, 8.8,
   8.9, 8.10, 8.11, 8.12, 8.14, 8.15, 9.1,
   9.2, 9.3, 9.4, 9.6, 9.7, 9.8, 9.9, 9.10,
   9.11, 9.13.1, 10.1, 10.2, 10.3, 10.4, 10.5,
   10.6, 10.7, 11.1, 11.4, 11.7, 12.2, 12.4,
   12.6, 12.7, 12.8, 12.9, 12.10, 12.13, 13.1,
   13.2.1, 13.2.2, 13.3, 13.4, 13.5, 13.6,
   13.7, 13.12, 13.13, 14.1, 14.3, 14.5, 14.6,
   14.7, 14.10.1, 14.10.2, 14.11, 15.1, 15.4,
   15.5, 15.8, 15.12, 16.1, 16.4, 16.5, 16.6,
   16.7, 16.8, 16.9, 16.10, 16.11, 16.12, 16.13,
   16.14, 16.16, 16.17, 16.18, 17.1, 17.2, 18.2,
   18.4, 18.6, 18.10, 19.2, 19.4, 19.6, 19.6,
   19.11, 19.13, 20.2, 23.1, 24.1, 25.2.1,
   26.2.1, 27.3, 28.1, 29.1, 29.2, 29.3,
   29.4, 29.5, 29.6, 30.1, 31.1.2, 32.1.1,
   32.1.2, 32.2, 32.4, 32.5, 34.1, 34.2,
   35.1.1, 36.1, 36.5, 36.6, 36.7, 37.1.1,
   37.1.2, 38.1.1, 38.1.2, p. 381, p. 383,
   p. 385, p. 390, p. 391, p. 395, p. 398,
   p. 399, p. 401
G. Berengo Gardin 4.15
Peter Blundell Jones 25.2.2
Nicolas Borel 7.5, 11.3, 13.10.2, 17.3,
   19.5.1, 19.5.2, 20.1, 20.5
Gerard Cadou/ADP 22.1.1, 22.1.2
Couturier 13.10.2
Christophe Demonfaucon 11.5
Michel Denancé 4.16, 19.14, 33.1
Favret et Manez 19.12
Georges Fessy 5.13, 20.4
Scott Frances 15.10
Aki Furudate 11.6
Gaston 15.3, 18.1
Khalfi 17.3
Peter Mauss/ESTO 36.4
J. M. Montiers 11.2, 15.9, p. 393
Valérie Pernard 19.3
Philippe Rouault 14.4
Deidi von Schaewen cover
Florian Sennlaub 7.4, 16.16, 19.1
P. Tournebœuf 18.9
Philippe Vandermaren 18.5
Christopher Wilson, *The Gothic Cathedral* 4.2.3, 21.2

All other photographs not mentioned here were kindly supplied by the architects and institutions listed in the foreword.